GW01605427

Taplow Moments

Taplow Moments

A Unique History

First published in Great Britain in 2015 by Words by Design

www.wordsbydesign.co.uk

ISBN: 978-1-909075-37-5

Typeset in Calibri

Contents

Foreword

The present Lady Wogan (I call her that to keep her on her toes), our one-year-old son Alan and myself – having taken the mailboat, in the ancient Irish tradition, from Dublin to Liverpool – arrived in the leafy environs of Taplow in late-1969. After eight years on Irish radio and TV, I was trying my luck with the BBC. Helen and I will always regard it as one of our luckiest chances that the only good friends we knew in Britain were 'Kits' Browning (son of General 'Boy' Browning and Dame Daphne du Maurier) and his Irish wife 'Hacker', once Olive White. They lived in *Tithe Barn* on Lake End Road, Taplow. We stayed with them while we looked for somewhere to put down our roots. And we've been here ever since....

We had early diversions to Farnham Common, Burnham and Bray but, seeing the error of our ways, moved back to our beloved Taplow in 1975, to *Hitcham Close*: a house we had long admired. Knowing Susan & Michael Stewart-Fry were moving to Jersey, we snapped it up before it even came on the market. Susan remains a close friend and now lives not far away.

It was the happiest of good fortunes that brought us here, where our family grew up, and Helen and I have spent the best of times with the best of neighbours. And no matter what the post code or the Post Office may say, we're proud to be residents of Taplow, Buckinghamshire....

Sir Terry Wogan KBE DL

Terry Wogan / 2013

Yours Truly

The Cottage, Rectory Road / 31st August 2014

I fell in love with history in 1959 when I was taken on a school trip to Berkhamsted Castle. Seven-and-a-half centuries disappeared in a flash as I imagined clambering up the motte to besiege the bailey in 1216. From this seed grew the realisation that history isn't just in the past. We are because they were, what is stems from what was. History is packed full of good stories about how and why. What's more, the stories are still unfolding: history is happening before our eyes. Taplow is tiny – the civil parish is just 2.75 square miles in area – yet it can tell more tales than most, not only of the headlines at Taplow Court and Cliveden but also of the everyday everywhere you look. Perhaps that's what drew us here.

I was born in Ealing in 1950, brought up in Wembley, educated at Latymer Upper School in Hammersmith and met Caroline in Harrow when I was a villain in pantomime (typecast again) and she was gracing the chorus line. We married in 1985, moved to Chalfont St Peter and came to Taplow in 1997 primarily because we wanted to live somewhere with a sense of place. She was a nurse and is now a nurse lecturer at the University of West London. I was an architect who evolved to spend 30 years as a management consultant during which I was fortunate to travel the world helping businesses to change. We became three in 2003 when we went to China to adopt our daughter Keira, now 12. It is the best decision we have ever made.

My father-in-law Eric Bidmead used to say that retirement was the best job he'd ever had. Now I know what he meant. My retirement in 2011 gave me three opportunities: to be a volunteer at the London 2012 Olympics (an adventure that continues as an occasional Royal Borough Ambassador), to join the executive committee of the Hitcham & Taplow Society and to try my hand as a wordsmith in order to keep the old brain ticking. I had long been dabbling with a biography of my father Eddy 'Smiler' Smales, whose lot in life was to film bits of history happening. *When You're Smiler* was published in October 2011 and soon I was ready for my next close-up: Taplow. I began working in earnest on *Taplow Moments* in January 2012 and a year later was persuaded to split my focus between it and editing the Society's biannual newsletter. I suspect Caroline hopes that will be enough to be going on with now 'The Big One' is done.

Nigel Smales

The Author / 2011

Dedication

To Caroline, the love of my life to whom I shall be eternally grateful for somehow tolerating my passion for history and the indulgent, single-minded, wee-small-hours dedication necessary for me to be an author-of-sorts.

To Keira, our beautiful ray of sunshine.

To all Taplovians: past, present and future.

Keira & Caroline / 2014

Acknowledgements

Who owns history? Those who write it down have a claim but this isn't my History. It belongs to all Taplovians who have been, who are and who are still to come. I am deeply indebted to those in the past who noted what was happening and what life was like, and to those in the present who chose not to covet their knowledge but to share it with such astounding generosity. I will be delighted if this book helps them and future Taplovians to treasure our heritage half as much as I do.

Three are first among equals: the eminent Sir Terry Wogan for so kindly looking back to look Foreword, the astounding Alistair Forsyth for his wealth of anecdotes and especially for his diligent proof-reading, and the incredible Karl Lawrence for his enthusiasm, constant encouragement and counsel.

I am also immensely grateful to Brian Ackland-Snow, Liz & Tim Anderson, Roger Andrews, Susan Andrews (née Lock), Chris Ashford, Barbara Askew, Emily & Matthew Ball, Michael Bayley, Pamela Bentley, Ingrid Bevan (née Thomas), Maggie Blakeslee, Marc Boden, Joanna Brooking, Tim Browning, Burnham Library, Peter Casey, Michael Chaloner (of Cliveden), Gillian & Rev Alan Dibden, John Dunleavey, Carol Farmiloe, Euan Felton, Ginny Felton (née Miall), Heather Fenn, Andrew Findlay, Michael Fletcher, Liz Forsyth, Richard Forsyth, Bryan Galan, Caroline Gillies, Gavin Gordon, Daphne & Rusty Grant, Helen & Aleyn Grellier, Arthur Grout, David Grout, Gillian & Robert Hanbury, Anne & John Hanford, Anthony Harding, Louise Hartman (née Green), Brenda & Tony Hickman, Gill Holloway, Paul Holt, Sheila & Brian Horton, Anne & Lionel House, Nicki & Paul Jeffries, Maud & Ken Johnson, John Kennedy, Muriel King, Richard King, Alan Langton, Philip Langton, Rosaleen Lawrence, Christine & Simon Leach, Duncan Leftley, Eva Lipman, David Long, Janette & Laird Mackay, Maidenhead Heritage Centre, Maidenhead Library, Giles de la Mare, Joy Marshall, Sarah & Tony Meats, Sally & Leonard Miall, Iris Midlane, George Milne, Stuart Montgomery, the National Archives at Kew, Heather & Warren Palmer, Keith Parry, Graeme Paskins, Julia Paskins, Sheila & Barrie Peroni, Nik Powell, Jim Rance, Tony Read, Dave Reeves, Bronwen Renwick, Jennifer Robertson, Sally & George Sandy, Morag & Mike Scarlett, Sue & Alan Senior, Alexander Shephard (of Hedsor), Hamish Shephard, Susan Silver, Adam Smith, Christopher Smith, Jo & Greg Stevenson, Lesley & Geoff Street, Tim Street, Lynette Szczepanik (née Murray), Vivien Thomas, Mary Trevallion, Jackie & Steve Vinden, Pamela & Joel Viollet, Daphne Walker, Victoria & Miv Wayland-Smith, Donna & Andrew Wells, Phillip Wells, Jon Willmore, Mike Yeadon (and his friends at *SGI-UK*).

Special thanks are also due to Lorraine Sutherland, former headteacher at St Nicolas' CE Combined School, to Sally Sharp and the Key Stage 2 schoolchildren of 2012: Ariana Aghoghovbia, Jamie Ashford, Alex Bainbridge, Edward Bennett, Eleanor Bunce, Jessica Cart, Renzo Casale, Arthur Cassells, Hannah Chapman, Lyra Cherry, Kai Cooper, Emily Costello, Grace Dixon, Jessica Edmonds, Molly Edmondson, Freya Esplun-Evans, Ronia Falana, Sophie Greenham, Olivia Hall, Katie Harris, Chloe Harvey, Arthur Herman-Heynes, Lucy Hill, Katie Hornett, Felicity Humphreys, Robert Hutton, Hannah Irwin, Poppy Jaminson, Monty Keates, Willow Kerr, Tom King, Thomas Knight, Robbie Lawrence, Esme Maree, Nicola Mayo, Lily Messenger, Rosie Middleton, Freya Molony, Lauren Murphy, Jennifer Neal, Louis Ness, Archie Norman, Joseph Oliver, Louis Plumley, Chloe & Lucinda Plummer, George Pole, Joe Pontin, Timothy Pretty, Serena Protopadadakis, Rosie Sellers, Anna Shanu-Wilson, Keira Smales, Alice Snoxell, Joshua Stow, Andrew Walker, Imogen Wallis, Scarlett & Theo Wayland-Smith, Mia Webb, Ciara Williams and Katie & Olivia Wrennall.

Finally, I must give tremendous credit and sincere thanks to Taplow Parish Council and to Tony Gray of Words by Design. On 25th February 2015, the Council was kind and generous to allocate a grant from its legacy fund that has enabled Taplow Moments to emerge in full colour from its primarily black-and-white chrysalis. And Tony's creative skills, perceptive advice and patience have once more been invaluable in pulling the fruits of my labour into a package to be proud of.

Setting the Scene

In the Blink of an Eye

The Old Churchyard / 3rd June 2012

It is ten o'clock in the evening. We are on what was consecrated ground: the old church of St Nicholas stood here for hundreds of years. By the light of our torches we can see to our right the magnificent **Taplow Court**, now in the care of Buddhists. A century ago it was home to an Olympic hero and before him to myriad lords of the manor who ruled the roost around here when it was the place for the powerful to play. To our left down the hill is **Bapsey Pond**, sacred to early Christians who were baptised in its waters and before them mystical to Ancient Britons since time immemorial. In the valley below Old Father Thames keeps on rolling along down to the sea: often Taplow's lifeblood, always its backbone. Rising steeply in front of us is **Tæppa's Mound**: an Anglo-Saxon earthwork piled high almost 14 centuries ago as the last resting place of the last pagan lord in these parts. And atop the mound is why hundreds of local people spanning five generations are here tonight. A beacon burns brightly up there to mark the Diamond Jubilee of Queen Elizabeth II. **Jamie Barnard** waves his Union Jack. Reverence and revelry, ceremony and community, today and all our yesterdays in the blink of an eye: Taplow Ancient and Modern.

Sarah Meats lives at ***Number Three*** in the High Street. She is a caterer with a rare talent for *canapés*. Maybe that's why her husband **Tony** likes his history bite-sized. If you do too, stop reading now. The rest of us are hungry for more. We will find not devils in the detail but delight. This story of Taplow is structured in a series of essays to enable 'skipping and dipping' if that takes your fancy.

All in the Mind

The Old Churchyard / 3rd June 2012

History is a time-machine. Mix in imagination and we can watch events in the past. Some moments in this History actually happened on the dates given. Others are spiced with sprinkles of imagination but always in historically factual context. All people mentioned really did (or do) exist and they really had (or have) the positions and responsibilities attributed to them at the time. Our first stop is just three years back when this History first saw the light of day as a *Powerpoint* slide presentation....

Little Eyes are Popping

St Nicolas' School / 23rd June 2009

This is Taplow Heritage Week. We are surrounded by over 200 children in the hall of **St Nicolas' Combined Church of England Primary School**. I start by asking the assembled multitude "What was the world like 12,000 years ago?" My carefully-rehearsed 7-year-old daughter **Keira Smales** takes her cue well. She puts her hand up and says "The Ice Age!" A picture of a never-ending ice sheet duly scrolls down the screen. An arrow points downwards to show where Taplow might have been hidden beneath the ice. In fact, glaciers never quite covered Taplow but they came close so the place must have been pretty chilly. And the picture serves its purpose: attentions are well and truly grabbed.

The next slide asks "Who was Taplow's first inhabitant?" I haven't told Keira the answer to this question so, when nobody pipes up, a picture of a mammoth appears. This is my cue to tell how the remains of a woolly rhinoceros, a musk ox and a mammoth were discovered in a gravel pit near Taplow Station in 1854. Little jaws are dropping and little eyes are popping. The children are ready to be whisked on a whistle-stop tour through 12,000 years of local history in 33 minutes. Well, perhaps not every single one of them, but my ruse works well enough. Silence reigns throughout as everyone gets a flavour of Taplow's fascinating story. A week later 6-year-old **Jamie Ashford** will still wide-eyed when he taps me on the elbow to ask "Is it really, really true that mammuffs were the first people in Taplow?" I'll be pleased to think that perhaps I have sown the seed in his young mind that history can be fun.

Having Fun with History

Taplow Village Centre / 4th July 2009

This is Taplow Heritage Day. **Marc Boden** and **Adrian** (**Miv**) **Wayland-Smith** thought we should have a little fun by gathering to enjoy an exhibition and a few glasses of wine. Or was it the other way around? We are surrounded by history. The **Village Centre** was formerly the Reading Room, built in 1894 by public subscription and extended almost eight decades later. This History appears in its originally intended form as a words-and-pictures wall display. It and other exhibits pale by comparison with the magnificent **Sheila Horton** murals depicting Taplow in the early-1990s. **Karl Lawrence** approaches. He has an idea....

The Cottage, Rectory Road / 31st August 2014

At Karl's invitation, the History evolved to become an enhanced *Powerpoint* presentation on 30th October 2009 at the Annual General Meeting of the **Hitcham & Taplow Society** (the Society). **Brian Smith** asked afterwards if I was thinking of turning it into a book. I said that I hadn't but I would. Now I have and this is it.

I started out with the perfectly sound notion that all good stories unfold in chapters. It makes the telling easier and the listening (or reading). The distinct incremental steps in Taplow's tale were quickly clear. Ancient comings and goings evolved the original settlement on high to take on first pagan then Christian significance. Medievals minded their manors as travellers wended west and back again. Royal favourites stirred up an elite social whirl. Taplow found itself centre-stage in the affairs of the nation. Focus sharpened to reveal real lives up on the common, in the village and down in the valley. Those who had been born to money were gradually replaced by others who had made it but pretended otherwise. The cycles repeated on a grander international scale; social whirlwinds spun at **Cliveden**, **Taplow Court** and ***Skindles*** rocking boats and setting trends. And finally – just within living memory – everything began to settle down to today's more egalitarian contentment. This framework affords me a natural sweep across the ages to celebrate individuals who are worthy of celebration for adding splashes of colour to local life and times.

Four other thoughts occurred as I've examined the fluff in Taplow's navel.

Firstly: **Tony Meats** has a point – dipping straight into detail makes it difficult to see the wood for the trees. Consequently in the second half of 2013 my tapestry was unravelled and rewoven to create the 'Big Picture' of the first two chapters – **Making and Shaping** and **Comings and Goings** – in order to give context to the more intricate threads that follow.

Secondly: nowhere stops abruptly at boundaries drawn down the years to define church or civil domains. Even today Taplow's ecclesiastical span doesn't match its extent as a South Bucks electoral ward. So where does the place begin and end? For convenience, my spotlight in 2009 shone on the trinity of Amerden, Taplow and Cliveden. I omitted much mention not only of neighbours such as Hitcham but also of the broader sweep of history in this little corner of Buckinghamshire and how parish boundaries have wandered over time. The wall display and slide presentations were limited by space and time constraints that now do not apply. This is the perfect opportunity to put things right by taking the occasional **Sideways Glance**.

Thirdly: History likes written sources. It turns its nose up when people tell tales. And yet – unless it is an eye-witness account – all history is verbal until somebody writes it down and thereby somehow magically makes apparent fact of what might be opinion. Even modern archaeologists can contradict: the estimated date for Taplow's first St Nicholas' Church slipped by some four centuries in the decade between 1995 and 2005. Did the latter conclusion relegate the former from fact to opinion? The fact is that History has a history of evolving, of historians not being on the same page. Some reject all except 'facts' even though they may not be what they claim. Some see possibilities that seem to add up but can't be proven. History is all the better for it, which is why it is wise to keep a pinch of salt handy and accept that what's being said can add value to what's been read. Consequently it is essential for this History to tell some of these **Tall Tales** for they add flavour and texture to the fabric of life, the universe and everything with their different perspectives, possibilities, myths and mistakes. And it is a must to explore telltale unsubstantiated sources under titles such as **Old Bayley Lore** and **Hurn's Turn**.

Finally: one of history's most valuable gifts is a shared identity that connects the dim-and-distant with what is happening right now. All of us are making history daily. Consequently my tales of the recent past and present have been enhanced by listening to locals. The children of St Nicolas' School have helped me with up-to-date snapshots summarised in the **Eyes of a Child** and the recollections of some of whom have lived hereabouts for decades are captured in **About Grout**, **Harding Happening**, **The Forsyth Saga**, **The Man from Auntie**, **So Long** and elsewhere.

If the sum total is not your cup of tea, have a word with Marc or Miv or Karl. They started it.

By Numbers

The Cottage, Rectory Road / 4th July 2013

I am old enough to remember 'old money'. For perhaps eight centuries until 1971, a pound was divided into 20 shillings and each shilling into 12 pence. Six pounds, eight shillings and tuppence was written numerically as £6/8/2 or £6 8s 2d, with the *d* deriving from the Roman *denarius* (the Angles introduced the *penny* but didn't make it a *p*), the *s* from the Roman *solidus* (later used for *shilling*, the value of an Anglo-Saxon cow in Kent) and the £ from the first letter of *libra* (a Roman pound weight of silver). Nobody alive today ever spent a *groat* (4d) or a *mark* (13s 4d) but people in this book did, and some will remember that until 42 years ago a *guinea* was a term used for a sum of £1 1s (£1.05 nowadays). When I mention money, I have added in brackets the rounded current value based on the most appropriate calculator of inflation available at www.measuringworth.com.

I have used a similar philosophy for measurements. Call me old-fashioned but I like it that we British are going metric inch-by-inch. Almost everyone in this book sized length and distance at 12 inches to the foot, three feet to the yard and 1,760 yards to the mile. Few would have had a clue (and fewer could have cared less) that an inch is 25.4 millimetres, a foot 30.48 centimetres, a yard 0.9144 metres and a mile 1.61 kilometres. The same applied to weight (a pound is 0.4536 kilograms) and to area (an acre is 0.4047 hectares). I won't tell you again.

The Diamond Jubilee Beacon

The Honourable
Dominic Grieve QC MP
with George Sandy

Claire Ashton Tait
and Juliet Lecchini

The beacon burns on
Tæppa's Mound / 2012

Victoria Wayland-Smith with her mother Hilary and daughter Scarlett / 2012

Taplow Heritage Day

Keira Smales suggests how her father might improve his display / 2009

Chapter One

Making and Shaping

In which Taplow came to be

Making It

Whys and Wherefores

The Old Churchyard / 6th January 2014

Let's begin at the beginning. There's no getting away from it: Taplow is here because it is high.

It is hard to separate History from Legend, fact from guesswork, but archaeological excavations in 1999 and 2005 suggest that the Taplow of today may have begun a long, long time ago. Let's imagine the moment....

A blink takes us back 10,300 years....

The glaciers came as far south as not-yet Beaconsfield. It is warmer now they are receding northwards. Down below in the valley early Mesolithic Man and a few of his mates are following the tracks of reindeer or whatever they hope will be on their menu tonight. Two of them climb the hill. They turn to admire the view and realise that up here any impending threats could be seen coming for miles. They separate to explore further. One squelches into a little stream. He follows its course to find something magic: a freshwater spring almost a hundred feet above the river. His shallow forehead disappears altogether as his bushy eyebrows rise to meet his hairline. He grunts softly to himself in surprise and delight then more loudly to call his pal over to admire his discovery. The excited expressions on their faces suggest that they have hit the jackpot: a high and easily-defensible plateau with the added bonus of running water. This is just the place to make camp, and so they do. And so will their descendants for many-a-moon.

These ancient visitors won't stay long anywhere but the complete tranchet axe and possibly another, the struck flints and charred hazelnut shells they'll leave behind here in the grounds of what will be **Taplow Court** may well be the oldest evidence of humans being in Buckinghamshire and amongst the oldest in England since the last Ice Age melted away. They are unaware that even more ancient hominids had been here before them.

Mother Nature

The White Stuff

South Lodge Pit, Mill Lane / 6th July 2008

Taplow clearly owes its being to its topography. What is now high was once very low, what is now solid rock was once alive. The chalk ridge on which Ancient Britons made their home began beneath the sea. When you next wind down **Mill Lane**, look to your right and blink back in time....

Deep in a Cretaceous Ocean / 80 million years ago

The microscopic skeletal remains of billions of marine plankton called cocolithosphores are settling on the bed of this vast, warm ocean just as they have for over 50 million years, just as they will continue to do for perhaps another 15 million. They accumulate at no more than one-and-a-half inches every 1,000 years. The low percentage of minerals in this mix indicates that this spot is far from land. The contours of the sea bed form a submarine channel which will be known as a *cuvette* or perhaps a *paleoscope*. This creates a current that sweeps away finer particles and thus concentrates the more granular phosphatic materials which consist of phosphate-filled and -coated foraminiferal tests (the shells of another microscopic marine animal), faecal pellets and phospatised macrofossil fragments, intraclasts and vertebrae remains.

What an incredible picture, but not half as amazing as what will happen when Africa arrives with a bang. This distant continent will begin to throw its weight around in another 30 million years or so. Its collision with Europe will force the Alps upwards and cause secondary geological upheavals in the Earth's crust which thrust southern England above the surface of the sea as it falls gradually by some 600 feet. Water and ice will sculpt the land for millennia until there is a river running eastwards from not-yet Oxfordshire, across what will be **Dropmore** and on through what will become Hertfordshire, Essex and beyond to where it will join a larger river – let's call it the Rhine – and flow north to find the sea somewhere east of 21st Century Newcastle-upon-Tyne.

South Lodge Pit, Mill Lane / 6th July 2008

Most see here an overgrown quarry. Some remember the enormous icehouse: a tall, thin egg-shaped brick structure demolished in the 1960s for being a safety hazard. A hundred years ago Grenfell staff packed winter ice from **Bapsey Pond** in there to keep cool the **Taplow Court** cuisine come the summer. Geologists wax lyrical that the exposed cliff face is the only known British example of Santorian-to-early-Campanian phosphatic chalk. Its unusual character was first recognised in 1891 by the Museum of Practical Geology in London. In 1905 Harold White and Llewellyn Treacher published an extensive paper describing the pit and its phosphatic deposits and fossils. And in 1987 it was declared a Site of Special Scientic Interest of great importance for stratigraphy and the geological history of Late Cretaceous palaeontology and sedimentology. It contains abundant fossils of encrusting annelids and oysters, burrows and foraminifera presented in several horizons along with bivalves, echinoids, belemites, ammonites and crinoids that settled on ancient seabeds at the dawn of time. Of course, most will be at sea with all this scientific stuff but the message is overwhelming: this is an SSSI that causes much excitement to those with the knowledge to be excited; long may it do just that.

Phosphorus is essential for life: in various forms it is a component of human and animal cell membranes and molecules, an excellent fertiliser and important in food processing and the production of steel, glass for lamps, fine china, toothpaste, matches and munitions. This last application sparked analysis of Taplow's chalk during both 20th Century world wars which confirmed a phosphate content of between 5% and 20% but concluded that extraction would be uneconomical in an area of only 300 yards wide by no more than a mile long. However, not half-a-mile upstream, a *Thames Water* pumping station enjoys the conveniently semi-secret site of a disused quarry in Taplow Court's western cliff....

Taplow Quarry / 6th July 1533

Chalk extraction may have begun here in the Roman era and will continue modestly for centuries more. Although too soft to be used as stone for building, Taplow's chalk is still a very valuable commodity. It can be ground down to make an alkaline fertiliser for neutralising acidic soils, or burnt to make quicklime for use in construction as mortar, cement or whitewash. That heavily-loaded barge is heading downstream to Hampton Court where its cargo of quicklime will be used to make mortar to bond the bricks of **King Henry VIII**'s palace. The watermen will be careful to keep it dry for they run the risk of not only having their skin, eyes and innards burned by this nasty stuff but also of fire and explosions because, when it reacts with water, enough heat is released to ignite anything combustible. It has long been used as a detonator for explosives or a blinding agent: **King Henry III**'s navy famously threw it downwind into the faces of his French enemies.

The Hard Stuff

Cliveden Cliff / Perhaps half-a-million years ago

The weather is so very nippy that glaciers have crept south to dam the ancient river near not-yet St Albans. An icy lake is getting deeper and broader. Something's got to give: suddenly the waters burst southwards between Berkshire's Winter Hill and Buckinghamshire's Cliveden Cliff to spread over the broad plain to the south before running eastwards to make a new estuary that will separate Essex and Kent. Over hundreds of thousands of years of alternate freezing and warming, water and ice will continue to shape the landscape. The river will gradually cut deeper to create a valley lined with stepped terraces of sand and gravel up to 25 feet deep and rarely less than 15 that is relatively free of mud and clay. This layer will be overlain with fertile loess or loam deposits that will become known as 'brick earth' for being perfect for making bricks. One particular gravel ridge will first provide a ford across the Thames at **Bray Rigle** (or *Rhydle*, meaning *ford*), the gravel bed of which will one day provide the foundation for a graceful railway bridge (whatever that is). Other gravel deposits will await the likes of ***Summerleaze*** and ***William Boyer & Son*** who will make it their business to dig them out for use as aggregate in concrete.

The second Taplow Station / 6th January 1891

Just 100 yards west of here and a few steps north is a quarry first carved over 50 years ago to extract gravel to build the railway embankment. Anyone passing this spot between 1854 and 1856 might have seen two gentlemen scrabbling on their hands and knees like schoolboys. It is likely that the Reverend **Charles Kingsley** knew Taplow through his wife Frances (Fanny), daughter of **Pascoe Grenfell** of ***Taplow House***. His fellow scrabbler **Sir John Lubbock** has seven younger brothers, two with Taplow connections which probably have their roots in those notable diggings over three decades ago: **Edgar Lubbock** is the current tenant at ***Springfield*** and in 1888 Henry Lubbock's daughter Cecil married **Dick Grenfell** of ***Hill House***, son of **Elizabeth & (Charles) Seymour Grenfell** of ***Elibank***. It's a small world.

Both the Reverend and Sir John have grown to eminence as archaeologists and much more besides. Kingsley became Regius Professor of Modern History at Cambridge University and later canon of Chester Cathedral while writing *The Water Babies* and other novels including one which has led to the founding of the only place in England to have its own exclamation mark: the Devon village *Westward Ho!* Lubbock is now an innovative banker, politician and polymath who as Member of Parliament (MP) for Maidstone invented Bank Holidays in 1871 and first advocated proportional representation in 1883. He is a past-president of the Linnean Society, a Fellow of the Royal Society, a Privy Counsellor, chairman of the London County Council and author of influential books including *Pre-Historic Times* in which he was first to distinguish the earlier and later Stone Ages by coining the terms *Paleolithic* and *Neolithic*. In 1900 he will be created 1st Baron Avebury in recognition for having saved its megalithic henge for posterity. Little did these gentlemen know it at the time but their excited exploits in Taplow's substrata were probably defining moments in their lives. Unearthing the remains of pre-historic creatures fuelled the thirst for knowledge that has driven them to fame and fascinated everyone from their friend Charles Darwin to our friend **Jamie Ashford**.

Further gravel extraction to widen the embankment has since extended the quarry into a reverse L-shaped excavation that extends north along **Station Road** to **Taplow Grammar School**. And now another party of gentlemen are busy at the toe of the L in the area Kingsley and Lubbock examined. However, this new interest is geological not paleozoological. They represent the

Ordnance Geological Survey, an organisation doing a nationwide study to get to the bottom of what Britain is made of. The rising, flattening and rising again of **Town Lane** as it runs up **Berry Hill** is a topographical clarity that will inspire **John Rhodes** to take the name Taplow for the eighth of ten Thames Valley river terraces.

Human Nature

Getting Stoned

The Old Churchyard / 6th January 2014

Taplow Terrace was long in the making. Mother Nature started the job around a quarter-of-a-million years back and took only half the time since to get it done. But it was worth all the effort. Archaeologists know that really ancient nomadic hominids explored the Thames Valley because hidden in the depths of the terrace are hundreds of their stone artefacts, many in excellent condition because they haven't been rolled and crushed under creeping glaciers. Palaeolithic tools and artefacts found locally include an antler pick and flint handaxes, blades, scrapers and flakes at **Taplow Court**, **Ten Acre Field**, **Hitchambury**, **Roque Meadow**, **Poplar Farm**, **Taplow Mill** and in the River Thames. It is incredible to think they were crafted more than 40,000 years ago, possibly even as far back as 200,000 years. And it is remarkable to imagine a farmstead that may have stretched across **Town Field** – now part of **Berry Hill Farm** – from the Paleolithic era to the late Iron Age.

The richest archaeological evidence of Mesolithic humans being hereabouts dates from about 9,000 to 8,000 years ago in the Colne Valley at Denham, Uxbridge and Iver. Tranchet axes and other flint and antler tools indicate activity at Taplow Court, Roque Meadow and down by the river. Other evidence at Marlow, Burnham, Wexham and Langley reveals that South Bucks was a pleasant place to be even way back when. East Berks too, where the nearly 600 hand-axes found in and around Furze Platt suggest a hive of industry, possibly even a permanent settlement. Flora and fauna varied as the climate and water levels fluctuated but the fast-flowing river teemed with fish. Beavers, otters and various voles lived in the reed beds along quieter stretches. Mammoth, musk ox and wood mice, red deer, roe deer and reindeer, aurochs (wild cattle), wild boars, bison and badgers, foxes, hares, horses and even elephants and Etruscan rhino came down to the river from the dense forests of alder and ash, birch, oak, elm, lime, hazel and holly, juniper and pine, yew and even water chestnut in the warmest times.

The Old Churchyard / 4,000 years ago

Mother Nature made Taplow. Neolithic human nature began to shape it perhaps a thousand years ago. Nobody stayed here for long. They came up from their nomadic settlements by the river to cut wood, keep watch or find brief refuge in wet weather when the myriad streams overflow.

Life is different now: pastoral and generally peaceful. Fired clay, charred wheat and barley, charcoal from oak, maple, ash, blackthorn and hawthorn, numerous sherds of pottery – including three from twisted cord decorated collared urns – and worked flint hammerstones, flakes, blades and scrapers will be left in tree-throw holes and intercutting hollows up here to provide rare evidence of early Bronze Age domestication.

In another thousand years a timber palisade backed by a raised walkway, a trench-built palisade, a ditch and rampart will enclose an area of 2.5 acres in which evidence will survive of roundhouses and rectangular structures. This hillfort will continue to be home for up to 200 people for perhaps another 200 years before being abandoned. It will stand empty for over 300 years until some time between 480 and 400 BC when early Iron Age Britons increase it to three acres by constructing a new U-shaped ditch and timber-laced rampart. Soon afterwards a section of the rampart including its gate will be deliberately destroyed by fire. Later a V-shaped ditch will surround the whole hillfort which will be remembered on 19th Century maps as a *British Camp*....

Happy Campers

The Old Churchyard / 12th January 2014

We'll call the camp **Taplow Castle**. It affords archaeologists wonderful opportunities for debate. Was the original late Bronze Age palisade for defence or for show? Did the elevated location of this hillfort indicate the social or military power of its occupants, or both? Was it abandoned due to a decline in river trade or to encroaching heather making heaths of deforested areas, or both? Did the early Iron Age enclosure extend southwards to the edge of the plateau to deliberately increase in its visibility and offer a symbol of power? Was this rampart burnt during an attack or for ritual reasons? And why make the hillfort multivallate by adding the third ditch?

History isn't certain but there's no doubt that the place had something wonderful. Silts settled onto the gravel to be compressed into impermeable clay layers upon which rainwater flows south to the edge of the ridge where it trickles from springs at an unusually high elevation: hence **Bapsey Pond**, closes called **Springfield**, **Stockwells** and **Wellbank** and the trickle that runs down **Rectory Road**. It must have been exceptionally convenient for Ancient Britons to find a reliable source of water up here where they could slake their thirst while feeling safe from their enemies. But that wasn't the half of it. For them such springs were supernatural, perhaps portals to the afterlife. History is brave enough to suggest that they regarded this hilltop as a mystical location blessed by the pagan gods, a site of religious and ritual significance that could be seen from miles around, and the view was awesome. It was a site to die for and perhaps to be buried at: the very model of Location Location Location until about 2,000 years ago, which is just about when the Romans arrived.

Sherds of poorly-preserved pottery deposited here and hereabouts throughout the Roman era suggest there was a settlement nearby, possibly at **Taplow Cricket Club** or within the (as yet) unexcavated bounds of the Castle. However it is likely there was a hiatus of occupation from around 200 to 460 AD. Thereafter the site seems to have been in use throughout the Anglo-Saxon era but perhaps not as a settlement. Although the ditches gradually eroded, they may still have been over six feet deep during that period and it wasn't until the 11th or 12th Century that they were finally filled in, perhaps around the time the Norman church was built.

Taplow Quarry

The White Stuff revealed / 2012

Shaping Up

Parish Patchwork

Taplow Castle / 16th November 1012

Like most counties, Buckinghamshire is already what it will be for a thousand years bar a few tweaks. It is divided into 18 *hundreds*, so-called for being land sufficient to sustain 100 men-at-arms and their households, each subdivided into *tithings* capable of supporting 10 such households. Perhaps the county's long, relatively slim shape originated 130 years ago when it was a buffer-zone between the sedentary Anglo-Saxons and the invading Vikings. **Alfred** (later **the Great**) raised a defensive force in the Chiltern Hundreds – then including Aylesbury as well as the usual suspects of Burnham, Stoke and Desborough – only for them to be marooned in the south-western corner of Danelaw for 23 years.

The Danes were dominant but not daft. Why change what worked? The mathematics aren't decimal perfect – Taplow is one of 13 tithings in the Burnham Hundred which covers a total of 100 hides (about 1,200 acres) – but the logical hierarchy does the job. The other tithings are Amersham, Beaconsfield, the Chalfonts of St Giles and St Peter, Chenies, Chesham, Chesham Bois, Dorney, Farnham, Hitcham, Penn and of course Burnham itself (with Upper Boveney). And that's how they'll still shape up in a thousand years except for two things: Hedgerley Dean and Seer Green will have split from Farnham Royal, and they will all be called *parishes*.

The northernmost of these tithings are along the southern edge of the Chiltern Hills, an area "covered with woods and groves of beeches so thick as to be impassable". In about 30 years, some scribe in **King Edward the Confessor**'s court will note that the forest is "a harbour of thieves... a refuge for divers sorts of wild beasts such as wolves, wild boars, wild oxen, robbers, outlaws and fugitives to the great annoyance and danger of all passengers". The Confessor will have Leofstan, Abbot of St Albans, lead efforts to clear tracks through the woods – pretty much along the lines of the 20th Century A40, A413 and A41 – but the Thames Valley will remain the much safer highway.

The southern tithings of Taplow, Hitcham, Burnham and Farnham already have their rather curious long, thin shapes which neatly divide different terrains between the communities so that each had a riverbank (for fishing and for osiers to make baskets, kiddles, fences and wattle to daub), water meadows (for rushes and summer grazing), arable land (for growing crops), higher, dryer land with freshwater springs (perfect places for villages), grassland (for pastoral grazing), common land (for rough summer

Maps 1, 2 & 3 – The Elongated and Evolving Parish
Long, Slim and Handsome

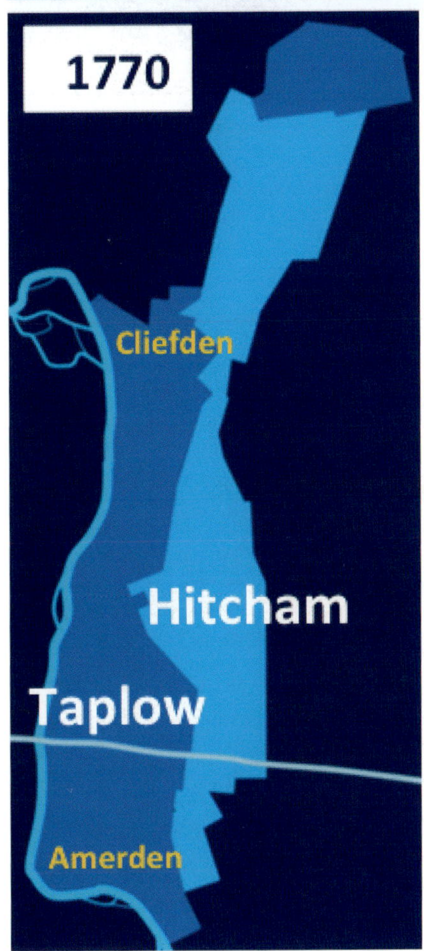

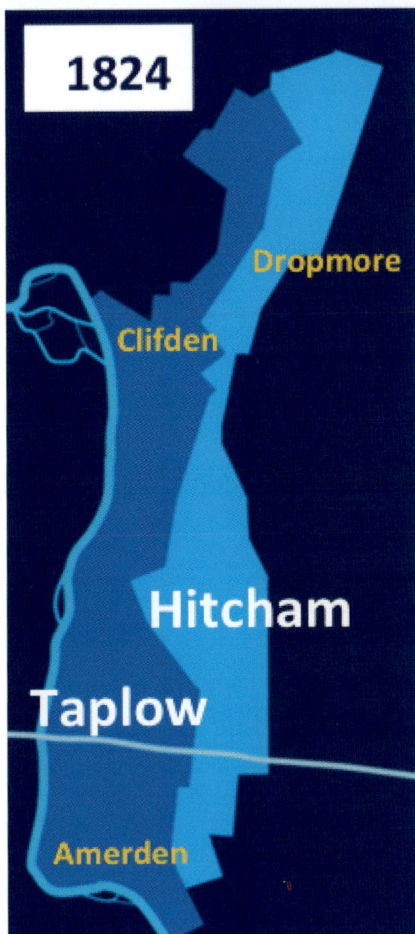

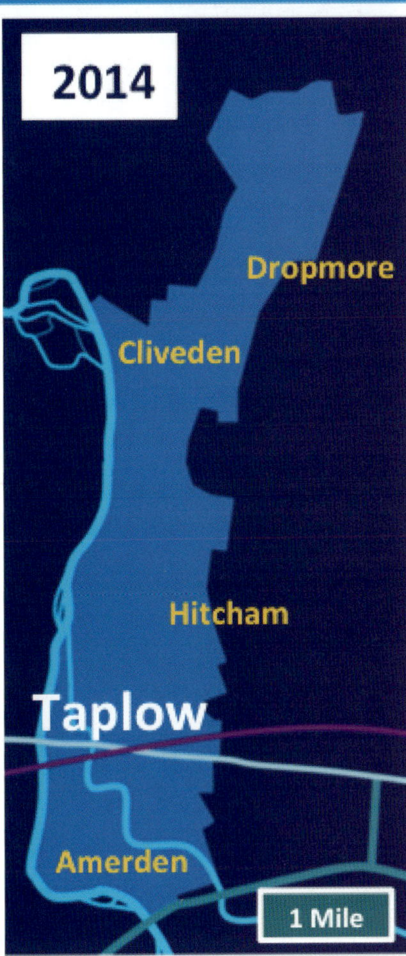

Primary Sources: Jeffreys' Map 1770 (amended for Inclosure Map s1779/1787), Bryant's Map 1824 and Ordnance Survey 2008

grazing) and woods (for fowl to peck, pigs to rummage, goats to gobble and humans to hunt game, take timber for tools and construction or collect turf and faggots for firewood). In Taplow's case, here is the root of its Amerden-Taplow-Cliveden trinity of valley, village and common, a convention that probably dates back to Neolithic times with added Anglo-Saxons twists of pragmatic disconnection [*see Maps 1, 2 & 3*].

Finding the Manor House

Taplow Court / 16th November 2013

At first glance, Taplow Village appears to conform to the usual English model. It is anchored at one end by an ancient castle where the Good Lord and his lordship lived side-by-side: History, Church and Manor in partnership.

Looks can be deceiving. Taplow has been conventional for only 400-and-a-few years. The change came in 1598 with the construction of the original **Taplow House**, probably the home of royal stewards and favourites. Local authority passed to the first **Thomas Hampson** in 1528. Ten years later he transferred his seat to the second **Taplow Court** which remained home for successive lords of the manor spanning three centuries.

Amerden Priory / 16th November 2013

The medieval heartbeat wasn't at **Cliveden**, which never had more than a hunting lodge or two before 1666 when it became for evermore a rich man's indulgence. Although it would be logical for Taplow Court to sit on the site of a previous manor house or houses, there is inconclusive physical evidence of a previous building on the site before the first few years of the 1600s. Amateur excavations in 1996 revealed a section of chalk block wall five feet wide and almost four feet deep. Associated 12th or 13th Century pottery may give a clue as to the age of this wall but not its purpose and although its size suggests it was part of something substantial, no documentary evidence supports the assumption that this was Taplow's manor house.

Some sources speculate that the secular hub of the manor may originally have been on the site of ***Amerden Ponds*** where a modern curved terrace has replaced ***Amerden Grove*** which may itself have superseded Amerden Mill (if it ever existed). However the prime suspect has to be here on a triangular island created in or soon after 1197 to protect a cell of monks from Merton Priory. ***Amerden Priory*** is now being lovingly restored by **Emily & Matthew Ball**. They think this and possibly ***The Other House*** next door might together have been ***Amerden Place***, first noted as the home of **Henry Manfield** in 1540 just two years after the dissolution of the Priory.

So Long – The Manfield Manor

Amerden House / 16th November 2013

This wonderful Whitlaw mansion has been home to veterinarian **David Long** for 42 years during which (according to **Iris Midlane**) he has become "the most knowledgeable man in Taplow". This walking, talking treasure trove of facts and carefully honed hypotheses begs to differ with his neighbours. He is adamant that today's ***Amerden Bank*** was "the stable quarters of a 15th Century house" and that while *Amerden Priory* is of great antiquity and may have been "in the Manfield family" it was never grand enough to be the seat of those wealthy medieval lords. So where exactly was this grand house? A miniscule mark on the Inclosure Map of 1779 suggests it stood to the east of today's *Priory* but, with typically definitive iffyness, David will only say it was "within the moated triangle". History can be irritating like that [*see Map 4*].

Sideways Glance

Chiltern Hundreds

Disraeli House, Aylesbury End, Beaconsfield / 11th July 2014

If the Chiltern Hills were a scary place before the Conqueror came, they were even worse after two centuries of Norman and Plantagenet rule. King Henry III appointed a Crown Steward and a Bailiff of the Chiltern Hundreds – by then just Burnham, Stoke and Desborough – to use whatever strong-arm tactics were necessary to bring their wild wooded hills under control. It was a thankless task. Not until 600 years later did things change at last to create the mix of woodland, grassland and occasional arable fields still evident today. And despite all that, Legend tells of wolves prowling the hills into the 18th Century and rare native English butterflies, birds, insects and flowers (including orchids). Even the freshwater fairy shrimp can still be found occasionally.

Nowadays the office of Steward and Bailiff of the Chiltern Hundreds has an entirely different connotation. As a constituent of the Burnham Hundred, Taplow sits unwittingly in a vehicle of legal fiction that enables an MP to resign his or her seat in the House of Commons, an act technically forbidden to this day by a provision dating back to 1624 when MPs could be elected against their will or even without their knowledge.

This change took centuries to unfold. As civilisation edged into the Chilterns, the need for forceful pacification dissipated and finally disappeared. The roles of the Steward and Bailiff were first combined then reduced to a sinecure and eventually in the 17th Century to a nominal position of honour affording no financial benefit. The title did little but gather dust until 1751 when Henry Pelham's government noted that the 1701 Act of Settlement disqualified MPs if they accepted "an office of profit under

Map 4 – Finding the Manor House
Within the Priory of Merton's Moated Triangle?

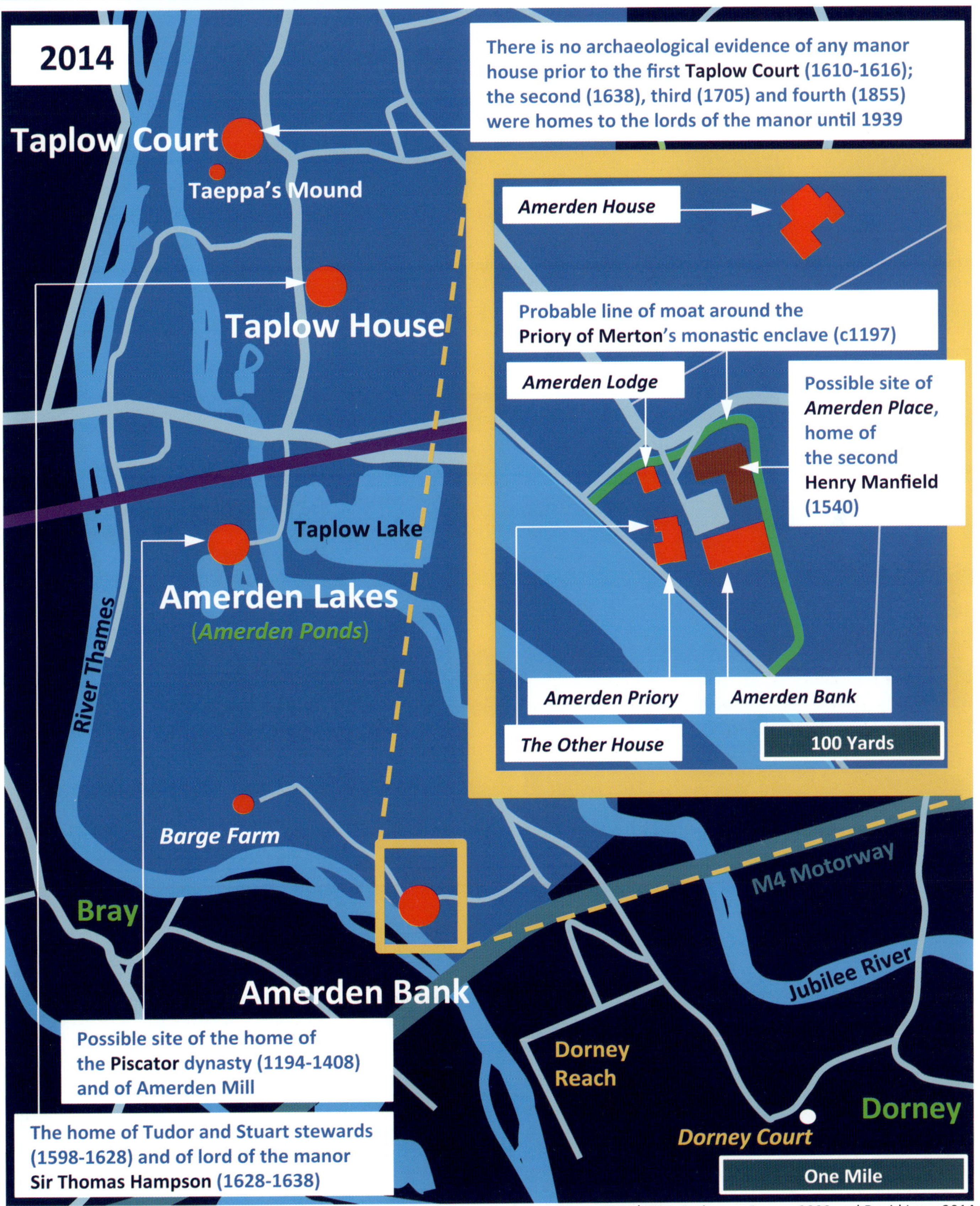

Primary Sources: Inclosure Maps 1779/1787, Ordnance Survey 2008 and David Long 2014

the Crown", an office such as the Steward and Bailiff of the Chiltern Hundreds. Here was the perfect procedural device to circumvent the 1624 prohibition, a 'departure lounge' for hundreds of MPs down the years. Any question of this being an honourable means of departure was removed by **William Gladstone** in 1861 but he didn't alter the convention that each appointee remains in office until such time as another erstwhile MP enters it – sometimes only a matter of minutes – or they apply to the Chancellor of the Exchequer to be released.

The parliamentary constituency of Beaconsfield now includes much of the Chiltern Hundreds. Despite today being relieved of his post as Attorney General, our current MP the Right Honourable **Dominic Grieve** QC has given no indication that he wishes to assume the rights and responsibilities of this ancient office.

Satellites, Slivers and Slices

Dividing the Spoils

The Gables, Pikels / 14th January 1891

The builder, self-styled architect, church organist and renowned parish clerk **James Rutland** is the epitomy of the Victorian amateur antiquarian. He has an unquenchable yearning to be a history-maker, or at least to learn all there is to know about why things are as they are and to preserve and promote that knowledge as widely as possible. Today he is poring over four maps that tell two tales spanning almost 90 years: one of the ways changing with the whims of those with wherewithall, the other of the apparently evolving extent of the parish.

Maps 5 & 6 – Changing Ways
From Jefferys to Bryant

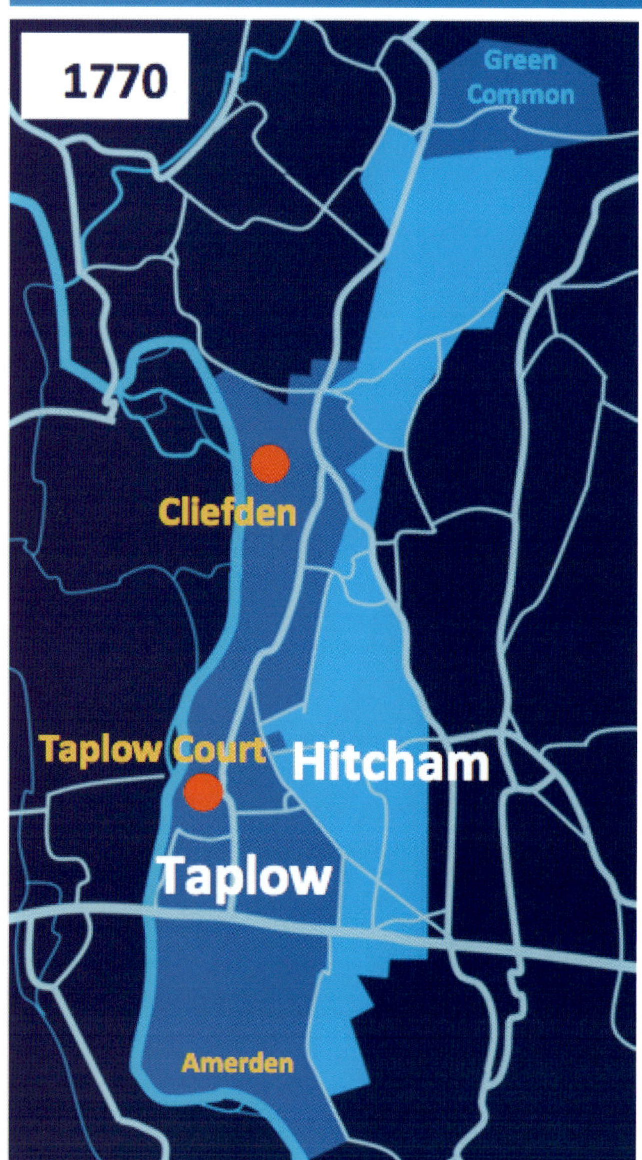

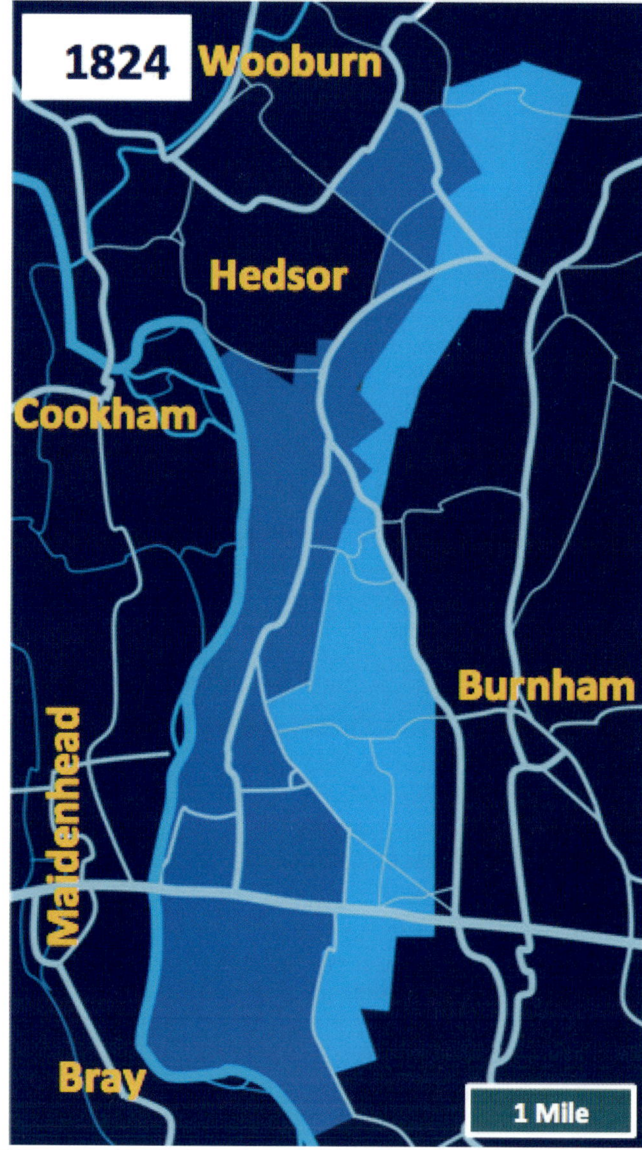

Primary Sources: Jeffreys' Map 1770 (amended for Inclosure Maps 1779/1787) and Bryant's Map 1824

The oldest of Rutland's maps is that of the County of Buckinghamshire published in 1770 by Thomas Jefferys, Geographer to King George III. It shows the old way north running from the Bath Road up Town Lane to Taplow Court to turn east along **Church Road**, north along **The Phygtle** and **Back Lane** then east past ***Hitcham Parsonage*** to meander north to meet the road from Burnham. For much of this route, the road prescribed the boundary between Taplow and Hitcham. Jefferys has lightly sketched in to the west what might be a lesser track or perhaps the first Lord **Orkney**'s more direct road from Taplow Court to ***The New Inn***. The Taplow Inclosure Map of 1787 confirms that this new road had superseded the old way as far as **Captain's Field** to the north-east of Clifden. There it turned west down to **Hedsor Wharf** and then up the Wye Valley through Wooburn while lesser tracks meandered across the commons through **Cabrook** and past **Skipcot**, Lillyfield and Woodlands Farms towards Beaconsfield.

If Arthur Bryant's 1824 county map is anything to go by, these age-old ways were not to the liking of Lord **Grenville**. Soon after he acquired Dropmer Hill in 1792, new roads were laid to route wayfarers west and north of his splendid new home at **Dropmore** which spans the parish boundary between Hitcham and Burnham. The old ways across the common to Cabrook were closed to the public. Some remained estate tracks while others were reclaimed by the woodlands and are lost forever [*see Maps 5 & 6*].

The elongated parishes and their disconnections still survive. Burnham encircles Dorney's wood, conveniently called Dorneywood. Boveney has two satellites: one of pasture sandwiched between Dorney and Burnham, the other merely a wood in northern Burnham. Hitcham is a whole by virtue of a narrow isthmus connecting its farmland with its wooded common land to the north. However, unlike Bryant's map, those drawn in 1787 and 1851 confirm Taplow's northern satellite, a half-mile by three-quarters patch of almost 200 acres comprising much of Dipple Wood and Green Common with ***Hodds Farm*** (originally *Didler's End*) as its western anchor. Rutland believes this shaping is a remnant of ancient communities dividing the spoils.

Dropmore House / 14th January 1934

Eton Rural District Council rules the roost around here. It is about to indulge in the traditional local authority pastime of tinkering with boundaries. Disconnections will be done away with and Hitcham shared between its neighbours. Taplow will lose half its satellite to Beaconsfield but gain the top end of Hitcham to connect its top and bottom. At this very moment, some draftsman is proscribing upon his maps its new eastern boundary which heads south from the halfway kink in **Green Common Lane** to transfer into Taplow ***Sheepcote Farm***, ***Hales Corner*** and the western half of Dropmore House and its grounds, formerly Hitcham Common. It skirts **Parliament Lane** to reach **Huntswood Lane** and then slices through the heart of Hitcham. It runs no longer down the bridle path to **Hunts Lane** and along the middle of Back Lane, **Station Road** and **Marsh Lane**. Instead it is nudged eastward to follow **Chestnut Drive** south, skip west to leave Old Hitcham School (not yet ***Cloverdown***) and ***Hitcham Rectory*** in Burnham, skirt the eastern edge of ***Hill Farm***, run down the far reaches of ***Lea Rig Farm*** and across **Hitcham Field** and **William Wood**'s nursery to zigzag onwards through the fields east of Marsh Lane. Those to the east of this line will have their letters delivered from Slough, those to the west from Maidenhead just as they have always been. When the Post Office imposes postcodes in the 1970s, much of the southern length of this 1934 line will prescribe where SL1 and SL6 abut [*see Map 7*]. Taplow will be in the latter, thus having the illusion of being within Maidenhead, an inconvenience for anyone after 1986 who makes the mistake of thinking **Cliveden Hotel** is in Berkshire.

Beating the Northern Bounds

Taplow Court / 26th October 1946

A large party is gradually assembling just inside the gates of **Taplow Court** under the leadership of the eminent Chairman of the Parish Council, Major **George Bond** of ***Hawthorn*** on the Bath Road. Our purpose today is to perambulate the northern boundary of Taplow to observe the ancient tradition of 'Beating the Bounds' [*see Map 8*]. As Parish Clerk, it falls to **Arthur Webb** of ***Priory Cottage*** to note names as everyone arrives. He already has on his list **Maurice Rance** of ***The Hollies***, **Victor Williams** of ***Rectory Farmhouse***, **Arthur Mewton** of ***Hill Farm***, **George Emmett** (Lady **Desborough**'s agent at Taplow Court) and Noel Wiseman (Emmett's Cliveden equivalent and of its *North Lodge*). And here comes **Marie (Minna) Pearce-Serocold** of ***The Red Cottage*** and her brother Colonel **Oswald Serocold**, now neither Chairman of the Council nor even a resident of Taplow but still at 81 as keen as ever to maintain its traditions for old time's sake. **Frederick (Digger) Gardner** the schoolmaster looks to have his hands full with a contingent of local boys but fortunately Inspector Tomlin and PC Christopher Goddard are here to maintain order. The official party departs at 1.30pm. Mr Webb doesn't trouble to take the names of the gaggle of followers who straggle on foot or on horseback in its wake. He is too busy explaining that the boundary of Taplow has not been formally circumnavigated these past 17 years and that nobody can recall the last time such a procession disturbed the peace of the countryside by beating drums. Major Bond points out that our course today will follow the boundary as nearly as public rights of way and private permissions will allow. Miss Serocold chips in that the boundaries of the ecclesiastical parish have long since varied from those of the civil parish that constitutes the current Eton RDC electoral ward.

The party pauses at the eastern boundary by Old Hitcham School in order that tradition can be honoured by bumping a boy. The poor lad doesn't seem to enjoy the experience as much as his pals. We set off northwards along Chestnut Drive (the footpath across what will one day be a golf course) to find Huntswood Lane where it meets the main Burnham-Cliveden road (**Taplow Common Road**). We head west past the junction with Parliament Lane, once the main road north from Taplow, and turn right into Taplow Lodge Paddock (the southern extremities of **Cliveden Stud**), right down the main road, left past ***Nashdom*** and left again into Dropmore Park. After such a dull and wet summer, it is absolutely delightful to stroll in the sunshine. The woods are positively gleaming in their autumnal hues. **Lord Burnham** waves a greeting as we skirt Dropmore House to exit his estate at **Oak Lodge**. We pass Dropmore School and take the footpath into Bristles Wood and past Ashen Coppice on our right. Somebody

Map 7 – Borderers: Taplow Edging East

Slicing Hitcham

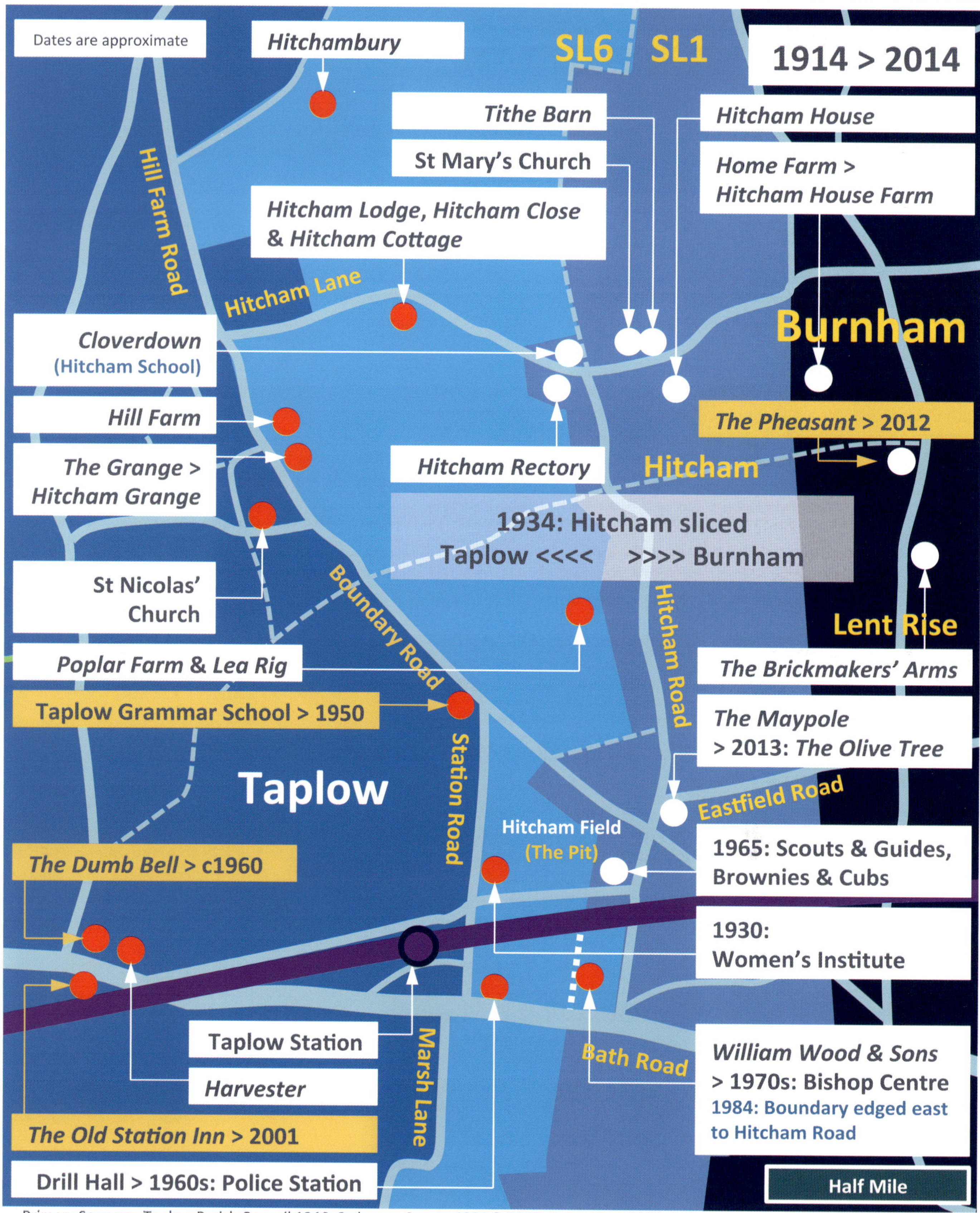

Primary Sources: Taplow Parish Council 1946, Ordnance Survey 1950 & 2008, Harry Hurn 2001, Robert Hanbury 2012 and Arthur Grout 2014

Map 8 – Beating the Northern Bounds

26th October – Approximately Twelve Miles

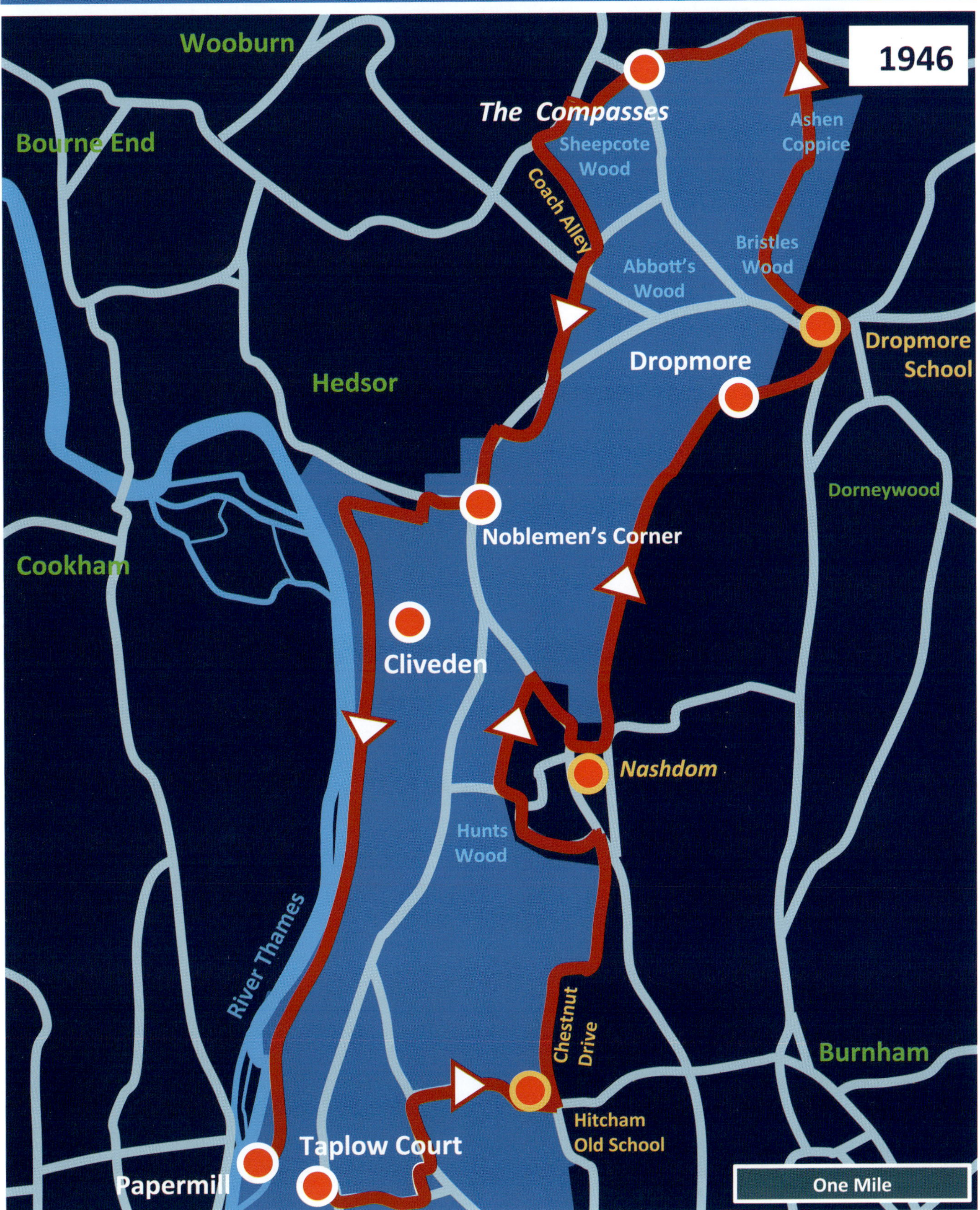

Primary Sources: Taplow Parish Council 1946 and Ordnance Survey 1950

says this footpath was once an ancient way from **Taplow Castle** to Bulstrode Castle at Gerrards Cross. If it's difficult to imagine Dropmore's tracks as thoroughfares until a century-and-a-half ago, it's harder still to picture the even more ancient ancestors in whose footsteps we now trudge. We reach **Green Common Lane** where Mr Webb nods north to **Dipple Wood** and east to the western fields of Woodlands and Hicknaham Farms. He explains that these parcels of land were once within Taplow's disconnected satellite which was lost to Beaconsfield in 1934 in exchange for half of Hitcham. It is a lot to take in but it's not far now before we reach the welcome of George Carey at ***The Compasses Inn***.

What a pleasure it is to take the weight off our feet and enjoy the Carey's generous hospitality. Refreshed by cups of his wife's hot sweet tea, we cross the road and take the footpath along the northern edge of **Sheepcote Woods** to emerge onto **Broad Lane**. At ***Roses Cottages***, we turn south-east down **Coach Alley** and south-west along Sheepcote Lane to detour briefly into Dropmore Park once more before returning to Grenville's western by-pass, long known as **Noblemen's Walk**, at its junction with **Hedsor Hill**. We pause for a moment while Mr Gardner explains to the boys that this is called **Nobleman's Corner** because at the formation of the United Kingdom in 1801 it marked the meeting point of three noble estates: Lord Grenville's Dropmore to the east, Lord Boston's Hedsor to the north-west and Lord Inchiquin's Cliveden to the south-west. As we resume our sojourn westward, we smile quietly to recollect the blank looks on the boys' faces. These illustrious gentlemen shaped all we see but evidently their names cut no ice with the youngsters of today.

We enter **Cliveden** by its Gas Works Gate (yes, Cliveden once had its very own gas works) and pause to admire the *Fountain of Love* before continuing west to the *Blenheim Pavilion* and down to the River Thames. The lowering sun sparkles in the water and plays on the yellowing leaves as we proceed along the riverbank past **My Lady Ferry**, ***Spring Cottage*** and onto the **Taplow Court** estate where at ***Joel's Lodge*** we turn right to **Taplow Paper Mills** where today's sojourn ends at 5.30pm. Mr Webb congratulates everyone for having walked approximately 12 miles and, ever diligent, reminds us of our agreement to reassemble in a week's time to perambulate the southern boundary....

Map 9 – Beating the Southern Bounds

2nd November – A Little More than Seven Miles

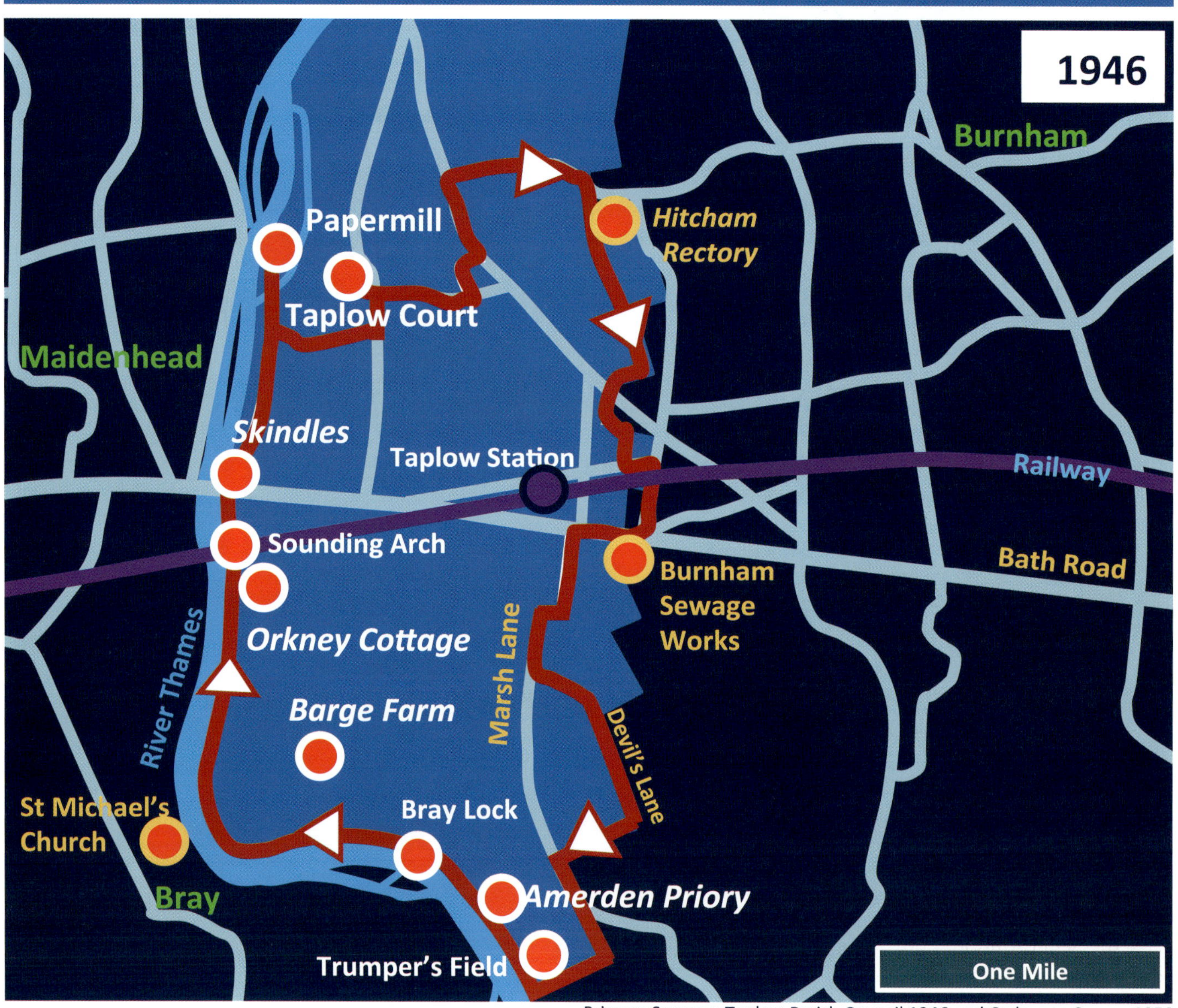

Primary Sources: Taplow Parish Council 1946 and Ordnance Survey 1950

Beating the Southern Bounds

Taplow Court / 2nd November 1946

And here we are again. Miss **Serocold** isn't too pleased with the unseasonably hot weather but she isn't one to shirk her duties. She strides out towards Old Hitcham School where she waits for us to catch up and chides **Major Bond** for his rather sedate pace. Last Saturday we went north from here; today we head south with Hitcham Rectory to our left [*see Map 9*]. As we walk along the spine of ***Lea Rig Farm***, old **Janie Dykes** waves a welcome but, much as we'd like to, there's no time to chat. When we reach the footpath by Hitcham allotments, we turn west to cross **Green Lane** and tread carefully through **Hitcham Field**, a rusty, dusty wasteland now the vicious whorls of barbed-wire have departed. We go under the railway about a quarter-mile east of **Taplow Station** to the **Bath Road**. Some of the cars must be going over 30 miles-an-hour but, brave souls one and all, we take our lives in our hands and scamper across. **George Emmett** wisely suggests we try not to breath too deeply until we leave behind Burnham Sewage Works.

It doesn't take us long to get upwind and we are quick to take deep draughts of the fragrant air as we turn south along **Marsh Lane** and south-west down **Devil's Lane**. A sharp left brings us back to Marsh Lane and we head south once more. We can soon see the trees surrounding **Dorney Court** away to the south-east but we turn westwards to find the River Thames at **Dorney Reach** where Mr Webb announces that we are at Taplow's most southerly point. He is blissfully unaware that Taplow's toe will soon be trimmed when its boundary is redrawn to retain **Trumper's Field** in Taplow whilst giving a new housing estate at Dorney Reach its rightful place in Dorney Parish. Colonel Serocold concedes that the line of the boundary south of the Bath Road has been hard to follow but now he is pleased to reassure us that Old Father Thames will now guide our way home. ***Amerden Priory*** stands serene in contrast to busy **Bray Lock** and isn't long before we stumble on the curious sight of a Maidenhead boundary stone on the Bucks bank. Was Bryant's map correct in suggesting that the towpath was once in Berkshire? The question remains unspoken for we come upon the most delightful sight of **St Michael's Church** in Bray standing serene beyond the sparkling river.

The tranquil spectacle continues to unfold as we skirt **Barge Farm** along the ancient towpath. The going becomes even easier when we reach ***Harefield***, the first of five mansions which watch our gentle entry into Taplow Riverside. ***The Red House***, ***Broomcroft***, ***Fair View*** and ***Riverbank*** are left behind to our right as we progress past ***Orkney Cottage*** and under Mr Brunel's Sounding Arch to arrive at *The American Restaurant, Bar & Hotel*: the riverside annex of ***Skindles Hotel***. As our host Mr Seechi entertains us to tea, Colonel **Serocold** enthrals by standing with his feet apart in the centre of the room and indicating with a wave of his tea cup that his left foot is in Bucks and his right in Berks.

We tarry longer with this curiosity than we should for we haven't far to go. After tea our party proceeds the last few hundred yards to **Taplow Paper Mills** on **Glen Island** where we see another Maidenhead boundary stone. One of the boys is astute enough to ask why these stones aren't in the middle of the river. The boy is not impressed with the Colonel's explanation that they were put here long ago and that's the way of it. The Major leads the way up the hill past the old ice house and we complete our perambulation of the parish at **Taplow Court** at 4.30pm after walking a little more than seven miles.

Beyond a Boundary

Maidenhead Bridge / 12th July 1987

You'd have thought a river might work well as a boundary – this is our land and beyond that wet bit is your land – but the concept was too much for Berks. Taplow has always been reasonable in asserting that its western boundary should naturally run along the centre of the Thames and, according to depositions made in 1633, to take its share of the responsibility for Maidenhead Bridge. Stuart scribes noted that "the inhabitants of Taplowe have usually searched & apprehended Rogues & Vagabonds usinge to lodge" under their end of Maidenhead Bridge, that "children borne.... under that part of the dry Arches.... have been baptised in Taplowe church [and] one that died was buried in Taplowe churchyard", and that in about 1613 when "12 Pirats [were] brought [as] prisoners by the Sheriff of Berkshire [they had] their yrons taken off.... near the Barge peere at the middle of Maidenhead bridge [before being] delivered to the Sheriff of Buckinghamshire whose men put other yrons on them and so had them towards London". In addition, since the late-1500s (and probably before) "the procession of Taplowe hath gone to the said Barge peere and there the minister of Taplowe hath usually read a Gospell without any contradiction" thereby demonstrating the Taplovian claim clearly but quietly.

God may have heard but the burghers of Bray and Cookham pretended not to. It never cut any ice in Berks that the bridge wouldn't have a hope without one foot in Bucks. These ancient mini-metropolises had coveted fishing, towing and mooring rights along the Bucks riverbank for centuries before Maidenhead eventually inherited this unreasonable possessiveness and in the 1770s sequestered a sliver of Bucks to land its bridge. This patch of barely two acres may originally have been a bankside island or two, although perhaps its triangular southern sliver was once a strand later built up and widened to become a boatyard for **Jonathan Bond the Elder** and soon the site of the new **Maidenhead Rowing Club** and eventually also of ***Taplow Quay***. The upstream tip of the patch was certainly an island – an angled inlet marked its extent for many years and was roofed in the 19th Century – which explains the wandering boundary that runs not through the ballroom but through today's *Valbonne* nightclub. In the old soldier Serocold's day it followed the rear curtilage of four cottages tucked between the ballroom and the western **Mill Lane** frontage. He could be forgiven for giving life to the tall tale but what possessed King George III and his Parliament to allow this sequestration? Perhaps they were distracted by the small matter of a colonial revolution on the far side of the Atlantic Ocean. No such excuse applied a short way upstream where the boundary sliced the slim Glen Island from top to toe, a split reinforced with new boundary stones installed in 1886 by **Sir Roger Palmer**.

If Taplow thought this was the be-all-and-end-all of Berkshire ambitions, it was very much mistaken. In 1965 Maidenhead attempted a takeover of western Taplow as far as today's Jubilee River, the Bath Road up to ***Dumb Bell Bridge*** and Amerden as far east as the lane from ***The Dumb Bell Hotel*** to **Amerden Bank**. And to make matters worse, Slough (then still in Bucks) coveted Burnham and Hitcham from the M4 north to Burnham cricket club and as far west as **Hitcham Road**. Fortunately the weight of reasoned objections persuaded the Boundaries Commission that it would be wise to reject both landgrabs in order to retain the vital Green Belt wedge between the burgeoning neighbours.

Berkshire wasn't to be sated. In 1974 it consumed a considerable chunk of Buckinghamshire comprising not only Eton but its bigger little brother Sloughalong with Langley, Datchet, Wraysbury and much of Burnham. Taplow found itself in the demise of **Beaconsfield District Council** which evolved six years later to become **South Bucks District Council** (SBDC) which three years ago nudged the Taplow-Burnham boundary from the centre of **The Bishop Centre** to Hitcham Road. However last year Berks was back, still hungry for more of Bucks – preferably all of it up to the M40 motorway, or at least all of Dorney and of Taplow too as far as a postulated new boundary wandering divisively to transfer the mill and village to Berks while leaving Taplow Court and Hitcham in Bucks.

As 21 years before, the fear was that Buckinghamshire's green tail would be sliced off. The neighbours argued that it "stuck out inconveniently into Berkshire". Locals countered correctly that "in fact, the unnatural excrescence is not Taplow and Dorney sticking into Berks but Slough sticking into Bucks". Both Parish Councils, local MPs, the Society and over 300 individuals registered strong objections to both proposed boundary realignments and advanced the popular counter-argument that it would be better for the county boundary to return to "the natural and time-honoured" line of the River Thames....

Maidenhead Bridge / 19th May 1993

And as far as Taplow is concerned, that is what has been decided today. Next year the bridge sliver and the western bank of **Glen Island** will finally be restored to Bucks. This adds to the recovery on 1st April 1992 of a north-west corner containing ***The Royal Standard*** and an erstwhile mink farm, a few acres that seem to have been lost to Wooburn some time between 1824 and 1851. The only 'slicing off' will be in the deep south when Taplow's toe is trimmed again to recognise the reality that **Trumper's Field**, long exiled by the M4 motorway, makes more sense ceded to Dorney Reach.

Seeds of Destiny

Taplow Village Centre / 18th January 2012

Had the decisions in either 1965 or 1987 been different, Slough and Maidenhead would have long since merged into one urban sprawl. It took the combined efforts of many to save our little slice of Green Belt to the extent it has been, although of course the struggle continues.

This completes the tale of how Mother Nature and the human nature of its inhabitants shaped Taplow, but it's not the whole story. Taplow was once a possession, home to a handful of peasants. For some, it was a place nearby. For most, it was on the way to somewhere else. This last was a force to be reckoned with: the power of passers-by coming and going by road, river and rail. At about 25 miles from London, Taplow was a hard day's march for those on foot, a comfortable ride on horseback or stagecoach and eventually a convenient commute or a pleasant day out by train. Some came to stay, more came to play, many more made their way west or back again. And what's more, Taplow was within easy reach of the Royal Ripple running from Windsor. Here are the seeds of Taplow's destiny we shall discover on our journey in the company of such as Harry Hurn....

Hurn's Turn – Meet the Family

Dulverton, Somerset / 18th June 2002

Harry Hurn writes from his West Country home to say he was born in Taplow in 1925 and lived there until 1949. He was baptised Frederick after his grandfather but has always been known by his middle name. His recollections provide a fascinating insight into the people of Taplow and the place itself when "summers were always golden, stretching to infinity, with frolics and rabbit chases among the corn stooks at harvest", when children enjoyed "swinging on the back of hay wagons as, drawn by the great shire horses, they trundled up to the farmyard", when "gas-lit winter evenings beside the fire [were] cosy and inviting", when "it was fun setting off on extensive day-long journeys of exploration through the woods and fields around us at all times of year.... hunting for chestnuts in **Chestnut Ride** each autumn, picking bluebells in **Hunts Wood** in the spring [and] on long summer days, basking in the sun, climbing trees, splashing in the water and fishing for sticklebacks and minnows" in the brook running south from **Taplow Mill** leat – then a sparkling stream, now little more than a ditch soon to be lost in the excavations for the Jubilee River.

Harry's family line is fragmented and farspread across the Burnham and Desborough Hundreds. They are in need of a spell check for various registrars made it up as they went along. Locally the family line can be traced back to **May Hern** in 1748. She may well have been the great aunt of the **William Hearn** who married **Harriet Brown** in 1788 to be the likely candidates for being grandparents to **Henry Hearn** who was born in 1824 in a cottage behind ***The Feathers Inn*** and lived there all his life.

The 1861 census has him as **Henry Hurn** but doesn't tell his tragic tale. Having lost his first wife Eliza and their three infant sons before he was 26, he married the teenage Mary Ann Monk within a year and had five more children only to die himself aged 40 just weeks before the first birthday of his youngest son **Frederick Everett Hurn**. Freddie was brought up by his mother and her second husband **William Wells**, a bricklayer from Beaconsfield. He could just about remember the death in 1867 of his 9-year-old elder sister **Alice Hearn** and counted himself lucky to have grown up at all let alone to be nightwatchman at Cliveden for the Duke of Westminster then for the Astors. His home was across the road from *The Feathers* in an old lodge long since replaced by Cliveden's glorious wrought iron gateway. He never knew why his stepfather always insisted on calling him by his middle name – which probably derived from Thomas Everett, tenant in 1720 of Gages Copps, then a 6-acre close immediately north of today's **Cliveden Gages** [*see Map 16*] – but it seemed right to pass it on to his son **Everett Hurn** who grew up to marry Violet Haydon of ***The Compasses Inn*** on Wooburn Common and to sire Kathleen, Harry and June [*see Appendix 1, Tree 12*].

Burnham High Street / 18th June 2013

Hearn & Son is closed. The butcher's shop was established in 1928 and run until recently by John Stephenson. Could the founder have been related to the Taplow Hurns? Spelling variations continued with **James Hearne**, probably Henry's elder brother or cousin, and his son **Francis (Frank) Hearn**, a farmhand who lived in the cottage behind **William Rance the Elder**'s butcher's shop (now ***Mulberry House***) until he died in 1906. He would have known whether Jack Hearne of Chalfont St Giles was a cousin. Between 1888 and 1923 this famous cricketer took 3,061 wickets for Middlesex and England including the first ever hat-trick against Australia (in 1899 at Headingley).

Naming of Parts

The Reading Room, Taplow / 18th June 1952

Eton RDC has been at it again, changing things because it can. New road signs have been installed over past couple of years. Harry reckons that's all very well but everybody was perfectly happy with the old colloquial names so why think up new official ones? We shall hear more from him and his family later but for now his job is to help us spot a few differences [*see Map 10*].

Harry leads the way down the steps to the road that has been known as **The Pightail** (perhaps for its curl at the end), **The Phygtle**, **The Pikel**, **Pikels** and more recently as **Pikle Lane**. He and his boyhood pal **Michael Good** had so much fun getting folk in a pickle by telling them the first syllable is pronounced *pie*. Our Parish Clerk **Walter Leyster** protested as long ago as 1941 when **Eton RDC** first "facetiously" proposed to call it the **High Street**, a name that might have made sense way back when we had a grocery-cum-bakery with a post-office, a butcher's and a dairy that had been a cobbler's, yet today all but *Budgen's* is history. And what's worse, this isn't the half of it....

Down the hill, **St Nicolas' Church** was itself subject to a subtle name-change in the late-1920s when its 'h' was lost during the rectorship of the Reverend **Francis Phillips**, a passionate devotee of Latin whose aim may have been to create distinction between the churches of Taplow and Hedsor. The road running east-west here has been called **Church Road** since before the church moved from one end to the other in 1828. It has never needed to be **Rectory Road** for people to find ***The Rectory*** that has stood by it for generations.

We move on to **Well Corner** at the eastern end of Church Road – sorry, Rectory Road – where it meets a road that marked the boundary between Taplow and Hitcham until the latter was split asunder 18 years ago. The southerly stretch was **Green Lane** until the new railway station opened in 1872. Ever since, it has been **Station Road** all the way from here down past the kink by **Taplow Grammar School** to the station. Now only the last leg is still Station Road and the whole of Green Lane is **Boundary Road** despite it no longer being the boundary. And why change the name of the northern stretch from **Back Lane** to **Hill Farm Road**? At least we can take some solace that Burnham Lane – until not long ago **London Road**, as it had always been – is to be **Hitcham Lane**; it does run through Hitcham village, after all.

We repair to the junction at the western end of the newly-dubbed Rectory Road. Looking southwards, **Town Lane** – once **Maidenhead Lane** – runs from here down **Berry Hill** to the **Bath Road**. Harry thinks Berry Hill was named for the *burg* at its zenith. If the derivation is good enough for Canterbury, what better way to remember **Taplow Castle**? However in 1997 **Lincoln Lee** of ***Berinus*** – otherwise known as N° 7 **Saxon Gardens** – will offer a typically whimsical handful of other options: was it Barrow's Hill (for Tæppa's Mound or barrow), Bury Hill (for the burials in the old graveyard), Berry Hill (for the wild blackberries), Strawberry Hill (as on an old postcard) or Bray Hill (for being the way to the old ford at ***Bray Rigle***)?

To the north is an epidemic of change for change's sake. The road from here up to Taplow Common has long been **Common Lane** but now Cliveden has become so famous there is sense in it becoming **Cliveden Road**. Further north, there is sense but no soul in **Noblemans' Walk** becoming **Heathfield Road**. Who knew that the close in the north-west corner of **Dropmore** is called Heath Field? For whom is it a destination? And why lose an echo of days gone by? Will everyone forget its junction with the road to Bourne End is **Noblemans' Corner**? This tale of Taplow will do its bit to keep the past alive by using road names that were contemporary at the time of the events it will witness down the years.

Map 10 – The Village: Naming of Parts

From Colloquial to Official

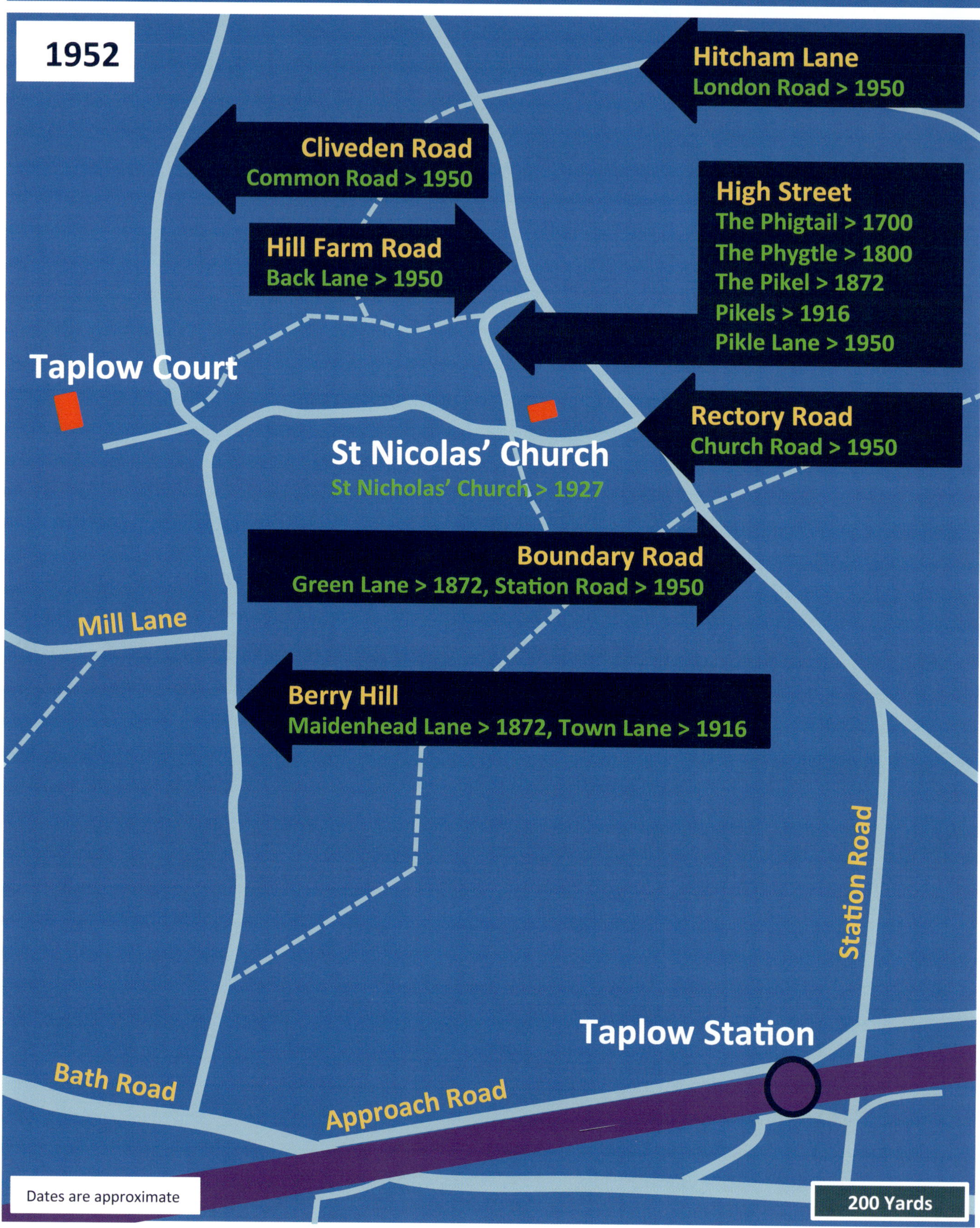

Primary Source: Ordnance Survey 2008

Taplow Court / 2009 & 2012

Taplow House/ 2009

Finding the Manor House

Amerden Grove / c1895

Amerden Lakes / 2011

Amerden Bank / 2011

Amerden Priory / 2011

The Top and Tail of Taplow

***The Compasses* stands on Taplow's northern boundary: Green Common Lane** (left) / 2012 & c1920

The M4 spans the Thames to define Taplow's southern boundary / 2011

Chapter Two

Comings and Goings

In which Taplow found its name and began to make history

Passing By

Not Stopping

Dumb Bell Bridge / 5th March 2012

It's the morning rush hour on the **Bath Road**. A ***First Great Western*** train flashes past over the bridge carrying commuters to London. Vehicles are nose-to-tail under it towards Maidenhead and crawling not a lot faster towards Slough. Thousands pass here every day. Few notice they've come and gone through Taplow. Fewer still realise that their cars and carriages follow footsteps trodden for centuries. Only the occasional historian has the inclination to imagine what life was like for ancient Taplovians, their neighbours and those who drifted in and out on the way there and back again along the Thames Valley. Here is someone who has done a bit of that....

Michael Bayley, Not a Historian

Westmorland Drive, Maidenhead / 5th March 2012

Here in his study surrounded by books and boxes of documents, **Michael Bayley** smiles benignly like Professor Albus Dumbledore indulging the innocent and incredulous Harry Potter. He breaks it gently that there is a lot to learn, not least that he refuses to be called a historian because his font of local knowledge springs from tales told down the generations of his family and their friends over hundreds of years. I beg to differ. His fastidious documentary research has added varying degrees of corroboration to what he has been told. His study of Cornish, Welsh and Breton etymology has enabled him to suggest interpretations for the remnants of the Britannic language that local farm labourers used in the middle Thames Valley until the late-19th Century, an ancient dialect that he believes still echoes in the traditional names of roads, fields and places. His conclusions will forever prompt debate but they make him a historian in my book. And this is my book. It is all the better for the added sparkle of Michael's gems even if some are cut and polished to his wonderfully whimsical taste...

Old Bayley Lore – The Really Ancient Way Back When

Once Ways West

Hitcham Lane / 6th March 2012

For generations before the Romans arrived, the Thames Valley provided a natural way to wend west without getting lost. Many came and went by river and sometimes ran aground on seasonal shallows hereabouts: the rapids at Hedsor could be so dangerous that they were the head of navigation when waters were low. Many more came and went along myriad tracks which converged at fords, ferries and *brivas*: porous brushwood causeways across rivers rather like human versions of beaver dams.

Michael believes there were two main ways west from London. One crossed the Thames at a place the Romans called *ad Pontes*, meaning *at the bridges* (so it is likely there was more than one), and the Saxons renamed *Stanes* – now Staines – meaning (*the place at the*) *stones*, perhaps referring to either residual stone bridge piers or boundary stones. The other way lay along the north bank of the Thames to the River Colne where it split into winter and summer options: the high way and the low way. The winter road took the drier high ground through Stoke, Farnham and Burnham to **Hitchambury**, continued to the gate of **Cliveden Woodlands** and zigzagged down the chalk escarpment into **Clemish Meadow**, across a ford or an island-hopping *briva* and headed for Hurley along the line of the modern Islet Road [*see Map 11*]. This avoided winter mud and floods but risked a journey through the tangled woods on the southern ridges of the Chiltern Hills where wild tribes lurked with menace in mind.

Forgotten Fields – Cropmarks on the Hill

Hitchambury / 6th March 2012

Despite its imposing scale, this grand house at the end of Hunts Lane has something of a transitory air. Nobody stays for long nowadays in its 26 "tasteful hotel-style bedrooms all traditionally furnished with TV". One can only imagine this as a busy nurses' home from the 1940s to the 1980s. Not even the man who had it built in 1909 lasted long. As a bishop's son, **Charles Selwyn Awdry** had the contacts to know that the Church of England wished to dispose of the dilapidated former rectory of **St Mary's Church**, Hitcham. As a partner in the successful newsagents and booksellers *WH Smith & Son*, he had the wherewithal to invest £7,629 (£4.1m) to acquire the site and its surrounding four-and-a-half acres. But as a major commanding the 6th Battalion of the Royal Wiltshire Yeomanry, he was posted missing during a retreat at Bapaume in the Somme Valley on 25th March 1918. Although his wife Constance remained hopeful that he had been taken prisoner, he was never seen again and eventually was presumed to have been killed in action. He would never know that his young first cousin grew up to be the Reverend Wilbert Awdry, creator of *Thomas the Tank Engine*.

The timber-framed, tile-clad old rectory had survived in various forms from the 16th Century – it is thought that **Awdry** retained a fireplace of that era – but perhaps the seed of 'not stopping' was sown in ancient times when some Neolith left his axe-head behind. **Michael Bayley** thinks **Hitchambury** may derive from *Uchel-am-Burrow* – meaning *the earthworks of the highest cultivated land* – and indeed aerial surveys suggest this might be the site of a very ancient British settlement. Or do the cropmarks indicate field enclosures or a ring-ditch? These uncertain and comparatively modest earthworks are perhaps not quite as old as **Taplow Castle**, the nearby fortification which has tended to overshadow its smaller neighbour. It is all too long ago to say whether the sites were occupied concurrently or consecutively and if Hitchambury was an overspill from Taplow Castle or the home of an entirely different family or tribe. Michael was told of a time when the people of Hitchambury were defeated by a 'conqueror' who forcibly relocated them to become servants at Taplow Castle. But who was this conqueror? Perhaps the story recalls the Norman Conquest or possibly the Roman one. Maybe it's a wispy folk memory of Belgae imposing their Iron Age will or of a land-grabbing Angle or Saxon lord. Whoever he was, the conqueror must have been a pagan because Britannic priests seem to have been allowed to stay on at Hitchambury to preserve the sanctity of the old place.

Map 11 – Old Bayley Lore: Ancient Ways West

Wishful Thinking or Inspired Guesswork?

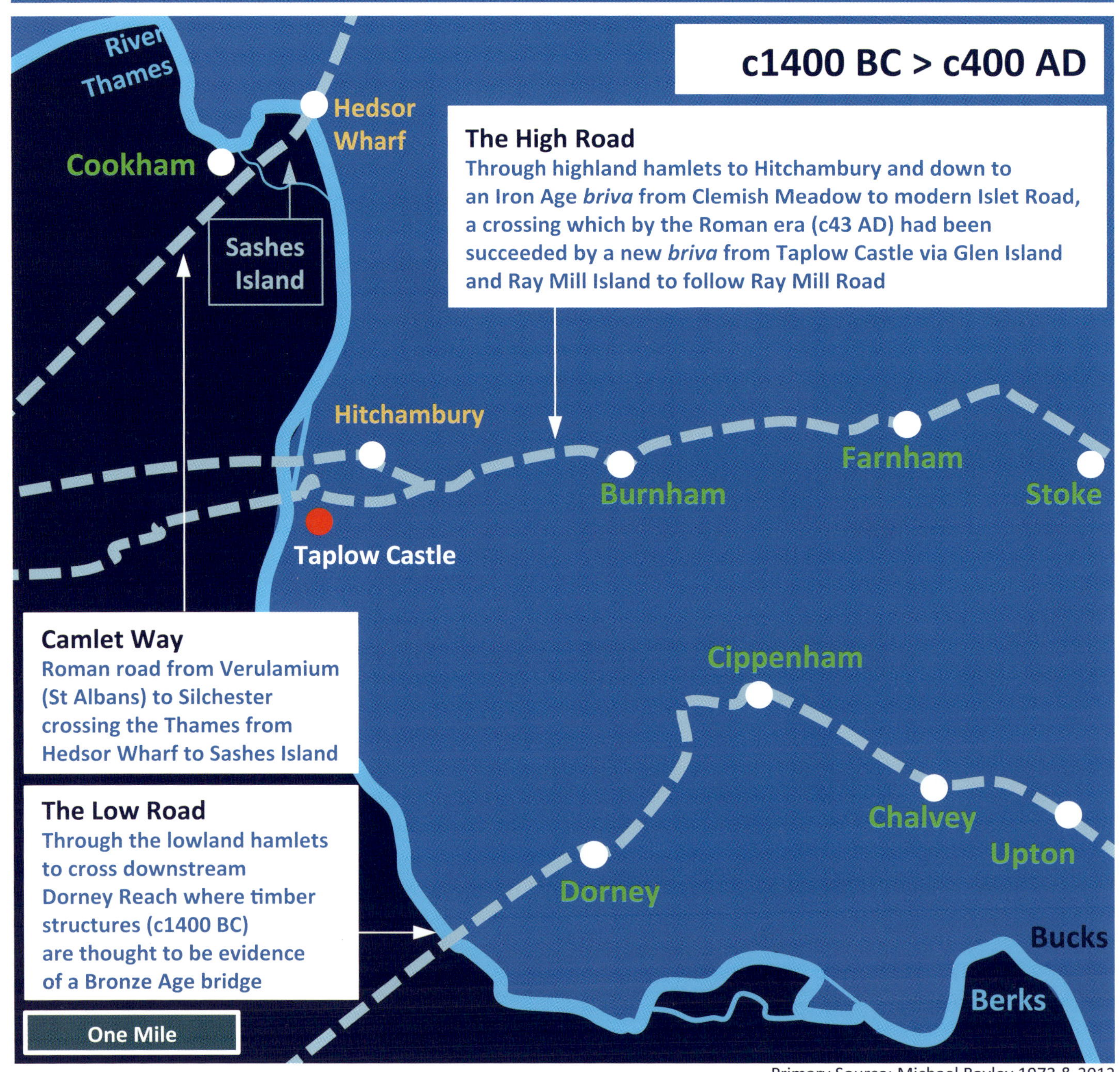

Primary Source: Michael Bayley 1973 & 2012

About Grout – Meet the Family

Hitchambury / 6th March 1932

Alfred Grout smiles as his wife Bertha fusses over the creases their nearly-nine-year-old son has already got in his cassock. He'll be surprised if Arthur is as smart by the time he gets down to **St Nicolas' Church** to sing in the choir. But he hasn't time to worry about that now: he has to drive Mrs Awdry and her daughter Lilian down to church.

Constance Awdry is bucking the trend. She will stay on at *Hitchambury* until she passes away in 1946. When Lilian marries in 1941 to Colin, son of poet and novelist **Walter de la Mare** of ***Hill House***, she will be content to retain a small apartment while the rest of the house is converted to accommodate Cliveden Hospital nurses. She engaged Alfred as her chauffeur in 1923 when Arthur was just six weeks old and enjoys seeing him and his elder brothers Philip and James playing about the place. It reminds her of when her own sons Charles, Selwyn and Henry had the run of *Hitchambury's* fields and woods. Phil will find pastures new in the Metropolitan Police and Jim in the Royal Air Force but Arthur will stay local all his life. He will move with his parents to N° 56 Milner Road in 1935 and from there with his wife Doris to N° 40 Bayley Crescent in 1950. They will still be there 64 years later.

Forgotten Fields – Droppings in the Valley

Dorney Lake / 6th March 2012

They are working hard to reinvent the **Eton College** Rowing Course as Eton-Dorney for the London Olympics. Thousands will flock to watch the rowing and canoeing events. Few will imagine that this flood plain was a hive of Neolithic activity perhaps as far back as 6,000 years ago. Excavations for this 'rowing trench' and for the **Jubilee River** revealed chisel arrowheads and sherds of Plain Bowl and Ebbsfleet Ware pottery indicating large-scale and long-term visitation.

The remains of hollowed-out tree trunk boats at Marlow and Bourne End confirm that the river was the highway of the day for trade and travellers alike. They made pottery at **Hedsor** and dug a ring-ditch east of **Barge Farm**. They dumped unwanted flints in a midden east of **Marsh Lane**, dropped flint artefacts and pottery while burying their dead by the river at **Glen Island** and left two more axe-heads in the river at **Cliveden** and **Amerden**. Somebody buried their dead in barrows at Cock Marsh in **Cookham** and off Poyle Lane in **Burnham**. Somebody lived in circular huts off Hag Hill Lane in **Lent Rise**. Their dwellings were up to 20 feet in diameter with sunken floors at least three feet deep and sometimes seven. They were roofed with conical timber constructions finished with turf and bracken. **Taplow Castle** could boast at least two equally desirable residences.

Heavy Metal

The Bronze Age

Taplow Castle / 8th March 2014

Somewhere between 4,000 and 3,250 years ago settlements in and around Dorney and Eton Wick left behind thousands of artefacts including flint arrowheads, sherds of pottery and animal bones, the oldest scythe yet found in Britain, a long barrow, a ring-ditch, a large rectangular structure and various ditches, pits, field enclosures and trackways, one of which was still used in the 1800s, and the 3,400-year-old oaken remains of a bridge across the Thames at **Dorney Reach**, almost certainly the oldest hereabouts and possibly reconstructed at least six times over 1,000 years [*see Map 11*]. There were burials on the flood plain between Amerden and Eton and possibly here too. Pits, pottery and metalwork including axes, spears and spearheads show somebody was busy by the river. Bronze artefacts including a crucible and ingot suggest long-term metalworking at **Lay Chequers** (south-west of Mill Lane's bridge over the Jubilee River) and somebody left sherds of grog-tempered pottery south-west of **Coldgrove Corner**.

Everything seemed to have been all sweetness and light for a while but, as the population grew, it all began to get rather crowded. Society became increasingly hierarchical and fractious. Metallurgy arrived. It was a double-edged sword. Bronze tools and implements made the daily grind of subsistence farming easier but Bronze Age Bucks was no longer a peaceful place to be if the socketed knife at **Dorneywood**, the axe-heads at Mill Wood above **Wooburn Green** and at **Slough Trading Estate** and all the spearheads, swords, rapiers, daggers and socketed axe-heads found in the Thames between here and Amerden are anything to go by. Many of these weapons had been deliberately broken or 'killed' perhaps as votive offerings to the gods in a time of rivalry and turmoil, to confirm peace between previously feuding neighbours or simply to show off with a gesture of strength.

The Iron Age

Lake End Road / 8th March 2014

Things went from bad to worse. Altogether there were at least 17 hill forts in Buckinghamshire during the 1st Century BC, including one here at Taplow and others at Bulstrode Camp at Gerrards Cross and Seven Ways Plain at **Burnham Beeches** (also called Hardicanute's Moat). And across the river there was a small farmstead in Maidenhead Thicket later dubbed Robin Hood's Arbour. Danesfield at Medmenham had echoes of Taplow for being by a natural spring high above a bow in the Thames.

Around 2,400 years ago there was some kind of an enclosure in the 300 yards between here and where the slip road sweeps up and over the M4 motorway. This and another at Denham may have been destroyed at around the same time as the timber ramparts at **Taplow Castle** were burnt. Perhaps this was when the farmstead east of **Berry Hill** was abandoned – a quern and various pottery and metalwork were left there, forgotten – but it isn't clear who did the damage to whom and why. Were these fights between ancient Britons armed with brown-gold bronze weapons? Or were the culprits the Belgic and Gallic tribes who came across the Channel with their cold blue iron weapons looking for a better place to be? Was the iron sword and its bronze sheath thrown into the Thames at **Amerden** as a votive plea for peace or did its owner die in an ambush before he could draw his weapon?

The Coming of Civilisation

Roman Arrivals

Taplow Castle / 100 BC (or thereabouts)

Things are a little clearer now in the big, wide world beyond the ramparts. Yet more foreigners have arrived from even further away. Most of these Mediterranean commercial travellers are after tin but some have made a few notes about South Bucks being the frontier between the *Catuvellauni* north of the Thames and the *Atrebates* to the south. Domestic pottery at Poyle Farm reveals the dual influence. While the jars are of a type used by both tribes, the cooking pots are of an exclusively *Atrebate* style. This suggests the southerners are top dogs just now.

Taplow Castle / 50 BC

The *Catuvellauni* clawed their way back into control before the Romans first took a fancy to the island they called Britannia. They were perhaps the strongest of Britannic adversaries to the second of Emperor Julius Caesar's invasions four years ago but they lost the will in battle and eventually turned tail. Somebody buried a fortune – probably 1,000 gold coins – at Whaddon Chase in Aylesbury Vale. Were they on the run from the all-conquering Romans? Most of the money had been minted by the *Catuvellauni*, the *Trinovantes* (of Essex) and the *Atrebates* but there were also coins of the *Durotriges* (of Dorset) and the *Corieltauni* (of Leicestershire and south Lincolnshire) which goes to show what a commercially integrated society spans southern England in these late Iron Age days.

Taplow Castle / 43 AD

Caesar was victorious but he didn't really conquer Britannia. He made a few notes about how fabulously imperial he was and went back home taking with him every last Roman. It suited him to cast Britons as barbarians but we couldn't care less. Britannia has pretty much gone its own sweet way for the past 97 years until Emperor Claudius sent his general Aulus Plautius to civilise us at the point of his sword and charge for the privilege. This is the real Roman conquest.

Tall Tale – Taplow versus Rome

Chertsey Riverbank / 9th March 2012

Local lore tends to confuse the second and third Roman invasions. An erroneous belief has grown that a contingent from Taplow fought under King Caractacus against Julius Caesar at the legendary Battle of Chertsey Stakes. It is either a myth or a mistake because this king and that battle are separated by almost a century.

History tells that the *Catuvellauni* fortified the north bank of a ford across the Thames with sharpened wooden stakes in an attempt to resist Caesar's second expedition in 54 BC. Nobody is quite sure exactly where this was. Some say Brentford, others Lambeth or here at Chertsey. *The Anglo-Saxon Chronicle* suggests that the warlike and quarrelsome inhabitants of Taplow fought and lost that year under King Cassivellaunus. It is possible (although less likely) that their grandsons and great-grandsons fought under Caractacus in 43 AD as he led the *Catuvellauni* and other tribes against the third Roman invasion. However these battlegrounds were miles away at the River Medway, where British chariots were made useless by specially-trained Batavi warriors who swam across to kill the horses, and somewhere on the northern Thames riverbank, where two invading forces came ashore to catch the Britons in a pincer movement without being inconvenienced by sharp stakes or indeed by any further determined resistance before Claudius caught up to lead the march on Camulodunum (Colchester, Essex), accept the surrender and take the credit.

Old Bayley Lore – The Merely Ancient Way Back When

The High Way

Coldgrove Corner / 10th Martius 155

How things have changed under Roman rules. Londinium has grown quickly as merchants set up shop to exploit the Empire's expansion. The invaders' aversion to wet feet has made the high road their favoured way west [*see Map 11*]. Their military might has reduced the threat of ambush and the ground up here is dry enough not to need stone paving. They have rather taken to Taplow Castle: the perfect place for a sleepover one-day's march from Londinium. A *centuria* of perhaps 80 legionnaries is on its way there now. On leaving Burnham, they ignore the old way to Hitchambury and instead stride smartly along not-yet **Hitcham Lane** to where it will meet **Hill Farm Road** to create **Coldgrove Corner**. There are bulls to the right of them and cows to the left.

The Romans aren't fussy about the field names hereabouts so they are missing out on a lot of fun. Over their right shoulder is a field the locals called *Gre-ty-kole-crow* (*the place of the young bull's hovel*), a name that will evolve to become Great Cold Grove. Up ahead on their left is *Laity-kole-crow-fa* (*the dairy by the young bull's hovel*). One day this will be Little Cold Grove and eventually the site of ***Coldgrove Cottages***, ***Church Cottages*** and **Buffins**, a housing estate which will take its name from *Bugh-fan* (*the place of the cattle*), the field immediately to the north-west.

The *centuria* marches straight ahead between *Laity-kole-crow-fa* and *Bugh-fan* to enter the east gate of the restored **Taplow Castle**. To the right is *Caer-tyow Vear-lle*, eventually Court Field but then *the big space of the houses of the fort* where locals live to serve the needs of the *Caer-ty* or *Fort House*. Perhaps they are of Hitchamburgian descent. The legionaries wheel left into *Chwarae* which will become Cherry Orchard and halt without wondering why there are no cherry trees here. For the Romans, this is a parade ground, the town square; for the locals it is *the stony place on the edge of the hill where the games are held*. An old oak in its north-east corner marks the zigzag way down the chalk escarpment to where the locals have long had a *briva* almost half-a-mile downstream from the original. In 1,855 years folk will recognise the line of this crossing as being via **Glen Island** to Ray Mill Island and **Boulter's Lock** then west along Ray Mill Road. The *centuria* has come to guard this bridge. It has changed the riverscape. An upstream pool spreads across the low grassland to the west (Widbrook Common). This is frozen now and the ice is thick enough for centurions to walk withour fear of falling through to another fortified settlement on what will be Sashes Island. Local boatmen are pleased the water is deep enough even in dry summers to cover the notorious rapids at **Hedsor** but still they moan that the surge through the narrow *pont* (bridge) in the *briva* makes navigation difficult. Some people are never satisfied.

Cherry Orchard, Taplow Court / 10th March 2012

With remarkable coincidence, Cherry Orchard is blessed with cherry trees planted near the modern Buddhist prayer hall by **Soka Gakkai International**, the current owner of **Taplow Court**. It is no coincidence that the oak which grew from the acorn that fell from the oak which grew from the acorn that fell from the oak which grew on the edge of the escarpment came to be called **Queen Elizabeth's Oak**, but don't be fooled. Its name probably derived from *Quidden-un-alaw-ys-beth*: *the holy one of the lily of the place beneath the tomb*. The lily remembers the yellow water iris once common in local water meadows, marshes and millponds. The tomb was of course Tæppa's. We will come to him shortly.

Taplow Bridge / 10th March 1212

The water rushes noisily through the brushwood but the earthen crust of the *briva* is a firm footing for pedestrians, handcarts and even mounted riders. To the west, not-yet Ray Mill Road fords streams running southwards from the thriving mini-metropolis of Cucheham (**Cookham**) where a weekly market and two annual fairs have been held for more than 100 years. About half-a-mile from the Thames we reach a deep weir pool and the little settlement of *N'oath-towan* (*the watercourse gravel ridge island*) in the manor of *Eal-llan-towan* (*the ox enclosure of the gravel ridge island*). English-speakers hear these as **North Town** and **Elentone**, eventually *Aylington* or *Ellington*.

The Picquigny family has held Elentone Manor since the Conquest. They will soon divide it in two separate subtenancies. William de Coleworth's portion will pass in 1306 to John le Despenser and thereafter will be known as Spencers. Henry de Elington will evolve his surname from his half and the hamlet that grows 500 yards downstream will be Soth Elentone, so-called not for its relative location but because it is *a place of service* to the manor. One day, **Maidenhead** will be the sum of these parts.

Roman Rules

Queen Anne's House, Berry Hill / 12th March 2012

There are those not convinced by **Michael Bayley**'s etymological interpretations but no doubt that the middle Thames Valley was quite happy to be romanised. There were villas at High Wycombe, Hambleden, Cox Green and at the foot of Castle Hill in Maidenhead where it is rumoured that a Roman mosaic tiled floor lies hidden deep below the roundabout. There was a Christian church on the site of St Peter's Church in Burnham and perhaps pagan temples where there are now churches in **Hedsor** and Taplow. A pewter ewer was found at **Cliveden**, there were burials at Bourne End, a cemetery by ***Bray Studios*** and kilns for making tiles at Altwood and potteries at Hedgerley, Fulmer and possibly in **Ten Acre Field** (Taplow Cricket Club) where a floor, wall, ditch, pottery, animal bone and metalwork suggests a hive of industry. This theory was reinforced in the 1970s when the stable block here at ***Queen Anne's House*** was being converted into a cottage. Excavations for new foundations revealed flint stones and shards that convinced builders employed by **Laura (Lynn) & Eric Pope** that a Roman villa had once stood there. The local Romans certainly knew how to party judging by all the broken pottery strewn about in Taplow village, near the station, at **Sheepcote Farm** up on Wooburn Common, at Taplow Court and especially in Ten Acres, so maybe there was a villa there too.

The 2nd or 3rd Century timber posts in the river at Hedsor suggest a substantial wharf or pile-dwellings. Some speculate that *Camlet Way*, a minor Roman road from Verulamium (St Albans) to Calleva Atrebatum (Silchester), may have crossed the Thames there, either by ferry or even over a bridge to **Sashes Island** where Roman swords and javelin heads have been found. Archaeological excavations have been unable to confirm the existence of a Roman road down to the wharf but didn't rule out that there might have been a pre-existing ancient British track. Similar timber pile remnants at Cookham Lock and the Amerden bank of **Bray Lock** may have supported a wharf or a stilt-dwelling. The discovery of remains of horses at these locations – a skull at Cookham, a complete skeleton at **Amerden** – raises the possibility that these were votive offerings, perhaps to speed travellers on their journeys. The Greek inscription on a cinerary urn sherd discovered in 1899 on the riverbed at Amerden suggests it contained the cremated ashes of a 'mule-physician', perhaps the very fellow who had despatched the unfortunate animals.

Being There

On the Frontier

Tæppa's Mound / 5th February 828

Taplow has been on the frontier for over 300 years. The protagonists have changed with each new century. First it was the East Saxons versus West Saxons, then Anglian Mercia versus Saxon Wessex, now it's Danelaw versus Saxon England. Matters are complicated by the fiercely independent *Cilternsæta* tribe, once likely cross-river rivals with the *Sunninga* to the south, now lurking with menace in the Chiltern Hills from where their echoes will resound softly in local lore for millennia.

Taplow Castle / 5th February 528

The Romans went home in the early-5th Century leaving Taplow eventually to become an outpost of the Middle Saxon kingdom which spanned Middlesex, South Bucks and Surrey. The land south of the Thames was called *Suthrige* – meaning *south region*, hence Surrey – which will lead to idle etymological gossip that the northern region must have been *Nuthrige*. However if Taplow ever thought it was in *Nurrey* or *Norrey* the idea didn't last long. What will is that the Thames is a frontier and Taplow is on it.

The late-5th Century was eventful for the south-eastern two-thirds of Britannia. In a thousand years the popular myth will be that England was already Anglo-Saxon. In fact Angles and Saxons rubbed each other up the wrong way for 300 years or so before the hyphen really took hold. Sometime between 455 and 470 the Middil Engle surge southwards into Aylesbury Vale may have got as far south as the Thames. And then in the 490s, Ælle led the South Saxon sweep west along the Thames Valley. If he was the first to be called *Bretwalda* (*Britain-ruler* or *Lord of Britain*), Britons didn't think much of the idea. He was defeated – perhaps at *Mons Badonicus* (the legendary *Battle of Badon Hill*) – by Ambrosius Aurelianus, King Arthur or whichever ancient British legend takes your fancy.

Old Bayley Lore – Name Games: Elentone & Aumberdene

Westmorland Drive, Maidenhead / 5th March 2012

Might the root of **Elentone** have been *Alaunodunum*? It is thought that Boyne Hill was crowned with a long lost earthwork enclosure that Romans might have decided was a *dunum* (*fortified encampment*). Or could Elentone derive from Ælle whose surge was stayed for twelve years by a garrison at Aumberdene (**Amerden**) under the command of his legendary adversary Ambrosius, and even that Ælle was killed in battle on Bapsey Field. This idea is attractively embroidered by the possibility that Aumberdene recalls Ambrosius. Or does it derive from *Aune-berw-den* or *Augh-berw-wy-din*, both variations on the theme of a *fort* (Taplow Castle?) and *frothy wild waters*? Or does a later version – Amerton – originate from it being held by Merton Priory? The only certainty is that nothing is certain but isn't speculation fun?

The Elusive Tæppa

Anglo-Saxon Explosion

Tæppa's Mound / 5th February 628

The 6th Century was relatively peaceful. The Middle Saxons came under the thumb of the East Saxons (of Essex) and South Bucks calmed down. Soon everyone was sowing and reaping, feasting, fighting each other and fearing the magical beasts of their imagination. There were settlements at Marlow, Medmenham, **Hedsor**, Hedgerley, **Dorney** and Taplow where the discovery of seeds of rivet (wheat bread), hulled barley, oats and rye indicates a thriving arable farm. Hedsor and Marlow had busy wharves. Dorney probably had a smithy and a heckle found there – its iron teeth set in a wooden block – suggests the carding of wool or flax to make cloth or linen.

Life was humdrum but happy enough for a few generations until it all got very exciting early in the 7th Century. A resurgence of old inter-tribal tensions was spiced with something new and strange: they called it Christianity. Æthelberht of Kent was acknowledged as *Bretwalda* by Rædwald of the East Angles and Sæberht of the East Saxons, each of whom embraced Æthelberht's new St Augustinian faith. The West Saxons and the Angles of Northumbria and Mercia knew their place. They kept their heads down and tolerated this triumvirate until Æthelberht and Sæberht both died in or around 616. The Anglo-Saxon world exploded. Rædwald seized his chance to quickly establish himself as the first Anglian *Bretwalda*. This was a pivotal move towards the emergence of Angle-Land – eventually England – but at the time the big issue was that Rædwald's conversion had been less sincere than Sæberht's, more to keep sweet with Æthelberht. This suited Sæberht's still pagan sons Sæxred, Sæweard and Sæxbald down to the ground. Their alliance with the increasingly powerful Rædwald gave them confidence to revive cross-river rivalry in the Thames Valley. Once more Taplow was back on the front line: an East Saxon sentinel watching West Saxon cousins over the water. The three brothers did something novel; they ruled by committee. It might have been good to talk but it seems their West Saxon neighbour Cynegils didn't think much of the idea. All three were killed in battle not long ago and somebody was buried in splendour beneath this mound in the south-west corner of **Taplow Castle**.

A Pagan Parting

Tæppa's Mound / 6th February 2012

Archaeological excavations in the grounds of Taplow Court in 1999 led **Elias Kupferman** to reinforce the ancient mystique of this place by suggesting that Tæppa's Mound may have been piled on or used earth and debris from one of perhaps three even more ancient Bronze Age burial mounds constructed here, possibly around 2,400 years ago. However he was unable to shed any further light on Tæppa himself: Taplow's first identifiable Local Hero if rather an elusive one. The name Taplow is said to derive from *Tæppa's Hleaw* – spellings vary but the meaning is always *Tæppa's Mound* – which is why it is thought he lay beneath it. **Mary Trevallion** believes that *Cartularium Saxonicum* suggests Tæbba might have been a personal name in such places as Derbyshire and Kent. However this collection of Anglo-Saxon charters gathered in 1885 makes no mention of Taplow's **Tæppa**. Was he a local lord or a warrior from elsewhere who led the defence against West Saxon attacks? What was his heritage? Whose side was he on in the greater scheme of things? History has no idea. Not even Legend has much of a clue. But uncertainty never troubled a certain 19th Century Taplovian....

The Past Master

Tæppa's Mound / 6th February 1891

James Rutland is an acquired taste respected by all for his laudable aims and determination to succeed but given a wide berth by some for being a bit of a know-it-all. Right on cue, he begins to explain how hard it was eight years ago in 1883 when he had no doubt the world needed to know what was secreted beneath Tæppa's Mound. The open-minded lord of the manor **Willy Grenfell** had been all for the idea but it was only with great persistence that Rutland overcame the reluctance of the Reverend **Charles Whately**, 42nd Rector of Taplow, to seek and secure the necessary permission of the Right Reverend John Mackarness, Bishop of Oxford, to proceed with the excavations at his own expense.

Rutland's plan was not to disturb either the graves surrounding the Mound or "the dead remains of an ancient yew tree [on its summit] whose knotted trunk [was] nearly six feet thick and whose age [was] estimated at possibly 600 years". Rutland's ten men began work on 15th October 1883 under the watchful eyes of Dr Joseph Stevens and Walter Money, both Fellows of the Society of Antiquaries, and Major Cooper-King, a fellow of the Geological Society. A six-foot wide cutting four-foot above ground level was dug horizontally into the Mound from the south and then vertically downwards at the foot of the yew. Meanwhile two other seven-foot square shafts were dug from the north and west. The cuttings revealed numerous irregularly dispersed relics of human workmanship spanning many centuries. The upper layers revealed several pieces of dressed chalk, possibly remnants of the Norman church, and fragments of coarse pottery, bones and bone tools, hammer stones and flints, cores and scrapers all thousands of years old: a jumble of history that will inform Kupferman's theory. Deeper down a fragment of Samian Ware was found along with a brick and a pair of bronze tweezers, both thought to be Roman.

After three days the first shaft was almost 20 feet below the summit of the Mound when the first fall of earth occurred. Rutland hoped that the roots of the yew would retain the earth but when more fell in next day he had the shaft hurriedly reinforced with timber planks and beams. When the first object – a spearhead – was discovered protruding from the wall of the shaft, Rutland descended to investigate only to be buried by another substantial fall. He was extricated with difficulty and that night the yew fell into the shaft. After the several days it took for Rutland to recover and for the remains of the yew and the splintered timber supports to be removed, work recommenced and was almost immediately rewarded by the discovery of lines of gold in the dark brown earth.

Rutland stands hands on hips looking up at the Mound, his face glowing with evident pride that he found within it the most astounding Anglo-Saxon relics yet discovered in the United Kingdom. Unfortunately some of the articles were broken – almost certainly by the collapse of the yew and much of the Mound – but he feels vindicated to have finally found Tæppa in his grave. Not much of him, Rutland admits, but fragments of his jaw, thigh and several vertebrae were there in the remains of a 12-foot-by-8 oaken chamber with a floor of fine gravel. The golden lines were thought to be the remains of an inch-wide gold brocade on a woollen garment extending diagonally from his shoulder. He must have been an honoured and prestigious pagan to be ritually interred at a site of such ancient religious significance. No Christian would have been buried with magnificent grave goods to make his going easier in the afterlife.

These fabulous relics are now in the care of the British Museum. The Mound has been restored to a happy hump bereft of its treasures. The past master climbs to its crest and strikes a pose with his legs astride to evoke verbal images of the mythological Wayland the Smith forging Tæppa's iron sword and of chieftains riding around the mound reciting elegies of praise for this heroic king. His Beowulfian flow is impressive. Even sceptics might be drawn irresistibly to this man's flame. No wonder he is honorary secretary to three societies – the Maidenhead & Taplow Field Club, the Thames Valley Antiquarian Society and the National Society for Preserving Memorials to the Dead – which seem to exist and survive solely due to his enthusiastic energy.

Little does Rutland know but the Field Club will fold later this summer having enjoyed eight successful years. It was founded on 18th September 1883 and thrived at a time when the discovery of Tæppa sparked enthusiasm for all things ancient among what *The Maidenhead Advertiser* called "a certain class of intelligent people". The declared aim of the Club – to collect and publish information on local antiquities – immediately attracted 55 members. Many more joined to enjoy "semi-scientific flirtations.... errant gossip in sylvan spots.... meanderings in ivy-clad ruins, with panoramic peeps across vale and plain" and picnics provided by the ladies. Naturally Rutland maintains the Club's journal in which he has recorded his fieldwork in Taplow and elsewhere.

He had the Thames dredged in 1884 and has since excavated beyond it with enthusiasm at Robin Hood's Arbour, Spencer's Farm and the Roman villa at Castle Hill. The rather hurried and unscientific execution of the latter in just five days of 1886 has done no harm to his reputation as an archaeological expert. He will be summoned to consider finds made when a gas main is buried beneath **Mill Lane** in 1893 and a cess pit is dug at **Hedsor Wharf** in 1895.

The Identity Question

Tæppa's Mound / 6th February 2012

Kupferman's excavations by the Cruciform Dairy not far to the south-east revealed a 4,000-year-old knife blade, an Iron Age brooch and pot, 3rd Century Roman coins and Samian pottery from Gaul, 9th and 10th Century Saxon pottery and medieval stone window jambs and blocks. This very strange mix of finds suggested two things: that Rutland had dumped there both the spoils from his excavations and the surviving remains of the Norman church, and that the amateur past master's over-enthusiastic and misguidedly slapdash efforts may have destroyed forever any reliable evidence of any possible earlier ceremonial burial and of exactly who Tæppa was and when he was interred. Guesses on the latter question usually range between 620 and 625. However there is no doubt his burial was of such astounding richness that it remains third only to the burials at Sutton Hoo (Suffolk), found in 1939 (possibly of Rædwald), and at Prittlewell near Southend (Essex) discovered in 2003 (possibly of Sæberht). Archaeological wisdom is that all three are contemporary to within a few years and that Tæppa's treasures were crafted between 590 and 610 AD. They comprise a unique intricately decorated heavy gold buckle, a pair of gilt bronze clasps (which had probably been attached to a belt), iron weapons (a sword, a knife and three spearheads) and two iron shield bosses, a 'Coptic' bronze bowl, a large bronze cauldron (two feet in diameter) of a type used in raiding Saxon warships, two wooden buckets with decorated bronze rims, two crescent-shaped bronze ornaments (thought to be part of a lyre), the remains of six drinking horns (two of them 18 inches long) with silver gilt mounts and finials, four green glass 'claw' beakers and several cylindrical antler gaming pieces.

The identity question still hangs in the air. Who might have been pagan and so important in or around the second decade of the 7th Century? Who would have wanted to establish their tribal or religious authority over this revered ancient site and its surroundings? Could he be the culprit who curtailed **Hitchambury**?

Whimsy extends to seven horizons. The discovery made the national newspapers which celebrated the "Viking's Tomb at Taplow": a "ludicrous appellation" according to **James Rutland** for whom the most popular candidate was Ælle, buried as the South Saxons retreated from *Mons Badonicus* in a vain attempt to claim the land as theirs. **Willy Grenfell** also advanced this theory despite it being probably some 70 years before its time or around 250 after it in the unlikely event that the deceased was Ælla of Northumberland. The comparison and contiguity with Sutton Hoo makes it tempting to wonder if he was an Anglian nobleman, perhaps a relative or *thegn* of Rædwald stationed on a far-flung outpost of his expanding domain. The artistic style of his artefacts and adornments led archaeologist SC Hawkes to suggest in 1986 that **Tæppa** was a Kentish prince or an ally of the Kentish king. This theory is reinforced by the discovery of the 'Coptic' bowl and of a sherd of an eastern Mediterranean late-Roman vessel found in the spoil, both potential indicators of foreign trade then associated with Kent. But if he was Kentish, wouldn't he have been Christian? Maybe not if he was Æthelberht's son Eadwald or some other young Kentish buck who had rejected the heresy of there being but one god and was seeking somewhere to stay heathen and free. Alternatively, could he be one of Sæberht's sons imitating Kentish extravagance, or perhaps simply the chap who built the mound not the body beneath it?

Eyes of a Child – Esme Maree, Scarlett Wayland-Smith & Keira Smales

St Nicolas' School – 23rd April 2012

Esme thinks Taplow has lots of history because we have Tæppa's Mount that Taplow is named after him. Scarlett explains that, in Taplow, there is a big Mound next to Taplow Court. There was lots of treasure buried deep down in the Mound. The treasure was old plates and cups with lots of gold and even the prince was buried there. Next to the Mound there is a big house and you can go and have a look at all the history. I think the Mound is special to me because you can have lots of fun on it like have races down it and do rolly-polly on it. Keira likes the Mound because it has an amazing history and in the snow it's fun to sled down it. She says that on top you can see over the wall and see Maidenhead. In the night you see all the lights and it looks like stars in the sky but on the ground.

Tall Tale – Stag Night

Tæppa's Mound / 6th December 628

The view from 15 feet up atop the Mound is better than ever before. At 80 feet in diameter and 240 feet in circumference, it is a worthy example of the ancient *tumuli* that crown many a British hilltop to command the land for miles around: a sure sign that while warlords may come and go the spirits of our land are forever unchanging.

The sky has been icy cornflower blue all day until the winter sun began to slip away beyond Bray. The south-western horizon was burnished gold then set afire in crimson flame that edged to an orange ember before the darkness cooled the night air to chill our cheeks. Now the inky black above us is sprinkled with a million twinkling stars but we have eyes for only one: *Merak* sparkles at the heart of the *Great Bear* constellation. It is the lower of the two stars on the right of *The Plough* that align to lead the eye to the *North Star*. Two nights ago the annual meteor shower near *Merak* heralded the festival of the stag-horned winter sun god Herne the Hunter. The climax will come soon with frenzied dances and clashing antlers, an ancient rite performed down the generations to bring fortune to the hunt.

A Christian Coming

The Accidental Saint

Tæppa's Mound / 6th December 635

If the Mound was intended to proclaim and protect the polytheistic world in the Thames Valley, it isn't a success. In fact, it will be its grand last shout. Taplow is now on another frontier: the cusp of Christianity.

A little way down the hill there is a large gathering around the pool that has been sacred since time began for being where no pool should be. Back in the summer a foreign holy man stood waist deep in the waters. Locals took turns to let him duck them beneath the surface. He called it baptism: a rite of acceptance of and into the Christian faith. Not everyone around here is convinced that just one God can be more powerful than all the pagan gods put together but the feeling is that we are witnessing something rather special here, something that will change the way of things forever.

One of the holy man's West Saxon disciples is sitting quietly by the pool. He confides that the new faith has had a bit of trouble spreading from its early roots in the south-east corner of Britannia. Although it has begun to make its mark amongst the Angles of Northumbria, Pope Honorius I decided Christianity wasn't catching on fast enough with the Mercians and he knew just the Frank for the job. A year ago the Benedictine monk **Birinus** was despatched reluctantly from Rome. Legend has it that shortly after setting sail across the Channel he realised he had left behind the holy sacrament he normally wore wrapped in a cloth around his neck. He calmly walked on the water back to the port, picked up the sacrament and returned completely dry to the boat where its crew immediately converted to Christianity.

A second serendipity soon followed. Birinus must be counting his blessings for Mercia can wait. He got only as far as *Dorcic* (Dorchester-on-Thames, Oxfordshire) where the fearsome Cynegils had good reason to come to Christianity at that very moment. Oswald of Northumbria would not ally with a heathen, not even against the dreaded Mercian menaces. The wily Cynegils took baptism, married his daughter Kyneburga to Oswald to cement their alliance and rewarded Birinus by making him Bishop of Dorcic and giving him the freedom to spread God's Word along the Thames Valley. Where better to start than Taplow?

Holy Places

Bapsey Pond / 6th December 2012

It is often forgotten that ancient Britons got the Christian message well before the Romans made it theirs. This original Britannic creed of Christianity came erroneously to be called the Celtic Church. It secured its patches not by fighting pagan beliefs but by accepting and evolving them. This was perhaps a more astute strategy than the more remote and rigid Roman Church which came to claim the high ground only to disappear when the Germanic invasions cast a new pagan cloak over Britannia in the 5th Century. However Roman Catholics learned a trick or two in the ensuing double millennia. The word of Pope Gregory was to draw people willingly to a new faith by adapting local mystic traditions and re-dedicating shrines. According to Legend, Birinus embraced Taplow's ancient pagan pomp and circumstance by adopting as a holy place for Christian baptism an apparently supernatural pool known ever since as **Bapsey Pond**.

It was clearly no mean diplomatic achievement for Birinus to secure not only a fusion of pagan and Christian beliefs but also the cooperation of the local community leaders with his novel ideas. He respected the fresh burial mound of a revered chieftain by leaving it intact – it was eventually crowned with a mystical yew tree – and the whole site was given new and vibrant life when Taplow's first church was built a few yards away.

Bapsey Pond / 19th June 1942

The waters of Bapsey Pond are once again being used for baptism. The ancient Norman font has been set up in the shade of an ivy-bound may tree for the Right Reverend Gerald Allen, Bishop of Dorchester, to baptise Anne Morrison and her baby brother John, the siblings Eileen and John Miller and a fifth child.

The Old Churchyard / 6th December 2012

This is where we started our journey. Once upon a time, this churchyard was new. Opinion differs on when that was. Seven years ago, its geophysical survey and resistivity tests led Marlow Archaeological Society to suggest the first St Nicholas' Church was of the Early English style, possibly built between 1190 and 1260. This contrasts with the conclusion reached by English Heritage ten years before that its geophysical survey coupled with parch marks on the grass indicated a much earlier church, possibly built in the 8th or 9th Century with walls six feet thick in places in the tradition of Kentish churches like St Mary's in the coastal hamlet of Reculver.

A hundred years ago Lord Desborough described the discovery of an Anglo-Saxon church which current churchwardens **Jennifer Robertson** and **Richard King** date more precisely to "around 640". Those who dismiss this as wishful thinking should perhaps beg this question: given that they built a wooden church of **St Laurence** at **Upton**, why would Anglo-Saxons not have done something similar at Taplow's more sacred site? This History is none the wiser. It will accept the possibility of there being a Saxon church for two indulgent reasons: it would confirm a seamless evolution of the site from pagan to Christian worship, and it would be nice to think that it might have been blessed by Birinus before he died in 649 and was canonised soon afterwards. Some say there are burials hereabouts which go that far back, but are they Christian? Perhaps they include descendants or friends of Tæppa whom **St Birinus** had to persuade to his way of thinking. Maybe they could say whether Legend has it right that Birinus died after being bitten by an adder in the Chiltern woods and that as a result no adder can survive within the sound of Dorchester's bells. Or maybe they would give us a different angle altogether.

A Century Partnership

St Nicolas' Church / 14th January 2012

If the churchwardens are right there has been a St Nicholas in Taplow for 1,372 years, or only for 742 years according to Marlovian archaeologists. That Norman church by Tæppa's Mound was described as being about 84 feet long by 20 broad and boasting handsomely-mullioned windows of painted glass. For almost four centuries various lords (and ladies) of the manor in the Manfield, Hampson and Orkney families were interred in its crypts and vaults. The belief that there had been a previous church was perhaps fuelled by its ancient square font, said to be older than the church and given pride of place on a circular column profusely decorated with carvings and coats of arms

It is 186 years since the second (or third) church was built here, a new location but not the same durability. It lasted a mere 84 years before being substantially replaced by the third (or fourth) which by the end of this year will have served its congregation for the small matter of 100 years during which it lost its 'h' (in around 1927).

Hundreds have squeezed in here tonight to begin this church's centenary celebrations by witnessing an engaging, semi-dramatised story of the lives of WS Gilbert and Arthur Sullivan and a performance of *Trial by Jury*, their second collaboration. In all, the assembled multitude has seen 16 actors, a 19-piece orchestra and a chorus of 74 Victoriana-attired locals sing and play admirably under the accomplished baton of the renowned **Gillian Didben**. Three of the soloists have long been in her tender loving care: Lucy Morris (the fainting Plaintiff) was formerly of Taplow Youth Choir, Gareth Watkins (the Defendant) a dedicated choirboy at Desborough Boys' School, and her son Mark Griffiths (the Learned Judge), Musical Director of the prize-winning choir *Coro* and Director of Junior Choirs at Trinity College of Music. Hearts were melted by the contributions of **Amelia** and **Florence Snoxell**, **Lily Begley**, **Jasmine Fone**, **Luisa Kent** and **Tamsin Ratcliff** as the Bridesmaids and by the Pageboys, **Daniel** and **Max O'Brien**. Grateful thanks are also due to the offstage team led by the Reverend **Alan Dibden**, our vicar resplendent in an open-necked shirt to match his open-toed sandals.

St Nicolas' Church / 9th December 2012

The church is packed once again, this time for a Festival Parish Communion on the nearest Sunday to the centenary of its consecration on 6th December 1912. What's all the fuss about? This is just a building which has been here for exactly 100 years and three days. The Right Reverend John Pritchard, Bishop of Oxford, tries to answer with a sermon of three intertwining themes: the importance of place, of people and of vision. St Birinus brought a vision of a just, compassionate and purposeful society which played a significant part in giving the people of Taplow a sense of common identity, of community and of continuity represented tangibly by our churches. The past is present all around us. Here and in the old churchyard lie generations of previous Taplovians. We are their future. Ours will be our children and theirs. This isn't the same place it has always been but it is the same old faith resurrected in new people in new surroundings.

My Lord Bishop ends with the words, "May the Lord bless you.... as you, the living stones, celebrate the old stones in the name of the Cornerstone, Jesus Christ our Lord". I don't have his strength of faith in God but I believe strongly that the Church and this church are important to our community. That is why any and all profits from this book will go towards keeping the current St Nicolas' Church in good repair for future Taplovians.

Eyes of a Child – Molly Edmondson, Poppy Jaminson, Monty Keates & Jennifer Neal

St Nicolas' School / 23rd April 2012

Molly and Poppy agree: their favourite place in Taplow would most definitely be the Church, with all its beauty and space it gives them wonders how people built it. The Church is one of Monty's favourite places because "we get to share our thoughts and pray". He loves the things we do there like all the services and the Nativity. Jennifer thinks the Church is very old. Lots of people go there at Easter, Harvest Festival and at Christmas. There is a vicar that works there. His name is Reverend Dibden, he is a good vicar.

A Thirty Partnership

The Rectory / 9th December 2012

The Dibdens had something of their own to celebrate this year: 30 years of marriage.

Gillian is a local girl. Her grandfather Saul Eason came from Canterbury via Islington, where he was a police constable, to Burnham where by 1911 he was landlord of *The Garibaldi*. His son Thomas earned pocket-money in his youth rolling the grass at Taplow Cricket

Club before growing up to be a self-taught pianist famous hereabouts for playing-by-ear in wartime bands. Gillian inherited this musical talent. She joined the choir at St Mary's Church (Langley) and went on to study piano and cello at The Royal College of Music until 1963 when she became a music teacher St Bernard's Convent School (Slough). During her 20 years there, her Chamber Choir won both National and International prizes in *Let the People Sing*, a competition sponsored by the European Broadcasting Union.

Alan had a rather appropriate birthplace for a man of the cloth. His family had long been farmers at Christchurch (then Hampshire, now Dorset) where his surname meant *the people who live in the hollow*. His upbringing was church-every-Sunday but it wasn't until he was studying law at Hull University that his heart set on a career as a cleric. After theological college in Cambridge, his first post was in Peckham, initially as deacon until his ordination in 1974 elevated him to the priesthood. He spent two very stimulating, impossibly busy years as warden and missioner of Pembroke House in Walworth before his ability not to send his interviewer to sleep secured him the post of Team Vicar at St Francis (Langley). Gillian was just up the road. They quickly became firm friends and slowly realised there was more to it. They married in 1982 and moved together to All Saints' Church on the cusp of Chalfont St Peter and Gerrard's Cross. Gillian's prowess was recognised in 1984 when she was appointed Head of Voice & Choral Music for the Berkshire Young Musicians' Trust. Her choirs many times won the Youth and Junior Choir sections of the *Sainsbury's Choir of the Year* competition, once beat all adult choirs to take the *Choir of the Year* award, won numerous prizes at the *National Festival of Music for Youth* and performed at the *School Proms* in the Royal Albert Hall.

Alan smiles now to recall that in 1990 he came to Taplow for the variety. The congregation he inherited from the Reverend **Jonathan Meyrick** ranged from the better-off to retired agricultural workers on state pensions. The Taplow Parish Charity was still active: it had originally been founded as a coal fund but was still important in giving support those in need. Now the socio-economic balance has shifted, especially in the last ten years as younger families with children have come to Taplow. Many of these youngsters have flourished under Gillian's direction. At the church, she found a soulmate in **Keith Weller**: St Nicolas' organist and choirmaster for more than 40 years until his death in 2005. Nowadays she shares church choirmaster responsibilities with organist **Neil Matthews**.

Having been named National Choir Director of the Year in 2002, she and **Philip Viveash** set up **Taplow Youth Choirs** in 2004 and won the *BBC Choir of the Year* four years later. TV choirmaster Gareth Malone came to watch and learn. Her outstanding services to youth choral music were recognised in 2009 by the award of an MBE. There are now four Taplow Choirs – Boys', Girls', Children's and Youth – and Gillian is also leader of the Marlow Community Choir.

Alan's responsibilities include being a governor of St Nicolas' School and an elder statesman in the **Jubilee River Group Ministry** in which five vicars span eight churches. St Nicolas has long been associated with **St Mary** (Hitcham) and **St Anne** (Dropmore). In 2008 they were joined in a new Group Ministry by **St Peter's** (Burnham), **St James the Less** (Dorney), St John the Baptist (Eton) and St John the Evangelist (Eton Wick) and St Andrew (Cippenham). The Church of England ordained its first female priests in 1993; by the summer of 2014, Alan and the Reverend Bill Jackson of St Peter's will be outnumbered by three female colleagues.

Taplow in the Dark

Old Bayley Lore – Name Games: Taplow

Westmorland Drive, Maidenhead / 5th March 2012

Did **Tæppa** ever actually exist? Or could Taplow's 12th Century name Tappelawe have derived from the ancient Britannic *Tir-Pel-lor*, meaning *the tumulus of the distant leader*? The phonetics fit perfectly for an unidentified but legendary lord who came with bravado only to fall in battle leaving nothing but a pile of earth and a misty folk memory revived by the imagination of a Victorian past master.

Which came first for **Bapsey Pond**: its name or baptisms by **St Birinus**? The Romans watered their heavy horses in a handy pond near **Taplow Castle** that locals called *Bur-Epow-Seiri-Pwll*, meaning *the pool of the horsemen of the earthworks*. Perhaps Birinus thought it must have been God's will that he found a pool in a pagan land with just the right name for the purpose he had in mind for it. But he was very much mistaken if he thought that by baptising a few important locals he had succeeded in persuading everyone to put aside their pagan beliefs. Ancient witchcraft still echoed into the 19th Century when the lace-making wise women of Taplow knew how to cure most ailments with natural potions and balms, and a bowl made from a human skull was found in Bapsey Pond when it was cleaned out in the 1960s.

Were the churches in **Hedsor** and Taplow dedicated to St Nicholas to trump preceding pagan ceremonies? Christians celebrate St Nicholas' Day on 6th December, previously one of the most important nights in the pagan calendar. Can it be mere coincidence that both churches are on sites that may have had ancient pagan importance that extended into the Roman era, or that *Merak* is known to Christians as the Star of St Nicholas? Anglicans celebrate St Birinus's Day on 4th September but Catholics do so on 3rd December: traditionally the anniversary of his death at Dorcic and coincidentally the eve of the festival of Herne the Hunter. What better signal that such heathen shenanigans would no longer be tolerated in Taplow?

Rubbing Along

Tæppa's Mound / 24th February 838

The rest of the 7th Century was quiet after all the excitement of Tæppa and Birinus. As an East Saxon outpost Taplow's primary duty appears to have been little more than pulling faces at the West Saxons across the river. Most of the action was miles away up north where the rivalry between the Angles of Northumbria, Mercia and East Anglia bubbled away to create Angle-land and call it England.

The 8th Century had its moments. The East Angles edged in only to be elbowed out and replaced as South Bucks overlords by the Mercians whose domain grew to extend from the Humber to the Thames. Perhaps Taplovians developed face-pulling into the noble art of gurning. The West Saxons retaliated by inventing Wessex. Several warriors were buried near where **Bourne End** will have a station. Wags will speculate whether they died in a border battle or waiting for a train (whatever that is).

The 9th Century has gone for novelty. Egbert of Wessex has superseded the predominance of Offa of Mercia to become the first king of all England. Angles and Saxons have finally hyphenated. Resolving differences by talking them over has become all the rage....

A Dash of Danish

Taplow Manor House / 24th February 871

History is making a note that **Astig** is lord of Taplow Manor. He is the first to be recorded as having this privilege and responsibility, the last for another 200 years. That makes him official. It won't do him much good. Taplow is about to become briefly Danish on his watch.

The first Danish raid was in 789 when they landed in Dorset, of all places. Four years later they descended upon the much more logical target of Lindisfarne Priory in Northumbria where they "made lamentable havoc.... by rapine and slaughter". Angle-land has been subjected to *Vikings* ever since – the term originally meant *an overseas expedition* but has come to apply to the raiders themselves – and now they don't even bother to go home. They've established a base on the Isle of Thanet from where they ebb and flow irritatingly up and down the Thames. Æthelwulf of Wessex fought off a flush in 851 at Acleah (probably Oakley), they made life hell in Surrey in 853 and now they're giving Astig and his neighbours that same treatment.

Forever England

Taplow Manor House / 1st October 959

The 10th Century has changed the way of the world. Tonight's a night for celebration. Raise high our horns and drink deeply of *strangan beore* (*strong beer*) and *hluttor ealu* (*clear ale*). Taplow has just spent its last two years on the frontier. England is one once more. Let's sit here by the fire to hear again how the past hundred years have unfolded....

The Vikings matured from raiders to invaders of Northumbria and East Anglia before returning with a vengeance in 870 to sweep up the Thames Valley to Reading and on to Cirencester. It was all too much for King Æthelred of Wessex who died in 871 leaving the problem to his little brother Alfred. The enterprising young man established 33 *burhs* (forts) across his domain to thwart the Viking surges. One was at *Sceaftesege* (which thankfully will be simplified as Cookham's **Sashes Island**). Sadly these efforts didn't much hinder his enemy. Legend says the Vikings stopped off to defeat local Saxons on the Berkshire bank at *Batlyngmede*. Alfred didn't make it clear in *The Anglo-Saxon Chronicles* exactly where this was. However, when the Cookham Lock cut is dug in 1829, workmen will discover swords, spears and skeletons thought to be the remains of warriors who died defending their stronghold after being defeated on the meadows to the south that Victorian historians will note as *Bartle Mead*, later **Battlemead**. Young Alfred seems to have missed the debacle, perhaps because he was rather busy taking a break in Somerset where (as everyone knows) he failed dismally in the inaugural *Great British Bake-Off*. He recovered to fight the Danes to a standstill by 878 and do a few other clever things administratively and academically to become a national hero as **King Alfred the Great**.

Taplow and its neighbours remained Danish until the victories of Alfred's son King Edward (the Elder) laid the foundation for his son King Æthelstan to unite all England again in 927. This happy state lasted only 12 years before turmoil returned. Northumbria was lost to the Vikings. Æthelstan's half-brother King Eadred pulled everything back together again only for it to fragment in local powerplays. Two years ago the country divided along the Thames with 16-year-old King Eadwig a puppet in the south and his 14-year-old brother Edgar equally nominally in charge of Taplow and the rest of the north. But today Eadwig has breathed his last (how did that happen?) and the country is to reunite once more under King Edgar I. Soon his kingdom will be so secure that he'll be remembered as Edgar the Peaceful. And we'll remember that it was from this day forward that we could all rest assured that there will always be an England (even if it is usually ruled by foreigners).

Danish All Over

Tæppa's Mound / 28th October 1016

It couldn't last. The 11th Century hasn't started well. The village huts are still smouldering. Having done their worst, the dastardly Danes are dashing westward to Wallingford and Oxford, burning and pillaging all the way.

How did it come to this? Everything was fine in the reigns of Edgar the Peaceful and his son King Edward (the Younger) but the young fellow's brother and successor Æthelred's inability to organise the English effectively to resist Danish incursions justly earned him the epithet 'the Unready'. Consequently England ended the 10th Century at odds with its Danish minority. The last decade has been a nightmare here in the Thames Valley and things have just got worse. Ten days ago Cnut defeated King Edmund Ironside at *Assandun* (somewhere in Essex) and dashed upriver to trash Taplow and everywhere else. One of the Danes lost an iron axe-head in the river near not-yet **Glen Island** on the way to a final, conclusive victory in the Forest of Dean.

Cnut is a wily general. He will prove to be a wise king, possibly the best England has ever had. Where he meets prudent and pragmatic leaders like our good Earl Godwin of Wessex, he will react accordingly. He won't try to fix what isn't broken. Consequently it will come as a relief for England to be Danish all over for 26 years.

The Original Royal Ripple

Sashes Island, Cookham / 28th October 2012

Although Alfred the Great fortified and probably fought in the middle Thames Valley, royalty really arrived in 975 when King Edgar I coveted **Cookham** and local *ealdorman* Ælpheah thought it would be a good move to cede it to him. Cookham's serendipitous coincidence of road and river had made it a valuble prize worth £50 (£3.6m) in 1066, twice as much as **Bray** and more than all the nearby Buckinghamshire hamlets put together. **Burnham** was then the only parish in South Bucks more populous and more valuable than Taplow but it was very small beer by comparison with the two Berkshire beauties which grew up to spend the 14th Century within the dowry of the Queens of England until being settled in turn on King Henry IV's son Humphrey, 1st Duke of Gloucester: Bray in 1399, Cookham in 1435. This didn't seem such a good idea in 1441 when Humphrey's wife Eleanor was condemned to life imprisonment for treasonable necromancy (raising the spirits of the dead). The manors reverted to King Henry VI on his Uncle Humphrey's death in 1447 only to be forgotten as His Lancastrian Majesty suffered first a mental breakdown in 1453 and then deposition eight years later at the hands of his cousin the Duke of York, eventually King Edward IV.

The more modest manors of Elington and Spencers lay between these mini-metropolises. These retained their names through the reacquisition of both moieties by John Pinkney in 1428 and their sale as one package in 1445 to John Norreys. His family will hold them for 171 years during which Maydenhedd will enjoy the business opportunities presented by the hooves, heels and wheels of passers-by that sowed the seeds for the town to embrace both manors and to overshadow previously more notable neighbours. The same commercial seeds flourished across the river where **Slough** hungrily consumed its venerable neighbours to leave Taplow the rural meat in an urban sandwich.

Tall Tale – An Unlikely Seat of Government

Taplow Common / 28th October 2012

The winding **Huntswood Lane** feels secretive. A bungalow hides behind an unruly hedge. A barking dog discourages exploration. Foliage crowds in with foreboding to make the lane even narrower. The trees get taller, the shade intensifies. There is a turning on the left: a green tunnel heading who knows where. This is **Parliament Lane**, but why? History reports that the *Witanagemot* (the Anglo-Saxon Parliament) of Æthelred the Unready met in Cookham in 997. Legend likes to think the *Witanagemot* gathered here occasionally during Egbert of Wessex's reign as *Bretwalda* from 825 to 839, but where? There on the left in the southern paddocks of **Cliveden Stud**? Or here on the right in the grounds of ***Burnham Lodge*** nursing home? Or not at all if you think this is another tall tale that has grown in the telling.

The Elusive Tæppa

Tæppa's Mound as James Rutland began his excavations / 1883

His method and discoveries, as reported in *The Illustrated London News* / 1883

Rutland busy with another indulgence: playing the organ / c1890

The Elusive Tæppa

Rutland (front right) **supervises the excavations** / 1883

How Tæppa's burial might have looked / 2014

Tæppa's Mound today / 2012 & 2014

Bapsey Pond

Millennium Baptisms: the Bishop of Dorchester baptises Anne Morrison with the waters of Bapsey Pond / 1942

Many years later, Brian Horton captured its mystery....

Keeping secrets / 2009

Revealing why it was once mystical to pagans for its mysterious elevation / 2012

St Nicholas then, St Nicolas now

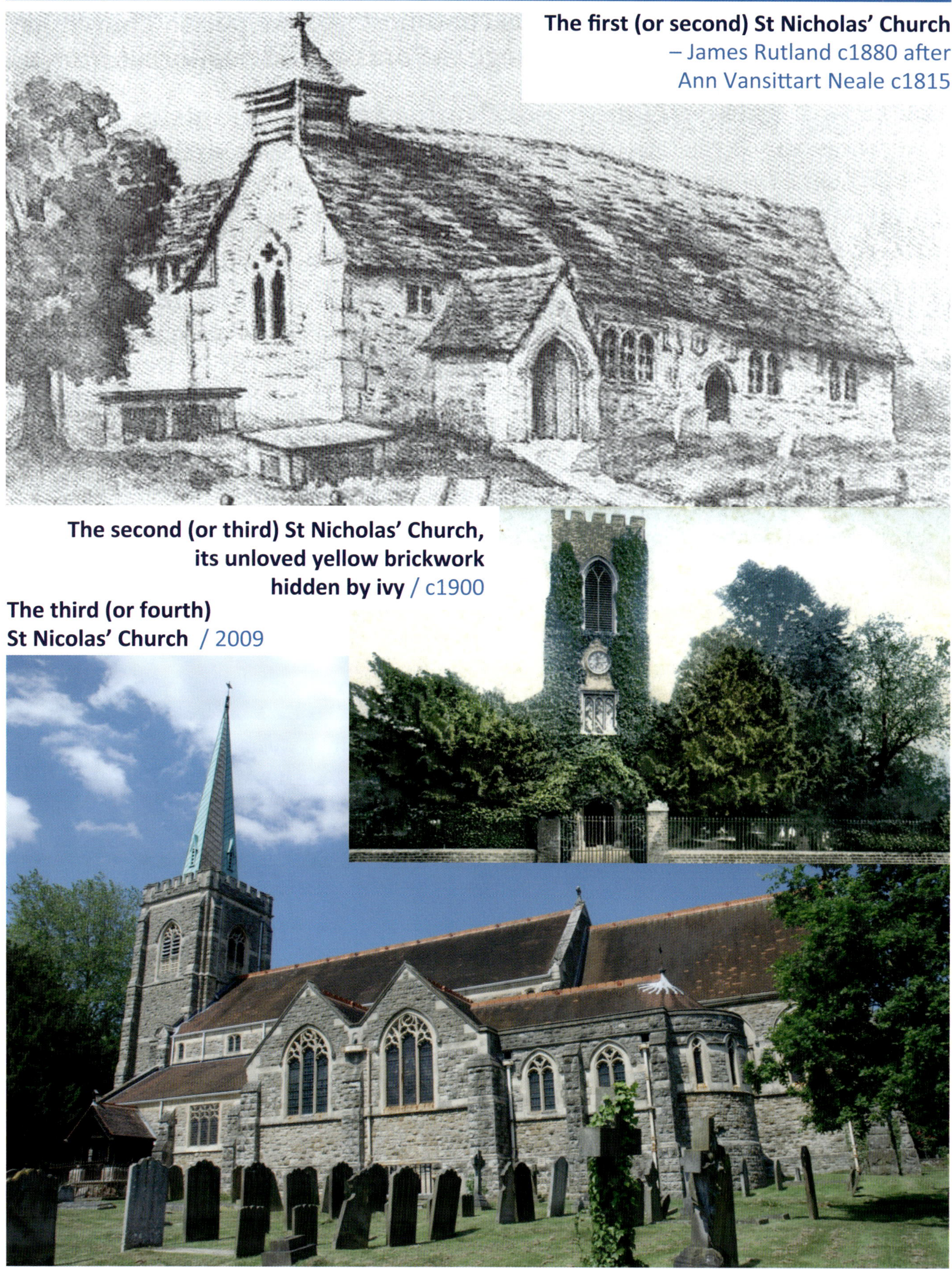

The first (or second) St Nicholas' Church – James Rutland c1880 after Ann Vansittart Neale c1815

The second (or third) St Nicholas' Church, its unloved yellow brickwork hidden by ivy / c1900

The third (or fourth) St Nicolas' Church / 2009

Reverend Alan Dibden, in the pulpit / 2014

A year of celebrations begin with a choral performance of *Trial by Jury* / 2012

Gillian Dibden with Gareth Watkins

Tony & Brenda Hickman, in costume

Chorus and Orchestra, in tune

St Nicolas now

A favourite place, most definitely – Molly Edmondson, Poppy Jaminson & Keira Smales / 2012

Medieval Meandering

Old Bayley Lore – Way Back When

The Low Way

Bray Rigle / 28th February 1212

For thousands of years, most travellers have preferred the safer summer road that once crossed Dorney Reach over an ancient bridge, one of the earliest in north-west Europe. Nowadays *The King's Street* – so-called for being the way Plantagenet monarchs travel west – wanders through **Upton** and **Chalvey**, edges carefully around the treacherous **Treacle Mines** (a derivation of the Ancient British *Tir Sigl Minen*, meaning *land of the quaking bog*) and on past **Cippenham Palace** to **Dorney**, past **Aumberdene** onto a causeway that will be the lane to ***Barge Farm***, across the *briva* to **Bray** and on westwards along another causeway. When the river is low, travellers might leave the higher winter road at **Burnham** to come down *Hogue Heol* (Hag Hill Lane) to converge with others on their way from Cippenham and paddle across the river here at **Bray Rigle**, the firm bed of which will eventually excite the great engineer **Isambard Kingdom Brunel** to use it to bear the ***Great Western Railway***. But Taplow won't have to wait over six centuries for its first bout of civil engineering. It will soon be tailored to the wants and whims of a king's little brother....

Sippenham Palace / 28th February 1252

Perhaps this place was a palace in the Norman era. It certainly became one in 1227 when **King Henry III** had it rebuilt for his then 18-year-old brother **Richard, 1st Earl of Cornwall** (and lord of Hitcham, as it happens). Naturally what this young buck needed most was a bigger deer park. His new neighbour Thomas de Lascelles was quick to oblige. Having inherited his father Duncan's bits of Burnham, he saw the prudence of ceding them in 1230 to the eminent young Richard whose taste for tinkering locally never tires despite his living at Wallingford Castle, going off on the Sixth Crusade to the Holy Land, claiming large chunks of France and ending up as King of the Romans (meaning the Germans). Top of his 'to do' list recently has been to divert the summer road along a new line all the way from Colnbrook to a new bridge over the River Thames [*see Map 12*]. Some say this makes sense since the old *briva* to Bray was washed away a while ago. Or is his real aim to spare his deer distress at the frightening sight and disgusting smell of weary travellers crossing his Sippenham estate?

King Charles I will appoint Thomas Witherings as Postmaster of Foreign Mails in 1632 and charge him to speed delivery of the post by building six 'Great Roads' radiating from London. The Great West Road will follow the course laid out for the benefit of dear Richard's deer. This will be rebranded the **Bath Road** in around 1705 when **Queen Anne** travels so often along it to frequent her favourite spa, and in 1908 my great-grandfather Hiram Morecroft's civil engineering firm will complete the reconstruction of the road from Chiswick to Maidenhead and the installation of mains sewers beneath it. One hundred years afterwards the road will have been re-laid many times but the sewers will still be doing what sewers do.

Troubled Bridges over Water

The first Maidenhead Bridge / 28th August 1269

It took three years to construct a causeway nearly a mile long with bridges spanning the Thames and five tributaries. They don't call it civil engineering yet but it is certainly impressive. No record confirms it but nobody would be surprised if My Lord Cornwall hasn't coughed up for the whole caboodle from the proceeds of his Cornish copper and tin mines. Who'd have thought that the wealth of far distant Cornwall would be spent tinkering with the Thames Valley? That'll never happen again, will it?

Travelling west, the first bridge crosses the Taplow Mill tailwater as it runs south to feed Amerden Ponds. The second is this Great Bridge over the river itself – the first **Maidenhead Bridge**, completed in around 1254 some 300 yards upstream from Bray Rigle and perhaps 30 yards north of the 1777 bridge that will still there 225 years later. The third bridge spans **Clappers Stream**, the fourth a culvert that flowes through Rat's Hole. The final pair cross the two natural branches of what will be excavated to create the **Cookham-Maidenhead-Bray Canal**, a useful waterway that in 1875 Victorians will rename York Stream – after Her Majesty's uncle Frederick, Duke of York – some say to avoid the increasingly posh High Street having to tolerate proximity to anything so work-a-day as a canal.

The third Maidenhead Maidenhead Bridge / 28th August 2012

Michael Bayley believes the bridges over the river have gradually crept downstream. He thinks the original was an ancient *briva* a little more than a mile north of here and that its successor – the *briva* below **Taplow Castle** – must surely be that noted in 1202 in the first written reference to a bridge hereabouts. Michael calls this **Taplow Bridge** to differentiate it from Maidenhead Bridge first noted in 1254. Perhaps 13th Century Taplovians could a pleasant circular walk west one way and back the other, an amenity that appeals nowadays with all the talk of a new footbridge being built from **Glen Island** to **Ray Mill Island**.

The first (much repaired) Maidenhead Bridge / 28th August 1382

King Henry III's authority to build the bridge included a grant of 'pontage': the right to raise funds for the upkeep of the bridge by levying tolls on goods passing over or under it. His son King Edward I was a leader of broad vision and great purpose, not the kind of fellow to tolerate anything getting out of control. His headlines about quashing the Welsh and hammering the Scots have tended to overshadow his efforts to make every little thing alright in his realm. The River Thames and its tributaries are no exception. He first granted pontage in 1280 to William de Berford but perhaps this chap pocketed the money because by 1297 the bridge was once more in such desperate need of repair that he was obliged to make a second grant in 1299. Forty years later it cost one penny (£3.73) to take a laden cart over or for a laden barge to pass beneath. The next two Edwards tinkered too – King Edward III made a further grant of pontage in 1339 – but the bridges have remained in such a sorry state now for as long as anyone can remember. Bridgemasters have the right to claim timber for repairs from royal estates at Windsor or **Cookham** but it is another matter altogether to exercise it during this troubled reign of the boy King Richard II. What with the creaking timbers and heavy tolls, it is no wonder that many people prefer to paddle across the river at **Bray Rigle** or ride a ferry first recorded here in 1352 and still run by the Babeham (or **Babham**) family of Cookham.

Such discomforts are not for us. We have paid two tolls today to avoid them: one at ***The Hermitage*** in Tappelawe to cross the brook at the eastern end of the causeway and another here at the chapel to leave the westernmost bridge and enter Maydenhuthe. Perhaps we should count our blessings that we have this and Tappelawe Bridge to choose from. Neither will last much longer, but their end will not be down to rotting timbers.

The second (much repaired) Maidenhead Bridge / 28th August 1612

Not long ago Maidenhead adopted as its seal a probably 14th Century image – but is that long-haired head a maiden, a saint or a portrayal of John Godayn whose name and the crytic *Can Tigern* surrounds the face? Who was this fellow? If the Latin

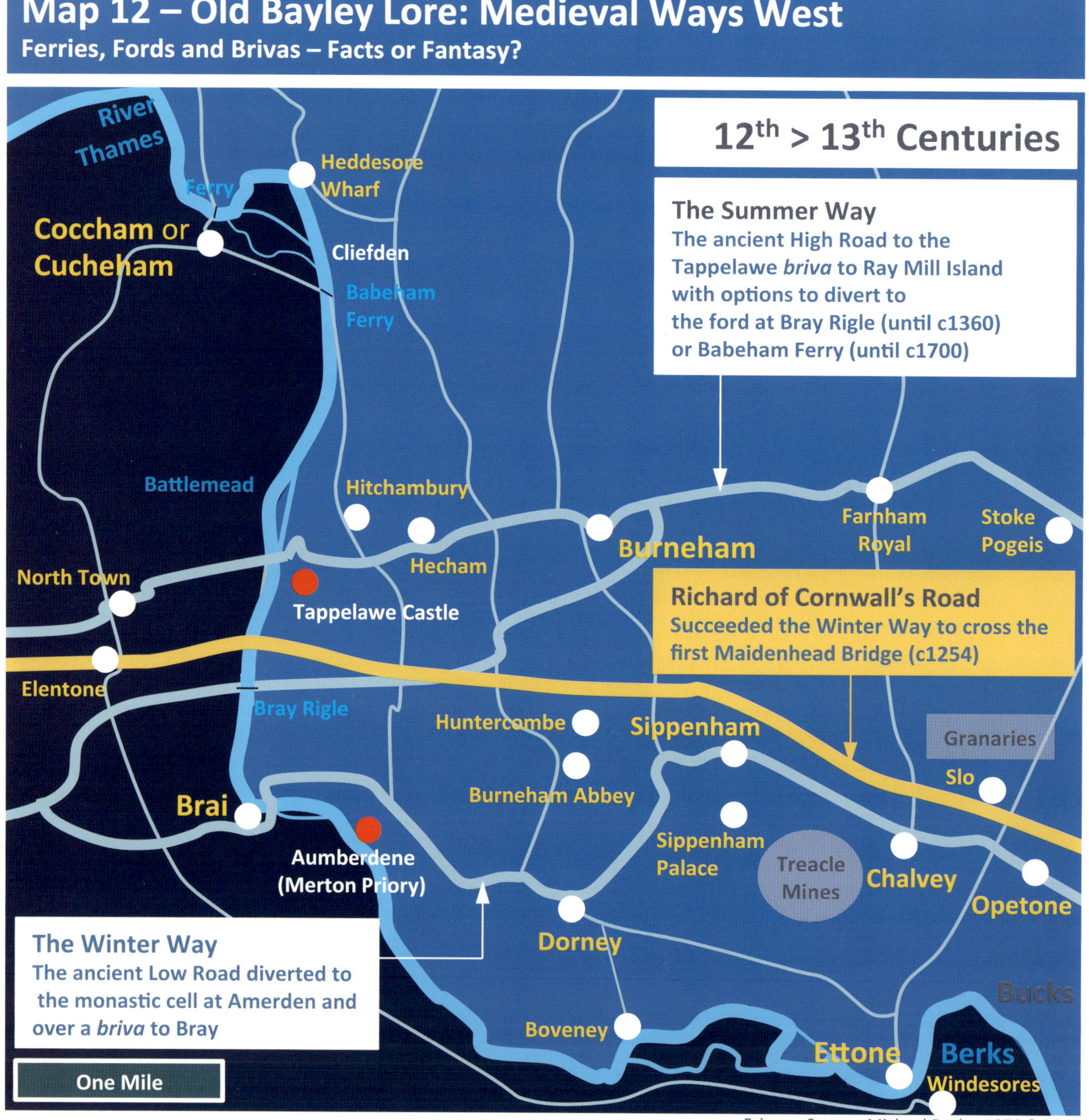

Primary Source: Michael Bayley 1973 & 2012

abbreviation means *Canon of Thiers*, perhaps he was a priest, yet no historical records will show him in the employ of the Church or the Crown. If it means *Cancer Tignarius – builder of trellises in large timber beams* – perhaps he was the engineer who built the original bridge or supervised one or more of its many repairs.

Parry and Thrust – Divergence

Maidenhead Library / 13th November 2013

Keith Parry of **Maidenhead Heritage Trust** isn't convinced that there was any bridge hereabouts before 1254. His thrust is that Cookham ferry was the main river crossing until the need to transport Cotswold wool to London motivated the construction of the first Maidenhead Bridge. And he has found no documentary evidence that there were ever two concurrent bridges. Does **Michael Bayley** base his belief that there were two bridges on Maidenhead records which show two concurrent bridgemasters? Sadly, having passed away last month just eight days before what would have been his 91st birthday, Michael is no longer here to explain that he has no doubt that Maidenhead Bridge had two bridgemasters, neither of whom had responsibility for Tappelawe Bridge since it was an asset of Taplow Manor, never of Maidenhead, and that just because something isn't written down doesn't mean it wasn't so. Here's a thing about history: two people passionate about the past but not on the same page. Who knows what is the truth, the whole truth and nothing but?

Going with the Flow

The third Maidenhead Bridge / 13th November 2013

As Old Father Thames flows below, it is easy to imagine it being a major thoroughfare in ancient times. However its variable depths and shoals, rapids and swift currents didn't always make for an easy ride. Consequently travellers and traders making their way west (and back again) often preferred to have their flat-bottomed barges hauled through the webs of navigable waterways on either side. These slow-flowing waters played a subliminal but significant role in shaping this little corner of the world....

Sideways Glance

Cippenham Palace

Chalvey Ditch / 17th August 1324

The water is low – it hasn't rained for months – but the royal barge has enough draught. King Edward II is relaxing under an awning with his favourite friend: Hugh Despenser, cousin of John of nearby **Elentone Manor**. They left Sheen Palace early this morning to be rowed almost 30 miles upriver and then punted the last three-and-a-bit miles up the brook to their destination, **Cippenham Palace**, where the king will pay his crew of seven a penny each (£2.62) for their day's work.

The spectacle seems serene and yet a shadow of foreboding seems to falls upon the king and upon Cippenham as the barge disappears from sight. How strange to shiver in this unforgiving heat. In three years Edward will be deposed by his wife Queen Isabella and her lover Roger de Mortimer. His successor **King Edward III's** reign of half-a-century will transform England into one of the most formidable military powers in Europe but he will have no time for Cippenham. The palace's history will get distinctly misty for over 200 years until it reappears as Cippenham Place, an Elizabethan manor house surrounded by what may originally have been an Anglo-Saxon moat. By the late-20th Century the site will be a municipal park.

Old Bayley Lore – Just Before Way Back When

Gone in a Flash

Amerden Ponds / 14th March 1342

The brook here is unusual. It flows from the mainstream as the tailwaters of **Taplow Mill** and is therefore the only tributary on the Bucks bank. All the other streams are fed from from springs in Stoke, Farnham, **Burnham** and **Hitcham**. The flow of water is managed by a number of weirs (from *werian*, meaning *to defend* or *dam up*) which create upstream pools of placid water that make excellent fisheries and provide power for watermills. They also make navigation safer up to the moment their single-gated flashlocks are opened to allow boats and barges to pass through.

Amerden Lakes / 14th March 2012

Here is a picture of modern tranquillity: a new curved terrace of seven exclusive townhouses protected from the world behind an iron gate. There are echoes of the past – the old millstream still runs to feed two fishponds formed all those years ago – but no sign of the flashlock, an evocative name that conjures up exciting images of boats flashing past. Downstream traffic did precisely that when it went with the flow. It was much harder work for upstream traffic which had to be hauled or winched through against the current. Actually a *flash* meant an *emptying*: an apt term since upstream water levels dropped dramatically and caused dangerous spates of water below the weirs. Flashlocks were unpopular with millers because the release of so much

Map 13 – Old Bayley Lore: Going with the Flow

Medieval Mills and Waterways

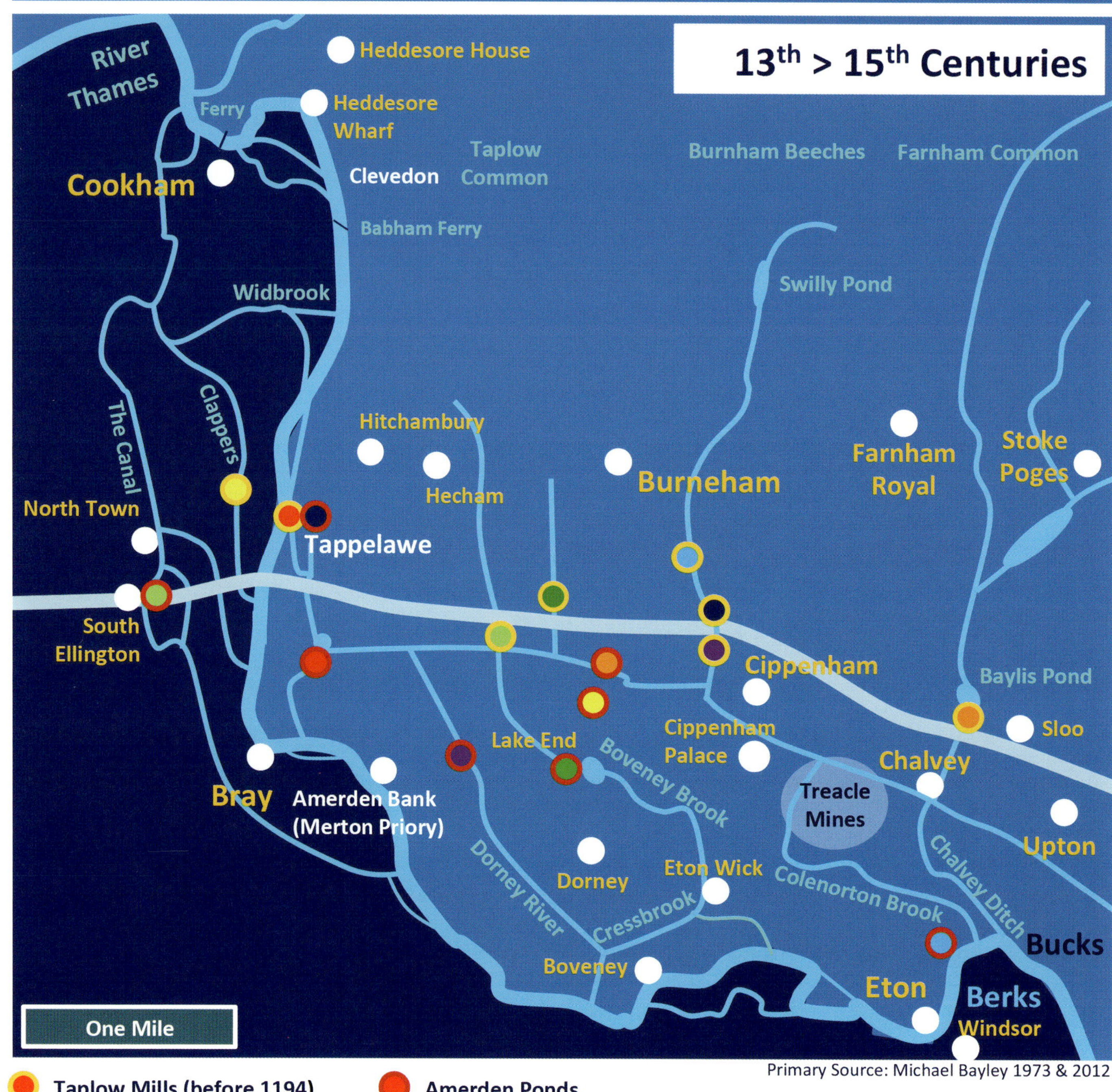

Primary Source: Michael Bayley 1973 & 2012

- Taplow Mills (before 1194)
- Raye Mill (c1346-1828)
- One Mile Mill
- Gy Mill
- Lammas Mill
- Aymill
- Two Mile Mill
- Farnham Mill
- Amerden Ponds
- Burnham Abbey (1265)
- Chapel Arches (1269)
- Dilehurst (until c1270)
- Eton College (1440)
- Taplow Castle (c1000 BC) & Tæppa's Mound (c620)
- The Ghostly Coach
- Huntercombe Manor (c1345)

water temporarily deprived them of the power that turned their waterwheels. And despite lock-keepers sounding horns to warn they were about to flash, the rushing walls of water occasionally washed away unsuspecting souls.

Nowadays Boveney Brook still skirts the western and southern edges of **Eton Wick** and other ancient waterways echo as reservoirs, ponds, brooks and ditches that chequer and criss-cross the flood plain [*see Map 13*]. Many have been obliterated by the recently-dug flood relief channel. The **Jubilee River** looks almost natural as it winds from the now defunct **Taplow Mill** to rejoin the Thames where Chalvey Ditch once did. None of the other mills survive. The One Mile mill became a pub, was rebuilt as *The Horse & Groom* and eventually reinvented as a day nursery near *Sainsbury's* superstore. The Gy, Lammas and Two Mile mills are long gone. Aymill enjoyed periods as Eymille and Eyemill before settling down as Hay Mill, its site is now a petrol station on Burnham Lane and what's left of its mill pond hides in a wooded recreation ground near Haymill Community Centre. Farnham Mill was replaced by a pub called *The Windmill* now itself remembered only by Windmill Road. Not far north, the watercress beds lasted into the early-1900s and *Beler-Llys* is still going as Baylis Pond. *The Treacle Mines* have been drained and forgotten beneath a housing estate and an *Asda* superstore.

What Did for Dilehurst?

The Pineapple, Lake End / 14th March 2012

A thousand years ago two streams drained from **Amerden Ponds**. One ran over a weir and past not-yet ***Barge Farm*** to rejoin the Thames near what became Headpile Eyot. The other ran eastwards to cross **Marsh Lane** – which is kinked at this point to lessen the risk of a flash hitting a wagon broadside – before dividing again into streams running east and south. The southwards stream ran down to **Dorney** while the eastwards stream met that running from **Hitcham** to flow west of *Westone* (West Town Farm) to another weir pool at *Llaca-Eyn* (*the mire of the uncultivated land*), the root of its modern name, **Lake End**. This pool – *Dyllo-Pwll* (meaning *unloading pool*) – was also fed by streams flowing from Hitcham and Burnham. It was probably the head of navigation of Boveney Brook and the likely location of *Dyllo-Hiris-Tre* (*the unloading village of the fishpond outlet*), the **Dilehurst** noted at *Domesday* as having nestled under the ultimately ineffective protection of King Harold's brother Leofwin, Earl of Kent.

Unfortunately the Conqueror's assessors neglected to record either exactly where Dilehurst was or whether it was in fact named for growing the herb dill. Excavations for the Jubilee River revealed evidence of an early-medieval settlement east of Lake End Road. Perhaps the small pool nearby is a remnant of this hamlet's *unloading pool*. The culprit may have been Richard of Cornwall for he had the Gy (meaning *water* or *stream*) dammed to create a fishpond at Hitcham, probably in the late-1260s. This indulgence reduced the flow of the stream so much that Gy Mill would no longer turn, **Cippenham** went thirsty, the unloading pool dried and Dilehurst died.

A Happy Medieval Meeting

Outside Maidenhead Library / 17th March 2012

The Berkshire bank was a mirror of the South Bucks floodplain with a subtle difference. Instead of being intersected by a number of streams flowing from different springs, the Berks landscape was of natural tributaries of the Thames flowing from upstream of Cookham along multiple courses to rejoin the river at various locations either side of Bray. It was probably in the 13th Century that the main tributary was made a navigable canal, the better to transport the popular decorated floor tiles made at Penn and Tyler's Green downstream to market in London, avoiding the mainstream rapids at **Hedsor** and the turbulent flashlock in the *briva* below **Taplow Castle**. Maidenhead may owe its location – perhaps even its foundation – to the happy medieval meeting of north-south trade being pulled and punted up and down the canal with travellers riding along Richard's new east-west road.

The course of the **Cookham-Maidenhead-Bray Canal** can be traced from Fleet Bridge – the old double-arch brick bridge on The Pound west of **Cookham** village – via North Town and under Ray Mill Road to divide into two branches. One skirts the edge of Town Moor looking little more than a dry cut for emergency flood relief. The other is a shallow stream trickling by the library. They reunite to find the Thames downstream of the M4 crossing. Was the original settlement of **South Elentone** (Aylington) on this island formed by the divergence and convergence of the two branches of the canal? Were the *maiden hythes* built on the banks of this island? **Michael Bayley** recalls signs for *Willow Wharf* on the wall of the Town Moor cut but it is hard to imagine this being a busy commercial waterway for hundreds of years until it finally closed for business in 1926. It is harder still to picture North Town being swamped by flashlock surges from Strand Water, one of at least four weir pools in the canal. Michael thinks Widbrook was dredged deeper or perhaps even dug from scratch some time before 1372 to divert surges from upstream flashlocks eastwards to the Thames. This channel sometimes appears at *White Brook* or *Wythebrok* and may have started as *Wy-Da-Berw-Eog* meaning *the water of the cattle seething with salmon*. If this rather picturesque name raises modern eyebrows, just think how surprised medieval cowmen must have been to see it flow in the opposite direction when a downstream flashlock was opened.

Going like the Clappers

Ray Mill Island, Maidenhead / 17th March 2012

A casual glance at the historical record might suggest that every weir, lock and mill was on the mainstream of the Thames. Two weirs were almost certainly on the river – in 1346 **William ate Raye** was noted as keeper of that at *Reyelond* (presumably **Ray Mill Island**) and by 1377 another had been built at *Hameldon* (possibly downstream of **Amerden Bank**) – but many mentions may in fact be of devices on the tributary waterways.

It is easy to be confused by what was where. The first written record of Ray Mill Island dates from 1304 when it was rented by **John atte Ray** (William's father?) but did he give his surname to the island or take it from it? His suffix might derive from *re*, meaning *clear* or *free* referring to the water or its flow, or to the island being granted to the miller free of charge, as it seems to have been by 1392 when he and Thomas Cruchefield jointly owned *Raye Mill*. However, since *rey*, *ray*, *raz* or *ras* are all variants meaning *millstream*, it is likely that John, the island and possibly even the whole area had already acquired their names from the *ray* 200 yards to the west, a lesser tributary of what became the Cookham-Maidenhead-Bray Canal.

In 1346 King Edward III's scribes noted *Reyemulles* being driven by this nearby *ray*, long since called **Clappers Stream** (from *clappya*, still Cornish for the chatter of a millwheel). The *ray* ran into the Thames by **Bray Rigle** where it drove Oldfield Mill until being diverted in the 1830s to its current outflow just north of Ray Park Road. The mill evolved into Ray Mill as it continued to operate until the 1830s – its mill pond still survives at the northern end of Clappers Meadow – but it had a twin sharing its name for much of its life. A map dated 1637 has *Raye Mill* at the downstream end of Ray Mill Island and it may have been rebuilt at least twice, first in the 1720s and then in the 1830s. Another account says the mill wasn't built there until the original one closed. Who knows which way the millwheel winds? Two things are certain: the mainstream mill closed in the 1920s and the modern *Boulter's Restaurant* was the miller's house not the mill itself.

The lower stretch of the canal – or perhaps a cut through Bray – might have been the *Braibrok* (Bray Brook) noted in 1328 where Richard ate Lock was appointed keeper of a weir. This Richard's suffix is likely to have been pronounced *loke*, meaning *a passageway for boats* and referring to the flashlock in the weir which could have been at or near to a *briva* remembered as *Sawgh-Kens*, or *the former backload bridge* (for packhorses?), the approach to which may still survive as *The Causeway*.

Maidenhead on the Map

Outside Maidenhead Library / 19th March 2012

Maidenhead has a kind of magic for myths, or are they mistakes?

It is often said that Maidenhead's name derives from *maiden hythe* meaning *first wharf* and easy to leap to the conclusions that both this wharf and the original Ray Mill were on the Thames and that the legendary chapel where a medieval hermit took tolls was on the Great Bridge over the Thames: the first Maidenhead Bridge. However there are two more lessons to learn today from **Michael Bayley**....

The first is that there many theories of variable credence for how Maidenhead's name came about. Only one relates to a wharf. Two derive from Old English in which *maegdena* meant *maiden* and *moed* meant *timber*, or maybe the place was a rubbish dump and a *midden* to the Saxons. Or perhaps the root goes back even further. Students of ancient Britannic languages are spoiled for choice. Over 100 years ago, the local historian **Stephen Darby** favoured *Mai Dun* or *Mawr Dun* (*Great Fort*), referring to **Taplow Castle**. Some widen the etymological debate to embrace *Mai-Eadhainn* (*Great Cauldron*, as in fort), *Ma-Din-Heng* (*place of the threatening fort*), *Ma-Din-Huth* (*place of the sheltered fort*) and *Ma-Din-Haidd* or *Ma-y-Din-Heth* (*place of the barley fort*). Others point not east but west to that earthwork enclosure on Boyne Hill for any or all of these sources.

These possibilities lead neatly to the very first written record of *Maideheg* in 1202 which appears to relate not to any riverside wharf but to a farm at the foot of Castle Hill. Folk tales of a farm there are given a smidgeon of credence by an aged yew tree in the middle of the modern roundabout just where it was traditional to plant one to protect a farmhouse from prevailing winds and provide a good, old-fashioned lightning conductor.

The most fanciful theory is that of the antiquarian **John Leland** who in the early 1540s noted travellers seeking a blessing for their journey by drinking holy water from a human skull in the chapel on the bridge. Maybe he had been drinking something stronger for he decided that this maiden's head was a relic of one of the British virginal handmaidens – estimates vary from 11,000 to 21,000 – who went on pilgrimage in the late 4th Century with the Romano-British St Ursula only to be martyred by Teutonic heathens at Cologne. The skull story holds little water but perhaps Leland's linguistic speculation added enough spice to the stew for *Maydenhedd* to make its first written appearance in 1548. Tudor spelling is notoriously arbitrary but perhaps the pronunciation has survived.

The second lesson according to Michael is that the famous chapel was built in 1269 at the expense of the Hosebund family of **Bray** (later of **Cookham**). It stood just up there on the bridge over the western branch of the canal which eventually became known as **Chapel Arches** while that over the eastern branch was Moor Bridge. However the chapel may have begun life as a toll booth to serve Hosebund commercial aspirations rather than the spiritual well-being of travellers. It was probably 50 years or so before the Church gave its blessing to the place by dedicating it to St Andrew. The chapel was rededicated to St Mary Magdalene in 1372 when **King Edward III** granted to corn merchant John Hosebund the right of chauntry enabling him to raise funds to maintain the bridge by charging those wishing to pray for a blessing on their journey.

Battles at the Bridges

The third Maidenhead Bridge / 20th March 2012

Who would have thought a family feud for the kingdom of England would have begun and ended with battles for the beleaguered bridge (or bridges) between Taplow and Maidenhead? These two skirmishes happened 13 years apart (exactly how is hearsay) and the protagonists were proxies but the final outcome was no less pivotal for that. The second turned out to be the penultimate act in the saga that saw **King Richard II** usurped by his cousin **Henry Bolingbroke**, 1st Earl of Derby. It might also offer an alternative medieval possibility for how Battlemead got its name for Danes chasing Saxons didn't fire the stone cannon ball that was found there 600 years hence.

Kingdom Come

Tæppa's Mound / 20th December 1387

The royal cousins have the country in turmoil. The bridges across the Thames below us are about to be centre stage in King Richard's battle for royal authority, and we have a grandstand view. While we wait, let's hear how things have come to this not so pretty pass...

Richard II is the son of **Edward, the Black Prince**. He was just ten years old in 1377 when he succeeded his grandfather **King Edward III** to the throne under the regency of Bolingbroke's father, the powerful **John of Gaunt**, 1st Duke of Lancaster, a yoke he finally shook off last year. But now with a French invasion feared the young king is confronted by the Lords Appellant, an aristocratic alliance led by Lancaster's brother Thomas of Woodstock, 1st Duke of Gloucester, and including a stellar cast of Richard FitzAlan (4th Earl of Arundel), Thomas de Beauchamp (12th Earl of Warwick), Thomas de Mowbray (1st Earl of Nottingham) and of course the ambitious Bolingbroke. Richard recently completed a *gyration* (tour) of the country but his failure to win to his cause a corresponding array of titles gave Gloucester the chance to bring matters to a head by demanding the dismissal from court of the royal favourite Robert de Vere, 1st Duke of Ireland. Richard summoned his friend post-haste from Chester. Ireland's army met Gloucester's yesterday outside the gates of London. The skirmish was brief but decisive. Ireland turned tail and his men are at this very minute down below us: a rabble rushing over **Maidenhead Bridge** and swinging around to destroy it. Thinking they are safe, they turn to wave and cat-call smugly across the river at their pursuers. Gloucester sends one of his men north to **Taplow Bridge** to confirm it is intact and undefended. Ireland sees his cunning plan is foiled and dashes west again in dismay. His rearguard battles briefly but cannot prevent the inevitable. Later today Gloucester will catch up with Ireland at Radcot Bridge and complete his victory.

Tæppa's Mound / 4th January 1400

Ireland fled into exile across the Channel. The Lords Appellant considered deposing King Richard but thought he might make a perfect puppet. They were wrong. He played his politics well, rode his luck and was rewarded when an invasion by the Scots united the country behind him. His authority restored, he had Maidenhead Bridge repaired and agreed a truce with France; the Hundred Years' War was middle-aged and needed a break. A fragile peace reigned at home and abroad until 1397 when Richard felt strong enough to exact a little revenge on his erstwhile antagonists. Arundel was beheaded, Warwick sentenced to life imprisonment and Gloucester died in mysterious circumstances while incarcerated in Calais in the care of his former conspirator Nottingham, who was rewarded by being elevated to 1st Duke of Norfolk. And when his Uncle John died early in 1399, Richard must have thought he was such a clever dick to exile his cousin Bolingbroke as well. He celebrated by popping over to spend the summer in Ireland. It was a mistake. Bolingbroke slipped back into Yorkshire and quickly won significant support. Richard landed in Wales and established himself at Flint Castle only to realise that the game was up. Bolingbroke was duly proclaimed **King Henry IV**. He celebrated by locking his cousin in the Tower of London and later at Pontefract Castle.

We have returned to our eyrie to witness the last act of this sorry saga made all the more confusing by a flutter of changing titles. A conspiracy to restore Richard has been gathering support, especially in Berkshire where the influence of Sir Bernard Brocas of Clewer is strong. Late yesterday a small group led by the usurped king's half-brother John Holland, 1st Earl of Huntingdon (formerly Duke of Exeter), sneaked into Windsor Castle to assassinate Henry IV only to find this so-called **Epiphany Rising** had been betrayed. Henry slipped away to London. Now his army is heading this way, hot on the heels of Huntingdon's nephew Thomas Holland, 3rd Earl of Kent (formerly Duke of Surrey), whose men fought a brief rearguard action at Colnbrook before retreating at the gallop. Here they come, hurrying west as fast as they dare over frozen ruts in the old road in much better order than Ireland's army 13 years ago. And they don't make the same mistake. They cross Maidenhead Bridge and quickly set fire to both it and Taplow Bridge. Then they prepare to stand and fight.

With the bridges destroyed, it will be a bloody stalemate for three days. Eventually the usurper's men will haul cannon up here on the frosty Buckinghamshire heights to bombard Kent's cohort on the Berkshire meadows below. And at last raiding parties will brave the icy water at Bray Rigle and Hedsor Rapids in sufficient number to catch Kent and his fellow conspirator John Montagu, 3rd Earl of Salisbury, in a deathly pincer on Battlemead. As his men are cut down, Kent will finally concede defeat and head west. He will reach Cirencester only for angry townsfolk to chop off his head and Salisbury's. Perhaps if Taplow and Maidenhead Bridges hadn't been destroyed in battle the heads of Huntingdon, Brocas and Thomas le Despencer, 4th Baron le Despencer (formerly Earl of Gloucester), would have been displayed on pikes there and not on London Bridge. Twenty-nine other conspirators will suffer a similar fate administered with vengeful brutality in Green Ditch, Oxford (where Broad Street will be).

St Paul's Cathedral / 20th February 1400

King Henry IV wants there to be no doubt that his cousin is beyond restoration. The late King Richard II is lying in state for all to see. Is it wise in these turbulent times for **Sir Adam Ramsay** of Hecham Manor to have accepted the honour of standing as esquire to the body of his erstwhile sovereign?

Abridged Restoration

The second Maidenhead Bridge / 20th September 1451

It wasn't easy or cheap to keep twin bridges in repair. It was harder not having any bridge to cross. The **Babham** family don't mind of course – many travellers preferred a nice dry ride in their ferryboats rather than a wet paddle across **Bray Rigle** or the ford where Tappelawe Bridge stood – but Maidenhead minded very much indeed. Its bridge was rebuilt and Richard Ludlow petitioned successfully in 1423 to become the resident hermit and toll-collector at **Chapel Arches**. He charged one penny (£2.94) for a loaded cart to cross the bridge or a loaded barge to pass beneath it. Naturally the townspeople wanted more of that and **King Henry VI** has been happy to oblige by issuing a royal charter to establish the **Guild of St Andrew & St Mary Magdalene** and grant it pontage in perpetuity to maintain the bridge and the right to a fishery for 50 feet either side of it. The first chaplain of the Guild is Thomas Mettyngham and John & William Norreys of Ockwells Manor are the first bridge keepers. The Guild will be dissolved by **King Edward IV** in 1547 and reinstated in 1581 when **Queen Elizabeth I** grants to Maidenhead its Charter of Incorporation.

Parry and Thrust – Confluence

Maidenhead Library / 13th November 2013

Fortunately **Keith Parry** concurs with **Michael Bayley** on many matters and adds various details....

The 1451 royal charter confirmed tolls that had applied since about 1423 and would continue to apply until the 17th Century. Crossing over the bridge cost a penny (£2.78) per cask of wine or hundred of cloth, a ha'penny (£1.39) for a cow and a farthing (70p) for five hogs, a salmon or a load of woad. Boats passing beneath had to pay tuppence-a-time (£3.92) because many bargees baulked at having to pay for an obstruction to their passage. The increasingly heavy traffic combined with the natural swell of the river and its flotsam to cause the bridge repeated damage. Time and again it was necessary to plead for royal authority to take oaks in order to affect repairs. Timber bridges were sufficiently rare by 1675 that the London-to-Marlborough road map prepared by the cartographer **John Ogilby** (or Ogilvy) made specific mention of Maidenhead Bridge being of timber – and at only 13-and-a-half feet, it wasn't wide enough for two stagecoaches to pass.

Taylor's Triumph

Robert Taylor's third Maidenhead Bridge:
234 years and counting / 2011

Quickening Pace

The Coming of the Coaches

The Orkney Arms / 29th March 1743

At last we have an inn on the Bath Road. ***The Orkney Arms*** is open for business. What took Taplow so long? Stagecoaches have been trundling past for generations, all heading for Maidenhead Bridge, all gasping for rest and refreshment. Has Taplow been such a hotbed of highwaymen so intent on parting passengers from their cash at the point of a pistol that they couldn't dream up a way to do it by giving service with a smile?

Traffic trundled by happily enough throughout the Tudor period and enjoyed the smoother ride afforded by **King Charles I**'s Great West Road from 1632 until 1642 when the Roundheads secured London's western approaches by breaking down **Maidenhead Bridge** and protecting it with armed barges. The 1660 restoration of King Charles II kick-started commerce and stagecoaches began to ply between London and Bristol. Nowadays fast coaches can do the journey in two days and slow ones take three but both are reliant on changing to fresh horses at regular intervals. Where better than here in this idyllic spot an uncomfortable three-and-a-half-hour ride on the fastest coaches from London? It is just the place to slake thirsts, take food and new horses and for slow coaches perhaps to enjoy an overnight stay. And yet Taplow has been slow on the uptake. The best it could offer until now was ***The Queen's Head***, a pleasant enough place but a little snug and a long haul for tired horses up a very steep hill.

Others have been quicker to spot the business opportunity. By the late-16th Century coaches had the choice between *The Greyhound* in Maidenhead, *The Red Cow* in the newly-combined village of Upton-cum-Chalvey and three inns on the Great West Road: *The Three Tuns* at Salt Hill, *The Crown* on the Stoke-Eton crossroads and *The Reindeer* nearby. By 1636 these earlybirds were competing with *The Black Boy* and *The Red Lion* at Wexham and *The White Hart* at Stoke Poges. And now Maidenhead inns are doing a roaring trade. Westbound coaches prefer to stay the night in town rather than risk being robbed after dusk in the notorious Maidenhead Thicket to the west of the town. *The White Hart* stables 50 horses and *The Sun Inn* 40, some of which are extra 'cockhorses' to help heavy coaches up and down Folly Hill (eventually Castle Hill). Rumour has it that an ostler at *The Sun* moonlights as a highwaymen and then sympathises with those he had held-up. That's the Berkshire Boys for you.

The Dumb Bell Hotel / 29th March 1786

Taplow is still disguised as Toplar on a new map of the London-to-Bristol road. Nobody is confused. This is the busiest stretch of road in the country. By 1834 Maidenhead will see almost 2,000 vehicles and nearly twice as many horses passing through every week, not to mention 1,500 sheep and other beasts. Most of them will come along here. *The Orkney Arms* is already a little goldmine [*see Map 14*]. So is ***The Dumb Bell*** since it opened not long ago courtesy of the enterprising Marlow brewer **Thomas Wethered**. Hands up who's surprised.

Turning to Stone

The third Maidenhead Bridge / 1st September 1777

Is a broom with a new handle and a new brush the same broom? Fifty years ago Daniel Defoe described barges loaded with up to 120 tons of dead weight hauling upriver cargoes of "coals, salt, grocery wares, tobacco, oils and all heavy goods" and gliding back down carrying malt, meal and vast quantities of timber. The second Maidenhead Bridge took such a battering. It had to be repaired so many times that the only original thing about it was its location, the only permanence a perennial economic headache – not least because the many periods out of action and the inconvenience and slowness of the parallel ferry resulted in significant losses of tolls and of indirect commercial income from the ever-increasing stagecoach traffic. The bridge required extensive repairs in 1734 and again in 1750 to the tune of £794 9s 2d (£11.2m) payable to **Stiff Leadbetter**, the surveyor of Eton College who in 1743 had remodelled **Taplow Court** for **William O'Brien, 4th Earl of Inchiquin**.

This Stiff fellow – named no doubt named for his English upper lip – has since gone on to be surveyor of St Paul's Cathedral and to become well-connected with the peerage for his work at such places as Fulham Palace, *Bulstrode Park* in Gerrard's Cross, *Langley Park* in Wexham, the Ratcliffe Infirmary in Oxford and especially at *Shardeloes* in Amersham and at *Syon House* in Brentford where he was trusted to execute the designs of Robert Adam. However his massive bill for bridge repairs was too much for Maidenhead which decided to build a completely new stone bridge a few yards downstream of the old one. It took 21 years of dreaming, discussing, designing and modifying before a proposal by **Robert Taylor** was finally authorised for construction by an Act of Parliament. Then there was another six years of pandemonium caused by ice, floods, running a temporary ferry and competing for elbow-room with the Bath Road's busy traffic before John Townsend of Oxford finally turned the sculptor-turned-architect's vision into a 13-arch Portland stone and brick reality [*see Map 15*]. The *voissoirs* around each arch are in Taylor's signature style: 'vermiculated rustication', each stone so deeply cut it looks like a mouse-nibbled chunk of cheese. Now at last he can look forward to being knighted in 1782 on being elected Sheriff of London and put behind him the logistical nightmare of overlapping his construction works with the re-engineering of the river by the Thames Navigation Commission. Seven new pound locks between Marlow and Sonning began operation in 1773 in the wake of the new **Boltus Lock** above **Taplow Mill** which replaced the original 1746 Bolter's Lock in 1772.

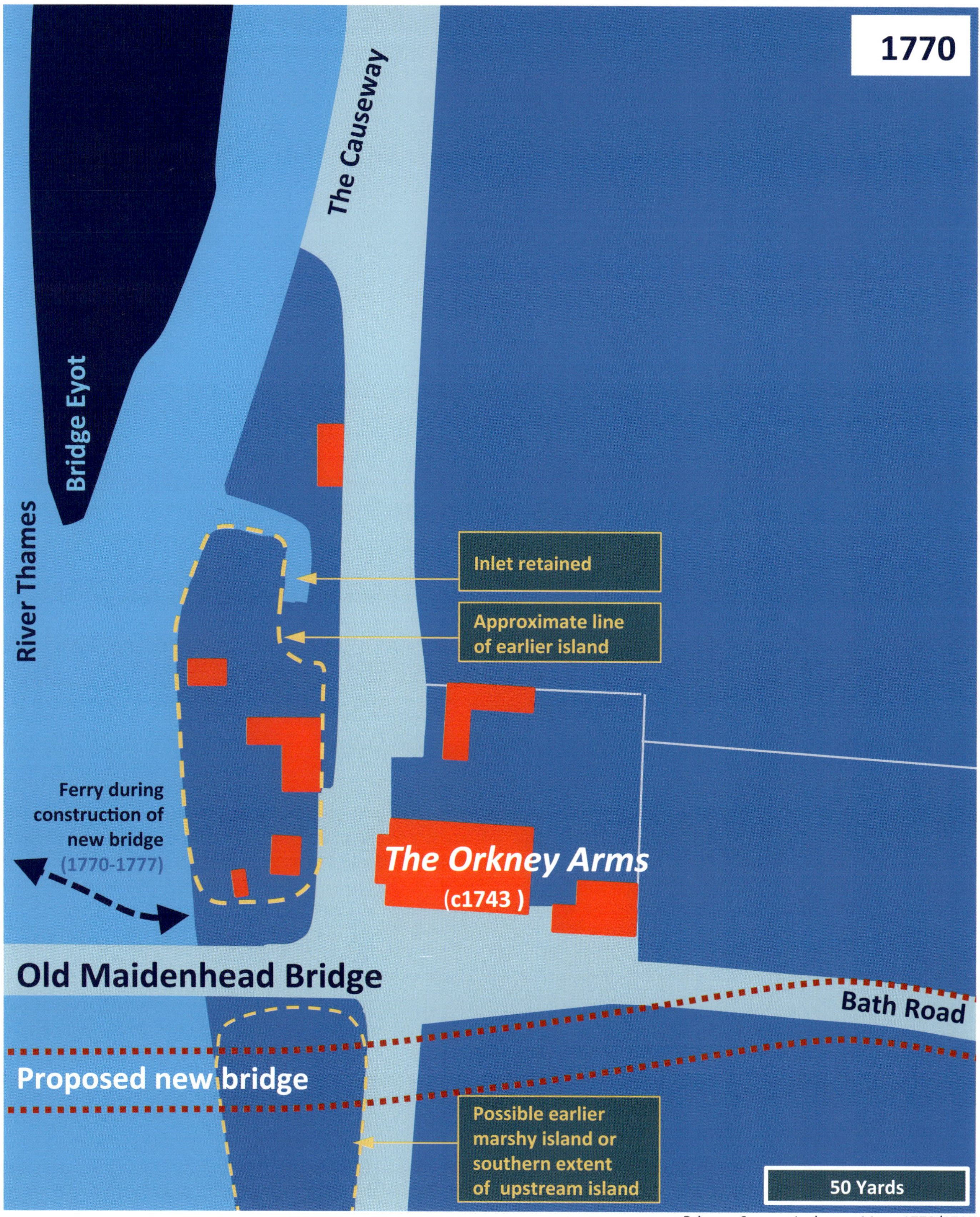

Primary Source: Inclosure Maps 1779/1787

Map 15 – Down by the Riverside: The Evolving Skindles

Still standing – *The Orkney Arms*, a coaching inn by the new bridge

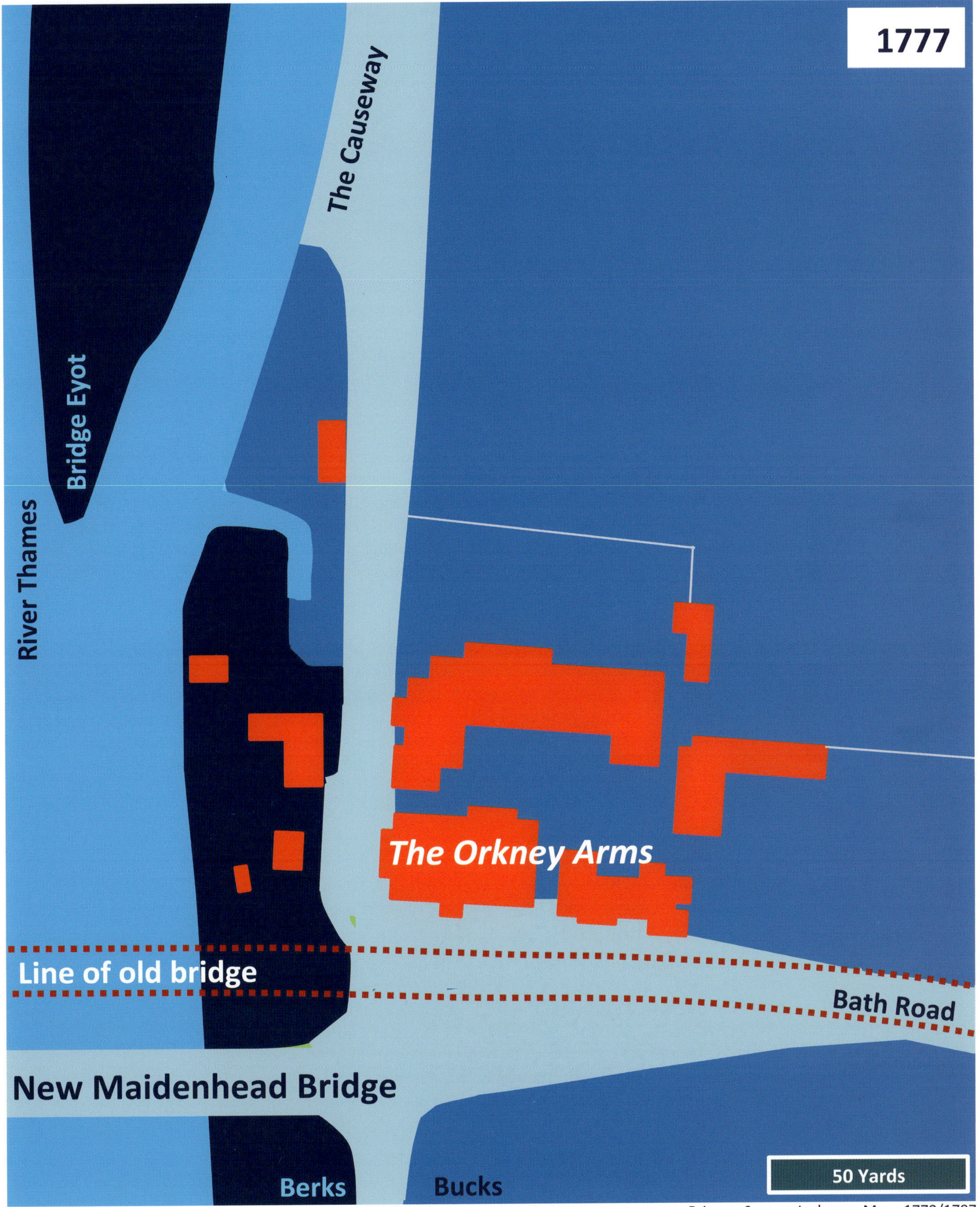

Primary Source: Inclosure Maps 1779/1787

The third Maidenhead Bridge / 1st April 2012

Perhaps Taplovians were relieved to have been deprived of a share in the old bridge and therefore of any obligation to contribute towards the final £19,000 cost of the new one (£169m) but there was a price to pay. It had never cut any ice in Berks that the bridge wouldn't have a hope without one foot in Bucks. Consequently Taplow gleaned no direct commercial benefit when the venture turned out to be a roaring commercial success. Tolls were significantly increased in 1777 – coaches and wagons were charged per horse, tuppence (90p) for the former and a penny-ha'penny for the latter, while each cow crossing cost a penny and each pig a ha'penny – and by the 1830s Maidenhead was taking £1,245 (£96,500) each year and (if Legend has it right) rather enjoying it. Although it always claimed not to be able to afford to pay back the original bondholders, somehow it always had plenty of funds to spare for the Mayor's Feast and, in 1797, to buy a round of drinks for 330 soldiers.

The Coming of the Railway

Glum Gooch

Maidenhead Bridge / 15th January 1838

Why is **Daniel Gooch** so glum? He has a fine vantage point up here on Robert Taylor's bridge to watch the arrival of a barge that has carried Robert Stephenson's famous locomotive *North Star* all the way from Newcastle-upon-Tyne. The 20-year-old engineer from Northumbria confides that his relationship with the famous engineer **Isambard Kingdom Brunel** still hasn't completely recovered from the events of 27th November last year when the very first ***Great Western Railway*** locomotives were delivered to West Drayton by canal. Brunel made plain his annoyance when he arrived a little late to discover that *Vulcan*, *Aeolus* and *Premier* had already been lifted onto the tracks without mishap under Gooch's supervision. Consequently the young man is disappointed but not exactly surprised that his role today is merely to watch and learn.

The barge glides into view at the far end of Bray Reach. Its load is so heavy the water laps the gunnels as it is slowly manoeuvred into position and safely moored. It takes an exceedingly long time to fit the lifting tackle to the locomotive to the satisfaction of Brunel, but at last all is ready. Everyone holds their breath in excitement as the team of horses takes the strain. The locomotive rises a few inches above the barge. The enormous ratchet clicks a notch. The horses haul again, the ratchet clicks. Haul and click, haul and click. Now *North Star* is being swung slowly over the riverbank. Suddenly there are two screams – the first metallic, the second human – and then an awful silence. The lifting rig has toppled sideways just missing Brunel but crushing an unfortunate labourer.

The mood is sombre now as *North Star* is lifted onto a specially-constructed carriage that eight enormous shire horses heave with great difficulty almost a mile along the Bath Road and up the newly-constructed embankment to a point where it can be lifted without further incident onto the railway tracks, loaded with coal and fired up to begin its first test run to West Drayton. Gooch leaves with just the hint of a gleam in his eye. Tonight he will write in his diary that "but for the loss of the man's life, I rather rejoiced, after the scolding I had had for doing the work at Drayton without him, that the accident should happen under [Brunel's] supervision". Gooch will rise to become lord of Clewer Park from 1859, Chairman for life of the *GWR* from 1865 and a baronetcy in 1866.

All Aboard for Taplow

The second Taplow Station / 15th April 2012

This is where the *Great Western Railway* really began when the wheels of *North Star* were first settled onto the tracks. It is likely that the locomotive was hauled up the gradual incline of Approach Road. If anyone asks what was approaching, tell them it was the future.

Anyone who wants to know how the original section of the *GWR* came about should read *First Stop Maidenhead* by Matthew Wells. It is a very good little book except for its title. In fact the first *GWR* passengers travelled the 22-and-a-bit miles from Paddington to their first stop at Taplow, not Maidenhead. The western terminus at the bottom of Berry Hill enjoyed many names during its 32 years of operation. In the early days it was known as Maidenhead (Dumb Bell Bridge) Station, Maidenhead (Riverside) Station or simply Maidenhead Station despite being half-a-mile short of Maidenhead. Passengers had to walk or take a horsedrawn carriage or coach the rest of the way. There are only two visible remnants of this original station: the former ticket office is now ***Walnuts Cottage*** and a bricked-up archway in the south-west abutment of **Dumb Bell Bridge** was the eastern of its three entrances.

Taplow was in the vanguard of the veritable explosion of railways across the country in the mid-18th Century. The first steam trains to carry passengers ran on the Stockton-Darlington line in 1825 and between Liverpool and Manchester five years later. These ventures convinced everyone that railways were the future. In 1833 a consortium of Bristol merchants appointed Brunel who set out personally to plan the route to London. His finished project would cost just over £3 million (£327m). It was no easy task, not least because of local sensitivities.

The original idea was to go via Windsor but two things nudged the line north. The main reason was the discovery of the solid bank of gravel laid down by the wandering river many millennia before: a geological serendipity that had already served for many years as the way to and firm base of the ford at **Bray Rigle**. In the 1830s it offered a perfect foundation for both the line itself and especially for Brunel's revolutionary brick bridge over the Thames. In addition, it was far enough away from Windsor Castle to quell concerns that puffing locomotives might disturb the royal peace. Nevertheless the *GWR* still fell foul of opposition from Dr John Keate, Master of **Eton College**, who feared that the railway would lead to an "increase in floods" that would endanger the life of the boys and that a station within three miles of his elite domain would "interfere with the discipline of the school, the studies and amusements of the boys, affecting the healthiness of the place and endangering even the lives of boys" (and no doubt bring plagues of frogs and countless other undesirables too). Consequently there were to be stations at Taplow and Langley but not at Slough. Maidenhead complained bitterly about the potential loss of stagecoach trade and bridge tolls – it was to be compensated for any losses over six years – but the incorporation of *GWR* in 1835 was the signal for construction to go full steam ahead. The first section of the line would terminate at Taplow until Brunel's bridge was completed.

Maidenhead (Dumb Bell Bridge) Station / 4th June 1838

Mr Bell of the *GWR* is proud to report that five days ago *North Star* carried 200 *GWR* executives and guests all the way from Paddington to Taplow at an average speed of 28 miles per hour. Apparently director George Gibbs issued everyone their tickets with such pomp and circumstance somebody joked that *GWR* must stand for *Gibbs' Wonderful Railway*. Bell chuckles conspiratorially but is cut short when he sees two plumes of smoke rising over the eastern horizon. Excitement mounts as *Apollo* and *Aeolus* puff into sight pulling parallel trains on which the *GWR*'s first fare-paying passengers are making the same journey. The noise is deafening as the two locomotives come to a halt and sound their whistles in celebration. The passengers spill onto the smoky platforms and mill about congratulating anyone who will shake them by the hand. Everyone is overcome by the wonderful atmosphere. The average speed of the locomotives today was a more sedate 25 miles per hour, their progress perhaps impaired by being laden with 1,479 passengers who together have paid £226 (£17,750) for the privilege of making the journey a mere 13 years into the UK's railway age. Three weeks later the *GWR* will announce it has already taken £4,576 (£360,000) in fares from 29,537 passengers.

Maidenhead (Riverside) Station / 4th May 1839

The Reverend Francis Witts, Rector of Upper Slaughter in Gloucestershire, takes up the story to tell of his journey to London. "The [horsedrawn] coach drove into the station yard where the passengers alighted, leaving their luggage with the coach which proceeded a little onwards and reached the level of the railway by a road constructed for this purpose. There [coaches] are placed each onto a railway truck, ready to be hooked onto the train when it comes to that point. Meantime the passengers receive a railway ticket to London which purports to be worth five-and-six (£21.11). The width of the rails being 7ft and consequently the coaches are as wide, each holding eight persons, or four in two breadths. The distance to Paddington [is] tranversed in 50 mins including stoppages".

The renamed station is certainly something to behold. Its first stationmaster Samuel Chettle has a staff of six running this, only the third station in the country after Euston and Birmingham to have raised platforms. Less than half-a-mile up the line there is a substantial engine house, a turntable and an ingenious arrangement that enables stagecoaches to be driven directly onto open wagons. To prevent any passengers from London worrying that they have travelled back in time – local time is three minutes behind Greenwich Mean Time – the clocks in the towers on both platforms are set to GMT. There are eight trains to and from Paddington each weekday and six on Sundays but it is an expensive way to travel. Semi-skilled workers earn about £1-a-week (£76.78) and agricultural labourers only about half that but the second class fare to Paddington is four shillings (£15.36) in an enclosed posting carriage or three-and-sixpence (£13.44) in a cold and dirty open coach. First class fares are six-and-six (£25.53) in a carriage or five-and-six in a coach. And there is no facility to accede to a recent request by Mr J Stearns for a 'season ticket' – such luxury won't come in until the 1850s – but by 1844 one train each way every day will charge just two bob (£8.73) for a second class fare in an open coach and soon afterwards *GWR* will be offering excursion fares at less than a penny-a-mile (35p).

The second Taplow Station / 4th May 2012

The novelty of the *GWR* eventually wore off but it continued as a commercial success despite an accident near the station on 4th December 1839 when wrongly set points caused the derailment of Driver Almond's engine but not his carriages. Luckily the only casualty was the guard, Mr Dawson, who lost the top of his finger. There was also a modicum of confusion about who was the first stationmaster. *First Stop Maidenhead* casts Mr Bell in this role but when Sam Chettle of **Hitcham New Town** was buried in St Nicholas' Churchyard in 1850 the Reverend **Charles Whately** noted in Taplow's Parish Register that the honour had been his.

When the first actual **Maidenhead Station** opened in 1854, Maidenhead (Riverside) Station tried to differentiate itself by being **Maidenhead & Taplow Station** and then in 1869 simply **Taplow Station**. It closed down three years later when this, the second and current **Taplow Station** opened where the old turntable and stagecoach terminal had once been. This must have been a blow for ***The Old Station Inn*** and for ***Cleare's Hotel*** but both hostelries continued to survive and thrive into the 20th Century.

The Graceful Leap

Brunel's Bridge / 1st July 1839

It was a challenge in more ways than one for the *Great Western Railway* to get over the river to Berkshire. Oldfield Mill had to go and the giant leap was made all the harder by the insistence of the River Thames Commissioners that the bridge be brick-built and without impeding the flow of the river in times of flood or the operation of the towpath on the Buckinghamshire bank. When Christmas cards are invented in four years, it will be unlikely that **Brunel** will send any to these fellows. However their obduracy played its part in giving the great engineer the chance to respond memorably in adversity.

The stone for **Brunel**'s bridge came from Yorkshire and much of the muscle from Ireland but local businesses, shops and inns boomed as the construction of the railway demanded labour, food, drink, clothes, iron, tools and especially gravel and bricks. ***The Brickmaker's Arms*** in Lent Rise will be a reminder that most of the bricks used to build the spectacular bridge over the river and the more prosaic arches under the railway were made in Burnham. The first were laid on the western scaffold of Brunel's bridge in October 1837 and everything went smoothly until the following summer when the eastern arch started to settle as soon as its scaffolding began to be removed. Everyone from influential politicians like Charles Jenkinson, 3rd Earl of Liverpool, to the *Railway Times* magazine and even the *GWR*'s Mr Bell were fiercely critical of Brunel. There were calls that the "dangerous" bridge "must come down". Brunel ignored the furore and calmly diagnosed the problem: the mortar hadn't had time to dry. The contractor, Mr Chadwick of London, accepted responsibility and rebuilt the distorted section. All went well in October last year when support was removed from the western arch. Brunel left the scaffolding in place to allay the fears of his critics that collapse was inevitable. Meanwhile he negotiated the acquisition of land from **Pascoe Grenfell** on which to extend the embankment from the station to the bridge.

The first locomotive tested the bridge on 12th April 1839 and was soon shunting Buckinghamshire gravel over the river to build the embankment on the Berkshire side. The scaffolding still remains in place but it gave no support as the first passengers trundled across the bridge earlier today. Mission accomplished: £37,000 well spent (£41.4m). Services will be immediately extended to Twyford.

Brunel's Bridge / 23rd April 2012

What a splendid sight is Brunel's masterpiece. Its overall length is 778 feet and its two main semi-elliptical brick arches were incredible for being the widest and flattest in the world. Each spans 128 feet with a rise of just 24 feet 3 inches. They are still held in awe for their artistic grace and stunning engineering. Maidenhead Railway Bridge was nominated as a UNESCO World Heritage Site and has just been upgraded to Grade 1 Listed status on the recommendation of English Heritage. It is undoubtedly one of the great engineer's finest achievements.

Perhaps Brunel allowed himself three surreptitious smiles: one in January 1840 when a flood washed away the scaffolding leaving the bridge intact, another a few months later when the line to Bristol was completed and the third in 1844 when **JMW Turner**'s painting ***Rain, Steam and Speed*** provided the *GWR* in general and him in particular with fantastic free publicity. The illustrious Impressionist painter captured all the drama and excitement of cutting-edge rail travel having been inspired on a journey from Reading to London when, according to a fellow passenger: "The old gentleman seemed strangely excited... jumping up to open the window, craning his neck out, and finally calling to her to come and observe the curious effect of the light. A train was coming in our direction through the blackness over one of Brunel's bridges and the effect of the locomotive lit by crimson flame and seen through driving rain and whirling tempest gave a peculiar impression of power, speed and stress".

Eyes of a Child – Esme Maree & Louis Ness

St Nicolas' School / 23rd April 2012

Esme thinks there was a Victorian inventor called Mr Brunel and he designed the bridge. It's a massive bridge made by a famous builder, says Louis, it is called 'the Echo Bridge'. There is an island in the middle of the river which is good for playing games on.

Louis continues: I like the River Thames at Taplow. I go there a lot. I like the path alongside the grass slope. I sometimes swim or go fishing there. It is a good place for a picnic. They do the Regatta there. Sometimes the rowers go past to the rowing club next door. If you keep walking you get to a gate and some nice houses and a rather pleasant lock. When (comic actor] David Walliams swam the Thames last year, he came past Taplow on 9th September. It was a Saturday morning so a lot of people were cheering him on. He stopped at the lock and when he got back in there were a police boat and canoes alongside him.

Sideways Glances

Making Tracks

Brunel's Bridge / 2nd June 2012

Most railways were being built with a gauge (space between rails) of four feet eight-and-a-half inches. Brunel's obsession was to build a line as flat as a billiard table on which passengers could take coffee and "write whilst going noiselessly and smoothly at 45mph". Consequently the *GWR* bucked the trend with a seven feet and a quarter-inch gauge but by the 1860s the need for conformity was winning the day. *GWR* had to change, at first by installing mixed tracks and in 1882 the need for greater capacity led to its decision to add an extra pair of tracks on its main lines. It took ten years from 1883 to widen bridges and embankments and lay the new narrow-gauge lines from London to Bristol. The new Taplow Station had two new platforms on its northern side by 1884 and the northward expansion of Dumb Bell Bridge was completed soon afterwards. Meanwhile, after considering the demolition of Brunel's bridge, the *GWR* engaged **Sir John Fowler** to replicate it on the upstream side. When the new span from Buckinghamshire to Oldfield Eyot (now **Guard's Club Island**) began operation in 1893 it exhibited such a distinctive echo that it came to be called 'the Sounding Arch' – or 'Echo Bridge' as Louis Ness prefers.

The Making of Maidenhead

Maidenhead Station / 2nd June 2012

Whether or not the hythes made Maidenhead, the coming of stagecoaches made it anew and the arrival of the *GWR* in 1838 remade it once more.

It all started badly. The road bridge toll was reduced in 1839 from £18 (£1,380) to £4 (£307). There were complaints that the new embankment was causing flooding at Boyne Hill. Stagecoach traffic fell from 70 a day in 1838 to none at all within five years.

However, the corner was already being turned. The rail link to London attracted an influx of people that by 1841 quadrupled the population to 3,315, doubled that by 1871 and doubled it again by 1901. Entrepreneurs from London quickly bought up all the old coaching properties to convert them to or replace them with shops and other business premises. These newcomers built the desirable residences, schools and churches that made Maidenhead middle-class. How strange that the railway still steamed straight through unstopping. An 1842 petition went unheeded for 12 years before the new branch line to High Wycombe began operation in 1854 and the rapidly expanding town finally had its first station on its side of the river. Maidenhead (Wycombe Junction) Station had been long-awaited but didn't last long because it wasn't on the main line. Consequently Taplow (by whatever name) remained the interchange from the *GWR* to the *Wycombe Railway Company* line which by 1864 ran through to Aylesbury, Princes Risborough and Oxford. This first truly Maidenhead station tried two other names – Maidenhead (Boyne Hill) and Maidenhead (Castle Hill) – before being closed after just 17 years when the current **Maidenhead Station** was opened in 1871 without the safety net of a bracketed suffix. The original station's ticket office is still there hidden behind its bricked-up arched entrances halfway up Castle Hill.

The Spur for Slough

Slough Station / 2nd June 2012

The prohibitive efforts of **Eton College** had no detrimental affect whatsoever. Within a week of its first run to Taplow, the *GWR* was stopping trains at **Slough** where passengers could buy tickets at *The Crown* and climb aboard despite the lack of any platforms. *North Star* also did a stint as a temporary ticket office until common sense prevailed and the original Slough Station opened in 1840. In the hope that it would become a royal terminus, it was built in a grand style with a broad approach road and **Queen Victoria** duly made her first railway journey from there to London in 1842. She enjoyed the experience so much that a branch line was built to Windsor in 1849 and Slough's pretensions to royal grandeur took a bit of dent. However it rode the punch easily enough. By the time the current station replaced the original in 1884, it could already boast another claim to fame: the first use of the electric telegraph to aid the capture of a murderer. John Tawell poisoned his lover Sarah Hill at Salt Hill in 1845 then fled on a train from Slough to Paddington only to be overtaken by a telegraph message and arrested on arrival.

The stagecoach trade had fuelled Slough's growth from a village clustering around stagecoach inns at *The Crown* crossroads to become a busy little town already nibbling at its older neighbours. The railway was the spur for its feasting, Upton-cum-Chalvey and Salt Hill the appetisers in the 1830s. Farnham and Stoke made a tasty dish around 100 years later and Britwell, Cippenham, Colnbrook, Langley and Wexham were all hungrily devoured in or after 1974 when the whole 'unitary authority' defected from Buckinghamshire to Berkshire.

Not the Slough of Despond

St Laurence's Church, Upton / 2nd December 1851

The faithful of Upton and Chalvey have worshipped together here in this little flint church since it replaced a wooden Saxon predecessor sometime before 1135. St Laurence set a precedent in around 1160 when it came into the care of the Augustinian priors of Merton. They liked the area so much that in 1197 they adopted Taplow's St Nicholas too.

These hamlets have always been a pair. It could have been no surprise when Richard Bulstrode merged them in the 15th Century to create **Upton-cum-Chalvey**. With Eton in the background and beyond that, shimmering in the haze, the imposing outline of the Conqueror's castle on its hill at Windsor, it must have made a memorable sight. However its days were already numbered by 1822 when it became the final resting place of the renowned astronomer Sir William Herschel, resident of Upton from where he discovered Uranus. Just 13 years later little St Laurence was abandoned for being too old and dilapidated for its growing congregation only to be saved from demolition by Mr Pocock, a sentimental benefactor keen to preserve it as the oldest building in Slough. What a good job he did because today, thanks to an appeal for funds to which Her Royal Highness Queen Victoria contributed £50 (£4,800), St Laurence's Church is being re-consecrated.

The idea of Slough was beyond imagination in 1324. **Old Bayley Lore** has it that the name first appeared as *Slo* in 1196 referring to a field or possibly a hamlet on the Stoke-to-Eton lane a little more than a quarter-mile north-west of Upton. It was recorded as *Sloo* in 1336 and *Slow* or *Slowe* in 1437. A *slough* is of course a *swamp* or *mire* and literary giants have dumped the place right in it. William Shakespeare went for comedy in 1602 with a *dun* (cart-horse) stuck in the mire near the setting of *The Merry Wives of Windsor*. Tragedy was John Bunyan's theme in 1678 when *The Pilgrim's Progress* had *The Slough of Despond* as an allegory for a deep bog into which the character Christian sinks under the weight of guilt for his sins. Thereafter many assumed that Slough's name was inspired by the notorious bog west of Chalvey known as **The Treacle Mines**. However its etymological root may just as well have been the *ysleow* (*granaries*) where grains and cereals for Windsor Castle and later Eton College were stored after harvesting from the "best corn-growing land in Berkshire, Buckinghamshire and Oxfordshire", the flat, brick-earth fields where Slough Trading Estate will take root in the 1920s.

Slough Trading Estate / 2nd June 1951

Perhaps it would all have been different if the authorities had heeded Lord Desborough's complaints in 1916 when war-damaged vehicles were brought back from Flanders and France to be dumped on the prime farmland along the railway between Burnham and Slough. They didn't. Rather than return this fertile land to its age-old purpose, industry descended upon it. The poet John Betjeman was so impressed with the result that in 1937 he invoked "friendly bombs" to do their worst. They didn't.

The Turning of Taplow

The Village Green / 2nd June 2012

The railway changed Taplow too. In the mid-19th Century it quickly turned from a sleepy seat of faded gentry into the place to be for well-heeled commuters and day-trippers eager to enjoy its riverside delights, and how Maidenhead had the cheek to usurp this revival of Taplow's air of exclusivity, a zephyr that has whispered for almost 1,000 years since the original Royal Ripple.

So there we have it: the story of Taplow writ large from the creation of its mystical elevated springs and its pagan importance through its Christian conversion and medieval convenience to become somewhere on the way to somewhere else and eventually, a little more than a hundred years ago, a honeypot for Stayers and Players. But we have hardly touched upon Taplovians. Almost everywhere hereabouts knows secrets about those who came before and went leaving legacies. Some are physical: Tæppa's Mound, houses great and small, the walls, the village green, the school, the church, the pubs, the river and its banks, the woods and green fields. This is all so much to admire but no more than the Where of it. Real appreciation of Taplow's heritage can only come through sharing the interwoven sagas of the Who, When and Why. The days are long gone when folks young and old would gather around the fire to listen as the local sage spun dramatic yarns of yore. Nowadays we have to make do with the written word. Perhaps this poor substitute will suffice....

Turner's Turn

Rain, Steam and Speed – JMW Turner 1844

North Star **approaching Maidenhead (Riverside) Station**
/ Reconstruction c1870

Maidenhead (Riverside) Station
/ Platforms 1839 & Ticket Office c1870

The Graceful Leap

Brunel's Railway Bridge / Under construction 1839 and in operation 1846

Brunel's Railway Bridge / 2011 & 2014

The Graceful Leap

The western span / c1912

The Sounding Arch / 2011

Two Bridges

The pair from the air
/ c1962

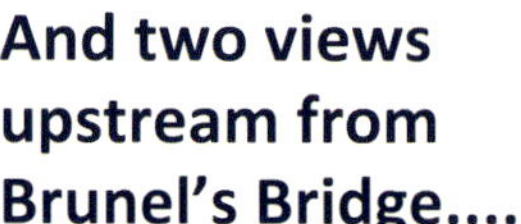

And two views upstream from Brunel's Bridge....

The eel bucks are in the channel between the Berks bank and Oldfield Island, and perhaps the skiffs moored on the Bucks bank just beyond Maidenhead Bridge are for hire from Jonathan Bond / 1850s

Some 30 years later, Oldfield Island has been tamed and the footbridge built over the bucks, probably by the owner of *Riverside* / 1883

In 1889, *Riverside* and its neighbour *Edendale* will combine to create a gentlemen's club which will be acquired in 1904 by the Brigade of Guards Boat Club

Chapter Three
Minding the Manor

In which Taplow went from being a jewel in the Crown into God's hands and back again...

The Royal Ripple Arrives

What History Says

The Cottage, Rectory Road / 6th June 2012

History summarises almost 500 years as follows....

In 1066 Taplow was "held by **Asgot**, a man of Earl Harold". After the Conquest, it could be found "among the lands of the Bishop of Bayeux". "Holding under the bishop in 1086 was Roger, who was succeeded by the Bolbecs and Turvilles" and yet it was also held "to the honour of Leicester and the duchy of Lancaster". **William de Turville** "subinfeudated" Amerden to **William Piscator** in 1194 and Taplow as a whole to the Prior of Merton three years later. Piscator's son Stephen "did homage for his lands in Taplow to the Prior of Merton" in 1213 and Amerden (with Cliveden) passed down four generations of his family to John Goldby who "alienated it" in 1408 and, after "several intermediate conveyances, it was obtained in 1433 by **Robert Manfield**". **King Henry VII** attempted to establish his ownership of Taplow only for the then Prior to resist the claim in 1500 by demonstrating that it "was held neither of the king in chief nor as of his duchy of Lancaster". Successive Manfields continued as tenants of the manor "after the Dissolution [in 1538, when Taplow] was attached to the honour of Windsor" [*see Appendix 1, Trees 4 & 5*].

Once again, a smattering of tasty morsels for **Tony Meats**, but are we much the wiser? History has a talent for begging questions. Who were these people to the manor born? What does their antiquated language actually mean? What have Merton, Leicester, Lancaster and Windsor got to do with it? And how did hereabouts fit into the big wide world?

The Conqueror's Coming

Brief English Days

Tæppa's Mound / 6th June 2012

Asgot is often confused with Astig despite their being separated by the best part of two centuries. It's his own fault for not leaving something more durable than a whisper that he may have built a new manor house on the site of present-day **Taplow Court**, possibly replacing an earlier Saxon dwelling which might have replaced a Roman villa (are you keeping up?). It is 946 years since Taplow was for the first time a jewel in the crown when it joined **Cookham**, **Bray** and **Hitcham** in being the proud possessions of the last truly English king of England.

Tæppa's Mound / 6th June 1066

Asgot stands in the lee of the yew tree on the ancient burial mound and gazes over the fields below. Cookham and Bray can claim royal patronage since the reign of King Edgar the Peaceful. Hitcham can do the same for it is held by Haming of Branston, a *thane* of the late **King Edward the Confessor**. Taplow ascended to these heights earlier today when Asgot's own lord Harold Godwinson, Earl of Wessex, was crowned **King Harold II**, probably in Westminster Abbey, possibly by the powerful **Stigand**, Archbishop of both Canterbury and Winchester who can count among his extensive landholdings some one-eighth of Thapeslau (Taplow). This controversial fellow is less of a spiritual animal than a political one. Despite being excommunicated by five successive popes, he has skilfully used his influence with the devout Confessor to feather his nest these last 14 years. Now he is at pains to ingratiate himself with Harold while keeping a weather eye out for what's happening across the Channel.

Later this year the arrival of the Normans will change Taplow for good, or not so good for the locals. It will remain 'Crown land' because everywhere will be. However when William the Conqueror sets up shop at Windsor Castle a seed will be sown a few miles upstream that will take 600 years to blossom. Being a neighbour to royalty will one day be the making of the place despite never being blessed by a suffix like **Farnham Royal**, so-called because its new lord Geoffrey de Mandeville will be granted rights to give King William I a glove and the privilege of supporting his arm at his coronation. Nice work if you can get it.

Long Norman Knights

The Bee, Burnham / 8th June 2012

As the new all-powerful sovereign, **King William I** decided that he owned everything, everybody and everywhere. He and his ilk were a class apart who ruthlessly enforced their dominance in a simple social structure: the Sovereign (William himself) was

Top Class, the Normans were Upper Class and the English were Lower Class if they were lucky. With tweaks here and there, Anglo-Saxon tithings became Norman manors that were bestowed in return for certain services, usually of a military nature. This evolved into sophisticated layers of feudal ownership and obligation within which each level bestowed land, privileges or benefits in return for allegiance, service or rent and taxes almost always paid in kind not coinage.

The system relied upon layer-to-layer *fiefs* (*agreements*) which included the right of tenants-in-chief to *subinfeudate* (essentially, *lease* or *subcontract*) selected rights and responsibilities to intermediary lords who in turn subinfeudated rights and responsibilities (not necessarily the same ones) to lesser Normans or, as time went by, to Lower Class locals who had learned how to be useful and to speak Norman French very politely. The two Upper Class layers were fluid – a tenant-in-chief of one manor might be the intermediary lord of the next and vice versa – but everyone knew their place. The (Norman) lords fought for all, the (mainly Norman) priests prayed for all and the (English) serfs worked for all. Lords managed their manors in seigniorial courts of which the Court Baron, the middle of three, continued to have jurisdiction in Taplow into the 19th Century. In general each manor was a parish and the church a parallel instrument of control and administration. Who before 1066 would have thought that God was Norman? Even the *advowson* – the right to nominate a person to an ecclesiastical position such as a parish priest – could be bought, sold or bequeathed, as could the position itself. Its value was vested in the *glebe land* allocated to support the priest, usually through being subinfeudated to others.

Buckinghamshire offers a good example of how it all worked. *The Domesday Book* records the county in 1086 as comprising 393 estates adding up a tad over 2,122 hides. A hide was an area of mixed arable land, meadow and woodland on which a free family could live comfortably: roughly 120 acres according to soil quality, measured by the amount an ox-team could plough. King William kept seven estates as *demesne* land for himself (almost 6% of the county) and delegated them to his trusted lieutenant Ansculf de Picquigny who as *Shire-reeve* (Sheriff) of Buckinghamshire kept any excess income after paying the annual fixed fee levied by the king to finance his running of court and country. Ansculf was also lord of Stoke Poges and 18 other Buckinghamshire manors as well as Sheriff of Surrey, later Baron of Dudley. Meanwhile Ghilo (Giles) de Picquigny held the manor of **Elentone**. These brothers were ancestors to the Pinkney family which in the late-17th Century invented **Pinkney's Green**.

The king divided up the rest of Buckinghamshire between 69 tenants-in-chief. By 1086 just 3% of these estates (1% of the land) were still in the hands of just a dozen previous owners. Once the dust had settled, Reinbald of Cirencester was the only local to keep his estates at Brai (**Bray**) and Cicheheam (**Cookham**), the richest bits around. As King Edward's chancellor, Reinbald's intimate knowledge of who had what wealth made him indispensable to King William for whom he continued as chancellor. By 1086 the number of estates in which he held an interest had leapt from five to 48.

Another 24 former Buckinghamshire landowners were sufficiently astute or obsequious to stay as tenants on 6% of the county's estates (not quite 2% of the land). Just one was local. Alric Gangemere swallowed hard and dug deep into his pockets to pay his new tenant-in-chief Milo Crispin for the privilege of continuing to farm land at Opetone (**Upton**) that had once been his. Crispin was also tenant-in-chief of Hucheham (**Hitcham**), Dornei (**Dorney**) and 31 other estates adding up to 6% of the county. They were held *to the honour of Wallingford* in recognition that Milo served his father-in-law Robert D'Oyly as the first *Castellan* (Constable) of Wallingford Castle where he resided from 1071 until his death in 1107. Milo's name was later anglicised as Miles.

For over 200 years this inn was called *The Crispin* in his memory; it became ***The Bee*** only recently.

A Jewel in the Crown

Taplow Manor House / 8th June 1087

If **Stigand** thought he was a clever old stick to win King William's favour, he was counting chickens. His value initially was that he knew the lay of the land and gave God's blessing to the invaders but it wasn't long before the new monarch rang the changes. He was deposed as Archbishop of Canterbury in 1070 and relieved of his holdings. His small slice of Thapeslau was reunited with Godwinson's majority chunk and passed to the Conqueror's half-brother **Odo** who was made Bishop of Bayeux in 1049 and Duke of Kent in 1067. The greater Thapeslau and Dilehurst were two of his 43 estates that amounted to 10% of Buckinghamshire [*see Appendix 1, Tree 1*].

The local feudal cake will grow to be five layers deep. At the outset, top of the shop under the king was Odo who saw the value of Thapeslau Manor drop dramatically from £9 (£950,000) in 1066 to a meagre £3 (£324,000) four years later but didn't much care. He was much too busy having the Bayeux Tapestry embroidered in Canterbury and upsetting all and sundry with his pomp and circumstance. He might have felt a bit better last year when ***The Domesday Book*** recorded Thapeslau – by now including what had been Stigand's – as having risen in value to £8 (£885,000). It extends for eight hides and one virgate (a total of about 1000 acres, a little over half the size Taplow civil parish will be in 2012) and boasts 24 grown men, 15 ploughs, 700 pigs and 1,000 eels, all held for the bishop by a mysterious but reliable **Roger**. Counting the eels must have been so much fun that the *Domesday* assessors forgot to note exactly where Stigand's erstwhile patch of Thapeslau actually was (**Amerden Bank** might be a good guess).

Sideways Glance

Domesday Numbers

Fulham Palace / 8th June 1179

Nigel the Poor, Bishop of Ely, was Lord High Treasurer to King Henry I. His son Richard fitzNigel has the same position under King Henry II. In writing his definitive treatise on royal finances and how to collect them, Richard notes that *The Domesday Book* was so-called not by the Normans but by the English for whom *dome* (pronounced *doom*) had meant *judgement* since Æthelberht of Kent had first written laws down over 500 years before, possibly longer. Consequently *Domesday* will become not merely the oldest 'public record' in England and probably the most remarkable statistical document in the history of Europe but also an early example of the English making light of their plight by laughing at it darkly.

Taplow Manor House / 8th June 1087

The counting is complete. *Domesday* assessors have noted everything might be taxed – people, land and other assets – together with changing values and ownership from being conquered in 1066 to being counted in 1086. Not everyone counts in the Lower

	Households	Value	Assets	Lords in 1066	Lords in 1086
Thapeslau (Taplow)	24 households (18 villagers, 4 smallholders & 2 slaves)	£9 in 1066, £8 in 1086	Arable 15 ploughs, meadow 3 ploughs, wood 700 pigs, 1 fishery (1000 eels)	Asgot for Earl Harold, also Stigand	Roger de Tourville for Odo
Dilehurst (probably **Lake End**)	16 households (14 villagers, 1 smallholder & 1 slave)	£6 in 1066, £6 in 1086	Arable 10 ploughs, meadow 2 ploughs, wood 300 pigs, 1 mill	Earl Loefwin, brother of Earl Harold	Gilbert Maminot (Bishop of Lisieux) for Odo
Hucheham (Hitcham)	11 households (8 villagers & 3 slaves)	£5 in 1066, £4 in 1086	Arable 6 ploughs, meadow 1 plough, wood 100 pigs, 1 fishery (500 eels)	Haming for King Edward	Ralf & Roger de Anvers for Milo Crispin
Dornei (Dorney)	10 households (5 villagers, 4 smallholders & 2 slaves)	£3 in 1066, £1.5 in 1086	Arable 3 ploughs, meadow 3 ploughs, wood 150 pigs, 1 fishery (500 eels)	Aldred for Earl Morcar	Ralf de Anvers for Milo Crispin
Bouneaie (Boveney)	1 household (1 villager)	£3 in 1066, £1 in 1086	Arable 2.5 ploughs, meadow 2 ploughs, wood 60 pigs	Siward for Earl Harold	Gerard for Giles, brother of Ansculf
Burneham (Burnham, including **Beaconsfield)**	37 households (28 villagers, 7 smallholders & 2 slaves)	£10 in 1066, £10 in 1086	Arable 15 ploughs, meadow 3 ploughs, wood 600 pigs	Ælmer of Wootton for King Edward	Walter fitzOtho
Esburnham (East Burnham)	7 households (6 villagers & 1 smallholder)	£6 in 1066, £5 in 1086	Arable 6 ploughs, meadow 6 ploughs, wood 100 pigs	Edric of Marlow, also Sæwulf	St Peter's Church, Westminster Abbey
Ettone (Eton, including **Hedgerley)**	23 households (15 villagers, 4 smallholders & 4 slaves)	£6 in 1066, £6 in 1086	Arable 8 ploughs, meadow 2 ploughs, wood 200 pigs, 2 mills, 2 fisheries (1000 eels)	Queen Edith, sister of Earl Harold	Walter fitzOtho
Windesores (Windsor)	26 households (1 priest, 22 villagers, 2 smallholders & 1 slave)	£15 in 1066, £15 in 1086	Arable 11 ploughs, meadow 40 acres, wood 50 pigs, 1 fishery	King Edward	Walter fitzOtho and 6 others for King William
Elentone (Maidenhead)	10 households (6 villagers & 4 cottagers)	£3 in 1066, £2 in 1086	Arable 4 ploughs, meadow 16 acres, wood 10 pigs, 1 fishery (500 eels)	Sæwulf	Giles, brother of Ansculf for Hugh Landric of Brime
Brai (Bray)	80 households (56 villagers, 7 smallholders, 3 men-at-arms & 4 slaves)	£25 in 1066, £17 in 1086	Arable 25 ploughs, meadow 50 acres, wood 60 pigs, 1 church	Reinbald for King Edward	Reinbald for King William
Cicheheam (Cookham)	67 households– (32 villagers, 4 smallholders & 31 cottagers)	£50 in 1066, £39 in 1086	Arable 25 ploughs, meadow 73 acres, wood 100 pigs, 2 mills, 2 fisheries, 1 church	Reinbald for King Edward	Reinbald for King William

Class, of course: only adult males in a peasantry four layers deep. At the top are freemen: rent-paying farmers who owe little or no service to the local lords and enjoy relative independence, security of tenure and the profits of their labour. Everyone else is a serf of sorts, tied to their manors and unable to leave without their lord's permission, not even to spend a day at a nearby fair or market. Most are *villeins* or villagers who rent a cottage and land from the lord but can keep any profit. Nearly as many are smallholders and cottagers noted as *bordars* (from Old French, the etymological root for *board* as in *board and lodging*) and *cottars* (from Old English), terms used inconsistently for those who rent a cottage and just enough land for subsistence, perhaps up to five acres. Slaves are lowest of the low: some are skilled tradesmen but all must do menial tasks as required.

The reliable Roger is examining a parchment on which a scribe has compared Thapeslau with its neighbours. There are no freemen hereabouts, so much the better for Roger and his noble ilk. He spots another inconsistency – meadowland is measured by the acre in Berkshire and by plough-team in Buckinghamshire – but knows no mistake has been made about Cicheheam. Although not quite as populous as Brai, its riverside location at the head of year-round navigation makes it twice as valuable for being the predominant local commercial centre, a veritable metropolis of greater value than all its Buckinghamshire neighbours put together. Reinbald the Chancellor must be counting his blessings but Roger is content enough that being by the river makes Thapeslau almost as valuable as Burneham despite having only two-thirds as many people.

The Leicester-Lancaster Line

That Mysterious Roger

The National Archives, Kew / 8th June 2012

Who was this mysterious Roger who knew a good thing when he lorded over it? *Domesday* has a total of 2,669 manors throughout England held as tenants-in-chief or intermediary lords by a horde of different Rogers, 223 of whom are noted simply as Roger. Just one was lord of all thirteen of Odo's Buckinghamshire manors (including Thapeslau) which together amounted to over one-fifth of his holdings in the county, but it's even more complicated than that. There were probably three Rogers in the local picture by 1086. Certainty gets lost in a swirl of tenancy layers, marriages, hierarchies and bestowals but the story may have gone something like this....

Roger de Anvers can be discounted. He shared the intermediary lordship of Hucheham with his brother Ralf whose descendants founded Danvers Manor in Little Marlow. Both the other Rogers had a Taplow connection.

Roger de Tourville was **Odo**'s man-on-the-manor as intermediary lord of Thapeslau (or Tapeslawe as it was soon recast). He had succeeded his father Anschetil as *seigneur* of Tourville-de-Campagne, a Normandy village now known as Tourville-sur-Pont-Audemer, and was granted an English seat at Westone in Aylesbury Vale which he modestly rebranded Weston Turville. As in the Lower Seine his neighbour was **Hugh de Bolbec** (or Bolebec), lord of Whitchurch, Great Kimble and much else besides. These families were united with the marriage of Roger's son **Geoffrey de Turville** to Hugh's daughter Isabel and again when their daughter Isabella married Hugh's grandson Walter de Bolbec. And Geoffrey's son Geoffrey de Turville married Gundred and sired the **William de Turville** who turned up in Tapeslawe around 1187 acting as if he owned the place.

What about the third Roger? The answer is one level up the layer cake. When the odious Odo fell from grace his half-brother **King William I** confiscated his English estates. The tenancy-in-chief of many (including Thapeslau) fell into the lap of a trusted elder second cousin of and wise counsel to the Conqueror. **Roger de Beaumont**-le-Roger is depicted with William and Odo in the 32nd panel of the Bayeux Tapestry wearing the very unfashionable beard and moustache that earned him the nickname *Le Barbe*. As *seigneur* of Beaumont-le-Roger and Pont-Audemer, he too had been a Normandy neighbour to Roger de Tourville, but a much bigger *fromage* than the Bolbecs. His son **Robert de Beaumont** had been rewarded for his leadership of the infantry on the right flank at the Battle of Hastings by being created Count of Lancaster. It might have been a good career move for Robert to be with the hunting party in the New Forest when the Conqueror's son King William II (Rufus) met his mysterious death in 1100. He immediately pledged allegiance to King Henry I and seven years later was created Earl of Leicester. Coincidence or what? So he is probably why various manors (including Tapeslawe) eventually emerged as being held *to the honour of Leicester and the duchy of Lancaster* [*see Appendix 1, Tree 2*].

There but not Aware

The National Archives, Kew / 8th June 2012

Robert de Beaumont's son **Robert de Beaumont**, 2nd Earl of Leicester, had a daughter Hawise who in or around 1150 married William fitzRobert, 2nd Earl of Gloucester. Their second son was called Matthew de Cliefden, which just might have been a nod of acknowledgement towards his grandfather's Buckinghamshire lands. The poor lad died without issue at just 19-years-old in about 1190 but the title skipped sideways to trickle down the fitzRobert line in the West Country to Sir John de Clivedon, Governor of Bristol in 1321, before getting lost in the Berkeley and St Loe families. Meanwhile the second and third Roberts of Leicester spent most of their time at Breteuil in Normandy until 1173 when the younger was dispossessed and imprisoned for being revolting to King Henry II. His Lancaster-Leicester titles and lands (including Tapeslawe) were restored in 1177 and he returned to Normandy until 1189 when he went off crusading with Richard the Lionheart only to expire on his way home. Having crusaded with his father, the fourth Robert of Leicester fought the French for Normandy and was incarcerated for his trouble. On his release **King John** rewarded him with a new Norman seat at Radepont. When he died in 1204 this and all his other titles and lands (including Tappeslawe) passed to his sister Amicia and her husband **Simon de Monfort**, 5th Earl of Leicester, in whose hands the package suddenly became something of a 13th Century hot potato.

King John confiscated the whole lot in 1207 for reasons unknown. It is tempting to think that, having just lost Normandy to King Philip II of France, holding Tappelawe might have been some consolation for John. By 1215 the package was more useful as a thank-you gift for the loyal support of Ranulph de Blondville, 6th Earl of Chester, who bequeathed it to his eldest sister Matilda of Chester and her husband John of Scotland, 7th Earl of Chester and 5th Earl of Huntingdon, only for it to revert to **King Henry III** in 1237. Their jealousy at his holding Tappelawe may have been one of the reasons that the nobility got fed up with King Henry. **Simon de Monfort**, 6th Earl of Leicester, thought he could do a better job of ruling England. He defeated the king at the Battle of Lewes in 1264, reclaimed the Leicester-Lancaster lands (including Tappelawe) and had an eventful year in 1265 when he called the first elected parliament in Europe only to be killed at the Battle of Evesham by an army led by Prince Edward Longshanks.

King Henry celebrated the resumption of his reign by appropriating de Montfort's title and estates (including Tappelawe) for his younger son who was created **Edmund, 1st Earl of Leicester and Lancaster**. These twin titles and the tenancy-in-chief of these many manors eventually passed to Edmund's grandson who was elevated by King Edward III in 1351 to **Henry of Grosmont**, 1st Duke of Lancaster and 4th Earl of Leicester and Lancaster. There is no reason to think the whole caboodle didn't pass in 1361 to his son-in-law **John of Gaunt**, 1st Duke of Lancaster, but as one of the most pivotal figures in medieval history he was probably much too busy to notice. For the record, he was also **King Edward III**'s third son, **King Richard II**'s uncle, regent and mentor, and (in his spare time) ancestor to half the crowned heads in Europe.

What with all these aristocratic excitements, this noble but neglectful Leicester-Lancaster line seems to have completely forgotten it held Tappelowe as tenants-in-chief. And so it seems did everyone else. It wouldn't be until 139 years after the death of Henry of Grosmont that some bright spark at the Duchy of Lancaster spotted this oversight but failed to make anything of it.

Spell Check – Les Nobles d'Angleterre

The Cottage, Rectory Road / 10th June 2012

The French pretenders from Normandy were confusingly inconsistent at spelling. The *actuelle Francais* Plantagenets of Anjou who followed did little better. That's what comes when those in charge talk a funny foreign lingo. Male Christian names were fairly reliable – thank Heaven for William and Walter – but female names were not. Petronilla might appear as Parnel, Amise as Amice or Amicia, Alice or Alyss as Hawise, Cecilia as Cecily and even Matilda as Maud (which made sense, didn't it?). Surnames were just starting out. The earliest usually derived from places of origin or ownership but most families had more than one place to be from, so **William de Turville** had the *alter ego* William de Puttenham for a Hertfordshire village just up the road from Weston Turville. The name Turville may have crossed the English Channel as *Turuille* and William's grandfather appears as *Geoffrey de Tureuilla* in the Berkshire Rolls of 1130. Work that out.

Personal names are generally used herein in a consistent form to clarify lineages. Place names have no such need. They appear as per the relevant period, glorious in their myriad iterations. Thapeslau or Thapelau (1086) evolved through Tapeslawe (1187), Tappelawe (1196), Tappelow (1291), Tappelowe (1379), Tappelow (1517), Topley (1562), Toplar (1675) and Taplowe (1720) to become Taplow (1737). Aumberdene (1194) experimented with Amerton (c1300), Hammerdon Ash (c1430), Hameldon (1510), and Amerden (from 1568) despite the occasional reversion to Amarsden Ash (1672). Cliefden (1213) tried out Clyvedene (c1280), Clevedon (1304), Clyveden (1513), Manfield Park (around 1573), Clevenden and Clevendon (both 1633), Cliffden Park (by 1666), Clifden, Clivden and Cleavden (all 1706), Cleifden (1720) and Cliefden or Clievdon (1860s) before settling on Cliveden (1880s).

The Bayeux Tapestry

Extract from Panel 32:
Roger de Beaumont (*Le Barbe*)
(Second from left,
to the right of William the Conqueror)

Mysterious Ways

Medieval Mastery

Prior Engagement

The Chapter House, Merton Priory / 18th June 1197

The **Priory of St Mary** was founded here about 83 years ago by Gilbert Norman, Sheriff of Surrey. Having arranged its colonisation from the Augustinian priory at Huntingdon, he quickly won the blessing of King Henry I and particularly of his wife, Queen Matilda. Its early pupils included in 1125 Nicholas Brakespeare who in 1154 became Adrian IV, the first English pope, and in 1130 Thomas Becket who was elevated to Archbishop of Canterbury in 1162. Having such august alumni has done much to speed the Priory's rapid rise as not only one of the most distinguished centres of religious learning in England but one with considerable political influence. Not even Becket's ultimately fatal falling out with King Henry II has diminished its standing.

Over the years successive priors have supplemented their religious and political prowess by developing an impressive commercial astuteness. The sixth, Prior Richard, is today giving audience to the aforementioned **William de Turville** who revels in the perennial absence of his tenant-in-chief **Robert de Beaumont**, 4th Earl of Leicester, for it allows him the freedom to deftly exercise his dab hand at liberating cash from the value of the Tappelawe estate. He has added a second water mill alongside the first, subcontracted both and in 1194 subinfeudated Aumberdene to an apparently local fellow by the name of **William Piscator**.

Aumberdene comprises 3 virgates and 2 acres (about 92 acres) of arable land with fishing rights in the Thames. Although it will not be noted as **Amerden Manor** until 1540, it is already a worthy holding, especially for someone whose surname means *angler* in Latin. The man himself is something new too. Piscator's elevation to a position of importance seems to have resulted not through royal favour or brute strength but from business endeavour to become a *bona fide* tenant who paid his dues and had the autonomy to do his own thing, including bequeathing his holding to his heirs.

Turville's purpose today is to take his business ambition to new heights: an intriguing commercial proposition to subinfeudate Tappelawe Manor to the Priory in exchange for a purse of silver. Silence reigns as the gentlemen hold each other's gaze. The taciturn Turville's face is a mask of ambivalence that hides his sense of triumph when Prior Richard looks away to mull yet again over the parchments he has studied meticulously beforehand. The prior has taken the bait: now the only issue is the size of the purse. After a little ritual haggling, the deal is done. As Richard considers which of his acolytes is most suited to build and lead a small alien priory at his new domain, Turville heads for home wearing a broad smile. His purse is bulging with 40 silver marks (£39,300) for himself and another three marks (£2,900) for his good lady wife Isabell. Tappelawe is in God's hands: truly He moves in mysterious ways.

Holy Island

Amerden Bank / 18th June 2012

Two surprises not 200 yards downstream of **Bray Lock**: a flock of sooty-brown swifts screams from the wood and swoops to skim the surface of the river to make a feast on the wing of the swarms of low-flying insects, and a beautiful white-painted, black-timbered, red-roofed house emerges suddenly from the riverside greenery like a maiden discovered.

Amerden Priory may be old enough to have been at least a part of what its name suggests. A monastic outpost of Merton Priory stood here for over three centuries on a triangular island created by diverting a flow of the Thames through a ditch dug to define its northern and eastern extent. The remains of the medieval moat can still be seen prescribing its eastern boundary with Amerden Caravan Park. Despite the hum of the nearby M4 motorway, there is a sense of the rural isolation the monks enjoyed as they went about their work. It is likely that their job was as much to look after estate business as the souls of the locals.

Covetous Cousin

Bolbec Castle, Whitchurch / 18th June 1212

Merton Priory had already 'appropriated' **St Laurence's Church** in Opetone (**Upton**). It did the same to **St Mary's** in Hecham (**Hitcham**) in 1210 but there is no evidence that Turville had any part to play in this. His sole interest seems to have been to install yet another layer in Taplow's matrix of ownership – from the Crown, which had more regal matters to distract it, through the light-handed Leicester-Lancaster line to the enterprising Turvilles and the astute priors – which will continue for 341 years with various sub-tenancy twists and challenges. The first has come in the shape of Turville's cousin **Herbert de Bolbec** who is attempting to claim Westone (and presumably Tappelawe) as his own [*see Appendix 1, Tree 3*].

The Bolbecs went a few notches up the social scale in the 1140s when Hugh de Bolbec's grandson Hugh built this castle in Aylesbury Vale and founded Woburn Abbey and its subsidiary Cistercian cell at Medmenham (an abbey in its own right by 1200). This Herbert was that second Hugh's great-nephew. Turville will need to be on his toes to smooth away the challenge with as few family wrinkles as possible and to be succeeded as intermediary lord of all Tappelawe in 1222 by three daughters: Petronilla, Cecily and Isabella. Primacy will pass eventually to **Petronilla de Turville** and her husband Simon de Crewelton who will make things simpler for historical scribes by taking his wife's surname. The Bolbecs will have one last shout when Herbert's son Gilbert tries to oust Petronilla in 1236. Thereafter their interest will wane away.

The Emerging Trinity

The Chapter House, Merton Priory / 18th June 1212

The Priory's cash must have come in handy for William de Turville but it is likely he had another motive. Successive priors enjoy royal patronage and political clout that will continue for generations. Keeping sweet makes even more sense now than it did 19 years ago, which may be why Turville has come up with another wheeze for Prior Walter. It is necessary for late William Piscator's son Stephen to pay homage to Walter in order to succeed his father as tenant of Aumberdene, an arrangement that will involve the prior granting Turville enough wood to repair the mills.

Amerden Ponds / 18th June 2012

History recognises **Stephen Piscator** as "**Stephen de Tappelawe** or **Stephen de Cliefden**" but does not reveal where he lived. It is possible that he shared the **Amerden Bank** triangle with the monks of Merton. However, as their tenant, he might have made his home here at **Amerden Ponds**: the perfect place for a fishery. And perhaps he or his progeny crafted the cruciform island in the eastern pond in gratitude for God's beneficence.

Cliveden / 18th June 2013

This first written mention of Cliefden in 1213 implies that it was an adjunct to Aumberdene and provides the original concurrent glimpse of the Amerden-Taplow-Cliveden trinity. Some historical references to Tappelawe Manor might be taken to distinguish it from Aumberdene and Cliefden while others suggest the fertile arable fields of Aumberdene and the near-treeless rolling chalk plateau of Cliefden together added up to Tappelawe. The latter is more likely in the 12th and 13th Centuries, when Norman fief layering was still prevalent, but things seem to have changed by 1533 when **Thomas Manfield the Elder** celebrated the centenary of his family's tenure of Amerden Manor and Clyveden by also taking tenancy of Tappelow Manor, apparently by then a distinct intermediate entity rather than an overarching layer.

Soon after 1230, Stephen divided his lands between his sons. The suffix of Geoffrey de Cliefden suggests which portion he enjoyed and implies that his little brother might have been William de Aumberdene. Geoffrey survived until at least 1253 but apparently never got around to starting a family or to building a house on his sparse land – perhaps that's why Cliveden never became a manor in its own right – and when he died his brother styled himself William de Cliefden. By 1300 he had been succeeded in the twin tenancies by his son William de Clyvedene and in the 1340s by this second William's sons: first Richard, then Nichole (Nicholas) [*see Appendix 1, Tree 4*].

Tall Tale – Not Rabbiting On

Cliveden Woodlands / 20th June 2012

In 1252 the thirteenth prior Prior Gilbert de Asshe obtained from **King Henry III** a royal charter for a free warren in Taplow. The charter was either renewed or a new one obtained in 1280 for a separate warren by William de Agmodesham (Amersham).

Does this indicate that rabbits were big business? Fluffy bunnies had first been brought to Britannia by the Romans but all died or were eaten by Anglo-Saxons or good old British predators. The Normans came with a second colony, and indeed the word *rabet* came to Old English from either the Walloon *robète* or the Old French *rabbotte* or *rabouillet* meaning *baby coney*. They were kept in highly-valued warrens for centuries before they escaped to run wild. However, *warren* derives from the Anglo-Saxon *warian*, meaning *to take care*, and care should indeed be taken because Normans and Plantagenets used the term *free warren* to mean a privilege permitting the holder to kill specific game within a stipulated area. Four ancient enclosures have been combined to create the modern-day **Cliveden Woodlands** immediately west of the junction of Hill Farm Road and Cliveden Road – running north, their names were Eight Acre Warren, Ten Acre Warren, Middle Warren and Long Warren – but it would be a mistake to think that rabbits were the only game in town.

Prize Fighting

The first (or second) St Nicholas' Church / 20th June 1286

Prior Gilbert is typical of his ilk: pious and holy on the one hand but commercially acute on the other.

Merton Priory was at the peak of its power in 1236 when the tenth prior Henry de Basinges hosted King Henry III and his parliament. One aspect of their business was to enact the Statute of Merton to allow lords to enclose common land provided sufficient pasture remained for their tenants. If Prior Henry took advantage in Tappelawe, he was prudent to keep a low profile. Gilbert had a different purpose in 1266 when he made sure some scribe noted his investing ten shillings (£270) to send Prince Edward Longshanks off crusading. However, royal goodwill has been of no help in an era of political nightmares surrounding the church of St Nicholas.

The wool trade has been thriving in and around Wiccomb for many years. By 1235, the place was wall-to-wall with weavers spinning a rough webbed cloth. Tappelow has seen enough of a spin-off to remain in the Priory's eye sufficient of a prize to be blessed by the building of a new church, either on virgin ground or to replace an Anglo-Saxon predecessor. Unfortunately this has led to disputes with **William de Turville the Younger**, son of Petronilla and Simon, and with two other houses of Austin canons. The trouble started some decade-and-a-half ago when Prior Gilbert exercised his advowson to appoint Gilbert de Paunton as the first Rector of Tappelow. This latest Turville may have been a stay-away landlord but out of sight wasn't out of mind for his Thames Valley investment and he contested this appointment with support in ecclesiastical law from William of Colingham, Prior of Chalcombe (Northamptonshire). Eventually Prior Gilbert's will prevailed only for him to fall out with **Missenden Abbey** which was in such dire financial straits that its abbot, William of London, was desperate to retain a pension from St Nicholas' Church to which it had no right. These arguments have paled into insignificance during this last year when Prior Gilbert has been obliged to resist an acrimonious attempt by Turville to terminate his Priory's tenancy of Tappelow.

The Old Churchyard / 30th June 2012

Colingham has a distinct whiff of being a religious precursor of 'no-win, no-fee' lawyers. What did Turville hope to gain by engaging him? Had he funded the new church or donated glebe land to maintain the Rector and did he feel this entitled him to select the man for the job? Had he promised the valuable position to someone else? And when he failed in this aim, was his attempted eviction of the Priory inspired by simple revenge or the business opportunities presented by the new Maidenhead Bridge? The tenacious Gilbert survived this trio of threats and could have been excused if he gave himself a pat on the back in 1291 when King Edward I's assessors valued Tappelow Manor at £6 10s (£256,000). The following year Pope Nicholas IV's ecclesiastical survey assessed the new St Nicholas' Church as a tad more valuable at £6 13s 4d (£263,000).

Losing these legal battles with Merton Priory didn't dent this latest William de Turville's status sufficiently to prevent his being Sheriff of Buckinghamshire and Bedfordshire for three years from 1288 or his son **Nicholas de Turville** succeeding him to this lofty position in 1293. Nicholas's interests in Tappelow and Penne were valued in 1296 at *one knight's fee*, sufficient to support a knight for a year in his feudal duty. In that same year, three other Turville cousins also held interests locally. Those of **Cecily de Turville**'s great-grandson George de Charneles (or Charnell) in Tappelow and Penne were also valued at *one knight's fee*, and her great-granddaughters Ella and Isabel de Herdeburgh (or Herdebone) jointly held interests in Tappelow worth *one-half knight's fee and one-eighth part of another*.

Nicholas was succeeded by his son-in-law Hugh de Turpleton and in 1361 there is a fleeting mention of the intermediary lordship of Tappelowe being vested jointly in Hugh's son Walter de Turpleton and in Ella's daughter Ella le Botiller, but then silence falls. Thereafter the residual Turville interests recede into obscurity except for modern whispers that the original Geoffrey de Tureuilla was ancestor to at least 25 generations descending variously to **Sir Winston Churchill**, Prince Charles, Princess Diana and David Cameron [*see Appendix 1, Tree 3*].

Gilbert's successor Prior Edmund de Herierd felt sufficiently prosperous in 1303 to acquire additional (but unidentified) land for Tappelow Manor. With the Bolbecs long gone and the Turvilles eventually going the same way, thirteen successive priors were able to relax in secure control of the manor for a couple of centuries.

However the relatively small size of Tappelowe and the continuity of Merton Priory's management made further fragmentation unnecessary, with one possible exception: in 1335 either Hugh de Turpleton or Thomas de Kent, the eighteenth prior, sold or leased an estate in Tappelowe to John de Alveton (Sheriff of Oxfordshire), William de Shareshull, Thomas de L'Angele and Hugh de Berewyk. They all represented Oxfordshire in King Edward III's Parliament and they acted jointly, possibly on behalf Medmenham Abbey for which Berewyk was holding land locally in 1349. But exactly which land was acquired by this consortium of gentlemen, from whom, in what form of transaction and what happened to it next? Silence is the stern reply – except for one whisper: the ninth Rector of Taplow (1370/73) was one John Shareshull, possibly son of William.

It is hard to imagine that silence reigned in 1500 when **King Henry VII**'s legal eagles stumbled across Tappelow on the books of the Duchy of Lancaster. Their claim for 13s 4d (£4,850) was resisted successfully by Prior John Gisbourne on the grounds that the interest of the Sovereign, the Duchy and indeed everyone else was long gone. Gisbourne's achievement must have been warm in the memory of his successors, Priors William Sayling, John Lacy and John Ramsey, who from 1515 shipped downriver first timber for the construction of Hampton Court and then gravel, chalk, burnt lime, bricks and tiles. With his commercial heyday in full swing, Sayling somehow found the time in 1517 to unite the parishes of Tappelow and Hecham. It isn't clear why. There was no economy of personnel. The Reverend Michael Mabson had already been the 26th Rector of Tappelow for 19 years and would continue for another 20 in tandem with a series of four rectors who had their 'living' in Hecham. Whatever the objective, it all became irrelevant in the mid-1530s. Sayling can have had no idea that Ramsey would be Merton Priory's thirty-first and last gasp. As the Dissolution gathered pace, the parishes were split asunder once again in 1537 and within a year the Priory was no more, a victim of royal politics.

Sideways Glance

Burnham and its Bits

St Peter's Church, Burnham / 23rd June 1266

The Norman royal ripple quickly reached **Eton** and **Burnham**. Both came into the proud possession of a royal favourite who, when appointed Castellan (Constable) of Windesores Castle in 1070, was rewarded with a suffix to become Walter fitzOtho de Windsor. Burnham passed to his grandson Walter de Windsor and was divided in 1204 between his sons-in-law Duncan de Lascelles and Ralph de Hodeng. The place is famed for playing at jigsaw puzzles. It has nine separate liberties (districts): Burneham, Esburnham, Brittilthrup, Bretywylle, Bouneaie, Sippenham, Lient, Westone and Wodeland. East Burnham, Britwell, **Boveney**, **Cippenham** and Weston already are or will eventually become distinct if modest manors. Brittilthrup is a prime suspect to become **Beaconsfield**. Weston may derive from *Gwesty-Towan* (meaning *gravel ridge inn*) which in the 15th Century will have a spell as Rokesby, named for Richard Rokeby, before becoming ***West Town Farm***. Woodland will remain just that for many moons but how does **Lent** sit in this carve-up?

Burnham Abbey / 23rd June 1271

Road realignment wasn't the be-all-and-end-all of Richard of Cornwall's pet projects. Twice he graced **St Mary's Church** at Hitcham with decorated floor tiles he had specially made in the renowned kilns at Penn: firstly to celebrate his wedding to Isabella Marshall in 1231 and then to give thanks for surviving a Scilly Isles shipwreck in 1242, a salvation also celebrated by the founding of Hailes Abbey (Gloucestershire). However his much grander expression of gratitude in 1265 wasn't universally popular. It was one thing to give thanks for having survived the battles of Lewes and Tewkesbury the previous year by founding **Burnham Abbey** and ceding to it the erstwhile Lascelles estates and two watermills: Gy Mill and Aymill. The trouble was that his gratitude knew no bounds and he didn't care who he hurt to show it. He made sure that every whim of the first abbess Joan of Rideware was fulfilled regardless of the consequences. The locals lost 20 acres of common woodland – perhaps at **Abbey Park**, north of Burnham – when they were enclosed for her flock's livestock. The Gy was dammed to provide a better fishpond despite critically depleting **Cippenham**'s drinking water and **Dilehurst**'s waterborne trade. A footpath from **Dorney** to **Burnham** was diverted to keep the riff-raff at arms length. And now the Abbey has been granted a royal charter that not only gives Burnham the right to hold a three-day fair of St Matthew each September but also transfers to Burnham the Thursday market that has been held at Dorney for over 400 years. It will still be going in the early-21st Century but on Wednesday not Thursday.

Burnham Abbey / 23rd June 1337

Joan's tenure at Burnham Abbey ended with a drama of a different kind in 1311 when one of her nuns was excommunicated for running away to be married. The unfortunate Margery of Hedsor was restored to the Abbey in 1317 when she convinced Joan's successor, Idonea de Audley, that her father had made her marry against her will. All's well that ends well of course but the Abbey's bit of bother involved not only the two abbesses but also layers of cardinals and two popes: Clement V to do the deed and his successor John XXII to undo it. Perhaps it exhausted papal patience. The latter was too busy to intervene in 1330 when Geoffrey de Bulstrode protested his right to Bulstrode Manor in **Hedgerley** by vandalising the Abbey's property and harassing its servants. The Abbey's holdings at the time included half of Burnham (and **St Peter's Church**), half of Beaconsfield, the church of **St James the Less** in Dorney and the manors of Holmer and **Stoke Poges** but the income added up to nowhere near enough to fund the legal battle. Idonea's only option was to borrow and then borrow some more. The dispute dragged on for over two years before finally being resolved in the Abbey's favour but the fight had been financially crippling. Pope Clement VI has turned a blind eye to Idonea's plight leaving **King Edward III** no option but to pardon the poverty-stricken Abbey's debt which now stands at a massive £57 6s 4d (£45,000).

The Bee, Burnham / 23rd June 2012

This is just the place to contemplate over a pint the name games that might have been.

Old Bayley Lore speculates that Burnham might have been more than the village (*ham*) on the stream (*burn*). After all, *Bur-wy-nan-am* meant *the wild water of the stream* [in the] *valley of the cultivated land*. **Boveney** was *the small island of the cow*, or *Bugh-Ven-Ynys*, and although it's rather a lot of meaning to fit into three short syllables, Cippenham might derive from *Sink-pen-am*, meaning *the chief corn-rich cultivated land village*. Everyone agrees that Dorney was an island in the marshes. Most accept that its name means *the island of bees*. There are other less well-known possibilities. In Old English, *Dorn-aue* meant *thorny floodplain*, and in Ancient British, *Dorge-yny* was *the earthwork hedged island*, a nod to its man-made floodbanks. All three explanations hold water: take your pick.

Huntercombe Manor / 23rd June 1342

Hodeng's half of Burnham descended to his grandson's aunt, wife of Sir William de Huntercombe, and is now held by their son Thomas de Huntercombe (another Constable of Windsor Castle). His son John de Huntercombe will complete the construction of Huntercombe Manor in about three years before being succeeded by three generations all called John de Huntercombe, the last of which will relieve the tedium in 1390 by passing the manor to his aunt Elizabeth de Huntercombe, wife of Philip Scudamore of Herefordshire. Their descendants will play spelling games with Skydamoor and Skydamour before settling on Skydmore as they enjoy the pleasure of Huntercombe for the next 216 years.

Tall Tale – Welsh Whimsy

Huntercombe Manor / 23rd June 1432

George Skydmore has just received news that his cousin Sir John Scudamore, Sheriff of Herefordshire, has fallen from royal favour. It seems Sir John has mellowed from quelling the Welsh to marrying one of them, and not just any old *fenyw* but Alys, daughter of his old enemy Owain Glyndŵr (**Owen Glendower** to the English). **King Henry IV** is so furious that he intends to strip Sir John of his stewardships of Monmouth Castle, Grosmont Castle and the White Castle. In years to come the legend will grow that Glyndŵr spent his last years disguised as a friar at Huntercombe. And when a large ornate lead coffin is found at Burnham Abbey in the mid-20th Century with no hint as to its occupant, there'll be speculation that this might be the last resting place of the last native Prince of Wales.

Handing Down Hecham

St Mary's Church, Hitcham / 26th June 1272

This church is already over 100 years old. The chancel was rebuilt in 1190 and will be further enlarged in 1340 which might be when it is blessed with nine stained glass windows depicting Ezekiel's vision of either of the nine orders of angels (or according to the 20th Century fantasist Erich von Daniken, the landing of aliens) – but why on earth here in Hitcham?

As a royal grandson, **Edmund of Cornwall** was never going to go short of privileges. Little does he know but today the lucky fellow inherits not only a tin-rich earldom but also the tenancy-in-chief of Hecham and the free warren originally granted in 1231 to Miles Neymut (or Neyrant). Hecham was Hucheham in those days and prized highly enough in 1233 for a big furore to blow up about who was Neymut's tenant-in chief. The protagonists were men of considerable clout. On one hand there was Edmund's father Richard, 1st Earl of Cornwall (him again), and on the other was Walter Mauclerk, Bishop of Carlisle. The bishop didn't have a prayer. He was deposed after five years as Lord High Treasurer and deprived of Hecham.

The original Hecham Manor House / 26th June 1382

The valiant soldier **Sir Adam Ramsay** has something to celebrate here in his fine house north-east of **St Mary's Church**. He has obtained King Richard II's confirmation of his right to a free warren.

When Edmund of Cornwall died without heirs in 1300, primacy over Hecham technically reverted to King Edward I (the crusader formerly known as Longshanks) and in 1337 to Edward, Prince of Wales and Duke of Cornwall. This worthy fellow – otherwise known as **The Black Prince** – is said to have dropped by for a sleepover in 1327, when he was on his way to Windsor get married. Perhaps he enjoyed his stag night there?

The tenancy of little Hecham was allotted in dower for the first of many times when Miles died. His widow Isabel married Reginald Beauchamp and the manor passed to their son Miles Beauchamp. In 1377 his great-granddaughter Isabel Beauchamp married Sir Adam. Unfortunately scribes will fail to note whether he or the Beauchamps built this, Hecham's original manor house. Perhaps such notarial neglect is the reason why Hecham will be cast in the role of *Sleeping Beauty* for the best part of the next hundred years.

Misty Haddesovere

The original Hedsor Manor House / 26th June 1382

Haddesovere is a pair with Hecham for its likely lordship at *Domesday* and for being a medieval secret.

The *Domesday* surveyors either missed the place entirely or more probably counted it within another manor. There are two candidates: Hanechedene (Cresswell, near **High Wycombe**), which with Well End was in the hands of Theowald under **Odo**, and Merlaue (**Little Marlow**), which like Hucheham was bestowed upon Ralf and Roger de Anvers under Miles Crispin. The latter is more logical since eight decades later it was held *to the honour of Wallingford* by Crispin's heirs in the line of his brother-in-law Nigel D'Oyly. Technically the D'Oyly family remain tenants-in-chief of both manors but this means little. It is doubtful if any of them know or care about either of these little gems. This should be no surprise. Nigel's son Robert D'Oyly had much too much else to worry about in the misty 12th Century, what with helping King Henry I's daughter Matilda fight her cousin King Stephen for his throne while trying to decide if he was a D'Oyly, a D'Ouilly or a Doyley. Eventually he will forget the whole spelling thing and instead take the name Osney for his home on the western edge of Oxford.

The Chequers Inn, Kiln Lane / 26th June 2012

Heddesore emerged from the mists in 1166 held by a Geoffrey who may have built the original manor house. He was succeeded about 800 years ago by his son who styled himself William de Heddesore and ceded a plot a few yards west of his house for the construction of **St Nicholas' Church**. William's great-grandson John de Heddesore sold the manor in 1305 to Ralph Loveday. His grandson John Loveday died in 1362 and by 1379 the manor had passed to Ralph Restwold the Younger. It remained in his family for 170 years during which it couldn't decide if it was Hedshore, Endesouere or Eddysore (which sounds painful).

The mists still swirl around the origins of St Nicholas. Did the Augustinian abbots of Missenden Abbey miss a trick? The church appears in its 13th Century Charter yet the Benedictine prioresses of Little Marlow exercised the advowson until the early-15th Century. Their priory was founded before 1218 by **Hugh of Wells**, Bishop of Lincoln (1209/35). Perhaps he also funded Hedsor's church. Maud d'Anvers was the second prioress (1230/37): her name suggests descent from the original Norman lords. The fourth, **Cecily de Turville** (1256/58), was the daughter of the lord of Taplow and the name of the tenth, Agnes de Clevedon (1291/98), suggests a close familial link to the local **Piscator** line or a looser one to the lords of Leicester.

Another pint helps the pondering on how **Hedsor** got such an unusual name. Hedsor Wharf had probably been there for centuries before it was first noted in 1195 so could *Hed-sor* simply combine the suffixes of Maidenhead and Windsor as *the wharf on the bank*? **Old Bayley Lore** offers other theories: that it derives from *Haed-Scorer* (*steeply sloping heath*), from *Hæddi's Ora* (referring to the riverbank village of Hæddi's tribe) or from *Hædda's Sgur* (referring to its clifftop location) or *Heddel-Esc-Or* (*tribe of the border water*, a reminder that the river was once the frontier between Wessex and Danelaw).

The Brass Age

Something Fishy

The first (or second) St Nicholas' Church / 30th June 1355

It is a fabulous sight, this brass cross set into stone indents carved some five years ago into the tomb of the 'London fishmonger' **Nichole (Nicholas) de Aumberdene**. Its design speaks subtly of such wealth and piety.

The third (or fourth) St Nicolas' Church / 30th June 2012

The magnificent cross has weathered well. It is now acknowledged as the earliest surviving civilian commemoration in brass. Such posthumous showing-off was something knights did, not upwardly-mobile merchants. Six-and-a-half centuries ago, Taplow became trend-setting all of a sudden. It wasn't the last time.

There's a whiff of intrigue about a fishmonger flying so high. Was he a Londoner who went west for the rural tranquillity and fish-filled waters of the middle Thames Valley? Or was he a local yokel who made good in the big city selling perch, pike, trout, salmon and such, home-grown in **Amerden Ponds**? Logic suggests the latter. Surely he must be Nicholas, son of the second William de Clyvedene who held Aumberdene too? Both estates will pass eventually to Nicholas's son-in-law John Goldby. His son, also John Goldby, will end the **Piscator** inheritance by *alienating* (*selling*) it as a package to John Newenham in 1408 [*see Appendix 1, Tree 4*].

Enduring Dynasty

The third (or fourth) St Nicolas' Church / 2nd July 2012

Taplow had been there in the Bronze Age and seen out the Iron Age. Nichole de Aumberdene had the original idea in or around 1350 but Taplow's very own Brass Age really began in 1433. It is the story of the Manfield family. Their tenure in Taplow lasted 263 years, possibly 271. Nearly all are commemorated in St Nicolas' Church on brass plaques, most with palimpsest inscriptions.

It took 25 years and several intermediate conveyances for Aumberdene and Clyvedene to wend their way from John Newenham to **Robert Manfield** (spelled *Manfelde* or *Manfyld* according to taste). Although neither his heritage nor his track record is on record, it seems safe to say he was a man of means and the first of a kind, a true outsider for whom Amerden was a country retreat, possibly a place to play. He didn't enjoy it for long himself but his dynasty was as durable as they come. In total ten Manfields – three Roberts, a Thomas, two Henrys, another Thomas, an Edward, another Robert and a final Edward – were lords of **Amerden** and **Clyveden** for over two-and-a-half centuries.

The second **Robert Manfield** styled himself Robert of Amerden and was much admired by King Henry VI who granted him a free warren in 1440 and appointed him the following year to the lucrative post of Victualler of Calais. He was elevated in 1445 to Master of the Mint and in 1451 to Master and Worker of the King's Monies with an annual salary of £10 (£179,000) from 1447 increased to £15 (£315,000) from 1452 and supplemented by a "pipe of Gascon wine" each year from 1453. In his spare time he was Steward of Colchester Castle from 1447 and Keeper of the Lions in the Tower of London from 1456. Whenever the King needed anything organised in Buckinghamshire, Manfield was the man he turned to: he was twice a knight of the shire. His twin estates passed in 1459 to his son, the third **Robert Manfield**, who after a brief term as the 20th Rector in 1462 set the style for his dynasty by blessing the church in 1465 with a handful of brasses in remembrance of his grandfather Robert, his parents Robert and Jane, and his father's three siblings Richard, Isobelle and John who had all died young in or around 1455, possibly of the dreaded plague. Robert also acquired **Burnham Manor** in 1478. It remained in his family's possession for three generations spanning over a century before passing to Richard Bavin.

The enterprising **Thomas Manfield** succeeded his father in 1500. It took a while for him to get into his stride but then there was no stopping him. He kept in the good books of **King Henry VIII** to obtain royal confirmation of the free warren in 1513 and to secure fishing rights in the Thames in return for repairing and continuing to maintain the weir and flashlock. Meanwhile he rebranded his northern estate as Clyveden Park alias Manfield's and his southern one as **Amerden Manor**. The latter was valued at £21 (£330,000) in 1523. The two estates descended to his son **Henry Manfield** in 1540 and to his son **Henry Manfield** in 1568 when the annual rent to the Crown for Amerden was £6 13s 4d (£2,200). ***Amerden Place*** was the second Henry's home and **Clyveden Park** his playground for all of 68 years during which he continued to install brasses in **St Nicholas' Church** until 1619 in commemoration of his grand-parents Thomas and Agnes, his parents Henry and Jane, and his own wife Hester. His sons spread across the river, **Thomas Manfield** to *the maner of Rayes* and **Sir Edward Manfield** to ***Bullocks*** at **Cookham** (now ***White Place Farm)*** upon his marriage to Maria Smyth. Sir Edward finally inherited his father's twin Buckinghamshire estates in 1636. His elder son **Robert Manfield** had a spell in the driving seat before his younger son **Edward Manfield** got the lot in 1671 [*see Appendix 1, Tree 4*].

However, the Manfield story wasn't as simple as it might seem. What really made the later of their ilk remarkable was that they remained dedicated Catholics at a time when it was fast going out of fashion. The tale of their tenure in Taplow has to be seen against the dramatic background of religious turmoil from the English Reformation, through the ups and downs of the Tudors and Stuarts, the English Civil War and the Puritan Protectorate that followed, all the way to the invention of constitutional Anglican monarchy in the last decade of the 17th Century. In the main, the great shift in England's religious, moral and political soul swirled around Taplow but how it got through can only be appreciated with an understanding of the context and proximity of events....

God's Landscape

The third (or fourth) St Nicholas' Church / 2nd July 2012

A cursory glance at history books might suggest that the English Reformation came about so **King Henry VIII** could divorce the aging Catherine of Aragon to marry the beautiful Anne Boleyn in the hope that she would bear a boy to succeed him. There is a lot more to it, and not just the royal libido. For the king, it was a matter of principle: he and not the pope was in charge of all things English. Some of his influential subjects had other ideas that spanned from a spiritual rejection of mystical idolatry to a downright resentment of the financial and political power the Church enjoyed. Perhaps this angst stretched back to the differences between the beliefs and morals of the Normans and the English, the Conqueror and the conquered. Norman lords and their Plantagenet successors used the church to assert their authority. The only way to God for the peasant populace was through layers of parish priests, bishops, archbishops and ultimately the pope in Rome (wherever that was). Then there were abbeys like Burnham, priories like Merton and other monastic institutions whose social impact was as much secular and social as spiritual. They all reinforced their aloofness by using God's secret language: Latin.

Faith was neither universal nor consistent yet many (perhaps most) were comfortable with Catholic mystique and content with the Church and its age-old customs. In 12th and 13th Centuries new churches were dedicated to **St Peter** in **Burnham**, **St James the Less** in **Dorney**, **St Mary Magdalene** in **Boveney**, **St Mary** in **Hitcham** and **St Nicholas** in both Taplow and **Hedsor**. Some replaced earlier Anglo-Saxon churches. That at Boveney had long been a place of worship for the bargees who plied the Thames and that at Burnham may have replaced an even earlier church dating back to 500 or possibly earlier. Nobles and their less wealthy neighbours were united in two things: getting by in this life and striving for salvation in the next. Having a religious calling seems to have ticked both boxes. Everyday folk in the fields and workshops knew the pious played politics for profit. It was the way of the world. For centuries the monks of Merton and the nuns of Burnham were effective lords (or ladies) of their manors – or perhaps not so effective if you take into account the profits of one and the debts of the other. Even the modest Benedictine priory of **Little Marlow** had an outpost of nuns in the woods on Hitcham Common – the offerings at **Cabrook Chapel** were valued at 10s (£7,750) in 1536 – but the roost was ruled by the Bishop of Lincoln and his parish priests.

See Here

Lincoln Hatch Lane, Burnham / 2nd July 2012

What's that about the Bishop of Lincoln? How did Buckinghamshire find itself in such a distant episcopal see? It's a long story that began (of course) in 635 with **Birinus** whose diocese of Dorchester included South Bucks. This see's history reflects the sway between Saxons and Angles. It was embraced by Saxon Winchester in the 660s, briefly independent in the 670s under Anglian Mercia, within Winchester again from about 690 to 875 before reviving as an independent Mercian see until 971 when it merged with the diocese of Lindsey. The bishop's seat remained at Dorchester until 1070 when the Conqueror transferred it to Lincoln and sat upon it his friend Remigius de Fécamp. The **Diocese of Lincoln** was massive: the biggest in England, extending diagonally from the Humber to the Thames. It survived intact until 1541 when the dioceses of Peterborough and Oxford were carved from it. The bishops of Lincoln watched their southern flock from **Wooburn Palace** until 1547. Buckinghamshire remained a disconnected fragment of the see until 1837 when it was taken into the Diocese of Oxford. It remains there to this day but the Lincoln link echoes locally in the odd place name like Lincoln Hatch Lane in Burnham, perhaps once the site of the bishop's most southerly hen house?

Hotbed of Heresy

The first (or second) St Nicholas' Church / Christmas Eve 1521

The first **Thomas Manfield** will spend the night paying penitence in thanks for the Saviour's birth. It has been an eventful year for righteous Catholics. John Longland, Bishop of Lincoln, has completed his inquisition tour of South Buckinghamshire where he found over 200 wayward souls, some of whom were quick to save their skins by pointing fingers at others, but he passed by Taplow and Hitcham. He knew he'd find no heretics here.

It is safe to say that when the first **Robert Manfield** settled in **Amerden** in 1433 most of the country was happy in its medieval Catholic cloak. However some had other ideas, some in places very nearby. Did this original Manfield realise that South Bucks had long been a hotbed of heresy? If he did, perhaps he was reassured that various bishops of Lincoln holding court at **Wooburn Palace** would conduct regular persecutions to exorcise the problem. If he was, he was counting chickens. In less than a lifetime, the boot will be on his descendants' other foot. And their descendants will find themselves out of step again a century after that.

South Bucks and the middle Thames Valley can claim to be one of England's original centres of theological dissent and pressure for social change. Perhaps the sense of ethical and moral independence that grew to be religious non-conformity has its root in the untamed Chilterns Hills where pagan beliefs still clung on either alongside Christianity or at best absorbed into its teachings. Or perhaps it was being halfway between London's commercial freedom and Oxford's intellectual perspective. Or was it just the British being belligerent? Maybe they had been taught to be by their succession of foreign rulers. Either way there were signs as early as the 12th Century that South Bucks wasn't doing things by the Good Book. **Hugh of Avalon** was Bishop of Lincoln from 1186 until 1200. His determined struggle with the many relics of heathenism in his diocese, not least the worship of a 'fountain' at **Wycombe** – the spring at Halliwell Mead on the Rye – was acknowledged by his rapid canonisation in 1220 as St Hugh, patron saint of swans, shoemakers and the sick. And during his period in the same office from 1235 to 1253, Robert

Grossetete took note of another aspect of English upset: resentment at church corruption and papal interference in secular matters.

Here's the rub: the first stirring of what came to be called Protestantism almost 300 years later. And it began not with a German monk but English peasants. Originally their gripe wasn't about Catholic doctrine and idolatry, although that was coming. The Oxford don and Buckinghamshire vicar John Wycliffe started the ball rolling in the late-14th Century by translating Holy Scriptures into English to give everyone direct access to the word of God and by challenging every convention the Catholic church held dear. His russet-gowned followers found fertile ground for their 'obstinate questioning' in the hill-country parishes in the north of the Burnham Hundred. By 1382 the 'uplandish folk' of Amersham, Chesham, Chenies and Chalfont St Giles were called *Lollards*, a word of uncertain provenance but possibly from *lollaert,* Middle Dutch for *to mutter* or *to mumble*.

The persecution of local Lollards has continued for generations but all the burnings, brandings and bearing of faggots or green badges of disgrace seemingly stimulated the spread of dissent. The founding of **Eton College** in 1440 added fuel to free-thinking. Time and again Bishops of Lincoln have found heretics everywhere from their Amersham heartland to Henley, Wendover, Beaconsfield, Burnham, the Missendens and eventually Dorney, Chalvey, Iver and Uxbridge – but never here, which explains why Longland let us be. Somehow the Manfields and Merton Priory have ridden the storm around them and kept Catholicism safe and sound in Taplow.

It can't last, and it won't. Soon everything will fall apart for the Priory and, although it will first float higher, eventually the bubble will burst for the Manfields too.

Minding the Manor: The Brass Age Begins

The Arms of the Priory of St Mary, Merton
Successive priors gradually superseded the Turvilles as effective tenants-in-chief of Taplow 1197-1538 to enjoy 'homage' for 'subinfeudating' manorial rights to the Piscators and Manfields

The brass commemorative cross of fishmonger Nichole de Aumberdene, last of the Piscator male line / c1350

Crowning Glory

Once More a Jewel

In the Gift of the Crown

The Chapter House, Merton Priory / 19th September 1533

King Henry VIII will remain ever faithful to Catholic teachings and yet his yen to be free from papal authority for what he sees as England's sake is unleashing a political and theological earthquake that will change England forever. Prior John Ramsey has sensed the way the winds are blowing and is seeking quick cash. **Thomas Manfield** is pleased to have leased Tappelow Manor from Merton Priory for 21 years at an annual rental of £13 6s 8d (£7,070) although the mills, islands and church advowson remain within the Ramsey's gift.

The Chapter House, Merton Priory / 19th September 1538

It is three years since Thomas Cromwell's assessors descended upon Merton to calculate the total value of the Priory's assets (including Tappelow, **Amerden** and **Clyveden**) at £960 16s 6d (£16.75m). The following year the king began dissolving monasteries, priories and abbeys and pocketing the proceeds. Prior Ramsey's pride and joy is being razed to the ground – in 1989 its remains will be interred below a Sainsbury's carpark and the A24 – and King Henry will recycle much of its stone to build Nonsuch Palace six miles down the road at Cuddington, a village being obliterating for his indulgent purpose. Tappelow will suffer no such fate: it has been taken *to the Honour of the House of Windsor* and is once more a jewel in the Crown. Manfield has emerged from the melee smelling of roses and paying rent for the trinity to the Crown instead of the Church. He will pass away in a year or so in blissful ignorance of how the future of Taplow will be shaped by this latest rush of the Royal Ripple.

Sideways Glance

Resigned to Reformation

Burnham Abbey / 19th September 1539

The sharpened nib of her quill hovers halfway from inkwell to parchment. Abbess Alys Baldwin pauses to pray for forgiveness. It is five years since her predecessor Mary Gibson resigned rather than submit to the Act of Supremacy which confirmed the Church of England's split from Rome. A drop of ink falls from Alys's nib to explode silently on her oak tabletop. She watches as it soaks into the ancient grain of the wood leaving an indelible stain to commemorate 274 years of Augustinian ascendancy. The last nine nuns have all signed the Deed of Dissolution. It only remains for her to do the same. With a deep sigh of resignation, she does what must be done. If pride wasn't a sin, she might be proud that hers is reputedly the last religious house to surrender.

Perhaps Alys will find some solace that God hasn't smiled kindly on His Majesty. Having hated heretics, he suddenly found himself branded as one and excommunicated by the Holy Father, Pope Clement VII. The shock waves of the Reformation will reverberate across England for over two centuries as the national faith edges gradually and painfully to become Anglican. The constitutional echoes will still ring almost 600 years hence.

The Church's largesse and the sale of its properties will top up Crown coffers to the tune of almost £1.5 million (£25,470m). Much of it will go to fund fights against the Scots and the French, some to pay ecclesiastical pensions and the rest to feather the royal nest or to keep sweet the king's coterie. **Thomas Manfield**'s boon is modest compared to most. As groom of His Majesty's wardrobe, the opportunistic William Tildesley will be well-placed to lease **Burnham Abbey** from the Crown and Little Marlow Priory has been granted to Elizabeth Restwold of Hedsor and John Tytley of Amersham who will sell **Cabrook Chapel** to the Borlase family of Marlow for ten shillings (£8,500). Cabrook will be variously Caybrook, Cadbrook, Craybrook, Cavebrook, Caresbrook, Carbrooke, Cray Brook and (by the 1770s) ***Chapel Farm*** as it survives within the Borlase Warren estate until being acquired in 1781 by a Mr Antonie, probably William Lee Antonie, former MP for Great Marlow.

Tudors and Stewards

Tall Tale – Clever Cleeves

The Old Public Slipway / 19th February 1937

King Henry VIII was quick to give something of Taplow to Anne of Cleeves. When 403 years ago she consented to the annulment of their marriage, he expressed his gratitude by giving her not only various properties including Surrey's Richmond Palace and Kent's Hever Castle but also, most generously of all, the riparian rights for a stretch of the Bucks bank from this slipway for perhaps 100 yards upstream. Such rights – the exclusive rights to fish, now abolished – were normally held under the Royal Franchise and rarely fell into private hands. There is no record that the erstwhile Queen Anne ever angled here but, as **Sidney (Paddy) Sutton Smith** discovered on 7th January when he completed his acquisition of ***Bond's Boats***, this once valuable commodity still remains vested in this river frontage.

The Turning Tables

Amerden Place / 19th February 1549

The regal reshaping has begun. Every table is for turning.

If **Henry Manfield** thought when he stepped into his father Thomas's shoes that he could rest on his ancestors' laurels, he was very much mistaken. He and his wife Jane Lovelace of Hurley knew within months of old King Henry VIII's death two years ago that being Catholic was going to be difficult in the reign of the ardently reforming **King Edward VI**. He has trodden carefully by making sure to pay his rent on time and by not grazing too many sheep on the common, the kind of encroachment that is causing so much social unrest elsewhere. And yet the Crown has terminated his leasehold of Tappelow Manor with six years still to run.

Was the decision made by 12-year-old king himself or by his uncle and Protector Edward Seymour, 1st Duke of Somerset? Has Manfield offended by objecting to church services being held in English, or to the use of *The Book of Common Prayer*? It matters not. Somerset will soon be deposed but Manfield has no friend to support him on the Regency Council. He can only pray that if he keeps his faith as quietly as a churchmouse he will be left in peace to enjoy his tenancy of **Amerden** and **Clyveden** under the jurisdiction of the royal steward **Thomas Jones**.

St Peter's Church, Burnham / 19th February 1559

The passing of King Henry VIII in 1547 heralded what will be seen as one of the nastiest periods in the history of the Church of England. Religious principles and prescribed ecclesiastical practice and doctrine have swung this way and that in the reigns of three Tudor siblings. King Edward VI made many Lollard dreams come true by having churches stripped clean of papist trappings. His half-sister **Queen Mary I** was equally passionately Catholic for five years during which she had them all put back again. **Queen Elizabeth I** succeeded her half-sister three months ago. She will be more politically pragmatic but no less reforming than her half-brother and her 45-year reign will be long enough to make it stick.

The church of St Peter has seen events more tumultuous than most. The vicar of Burnham, Reverend John Mallet, spoke out so strongly against the Dissolution that King Henry had him executed in 1542. Thereafter this was the place for successive monarchs to set an example in the middle Thames Valley. King Edward had St Peter stripped of "superstitious images" and "evidence of popery" in 1549 and the following year presented **Richard Davies** who, only months after Queen Mary took charge, got himself into trouble for either being married or "seditious preaching" (or both). He didn't take the hint. Within a year Mary deprived him of his office and had St Peter restored to its former Catholic glory. Elizabeth has quickly restored Davies (complete with wife) and instructed that the newly installed idolatrous trappings be stripped away once again. It is all as confusing for the congregation as it is profitable for local artisans and tradesmen.

Manfield Park / 19th February 1573

The church of St Nicholas probably went through similar turmoil. Each monarch persecuted those who didn't share their creed and so did everyone else. Hatred was rife. Life was anything but a walk in the park for dedicated Roman Catholics in an ever more Protestant England. The former heretics now held the high ground. The religious rights of one day were wrong the next.

Henry Manfield's prayers were answered. His tenure of Amerden and Clyvedene survived Edward's reign unscathed. And if he breathed a sigh of relief in Mary's time, he did it discretely enough not to annoy Elizabeth who in 1561 was happy enough to receive payment of his annual rent for Amerden in the sum of £6 13s 4d (£1,840). Manfield might not have been delighted to discover the following year that his new neighbour at **Burnham Abbey** was the passionately puritan Paul Wentworth MP, an avid and feared "smeller-out" of papists, but he hung onto his faith and his estates and passed them to his son in 1568.

The second **Henry Manfield** celebrated by giving Clyveden a new name – **Manfield Park** – and over the last five years tripling its estate from 50 to 160 acres and adding a second lodge. Clearly he doesn't have his father's gift for keeping a low profile. Now someone else is translating the word of God and it sounds to him very different indeed. He and his wife Hester will suffer years of persecution for continuing to believe what has been believed for generations. He will be punished for nonconformity during purges in 1581, 1587 and 1608. She will be required to pay a monthly fine of £20 (£4,260). And in 1611 *Bullocks* will be sequestrated from their recusant son **Sir Edward Manfield**.

Queuing up for Topley

Whitehall Palace / 19th February 1587

This mid-Tudor merry-go-round was also evident in secular matters. King Edward VI's installation of Thomas Jones as steward of Tappelow Manor in 1549 marked the beginning of an increasingly crazy 81 years during which (according to a 1562 map) the manor assumed the alias Topley. King Edward nudged Jones aside within a year to appoint William Ferror (or Turner) to a term of office of 21 years. He lasted just six. Queen Mary I reinstated Jones in 1556 on a 30-year tenure in return for an annual fee of £13 6s 8d (£3,640). These switches might indicate the respective religious persuasions of the two gentlemen and their sovereigns but it seems that Jones wasn't too Catholic for Queen Elizabeth I's taste for she left him in place. Or perhaps she was just too busy trying to decide whether or not to wed and to whom.

It was a decade before Her Majesty realised the full value of Topley. The manor makes a mint from its quarries. It has long sent chalk, burnt lime and gravel to Hampton Court and Windsor Castle and will continue to do so until at least 1680. Its stewardship is a much sought-after position, so much so that in 1570 she negotiated a contract with John Lely (or Cely) and

John Whynniard to succeed Jones when his tenure expired in 1586. As it happened, Jones died two years before his time was up but he didn't do too badly, especially as his wife Ursula confirmed his Catholicism by installing a brass in **St Nicholas' Church** that reveals she had been imprisoned for her faith. The two Johns settled down to their sinecures only for Elizabeth to be at it again with an even more complicated two-layer arrangement whereby Captain Richard Pickman will pay Richard (or Roger) Morgan and Thomas Bradford the sum of £5 18 3d (£3,400) annually for the post which won't fall vacant until 1608 [*see Appendix 1, Tree 5*].

The third Taplow House / 19th July 2012

It is thought that the original **Taplow House** was built in 1598 with brick ovens in its basement and the convenience of running water from its springs: a grand new addition indicating how far the Royal Ripple had reached from Windsor by the end of the Elizabethan age. In its guise as Topley, Taplow offered the elite exactly the right combination of exclusive luxury, independence and proximity to the royal heartbeat. But who first enjoyed the comforts of this well-appointed dwelling? He must have been a man of considerable wealth and influence for Elizabeth to have given him leave to build such a desirable residence. The prime suspect is Pickman, a firm favourite for keeping Berwick from the Scots. Did Bess send a bouquet of tulips as a house-warming gift and let Legend take it from there?

Pickman's patience ran out in 1601 when he subcontracted his place on the waiting list. John Treharne and Roger Tenne parted with £100 (£19,300) for the privilege of a 30-year term at an annual rental of £13 6s 8d (£2,570) payable to Morgan and Bradford who must have been very happy to anticipate more than doubling their money. These various intricate contracts are on record but not whether Pickman, Treharne or Tenne actually did succeed Whynniard and Lely to the stewardship or the precise nature of the intermediaries Morgan and Bradford. It is tempting to imagine the Queen was pocketing the proceeds from her very own options market. If so, what a clever Queenie she was.

Tall Tales – Good Queen Jests

The fourth Taplow Court / 19th July 2012

Good Queen Bess has a knack of inspiring Legend's imagination. It has her as a young princess planting the magnificent tulip trees at Taplow House, later being held under house arrest in **Taplow Court** at the pleasure of her sister **Queen Mary** and eventually returning there as the Virgin Queen to plant ***Queen's Elizabeth's Oak***. This oak was noted on Ordnance Survey maps until 1933.

Grains of truth are thin on the ground.

The story of Elizabeth's house arrest at Taplow Court stands little scrutiny. It is possible that she enjoyed a sleepover in Taplow while on her way between imprisonments in the Tower of London and at Woodstock in 1554, or perhaps when she was brought to Hampton Court in 1555 to meet her new brother-in-law Prince Philip of Spain. And as this period coincides neatly with the stewardship of William Ferror, it is tempting to think it was then she found reason to have him replaced as soon as the opportunity arose. However there are two problems with this theory. Firstly: it isn't credible that any such visits could entirely escape the attention of otherwise diligent scribes who recorded Elizabeth's every movement. And secondly: just where would she have been accommodated? Neither Taplow House nor Taplow Court existed during her sister's reign. There is no more than presumption that any medieval manor house preceded the latter. However, here's a twist: Henry Manfield the Elder held Taplow during Mary's reign. As a dedicated Catholic, perhaps she trusted him to keep her sister for a few days in closely-watched comfort at ***Amerden Place***. Perhaps his hospitality made sufficient impression for the pragmatic Elizabeth to leave him *in situ* on her accession to the throne.

The story of the oak is hokum. There are four oaks of varying ages here now. They may have sprouted from little acorns that fell from ancestors that might date back to the one which shaded Romans but the most ancient is nowhere near 400 years old. It is possible that Elizabeth dropped in to check that her latest steward was up to scratch and that she marked the occasion by planting a tree or two, but why here? Even though it is feasible that an English oak might have survived 350 years, could it be that modern eyes see Taplow Court and assume something similar was there then?

The third Taplow House / 19th July 2012

At first glance the story of the tulip trees has a faint whiff of credence. Elizabeth was still alive when the first Tappelow House was built and here for all to see from the southern terrace is a fine specimen with a plaque saying "This tree believed to be planted by Queen Elizabeth I". Any second glance is not so kind. The plaque contradicts itself by confiding that tulip trees were "Introduced to Great Britain in 1650" and giving the "Estimated date of planting" of this particular tree as "1770 to 1775". However, its less perfectly-formed neighbour is thought to be older, which would be spectacular given that there are few tulip trees anywhere more than 200 years old.

Although it is feasible that the first *Liriodendrum tulipifera* may have been brought to England from its native North America during Elizabeth's reign, official sources tell different tales. **The Woodland Trust** reports its arrival "perhaps as early as 1630", **The Chilterns Conservation Board** offers 1650 and **The Royal Botanic Gardens** at Kew says 1688 despite the usually accepted claim that Henry Compton, Bishop of London, received the gift of one at Fulham Palace "before 1680". Take your pick from these dates which all supersede Elizabeth who died in 1603. However, if all this myth-blowing is hard to swallow, take heart: The Woodland Trust acknowledges one of these at Taplow House as being "possibly the oldest tulip tree in Britain" so it is just within the bounds of possibility that it may have been seeded or grown from a cutting of an earlier tree that may have been planted in Elizabeth's dotage if not in her youth.

Sideways Glances

The Royal Ripple

St Mary Magdalene's Church, Boveney / 19th February 1520

Taplow in its various aliases isn't the only place to enjoy the benefits of being near to the royal residence at Windsor. Other rich and well-connected folk are beginning to set up shop nearby.

In 1486 **King Henry VII** appointed Sir Reginald Bray (or Reynold Braye) as Chancellor of the Duchy of Lancaster. In his spare time he designed both St George's Chapel at Windsor Castle and the Lady Chapel at Westminster Abbey. He was lord of one of the manors at Weston Turville (that place again) but didn't enjoy the long and risky journey to Windsor through the Chiltern wildwoods. It was probably while he was house-hunting in 1500 that he or some clever clerk discovered the Duchy had an interest in Taplow. When he failed to make that stick, he settled for being granted the manor of **Boveney** in 1502. Unfortunately the excitement must have been too much for him: he died the following year.

Boveney passed to his nephew Sir Edmund Bray, such a well-connected courtier to King Henry VIII that he is at this very moment away attending to his royal duty as one of the impresarios organising His Majesty's meeting near Calais with King Francis II of France. This flashy show of friendship will become known as *The Field of the Cloth of Gold* for how the monarchs compete in extravagant and profligate showing-off. Sir Edmund will lease a portion of Boveney to Sir William Cowper, Collector of Customs at the Port of London, for a penny-a-year (£2.25). And when he is elevated to the peerage in 1529 as 1st Baron Bray of Eaton Bray, Bedfordshire, he will sell the lot to Richard Hill, sergeant of the royal wine-cellar.

Dorney Court / 19th February 1543

Hill acquired **Dorney** at the same time. Since being bestowed by the Conqueror with Hitcham upon Milo Crispin and his tenant Ralf (de Anvers), the manor had passed through seven families, one of which built ***Dorney Court*** in around 1440. None were as adept as wine-sergeant Hill at making enemies. He caused great commotion in 1530 by enclosing common land at Dorney Wood and failing to evict a band of "divers arrant theves" who made it their base to rob travellers, steal sheep and cut the legs off cattle. In 1531 he enclosed and ploughed land at Hedgerley Hill owned by Thomas Woodford of Britwell Manor. It must have come as a relief to the locals last year when his son James Hill sold Dorney to the upstanding Sir William Garrard, a fine gentleman who will serve as Lord Mayor of London in 1555.

Dorney will pass to Sir William's sons William and John and then to their sister Martha and her husband **James Palmer** (later Sir James) who will have three claims to fame: his home, his artistic skill and his pineapple. Dorney Court will still be held by his direct descendants in 470 years. Many will think it one of the most haunted houses in England. Some will report that a ghostly cavalier gives an excellent guided tour. Makers of at least 25 different movies or television programmes will delight in sharing its spectacle. More serious students of history will recall Palmer himself as a respected artist and miniature painter, initially a trusted courtier and confidante to the first two Stuart kings and latterly a close friend and mentor to the third in his darkest days of exile during the Protectorate. And yet he will be of less renown than his pineapple. Not just any old pineapple but the first ever to be grown in England. The story will be told of how Master Rose, a gardener at *Dorney Court*, put leaf cuttings from a 1661 Whitehall banquet into a dish of water and worked a spot of horticultural magic to produce a ripe fruit. The achievement will be forever remembered by ***The Pineapple*** pub nearby in Lake End Road.

The second Hedsor House / 19th February 1584

The Restwold family of **Hedsor** and The Vache, Chalfont St Giles, had long been prominent in the Thames Valley and as MPs for Cumberland and Westmorland. Anthony Restwold might have thought it just reward when in 1540 his wife, a lady-in-waiting to Catherine Howard, saw her mistress become the fifth wife of King Henry VIII. Unfortunately for the lord of Hedsor, Queen Catherine lost her heart to at least two young courtiers and her head to her cuckolded husband in 1542. Restwold's wife's complicity with her mistress's dalliances damaged his reputation irreparably and it got worse in 1549 when his ignominy or penury obliged him to end his family's long and illustrious tenure at Hedsor by selling it to Sir Edmund Peckham, lord of Denham and **King Henry VIII**'s last, **Queen Mary I**'s only and **Queen Elizabeth I**'s first Master of the Mint.

Peckham was also a Privy Counsellor throughout Mary's reign, a responsibility which distracted him enough to lose interest in Hedsor. He alienated **Hedsor Wharf** in 1555 with its "land and fishery appurtenant" to **Richard Over** (ancestor of 20th Century local historian **Luke Over**) and let Hedsor itself go in 1557. The new owner Ralph Hawtrey of *Chequers* at Ellesborough eventually sold to Rowland Hynd who recently completed construction of a new Tudor manor house and the restoration of **St Nicholas' Church**. It won't be long before he takes over the Wharf from Over, styles Hedsor as Edsor and splits it between his daughter Anne Dethick and his son Rowland Hynd the Younger. In 1637 Anne will sell her half of the estate to William Price who will set about remodelling Hedsor House to his taste while the other half of the manor passes to Anne's and Rowland the Younger's niece Elizabeth and her husband William Chilcot. They will reunite the manor in 1670 by acquiring the half with the house from Price's son William.

The original Hitcham House / 19th February 1603

Hichen Manor passed down the generations to **Elizabeth Ramsay** and her husband **Sir Nicholas Clarke** (or Clerke) who built on the site of the old manor house a new mansion in the Tudor style and called it simply **Hitcham House**. When the aged **Queen Elizabeth I** came to call last summer she observed that his son and successor **Sir William Clarke** "so behaved himself that he pleased nobody, but gave occasion to have his misery and vanity spread far and wide". Clarke survived the scorn of the Virgin Queen and will go on to please **King James I** well enough that in 1618 he will be granted leave to try accused criminals at his very own Courts Leet, a departure from the longstanding arrangement whereby the Burnham Hundred held such courts wherever made sense for its sheriff. He will also be credited with influencing James to order clearances and enclosures in the Chilterns to expand sheep-farming and make travel safer, and possibly with persuading him to grant Maidenhead the right to take timber from Windsor to maintain its bridge.

Hitchambury / 19th February 1627

This 'Parsonage House' a little more than half-a-mile north-west across the fields from Hitcham House is the residence of the Reverend Robert Lloyd who as Rector enjoys an imposing "house of seven bays built all of timber and covered with tiles and all being chambered over and boarded and the whole building contrived in two storeys and siposed into 15 rooms".

Huntercombe Manor / 19th February 1607

John Skydmore of **Huntercombe** was a gentleman usher to **King Henry VIII** for 30 years. The manor descended through three generations to Philip Skydmore, the third of that name and last of the line of Walter fitzOtho, the original Norman castellan of Windsor Castle. He sold it a few months ago to Sir Marmaduke Darrell, Cofferer (Paymaster) to the household of King James I.

Burnham Abbey / 19th February 1624

Richard Hill wasn't the only servant of King Henry VIII to grab the chance of a country seat. As groom of His Majesty's wardrobe, the opportunistic William Tildesley was perfectly placed in 1539 to become the first lessee of the erstwhile **Burnham Abbey** and its estates. His home improvements included the demolition of the Abbey church. After he died in 1563 his widow Helen Tildesley married the notorious Paul Wentworth and set about the 'inclosure' of common land at Abbess Park, presumably to keep sheep to produce wool for Wycombe's weavers. She was again widowed in 1593 and three years later had to fight alone against Robert Woodford of Britwell Place over rights of common at Abbess Park (later Abby's Park and eventually ***Abbey Park Farm***). She finally sold the lease in 1610 to another MP, Sir Richard Lovelace of Hurley, a great-nephew of Jane, wife of the first Henry Manfield. Sir Marmaduke recently joined with his son Sir Sampson Darrell MP to acquire the leasehold for the latter's daughter Ann. Sir Sampson has held Fulmer since 1607 and acquired **Burnham** from Nicholas Bavin in 1610. **Upton** will complete his picture in 1630. The Abbey estates will eventually pass from Ann Darrell to Sir John Wintour and in 1675 to William Samuel.

Cippenham Manor / 19th February 1624

Cippenham was briefly home to the politician and statesman Thomas Cecil, 2nd Baron Burghley, before being acquired in 1604 by its current incumbent **Sir Edward Coke** (pronounced *Cook*), Attorney General to King James I and (from March next year) to **King Charles I**. He is currently drafting *The Statue of Monopolies* which will restrict the Crown's right to grant patents. In 1628 he will define in *The Petition of Right* specific liberties which the Crown cannot infringe. Sir Edward will then retire to relax by drafting *The Institutes of the Lawes of England*. The second work will stand alongside *The Magna Carta* (1215) and *The Bill of Rights* (1689) as one of the United Kingdom's three fundamental constitutional documents. The third will become the foundation of common law across the world. And the three together will add up to arguably the greatest contribution by a single individual to not only the legal and constitutional framework of England (and Wales) and (eventually) the whole United Kingdom but also to those of the United States of America and the Commonwealth of Nations (whatever they may be).

Fit for Favourites

Stuart Steward

The original Taplow Court / 3rd June 1612

It is nine years since King James VI of Scotland succeeded Queen Elizabeth I to become King James I of England (and Wales). He considered combining his domains as Great Britain but settled for being a king of two kingdoms. It was a year before he saw through all the smoke and mirrors involved in his predecessor's steward-in-waiting games at Taplow, cancelled all previous arrangements and granted lifelong stewardship of Taplow Manor to **Sir Henry Guldeforde**, a trusted courtier from Hempsted in Kent who was probably descended from a previous fellow of the same or similar name who had been King Henry VIII's Master of the Horse. The confusion might arise from the various spellings *Gilford, Guildford* or *Guildeford.*

This first Stuart steward is delighted to reside at **Taplow House** as he strives to make a commercial success of the land and its river, not least with a build-to-let venture of considerable ambition. Taplow Court took some three years to construct, possibly at the considerable cost of destroying all remains of any previous medieval manor house and any evidence of its possible Saxon predecessor. The new house was occupied by its first tenants in 1610. Sir Henry must have thought 'Job done' but now he (or his son Edward) is obliged to find new tenants. What a shame that in 1616 Taplow Court will be destroyed by fire, perhaps because the new but unrecorded tenants celebrate their good fortune by trying to burn candles at both ends.

Holding Court

The original Taplow House / 16th December 1629

Like his father before him, **King Charles I** is one for showering favours upon those who favour him. Last year he bestowed Taplow House upon the grateful **Sir Thomas Hampson**. Today Hampson and his son Thomas have acquired Taplow Manor from Sir Henry Guldeforde and his son Edward [*see Appendix 1, Tree 5*]. The elder Hampson is a senior civil servant of some repute who came to the approving attention of King James I as Master of the Statute Office and an enthusiastic advocate of speculative joint-stock companies, a popular commercial ruse invented by the Elizabethans as a means to fund overseas trade, settlement and sheer piracy by attracting 'adventurers' to invest considerable sums in the hope of reaping a substantial profit in due course. Sir Walter Raleigh used the ploy in the 1580s to finance the first attempt to colonise Virginia. The failure of the settlement at Roanoke didn't deter the Stuarts. *The London Company* was founded in 1606 and King James I duly granted it a charter to establish a 'plantation' in Virginia, hence it becoming commonly known as *The Virginia Company of London* or simply *The Virginia Company* and eventually *The Company*. Despite shares of stock in *The Company* being priced at £12 10s (£2,400) each – the equivalent of one horse, two cows or 177 days work for a skilled craftsman – they were eagerly snapped up by gentlemen adventurers. The largest single investor was Thomas West, 3rd Baron de la Warr, whose name – pronounced *Delaware* – has been given to a river and will eventually bless a crown colony in 1664 and the state which succeeds it in 1787.

Hampson is well-connected enough to have no need to call in favours from his neighbour **Sir Edward Manfield** but there is an intriguing link through Manfield to *The Company*'s treasurer Sir Thomas Smythe and to Lord de la Warr. It is likely that Sir Edward's first wife Maria Smyth was the former's daughter and his second wife Frances Knollys was the great-niece of the latter's wife Anne (and of Anne Boleyn). It's all wheels within wheels wherever you look [*see Appendix 1, Tree 4*].

The second Taplow Court / 3rd June 1640

From its construction in 1598 until 1638 the local heartbeat was at **Taplow House**, home of the last Elizabethan steward and then of Guldeforde and the first Hampson. Taplow Court came and went in six years and was still a burnt-out ruin when King Charles bestowed its estate upon on Charles Harbert in 1630 [*see Appendix 1, Tree 5*]. Hampson was revelling in the royal spotlight at the time and was determined to stay in it. He warmed up in 1633 by adding an aisle to **St Nicholas' Church**. Two years later he acquired the manor from the historically elusive Harbert and began building Taplow Court anew. It seemed when it was completed two years ago that the Royal Ripple had returned for good and the future was bright. Now folks are not so sure. The Scots are revolting. His Majesty needs funds to fight them. A month ago he caused uproar by dissolving his recalcitrant parliament for demanding political reform in return. Looking forward in hope might have to be put on hold.

Tall Tale – Virginia in Mind

Taplow House / 3rd June 2012

Some say Sir Thomas Hampson was Colonial Governor of Virginia, perhaps even the first. He wasn't.

Eight "loving and well-disposed Subjects" are named on *The Company*'s charter. Perhaps Hampson has been confused with one of these founders: Thomas Hanham, son-in-law of Lord Chief Justice Sir John Popham, the power behind the venture. Hampson may have been an adventurer, but that is as far as it went. *The Company* elected Edward-Maria Wingfield as its first President of the Council in 1607. Three years later Lord de la Warr was first to be officially styled Governor of Virginia, a post he held until being succeeded in 1618 by plantation owner Sir George Yeardley. The Crown took over the Colony in 1624. Sir Francis Wyatt was both the last Governor of *The Virginia Company* (1621/24) and the first Crown Governor of Virginia until he was interrupted by Yeardley (1626/27) and Sir John Harvey (1628/39). Wyatt served a further three years before being succeeded by Sir William Berkeley (1642/52) and Richard Bennett who stepped down in 1655, the year Hampson died without ever having held the esteemed office.

Taking Taplow as a Title – The First Baronet

The second Taplow Court / 3rd June 1642

What a surprise that was. Who could have expected **King Charles I** to drop by today to admire the palatial new **Taplow Court** and elevate its owner to 1st Baronet Hampson of Taplow? However, should this be a cause of celebrations or commiserations for his lordship? Being a baronetcy is something new for Taplow but it is a mixed blessing for the man in charge. The timing leaves much to be desired. Civil war is simmering and – despite the king's accolade – Hampson is still dithering about whose side it will be best to be on. Maybe that's why his home will suffer damage at the hands of both Cavaliers and Roundheads.

The World Falling Apart

Hold Everything

Amerden Place / 14th November 1642

These past 17 years have been a blessing for the Manfields. The greater tolerance of King Charles I has permitted them to practise their Catholic faith in peace. Despite having suffered as a recusant during **King James I**'s reign, **Sir Edward Manfield** recovered sufficient standing by 1636 to be granted freedom to travel throughout the kingdom and there was no impediment that year when he inherited the leasehold of **Amerden Manor** and **Manfield Park** from his father, the second **Henry Manfield**. Unfortunately Sir Edward enjoyed his twin estates only briefly before his death two years ago when they passed to the fourth **Robert Manfield**, his son by his first wife Maria [*see Appendix 1, Tree 4*]. It is a trying time. The boy has not yet reached maturity and now the world has fallen apart: social, religious and political divides have sharpened; fun has gone out of fashion with a passion.

Parliament is dominated by Puritans who reject not only Catholic idolatry and 'popish superstitions' but anything they think might have pagan origins, including the celebration of Christmas and saints' days. For them, self-denial is the in-thing, happiness is being unhappy and everyone must share their pain. Things came to a head in January when they told the king that he was throwing his weight around a mite too much. He responded by having five MPs arrested. One was a Buckinghamshire boy: John Hampden of Great Hampden in Aylesbury Vale. Within a week over 2,000 Bucks petitioners marched in protest to London in an incredible spontaneous display of loyalty and support. That was the spark which lit the fuse. From that moment everyone had to take sides, and that was why the King came to covet **Sir Thomas Hampson**'s support.

Not long ago Robert Manfield would have been delighted to entertain a royal prince's passage through Taplow. Now he fears there will be hell to pay. Civil war finally exploded three weeks ago at the inconclusive Battle of Edgehill. King Charles captured Banbury on 27th October and entered Oxford to cheers two days later. And in the first few days of November, Cavaliers led by the king's nephew Prince Rupert, Count Palatine of the Rhine, swept down the Thames Valley to take Abingdon, Aylesbury and Maidenhead. Undeterred by failing to capture Windsor, Rupert changed tack, clattered triumphantly over Maidenhead Bridge into Taplow and dashed to victory at Brentford two days ago and a stalemate at Turnham Green just yesterday. He was eager to rally for an attack on London but his uncle over-ruled him. Now the Royalist army is withdrawing along the Great West Road to the safety of Oxford for the winter.

Sideways Glance – A Very Deboyce Typpling

St Peter's Church, Burnham / 14th July 1645

It was Prince Rupert's surge in 1642 that prompted the Roundhead Lord Lieutenant of Buckinghamshire Philip Wharton, 4th Baron Wharton, to break down Maidenhead Bridge and quarter troops in Burnham. South Bucks has since been strongly Puritan and Parliamentarian under his firm hand. There have been rumours that Oliver Cromwell gathered himself at Braywick for a time and that Wharton or his father-in-law Arthur Goodwin has converted one of Wooburn's mills to make gunpowder. There were three skirmishes at **High Wycombe** between 1642 and 1643 and another earlier this year, and in 1643 Goodwin made an unsuccessful attempt to seize Brill in Aylesbury Vale and Hampden was fatally wounded in a skirmish at Chalgrove Field near Oxford.

That's the long and the short of the First English Civil War hereabouts – until today when news arrived that Cavaliers who "carried off men and horses from Cippenham" have got clean away because the Roundhead Lieutenant Ryder and "divers others of his troopers" have been "typpling in a very deboyce manner". You have to laugh.

Tall Tale – Royal Farewell

Maidenhead High Street / 16th July 2012

Maidenhead Heritage Centre enjoys the possibility that exactly 365 years ago today on 16th July 1647 **King Charles I** was brought from house arrest in Caversham to say goodbye to his three younger children, James, Henry and Elizabeth in Maidenhead before being taken to meet first his executioner and then his Maker. Legend leavens the tale with the people strewing flowers into his path as he walked to *The Greyhound Inn* while Oliver Cromwell was much moved to watch proceedings from an upstairs window.

History pours cold water on all this. During the two years before his execution at Whitehall on 27th January 1649, Charles was held prisoner at eight different locations, none in or near Caversham. He was subjected to the hospitality of the New Model Army at Newmarket (Cambridgeshire) for much of the summer of 1647, including 16th July. However, he did spend a while that autumn at Hampton Court before his year on Isle of Wight at Carisbrooke Castle. Wouldn't it be nice if Legend has it right – apart from the date and the claim about Caversham – and he did have an awayday from Hampton Court to Maidenhead? Did he begin the last leg of his journey to his ultimate incarceration at St James's Palace by crossing Maidenhead Bridge to ride along the new road Witherings had built? If so, surely he wouldn't have missed the opportunity to wave farewell to Taplow.

History does record that *The Greyhound* had hit the headlines in 1603 when a trial held there found Sir Walter Raleigh not guilty of conspiring against **King James I**. It did so again in 1746 by being destroyed by fire, which is why *NatWest Bank* now stands where it did, and why today's *Greyhound* is around the corner in Queen Street.

Holding On

The second Taplow Court / 3rd December 1655

These are troubled times. The Puritans are making things very uncomfortable. It is hard for Anglicans. **Sir Thomas Hampson**, 2nd Baronet Hampson of Taplow, is counting his blessings that he has inherited Taplow Court from his father without incident. It is harder for Catholics. Sir Thomas the Younger is discretely elsewhere as his neighbour the fourth Robert Manfield quietly celebrates a secret St Birinus's Day mass in St Nicholas' Church with his young half-brother, the second Edward [*see Appendix 1, Trees 4 & 5*].

Soon after Cromwell became Lord Protector in 1553 he responded favourably to a claim for three oaks to rebuild **Maidenhead Bridge** but the Puritan Commonwealth wasn't at all comfortable for residual Catholics and Royalists locally. **Huntercombe** was confiscated from Marmaduke Darrell (grandson of the first) in 1649 and bestowed upon the Parliamentary cavalry captain **George Evelyn** whose cousin, the renown diarist John Evelyn, observed it was "a pretty seat in the forest". **Sir Edward Coke**'s illegitimate grandson **Robert Villiers** clung onto **Cippenham** by adeptly becoming a Presbyterian all of a sudden. Villiers was the third of this slippery chap's four surnames. He had been Wright and Howard and eventually became Danvers – actually "Robert Villiers alias Danvers" – before finally fleeing to France to escape his creditors.

The fourth Taplow Court / 19th July 2012

The Manfields and the Hampsons were too true to their faiths to be so slippery but they trod lightly throughout the straight-laced and dour days of Cromwell's Commonwealth. Some repairs were necessary to Taplow Court but the only mention of **Amerden Manor** and **Manfield Park** was in 1647 when these "lands of a Papist" were valued together at £150 (£665,000). Perhaps it was these troubles that caused Taplow (or Topley) to adopt the alias Toplar before 1675 when it was captured on **Ogilby**'s map.

Tall Tale – Not Only Bray's Bailiwick

St Michael's Church, Bray / 19th July 2012

The traditional satirical song *The Vicar of Bray* was written between 1714 and 1727. It tells how its hero survived throughout the religious and political ups and downs in the days of Charles II, James II, William-and-Mary, Anne and George I with a chorus of "I will maintain unto my dying day, sir, that whatsoever king may reign, I will be the vicar of Bray, sir".

Five reverends graced Bray between 1621 and 1709. Edward Boughton was replaced in 1640 by Anthony Faringdon. No vicar was in post between 1642 and 1649. Oliver Cromwell installed his own chaplain Hezekiah Woodward until he was 'deprived' at the fall of the Commonwealth. Boughton enjoyed his own personal restoration in 1660 just months before expiring. Edward Fulham was succeeded in 1665 by Francis Carswell who served for 44 years. Boughton's comeback and Carswell's longevity might make them prime suspects for inspiring the song, but could the tale have a Taplow twist?

The Old Churchyard / 19th July 2012

History believes that musical tribute was likely to have been an updated version of an earlier ballad about the similarly turbulent Reformation period during which Bray was served by the Reverend Symon Aleyn from 1540 until 1588, a span of four sovereigns: the conditional Catholic Henry VIII, the zealous reformer Edward VI, the passionately traditional Catholic Queen Mary and her half-sister Queen Elizabeth I whose revived reforms were the foundation of the Anglican Church. However some say this chap's name was actually Symon Symonds – a claim that raises the old eyebrows for Merton Priory 'presented' **Simon Symonds** to Taplow in 1537. This 27th Rector survived Henry and four years of Edward before being replaced in 1551 by George Curzon whose 'living' spanned the end of Edward, all of Mary and nine years of Elizabeth. The two concurrent clerical Symonds are an amazing coincidence. Some clergy held a handful of rectorships; could Symon of Bray and Simon of Taplow simply have been one and the same? Or perhaps the original ballad gave a nod to both?

Merton also 'presented' Robert ap Griffith at Hichen (Hitcham) just weeks before its dissolution in 1538. He survived in his 'living' until being 'deprived' in 1553 on the ascension of Queen Mary whose rush of rectors at St Mary's Church concluded in 1556 with the 'presentation' of the third: John Ball. Perhaps he took a leaf from the book of clever Curzon who somehow juggled both changing regal requirements and the evident Catholicism of his major benefactor Henry Manfield. Did Curzon concur with Manfield's beliefs or bend to them for expediency? When Queen Elizabeth restored Richard Davies at St Peter's in 1559, he found his neighbouring rectors still sitting pretty: Curzon until 1567 and Ball until 1569. Clearly some were better than others at turning the right cheek at the right moment.

Curzon's persistent ability to change his spots enabled him to endure the three reigns which lurched most dramatically from pillar to post. However William Edmunds offers stiff competition for the prize for theological agility. As the 31st Rector of Taplow for 45 years from 1625, he began and ended his term an Anglican either side of the mid-century Puritan peak of intolerant pique in the form of Commonwealth minister Thankful Owen (a contribution for which he is not thanked on the carved record of Rectors and Vicars in St Nicolas's western lobby).

Minding the Manor: Manfields and Hampsons

The Manfield Arms

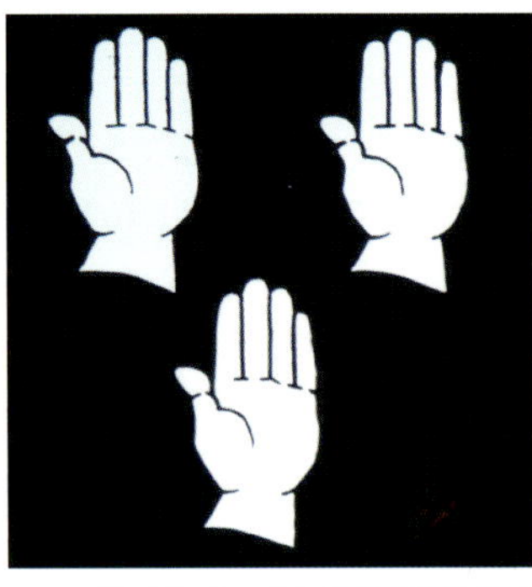

The Hampson Arms

This motif of three hemp brakes decorated the c1630 screen to the Hampson chapel in the medieval St Nicholas' Church

Thomas Manfield (d1540) and his wives Agnes & Katherine, commemorated in brass in St Nicolas' Church / c1575

The Dashing Duke

Buckingham's Cliefden....
– Colen Campbell
Vitruvius Britannicus c1717

....still going strong / c1785

George Villiers, 2nd Duke of Buckingham – Sir Peter Lely 1675

Chapter Four

Commanding Attention

In which Taplow stepped into the national spotlight

Days of the Dashing Duke

George Villiers, 2nd Duke of Buckingham

Making Merry

Cliveden Terrace / 3rd September 2012

Everybody thought in 1649 that there was a lot to be said for being a republic. It was a little while before it dawned on almost everybody that nobody could work out what it was. Righteousness had seemed so right but it didn't turn out to be much fun. All the bearing it and not grinning turned out to be tough. Everybody kept it under their cockle hats that the Puritans had won the war but lost the peace. Nobody wanted to upset Cromwell – he had some pretty revolutionary ideas (and maybe they'd come in useful one day) – but when he died in 1558 everyone got to talking about how the bad old days had been alright really. And in 1660 they decided how fortunate it was that **King Charles II** had been waiting patiently in exile for eleven years, and that his Restoration would be just the tonic Taplow needed. How right they were, although it didn't start too well. The second **Sir Thomas Hampson**'s celebration party must have got out of hand. **Taplow House** was burnt to the ground in 1660.

The second King Charles has a reputation for being *The Merry Monarch*, an epithet conferred by his friend the poet John Wilmot in a bawdy but affectionate verse that ends "... a merry monarch, scandalous and poor". John Evelyn summed him up as "a prince of many virtues and many great imperfections". His mentor in gaiety, frivolity and indulgence was Lord Buckingham, the erstwhile Cavalier who had been his companion in exile in the Netherlands. The Dashing Duke returned home to set the style for his friend's reign by being the archetypal Restoration rake: "a politician, diplomat, poet, playwright, amateur chemist, gambler, adulterer and murderer" who scandalised and titillated Restoration England as a leader of fashion and opinion with a charismatic charm, rapier wit and headstrong arrogance. Gilbert Burnet, Bishop of Salisbury, denounced him as "the main blame of the King's ill principles and bad morals [for] pleasure, frolic or extravagant diversion [were] all that he had laid to heart". And although it tried to cover its tracks in the guise of Toplar, Taplow was his stage.

Cliffden Terrace / 3rd September 1666

There is a great pall of smoke on the eastern horizon: London's burning. Lord Buckingham couldn't give a fig. He may have discovered **Manfield Park** in his innocent pre-Civil War youth, perhaps as a guest of **Henry** or **Sir Edward Manfield**. Now he has made it his, restored its name as ***Cliffden Park*** and has unleashed the architect **William Winde** on replacing one of its lodges with an enormous and sumptuous mansion designed to his lavish taste. He loves to party and where better for a Duke of Buckingham than a luxurious new Buckinghamshire home perched high on the rolling chalk escarpment above the Thames?

Winde's work is nearly done. The four-storey house stands proudly on its 25-foot arcaded terrace looking out over the newly-modelled 400-foot 'step' down to the silvery sliver of the River Thames far below – like Taplow itself, its elevated location made practical by natural springs. The Duke intends Cliffden as a "Palace on the Thames [with] both the pleasures of the chase and the pleasures of the flesh in mind". It won't be long before it is for the first time at the nation's political heartbeat as His Grace entertains four other royal favourites who are effectively King Charles's government. Collectively they will be known as ***The Cabal Ministry*** for being a group sharing power and for their initials – C for Thomas Clifford, 1st Baron Clifford of Chudleigh, A for Henry Bennet, 1st Earl of Arlington, B for Buckingham, A for Anthony Ashley Cooper, 1st Baron Ashley of Wimborne St Giles, and L for John Maitland, 1st Duke of Lauderdale. And that won't be the half of it. Cliffden will also see such heady days as an exclusive retreat for Buckingham's rich and famous friends in ***The Merry Gang***, an elite renown for notoriously extravagant frolics of every kind imaginable. Its leading lights will be Henry Jermyn, Charles Sackville, John Sheffield and John Wilmot (otherwise known as the earls of St Albans, Dorset, Musgrave and Rochester), Sir Charles Sedley and three playwrights: William Wycherley (*The Country Wife*), George Etherege (*She Would If She Could*) and Henry Killigrew (of *The Savoy Theatre*).

High Flying, Not Always Adored

The first Cliffden House / 3rd September 1674

Can this be true? Buckingham has retired from public life and is working at being a good boy. He has settled down with his wife Mary, attends church regularly and has paid off what debts he can afford. It won't last, of course, but in the meantime what better place than Cliffden to relax and reflect? After all, John Evelyn will describe the estate in 1679 as "that stupendous natural Rock, Wood and Prospect [with] buildings of extraordinary expense, the cloisters, descents, gardens and avenue through the wood, august and stately. 'Tis a romantic object [that] altogether answers the most poetical description [despite] the land all about wretchedly barren, producing nothing but ferne".

This **George Villiers** is the third of that name. His grandfather emerged from Leicestershire to sire twin dynasties that will see fame and intricate connection to myriad movers and shakers down the ages. The first George's son Sir Edward Villiers was Master of the Mint to King James I. His daughter Elizabeth joined the Turville line when she married into the Boteler (formerly Botiller) family and his son John Villiers, 1st Viscount Purbeck, married Frances, daughter of **Sir Edward Coke** of Cippenham. His grandson Sir Edward Villiers will be entrusted with educating as Anglicans the Princesses and future Queens Mary and Anne, daughters of King James II and his first wife Anne. His great-grandchildren include the worthy statesman-to-be Edward Villiers, 1st Earl of Jersey, and the beautiful **Barbara Villiers**, 1st Duchess of Cleveland, Charles II's favourite mistress by whom he has had at least five (possibly six) illegitimate FitzRoy offspring. These dynasties will sire **Queen Elizabeth II**, Princess Diana, Confederate General Robert E Lee and no less than 17 Prime Ministers including **William Wyndham Grenville** of Dropmore, David Cameron and regular Taplow socialites **Arthur Balfour** and **Sir Winston Churchill** [*see Appendix 1, Tree 6*].

The second **George Villiers** became a favourite of James I. He was created **1st Duke of Buckingham** in 1623 only to be assassinated five years later when his son of the same name was just four months old. An unfortunate beginning, but young Buck's fortune soon took a turn for the better. He was brought up in the court of **King Charles I** as a close friend of the sibling princes who are now **King Charles II** and James, Duke of York. Time and again he rose to incredible heights and plunged to the depths of despair. His nadirs have been two spells of imprisonment in the Tower of London: first in 1658 when suspected of plotting against Lord Protector Oliver Cromwell, then again nine years later when accused not only of "treasonable intrigues" against Charles II but also of having cast the king's horoscope. And yet within weeks of his release in July 1667, he reached the zenith of replacing Clarendon as the king's chief minister, a position he held until January this year.

Lord Buckingham was just 15 in 1643 when he gained a reputation for military bravado by helping the Royalists retake Lichfield from the Roundheads. His dashing image was enhanced no end by miraculous escapes from three later defeats. During the first in 1648 at Kingston-upon-Thames, with his brother Francis lying dead nearby and his own back against an oak tree, he heroically vanquished six Roundheads and lived to fight another day. The opportunity came months later at St Neots in Huntingdonshire where against all the odds he escaped to join Prince Charles in The Hague. He repeated the trick by spiriting himself from Worcester to Rotterdam in 1651 only to find the prince – by then King Charles II to non-Puritans – had trumped him by hiding in an oak tree at Boscobel, avoiding capture for six weeks on the run and finally slipping across the Channel to Normandy.

His estates were restored by King Charles II in 1662 when he was said to be the king's richest subject, probably one of the most influential and certainly one of the most ambitious. He had a few adventures at sea during the Second Anglo-Dutch War in 1665 but this foray was just a brief distraction from his new excitement: a love life of astonishing audacity and scandal. His amorous advances to the king's sisters Mary (in 1656) and Henrietta (in 1661) got him deeply into the royal bad books. Between these exploits he fell madly for another Mary, daughter of his erstwhile enemy Thomas, 3rd Lord Fairfax, to whom his confiscated estates had been given in 1647. She was betrothed to Philip Stanhope, 2nd Earl of Chesterfield, but he wooed and wed her in weeks.

Buckingham dabbled in chemistry and was drawn like a moth to a flame to political intrigue. He made many firm friends but also more enemies than was wise. He came to blows in the House of Lords with Henry Pierrepoint, 1st Marquess of Dorchester, and made matters worse by refusing to apologise. Not only Clarendon but also James Butler, 1st Duke of Ormonde, his son Thomas Butler, 3rd Earl of Ossory, and Sir William Coventry all felt his sharp and skilfully-aimed political elbow and seethed in his shadow. Others watched in fear they might be next. The Dashing Duke couldn't care less. He had something more important to attend to: the entirely unofficial strategic management of the love affairs of the not-quite-17-year-old actress (Eleanor) Nell Gwyn. His plan was to increase his influence over Charles II by providing him with a new and entertaining distraction but the scheme ran aground when the beautiful Nell demanded £500-a-year (£73,600) to be kept. Buckingham had enough trouble with his own dalliances. In 1668 his rapier fatally wounded Francis Talbot, 11th Earl of Shrewsbury, in a duel over his affair with Shrewsbury's wife Anna Marie. Legend will prefer to ignore that she was in France at the time and instead say she witnessed the confrontation disguised as a page and then slept with her lover still in his bloody shirt.

His rivals resented Lord Buckingham making friends with King Louis XIV of France during treaty negotiations and his persuading King Charles to favour religious liberty with the *Declaration of Indulgence* in 1672. It was these successes that finally polarised opinion strongly enough for Arlington to outmanoeuvre and overthrow him for promoting alliance with France (he was carrying the can for the king), for arbitrary government (which was fair enough), for continuing his scandalous affair with the Countess of Shrewsbury (which he was) and for "popery" (a gratuitous slur).

Final Flings

Cliffden Terrace / 9th September 1687

It is not quite five months since the death of Lord Buckingham: a "chymist, fiddler, statesman and buffoon" (according to the poet and playwright John Dryden) who was "always in the wrong" and yet could never be ignored. Party politics is in its infancy. First the 'Court Party' – which supports the Crown (and will become the Tories) – and then, when he fell out of royal favour, the 'Country Party' (eventually the Whigs) have been eager for his charisma to aid their causes. He resisted these temptations but events have occasionally riled him enough to return to the public stage. None of his three interventions met with success. Religious tolerance was pushed a step backwards in 1675 by the *Test Acts* which imposed various civil disabilities on non-Anglicans. He was obliged to relax in the Tower once more for a few months in 1677 and two years later was close to being arrested for accusing Lord Chief Justice Sir William Scroggs of favouring the Catholics implicated in the fictitious Popish Plot. Otherwise he has been content to watch from the wings and live life slowly.

What he didn't do was to pay for Cliffden, nor care for it well. Burnet rues that Buckingham "could never.... govern his estate, though then the greatest in England". And yet it is likely that **Robert Manfield** didn't much mind. Long years of Puritan persecution had left his family in a parlous state. He was probably delighted to put his pride and joy at the disposal of a royal favourite with a refreshing religious tolerance and apparently deep pockets. It isn't hard to imagine that he basked in the reflected glory as His Grace enhanced Cliffden with **Winde**'s creation. Buckingham's debt passed in 1671 to Robert's half-brother **Edward Manfield**. Despite being increasingly financially embarrassed and obliged to ease his cash flow by mortgaging **Amerden Place** to William Rawstone and letting fishing rights in the Thames for £8 (£1,490) a year plus a salmon, he too opted for smiling sweetly, saying nothing and hoping for the best [*see Appendix 1, Tree 5*]. The duke responded in kind for nine long years until 1680 when he had another bout of being a good boy in which he paid some of his debt to Manfield and reconciled with his old pal King Charles. However it wasn't long before failing health and finances caused him to retire to his manor at Helmsley (Yorkshire), this time for good. And after Charles' death in 1685, it was wise for the old fellow to keep some distance between himself and the new monarch, the openly Catholic King James II.

Cliveden Terrace / 9th September 2012

Buckingham didn't survive to see the deposition of James II, the last Catholic King of England. Edward Manfield did. **Cliffden** was restored to him within a year of King James being replaced by his daughter Queen Mary II and her Dutch husband **King William III** in *The Glorious Revolution* of 1688. This suggests that either Buckingham had never paid in full for Cliffden or that Manfield got his heirloom back for a knockdown price. Perhaps it was this latest and last of Taplow's Manfields who commemorated the Dashing Duke by setting into the lawn by Cliffden's east wing a pattern of flints shaped as a rapier and the date 1668, though to be a reference to his duel with Shrewsbury. Naturally this relatively intimate domain has long been called the Duke's Garden.

Buckingham's had been a shooting star that flared brilliantly but briefly, yet with lasting effect. His effervescent social whirl had been and gone for now but it had sown seeds which would grow and blossom for 250 years after his death. Taplow was set irrevocably on course from a pleasant rural backwater into the uncharted mainstream of being a place for the powerful to party. However, Manfield wasn't invited. He tried his best to follow in the Good Lord Buck's profligate footsteps by staging a horse race for *Lord Lovelace's Plate* on Toplar Heath in 1689. John Lovelace, 2nd Baron Lovelace, was of a line that had held Hurley for generations and **Burnham Abbey** briefly earlier in the century. As an infamously whiggish party animal and inveterate gambler of some pedigree, he had about him an echo of the Villiers style. Manfield was a distant cousin through their mutual great-grandmother Jane but he just couldn't afford to keep pace let alone set trends.

Sideways Glances

Trysting Times

Philibert's House, Holyport / 3rd September 1681

Lord Buckingham was right in thinking Nell Gwyn would be to King Charles's taste. Their affair began by chance in the spring of 1668. Whenever he was in residence at the castle, His Majesty installed Nell and their son Charles Beauclerk at *Burford House* in Windsor's Home Park, which is why the boy is styled the Earl of Burford. Some say that when Buckingham was in the king's favour, he would ride from Cliffden to Windsor to feast with his royal friend at *The Duke's Head* in Peascod Street before slipping out there together to dally with Nelly. Nowadays Charles and his Nell tryst here at the home of the trusted William Chiffinch, Keeper of the King's Closet. Today the trio have matchmaking in mind and, wheels within once more, Chiffinch's daughter Barbara will soon marry Buckingham's cousin **Edward Villiers** [*see Appendix 1, Tree 6*]. This young man's star will shine on the accession of William-and-Mary. As he rises to be ambassador to France, 1st Earl of Jersey and Lord Chamberlain to both King William III and **Queen Anne**, he will be permitted in 1692 to lease the Burnham Abbey estates. They will remain in the Villiers family for 143 years.

Shuffling Hitcham

St Mary's Churchyard, Hitcham / 3rd September 1681

Hitcham had sat happily for over 300 years in the hands of the Neyrant-Beauchamp-Ramsay-Clarke line but **Sir John Clarke** had a spot of bother with his cash flow. Letting **Hitcham House** as a monastery with 'stew ponds' for fish hadn't made things much easier so in 1660 he decided the time was right to cash in on Windsor's likely Restoration resurgence. Only it wasn't so simple. Some ancient legal provision required royal assent to a special Act of Parliament permitting him to sell Hitcham to **Sir Charles Doe**, a London financier. Doe was doing rather well. He also acquired **Upton** from the Darrell family in 1662 and rose to be Sheriff of London in 1666, which wasn't great timing. Fancy attaining such an eminent post just before some pudding started the Great Fire of London. Doe reacted with impressive ingenuity and courage to save *Goldsmith's Company* treasures from being consumed in the conflagration but Lady Luck didn't smile upon him: his fortune went up in smoke with most of London. Consequently in 1670 his widow was obliged to sell Hitcham to Edward Fulham and to begin a long but losing battle to keep hold of Upton.

Fulham was canon of St George's Chapel at Windsor Castle from 1660 until 1694 but he enjoyed Hitcham for only three years before selling it to the well-connected **Sir Edward Nicholas**. His father, also Sir Edward, had been secretary to **George Villiers, 1st Duke of Buckingham**, and subsequently Principal Secretary of State to **King Charles I** from 1641 and then to his son King Charles II until 1662. This dedication to the Royalist cause had reduced the elder Sir Edward to poverty when his estates were sequestrated by Parliament. He was obliged to spend long years in exile with the younger Sir Edward who earned his keep tutoring the children of Charles II's original chief minister Edward Hyde, 1st Earl of Clarendon, whose daughter Anne would be the first wife of the future **King James II**. The latest Sir Edward enjoys Hitcham so much that, having already added new barns to glebe estate, this year he contributed three-quarters of the cost of building the brick wall around **St Mary's Churchyard** (it will still be standing in 323 years) and will shortly begin the enlargement of the parsonage.

Teacher's Pets

Baldwin's Bridge, High Street, Eton / 3rd September 2012

A neighbour of Sir Edward at Hitcham had an even more celebrated impact at Eton College. **John Newborough** made a significant contribution to the school's physical appearance and enviable reputation during his 21 years as its Master from 1690. The fruit of his spending £8,000 (£166m) in remodelling the chapel and building the Upper School is still evident today but perhaps his greatest achievement stemmed from his remarkably progressive approach to education. Three of his pupils grew up to play substantial roles in defining and dominating British politics during the first half of the 18th Century. Sir William Wyndham was Queen Anne's Secretary of War and then Chancellor of the Exchequer before his Jacobite tendencies caused his political retirement in 1714. Sir Robert Waplole was Great Britain's first Prime Minister (PM) from 1721 to 1742. Viscount Charles Townshend was Walpole's political ally and eventually also his brother-in-law before putting aside foreign affairs in 1730 to earn his nickname 'Turnip' Townshend for driving the agricultural revolution which eventually sowed seeds of nutrition and wellbeing essential for the industrial revolution.

Sir Dennis Hampson, 3rd Baronet Hampson

Friends and Enemies

The fourth Taplow Court / 14th September 2012

How **Edward Manfield** must have envied his neighbours the Hampsons down at Taplow Court. They had no problem keeping pace. The national turmoil had hampered any ambitions the second **Lord Hampson** might have had to rise to his father's pre-eminence in the statutory affairs of the nation but his second marriage – to Mary Dennis, the great-granddaughter of the famous Elizabethan naval hero **Sir Richard Grenville** – secured his place in local high society and provided the platform for his son to rise even higher. **Sir Dennis Hampson** succeeded in 1671 as 3rd Baronet Hampson and lord of Taplow Manor (still cast as Toplar) [*see Appendix 1, Tree 5*].

With the peculiar exception of Hitcham since 1618, Courts Leet were held for the whole of the Burnham Hundred until **King Charles II** extended this privilege to both **George Evelyn** at **Huntercombe** and Sir Robert Gayer at **Cippenham**. It would be logical to assume that, as MP for Wycombe and Justice of the Peace for the Burnham Hundred, Sir Dennis would have been similarly honoured. Such courts were being held in Taplow by the early-18th Century and there is an earlier record of the lord of Taplow's efforts to bring locals into line. In 1683 he led "a party of horse" which broke up "a little meeting near Wooburn". Despite being discovered "sitting peaceably together", all 23 men present were indicted for riot, found guilty at Aylesbury and sentenced to hard labour until they paid a fine of "a noble a-piece", a gold coin worth 6s 8d (£47.50).

The likely 'crime' of those assembled was to be Friends of the Truth, a society of dissenters known as 'Quakers' since 1650 when its leader George Fox bade magistrates accusing him of religious blasphemy to tremble at the Word of the Lord. **Richard Aldridge** was the first Quaker to be recorded locally – in 1655 at ***Brook End*** on the edge of **Dropmer** – but since before 1678 the Friends' favourite haunt was the remote farm of John Jennings sometimes noted as *Starveall* for being hard to scrape a living on. He was probably related to the Samuel Jenings of Aylesbury who in 1680 took his Friendship faraway across the Atlantic to the New World where he became Speaker of the New Jersey Assembly in 1707. ***Jennings Farm*** was a perfect place for Friends to meet in secret because they could quickly make themselves 'out of reach' by crossing the parish boundary from Burnham into Beaconsfield. Clearly in 1683 the ploy didn't outfox the vigilant Hampson who seven years earlier would have been pleased to report that among 149 Taplovians there was not a single dissenter and only five Catholics, all probably in the Manfield household. It would be six years before **King William III** changed the rules forever. Religious tolerance became official and Jennings Barn approved as "a publick meeting house for religious worship".

No Battle at the Bridge

Tæppa's Mound / 14th December 1688

It is the wee small hours and freezing cold up here under the old yew tree. Down by **Maidenhead Bridge** a contingent of Irish troops are at the ready. They spilled over the bridge a couple of days ago, made it impassable (with help from Jacobite locals) and set up their gun emplacements. Clearly their commander Patrick Sarsfield, 1st Earl of Lucan, is expecting trouble so Taplovians are staying well out of the way. Somebody grumbles that it was only nine years ago that the bridge was repaired with 20 trees that took three years of pestering to prise out of stingy old King Charlie, and now look what they've done to it. Somebody else complains that he is missing the point and it isn't the bridge that matters but what happens next. Everyone stifles a laugh. It settles the nerves for a few moments.

The worry is that another civil war is just around the corner. Nobody wants that but the opinions of those who decide such things are sharply divided. When Charles II died three years ago, Tories argued that it was his brother's birthright to reign despite his Catholicism. Whigs were passionate that his faith made him unacceptable. The Tories won the day and the Duke of York was duly crowned as King James II. That seemed fair enough until just six months ago when his Italian second wife Mary presented him with a new James: a Catholic son and heir. Suddenly the fine balance was tipping the way of the Whigs. The boy will have primogeniture over his elder Anglican sisters Mary and Anne. Many had been prepared to tolerate a Catholic king for the time being but not for ever and ever, amen.

There have been whispers that Parliament secretly offered the throne to Mary and her Dutch cousin and husband William of Orange who as **King Charles I**'s grandson has his own strong claim to the throne. The whisperers were right. Dutch Billy landed at Brixham in Devon six weeks ago and ever since all the talk has been about which side to be on. Some are excited to hear that he was cheered all the way to Reading where five days ago (with help from non-Jacobite locals) a small force of 250 Dutchmen chased 600 Irishmen out of town. Most are sitting on the fence watching with bated breath and wondering how strange Holland must be to have somewhere coloured orange.

Suddenly the beat of drums drifts across the river. An old ex-military man says they are sounding the retreat, and that is just what the Irish do. But they have been tricked. The drummers are Dutch. Now the bridge is too. Daylight creeps over the horizon to reveal thousands of troops milling on the Berkshire bank: not only Dutchmen but also Englishmen who have come over to **William-and-Mary**. A few brave locals venture cautiously down the hill to offer assistance as they begin to repair the bridge. It's always wise to help soldiers when their enemies aren't looking. Once the bridge is safe, they stand back – and here comes ***The Glorious Revolution***! It is impossible not to admire William as he rides over the bridge on his white palfrey. And what a sight is his guard of honour: scores of black men from the Dutch colonies all dressed in white with turbans and feathers!

King James has already attempted to flee the country only to be captured in Kent. It won't be until the New Year that gossip says he has been allowed to slip away across the Channel, a departure that can reasonably be taken as abdication. William-and-Mary won't last long – Queen Mary II will reign for just five years before she is taken by smallpox and William III will be king for only thirteen – but they'll changed the country forever, starting in a year and two days with the *The Bill of Rights* and the invention of constitutional monarchy.

Taplow can claim no credit for this pivotal change in the way of things but watching William go by in triumph and expectation has been something special: rather like having a 2012 Olympic torch parade without the torch.... or the Olympics.

The Coming of the Scot

George Hamilton, 1st Earl of Orkney

Taplow Together Again

The third Taplowe Court / 1st May 1707

Lord Orkney has for many years been an enthusiastic supporter of the union of Scotland with England (and Wales). Last year the two parliaments passed the necessary **Acts of Union**. Today he took his seat in the House of Lords to see these acts become effective. He will serve as a Scottish peer in Great Britain's first parliament for 30 years. And as the nations unify, so Orkney has begun to replicate the trick in Taplow....

Amerden Towpath / 16th September 1720

Slow hoofbeats herald the arrival of a fine gentleman on horseback. A few miles downriver in London hundreds are facing ruin in a shuddering financial crisis. *The South Sea Bubble* is threatening to tear the country's financial foundation apart just as Taplowe is one again. Orkney rides past with a smile. **Taplowe Court** and **Cleifden** will remain a pair for another 104 years and he has just acquired **Amerden** (and its towing and fishing rights) from Sir William Scawen, co-founder and former governor of the Bank of England. No wonder he looks a happy man.

The Old Churchyard / 18th September 2014

In modern parlance, Lord Orkney believed that Great Britain is 'Better Together'. He can rest easy for, in its referendum today, Scotland agreed.

A Mystery of History

The fourth Taplow Court / 11th November 2013

Where and when did Orkney begin his Taplovian assembly? **Sir Dennis Hampson** finished his family's 72-year stay by selling him Taplow Manor in "around 1700". The mystery swirls around when he acquired Cliveden. One source tell a simple story: he bought it from **Edward Manfield** on 28th October 1696. Another relates the more complex tale about **Budd Wase** of Datchet....

The elusive Wase had very different reasons to Orkney for wanting to be within Windsor's Royal Ripple. His lordship was a man of the moment: a high-born, well-connected Scottish army officer who moved in for pleasure. Wase seems to have been out for a profit. History first noticed him in 1681 when he sold an estate in Petworth (Sussex) to buy the manor of Datchet where he laid low until embarking on a series of apparently speculative deals, the first of which was the 1696 acquisition from Manfield of ***Bullocks*** alias *White Place Farm* in Cookham. Could this transaction have included Cliveden or later be thought to have done so? Not if the rest of the tale holds water: he sold *Bullocks* in 1703 and acquired not only ***Amerden Place*** from William Rawstone's heirs but also Cliveden from Manfield. Soon afterwards, Scawen took Amerden off his hands and in 1706 he sold Cliveden to Orkney [*see Appendix 1, Tree 5*].

Which tale is true: with Wase or without him? If he was in the chain then the speed, enormity and turbulence of these transactions suggest he may have been acting for a rich investor such as his old neighbour at Petworth House: Charles Seymour, 6th Duke of Somerset, had married into the fabulously wealthy Percy family and could afford a flutter. And two things add a little credence to the idea of his being at least an intermediary. Firstly: Orkney invested heavily in rebuilding **Taplow Court** before 1705 when **Queen Anne** came to enjoy its extravagant neo-Norman saloon in the style of the interior of Kirkwall Cathedral. Why would he have entertained Her Majesty anywhere but his principal residence? Secondly: the oldest record of his possession of both Cliveden and Taplow Court seems to have been late the following year....

The third Taplowe Court / 11th November 1706

Lord Orkney is writing to his brother Archibald Hamilton (future Governor of Jamaica) to confide "I have got two old homes on my back.... A good part of the Monney has been borrowed to buy it.... tho I Haite the thought of paying interest.... and now to begine to build one's needs". Since much of the work at Taplowe Court has already been completed, it might reasonably be inferred that Orkney has only recently acquired Clifden and that his ambitions for it will be postponed by the escalating conflict on the Continent. Perhaps it was Somerset or Wase on his behalf who has lent Orkney the 'Monney' to buy it and 'build one's needs'. Wase may be made for life by his wheeling and dealing but – despite hating "the thought of paying interest" – his lordship can show him a thing or two about living life to the full. They say he has consulted the Parisian landscape architect **Claude Desgots** on plans for new avenues. The main access from Hedsor Hill to the north will soon be lined with lime trees to enhance the progression towards the house which the architect **Thomas Archer** will enhance with curved corridors leading to symmetrical wings.

The third Taplowe Court / 29th March 1720

Here perhaps is the root of Orkney's content: today, on the occasion of the marriage of his daughter and heir Ann to her cousin **William O'Brien**, he took the precaution of arranging the settlement of both estates upon them under the trusteeship of Sir

Thomas Clarges, 2nd Baronet, and John Campbell, styled Lord Glenorchie. Yesterday he let Cleifden for a year to Richard Reeth and William Rawlins with a view to funding the grand ideas that landscape architect **Charles Bridgeman** has in mind: a 'plain' parterre and woodland walks to the north of the house, a pheasantry and a system of avenues and rides to the south, including the tree-lined Green Drive.

The Original Orkney

The Blenheim Pavilion, Clifden / 16th September 1727

As the fifth son of William Douglas-Hamilton, 1st Earl of Selkirk, and Ann Hamilton, 3rd Duchess of Hamilton, **Lord George Hamilton** was destined for a military career; events unfolded neatly for it to be one of great challenge and achievement. In the days when he was a colonel in an Irish regiment of foot, the 7th Foot (Royal Fusiliers) and eventually the Royal Scots, Hamilton served under and became close friends with **King William III** as he confronted twin threats: one within as Jacobites manoeuvred for the restoration of King James II, the other across the Channel where King Louis XIV of France held the balance of power in Europe and wanted more. As Prince of Orange, William had instigated the League of Augsburg against Louis in 1686. When he also became King of England in 1689, the League evolved into the Grand Alliance. The Scot fought alongside William against Irish Jacobites and the French at the Boyne (1690) and Aughrim (1691, where he was wounded, and against the French at Steenkeerke (1692), Landen (1693) and Namur (1695), where he was badly wounded.

King Billy didn't do things by halves when it came to showing appreciation. He rewarded his pal with promotion to Brigadier-General, by arranging for him to take as his bride Queen Mary's lady-in-waiting **Elizabeth Villiers** – an exceptionally astute and sharp-witted woman with a reputation for political intrigue and being "extreamly medling" in affairs of state – and on 3rd January 1696 by raising him to the Scottish peerage in triplicate as **Earl of Orkney**, Viscount Kirkwall and Baron Dechmont.

Queen Anne succeeded her brother-in-law in 1702 and Orkney returned to his heroic adventures in the fight against France, Spain and Bavaria under the command of his wife's cousin **John Churchill, 1st Duke of Marlborough**. He fought with courage and tenacity in every battle and siege during the Nine Years' War and the War of the Spanish Succession, conflicts that redesigned Europe. At the Battle of Blenheim (actually Blindheim in Bavaria) in 1704 he attacked the heavily defended village churchyard with eight battalions of foot and, despite having his horse shot from under him, his "sheer bluff and deceptive self-confidence" tricked a superior French force – reputedly of 800 officers and 8,000 men – into surrendering. He performed with distinction in relieving the siege of Liège (1705), at Ramilies (1706), at Oudenarde and Tournai (1708) and at Malplaquet (1709), a battle so bloody that he hoped "in God to be the last he may ever see". God listened and was kind. Participation in the sieges of Douai (1710) and Bouchain (1711) – where he was promoted General of the Foot – brought an end to his years in the field.

Marlborough rewarded eight of his generals with sets of six ***Art of War* tapestries**. Orkney hung his at Clifden and commemorated his greatest battle by having the Palladian architect **Giacomo Leoni** grace the grounds with the construction of the Blenheim Pavilion looking down on trees planted in the pattern of the armies. His military career continues in strategic and ceremonial matters and, just three weeks before his death on 29th January 1737, his long and distinguished service will earn him the honour of becoming the very first Field Marshall in the British Army.

The Sociable Orkney

The third Taplowe Court / 16th September 1729

Buckingham had been a master at entertaining the elite but Orkney needed no lessons in this respect nor in being everybody's constant friend, a talent the old Buck sorely lacked. The earliest evidence of this latter attribute might be Orkney's marriage. His wife Elizabeth had served under King Billy in the same way her first cousin **Barbara Villiers** had served under the Dutchman's uncle **King Charles II**. Her reward was to be awarded in 1689 almost all of **King James II**'s lands in Ireland: some 90,000 acres. However, less than one-fifth of the income found its way into the new Lady Orkney's silken purse once the erstwhile monarch's mistresses had been paid their dues and it was only ten years before Parliament quietly revoked the grant. At around £6,000 (£880,000), their annual income was relatively modest for a courtier of Orkney's stature. No matter. Like her cousin Barbara, Elizabeth was a half-niece of the 2nd Duke of Buckingham and Orkney was the great man's third cousin, so they knew all about keeping it in the family. It is likely that both Lord and Lady Orkney had come to Clifden as children – they may even have first met there – so it must have felt like going home when they acquired the place, whenever that was exactly.

By the time his mentor King Billy died in 1702, **Orkney** was about as well-connected as could be. When he and Elizabeth entertained **Queen Anne** at Taplow Court in 1705, he waited on Her Majesty personally at dinner. He is not noted as repeating the compliment in 1726 when **King George I** enjoyed his stay here, nor when the dowager Queen Caroline did so a few months ago. Perhaps age is catching up with him but his talent as a splendid host will never fail him. And he can look back with pride that his trusted friendship with His Majesty has been rewarded in quadruplicate. In 1714 he was appointed for life to three lucrative positions – Lord Lieutenant of Lanarkshire, Governor of Edinburgh Castle and Crown Governor of Virginia. He has risen to the first and second challenges but can't be terribly good at the third because he has never been to Virginia and never will. The fourth appointment – as Gentleman of the King's Bedchamber – was the pinnacle for being purely personal.

The Political Orkney

The Octagon Temple, Clifden / 16th September 1735

The conversion of Clifden from barren hilltop to verdant woodland is nearing completion. The landscapist **Charles Bridgeman** has lined with lime trees its southern approach along Green Drive and its eastern boundary with Taplow Common, devised woodland ways including the Yew Tree Walk and carved a rustic turf amphitheatre into the cliffside. Leoni has returned to create this gazebo, the latest of Clifden's follies, which commands a magnificent view of the Thames sparkling in the sunshine 200 feet below. All seems so quiet, calm and content.

Lord Orkney is a prime example of how quickly many Scots have taken advantage of the creation of Great Britain to contribute their own nobility, ambition, energy and intellectual capability to the emergence of this bright new 18th Century nation. It is a mark of his skilful and tactful diplomacy that he can now count not only King George II among his friends but also those in two factions who oppose him with the same passion they opposed his father.

One faction has been family. His sister Catherine was married to John Murray, 1st Duke of Atholl, chief of Clan Murray. The brothers-in-law fought alongside each other at Malplaquet but didn't share political opinions. It wasn't only the unionist question that divided them. Atholl felt passionately that King James II's son James should succeed Queen Anne in 1714. Orkney preferred to accept **King James I**'s great-grandson George, Elector of Hanover, as **King George I**. Atholl was implicated in the Jacobite rebellion of 1715 and his sons George, William and Charles Murray led an army of Scots and Spaniards at the Battle of Glen Shiel during the rising of 1719. As his appointment to the King's Bedchamber demonstrated, Orkney survived this familial link to fomenting rebellion with his standing not only intact but enhanced.

The other faction pertains. It is about politics, personality, pamphlets and persuasion. Constitutional monarchy is still finding its feet. If ministers have a right to be heard but not to govern, how did Sir Robert Walpole come to exercise so much control over the realm of the first and second King Georges? Everyone thinks they know best. Political alliances are fractious and often fluid. Walpole's unpopularity has driven some of his fellow Whigs to turn Tory and others to gravitate to **Richard Temple, 1st Viscount Cobham**, and become styled as *Cobham's Cubs* or *Patriot Whigs*, effectively a third political force. And yet whether they are Whig, Cobhamite or Tory, Orkney is everyone's rock. During **Queen Anne**'s reign he remained friends with her leading ministers Robert Harley, 1st Earl of Oxford and Earl Mortimer, (a Whig who went Tory) and **Henry St John, 1st Viscount Bolingbroke** (a Tory with Jacobite tendency), even after they fell out with each other. And throughout the reigns of both Georges, he has enjoyed hosting those of ***The Scriblerus Club***, a group of perceptive Tory and disaffected Whig intellectuals and like-minded literary lights whose sophisticated social and political satire aspires to make opinions and break reputations [*see Appendix 4*]. Over the years Orkney has chewed the social, political and constitutional cud with this loose-knit group consisting at different times of the Lords Oxford and Bolingbroke, Jonathan Swift, John Gay, William Congreve, Alexander Pope, John Arbuthnot, Sir Richard Steele, Joseph Addison and Sir John Vanbrugh [*see Appendix 4*]. His guests could always find Enlightenment on the agenda – civil liberties, the separation of church and state, freedom of religion, expression and trade – and Bolingbroke introduced the French philosopher Voltaire to the circle during his nearly-three-year exile in England from 1725. Somehow the ever-accommodating Orkney successfully juggled inflated egos and rivalries as **Taplow Court** tended Tory while **Clifden** went Whiggish. Taplow is well and truly established politically and socially as THE place to be and to be seen for 200 years hereafter.

The Orkney Inheritance

Tæppa's Mound / 6th February 1737

The great and the good are gathered below in St Nicholas' Churchyard to witness the interment of Lord Orkney. He has made provision for each of his servants to receive £30 (£77,100). In addition, his housekeeper Sarah Lee will enjoy an annual pension of £20 (£51,400) and his *valet de chambre* Gilbert "all [his] wearing apparell, new and old". In all he and his heirs will grace Taplow for 152 years. George's passing closes the first chapter in their story but national dramas will make many guest appearances as Ann, Mary, Mary and Thomas play out their chapters of the family saga before Taplow's deceptively tranquil and idyllic backdrops.

Orkney could trace his extra-marital lineage back to King James IV of Scotland. He had no sons but his Scottish title passes to his eldest daughter who now becomes **Ann O'Brien, 2nd Countess of Orkney**, and Taplow goes too – all except a piece her father has ceded to a Scottish cousin to build his English country home. The title will do something unique by passing through three consecutive female generations: in 1756 from Ann to her daughter **Mary O'Brien, 3rd Countess of Orkney**, and in 1790 to Mary's daughter **Mary Fitzmaurice, 4th Countess of Orkney**. It will revert to the male line in 1831 in the person of the second Mary's grandson **Thomas John Hamilton Fitzmaurice, 5th Earl of Orkney**. The title to Taplow will follow the same line as the Orkney title with the exception that the widowers of both Ann and the first Mary will remain *in situ* after their wives pass away.

The sequence might seem simple enough but, by the time the bloodline reaches its fifth generation, it will be more Irish than Scottish. And as Ann has and the first Mary will wed first cousins, it might be a little too close knit for comfort. Ann's husband **William O'Brien, 4th Earl of Inchiquin**, is the son of her mother's sister **Mary Villiers**. Their four sons will all die in infancy, two of them within weeks of each other in 1726. The first Mary O'Brien was born deaf and dumb in 1721. At 32 she will be married by signs to her father's brother's son **Murrough O'Brien, 5th Earl of Inchiquin**. Their only daughter, the second Mary O'Brien, will keep up the Irish link but reduce its genetic potency when she weds **Thomas Fitzmaurice**, a grandson of an earlier Thomas Fitzmaurice, the Hiberno-Norman Earl of Kerry. His brother William Petty, 1st Marquess of Lansdowne, will be an eminent politician who will become 2nd Earl of Shelburne in 1761 and Prime Minster in 1782/83. Mary and Thomas's son **John Fitzmaurice, Viscount Kirkwall**, will predecease his mother hence the passing of her title and estates to his son Thomas, the fifth Orkney [*see Appendix 1, Tree 7*].

Sideways Glances

Doctor in the House

The original Hitcham House / 23rd September 1728

Hitcham stumbled a little on its way from **Sir Edward Nicholas** via his son Edward Nicholas and the Reverend Stephen Weston to Samuel West who sold it in 1715 to the Reverend **William Freind**, rector *in absentia* of two parishes – neither of them local – who months before must have been very pleased to have won the very tidy sum of £800 (£64,000) in a national lottery. Sadly for him, what goes up will come down. He did just that with an almighty thump when the *South Sea Bubble* burst and his fortune went with it. Fortunately for Hitcham, his brother the eminent **John Freind** came to the rescue. It seemed a natural move for a man of John's precocious talents yet – perhaps due to rumoured estrangement with his wife Anne – he spent little time at Hitcham until returning this year to find his last resting place in **St Mary's Churchyard**. He will be remembered for his ups as a physician and his downs as a Jacobite.

The roots of both began at Oxford where he was drawn to intellectual circles in which two Scots – David Gregory and Archibald Pitcairne – advocated the application of Newtonian natural philosophy to physical and social wellbeing. The first fed Freind's fervent belief in traditional learning and medical practice. The second convinced him that reason must combat what he saw as the growing religious dogmatism of Presbyterianism under King William. He travelled to Paris, where he befriended both the erstwhile King James II and his son James, later known as the Old Pretender, and to Flanders, where, while serving as an army physician, he grew close to two passionate Jacobites: Charles Morduant, 3rd Earl of Peterborough, and James Butler, 2nd Duke of Ormonde. And on his return his long association with **Bolingbroke**, Swift and Arbuthnot may well have seen him in with the Tory in-crowd at **Taplow Court**.

He was accepted into the Royal College of Physicians in 1716 only for his career to take a turn for the worse soon after he relieved his brother William of Hitcham. In 1722 he was implicated in a plot to overthrow King George I and imprisoned in the Tower of London. If he was a conspirator he had been wily enough to ensure there was no solid evidence beyond his friendship with the instigator Francis Atterbury. Within months of his release yet another of his influential friends – George Granville, 1st Baron Lansdowne – secured his election as MP for Launceston (Cornwall). Meanwhile he penned many scientific theses, most notably *The History of Physick* (published in two volumes in 1725 and 1726), persuaded Voltaire to Newtonian philosophy and argued against inoculation – but not with King George II's wife Queen Caroline since he became her personal physician. Suddenly the Jacobite is Hanoverian. How did that happen?

Sadly **John Freind the Younger** will not follow in his father's eminent footsteps. Within 18 years he will exhaust his inheritance and oblige his uncle **Robert Freind** – headmaster of Westminster School – to obtain a court order to prevent him from "cutting down timber and otherwise diminishing the value of the estate to meet his own, possibly extravagant, expenses". Just as well for Hitcham that the manor will pass to Robert's son the Reverend **William Freind**, Rector of Witney (Oxfordshire) and later Dean of Canterbury, and then in turn to William's sons Robert Freind and the Reverend **William Maximillian Freind**, Rector of St Andrew's Church, Chinnor (Oxfordshire).

Naughty Neighbours

Down Place, Water Oakley / 23rd September 1736

Taplow cannot claim to be the only place locally where the elite whirl socially. Many Scriblerians are also members of ***The Kit-Cat Club*** which perhaps has roots in securing the Hanoverian succession but is now notorious for its more frivolous and rather raucous gatherings at which members toast in turn all the beauties of the day. And for at least 20 years they have enjoyed being naughty here at the home of the recently deceased Jacob Tonson, a bookseller who matured to be the first modern publisher whose releases include the works of Shakespeare.

The informal Whiggish beginnings of *The Kit-Cat Club* are obscure but by 1700 its meetings were held at *The Cat & Fiddle*, a convivial London hostelry that will survive until the 1870s when it will make way for the Royal Courts of Justice. Some say it was the delicious mutton pies served by its landlord Christopher (Kit) Catling that gave the club its name. There is no debate that it owes its reputation to the well-connected Tonson who organised club meetings in various houses and hostelries before settling here at *Down Place* which in the 20th Century will enjoy a different kind of fame as *Bray Studios*. In addition to the Cliveden set, his fellow reprobates have included the trend-setting patron of Palladian architecture Richard Boyle, 3rd Earl of Burlington, the renowned soldier and politician James Stanhope, 1st Earl Stanhope, Thomas Pelham-Holles, 1st Duke of both Newcastles (who will twice be Prime Minister in the 1750s), Sir Godfrey Kneller (the portrait painter who captured 43 Kit-Cat members on canvas), Charles Seymour, 6th Duke of Somerset, and two of the co-founders of the Foundling Hospital: Lionel Sackville, 1st Duke of Dorset, and Charles FitzRoy, 2nd Duke of Grafton (one of many illegitimate grandsons of Charles II and Barbara Villiers).

Tonson's demise will see *The Kit-Kat Club* trumped by ***The Hellfire Club*** with its reputation for all sorts of naughtiness from bacchanalia to devil worship in the caves of West Wycombe and the ruins of Medmenham Abbey. Sir Francis Dashwood, 15th Baron le Despencer, and Robert Vansittart (Recorder of Maidenhead, later Regius Professor of Civil Law at Oxford) had local roots and might well have been familiar with the pagan lore that still echoed in the Chilterns. Other members included George Dodington (friend of Frederick, Prince of Wales, and reputedly an anti-Jacobite spy), the painter and satirist William Hogarth and the politicians Thomas Potter and John Montagu, 4th Earl of Sandwich (inventor of the sandwich).

Although there will be no records of either of these crowds coming to Taplow too, it is hard to imagine they don't drop by to sample its delights in their calmer and more intellectual moments. They certainly move in the right social circles.

A Man of the Moment

The Orkney Arms

George Hamilton, 1st Earl of Orkney
– Martin Maingaud 1724

Cliveden's Blenheim Pavilion and Octagon Temple / 2011

An imaginative view of Cliveden (centre) **and Taplow Court** (right) – William Tomkins c1767

Irish Highs

William O'Brien, 4th Earl of Inchiquin

The O'Brien

The third Taplow Court / 6th February 1737

The **Orkney** title stays with the ladies but the Inchiquins are something to behold. They attract honorific titles like bees to a honeypot. Lady Ann's husband, her cousin **William O'Brien**, isn't merely **4th Earl of Inchiquin**, a small seat in south-western Ireland's County Clare. He is *the* O'Brien, Chief of the Name, Prince of Thomond, Lord of Dál gCais, 9th Baron Inchiquin and, since 1725, a founder Knight Companion of the Order of the Bath.

The O'Brien can count among his ancestors Brian Boru, the 10th Century High King of Ireland, and Murrough O'Brien who had been rather pragmatic in 1541 when the Irish parliament bestowed the title King of Ireland on Henry VIII. This deal had involved no loss of Ireland's unity and independence for its nobility was granted the same rights of primogeniture as English knights. Not everyone went as far as Murrough who swapped being the last Catholic King of Thomond with being the Anglican 1st Earl of Thomond and 1st Baron Inchiquin. Thereafter the Thomond title reverted to his nephew Donough while the barony of Inchiquin passed to his son Dermod and down generations which increasingly edged into the English spotlight [*see Appendix 1, Tree 8*].

William's great-grandfather was another Murrough O'Brien who had fought for the English Parliament against the Irish Rebellion of 1641 and was made first governor and then president of Munster as he strove to keep Anglican ascendancy. By 1647 he was master of the south of Ireland but tending rather more Royalist. Murrough's powerbase crumbled in 1649 when Cromwell invaded and in 1650 he slipped away to join **King Charles II** in exile. His loyalty was rewarded in 1654 by his elevation to 1st Earl of Inchiquin. He served the French in Catalonia, plotted Cromwell's assassination, converted to Catholicism and was on his way with his son William in 1659 to help Portugal retain its independence from Spain when they were captured by the Ottomans who ruled in Algiers. Charles II successfully petitioned for Murrough's release in 1660 and had Parliament pay a king's ransom to extricate his son from captivity. With his lands restored, the young William succeeded as 2nd Earl of Inchiquin in 1674 and repaid his sovereign by commanding English forces in Tangiers for six years and spending the last years of his life as Governor of Jamaica. His son William gave **King William III** fervent support and served both **Queen Anne** and **King George I** as a Privy Counsellor and Governor of County Clare. Being in such elevated circles led to his marrying Mary Villiers and they were blessed with yet another William O'Brien, the one who began this tale. His wife Ann is now spoiled for choice as both Lady Inchiquin and Lady Orkney.

Sadly some are jealous that William and Ann make a devoted and magnetic couple with many friends. The snooty and acerbic social critic Lady Mary Wortley Montagu will describe Ann as "fat and wrinkled". Even her friend Jonathan Swift will be heard to remark that she "squints like a dragon" but he'll paint a truer picture by adding that she is "the wisest woman I've ever known". Her husband Lord Inchiquin is a diplomatic socialite and a fine political pioneer despite having a stutter that will prevent him from ever giving a speech in the House of Commons during a total of 25 years as a Whig MP for Windsor, Tamworth, Camelford and Aylesbury in turn. In 1740 as he enjoys a year as Grand Master of England's first Masonic Grand Lodge, his annual income of £9,000 (£1.14m) from estates in Cork and Clare will enable him to engage **Stiff Leadbetter**, surveyor of **Eton College**, to remodel Taplow Court by enclosing his father-in-law's neo-Norman hall in a Georgian package. The following year he will be appointed Governor of County Clare for life and in 1753 he will be admitted to the Privy Council of Ireland. After Ann's death in 1756, he will continue to live an active life at Taplow Court for 21 years. He will marry again in 1761 – to Mary Moore, daughter of Stephen Moore, 1st Viscount Mountcashell – and pull powerful strings when the need arises, not least in 1768 when, to prevent undesirables from trespassing in his gardens, he will obtain an Act of Parliament prohibiting the mooring of boats in the mill leat.

A Royal Residence

The Parterre, Cliveden / 1st July 2012

The term 'His Majesty's Loyal Opposition' wasn't coined until 1826 but Cliveden can claim to have been in on the act. It began as **Buckingham**'s personal pique in the days when he seethed out of favour in exile at Cliffden. In the first Lord Orkney's time, conversations at Clifden and elsewhere sparked Scriblerian satire as it sharpened from spiteful ridicule to intellectually critical essays. Those penned by the likes of Pope and Bolingbroke explored such constitutional theories as the need for and machinery of the democratically mature concept of having a continual, dissenting and inquisitorial parliamentary opposition holding government to account without fear of accusations of treason. The next and perhaps one of the most important phases of its genesis was during the 1737/51 tenancy at Clifden of **Frederick**, **Prince of Wales**, who paid £600-a-year (£1.46m) to Lord Inchiquin for the privilege.

No Georgian king ever thought much of his heirs. **King George II** thought so little of his eldest son that he banned him from court without realising until too late that this would make him the focus of opposition to His Majesty and the Prime Minister, the hated Sir Robert Walpole. **Bolingbroke** captured the counterpoint in his 1738 essay *On the Idea of a Patriot King* which cast the Prince of Wales as "the common father of his people" in implied contrast to King George, who many thought to be more interested in Hanover than Great Britain.

The Ilex Grove, Cliveden / 1st July 1740

There can be few better places for 'Poor Fred' to find refuge than Clifden. He can spend the morning dealing with his business affairs at *Carlton House*, his London home, take luncheon and then a coach for just three hours and 20 minutes to be here with his family for dinner. This is the perfect place for him to enjoy playing cards, games and his cello, fishing, shooting, riding, rowing and especially hosting friends like Lady Orkney and Lord Inchiquin in sheer extravagance. Next year he will show his appreciation to Inchiquin by sponsoring him for six years as MP for Camelford (Cornwall). He treasures the intellectual company of artistic fellows such as Swift, Pope, Henry Carey (*God Save The King* and *Sally in Our Alley*) and Lady Orkney's distant cousin Henry Fielding (*Tom Jones*), but he loves nothing better than fomenting a hotbed of political opposition to his father with William Pitt (the Elder) and George Grenville, both up-and-coming anti-Walpole Patriot Whigs who might have what it takes to be future Prime Ministers. Perhaps they stroll through the grounds in conversation and divert for refreshment in ***The New Inn*** (not-yet ***The Feathers*** by any incarnation).

It is such a joy for Princess Augusta of Saxe-Gotha to feel warm again after the awful winter just past which saw "the coldest day in the memory of man" on 16th January, snow thick on the ground until March, more falls in April and May, and outbreaks of scurvy here and there due the lack of fresh vegetables. But today Prince Frederick's young wife can put all that hardship behind her as they walk through Bridgeman's Ilex Grove in excited anticipation of this afternoon's entertainment....

The Amphitheatre, Cliveden / 1st July 1740

After taking tea, guests gather to witness the first performance of *Alfred*, a masque by two Scots – the poet James Thomson and the dramatist David Mallet – assisted by the Prince's secretary George Lyttleton (later 1st Baron Lyttleton). The setting: the dramatic amphitheatre **Bridgeman** had cut into the cliffside in 1723. The theme: Alfred the Great and his victories over the Vikings, so topical given all the arguments about Walpole's leadership of the unfolding naval war with Spain. The crescendo: the first performance of ***Rule Britannia***, a poem penned by Thomson and set to music by the English composer Thomas Arne.

Fooled Britannia

The Parterre, Cliveden / 1st July 2012

History likes to think that *Rule Britannia* was first heard at Cliveden on 1st August 1740 at a celebration of the third birthday of Princess Augusta the previous day. This claim contrasts with *The London Daily Post & General Advertiser* which reported on 5th July 1740 that *Alfred* was performed "on Friday last, upon a theatre in the garden composed of vegetables and decorated with festoons of flowers at the end of which was erected a Pavillion for the Royal Household of the Prince and Princess of Wales, Prince George and Princess Augusta". It continued that "the Prince of Wales was so well pleased that he commanded the same to be performed on Saturday with the addition of several pantomime scenes from Mr [John] Rich's Entertainment" and *The Judgement of Paris*, a masque by William Congreve set to the music of Giuseppe Sammartini. The combination of a larger cast, orchestra and audience demanded the grander stage of the Parterre where the setting gave *Alfred* a wonderful but worrying backdrop. The south-western horizon disappeared as a dark and foreboding bank of cloud swept in to deposit a deluge on the valley below. The performances were "begun but the rain falling very heavy obliged [the assembled company] to break off before it was half over" to enjoy the conclusion of the entertainment in the dry of the house. Once more the cockles of everyone's British hearts were aglow with privilege, pride and patriotism, emotions that were rekindled later that year when *Rule Britannia* had its first public performance at a dinner to celebrate the safe return of Vice-Admiral Edward (Old Grog) Vernon after his capture of Porto Bello (Panama) and all its Spanish silver.

Tall Tale – Having a Ball

The Parterre, Cliveden / 1st July 2012

Prince Frederick was attracted to cricket by gambling but fell in love with the game as an occasional player and an enthusiastic spectator, gambler and patron. In 1731 he attended the match on Kennington Common between Surrey and London which may have been the first to charge admission – but only to other people, of course. And in 1733 at Moulsey Hurst (now West Molesey, Surrey) he awarded a silver cup – the first ever cricket trophy (other than cash) – to a combined Surrey and Middlesex team that defeated Kent, the best team in the country. His death in 1751 at the unfortunately early age of 42 was a big blow to cricket, which lost his enthusiastic patronage, and to Clifden, which had rather enjoyed being a royal residence.

It is widely believed that the culprit was cricket, or at least a cricket ball which hit him while playing with his children at Cliveden some time before and caused "an abscess in the breast" that eventually burst and killed him. It is medically feasible that such a blow could have caused an abscess on the lung, or more likely a punctured lung, which might well have become fatally infected. However, here's the killer (excuse the expression): Fred's physician **John Webster** exonerated the offending ball by recording that it struck Fred on the head, not the chest, and that the poor fellow had influenza which became pneumonia.

Legend says that King George II was informed of the death of his heir when playing cards with his mistress. He continued the game without comment then said "I have lost my eldest son but I'm glad of it", an attitude that may explain the general public distaste for the Hanoverians which was captured in an anonymous ode....

Here lies Fred, who was alive and is dead,
Had it been his father, I had much rather,
Had it been his brother, still better than another,
Had it been his sister, none would have missed her,
Had it been the whole generation, still better for the nation,
But since 'tis only Fred, there's no more to be said.

The New Inn thought differently. It commemorated its favourite customer by becoming ***The Three Feathers***, an emblem borrowed from the Prince of Wales's heraldic badge to recall Poor Fred's yen for refreshment.

Taking Taplow as a Title – The First Viscount

The third Taplow Court / 7th February 1747

Taplow continues to be in the vanguard of changes to the bigger picture. Ireland will not join Great Britain to create the United Kingdom until 1801 but, like Jonathan Swift, Inchiquin is already showing the way for the Irish elite to make significant contributions to the dramatically developing British way of things. His wife's sister Henrietta went Irish too in 1728 when she married John, son of Charles Boyle, 4th Earl of Orrery, a neighbour at *Britwell Court* since 1713. And his own sister Mary's son **James FitzGerald**, 20th Earl of Kildare, flew even higher up the social scale today when he married the 15-year-old Lady Emilia Lennox, daughter of King Charles II's illegitimate grandson Charles Lennox, 2nd Duke of Richmond. King George II is so taken by this young Irishman that he has from this day forth created him **Viscount Leinster of Taplow** in the English peerage [*see Appendix 1, Tree 8*].

FitzGerald will out-title his Inchiquin cousins by some distance. He succeeded as Earl of Kildare three years ago and will be created Earl of Offaly and Marquess of Kildare in 1761 and Duke of Leinster in 1766 to make him the premier duke, marquess and earl in the Irish peerage. And when he serves with the Royal Irish Artillery, he will rise from Colonel in 1760 to Lieutenant-General within a decade. But of all his titles, surely the one he'll treasure most will be his English one. He has no residence locally so it can only be presumed that he has selected his suffix to acknowledge his love of Taplow Court. How excited this must make his Uncle William and Aunt Ann.

The Coming of the Scots

The Elibank Plot

Elibank, Church Road / 10th November 1752

Lady Ann might have had a little excitement of a different kind if she had seen the coded letter 'Pickle' sent six days ago from Boulogne to the Prime Minister, Henry Pelham. Having fellow Scots just around the corner at ***Elibank*** has been all very pleasant. Will she feel the same when she hears that her new neighbour **Alexander Murray** and her own nephew Lord George Murray are implicated in ***The Elibank Plot***, yet another Jacobite conspiracy to claim **King George II**'s crown for the Young Pretender, otherwise known as King James II's grandson Bonnie Prince Charlie?

The Elibank Plot and the house called *Elibank* are like brothers born in secret to fly so high. Their origins will be lost in the mists of time but both are thought to be named after the estate by the River Yarrow near Selkirk in the Scottish Borders, which had been acquired around 1594 by Sir Gideon Murray who went on to be treasurer for Scotland. His son Sir Patrick Murray became 1st Lord Elibank in 1643 and his Royalist great-grandson, yet another Sir Patrick, fought in the Civil War alongside James Graham, 1st Marquess of Montrose. Two generations later, it is likely that **Alexander Murray, 4th Lord Elibank**, knew Lady Ann's father George from Edinburgh or that they met as fellow Scots in London society. Perhaps the first Lord Orkney suggested to the fourth Lord Elibank that Taplow is just the place for a Scots border laird to have an English country seat for his family to lay their weary heads. The house reflects the style of Sir John Vanbrugh and may even have been built according to a sketch design by the famous architect before his death in 1726. However his lordship's passing in 1736 meant that, by the time the year 1737 was cast into the rainwater heads of *Elibank*, it was his sons Patrick, George, Gideon, Alexander and James who had the benefit of the finished article and its easy access to life.

The Plot was probably the idea of the younger Alexander in cohorts with his fellow clansman (but no relation) George, the sixth son of Ann's paternal Aunt Catherine and her husband John Murray, 1st Earl of Atholl. There is limited evidence but, if Pickle's florid testimony is to be believed, the aim of the Plot was for an elite force of over 200 Jacobites to seize St James's Palace this evening, capture the king and his family and hold them hostage in France until he abdicated – or to poison them, and perhaps even to storm the Tower of London as well. Pickle was Alistair Ruadh MacDonnell of Glengarry, a spy in the Young Pretender's Parisian enclave. He got himself into a pickle on the details but word has spread that the conspiracy had been betrayed. Nobody will be sneaking into the Palace tonight with malice intent and Stuart ambitions will soon finally run out of steam. Ann of Orkney and William of Inchiquin may breathe sighs of relief that rebellious relations will no longer wrinkle their comfort in the Hanoverian good books [*see Appendix 1, Tree 15*].

Murray Hints

Elibank, Rectory Road / 10th October 2012

The five sons of the fourth Lord Elibank were remarkable men. All escaped the jaws of disaster. Taplow was the English home from home of their branch of Clan Murray for at least 70 years.

Patrick Murray was just 21 when he qualified in 1723 as an advocate in Edinburgh and 34 when he succeeded to his father's title as **5th Lord Elibank**. His disaster came five years later when he was serving as a lieutenant-colonel in Colonel John Wynyard's 4th Regiment of Marines which was decimated in its efforts to take Fort San Lazaro in the Spanish port of Cartegena (in present-day Columbia). Two-thirds of Vice-Admiral Edward Vernon's 27,000 men were killed, wounded or taken ill failing to achieve their objective. Murray recovered quickly to gain an enviable reputation back home as a financial wizard, socialite and friend of Samuel Johnson. James Boswell described him as "a man of great genius, great knowledge, and much whim". According to Alexander Carlyle, he was "one of the most learned and ingenious noblemen of his time" with "a mind that embraced the greatest variety of topics and produced the most original remarks". David Hume thought him a prime mover in an 18th Century outburst of intellectual, moral and scientific thinking that became known as the Enlightenment. No wonder he fitted in so well in Taplow.

George Murray's disaster was at sea in a squadron of six ships under the command of George Anson, 1st Baron Anson. Their objective was to sail to Manila in 1740 to plunder whatever Spanish ships they could find. High seas and diseases made life hell or ended it nastily. The squadron rounded Cape Horn to be dispersed in violent storms. Disorientated and with their crews severely debilitated, Murray assumed captaincy of *HMS Pearl* and sailed with *HMS Severn* back into the Atlantic and home via Rio de Janeiro in 1742. Three other ships were lost but incredibly Anson sailed *HMS Centurian* around the world via China and captured along the way a Spanish galleon laden with gold and silver. It was 1744 before they found safe haven at last in Portsmouth. George suffers from being confused with his brother Alexander's plotting pal George Murray who commanded the Jacobite army's advance from Edinburgh to Derby in 1745 and its right wing in the Battle of Culloden the following spring.

As chaplain of the 43rd Highlanders, the Reverend **Gideon Murray** had to convince everyone that God was on their side even when the evidence suggested otherwise. Regimental morale was shaken to the core in 1743 when three deserters were shot and in 1745 when they suffered heavy losses performing heroically as the Battle of Fountenoy (Belgium) was lost to the French. But Gideon must have done a good job because he was promoted in 1749 to Chaplain-General of the British Army. Clan Murray's tenure of *Elibank* ended in 1811 when Gideon's eldest son **Alexander Murray, 7th Lord Elibank**, surrendered it in trust to the original Lord Orkney's great-great grandson **John Fitzmaurice, Viscount Kirkwall**.

Alexander Murray, the fourth of the five brothers, is easily confused with his father, the fourth Lord Elibank, or his nephew, the seventh, which is unfortunate for them because he is undoubtedly the black sheep of the family. His disaster was an inability to channel his energy and ambition to better effect. His various grievances including the Highland Clearances may have had justification but the volatile and aggressive way he expressed them fuelled his reputation as a troublemaker. He was arrested for rioting at Westminster in 1750 and emerged bent on revenge from four months in Newgate Prison the following year. When *The Elibank Plot* came apart at the seams, he fled to exile in France but was eventually forgiven by King George III and allowed to return home in 1771. The fact that he is buried in the old St Nicholas' Churchyard suggests he spent his dotage at *Elibank*.

Patrick may have been the sage but his youngest brother **James Murray** was the success as a soldier and Empire builder. He was severely wounded at Ostend (Belgium, 1745) but recovered to perform outstandingly at Lorient (Brittany, 1746). He fought against the French with such distinction as a lieutenant-colonel at Rochefort (Brittany, 1757), Louisburg (Nova Scotia, 1758) and Quebec (1759) that he was made Governor of Quebec in 1759 and then of Canada four years later. But still he wasn't done. During eight years in Minorca until 1782 he rose to be its governor and concluded by commanding Fort St Philip during a seven-month Franco-Spanish siege. He was thereafter promoted to general but known to all as 'Old Minorca' Murray.

Sideways Glance

Boston Manor

The third Hedsor House / 10th October 1775

The old manor house is looking rather dilapidated now. It is hard to imagine what it looked like in the 1640s when William Price the Elder completed enhancing its Tudor elegance with Stuart sparkle. It has passed from William Chilcot to his widow Mary, who died in 1720, and to a Captain Parker who was excited by a plan drawn up in 1749 for his Orkney-Inchiquin neighbours and their royal tenants at Clifden.

This involved extending Clifden's Grand Avenue north into the Hedsor estate and the introduction of two circuses: one where the Avenue intersected Hedsor Hill on its way west down to **Hedsor Wharf**, the other a quarter-mile to the east on the Wooburn-to-Taplow road. And the old woodland track from this second circus east to **Cray Brook** would be replaced by two new avenues radiating north-east to **Dropmer Hill** and south-east to **Rose Hill**. The scheme was too ambitious by half. William of Inchiquin succeeded in funding improvements within Clifden itself and three of the new roads made it onto Jeffery's 1770 map perhaps more in anticipation than accuracy. Hedsor's limetree-lined avenue will survive as a private woodland walk but the south-east and north-east radiants remain aspirational not actual. The western circus will appear eventually, but not for another six score years and more for the enjoyment of an American: a concept difficult to comprehend at this time of colonial conflict.

Hedsor passed via Parker's widow Elizabeth to the brothers Richard and Thomas Bowyer who in 1764 welcomed the return of the Royal Ripple when they sold the estate to **William Irby, 1st Baron Boston**, son of Sir Edward Irby, 1st Baronet of Whaplode & Boston, once MP for the longstanding family home of Boston in Lincolnshire [*see Appendix 1, Tree 10*]. Irby's maternal grandmother had been Irish but he bucked the local trend by otherwise being all-English. He had been a Page of Honour to both the first two King Georges before spending eight years as equerry to **Frederick**, **Prince of Wales**, and then 26 years as Tory MP, for first Launceston then Bodmin, which overlapped 36 years as Vice-Chamberlain and then Chamberlain to Augusta, Princess of Wales, until her death three years ago. It was she who ensured his elevation in 1761 from 2nd Baronet with the Whaplode to 1st Baron without it: such a relief.

The Princess and her children had fallen in love with the area during their happy time at Clifden. It is thought that she used Hedsor as a minor residence and that she may have assisted Boston with its acquisition in part to keep it during her last years as a haven from critical public gaze. Her unpopularity was an unfortunate legacy of her husband's feud with his father fuelled by malicious rumours of an unlikely affair with John Bute, 3rd Earl of Bute, secretly tutor to her eldest son George and, albeit briefly, his first chosen Prime Minister after he ascended the throne as King George III.

The old-fashioned house holds no sentimental value for **Frederick Irby**, **2nd Baron Boston**. It is little more than six months ago that he inherited the place from his late father and he has already commissioned Augusta's friend **Sir William Chambers** to build a brand new modern mansion a little to the south-east. It is said that King George and Queen Charlotte selected the site of the new house for its magnificent views west and south along the Thames Valley.

Chambers is one of the most influential architects of the day: a founder member of the Royal Academy famous for his blend of Neoclassical and Palladian styles at *Somerset House* in London and much favoured for helping the dowager princess as a major benefactor to Kew Gardens where he designed the Chinese pagoda. When he completes his creation in 1778 the fourth *Hedsor House* will become home for the second Lord Boston and home from home for their Royal Highnesses. His Majesty will show his appreciation in 1780 by making Boston a Gentleman of the Bedchamber.

Murrough O'Brien, 5th Earl of Inchiquin

Coming Home

The third Taplow Court / 25th July 1777

A carriage sweeps by carrying Lady Orkney and Lord Inchiquin on the last leg of their journey from Ireland where they have lived for almost a quarter-century. The deaf and dumb **Mary** has been **3rd Countess of Orkney** since her mother Anne died 21 years ago but now at last – bereft at losing her father but perhaps a little excited to come back to her childhood home – she is returning as mistress of Taplow Court.

As a young man Morough O'Bryen served in the Grenadier Guards in Germany and carried the colours in 1747 at the Battle of Lauffeld (Netherlands). He married his cousin Mary in 1753 and retired from the army the following year to live on his family's estate in Rostellan (County Cork) where it is said that his wife had once approached their new-born daughter Mary armed with a stone. Her maid was aghast that she meant the baby harm only for her to drop the stone with a loud crash that made the child cry, thus confirming she didn't share her mother's impairment. Morough has by all accounts conducted himself impeccably to help Mary cope with her disabilities and has these last 11 years represented Clare and Harristown as an Irish MP. Mary's father was his uncle and he now succeeds him as **5th Earl of Inchiquin** [*see Appendix 1, Tree 7*]. Time will tell that his taking over at Taplow Court and Clifden will give him a whole new lease of life and new ways to spell his name.

If the remarkably respectful letter Inchiquin wrote to **Lancelot (Capability) Brown** is anything to go by – signed "Your most obedient humble servant, M O'Brien" – his Uncle William had already begun discussions with the renowned landscape architect about remodelling the grounds at Taplow Court. Morrough will take up the project with unbridled enthusiasm and will also look north to the "ill kept" Clifden. The premature death of Prince Edward, Duke of York, ended any possibility that he might succeed his father the Prince of Wales as its tenant and it proved impossible to find anyone willing to pay a much-reduced annual rent of £200 (£381,000), just one-third of that paid by Poor Fred. Perhaps people were put off by having to find an additional £140-a-year (£217,000) "to keep the gardens in order". Now Murrough will have Brown eradicate Bridgewater's straight sightlines to give a sense of surprise to Leoni's follies.

These are halcyon days for the fifth Lord Inchiquin and his wife. Their daughter **Mary O'Brien** is healthy, happily married to **Thomas Fitzmaurice** and the mother of an infant son John. With the Orkney and Inchiquin lines seemingly secure, it is time for him to join the social whirl. He has a zest for life and is already well-connected. Three of his closest friends are Sarah Siddons, Sir Joshua Reynolds and Edmund Burke: a great actress, a great artist and a great statesman. So struck was Murrough when he first saw Siddons onstage in Cork that he graced Rostellan with a monument to her and the moment they met. So taken was she by his gregarious nature and amiable disposition that they quickly became firm friends. Reynolds painted his daughter Mary's portrait four years ago and the gentlemen love fine dining at the Royal Academy and ribald sessions of drinking, gambling and gossiping. And Burke – who shares Murrough's Irish roots and his love of eloquent philosophical and political debate – is almost a neighbour: his home is but a few miles away at *Gregories* in Beaconsfield.

Remembering Rotation

Berry Hill Farm / 5th December 2013

Summerleaze is digging a very big hole between here and Station Road. Residents on **Boundary Road** are fed up with the dust created by the gravel extraction which is also removing another layer of Taplow's history. This used to be **Town Field**, possibly one of three open fields in the old days when soil was kept up to scratch by crop rotation. The others were **Buffins** to the north of the Village and **Berry Hill Field** to the west.

Things had evolved by the early-18th Century. Although a number of copyholders farmed certain closes or strips here and there, the land appears to have been managed in two parcels: one farmed for the Lord of the Manor, the other to provide the Rector his 'Living'. As its name suggests, *Home Farm* centred upon **Taplow Court** and stretched along the riverbank north to the Cliveden woods and south to Amerden Bank. By then, the floodplain area of Berry Hill Field has its own name: **Upper Thames Field**, a distinction now emphasised by the Jubilee River. To the east was a large triangle – effectively Buffins and Town Field – bounded by today's Cliveden Road and Berry Hill on one side and by Boundary Road and Hill Farm Road on the other. This seems to have been *Taplow Hill Farm* in the 18th Century, when it was held in 1737 by Thomas Cuningham and William Mount and in 1757 by Bristol sugar-baker **Andrew Pope**, and later possibly *Tythe Farm* then *Glebe Farm* before eventually becoming ***Rectory Farm***.

It isn't clear if these two farms originally included any of Amerden, some of which was glebe land but most held by the manor. The picture had sharpened by the 1840s when **George Norrington** held *Home Farm*, his father **William Norrington** held *Glebe Farm* until being succeeded by his son-in-law **Richard Briginshaw** whose elder brother **William Davis Briginshaw** held ***Amerden Farm*** while **George Cross** held ***Barge Farm***. Could Cross have felt the odd one out?

Perhaps Lord Inchiquin experimented with fashionable four-field-rotation at *Home Farm*. If so, he seems not to have reaped the benefits of agricultural revolution he was after....

Coveting the Common

The Houses of Parliament, Westminster / 5th December 1779

Murrough O'Brien watched with interest earlier this year when another neighbour, the Reverend **William Freind**, secured **Hitcham**'s inclosure award. If he thinks today's Act of Parliament will do just that for him, he reckons without the Reverend **George Hamilton**. The way the award defines who has what rights over which land won't be at all to the Rector's liking. The Reverend Richard Wells of Maidenhead, Henry Emblin of New Windsor and John Mitchell of South Weston have been appointed as commissioners. They will meet in due course at ***The Orkney Arms*** to consider any claims against the award that might be submitted by local proprietors. Hamilton is especially concerned his lordship has designs upon the glebe land opposite the Rectory: *Homestead* orchard and garden are occupied by blacksmith John Read and the adjacent **Pater Noster** by the widow **Elizabeth Brown**. He will have his curate Frederick Browning pore over the Act and its appended maps in readiness for him to join with **Andrew Pope** and other copyholders such as **George Johnstone** and Robert Woodford to make their representations.

Going Out

The Artillery Ground, Finsbury / 15th September 1784

There must be 200,000 people here in the Honourable Artillery Company's cricket ground just north of the City of London to witness a great event: the first successful manned hydrogen balloon flight in Great Britain by the dashing Italian dare-devil, Vincenzo Lunardi. Lord Inchiquin is here in the exalted company of Sir Joshua Reynolds, Jane & Edmund Burke and their son Richard, the musician and historian Charles Burney (Fanny's father) and the politician, author and topographer Henry Wyndham. As he passes, Sylvester Douglas, 1st Baron Glenbervie, confides to a friend that Inchiquin is "handsome and not agreeable... a true Paddy of high rank, spouting hackneyed verses, talking a good deal... adulatory to excess and mixing a sentimental sort of compliment to yourself and your friends with a sort of bluff commonplace frankness not half or quarter witty and very nearly quite vulgar". The friend smirks that Inchiquin has a reputation for being "a six-bottle man". Someone else interjects that his being "a happy fool, lively as a lark" must have its virtue for his social circles include witty and influential theatrical and literary doyens like David Garrick, Fanny Burney, John Hawkesworth, Samuel Johnson, James Boswell and another lyrical Irishman, Oliver Goldsmith. The artist and diarist Joseph Farington agrees: he thinks his good friend Inchiquin's "open and cheerful manner banishes reserve and makes every society into which he goes pleasant".

The gossip is cut short by the appearance of Lunardi who has a dog, a cat and a caged pigeon in his basket but can wait no longer for his friend George Biggin. His balloon is still not completely filled as it rises to wild cheers and drifts northwards. The excitement only subsides when the balloon has disappeared from sight on its 24-mile sojourn into Hertfordshire but the glorious day is far from over for Inchiquin and friends. After watching in amusement as a mob inconvenienced the leading Whig politician Charles Fox by taking the wheels off his hackney coach, the happy band repairs to the Tower to see the lions and then to have dinner at Sir Joshua's house in Leicester Fields (not-yet Leicester Square). They listen patiently as Inchiquin reminds them once more that at King George's invitation last year he became one of the founding knights of the Order of St Patrick, and that only a few months ago he and George, Prince of Wales, had been elected to Brooks's Club together.

Reynolds and His Majesty detest each other with a passion and yet the consummate diplomat Inchiquin has deep friendships with both. Reynolds is cosmopolitan, the king provincial, Inchiquin either according to his company. He shares the king's love of country pursuits. They hunt together in Windsor Great Park and after dinner at each other's homes and at Burke's they enjoy nothing more than chewing the cud about farming. Talk of the king taking a lease on Clifden has come to nothing. His Majesty is spoiled for choice, he can enjoy Hedsor or Taplow whenever he likes, but it was a bit of a blow for Inchiquin who is gradually running up debt despite still having extensive Irish estates in Cork and Clare that are now reaping £18,000 (£30.9m) each year. In contrast the annual income from his Taplow estates is a modest £1,200 (£2.1m). The Orkney-Inchiquins do well at keeping up appearances but the coffers aren't exactly overflowing and they are definitely feeling the pinch. Having both **Taplow Court** and **Clifden** is a bit too much of a good thing. They have been obliged to let the latter go a bit.

Lady of Letters

The second Taplow House / 17th September 1783

Jane Vigor (Viger or Vigo) was a remarkable lady, not least because 32 years ago she and her late husband William completed building ***Taplow House*** anew. They lived there quietly until his death 16 years later. Jane stayed on until 1774 when she let the place to William Mowbray only to surprise herself by finding fame with the publication of the charming, gently humorous, sharply perceptive and wonderfully entertaining letters she had written to friends in England from the courts of Tsar Peter II and Empress Anna Ivanova of Russia between 1728 and 1740. Suddenly she was known of by almost everyone who was anyone, well-liked by many but forever known well by few.

Jane was the daughter of the wealthy Reverend George Goodwin of Methley, near Leeds in West Yorkshire. In 1728 she married family friend Thomas Ward who had just been appointed British consul-general to Russia. He was soon also the first agent for the Russia Company and in control of a monopoly on trade between Great Britain and Russia. These twin responsibilities, his fluent Russian and their easy sociability led to him and his wife becoming intimate friends of the Empress Anna. Jane had a gift for friendship and was able to write about historical figures as human beings. She was also incredibly resilient in recovering from the loss of two husbands and at least two children.

Thomas died in 1731. Later that same year his widow married his secretary Claudius Rondeau, a French protestant *émigré* to England. Their first child was stillborn. Jane was pregnant again in October 1739 when Claudius passed away. She set out on her journey home in the company of **William Vigor**, a successful Quaker merchant. Having travelled far in a sledge one day across snow-covered Polish Prussia, they arrived exhausted at Memel to find its inn full of soldiers. A stranger called Meyer offered them accommodation in his own home, his generosity inspired by the experience of his son who had fallen ill with smallpox in England the previous year and owed his life to a kind clergyman who had taken him into his home to recover. Jane was astounded to realise that young Meyer's benefactor was her own father.

Her daughter Claudia arrived in May 1740 but survived only three weeks. William consoled her, their relationship blossomed and he was soon her husband. It was to be third time lucky for they shared a convivial nature, a love of learning and of conversation, a calm benevolence and a dislike of show and ostentation. William was very friendly with the Penn family of Jordan's near Chalfont St Giles. It was a natural move for them to leave London for South Bucks. After 23 years in Taplow, friends in Windsor suggested she should live near them and, once she had moved there, she was persuaded to publish her *Letters from a Lady* in 1775. Suddenly at the age of 76 she was in the public eye and the apple of it but, as always, modesty best became her. She continued her charitable efforts to the end and is returning today as stipulated in her will "in as private a manner as possible" to rest in peace alongside her late husband in St Nicholas' Churchyard. She has left her money to her servant Anne Smith and for the education and care of Eleanor, the daughter of local labourer William Allen. *Taplow House* will pass to her husband's niece **Ann Viger** but she will take little interest in it.

Inclosing the Common

The Three Feathers, Taplow Common / 8th February 1787

The woodland walks at Taplow Court are **Lord Inchiquin**'s do-it-yourself distraction as he throws himself into finding economies through improved farming methods including mechanisation. And at last, after seven years of wrangling, today's Act of Parliament finally allows him to inclose bigger patches to play on. It will change the face of Taplow by reallocating 685 acres.

Not even the glowing log fire can lift the darkness from the weatherworn face of 64-year-old **William Aldridge** as he complains to nobody in particular that, now Inchiquin has exclusive use of Taplow Great Common either side of the Taplow-to-Wooburn road, he'll no longer be able to turns his Christmas pig loose to root in the woods roundabouts. Now Inchiquin has ***The Gages*** and the close to the south (which will one day be the site of a hospital) and hundreds of acres of common land, Aldridge mutters. How much does he need?

The Rectory, Church Road / 8th February 1787

Reverend **George Hamilton** made no objection that certain tracks, including two that converge at ***The Three Feathers***, are to be upgraded to 40-foot wide roads and three sites are to be set aside for the excavation of gravel to surface the roads or chalk to make quick lime for mortar and the like. And he takes some solace that Inchiquin has assigned to the poor of the parish an allotment of an additional three acres together with six ***Taplow Common Cottages*** with an annual letting value of £36 4s (£62,100) of which £20 (£34,300) will be contributed to the Taplow Coal & Clothes Clubs and £4 (£6,700) to the Dropmore Coal Club with the remainder being expended in rates and upkeep.

However, other aspects of the award will remain a sore point for years between the 38th Rector and his lordship. Inchiquin is to have exclusive use of **Upper Thames Field** to north of the Bath Road and both **Long Meadow** and **Lower Thames Field** to the south of it. No longer will villagers be allocated arable land to rotate in strips. Instead three large fields – **Buffins** to the north of the village and **Town Field** and **Amerden Field** to the south – will be divided into larger blocks to be fenced and farmed by Inchiquin and 13 others. His lordship believes the Rector can take a comfortable living from 175 acres of glebe: 80 acres in Town Field, 60 scattered around Amerden Field and 35 in Buffins. **Nathaniel Newberry** has done well: he will hold some 25 acres in three closes. **George Johnstone** has two totalling about 5 acres. Small closes along the west of Town Field are assigned to **Elizabeth Colsell**, **Giles Colsell**, Elizabeth Galley and **George Davies** of New Windsor. Even smaller ones are to be allocated to Hitcham rectory, **Cate Pope** (daughter and heir of Andrew), R Styles, M Joslin, **Henry Colsell** and **Ann Viger**, whose holding is a remnant of her Uncle William's tenure at ***Taplow House***. And just 500 yards south of *The Three Feathers* a half-acre sliver along the eastern verge of not-yet Cliveden Road has been allocated to somebody called **Wogan**. Now there's a name to be banjaxed by [*see Maps 16, 17 & 18*].

Bound for Botany Bay

Aylesbury Assizes / 23rd July 1790

It is over five years since George Nugent-Temple-Grenville, **Earl Temple**, was created 1st Marquess of **Buckingham**. Today he presides as Chairman of the July Quarter Sessions for the Peace of Bucks. The clerk's records will show that **Thomas Sambourn**, "a young man of Taplow.... was tried for breaking into the temple, in the gardens of the Right Honourable the Earl of Inchiquin, at **Taplow Court** and taking from there 12 bound books, when he was found guilty and sentenced to be transported to Botany Bay for seven years". Lord Temple accepted testimony that "though not yet 19 years of age.... this artful villain reigned [as] the terror of the Village in which he lived, and of the neighbouring parishes of Cookham, Bourne End etc and has been guilty of almost every species of villainy".

Tom the Terror will be transported to New South Wales by the Third Fleet, almost certainly on one of eight ships which will set sail on 27th March 1791: one from Portsmouth, the others from Plymouth. Three other ships will join the fleet which in total will carry 2,057 convicts, 182 of whom will not survive the voyage. Their destination will not be Botany Bay, by then considered unsuitable for settlement, but Port Jackson where the city of Sydney is already beginning to grow.

The Luck of the Irishman

The third Taplow Court / 24th July 1792

Serendipity sometimes strikes in the darkest times and it has twice for Lord Inchiquin.

Three years ago with his wife Mary terminally ill, Murrough welcomed to his home Thomas Carter, a young man who had recently returned to England from India with a considerable sum he had earned singing at a benefit concert in Calcutta. Did the ailing lady know that Tom was probably her beloved husband's illegitimate son? Did she guess that Murrough had dented his impeccability with a little wandering back in 1766? It is likely that she died in May 1790 without ever knowing the truth about Tom, or that he lent his entire nest egg to his father to pay off a pressing debt. Next year Tom will marry Mary Wells and go on to have success as a singer at high society gatherings and later as a coal merchant content that he has helped his father keep the wolf from the door until tomorrow when a second slice of good fortune chases it away forever.

Gregories Court, Beaconsfield / 25th July 1792

It is pouring with rain yet again but the dreadful weather won't stop today's celebrations at Edmund Burke's fine mansion where his 69-year-old friend and widower **Murrough**, **Lord Inchiquin**, has married **Mary Palmer**, the 41-year-old spinster niece of Sir Joshua Reynolds. They had been acquainted throughout his long friendship with Reynolds – she had long been the eminent painter's housekeeper, well-loved companion and fellow artist at Leicester Fields – but it seems that the idea of being together has occurred to them only since her uncle passed away in February.

Mary must have been impressed by Murrough's strength despite his years when he was one of the pall-bearers at Sir Joshua's funeral in St Paul's Cathedral. Rumours abound that she has inherited £40,000 (£4.25m) from her uncle and intends to allocate half immediately "to relieve him from his encumberances". Such a sum would be enough to free Inchiquin of his creditors and thus save Clifden. How could he not be eager? However this is not the whole story. He has arranged for her an annual pension of £3,000 (£319,000). And she praises him with the words: "There is not such another man in the world; he is the best man in it. In trifles he is irritable in the extreme, but in everything of moment calm and firm, bearing whatever may happen with fortitude". This may be a marriage of convenience but it is clearly one based on genuine respect and affection. Murrough O'Brien is a very lucky lord.

Something's Burning

The Grand Staircase, Clifden / 20th May 1795

Murrough isn't feeling so lucky now. Clifden is ablaze. The sight is both awesome and awful. His daughter **Mary Fitzmaurice**, **Lady Orkney**, stumbles to safely down the grand staircase from the terrace. She was entertaining her father and his new wife Mary to dinner when a maid knocked a candle against the curtains while turning down her mistress's bed or reading in her

Map 16 – The Common: Inchiquin Inclosures

Dividing the Spoils

Primary Source: Inclosure Maps 1779/1787

Map 17 – The Village: Inchiquin Inclosures

Dividing the Spoils

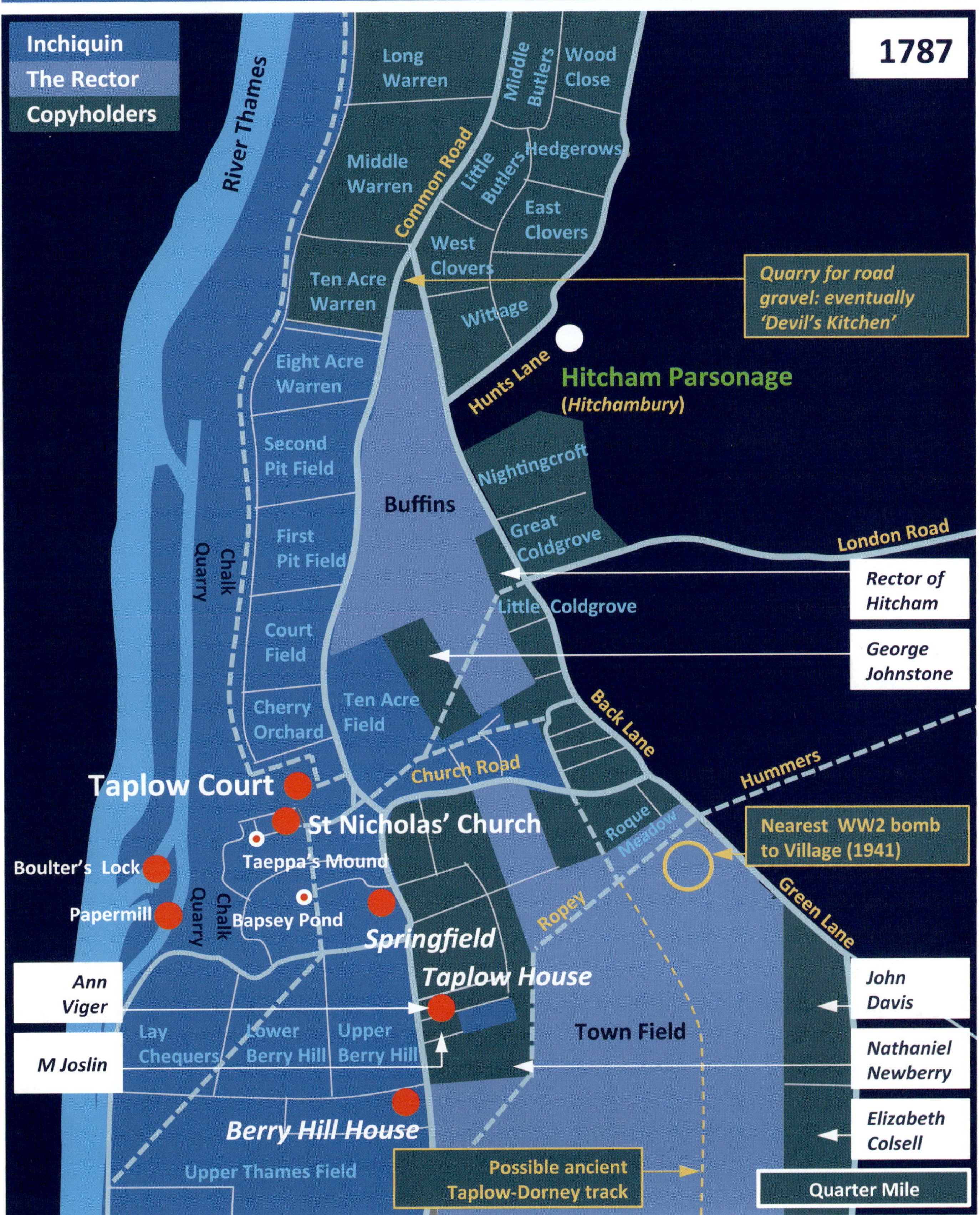

Primary Source: Inclosure Maps 1779/1787

Map 18 – The Valley: Inchiquin Inclosures

Dividing the Spoils

Remains of woolly rhinoceros, mammoth & musk ox (discovered 1854)

Elizabeth Colsell

1787

George Colsell

Elizabeth Galley

R Style

River Thames

Upper Thames Field

Town Field

The Orkney Arms

Foxholes

The Dumb Bell

Withy Close

Pits

Bath Road

Bucks Close

Ten Acres

Great Western Railway (1838)

Nathaniel Newbury

Henry Colsell

Cow Leys

Possible ancient Taplow-Dorney track

Latchmore

Lower Thames Field

Long Meadow

Amerden Field

Quarry for road gravel

George Johnstone

Marsh Lane

Devil's Lane

Late Andrew Pope

Dorney Corner

M4 Motorway (1964)

Barge Farm

Coneygears

Great Hack Field

Little Hack Field

Home Meadow

Barn Close

Late Steech

Amerden Bank

Dorney Piece

Amerden Marsh (Ash Field)

Inchiquin

The Rector

Copyholders

Quarter Mile

Primary Source: Inclosure Maps 1779/1787

own. George, Prince of Wales, can see the fire from Windsor but sends no aid despite knowing that Lady Orkney has no means to pump water. With friends like that, who needs enemies?

All had seemed so pleasant for Murrough and his pair of Marys after their recent traumas. His daughter had married well, or so it seemed. **Thomas Fitzmaurice** was the son of another distinguished Anglo-Irish Parliamentarian, John Petty-Fitzmaurice, 1st Earl of Shelburne, and the younger brother of William Petty, 2nd Earl of Shelburne, who was PM in 1782/83 [*see Appendix 1, Tree 7*]. Before his marriage in 1777, Thomas had dabbled in politics as MP for first Calne (Wiltshire) then Wycombe before focusing full-time on his commercial interests from 1779. His business was linen. He had fabric woven on his estates in Ireland and bleached in his factory at Lleweni Hall near Denbigh (North Wales) which he had erected in 1776 at a cost of £20,000 (£36.5m). He opened a shop in Chester and according to *The Gentlemen's Magazine* such was his success in manufacturing and retailing quality linen in the mid-1780s that he was dubbed "the Royal Merchant".

Perhaps this was a spot of journalistic exaggeration or perhaps Fitzmaurice had got a little too clever by half for, by the time his wife Mary succeeded her mother Mary as 4th Countess of Orkney in 1790, his business had fallen on hard times. He was struggling to pay his creditors the required £5,000 (£7.6m) a year. He and Mary have rather neglected **Clifden** but, when they failed to let it at an acceptable rate, their only option was to come to live here, constantly seeking economies.

The new Lady Orkney is just five years younger than the Mary who has become her stepmother. She was happy for her father to have found such a strong and vibrant shoulder to lean on and the Inchiquins returned the favour when she was widowed in 1793. Murrough and the Marys have continued to get together regularly and tonight was one such occasion. Now they stand aghast as the 129-year-old house is reduced to ashes in just four hours. Many heirlooms will be lost to the flames or to plundering locals and Lady Orkney will be without a change of clothes for the next day. Only the east wing will survive unscathed. She will make this her home as she counts losses estimated at £50,000 (£61m). Her father will have John Nash and George Repton design a new house in 1805 but it will never be built. Her only consolation will be to have Peter Nicholson build a 'gothic summer house' by Cliefden Spring. The burnt-out shell of Clifden will stand forlorn for 29 years.

Tall Tale – The Going of the Tapestries

The Great Hall, Clifden / 20th May 2012

There are conflicting stories about the fate of first Lord Orkney's fabulous ***Art of War* tapestries**. Some say they were saved, others that they went up in flames. All agree that the three here now were bought 98 years later by an American in Paris. Which is tall tale and which the truth?

Something's Burned

The remains of the second Hedsor House / 20th December 1795

Nobody can believe the events of this year – old Clifden destroyed by fire in May and **Sir William Chambers**' grand, brand new Hedsor House suffering the same fate a few months later. Both are shells beyond any prospects of habitation. Like gravestones, they are sad reminders of what was. And today is something of a funeral, a gathering to pay last respects and say goodbye.

The Reverend Ralph Leycester, Rector of Hedsor, is consoling his lord of the manor **Frederick Irby, 2nd Baron Boston**, and his wife Christian. Their neighbours the **Inchiquins**, the **Orkneys** and the **Grenvilles** are all here too. **King George III** and Queen Charlotte have sent their apologies: they are said to be almost as devastated at the loss of Hedsor as their friend Boston. Lord Grenville will come to his friend's aid by making available to him a plot of land for him to build a home within the parish of Hitcham but conveniently located on the edge of Taplow village.

A Good Living

The Rectory, Church Road / 20th December 1799

Twelve years of argument have seen off three rectors but Thomas Langley can give quiet thanks to St Nicholas that the Reverend Archibald Hamilton Cathcart has finally agreed to accept land in lieu of tithes and Lord Inchiquin's enclosures have been confirmed at last by an Act of Parliament. Thomas has been curate at St Nicholas' for over seven years. He confides that it had been all too much for the Reverend **George Hamilton** when the inclosure award threatened his living in 1787, and that while Inchiquin was always pleasant in his dealings with the Reverend William Paxton, he was intransigent when it came to money matters. Paxton's death towards the end of 1795 heralded a year of turmoil. It wasn't until April 1796 that Reverend Cathcart was 'presented' at the 40th Rector only for him to be gone before Michaelmas at the end of September. The official story was that, by taking up the rectorship of Kippax and Methley in Yorkshire (coincidentally the birthplace of Jane Vigor), Cathcart hopes to clear his way to being Prebendary of York. Gossip has it that he and Inchiquin couldn't abide each other. Maybe it was a bit of both. Yet somehow he retains the rectorship here despite rarely putting in an appearance. Some say his being the younger son of a baron is an advantage.

The Rectory, Church Road / 20th December 1805

The Reverend **Edward Vansittart Neale** is a very happy Rector. Now the tension with the lord of the manor is a thing of the past, he will enjoy a very nice 'living' for the next 45 years. The Rector's family is of Dutch origin. His great-grandfather Peter hailed from Sittard in the southern Netherlands to business success with both *The Russia Company* and *The East India Company*. Peter's son Arthur followed in his father's footsteps and – after youthful frolics at The Hellfire Club – Arthur's sons have trodden other paths to eminence. Robert was Regius Professor of Civil Law at Oxford University, Henry (of *Foxley's* in Bray) rose to be Governor of Bengal and Edward's father George did so well with *The East India Company* that he was said to be worth £150,000 (£274m) in 1776 when he settled at Bisham Abbey. Other Vansittarts have or will excel in politics, the church, foreign affairs and trade, the law, banking and the armed forces, none more so than Henry's son Nicholas who will be Chancellor of the Exchequer for longer than anyone in the 19th and 20th Centuries (11 years from 1812).

The Old Rectory, Rectory Road / 20th December 2012

Why did the Reverend Edward take the surname Neale (or Neal as it was styled in the Parish Register until 1808)? His wife Jane's maiden name was Gardiner and his mother Mary was a Boddam so it was no nod to his immediate females. Was it Christian modesty or a desire to avoid comparison that made him conceal his connections to the vaunted Vansittarts? The association didn't trouble his Taplow-born son **Edward Vansittart-Neale** who cultivated the hyphen as he grew up to be a Victorian barrister innovative in social reform, adult education and cooperative societies.

Pride before a Fall

The third Taplow Court / 2nd October 1801

Murrough O'Brien is admiring himself in the mirror. Doesn't he suit his new livery? It was all very well when King George III elevated him to 1st Marquess of Thomond in the Irish peerage at the end of last year. And it has only been with the exasperated support of the new Prime Minister Henry Addington that he has finally got his just deserts by being made Baron Thomond of Taplow in the English peerage. But wasn't it worth all the effort?

He had long aspired to higher rank and a salary to go with it. He first lobbied for an Irish marquessate in 1786 before setting his heart on British peerage. In 1794 he confided that he could do with a place of profit and that a seat on either the Treasury or Admiralty boards would not go amiss. He cherished the support of the influential Sir Thomas Dundas, 2nd Baronet, but was frustrated by the deaf ears turned with amazing grace by William Bentinck, 4th Duke of Portland, and the Prime Minister **William Pitt the Younger**. In 1797 he settled reluctantly for the consolation of becoming MP for Liskeard (Cornwall) and was rewarded two years later when Portland suggested that King George might appreciate his support for the idea of a new United Kingdom of Great Britain and Ireland.

Inchiquin needed no second invitation. He believed sincerely that Ireland would be safer if France could be prevented from interfering and, even better, if it were to join with England, Wales and Scotland in the United Kingdom. He invested his considerable influence towards this goal. When the **Acts of Union** were passed last year he was rewarded with his Irish peerage, an accolade he accepted with mixed feelings: the satisfaction of being regally appreciated and the disappointment of it not being the full English. A little more lobbying was required before the king said to Portland "He has been ill-used, but he shall not suffer for it; make out a writ for an English barony".

Grosvenor Square / 10th February 1808

The newly dubbed Thomond resorted once again to statuary to show his appreciation. The 1804 Coadestone statue of **King George III** as a Roman emperor stands proudly in the centre of an oval lawn in front of **Taplow Court**. Perhaps such a show of gratitude and affection stuck in the craw of the Prince of Wales who last year decided to cut Thomond dead socially for having the audacity to invite to dinner his brother and hated rival Prince Ernest, Duke of Cumberland. The old man was never the sort to fret about such an insult but sadly he hasn't had the time to avenge it. He died here today when he fell from his horse and was crushed by a market cart. His title will pass to his nephew **William O'Brien**, son of his brother James.

James Thomson / c1740

Thomas Arne
– Johann Zoffany c1760

Frederick, Prince of Wales
– Jean-Étienne Liotard 1754

Cliveden Amphitheatre / 2011

Illustrious Neighbours

Patrick Murray, 5th Lord Elibank
– William Anderson / 1862

The Vigor Family:
Jane, Ann, Joseph & William with (probably) John Penn
– Joseph Highmore 1744

Elibank / 2009

Murrough and his Marys

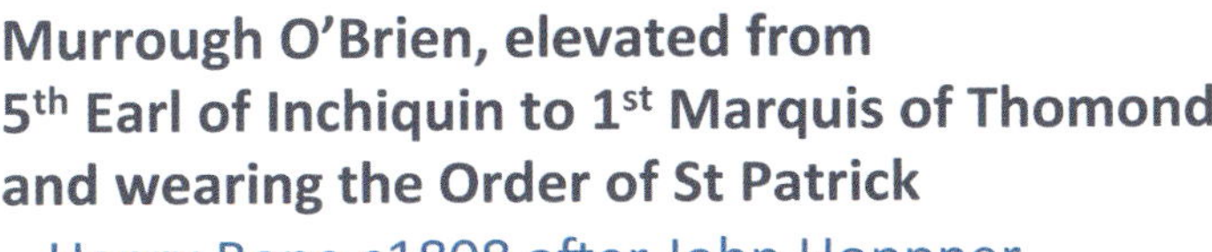

Murrough O'Brien, elevated from 5th Earl of Inchiquin to 1st Marquis of Thomond and wearing the Order of St Patrick
– Henry Bone c1808 after John Hoppner

Lady Mary O'Brien – Sir Joshua Reynolds c1772
Lady Mary O'Brien – after Thomas Lawrence 1800
Her age at the time of these portraits (22 and 45) suggests that both are of Murrough's daughter before and after she succeeded as 4th Countess of Orkney – but either or both may be of his first wife, 3rd Countess of Orkney, possibly painted 'after' earlier works
Mary Palmer – Sir Joshua Reynolds (her uncle) 1785
She became Murrough's third Lady Mary O'Brien when they married in 1792

Illustrious Neighbours

William Wyndham Grenville, 1st Baron Grenville
– John Hoppner 1800

Pascoe Grenfell
– Sir Martin Archer Shee 1818

Two New Normans

Grenville and Grenfell

Distant Cousins

Taplow House / 20th October 2012

At first glance the two newcomers were very different: one had made money, the other was made of it. One's family was Cornish metal merchants. The other's was Buckinghamshire blue-blood long in the national political elite. And yet it is possible that **Pascoe Grenfell** and **William Wyndham Grenville, 1st Baron Grenville**, shared a common ancestry. If they did, it went way back: probably to Grainville-la-Teinturière in Haute-Normandie and beyond [*see Appendix 1, Trees 1, 9 & 16*]. And some say a few of the Conqueror's genes crept in somewhere. They usually did. However this pair of possible cousins had contrasting fortunes when it came to raising a family. Grenville was the end of his line for he had no children. Grenfell had eleven who at the last count had given him over 340 direct descendants. They and their myriad Grenfell cousins are everywhere nowadays having spread from their Cornish origins throughout the UK and away to Australia, Canada, Mexico, Brazil and the USA.

In 1895 the Reverend Roger Granville claimed to have traced his line back to Rognvald the Mighty, a 9th Century Norwegian jarl whose great-times-three grandson Hamon Dentatus (the Toothy) fought for control of Normandy in 1047 but lost out to his third cousin William who had the edge when it came to conquering. Toothy's son Hamo Dapifer recovered to be Sheriff of Kent and lord of many manors there and in Essex. His son Richard fitzHamon de Grainville married Isabel, daughter of Walter Giffard, Duke of Buckingham. In the 15th Century the lesser progeny of Sir Thomas Grenville spread into the West Country and South Wales while their first-born siblings enjoyed their seat at Wootton Underwood in Aylesbury Vale, the ancestral home of a series of sheriffs of Buckinghamshire and Bedfordshire that eventually produced William Grenville who in 1792 will begin to transform **Dropmore** from a wilderness to a paradise.

Other family lines experimented with spelling; amongst many others they tried for size Greynville, Glandfelde, Greenfield, Grendfield and Grienfield. Somewhere in the mix were Richard de Glanville (who founded Neath Abbey in 1130), Sir Roger Grenville (captain of Henry VIII's *Mary Rose* when she sank off Spithead in 1545) and his son Sir Richard Grenville (cousin of Sir Walter Raleigh and Sir Francis Drake, admiral of the fleet that took New World settlers to Roanake Island in 1585 and hero of *The Revenge* which valiantly fought alone against 53 Spanish galleons in 1591). The Cornish branch becomes clearer as it extends from Sir Thomas de Granville (who died in 1513 at Stow in Devon) to Pazko Grinfil of St Just in Penwith (who pledged his allegiance to the Lord Protector Oliver Cromwell in 1658) and Paskow Grenfield (born in 1692 at Penzance). His sons Pascoe and William took Grenfell as their name and made it known in the big, wide world. They were successful merchants of Cornish copper and tin ores and products. Pascoe also became Commissary to the States of Holland and four times mayor of Marazion only for his son Pascoe Grenfell to stride even further into the spotlight – not least by making **Taplow House** his home in 1794 and having **Joe Springall** laying out the grounds and tending to the tulip trees. Good Queen Bess would be pleased if these really were her work. It is more likely they were Joe's.

Pascoe Grenfell & Sons

The Copper Age

Temple House, Bisham / 30th November 1802

The world's richest Welshman died today. It could be said that **Thomas Williams** of Llanidan (Anglesey) set Pascoe Grenfell a fine example of how not to live life and behave in business. It can't be denied that the pair began and sustained the Copper Age in the middle Thames Valley.

Williams was originally a lawyer who, in around 1779 more by accident than design, had become the managing partner of the Parys Copper Mine in Anglesey. He established himself as the undisputed 'Copper King' through a ruthless determination to shape his products, his operation and his marketplace in order to profit at all costs. He tirelessly fought cartels and competitors, often by acquiring them as he did Bisham's Temple Mills in 1788. His industrial and organisational innovation created an efficient vertical commercial operation that mined ore in North Wales and Cornwall, smelted it in Bisham, Swansea and St Helens (Lancashire), and manufactured and finished copper and brass products in West Glamorgan, Flintshire and at Wraysbury (then in Buckinghamshire). Matthew Boulton of *Boulton & Watt* steam engine fame regards Williams as "the despotick sovereign of the copper trade [and] a perfect tyrant.... not over tenacious of his word and will screw damn hard when he has got anybody in his vice". These characteristics were evident when he invested £70,000 (£99m) in making copper trinkets to be used to buy slaves in West Africa, and in 1788 when the government debated a motion to prevent British ships from continuing in the slave trade, he petitioned strongly against it. Another of his clever ideas was to produce copper bolts to fix copper sheeting to timber naval vessels and sell them to both friend and foe. And he also ran his own mint, as if he wasn't making enough money.

The second Taplow House / 30th November 1802

Pascoe Grenfell came to London in the mid-1780s as an agent for his father and uncle. He was just 25 when in 1786 he married his cousin Charlotte Granville who died in 1790 four weeks after the birth of their third son, **Charles Pascoe Grenfell**. Suddenly he was a widower with four children to care for. Williams had long been impressed by the young man's experience in the copper and tin industry. He seized the moment to make Grenfell an offer he couldn't refuse. The Cornishman soon rose to become principal manager of the Welshman's company.

Williams had settled at *Temple House*, a fine mansion he had built for himself at Bisham, and in 1790 began 12 years as MP for Great Marlow, a role he shared from 1796 with his son Owen. Did the elder Williams introduce Grenfell to the area, or was there some family link with his great-uncle William Borlase, a Cornish geologist and antiquarian who may have been related to the Marlow branch of the Borlase family? Grenfell's move to Taplow in 1794 brought him into new social circles and four years later to a second marriage. Georgiana St Leger gave him six daughters and two sons – Riversdale William Grenfell and Pascoe St Leger Grenfell – who with their half-brother Charles Pascoe Grenfell set a family trend for requiring the use of all their Christian names in order to have a chance of telling one from another [*see Appendix 1, Tree 16*].

Grenfell will emerge with credit from the shadow of the domineeringly successful Welshman to pursue parallel careers in politics and in business. He has recently acquired Shoppenhangers and Ives (Boyne Hill) and will this year take two strides by launching an independent copper trading business in London contracted to Owen Williams and by being elected to serve alongside him as MP for Great Marlow. He will add Bray to his local landholdings in 1818 as he establishes an enviable reputation as a zealous slave trade abolitionist, a great authority on finance, a vigilant observer and critic of the Bank of England and a loyal ally of three notable English Whigs, Samuel Whitbread, Samuel Romilly and Henry Brougham, and three prominent Irish ones, Henry Grattan, George Ponsonby and the famous playwright Richard Sheridan, author in 1777 of *The School for Scandal*. His business will expand to Swansea, Liverpool and Flintshire and in 1820, as he begins six years as MP for Penrhyn, he will diversify by founding his own firm, ***Pascoe Grenfell & Sons***, to manufacture copper products in Swansea. And in 1829 he will become governor of the *Royal Exchange Assurance Company*, an eminent post he will hold until his death in 1838.

Family Fortunes

The Old Churchyard / 27th January 1838

It is four days since Pascoe Grenfell breathed his last at his London home of N° 38 Belgrave Square. Today his three sons are here to witness his interment in the family vault by the ruins of the old St Nicholas' Church. All three will make significant achievements in life. **Charles Pascoe Grenfell** has been a director of the Bank of England since 1830 and will continue in that position until 1864. Pascoe St Leger Grenfell will succeed his brother Riversdale William Grenfell at the helm of the family firm in 1844. They will sell ***Taplow House*** later this year to Murrough O'Brien's nephew and successor **William O'Brien, 2nd Marquess of Thomond**, who will sprinkle Springall's creation with sequoias, oaks and other marvellous trees while **George Basevi** remodels the house. The Doric columns in the entrance hall and the staircase, with its elaborate chiselled brass balusters and exquisite wrought ironwork, will be cautiously credited to this reputable architect.

The Old Churchyard / 27th October 2012

The mid-19th Century was a time when rapid expansion and innovation in trade and colonialism really coalesced into Empire. British commercial ambition had long been built on borrowing and investment. Both depend on a sound financial environment in which there is confidence in the currency, the economy is stable, promises are trustworthy and returns can be relied upon. That was where Charles Pascoe Grenfell came in, especially after 1844 when the Bank of England was given sole rights to issue banknotes and their value was tied to the gold reserve. The quiet contribution of Grenfell and his ilk to the UK's ascendency is easily overlooked. It shouldn't be.

In 1819 Charles married Lady Georgiana Molyneux, daughter of William Molyneux, 2nd Earl of Sefton, who gave him four healthy children before her fifth pregnancy ended tragically for both mother and the daughter who shared her Christian name. He never married again but instead sought solace in a successful career in banking, business and politics. Soon after his father died, he became a director and eventually chairman of the *London, Brighton & South Coast Railway* before turning to politics in 1847 when he was first elected as MP for Preston, a constituency he was to serve for 13 of the next 18 years. His elder son Charles William Grenfell married Georgiana Lascelles and had five children as he served in the 2nd Middlesex Militia and as MP for Sandwich then Windsor (1847/59). His younger son **Henry Riversdale Grenfell** represented Stoke-on-Trent (1862/68), served as a Justice of the Peace and Lord-Lieutenant of the City of London and then went one better than his father by becoming Governor of the Bank of England (1881/83).

Under Pascoe the Younger, *Pascoe Grenfell & Sons* grew to dominate Swansea where more than 600 furnaces smelted half the world's copper ore. As a benevolent employer, he built model housing for his 800-plus employees and had not one single strike or lock-out in more than 30 years. As a great benefactor to the city, he built a concert hall, All Saints' Church and schools for over 1,000 children. There was no doubt method in his philanthropy – his leadership of the development of Swansea's harbour and docks was a boon to his own shipping line as it transported raw materials and finished products – but his active humanitarianism was admired by his contemporaries and especially by his nine children. His daughters Madelina and Mary won immense respect and affection for the zeal and dedication with which they funded local churches and hospitals, and Mary devotedly nursed the poor. And his son Field Marshall Francis Wallace Grenfell achieved national fame for his heroism in South Africa (1873/79) and his military leadership in Egypt (1882/99).

William Wyndham Grenville, 1st Baron Grenville

The Greatest Stage

Dropmore Park / 15th April 1792

Lord **Grenville** smiles as he stands back to admire the two cedar trees he has just planted on this, the first day of his life at Dropmore. Buckinghamshire has long been his family's home. Now this sparse little bit of it is his.

Grenville is related either by blood or marriage to just about anybody who is, was or will be somebody, including royalty. His mother Elizabeth Wyndham was even very distantly related by marriage to the Inchquins. His father-in-law Sir William Wyndham had been an ally of **Bolingbroke** as an MP for Somerset with a Jacobite tendency. His great-uncle, the great Whig icon **Richard Temple, 1st Viscount Cobham**, mentored *Cobham's Cubs* including his father **George Grenville** and his maternal uncle **William Pitt the Elder**, 1st Earl of Chatham, both of whom served terms as PM in the 1760s [*see Appendix 1, Tree 9*]. His paternal uncle Captain Thomas Grenville died in 1747 fighting the French at the Battle of Cape Finisterre, a victory which helped secure British naval ascendancy. His elder brother George spent five years as MP for Buckingham before succeeding as **Lord Temple** in 1779 and in 1784, having been a Privy Counsellor for two years, he was created 1st Marquess of Buckinghamshire. And once the noted architect **Sir John Soane** has completed the extension of ***Berry Hill House***, his widowed sister Lady Charlotte Williams-Wynn will be just a short ride away.

These Grenville gentlemen have been some of the biggest players on the greatest stage in the country during a period of significant international turbulence in which the competing ambitions of France, Spain and Great Britain have led rulers to rile their people and the people to change the rules. Pitt the Elder will be seen as the first real British Imperialist but George Grenville will carry the can for thinking it only fair in 1765 that New World colonists should share the cost of a seven-year war fought to keep them from becoming French. Their outrage and his aggressive foreign policy combined to convince George III to dismiss Grenville but one thing had already led to another and the king had the American War of Independence on his plate. It was far away but emotionally close to home. It rocked Great Britain's very being.

It is ten years since William Grenville was elected as Tory MP for Buckingham and nine since his cousin **William Pitt the Younger** became Prime Minister. Things were just getting back on an even keel when the French were revolting in 1789. Britons had a grandstand view as their nearby rivals tore themselves apart. This was all very nice to see but the smug mood is changing all too quickly to fear and trepidation now the French seem intent on exporting revolution. Grenville served as Paymaster of the Forces, Speaker of the House of Commons and Home Secretary before being elevated two years ago to the House of Lords as 1st Baron Grenville. He has weathered the unkind wit of his cousin Lady Hester Stanhope making much fun of his 'broad bottom' – a tease pertinent for both its physical accuracy and its hark back to his father serving in Henry Pelham's coalition government which was satirised in 1744 by caricaturist James Gillray as the 'Broad Bottom Ministry'. Last year he became Leader of the House of Lords and Foreign Secretary, positions he will hold throughout the coming decade of French Revolutionary Wars. He will be steadfast in his belief that Great Britain's most valuable contribution is to support continental coalition armies with naval action, and always a man of great resilience and dexterity able to somehow juggle national interests with his own need to savour the loves of his life: a lady called Anne and the woods of Dropmore.

Away to the Woods

Dropmore Park / 15th April 1796

There are dark clouds of war over Europe but Lord Grenville will allow nothing to cast a shadow over his happiness today in this "wild track of woodlands and heath", this "bleak and barren spot where.... neither tree nor shrub and scarce a blade could be seen" which he intends to make a paradise. Some call it *One Tree Hill*, to others it is *Drapmore Hill* or *Dropmer Hill*. It was once *Droppingwell*, a name first noted in 1368 which is thought to derive from a much less poetic feature: the sink holes on the heath, some up to 15 feet deep, where underlying chalk had dissolved causing subsidence of surface clays [*see Map 19*].

Grenville's face glows as he tells the tale of how, during schoolboy rambles from Eton and while enjoying Orkney hospitality with his father George at ***Clifden***, he fell in love with the place for its wilderness and set his heart on making his home in these woods. In January 1792 he reached agreement with John Popple of Burnham to lease three acres of common land belonging to Burnham parish and then took possession of 30 adjoining acres around *Dropmore Lodge*: "so mere a cottage [that requires] some small addition to it in order to make it at all habitable". Three months after planting those first cedars he married **Anne Pitt**, the first cousin of his own first cousin William Pitt the Younger. It was a marriage of convenience that grew to be a marriage of hearts: they shared Christian values, simple tastes and her large dowry. "The mildness and gentleness of his nature, temper'd with a firmness that belongs to a manly character" gradually mollified her sharp temper. Her tendency to indolence was overcome by his "zeal and earnest application" and she joined his mission with enthusiasm. They engaged the architect **Samuel Wyatt** to replace the original lodge with *Dropmore House*, an elegant brick and timber mansion faced with painted stucco to give an appearance of Italian stonework.

The Grenville's grand horticultural venture was delayed by an exceptionally heavy and persistent deluge from July to September and it was another month before the sodden ground had dried enough for planting to begin. On 6th November they took delivery of 2,000 birch saplings, a present from his brother Lord Temple. The following day Lord Grenville sent a letter of thanks confirming the arrival of the trees and adding that they were unpacked "in the middle of such a fog as I have never seen before. They will answer admirably well for my purpose and will make a great figure on my hill in the course of the next century or so". He and Lady Anne spent the December fretting that storm-force winds would blow the birches away. They may have been the icing on the fraternal cake for it seems that Temple had paid £3,000 (£4.6m) to fund his brother's acquisition of the 30 acres from the Copper King's younger son **John Williams** of *Shardeloes* at Amersham.

Luckily 1793 brought perfect conditions for the Grenvilles to join the agricultural revolution. They have been working hard to improve soil conditions at ***Brook End*** and elsewhere by digging in as much manure and soot as they could acquire – what a job it was to have it ferried on barges upriver to Hedsor Wharf and hauled inch-by-inch up the steep hill by a waggon-and-eight – and they've scoured the country for the very best seed and livestock. New trees keep coming: a Cedar of Lebanon planted two years ago is the first in an avenue that will grow to half-a-mile long. One hill has been lowered to afford a better view of Windsor Castle and another raised so Harrow may be seen from its crest. Grenville announces with amusement that this is called Root Hill for being made of tree stumps and gravel but he doesn't explain why an old Etonian would want to see Harrow. He is too busy planning his next projects: new roads to divert travellers away from *Dropmore House* and a subterranean ice house that will be insulated with hay and filled in winter with ice from estate ponds [*see Map 20*].

Map 19 – The Common: Before Grenville
Still a Wilderness

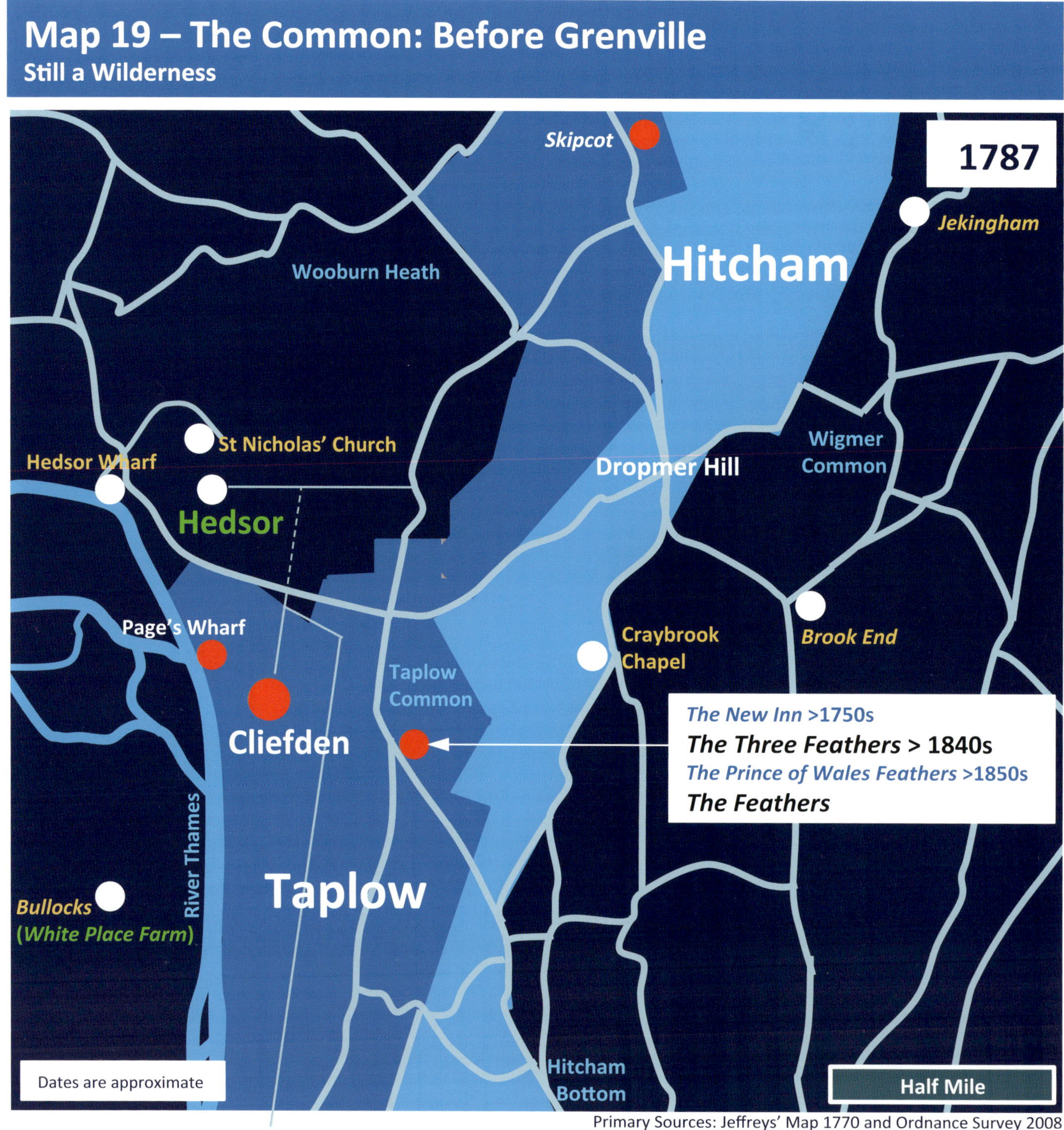

Primary Sources: Jeffreys' Map 1770 and Ordnance Survey 2008

Triumph and Disaster – United Kingdom, Divided Faiths

The Houses of Parliament, Westminster / 1st August 1800

Lord **Inchiquin** is here to congratulate the Williams **Pitt** and **Grenville** on the passing of the second of two acts that on the first day of next year will create the United Kingdom of Great Britain and Ireland. Grenville has long believed fervently in freedom of religion and passionately supports Pitt's promise of Catholic emancipation throughout the new UK. Ever since France sent troops to support the Irish Rebellion of 1798, he has felt that union was only way to restore order, end sectarianism and ensure Ireland would not be a staging post for a French invasion.

Inchiquin can't stop smiling. Would the anticipation of his forthcoming elevation in the Irish peerage be diminished if he knew that this first tumultuous crescendo in Grenville's many-splendoured career will shortly be succeeded by a discordant sforzando? The cousins will resign on the point of principle on 16th February 1801 when King George declines to accept Catholic emancipation because he feels it would violate his Coronation Oath.

The French Revolutionary Wars will finally end in March 1802 only for a more familiar kind of war to break out 14 months later. Napoleon Bonaparte's seemingly irresistible surge to spread his French empire across Europe will be frightening but not in the least confusing. No more moral navel-gazing about who makes the rules. It will be backs-to-the-wall for the British and that they know. King George III will turn once more to Pitt the Younger in May 1804. Having in Opposition edged towards the Whigs,

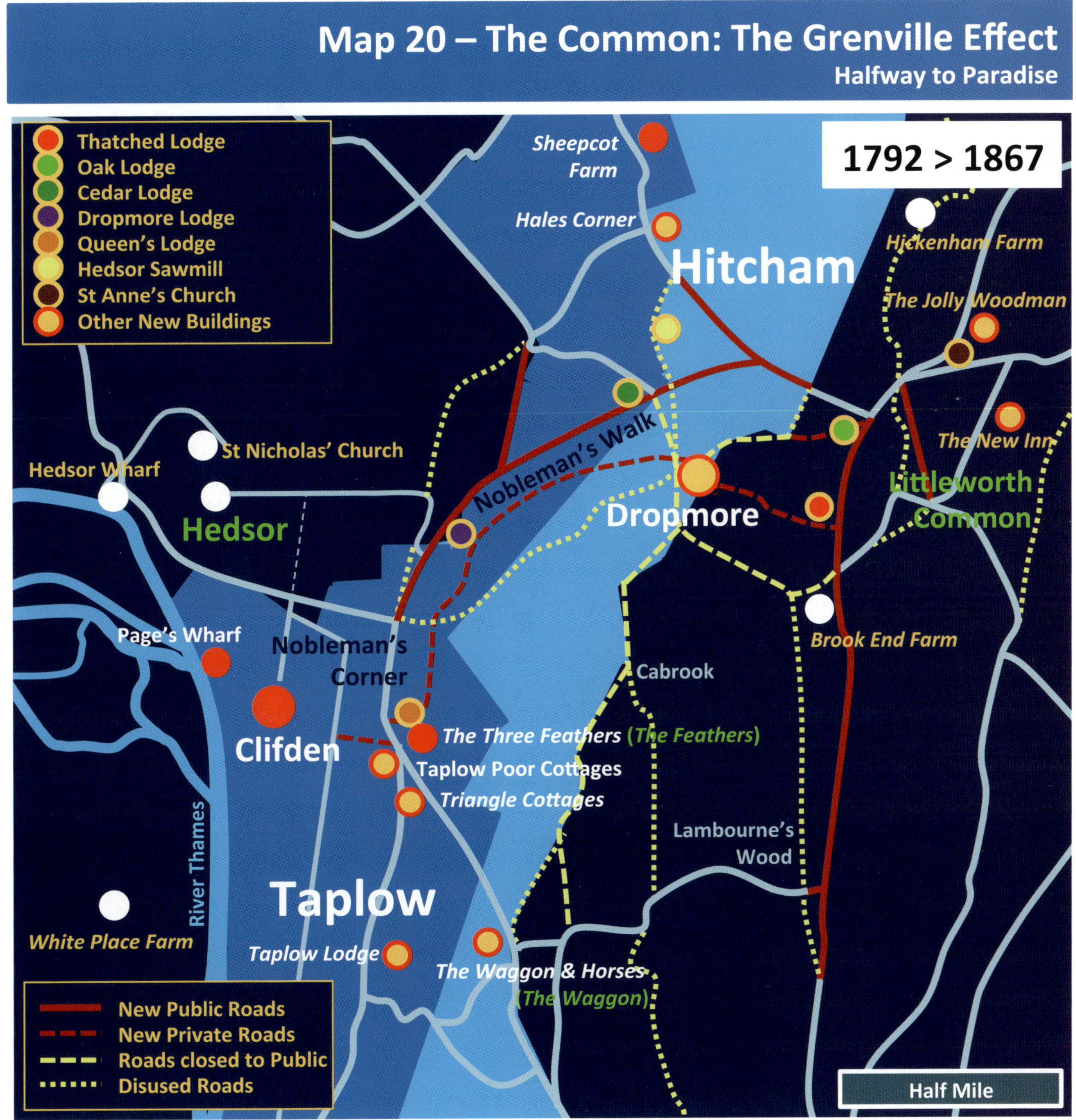

Primary Sources: Bryant's Map 1824 and Ordnance Survey 2008

Grenville will not join his cousin's second government but who will the king turn to in January 1806 when Pitt's poor health finally catches up with him and the country is left leaderless with the threat of Napoleonic invasion at its height?

Expanding the Empire – Hitcham

The remains of the original Hitcham House / 15th September 1804

Hemmed in as they are to the west by Hedsor and Clifden, the Grenvilles have begun to spread south and east to increase his electoral advantage and guarantee the tranquillity of their domain. Lesser mortals have warmed to the reflected glory of the great man or perhaps to his readiness to pay a good price for their estates. John Symonds of *Britwell Court* was first to succumb in 1794. He bought ***Chapel Farm*** from William Lee Antonie in 1795 and the following year secured some of Hitcham by means of a land swap and acquisitions of glebe land. Later this year the Reverend **William Maximillian Freind** will be unable to resist taking £17,500 (£20.25m) for the rest of Hitcham Manor and sundry other land. Although it is said that *Hitcham House* once boasted portraits from the time of King Charles I, the Commonwealth and King Charles II, there will be no record of whether they were included in Grenville's acquisition.

Lord Grenville has never been on quite such relaxed and intimate terms with George III as his noble neighbours – the price of being a political animal, no doubt – but they enjoy cordial relations with each other and often share strategic interests. Grenville has combined effectively with Lord Boston and Lady Orkney to make sure that two canal schemes to link the Thames with the Grand Union Canal got lost in the long grass: the first from Hedsor to Hillingdon, the second from Boltus Lock to Cowley.

He was content to sell Britwell to Boston only to find himself in friendly competition with his friend when they both opened public schools, the first in the area. Boston's at Britwell Court was a pre-Eton prep school but Grenville was more ambitious. His school in ***Hitcham Manor House*** offered an alternative to Eton. Having visited the school earlier this year, Joseph Farington recorded its headmaster Dr Gretton speaking of his good fortune at being paid £700 (£361,000) a year to have 26 boys under his tuition, and also remarking candidly that "the bane of public schools is that the parents of many of the boys fill their pockets with bank notes, and opportunity is allowed for the expenditure of it viciously", that "the youth at Eton are dissipated gentlemen; those at Westminster dissipated, with a little of the blackguard; those at St Paul's the most depraved of all" and that "Rugby was on a bad footing (because) many are sons of manufacturers at Birmingham, Wolverhampton &c, who having little sentiment of the disgrace of anything dishonourable, act as their inclinations lead them".

Sadly the inclinations of Gretton's pupils led them astray and their *alma mater* was destroyed in a fire soon afterwards. The 14th Century home of the Ramsay, Clarke, Nicholas and Freind families is no more than a charred timber frame and precarious piles of smoke-blackened bricks. Perhaps the memory of the sad sight will galvanise Grenville in 1811 to join others in subscribing to supplement the £500 (£643,000) left in 1796 by Lady Anne Ravensworth of *Britwell Court* (widow of Henry Liddell, 1st Baron Ravensworth) to open the first National School on **The Gore** at Burnham in order to provide religious learning and basic reading and writing to pupils from Burnham, Hitcham and Taplow. This tri-parish school will survive until the National School in Taplow is expanded and new elementary schools are built in Burnham and Hitcham. It will close in 1871 and be converted by local builder George Almond into two pairs of cottages with a new third pair at the northern end to create a little terrace that will still be there in 2012.

Triumph and Disaster – Abolition, Resignation

The Prince of Wales Feathers Inn / 25th March 1807

It is precisely 407 days since King George asked Lord Grenville to lead a coalition government dubbed the 'Ministry of All the Talents'. High hopes matched the grand title but it has achieved precious little – neither Catholic emancipation nor peace with France has been attainable – and yet today is a day to celebrate. A messenger has just stumbled across the road from Cliefden's main gate and through the open door of ***The Prince of Wales Feathers Inn*** with the news that Parliament has just voted to abolish the slave trade. Abolitionist leaders William Wilberforce and Thomas Clarkson have often visited the Prime Minister at ***Dropmore*** to persuade, propose strategy and perhaps even to assist in drafting the necessary legislation, but everyone is still astounded that the act has been passed by an overwhelming majority of 267 votes.

The United Kingdom is not the first country to declare the slave trade illegal. France did so in 1789 only to reverse the decision in 1804. Denmark and Norway did so in 1792 but their ban didn't come into effect until 1803. And besides, none of the above had what it took to really, really make a difference. Napoleon is invincible in Europe but Britannia rules the waves and, once her mind is made up, it is not in her nature to waive the rules. Fines of £100 (£102,000) will be imposed for every slave found aboard a British ship and the Royal Navy is to be authorised to free slaves from all ships, British and otherwise. And yet in just six days will come the stunning news that spiteful political in-fighting has brought down Grenville's government. With his second crescendo brought to the same abrupt halt as the first, he will find solace once more at Dropmore.

Home Comforts – Design for Living

Dropmore House / 15th September 1808

The architect **Charles Tatham** has completed three years work expanding and improving *Dropmore House*, perhaps using some of the bricks rescued from the ruins of the old *Hitcham Manor House*. The Grenville's grand home has six receptions rooms and over 20 bedrooms all elegantly finished and graced with valuable Sevres china, fine art by such as Thomas Gainsborough and Sir Anthony van Dyke and many rare books and manuscripts including Grenville's own translation of Homer and *The Dropmore Papers*, his cabinet correspondence during the French Revolutionary Wars.

Expanding the Empire – Burnham

Allards Manor House, East Burnham / 15th September 1812

Grenville is gradually expanding Dropmore Park through acquisition of other adjacent manors and the enclosure of common land stretching across **Wooburn**, **Hitcham** and **Littleworth Commons** and the areas of **Taplow Great Common** that Lord Inchiquin had fought so long to enclose. Having recently acquired the scattered **Burnham Abbey** lands from the executors of the late **George Villiers**, he is now negotiating with John Popple a reversion that will entitle him to relocate **Huntercombe**'s beautiful wrought iron *Evelyn Gates* to grace the Italian Garden at ***Dropmore***. They will still be there in 200 years.

Popple's wife Arabella is the last of the Eyre family which has held Allards (including Burnham Beeches) since about 1500 and Huntercombe too since 1705. Grenville and Popple are thick as thieves, not least because of their recent alliance with Sir Robert Harvey of *Langley Park* to prevent the Berkeley Hunt and its foxhounds causing damage, a precaution necessary because (according to Popple) "we are all anxious to raise a stock of pheasants" (presumably to shoot in their own hunts, so the birds weren't reprieved for long).

Peace at Last

Dropmore Park / 21st June 1815

The woods are damp and dripping. William Wilberforce senses a movement to his right and turns to take in the marvellous sight of a green woodpecker crouching low as it forages for ants. The bird looks him warily in the eye as he watches in awe. Suddenly a scream disrupts the moment and a flash of electric-blue and white spurts across the scene. Wilberforce can't help but follow the flight of the jay and when he glances back, the woodpecker is gone. He smiles with quiet irony only for his reverie to be interrupted again, this time by a young lad crashing through the undergrowth to bring the astonishingly good news from **Lord Grenville** that three days ago the heroic Lord Wellington defeated the upstart Napoleon on the fields of Waterloo in Belgium. Wilberforce reflects that his countrymen have been at war with the French for the best part of 23 years; can it really be that there is peace at last?

Home Comforts – Natural Harmony

Dropmore Aviary / 15th September 1831

The greater Grenville domain now extends over more than 2,600 acres with Dropmore at its heart. The circular 600-acre park has one of the United Kingdom's earliest arboreta with over 4,000 trees of 200 species including a pinetum that is the biggest collection of conifers in the country and considered the finest in Europe. The pines shelter rare species of ferns, laurels, azaleas and rhododendrons, all carefully acquired or gratefully received as gifts. The ornamental lake is well-stocked with fish which when caught by his lordship are carefully marked and thrown back. Silt from the lake is used to mulch trees starved by the poor soil. To the west of the house is a 200-yard wall dressed with long runs of pergolas, decorative trellises and, since 1820, this twelve-foot high three-winged aviary elaborately decorated with cupolas and enclosed by a red cast-iron trellis with blue and green Chinese ceramic tiles on its base, columns and frieze. To the south, the formal gardens dance with colourful flowers set around a grotto, a pool, a rockwork arch, two Greek temples, a Chinese pavilion and a dairy where guests can watch fresh milk being drawn. And there is *Tippo's Tomb*. One can only wonder how this dog, the lone survivor of a shipwreck off Tenby, came to be laid to rest at Dropmore.

There is ample rough grassland for grazing cattle, sheep and pigs at farms within Dropmore – ***Brook End***, ***Abby's Park*** and ***Chapel Farm*** – and others further afield such as *Jekingham*, *Jennings* (*Starveall*) and ***Skipcot*** (*Sheepcote*). Lady Anne is indulging her romantic vision of the simple life in the rustic and picturesque design and construction of ***Cadbrook Cottage*** and the lodges that preside over Dropmore's various gates. She has even incorporated old carved chests and blocks used for printing cotton in the fabric of that by the north-east gate which was *Swiss Lodge*, is *Dropmore Lodge* and will be ***Oak Lodge***. The eastern boundary boasts two other gates either side of *Brook End Farm*: the southernmost – *Pale Gate* (or *Green Gate*) – has no lodge but ***Thatched Lodge*** (also known as *Wicker Work*, *Burnham* or *Brook End Lodge*) presides over Dropmore's main gate. There are another two gates on the western boundary: *Cabrook* or *Keeper's Lodge* will be ***Dropmore Lodge*** and, further up ***Nobleman's Walk***, ***Cedar Lodge*** (or *Wooburn Lodge*) watches over what is effectively the tradesmens' entrance because it is closest to the house. Still the Grenvilles aren't finished: with Popple's passing ***Allards*** and *Huntercombe* have finally reverted to them after a wait of 19 years. His lordship will be quick to plant at *Huntercombe* two magnolias, a Venetian stomach tree and his widowed sister Elizabeth Proby, Countess of Carysfort, which she will enjoy until her death in 1842. After her husband's passing in 1834, Lady Anne will let her leasehold of Burnham Abbey lapse and she will demolish *Allards Manor House* while retaining the rest of their holdings and her matriarchal role in the locality for 29 long years thereafter. She will come to rely heavily upon **Philip Frost**, a Cornishman from *Boconnoc* who first joined the gardening staff at Dropmore as a 15-year-old in 1822. Frost left five years ago and is now a foreman at the Botanic Gardens in Chelsea but will return next year to succeed Mr Baillie as Head Gardener, a position he will hold for 55 years until his death in 1887.

Home Comforts – A Dream Realised

Dropmore House / 25th August 1839

Lord Grenville remained politically active in Opposition until 1823 when a stroke led to his retirement from the national stage. His public impact had had its day but his imagination had not. He spent most of his last 11 years at ease in the wooded parkland he had created, always thinking up schemes to make it even better. When plans emerged in 1829 for the demolition of London Bridge, it was suggested to his lordship that he might like to have two of its smaller arches. He shared the dream with Lady Anne only to pass away in 1834 without seeing it realised but now his widow has finally had one of the old bridge's stone alcoves reconstructed as a grotto at Dropmore. And when the young **Queen Victoria** pays a visit in a few years, she will be delighted to see his aviary "filled with singing canaries". Grenville is rightly revered for ending the slave trade. He should also be remembered for making Dropmore a delight.

Return to Indolence

The History Hut, Burnham Beeches / 25th August 1853

It is 15 years since Harriet & George Grote first came to live at East Burnham and three since they moved to this smaller home they had built to their tastes. She is a biographer, he a classical historian: hence the name of their home. They share a philosophical radicalism with their guest John Stuart Mill, who listens carefully to her tale of woe.

They say Lady Anne was at Dropmore recently "going about in a bath chair or, in bad weather, in a miniature chariot known as 'The Box', drawn by her little grey pony Polly". Nowadays the old lady prefers life at *Boconnoc* near Lostwithiel in Cornwall. She rarely visits her Buckinghamshire estates and they have been badly neglected. Nobody farms at *Chapel Farm* at **Cabrook** any more. Estate roads are in a poor state of repair; so are the cottages and lodges. Tenants are denied common rights to cut peat or coppiced wood for their fires.

As an economist, Mill had been in favour of inclosure but Harriet's knowledge and sense of injustice weighs heavily on him. Her first-hand experience of the problems caused by loss of common rights will influence his efforts to preserve common land and lead directly to his involvement in the creation of Epping Forest in 1878. No doubt Lord William Grenville would have been pleased with the consequence of his widow's return to indolence in her dotage.

Grenville's Delight

Dropmore House – J Gendall 1823

Gathering Clouds

John Hamilton Fitzmaurice, Viscount Kirkwall

Dark before Dawn

Elibank, Church Road / 24th May 1811

Lord Kirkwall can breathe more easily now. The long and acrimonious legal dispute with his step-grandmother-in-law **Mary O'Brien**, the dowager **Marchioness of Thomond**, has been resolved in his favour and he has finally received the £4,000 (£3.77m) he has always believed was due to him from his grandfather's estate. This will be enough for him to recover from his bankruptcy. Today he has acquired ***Elibank*** in trust from **Alexander Murray** and tomorrow he will recover Taplow and *Amerden Farm*. Surely this silver lining heralds a new dawn?

Thomond's parting three years ago put a considerable strain on his Marys, widow and daughter. The Marchioness was initially so distraught that **Mary Fitzmaurice, 4th Countess of Orkney**, sympathetically avoided mention of her right to Taplow Court and forbade her son Lord Kirkwall from doing so. In time, the elder Mary gradually recovered to resume painting and doing do her best for her the memory of her uncle, Sir Joshua Reynolds. Her persistence has resulted in John Flaxman's statue of Reynolds being placed beneath the dome of St Paul's Cathedral and a late self-portrait being hung at Windsor Castle by the Prince of Wales, now the Prince Regent and well on his way to being King George IV. But she remained either blithely unaware of her step-daughter's difficult financial circumstances or carefully ignored them despite Clifden being uninhabitable and Kirkwall suffering bankruptcy.

The young man had started out well enough by buying himself into Parliament as MP for Heytesbury (Wiltshire) in 1799 and then transferring to represent the nearby constituency of Downton under the influential sponsorship of Jacob Pleydell-Bouverie, 2nd Earl of Radnor. He built a solid military career rising from a lieutenant in the Buckinghamshire Yeomanry in 1797 to a lieutenant-colonel commanding the Denbigh Militia in 1808 only for the burden of debt left by his father to gradually become too heavy. It might have been different if he hadn't broken his engagement to Mary Jane Ormsby in 1802 to marry Anna Maria, daughter of John Blaquiere, 1st Baron de Balquiere, who had taken a house in Taplow with the match in mind. His wife's annual income was £600 (£694,000); as heir to the Godolphin fortune, his former fianc**é**e's was £8,000 (£9.25m).

Three years later Kirkwall kept solvent only by two drastic measures: he sold *Lleweni Hall* and a nearby estate in Flint, and with his parents as trustees, he took out a £20,000 (£21.5m) mortgage on Taplow Court from *Thomas Coutts* of The Strand. Bad went to worse in 1806 when he lost his seat in Parliament, in 1808 when he lost not only his esteemed grandfather but also his father's once-busy bleaching works, and in 1809 when his mother assisted him in securing a further security of £30,000 (£29.2m). He was desperately in need of a place for his wife and their infant son Thomas to call their own. Their plight obliged Lady Orkney to make the most of her holdings. Two years ago she let ***Berry Hill House*** to the noted Anglo-Irish MP General **Francis Needham** who has set about enhancing the place with a splendid mansion set in ornamental gardens. Unfortunately the £216-a-year (£204,000) Needham is paying isn't enough for Kirkwall who finally ran out of patience last year and began the legal action against the Marchioness.

This drastic step will indeed be a new beginning. Kirkwall will recover his financial standing sufficiently to be MP for Denbigh for six years until 1818 and to become a trustee of *Norwich Union Insurance Company* from 1817. He will speak only once in Parliament – a tribute to the Duke of Wellington in 1814 – but will earn respect for being staunch in his support for the Tory government of Prime Minister Robert Jenkinson, 2nd Earl of Liverpool, and in opposing Catholic Emancipation.

The Coming of Sir Georgeous

Garraway's Coffee House, City of London / 10th July 1821

Lady Orkney was rocked twice in a few weeks last autumn. It was hard enough on 10th September 1820 when her 70-year-old stepmother Mary, Lady Thomond, died at *Bayliss House* in Slough, her home since 1815. It was devastating on 23rd November to lose 42-year-old **John**, **Viscount Kirkwall**, her only son and heir. She was left alone to guide her 17-year-old grandson **Thomas John Hamilton Fitzmaurice** as he succeeded to his father's title. And yet now the new Lord Kirkwall is hurrying confidently east along Cornhill. At the Royal Exchange he turns right into the narrow Change Alley and is ushered into what is said to be "a place of great mercantile transactions" where "people of quality" meet in the rooms where in 1658 tea was first sold in England.

Kirkwall is acting for his dowager grandmother to oversee the sale of the **Cliefden** estate in five lots. In the past weeks his agent **Harry Tyre** has shown a number of interested parties around the house and its 380 acres. Many have been taken by the 'gothic summerhouse' built in 1813 by **Peter Nicholson**. Sadly Her Ladyship will enjoy taking afternoon tea there no more. The reknown auctioneer George Squibb of Savile Row cracks his gavel. The room falls silent. It seems only seconds before the business is done: **Sir George Warrender** MP is the new owner of Cliefden. Sir George is known as 'Sir Georgeous' for his handsome features or 'Sir Gorge Provender' for his reputation as a *bon viveur*. He and its vendor and new neighbour will become good friends during the three years that the conveyance is delayed until Kirkwall comes of age, perhaps because he will see something of himself in the young man. Sir George was just 17 in 1799 when he inherited a baronetcy and considerable wealth vested in property and mercantile rights in Edinburgh. He became an MP eight years later and is now serving Sandwich (Kent), his third constituency, as Lord of the Admiralty. He will become a Privy Counsellor next year and two more constituencies will enjoy the privilege of his representation before he retires from Parliament in 1832.

Separate Ways

Canning's Oak, the second Clifden / 24th June 1826

The partnership is over. **Taplow Court** and **Clifden** are going separate ways. **Viscount Kirkwall** had no option but to mark his recent marriage to his neighbour **Charlotte Irby** by taking a £15,000 (£18.3m) mortgage on the Taplow Court estate, repayable over an incredible 1,300 years and arranged only with the help of eight trustees: his brother William FitzMaurice, his new wife, her father **George Irby, 3rd Baron Boston** of **Hedsor**, her uncle Captain Frederick Irby, Mark Sawim, Christopher Tower, George Dawkins-Pennant MP and Henry Peachey, 3rd Baron Selsey. And yet despite these financial worries, his marriage will be happy and blessed with eight children [*see Appendix 1, Tree 7*].

The contrast at Cliefden is sharp. Warrender's marriage to Anne Boscawen is childless and unhappy but he suffers no financial deprivation. He wasted no time in engaging the Scottish architect **William Burn** to design a new two-storey mansion incorporating what he could of the original structure. Three new entrances have been created: one opposite ***The Three Feathers***, another further south at ***Woodgate Lodge*** and Green Drive now extends south to another lodge. The result is magnificent: the perfect setting for entertaining on a grand scale. But he is forgetting his guest. Where is George Canning?

The Foreign Secretary and Leader of the House is where he can always be found – sitting in the shade of an old oak tree contemplating the glorious view across the Thames. Canning has much on his mind. He has overcome great opposition to do more than any other foreign statesman to make Latin American independence a reality. As he will explain in the House of Commons in December: "I called the New World into existence to redress the balance of the Old". Now his challenge is to secure the UK's political and economic interest in the region. However, a new priority will soon demand his attention. Next April, he will step into the shoes of the ailing Lord Liverpool only for his own health to fail him at just 57-years-old. His death in August will mean he will remembered less for his astute and far-reaching foreign policy than for serving the shortest term a PM has ever or will ever serve: a mere 119 days. The tree will last much longer: *Canning's Oak* is said to have been here before the Dashing Duke arrived in 1666 and will be by far Cliveden's oldest inhabitant when it finally falls on 5th May 2004.

Sir Gorgeous will miss his old friend and namesake, but not enough to prevent him making the most of Cliveden. Although his hospitality is a mix of extravagance and economy – his cuisine will be of the highest order but the "warming department will be neglected" – his rules are simplicity itself: "dine at 7 and breakfast at 10; all the rest, do as you please". Despite deciding not to proceed with the proposals of Conte Alfred d'Orsay for the redesign of the parterre, he can look forward to receiving from Queen Adelaide, wife of King William IV, the compliments that Cliefden is "one of the most charming places [she has] ever beheld" with gardens "of the highest order and beauty" and "your people kind and attentive".

Thomas Fitzmaurice, 5th Earl of Orkney

Making Ends Meet

Stockwells, Town Lane / 25th November 1828

The grandson continues to steer his grandmother Lady Orkney as she struggles to make ends meet by selling off or leasing out her land. His mortgage has provided him sufficient liquidity to invest in the construction of two mansions: ***The Elms*** has been built here on ***Stockwells***, a close off **Town Lane**, and *Hill House* on **Church Lane** is leased to Robert Myrtens Bird of the Bengal Civil Service. Bird will recover from the death of his wife Rebecca to marry his neighbour Pascoe Grenfell's daughter Henrietta in 1848. *Hill House* will spend many years as ***Taplowhill House*** before eventually settling on ***Taplow Hill***.

Berry Hill House, Town Lane / 25th November 1833

Having finally succeeded as the latest Lord Orkney two years ago [*see Appendix 1, Tree 7*], it is now Thomas FitzMaurice's challenge alone to try every which way to keep himself in the manner his family had long been accustomed. In August he conveyed Taplow Court to the settlement of his Sligo estate in order to secure incomes for his children. He is pleased that **Francis Needham**, for ten years 1st Earl of Kilmorey in the Irish peerage, was as good a tenant of ***Berry Hill House*** in death as he was in life. Last year the old soldier's will placed that estate in the hands of trustees and it is now home to **Charlotte Tonson**, the Dowager **Lady Riversdale**. She has strong local connections: her late husband Irish peer William Tonson, 2nd Baron Riversdale, may have been the great-nephew of Jacob Tonson of ***Down Place*** and her aunt Georgiana, **Pascoe Grenfell**'s second wife, was so taken by her title that she borrowed it for their eighth and last child Riversdale William Grenfell.

The Coming of Gas

Mill Lane / 26th November 1834

Things are looking up even more for Orkney: he has just pulled off what might be his best financial deals yet. One will result in dramatic and durable physical change as the *GWR* digs gravel out here and piles it there to build a massive railway embankment. The other will damage Taplow's environment in a different way....

Maidenhead is getting bigger. Gas is the latest big thing. Preston started it in 1816 when its streets were bathed in gaslight. The metropolitan neighbours want some of that, especially if all the unpleasant industrial activity and odours are secreted elsewhere. Taplow's riverside is nearby but out-of-the-way, across the river and behind a wooded island. The coal from which gas is extracted can be delivered by a stream of barges and Orkney needs the money too much to fuss about the inconvenience. He has just leased a one-third acre parcel of riverside land to WB Stears. Within a year the ***Maidenhead Gas Light & Coke Company*** will be releasing gas from coal by pyrolysis and storing it in a telescopic gasometer which forces the gas under pressure into a network of underground distribution pipes.

Harding's Happenings – Carting the Coke

Marsh Lane / 26th November 1946

Nine-year-old **Anthony Harding** has no idea how coal turns to coke. All he knows is that his dad Frank trusted him with a half-crown (£15.25) to pay the gasworks for four bags of the stuff. And now he has to grit his teeth and haul his two-wheeled handcart home to Marsh Lane with its precious cargo. His future wife Mary is doing the same in Slough. It's a tough old world.

Cooking on Gas

Mill Lane / 26th November 2012

Gas production continued on the riverside site through a long commercial evolution – to the *Maidenhead Gas Company* in 1876, through the acquisition of the *Burnham United Gas & Lighting Company* in 1904 (Burnham High Street had been gas lit since 1878) to being overtaken in 1925 by the *Uxbridge, Wycombe & District Gas Company* which was itself acquired in 1936 by the *South Eastern Gas Corporation*. A resident manager lived on the site: censuses spotted William Whatmore in 1871 and **George Wood** in 1881. The latter was in charge for more than 30 years during which in 1893 he presided over the expansion of the site that put the kink in **Mill Lane** and built the forbidding brick wall still there today. He installed new plant to make carburetted water gas in 1898 and added a new retort house five years later, modernisations which enabled gas output to increase from 60 million cubic feet in 1900 (the earliest recorded figure) to 100 million in 1910, 169 million in 1922 and 250 million in 1949, the last year of production when the site was nationalised and converted to a holder station. It was kept ready for winter emergencies until being finally decommissioned in 1954 and eventually dismantled some ten years later. A new gasholder was erected on this triangle of land across the road in the mid-1960s. The site was 'mothballed' perhaps ten years ago but may have been used then or since by *Transco* (*British Gas* by any other name) to store radioactive substances and hazardous waste before eventually being made redundant. What dangers still lurk on the triangle and its long-derelict riverside neighbour as they await redevelopment decisions by their current owner *National Grid*?

Every Which Way

Clifden Mills / 27th November 1840

Orkney's next money-making move looks to be a good one. **Charles Venables** is just leaving a cordial meeting having agreed to lease ***Clifden Mills*** for mechanised papermaking. His lordship hopes this will inject new life into these mills and also ensure the viability of the fourth as the only cornmill for his major tenant farmers **George Norrington**, **George Cross** and **William Davis Briginshaw**. Together these three fellows farm well over half his land. Mutual dependence is vital. Norrington is perhaps the least dependent – he leases only two-fifths of his 248 acres from Orkney, the remainder being the Rector's glebe lands which he took over from his father William some years ago – but he is locked in by his leasehold of the cornmill. That's so far so good.

Berry Hill House, Town Lane / 27th November 1845

The Anglo-Irish foothold on Berry Hill is strengthening. The Kilmorey trustees have agreed to pay an additional £46 (£2,700) per year to increase the ***Berry Hill*** estate by a quarter to almost 32 acres. The additional land will be occupied by Needham's youngest daughter Mabella and her husband John Henry Knox, son of Thomas Knox, 1st Earl of Ranfurly, rather than by her elder brother **Francis** (Black Jack) **Needham**, 2nd Earl of Kilmorey, who two years ago at the age of 50 scandalised society by eloping with his 20-year-old ward Priscilla Hoste.

Springfield House, Town Lane / 27th November 1845

It was probably the first Lady Mary, the current Lord Orkney's great-grandmother, who leased this close of four-and-a-half acres to the Whitlaw family. Perhaps ***Springfield House*** was built for **Francis Whitlaw** who in 1789 let certain unspecified fishing rights to George White of Bray and Edward Adams of Maidenhead. Now his nephew **Charles Whitlaw** intends to replace the old house with a splendid Italianate mansion designed by **Charles Barry** during a break from supervising the construction of the Palace of Westminster, otherwise known as the Houses of Parliament. How Orkney must be licking his lips in anticipation of increasing the land rental to £71 (£85,500) well before Whitlaw's new home is completed.

Clifden Mills / 27th November 1847

His lordship is nearing the end of his tether. Despite trying every trick to balance his books, his parlous financial plight is becoming an increasing preoccupation. And in his desperation Orkney is squeezing his tenants even more. The Venables brothers haven't quite finished their refurbishment of the mills but his lordship has already served notice that their annual rent will be raised to £500 (£545,000) with a further uplift of £20 (£19,000) scheduled for 1855.

Church Road / 27th November 1847

And still Orkney squeezes. He will be quick to increase **Richard Briginshaw**'s rent for ***Rectory Farm*** now that the farmer has enough capital to build a bigger home incorporating his grandfather John's small cottage (which in 160 years will still be doing a stalwart job as a utility room). And next year he'll persuade William Payn and other trustees to allow him to end their interest in ***Elibank*** so he can lease it without complication to his brother **William Fitzmaurice**. Time will soon tell that this catalogue of last-gasp gambles won't be enough. Stormclouds are gathering on the horizon.

The Coming of the Lancers

The third Taplow Court / 22nd November 1838

Civil unrest simmered worryingly in 1803 as the Napoleonic threat loomed ever larger. Despite having retired from the political arena some years before, Lord Grenville's brother the **Earl Temple**, 1st Marquess of Buckingham, grasped the nettle to establish the Buckinghamshire Yeomanry Cavalry comprising three regiments of small farmers led by their landlords in military guise. The 1st (Southern) Regiment was able to boast a troop of brave Taplovians which stood at the ready to keep the peace by force.

The eventual defeat of France in 1815 and the recovery of the economy left local militias a luxury few could afford. The 1st and 3rd Regiments of the Bucks Yeomanry were disbanded in 1827 and the 2nd survived only with the sponsorship of Richard Temple-Nugent-Brydges-Chandos-Grenville, 2nd Duke of Buckingham & Chandos – evidently his pockets were as deep as his name and title were never-ending – but when the discontent of agricultural workers escalated into the so-called 'Swing Riots' of 1830, the 2nd Regiment was in urgent need of reinforcement. The valiant **Lord Orkney** – then still **Viscount Kirkwall** – found welcome distraction from his financial worries by raising a new troop of local yeomanry with himself as its Captain Commandant. The South Buckinghamshire Yeomanry Cavalry – now known unofficially as the ***Taplow Lancers*** – was soon called into action to arrest suspects at Prince's Risborough. Today the proud yeomen are standing at attention in Cherry Orchard to hear Orkney make an important announcement. Civil unrest has subsided in recent years. Consequently the War Office has decided to withdraw funding from local militias, including the Lancers. However he proposes that the troop may wish to remain at the ready without government pay or allowances.

After a moment's silence, the men mumble briefly amongst themselves before nodding to Sergeant **William Norrington** who speaks up to confirm everyone's assent. As his lordship's steward, Norrington has already gauged the general feeling of the troop, and in anticipation of their decision, Orkney has been at pains to acquire half-a-dozen *Brown Bess* flintlock muskets. These heavy weapons are rather old-fashioned now but they can still be effective if properly maintained. There is a cheer as he signals Norrington to hand them out and the happy mood continues as his lordship hands out the shot he uses for hunting and the men practise muzzle-loading and firing into the sunset. A flock of birds rises squealing from the woods on the escarpment. As he fits his bayonet, Trooper **Richard Simmonds** (or Simmons) wonders to himself if it would be worth a walk over there later to see if any game has been hit. But military matters must come first. He fits his bayonet and raises a laugh by thrusting it into an upright bale of straw with a particularly nasty snarl. Discipline breaks down completely for a few moments when Trooper **William Saunders** accidentally cuts the string that holds his bale together and straw flies everywhere. These friends are soon to be brothers-in-law. Dick married **Thirza Pagett** two years ago and Billy will wed her sister Sarah next year.

Queen Victoria will reward the Lancers for their persistence in 1845 when she makes their regiment royal. The 2nd Royal Bucks Regiment of Yeomanry will be mobilised three years later when the Chartist movement for political reform threaten disturbances at Slough but it will came to naught. On this occasion, the eager Lancers will be stood down without seeing any action but giving up won't be in their nature. They will continue to parade for another generation. Orkney will be succeeded as Captain Commandant in 1863 by Nathaniel Lambert of Denham Court – a mine-owner, later Liberal MP for Buckinghamshire – and from 1867 a new Orkney echo will resound when Lieutenant **Alexander FitzMaurice** is appointed second-in-command. The Lancers' zenith and nadir will be just two years apart. Their proudest moment will in 1869 when they parade at the Windsor Volunteer Review; the saddest in 1871 when, having dwindled to just five men – Sergeant **William Rance**, Corporal **Richard Cleare** and Troopers **John Cleare** (son of Richard), **Henry Davis** and **Charles Cross** (son of farmer George) – the troop will be finally disbanded. The regiment itself will continue and in 1889 it will have yet another new name – The Royal Buckinghamshire Hussars Yeomanry – but later Taplovians with a military bent will tend towards Berkshire.

George Sutherland-Leveson-Gower, 2nd Duke of Sutherland

Pheonix from the Ashes

The second Cliefden / 27th June 1849

On 21st February as he was counting the pennies and hoping desperately that the pounds would take care of themselves, Lord Orkney was hit by the devastating financial and personal blow of losing his friend and neighbour **Sir George Warrender**. He is relieved now to be a guest of the new owner of Cliefden. George Sutherland-Leveson-Gower, **2nd Duke of Sutherland**, paid Warrender's brother John £24,850 (£27.4m) for Cliefden plus an additional £9,566 (£10.5m) for its 'effects'. The assembled lords and ladies in all their finery need no nudge to correctly pronounce His Grace's family name *Looson-Gore* as they witness Henry Howard, Dean of Lichfield, exercise a special licence from the Archbishop of Canterbury to join the duke's son and heir George in Holy Matrimony with Anne Hay-Mackenzie, Countess of Cromartie and the great-granddaughter of **George Murray, 6th Lord Elibank** [*see Appendix 1, Trees 10 & 15*]. If it occurs to anyone what a small aristocratic world it is, they won't have long to dwell on the coincidence....

The second Cliefden / 15th November 1849

The family is in Scotland. Their servants are at church at a thanksgiving for surviving a severe outbreak of cholera. The fire is out of control. Once again the flames will be seen from Windsor but, unlike her uncaring Uncle George 54 years before, **Queen Victoria** will despatch her fire brigade to assist. Not even this royal intervention will prevent everything except the original 1666 terrace being destroyed.

Sutherland will waste no time in commissioning a famous architect to rebuild Cliefden. **Charles Barry** is already gracing Taplow with ***Springfield***, now close to completion. He will take time out once more from building the Palace of Westminster to inspect the ruins and conclude that workmen carrying out repairs had left the end of a wooden joist protruding into a chimney from the hearth in the servants' hall: the joist overheated and the second Cliefden is history. Barry's first design for the third will be "set aside for commercial reasons". Undeterred, he will be inspired by the outline of the earlier Cliefdens to create a splendid Italianate villa which will be ready for His Grace's enjoyment in 1852. The brick structure is rendered in Roman cement – a mixture of slaked lime and volcanic ash – and its embellishments expressed in moulded terracotta. Decorative urns and pilasters abound. A heavy balustraded cornice tops an arcaded ground floor. Above this are two storeys crowned with a parapet into which are embedded Latin inscriptions composed by the future Prime Minister **William Gladstone** to laud **Buckingham**, Cliefden's founder, **Sutherland**, its latest benefactor, and Barry, its architect. Once again two curving corridors lead to wings where extra guests can be accommodated. The graceful symmetry is reinforced by stone staircases descending from the terrace to the parterre.

Tall Tale – Falling Out

The third Cliveden / 15th November 2012

It is reasonable to assume that 'Looson-Gore' and Barry might be pleased to see thousands still enjoying this largely unchanged exterior 160 years later. However, perhaps His Grace would still not be available to share the pleasure with his architect....

The completion of the third Cliveden coincided with Barry being knighted by Queen Victoria in recognition of his ongoing achievement at Westminster. Amid all this excitement, it wasn't well known that His Grace had fallen out badly with Barry over his fee. And to make matters worse, although by 1855 he had eventually paid his famous architect a sum amounting to 5% of the construction cost of Cliveden, Sutherland was indignant to receive an additional bill for £105 6s (£8,585) to cover his travelling expenses. He wondered aloud if it had been necessary to make every journey by coach-and-four but paid the bill under protest, complaining that "if these charges were not so provoking, they'd be ridiculous" and instructing his staff that he would "never again be available" to Sir Charles.

Eyes of a Child – Louis Plumley

St Nicolas' School / 23rd April 2012

My favourite part of Taplow is Cliveden. Last time I went in the maze with **Tom King**. When we got there, we warmed up to get ready to go in. We had a little run around, got stuck and had fun. We kept changing directions. I cut myself. It didn't hurt much so I got up and carried on. I've still got that cut today. After a rough journey we made it to the middle and celebrated and took a long time to get out. We then challenged people to play football. I scored backwards. That's what I like about Taplow.

Taplow Court

The third Taplow Court
– JP Neale 1821

Orkney Over and Out

Taplow for Sale

Garraway's Coffee House, City of London / 10th August 1852

It is a quarter before noon. **Lord Orkney** is hurrying into *Garraway's* once more. He is greeted by his agent Mr Ford who is not surprised at his nervous and perhaps slightly embarrassed air for, as **Clifden** has waxed, **Taplow Court** has waned and the wolf of bankruptcy is finally at his door. Four years ago he secured a further £7,500 (£8.3m) mortgage from Edward Marjoribanks and Sir Edmund Antrobus, bankers of The Strand. It wasn't enough. In 1850 with debts totalling £44,000 (£56.6m) he submitted a bankruptcy petition to the Lord High Chancellor, Charles Pepys, 1st Earl of Cottenham, who authorised the appointed trustees Sir Edward Alderson, James Farrer and Privy Counsellor John Campbell, 2nd Marquess of Breadalbane, to grant payments to Orkney's primary creditors – £925 (£1.1m) to Mark Sawim and £8,850 (£10.6m) to Marjoribanks and Antrobus – plus release of a further £13,225 (£15.8m) to cover Orkney's immediate needs and demands from other creditors. However the Lord Chancellor's terms left him no option but to sell at auction today "upwards of 950 acres" – actually 941.64 acres comprising almost 928 in Taplow, ten in Hitcham, three-and-a-half in Cookham, half-an-acre in Dorney and a tiny patch in Bray.

The smoky, walnut-panelled first-floor room is crowded with gentlemen diligently examining the offer papers prepared by *Farebrother, Clark & Lye*, a noted firm of land surveyors and auctioneers with offices in Lancaster Place. Maybe it was My Lye who made almost 942 acres into "upwards of 950". Many have visited **George Norrington** to inspect these papers. Others have viewed them at the offices of four London solicitors. The descriptions of the 43 lots and their tenants give a fascinating insight into the fabric and society of Taplow today. Taplow Court and its "Pleasure Grounds", ***Elibank*** and ***Springfield*** are all presented in mouth-watering detail, as is the Manor of Clifden and its "Renowned Springs & Ornamental Fishing Villa".

Currently Orkney holds 360 acres in hand (just over one-third of Taplow) and lets the rest to copyholders and tenants, most of it (over half the whole) to three farmers: **William Davis Briginshaw** at ***Amerden Manor Farm*** (219 acres), **George Cross** at ***Barge Farm*** (176 acres) and **George Norrington** at ***Home Farm*** (96 acres). Norrington's brother-in-law **Richard Briginshaw**'s 152 acres of glebe land are not up for sale today. Richard's brother and Cross each have all their eggs in one basket and will end the day with different landlords. Other significant *in situ* tenants include the **Venables** brothers at ***Clifden Mills***, **Charles Whitlaw** at ***Springfield House***, the Dowager **Lady Riversdale** at ***Berry Hill House***, **William Skindle** at ***The Orkney Arms Hotel*** and the **Wethered** brothers at ***The Dumb Bell Hotel***. Various other houses, cottages, closes and meadows are noted as being spread amongst 35 other tenants including the ***Maidenhead Gas Light & Coke Company***, the village baker Thomas Hughes, the publican Lydia Austen and two blacksmiths – Thomas Jones by ***Maidenhead (Riverside) Station*** and **George Stevens** at **Carkins Meadow**. Some have had the privilege of viewing some of these properties "by leave of the tenants" and of obtaining tickets to do the same at Taplow Court. The excitement at being here is tinged with sadness at how hard it must be for Orkney to part with these gems, his family's pride and joy for five generations.

There are a few familiar faces. Norrington is talking with fellow Taplovians **William Rance**, **William Skindle**, **Henry Simmons**, **Edward Winslow** and **Harry Tyre**. These last three gentlemen hope to make successful bids for the freehold of the homes which they currently rent, and Harry's wife Rose will be delighted if he not only can make ***Bapsey Lodge*** their own but also if **Charles Pascoe Grenfell** acquires Taplow Court. Rose served Mr Grenfell's father at ***Taplow House*** for 34 years – initially as the boy's nursemaid – and the fact that she still enjoys his gratitude and affection holds the promise that Harry will retain his position as the Court's estate agent. Harry looks around to assess the competition. A Maidenhead thicket of **James Lovegrove**, **Thomas Bell** and James Pearce share a joke. And is that Henry Darvill of Windsor with **James Webb** of Burnham and Mr Bennett of the gas company? A distinguished gentleman is deep in conversation with his agent. Another six or seven agents are trying to keep themselves to themselves. Mr Bell is representing **Charles Whitlaw** but for whom are the others acting?

A ripple of anticipation runs through the assembled company as Grenfell enters with the **Duke of Sutherland**. Perhaps these eminent gentlemen have come to some private agreement over which lots each will bid for. The clock strikes twelve. The auctioneer steps up on his dais, calls for silence and begins the business of the day. Everything happens so quickly. The auctioneer somehow sees every raised eyebrow or slight nod and rat-a-tats his acknowledgement of the bids in a piercing nasal twang. He punctuates each sale by bringing down his gavel with a sharp crack. It is the sound of the end of an era.

By late afternoon, a new one has begun. The auctioneer announces that all the promises to pay add up to a massive £102,415 (£111.91m) less the £2,000 (£2.2m) that Orkney somehow owes himself for Lot 18, *Elibank*; clearly the excitement has got the better of the poor chap. Nine-tenths of Taplow is now shared by a triumvirate representing three pillars of high society. Sutherland took his leave having secured five of the first six lots for the trifle of £24,060 (£26.49m) in 'Old Money'. He had added to Clifden a total of 202 acres to the east and south of the heartlands around the house, thus bringing the estate close to its 2012 extent and shape. Meanwhile the 'New Money' of Whitlaw has made him the effective lord of the south. Mr Bell invested on his behalf £24,840 (£27.35m) to acquire over 400 acres of fertile land at *Amerden Manor Farm* and *The Barge Farm* as well as the freehold of two parcels of Upper Green Common in **Hitcham** and his home, *Springfield*. And with perfect symmetry, Grenfell's blend of 'Old Family / New Money' has taken Taplow's centre ground in exchange for £31,770 (£35.06m) spent on nine lots comprising almost 220 acres including Taplow Court and the mills.

It isn't long before clerks pass around copies of two tables which summarise the sales. The three leading lights – Grenfell, Sutherland and Whitlaw – acquired 19 lots covering 89% of the ground. Someone whispers that the distinguished gentleman whom no one knew was **John Noble**, the paint and varnish manufacturer for whom his agent Edward Grove has spent £8,750 (£9.63m) to acquire three lots amounting to half of the remainder: *Berry Hill House*, *The Dumb Bell Hotel* and **Bridge Field** add up to an intriguing mix of potential grand home, going concern and nest-egg. The other 21 lots are shared between six everyday Taplovians, eight nearby neighbours (including one commercial company), five agents acting for others unknown and a certain **Zadok Aaron Jessell** of N° 1 Savile Row. This enterprising diamond, pearl and coral merchant has secured the very complex package of ***The Orkney Arms*** which boasts a bar, two parlours and two coffee rooms on the ground floor with a taproom in a former cottage to the rear, three large sitting rooms and three principal bedrooms on the first floor with nine more bedrooms above. It has a pleasure ground, a kitchen garden, a meadow and Horse Radish Paddock plus three other cottages on Mill Lane: one used by staff, another with a garden let to George Heath and a third with a boathouse and yard all let to **Jonathan Bond**. Jessell will complete his acquisition on 22nd November 1852. Four months later he will hedge his investment with a covenant by which Grenfell secures a reversion.

Taplow for Sale – Acquisitions by the Leading Lights

Purchaser (Agent)	**Lot Description** (2012 Location)	**Tenants** (Portioned by Acre)	**Total Area** (Acres)	**1852 Price** (£)	**2012 Price** (£)
Charles Pascoe Grenfell	Lot 1 – 'The Manor of Taplow: Taplow Court Mansion & Pleasure Grounds', including ice house and certain closes (Taplow Court)	George Cross & John Nason (6.00), George Lambourne & William D Briginshaw (10.00)	101.61	12,000	£13.21m
	Lots 7 & 8 – Parliament Close & adjacent parcels (east of Hill Farm Road either side of Hunts Lane)	George Norrington	58.00	3,420	£3.85m
	Lot 19 – Ten Acres (Taplow Cricket Club)	George Cross	7.96	800	£0.88m
	Lot 26 – 'Clifden Mills' (Taplow Mills) including 3 paper mills, a flour mill, various cottages and outbuildings, several small aights, ozier beds & Cookham Lock meadow	Charles Venables (5.00), George Venables (0.91), Richard Lovegrove (2.06), George Norrington (1.25)	9.64	11,000	£12.11m
	Lots 27 & 29 – The Leychequer (disused gasometer & paper storage sites & car park)	George Cross	20.57	1,960	£2.16m
	Lot 33 – Foxholes & Berry Hill Field (Lansdowne Court & adjacent parcels)	George Cross (18.98), William Skindle (2.84)	21.82	2,260	£2.49m
	Lot 41 – Meadow (Bray)	Charles Mickley	0.09	330	£0.36m
		Total for Grenfell	**219.69**	**31,770**	**£35.06m**
Duke of Sutherland	Lots 2 & 3 – Cliveden Woodlands	George Cross (68.03), Richard Lovegrove (0.98)	128.13	13,400	£14.75m
	Lots 4, 5 & 6 – 'The Manor of Clifden', including Four Cottages (actually east & south portions of Cliveden estate)	George Cross (24.83), William Saunders & John Montague (0.31), William Buckland (0.39), Daniel How (0.22)	74.19	10,660	£11.74m
		Total for Sutherland	**202.32**	**24,060**	**£26.49m**
Charles Whitlaw (Mr Bell of Bow Churchyard)	Lot 25 – 'Springfield House, a beautiful Italian Villa' (junction of Berry Hill & Mill Lane)	Charles Whitlaw	4.66	2,340	£2.57m
	Lot 39 – 'The Barge Farm' (from the River Thames to the lane with no name)	George Cross (27.41), William D Briginshaw (9.44), Miss S Wilder (0.13)	196.33	10,250	£11.29m
	Lot 40 – 'The Manor of Amerden' (from the lane with no name to Marsh Lane)	William D Briginshaw (204.80, of which 3.06 in Hitcham and 0.54 in Dorney)	207.40	12,000	£13.21m
	Lots 42 & 43 – Two parcels in Hitcham (Upper Green Common; probably across Marsh Lane)	George Holly (4.28), Richard Meads & Charles Bovington (2.78)	7.06	250	£0.28m
		Total for Whitlaw	**415.45**	**24,840**	**£27.35m**
		Total Acquisitions by Leading Lights	**837.57**	**80,670**	**£88.9m**

Source – *Farebrother, Clark & Lye* sales particulars held by *The Centre for Buckinghamshire Studies*, Aylesbury

Taplow for Sale – Acquisitions by Others

Purchaser (Agent)	Lot Description (2012 Location)	Tenants (Portioned by Acre)	Total Area (Acres)	1852 Price (£)	2012 Price (£)
John Noble (Edward Grove of Kennington Common)	Lot 34 – *Berry Hill* Mansion House & Grounds with outbuildings (Berry Hill estate)	Trustees of the late Earl of Kilmorey for Lady Riversdale	31.54	5,750	£6.33m
	Lot 35 – *The Dumb Bell Hotel* or *Bell & Crown Railway Hotel* (*Harvester* & adjacent car sales)	Owen & Laurence Wethered of Marlow	4.45	1,500	£1.65m
	Lot 38 – Bridge Field (Ellington Road)	George Norrington	16.19	1,500	£1.65m
		Total for Noble	**52.18**	**8,750**	**£9.63m**
Other Taplovians					
William Rance	Lot 10 – Little Coldgrove (*Coldgrove Cottages, Church Cottages* & part of Buffins)	George Norrington	1.18	115	£0.13m
George Norrington	Lot 11 – Two Cottages (*The Old Cottage*)	Richard Simmons & Thomas Avery	0.38	170	£0.19m
Edward Winslow	Lot 13 – 'Handsome Detached Villa' (north-east corner of Wellbank)	Edward Winslow	1.68	1,160	£1.28m
Henry Simmons	Lot 14 – House, Workshops, Timber Yard & Meadow (north-west corner of Wellbank)	Henry Simmons	1.61	460	£0.51m
Lord Orkney (Mr Ford)	Lot 18 – *Elibank House*, Outbuildings & Meadow (*Elibank House, The Old Coach House, Elibank Court* & School Playing Field)	George Norrington (2.96)	5.64	2,000	£2.2m
Harry Tyre	Lot 23 – 'Picturesque Cottage' with stable & garden (*East Bapsey* & *West Bapsey*)	Harry Tyre	0.66	600	£0.66m
		Total for Other Taplovians	**11.75**	**4,505**	**£4.97m**
Other Locals					
Mr Soundy of Henley	Lot 9 – Nightingcroft and adjacent parcel (east of Hill Farm Road)	George Norrington	13.14	840	£0.92m
Henry Darvill of Windsor	Lot 15 – *The Oak Beer Shop* with House & Garden (Priory Cottage)	Lydia Austen	1.03	610	£0.67m
Thomas Bell of Ray Mill, Maidenhead	Lot 16 – House, Shop & Bakehouse plus Two Cottages (north areas of *The Oak & Saw, The Old Manor House, The Cottage* & *Farm View*)	Thomas Hughes (0.51), Sarah & Anne Langfield & Thomas Fenner (0.08)	0.60	610	£0.67m
James Webb of Burnham	Lot 17 – Cottage & Storehouse (north-west corner of Cedar Chase)	Widow Brown, Ann Kent & James Webb	0.13	510	£0.56m
WR Fletcher (JE Langton of Maidenhead)	Lot 20 – Meadow (wood between *Hill House* & Taplow Cricket Club)	Thomas Greenhalf	0.78	180	£0.2m
James Lovegrove of Maidenhead	Lot 24 – Timber Yard, Two Cottages with Gardens & Orchard (south of lane to Taeppa's Mound)	Edward Darling & George Cross	1.25	385	£0.42m
Maidenhead Gas Light & Coke Co	Lots 28 & 30 – Garden plus Gasworks (together comprising disused riverside gasworks)	Thomas Wynn (0.33), Maidenhead Gas Light & Coke Co (0.30)	0.63	430	£0.47m
James Pearce of Maidenhead	Lot 31 – Two Gardens (*The Wharf*)	Thomas Wynn & Jonathan Bond	0.41	125	£0.14m
		Total for Other Locals	**17.97**	**3,690**	**£3.13m**
Agents					
(John Gadsby of St Pancras)	Lot 12 – Little Meadow (*Wellbank Cottage* & *Lindens*)	Edward Winslow	0.94	160	£0.18m
(JG Sambrooke of Eaton Place)	Lot 21 – *Prospect House* (*Hill House* & *Old Malt House*)	Ann Dancer	0.46	750	£0.83m
(W Meyrick of Parliament St)	Lot 22 – Carkins & Blacksmith Shop (*Eriska* & west Saxon Gardens)	Joseph Saunders (2.67), George Stevens (0.14)	2.81	640	£0.7m
(Robert Russell of Cannon St)	Lot 36 – Arable Land & Blacksmith's Shop (south of Bath Road between Amerden Lane & Jubilee River)	George Cross (5.30), Thomas Jones (0.06)	5.36	640	£0.7m
(RH Witty of The Strand)	Lot 37 – Buck's Close (south of Bath Road between Jubilee River & Ellington Road)	George Norrington (4.78)	4.78	490	£0.54m
Another					
Zadok Jessell of Savile Row	Lot 32 – *The Orkney Arms Hotel* with cottages, gardens, meadow & paddock (*Skindles* with adjacent car sales & paddock)	William Skindle (8.34), George Heath (0.08)	8.42	2,120	£2.33m
		Total for Agents & Another	**22.77**	**4,800**	**£5.28m**
		Total Acquistions by Others	**104.64**	**21,745**	**£23.01m**

Source – *Farebrother, Clark & Lye* sales particulars held by *The Centre for Buckinghamshire Studies*, Aylesbury

Garraway's Coffee House / c1872

Sir Charles Barry / c1850

'Looson-Gore' / c1810

Approaching Cliveden from the Grand Avenue / 2009

Sutherland's Pleasure

Cliveden Parterre & Terrace / 2012

Chapter Five

Ruling the Roost

In which Taplow trinity was redefined

All Change

Watersheds and Other Shifts

The Cottage, Rectory Road / 12th August 2012

Places change so incrementally over the years that it can be hard to identity specific threshold dates after which things were never the same again – and yet Taplow had two just 14 years apart. The first watershed was on 4th June 1838 when the ***Great Western Railway*** chuffed from Paddington. The second was on 10th August 1852 when the fifth **Orkney** sold Taplow.

Together, these watersheds redefined the social fabric and in doing so brought the age-old triptych of Cliveden, Taplow and Amerden into sharp focus. The first brought commuters to stay and day-trippers to play. The Industrial Revolution arrived with Education close on its heels. Ordinary people were at last a force to be reckoned with. The second echoed the nationwide mid-1800s waning of the 'Old Gentry', which inherited land and property it could no longer afford to keep, and the waxing of the 'New Gentry', whose commercial success had made money they wanted to spend on land and property so their new-found status would be evident to all and sundry.

Cliveden still remained the former, now at the highest and most durable level. **Taplow Court** and **Amerden** were the latter. These three elites wove contrasting threads into Taplow's tapestry over the next hundred years. One ran from a banker to a man for all seasons, another from a surgeon to a mistress of all she surveyed and a third from the richest Englishman to the richest American. Let's meet those who ruled the roost....

Triptych

The third Cliveden
(built 1852) / 2012

The only *Amerden House*
(built 1874) / 1884

The third (remodelled) Taplow Court
– George Lipscomb 1847 (rebuilt 1855)

The Grenfells at Taplow Court

Charles Pascoe Grenfell

Carry On Banker

The third Taplow Court / 12th August 1852

Charles was just six years old when his father **Pascoe Grenfell** brought him to ***Taplow House*** in 1794. For 58 years his family's star had risen ever higher while somehow still remaining in the social shadow of the Orkneys. He married in 1819 to Lady Georgiana, daughter of William Molyneux, 2nd Earl of Sefton; she gave him two sons – **Charles Pascoe Grenfell** and **Henry Riversdale Grenfell** – before passing away 26 years ago [*see Appendix 1, Tree 16*]. He has lived in London for most of his adult life, currently at N° 38 Belgrave Square, but his childhood love of Taplow has never waned, not even during the 14 years since his father passed away. And now at 64 and just two days since that eventful afternoon at *Garraway's*, he is coming home as the new lord of the place. How sweet that must be. Grand plans are already forming in his mind as he explores his new domain.

The fourth Taplow Court / 12th August 1855

Surely Taplow Court was the perfect home for one of the country's most eminent bankers? Not quite perfect enough, it seems. Charles wasted no time in beginning three projects to put things right to his way of thinking.

Most ambitious is the substantial remodelling of the house not as some will say by **Sir Charles Barry**, nor by NJ Cottingham, who drowned before he could begin the work, but by **William Burn**, whose reputation as an architect survived the conflagration at Clifden. Works are nearly complete on creating this fourth neo-Tudor edition of Taplow Court which retains the neo-Norman saloon along with the original Orkney's early-18th Century vestibule and porch.

The second project involved some clever politicking. The unruly ruins of the old **St Nicholas' Church** rather spoiled the southerly view from his drawing room. They had to go. The objections of the new Rector, the Reverend **Charles Whately**, were neatly assuaged by exchanging this adjacent church land for a plot on **Back Lane** where he is funding the construction of ***Church Houses***, six almshouses for the poor of the parish. Their rents will contribute some £30-a-year (£20,000) towards church expenses.

The third project had Burns landscaping 30 acres of formal garden around the house and renovating the walled gardens where melons, peaches and grapes are kept warm with hot water pipes. **Bapsey Pond** has been given a good tidying-up. Two skulls and an old sword have been dug from the mud as it was lined with brick and the spring that feeds it was culverted to clean up its water supply. A cedar walk along the crest of the escarpment will be a nice touch. He will enjoy looking down on his expanding Berkshire domains: he has already supplemented *Ives* and *Shoppenhangers* (inherited from his father) with *Ockwell's* and *Kimber's* (acquired in 1846) and will add *Lowbrook's* (1856), *Cresswell's* (1860), *Philbert's* (1863) and *Foxley's* (1864) to make him owner of most of Maidenhead.

Meanwhile, **Lord Orkney** has found ***Elibank*** a treat too far for a bankrupt. Charles is only too happy to oblige his struggling neighbour by taking it off his hands. Orkney won't lose touch with the area. He'll adjourn to a small house on Widbrook Common – he will call it ***Cliveden View*** oblivious to the wistfully poignancy the name conjures – where he'll watch from a discrete distance as Charles sets into place a complicated tenure for *Elibank* involving trustees, tenancies and intra-family conveyances presumably designed to keep taxes and duties to the minimum.

Cryptic Crosswords

The Old Churchyard / 12th August 1969

A hole has appeared in the grass. The Diocese of Oxford is looking into it.

When Charles Pascoe Grenfell had the Norman St Nicholas demolished in 1853, a stairway and corridor was built to give access to the crypt beneath and then sealed to protect the lead coffins containing the remains of the **Hampson**, **Orkney** and **Inchiquin** families. Coronets and honours still adorn their coffins. Now for the first time there is the opportunity to make a detailed photographic record of these relics before the crypt is once more closed, sealed and hidden again from view.

The Old Churchyard / 12th August 2012

A hole has appeared in the grass. The Diocese of Oxford is nowhere to be seen.

It seemed such a good idea in 1996 for the Old Churchyard and **Tæppa's Mound** to be declared a Scheduled Ancient Monument. And yet now – just weeks after the churchyard was packed with QEII Jubilee crowds and perhaps weakened by them – part of the crypt's ceiling has collapsed. The Diocese and English Heritage shrug shoulders and avoid discussing which of them should do what. The matter is complicated by questions about whether anyone can do anything without the permission of (Oliver) Peter St John, 9th Earl of Orkney (grandson of the 5th Earl of Orkney's youngest son James) who as a Canadian citizen has no connection with his Taplow roots.

Water Performance

Taplow Court Escarpment /12th June 2012

Taplow Court has a secret world. The wooded escarpment is a haven for wildlife. Is that a badger's sett there below the upper chalk cliff? Surely foxes wouldn't want holes that big. That rat-tat-tat must be woodpeckers at work. Could this steep traverse path or one like it really have led down to the *briva* hundreds of years ago? The peace is startled by shrit-it-it cries. Two electric blue flashes zip away across the shallow, still water to the soggy almost-eyot of Clemish Meadow. Good day to you too, Mr & Mrs Kingfisher. Isn't this natural tranquillity delightful?

The path arrives at the riverside where two surprises await. What's that utilitarian brick blockhouse, and why a single-track road and not a well-trodden footpath along the bank of the mill leat? A sharp left turn and here's the old quarry crammed with more utilitarian buildings surrounded by an unwelcoming metal grille fence and gate. What might it have looked like in the 16th Century when quarrymen busily clawed chalk from the cliff, burnt the lime and loaded it onto barges bound for Hampton Court? The thought is shattered by a gruff "Can I help you?" with sufficient 'edge' to suggest that help is not on offer. Fortunately this wary ***Thames Water*** engineer is mollified by my reassurance that I have permission from **Mike Yeadon** to explore as long as I stay on SGI land and don't enter his enclosure. And in no time, we are chatting happily and learning from each other.

The engineer says there have been freshwater boreholes along this riverbank for at least 170 years. The oldest of the nine currently in operation was drilled in 1948 by the *Burnham, Dorney & Hitcham Water Company* (founded 1891) which had acquired from **Lady Desborough** the rights to source the water and also to Taplow Village and ***New Taplow Paper Mills***. Later boreholes were drilled by its successors the *Middle Thames Water Board* and *Thames Water*. The deepest goes down 400 feet. Together they now supply water to two million people. Did he know that the old cornmill used to pump water to Taplow Court or that in the 1860s another of **Charles Pascoe Grenfell**'s projects was to install underground pipes to supply fresh water from the original boreholes not only to his home but also to houses in the village. No, but it fits, he says, because the water pipe under **Rectory Road** is very old. Still in good working order, he adds quickly. The surface trickles down there come from natural springs, not our pipes. He's not wrong.

William Henry Grenfell

Man for All Seasons – A Sporting Life

The fourth Taplow Court / 12th October 1891

As if things weren't as wonderful as could be back at Taplow Court 36 years ago, Charles Pascoe Grenfell's son Charles William Grenfell gave him a grandson who has grown up to be Willy Grenfell, a true man for all seasons [*see Appendix 1, Tree 17*].

In an era when 'being a sport' is paramount there can be few who 'play up and play the game' more impressively than **Willy Grenfell**. He earned a reputation for being a "young daredevil" at Harrow School where he played First XI cricket, won the foils competition and ran a mile in 4 minutes 37 seconds, a school record that will stand for 67 years. He was a founder member of **Maidenhead Rowing Club** in 1876 and its first captain. He kept up the pace at Balliol College, Oxford: he won at foils again and, having hosted his eight at Taplow Court as they practised on his stretch of the Thames, he rowed for the University against Cambridge in the dead-heat Boat Race of 1877 and in the easy victory the following year. He was Master of the Draghounds, remains the only person to have been concurrently president of both the Oxford University Rowing Club and Athletic Club and yet still found the time to excel at Alpine climbing by ascending the Little Matterhorn, Matterhorn, Monte Rosa, Rothorn and Weisshorn in eight days and the Matterhorn three times by different routes.

Willy's sporting prowess wasn't impaired by his spending six years from 1880 as a Gladstonian Liberal MP for Salisbury (Wiltshire). In 1881 he became the only MP ever to row in the Grand Challenge Cup at Henley Royal Regatta. He returned to Henley as a steward the following year and quickly took a leading role in defining exactly what *amateur* means when it comes to rowing. Stroking an eight across the English Channel in 1883 kept the adrenalin flowing until a year later he swam across the pool below Niagara Falls – naturally as near to the thunderous cascade as possible. He was a founder member of the Thames Punting Club in 1885 and somehow fitted four notable achievements into 1888: neither his new wife **Ethel Fane** nor a snowstorm could prevent him once again swimming across Niagara to prove to a sceptic that he had done it the first time; when he was hiking in the Rocky Mountains and his companion strayed from their camp and perished, he survived entirely alone for two days during which he passed the time by reading the works of Milton by candlelight; he served admirably as a special correspondent for *The Daily Telegraph* in the Sudan where, armed only with an umbrella, he is said to have outrun a horde of advancing tribesmen; and he won both the Upper and Lower Thames Single Punting Championships, a trick he twice repeated before retiring unbeaten. If he was disappointed to be able to take part in (and win) only the Upper Thames Championship this year, he can console himself that in 1889 he overcame blisters and violent muscular contractions to scull 105 miles from Oxford to Putney in 22 hours despite not having sculled at all for two years.

The admiration in which Willy is held locally was evident four years ago when he married Ethel, daughter of diplomat and poet Julian Fane, the son of John Fane, 11th Earl of Westmoreland. When Willy and Ettie returned from their honeymoon, they were met at Taplow Station by tenants and employees who hauled their carriage up Berry Hill as a gesture of fealty.

Willy will shortly bless Taplow Court with a *stické* court where he can play his favoured form of indoor tennis. Few will be surprised that the court will become a model for the sport which will evolve to become lawn tennis. Many think the man is probably the best all-round sportsman in the world and none other than his erstwhile neighbour George Sutherland-Leveson-Gower, **3rd Duke of Sutherland**, regards him as "the absolutely finest man I know". Who would argue? And surely there are more achievements to come, but is there something ominous lurking in the shadows?

Tall Tale – Witch's Brew

Bapsey Pond / 12th October 1891

Pagan lore still runs strong in the locals even now. There are rumours that black masses were held only a few years ago in the woods between the cricket club and ***Elibank***. And that an old lace-making lady who may have lived in the 1850s at what will become ***The Old Cottage*** would whisper that **Charles Pascoe Grenfell**'s interference with the sacred Bapsey spring was a desecration that deserved no less than a witch's curse on his family to decree that the estate would never pass from father to son.

Was the old banker shaken when young Charles William Grenfell, his only son and heir, died in 1861 at just 38 years old? Was the curse why Willy's uncle **Henry Riversdale Grenfell** divided his time between his homes in distant Somerset and at N° 15 St James's Place in London? Perhaps the family breathed more easily in 1867 when young Willy succeeded to his grandfather's estate: more than 3,000 acres of Buckinghamshire and Berkshire worth "under £180,000" (£136m). The lad was just 11-years-old and the future was bright, wasn't it? Or was it an omen when in 1883 the yew tree on **Tæppa's Mound** fell over? Traditionally a yew guards against witchcraft, after all. Willy and his brothers Claude and Charles wouldn't dream of needing the protection of a yew tree of all things. Until their maturity, the boys were under the guardianship of their Uncle Henry who also looked after Taplow Court for Willy. In 1884 Henry took the precaution of uniting with his three nephews and his sister Louisa's husband Theodore Walrond to establish a Grenfell trust to hold the Manor of Taplow but since Willy and Ettie now have two young sons – **Julian** and Gerald William (known as **Billy**) – and a third, Ivo, will soon follow, the succession is secure. Isn't it?

William Grenfell: Man for all Seasons

1890

Ethel with Billy & Julian / c1897

1895

Bapsey Pond: The Offending Culvert / 2012

The Whitlaws at Amerden

Charles Whitlaw the Elder

Wither Whitlaw?

Springfield, Town Lane / 12th October 1852

Charles Whitlaw has a Taplow connection – the **Francis Whitlaw** noted here at ***Springfield*** in 1789 was probably his uncle – but how come he can afford to acquire so much of it? His father-in-law William Ward was well-off enough in 1839 to be living in Cornwall Terrace by Regent's Park so Whitlaw's wealth was probably his wife Anne's. And yet her marriage settlement included a portfolio of consolidated stock represented in part by property in Amerden, which indicates a degree of affluence on his part and confirms his local link. So what's the story?

So Long – A Quacking Tale

Springfield Cottage, Berry Hill / 12th October 1982

Another **Francis Whitlaw** thinks he knows. This Francis is the grandson of Selina & Charles the Younger, the great-grandson of Anne & Charles the Elder and probably the great-times-three great nephew of his late-18th Century namesake. His guest and bridge partner **David Long** lives at ***Amerden House*** which Charles the Younger had built in 1874 and was home to Selina for 66 years until 1940. David smiles as Francis asserts that his great-grandfather was a quack....

Tall Tale – Carry on Surgeon

30 Argyll Street, Westminster / 12th October 2012

Francis wasn't quite right. According to the Royal College of Surgeons in Edinburgh, his great-grandfather **Charles Whitlaw** qualified in 1829 to practice the arts of Anatomy, Surgery and Pharmacy. However, this surgeon's uncle of the same name was a quack of the first order. And eventually **Charles Whitlaw the Eldest** came to do his quacking right here, just across the road from where *The London Palladium* has stood since 1910. This was his home from 1837 until his death in 1850 and the last clinic where as a 'surgeon' he treated patients in patented medicated vapour baths. Before going further with the nephew's story, we must get to know this uncle....

30 Argyll Street, Westminster / 12th October 1844

These are salad days for naturalists. Charles Darwin will of course steal everybody's thunder in 1859 with *On the Origin of Species*. Charles Whitlaw is a man of a parallel and no less vital vision with his promotion of homeopathy and natural treatments in the fervent belief that a healthy life has its roots in rich, well-cultivated soil and the plants that grow in it. Such tenets had their own roots at *Yester House* (near Gifford, East Lothian) where he had been introduced to the wonders of botany by his "agriculturalist" father William Whitly. Having been inspired by the works of the Swedish botanist and physician Carl Linnaeus during two years studying horticulture, landscape gardening and botany in Edinburgh, he set off across the Atlantic to seek his fortune. His surname toured all possible spellings in Canada, where his adventures began, and in New York where he settled in 1794 to practise garden design, establish a nursery and cultivate a reputation as a "medical botanist" based not on academic qualifications but on patents. He claims to have obtained "knowledge of the medicinal and other virtues of plants [while travelling in] the West Indies, Spanish America, the United States and Canada [and] among many of the North American Indians, especially the Creeks" and to have received "great assistance from a native Indian [who taught him] knowledge of plants and skill in the healing art". Perhaps this "native" was instrumental in his "important discovery of a native vegetable possessing in the highest degree the qualities for the preparation of cordage, thread and linen cloth". In 1812 he took out a US patent on processing the fibres of this "vegetable" – in fact, a nettle – as a substitute for hemp and flax. The nettle was given gravitas by being named *Urtica whitlawii* and his reputation sufficiently enhanced that in 1814 he was able to sell half the patent for the very tidy sum of $20,000 (£190,000) – or $30,000 (£285,000) according to another source – and head for London to be proposed for election to The Linnaean Society. If it was a blow to be 'black-balled', the ebullient Whitlaw was undeterred. He returned to America to deliver a very profitable series of lectures on botany illustrated with illuminated transparencies painted on glass by Dr Robert Thornton. He was styling himself "Professor of Botany" by 1817 and two years later decided to try his luck once again in London with a new venture.

In 1820, he published in *The Times* an advertisement headed "For the CURE of the SCROFULA – WHITLAW'S AMERICAN EXTRACT" which encouraged sufferers to attend his clinic at N° 87 Great Russell Street to be treated in his "patented medicated vapour baths". By 1822, the Asylum for the Cure of Scrofula & Glandular Diseases expressed satisfaction with "the efficacy and utility of [his] remedies" for this tuberculous bacterial infection of the lymph nodes in the neck and assigned Dr Isaac Puddick to work alongside him at his new clinic in Bayswater Terrace. And in 1824, having observed 670 cases over three years, the Asylum concluded that it was "justified in giving every publicity to a system of medical discipline which [is] capable, not only of disarming the disease of its terrors, but even of eradicating it from the constitution altogether". The Asylum duly granted Whitlaw's clinic charitable status and he continued to build his reputation with various publications and lectures on how a combination of "vegetable decoctions, a suitable plan of diet and regimen and the medicated vapour baths" can successfully treat not only scrofula but also "liver complaints, gout, rheumatism, asthma, debility and all other disorders arising from derangement of the digestive organs" and "the causes and effects of inflammation, fever, cancer [and] nervous affections".

There was continued hostility from the formally educated medical elite, but his business boomed and a number of times he moved his clinic to better premises, first in Soho and later at two addresses in Finsbury just north of London's 'Square Mile'. In 1831, he could afford spend $900 (£17,100) to import 13 boxes of medicinal herbs from Ohio. And despite accusations of illiteracy, he took to the written word with *Whitlaw's New Medical Discoveries with a Defence of the Linnaean Doctrine* (1829), a work incorporating an English translation of Linnaeus' 'Canons' from his 1749 treatise *Materia Medica* which will become an authoritative reference book for physicians for its catalogue of the dietetic and medicinal benefits that he claims can be derived from different plants. And later he turned his enquiring mind to natural fabrics, specifically to the Biblical prohibition of garments "mingled of linen and woollen" (Leviticus 19:19). Perhaps his interest had been sparked in conversation with the fifth Orkney, the erstwhile linen lord. In 1838 he published *The Scriptural Code of Health with Observations of the Mosaic Prohibitions* to offer not only confirmation that linen and wool could indeed work together to cause fatigue, fevers, inflammation, blisters, dehydration and death but also an explanation for the phenomenon. This will eventually be recognised as the discovery that wool electrons are rejected by linen molecules resulting in static electricity. It was a revelation that excited men of science but upset men of the cloth who were unhappy at the mystical word of God being given the blessing of Science and affronted by Whitlaw's assertion that the nervous system, circulation, heart and brains all "work electromagnetically".

Although he is now 73, Whitlaw is once again seeking new opportunities. With the finely-tuned marketing strategy he developed in his youth, he wrote on 1st May this year to "His Excellency" Thomas Ford, Governor of Illinois. He came quickly to the point – the "scourging disease of milk-sickness" from cattle – and then established his credentials by claiming to have been "a close observer of Causes and Effects in Nature during the last fifty years, [to having] had the honor of lecturing [in New York in 1826 to] His Excellency De Wit Clinton (sic) and a large class on Agriculture [and to his being] highly flattered by the intimation that I had been the humble means of affecting much good". His letter returned to the key issue by sharing observations made over many years that America's "virgin soil [has] become sour... unhealthy... and deficient in the necessary constituents of salts, alkalies, carbon and hydrogen" with the result that "the animals [have become] diseased and the grain unwholesome". He developed his theory that "cows and stock generally" had become susceptible to milk-sickness as a result of feeding "largely upon.... noxious plants [and] poisonous weeds" not indigenous to America. He went on to proclaim that, "with a view to lessen this growing evil and impress upon the minds of your farmers the necessity of paying more and judicious attention to the cultivation of their lands, I intend delivering at Cincinnatti and Pittsburgh a course of lectures in which I purpose making them thoroughly acquainted with every poisonous plant at present in the fields of this Country and the means of eradicating them". And he concluded by humbly requesting the Governor's "influence in persuading the intelligent in the Agricultural class in your neighbourhood to become my pupils on this occasion" and by adding that he would "esteem it an honor could I number you among my subscribers".

Twist in the Tale

Orkney Cottage, River Road / 12th October 2012

Uncle **Charles Whitlaw (the Eldest)** certainly had the gift of the gab. He was not merely an innovative scientist but also adept at making his name and his living from being one. An American recalled "once seen and heard, his image could never be obliterated. His portly person, ruby face, and broad Scotch accent, with a tone of confident assurance which told of perfect self satisfaction, made an indelible impress on my youthful mind." Clearly, he was the David Bellamy, Brian Cox, Patrick Moore and Alan Titchmarsh of his day all rolled into one. However, neither his science nor his style went down well with the medical establishment. More than a few eminent physicians risked his eloquent wrath by branding him a charlatan and a quack. In America, Dr David Hosack was "malicious" to question his character in 1825 and at home Sir Astley Cooper was "facetious" to question his medicine. Both gentlemen had grounds for scepticism – not least when a number of the Scot's asthma patients died after smoking *Lobelia inflata*, also known as *Indian tobacco* or *pukeweed*, to treat respiratory and muscle disorders – but perhaps their disdain was due as much to snooty superiority as scientific certainty. Would they moderate their stance now that some of Whitlaw's other ideas have become accepted wisdom? Theologians no longer reject that the human body is driven by electrical energy; instead they embrace the concept as evidence of God's wisdom. And many advocates of healthy living would warm to all or part of his *Plan of Diet and Regimen* which promoted fresh air and water, taking vapour baths and exercise and eating vegetables (boiled or raw) and starch-rich grains (wheat, oats, barley, rice, sago and tapioca), allowed dairy food, lean meat, fowls, fish, shellfish, coffee and tea in moderation, recommended against fruit and pickles (for their acidity), potatoes, salt and water contaminated by iron or lead pipes and strictly forbid fat and fatty meats (pork, goose or duck), rancid butter, decayed cheese and other greasy substances.

Some recommendations hit the spot, others miss it by a mile yet, for all his faults, it would be fun if this visionary Whitlaw was the Taplovian. He wasn't. However, it is easy for Whitlaw lore to mix the pair. Both were born in East Lothian in Scotland: the uncle in 1771, the nephew (recorded Chairls as a good Scots registrar might) on 23rd August 1805 to Isobel (née Butters), wife of gardener George Whitlaw. The nephew assisted the uncle at his clinics – indeed, that at N° 14 Finsbury Square seems also to have been his home. And the nephew's wife Anne died in 1899 at another Argyll Street, that in Kensington not Westminster, before being buried at St Nicholas' Church in Taplow.

It would be no surprise if the nephew's qualification as a surgeon added a certain professional credibility to the uncle's quackery, but it didn't last beyond 1836 when the pair fell out over *Lobelia inflata*. The uncle left for Argyll Street and in 1837 their sharp differences were played out in the pages of *The Lancet*. They never spoke again. The nephew was living in Paddington in 1841 and 1844 when his sons **Charles** and **George** were born, and a few years later he could be found as tenant of the original ***Springfield*** – but what brought him to Taplow?

It is likely that his father George, Charles the Quack and the **Francis Whitlaw** noted at ***Springfield*** in 1789 were brothers, all apparently with 'green fingers', and that the latter was recruited to assist on the **Taplow Court** estate through the familial link between **Mary O'Brien, 3rd Countess of Orkney**, and her cousin George Hay, 6th Marquess of Tweeddale and laird of *Yester*. This could explain how he knew of Taplow and, in 1852, the surgeon put down firm roots by investing his wife Anne's wealth to acquire both *Springfield* and Amerden. They and their two boys settled in ***Springfield Cottage*** until the new *Springfield* was completed. Since Taplow knew of no other Charles, the father and his namesake son were naturally differentiated as the Elder and the Younger. Sadly the Elder's salad days here were shortlived. **David Long** believes that Taplow has him to thank for its wealth of cedars but there is no record of the fertile Amerden farmland being subjected to the special science of agriculture and nutrition promulgated by **Charles Whitlaw the Eldest** (the quack). All seemed well until 1860 when Anne gave **Charles Whitlaw the Elder** (the surgeon) a daughter: Annie Mellicent Whitlaw. Perhaps the shock was just too much for he passed away the following year at only 56. His lasting legacy to Taplow was ***Orkney Cottage***, a new house built by Brunel's bridge in 1856. Perhaps this was intended for Charles the Younger. Instead it became a valuable family asset.

Charles Whitlaw the Younger

Carry on Counsel

Amerden House / 12th October 1883

Charles Whitlaw the Younger married in 1867 to **Selina Frances Ingpen**, daughter of Robert Ingpen, a Lambeth bank manager. Selina's marriage settlement noted her rather curiously as being a "spinster and infant of eighteen years and upwards" as it conferred upon her ***Orkney Cottage*** and ***Barge Farm*** including its farmhouse, outbuildings and 190 acres, 2 roods and 23 perches "or thereabouts" of land plus exclusive towing rights from Amerden Dyke to Maidenhead Bridge. They spent much of their first year of marriage apart, she studying at a university in Germany and he preparing to be called the Bar in 1869. Since then he has spent most weeks in London while Selina remained at *Springfield* so perhaps it was she and not he who hatched schemes to make a success of his inheritance, not by working the land but by making it work for them. The Amerden fishing rights are easy to let to enterprising locals and *Orkney Cottage* was the model for their tempting gentlemen of substance to enjoy rural riverside tranquillity easily accessible by train from London. ***Amerden Grove*** followed in the late-1860s, replacing the old mill by Amerden Ponds. James Franklin of Ewelme in Oxfordshire didn't make much of a success of running ***Amerden Bank*** as a hotel but the Whitlaw grand plan took a leap forward in 1874 when *Springfield* was let on a long-term tenancy and seven Amerden fields were sold to **Charles Palmer** of ***Dorney Court***. Charles and Selina moved here to their brand new home at ***Amerden House*** where she has given him two children, Rosa (now 8) and Charles Francis Whitlaw (3). And now ***River Bank*** and ***Fair View*** are available to let to those of independent means.

Charles the Younger's brother George almost followed in his footsteps to the Bar. He was a student of Middle Temple before graduating from Cambridge – as a Bachelor of Arts in 1866 and a Master two years later – and steering a different course to be noted two years ago at only 38 as a "retired unbenifacted clergyman" of Kensington. Meanwhile, local family ties have been strengthen by the marriage last July of the brothers' little sister Annie to Charles' wife's cousin John Ingpen, a Putney solicitor. They will soon be neighbours in Dorneywood [*see Appendix 1, Tree 19*].

The Peers at Clifden

Harriet Sutherland-Leveson-Gower, 2nd Duchess of Sutherland

Carry On Duchess

The Parterre, Clifden / 13th August 1863

His Grace the **Duke of Sutherland** had his luxury seat at *Trentham Hall* in Staffordshire and "the most valuable home in London" at *Stafford House* in St James's but George 'Looson-Gore' couldn't wait to start embellishing his broader canvas at Clifden [*see Appendix 1, Tree 10*]. He wasn't a man for half measures....

The parterre had become "a prairie". The head gardener **John Fleming** has expanded it to six acres and transformed it with 16 formal flowerbeds planted with different coloured sedums and edged with box hedging and yew topiary. The Duchess, Lady Harriet (daughter of George Howard, 6th Earl of Carlisle), is delighted to see her monogram recreated in sempervivums and echeverias. Fleming's innovative and stylish use of durable and easy-to-maintain dwarf foliage plants is already setting a popular horticultural trend known as 'carpet bedding'. He and his 21 hands don't neglect the less dramatic aspect of their art: the 16 acres of lawn are kept looking a picture and all the vegetables and flowers the house needs are grown in the five-and-a-half acre kitchen garden. All agree he is worth every penny of his annual salary of £100 (£81,750).

Meanwhile two architects have been at work. **George Devey** has remodelled the fourth Lady Orkney's riverside summer house to make it ***Spring Cottage*** and designed ***Seven Gable Cottage*** and three other 'vernacular' half-timbered cottages, a dairy and a boathouse while **Henry Clutton** has added a few modern conveniences and enhancements about the house. **William Gladstone** composed the frieze which encapsulates Cliveden's history and **Auguste Hervieu** adorned the stairwell ceiling with *The Four Seasons*. A high brick wall on the northern boundary hides the minor industry of a gasworks that provides the domestic luxury of light and heat but one project didn't go at all smoothly: in April 1860 the poor construction of a number of fireplaces and the consequential fire damage resulted in the dismissal of a certain F Roberts who was held culpable despite claiming he was elsewhere at the time. Clifden had had its fill of being destroyed by fire. Remedial works were instructed but Lady Harriet thought it best not to worry her ailing husband. He died none the wiser in February 1861 just months before completion of another project, this one a triumph. Clutton invested over £3,000 (£2.5m) in making the only significant change to the southerly aspect of Barry's design by adding an ornate 100-foot clock tower, actually a water tower with clocks. Visitors to Cliveden in 150 years will see everything else as it was in 1861 and water taps will still be fed from the 5,000-gallon water tank high in Clutton's tower.

The Duchess continues to live at the house for part of each year. She has long been considered rather radical for an aristocrat and enjoys the company of a wide range of friends. Clifden is a magnet for Whig grandees including Gladstone (currently in his second term as Chancellor of the Exchequer) and others of an artistic bent such as the Poet Laureate Lord Alfred Tennyson, the gardener and architect Sir Joseph Paxton and the fashionable sculptor Carlo Marochetti. She is now entertaining her sister Blanche's daughter Lady Lucy Cavendish who strolls beneath her parasol to the balustrade, looks out over the parterre and down to the Thames and whispers "When one lives in Paradise, how hard it must be to ascend in heart and mind to Heaven".

Perhaps the Italian revolutionary leader Giuseppe Garibaldi will be Harriet's most sensational catch. Next April, having received a rapturous welcome to London, he will retire to enjoy the delights of Clifden where he will leave a souvenir – a tree in the Ilex Grove by the Clock Tower (it will still be there in 2012) – and daringly smoke a cigar in Harriet's boudoir. Queen Victoria will tut-tut that her former Mistress of the Robes should succumb to such "follies".

Lady Harriet is very close to the Queen. She has attended Her Majesty for 15 of the first 24 years of her reign and was her solitary companion for several weeks after the death of Prince Albert in 1861. Victoria first came to admire the just-finished third Cliveden in 1854 and again in 1857. Perhaps the relaxed atmosphere of these occasions encouraged the ladies to recall with quiet amusement the 'Bedchamber Crisis' of 1839 when Sir Robert Peel, the prospective Tory Prime Minister, requested that Harriet and other Whiggish royal companions should be replaced. Victoria refused, Peel refused to form a government and – much to Her Majesty's liking – William Lamb, 2nd Viscount Melbourne was restored to power.

The Coming of the Queen

The Servants' Hall, Cliveden / 26th May 1866

Where are we going to put them all, Sophia Badcock the housekeeper wants to know. Let's just make sure Her Royal Highness is comfortable, says Charles Pincott the butler. Then we'll worry about the rest. George Rose the youngest footman is sent scuttling to the kitchen to tell Mary Penson the cook that the royals will want breakfast each day at 9.30, luncheon at 2, tea at 5 and dinner at 8.

A crisis is looming at Westminster. Parliament is debating the Reform Bill tabled by Prime Minister John Russell. His party – the Liberals – are split. The Tories are making mischief. **Queen Victoria** was in Balmoral. Where better than Cliveden for her to keep in close touch with proceedings while not actually being part of them?

Naturally, Lady Harriet has obliged by making her home available. Naturally, Her Majesty has taken the precaution of bringing with her an intimate party of 90 comprising three princesses, a prince and a piper, a duchess, a duke and a general, her companions Flora Macdonald and John Brown (each with their own companions), two doctors, two governesses, eight policemen, three dressers for herself and three more for the princesses, five footmen and 55 other servants plus the small matter of eight carriages, ten horses, twelve ponies and dogs without number. How she will enjoy getting away from it all for the nine days she is here. She will write to say how much she enjoyed the "quiet, beautiful woods" and the gardens, "a delight", and to convey her gratitude for the services of the "attentive Groom of the Chamber" and the "nice old coachman [who] kindly showed us around everywhere" including Cookham, Marlow, Wooburn and Burnham Beeches.

Cliveden Round Garden / 13th August 2013

When does an orchard become a garden? Perhaps it was **John Fleming** who with typically artistic flair laid out this 250-foot diameter garden as much for the Sutherlands to enjoy walking here as for tasting its fruit. Then it was highly ornamental with apple, plum, cherry and pear trees and strawberry, blackberry and redcurrant bushes trained up and over perhaps 180 seven-foot-high iron hoops. Now the garden is being restored under the direction of Cliveden's Senior Ranger **Tim Craufurd** who thinks it was probably abandoned during or soon after the Second War.

Hugh Grosvenor, 1st Duke of Westminster

The Richest Englishman

Clifden Terrace / 13th August 1882

Two years after Her Majesty's departure, Harriet was obliged to discover just how hard it was to leave Paradise behind when she ascended to Heaven. Clifden was quickly acquired by her daughter Constance's husband Hugh Lupus Grosvenor, then in his twenty-first year as Whig MP for Chester. When his father died within a year, Grosvenor became 3rd Marquess of Westminster and inherited *Eaton Hall* in Cheshire – then valued at £152,000 (£116.4m) – and an annual income of £115,000 (£8.8m) from family land in Mayfair and Belgravia [*see Appendix 1, Tree 10*]. Naturally he invested a little of this largesse in enhancing Clifden further. Among his additions to the house and gardens are the *porte cochere* on the north front of the mansion, a new stable block and the dovecote, all designed by **Henry Clutton** in or around 1870.

Like others at Clifden before him, Westminster is a royal favourite. **Queen Victoria** invested him as a Knight Companion of the Order of the Garter in 1870 and four years later elevated him to **1st Duke of Westminster**: the only non-royal dukedom she will create in her long reign. In 1880 she made him a Privy Counsellor and Master of the Horse but he was a man of many other parts. He went on to be Lord-Lieutenant of Cheshire, High Steward of Westminster and the first Lord-Lieutenant of the County of London. Meanwhile Constance was claimed by *Bright's Disease* (nephritis) in 1880 having borne eleven children, eight of whom survived to adulthood.

His Grace has recovered to marry again last month at his seat of Holkham Hall in Norfolk. This is his first opportunity to introduce his new wife to Clifden. The former Katherine Cavendish is the 24-year-old daughter of William Cavendish, 2nd Baron Chesham. Being 33 years his junior, she will be able to give him four more children. Perhaps tonight's the night for the first, Lady Mary, will be born nine months today.

Eyes of a Child – Jack Churchill

Clifden Reach / 13th August 1889

The Churchill boys are staying for a few days. It has been a wonderful day on the river. At 15, Winston is no novice with oars and poles. His nine-year-old brother Jack needed a little more help to learn rowing and punting from **Ben Cooper** whose job combines responsibilities as a gamekeeper and as a waterman with entertaining His Grace's guests. He has enjoyed teaching the lads the ways of the water but will be surprised this evening when they take him for a thank-you meal in Maidenhead that young Jack is already adept when it comes to smoking cigars.

The Temperant Philanthropist

The Guinea, Mayfair / 13h August 2012

The Victorians didn't invent committees but how they cherished them for getting good things done. They admired greatness in business and on the battlefield and they loved high-faluting titles yet the way to be seen as great and good was to be on or in committees, councils, associations and societies – or even better, to be chairman of this and president of that and to quietly use your wealth to oil the wheels of social well-being. Anyone with an aversion to lists might want to skip the next couple of sentences which demonstrate how His Grace is defined by the committees on which he served. At one time or another Westminster presided over the Royal Society for the Prevention of Cruelty to Animals, the Metropolitan Drinking Fountain & Cattle Trough Association, the Royal Agricultural Society, the Gardeners' Royal Beneficent Society, Hampstead Heath Protection Society, the Council for the Promotion of Cremation, the United Committee for Prevention of the Demoralisation of Native Races by the Liquor Traffic, the Early Closing Association, five London hospitals and the Queen's Jubilee Nursing Fund, an organisation that provided district nurses for the poor and through which he became associated with Florence Nightingale.

Having only recently invested £3 15s (£363) to have Maidenhead outfitter James Moore tailor a very smart suit for **Ben Cooper**, in 1893 this richest Englishman sold Cliveden to the richest American. As was often the case, his immense wealth was tied up in property and he needed the liquidity to make provision for his many children. In the last years of his life he supported the Seats for Shop Assistants Bill and, despite having disagreed passionately with **William Gladstone** over Parliamentary reform and Irish home rule, was only too willing to preside with equal passion over the memorial committee for the great Prime Minister. And by the time he died in 1899, his business acumen and astute development and management of his estates had made him by far the wealthiest man in England with assets of more than £6m (£5,255m). He had always been propriety personified: his Cheshire racing stable bred four Derby winners but he never gambled, and as a teetotaller and keen advocate of temperance he was survived by only 8 of 47 public houses in Mayfair and Belgravia. We'll drink to that. Just as well we're in this snug 337-year-old pub leased from the Grosvenor estate by *Young's Brewery* since 1888.

Cottages and Clocktower

Harriet, Duchess of Sutherland
– Franz Winterhalter 1849

Hugh Grosvenor,
Duke of Westminster 1878

Cliveden's Clocktower, *Spring Cottage* and *Seven Gables Cottage* / 2011

Chapter Six
Meeting the Neighbours

In which everyday Taplovians emerged from the shadows

Olden Days

Look Back to Go Forward

Taplow Village Centre / 28th October 2012

History prefers headlines and those who make them. In olden days, it rarely took notice of ordinary Taplovians. As lords of the manor the Grenfells still held administrative, financial and moral sway over Taplow. And as major landowners they, the Whitlaws and the Cliveden peers were also major employers. But the way of the world was changing around them. To understand how, we must look back before we can go further forward. The past really was....

Another Country

Ordinary People

Bapsey Green / 28th October 2012

In medieval Tappelowe, Aumberdene, Clyveden and Hecham, somebody was busy looking after the local nobility, serving and clothing them, cooking and cleaning for them. And others were fishing the river and ponds, cultivating the fields, cutting the woods or toiling in the mills and the quarries or tending all the chickens, geese and ducks, horses, rabbits, sheep, cows, goats and pigs. Whoever they were, these country folk got on with their everyday lives as best they could. Most did what they were born to, if they were lucky. The unlucky had to survive any which way they could.

Where did they live? Was there a medieval Tappelowe village? Wispy aerial photographs of **Taplow Cricket Club** seem to indicate some settlement in its south-west corner and the odd tall tale tells of previous buildings on the site of ***Queen Anne's House***. It would be logical for any cluster of dwellings to gather around the old church or here at Bapsey Green on the doorstep of the original village pub and at the gates of the manor house. Perhaps all evidence of any early village is lost beneath later houses and the south-eastern outbuildings of **Taplow Court**.

What was life like? Typically since Norman times each *cottar* was allocated a strip of land within a communal or 'open' arable field to grow food to subsist and each *villein* enough to subsist and to pay his lord rent in kind. Each peasant was also permitted according to his status to graze a certain number of animals on the common. In return for these privileges, all but freemen had also to toil on their lord's land or on the rector's glebe land. The law was what the local lord said. Arguments over allocations, jurisdictions or anything else were settled at the Courts Baron under his authority. Criminal matters were dealt with haphazardly until the 1280s when King Edward I tried to impose a more universal system in which Courts Baron managed feudal matters and accused criminals were tried by jury in Courts Leet. Until the 17th Century, all legal matters in the Burnham Hundred were dealt with at a single court run collectively by the various lords, or more likely by the steward or bailiff of whoever was top dog.

Courts Baron were the way of the rural world until the Victorian era but there was something of a shake-up after the **Black Death** devastated the country in 1348-1550. No records confirm the nature and scale of the impact of the Black Death locally. Maybe all the local scribes succumbed. Perhaps the hamlet of Linlei was wiped out at ***Lillyfee Farm*** on **Wooburn Common**. And possibly much of Tappelowe too, including the brassy **Nicholas de Aumberdene**, but impossible that its aftermath did not have an effect on South Bucks. Estimates vary considerably but some suggest the plague cut England's population by half, possibly more. Suddenly any fit labourer was worth his weight in groats if not gold but he wasn't paid as such. This caused nationwide social unrest that finally came to the boil with the Peasant's Revolt in 1381 and within a few years massive social changes were happening nationwide. Serfdom had gone. Everyone could be a copyholder, meaning they held a copy of an agreement with their lord confirming their tenure of whatever land, property or rights they could afford to pay rent for. And they could bequeath this tenure to heirs who could pay the necessary *heriot* to the lord of the manor, in effect a death duty dating from Anglo-Saxon times. Those who were left were better fed; the spiral of decreasing soil fertility and increasing population was at an end and once things settled down the cost of living fell. There was land available for sheep; their wool and the cloth industry were to make England rich. Wages had risen; people with pennies in their pockets had greater freedom of decision. The clergy had been decimated; people had to find a more personal relationship with God. And for the first time in over 300 years, those in charge spoke not French but English, the language of everyday people.

At first glance things stayed much the same in Tappelowe and Hecham – the lords were still sitting pretty – but the seeds of change had been sown. Englishmen were realising greater rights to plough their own furrow and accepting the responsibilities that went with it. There was still plenty of work to do in the shadows but also occasional instances of ordinary folks emerging into the spotlight. One way to become notable overnight was to die dramatically. The unfortunate **Giles Chertsey** did just that in 1379 when he was killed by a mudslide at Tappelowe quarry. The Goodwin family of Wooburn found a better way. They rose in four generations from peasant farmers to major landowners, church benefactors, Members of Parliament and knighthoods.

The quarry stills exists here below Taplow Court's western cliff, a conveniently semi-secret site for a Thames Water pumping station. Chalk extraction may have begun here in the Roman era. The chalk is too soft to be used as stone for building but it was still a very valuable commodity. It could be ground down to make an alkaline fertiliser for neutralising acidic soils, or burnt to make quicklime for use in construction as mortar, cement or whitewash. Next time you go to Hampton Court, remember that its ancient bricks are bonded by Taplow mortar. Quicklime was also used as a weapon, either as a detonator for explosives or a blinding agent – as exercised by **King Henry III**'s navy – so even without landslides, Master Chertsey and his mates ran the risk of not only having their skin, eyes and innards burned by this nasty stuff but also of fire and explosions since when it reacts with water, enough heat is released to ignite anything combustible.

The Brickmakers' Arms, Lent Rise / 31st October 2012

Others were also playing with fire as they moulded and baked brick-earth in kilns at Poyle and Lent Rise to make bricks and tiles. The **Lent Rise** brickworks were on the sites of modern-day Lent Rise School and the Methodist chapel at the junction of **Nearways** and Lent Rise Road. The ancient industry is remembered in the name of this pub. There were also brickworks at Holtspur north of **Wooburn Green** and at Hedsor near ***The Chequers Inn***.

The Jolly Woodman, Littleworth Common / 31st October 2012

The name of this pub reminds us that another asset grew on trees. Or rather, it was the trees themselves. South Bucks had perhaps the best beech woods in the country. Coppiced beech, whitebeam and ash were just perfect for making furniture and fellies (wheel rims) and Bucks boys became brilliant at turning green (unseasoned) wood to make cylindrical elements like chair legs and tool handles. This traditional skill continued into the 1900s when in the Chiltern Hills around **High Wycombe** it was uniquely called *bodging* in defiance of Shakespeare's use of *bodge* to mean a temporary and usually clumsy job of repair.

It is hard now to understand how economically important the woods were. Oak was abundant and highly prized for all kinds of construction, especially boat-building. Acorns and beech-mast were excellent winter-feed for livestock. Juniper berries were used for gin-making and, like rowan berries, for food-flavouring. Wych elm was used to make wheel hubs, boat keels and rudders, coffins, floorboards and eventually underground water pipes. Many other trees could be used for construction. Some had medicinal value in their berries, bark or sap. And a few such as rowan and yew were magic or mystical. Yew was perfect for making longbows and ash for arrows which had heads and flights stuck on with birch glue. Maple sap made syrup or wine and its wood was just right for carving into harps and other musical instruments. Hazelnuts were nutritious and it was believed gave wisdom and inspiration. Willow was multi-purpose: its bark made fertiliser, its catkins were attractive to honey-making bees and could be mashed to make food, its osiers (shoots) were just right for making baskets, kiddles (fish traps), wicker, fences and frames for coracles or wattle-and-daub houses and its wood for making charcoal, brooms, tools, furniture, flutes, whistles, wands, paper, rope, string and (eventually) cricket bats.

Village Variations

Bapsey Green / 9th November 1612

The green is as big as it ever will be – hardly big enough to qualify as a village green but nevertheless the hub of the village, such as it is. Just over there is a 200-year-old thatch-and-plaster cottage. A cluster of more modest cottages skirts the southern edge of the green to straggle west down the lane to the Saxon mound and spill perhaps 50 yards down the hill to the junction with a lane running east which has a few more cottages on the right about 100 yards along – where ***Taplow Hill Cottages*** will be come the 1860s. And 60 yards to the north of the green is an impressive view of Sir Henry Guldeforde's pride and joy: Topley Court.

Across the road is a footpath running east through the wood along the southern edge of **Ten Acres** before twisting right and left to emerge into **Pater Noster**, a pasture with a spring in its north-west corner that feeds a pond. This natural source of fresh water has become a magnet for a cluster of timber-framed cottages. Just beyond the pond on the right is a thatched farmhouse, perhaps 10 or 15 years old. A young woman is carrying two pails of water from the pond into its open door. Could she know **Sarah Jeffrey**, wife of the scrivener-cum-composer John Milton of Cheapside in London whose almost 4-year-old son **John Milton** will become a poet of enduring renown? There are many Jeffreys of various spellings hereabouts and the 1863 edition of *Kelly's Directory* will claim Sarah is buried in the old churchyard. Could she be related to the **Mary Jefferies** who will marry the first **John Briginshaw** hereabouts, or to the **Paul Jeffries** who in 400 years will live at ***Pax Cottage***?

At the curl of The Pightail / 9th November 1612

A few yards farther on is the elbow of a broader track turns sharply from east to north, a curly twist for which it is called **The Pightail**. Up the hill to the left a farmer's lad whistles a happy tune as he leaves another tiny cottage. Across the road a glazier is repairing the leaded lights in a row of three cottages now some three years old. Soon two more cottages will be added to the northern end of this row. Could it be that this junction with its nearby source of fresh water is already on its way to becoming the new heart of the village?

Rutland's Register

At the curl of The Pightail / 9th November 1612

Who are these people? People and places can't yet be matched but the first real change in the balance between the lords and the locals is under way. Many parishes have started noting the baptisms, marriages and burials of ordinary people. Having served all but three years of the four decades he will be Rector of Taplow, the Reverend **John King** began to do just that in 1604. The Reverend Robert Lloyd did the same for Hitcham four years later.

Each record in Taplow's Parish Register is as brief as can be but already they tell a tale or two, especially about Richard Russel and Frauncisci Becke. King's first entries note the baptisms of Russel's son Thomas on 29th May 1604 and Becke's son Jacob five weeks later. His successor the Reverend John Rawlinson gave witness to the first life to begin and end on record – Russell's second son Solomon was baptised on 2nd October 1608 and buried a week later – and only the day before yesterday he buried Dennis Becke just four days after baptising her baby son John. It is unlikely her grieving husband cared his name has been anglicised as Francis. Spelling inconsistency has also afflicted the royal steward: King baptised "Thomas son of Henrici Gilford" in 1605 and six years later Rawlinson presided at the baptism of "John son of **Henry Guldeford**, Knight". Happily not all is doom and gloom: the first recorded marriage was that of Marie Smith and **Richard Palmer** on 20th June 1616 a little less than three years after he had buried his first wife Jane.

At the curl of The High Street / 9th November 2012

History is indebted for this 400-year-old detail to **James Rutland** who during 32 years as Parish Clerk from 1875 transcribed Taplow's old Parish Register and maintained current records in a single volume. Sadly he was unable to locate the original pages from 1616 to 1710 but his dedication and diligence enables us to glimpse those whose lives and interactions shaped Taplow before national censuses started to colour in detail from 1841. His records reveal an evolving social pyramid with an ever-expanding waistline....

Out for the Count

Having Faith

Fulham Palace / 9th November 1676

The Restoration hasn't made religious differences disappear. In fact, it has added new dimensions. The mood is for middle-of-the-road Church of England but gremlins lurk on either side. **King Charles II** persecutes non-conformists and claims to be C of E but rather indulges Catholics. The growing fear is that he might not only revert to claiming divine right and imposing papist supremacy but could also fall under the thumb of the increasingly dominant King Louis XIV of France. Archbishop of Canterbury Gilbert Sheldon decided it would be prudent to get an idea of the challenge facing the Church of England. He instructed Henry Compton, the new Bishop of London, to conduct a nationwide ecclesiastical census comparing the number of adult male Anglicans in each parish with the number of 'popish recusants' and 'dissenters'.

As he carefully consolidates the results of the survey, Compton realises that it leaves much to be desired. The priests who carried it out have been inconsistent in their diligence and accuracy about such matters as when a boy became an adult, how to count Catholics, Quakers and Baptists who habitually avoided them like the plague and how to gather reliable responses when their subjects' yen for a quiet life might have encouraged them to say what they thought the priests hoped to hear.

Taplow Village Centre / 9th November 2012

The schedule may involve rather too much guesswork for modern analysts but it provides an idea of the relative and total local populations in 1676 – with a limited comparison to 1523 – and reveals a dearth of Catholics and a fairly widespread distribution of non-conformists everywhere except here. Taplow was still free of dissent in 1709 and in 1851, by which time there were none in Hitcham either although Burnham, Dorney and Littleworth had Methodist, Wesleyan or Congregationalist Chapels.

Bishop Compton's Ecclesiastical Survey 1676

	Church of England	Non-conformist	Catholic	1676 Total	1523 Total
Hedgerley	38	4	0	42	
Hitcham	51	4	0	55	13
Hedsor	61	9	0	70	
Dorney	83	6	2	91	34
Taplow	144	0	5	149	
Farnham Royal	159	24	1	184	33
Wooburn	200	12	0	212	
Burnham	436	4	0	440	80
Beaconsfield	637	12	0	649	
Total	**1811**	**75**	**8**	**1894**	

Source – National Archives

The Sum of Civil Power

Stowe House, Buckinghamshire / 9th November 1798

Living across the Channel from the revolting French this past decade has led to two social novelties as Great Britain evolves towards becoming the United Kingdom. The first – a yeoman militia – will last on and off for almost eight decades. The second – a national census – will still be going in 2011.

In 1794 the Volunteer Act required "gentlemen of weight or property" to establish volunteer military formations in readiness to resist the feared invasion by French revolutionary forces and to subdue any civil disorder. Now **Lord Temple** has gone further by having John Penn, High Sheriff of Buckinghamshire, conduct the ***Posse Comitatus*** (meaning *Civil Power*) to identify all resources in the county that could be called upon should the need arise, and especially all men from 16 and 60 who are neither Quakers, clergymen, physically incapable nor already in the military. This table compares a summary of the returns for Taplow and five neighbouring parishes with those of Burnham Hundred as a whole and with the County.....

Posse Comitatus 1798

Location	Boveney	Burnham	Dorney	Eton	Hitcham	Taplow	Burnham Hundred	Buckinghamshire
Parishes							28	263
Men	36	167	53	340	32	78	3,053	23,547
Horses							1,720	13,854
Carts							714	6,125
Waggons							294	3,056
Watermills							14	97
Windmills							1	25

Source – Centre for Buckinghamshire Studies, Aylesbury

Meanwhile the *Posse Comitatus* will be a blinding flash of the obvious for Prime Minister **William Pitt the Younger**. He will see immediately that it makes much sense for a national leader to know how many he was leading and how many needed feeding. His government decided to count people, families, houses, baptisms, marriages and burials, and to note who did what for a living but not their names. The first census will be taken in England, Scotland and Wales in 1801 and again on the same model every ten years until 1831. This table compares the total returns of our six local parishes over that span....

Comparison of Population of Neighbouring Parishes in 1801 and 1831

Parish	Boveney	Burnham	Dorney	Eton	Hitcham	Taplow	Total
1801	165	1,354	190	2,026	200	422	**4,357**
	+42 (+25%)	+576 (+43%)	+78 (+41%)	+1206 (+60%)	+32 (+16%)	+225 (+53%)	+2159 (+50%)
1831	207	1,930	268	3,232	232	647	**6,516**

Victorian Values

The Gables, The Pikel / 9th November 1891

Georgian censuses introduced nationwide span and the Victorians added further new dimensions – names of individuals were first recorded in 1841 and gradually the thoroughness and sophistication of census-taking increased to open much deeper perspectives into everyday lives. Consequently **James Rutland** can compare the census taken in April this year with figures from 1851 in order to understand how the coming of the railway has impacted the populations of Taplow and Hitcham.

Table 1 reveals that the total population of Taplow has grown by a quarter over 40 years during which there has been a dramatic shift from the Taplow-born, down from four-tenths to just over a quarter, to those drawn from afar, up from less than one-third to well over four-tenths. These proportions are broadly reflected in the Village where increases in the number of newcomers can be explained by the influx of wealthy residents together with domestic staff and commercial trades eager to 'follow the money'. The greatest magnet is in the Valley where faraway folk have tripled and only one-fifth are Taplovians, clear evidence of the increasingly cosmopolitan nature of life along the Bath Road and down by the river. There are even newcomers on the more parochial Common where the balance is now a broadly equal three-way split.

1 – Taplow: Comparison of Origin and Location of Population in 1851 and 1891

Hitcham New Town took root in the 1830s during the construction of the railway. Table 2 indicates that the number of Hitcham's Valley People has grown fivefold, an increase driven by new Taplow Station and its goods yard. However, since two-thirds were born in Hitcham parish or nearby (within a day's walk), this is due to a very local relocation rather than an influx of outsiders. In contrast, half those in Hitcham Village are newcomers, mainly in service at ***Blythewood***, and only one-sixth are Hitcham-born. Up on Hitcham Common, the population has fallen by a quarter due in part to the New Town magnet and in part to Dropmore being less of a hive of rural activity than in the Grenville era. The proportionate increase in folk from not far away might be explained by gaps being filled by those seeking refuge from creeping industrialisation.

	Common		Village		Valley		Total		Percentage	
Origin	**1851**	**1891**	**1851**	**1891**	**1851**	**1891**	**1851**	**1891**	**1851**	**1891**
Taplow	44	75	163	115	70	48	277	238	39.3%	27.1%
Nearby	47	73	101	116	75	70	223	259	31.7%	29.4%
Elsewhere	33	70	127	189	44	124	204	383	29.0%	43.5%
Total	**124**	**218**	**391**	**420**	**189**	**242**	**704**	**880**	**100%**	**100%**
Percentage	17.6%	24.8%	55.5%	47.7%	26.9%	27.5%				

Source – National Archives Censuses (1891 excludes 137 pupils at Taplow Grammar School and 12 visitors)

2 – Hitcham: Comparison of Origin and Location of Population in 1851 and 1891

	Common		Village		Valley		Total		Percentage	
Origin	**1851**	**1891**	**1851**	**1891**	**1851**	**1891**	**1851**	**1891**	**1851**	**1891**
Hitcham	31	16	26	21	28	107	85	144	36.0%	29.3%
Nearby	27	31	40	36	21	106	88	173	37.3%	35.1%
Elsewhere	20	11	28	64	15	100	63	175	26.7%	35.6%
Total	**78**	**58**	**94**	**121**	**64**	**313**	**236**	**492**	**100%**	**100%**
Percentage	33.1%	11.8%	39.8%	24.6%	27.1%	63.6%				

Source – National Archives Censuses (1891 excludes 20 pupils at The Beeches School)

Rutland now examines the up-to-date data to understand what people do for a living.

Taplow has 205 dwellings in all: 92 in and around the Village (including the Grammar School and its nearby string), 50 on the Common and 63 in the Valley. Almost half the population is directly employed by a little more one-tenth who are independently wealthy or commercially successful. According to Table 3, only one-tenth of income-earners work the land, half as many again keep it looking good and almost one-third are in domestic service. The most significant growth has been on the Common where myriad maids, gardeners, grooms, gamekeepers and the like gather around **Cliveden**. Elsewhere staffs are smaller but everyone who is anyone has one, even small businessmen and senior employees.

3 – Taplow: Comparison of Occupations by Location of Population in 1891

Occupations		**Common**	**Village**	**Valley**	**Total**	**Percentage**	
Building	Builders, Painters & Carpenters	5	11	2	18	2.1%	3.9%
Commercial	Bankers, Stockbrokers, Businessmen, Retailers, Publicans, Hoteliers, Gas & Coal Workers, Insurers, Clerks, Dressmakers & Needlewomen	8	25	22	55	6.3%	11.9%
Gardening	Gardeners & Garden Labourers	26	32	11	69	7.8%	15.0%
General	Labourers	2	12	4	18	2.1%	3.9%
Horses	Fly Drivers, Coachmen, Stable Lads, Grooms & Blacksmiths	6	28	9	43	4.9%	9.3%
Independent	Pensioners, Retired Officers & those 'Living on their Own Means'	5	18	8	31	3.5%	6.7%
Land	Farmers, Farmhands, Shepherds, Cowmen, Dairymaids, Estate Agents, Huntsmen, Gamekeepers & Nightwatchman	16	13	18	47	5.3%	10.2%
Papermills	Millwrights, Papermakers & Labourers	8	0	2	10	1.1%	2.2%
Professional	Rector, Sexton, Teachers & Policeman	0	14	1	15	1.7%	3.3%
Railway	Railway Policeman & Labourer	0	0	2	2	0.2%	0.4%
River	Boat Builders, Boat Proprietors, Watermen, Ferryman & Fisherman	1	0	13	14	1.6%	3.0%
Service	Domestic Servants, Nursemaids, Laundresses, Housekeepers, Caretakers & Errand Boys	22	80	37	139	15.8%	30.2%
	Income-Earners	**99**	**233**	**129**	**461**	**52.4%**	**100%**
Adults	Wives & Families	45	88	55	188	21.4%	
Children	Scholars & Babies	74	99	58	231	26.2%	
	Dependents	**119**	**187**	**113**	**419**	**47.6%**	
	Total	**218**	**420**	**242**	**880**	**100%**	
	Percentage	24.8%	47.7%	27.5%		100%	

Source – National Archives Census (excludes 137 pupils at Taplow Grammar School and 12 visitors; an estate agent was an estate manager not somebody who sold land or buildings)

Hitcham now has 110 dwellings altogether: 74 in the Valley, just 12 up on the Common and 24 in the Village and on the edge of Taplow. Table 4 shows that only one-seventh of the population earn their living on the land in a parish where the land has been the livelihood for centuries. The occupational shift is evident in that one-third of all income-earners (more than half of those in the Village) are in domestic service or keeping the gardens at large houses, primarily ***Blythewood***, and the ***Great Western Railway*** employ one-sixth of all income-earners (almost one-third of those in the Valley) plus many of the building tradesmen and general labourers on an ad-hoc basis.

4 – Hitcham: Comparison of Occupations by Location of Population in 1891

Occupations		Common	Village	Valley	Total	Percentage	
Building	Builders, Bricklayers & Carpenters	4	2	7	13	2.6%	6.5%
Commercial	Businessmen, Retailers, Publicans, Clerks, Dressmakers & Needlewomen	3	5	8	16	3.3%	8.0%
Gardening	Gardeners & Garden Labourers	7	9	7	23	4.7%	11.6%
General	Labourers	2	2	22	26	5.3%	13.1%
Horses	Fly Drivers, Coachmen, Stable Lads, Grooms & Blacksmiths	1	5	6	12	2.5%	6.0%
Land	Farmers, Farmhands, Cowmen & Shepherds	9	14	5	28	5.7%	14.1%
Professional	Rector & Teachers	0	2	3	5	1.0%	2.5%
Railway	Engine Drivers, Porters, Platelayers, Signalmen, Clerks & Labourers	0	0	33	33	6.7%	16.6%
Service	Domestic Servants, Nursemaids, Laundresses, Housekeepers, Caretakers & Errand Boys	4	26	13	43	8.7%	21.6%
	Income-Earners	**30**	**65**	**104**	**199**	**40.5%**	**100%**
Adults	Wives & Families	12	20	74	107	21.5%	
Children	Scholars & Babies	16	36	135	187	38.0%	
	Dependents	**28**	**56**	**209**	**293**	**59.5%**	
	Total	**58**	**121**	**313**	**492**	**100%**	
	Percentage	11.8%	24.6%	63.6%		100%	

Source – National Archives Census (excludes 20 pupils at The Beeches School)

From the Shadows

Eyes of a Child – Jennifer Neal & Keira Smales

St Nicolas' School / 23rd April 2012

Jennifer thinks the **St Nicolas' Church** graveyard is very big. There are lots of graves in there, she says, some of them so old they have broken. Keira likes the graveyard. It is nice and relaxing. You can admire the ragged wall with all the ivy curling round it. All the graves let you find people who used to live here. It makes you think about Taplow's past and recent dates.

Neighbourly Beginnings

The New Churchyard / 16th November 2012

As I've explored the Parish Register, the censuses and as many old *Kelly's Directories* that I could lay my hands on, previous Taplovians have emerged from the shadows. Now when I walk around the churchyard, I feel I am among friends. Here lie the Briginshaws and Norringtons, married in the old St Nicholas' Church and buried by the new beneath a phalanx of six gravestones. They are neighbours in death; their matriarchs were Neighbours in life.

The Old Churchyard / 16th November 2012

John Briginshaw the Elder is first noted in 1746 as a St Nicholas' Churchwarden and later with the profitable responsibility of farming the Rector's glebe land. He may have hailed from Halton near Wendover to marry **Mary Jefferies** of Wooburn at Windsor in 1749 and have seven children in Taplow within 12 years. By 1795 he was at *Tythe Farm* where he died two years later aged 90. His widow was laid next to him in the Old Churchyard in 1809 and they were joined over the next 33 years by six of their children, their daughter-in-law Elinor (née **Neighbour**) and Mary's spinster sister Sarah Jefferies. Their gravestones once stood proudly. Now they lie flat, possibly as a result of the disruptions when Tæppa's Mound was excavated in 1883.

Nearby are the even older Neighbours from whom the matriarchs sprang. The moss can be brushed from the inscriptions on some gravestones to reveal who lies beneath. **Davis Neighbour** held ***Home Farm*** in 1762 when married Lydia Lonon. His brother **John Neighbour the Elder** married her sister Ann Lonon two years later. By then the tiny cottage we saw 400 years ago had been joined to make a terrace of three cottages and eventually six. The brothers were both churchwardens and overseers of the poor. It isn't clear if either or both the brothers lived in the terrace but one or both held their copyhold so they naturally came to be called ***Neighbour's Cottages***.

The elder John Neighbour died in 1809. The inscription on his gravestone in the Old Churchyard reads: *A sudden change! He in a moment fell and had not time to bid his friend farewell. Think nothing strange, change happens to us all. His lots today to*

Morrow thine may fall. What took Old John so suddenly? Which philosophical friend thought so wistfully and so wise?

Neighbour's Cottages, Back Lane / 16th November 1808

Lydia & Davis Neighbour had twelve children, eight of whom have grown to adulthood. He has today led his sixth and youngest daughter Lydia Neighbour up the aisle of St Nicholas' Church to marry **William Norrington**, originally of Wiltshire, now in the employ of Lady Orkney and an overseer of the poor, for which he earns £20-a-year (£21,400). By 1825 he will be steward of the **Taplow Court** estate and holding ***Home Farm***. His son **George Norrington** will be a farmer, miller and pillar of early-Victorian Taplow.

In 1790, Davis & Lydia's second daughter **Elinor** (occasionally Elenor, eventually Eleanor) married **John Briginshaw the Younger**, son of Mary & John, who farms at ***Amerden Bank***, sometimes noted as *Amerden Manor Farm*. Three of their sons merit mention. In three years **William Davis Briginshaw** will marry Sarah, widow of Elinor's cousin **John Neighbour**. He and William Norrington will be Taplow tax assessors or collectors until 1831 and possibly beyond. He and George Norrington will be churchwardens from before 1838 until after 1857. His brother **John Briginshaw** will marry Mary Maria Hammaton of Bray in 1820 and succeed to *Foxley's Farm*; they will continue the family tradition of confusing genealogical research by giving the first of their ten children the unusual name of John Briginshaw (1821-1861). Fortunately that will be over in Berks. Back in Taplow in 1837 **Richard Briginshaw** will wed **Grace Norrington**, daughter of Lydia & William, and within four years will be at ***Rectory Farm***, previously *Glebe Farm* and, before that, *Tythe Farm*.

In 1800, Lydia and Elinor's middle sister **Elizabeth Neighbour** married **Thomas Gurney**. The destiny of their line will be in retail. Their daughter **Mary** will marry the Taplow Court gardener **Edward Darling** and become the village shopkeeper. The shop will remain in the Gurney family until the late-1930s. In 1837 their grandson **William Gurney** will marry **Elizabeth**, daughter of **Eliza & William Rance the Elder**, the village butcher and also a farmer.

This Neighbourly genetic matrix will extend for up to five generations. It will be impossible not to stumble across various branches of it as we journey through Taplow's times [*see Appendix 1, Tree 20*].

Amerden Bank / 16th March 1841

William Davis Briginshaw is examining the Churchwardens' Account dated the 8th of this month. He notes with quiet satisfaction that while Lord Orkney's freehold land has an annual value of £477 15s (£611,000), the value of land held copyhold by his family is £861 12s (£1.1m) – that's £372 12s (£475,000) he holds himself, £354 (£453,000) held by his brother Richard at ***Rectory Farm***, £97 15s (£125,000) and £23 10s (£30,000) by his cousins George Norrington and **William Davis Neighbour** (son of Ann & John) and £13 15s (£17,000) by his uncle William Norrington. On his death in 1860 WDB will leave his copyhold to his nephews William and (yet another) John Briginshaw, sons of Grace & Richard, and spread £15,000 (£13.2m) between them and 73 other friends and relatives.

Spell Check – Freinds and Neibours

Neighbours, Hill Farm Road / 16th November 2012

The Freinds noted in Hitcham for 79 years until 1794 weren't the only family to suffer the vagaries of 18th Century spelling. **Davis** and **John Neighbour the Elder** are probably the younger siblings of **Margaret** and **Ann Neibour** who in 1754 married Edward Shepherd and Thomas Louch, and their wives Lydia and Ann Lonon seem to be daughters of Ann & John London who were first noted in 1740 when their son John was baptised. A miller called William Shekel married in 1748 and had a baby son John Shackle who died the following year. Even their eminent neighbours the O'Briens of Inchiquin appear in Parish Register as O'Brian and O'Bryen and elsewhere as O'Bryan.

Possibly the most intricate string of wayward spelling began in 1719 with the appearance of **Robert Lambourn** who was **Robert Sambourn** at his daughter Mary's baptism the following year. Was he the father of **Joseph Lamburn** whose wife Elizabeth gave birth to Sarah in 1747? Elizabeth & Joseph were **Samburn** four years later when they buried Sarah but Lamburn again in 1753 when their new daughter Sarah was baptised only to be **Sambourn** by the time the infant was buried the following year. They were Lamborn in 1756 at the baptism of their daughter Rebecca and he went to his grave in 1801 as Lamburn. A different Joseph Lamburn's daughter Ann had her "baseborn son" **Thomas Sambourn** baptised on 26th January 1772 only to pass away eight years later (if she was still Ann Sambourn) or nine (if she was Ann Samburn). No wonder the orphan Tom grew up to be the convict transported in 1791 to New South Wales. Meanwhile Robert's line extended to either or both the railway porter **Stephen Lambourne** (1855) and labourer **Jessie Lambourne** (1892) but probably not to George Lambourn who between 1836 and 1857 became **George Lambourne**, the timber merchant who gave his name to **Lambourne Wood**. It seems that this last fellow came from the Isle of Wight just to confuse matters.

Sad Snapshots

Persons Unknown

The Old Churchyard / 3rd December 1787

My whimsical wander with the departed has taken me further back into the past. St Nicholas' Church is packed for the funeral of the Honourable Reverend **George Hamilton**. Those who can't squeeze inside are waiting to pay their respects to the late Rector and Parish Clerk as he is laid to rest. Everyone else is silent but **William Hearn** is in a mood to gossip. He wonders in a loud whisper whether Lord Inchiquin and Lady Orkney will grace us with their presence, what with all the objections the good Reverend raised about the recent inclosure award. Nobody responds. He suspects all the worry about inclosures might have hurried the old chap to his end. Nobody comments. Hearn goes on to speculate that, what with him being a Hamilton and all, might the Rector have been related to the Countess's grandfather?

Somebody points out that, since he was the fourth son of James Hamilton, 7th Earl of Abercorn, his heritage is not Scottish but Irish. Hearn observes with a twinkle in his eye that he knew Hamilton wouldn't be English even if he sounded it because our betters never are nowadays. And anyway around here the nobs are as much Irish as they are Scottish. When nobody takes the bait, Hearn takes a different tack. He remarks with wry grin that Hamilton's rectorship was a risky time for 'persons unknown'. He has something there. Having served this parish these past 34 years, the Reverend Hamilton has had in the last 20 the dubious privilege of burying seven such unfortunates who have met their Maker while travelling through Taplow. Incredibly only three other unknowns have suffered the same fate since 1710 and there will be only two more in the next six score years: one in 12 months time and the other not until 1904 when a poor fellow will be found dead in one of the ***Rectory Farm*** barns on what will one day be the Village Green.

At least two travelling paupers will survive long enough to avoid being 'unknowns'. John Lloyd will expire "thro want and inclemency of weather" in December 1802. And in the dead of a winter's night in 1897, the wealthy coal merchant **Richard Webster** of **Hill Farm** will come across 45-year-old Rosa Grimsdale lying in the road "in a dying state". He will take the poor woman to the compassionate **James Rutland** who will convey her in his carriage to the Slough Union workhouse where she will die with dignity.

Someone reminds Hearn that these sad stories contrast with a happy one from 1721 when a baby boy was found abandoned by Maidenhead Bridge. Before he is hushed by the arrival of the funeral cortege, Hearn retorts that, if the lad thought being given the name William Bridge left a little to be desired, he could count himself luckier than the more recent unfortunates.

A Plague upon Them

The Old Churchyard / 3rd December 1787

Eighteen gravestones dating from 1671 to 1738 catch the eye for the skull-and-crossbones carved upon them. Do these deadly images indicate the last resting place of victims of the plague or are they a stonemason's ruse to deter prospective graverobbers? Can any mason be trusted whose inscriptions report that one of the **Andrews** family *dyed* in 1672, another *deseced* in 1675 and a third *deceaced* in 1678?

Infant Mortality

The Rectory, Church Road / 4th December 1801

This morning the Reverend **Edward Vansittart Neale** presided over the burial of 14-month-old Martha Austin. Now in the quiet lamplit evening after completing his latest entry into the Parish Register, he looks back through its pages to count at least 160 children and infants from 105 families buried in the old St Nicholas Churchyard during the last 90 years of the previous century. Almost every one of the 80 families now resident in the parish has lost at least one child. The **Aldridge** family has been hardest hit having suffered seven fatalities in all, including three – Sarah, Susanna and William – between 1747 and 1751.

The Rector's review reveals that most fatalities came in three waves: 31 youngsters died in the ten years to 1742, 19 in the four years to 1751 and 16 in the three years to 1793 including five in 1791. There were also three infant deaths in 1758 and four in 1764. Such grouping suggests outbreaks of disease. Cholera is still rare, especially in rural areas – there will be no major epidemics in the UK until 1831 – but smallpox, measles, chicken pox, scarlet fever, influenza, pneumonia, whooping cough, typhus, typhoid and puerperal sepsis take turns to decimate the population. And of course the young were and still are especially susceptible.

Every death is a tragedy but six stories are particularly poignant. The infant **Robert Sambourn** (or is it Lambourn?) and his father of the same name died within six weeks of each other early in 1731. The schoolmaster John Loveland was taken in 1750 by whatever had inflicted his charges. Elizabeth & Samuel Theed lost not only their daughter Anne in 1758 but also their own lives. In 1797 the infant twins John and Ann Treemer died within a week of each other and five-year-old Elenor Emson "died in consequence of the bite of a mad dog". But the saddest tale of all is that of the Craft family. Thomas Craft lost his children Elizabeth, John and William in 1742 and died himself within a year, perhaps of grief. His widow Elizabeth lost her fourth child Gatharitta (Gatty) in 1744 and herself passed away in 1752, perhaps of utter despair.

The Rectory, Church Road / 27th December 1817

As the Reverend Neale prepares to make another sad entry in the Register, he reflects back to the three years from 1809, when 16 more children from 12 more families were taken by an outbreak of scarlet fever, and to the seven children who died in 1812, the worst year on record. Clearly growing up has continued to be an achievement more of luck than judgement. And yet the population of the parish will increase by more than half in the thirty years to 1831. Perhaps a clever thing called vaccination has something to do with it. What a shame that he must record today that 15-month-old **Mary Ann Darling** "died of small pox, not vaccinated".

Accidents Will Happen

The New Churchyard / 12th January 1879

They say most accidents happen in the home. Not in Taplow they don't – not the fatal ones anyway – but keeping **Cliveden** in trim was a risky business as the painters James Randal and Charles Griffiths discovered in 1743 when they were "killed falling from Cliffden House". History repeated itself "at Cliefden" 95 years later when another painter, Thomas Woodward, and his glazier workmate William Swannock went the same way. Work was also the death of papermakers William Smart and William Beazley who died in an unspecified accident at Taplow Mills in 1815.

Horsepower could be lethal. The old-fashioned kind did for Stephen Powney in 1797 and **James Wells** in 1829. Powney was killed "by a wagon going over him" and Wells "by a kick from a horse". It is unlikely to have been any consolation that he was the first to be buried in the new St Nicholas' Churchyard. And the new-fangled steam-driven horsepower took its toll in 1877 when Henry Maltby was killed on the railway at Maidenhead Bridge. Perhaps he paid the ultimate price for trying to avoid paying the road bridge toll. And in 1902 William Crutch of **Hitcham New Town** and his young friend George Gibbons of Taplow Mills will meet their ends by being "smothered when buried in **Roque's** chalk pit" near Taplow Grammar School. Why would a farmhand and a papermill labourer be in this age-old quarry that will be eventually lost to gravel extraction?

The not-quiet 3-year-old Edwin Holem is the odd one out. He died at home on **Taplow Common** a few days ago when he "choked on a potato". As the poor lad is laid to rest, nobody is so unfeeling to mumble that he has had his chips.

Watery Graves

Maidenhead Bridge / 30th June 1907

It is no surprise that somewhere by a river has seen a few drownings down the years. Some were undoubtedly accidents. There is no reason to think that busy miller Stephen Darwell didn't tumble into the mill race by mistake in 1744. And what could be unusual about William Pascoe and **Charles Palmer** falling off their boats on Bray Reach in 1800 and 1891, or Horace Moore and Henry Quick doing the same at Amerden Grove in 1876 and near Ray Mead in 1897? Even when Matthew Barber fell into the old Boulter's Lock at Taplow Mill in 1820, it could surely be put down to the innocent carelessness of a 7-year-old.

Other deaths are more suspicious. How did 81-year-old Mary Cattle come to be trapped in the weir in 1835? Had she despaired and decided to end it all? Even worse were the deaths of three infants in which foul play might have had a hand: the body of the infant Elizabeth Stanworth was discovered in 1807, the not-quite 2-year-old George Andrews was found floating near Maidenhead Bridge in 1880 and an unknown one-week-old lifeless baby was pulled out of the dark waters in 1897.

Otto Eltrick (43) and Emily Maclean (38) were paying guests at ***The Dumb Bell*** until a few days ago when they both drowned in Cliveden Reach. An inquest avoided speculation on whether this couple died in a lovers' suicide pact. Their post-humous claim to fame will be as the last people to be buried by the Reverend **Nicholas Garry** before the Rector himself passes away at 76.

The two most intriguing drownings occurred not in the river but in a pond....

The New Churchyard / 30th June 1843

Hundreds have gathered for the burial of poor **Caroline Norrington** [*see Appendix 1, Tree 20*]. Her father William and her brother George lead the mourners. It is so quiet you could hear a pin drop. Even the birds have ceased their song. Only a few stifled sobs occasionally break the heavy silence.

Some are reliving the awful moments when they saw Caroline floating face down in the same tranquil pond at ***Rectory Farm*** where her nephew **Richard Briginshaw** drowned not quite two years ago. The poor lad was only three. It had been all too much for his mother Grace, Caroline's sister. Some said it was the grief that did for her when she died last November at just 27. The gloom still hangs over her young husband Richard but it was he and his carter John Lewis who took the initiative to wade chest-deep into the water to recover the body. When he saw it was daughter, old William gasped in such anguish that the sound hit everyone all like a thud in the heart. The dutiful George stepped forward to take his sister's limp body from Richard and John and carry it to the farmhouse.

The stoic and resonant voice of Reverend **Neale** calls the mourners back to the present to lead them in prayers for Caroline's soul. Nobody will say what everyone is thinking: little Richard's death had been a sad accident but how could his 29-year-old aunt have suffered the same fate so soon afterwards? The question will hang in the breeze for ever and ever. Amen.

Hurn's Turn – Pond Life

Pater Noster Pond / 30th June 1936

Like Bapsey, the willow-ringed pool never runs dry, not even in this hot, dry summer. In the spring Harry watched fascinated as hundreds of tiny frogs made their first exploratory journeys into the world.

If he were to come back in 80 years, he'd find the pool filled in – its place taken by a shed in the corner of St Nicolas' School playground – but the spring that fed it will still be there, mostly kept under control by a deep well in the garden of ***School House***. However it will occasionally cause a very soggy spot at the top of the Village Green and may be the reason why in early-2013 a hole suddenly appears in the car park of ***The Oak & Saw***.

Suspicious Minds

The New Churchyard / 30th June 2013

In recent years Taplow has featured often in television dramas such as *Endeavour*, *Midsomer Murders* and *Foyle's War* yet the scriptwriters of these *who-dun-its* have failed to pick up on our own peculiar departures. In 1833 butcher **John Aldridge** "destroyed himself near the (new) church" by cutting his throat, which can't have been easy to do. It is such a shame. The Aldridge family have been in Taplow for at least 120 years. Was he ousted by his new landlord, perhaps by having his rent increased beyond his means? Or is there something sinister at work? And then was John Burford, who in 1845 "hung himself in a cottage at ***The Elms***", and Sarah Gomm who for reasons unrecorded "died in the train between Slough and Taplow" in 1858. All very strange: were these suicides or homicides?

Pubs were particularly dangerous places. When the 46-year-old poverty-stricken farmhand Henry Baggs "died suddenly at ***The Oak & Saw***" in 1869, it was probably just a heart attack. And maybe some awful illness caused the deaths of the infant Amos siblings Cecil (14 months) and Florence (6 weeks) at ***The Old Station Inn*** in 1905. However there can be no possibility that natural causes took John Swears, who "poisoned himself at ***The Dumb Bell***" in 1843, or **Robert Lane**, who "hung himself at ***The Orkney Arms***" in 1857. Perhaps the service was depressingly slow.

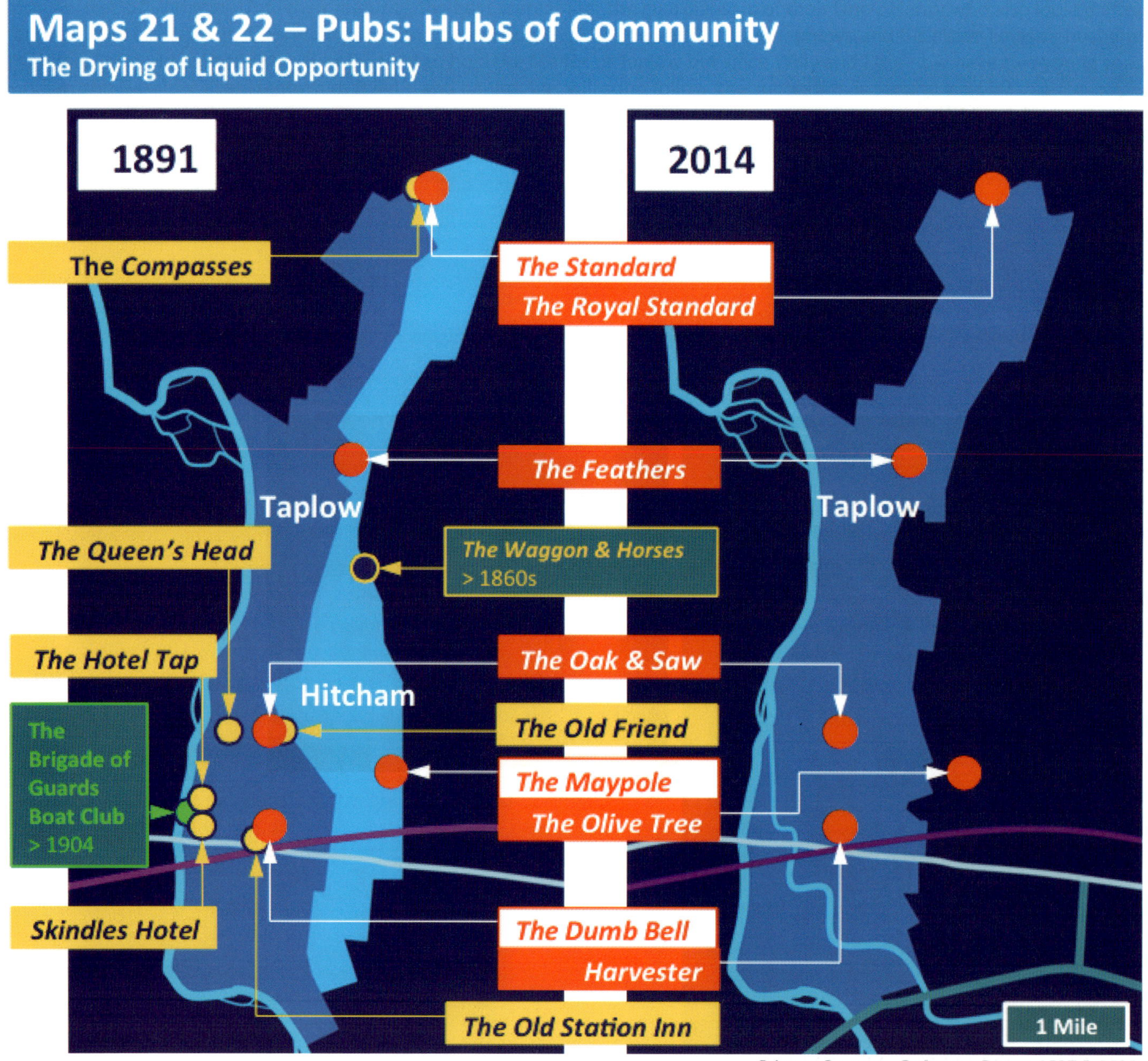

Primary Sources: Ordnance Survey 1897 & 2008

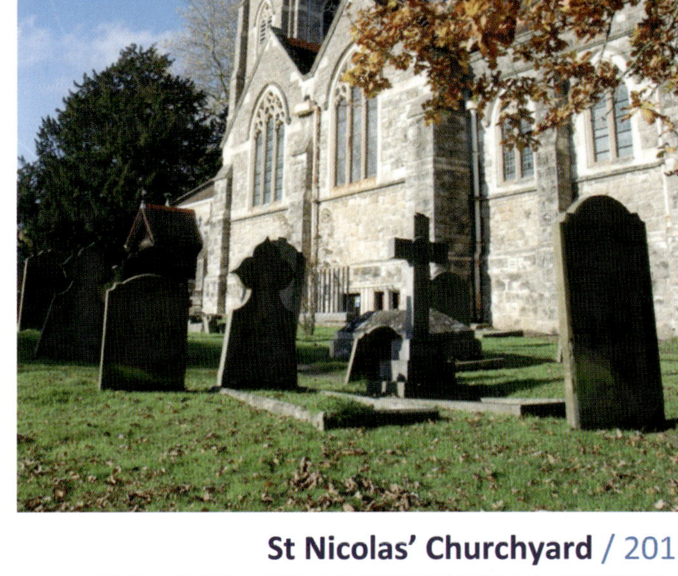

St Nicolas' Churchyard / 2012

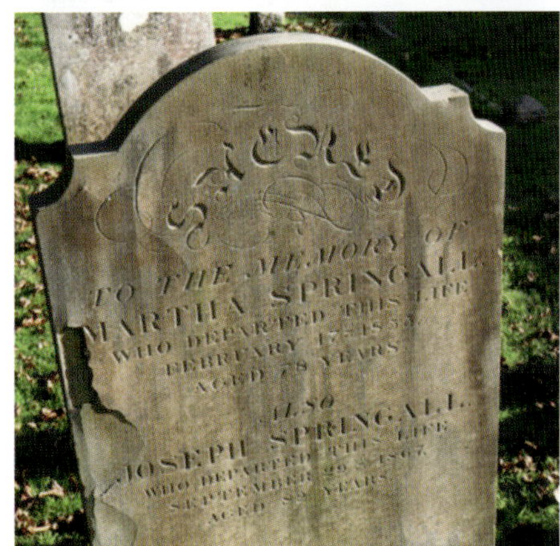

The New Trinity

Everybody is Somebody

Taplow Village Centre / 24th November 2012

The sum of the Parish Register and the censuses is that everybody was somebody at last. The records of the diligent Victorians reveal that their social fabric had become a layered patchwork which broadly reflected and gave depth to the new trinity: the Common People on the erstwhile common lands who kept **Cliveden** and **Dropmore** ticking, the Village People clustering around **Taplow Court** and **St Nicholas' Church**, and the Valley People living along the **Bath Road**, down by the riverside and on the **Amerden** acres. These 19th Century Taplovians shaped much of what still remains today, but something has changed. Back in 1891, 1,029 souls could find refreshment in any of ten hostelries (and a gentleman's club) without staggering from the civil parish. All survived into the 1900s when a strange thing began to happen: the more we multiplied, the less thirsty we became. The 2011 census found 1,669 of us but only three pubs – ***The Oak & Saw***, ***The Royal Standard*** and ***The Feathers***, the last really a restaurant – and a *Harvester* restaurant with a vague memory of another, ***The Dumb Bell*** [*see Maps 21 & 22*].

Have we lost something more intangible than a wealth of liquid opportunity? These pubs were hubs of the community. Where better to get to know the locals in those good old days than over a pint or two?

Outside The Feathers / 15th June 1891

Our accomplices on the first stage of our expedition will be Alfred Coe, a coachman at Cliveden who has been given permission to convey us on our mission, and his friend **Frederick Everett Hurn**: Cliveden's nightwatchman [*see Appendix 1, Tree 12*]. Freddie lives just over there in the lodge from which gatekeepers have watched over Cliveden's new main entrance since before 1838. After dark tonight, he will make his rounds of the house from cellar to the top landings, clocking in at every stage, moving with a slow measured tread the better to keep the floorboards from creaking too much. But first things first: Alfie clicks and flicks the reins, his horses take the strain and our coach begins to trundle up the hill....

Pubs: Still the Hubs of Community?

The Oak & Saw / 2009

The Royal Standard / 2012

The Feathers / 2009

The Common People

Highlanders

A Chance Meeting – Four of the Best

Noblemens' Corner, Taplow Common / 15th June 1798

Willam Aldridge and Ned Timberlick have scraped a living here on Taplow Great Common for years. The inclosures made things difficult and they aren't getting any better....

According to Will, there has been a crossroads here in the north-east corner of Taplow Parish since Good Lord Jesus was in swaddling clothes. One road went west to **Hedsor Wharf** and another south to ***The Prince of Wales Feathers*** where it branched to Burnham and Taplow. The third wandered north to branch west down to Wooburn and onwards up to Beaconsfield while the fourth forked north-east across **Dropmer Hill** to **Littleworth Common** and south-east through the woods to **Cabrook**. The grand Orkney plans for there to be a circus here never came to pass and all four quadrants are now enclosed as granted by act of Parliament eight years back. Three are still heavily wooded. The fifth Lord Inchiquin's sheep graze in the rough pasture of the fourth, **Captain's Field** to the south-west.

Ned thinks it's bad enough that Lord Grenville cares so much for his privacy at **Dropmore** that he has closed the tracks across the common that meet at Cabrook: one from here, the second from **Rose Hill** and the third which winds its way from Littleworth Common past his new mansion. The road north from here has been realigned through **Johnson's Coppice** and **Sheepcote Wood** to meet a new road across Wooburn Common running some way north of its old route.

The woodsmen are interrupted by the approach of three carriages and a horseman on a fine stallion. From north and south come the old faces, from east and west the new....

The Orkney-Inchiquin time in Taplow stretches back almost a century. The fifth **Lord Inchiquin** and his Lady Mary are travelling with his daughter the fourth **Lady Orkney** from ***Gregories Court*** in Beaconsfield where they have been entertained by **Edmund Burke**. Their journey has just reached the gate to ***Hedsor House***, home for nearly 20 years of **Lord Boston** who first came to Clifden as an infant when his father was equerry to the Prince of Wales. Having lunched with the Royal Family at Windsor, Boston is now passing ***The Prince of Wales Feathers***. It is barely six years since **Lord Grenville** began putting down roots in **Dropmore Park**. He is heading for Hedsor Wharf where he will supervise the unloading of a consignment of soot to be used to fertilise his growing forest. **Pascoe Grenfell** is the exception. The businessman has neither peerage nor carriage. He is riding on horseback from Bisham up the hill from Hedsor Wharf on the way to ***Taplow House***, his home for four years.

The rider slows his steed. The coachmen rein in their teams. The foursome nod cordial greetings to each other as they pass their separate ways with the future in their hands. This junction will be known as ***Noblemens' Corner*** for being at the point at which the estates of three peers meet: Lords Inchiquin, Grenville and Boston of Cliveden, Dropmore and Hedsor [*see Appendix 1, Trees 7 & 9*]. Ned and Will reckon that's as good a name as any for the whole common now. And what really gets their goat is that people call Grenville's new road north ***Nobleman's Walk***. Nobs, splutters Ned, they can turn corners when it suits them but how many ever walk anywhere?

What would poor Ned think to see *Nobleman's Corner* feature in *The Card* (1952), a film (whatever that is) starring Alec Guinness, Valerie Hobson, Glynis Johns and Petula Clark?

Hedsor Revival, Dropmore Divestment

Taplow Common / 15th June 1891

It is hard to believe there are lordly estates on both sides of us – Dropmore to the right and Hedsor to the left. We chuckle to think what **Lady Fortescue** and Lord Boston would say if they knew that, to us, they too are Common People.

Hedsor went into a kind of hibernation after the original house burned down in 1795. **Frederick Irby, 2nd Baron Boston**, didn't forget his estate – he commemorated the victory at Waterloo in 1815 by building a folly there – but his son **George Irby, 3rd Baron Boston**, wasn't much interested. It wasn't until 1865 that his son **George Ives Irby, 4th Baron Boston**, finally got around to having the architect **James Knowles** design a new house in grand Italianate style with an unusual central domed hall. The fourth *Hedsor House* was completed in 1868 only to get a sad reputation in its early days. The 4th Lord Boston enjoyed it for little more than a year before he went to meet his Maker – Alfie says we should ask his fellow coachman Willie Cleal about that story when we get down to ***The Grange*** on the edge of Taplow village – and his son **Florance George Henry Irby, 5th Baron Boston**, didn't last long either [*see Appendix 1, Tree 7*].

The current incumbent, **George Florance Irby, 6th Baron Boston**, was just 16 when he inherited the house and its 562 acres in 1877. Nobody can recall which of the Florances added four large ornamental domes on each corner of the roof. The latter served briefly as Lord-in-Waiting (Government whip in the House of Lords) in the 1880s and is a Fellow of the Society of Antiquaries and of the Geological Society. Alfie has heard that his wife Cecilia often finds him studying astronomy, botany, entomology, archaeology and such like deep into the night. Freddie smirks that if you were a fellow with a girl's name you wouldn't go out much, would you?

As we take the left fork across Hitcham Common (not-yet ***Sheepcote Lane***), we contrast the fortunes of two of Lord Grenville's satellites. **Hitcham** was drawn into Burnham's orbit and rather eclipsed as **Littleworth Common** emerged into the daylight. Its name reveals how poorly valued it had been in days of yore when its common name was Widmore (or Wigmore) but it was the perfect place for a hamlet to grow to serve Dropmore. It really came into its own after Grenville's sister Hester's younger son **George Fortescue** inherited Lady Anne's estates in 1863 [*see Appendix 1, Tree 9*]. Within three years he had carved 1,735 acres from Taplow, Hitcham, Burnham and Dorneywood to create the new ecclesiastical parish of **Dropmore & Littleworth Common** and grace it with **St Anne's Church**, named for his aunt. He was himself commemorated in 1877 by the addition of a transept.

Shame it's been downhill for Dropmore ever since, observes Freddie wryly. He exaggerates of course but there is more than a grain of truth in his humour. Despite the sale in 1872 of *Sheepcote* and *Hicknaham Farms*, the former Grenville estates still spread over 2,509 acres when they passed in 1877 to George's son **John Bevill Fortescue**. He prefers life at *Boconnoc* – yet another Taplow connection with Cornwall, says Alfie – and leaves his mother **Lady Louisa** (née Ryder) to manage Dropmore in his stead. What a shock she caused in 1879 by offering for sale 49 lots of land and property including 540 wooded acres her agent described as land "suitable for the erection of superior residences". Thank Heaven for the Surrey tea broker and philanthropist Sir Henry Peek MP. He had saved Wimbledon Common in 1864 and when Francis Heath drew his attention to the danger that this "precious remnant of wild woodland" would be lost, he repeated the trick by acquiring **Burnham Beeches** and selling it to the Corporation of London in 1880 thus protecting it forever as a public open space and wildlife reserve.

The Fortescues can't claim philanthropy on that scale, says Alfie, but there's something be said for them all the same. The son has recently funded the construction of an elementary school in Hitcham and the mother seems content to keep even 'superior residences' out of Dropmore Park. And in 1897 over 300 locals will celebrate Queen Victoria's Diamond Jubilee at Dropmore "by kind permission of Lady Louisa Fortescue". A service at St Anne's Church will followed by races for all age groups, a *Punch & Judy* show and side shows, donkey rides, music by the Hitcham, Burnham & Taplow Brass Band, a "monster tea" and cricket matches between Dropmore Park and their rivals at Burnham Priory, ***Blythewood*** in Hitcham and **Taplow Grammar School**.

Howard's Way

The Compasses, Wooburn Common / 15th June 1891

That's enough of that, laughs Freddie, it's time for a pint. Before us is a terrace with pubs at either end: ***The Compasses*** to the north and ***The Standard*** to the south. The sight brings to mind a picture of two rather tipsy pals sandwiching a couple of more sober friends. We are sober now but don't plan to stay that way.

Freddie leads our little party determinedly into *The Compasses* where the landlord **James Howard** welcomes us with a broad grin and tankards of *Weller's Entire*. As we savour the slightly sweet roasted chocolate flavour of this porter, Jim tells us that the pub has been in the hands of the Weller family of the ***Amersham Ales*** brewery for as long as anyone can remember. It was called ***The Three Compasses*** when he, formerly a labourer, and his wife Eliza took over more than 20 years ago but now he is 71 and she 68 they need the help of his little brother George, a mere 66. Freddie explains our mission to explore and our supplementary goal of drinking Taplow dry. Eliza asks why then have we come to this spot in the parish of **St Paul's Church**, Wooburn. Her puzzlement is no surprise. Nobody around here knows where they are, what with all the juggling of boundaries and the loss of the match between civil and ecclesiastical parishes. Back in 1824, we'd have been in Taplow but now we're in civil and ecclesiastical Wooburn but a few steps south at ***Hodds Farm***, **Richard House** is in the civil parish of Taplow and the new ecclesiastical parish of St Anne's, Dropmore. For the farmer William Lever and his son Walter at ***Sheepcot Farm*** 300 yards farther on, it's the strange mix of Hitcham and St Anne's. And yet the census counts the Reverend John Shackle, vicar of St Anne's Church, in the civil parish of Burnham and the ecclesiastical parish of St Peter's, Burnham. Work that one out.

Looking ahead, first Henry Platt and then Samuel Haydon (or Hayden) will take over ***The Compasses*** and by 1901 it will have expanded into its adjoining cottage. Sam's niece or cousin Violet Haydon will marry Freddie's son **Everett Hurn** in 1921 and eight years later the inn will be acquired by *Benskins & Co* when the Watford brewers pay the Wellers £350,000 (£85m) for *Amersham Ales*. By then both pubs, *Sheepcote* and *Hales Corner* will also be counted in Taplow. There are blank looks all round. We've hardly started to tipple yet and already confusion reigns. However the knowledge that it will still be raising eyebrows in 120 years reassures us that we need give it no more heed today.

We change the subject: let's hear about the neighbours. Eliza obliges. It is a tight-knit community. The Common People aren't engaged only at **Cliveden** and **Dropmore**. Her son **Sam Howard** and Reuben Ludgate live in the two cottages sandwiched between the pubs. Both work in the Wooburn papermills with their brothers **Jimmy Howard** and Joe Ludgate and their friends Richard Goode, George Healey and George Craft. James's brother **David Howard** is a wood dealer on Hitcham Common and George's son **Fred Howard** is a farmhand and odd-jobber who with Dan Guilder and George Gee finds work for Joseph Tyrell at *Castleman's Farm* or at *Hodds* or *Sheepcot*. There are more Howards in Hedsor and Hitcham and more Houses and Healeys hereabouts too – like **Henry House** at ***Abby Park Farm*** and Richard's father **William House** who has retired to lodge with George Healey in ***Salter's Row***, a group of cottages built near *Hodds* almost 30 years ago for or by **Tom Salter** who used to be at *Castleman's*. His carpenter son Tom still lives there aged 67. That's all as it should be, says Eliza, but there is talk of something fishy going on at *Sheepcot* where a retired accountant called William Smedley has been sniffing around. We suspect there's more to this story than meets the eye.

Stevenson's Rock

The Compasses, Wooburn Common / 11th September 2012

This former pub has been home to **Johanna & Greg Stevenson** for 18 years. Having researched diligently and indulged me with some refreshment in *The Royal Standard*, he takes up the story....

The Howards had been hereabouts since at least 1687. James & Eliza's son James ran *The Bell* in Wooburn until his death in 1882 and within a year his widow married his brother William and family tradition continued down in the Wye Valley. Up here on the common, George Camp took over *The Compasses* from Haydon and in 1905 enjoyed the publication of this accolade: "This house affords comfortable bar-parlour accommodation.... many are the testimonies given by customers to the civility and promptitude with which their requirements are met". Strangely, these much-trumpeted "testimonies" didn't secure his future. He was succeeded by Frederick Allerton, Arthur Stevens, Lewis Bryant, Charles Taylor and Clifford Clayton before Benskins took over and installed Fred Stanford as licensee to be succeeded by Bill Sawle in the late-1930s and by George Carey early in the Second World War.

Carey was a case. He made enough money selling black market petrol during the war that by 1948 he could afford to acquire *The Compasses* from *Benskins* only to be caught two years later with petrol in his beer. He had little option but to sell the place for £1,950 (£201,000) to Gerald Stevenson (possibly a relation) who turned it into a cafe with tables on either side of the road. The cafe closed in the early-1960s and, having outlived the competition, *The Royal Standard* expanded north into its adjoining cottage. When Gerald's widow Maisie died in 1975, *The Compasses* passed to their son Christopher Stevenson and, 19 years later, to his son Greg.

Setting the Standard

Wooburn Common / 15th June 1891

It is time to move on. James Howard seems reluctant to bid us farewell. He reminds us that he is licensed to sell spirits whereas ***The Standard*** is merely an alehouse. He is a tad dismayed when we say this is music to our ears. We drain our tankards and stride towards our second port of call. Alfie whispers that *The Standard* changed hands seven years ago when it all became too much for 74-year-old William Goodall and that, although her husband Charlie now is the official publican, it is his young wife Georgina Dean who runs the place. And there she is pulling our pints and explaining with a wry smile that her Charlie prefers to potter about keeping people's gardens in trim while she keeps their customers satisfied. We are keen to know how two pubs can survive in this remote corner of the common. Georgina sniffs and says she and Mr Howard do very nicely thank you, and so does *The Pheasant* not a quarter-mile away at Beggar's Hill (not-yet **Bergher's Hill**).

She pours us pints of *Brakspear 'Double Drop' Bitter*. Local brew, she says, made in Henley. Got a lovely tang, adds Charlie. The conversation wanders naturally from beer to that other English stalwart: the weather. Last winter was awfully long and cold with four heavy falls of snow between November and May. There were times when the ice on the Thames was thick enough for people to walk across to Maidenhead. The worst snowstorm in mid-March killed 220 people nationwide, wrecked 65 ships in the Channel, buried trains in the West Country and blew down half-a-million trees. Georgina says snowdrifts piled up to the eaves of *The Standard*. The stables at Clifden were buried so deep it took two days to dig the horses out. Charlie remembers that some newspaper called it a *blizzard* but why should Freddie's neighbour, the old garden labourer Jimmy Blizzard (of ***Woodgate Cottages*** near ***Taplow Lodge***), get the blame for a snowstorm? Alfie reckons the word comes from the German *blitzartig* meaning *like lightning*. Freddie says that's what comes from having foreign royals.

We don't need outsiders to give us funny words, smiles Charlie. Willie Goodall told me the common hereabouts used to be called **Pincushin** because the womenfolk earned 'pin-money' making lace; there were 14 still at it in 1841. Those were the days, laughs Georgina as she rinses the beermugs. She will preside at *The Standard* for another 41 years, the last 16 as a widow. Thereafter her hostelry will tweak its name to be ***The Royal Standard***.

High Pastures and Pastimes

Green Common Lane / 15th June 1891

Gamekeeper Robert Elliker strides west-to-east down the spine of Taplow's northern satellite. It's neither here nor there that it falls within the ecclesiastical parish of St Anne's, Dropmore. The land is still in the civil parish of Taplow so still benefits Taplovians. According to Elliker (and eventually **Michael Bayley** too), for centuries old men and young boys left their villages each spring to drive livestock up here to the high ground [*see Map 23*]. The cattle and goats would feast on the new growth of grass and leaves in the woodlands while these itinerant Taplovians camped amongst the furze in a group of closes to our right called *Hodds*, derived from *hafods*, a local dialect word for *summer dwellings* known elsewhere as *bothies* (*basic shelters*) or *sheilings* (*remote summer dwellings*). And that's how ***Hodds Farm*** got its name.

To the left is a close called **Hinchmore** (which Bayley says may derive from *Hinjy-Ma-Wy* meaning *the crossroads place of water*), beyond it **Kitchen Dean** and to the east is **Dipple Wood**. These two names tell similar stories. A *dyppa-wy-le* was a water-filled hollow where a bucket on a pole could be dipped into clear water beyond the cattle-trodden muddiness by the bank. There was just such a place at *Kitchen Dean* (from *keech* or *keach* meaning *to fetch* or *collect water*) where the itinerants watered in the depths of what was until recently *Dipwell Wood*.

Some say the kink in the lane was once part of an ancient footpath running from Cippenham through Burnham and Beaconsfield to Penn. To the north on the edge of the wood is Elliker's home: ***Dippwell Lodge***. To the south-west is **Lilly Field**. Its name derives from *Lyes-Le Vear-Lle* – meaning *the big space of many people* – a reminder that once the valley fields had been harvested mothers and girls would join their menfolk to make butter and cheese up here on the common. Many stayed until Michaelmas (29th September) when games and pastimes were played in Lily Field, often in competition with other villages. This end-of-summer celebration was the perfect opportunity for boys to meet girls to whom they are not related, or at least only distantly. This custom has survived from semi-nomadic Bronze Age times and (according to **Bayley**) will still be the way of the world in Chalvey, Cippenham and Dorney until the late-1930s when their commons are requisitioned for munitions dumps.

The first (or second) St Nicholas' Church / 15th June 1758

The sun is shining warmly as the happy couple emerge from the cool of the old church. Mary Lockitt of this Parish looks sweet arm-in-arm with her new husband **Henry Gurney** of Hedsore. Did they begin their courting last Michaelmas up on the high pastures? Henry is the first Gurney to be recorded in Taplow. He won't be the last.

An Odd Story – Six Generations of Houses

Hodds Farm / 15th June 1891

Elliker leads the way back to *The Standard* telling the tale that Bryant's Map of 1824 noted *Hodds Farm* as *Didler's End*, possibly because its five acres were tenanted to **William House**, a *higgler* (general dealer) with a nose for sharp business deals. It has taken most of his 40 years for **Richard House** to put his father's past behind him. If the gamekeeper finds that amusing, what would he say if he could see 112 years into the future....?

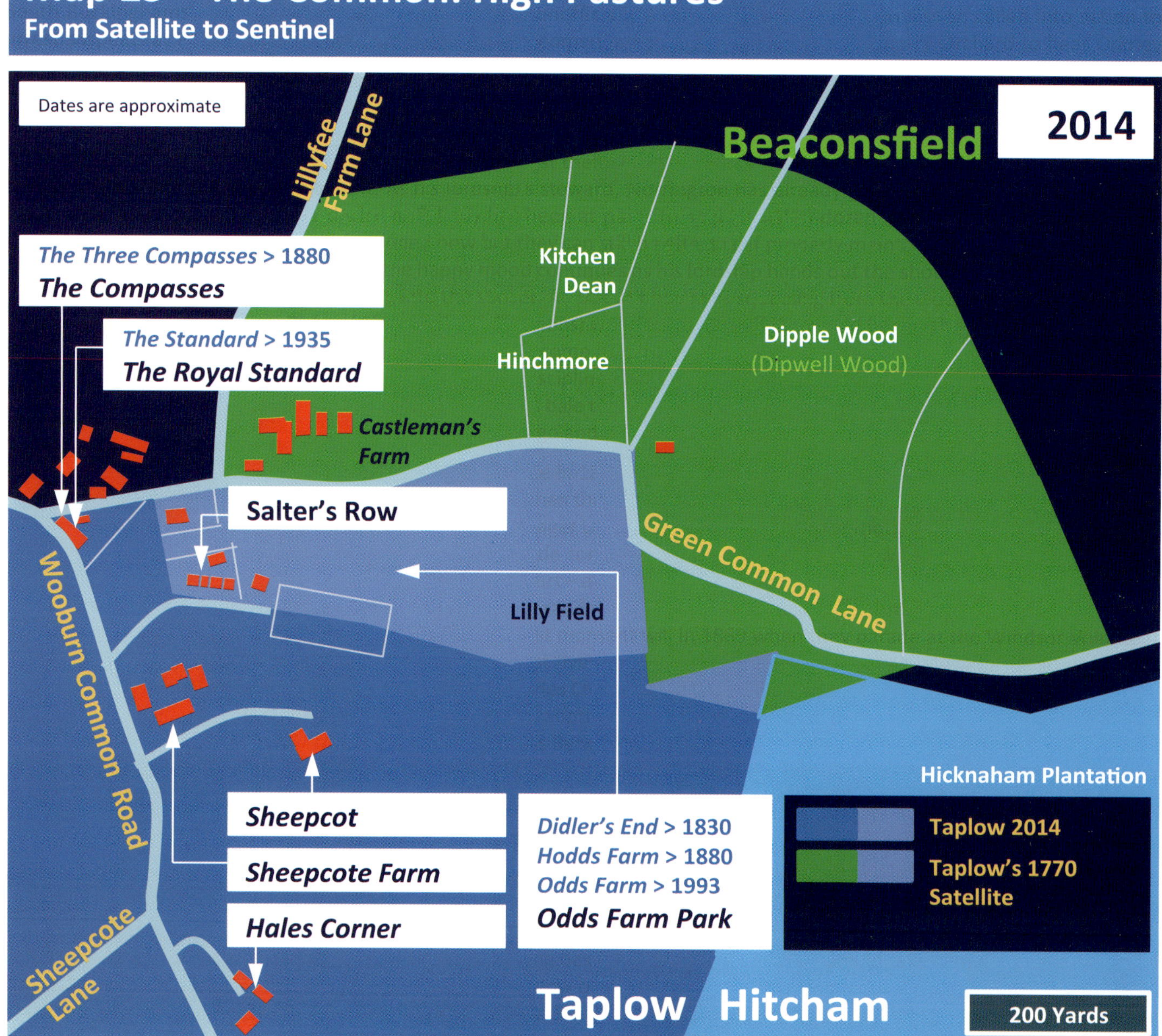

Primary Sources: Inclosure Maps 1779/1787, Ordnance Survey 2008 and Michael Bayley 2012

Odds Farm Park / 8th March 2013

There are nearly 200 farm attractions in the UK. Taplow's is "leading the way in terms of innovation, quality and customer experience". *Odds Farm Park* is *Farm Attraction of the Year 2013*, an accolade awarded annually by the National Farm Attractions Network.

Jackie & Steve Vinden opened *Odds Farm Park* 20 years ago as a Rare Breeds Centre. It has since evolved to employ about 50 people and to provide a unique mix of animal contact, education and leisure. The latest innovation is a giant indoor playbarn complete with cafe and espresso bar. Many local children have grown up not knowing what to do first – pet piglets, have a go at mini-golf, feed lambs, goats and rabbits, ride the tractor-train or dash past the duck pond to the adventure playground.

Jackie is the sixth generation of the House family at *Odds Farm* [*see Appendix 1, Tree 13*]. Her father **Lionel House** tells the tale that the land was owned by Portland Estates whose local manager offered his great-grandfather Richard the chance to acquire and expand the farm in the 1890s. His elder sons Dick and Joe moved to Oxfordshire where in 1913 they started a successful motor bus company running services between Henley, Reading and their home in Watlington. Their brother Freddie (sometimes known by his second name, Charles) and twin sister Annie (known as Dolly) took over Hodds Farm soon after the Great War.

Beaconsfield Magistrates' Court / 7th February 1964

Freddie House is 72 and able to walk only with the aid of two sticks but he is as determined as ever. It is more than 30 years since he first allowed 'fair folk' to live in their caravans at Odds Farm. There are 58 caravans there now spread over three sites either side of the district boundary, one in Beaconsfield Urban District and two in Eton Rural District. The two councils have over the past few years tried every legal avenue to have the number of caravans on the Beaconsfield UDC site reduced from 22 to 13 and to close the Eton RDC sites altogether and relocate the 36 caravans to a site in Datchet. Freddie and his 74-year-old sister Dolly thought they had won the case last August when Keith Joseph, Minister of Housing & Local Government, found in their favour only for the councils to bring before the magistrates a revised proposal to reduce the number of caravans to 22 in total.

Freddie argues his case with rare verbosity and vehemence. "It is an abominable shame," he shouts, "a wicked shame that you want to take these people from my site and put them on yours. It would be a sin and a shame to uproot [them]. We want to live and let live". Despite all attempts to stop him, he quotes at length a poem and finishes by saying "There's One above who knows all and there will be a day of reckoning". When challenged if he has the £22,000 (£889,000) necessary to put the sites into proper shape, he responds "What? You want your brains testing! I'm not telling you what I've got, but I am saying I can afford to bring them up to standard".

His passion succeeds in convincing the court to direct that, on condition that the sites are upgraded, all caravans can remain on the Eton sites but the number on the Beaconsfield site must be reduced from from 22 to 13. Freddie is pleased with his day in court and the right to rental income from 49 caravans. However nobody will be surprised that the upgrade never quite happens before he passes away or that Dolly will claim paying heavy death duties on his estate prevents her from doing what's required.

Odds Farm Park / 8th March 2013

The farm passed in the early-1970s to Dick's son **Arthur House**. Being busy with the buses, he employed Lance Pithers to run what was by then a dilapidated dairy farm of 140 acres and consolidated the three caravan sites into one equipped with mains services to accommodate 49 'mobile homes'. When he was obliged to sell the bus company in the late-1980s, Arthur persuaded Joe's grandson Lionel to take over the farm. Lionel and his wife Anne had been farming at Cublington in Aylesbury Vale but they jumped in at the deep end in 1989. Dairy farming was no longer economic so they renovated Odds Farm to breed beef cattle and offer bed-and-breakfast. Further change was soon in the air. The seed was sown when the family visited friends who had a Rare Breeds farm in Pembrokeshire and the rest is history. *Odds Farm Park* now occupies half the land while Jackie's brother Derek farms the rest.

Pastoral Symphony

Noblemen's Walk / 15th June 1891

We decide to see how Lord Grenville's new road is faring. One day it will be **Heathfield Road** but it is still ***Noblemen's Walk*** to us. Of course, it's not so new now. It's almost a hundred years old and even we don't walk it, let alone the nobility.

Beyond ***Cedar Lodge*** we reach a dip in the road and begin to descend into it. Suddenly Alfie reins in his pair, puts his finger to his lips to signal for silence then points up ahead. Initially we can see nothing except the multitude of greens, browns and yellows of the sunlit woodland. A movement catches our eye. A small herd of roe deer are browsing amongst the foliage. Despite being nearly red now summer's here, they blend into the background so effectively they are almost invisible. This is a rare sight now in southern England although a little less so in these parts. We watch them in admiration. After a while one of the horses snorts impatiently as if to say he wants to be on his way. The deer disappear westward into **Johnson's Coppice**. Alfie clicks and flicks again and we're off once more through the glorious woodlands. There are still fallen trees here and there, casualties of the March storm, but the woods are healing themselves miraculously.

On our left is ***Dropmore Lodge***. It is many years since **Lady Louisa Fortescue** made this Dropmore's main entrance and installed a heavy wooden gate crowned with a large spike. William Avenell is on the veranda playing his concertina as usual. He's worked at Dropmore as a gardener for 26 years, says Alfie, but likes nothing better than to sit up there in the shade teaching the estate girls to dance to his music. Only his wife Charlotte doesn't approve, smiles Freddie. She doesn't mind so much that he supplements his wage of half-a-crown-a-day (£53.25) with whatever he can pick up playing at ***The Feathers***. And I've heard she was pleased as punch when the **Duke of Westminster** gave her a sovereign instead of the usual penny for opening the gate as he was leaving for Cliveden.

The Bevill You Know

Dropmore Lodge, Noblemen's Walk / 9th January 1899

Only seven of Charlotte & William's 15 children have survived beyond infancy. Lily Avenell was nine-years-old in 1885 when she left home to go into service. Her visit to her parents is interrupted by their boarder, gardener **Jimmy Cooper**, who bursts in with the news that her ladyship has passed away. The rhythm of life at **Dropmore** is about to change....

Summers will be busy with **John Bevill Fortescue** and his wife Dorothy in residence [*see Appendix 1, Tree 9*]. The estate cricket team will continue to play at ***Brook End Farm*** and the park will be open to local people on three days each week. Schoolchidren will be brought to see the Pinetum and the rhododendrons, and to enjoy parties and races at half-term. And in the long evenings, at weekends and during the holidays, they will play in the woods, stumble upon the 'Gingerbread' cottages at Key Brook or Kay Brook (formerly **Cabrook**), swim in *Quavers* and *Limes* pools on **Littleworth Common** or gather at ***Dropmore Lodge*** in often rewarded anticipation that visitors might throw pennies if not sovereigns from the carriages.

In sharp contrast, winters will be spent in limbo awaiting the Master's occasional and sometimes unexpected arrivals. He will engage Detmar Blow and Ferdinand Billerey in 1906 to exercise their French 18th Century architectural expertise on remodelling the house, but it will prove something of a false dawn for the winter twilight will persist.

Dropmore will hit the headlines in 1919, when JBF reduces his great uncle's domain by about 1,000 acres, and in 1922, when an aeroplane *en route* to Farnborough gets lost in failing light and mist and crashes into the woods near *Kaybrook Farm* killing its pilot, Flying Officer Geoffrey Robinson, and his passenger, John Mitchell. The large ear trumpet that JBF brings to church in his dotage will fascinate the local lads but serve to emphasise how far Dropmore has slipped into the shadows of Cliveden and even Taplow Court. And when the old fellow dies in 1938, St Anne's bells will toll for more than his passing: it will be the end of an era for his son **George Grenville Fortescue** will have no option but to put the rest of estate up for sale to pay death duties.

Staffers

Royal Refreshment

The Feathers, Taplow Common / 15th June 1891

On the left is Dropmore's newest gate, added in 1867 at its southern extremity for **Queen Victoria** to ride through as much of the park as possible on her way to visit her friend Lady Louisa – which would be why its gatehouse is ***Queen's Lodge***, home of Jacob Street. He gives a wave but we haven't time to chat. Our third stop is in sight. It's about time; our thirsts have been sharpened nicely by the warm sunshine. **Freddie Hurn**'s wife of four years, Sophia (née Wheeler) of Wooburn is waiting outside *The Feathers* to introduce us to their two-year-old son Everett and Alfie's wife Jane has brought young Alfred, Harry, Eva and Arthur from their nearby home at *Farm Cottages*. The Dropmore gamekeeper John Bradshaw arrives from ***Cabrook Cottages*** and the children dance a reel to a concertina played by his assistant George Avenell, the spit-and-image of his father William. The happy sight contrasts with the sad thought that Sophia will pass away two years from now leaving Freddie to bring up little Everett on his own. It is some consolation that in 1901 he will marry her youngest sister Clara.

Alfie's brother emerges from the inn. Arthur Coe has been landlord here for 16 years. He was only 21 when he came from Balham in Surrey to take over *The Feathers* and now his coachman brothers have joined him out this way. His being in the know locally led to Willie coming from Lambeth to *The Jolly Woodman* where his wife Helen is the publican. And not so long ago he wangled an opportunity for Alfie and Jane to leave smoky Earl's Court and come to breathe the country air.

I know what you need, says Arthur, a *Jenner's N° 3* each, a nice sensible light ale from Southwark, my neck of the woods. As he ushers us inside where his pretty wife Margaret is pulling our pints, he tells us with evident pride that his inn gets its name from the coat of arms of the Prince of Wales. Freddie chips in that he's heard the Black Prince stopped off for a quick stiffener at a couple of local hostelries when was on his way to marry Philippa of Hainault at Windsor in 1327 – first at *The Black Lion* at Well End and then here. It would be nice if that was true, says Maggie – after all, the Prince was tenant-in-chief of Hitcham Manor – but *The Black Lion* dates from 1863 when it was *The Old Lion*, which puts paid to it having such an ancient royal link. And her home's royal vintage is fresher too. She reckons it was originally ***The New Inn*** until becoming ***The Three Feathers*** as a nod to the ill-fated Prince of Wales. Arthur chimes in: they say Poor Fred used to pop in for the occasional fillip while he was at Clifden. Of course he did, smiles Maggie.

Are you confusing it with *The New Inn* on Littleworth Common (which was first noted in 1841 and won't be *The Blackwood Arms* until 1971)? Not according to Jeffreys' Map of 1770, says Arthur. And anyway, by 1847 this place had reopened as ***The Prince of Wales Feathers***, an alehouse like *The Standard* until the licensed victualler William Light took over in about 1850 and abbreviated the name to *The Feathers*. Back then, he had competition from ***The Waggon & Horses*** just half-a-mile down the road (on the corner of not-yet **Nashdom Lane**) where Sam Marshall did well enough to be able to take over ***Hitcham Bottom Farm*** a few years later. Soon afterwards John Alder rebranded it *The Waggon* only for the wheels to fall off during the 1860s. Arthur grimaces at Freddie's joke and suggests that the success of John Swan, his predecessor at ***The Feathers***, might have had something to do with *The Waggon* waving farewell.

That's enough about then, says Freddie, what about now? Is it true that, when Queen Victoria's son and heir Prince Edward comes to visit the abstemious Duke of Westminster at Cliveden, he slips away from His Grace's alcohol-free zone to refresh his courage in here? Margaret smiles knowingly but can't possibly comment except to say that, if we see Bertie (as the Prince's pals call him), we should ask whether his patronage inspired the inn's name or if the link goes way back to 'Poor Fred'. Arthur cuts short the chuckles with a nod to the door: our guests have arrived....

Service As Usual

The Feathers, Taplow Common / 15th June 1891

Freddie has arranged for us to meet employees from each of the three estates, and here they are – **John Jaycock** of **Cliveden**, George Martin of **Dropmore** and William Flatt of **Hedsor**. All are locals – Jaycock hails from Taplow and the others from Burnham – but they have very different roles in making their employers' lives comfortable.

Just as we are making sure they have full glasses, we are interrupted by the arrival of four old pals who live just across the road. Freddie Hurn shakes his stepfather **William Wells** by the hand. John introduces his father Richard Jaycock with a joke that his dad used to call himself a carpenter but now says he's a rustic worker, whatever that means. And the young barman Arthur Holem seems a little embarrassed for his father Edwin to watch him at work. The fourth old fellow, labourer **George Jeffries**, tells us that their little terrace of six 'poor houses' known as **Taplow Common Cottages** is home to 28 people. John Clements, another gardener, and Richard's widowed sister-in-law **Jane Jaycock** are heads of the other two households.

When everything eventually settles down, we ask our guests one-by-one to tell us what they do.

John prompts a sage nod from Richard by saying there are a lot of his lot around these parts. In the 83 years since his great-uncle John had little Elizabeth baptised at the old St Nicholas' Church another 69 Jaycocks have been baptised, married or buried in the parish and there were and are plenty more nearby. Eleven live work at Cliveden. In addition to his father, there are his wife Mary, his mother Sarah, his sister Grace and his aunt Jane who all work together in the laundry. His cousin Ernest is a groom, his nephew William Courtney an errand boy and he himself is one of 12 gardeners who work under Frank Westron keeping the grounds pristine. And then there are the three youngsters at school.

George isn't impressed. His family go back further in Taplow – his ancestor James Martin married at St Nic's as far back as 1721 – and there are 15 of them at ***Brook End Farm*** where he is a dairyman, his wife Zilphah a dairymaid and his brother John a farmhand. The cows are all in a day's work for George but having six children under 12 makes life hard. He reckons John and his wife Ellen have it easy with their brood of only five, especially now the eldest two are earning their keep as garden-boys.

Billy Flatt is a man of the moment. It isn't long since the gasworks was installed at *Hedsor House* and it's up to him to make sure it everything works safely. He has reason to be confident that Lord Boston values his engineering skills highly, so why does he look slightly embarrassed? The reason is soon clear; proud as they are of their four children, he and his wife Georgina couldn't do without their housemaid, 15-year-old Kate Newell of Wooburn. He responds to the rise of envious eyebrows by joking that his Cliveden counterpart John Willows and his wife Rebecca have eight children to help around the house.

His humour falls on stony ground. It's time for us to take centre stage by summarising our very rudimentary survey of how many it takes to run country estates nowadays. Put simply, just three people – **Lady Fortescue** and the **Lords Westminster** and **Boston** – together have some 125 employees who in turn support a similar number. Of the one-third with domestic duties, only one-third were born nearby and recruited locally. This compares with three-quarters of those who work outside in the gardens, fields, stables, coach-houses and kennels. And speaking of kennels....

A Perfect Specimen – Setting a Precedent

Taplow Lodge / 15th June 1891

This is the last trip we'll make on Alfie Coe's coach. We stop to drop off John Jaycock at his home, ***Windsor Lodge***, just north of the kennels where Cliveden's foxhounds are kept by two huntsmen, George Farr and his assistant George Devonshire. The dogs are barking fit to burst as John introduces us to these two Georges and their friend Henry Hellier, the whipper-in of hounds who lives not far away at ***Green Drive Lodge***. It's hard to hear ourselves speak as we ask about the very grand mansion we glimpsed through the trees on our left a few moments ago.

The elder George says ***Taplow Lodge*** was built in 1794 for Patrick Craufurd Bruce, MP for Evesham (Worcestershire) and well-connected enough to marry off his daughter Jane in 1811 to Cornwallis Maude, 3rd Viscount Hawarden. After Bruce died in 1820 he was succeeded by **Edward Tunno**, MP for Bossiney (Cornwall). His gardener **Jasper Holland** attracted the attention of *Gardener's Magazine*, which published his treatise on the cultivation of melons in 1831, and of the renowned horticulturalist and garden designer John Loudon who featured the garden in his *Gardening Tours* series the following year. However Jasper could take no credit in 1842 when the *Windsor & Eton Express* commended Mrs Tunno's dahlias.

Sadly George reckons there's been something of a cloud over ***Taplow Lodge*** ever since the early-1870s when a fellow called Joseph Maynard renovated it lavishly in the Elizabethan style, went bankrupt as a result and had to sell up in 1877 to the Lancastrian cotton magnate **Edward Whaley**, only for him to breathe his last a couple of years later. They say bad luck comes in threes but Whaley's widow Elizabeth has lived there happily enough ever since.

Young Georgie chips in to say that Widow Whaley has four servants, none of them local, and when he was roped in to help unload some furniture some time back, he was astounded by the majestic staircase and the dining room which somebody said was 'the perfect specimen of an Elizabethan room'. It must have been 30 feet long by 12 or 13 wide. There was a dado of oak panelling round the walls with green velvet above partly covered by fabulous tapestries depicting rural scenes. And above the carved oak fireplace was an enormous oil-painting of the Virgin Queen, her gaze so striking young Georgie felt she would tick him off if he so much as whispered out of turn. And the cellar was even scarier, a maze of bare-brick passageways with cobbled floors. It wouldn't surprise him at all if it's true that there's a secret tunnel to Cliveden.

Elizabeth Whaley will live at *Taplow Lodge* until her death in 1907 sparks a big family argument about whether the portrait is part of the house, bequeathed to her grandson Herbert Whaley, or a chattel that may be removed by her daughter, by then Mrs Roehrich. In 1908 the Chancery Division of the High Courts of Justice will set a well-worn precedent by deciding for Herbert. Legal eagles should search for Whaley versus Roehrich and revel in yet another Taplow legacy.

Hurn's Turn – The Devil's Kitchen

Top of the A / 15th June 1952

Taplow has been described as an A with **Rectory Road** its crosspiece and **Cliveden Road** and **Hill Farm Road** its converging sides. There was a quarry at the point of the A where for centuries gravel had been excavated to surface local roads. Although no longer used by the 1930s, it was still a big overgrown hole, a dark and scary place even in the daylight. Harry and his young pals knew it as ***The Devil's Kitchen*** and towards dusk would scuttle past as fast as their legs could carry them.

The Common People: Decline and Revival

1994

2012

***Taplow Lodge* and the CRCMH fell into a long dereliction before being replaced by Orkney Court and Cliveden Gages**

2001

2012

The Common People: Boston Manor

Hedsor House / 2013

St Nicholas' Church, Hedsor / 2012

The Arms of the Barons Boston / 1790

The Common People: Grenville's Legacy

Cedar Walk & *Cedar Lodge*
(now *Johnson's Coppice*) / c1925

The Evelyn Gates,
originally of Huntercombe Manor / c1925

Dropmore House / c1925

The Common People: Grenville's Legacy

Dropmore House / 2011

Evelyn Gates & The Aviary, dilapidated / 2011

The Common People: An Odd Story

The House family, squirrel shooting / 1951

Odds Farm Park / 2013

Odds Farm / c1925

Steve & Jackie Vinden, Anne & Lionel House/ 2013

The Village People

Westenders

At Her Majesty's Pleasure

The Queen's Head Hotel, Bapsey Green / 18th June 1891

Queen Anne's visit to **Taplow Court** in 1705 was something to remember. She expressed her gratitude for the Orkney's hospitality with a gift of four enormous stone urns decorated with armorial reliefs. Three still grace the grounds; the fourth is at the end of the Long Walk at Cliveden.

They say the enormity of the royal retinue matched that of the urns. Taplow Court didn't have enough bedrooms for everyone so some, perhaps Her Majesty's ladies-in-waiting, were accommodated here at Taplow's oldest inn, built on the site of the thatch-and-plaster cottage we saw in 1612 – the perfect place to begin the second leg of our pub crawl. They say it celebrated by becoming *The Queen's Head Hotel*, smiles our host Willy Sargent, and was doing well enough as a coaching inn that by 1824 the brewing brothers Henry and John Langton of Maidenhead acquired the leasehold from Viscount Kirkwall. The following year the Langtons were also noted as licensees of 26 other inns including *The Complete Angler* in Bisham (not *Compleat*), *The Palmer's Arms* and *The Bells* in Boveney (not Dorney), *The Hind's Head*, *The Nag's Head* and *The George* in Bray and *The Bull*, *The Vine*, *The Green Dragon*, *The Quart Pot*, *The Red Lion*, *The Saracen's Head* and *The Maiden's Head* in Maidenhead.

Willy goes on to say that things have been difficult since the coming of the railway. Oh do give over, says his wife Cate. We hire out horses, pony traps, carriages and dog carts. We take in boarders at five or ten bob-a-week (£163 or £326). And if money's too tight to mention, she adds with a twinkling eye, we make things meet by selling my Willy's homemade hair restorer.

The Sargents should be complimented on their fine cellar – their draught of *Langton's Old Ale* is rather tasty – but it won't be long before the Langtons sell the place to *Worthington & Co* of Leicester. Cate and Willy will move to ***Dorl Cot*** on ***Back Lane*** to turn his sideline into their main line of business. Meanwhile *Worthington* will install William Murray as landlord but to no avail. Soon after ***Langton & Co*** is acquired in 1906 by its competitor ***Nicholson & Co*** – in about a century, *Nicholson's Shopping Centre* will be built on the site of William Nicholson's Maidenhead brewery – Lord Desborough will get fed up seeing drunks sleeping off their Saturday nights on Bapsey Green. He will have a word in the right ears and ***The Queen's Head*** will end its 200 years as a pub and become ***Queen Anne's House***, the private residence of Colonel George Thesinger of The Rifle Brigade. Eventually it will be home to Franckenstein....

At His Majesty's Pleasure

St James's Palace, Westminster / 26th July 1938

Of course the gentleman in question wasn't the fictional Frankenstein created in 1818 by Mary Shelley but the very real Baron Georg von und zu Franckenstein, Austrian Ambassador to the Court of St James for the past 18 years. The diplomat quickly won the confidence of politicians with his financial acumen and the esteem of high society with his aristocratic yet modest manner and by hosting concerts and masked balls. He was held in such high regard that blind eyes were turned when King George V's cousin Princess Louise paid him discrete visits at home. His recent dismissal by the Nazis has prompted King George VI to dub him today a knight of the realm. **Sir George Franckenstein** will be pleased to complete his Anglicisation within two years through his marriage to a young English lady, Editha King, and his becoming a British subject. Clearly his time in Taplow sowed the seed.

The Coming of Cricket

The Queen's Head Hotel, Bapsey Green / 1st November 1850

It is a dark and cold winter's evening but the Williams **Rance** and **Skindle** have warm, sunny summer days in mind as they are welcomed into ***The Queen's Head*** by the cheery faces of friends and neighbours. Landlord Tom Greenhalf is savouring his ale with his namesake and fellow publican Tom White of ***The Palmer's Arms***. The farmers and cousins **William Davis Briginshaw** and **George Norrington** are enjoying a joke with the blacksmith **David Harris**. And there are carpenter John Tubb, farmhands **John Cordery** and **Thomas Simmons**, **Ambrose Oliver** (a railway contractor of Hitcham) and three outsiders labouring locally surnamed Hamerton, Luker and Mitchell. The declared purpose of these assembled gentlemen is to become the co-founders of **Taplow Union Cricket Club**. By May next year they will be joined for the first match of their first season at Ten Acres opposite Taplow Court by **James Rutland** and seven others including **William Simmon** (a Taplow-born gardener of Bray) and farmhands Middleton, Plummer and Amery.

These pioneers evidently enjoy the prospect of scoring runs and taking wickets but they won't excel at taking names with any consistency. Reference to the 1851 census will suggest that Tubb was Tabb, Amery was Avery and both Simmon and Simmons were Simmonds but it won't tell which of three brothers played the game: Robert or **Thomas Avery**, Philip or **Thomas Plummer** and James or David Middleton (of Dorney). This laxity of nomenclature also applies to their ground: **Ten Acres** is but eight-and-a-bit acres. **Michael Bayley** will scoff at any suggestion that somebody got their sums wrong: he will say its name derives from the ancient British *Tir-ner-argae*, meaning *the enclosure of the lord of the manor*.

Taplow Union Cricket Club, Ten Acres / 29th September 1853

The season has seen Taplow's cricketing pioneers travel on a horsedrawn carriage to play at Wycombe and Colnbrook. It has ended today with a match against Edward Winslow's Party, a team comprising seven Winslows, three Stewarts and a Sperling. Taplow made a grand total of 44 all out – Tom Simmon top-scoring with seven – and their opponents replied with 41. A Taplow victory by just three runs, won by the bowling of Harris, who took six wickets, and the Simmon brothers, who took two each. They thwarted the stalwart **George Winslow**, who top-scored with eleven, and James Stewart, stranded on nine not out when Will Simmon bowled the elder **Edward Winslow** of ***Well Bank*** for four: a thrilling finish recorded on what will be the club's oldest surviving scorecard.

Taplow Cricket Club, Ten Acres / 29th September 1888

Over the next few years the fixture list increased to include games at Beaconsfield, Iver, Marlow, Slough, Stoke Green and Wargrave. Members paid 3s 6d (£12.64) per season and one shilling per match (£4.08) but this was nowhere near enough to cover expenses – balls cost seven-and-six each – and additional subscriptions were gratefully received from the gentlemen of the village. Members continued to gather for formal meetings and informal refreshment but a full toss from the ground in ***The Queen's Head*** for the surroundings here were less convivial. A tent played the part of a pavilion and the 'sporting' nature of the rough hewn pitches made matches notoriously unpredictable. But did that spoil the fun? Of course it didn't.

Much fun was had earlier this season when **Taplow Cricket Club** played **Ally Sloper's XI**, a very strange team from Maidenhead captained by Sloper himself – actually a certain T Emmett with a strawberry nose, a tall white hat covering his bald pate and a bottle of 'unsweetened' halfway out of his coat-tail pocket. He opened for the visitors and made 14 of the 26 amassed by his less gifted team-mates, all of whom were dressed as women complete with heavy make-up. It takes all sorts. Taplow replied with a handsome 99. Were the Slopers hampered by their long skirts or by the intoxication of the moment?

The Good Butler

Bapsey Green / 18th June 1891

As arranged, Mr Grenfell's 31-year-old butler **Barrett Good** is waiting for us outside *The Queen's Head* [*see Map 24*]. This Essex lad left school to enter service with the family as a page to his master's grandmother Georgiana. He has already held his present post for over ten years and he will continue in it until his death at 84 in 1945. Ever the perfect butler, he will be appointed a member of the Royal Victorian Order by **King Edward VII** and decorated by the King of Siam. Nowadays he spends most of his time up at Nº 18 New Cavendish Street, the Grenfell London home, so he is looking forward to this evening when he will be reunited with his wife Mary and their infant son William at *Taplow Court Lodge*. They will be blessed with two more sons: Harry in 1893 and Herbert in 1900. Harry's son **Michael Good** will be born in 1925 to be Harry Hurn's best boyhood pal and in 1982 to rest forever after in St Nicolas' Churchyard.

The gentleman's gentleman's duty today is to acquaint us with those who live in this, the west end of the village. He begins by remarking that, while they say an Englishman's home is his castle, in fact it's more subtle than that. There is perhaps a trait among English gentlemen to look down on anyone who talks themselves up and look up to anyone who lets their home do their talking for them. The spate of up-and-coming newcomers a generation ago spoke volumes, and the trend continues....

Another Kilmorey Connection – Darling's Cottage

Darling's Cottage / 18th June 1891

We walk down the lane towards **Tæppa's Mound** and stop outside two pretty adjoining cottages on the south side. Back in 1852 the farmer **George Norrington** lived in the easterly one. However today it is the westerly cottage we want to hear about for doesn't ***Darling's Cottage*** have a whiff of scandal? Its name reminds us that it was the home of **Edward Darling** – not only head gardener at **Taplow Court** for much of the mid-19th Century but also the husband of **Mary Ann Darling** (née **Gurney**) who started the village shop and post office – but there's no scandal in being a Darling [*see Appendix 1, Tree 14*]. Good is adamant that there was no scandal of any kind. Yes, its tenant Joseph Hoffman – an importer of foreign luxury goods – disappeared in 1876 without paying his rent. And yes, it was hard to believe that Hoffman had not 'bolted' but merely "gone abroad to sift the matter of having lost a considerable sum of money thro' his foreign agents". But this was merely an inconvenience for Mr Grenfell and the Kilmorey connection revived to save the day.

Having served with the 12th (Prince of Wales) Lancers in the Crimea at Sevastopol in 1855 and later in India, Major **Robert Needham** (second son of 'Black Jack', the 2nd Earl of Kilmorey) had returned in the early-1870s to settle in his grandfather's home at ***Berry Hill House***. And his nephew Lieutenant-Colonel **Henry Needham** of the Grenadier Guards just happened to be eager to take up the lease of ***Darling's*** at a very healthy annual rent of £75 (£6,200), reduced to £67 (£5,900) in 1881. Henry still lives there and in four years he will renew his lease and take another on ***Bapsey Cottage*** for a total of £100-a-year (£10,100). Come 2011 *Darling's* will have united with its neighbour to become ***May Cottage***, home of ***SGI*** estate manager **Mike Yeadon**.

Cold Comfort – The Thatched Cottage

Bapsey Green / 18th July 1891

We retrace our steps to stop outside ***The Thatched Cottage***, a misleadingly modest name for the rather extensive residence on the south side of Bapsey Green. Its owner has an extensive name to match. Alan de Tatton Egerton hails from Tatton Park in Cheshire where he is MP for Knutsford. He first came to Taplow in 1877 to briefly sublet *Darling's* from Needham before relocating to this house and changing its name from ***Taplow Cottage***. He will succeed his elder brother to become 3rd Baron Egerton in 1907 but is currently noted as an innovative civil engineer with a keen interest in railways, engineering and the development of cold storage. He will be appointed the first president of the UK Institute of Refrigeration in 1899.

Another new identity will strike Egerton's home during the Great War when a steam traction engine struggling up the hill sends out a shower of sparks to set alight to the thatch. It will be restored as ***Bapsey Lodge*** and eventually ***Bapsey House*** to be acquired in 1978 for £55,500 (£454,000) by **Patty & David Stanning** – he a Gerrards Cross solicitor – who will split it into two, retain ***West Bapsey*** and sell ***East Bapsey*** to **Lesley & Geoff Street**. The timber-framed, timber-clad ***Bapsey Cottage*** overlooking the cricket pitch will survive until 1966 when **Raymond Lock** replaces it with the first ***Wickenden***.

Springfield Fellows

Springfield, Town Lane / 18th July 1891

Church Road joins Town Lane a few yards down the hill. There is is fine view from the junction across **Carkins Meadow** to Windsor Castle some six miles away. Further downhill, there's Billy Lemon at the door of his cottage chatting with Gilbert Clare. Billy tends the grounds of ***The Elms*** for William Casberd-Boteler, a retired Royal Navy Commander who enjoys the mansion which Charles Matthews either substantially extended or completely replaced some 30 years ago on land held by the Whitlaw estate. Gilbert lives next door at ***Springfield Cottage***. Rising above that are the gables and chimneys of ***Springfield*** itself, from 1873 until recently the home of Lieutenant-Colonel **Sir John Edmund Harvey**.

After years abroad serving with the 41st (Welch) Regiment of Foot in the Mediterranean, the Crimea, the West Indies and India, Sir John and his wife Lady Octavia divided their time between his family's seat at Thorpe in Norfolk and Taplow where they leased *Springfield* from **Charles Whitlaw the Younger**. For a time ten years ago they sublet the place to Theodore Walrond, husband of Willy Grenfell's Aunt Louisa, who installed there in the care of a governess Victoria and Georgina, his daughters by his late first wife Charlotte, daughter of Riversdale William Grenfell [*see Appendix 1, Tree 16*]. The Harveys returned and their son **Sir John Robert Harvey** married Nora Adams of Bray in 1888 only for tragedy to strike three times the following year. Nora died in India giving birth to twins – little Norah survived, the new John didn't – and John the Elder passed away at *Springfield* just before Christmas.

The younger John was eight when his parents first brought him to *Springfield*. He has grown up to follow his father's military footsteps in the East Norfolk Militia, as a ranker in the 16th (Queen's) Lancers and now as a lieutenant in the 5th Royal Irish Lancers. He will become a bit of a military hero as he serves with distinction during the Second Boer War in South Africa, first with the 43rd Suffolk Hussars and then the Imperial Yeomanry, in which he'll rise to lieutenant-colonel and be created Companion of the Distinguished Service Order in 1902. After a term as the mayor of Norwich, he will return to action in the Great War commanding the 4th Battalion Norfolk Regiment at Gallipoli and later serving in France.

The Harveys were the kind of reliable, reputable people the Whitlaws would want as tenants but it still cut a dash when Amy & **Edgar Lubbock** of distant Lincolnshire took over the tenancy of *Springfield* from the widowed Octavia. Lubbock is of impeccable stock and credulity. His father was Sir John Lubbock of the bankers *Robarts, Lubbock & Co* which will merge with *Coutts & Co* in 1914. He is the youngest brother of **Sir John Lubbock the Younger** (who discovered Taplow's mammoth in 1854) and the uncle of **Cecil** (daughter of his brother Henry) who in 1888 married stockbroker Riversdale Francis John **Grenfell** (conveniently known as **Dick**). He has long been a director of the brewers ***Whitbread & Co*** and recently became a director of The Bank of England, which is why he needs a place within striking distance of London. But Barrett Good reckons none of this is why he is famous.

Every schoolboy knows Lubbock as a footballer who in 1870 played for England in all five 'representative internationals' against Scotland, two years before the first officially recognised international match. The following year he played for The Gentlemen of Kent versus Marylebone Cricket Club, scoring 54 runs in one innings and twice being dismissed by none other than WG Grace before playing for The Wanderers in the very first Football Association Challenge Cup Final in 1872, a 1-0 victory over The Royal Engineers. He has since played for The Old Etonians in three further FA Cup Finals, losing to The Royal Engineers (1874) and The Wanderers (1875) but emerging victorious over Clapham Rovers (1879). The 1874 match was decided in a replay in which Edgar and his brother Alfred became the first siblings to play together in an FA Cup Final. Edgar was described in the 1875 Football Annual as "still unrivalled as a back" by none other than Charles Alcock, the Old Harrovian secretary of the Football Association who 'invented' the FA Cup. This man was a sporting colossus. It will be a disappointment to the local lads when the tenancy of *Springfield* is taken by an old soldier, Major-General William Truman of the 7th (Princess Royal) Dragoon Guards.

York Road Football Ground, Maidenhead / 18th July 2012

The Lubbock story can't be left without a nod to **Maidenhead United Football Club**, just plain Maidenhead FC when it was founded in 1870 and moved to its current ground in York Road the following year. The club played its first game in the FA Cup five weeks before The Wanderers, beating Marlow 2-0 on 11th November 1871 while Lubbock's team had a walkover when

The Village People: Westenders

***The Thatched Cottage* overlooking Bapsey Green** / c1912

....evolved to become *Bapsey* and eventually *East & West Bapsey* / 2012

The second *Wickenden* / 1991 (on the site of *Bapsey Cottage*)

***The Thatched Cottage,* Berry Hill** (once home to Joe Springall) / 2009

May Cottage (formerly *Darling's*) / 2012

Queen Anne's House
(formerly
The Queen's Head Hotel)
/ 2012 & 1904

Hill House
(formerly *Prospect House*
& *Prospect Lodge*) / 2012

Taplow Hill
(formerly *Taplowhill House*) / c1930

Map 24 – The Village: Westenders
Ancient & Modern

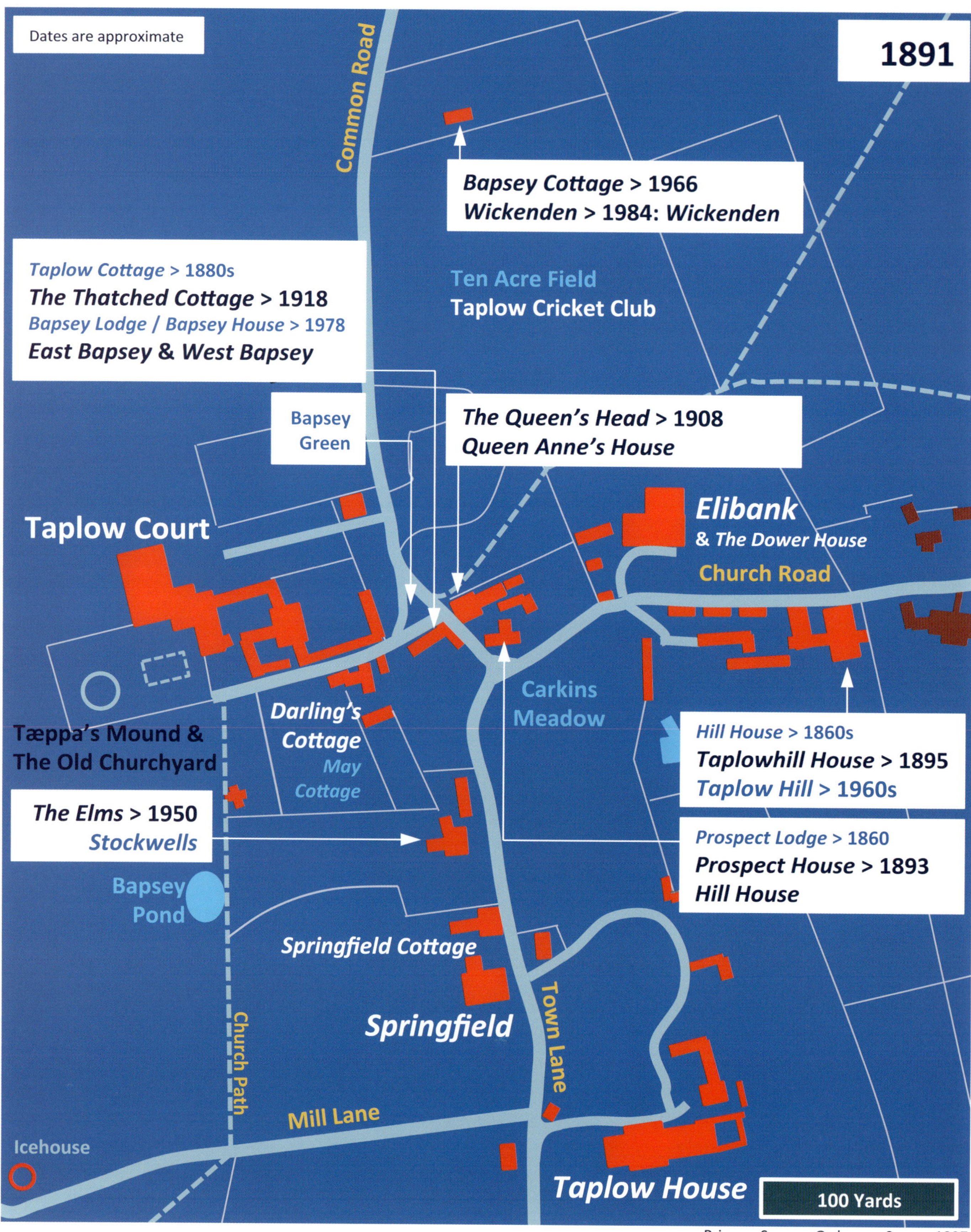

Primary Source: Ordnance Survey 1897

Harrow Chequers couldn't get a team together. Sadly in the second round Maidenhead went down 0-3 to Crystal Palace on 16th December, the day Lubbock and The Wanderers made their FA Cup debut in a 3-1 win over Clapham Rovers. The FA has acknowledged that York Road is "the oldest senior football ground continuously used by the same club".

The Coming of a Croquet Champion

Taplow House, Town Lane / 18th July 1891

Beyond ***Springfield*** is a thatched cottage, once the home of ***Taplow House*** head gardener **Joe Springall** and later of his son. Joe the Younger inherited his father's green fingers and exercised them for **Charles Whitlaw the Elder** at *Springfield*, probably at *Taplow House* and ***Berry Hill House*** too. In 105 years, **Brenda Burns** will give new life to the twee antiquity of the place when by having it re-thatched. By then it will long have been the last surviving thatched dwelling in Taplow with every right to have inherited the name ***The Thatched Cottage*** since Egerton's home discarded it.

Taplow House is just across the road. When it was offered for sale at auction in 1875 after the death of **William O'Brien, 2nd Marquess of Thomond**, the auction booklet made much of its Louis XVI-style drawing room dominated by the superb fireplace with marble hearth and carved wood mantel, and the beautifully marbled and tessellated floor in the outer and inner halls. The booklet mentions many notable features – the thatched outer larder, the conical icehouse and the butler's room complete with fireproof strongbox – but not that the walled gardens of the house had been blessed with some six-feet of topsoil, all brought in by horse-and-cart and spread by man-and-wheelbarrow. The successful bid was received from a certain **Neville Ward** of whom History will say little except that the Cedar of Lebanon he planted almost ten years ago promises to be a fine compliment to Thomond's sequoias. Ward will be followed at *Taplow House* first by the widow Alice Barrow and her son, three daughters and nine servants and then by Lieutenant-Colonel **William Baring du Pré**.

High Wycombe Town Hall / 6th December 1923

This well-connected gentleman has local roots. His grandfather the Reverend William du Pré, vicar of Wooburn, was descended from Josias du Pré, the former Governor of Madras who in 1779 built the luxurious *Wilton Park* in Beaconsfield. His grandmother Emily was a daughter of the banking Baring Brothers. His great-aunt Catherine du Pré married Pascoe St Leger **Grenfell**, which gave him a distant familial link to Willy Grenfell. And his daughter Elizabeth will marry Richard Yarde-Buller, 4th Baron Churston, whose father John was born at ***The Grange*** on Back Lane in 1873.

His military career spanned three regiments from the Second Boer War to the Great War, a period during which he founded Beaconsfield Golf Club in 1902 and became a Justice of the Peace and High Sheriff and Deputy Lieutenant of Buckinghamshire. Having been a strong opponent of women's rights while serving for nine years as MP for Wycombe, he has today lost his seat to a woman: Vera Woodhouse, Lady Terrington to be precise. While his political career will never recover from the comeuppance, he will find solace by excelling at croquet to win many tournament victories including the British Open Championship twice.

The Spreading Grenfells

Hill House, Town Lane / 18th July 1891

The butler turns to look up at ***Hill House*** reaching for the sky behind us. It has been in the extended Grenfell family for over 40 years and is now home to Cecil & **Dick Grenfell**. And not 100 yards along **Church Road** is ***Elibank*** where that gentleman's merchant banker father (Charles) **Seymour Grenfell** (Willy Grenfell's half-second-cousin) will remain until his death in 1924 the primary beneficiary of the family trust set up by **Charles Pascoe Grenfell**.

Ever the soul of discretion, Good is silent on whether the rumour is true that there is a tunnel from *Elibank* to **Taplow Court**. Instead he delights in reeling off a list of noteworthy Grenfells beginning with his master's uncle and former guardian **Henry Riversdale Grenfell**, Liberal MP for Stoke-on-Trent (1862/68) and Governor of the Bank of England (1881/83), and his nine half-uncles, sons of Pascoe St Leger Grenfell, who have begun military careers in which three will be killed in action. Then comes a clutch of cousins: Edward Grenfell (son of Henry), the future 1st Baron St Just, not yet a partner in the investment bank *Morgan Grenfell & Co* or Unionist MP for the City of London (1922/35); John Pascoe Grenfell, somehow an admiral in the Brazilian navy; John Granville Grenfell, Commissioner of Crown Lands in New South Wales where he was killed by bushrangers; Commander Harry Tremenheere Grenfell, who survived being severely wounded in Turkey to command the paddle steamer *HMS Cockatrice* during the Egyptian War; Major-General Francis Grenfell, currently *Sirdar* (Commander-in-Chief) of the Egyptian Army and future 1st Baron Grenfell; the twins Francis Octavius Grenfell, who will be awarded the Victoria Cross in 1914, and Riversdale Nonus Grenfell, both of whom will fall in the Great War; and the former Marie Grenfell (daughter of George St Leger Grenfell) who lives little more than 100 yards away [*see Appendix 1, Trees 16 & 17*].

Something's Brewing – Serocold Comforts

Prospect House, Town Lane / 18th July 1863

The Great Western Railway has brought something new to Taplow and Hitcham: commuters. Commuting isn't cheap. Many of those attracted by the rural beauty and tranquillity of the countryside and the ease of railway access to the metropolis are wealthy businessmen. Some travel daily to London, others stay during the week at their London homes or clubs and return to their families at weekends. One such newcomer is **Charles Pearce-Serocold**, senior partner in the Clerkenwell brewers ***Reid &***

Co. His interest is less to do with the brewing of beer and more with the commercial advantage of acquiring interests in profitable pubs such as *The White Hart* in Theobald's Road, *The Man-in-the-Moon* in Chelsea and *The Hole-in-the-Wall* near Hatton Garden.

Both brewing and Taplow are a big departure from Pearce-Serocold's Cambridgeshire roots. His forebears have long been lords of Uphall Manor in Cherry Hinton or rectors of St Andrew's Church like his great-grandfather Walter Serecold and his father Edward Pearce-Serocold. His maternal grandfather William Pearce had come to Cambridge from Cornwall to be Master of Jesus College in 1789, Dean of Ely in 1797 and to hyphenate with Walter's daughter Anne. Could this (yet another) Taplow connection with Cornwall be how he met his wife Marie (Willy Grenfell's half-fourth-cousin) and how they together found Taplow?

In the few years they have been here Charles and Marie have changed the name of their home from *Prospect Lodge* to ***Prospect House***. It certainly has a fine prospect of cross the Thames Valley to Windsor. However their gaze nowadays tends to be drawn eastwards along Church Road to something closer to home. The ***Taplow House*** cattle chew the cud in **Carkins Meadow** before being milked in the cowsheds that in 150 years will be an annexe to ***Upper Bumbles***. Beyond Carkins is a cluster of cottages and workshops where the carpenter **William Simmonds**, the bricklayer Alfred Bailey and the blacksmith **David Harris** live and ply their trades. Beyond them stands the well-appointed red-brick ***Taplowhill House*** from whence the Birds have flown to be replaced until recently by another commuter, the barrister Edward Conant, his wife Gertrude and their ten children and seven servants. Now it is being refurbished for the Pearce-Serocolds. Here lie seeds of glorious confusion for in 30 years (after **Dick Grenfell** decides that ***Prospect House*** has better prospects as ***Hill House***) *Taplowhill House* will revert to being ***Taplow Hill*** except in conversation. Are you paying attention at the back? But of course nobody will be confused at the time because they know who lives where.

Church Road / 18th July 1891

Taplow Hill Cottages and their workshops have now all been acquired by Pearce-Serocold to accommodate his entourage and their families. Under-gardener James Brooks is from Stoke Poges, the others all hail from far distant parts – Thomas Caffyn the butler from Surrey, coachman Ellis Dellar from Cheshire, gardener James Charlton from Hampshire and of eight domestic servants, only Ellen Deane is from Buckinghamshire. This contrasts with **Charles Seymour Grenfell**'s staff at ***Elibank*** across the road left where Richard Martin the footman is from Maidenhead's Boyne Hill, all five female domestic servants are Buckinghamshire-born and the gardener **George Horton** at ***Elibank Lodge*** is from Burnham.

Cedar Chase / 18th July 2012

It is possible here in the clearing to imagine hordes of Pearce-Serocold children running amok 140 years ago. Looking uphill to the mid-1960s *Span* development of **Cedar Chase**, it is much harder to picture *Taplow Hill* up there on the right with those more workaday buildings to the left on the western boundary with Carkins which now accommodates ***Eriska*** and the western houses of **Saxon Gardens**.

Charles, Marie, their (eventually) ten children and twelve servants lived contentedly in their newly-modernised home for 44 years. In their dotage the happy couple took to spending their winters in Bordighera on the Italian Riviera. They both passed away there in 1904 – he in January, she in April – before being commemorated in the lobby of **St Nicholas' Church** by a pair of stained glassed windows portraying *Faith* and *Fortitude*.

His father's brewing background led to **Oswald Pearce-Serocold** being instrumental in two unions. The first was personal: he married Gwendolyn Combe of rival brewers *Combe Delafield & Co.* The second was business: *Reid* and *Combe Delafield* merged with *Watney & Co* in 1898 to become ***Watney Combe Reid & Co***. His younger brother Eric returned home in 1902 from the Second Boer War in South Africa to suffer a double tragedy. His wife Beatrice Rice died in 1906 giving birth to their second daughter Anne-Marie who didn't survive a year. He recovered to marry Blanche Stanley who could claim descent through eight generations from **King Charles II** and his mistress **Barbara Villiers**. An extended and tenuous royal circle was completed in 1923 when his fourth-cousin Elizabeth Bowes-Lyon married Bertie, the second son of **King George V** who succeeded to the throne in 1936 as **King George VI** [*see Appendix 1, Tree 18*].

Eastenders

A Good Living

The Rectory, Church Road / 30th October 1891

The two ends of the Village are only 200 yards apart yet it is a strange journey from one to the other through a channel enclosed between parallel eight-foot high brick walls. Only *Elibank Lodge* peeps out. Occasional doors and gates hint at unseen residences but *Elibank* on the left and *Taplow Hill* and ***The Rectory*** on the right all keep their secrets from passers-by.

James Rutland is waiting for us by the old village pump, still in good working order although much less used now that most houses are connected to the water supply from Taplow Court [*see Map 25*]. He greets us with a firm handshake just as the Reverend William Sawyer emerges from *The Rectory* with a wave goodbye to his wife Edith and their baby daughter Violet. The 43rd Rector smiles a pastoral greeting to us and heads busily towards the church with his surplice flying behind him. Rutland reckons he has reason to be thankful. Taplow's rectorship is very attractive with a 'living' of £380-a-year (£247,400) from 183 acres of glebe land. And within four years it will grow to £450 (£288,500) and 190 acres. No wonder Sawyer's predecessor enjoyed the benefits for 40 years....

The Rectory, Church Road / 30th October 1883

Here they come now, two pillars of local wisdom: the Rector and his organist, not always in tune. And yet today the Reverend **Charles Whately** and Rutland put aside their differences over the latter's disruption of the old churchyard and its ancient mound to perform the ceremony of holy matrimony between Fanny, daughter of the butcher **William Rance the Elder**, and **Sidney Budgen** of Windsor, the grocer son of grocer **John Budgen** [*see Appendix 1, Tree 14*]. The Rector is 67 now and eager for the quiet seclusion of his home for, in 56-year-old Rutland's company, the uphill walk from the church feels as long as that the good Lord Jesus took in the desert.

A Farm No Longer

Rectory Farm, Church Road / 30th October 1891

Rectory Farmhouse is now the home of the 42-year-old widow Helen Bellamy. Rutland recalls that the farm thrived in the days of **John Briginshaw** and his son **Richard** when one or other turned **Pater Noster** meadow into a farmyard. It is now crowded with pigsties, cow-briars and barns, the largest of which is said to have its roof supported by trusses rescued from the old church. The shadow of the tragic deaths in the early-1840s hung over Richard and things went further awry after he died in 1864 at just 51-years-old. His widow Elizabeth struggled to run the place until the early-1870s when her son William took over, but not very well. He and his wife Ann have for the last ten years lived with her mother in Windsor. The word is that he was a travelling

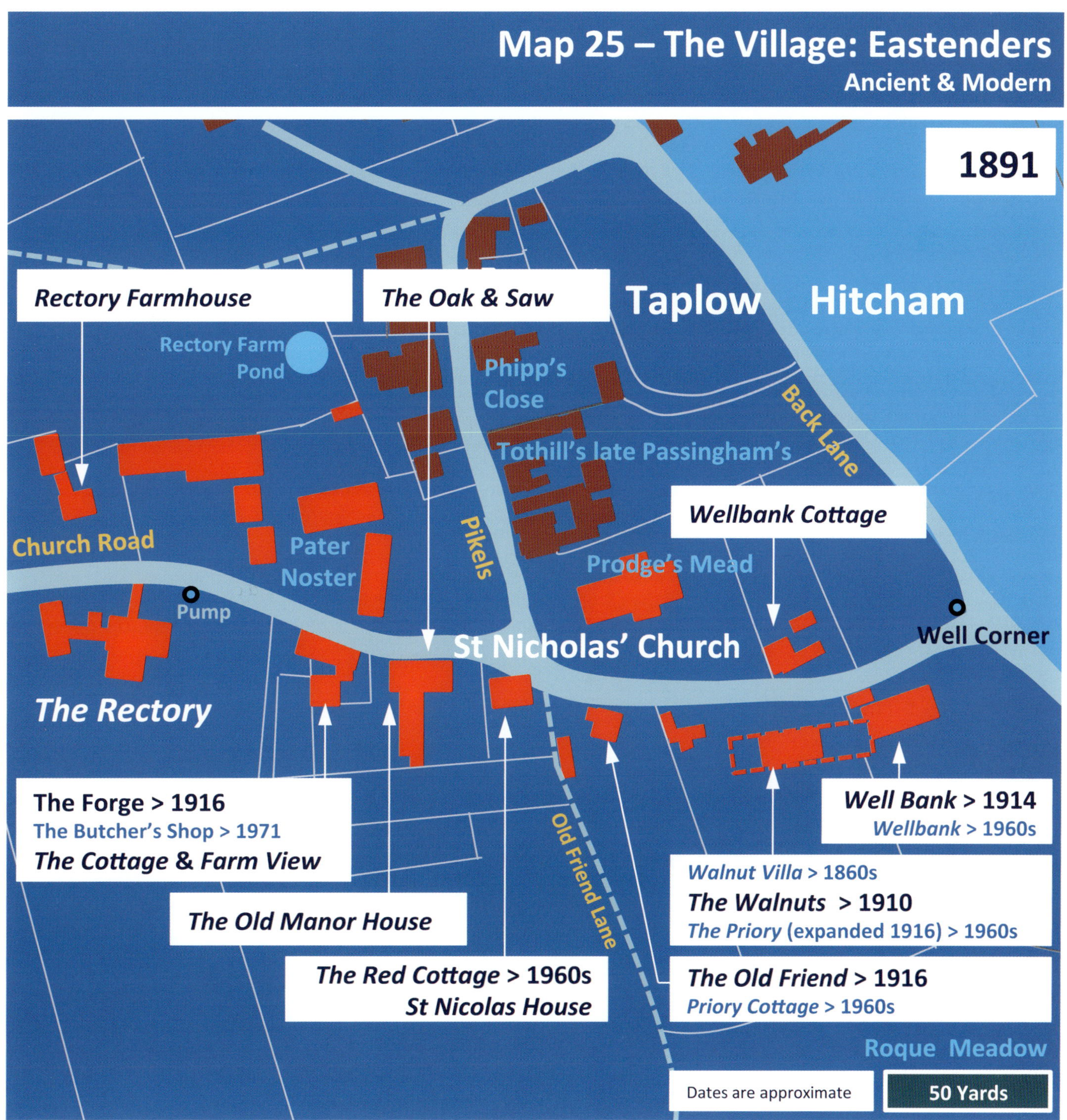

Primary Source: Ordnance Survey 1897

salesman of some kind and now has ideas about becoming a coal merchant. Meanwhile **Willy Grenfell** has let Rectory Farm's lands and its farmyard to **William Rance** and the house to Mrs Bellamy.

Nobody knows much about this fine lady except that she moved down from Edgbaston some years ago after her wool merchant husband William Bellamy died leaving her and their two children comfortably off. It will be much the same when she is succeeded here by William Wallace French. Nobody will know much about him either. Perhaps his Midland origins indicate a familial link with Widow Bellamy. Perhaps his being a paper manufacturer suggests he'll have professional interests in ***Charles Venables & Co*** which has continued at **Taplow Mills** since the man himself passed away in 1880. Most likely this pair of briefly appearing Brummies will remain enigmas forever.

Rectory Farm, Church Road / 30th October 1918

Two more Midlanders are having a very different impact. **Walter Baldwin** has a long family history in Birmingham where his grandfather founded the papermakers *James Baldwin & Sons Ltd* in 1829 and rose to serve as mayor of the rapidly growing city in 1853. By the late-1880s Walter settled in Bloomsbury to open new markets in London for the company's specialities of gun wadding and square-bottomed paperbags for grocers and fruiterers. He and Liley moved some ten years later to ***Rectory Farmhouse*** where their daughter Daphne was born in 1902 and Liley's companion Alice 'Obbie' Osborn took on the extra responsibility of being the child's governess. Nowadays Walter divides his time between Taplow and his London business address at N° 182 Upper Thames Street while Walter's brother Harry keeps a watchful eye on their nephews James and Harold Baldwin as they run the company.

Liley and Walter were quickly accepted into Taplow although they did cause something of a stir a couple of years ago by adding an extension to *Rectory Farmhouse* without permission from either Lord Desborough or the Rector. What made matters worse was the prefabricated nature of the extension which it seems Walter's Uncle William sent from Canada. The Reverend **Francis Phillips** is particularly aggrieved. His first reaction was to give notice to determine the Baldwins' tenancy, his second to withdraw it and grumble. Ever since, Walter has waited while Phillips fumed. The matter has come to a head again with the Rector instructing *Egginton's* the solicitors to send an ultimatum that "steps will be taken to remove the structure". It will only be with some difficulty that Walter finally succeeds in mollifying the Rector's angst by paying an undisclosed sum in 'compensation'.

Tall Tale – A Site for Saws

Rectory Road / 30th August 2012

Nothing remarkable here across the road from where the old farmyard used to be – just a village pub, an adjoining cottage with another attached and a pair of double-fronted cottages to the west, all decked out in Union Jacks and red-white-and-blue bunting to celebrate the QEII Jubilee and the 2012 Olympics and Paralympics. But wait a while....

These buildings share a secret. Well, two actually – but who else cares that *The Cottage* has been my home-sweet-home since 1997? The much more interesting secret is hinted at by the pub's sign. The oak tree, ship and saw reflect devices in the coat of arms of **George Hamilton**, **1st Earl of Orkney**, or more precisely a combination of heraldic devices on the coats of arms of Clan Douglas for his noble father and Clan Hamilton for his even more noble mother. The second is an oak tree penetrated transversely by a frame saw. The first includes a sailing ship, the product of sawn oak. The heraldry preceded noble George but perhaps it inspired him and his heirs to make their mark on this little patch of Taplow....

Legend has it that the first Lord Orkney used his privileged position as a friend of royalty to acquire damaged warships and have them towed up the Thames to be broken up and their salvaged timbers used to construct houses or river barges or for fuel. And maybe this became a family tradition. And maybe (running west to east) the result is ***Farm View***, ***The Cottage***, ***The Old Manor House*** and ***The Oak & Saw***.

A Site for Saws – Second Chances

Church Road / 30th October 1891

The whole four-part timber-framed package was acquired by Thomas Bell of Ray Mill in 1852. The westerly pair of two-up-two-down semi-detached cottages are said to date from 1756; they are unusual for being double-fronted. By 1841 the westernmost cottage destined to become *Farm View* was home to **Thomas Fenner**, a gardener, his laundress wife Mary and their eight children while two pauper lace-maker sisters, Sarah and Ann Langfield, were next door at not-yet *The Cottage* with their bricklayer lodger, **Harry Hearn**. Bell was content to leave these tenants undisturbed until nearly six years later when the Langfield sisters passed away. Both were well into their eighties. Such was Ann's grief that she survived Sarah by just 25 days. Was it one of these old lacemaking ladies who cursed the Grenfell family? James Rutland thinks not; they both had Christian burials, after all. He is eager to tell us what happened next....

Church Road / 6th February 1858

It is just two days since Ann Langfield was buried but James's father **Thomas Rutland** already has designs on her cottage. Having given him 13 children and lost three of them as infants, Tom's wife Rebecca died last January when they were both 57. It was a big blow but he is nothing if not resilient. In October he married Charlotte, the 45-year-old spinster daughter of his fellow carpenter Richard Carey of Maidenhead North Town. And while he had the new broom handy, he also decided to leave papermaking behind for the more sedentary responsibilities of Taplow's Parish Clerk. He has to give up his cottage at Taplow Mills but that's alright, says Tom. Mr Venables didn't get where he is today by doing favours, not even for such a stalwart employee. And anyway, even late-middle-aged newly-weds want a home to call their own. All he needs is for his son to give him a few ideas about what can be done to dust off the Langfield cobwebs.

James Rutland is doing very nicely thank you as a builder and self-styled architect. He usually has at least half-a-dozen men on the go, building this, altering that. He plans to add onto the back of the century-old cottage a kitchen and a privy draining to a new cess pit. They're all the rage, he says. Tom interrupts to prevent his son getting too graphic. We get the picture and limit ourselves to agreeing that **Tom Fenner** next door might appreciate a privy too. After all, he and his wife Mary have eight children. The Fenner family have been in Taplow for over a century and Tom may be the second or third generation to live in his home.

The younger Rutland gives the elder a withering look. Tittle-tattle isn't his thing. He is growing impatient to turn the conversation back to his favourite topic: his ambitious ideas. James is clearly a chip off the old block but with more besides. He learned carpentry from his father at the mill and has obviously inherited his practicality and imagination but, whereas Tom applied these attributes to the construction and maintenance of papermaking machinery, James has bigger fish to fry. Taplow is growing, he says. The railway is bringing gentry with money to spend. They want comfortable homes and so do all the people who serve them. What they need is a builder they can rely on. Who can he have in mind?

The second (or third) St Nicholas' Church / Christmas Day 1876

The church is packed to celebrate not only the Saviour's birth but also the second marriage of 62-year-old Tom Fenner. As the congregation sings with gusto the traditional hymn *All People That On Earth Do Dwell*, thoughts drift back to the dark days of last June when we saw two neighbours – 75-year-old **Tom Rutland** and **Mary Fenner** (68) – buried within four days of each other. The Rutlands had been married for 18 years, the Fenners for well over 40. How sweet that the cloud has a silver lining for now our sadness had turned to joy that our green-fingered old friend has found new love in the shape of Jane Barnes, a sweet young widow of 53. It won't be long before the new Mr & Mrs Fenner move to N° 6 ***Church Houses*** and the widow Charlotte Rutland moves into Fenner's old home leaving hers free for blacksmith **David Harris** to forge ahead.

A Site for Saws – Forging Ahead

Church Road / 30th January 1877

Taplow will never match its neighbour for industrialisation – there have been two iron foundries in Burnham for many years – but anywhere that has nearly as many horses as people will always need an unlimited supply of horseshoes. There were three blacksmiths here five years ago. The former Bray baker **George Butler** was in prime position down at the old station yard. He ran the smithy there for only ten years or so but, by the time the old station closed five years back, he had made such a fortune that he could retire to live in luxury at ***Charlton Villa*** despite still being in his thirties. **William Hooper** learned his trade from his father in Burnham and will follow in his footsteps happily enough for another couple of decades just up the road from the grammar school. David Harris has been hammering away for 30 years – first in a small forge just north of the new church and from the mid-1850s succeeding **George Stevens** in the smithy by ***Taplowhill Cottages***. And now Butler's retirement and the coming of age of his second son **Richard Harris** have given him an opportunity to expand. Time will tell if it is a good move.

Church Road / 30th October 1891

Rutland concludes that time has told, and Harris had it right. In the early-1880s with all their nine children having reached maturity, David and his wife Charlotte retired to Burnham leaving the forge to Richard and his elder brother William who returned home from being a journeyman gunmaker under Charles Clark in Bray. The pair built a new and larger forge behind William's western cottage accessible from a yard to the rear of Richard's eastern one which became known as ***The Forge***. Are their wives happy their homes have interconnecting doors both upstairs and down? All seems well: Ellen has given William two children, Gertrude and Frederick, and Ada has given Richard twins, Winifred and Constance.

This domestic intimacy will not survive beyond the late-1890s when Ada and Richard will take their still-growing family to live at N° 10 **Fair View** in Hitcham New Town. Ellen and William will replace them at *The Forge* and their house will be let to coachman Frank Taylor, his wife Rosina and their four children. Perhaps they will call it ***Farm View***. Meanwhile the fraternal Harris partnership will continue until the Great War.

A Site for Saws – Loafing About

Church Road / 16th June 1861

The third portion of Bell's package is a puzzle of a place. It started life almost 400 years ago as a timber-framed barn or humble dwelling set back from the street in an L-shaped parcel of land "to a total of 36 perches" (almost a quarter-acre). Sometime later a separate cottage was added on the frontage. This had a rather urban feature: a brick-floored kitchen in a half-sunken cellar to the rear. The next chapter opened when, perhaps in the 1820s, an adjoining terrace of four two-up-two-down cottages was built abutting this original cottage. Elizabeth Castle takes up the story....

I don't know if it was then – but if not, by 1841 – my father Thomas Hughes merged the westernmost of this row with both the cottage and the barn to make his bakery. We lived with my mother Charlotte in the newer cottage. The older one was converted to be the shop with the bakery behind it and the flour-filled cellar beneath it. Back then father employed two young live-in lads to help him. Now my husband James has a young man and a 15-year-old girl to help him.

James Castle was born in Bray and worked as a *GWR* porter at Southall Station and then at Taplow. He and his first wife – another Elizabeth – had two children before she passed away ten years ago leaving him to bring up Charlotte (then aged 8) and Alfred (just 2). He confides that his second Elizabeth had been rather concerned in 1852 when Thomas Bell acquired the freehold of her father's bakery. The worry was whether he had big ideas that might not include her father. James seems rather pleased that he had grabbed three opportunities with both hands by marrying Elizabeth, getting his new father-in-law to teach him baking and persuading Bell to let him take over the lease with but a small increase in rent.

Today is a day for celebration for Elizabeth & James. The Reverend **Charles Whately** has just baptised little Lizzey. Kate is still a baby being entertained by her sister Clara (4) and her half-brother Alfred (13) in the orchard which slopes back from the bakery and extends some way west behind their neighbour Tom Rutland's yard to afford a beautiful view across the glebe land to the south. How does Elizabeth manage such a large family? She smiles and looks at her husband. They will have at least four more children, making eight of their own plus Alfred and the elusive Charlotte. None of them will take over the Castle bakery for, despite competition from the Gurneys, James will bake here for nearly 50 years. He will be almost 80 when he retires to Maidenhead in the 1890s and will even then be roped in to train other bakers. His children will find new lives elsewhere: Alfred and James will follow in his footsteps as bakers but far away in Clacton and Lewisham; Clara will marry a coal merchant and Kate a chimney sweep, both in Penge; Lizzey will go into service in London and Jessie into dressmaking in Beckenham; Ernest will be a groom and cab driver in Burnham and Herbert (using his second name, Edwin) will also drive a cab in West Ham before going on to drive a tram. Such will be the ripples of life in the busy, busy late-19th Century.

Sweet Sisters

The Sweetshop, Church Road / 30th October 1912

Rose Deacon shakes her head. The original tenants here were Dinah & George Macdonald. Why did they open a grocer's shop, she says from behind her confectionery counter, when there's *Gurney's* just up the road? Her sister Elizabeth West thinks this little place is just right for a sweetshop though. And as if to prove it, an 11-year-old girl comes in to buy a quarter of broken butterscotch. She pays her ha'penny and skips out to enjoy her crunchy treat. Elizabeth laughs and says Betty's father Philip Bellingham-Smith should know about that sort of thing, what with him being an importer of sugar, molasses and such stuff. He lives next door in what was the Castle family bakery.

Fred West the carpenter taps on the window and waves a cheery greeting to his daughters before heading off to his cottage on Station Road for his tea. He and his wife Elizabeth welcomed Rose into their home when she was widowed more than a dozen years ago but it suited everyone when she and her sister came to the sweetshop. They don't know if it was their landlord Sydney Griffin who bought the former bakery just before the turn of the century, called it ***The Old Manor House*** and capitalised by building this little shop on its western flank and the two pairs of semi-detached cottages called **Elm View** in its orchard behind **William Harris**'s forge, but he certainly owns all six places now. And they have no idea that the spoil from the foundations of these new houses had been used to make two levels in the sloping garden behind *The Old Manor House* and to fill the old flour cellar beneath the bakery. In the early-1990s, **Liz Forsyth** will sink up to her hips in a hole in that garden, the opening to an impressive Victorian brick cess-pit, and in 2005 her husband **Alistair** will have 20 tons of earth removed from that cellar to make it a fine wine cellar. He will discover there a fireplace, a window frame, graffiti scrawled in 1812 and a beer bottle embossed ***Langton's****, Maidenhead*.

When the sisters took over the shop, the Elm View cottages were home to gardener Tom Chamberlain in N° 4 with his wife Minnie and their son, the district nurse Elizabeth James in N° 3, two coachmen – Fred Taylor and Fred Little – and their wives Sarah and Alice in N° 2 and labourer John Pound in N° 1. Now **William Fenner**'s widow Mary has retired from ***The Old Friend*** to live in N° 2 with her sister Fanny and brother-in-law Ben Box, a retired shepherd. Charlotte & Arthur Empson are in N° 1, Sarah & Joe Paxton in N° 3 and Annie & Edwin Stannett in N° 4 with their son Francis and daughters Bessie and Lucy. Elizabeth adds that the men are all gardeners and don't forget the new district nurse **Margaret Rome** lodges with the Paxtons.

William Harris the blacksmith has been at ***The Forge*** for years, says Elizabeth, only now he's a farrier, a specialist in looking after horses' hooves. He hoped his son Fred would follow in his shoes but the young man is a motor engineer – a sign of the times, Rose observes sagely. Two little girls bounce into the shop with a farthing each to buy something special. Six-year-old Lucy Stannett knows exactly what she wants – two ounces of *Mackintosh's Celebrated Toffee* – but 8-year-old Annie Taylor takes a little longer to decide she needs some liquorice. Please may I have two ounces of *Pontefract Cakes*, she asks politely. Rose carefully makes sure the girls' delights are slightly overweight and waves them on their way before confiding that it must be hard for Annie's mother Rosina. It is three years now since she lost her husband Frank, a coachman like this brother Fred, and she's left to look after their eight children in the small cottage on the far side of the Forge. Sarah, her eldest at just 15, earns a few bob as a dressmaker's assistant but goodness knows how Mrs Taylor makes ends meet. And goodness knows why, after Elizabeth moves away, Rose will choose to confuse historians by first reverting to her maiden name as Miss West and eventually deciding to be known as Ada, her second name.

A Shrewd Investment

The Dumb Bell Hotel, Bath Road / 27th June 1918

The auctioneer acting for solicitors *Giddy & Giddy* brings down his gavel with a sharp rap. **Walter Baldwin** of ***Rectory Farmhouse*** gives his wife Liley a satisfied nod. His bid of £1,800 (£408,100) has been successful in acquiring six properties from his friend and business associate Sydney Griffin. Walter hopes they will retain their value as a nest-egg for Liley as post-war deflation shrinks the economy. ***The Old Manor House*** is currently valued at £875 (£198,400) and its tenant Baron **Arild Rosenkrantz** pays an annual rent of £25 5s (£1,075) plus £22 5s (£645) to cover rates. The four cottages in **Elm View** are valued in total at £700 (£158,700) and each tenant pays £20 16s (£885) annually to cover rent and rates while Rose West pays £15 12s (£665) each year for the confectionary shop, which is valued at £225 (£51,000). Baldwin will complete the conveyance on 7th August. The pound buys 40% less than it did when war was declared. He expects the trend to continue and hopes the properties will retain their value sufficiently to be a nest-egg for Liley.

Rectory Farmhouse, Church Road / 29th April 1924

Liley Baldwin is much relieved. After months of legal wrangling over every petty detail the solicitor Josiah Kilner has finally completed the purchase of Nos 3 and 4 Elm View for £650 (£166,300). Two years ago she was hoping for £750 (£185,600) but now she is pleased to put the matter behind her. Her nest-egg has weathered the storm very nicely. Obbie Osborn recalls the sales: in 1919 the church organist **Percy Goulden** bought Nos 1 and 2 Elm View for £675 (£142,400), the stationmaster **John Grigg** paid £950 (£235,100) for *The Old Manor House* in 1922, last year the Rector helped the schoolmistress **Agnes Tanner** to pay £310 (£80,800) for Ada West's sweetshop and, once Kilner's money is taken into account, Walter's £1,800 has grown by over 46% to realise a profit of £835 (£213,600) in six years, and this despite a further 12% deflation over that period.

The ladies fall silent. Both are thinking what a shame Walter isn't here to be congratulated. He was only 59 when he died in 1921. Obbie deftly lightens the mood by remarking how glad she is that Mr Grigg has restored the name of *The Old Manor House*. Her timing is well-judged as usual. Liley laughs and agrees that she can't think what possessed Emily Hampton to call the place ***Goblins*** during her three years there from 1918. Obbie thinks better of remarking that the stationmaster gets his top hat out for the gentry but doesn't recognise the commoners. Neither she nor Liley can imagine that *The Old Manor House* will still be home for John Grigg's daughter into the 1960s when the sweetshop will be a cottage called *Flexbury* until being recast once more as ***Mysteria***.

A Site for Saws – King George's Realm

The Oak & Saw, Church Road / 30th October 1891

For the second time we come upon a pair of beerhouses just a short stagger from each other. ***The Oak & Saw*** and ***The Old Friend*** are separated only by a small close and **Old Friend Lane**, an ancient footpath – effectively a southerly continuation of **Pikels** which once led to Dorney but now offers only the choices of turning left onto **Ropey** to head for Hitcham or right across **Town Field** and down to the foot of Berry Hill.

We head for the first of the two and consider our next decision. What should we have to drink? The landlord **George King** is very patient: the choice is ale, beer, porter or stout. All vary according to the alcoholic content, the amount, type and preparation of hops, malt and barley used and brewing techniques such as mashing, aging (in vats or casks) and fining (for clarity). Ale has fewer hops and pale ale less malt or barley than mild ale or brown ale. Beer is hoppier than ale and is therefore more acidic, giving it a relatively bitter taste and its name. Porter was originally a blend of dark brown ale, pale ale and 'stale' or well-matured ale that became popular with London porters. As its name suggests, 'stout' is strong porter. We've had a porter, a bitter and a light ale. George's wife Elizabeth prescribes *Young's Double Brown Stout*. Don't tell the brewery, says George. *Nicholson's* wouldn't be happy but a friend of mine works for *Young's Brewery* in Wandsworth and some of the locals are rather partial to this. We aren't surprised.

This pub is the fourth part of Thomas Bell's 1852 acquisition. It was once the three easterly cottages in the terrace of four. We feel part of history as we sit in the private bar supping our pints of heavy-dark stout crisp with roasted malted barley surrounded by equally dark wooden beams that may have seen service during the Battle of Trafalgar in 1805 or some other thrilling maritime adventure. And there's more here than the story of ships' timbers and Orkney heraldry. If there's another pub in the country called *The Oak & Saw*, we've yet to hear about it.

George thinks he is the fourth landlord of *The Oak & Saw*. The first was probably John Pusey of Renfrew who somehow reached Taplow via Burnham and Chalfont St Peter. George doesn't know if it was Pusey, Bell or his successor as freeholder who converted the cottages into the pub. He does know that Pusey didn't hang around. In the early-1870s the wandering Scot moved on to a cottage in **Station Road** and a new career as a fly proprietor. His successors didn't last long either – **William Bond** died aged 51 in 1876 and his widow Caroline two years later at 48 – but George and his wife Elizabeth have been here for 13 years now and will be for a good few more. Three of their four children are still at home – John (20) is a clerk, Emily (15) an apprentice dressmaker and Ada (11) a 'scholar' at school. Their young groom Arthur Mendham is eager to tell of all the talk that Mr Pearce-Serocold wants to buy the adjacent close but George says you know how chins round here will wag in the slightest breeze.

Hurn's Turn – A Quiet Drink

The Oak & Saw, Church Road / 30th October 1932

Harry's mother **Violet Hurn** is heading for the butcher's when a cockney lady visitor bustles out of ***The Oak & Saw*** and into her path. It's too quiet fer me in there, says the stranger without being asked. I like a beer 'ouse that 'as a bit o' life to it. Blimey, it's like bein' in church. And she's right: it's the last pub in the village but Charles Winfield and then his son Sid have presided over its decline into such a sombre place. The front door opens onto a dim and dreary corridor leading to three small dark rooms: the saloon bar at the back and the public bar on the right opposite the private bar, which is used for meetings and for the Slate Club to collect monthly dues. Sid's mongrel Teg is a fine reminder of the wisdom of letting sleeping dogs lie. He spends his waking hours terrorising customers in the pub or other village dogs when he's out on the prowl. *Nicholson's Brewery* can't be happy with the takings. No wonder Sid tries to earn a few extra bob by working one of the old gravel pits, only he can't make much with only a small cart and just the one horse which he pastures in Irby's field (where **Boundary Road Stables** will be in 60 years). Everett Hurn will be pleased that the Canadians from Cliveden Hospital will be around to liven up *The Oak & Saw* by the time Harry is old enough to join him for a pint towards the end of the Second War.

Tall Tale – A Broken Bond

The Oak & Saw, Church Road / 4th March 1996

The last customer has finally supped up and slipped out. Landlord **Peter Casey** has locked up and is now sitting at the bar with Sue Robinson planning the menu for Mother's Day the Sunday after next. A sudden cold shiver shudders them both. Reflected in the mirror behind the bar, a woman in Victorian attire walks behind them from the ladies' toilets to the kitchen. They turn but there's nobody there.

Some weeks before, Sue found the floor of the ladies' toilet carefully carpeted with neatly folded bar towels. More than once, Peter discovered gas taps left on in the kitchen. Next time Pete will threaten loudly to call in the exorcist if it ever happens again. It never will and nobody will ever again glimpse this Victorian lady. Could this apparition have been **Caroline Bond**?

No Silent Night

The Oak & Saw / Christmas Day 1996

It is the wee small hours of Christmas morn. Peter is by the bar winding down from a long evening. He is blissfully unaware that, outside, having seen the light still on, two wanderers wonder if there is room at the inn. **Richard Forsyth** and his pal **Olly Meats** need no manger to lay their heads – but another noggin each of Christmas cheer would go down particularly well. They peer hopefully through the frosted bay window of the pub. Surely, if they can catch Peter's eye, he will offer them glad tidings and liquid comfort and joy....

Suddenly, Peter's reverie is shocked by a loud crash. He looks up to see the window has fallen in and smashed over tables and chairs. Two figures struggle not to follow the shards of glass scattering across the floor. They escape into the night, unidentified until a father comes sheepishly into the pub next morning to offer to pay for the damage.

Hurn's Turn – It Won't Wash

The Red Cottage / 30th October 1938

Our friend Freddie's 12-year-old grandson **Harry Hurn** is sitting on the pavement outside *The Oak & Saw* with his mouth wide open in awe as he watches **Marie Serocold** emerge from St Nicolas' Church and cross the road to her front door. Once she is safely inside ***The Red Cottage*** and out of earshot he observes quietly that she moves like a barge in full sail. We smile that such a young man should have such a perceptive turn of phrase but we have to agree that Miss Minna (as she is known) really is a most formidable figure.

Harry tells a lovely tale which goes to show Arthur Mendham really did have his ear to the ground. The story goes that in 1891 a Mr **Jeffreys** had acquired from **Willy Grenfell** that close between *The Oak & Saw* and ***The Old Friend*** with the intention of building a laundry. The village moguls (as Harry describes them, having read Rudyard Kipling) had no wish to see their linen (dirty or clean) hanging out for all to see. He was persuaded to exchange the site for one in **Station Road** where he built a pair of semi-detached cottages, one for himself and his wife with the laundry and the other, ***Baggot Cottage***, for his mother. It was **Charles Pearce-Serocold** who came to the rescue. He made it all possible by buying the close and building there *The Red Cottage*, a delightful home from 1893 for three of his daughters – the Misses Minna, Caroline and Rose [*see Appendix 1, Tree 18*]. As the years went by, there were a few who thought it too grand to be a cottage; they tried out *The Red House* but Miss Minna preferred the diminutive, so *The Red Cottage* was 'official'.

The Old Rectory / 2009

The New Rectory **starring as a 1960s set for the TV series *Endeavour*** / 2013

Rectory Farmhouse / 2012

The Village People: Eastenders

The Site for Saws / c1912, 2009 & 2012

The Cottage / 2011

2009

The Oak & Saw **recalls the Hamilton Arms and the Orkney Arms, which itself derives from the Douglas Arms**

The Oak & Saw / c1912

The Village People: Eastenders

St Nicolas House (formerly *The Red Cottage*) / 2009

Wellbank Cottage / 2012

Tall Tale – Spinsters on Show

The Red Cottage, Church Road / 30th October 1948

The story goes that, despite having plenty of land to play with, Miss Minna's father had ***The Red Cottage*** built close to the road in order that prospective suitors would have a splendid opportunity to see his three daughters were each in need of a husband. If this was the plan it worked well for Rose and Caroline, who married Robert White in 1903 and George Pache in 1905, but Miss Minna was beyond temptation. As ladies of independent means were wont to do, she busied herself as a pillar of the church, the Parish Council, the Women's Institute, local history and helping at the Duchess of Connaught Hospital during the Great War. She continued these efforts to and through the Second War whilst remaining a happy spinster until her death a few months ago.

Old Friend Fading

The Old Friend, Church Road / 30th October 1891

It's not far to our next watering hole. ***The Old Friend*** awaits us just a few paces away, and who should we see behind the bar but **William Fenner**, son of Thomas the gardener. What a small world it is. Will's wife Mary brings us bottles of old mild ale made at the ***Brown & Terry Brewery*** in Burnham (formerly *The Rose Brewery*). And very tasty they are too.

As we savour their coppery-dark sparkle and burnt nuttiness, Will gives us a potted history of his pub, a small cottage until sometime before 1835 when Robert Austen opened a beershop here called ***The Oak***. His family had been in Taplow for 40 years, possibly longer, and he ran the place successfully until his death in 1840 when his widow Lydia took over. Mary whispers that there was a bit of a scandal with a tragic end in 1847 when Lydia's 15-year-old daughter Frances had an illegitimate daughter Anne only for the poor child to die within a week. Will tells of a different drama. Lydia still had four of her eight children with her in 1851, not to mention a houseful of lodgers, but things took another turn for the worse the following year when the enterprising Henry Darvill of Windsor bought *The Oak* and increased the rent beyond Lydia's means. The licensed victualler Charles Steel came from Stepney to grab his chance only for him and his wife Maria to find *The Oak & Saw* opening up on their doorstep. We chuckle at the thought of the two similarly named hostelries almost side-by-side. No wonder *The Oak* became *The Old Friend* as it grew up to be a proper pub. Like Austen before him, Steel was succeeded by his widow Maria in 1871, and Henry Ogden succeeded her in the late-1870s.

How long can the two pubs survive in such close proximity? Will is optimistic – he has three very respectable lodgers in a governess, a tutor and a butler – and indeed he'll see off King and hold his own against Henry Baldwin, King's successor at *The Oak & Saw*. However by 1911 Baldwin's successor Albert Boore will have the edge due to his sharper business acumen and the enterprise of his two eldest sons Albert, 16-years-old and already driving the pub's motor cab, and George, a busy barman at just 14. And when opening hours are restricted, taxes are increased, drink is diluted by law and young men trickle off to the trenches the fight the Great War, Jonathan Jutton will struggle to keep *The Old Friend* awake.

A rather bedraggled young man comes in. Will Fenner introduces us to **Frederick Paget**. There are a few of his ilk hereabouts. If we count the Padgets, Padgetts and Pagetts as well, 47 have been noted in Taplow's Parish Register since their first entry in 1811 and five more will be buried here by 1900. When he took the census on 4th April, James Rutland noted this particular Paget living alone in a 'shepherd's hut', one of the 18th Century timber outbuildings that line the eastern side of the top end of *Old Friend Lane*. We wonder how he survived last winter's freezing cold in there but Fred seems a bright enough soul and ready at Rutland's suggestion to tell us about his well-to-do neighbours....

Well Corner

Wellbank, Rectory Road / 30th October 2012

At its eastern end, **Rectory Road** meets **Hill Farm Road** going uphill and **Boundary Road** down. They used to be **Church Road**, **Back Lane** and **Station Road**. Before that, the whole length of Back Lane and Station Road from north of **Buffins** to **Hitcham Road** seems to have been a tranquil bridle track called **Green Lane**. Nowadays an enigmatic dead-end driveway hints of once going somewhere south-west. What else is there to say? Quite a lot, actually – there is a clue in the name of the 1960s development on the south of Rectory Road. It isn't **Wellbank** on a whim....

Well Bank, Church Road / 30th October 1891

Fred Paget turns at the end of Church Road and looks back west towards *The Old Friend*. The close to our right – that's the north, he adds helpfully – used to be **Prodge's Mead** until the church was built at its western end. What's left became **Little Meadow,** although it's long been an orchard. The well in its south-east corner is why this junction is known as Well Corner. And across the road there was once was a small cottage in the north-east corner of **Roque Meadow** – which may once have been Roffe's Meadow and was mistranscribed as Rogue's Piece by some miscreant mapmaker – that some say was the home of a local constable for the village lock-up was built next to it in 1791. Just as well, smiles Fred, this was already **Well Corner** or p'raps it'd be Lock-Up Corner now.

The old cottage and its lock-up had been replaced by a "handsome detached villa" by 1852 when its sitting tenant **Edward Winslow** acquired the freehold at Lord Orkney's sale. At that same time the carpenter-cum-wheelwright **Henry Simmonds** acquired the adjacent close where he replaced a small house and its workshops with ***Walnut Villa***, so-called for the row of beautiful trees that still line Church Road. Rutland reckons that in the past 70 years there must have been 50 births in the Simmonds and Simmons families; the spellings vary, but they're all related. Henry is unusual for being an employer. Most of his family were or are labourers of some kind – in the 1850s his garden-labourer father John and farmhand brother Richard all lived within 100 yards of him – but if you went up to Taplow Common and threw a stone, you'd be bound to hit one of their relations.

In the late-1860s **John Noble** acquired ***Well Bank*** and leased it to **Henry (Harry) Arlett Woolfryes**, a Wiltshire surgeon and dentist who still practises in Marylebone. He sublet *Well Bank* for a while in the early-1880s to the East India merchant Silas Martyn but nowadays commutes back to Taplow by train from Paddington each weekend after staying at his club during the week. *Walnut Villa* had become ***The Walnuts*** by the time Noble acquired that too. His tenant now is Henry Buckmaster, a gentleman of Kensington "living on his own means" with his lady wife Dorothy. Both households have a cook, a housemaid, a coachman and either a butler or a footman. Clearly the coachmen are highly prized for each has his own cottage: Woolfryes' across the road and Buckmaster's by *The Old Friend*.

By 1911 stockbroker Edgar Stephens will have taken up residence at *The Walnuts* and renamed it ***The Priory***, a switch that will confuse later generations into thinking the site had a monastic past. And within three years John Noble's youngest son Percy will have settled at *The Priory* and Woolfryes' successor **William Butler** will have contracted the name of the house next door to ***Wellbank***.

Hurn's Turn – Never a Priory

Church Road / 30th October 1939

According to Harry's father **Everett Hurn**, **Percy Noble** was "a single gentleman with a particular predilection for young and handsome footmen". As John Noble's seventh and youngest son, Percy returned to his childhood home when he inherited the freehold of both *The Priory* and *Wellbank*. The first wasn't grand enough for a fellow of his means and lavish tastes. As soon as Butler's brief tenancy came to an end, he demolished ***Wellbank***, extended *The Priory* into the vacant space and added a drive for coaches to arrive though one gate and depart from another. He acquired the southern parcel of **Roque Meadow** from the Church Commissioners in 1919 to create a large a lovingly landscaped garden, installed his chauffeur Harry Hazeldene in the old *Walnuts* coachman's cottage, renamed that **Priory Cottage** and had ***The Old Friend*** converted as a home for his head gardener Edwin Plumridge. Once all that was done, he settled down to what he did best: partying. Almost every weekend he had a houseful of guests enjoying parties and fare elaborately prepared by his cook and served by the aforementioned footmen under the direction of his butler Mr Thame, who lived with his family across the road at ***Wellbank Cottage***.

Mr Noble's funeral last year was equally memorable: a big affair with a full choir, the bishop and all the local dignitaries congregating in the church: not a bad show for a non-believer. Now *The Priory* stands empty and the coachman's cottage is gone. There is no Mr Plumridge to stop Harry and his pals from scrumping pears from the trees espaliered to the brick wall along **Station Road**. And now, every day on their way to and from school, they delight in scrambling though the thick piles of leaves searching for the delicious nuts, so big, meaty and sweet, that have fallen from the line of walnut trees along **Church Road**.

Highstreeters

Last Rites, New Beginnings

The first (or second) St Nicholas' Church / 11th July 1828

Two years ago the surveyor William Lane of Eton estimated it would cost £1,900 (£1.46m) to repair our crumbling old **St Nicholas' Church**. The Reverend **Edward Vansittart Neale** advised that the Rectory had only £300 (£230,500) to spare but it seemed that Kirkwall would save the day with a promise of £1,000 (£0.79m). It was a false dawn. That very same year Kirkwall took as his wife the lovely **Charlotte Irby**, daughter of **George Irby**, **3rd Baron Boston**, and all of a sudden he had better things to do with what little cash he had. He offered instead a parcel of land for a new church to be built. This was a neat trick. The demolition of the old church will improve the view from Taplow Court's drawing room and the congregation will no longer disturb the peace every Sunday.

And so today will see the second-last baptism in this old church which has stood here since about 1197, possibly on the site of an ancient predecessor. It is amazing to think that this may have been consecrated ground for over 1,100 years. Appropriately the blessed child is Kirkwall's 4-day-old second son **Henry Warrender Fitzmaurice**, named for Sir George who is now a firm enough family friend to be one of the boy's 'sponsors' (godfathers). Come 10th August, the last child to be baptised here will be Thomas Buckland, the four-week old son of Elizabeth & William Buckland, gamekeeper at **Taplow Court**.

The second (or third) St Nicholas' Church / 11th July 1828

After the service some of the congregation take the time to walk to the other end of Church Road to see the new church at **Prodge's Mead**. Nobody is much impressed by the plain yellow stock brick building in the neo-Gothic style of the day. Unfortunately it looks like it has been built on the cheap despite costing all of £3,400 (£4.1m) and will quickly get a reputation for being the ugliest church in Christendom. This won't trouble either **Richard Pagett** or **James Wells**. On 14th September 1828 the former will be the first child to be baptised there, much to the joy of his parents Sarah & Thomas, a farm labourer. And on

30th March 1829 the latter, a 24-year-old farmhand, will be the first person to be buried in the new churchyard having been killed by a kick from a horse at Amerden Farm.

The second (or third) St Nicholas' Church / 9th March 1865

The Right Reverend Samuel Wilberforce has graciously come to consecrate the new chancel added to the church at the expense of the Reverend **Charles Whately**. As son of William the abolitionist, the Bishop of Oxford is familiar with Taplow and too polite to comment on the rather modest appearance of this new St Nicholas. Other more objectives observers will not be so kind....

The second (or third) St Nicholas' Church / 6th December 1891

James Rutland grants that old Whately did what he could but confides sadly that this year's edition of *Kelly's Directory* is not wrong to note his church as "small and plain" with an "embattled tower, a clock and three bells". Perhaps it should have noted the stained glass window added to the chancel in 1867 to commemorate **Charles Pascoe Grenfell**. And perhaps, he remarks with evident pride, future editions will report that £157 10s (£102,500) was raised this year by public subscription to install behind the altar a new stained glass window depicting the Nativity, the Crucifixion and the Resurrection of Our Lord Jesus Christ.

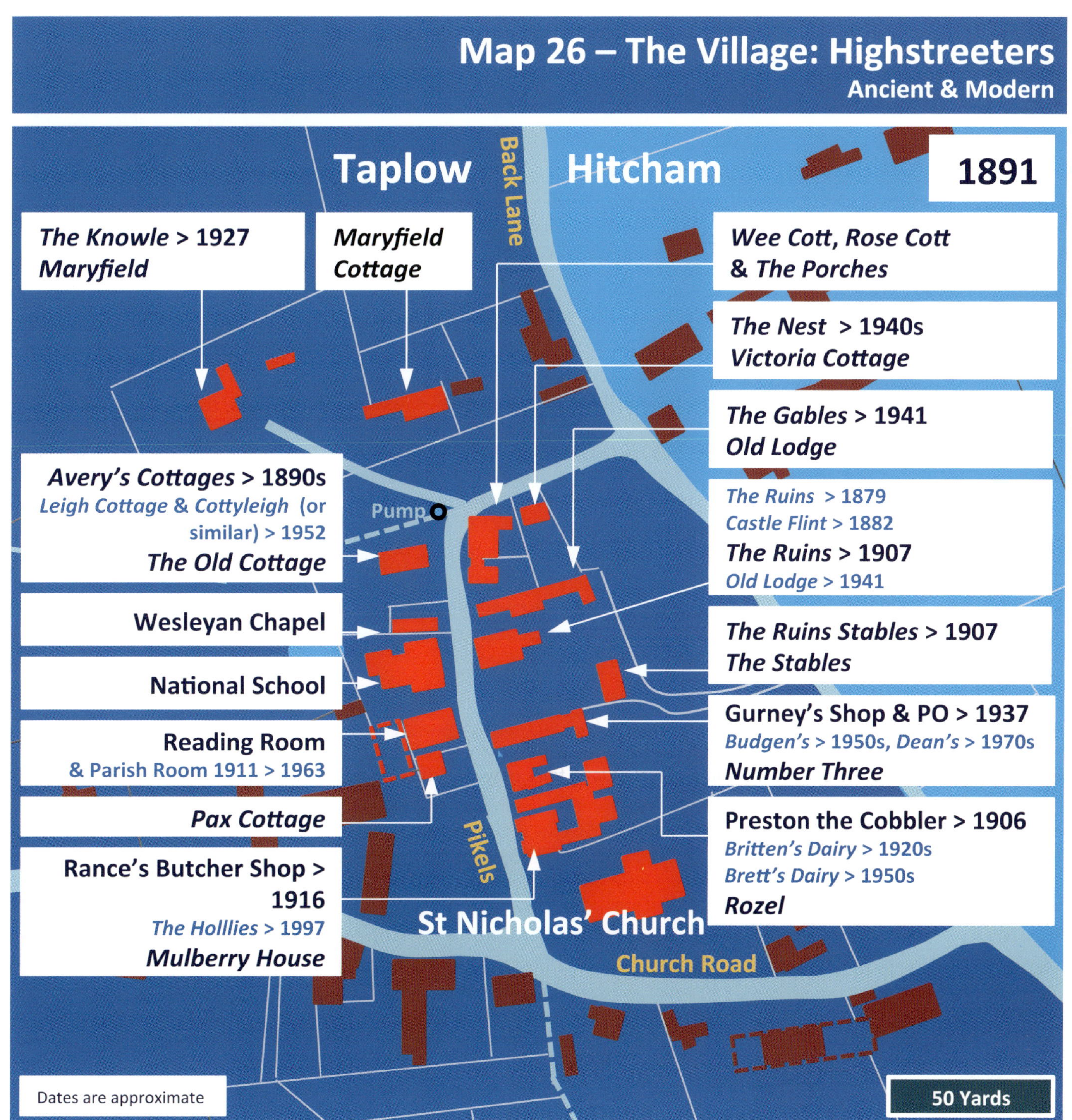

Primary Source: Ordnance Survey 1897

The Passing of Passingham's

Pikels / 6th December 1891

As we leave St Nicholas' Church and turn right up **Pikels** [*see Map 26*], Rutland explains that most of the parcels of land in the parish which aren't glebe are held by Willy Grenfell as the lord of the manor and let copyhold to 'customary tenants'. Their tenure is secure subject to payment of an annual rental plus various duties and fees to effect any change in or transfer of the title. Nowadays Grenfell's estate steward Edward Lodge handles all the paperwork involved and charges accordingly. In the old days his predecessors as the lord's steward presided at quarterly *Courts Baron* which would levy upon each supplicant a *heriot* (a death duty) and a *fine* (an administration fee) for its trouble in executing all the legal niceties.

Rutland pauses outside the butcher's shop. Many plots, he says, were named for their copyholders. These names often persisted long after they had gone. This shop, for example, is in the south-west corner of a T-shaped one-acre plot that may have been a Roman clay pit more than 1,000 years before becoming **Tothill's late Passingham's** in recollection of a transaction between long-forgotten copyholders. The shop will eventually be ***Mulberry House*** and it will share the plot with ***Rozel*** and ***Number Three*** on the **High Street** side and with ***Clent House*** on ***Hill Farm Road***. Our guide takes us back 128 years into the past to help us learn by example how *Courts Baron* administered the civil law of the land.

The Queen's Head / 29th April 1763

As steward for **Mary O'Brien**, **3rd Countess of Orkney**, John Crastor will preside on her behalf at this quarter's Court Baron. He takes his place behind a heavy oak table and smooths out the Court Rolls in which the formal proceedings of Taplow Manor are recorded. He opens formalities by introducing two local copyholders – Christopher Bracegirdle and **Giles Colesell** – who will act as Homage Jury to ensure all is in order. Mr Bracegirdle's father, the Reverend George Bracegirdle, was Rector here from 1742 until 1759. He is said to have accused the farmer **Christopher Brown** of either losing or spiriting away the pages in the Parish Register which covered the years from 1616 to 1710. Did they record some indiscretion that Brown preferred to keep secret?

The business of the day is to execute the will of the late **John Davis** who has bequeathed Tothill's late Passingham's and a meadow in Hitcham formerly held by Richard Sharp to his son **John Davis the Younger** subject to his paying a *heriot* of two guineas (£270), a *fine* of 14 guineas (£1,880) and £10-a-year (£1,280) rent to his cousin Elizabeth Row and her sons Robert and John plus 'rents and profits' to his daughter Mary Whitecar and in default to **Elizabeth Coalsell**. What a tangled web they weave.

The Queen's Head / 16th March 1807

The Court Baron is called to order by James Payn, steward for **Murrough O'Brien**, **Marquis of Thomond**. He nods to the Homage Jury of **Pascoe Grenfell** and **William Davis** and begins by recalling the Court Baron on 2nd November 1801 which gave authority for George Davis (younger son of **John Davis the Younger**, now a locksmith of New Windsor) to pass "the use and behoof" of Tothill's late Passingham's, the Hitcham meadow and another eight acres of arable land in Taplow to his elder brother Richard Davis of Lewknor (Oxfordshire). Secondly, the steward exercises due procedure to effect the sale of the copyhold of these parcels to **John Briginshaw** of Taplow. And finally he turns to supplementary matters. The subtenancy of the eight acres is passed to William Vintner from **Elizabeth Colsell**, wife of Edmund Rowls, and those of Tothill's and the Hitcham meadow are confirmed as remaining with a baker by the name of John Row. The meadow will be the site of ***Hitcham Close*** and the eight acres includes the eventual site of **Taplow Grammar School** and ultimately of a block of flats called ***Hillmead Court***.

Payn also confirms the subtenancies of the three "messuages or tenements" on **The Phygtle** frontage: a washhouse, a bakehouse and a tailor's shop and workshop in a two-year-old property called ***Dunvegan***. It is clear that Widow Baker does the washing and the other two subtenants are Robert Douglas and **Thomas Brown** followed by **John Brown** but we are hazy on whether Douglas stitches and the Browns bake or vice versa. And how are the barn, stable and yard and the orchard at the rear of the site distributed between these tenements? Perhaps we fell asleep.

The third Taplow Court / 2nd November 1833

Our absent host **Thomas Fitzmaurice**, **5th Earl of Orkney**, has delegated responsibility for this Court Baron his steward John Lowe and the Homage Jury of **Sir Charles Harcourt Palmer** and William Payn. When he died on 1st April, **John Briginshaw the Younger** left £2,400 (£3.24m) to his wife and children plus "certain customary or copyhold hereditaments". His will was proved in London on 2nd July leaving the task today to administer the transfer of the property as bequeathed to his son **William Davis Briginshaw** of ***Amerden Manor Farm*** subject to payment of a *fine* of £103 (£9,023) to Lord Orkney and "one clear annuity or yearly rentcharge of £36 (£2,981) in lawful English money" to John's widow **Eleanor Briginshaw**, daughter of **Lydia & Davis Neighbour** [*see Appendix 1, Tree 20*]. Three of the "hereditaments" present little complication – the Hitcham meadow, the eight acres in Taplow formerly sublet to William Vintner and another nine acres of arable land – but the three tenements on Tothill's have become five in the 28 years since it was last before the Court and four of them have seen a change of tenant since July.

The deceased's son **Richard Briginshaw** has passed his lease on the baker's shop to Richard Boulds and Lord Orkney's groom James Jennings has retired to succeed the Reverend **Edward Neale**'s coachman Benjamin Mason at ***Dunvegan***, which must have ceased its days as a tailor's shop some time ago. **Widow Brown** is still in place but Widow Samson has succeeded Widow Fountain, but which is the washerwoman and what does the one that isn't do for a living? And **William Rance** has taken over his lease on the butcher's shop held by **John Aldridge** until he "destroyed himself". It is possible that Rance has roots in Taplow – in the eight years from 1711, William Raunce of Cookham had three children baptised in St Nicholas' Church and two buried in its graveyard – but the man himself has come from **Wooburn Green** with aspiration in abundance.

The fourth Taplow Court / 9th June 1863

Despite being the biggest farmer in these parts, **William Davis Briginshaw** seems to have had a bit of trouble in 1855 when the Official Receiver took possession of the eight-acre parcel and "sold it.... to Algernon Sydney" only for timber merchant **George Lambourne** to pay Briginshaw £1,000 (£900,000) for the site in 1857. How did that work? We shall never know, but it wasn't long before a mansion called ***The Limes*** was being built there not far from Lambourne's home at ***Cranford House***. When Briginshaw died in 1860 he bequeathed the copyhold of Tothill's and the Hitcham meadow (now arable land) to his nephews William Briginshaw and John Briginshaw of *Crown Farm* at Englefield Green in Surrey subject to a "yearly rent-charge" of £13 (£11,500) "to **Eliza Davis** during her life should she be living in his service at the time of his decease".

These distant Briginshaw nephews have had their chance; now Rance is grabbing it. Having for three decades been subtenant of the Hitcham meadow and one of up to five of the tenements on Tothill's, at last he has come before Frederick Ward, steward to **Charles William Grenfell**, to acquire the customary tenancy of both the meadow and Tothill's for the sum of £750 (£613,000).

Rance Advance – Having a Butcher's

Pikels / 6th December 1891

Being the village butcher must have been a lucrative business. **William Rance the Elder** had enough spare cash to diversify ino farming and dabble in speculative property development. The acquisition of **Little Coldgrove** in 1852 and the construction of the original six ***Coldgrove Cottages*** wasn't a one-off. He also owned cottages in **Bourne End** and near ***The Pheasant*** at **Lent Rise**. Sadly this commercial success was no antidote to tragedy. In the winter of 1853/54, William and his wife **Eliza** saw three little daughters die: Eliza was six, Mary Ann not quite three and Frances just a babe of eleven months. Whatever it was, this same epidemic also carried off William Light of ***The Feathers Inn***, Anna Sanders of ***Taplow House***, **George Granville Grenfell** and **Charlotte**, **Lady Riversdale**.

Once Rance was master of Tothill's, he wasted no time in clearing room to build himself a new home with his butcher's shop on the left of the frontage and an abattoir to the rear. He retained the other buildings to the north. Charles Campion had his dairy in the western of a pair of cottages set back from the road and parallel with it. Having been displaced from ***The Oak*** beershop, the widow Lydia Austen ran an undefined retail establishment in the other while Mary Newman had taken over the washhouse to the rear. And up the hill bounded to the north by **Phipp's Close** – noted as "land formerly belonging to **Rachael Newberry**, Widow" – was the former ***Dunvegan***, by then a combined grocery shop, bakery and sub-post office that passed in the early-1870s from **Mary Ann Darling** to her nephew **William Gurney**.

We reach the butcher's shop window to see three teenagers hard at work. Edith Paramor, a bookkeeper from Margate, is supervising two boys arranging a display of meats. Rutland says that's local lad **Tommy Plummer** on the pork chops and Charlie Gerrard of West Wycombe with the legs of mutton. It's their boss the master butcher who we've come to see. **William Rance the Younger** appears and waves his cleaver by way of a greeting. It seems like only yesterday that his father William died. Rutland can't quite believe that it was 11 years ago and adds wistfully that the elder William was "a good, kind friend and neighbour" who he succeeded as the local census enumerator. No wonder no-one knows better than him who's who and who's where in Taplow society.

The younger William is no longer quite so young. He is 45 now and has had plenty of time to step comfortably into his father's shoes as the village butcher and a pillar of the community. He farms 200 acres, on which he employs 12 men and 3 boys, and owns or holds intermediary tenancy of numerous cottages in and around Taplow. In a few years, three houses – **Hitcham Cottage**, **Hitcham Close** and **Hitcham Lodge** – will be built in the Hitcham meadow his father acquired with Tothill's. Why is such an eligible fellow still a bachelor? He blushes as he reveals that he will marry at the end of September. What a lucky man he is to have been introduced to Louisa French of Marylebone. She is his junior by 19 years and will bear him three sons and two daughters before the turn of the century. There's nothing like up for lost time.

Butcher's Hook

The former Forge, Church Road / 6th December 1937

Arthur Saunders was doing well enough as Whitlaw's tenant at ***Barge Farm*** and at his butcher's shop at N° 9 Queen Street, Maidenhead. He didn't have the advantages enjoyed by his friend William Rance the Younger in serving such as the Astors, the Desboroughs and the rest of the rich and hungry Taplow high and mighty. But when ill-health began to get the better of William in 1916, Arthur took over the business and charmed Edith Paramor into accept his offer of employment. This was a masterstroke. Not only did she know each customer's every need but she used her Taplow connections to help Arthur acquire the old Harris forge and convert the room on the left of the frontage into a butcher's shop. Meanwhile **Louisa Rance** closed her husband's shop and gave her home a new name: ***The Hollies***. Arthur continued to run his Taplow shop under Rance's name until 1918 when William died and he switched to his own. And by 1923 he had leased a farm in Holyport to raise his produce, moved his Maidenhead shop to N° 26 Queen Street and was doing well enough to install telephones in all three properties. His Taplow number was Burnham 41 for over 40 years.

Arthur is a tall thin man with a white beard retained since days long ago when beards were fashionable. The only other beard Harry Hurn knows of was worn by King George V, which makes Arthur's all the more impressive. The shop is smaller than William's and the sides of beef and whole sheep and pigs hanging from hooks on the ceiling beams make it feels crowded even without customers. There is plenty of space to lead animals down the side of the shop for slaughter in the old smithy at the rear. Louisa's grandson **Jim Rance** will soon earn a bob or two as a butcher's boy by running errands, helping in the slaughterhouse by inflating carcasses with a stirrup pump to prepare them for butchery and riding with the old fellow in his *Ford* van to deliver cuts to customers including the Astors at Cliveden. He will chuckle to recall Miss Paramor as 'Uncle Popcorn', a nickname inspired by her being a rather large lady with more than a hint of a beard who sits intimidatingly "at the receipt of customs" in a little screened-off cubicle in the rear corner of the shop taking payment and keeping count. She is perfectly positioned to keep an eye on things from her home at N° 2 **Elm View** which she and her sister Emma have rented from **Percy Goulden** since Harry's grandmother Clara died in 1933.

Towards the end of the Second War, Arthur will retire to an apartment in ***The Hermitage*** leaving the business to his son **Jack Saunders**. The Taplow branch will be run by another Harry who Harry Hurn will describe as "round, hearty and red-faced as butchers should be" and deft at sharpening his knife on the steel and slicing "a leg of mutton from a carcass as smoothly as cutting butter". The shop will change little – Uncle Popcorn will still be in charge of finances – but things will be different behind the scenes with the old smithy reduced to a smaller slaughterhouse with its floor sloping to the drain.

Rance Advance – Shopping Centre

High Street / 31st March 2013

A quiet narrow road made narrower by cars parked down one side. On the right is a large double-fronted villa, then another and a third house which can't hide its origins as a shop. On the left the Village Green hides behind a high hedge, then there are three stairways: the first to ***Pax Cottage*** (built before 1853 by the Diocese of Oxford to provide a home for the verger of St Nicholas' Church), the second to the **Village Centre** (built in 1894 as the **Reading Room**) and the third to a car park (where **Taplow National School** stood from 1848 to 1965). So not a High Street, yet that's what it's called. When it was, it had only a nickname: Pigtail, Pikel, whatever. Can you imagine it as Taplow's shopping centre?

Perhaps **Brian Ackland-Snow** could. Sadly, news has just come through that he died yesterday. As a movie art director, he could transform almost any setting to almost any period. In 1997, he and his wife Carol acquired ***The Hollies*** – once Rance butcher's shop – and recast it as ***Mulberry House***. During the eight years they lived there, convivial company and a glass or two of a nice white might occasionally persuade him to give pride of place on the mantelpiece to his *Oscar* in Best Art Direction for *A Room with a View* (1985).

Next door were two cottages which **William Rance the Elder** built in the mid-1870s to replace the older tenements once occupied by George Campion, Lydia Austin and Mary Newman. His original tenants were still *in situ* in 1891. Bootmaker **Joe Preston** had hailed from Norfolk in the mid-1860s, married a Wooburn girl called Elizabeth and had three children in one of ***Taplowhill Cottages*** and four more after moving here. His family fortunes contrasted to his neighbour **Francis Hearn**, one of Rance's farmhands, who had lost his wife Mary Jane and their three eldest children. Ann, his youngest, by then 11, was still with him and his second wife, another Ann. Two Williams lodged with them: Jones the gardener and Saunders the shepherd.

Preston continued cobbling here until his death in 1906 when his home and shop became **Ted Britten**'s village dairy complete with a briar to the rear where cows were milked. The dairy was taken over in the mid-1920s by **Arthur Brett** who bottled the milk he received in churns for Hill Farm. **Harry Hurn** says he never let an employee do the job so nobody would know how much water was added to the milk. While he drove their carts out to deliver the milk, Mrs Brett busied herself in the little sweetshop at the back of the house by the stables where schoolchildren could leave their bicycles during the day.

Brett's dairy continued until after the Second War. By 1960 it was a house called ***Rozel*** and home to **Ann & Anthony Paines**, he a solicitor, and later to Ann & Bruce Durham. It was bought in 1978 by **Sally & George Sandy** whose successors, Wendy & Vincent Finnegan, had the misfortune of watching a large hole appear in their garden, apparently when an old well or cesspit collapsed. *Rozel* has led a quieter life ever since.

The third house has had more roles than most thespians. It has played a tailor's shop and a retired butler's home, starred for many years the village shop and post office, had turns as a *Budgen's*, a delicatessen, a mail order headquarters and a shop again before becoming a home once more in 1979. Let's take up the tale of the starring role....

Gurney's Turn – Open All Hours

The Village Shop, Pikels / 6th December 1891

William Gurney and his younger cousin **Edward Okey Gurney** run the grocery, bakery and sub-post office. Perhaps their name derives from an ancestor who was the local gurning champion 1,000 years ago. Plenty of their ilk are scattered across South Bucks and they have been flirting with Taplow for some time. We have already heard that in 1758 **Henry Gurney** of Hedsore married Mary Lockitt and in 1800 their son or grandson **Thomas Gurney** (of Chalfont St Giles) married local girl **Elizabeth Neighbour** (daughter of Davis). James Rutland recalls that in the late-1830s the latter couple's daughter **Mary Gurney** took over the Richard Boulds bakery, started to sell groceries as well as bread, added a sub-post office and still found time to marry her Darling.

Rutland smiles at his little joke before telling how two changes of hearts in the mid-1840s led to the Gurney emporium in what was once *Dunvegan*. Mary's **Darling** was one and the same **Edward** who rose to be head gardener at Taplow Court. This opened the way for her cousin **Mary Ann Gurney** to leave her position as the schoolmistress in Hitcham and take over the shop with her younger brother **George**. She was 44 when in 1855 she married her own **Darling**: this one a **William**, the 43-year-old brother of the green-fingered Edward [*see Appendix 1, Tree 14*]. However, neither wedded bliss nor branching into baking bread and running a sub-post office eased her iron grip on the business. By 1863 Maidenhead Post Office was making two daily deliveries of letters and one collection. Nowadays it makes three deliveries to the Gurneys, who need only a person's name on the envelope to do the rest, and collects four times a day from post boxes at Taplow Common, Taplow Hill, *The Dumb Bell* and the station.

Mary Ann was astute to delegate doing to family or trusted employees. There was a procession of George's children: Elizabeth and George then Caroline, who added a millinery sideline, and Katherine (Kate) who became the sub-postmistress, a responsibility she still holds today and will do so into her dotage 20 years hence. And they have employed just three bakers in 30 years: first Tommy Hare of West Drayton, then his brother Billy for many years, and now Henry Osborne of Maidenhead is on the job. There he is now: white as a ghost from heaving flour into the storeroom.

It's time for a snack. Going into *Gurney's* is like crossing the threshold into the big, wide world. What a fantastic place full of colour and the most fabulous aromas. The evocative smell of baking bread predominates but subtler sensations evolve as we wander from exotic tea, cocoa and coffee past wonderfully whiffy cheeses to fragrant soaps, sticky-sweet preserves and sour-sharp pickles. Edward waits patiently behind the counter as we take it all in. We are almost apologetic to ask for just bread and cheese but we need something portable. We take it outside and sit to eat on the steps up to the village school. The crusty bread is soft, light and still warm inside and the cheese is cool and creamy: the simple tastes of Taplow, such delicious contrast.

William's distant cousin **Mary Gurney** waves him goodbye on her way back to **Dropmore** School. She has been schoolmistress there since 1881 but her poor health over the past year has twice caused the school to be closed. There will be more closures in the New Year as epidemics of mumps, influenza and scarlet fever keep the youngsters away. William will count his blessings that his children William and Mary survive. The teenagers run out of *Gurney's* and down the hill and into the butcher's shop as if they own the place. And in a way, they do for **William Rance the Younger** is their uncle. Clearly their father made a wise move to secure the Gurney tenancy by marrying their landlord's sister **Elizabeth**, and she's not the only Rance daughter to have combined business with pleasure: eight years ago Fanny wed **Sydney Budgen** in St Nicholas' Church. The groom's father **John Budgen** is a grocer like the Gurneys. He opened his first shop in Maidenhead in 1872 and is now busy building the chain. His son is already following in his father's footsteps. Sydney and Fanny's sons John and William will do the same. And the Gurney family grapevine will remain strong enough into the mid-1930s for the Budgen boys to hear, when **Flora & Edward Gurney**'s son **Edward** passes away, that his widow Frances feels it is all too much to keep *Gurney's* going. In 1937 they will make it a ***Budgen's***, a small step in the long journey to 2012 when the company will have well over 200 stores and more than 6,000 employees.

About Grout – On Your Bike

Budgen's, High Street / 6th December 1939

Phil Grout's first job was doing odd-jobs for *Gurney's*. Now his little brother Arthur is *Budgen's* telegram boy. He enjoys the job except for one thing: nearly every day, just minutes before he is supposed to clock-off at six o'clock, the telegraph starts to click urgently and he knows he'll soon be on his bike. It's not so bad if the telegrams are for the gentlemen for whom his dad Alfred maintains motor cars – **George Bancroft** at ***Elibank***, **Victor Williams** at ***Rectory Farmhouse***, **Walter de la Mare** at ***Hill House*** or **Oswald Serocold** at ***Taplow Hill*** – nor if he has to deliver elsewhere around the Village but all too often he has to peddle all the way to ***Parr's Cottage*** for **Joyce Grenfell** or, even worse, to Cliveden for the Astors. Oh well, he sighs, maybe I'll get a tip or two.

This beginning will set Arthur's course in life. Except for his service in the Royal Navy during the Second War, his career will take him to three retailers: *Budgen's* in Maidenhead, *Warren's* (briefly in Taplow, for many years in Slough) and finally *Daniel's* in Windsor.

Meet the Meats

Number Three, High Street / 6th December 2012

Perhaps *Budgen's* employees nowadays are a little more customer-friendly than Lawrence Roadnight who ran the Taplow store in the late-1950s. He never seemed to stock anything that **Lorna Miall** wanted and would make matters worse by telling her there was no demand for whatever it was she wanted to buy. No wonder then that the company eventually decided village shops had had their day: supermarkets were the big idea. Ann & Bruce Durham of ***Rozel*** thought the old place would make a fine delicatessen but Taplow wasn't quite ready for country pâté and smoked salmon. After a few years, *Dean's of Twickenham* concluded it wasn't ready for a mail-order centre employing 30 staff, although locals were amused to see outsized ladies traipsing up from the station having seen the place advertised in *The Daily Telegraph*. *The Old Tudor Village Store* didn't last long either. The place was no more than a shell with one cold water tap and an 1887 baker's oven when **Sarah & Tony Meats** made it their home in 1979. As an architect of grand vision, Tony tried to rebel against house-naming convention by calling it N° 3 High Street. This numeric was rejected so it is ***Number Three***. How very droll. Locals encouraged them to reopen the shop but wouldn't guarantee the Meats an income to tide them over. Sarah thought about opening a cafe but met strong opposition from certain neighbours who shall remain nameless. She smiled sweetly and carried on catering, both things she does rather well. The house enjoys reviving its 'whodunit' role from time to time in television dramas such as *Foyle's War* and *Midsomer Murders*.

Let There Be Light

Pikels / 6th December 1891

We hear footsteps behind us and turn to see **John Siggers**, now in his twentieth year as master of **Taplow School**. John looks familiar. Wasn't he amongst the cricketers in ***The Queen's Head*** last summer? Diligent as ever, he has left his responsibilities as cricket club secretary to show us his professional domain. But first he spins a yarn of how it all came about....

The Rectory, Church Road / 19th April 1848

The Reverend **Edward Vansittart Neale** and his churchwardens **William Davis Briginshaw** and **Harry Tyre** have two very important guests: Charles Pepys, 1st Baron Cottenham, is Lord High Chancellor and the Right Reverend Samuel Wilberforce is the Bishop of Oxford. These five gentlemen are here today to sign the trust deed which will convey land and establish a committee to build and run the Taplow National School. The light of education has been a long time coming and it won't yet be compulsory but where there's a will there's a way.

For many years, Sunday school had been the only opportunity for children to learn more than their parents could teach them. If they were lucky enough to have a good and broadminded teacher, they might pick up some basic reading and writing along with the Lord's Prayer and their scriptures. Things improved a little in 1811 when the tri-parish school opened on **The Gore** between Hitcham and Burnham and by the 1840s there were at least three independent 'dame schools' in and around Taplow, so-called for being run by untrained 'dames' and noted as **Clayton's**, **Jaycock's** and **Williamson's**. This wasn't good enough for the Rector. Last year Neale directed his curate and son-in-law the Reverend Alfred Strettell to undertake a Church Inquiry which has revealed there are 39 boys and 53 girls attending Sunday school at St Nicholas' Church. Many but not all of these children are also counted in the 44 at the tri-parish school, the 10 older boys attending Strettell's evening school and the 49 girls and 16 infant boys being educated at the dame schools. Strettell singled out that run by gardener's wife Sophia Williamson who charges fourpence-per-child-per-week (£1.40) despite being "a very inefficient teacher [who] keeps her scholars in no kind of order".

Last October, Strettell wrote to the Church of England's National Society for Promoting the Education of the Poor to ask for a grant to supplement the £215 (£242,000) already promised by parishioners. The Society awarded £25 (£28,200) in February. Now a parcel of glebe land has been allocated in the north-east corner of the **Pater Noster** pasture, work will soon commence on the construction of a Jacobean-style schoolmaster's house and a single-classroom school for boys and girls aged between 3 and 13. These buildings with slate-tiled roofs will all be of red brick, diapered with blue-black bricks, with door and window surrounds of stone. Their capital cost will rise from an estimated £375 (£422,200) to an actual £480 (£540,500) but Strettell's tireless endeavours will succeed in raising the money through further subscriptions, donations, grants, the levy of 'school pence' – a weekly charge of just tuppence-per-child (75p) – and 'if necessary' an annual sermon to raise a collection.

What would old Mary Blizzard think of it all? She was a schoolmistress at the tri-parish school and thereafter ran a 'dame school', yet her chief claim to fame is still to come. She might be rather proud of being the only centurion in Taplow's Parish Register when she passes away at 101 a couple of years hence.

Taplow School, Pikels / 6th December 1891

The school has been expanded twice since the original classroom was built. The infants' classroom was added in 1854 and the second classroom for older children in 1870, when gas lighting was also installed along with flannel curtains to quell echoes and divide classes. These improvements have been made possible by the development of a certain civic cohesion based on the philanthropic instincts and practical convenience of the local gentry, who see value in subscribing between five shillings (£15) and £10 (£600) each year to have a more enlightened local workforce. These contributions and the grants obtained by successive rectors and curates from the government and the church made it possible for the payment of school pence to be reduced twice – initially in the late-1850s when the weekly charge for all but the first two children in each family had been reduced to one penny (25p), and again in 1870 when no charge was made for any child whose attendance record was good.

It is likely that the first schoolmaster was Henry Ford who the 1851 census found lodging with **David Harris** the blacksmith. He was succeeded by in 1863 by **John Wright**, in 1869 by William Amies and in 1872 by **John Siggers**, just 24 when he was appointed master of what the 1870 Education Act had redefined as an Elementary School and subjected to regular government inspections. All were helped immensely by the Rectors Neale, Whately, their curates and a series of 'monitors' – actually locally-recruited former pupils, effectively teacher apprentices – including George Campion, **George Cordery** and **Martha Springall**. Siggers had a staff of three – infants' teacher Miss Phillimore and two monitors, **Mary Cordery** and George Dance – but his school was quickly found wanting in everything but needlework.He improved matters significantly. Within a year attendance grew from 67 to 96 out of a possible 100 but Her Majesty's Inspector was not impressed by test results and the government grant of six shillings per pupil per year (£13.80) was cut accordingly. **Julia Siggers** came to the rescue. Standards began to improve considerably after she joined her husband in 1878 and together they turned the corner. In 1882 the inspector reported that "The school is in better case than I have yet found it. A great deal of the success is due to Mrs Siggers' exertions". The school will soon grow to be big enough for 150 pupils in 1895 (136 in attendance) and then 200 in 1897 (180 in attendance).

Mrs Siggers confides that attendance has always been an issue. If it isn't a real illness that keeps children away, it's an invented one – she was astonished a year or two back when a local farmer (who she declines to name) invented a measles epidemic to frighten his employees into keeping their children away from school and in his fields. And of course there are always parents who need their children to help at home or with some urgent task, especially at harvest time, and others who just couldn't afford the school pence every week. This last reason won't apply ever again now elementary school is at last free for everyone.

However, the Siggers are pragmatic; this will be one less reason for poor attendance but they know it will still be prudent for them to manipulate the opening of the school in sympathy with the agricultural calendar.

James Rutland interjects to give an example of how dedicated his friends are. He shows us the entry in the school log for 12th March 1886. It reads "Mrs Siggers returned to her duties in school having been absent since 1st March through an illness in the family". John and Julia had buried their 8-month-old son Harold on 8th March yet his written record was entirely factual and free of opinion or emotion, just as required by the authorities. They studiously avoid our admiring glance.

Rutland takes his fob watch from his waistcoat pocket and declares his time with us is done. He must away to prepare for a meeting this evening. We are intrigued by the gleam in his eye and beg him to let us into the secret. It's all very well that the youngsters learn reading, writing and arithmetic at school, he says, but education can't stop there. Knowledge is the key to the fulfilment of potential. Adults have a never-ending need to expand their knowledge of the world and its affairs. There are plans afoot for a new reading room and the agenda for tonight is how to fund the venture.

And with that, Rutland shakes our hands warmly and is away up the hill to his home at ***Ye Gables***. We are sorry to see him go but rest assured that his gathering of local worthies will set the ball rolling for the collection of subscriptions and donations that within three years will raise sufficient funds for a fine **Reading Room** to be built in the corner of the **Pater Noster** meadow just south of the school. It will be equipped with a library of over 100 volumes and daily newspapers available for all. Everything will be in the safe hands of its secretary, the ubiquitous John Siggers who will continue as Taplow's schoolmaster until 1919 after having retired five years earlier only to be recalled when his successor, George Leake, is called to serve in the Great War.

The Gables and the Mysterious Ruins

Allington Cottage, Hill Farm Road / 13th August 2012

I have come to borrow the Parish Register from **Brenda & Tony Hickman**. She asks if my research has shed any light on "the mysterious Ruins". It has, but not a lot. However, everything comes to those who keep digging...

The garden of Old Lodge West, High Street / 10th August 2013

Marc Boden's birthday party is in full swing. He and his wife Marianne bought this house from widower **Cyril Staley** in 2003. It was once the western end of ***The Gables*** which Cyril believed was built before 1763 and has since grown eastwards, divided into two, reunited as one – called ***Old Lodge*** from 1941 – divided again into two dwellings one of which was extended further eastwards then divided into two to make three altogether. And according to Cyril, ***The Ruins*** stood right here from before 1871 until 1941, except that it had been *Old Lodge* since before 1908.

If all that is hard to swallow, have another drink, take a deep breath and digest the evidence. The 1787 Taplow inclosure map shows an orchard between the muddle of buildings on **Tothill's** and a house to the north standing alone on **The Phygtle** frontage. The orchard was part of a parcel of land called **Phipp's Close** held freehold by the Manor of Taplow. The inclosure map didn't note it as being within the 25 acres held copyhold by **Nathaniel Newberry** but between 1801 and 1814, possibly before and after, it was held by his widow Rachael. Perhaps the Newberrys built the house on its northern edge that would become *The Gables*. Perhaps they built an adjacent house in the orchard which fell into ruin.

The 1861 census has this as yet unnamed house on The Phygtle as home to Mary & **James Rutland**. By then it had been extended east and the western solar was her stationer's and draper's shop. When a new organ was installed in the chancel of the new St Nicholas' Church in 1866, the old one found its way into Rutland's home in order that he could rehearse his hymns for the Sunday services. Perhaps this nifty trick inspired the rumour that his role as a local builder gave him opportunities to use materials taken from the old disused church or from St Mary's Church in Hitcham to build, alter or extend this home, or at least to furnish it with oak panelling, stair railings, timber beams and stained glass reclaimed from these holy sources. This may not be a tall tale at all. After it was vacated in 1828, the old church stood in an increasingly dilapidated condition for many years and wasn't finally demolished until the early-1850s, a time when Rutland in his mid-20s might well have taken advantage of anything that could be reclaimed from its remnants.

Copyhold of the orchard appears to have passed from Widow Newberry via William Austin, Matthew Smith and Thomas Marshall to Rutland who acquired it in February 1871 thanks to a mortgage from his friend **William Rance the Elder**. Later that year *The Ruins* made its first appearance in the census, which noted it as an unoccupied dwelling. Could Rutland have restored an existing ruin or built a new house on the site of a previous one? When Mary died the following year, he lovingly built her tomb in the old churchyard with his own hands before finding solace with his second wife Helen by giving their home a new name: *Ye Gables*, later *The Gables*.

In 1879 Rutland and Rance obtained licence from William Grenfell on behalf of the trustees of the Manor of Taplow to lease *The Ruins* to **Henry Arthur Herbert** for 60 years commencing the previous September. Herbert was an Irish gentleman of considerable note who like many of his ilk favoured English country seats in and around the Thames Valley. Like Grenfell, his family fortune derived from copper and his family home, Muckross House in Killarney, had been designed in 1843 by **William Burn** who had since remodelled Taplow Court. He had flown high in the military as a captain in the Coldstream Guards and a major in the London Irish Rifles before turning to politics in 1866 when he succeeded his father to the 47,000 acre Muckross estate and as MP for Kerry.

Their rental terms suggest a commercial astuteness on the part of the Taplovian friends – £50-a-year (£4,450) until 1888, rising to £75-a-year (£7,300) until 1898, £90-a-year (£8,750) until 1918 and finally £100-a-year (£4,250) until 1938 – but their cunning plan would come apart at the seams. The Rance interest in *The Ruins* seems to have ended with William the Elder's death in 1880 yet all must have seemed fine to Rutland in 1881 when his illustrious tenant retired after 14 years as an MP and was appointed High Sheriff of Kerry. The census that year counts Herbert and his wife Emily, three children and seven servants at ***Castle Flint*** (their name for ***The Ruins***) and the following year Herbert also leased much of *The Gables* leaving the Rutlands in eastern part with certain rights of use over other areas including his carpenter's shop and outbuildings. However, settling in Taplow wasn't to Emily's taste. She preferred the charms of a certain Charles Greenfield. Her husband saw no option but to divorce her. The unfortunate affair and later Parkinson's disease hit Herbert hard, he neglected Muckross and by 1897 it was insolvent.

William Rance the Younger played no part in 1885 when with Rutland's assent Herbert sold his leasehold to Captain **Frederick Fearon** who unlike his predecessor managed to overcome his own family tragedy to enjoy his dotage in Taplow. As the son of Robert Fearon, Major-General of the 31st Regiment of Foot, he was always going to be a military man. He served with distinction during the 69th (South Lincolnshire) Regiment posting to Malta from 1848 until 1851. While he was there, he married Isabel Bremer and had a daughter, Edith. After retiring from the army, he took a position as a chartered company secretary with a Canadian trust company and was first noted hereabouts in 1873 when Edith's marriage certificate places him at ***The Cottage***, wherever that was. Isabel died soon afterwards but Frederick recovered to marry again in 1882. It could have gone very wrong – he was a middle-aged man of 54 and his new wife Amy Martin of Kensington a sweet young thing of 23 – but they lived happily in Taplow until his death in 1902.

Exactly where they lived is another matter. Initially *Castle Flint* reverted to being *The Ruins*. In 1889 they leased from **Cecil Irby** of *Hitcham Grange* a roadway providing access to *The Gables* and *The Ruins* from Back Lane, and by 1891 they had built by this roadway ***The Ruins Stables*** and installed there coachman Johns Adams, his wife Jemima and six children. However, the 1901 census places the Fearons where *The Ruins* should be, between *Gurney's* and *The Gables*, but in *The Cottage* – an intriguing twist which suggests they had given their home yet another name. Fearon was either too boring or too clever for anyone to take any more notes. The widowed Amy remained in residence until 1903 when Fearon's daughter Edith Hordern paid Rutland £86 (£5,000) to accept surrender of the property.

The Rutlands decided to renew *The Ruins* as ***Old Lodge***. Within a year of her husband's death in 1907, Helen Rutland sold *Old Lodge* to the sisters Agnes Griffis and Gertrude Blackborow. The 1911 census noted the latter living at ***The Toft*** – possibly *The Stables* – and the artist brothers **Harold** and **Horace Gordon** at ***The Studio***, apparently Rutland's former carpenter's shop adjoining *The Gables*. Within a year the sisters leased *Old Lodge* to the diplomat **Sir Maurice de Bunsen** who remained in residence until the early-1920s when they were succeeded as tenant by **Eva Davidson**. In 1924 the sisters acquired the freehold from the Grenfell trustees and sold it to the solicitor **Noel Dowson**, a partner in his father Cecil's practice a N° 7 St James' Place, Westminster. **Cecil Dowson**'s local connection dates back until at least 1882 when he drafted the last will and testament of **Charles Whitlaw the Younger**. By the 1920s he was living at ***Guildersfield***, watching with interest as his son acquired *The Gables* and demolished *The Studio* and outbuildings to add an integral eastward extension. In 1941 Dowson the Younger sold both *The Gables* and *Old Lodge* to ***Whitbread*** director **Jack Martineau** who knocked down the latter to make a better garden and transferred its name to the former to make it *Old Lodge Cottage*. It was simply *Old Lodge* 22 years later when he gave it as a nest-egg to his son Charles Martineau complete with a trusted tenant in the person of the recently-widowed **Anne Young**.

Old Lodge can thank Charles for its eventual fragmentation. In 1975 he applied for planning permission to divide the house into two separate dwellings. Wheels turned slowly until 1981 when ***Old Lodge East*** was sold to Joy & Gordon Owen and ***Old Lodge West*** to **Frances & Cyril Staley**. The Staleys split their home some nine years later into a reduced *Old Lodge West*, which they retained, and ***Old Lodge***, which they sold to **Theresa & Jeremy Thompson**. And then in 1996 the Thompsons succeeded the Owens and **Christina & John Prestidge** settled at *Old Lodge* until selling it in 2011 to **Pamela & Joel Viollet**....

Tall Tales – Staleys Making Waves

The garden of Old Lodge West, High Street / 10th August 2013

Pamela has a note written by Cyril which interprets a Deed of Enfranchisement dated 14th August 1924 to suggest that *The Ruins* was the remnant of Taplow Manor House. He was mistaken. The Grenfell trustees held the freehold of much of the Manor and received annual rent-charges from tenants to whom various parcels of land were let copyhold or leasehold. Marc now has the relevant Deed. It confirms that the trustees were realising a manorial asset with the sale of the freehold of *Old Lodge* for £237 6s 8d (£61,000) to its copyholders Agnes and Gertrude. Much more intriguing is to wonder how **Willy Grenfell** felt about the sisters making a tidy profit by selling it immediately to Noel Dowson for £2,000 (£512,000). All would of course fall into place if, as suspected, Willy and Noel were distant cousins.

Tony Meats recalls that Cyril was never civil to him again after his was one of the more articulate of several objections which in 1991/92 scuppered the Staley plan to build a new house where *The Ruins* had stood. Or maybe the upset resulted from Tony's evident incredulity when Frances claimed to have seen a vision of the Virgin Mary in the High Street. He muses whether the Holy Mother was dismayed to be too late to buy a bargain *simlah* at *Dean's*.

Through the Church Gate / 2012

Mulberry House (formerly *The Hollies* and, before that, *Rance's Butcher's Shop*) / c1929 & 2009

The Village People: Highstreeters

Gurney's Shop & Post Office / c1910

Number Three
(formerly *Gurney's, Budgen's & Deane's*)
with *Rozel* & *Mulberry House* beyond

Number Three*: starring on TV as a pharmacy in *Midsomer Murders / 2012

Gurney's Shop & Post Office / c1890

Pax Cottage / 2015

Old Lodge West (formerly *The Gables*) / 2009

Old Lodge / c1976
(before subdivision)

The Old School / c1960

The Old Cottage
(formerly *Avery's Cottages*
and other names) / 2009

The Village People: Highstreeters

***The Nest*, with *Grange Lodge* beyond** / c1950

Victoria Cottage
(formerly *The Nest*) / 2015

***Wee Cott* & *Rose Cott*....**
....adjoining *The Porches* / 2015

When they were five and 200 / c1905

Hearn's Turn – Old Friends

At the curl of Pikels / 6th January 1892

We wait by the village's second old pump which is supplied by a culvert from **Taplow Court**. The water is frozen solid but we are treated to a warm smile from **Francis Hearn** as he marches up Pikels from his home by the butcher's shop. Call me Frank, he says. And before we ask, yes, despite the spelling difference, our friend Freddie Hurn is somehow a cousin. And before we begin, what do we think of the Parish Clerk? While **James Rutland** rather likes things and even people to be in an orderly state, preferably of his design, his strong appreciation of local history and current affairs and his diligence in recording it all are valuable attributes that smooth his rougher edges and will stand the test of time. We conclude that he is indeed a fine gentleman of a kind every community needs. Frank nods in agreement; strong medicine is always best in small doses, he says with a smile before changing the subject....

If we're interested in current affairs, Frank thinks we'll be pleased to see something different. Rutland has introduced us mainly to the gentry and the tradesmen who serve them – in other words, to people who employ people. Now we are where the workers live. He asks how many dwellings we can see. Eight, we say, not including Mr Rutland's. They are home to 25 folk altogether, Frank says, including nine children and a dozen wage-earners.

Across the road, ***Grange Cottage*** stands alone – an exception for being the residence of an educated man. In his youth, **Walter Leyster** set off from Ireland, land of his birth, to Africa where he was a missionary for some years before coming to England in the late-1870s to teach at **Taplow Grammar School**. Perhaps it reflects the content of Walter, his wife Isabel (Hettie) and their boys Herbert (9) and Gordon (4) that they will soon move to a larger cottage nearby and name it *Ye Nest*, later modernised to ***The Nest***. After he retires from teaching he will continue for many years as Taplow's Parish Clerk, Verger and honorary if rather imaginative historian, forever fascinating youngsters with his tales of life among the African tribes. He will remain very active well into his nineties when during the Second War he will enjoy conducting a Canadian grandson on tours of the village he loves so well.

The other homes hereabouts are those we saw 300 years ago. A few yards to the south are ***Springall's Cottages***, a name to conjure with. How did **Joe Springall the Younger** graduate by the 1860s to be 'house proprietor' for this trickle of five homes? Did he or his dad make so much by gardening that he could afford to invest in property, or was the copyhold of these cottages held by one of his employers, possibly **Charles Whitlaw the Elder** of ***Springfield***, later of Amerden? The southerly trio are home to herdsman George Bayliss, waiter Billy Harvey and coachman **Robert Johnson**. Harvey's house is called ***Ye Porch***; it will eventually embrace its adjoining neighbours to become ***Ye Porch Cottage***, ***Ye Porches*** and finally ***The Porches***. Building labourer **Henry Horton** and Joe's 73-year-old widow **Hannah Springall** live in the slightly younger pair to the north which will stay just good friends as ***Rose Cott*** and ***Wee Cott***.

Until 20 years ago, Wesleyans used to preach under a chestnut tree at the curl of Pikels. Now they have a corrugated-iron-clad chapel just north of the Elementary School. Once the Lent Rise Methodist Chapel opens in 1897, Taplow's will be converted to a private house until becoming so dilapidated that it is pulled down in the mid-1930s leaving only two or three foundation stones with initials and dates in the garden of the old thatched farmhouse we saw almost 300 years ago. This had been divided in the late-18th Century into two known by 1840 as *Avery's Cottages*. Local lore tells a tale of each. A coffin-maker lived in the western one where he slept in the most comfortable of his creations to save the undertaker trouble if he was taken in the night. Its neighbour was home to **Ann Avery**, an old lace-making wise woman who was housekeeper for the bachelor **William Davis Neighbour**. When he died in 1846 his will provided for **George Norrington** to give her "about Christmas each year, a fat pig of weight tenscore at the least".

Perhaps the cottages were then in Norrington's gift as well. Over the years, Ann's brothers Levy and Thomas joined her, and Tom was still there ten years ago. Nowadays one is home to the farmhand **George Simmonds**, his wife Sarah and their infant children Ellen and William. The other is empty. In years to come, these dwellings will enjoy a series of names before uniting (probably around 1940) as the oldest surviving freestanding house in Taplow. It will have just one serious competitor in its claim to be Taplow's oldest surviving dwelling. It is all so long ago now and too close to call but the tiny cottage up the hill is certainly contemporary. However it lost its independence in the early-17th Century as the Neighbour family grew organically northwards to create their terrace of six. We shall learn more of its story shortly.

At the curl of Pikels / 22nd April 1901

A grand house stands proudly up on the knoll to the north. It is home to **Walter Millington**, a wholesale stationer from Sydenham for whom it may have been built in 1890. Perhaps he has since discovered that ***The Knowle*** has been built just where a spring emerges after heavy rains. Millington has converted the nearby barn as his coachhouse and the eastern of ***Avery's Cottages*** is now ***Ye Cotty Legh*** and home to coachman Alexander Parker, his wife Julia and their baby daughter, and her mother Louisa, a widow "living on her own means". Louisa's late husband Charles Dorset had clearly put a little away during the almost 30 years in which he rose from being a domestic servant to butler at ***The Walnuts*** for wheelwright **Henry Simmonds** and then the independently wealthy Henry Buckmaster.

By 1911 the former Parker place will be ***Cottylegh*** and unoccupied. George Simmonds next door will be calling his home ***Leigh Cottage***, a name it will retain into the 1930s when Harry Hurn will remember George as a tottery little old man with a frame as crooked and aged as the lavender bush by his front door. Now **Pamela Bentley** takes up the story....

A Purring Bentley

The Old Cottage, High Street / 22nd March 2007

Lady Beatrice Pole-Carew was the daughter of James Butler, 3rd Marquess of Ormonde, the granddaughter through her mother Lady Elizabeth of Hugh Grosvenor, 1st Duke of Westminster (once of Cliveden) and the widow since 1924 of Lieutenant-Colonel Sir Reginald Pole-Carew of the Coldstream Guards, former MP for Bodmin and Deputy Lieutenant of Cornwall [*see Appendix 1, Tree 10*]. She had been lady-in-waiting to Queen Mary, wife of King George V, was a friend of the Astors and would be of Joyce Grenfell too. Her son Sir John Carew Pole, 12th Baronet Pole, having changed his name by deed poll in 1926, the following year acquired ***The Knowle*** from the recently widowed **Mary Webster** and added a new servant's wing to make it a suitably comfortable home for his mother. This and the three other properties included in the acquisition were all rebranded over the next few years.

The Knowle immediately became ***Maryfield***, named for Lady Beatrice's daughter and lifelong companion **Marye Pole-Carew**, its coachhouse was recast as ***Maryfield Cottage*** and ***Cottylegh*** was soon ***Ye Cottleigh*** and home to Lady Beatrice's sister **Lady Constance Butler**. Old George stayed on as sitting tenant at ***Leigh Cottage*** until his death when his home and *Ye Cottleigh* were united as ***Old Taplow Cottage*** where Lady Beatrice joined her sister when *Maryfield* was requisitioned during the Second War as the headquarters of the Dutch General Staff in exile. On her death in 1952 *Maryfield* and its friends passed to Marye and her sister Victoria du Cane. Marye installed herself in *Old Taplow Cottage* and simplified its name to ***The Old Cottage***, Pamela's pride and joy since 1967. In these four decades, Pamela has served 15 years on Taplow Parish Council (two as Chairman), 11 as a District Councillor and 8 as a County Councillor. She also spent many years as a governor of the high school that will become Burnham Park Academy in 2013.

Tall Tale – Falling Off a Wain

Maryfield Cottage, High Street / 1st November 2002

Leonard Miall has always been a sucker for tall tales and brilliant at telling them. As everyone enjoys his 88th birthday party, he confides conspiratorially that it must have been around 1820 when a load of heavy chestnut beams "fell off the back of a wain in Taplow". They were on their way to *Stratfield Saye* – the Hampshire stately home then being refurbished for Arthur Wellesley, 1st Duke of Wellington, iconic hero of the Battle of Waterloo and much else besides – but they found themselves spanning the barn which *The Knowle* sequestered as its coachhouse. It is now *Maryfield Cottage*, home to Leonard and his wife Sally.

One of these beams has the name ***Rubicon*** painted on it. Could this be the ship from which the timbers came? No British vessel has ever been registered in that name but it was given to a transAtlantic merchantman built in 1810 at Newburyport, Massachusetts. This American *Rubicon* was damaged catastrophically in 1816 when she struck an iceberg off Newfoundland. She lost her stem and other large structural timbers in the collision as well as most of her cargo but other ships saved her to be repaired in Boston and resume her travels. Her rescuers included a Liverpool brig. Could she or another British ship have salvaged these timbers? It's a long shot in every sense but so tempting to take Leonard's tasty bait hook, line and sinker.

Borderers

Living on the Edge

Back Lane / 6th January 1892

As we emerge from the top end of Pikels, **Frank Hearn** jokes that we'd better be careful here. We're teetering on the edge of Taplow and wouldn't want to fall off [*see Map 27*]. The nine houses (and 56 people) across the road are actually over the parish boundary in Hitcham. They're so close to Taplow we think of them as just as much part of the village as the 22 houses (and 93 people) on this side of Back Lane.

Elmbank Cottages

Back Lane / 6th January 1892

As we look north towards **Coldgrove Corner**, on our left is that terrace of six which grew from its small beginning to be ***Neighbour's Cottages***, then ***Norrington's Cottages*** for **Davis Neighbour**'s son-in-law **William Norrington** and now ***Elmbank Cottages***, home to 24 people – five less than a decade ago, four times as many as there will be in January 2012.

Thirza Simmonds is waiting for us in the shade outside the door of her home at N° 6, the most northerly of the cottages. She has lived here ever since marrying farmhand Richard Simmonds in 1836 – that's 56 of her 75 years, she's quick to tell us. He was a good man, she says. He took in my year-old illegitimate son Abraham and raised him as his own with the 11 children we had together, four of whom now lie with him in the churchyard where he's been these last 20 years. We remind her that we met Dick 53 years ago on parade with the Taplow Lancers. Yes, he always liked playing soldiers. She doesn't give a fig that a procession of confused curates and clerks have transcribed her unusual Christian name as Thirza, Thurza, Thurzah, Thursa, Thurjah or Thura over the years. Can't read nor write, she shrugs, never needed to. I've got my daughter Emma here to look after me.

Her 68-year-old widowed sister Eleanor (Ellen) Newman emerges from her home next door to find out who's come to call. Thirza smiles and says meet my little sister, Taplow born-and-bred like me. Aren't we the pick of the bunch, us Paget girls? Their near-toothless grins leave a little to be desired. Ellen married labourer John Newman in 1845. Our first four children were born over in one of the ***Taplowhill Cottages***, she recalls. After baby Rosina died in 1853 we moved to Maidenhead and John got a job on a Cookham coal wharf. We had two more children before coming home nearly 20 years ago. John died in 1887 but we're alright, says Ellen, me and Thirza aren't short of family hereabouts. Our cousin **George Simmonds** and his family are round the corner at N° 2 ***Avery's Cottages*** and Dick's sister **Fanny Paget** is just up the road in ***Church Houses*** with her daughter Laura and her son Ebenezer. You'll see them if you're going that way.

We ask about their neighbours. Ellen reckons it is more than 30 years since Kent-born carpenter and builder Philip Wakeman and his wife Louisa came to live at N° 1, the original cottage that sticks out at the far end, the one that might be as old as *Avery's*. She's either James Rutland's sister or his cousin. Two of their sons are still at home: William is a stableman and Sidney a carpenter like his father. Gardener Fred Willis and his wife Charlotte are at N° 3. He finds a lot of work for the young Oxfordshire lads Joe and Bert Busby who lodge at N° 4 with spinster **Ann Kent** (68). She's a one, says Thirza. Everyone calls her *That Bible Woman* for quoting from the scriptures at every opportunity. I expect she encourages the Busby boys by sending them out each day with *2 Thessalonians 3:10* ringing in their ears: "The one who is unwilling to work shall not eat". And talking of the scriptures, adds Ellen, we mustn't forget the parish sexton John Haseman who lodges with cowman Jonathan Smith and his wife Myriam at N° 2. There's a tale, says Thirza: the sexton was a bricklayer's labourer in Caversham before he lost his wife Eliza and found God. Haseman will find a second happiness with her daughter Emma, the church cleaner. He will be 65 and she 57 when they marry in 1898 three years after bidding farewell to Thirza.

Back Lane / 28th December 1928

The terrace was still called *Elmbank Cottages* in 1911 when the six were four. The northerly pair had become one, then unoccupied. Oxfordshire cowman Algernon Filbee (43) and Cumbrian farmhand John Clark (80) and their wives – both Margarets – lived in the middle pair, the former kept company by a son and granddaughter, the latter by three children. The southerly pair had also united and was home to Emma & John Haseman who it seems were well placed the following year to do some Rutland-style recycling by lining the dining room with panelling rescued from St Nicholas' Church. But what was their relationship with the mysterious Clara Muirhead? Who secreted behind this panelling a bundle of papers including an emergency passport issued to Clara to allow her to escape from Hamburg following the outbreak of war in August 1914? This intriguing relic was discovered in 1963 by Ian MacLeod, who wondered why would she hide her passport and then forget it?

The story of Herbert Ide Keen is equally intriguing. This American agricultural machinery engineer first came to the UK in 1909 to manage the European operations of the *Allis-Chalmers Manufacturing Company*. Having lived since 1911 in ***Ye Porch Cottage***, he moved into the southerly of ***Elmbank Cottages*** in 1918 only to be relocated to Paris within a year. And that would have been that if it hadn't been for his long dispute with the US Internal Revenue Service which will shortly conclude with the adoption of principles that will inform tax laws for expatriate Americans for 100 years and more. He was only a temporary Taplovian but, like the Whaleys of ***Taplow Lodge***, he still managed to make his mark on the legal workings of the world.

The name change came in 1919 after the terrace was acquired by a 25-year-old architect who is the prime suspect for calling the northerly cottage ***Greensleeves***, keeping ***Elmbank*** for the smallest in the middle (formerly Filbee's) and resurrecting ***Neighbours*** for the southerly one which he expanded into Clark's. This chap's name – William Frederick Victor Morduant Milner – was as long as he was tall, all six-feet-six of him. He went by the much less daunting name of Derek, all the better to fit beneath the low ceilings of *Greensleeves* where he became something of a recluse. His half-sister Doreen and her husband Victor Hope, 2nd Marquess of Linlithgow (later the longest serving Viceroy of India from 1936 to 1943), had a son Charles who recalled his Uncle Derek "remoting himself to a cottage" not far from where his father Sir Frederick Milner, 7th Baronet, erstwhile MP for York then Bassetlaw, rented *Taplow Lodge* from **Lord Astor**.

Horace and **Harold Gordon** relocated from ***The Studio*** to become Milner's tenants in *Neighbours* some time before 1921 when they installed two internal painted windows there. Today the brothers are marking their recent acquisition of all three dwellings for £1,300 (£320,000) by secreting behind the frame of one these windows a note of despair that reads "Two struggling artists put in this window in 1921, ruined by the damned war, disgusted with the vulgarity of the age". One window depicts the artist Raphael, the other the poet **John Milton** whose mother (according to unconfirmed legend) hailed from Taplow. Perhaps for the Gordons they were two icons of a better age.

Hill Farm Road / 14th June 2012

What were six homes then four then three are now two and home to six.

Harold Gordon made his home in *Greensleeves* and let out *Elmbank* and, after Horace's sad death in 1929, *Neighbours* too. His artistry is in metalworking, a craft that until the late-1950s he practised in a little brick outbuilding behind *Neighbours*. Some of the doors in *Neighbours* still swing on Harold's hinges just as they did when the place was let at a very high rent to a series of writers, theatre and film folk. One brought so much infamy to the house by not paying her bills that Harold felt obliged to change its name to *Cherry Tree House*. It had been restored as *Neighbours* by the time Harry Hurn recalls (in no particular order) it being home to the actress Ann Todd and her husband the author Nigel Tangye, to the influential romantic novelist and screenwriter Elinor Glyn who in 1927 had coined the soubriquet *The It Girl* for actress Clara Bow, and to an American screenwriter with *Warner Bros* who paid Harry sixpence-an-hour (£4) to grub weeds from the gravel paths.

The Village People: Borderers

Once six Elmbank Cottages, now *Neighbours* / 2012

.... and *Losuce* (formerly *Greensleeves & Elmbank*) / 2009

Coldgrove Cottages / 2009

Church Cottages / 2009

Hitcham Grange/ 2009

Map 27 – Borderers: Living on the Edge

Friends and Neighbours

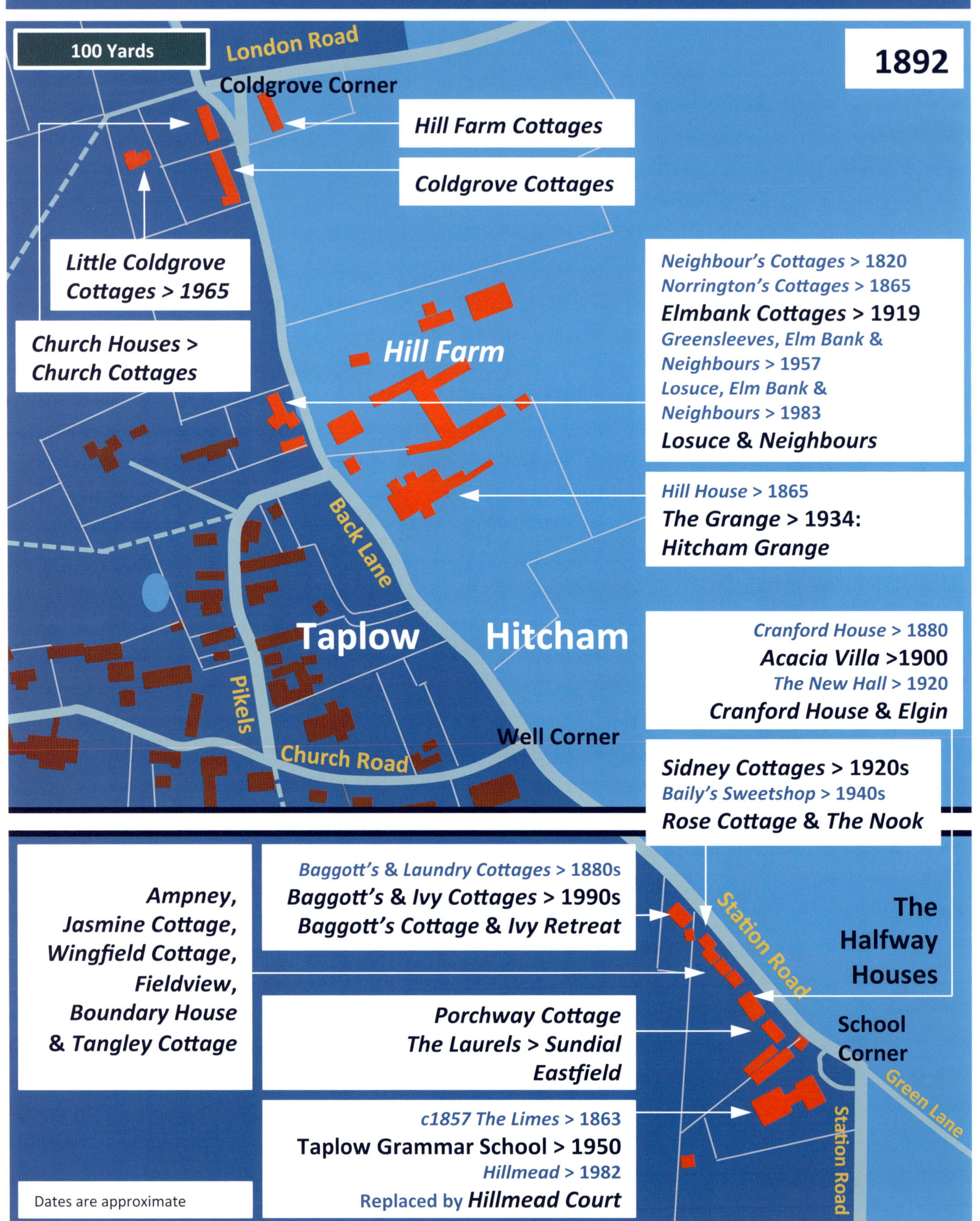

Primary Source: Ordnance Survey 1897

Eventually *Neighbours* passed to Ian MacLeod (discoverer of Clara Muirhead's papers), **Michael Goss** (a valued source) and via others to **Heather & Warren Palmer** (discoverers in 2005 of the **Gordon** brothers' despairing note) who after nine years there today completed the sale of the house to movie art directors **Rebecca** & **David Hindle**. Having spent about 70 years as ***Greensleeves***, ***Neighbour's*** northern neighbour was recast as ***Losuce*** in the 1950s (perhaps by a certain B Spivack) and embraced ***Elmbank*** three decades later. It is nearly eight years since **Janette & Laird Mackay** made it home but they still can't explain their cottage's unusual name.

Coldgrove Corner

Back Lane / 6th January 1892

It is 1,737 years since we imagined standing here to watch that Roman *centuria* march by. To the south-west, **Little Coldgrove** can boast 16 houses in which 67 people including 30 wage-earners and 20 children live within a stone's throw of each other. Three women work. The 27 men who are employed include Isaac Pengilley, an agent for *The Prudential Assurance Company* agent, three horsemen and 23 others who labour on the land, in gardens, in various building trades or wherever muscle is required.

Coldgrove Cottages was a 1850s build-for-rent venture by **William Rance the Elder** still owned copyhold by his son and now home to 30 including 11 wage-earners and 12 children. The southernmost of the terrace of six has been extended to become ***Dorl Cot***, standing empty right now. At the far end, ***Grove Villa*** has been added for Pengilley. In between live gardener Charlie Shewell, coachman **William House**, farm labourer David Grace, cowman John Wise and **James Bond**, a Bray cabman never shaken but stirred around 1880 to lodge with the Newmans and woo **Mary Cordery**, then of the northernmost of ***Springall's Cottages***. Her retired farm labourer father John and her garden labourer brother Richard live with them and their neighbours have three other working lodgers: farmhands Tom Harper and Amos Newell with Grace and carpenter Harry Wakeman at House's house. Harry is Philip's son and William must surely be related to the Houses at ***Odds Farm***.

Shallow bay windows and some red-brick coursing were the elder Rance's only indulgences as he cut his speculative cloth to suit the pockets of working men. In contrast, the terrace of six ***Church Houses*** was built for the poor of the parish in 1853 at the expense of **Charles Pascoe Grenfell**. Their tall chimneys, tiled dormers and porches, leaded lights and herringbone brickwork touches hint that he wanted to impress, all part of the deal that enabled him to improve his view from Taplow Court by removing the ruins of the Norman St Nicholas' Church. There are 19 folks here including 14 wage-earners and one child. The Bible Woman's brother, garden labourer **Abel Kent**, is at N° 1. Next door, **Fanny Paget** is a needlewoman like her elder daughter **Laura Brown** and her son **Ebenezer Paget** is a blacksmith. **Lucy Plummer** at N° 3 is a charwoman at ***The Grange***; gardener William James lodges with her. Bricklayer's labourer **Tom Horton** has four working sons at N° 4; Tommy and Billy work with their father while Fred and Arthur are general labourers like their neighbour Tom Willis. And amazingly at N° 6 is our old friend **Tom Fenner**, still with his wife Jane and still pottering in the gardens he has tended for so long despite being all of 80.

Another 18 people somehow squeeze into the three ***Little Coldgrove Cottages*** behind *Church Houses*. Five are wage-earners: at one end, Fred Perrin and his lodger **George Grantham** are labourers, at the other William Hunt is a carpenter and in between is cowman **John Butler** with his lodger Henry Rose, a garden labourer. Hunt has five children, Rose three and Grantham one.

In 120 years, *Dorl Cot* will be ***Harbinger***, *Grove Villa* will be ***The Ivy House*** and *Little Coldgrove Cottages* will have been lost to the garage court behind ***Church Cottages***, formerly *Church Houses*.

Stranger in the Waiting Rooms

Church Houses, Back Lane / 6th January 1871

Laura Brown is just 23 but her story is already a long one. She begins with her family background. The Brown and the Browne families are likely to have been related genetically if not by the spelling of registrars. Many are noted as paupers, the luckier men found work as agricultural or general labourers, their ladies as charwomen, needlewomen or lacemakers. Together they will appear in Taplow's Parish Register during the 18th and 19th Centuries more than twice as often as any other family. How they spend their spare time is evident because 87 of those 201 entries are baptisms.

John Brown died a pauper at 49 leaving 4-year-old Laura the middle of three infant sisters. At 14 she was living with her mother Fanny, two sisters, two step-sisters, a step-brother and her carpenter stepfather **Abraham Paget**, Thirza's illegitimate son. Now Laura's sisters and Abraham are gone and Fanny has moved her three Paget children and Laura into N° 2 *Church Houses*, the home of her 83-year-old father **John Simmonds**, who has a small but comfortable pension from a former employer. Fanny and Laura earn their living as needlewomen. The young woman confides that her neighbours in *Church Houses* are all so old and most with not so much as two brass farthings to rub together. Elizabeth Allum has been in Taplow for at least 50 years. She and Mary Keywood are at N° 6 with Elizabeth and Mary Bristow at the other end of the terrace. A playful smirk flashes across Laura's face as she whispers that these two pairs of seventy-something sisters with the same Christian names make perfect matching bookends. Fanny smiles at her daughter's way with words before adding that Hannah Baggs and Harriet Squires in N° 3 are even more ancient and so decrepit they are looked after by a live-in nurse, Susan Gibson. Laura chips in that even Susan is older than her mum, and Mary Smith in N° 5 is oldest of all at 90. Everyone is on parochial relief except the Simmonds household and the Greens at N° 4. July Green still earns a crust at 62 by running errands while her teenage son Sam is a gardener's boy and his elder brother George an under-gardener. Laura might be sweet on 30-year-old George if he ever gave her any encouragement.

Fanny remembers that, when William Goodchild became too old and creaky in his late-70s to support himself and his wife Mary with his gardening, they had both been sent off to the **Eton Union Workhouse** in Upton. And what made it worse was that, after a lifetime together, they were in separate dormitories. The Goodchilds were reunited only in St Nicholas' Churchyard where she was laid to rest in 1863 and he four years later. Laura thinks it must be the right thing for the Parish to waive rents and give financial relief as necessary to keep as many of the local old folk in **Church Houses** as long as it can. The girl came as a stranger into God's waiting rooms; now she is growing up. Perhaps she will even miss Mistress Squires when she is taken off to the Eton Union in a couple of years. And perhaps she will put a few flowers on the old lady's grave when she is brought back to be buried in the churchyard in 1875.

St Nicolas' Churchyard / 6th January 2013

The 1911 census shows that Laura Brown was still a spinster at N° 2 *Church Houses*, and that Lucy Plummer was still a widow next-door at N° 3. The only differences are that they were both living alone and both earning a living as charwomen at *The Grange* and *Hill Farm*. However, a walk around the churchyard is revealing. Lucy was a charwoman all her life yet she saved enough to invest in a tall cross as her memorial, sadly now broken. And nearby is the grave of **Francis Hearn** and his wife Ann. He couldn't have earned much as a 'farm servant' but his 1906 headstone is as impressive as those of the much better-off Norringtons and Briginshaws. If employees couldn't match employers in life, it seems they could do so in death.

Over, Not Out

Back Lane / 6th January 1892

Frank Hearn is otherwise engaged today, pointing out that Laura Brown has new neighbours over the road in Hitcham but somehow not out of Taplow. The rather demonstrative, ornately crafted WHG on the frontage of ***Hill Farm Cottages*** leaves no doubt that four years ago **Willy Grenfell** funded the construction of this terrace of four. Why would the lord of Taplow build houses for ***Hill Farm*** workers in Hitcham? Was his investment philanthropic or commercial? Dorney-born **Charlie Bunce** lives at N° 1, does what he is told by farm bailiff Charles Winfield at N° 4 and pays rent to Grenfell. Beyond that, he has no idea how it all works. He is however happy to report that Esther & George Futter are at N° 3, Henry Smith is at N° 2 and altogether 24 people live here including 10 children, himself and seven other farmhands.

The Enterprising Webster Clan

Hill Farm, Back Lane / 6th January 1892

Three Burnham teenagers are heading for *Hill Farm*. William Addaway is a 14-year-old farmhand who lodges with the Futters. His brother Charles (16) and Ada Coker (18) are domestic servants in the house itself. As he opens the gate for us, Will jokes that old **Dick Webster** has run the farm since the Saviour wore swaddling clothes – well, since the 1830s, which amounts to much the same thing. He's 81 now and leaves his son John the Third to run the place with only a little interference.

Farmer **John Webster** smiles at Will's cheekiness and explains that a numbering system can help when your family has four Johns in five generations including his 10-year-old nephew **John Richard Webster**. It all started hereabouts with his great-grandfather **John Webster**, an Aberdonian doctor of medicine who in 1746 upset his family by tending wounded Government soldiers in the aftermath of the Battle of Culloden. Although he was far from being the only anti-Jacobite Scot, he thought it prudent to travel with the Duke of Cumberland to the safety of England where he was rewarded for his loyal service to the Crown by being appointed family physician to **Frederick**, **Prince of Wales**, his wife Princess Augusta of Saxe Coburg and their eight children, the second of whom would grow up to be King George III. It was in this responsible and trusted position – but not necessarily while at Clifden – that he tended to His Majesty when his royal person was injured by the errant cricket ball of legend.

Other local lore swirls around memories of Dr John and his son, another **John Webster** born around 1763. John the First is said to have planted the three oaks at Cliveden known as 'Webster's Oaks'. Frank is much more entertained by the story that John the Second was the first person ever to arrest a peeress for debt, not least because the lady in question was none other than **Mary Fitzmaurice, 4th Countess of Orkney**. In the 1780s this enterprising fellow leased ***Barge Farm*** from Lady Orkney for £160 per annum (£18,000) and flourished as a farmer, seedsman and corn dealer. He made a fortune supplying corn to the army during the Peninsular War – he had a turntable installed at *Barge Farm* so barges could sail up the creek to be quickly and safely spun around, loaded and dispatched, and there are tales of Burnham being clogged as his wagons were readied for the road to Portsmouth – only to have much of it drain away as various coaching companies, hunts, stables and rather too many land-rich cash-poor nobles failed to pay for the corn he supplied. One of the latter was Lady Orkney who owed John the Second £800 (£89,000). That was a lot of corn she hadn't paid for. However he had friends amongst locals who perhaps shouldn't have but did confide where she would be when. He had friends in high places – the Grenvilles at **Dropmore**, for instance – who perhaps shouldn't have but did set the Parliamentary agenda. He waited with a postchaise at Westminster until a bill was passed into law to enable him to arrest his quarry, then he chased after her, caught up with her at Dover and made his arrest. She secured her freedom and saved her embarrassment by signing a cheque which was honoured by the bank, much to Webster's surprise and relief. He was saved from bankruptcy and able to settle down to a quieter but very comfortable future as a corn dealer and grass seedsman. His victory over Lady Orkney might have encouraged his debtors to pay for he never experienced such critical cashflow problems again.

John the Second's private life is almost as intriguing. He married Frances (Fanny) Bayley (née Hoare), already the mother of four children by her late husband Thomas Bayley. The eldest of these children, another Thomas, will be great-times-three-grandfather to our friend **Michael Bayley**. After Fanny died in 1801, he sired another eight children by his second wife **Elizabeth**

Hearne. Frank reckons that when John died in 1850 aged 87, his wealth and landholdings in Burnham, Cippenham and Cookham were sufficient to make his eleven surviving offspring very content indeed.

Old Dick Webster was John the Second's fifth child. In 1841 he married **Mary Ann Cross**, sister of **George Cross the Elder** of Amerden's ***Barge Farm*** [*see Appendix 1, Tree 21*]. Within 20 years, he had taken the tenancy of ***Hill Farm***, more than tripled its size to 960 acres and built a workforce of 30 men and 20 boys only for the high life to get in the way. How he enjoyed spending his inheritance on good living and sporting pursuits, chiefly hunting this and shooting that. The farm has shrunk to less than half its peak but still turns a handsome profit in good years. Dick's third son **George Webster** still lives here with his wife Mary (also his cousin, she being daughter to his Uncle William), their boy John (the Fourth) and baby Kathleen. He is now a coal merchant with his elder brother **Richard Webster** who married Emily, the sister of his own sister Emily's husband George Headington. Richard did well farming at Shoppenhanger's in Bray and has recently gone into partnership with **Robert Plummer** as *Coal, Coke & Salt Factors and General Forage Merchants* in Bray, Cookham and Maidenhead. It's not a catchy strapline but they're selling stuff everybody needs. Meanwhile the word is that his brothers John the Third and George have a new venture in mind....

Hill Farm Road / 6th January 2013

In the early 1890s, this pair of Websters took over the ***Brown & Terry Brewery*** in Burnham along with *The Rose* pub. Within a year or two they were supplying ales, stouts and beers to most of the inns in Burnham and many around about, much of it delivered by Jess & Joe Harris. These Burnham brothers are said to have had a phonograph playing loudly on their handcart at night to give the impression to potential robbers that there were more than two of them. And if their ruse didn't work, perhaps they kept safe by giving footpads information about the gentry.

Wheeler's & Co of Wycombe offered to buy the Websters out in 1905. They were quick to cash in. George invested the proceeds in acquiring ***The Knowle*** from **Walter Millington** but he had enough to spare in 1913 when the opportunity arose to buy back *The Rose* despite being prevented by covenant from brewing there again. When he died in 1926, George left the tidy sum of £21,220 (£5.5m). Seven years later, John the Third went to a better world leaving £21,056 (£5.7m).

Their brother Richard had done the business too. When ***Webster & Plummer*** was eventually dissolved in 1902, he concentrated on being a coal and corn merchant. If early-20th Century photographs of Maidenhead are anything to go by, he had learned a little about the importance of branding. ***Richard Webster & Sons*** advertising signs are plastered everywhere. No persuasive buy-me messages, just presence. It worked. He dominated the local market for coal or corn. How can we be sure? Here's a clue: he was worth £17,092 (£4.2m) when he died in 1930.

Boston Bolthole

The Grange, Back Lane / 6th January 1892

Grange Lodge faces across **Back Lane** into **Pikels**. Maria Meads is waiting for us by her front door, just as her younger sisters **Thirza Simmonds** and Ellen Newman promised she would. We recognise the toothless Paget girl grin. Her husband Robert died in 1886 having been a garden labourer at **Taplow Court** for over 30 years. Now she lives here with her youngest son Fred who does a similar job under head gardener Daniel Paxton. We tell her that Alfie Coe said to ask for Willie Cleal, the coachman here. Oh yes, she says, Willie and Dan have been here years. He knows a thing or two about the Irby family and especially ***The Grange***. She directs us to the stables on the far side of the house. Along the way we meet Fred who has been hard at work with his new lightweight cylinder lawnmower, just perfect for cutting the grass, he says. When we find him, Willie is happy to take a break from polishing tack to share his knowledge. It is a saga of delight, despair and doldrums....

This was the plot of land that **Lord Grenville** offered to **Frederick Irby, 2nd Baron Boston**, after ***Hedsor House*** burned down. He found solace by building a new home here around 1800. It served as the family's country seat for three generations. The third baron (from 1825) and the fourth (from 1856) both spent much of their youth here, as did the latter's sister Charlotte who in 1826 married her Taplow neighbour **Thomas Fitzmaurice**, Viscount Kirkwall, later **5th Earl of Orkney**.

The 4th Lord Boston went from the delight of seeing his son **Florance George Henry Irby** get married to the beautiful Augusta Caroline Saumarez in 1859 to the despair six months later of losing Fanny, his wife of 30 years, and back to delight in 1861 when at 59-years-old he married his daughter-in-law's 22-year-old equally beautiful sister Caroline Amelia Saumarez [*see Appendix 1, Tree 7*]. Meanwhile two grandsons arrived, **George Florance Irby** in 1860 and **Cecil Saumarez Irby** two years later, both born at ***The Grange***, or ***Hill House*** as it was then and had been since its construction. How did that work, given the merry-go-round of this name at the far end of **Church Road**? It can be no surprise that one or other of these illustrious Irbys put poor postmen out of their misery by giving their home a more distinctive name. Frank whispers that it might have helped if they had chosen less complex names for themselves as well.

The effervescent Amelia breathed new life into her George and in return he gave her a daughter, Maud. Sadly their second daughter Dorothy survived only a few days in 1865. Amelia sought solace by encouraging her husband to build *Hedsor House* anew. Their sumptuous home was completed in 1868. It was a memorable achievement – unusually modelled on the Italian Villa style and featuring as its focal point a stunning domed hall rather than the traditional open courtyard – but the delight was all too much for George and within a year Amelia was a widow at 30. She diverted her energy into acquiring the land for and later building a fine church in Lavender Hill, Battersea, dedicated to the Ascension of The Lord. And after Maud died in 1873, she took holy orders as a Benedictine nun, Mother Mary Caroline.

Florance succeeded as **5th Baron Boston** and divided his time between Hedsor and his London residence in Belgrave Square while leaving *The Grange* in the doldrums, an interlude which appeared likely to extend in 1877 when his son George inherited his father's estates and his title as **6th Baron Boston**. However the new 16-year-old Lord Boston was well advised to let *The Grange* for some years to John Yarde-Buller, 2nd Baron Churston, while his younger brother finished school and went off to military adventures with the 7th Battalion of the King's Rifle Corps. It was restored to the family fold in 1885 as home to Cecil and his new wife Florence Dormer. Now their first son Greville is two-years-old, their every need is catered for by seven domestic servants including one of Paxton's five children and both of Cleal's.

Greville and his younger brother Cecil will in turn succeed their Uncle George as Barons Boston but on their father's death in 1935 they will put the house – by then ***Hitcham Grange*** – up for sale only to find no takers until Lord Desborough acquires the property to prevent it being pulled down and the site developed.

Not Scrumping

Back Lane / 6th January 1892

We set off down **Back Lane** again. Past **Pikels** there are three orchards on our right. It is only with difficulty that we resist the temptation to go scrumping.

The furthest down the hill belongs to ***Well Bank***. In years to come it will be split into three. In 1922 St Nicholas' Churchyard will expand into its western half, in part to accommodate the War Memorial. In the early-1930s its north-eastern end will be donated by **Percy Noble** for the construction of ***Elizabeth Cottage*** at the expense of Lord Desborough to commemorate **Elizabeth Grenfell**, wife of his cousin **Charles Seymour Grenfell** of ***Elibank***, to provide a home and surgery for the district nurse. Some 70 years from now, the south-eastern quarter will be occupied by ***Lindens***, the home of **Herbert Chaplin**, an aeronautical engineer famed for his work with *Fairey Aviation* on the design of the dropnose for *Concorde*, an iconic supersonic passenger aircraft. Taplovians will treasure the memory of his son Stanley's wife Pat Chaplin running Taplow's last sub-post-office in ***Wellbank Cottage*** complete with a pilot's chair for customers to relax in.

The second orchard at the slimmer eastern end of **Tothill's** belongs to **William Rance**. Any last chance of scrumping will be gone forever once ***Clent House*** is built there. The first up here belongs to the **Irbys** of ***The Grange***....

Back Lane / 6th January 1938

Evelyn Irby is a problem [*see Appendix 1, Tree 7*]. The eldest child of Florence & Cecil Irby had no intention of meeting her parents' expectations to marry well nor of marrying at all. Worst still, she wanted to earn her living as a sculptress, not as a librarian at the Ministry of Labour. She never got her way but neither did they and life is easier now. Three years ago *Hitcham Grange* passed to her little brother **Greville Irby** who took pity on her plight and last year had a new home built for her in its orchard. It will be said that *Greenham* is one of only two new houses built in Taplow Village between the world wars of the 20th Century. Evelyn will give a portion of its grounds to her gardener Arthur Kitchiner for him to build a small bungalow called *Elsafra* and move there from ***Grange Lodge***, which will be demolished. In her dotage, she will be seen sitting on her balcony sculpting to her heart's content or observing what Taplow is up to through a brass telescope, perhaps the first local Neighbourhood Watch? Her home will eventually and appropriately grow into a new name: ***The Orchard***.

When she buys *Elsafra*, artist Sheila McWilliam will have architect Charles Land of *Wellbank* rebuild it and change its name to ***Allington Cottage***, so-called for her love of Anthony Trollope's *The Small House at Allington*. Her successors Pat & Michael Brining will sell it to **Brenda & Tony Hickman** in 1981.

The Kissing Gate

Station Road / 6th January 1892

The lane becomes **Station Road** at ***Well Corner***. We continue downhill to emerge from the cool shade of overhanging trees into the bright afternoon sunshine spilling across **Town Field** to the south-west. **Jane Poole** and Mary Ann Hubbard are walking towards us along **Ropey**, the footpath that leaves **Town Lane** just behind ***The Dumb Bell*** to run diagonally across Town Field, meet the bottom end of **Old Friend Lane** and skirt the railing that marks the southern edge of **Roque Meadow**. Frank winks at us and positions himself by the kissing-gate where Ropey arrives at Station Road. He has known these two ladies since childhood and intends to levy the traditional price for passing through the gate – and of course they pay happily. They are on their way from Maidenhead to their homes in Hitcham, and from here they will follow **Hummers**, the footpath that runs eastward all the way to ***The Pheasant*** at Lent Green. Their husbands both work for George Hanbury – **Tommy Poole** is a cowman at ***Hitcham Farm*** and Ted Hubbard a gardener at ***Blythewood*** – so we take the opportunity to ask about the modern lord of Hitcham....

Sideways Glance

Something's Brewing – Blythewood Spirits

Tithe Barn, Hitcham / 7th June 2012

Robert Hanbury is feeding me history. Our conversation has gone on for longer than expected – there's a surprise – and his wife **Gillian** has served an unexpected lunch of delicious soup and tasty sandwiches. What kindness.

Robert is the great-grandson of the man who built ***Blythewood***, now ***Hitcham House***. By 1966, this latest Hanbury had had enough of "being in computers in Africa". He returned home to a job near Heathrow and life with Gillian in *Laundry Cottage* while they spent three years and a small fortune on second-hand bricks to renovate (in fact, almost completely rebuild) this late-17th Century tithe barn and make it their home. Now for more of the Hanbury soup....

Blythewood / 7th January 1892

George Hanbury's ancient ancestry was French via Worcestershire in the 13th Century and Wales in the 17th Century. By 1720 his Welsh Quaker great-great-grandfather John Hanbury had established himself in London as the greatest Virginia tobacco merchant of his day, a position he enjoyed until his expansion into northern Pennsylvania was frustrated by the French in 1755. John's grandson Osgood Hanbury continued the tobacco business until 1770 when he began a diversion into banking by investing £5,000 (£10.1m) into *Hanbury, Taylor, Lloyd & Bowman* (a corporate banking ancestor of *Lloyds TSB*). Osgood's son Sampson Hanbury remained friendly with the Friends but let his own devotions lapse after 1788 when he became the major shareholder of *Truman's*, a brewery which had done well in the hands of five Truman generations – the third of which, Ben, really did more put hops in his porter. The firm enjoyed dramatic growth as Sampson and his nephew Thomas Buxton made it ***Truman Hanbury Buxton & Co***. In 1800 Sampson treated himself to *Poles*, an Elizabethan manor house near Ware where he lived in quiet splendour. This Hertfordshire house has been recently rebuilt and will spend 63 years as a convent until in 1990 it becomes a golf and country club called *Hanbury Manor*, a name never used by the Hanburys.

Sampson's son Robert took over the family business. That had been his son George's destiny too until he fell for Mary Trotter, a young Quaker who refused his attentions due to his brewing the demon drink. He duly sold his shares in the family company, became an independent hop merchant and married her in 1857. It was some years before Mary discovered what hops were used for. By then she and George were living happily at Hitcham in *Blythewood*, a very grand gothic revival mansion designed for them by the architect **Roger Smith** and completed in 1867 along with *Home Farm* and various cottages and lodges. Smith's extensive landscaping projects for Hanbury included lining the pond in concrete, an improvement that may well have reduced the flow of the stream sufficiently to put paid to the operation of *One Mile Mill* by the Bath Road. The estate's privacy was improved by sinking ***Hummers*** out-of-sight in a gully and and closing **Love Lane** entirely. This delightfully-named thoroughfare was effectively an extension of **The Gore** which ran south from the kink in **London Road** to who knows where. Its closure was agreed at the General Quarter Session at Aylesbury on 30th December 1867 when one of the justices was a certain Right-Honourable Benjamin Disraeli, Chancellor of the Exchequer. This political giant had spent the previous two years engineering the overthrow of his great rival William Gladstone and the introduction of the Reform Act which enfranchised working men for the first time. He celebrated this historic achievement by closing a footpath but (so far as we know) never suspected that London Road would eventually become **Hitcham Lane** [*see Map 28*].

Why did Hanbury pick Hitcham? The obvious answer is the ease of railway access to London but the local roots of family and friends may have played a part. Mary was the grand-daughter of Thomas Liddell, 1st Baron Ravensworth, of *Britwell Court* and George's grandfather's social reforming zeal had brought him into the circles of William Wilberforce and probably to Lord Grenville at *Dropmore*. Perhaps they heard through one or both of these social grapevines in 1863 that **George Fortescue** was looking to realise a little of his family fortune by selling off a chunk of the Grenville estate.

It wasn't only with his home that George Hanbury made his mark. He was quick to become a Justice of the Peace and to join Sam Quick, landlord of ***The Maypole***, and the Reverend George Frewer, Rector of **St Mary's**, in contributing generously to ***Hitcham Elementary School*** which in 1872 had an attendance of 75 of 97 children in the care of schoolmistress Alice Taylor. The school will continue here until 1927; it will be used by the Scouts throughout the 1930s and will eventually become a house called ***Cloverdown***. The village will for many years have its own post office on the corner of what will be Hitcham Road and Byways. After serving as High Sheriff of Buckinghamshire in 1875, perhaps with a nod and a wink to his brewing competitor neighbour **Charles Pearce-Serocold**, Hanbury turned his hand once more to local philanthropy by funding the Burnham Mission Hall in 1880 and workmen's reading rooms in both Hitcham and Burnham, the latter celebrated by the Blythewood Band playing at its inauguration. He co-founded Paddington Green Children's Hospital in 1883 and five years from now he will cede to St Mary's a field opposite the school for the construction of a new rectory. This will help the Reverend Edward Carter to recover from the embarrassment of the heavy mortgage he had taken to fund the expansion of ***Hitchambury***, but not without the sale of the parsonage and adjacent glebe land for £7,629 (£5.25m), enough for his successor to invest in an extremely comfortable if moderately less grand residence nearer to the church in 1908.

Soon after George's death in 1911, his son the eminent banker **Lionel Hanbury** will perform a different kind of trade by acquiring the land on which the old manor house had stood enabling the newly-refurbished *Blythewood* to be recast as *Hitcham House* and *Home Farm* as ***Hitcham House Farm***. And in 1974 St Mary's will appear as the Reverend Flasher's church in *Carry On Dick* before Tony Hickman designs and supervises the construction of its new parish hall in the early-1980s.

Our Home

Nashdom / 7th June 1912

The Hanburys have new neighbours. Less than a mile to the north of *Hitcham House* near to the site of ***The Waggon & Horses*** stands a grand neo-Regency mansion fit for a Russian prince and his Scottish princess renowned for her love of entertaining. **Prince Alexis Dolgorouki** is a direct descendant of Yuri Dolgorukiy, the founder of Moscow in 1129, of the Rurikid dynasty which ruled Russia until 1605 and of Count Vassili Dolgorouki who was tortured and beheaded in 1739 for forging the will of Tsar Peter II. As Secretary of State, he had been forced into exile after 1881 when Emperor Alexander II was assassinated to prevent

Sideways Glances....

The original Hitcham Manor House / c1800

The Tithe Barn / 1967 & 2012

St Mary's Church / 2012

Hitcham House (formerly *Blythewood*) / 2012

George Hanbury / c1900

Nashdom / 2009

Fanny & Alexis Dolgorouki / c1912

Happy Families

The Websters & Friends at Burnham Beeches / c1900
Standing: Jack Bradford, Emily Webster, Fan Bayley, Harry Baldwin (of Burnham's *Britannia Foundry*), Edith Bayley, George Webster & Fred Bayley
Sitting: John Webster, Mrs Barnet, Mrs Bradford & Daisy Webster

George & Mary Hanbury & Family at *Blythewood* / c1900

Map 28 – Borderers: Sideways Glance

Hitcham Going South

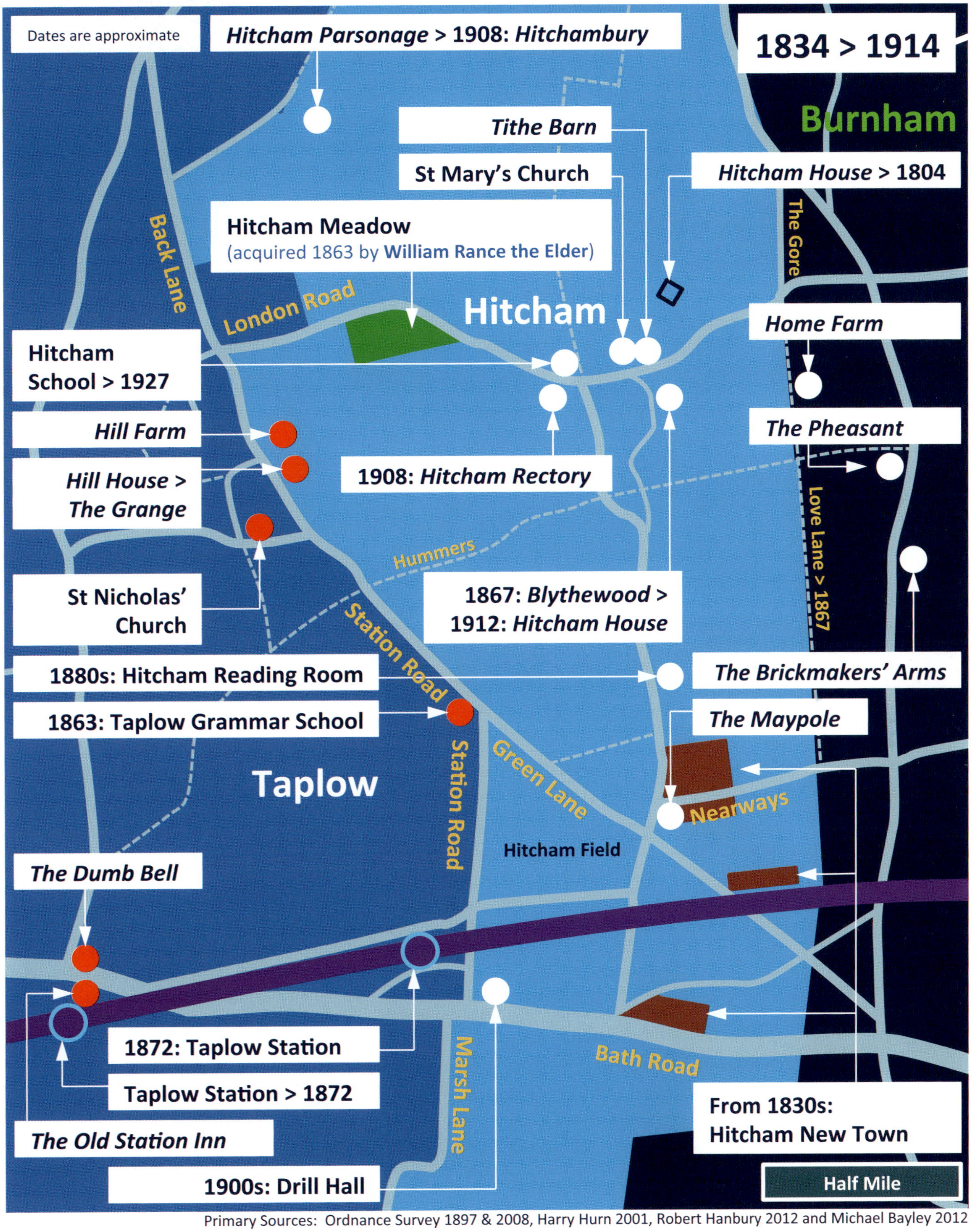

Dates are approximate

Hitcham Parsonage > 1908: *Hitchambury*

1834 > 1914

Burnham

Tithe Barn

St Mary's Church

Hitcham House > 1804

Hitcham Meadow
(acquired 1863 by **William Rance the Elder**)

Back Lane

London Road

Hitcham

The Gore

Home Farm

Hitcham
School > 1927

Hill Farm

The Pheasant

Hill House >
The Grange

1908: *Hitcham Rectory*

Love Lane > 1867

Hummers

St Nicholas'
Church

1867: *Blythewood* >
1912: *Hitcham House*

Station Road

1880s: Hitcham Reading Room

The Brickmakers' Arms

1863: Taplow Grammar School

The Maypole

Taplow

Station Road

Green Lane

Nearways

Hitcham Field

The Dumb Bell

1872: Taplow Station

Taplow Station > 1872

Marsh Lane

Bath Road

From 1830s:
Hitcham New Town

The Old Station Inn

1900s: Drill Hall

Half Mile

Primary Sources: Ordnance Survey 1897 & 2008, Harry Hurn 2001, Robert Hanbury 2012 and Michael Bayley 2012 his constitutional reforms. He was 50 and the heiress Frances (Fanny) Wilson 48 before they found solace in their 1898 marriage and in their adoption of Sacha, a little Russian girl who they "treat in the kindest way and dress in the daintiest garments".

Fanny's father Fleetwood Wilson made his fortune trading in Brazil in partnership with his brother Sir Edward Wilson. She and her prince have residences in France, in London at N° 46 Upper Grosvenor Street and at Old Mar Castle, which they have restyled Braemar Castle. But of course they needed a house in the Thames Valley for weekend river parties and to provide a luxurious setting suitable for exiled royalty to seethe in comfort at the influence that Grigori Rasputin has over Tsar Nicholas II. It is possible they discovered Hitcham through knowing Henry Gage, 5th Viscount Gage, a close friend of the Grenfells. The result is ***Nashdom***, which means *Our Home* in Russian. It was designed "in the spirit of Versailles [and] reminiscent of Roman palaces [with] brilliant manipulation of space and levels" by Edwin Lutyens, who some will decide is "the greatest British architect", and was completed in 1909. It boasts a range of useful features including new-fangled electric lighting, a resident staff of ten servants led by a 75-year-old butler, an alabaster relief of Princess Fanny and, over the main fireplace on the first floor, a decorated map of the area with an arrow indicating wind direction. Every home should have one.

Sadly they are not long for this world – they will meet their ends in France, he in 1915, she four years later – but will be reunited in the graveyard of St Mary's Church, Hitcham. Fanny will leave almost £47,797 (£10.1m) only for *Nashdom* to wander through legal uncertainty until 1926 when Dom Denys Prideaux leads a Benedictine monastic community from Pershore Abbey in Worcestershire. He will be succeeded as Abbot of ***Nashdom Abbey*** by Dom Martin Collet until 1948 and Dom Augustine Morris until 1974. The latter will preside over the addition of a new wing in 1968.

Despite being an enclosed and mainly silent community, it will have a lot to say about things religious in the big wide, world. Lutyens' restrained harmony will be the perfect cloak for an intellectual powerhouse of radical Christian thinking which will be described as Anglican, Anglo-Catholic and "traditional Anglo-Papist" as it seeks to build bridges with Rome and even to reunite with the Holy See on a modern model. Its monks will include a world expert on Canon law, a principal adviser to the Archbishop of Canterbury, Europe's leading authority on Spanish medieval literature and the highly-regarded liturgical scholar and ecclesiastical politician Gregory Dix, its prior from 1948 until his death in 1952. He will be an unusually quotable for a supposedly silent monk for remarks such as: "I really don't see why you should be surprised at the conduct of your fathers-in-God. After all the sign of a Bishop is a crook and of an Archbishop a double-cross". He will describe bishops as Edwardian for they are "strictly Edward VI in theology, strictly Edward VII in mental equipment and strictly Edward VIII in their views on marriage". The Right Reverend Kenneth Kirk, Bishop of Oxford, will remember him as "the most brilliant man in the Church of England".

Some will say the Abbey's edge softened in Morris's later years and under his successor Dom Wilfrid Weston until 1987 when the Benedictines depart for Elmore Abbey near Newbury. After aspirations in 1988 as a hotel and in 1989 as a conference centre cum 'health hydro', Nashdom will once more be lost in the wilderness until 1997 when the house is renovated to accommodate 15 luxury apartments with 13 more in a new East Wing – a different kind of enclosed community enjoying a solarium, a gymnasium and the restored 17-acre grounds complete with a tennis court and a heated outdoor pool.

Inbetweeners

A Minor Alma Mater

Upper Station Road / 7th February 1892

The view downhill from the **Ropey** kissing-gate is one of contrast. The phalanx of 50-foot elms marching down the Hitcham side of Station Road makes the string of houses on the Taplow side seem like toy sentinels watching over Hitcham's foreign fields to the east. The effect is exaggerated because the first houses we can see are single-storey.

As we approach, **Frank Hearn** says these are somehow 'halfway houses' for being in neither the Village nor the Valley. He thinks two – ***The Limes*** and ***Cranford House*** – may be of Georgian vintage. The latter was certainly here in 1852 to be acquired by James Pearce. Now it is *Acacia Villa* and home to music teacher **Elizabeth Lambourne**. She and her late timber merchant husband **George** have lived there for many years, probably since before 1857 when he acquired *The Limes* from **William Davis Briginshaw** but there's no telling if Farmer Briginshaw built the mansion or bought it. The upshot is that **Edward Dyke** came from Wiltshire in 1863 to turn it into a school with classrooms and dormitories added at the back. It began as Upton Cross School and that may still be its official name but everyone calls it **Taplow Grammar School**, including Mr Dyke who remains its principal. Right on cue, here come two schoolboys to tell us all about this neck of the woods....

George Hebbes is chattering to his brother Henry about **William Gurney** who they saw in church last Sunday. He was one of the older boys when I started here, says George. Six years ago he caused havoc when he ran away to sea. His younger brother Albert ran up to tell their Uncle William, the Village grocer, and soon it was the talk of the town. The boy's mother runs the family bakery and corn chandlery in Amersham but he didn't much fancy life as a shopkeeper. Somehow he got to Glasgow and tried to sign on join the crew of the *Ben Larigg*. When the captain found the lad was only 14 he sent him packing but was happy to take him on a couple of years later and he's been sailing the world ever since.

The Hebbes brothers are the only local lads of the 138 pupils from 8-to-18-years-old currently at the school. Their father George, a corn and coal merchant in Burnham, and their uncle Henry, the Haymill miller, are typical of the small businessmen, middle-managers, colonial administrators and junior officers who have responded to one of Mr Dyke's advertisements in *The Times* such as that published on 4th March 1880....

"EDUCATION - TAPLOW GRAMMAR SCHOOL, Maidenhead, 20 miles from London. 30 guineas (£20,500), no extras, no charge for laundress or books. Extensive premises well adapted and healthily situate: 20 acres of grounds, affording every facility for out-door recreation, cricket, bathing &c. Pure milk and vegetables from school farm. Preparatory department. Principal has been a successful tutor for many years. No corporal punishment. No quarter's notice".

How does an educated man put Taplow in Maidenhead? The reason is simple. Maidenhead is well known and its image more important than tedious factual accuracy. The commitment to administer no corporal punishment is unusual and has perhaps encouraged boys to follow their fathers' dreams of their being educated in the way of the great British public schools but rather more economically. Ever since the late-1860s, Mr Dyke has had well over 100 boys in his care, some as young as 4-years-old. Most of his charges are from London but he attracts others from right across the UK and British subjects from faraway places. Right now he has boys born in Austria, France, Germany, India, Natal, Persia, South America and Switzerland not to mention those from Ireland, the Isle of Man and Jersey in the British Isles. And in the past they have come from Australia, China, Guernsey, Jamaica, Mauritania, Russia, Trinidad, the USA and even one born at sea.

Frank is frowning. Mental arithmetic is in process. A raise of his eyebrows signals the sum is complete. So that means, he says slowly, that old Dyke rakes in something like £4,300-a-year (£2.8m) compared to my measly £75 (£49,000) as Mr Rance's farm foreman? No wonder he's been able to lease not only the Hitcham glebe farmland across the road but also to acquire either the leasehold or freehold of property in **Station Road**, **Fairview Road**, **Lent Rise** and Lent Green and in Forlease Road, Maidenhead. When he retires in a year or two, Dyke will continue to live locally until his death in 1914. Meanwhile Alexander Lane and the Reverend Alfred Bachelor will take over as joint Principals until Lane's departure leaves Bachelor in sole charge. Sometime after 1907 he will be succeeded briefly by William Wyndham-Smith and in 1912 by joint Principals Kenneth Waterlow and James Hargreaves who, in the mid-1920s, will be left to continue alone with his daughter Patricia, the only girl in the school. He will hand over in 1939 to William Williams.

The Halfway Houses

Upper Station Road / 7th February 1892

George Hebbes is 14-years-old and bright as a button. He says we mustn't forget how far that money goes. In addition to Mr Leyster, who walks down from the village with his black gown flapping behind him, Mr Dyke has five assistant schoolmasters, the matron Miss Kate Harrington and her nine domestic staff living at the school. He also employs many of the little community of 59 souls along here, either directly or indirectly. The first two houses belong to him: his coachman **Joe Talbot** is at ***The Lodge*** and his launderess **Hannah Jaycock** is next door. Her late husband William used to be Mr Dyke's gardener; their youngest son Charlie is his errand-boy and their eldest Will is the school caretaker and handyman. And further up the road his groom Tom Easton is in the southernmost of ***Sidney Cottages***. Henry interrupts to say that, being single-storey, *Sidney Cottages* should be called *Sidney Bungalows* according to his friend Frederick Briggs who was born in India where the word *bungalow* comes from. George ignores his little brother. And in between, he continues, there's our music teacher Mrs Lambourne, the current school gardeners **Fred Bovington**, Henry Sales and Harry Hooper, carpenters **Billy Simmonds**, Henry Collett and Tom Swabey, who help young Mr Jaycock, and Caroline Swabey and her daughter Maggie, who help Mrs Jaycock with the laundry.

Frank's penny has well-and-truly dropped. As 9-year-old Arthur Hooper dashes past spinning his hoop, he muses that the boy's blacksmith father **William Hooper** must do a roaring trade at his forge behind *Sidney Cottages*, what with all the carriages and horses that come-and-go hereabouts needing their shoes, hooves and tack kept in trim. And although her husband John passed away not long ago, Isabella Pusey must be making a mint as her sons William, George and John drive their flies to-and-from the station. Henry Rich the butcher and James Chambers our village policeman are odd ones out in that they have little if any direct link to the school. Henry learned his trade from William Rance the Elder and still works for the Younger, so Frank can see why he lives not far away, but what on earth is a copper doing here?

Henry Hebbes is only 12 but he knows the answer to that. When the Buckinghamshire Police Force was founded in 1856, Taplow fell into the Burnham precinct of the Slough Division under the command of Superintendent John Symington and, while he can't recall the name of the sergeant in charge at Burnham, he is certain that Police Constable William Denham was installed to keep the peace hereabouts. PC Chambers succeed him in the late-1870s. Frank chips in with a childhood memory of PC Denham in his frock coat and a top hat strengthened with cane to enable him to stand on it to peer over high walls. He wonders if it is true that Denham was seen wielding a cutlass instead of his usual stick when an election in Burnham became rather unruly.

A distinctly Welsh baritone voice calls the boys' names. We turn to see one of the assistant schoolmasters waving them to come into school. George says it's Mr Jones. Henry adds that he's from Llanryst, wherever that may be when you can say it. The boys grin and they're gone.

A Fine Rendering

Elibank / 26th April 1894

(Charles) **Seymour Grenfell** smiles with quiet pride and a little amusement as he reads this week's *Maidenhead Advertiser* report on two grand concerts "on Wednesday last... in the spacious gymnasium and lecture-hall of Taplow Grammar School... under the patronage" of Lady **Louisa Fortescue** (of **Dropmore**), Mrs **Mary (Mamie) Astor** (of **Cliveden**) and Mrs **Ethel Grenfell** (of **Taplow Court**) "and other notabilities". His pride is founded in the reference to his daughter Miss Cicely Grenfell, a young lady of "local habitation and notable fame brought down the house with her fine rendering on the violin of Gounod's *Ave Maria*". His amusement is in anticipating his wife Elizabeth's reaction. He passes her the newspaper and watches her face carefully. One eyebrow rises slightly at the curt description of ***Elibank*** as "local habitation". Her eyes widen as she realises she is an "other notability". She can't resist observing that at least – unlike certain "other notabilities" – she didn't think that the principal performer Miss Amy Sargeant is the daughter of William Sargent, landlord of ***The Queen's Head***. Charles isn't so sure but keeps his counsel.

Hurn's Turn – No Longer on the Edge

School Corner / 7th February 1937

Freddie Hurn's son Everett takes up the story....

This has been a three-way corner for as long as anyone can remember, he says, but things are different now. Once the muddy and rutted Green Lane ran uphill and down from this junction where it met another track running south along the parish boundary to the arch under the railway embankment. When the new station opened in 1872 this southerly track and the northern stretch of Green Lane were widened and re-invented as **Station Road** because that's where it went. Now after all these years the southern stretch of Green Lane is being upgraded for important people with cars to drive along. Everett isn't sure if they were important before they acquired their cars but they behave as if they are now they've got them.

A car pulls out of the gates of Taplow Grammar School. Headmaster James Hargreaves is at the wheel, his daughter Patricia beside him. Back in the 1920s she was the only girl in the school then and perhaps ever. Hargreaves heads down Green Lane and turns right onto Hitcham Road. He'll be going to Fairview, says Everett. The school has taken over ***May Cottage*** as a sanatorium for sick boys. They've put a corrugated-iron roof down one side to give shelter to a terrace for open-air treatment. One day this will be N° 60 Fairview Road.

We turn north and head up the northern stretch of Station Road. The first house past the School was once the school's coach house. **Joe Talbot** and his family live next door. He was once a coachman but now runs a taxi service often used by villagers to get down to the station – but only rarely by cheery **Cecil Dowson**. Despite being close to 80-years-old the old fellow always walks from ***Guildersfield*** to the station with a half-smoked cigar clenched in his teeth and an umbrella either swinging or unfurled and held aloft if the Heavens have opened. His son **Noel Dowson** emerges from ***Old Lodge*** to join him and together they march to *Wyman's Bookstall* where buy their newspapers before travelling to the offices of their family firm, ***Dowson & Sankey***, solicitors of St James's. Only if the day has been tiring and the weather is wet will accept a ride up the hill on the way home.

Next to the Talbots at ***The Laurels*** lives Miss Lovat with a companion and 20 cats on an allowance disbursed by the Rector from the Distressed Gentlefolks Society. She is a timid, kindly eccentric reputed to be connected to a notable Scottish family and to be rather fond of "a little drop of something to do you good, dear".

We pass ***Cranford House*** and come to the home of three elderly Blythe sisters. Everett's son Harry thinks them real characters, the sort of people one would only expect to meet in novels, the acknowledged aristocrats of the road. Just as he adds that Miss Ethel had been honoured with an OBE for her service during the Great War, the three dear old ladies emerge and head for the church. They are dressed in black in a fashion at least 20 years out of date. The tall and stately Misses Ethel and Alice walk side-by-side with the tiny Miss Agnes behind them under the shade of a parasol with a fringe of bobbles. They nod their greetings to Grandfer Stannett who lives a few doors along with two of his daughters and grandson Jackie. As usual, Grandfer has a knee pad of red rubber tied around his right knee. He's an old-fashioned gardener over at Hitcham Rectory, a rather severe, honest nonconformist with strict views on life, an attitude which makes it all the more fun for Harry to scrump the blackberries he grows on his back fence.

If it's not the blackberries he's after, smiles Everett, it's the apples in the back garden of *Cranford House*. The thought puts him in mind of little Olive Otway who lived there at *Blenheim*. It must be ten years ago that Mr Hargreaves caught her blackberrying in the school field and chased her out. And it must be more than 15 years since Miss **Simmonds** opened ***The Tuck Shop*** in Tom Easton's old place, the southern of ***Sidney Cottages***. Ethel & Bobbie Baily took over in a few years back. There can be no stronger supporter of *The British Legion* than Bobbie who was the butler up the road at ***The Priory*** until being severely wounded during the Great War and left with a hunched back and only one arm. As usual on sunny days like today, the warm and friendly fellow is sitting in his garden with his headphones on listening to one of the first wireless sets in the road. When the boys at the Grammar School have their break, he will be ready to take their pocket money in exchange for tins of fruit, biscuits, soft drinks and their favourite treat – *Lyon's* lime sweets.

The string of 'halfway houses' is completed by the Jeffreys pair at the northern end, built in the early-1890s. Within a few years, the experienced **Hannah Jaycock** moved up the road to take over the laundry here. It's still going, catering for the school and for the big houses where no laundry maid is kept. Heavy wicker hampers arrive every Mondays and until Wednesday four or five women stand at the worktubs inside the long window, all chattering like sparrows as they scrub the wash with stiff brushes and hang it out to dry on long lines strung across the garden. They spend Thursdays and Fridays at long tables pressing the clean laundry with flat irons heated on a coke stove in the middle of the room. And on Saturdays they pack it all back in the hampers and send them home. Among the washerwomen are little old Mrs Wheeler and two of her daughters. She claims descent from the Romany tribe and is very proud of never having washed her long dark hair in her life; she keeps it clean and fresh by constant brushing – a tip that might not go amiss in 70 years when the laundry has become ***The Ivy Retreat***, a health and beauty treatment centre run by **Louise Symons**.

The former glebe land over the road once leased to **Edward Dyke** of the Grammar School was acquired from Hitcham Rectory in 1920 by **Janie Dykes**, a Scot with no relation to the headmaster. Soon afterwards she built a bungalow for her farmhands and ***Lea Rig*** for herself and her late husband Jackie. She lives there alone now with her son **Andrew Dykes** and his wife in the bungalow. They sow their fields with oats, barley or wheat rotating with potatoes, kale and mangolds. The ashes of last year's fire can still be seen in the north-west corner of the field to the south of **Hummers** footpath. Four huge wheat ricks were set alight, probably by a tramp while lighting his pipe. Nobody can ever remember seeing such a blaze. After the first night, the flames settled down into a solid mass glowing like molten gold and smouldering for weeks. Something else is still smouldering, says Everett. Most people still haven't got used to the carving up of Hitcham's civil parish between Taplow and Burnham in 1934. *Lea Rig* is in Taplow but its driveway comes out onto Lent Rise Road, part of Burnham.

School's Out

The Lodge, Station Road / 22nd March 2008

Janie sold *Lea Rig Farm* in 1950 for £9,000 (£845,000) to a chap called Ballard, a garage proprietor who ten months later will take £11,850 (£1m) for it from **John Shepherd**, a very tidy profit of 18% even after allowing for economic deflation. That same year, unable to afford to provide facilities such as science laboratories required by the 1944 Education Act, its principal William Williams was obliged to close **Taplow Grammar School**. Soon afterwards, starved of boys with pennies in their pockets, the widowed Ethel Baily turned ***The Tuck Shop*** back into a cottage with a new name, ***The Nook***, the School's outbuildings were demolished and what was once *The Limes* converted to flats and renamed ***Hillmead***. By then, **Everett Hurn** had moved out of Taplow, although he came back to tend ***The Rectory*** garden each day and to be buried in St Nicolas' Churchyard in 1963.

This cottage was the School's lodge, occupied in 1891 by coachman **Joe Talbot**. Now it is home to **Esther & Jonathan Willmore** and, since the early-1980s, the last remnant of the School which was demolished and replaced by ***Hillmead Court***, a new block of flats that recycled the old mansion's most recent name. Jon looks uphill to Hummers and is saddened to see that the storm last night blew down an old chestnut tree. Despite it being Easter Saturday the footpath is quickly cleared with the help of volunteers and a chainsaw borrowed from the riding stables. As John Shepherd the Younger repairs the fencing, Jon recalls another Saturday 40 years ago....

Eyes of a Child – Jonathan Willmore

Hummers Footpath / 22nd March 1958

Young Jonathan saw the sign – *Beware of the Bull* – but it looks so decrepit nowadays that, just like everyone else, he ignored it. Perhaps that wasn't so wise for up ahead in the leafy shade of an old chestnut tree there stands a formidable presence rather closer to the path than is comfortable for anyone on it. John Shepherd the Elder's prize bull hears the boy approaching and turns his head with the apparently leisurely menace of a beast used to having its own way. Jon stops in his tracks, his heart beating fast. Should he retrace his tracks, dash onwards to Lent Rise or stroll past pretending nonchalance? He opts for the latter strategy only to break into a helter-skelter sprint as soon as he is past the animal which, of course, couldn't care less.

On the Verge

Boundary Road / 7th August 1986

Hundreds of elms once graced Taplow. **Arthur Grout** reckons those hereabouts must have been home to a murmuration of 100,000 starlings which would take off simultaneously and wheel across the skies in an awesome compact cloud. Sadly every tree was lost to Dutch elm disease in the ten years from 1972. It is nearly four years since **Bob Hanbury** galvanised the **Hitcham & Taplow Preservation Society** into action to restore something of what was along the eastern verge of Boundary Road.

The first step was to obtain written approval or at least confirmation of no objection from all the statutory bodies: the Highways Department, the Post Office (for its telephone lines) and the gas, electricity and water boards. And then in the autumn of 1983, working parties swung into action – first to prepare the planting sites by applying weedkiller and then, a few months later, to dig holes big enough so the subsoil could be broken up to give every tree the best chance of survival. A total of 42 trees have been planted in four years. There are 18 different species: hands up who can tell larches and the liquidambar from walnuts, the willow and the kayaki (*Zelcova serrat*).

Most people were pleased but some were not, smiles Bob. One resident protested vociferously to his newly-enjoyed view being impaired. Another emerged after dark to dig up recently planted trees. The southern stretch has presented most problems due to its increased exposure and a grass fire which started on the allotments and destroyed a number of trees. But Bob's biggest challenge has been going up and down the hill to give each young tree a gallon or two of water each week throughout the summers. And now today's work is complete, he is looking forward to watching the line of trees flourish in years to come. What he doesn't yet realise is that he has built himself such a reputation that his expertise will be called upon again in 1991 when 15 trees are planted on the Recreation Ground.

Amid the Diggings

Lower Station Road / 7th February 1892

George Pusey and his horse-and-fly await us outside his house. We climb aboard, he clicks and flicks the reins and we're off on the next stage of our journey, turning right at the **Grammar School** into lower **Station Road**, the stretch that will still have that name after 1950.

George nods towards the vast reverse L-shape depression to the west. It was from this quarry in the south-west quarter of **Town Field** that millions of tons of gravel were dug to build and then widen the railway embankments here and through Maidenhead. The workings began in the 1830s and continued on and off for over 30 years. It was somewhere at the toe of the L that the remains of the woolly rhino, mammoth and musk ox were unearthed in 1854. George adds that a number of gentlemen have been seen poking around there recently – all very official they looked, and of great interest to Lord Boston and Mr Rutland who both came down to talk with them as they pored over maps, dug pits, made notes and carted samples away – so he went to peruse the newspapers in the Reading Room to see if he could see what's what. Something called the **Ordnance Geological Survey** is apparently doing some kind of nationwide study of what Britain is made of – and what's more, one fellow by the name of **John Rhodes** is getting excited about the **Thames Terraces**, whatever they are.

Hitcham Field is to our left. Diggings there have left a cliff where sandmartins burrow. Up ahead a track runs along the bottom of the embankment, a remnant of its construction, and a railway siding slopes steeply down a cutting from the main line to ***Cade's Coalyard***, the pens and briars where livestock waits on its way to market and the stables and coachhouses where the big houses keep horses and carriages. A spur doglegs back east, crosses the track – the **Women's Institute** hasn't yet been invented so nobody has a clue that one day this will be **Institute Road** – and eases round a curve to end parallel with Hitcham Road. As its name suggests, Hitcham Field is still in Hitcham. It will remain so until most of it defects to Taplow in the 1934 boundary changes. In 68 years this too will be excavated for the gravel that lies beneath. But first it will have another tale to tell....

Harding Happening – Riding the Rails

Hitcham Field / 7th February 1946

During the war, railway passengers dubbed Taplow 'the barbed-wire capital of Britain'. They could look down from their trains to see *Hitcham Field* packed with great piles of the stuff piled 15 or 20 feet high. The vicious whorls are gone now – sold off to Argentina, so they say – leaving the whole field carpeted in dusty orange rust. Eleven-year-old **Anthony Harding** doesn't care. He and his pal **Michael Mann** have sneaked in here to play on the bogeys which still run along the remains of the narrow-gauge tracks once used to move the barbed wire to the old siding. It's a good job no jobsworth has yet invented health-and-safety.

The Beaujolais Brothers

Grovefield Hotel, Taplow Common Road / 24th November 1974

Philip and **Alan Langton** have something to celebrate. This morning in their *Reliant Scimitar SE5* they won the third 'open' *Beaujolais Run*, a contest in which lovers of both fast cars and fine wine vie to be first from Burgundy to London with a case of freshly-bottled *Beaujolais Nouveau*. What a way to put their new business on the map.

It is new for them, of course, but ***Station Garage Taplow*** (*SGT*) has been going for 56 years. They say **Edwin Johnson** came home from the Great War to rent a couple of the old coachhouses where he maintained motor cars and ran excursions in ***The Taplow Queen***, an eight-door bus with a canvas roof that could be folded back so its 16 passengers could enjoy the thrill of the road. Soon Edwin was garaging his small fleet of taxis, lorries and buses in the former stables and coal sheds, selling petrol in their forecourt and piling the likes of **Taplow Cricket Club**, Burnham Rifle Club and others into *The Queen* at weekends to carry them off to play away. The business lasted well enough until after the Second War when its founder passed away. Bigger competitors were better located on the Bath Road. *SGT* struggled until 1959 when a gambling debt was settled in *The Oak & Saw* and its new owner – *Station Garage Amersham & Chalfont* – gave it new life repairing *Rolls Royces* and *Bentleys* throughout the 1960s

Philip was a photographer with cars in his heart. He acquired *SGT* in 1971 and the following year took into partnership his brother Alan, until then a manager at ***Maidenhead Autos***. Their life in the fast lane together started in a caravan on the forecourt where the boys lived for nine months while the frontage was rebuilt, some of the old sheds were converted into workshops and the railway siding and its coal chute down the embankment were removed. The pace picked up when national newspapers featured photographs of them exchanging a *Rolls Royce* for a wad of banknotes from Max 'Superhod' Quartermain of Burnham, a fellow famous for earning more carrying bricklayers' plaster than did Harold Wilson for being Prime Minister.

Bigger competitors are better located on the Bath Road. ***Skindles Garage*** began as a repair shop with a couple of petrol pumps and evolved to an *Esso* petrol station and eventually into Martin Bending's *Volkswagen* sales (on the way to being *Windrush VW*). Alan's old boss Malcolm Wallace had the ***Taplow Motor Co*** by ***The Old Station Inn*** before acquiring ***The Dumb Bell*** across the road in the late-1950s, when the old inn and its garage were demolished and replaced by *Maidenhead Autos* (which will one day be *Sytner BMW*). And yet the Langton boys are carving out a unique market by selling and servicing an eclectic range that will grow to about 20 marques including *Alfa Romeo*, *Lotus*, *Mitsubishi*, *Morgan* and *Subaru* cars plus *Kawasaki*, *Silk* and *Triumph* motorcycles. Customers such as Ernie Wise, **Terry Wogan**, **Helen Grellier** (of ***Victoria Cottage***) and **Norman Stevens** (of ***Berry Hill Farm***) will appreciate their keen eye for cars and a relaxed style typified by their leaving vehicles unlocked on the forecourt when everyone adjourns for lunch in ***The Oak & Saw*** – but only if Alan phones ahead to order sandwiches, otherwise it will be crisps or nothing.

In its best year, the company will sell 600 motorcycles and 1,200 cars. At its peak, it will employ 70 local people. Long-serving stalwarts will include John McNaught, Jane Godfrey, Brian Clarke, Melvyn Perks, Julian Milne (later a Maidenhead car dealer) and Mike Goldsworthy (later at **Taplow Lake**). Alan will smile to recall the workshop lads going on strike when he agreed to sell the fibreglass, three-wheeled *Reliant Robin*. His children will never forgive him for taking one as his company car.

Station Road / 7th February 2014

SGT has had its day. The Langtons sold its site last year. Its journey from cowsheds and coaldust to cars aspired to 44 flats in 2003 and will soon see 66 flats in **Lansdowne Place**. If their dreams come true, there may also be 14 'affordable' cottages opposite the Scouts' & Guides' Huts. They call it progress.

All Steamed Up

Taplow Station / 7th February 1892

George Pusey halts his fly where **Station Road** meets the track in the lea of the embankment. At the far side of *Hitcham Field*, people are busy unloading goods onto carts from flatbed trucks left at the end of the siding by a locomotive which is now puffing back towards the dogleg. That's *Europa*, says George, one of the last of Sir Daniel Gooch's locos, a saddle-tank *Ariadne Class* Standard Goods 0-6-0, been in service nearly 40 years. She stops with a gasp and seethes steam as if gathering energy to climb up to the main line. The cattle jostle nervously in their pens. Two GWR pointsmen manually switch the siding's points. *Europa* whistles, jerks into motion once more and grunts up the incline.

George jerks the fly into motion once more and turns right to climb the hill to Taplow Station. Now we can take in the whole railway scene. This is where the *GWR* began over a half-a-century ago when they hauled *North Star* up what is not yet called Approach Road to be lifted onto the tracks for the first time. Most passengers go from here to Paddington and back, so flies and carriages usually drop-off by the ticket office on this side of the tracks and pick-up from the southern side. The narrow-gauge local lines are nearest to us. On the main line mixed-gauge tracks beyond, a locomotive pulling an express from Newton Abbott and Bristol seems to float in a wreath of steam as her enormous eight-foot driving wheels begin to ease her away from the platform, her last stop before Paddington. That's *Tornado*, says George, the last of William Dean's *Rover Class* 4-2-2 *Iron Duke* Renewal, just three years old but her days are numbered because the *Great Western Railway* will complete tearing up its old broad-gauge tracks next year. We watch in awe as *Tornado* rolls gracefully towards the eastern horizon seducing our eyes to the vast goods yards either side of the tracks. *Europa* is just cresting the rise on the north side, her effort and achievement celebrated by a high-and-wide pall of billowing black smoke tinged with a silver lining of white steam as it reaches for the blue sky above. The main goods yard is on the south side. A cloud of dust seems to hang over its massive coal bunkers. This work-a-day and grimy scene will be transformed by 2014 when Alan Langton will be selling mini-cars by its entrance and further along Chris Wartho will run *SGT Services*, an after-sales offshoot of the original.

As *Tornado*'s clouds begin to clear, her erstwhile passengers surge out of the station eager for horse-drawn transport to speed them on their way. The southern concourse is hectic with hackney carriages for hire and even here on Approach Road coachmen from the big houses jostle for position to save their masters and mistresses from having too far to walk.

Taplow Station / 7th May 1912

Lord Desborough should be here to see ***Taplow Court*** steam past. Having been constructed at Swindon by the innovative GWR Chief Mechanical Engineer GJ Churchman, this *Saint* Class 4-6-0 locomotive 2950 is being taken into service at Old Oak Common. She will pull passenger coaches from Paddington to Bristol and back until September 1952.

All Change

Taplow Station Yard / 7th February 1968

This used to be such a busy place, especially during the war when Canadian Army tanks would wait with menace in the arc south of **Taplow Station**. The slope up to the tracks was reinforced with concrete and steel so tanks could trundle off trains for storage either here, or more usually at 'the dump' on Slough Trading Estate, until they retraced their tracks to be taken wherever the action was. And there was plenty of action when nosy youngsters like **Anthony Harding** had to be chased away to avoid their appearance on film with Margaret Lockwood as she arrived to catch a train in the spy thriller *Highly Dangerous* (1950). And yet five years ago, the goods depot was handling only 5,000 tons of freight each week, the lowest volume of any depot noted in Dr Richard Beeching's report *The Reshaping of British Railways* (1963). Closure was inevitable. Two other uses continued – the coal distribution depot and the training centre for *British Rail* road vehicle drivers – and it enjoyed a new lease of life as home to the *Great Western Society*'s early acquisitions of historic rolling stock. However last November these exhibits were transferred to their permanent home at Didcot, the training centre will go next year and Taplow's last shunting engine will follow in a decade when the coal depot closes. The Old Station Yard will be left to find employment in the sales, maintenance or breaking-up of cars.

Meanwhile the station will feature on the cover of the album *Back to the Future* (1973) by *Man* and its south car park and Platform 1 will feature in the TV series *Shillingbury Tales* (1981) and star on the silver screen as Cambridge Station in *Chariots of Fire* (1981). And Platforms 3 and 4 will have a bit part as Northallerton Station in the TV series *Catterick* (2004).

Gone but not Forgotten

Taplow Grammar School / c1940

The Maypole / 2012

***Station Garage Taplow*: Alan & Philip Langton with customer Ernie Wise** / c1983

The Valley People

Sideways Glance

A Quick Half

The Maypole / 7th February 1892

George asks if we're ready for a quick half in Hitcham. If this seems a strange place to start the third stage of our pub crawl, any half-hearted objection to venturing out of Taplow quickly disappears in the cool, dark public bar as our cool, dark half-pint of ***Truman Hanbury & Buxton*** oatmeal stout disappears inside us. Sam Quick reckons his pub might originally have been called *The Retreat* but it's all guesswork as far as he's concerned, him being from Somerset and all. He's pleased everyone dances around ***The Maypole*** now and would we like another?

We'd better not. We're here to hear how Hitcham has changed. Sam's wife Caroline says how lucky we are because five fine fellows sitting over there know all there is to know. **Tom Neighbour** is a 65-year-old agricultural labourer who has lived in New Town for more than 40 years. We met **Tommy Poole**'s wife Jane earlier. He is a 46-year-old cowman on ***Home Farm*** whose family has worked the land for generations. **Will Lambourne** (34) and **Joe Bunce** (22) both live down in **Marsh Lane** and **Alf Jaycock** (32) on the **Bath Road**. They share deep local roots and ***GWR*** employment as a nightwatchman, a platelayer and a porter respectively. All are related to their namesakes we've already met. Ales of their choice to set their chins wagging....

Tom says that the parish of Hitcham is as long and thin as Taplow. Wherever you are, it's likely you can see both its east and west but it's five miles if it's a foot from its high top at ***Hales Corner*** and ***Sheepcote*** to its boggy bottom at the end of Marsh Lane. Like Taplow it was woods and the common up top, pasture in the middle and arable down south. **Hitcham New Town** began with Grenville's land-swap in 1796 – its first inhabitants included carpenter Joshua Pond, labourer Joseph Pitt, their wives and 14 children – and expanded after the railway came to be an urban slice sandwiched between the pasture and the arable.

Tommy reckons it's a different world up on the common where the Ludgates, Martins, Howards and Houses plod on their own sweet way and, although old Hoppy **Hanbury** has been busy with ***Blythewood***, he has kept the village much to itself. All the talk up there is of the Reverend Frewer catching the school assistant Blanche Rogers behind some hedge having a kiss-and-cuddle with Teddy Lloyd, one of Hoppy's grooms.

The conversation moves south to where the big changes have happened. Alf reckons it must have been one of her Fortescue relations who suggested to the dowager **Lady Grenville** that the coming of the railway was an opportunity too good to miss because it was around 1840 that we suddenly saw new houses being built down here. Tom says there was only a dozen-and-a-half in 1851 when he used to wile away an hour or two playing dominoes in here. There'd be the Chelsea Pensioners Tom Meads and Billy Bristo, father and son coal merchants **Tom** and **Tommy Plummer**, and that railway contractor **Ambrose Oliver** whose wife Catherine would bang on the door when she thought he'd been off the leash long enough. Those were the days, he says with a melancholic smile; long gone, retorts Joe with a wry observation that it was too good an opportunity for Hoppy to miss, wasn't it? Now there must be nearly six times as many houses if you include those at **Fair View** and by the Bath Road. He reckons Jimmy Cox is a good example of how people have adapted – he is a platelayer but his family go way back as farmhands – and now about one third of the menfolk here work for the *GWR* as engine drivers, porters, platelayers, pointsmen, brakesmen, signalmen, clerks and all. Whole families are 'on the railway': Fred Sawyer and his father Bill and his uncle Jim, for instance.

Will adds that other locals stick to their trades: **George Jeffries** is a carpenter, **Henry Jeffreys** an odd-jobbing labourer and Anne Etchells a needlewoman. But Anne's daughter Edith is a telegraphist, says Tom, and you can't get much more modern than that. And the railway brings trade to various independents like William Williams and his sons Billy and Henry, who do much of the painting and plumbing at the station and in the goods yard. The Howard clan has found its way down here too, laughs Joe: old **Dick Howard** still oddjobs at 62 and his sons Willie and Jim are doing well enough as a gardener and the New Town grocer. Alf pipes up that we've even got our own posh boys' school: *The Beeches*, run by Mademoiselle Frances le Mauge. How very *francais*, jokes Will. From Knightsbridge, counters Alf, but some of her 20 pupils come from exotic places like Ceylon and Uruguay so she's hot on Mr Dyke's heels. Yeah right, chuckles Sam, now would we like another? Oh, go on then. After all, no point in visiting Ezra Green at ***The Mile House*** – or is it ***The Horse & Groom*** – because it'll be over 100 years before it leaves Hitcham for Taplow, and by then it'll be a day nursery next to a *Sainsbury's* supermarket (whatever that is).

A Slow Blending

The Maypole / 7th February 2013

The old black-and-white pub is shut. Not closed until opening time. Shut. The doors of are locked dead tight, the windows blinded by metal sheets. Later this year it will revive as ***The Olive Tree***. Let's hope the new name brings new life. Over at Lent Rise, ***The Brickmaker's Arms*** is still going but ***The Pheasant*** isnt so lucky: a half-hearted attempt at renovation will soon give up and it will be replaced by two houses.

Hitcham New Town isn't easy to discern at first glance. It has rather blended into the edge of expanding Lent Rise which itself has been swallowed by Burnham. It takes a little imagination to picture New Town's evolution. It began as three outposts amidst tree-lined fields. The original houses trickled down the eastern side of **Hitcham Road** from *The Old Reading Room* to ***The Maypole***. They were soon joined by the semi-detached cottages of Fair View running parallel with the railway and by a cluster of cottages on the **Bath Road** east of its junction with Hitcham Road. This trio gradually grew together. The fair view across fields from Fair View (now **Fairview Road**) was filled by the houses on **Maypole Road**, **Eastfield Road** (formerly **Nearways**), **Byways** and **Hanbury Close** – which might have been Hanbury's Close had not Robert Hanbury pointed out that, once the land had been compulsorily purchased, it was no longer his possession. A small industrial estate still thrives on one side of the railway while on the other the eclectic **Bishop Centre** retail park will soon be reinvented big, brash and infiltrated by an apostrophe (as The Bishop's Centre) and a new *Tesco* (just what we need: another supermarket).

About Grout – Camaraderie

Bayley Crescent / 24th July 2014

Doris and I had been married two years when we moved here to N° 40 in 1950, says **Arthur Grout**. The Crescent got its name for being built in an orchard owned by Tiggy Bayley, a local farmer somehow related to **Michael Bayley**. The fruit trees on the green made good goalposts, adds Arthur's son David, and us kids loved to string rope bridges between them. Everyone knew everyone else. Nobody locked their front doors and we were always in and out of each other's houses. Or meeting in ***The Maypole***, smiles Arthur. My dad Alfred took me there first in the late-1930s. It had its own boxing ring then. The landlord Fred Gibson was a character: he refused to serve any strangers who weren't in uniform. And later I enjoyed the odd pint with my neighbours Frank Boulton and Tom McLoughlin. Frank was a lorrydriver with *Cleare's* known to all as 'Mr Muscle Man' and Tom a lovely Irish navvy with a brogue you could cut with a knife; his wife Peggy used to 'do' for **Lady Page** at ***Hitcham Lodge***. There was Jimmy Wakefield the barber where ***Dhariwal's*** is now and Janet Moon ran Lent Rise Post Office at the top end of Eastfield Road. That's where David got his first job delivering newspapers.

Lowlanders

Second String

Marsh Lane / 7th February 1892

We've learned that if anyone knows what's what and who's who, it's a fly-driver – so who better than **Jesse Hipgrave** to take us on the next leg of our journey? Here he is now, his clattering up the rise to the southern concourse of the station. As we climb aboard, he claims he'll give us a ride a whole lot smoother than that young Georgie Pusey.

We set off south, dash over the Bath Road and head down **Marsh Lane** across the flat countryside that has hardly changed in centuries. In 42 years, the fields on either side will all be in Taplow. Today we are on the edge. To the east is Hitcham, to the right Taplow – or **Amerden**, to be more precise. We turn right and left at the kink in the lane where the old lateral ford used to be and after a few hundred yards arrive at the homes of our friends **Joe Bunce** and **Will Lambourne**. Their neighbours here are blacksmith William Hutchins, *GWR* signalman Isaac Batts and **Isaac Lambourne**, Will's brother and a railway platelayer like Joe.

Within a few years, this cluster of cottages will be the anchor for a 100-yard cul-de-sac called **Ye Meads** extending eastwards and a string of houses which will creep northwards along the eastern edge of the lane to become an elongated reverse mirror image of Boundary Road: Hitcham's sentinels watching west over Widow Whitlaw's world.

Harding Happening – Meeting the Neighbours

Marsh Lane / 7th February 1952

Anthony Harding isn't happy. His mum insists on calling him Tony. When he grows up, so will his wife Mary. Perhaps he will cheer up as he introduces his neighbours....

The large house at the top of Marsh Lane is ***Marshmead***, home of **Eileen Matthews**, the doyen of Taplow Horse Show. Sometimes her widowed mother – a director of the printing company *Hutchinson's* – used to let her housekeeper Dora take Tony and his pal **Michael Mann** in a pony-and-trap to Burnham Beeches. The Matthews family own the next two houses, *Kingsdown* and ***Caversham***. Tony's father Frank, an aircraft maintenance engineer, has rented *Caversham* since 1937 when the lad was three weeks old.

Further down the lane is *The Oaks*. Don't tell the owners, whispers Tony, but sometimes when they're out Michael and I take a dip in their swimming pool. Then there are some bungalows: Michael lives in one and Mrs Studdart in another with her two sons Bruce and Cedric. Bruce is an ornithologist who rings birds. A couple of years ago, when a heron was nesting in the fir tree in ***The Devil's Kitchen***, Bruce sent Tony shinning up there to bring down the baby for him to ring.

The local celebrity lives at ***Wynn Green*** just beyond the kink. **Ronnie Binge** was originally a cinema organist. He went on to play the organ in Annunzio Mantovani's first band: *The Tipica Orchestra*. After the war, he rejoined Mantovani to develop his orchestra's 'cascading strings' signature sound. Last year was a good year. His arrangement of *Charmaine* catapulted Mantovani to worldwide fame as he composed the first of his own signature pieces. *Elizabethan Serenade* will win an *Ivor Novello Award* and become famous as the theme for the BBC radio series *Music Tapestry* and as the play-out for the *British Forces Broadcasting*

Service. Ronnie will go on to compose film scores and many fondly-remembered tunes including, in 1963, his second 'greatest hit', the slow waltz *Sailing By*, which will take its place in British radio heritage as the introduction to the late BBC Radio 4 shipping forecast broadcast at 0048 GMT each day. *Wynn Green* won't be graced with a blue plaque like his childhood home in Derby.

Beyond **Devil's Lane** is a pair of wooden cottages. The western one is home to Ted May who looks after the garden at *Marshmead*. His neighbour **Arthur Morrell** sits on his outside loo ready to take potshots at any passing rat. Next door in a bungalow is ***Philpott's Shop***, a general store with an orchard behind where the local lads love to go scrumping. Further down the lane past the scaffolder's yard is **Ye Meads** where the locals held a street party to celebrate VJ-Day. On the corner is ***Ye Meads Hotel***, originally built as a boarding house for visiting railway workers, now in the charge of the Latrelle family. Anthony chuckles to recall the antics of two of the lads who live there. **Ernie Joliffe** and Bob Tarrant clambered up onto the balcony to peep into the bathroom window only for the balcony to collapse. In 1968 Ernie's little brother Geoff will open a clothing hire business in Marlow. And in 2013 Geoff's son Ben will be top of the US charts as a drummer with *Young Guns*. By then, it will be 23 years since the Joliffe's old home was converted into the four flats of ***Ye Meads House***.

Next stop is at *Heatherdale*, home of David Clifford whose father – a chemist at the *Pyrene* fire extinguisher factory in Brentford – will invent *Nulon*, a dab-on liquid to prevent ladders in nylon stockings running further. It will be over 40 years before Tony and David meet again when the latter is running a mobile phone shop in ***The Bishop Centre***. And finally we come to smallholding where **Jack Peck** keeps cows and greyhounds. When he is otherwise engaged, Anthony and Michael like to sneak in here to play on and under the bales of straw in the old barn. A couple of summers ago, they watched secretly as Jack tended a cauldron boiling over a fire behind the barn. It took them a while to realise that he was throwing in the chopped-up carcass of a stillborn calf to make a meaty jelly to feed to the dogs.

Grant's Plant

Willowcroft, Ye Meads / 7th April 2014

This bungalow has been home to **Daphne** & **Rusty Grant** for 60 years. The view from their living room across to Devil's Lane is the same as it has always been thanks to the successful fight in 1975 to prevent 52 houses being built out there.

Both the Grants have served as Parish Councillors and Rusty on the Society's committee. In the early days they knew Jack Peck well as a man who could mend anything. If it was broke, he could fix it. Well, not quite, smiles Rusty. When he built himself a greenhouse, he couldn't fix it that he hadn't made the door big enough to get his wheelbarrow out.

Rusty's brother Ray bought this land around 1950, just about the time he was starting ***Grant Plant Hire*** and storing heavy plant such as excavators in ***Morlew Yard***, the old wheelwright's yard out on Marsh Lane where the Scouts met during the Second War. Rusty joined him in the business and Jack's son Vic Peck worked for them before moving to ***Summerleaze*** when it was excavating what became **Taplow Lake**. Although the brothers soon set up their company headquarters in Maidenhead they retained the yard for many years. It is now the offices of *Bull Developments (Maidenhead) Ltd*.

In the old days, Rusty and Daphne walked or cycled everywhere. The nearest bus stop was down in Dorney Reach from where they could catch the *Blue Bus* into Windsor to go to the pictures or the theatre, knowing that they would have to walk four miles home. When their son Andy was little, they got to know Alfred (Fred) Bestall who had a top-floor room at ***Ye Meads Hotel*** where he wrote and illustrated his ***Rupert the Bear*** stories for *The Daily Express*. Soon after Bestall retired in 1965 he moved to Surbiton where he named his home *Beaconsfield House*. Nowadays Andy's *Rupert* annuals are in his parents' loft while he runs *Grant Plant (Maidenhead) Ltd* in Furze Platt.

Widow Whitlaw

Amerden House / 7th February 1892

Amerden House is just half-a-mile to the south but there's no short way to it except across the fields. We will have to take a mile-and-a-half detour back up to the Bath Road, left by the railway embankment into ***Amerden Lane*** and down the long private lane with no name past ***Barge Farm***, once the medieval spine of southern Taplow for being the direct route between St Nicholas' Church and Merton Priory's outpost on Amerden's moated triangle.

Just before we reach the triangle, Jesse wheels left into the woods of Home Meadow, for 18 years now the grounds of *Amerden House*. Martha Whitfield is waiting for us at the end of the curving driveway. She looked after the house last year while her mistress **Selina Whitlaw** spent some time in Chertsey with her brother-in-law George to recover from the loss in 1890 of her husband **Charles Whitlaw the Younger** [*see Appendix 1, Tree 19*]. Martha explains that the master left £42,464 (£27.5m), most of it held in two trusts bequeathed to his brother George and his widow Selina who will shortly delineate their domains: she to the north, he to the south of a cinder track they will lay from Marsh Lane to Amerden Bank. Despite being a shy, largely invisible and therefore mysterious force, Selina is perfectly capable of ruling the roost down here alone. She will astutely keep sweet with her tenant gentlemen and stand tall as an influential if elusive pillar of the broader Taplow community as she holds sway over Amerden for an incredible seven decades, two as a wife and five as a widow.

In the meantime, George's land will be sold after his death in 1911 to **George Trumper**, a ***Great Western Railway*** director for whom from 1904 to 1926 a station on the Brentford branch line will be called *Trumper's Crossing Halte*. Trumper will never live locally but his name will survive beyond 1950, when Ray Grant buys three plots including one for his brother's bungalow, and

Amerden : Fields of Dreams / 2014

Amerden House / 2014

until 1992 when, having been isolated three decades before by the M4 motorway slicing through the toe of Taplow, **Trumper's Field** will be ceded to **Dorney Parish**.

Wimereux, France / 19th June 1910

There are tales of Selina's obsessive nature, of how day-in-day-out for years, with the illustrations of Randolph Caldecott as her inspiration, she carved her nursery rhyme frieze up the staircase of *Amerden House*. Some will say she refused to let her son Charles Francis Whitlaw live in or anywhere near "racy Maidenhead" in his youth for fear he would be misled by its Edwardian indulgences. Perhaps it is fear that has led her to escape to this house in the countryside near Boulogne in order to keep her daughter Rosa beyond temptation. They have found pleasant distraction in the company of the 'Idyllist' English artist Lionel Smythe and his wife Alice. Smythe will have such an impression on Rosa that she will imitate his style and, after his death in 1918, co-author a book on his life and work with his step-brother William Wyllie, an artist famed for his maritime themes. Thereafter Rosa's artistic aspirations will take second place to her life's work: being her mother's constant companion.

So Long – Name Games: Amerden Lane

Amerden House / 19th March 2014

The old cinder track was eventually adopted and tarmaced by Eton Rural Distict Council which, in its mid-20th Century mission to bring order, sowed confusion by calling the new road **Amerden Lane**, a decision which has led to some assuming that the old track up past ***Barge Farm*** to ***Arch Cottages*** is also Amerden Lane. It isn't and it never was. The real Amerden Lane runs from the **Thames Valley Adventure Playground** to ***Wey Lodge*** and on parallel with the embankment to *Arch Cottages*, only this last section has by a combination of neglect and appropriation become no more than a footpath.

So Long – Leap of Faith

Amerden House / 10th April 2014

While the cinder track divided them, **Selina Whitlaw** and her brother-in-law George shared another road. **David Long** explains that after her husband's death in 1890 "she went over to Rome". In fact, it is possible that her heart was always there and that Charles the Younger's passing freed her to be true to it. Her family – the Ingpens – had a strong Catholic streak and, strangely for a man of seemingly Scots Presbyterian heritage, so did George Whitlaw. It appears that the reference to him in the 1881 census as an "unbenifacted clergyman" was a euphemism for his being a papal knight, no less. Where, when and why did he make this leap of faith? Did Selina follow him or had he follow her? No wonder she kept herself to herself as she added her very own Catholic chapel alongside the billiard room at *Amerden House* and painstakingly carved its panels with her own hands.

The Ingpens had a secular role too. In 1948 Roger and Arthur Ingpen joined with Edgar Syers, **Cecil Dowson** (of ***Guildersfield***) and his son **Noel Dowson** (of ***Old Lodge***) as trustees of ***Amerden Properties Ltd*** which in 1956 retained ***Amerden House*** and its gardeners' cottages while selling *Barge Farm* to the gravel company ***William Boyer & Sons*** which only just pipped **Robin Prior** of ***Summerleaze*** to the purchase

Barge Farm for a Reason

Barge Farm / 7th February 1892

The Crosses have always been easy enough for the Whitlaws to bear. **George Robert Cross the Elder** was the sitting tenant at *Barge Farm* in 1852 when **Charles Whitlaw the Elder** acquired Amerden. **George Robert Cross the Younger** took over the tenancy from his father in 1875 – having the same name made the paperwork so simple – and five years later renewed his lease here and extended it to include most of ***Amerden Farm*** for a total annual rent of £780 (£68,000) until 1896. The farmer has a tale to tell of the Amerden riverbank....

The towing rights go back centuries, he says, but they've been a bone of contention since 1751 when the **Thames Navigation Commission** came into being and kept changing its mind. Lord Inchiquin as riparian owner claimed the right of supplying horses and towing along this reach, a right he delegated for a fee to John Lucas, my long-ago predecessor at *Barge Farm*. At first, the Commissioners went along with that by granting Inchiquin a "preference", only to prevent him exercising it by building a six-foot high oak fence along the towpath to keep Lucas's men off it. Then it granted Inchiquin a towing contract from Windsor Bridge to Boulter's Lock, only to cancel it and threaten to erect a raised timber towpath in the middle of the river. It didn't happen.

Things quietened down until 1789 when the towing rights passed from **William Aldridge** to **John Neighbour**. Bargees complained his charges were too high. A roller was built so barges could go upstream past Parting Eyot (where **Bray Lock** is now), only for it to be "cut down in the night". A reward of ten guineas (£740) was offered for information as to who might do such a dastardly deed but nobody ever claimed it. As if they would. Neighbour was ordered to reduce his charges to 13s (£46) for handling a "single Newbury siz'd barge" not exceeding 128 tons (109 feet long, 17 feet wide with a draft of 3 feet 10 inches) from Amerden Ash to Boulter's. He retaliated by keeping fewer horses at the ready. The Commissioners threatened once more to build a towpath on the riverbed. Still it didn't happen.

Bargemasters complained bitterly in 1808 of "great inconveniences, obstructions, delays and increased expences". The Commissioners offered £800 (£854,000) for the strip of land from ***Moat Farm*** to Maidenhead Bridge. Lord Kirkwall apologised on behalf of his mother the fourth **Lady Orkney** and promised that things would get better. They didn't.

Kirkwall forestalled more complaints of delays in providing horses and abuses of his monopoly in 1821 and again in 1843, by which time he was the fifth Lord Orkney. Nine years later he sold the problem to Widow Whitlaw's granddad. He was happy for my dad to continue with the rights and responsibilities. Just before he died I got into deep water with the **Thames Conservancy**, which had succeeded the Commission in 1866, for stopping a bargee from towing himself. It would've soon been water under the bridge if he hadn't been in the employ of Walter Hore-Ruthven, 9th Lord Ruthven of Freeland. With a title like that, he had a cheek to accuse me of obstruction, says an evidently cross Cross. When I did it again two years later, I got no more than a ticking off.

We thank Farmer Cross for his history of barging and head north up the lane with no name. Farmhand Henry Atkins waves a greeting. His son used to be a Harry but (much George's amusement) now prefers 'Henry Junior'. Thinks he's American, laughs Jesse. The father lives at *Rose Cottage* and the son in one of *Barge Farm Cottages*.

That Magnificent Man and his Flying Machine

Amerden Bank / 7th February 1910

The Crosses are gone. An Irish gentleman by the name of Arthur O'Conor has taken over ***Barge Farm House***. He has no known historical validity except farming's not his game. The same can be said for the charismatic Scot at ***Amerden Bank***. They say he's building a flying machine....

People have forever been in a flap about flying and that's how **George Davidson** started. This fourth son of the laird of Inchmarlo by Banchory in Aberdeenshire built a machine in the 1880s that would flap its wings and fly, only it didn't. The unfortunate pilot rowed for all he was worth but the wooden craft barely rose from the ground before crashing in a tangled heap. Davidson became convinced that the necessary lift could be created by downward thrust. In 1896 he applied for a patent on his *Air-Car*, a vertical take-off monoplane as big as a double-decker bus powered by 22 fans mounted horizontally in the wings. Models were tested at Banchory in 1897 but the project foundered for lack of funds.

The frustrated Davidson prophesied the following year that it would soon be possible to have afternoon tea in London and then fly to Manchester in time for dinner, or to soar into the air to drop loads of dynamite on enemy countries. Thereafter he diverted his energies into his mining business until the 1903 flights by the Wright brothers reawakened his aeronautical ambitions. He set off for the USA with the design talent of Alliott Verdon Roe and a pocketful of cash invested by the automobile manufacturer Sir William Armstrong-Whitworth. By 1906 he was in Denver building a new version of the *Air-Car* with just two steam-powered fans, one in each wing. Despite parting company with Roe, Davidson was still dreaming that it would carry 100 passengers from Chicago to New York. It didn't get off the ground. The first full-sized *Gyropter* blew to pieces in 1908.

Undeterred, Davidson came to Amerden three years ago to build a new version of the *Gyropter* with which he hoped to win the £10,000 (£910,000) prize offered by *The Daily Mail* for the first flight from London to Manchester. Progress has been delayed by cashflow and Davidson was disappointed when the Frenchman Louis Paulhan won the prize in April last year. He remains convinced that, although the monoplane and biplane are "marvels of ingenuity", they will not be as successful as his flying machine which has mechanical rotary wings that will do the same work as wings of a bird. Having invested £12,500 (£1.1m), construction of the new *Gyropter* is well advanced – it is a double-decker, triple-wing biplane with lifting fans in the centre pair of wings – and a model has been put on display at London's *Olympia* exhibition centre in the hope of attracting more investment in the project. The brochure aspires that the flying machine will carry 20 passengers from London to Manchester in 3 hours at speeds in excess of 100 miles per hour.

George Davidson is a charismatic eccentric of such admirable vision and resilience that he puts many in mind of two endearing British traits: he embodies 'the Triumph of Hope over Experience' and might just be remembered for 'Glorious Failure' rather than as an aeronautical pioneer ahead of his time. Roe and Armstrong-Whitworth will find their places in aeronautical history. Their companies *AV Roe & Co* (known as *AVRO*), the *Sir WG Armstrong Whitworth Aircraft Company* and *Vickers-Armstrongs Ltd* will design and build many of the British military aircraft that serve in the coming World Wars. Experiments with downward thrust by Davidson's French and Danish contemporaries will evolve into the helicopters first flown successfully in the 1920s and his efforts at Amerden will be forgotten by all but enthusiasts and the odd local.

Whine to Savour

Amerden Grove 7th February 1892

Jesse Hipgrave steers his fly left across the brook that emerges from a culvert under the embankment to feed two teardrop pools, once mill ponds or weir pools and maybe **Nichole de Aumberdene**'s fisheries. With these peaceful waters nearby, it is a surprise to hear that the house has something rather exclusive: a private swimming pool, Taplow's first. Straight ahead is ***Amerden Grove***, variously also known as *Amerden Lakes* or *Amerden Ponds*. Its gables and ornate chimneys rise proudly above trellises hanging with exuberant roses to give it the feel of being Taplow Court's secret little brother. The scene is so inviting and the idea of seeing the ultimate luxury of a swimming pool so exciting, it is hard to follow the arc of the pond to arrive at a boathouse where **Sir Henry Rae Reid** awaits with his wife Louisa and her son Herbert Budd.

Rosa & Selina Whitlaw / c1906

A model of George Davidson's dream machine / c1906

The Lords Burnham: Edward & Harry Levy-Lawson – Sir Leslie Ward / 1873 & 1893

White Place, Eastbank & Orkney Cottage (originally *Orkney Cottage*) / 2012

Amerden Grove / c1895

Sir Henry is a fourth baronet, originally from Ewell in Surrey. He has a fine reputation for competitive pigeon shooting and for his partnership in *Rayden & Reid*, a Pall Mall wine merchant to those with discerning palates and wallets to match. He invested last year in two cases of *Chateau Latour 1865*. One case is laid down for a valued customer. Having rested, a bottle from the other is Sir Henry's treat for us today. He cradles his glass lovingly, lifts it high to see its deep ruby red glow in the sunshine and lowers it once more to make much of the whiff of eucalyptus in the 'nose' of this classic vintage Bordeaux wine. He takes a gentle sip and lets its harmonious fleshiness caress his tongue and linger. We take the hint and do the same. We expect the best in Taplow.

Our host's home is built on the site of what may have been the old Amerden Mill before being converted to a home by the time it was acquired with the rest of Amerden by **Charles Whitlaw the Elder** in 1852. It was let for a while to William Tomkyns, a young gentleman of independent means, before Sir Henry took up the lease in the late-1860s. He engaged an architect called Richard Tress to clear the site and build the lovely residence we see today. Tress lived here during the early-1870s to supervise the project. Sir Henry has been here ever since. He is keen to claim it as being the site of the original Taplow Manor House, perhaps **William Piscator**'s 13th Century home. He wonders if perhaps Piscator's eldest son Geoffrey de Cliefden lived where **Taplow Court** now stands while his youngest, William, continued here and the place passed by the mid-1300s to his grandson Nichole de Aumberdene. Doesn't ***Amerden Bank*** have a more likely claim? Sir Henry doesn't refill our glasses. It is time to go.

Read All About It – First Edition

Orkney Cottage / 7th February 1894

Selina Whitlaw can rest easy. **Arthur Kennedy** looks like he will be another long-term tenant at ***Fair View*** and her income from her farmlands and mansions is more than sufficient for her to let matters lie. Nobody is happier with that strategy than **Harry Lawson**, the erstwhile MP for St Pancras West and Cirencester.

Harry was just 14 when his father rented ***Orkney Cottage*** in 1876 for £65 per annum (£5,300) to begin a trend that spanned 110 years in which a succession of Taplovians sought to inform and influence the public through their newspapers. His father **Sir Edward Levy-Lawson** had been editor and effectively in control of ***The Daily Telegraph*** since 1855 and its sole owner since taking over from his father Joseph Levy in 1885. And nearly three years ago when **Eliza Howard** of ***The Compasses*** told us about that fellow Smedley "sniffing around" up on the common, he was acting on Sir Edward's behalf to acquire not only ***Sheepcote Farm*** – complete with Walter Lever as its sitting tenant – but also (and more to the point) a new home in Beaconsfield incorporated two years ago into his title as Baronet of Hall Barn. He will be elevated in 1903 to **1st Baron Burnham** and realise a return on his asset in 1914 when **Gertrude Aird** invests her inheritance to build ***Sheepcote Manor*** next to ***Sheepcote Farm***. Her father Sir John Aird is currently MP for Paddington and a civil engineer noted for relocating the Crystal Palace from Hyde Park to Sydenham and thereafter building numerous docks, railways and reservoirs. He will complete construction of Egypt's first Aswan Dam in 1902. Neither Sir John nor his daughter has any idea that one of barns at *Sheepcote Farm* will briefly perform as a theatre before all three are converted for residential use in the early-1980s.

The tenancy of *Orkney Cottage* passed in 1892 to Harry Lawson who has retained his commission in the Royal Buckinghamshire Yeomanry and represents St Pancras West as both its Liberal MP and London County Councillor. This combination of military and political service will be his lot as he rises to the rank of Lieutenant-Colonel in the Royal Buckingham Hussars and serves terms as mayor of Stepney, Deputy Lieutenant of Buckinghamshire and twice as MP for Mile End. On the outbreak of the Great War, he will resume his military career as Honorary Colonel of the 99th (Bucks & Berks Yeomanry) Brigade until 1916 when he succeeds his father as **2nd Baron Burnham** and sole proprietor of *The Daily Telegraph*, a responsibility that will bring a delicate challenge. He will achieve a fine balance by declining ministerial office in order not to compromise his newspaper's political independence while continuing to play an active political role in the House of Lords, not least as chairman of the Standing Joint Committee on Education as it formulates new pay scales for teachers. He will be elevated in 1919 to be **1st Viscount Burnham** before taking the chair at a series of International Labour Conferences in Geneva and of the first World Press Conference in 1927. After selling *The Daily Telegraph* to *Allied Newspapers* in 1928, he will remain involved in its management until his death in 1933 and his family will retain its interest until 1986 when it is sold in to the Canadian press baron Conrad Black.

Come All You Fruitful

River Road / 7th February 1901

The Amerden riverbank is such an asset. Clearly Selina Whitlaw believes it would be a pity not to make the most of it. ***Orkney Cottage***, ***Fair View*** and ***River Bank*** (later ***The Riverbank House***) have been joined on **River Road** by three homes for businessmen – insurer Leslie Baynton, dental surgeon Jack Humphreys and launch owner William Gardener – and four more are under construction. Within a few years stockbroker Edward Micklem will be at ***The Red House*** and two independently wealthy ladies – Edith Andreas of Nottinghamshire and Janet Goodall of Australia – will have taken tenancies at ***Broomcroft*** and ***Bayebrown*** (or ***Bayes Brown***, later ***Harefield***).

Tall Tales – Falling off a Train

Maidenhead Bridge / 19th August 1932

Bill Brown rests his elbows on the downstream parapet of the bridge which reaches to our left to embrace his home, ***Bridge Villa***. His employer **George Bond** lives next door at ***Sunnyside***. He looks down proudly on ***Her Majesty*** – he's been her skipper now for a year or two – but his real purpose today is to keep a discrete eye on **Sydney Tanfield** as he manoeuvres his new launch away from the jetty. Tanfield is the latest of Mrs Whitlaw's tenants at ***Orkney Cottage***. Nobody knows much else about him except he's some kind of financier and it looks as though he'll leave something to remember him by. Bricklayers are hard at work building a high wall around his home.

Sydney and his wife Madeleine weren't the only parents to be horrified last spring by the unfolding saga of the Lindbergh kidnapping in America. The famous aviator Charles Lindbergh's little son Charles was abducted and, after seven weeks of searching and a series of ransom demands for his return, the child's body was eventually found not far from his New Jersey home. Tanfield thinks the loss of his river view is a small price to pay for the security his new brick wall will provide, and he cares not a jot that Bill thinks it makes his home look like a fortress or a prison.

White Place, River Road / 19th August 1938

Bill's bosses have had enough. The directors of ***Bond's (Maidenhead) Ltd*** have decided that Tanfield's bankruptcy leaves them no option but to exercise a lien on a launch for which he had not paid in full. The Tanfield tale is hard to believe....

He is an extremely nefarious fellow who likes to let it be known by word and deed that he is a millionaire despite hardly ever paying a bill. Until now, everyone took him on trust except the astute **Selina Whitlaw**, who in 1934 sold *Orkney Cottage* not to him but to Madeleine, and **William Wood**, whose firm laid out their new garden around the home they renamed ***White Place***. The suspicions really began when Tanfield 'bought' a Cotswold quarry and a load of the famous yellow stone "fell off a train" down the embankment to be used to construct a garage for his dozen *Rolls Royces* with flats above for four chauffeurs, a lodge on Amerden Lane, a *Wendy House* for his children (eventually a home called ***The Bothy***) and a potting shed that will become ***Crosswinds***, in the 1950s the childhood home of **Brenda Passmore**. And then last April it emerged that he had lent his own money to Golders Green fur-dealer Abraham Kacher to buy from him *White Place* and its contents. Soon afterwards, as Kacher changed his name to Abraham Katz and then Arthur Kershaw, valuable furniture, paintings and jewellery went missing from *White Place*. So did Madeleine, since found too ill to move from a Paris hospital. It will be revealed in court next spring not only that Tanfield has debts of £45,544 (£9.8m) but also that he was tried for but acquitted of fraud in 1931....

Allington Cottage, Hill Farm Road / 19th August 2012

Brenda Hickman (née Passmore) recalls hearing that, having spent seven years in jail, **Sydney Tanfield** celebrated his release with a big party at *Skindles* only to die soon afterwards. And when in the late-1960s **Liz & Tim Anderson** discovered Madeleine Tanfield's secret still-locked wall safe, there was nothing at all to be found in any of the blue-silk-lined drawers of the beautiful mahogany cabinet inside.

No Airs and Graces

The Old Station Inn, Bath Road / 7th February 1892

Jesse Hipgrave slows his fly as we approach the arch under the railway embankment. He points out ***Horse Harness Cottage***. That's where the first railway passengers could hire horsedrawn carriages. And there's my home, he says, over there at the top end of ***Arch Cottages***. He waves to his wife Florence by their front door. Lionel, their eldest, sits at her feet. Baby George sleeps in a cot made from a tea chest. Her rounded figure suggests she has another on the way. We leave behind the broad Amerden expanses and plunge into the darkness of the tunnel under the embankment to emerge into a jumble of cottages, unruly workshops and sheds that now clutter the old station forecourt. The sight brings home how half-a-century ago the railway cut Amerden off from Taplow, making it almost a separate world.

Jesse halts his fly by ***The Old Station Inn***. In years to come, some will say this is the old 1838 station converted to a pub. That's not quite right. It was built in the 1840s as an adjunct to the station, a permanent replacement for ***The Old Tin Shanty***, a shack which had sprung up by the old station to offer refreshment to Brunel's navvies after their hard day's toil. By 1851, railway porter George Camping of Henley had reinvented himself here as a 'beerhouse keeper', a new lease of life he enjoyed for probably 20 years until Oliver Perkins took over. It wasn't so long ago that Jim Akerman sowed the seed of confusion by giving the place its new old name.

Jim greets us on the veranda. His little daughter Kate looks up warily through eyes as big as saucers as her mother Jane leads the way inside and asks what we fancy. That one please, *Healey's Family Bitter Ale* from Watford, fresh to the tongue and light on alcohol because we need to be sharp, not least to ask how this little place survives. Jim smiles and says there has always been, still is and always will be a definite divide between the travelling public who favour ***The Dumb Bell*** and the coachdrivers and railway workers who fight for elbow room in here. And that's all well and good. There's plenty of working men who need a drink without airs and graces. Here's one now....

The new arrival catches the end of Jim's line and jokes that he's right about Jesse: he's got no graces, but I'm heir to a fortune. In your dreams, laughs Jesse. Meet Tommy Gallop, he says, my neighbour at *Arch Cottages*. Most folk around here rely on him to break and train their horses into various lines of work. He's got the name for it, see? The boys share a grin and savour their pints as Tommy tells us about **George Butler**. He's done alright, has George. Started out running the smithy here in the old station yard and made enough to build ***Charlton Villa*** there and, some years later, ***The Neuk*** next door. Now he rents them out to two newcomers – the wealthy banker Aaron Levy of Bloomsbury and Arthur Becker, a retired colonel of some Indian cavalry regiment – while he lives on the proceeds in a small cottage next door to the inn. Levy's middle-aged sons John and Alexander style themselves as 'precious house brokers'. Jesse laughs at this neat summing up of what's happening hereabouts.

The Valley People: Time for a Quick One

The Old Station Inn,
(Rebuilt 1931) / c1980s

Cleare's Hotel: originally and eventually ***The Dumb Bell*** / c1860 & c1935

Harvester Restaurant
(with a vague memory of its past)
/ 2015

Life's a Breeze

The Old Station Inn, Bath Road / 7th February 1911

Jesse Hipgrave still lives at ***Arch Cottages*** but gave up his fly some years ago to work on ***Barge Farm***. He introduces us to **Annie Portsmouth** who now runs this old beerhouse. Not that there's much money in it, she says, but they came here from Slough because being here on the busy Bath Road is the perfect place for her husband Alfred, a former *GWR* engineer, and his brother John to build their motor repair business. Motor cars are the future, you see. Alf reckons soon everyone will want one and they'll need people like us to keep them running. He and Annie have eight children. Most are in ***The Cottage*** where 13-year-old Alfie keeps the youngsters in order. And ***The Bungalow*** is big enough for Martha & John, their four boys and Billy Carnell, a chauffeur who boards with them. John is keen to show off his latest toy – a brand new *GWK Light Car* fresh from the new *Grice, Wood & Keller* works at Datchet. The Portsmouth brothers have begun an auto-trade tradition that will last 100 years and more. Meanwhile Alf's six-year-old son Bill will grow up to be a Maidenhead fishmonger-cum-car-salesman and in 2000 Jesse's grandson Martin Barlow will be at ***Horse Harness Cottage***.

A Sad Storie

The Old Station Inn, Bath Road / 22nd August 1961

The testimony of landlady Mary Lanz will confirm that Peter Alphon was here earlier this evening when Michael Gregsten and Valerie Storie were talking quietly together. She has no idea what is happening in a cornfield not far away....

Dorney Reach / 22nd August 1961

Michael and Valerie work at the Road Research Laboratory in Slough. They have long been lovers. A year ago, he returned to his wife Janet only for Valerie to prove too tempting. As the summer gloaming fades and their excitement rises, their tryst is ruined by a 'cockney' tapping on the window of their *Morris Minor* and thrusting a large black revolver into Michael's face. This is a hold-up, says the cockney. If you do as I tell you, you will be alright. They won't be. The cockney will hijack their car and force them to drive aimlessly for hours during which they learn that he knows *The Bear* in Maidenhead. Early tomorrow morning, he will kill Michael, rape and shoot Valerie five times and leave her for dead in a lay-by at Deadman's Hill between Bedford and Luton. Although Alphon will admit to the murder, James Hanratty, lately of Wembley, will be convicted and hanged for the **A6 Murders** early next year. DNA tests in 2002 will confirm the verdict to be correct while leaving the motive open to speculation.

Cleare Way

The Dumb Bell Hotel, Bath Road / 7th February 1892

No need to board the fly now. Jesse leads the way to our next port of call, just a short walk across the Bath Road....

Outbuildings spill either side of ***The Dumb Bell*** telling a tale of incremental expansion over more than a century. Mary Payne is waiting for us on a bench by the main door. Baby Daisy gurgles happily on her lap. Nursemaid Lizzie Giles of Eton softly hums a lullaby as she gently rocks 2-year-old Lilian's wickerwork baby carriage. Mary puts finger to her lips for silence, reveals her Scottish origins with a whispered *Fàilte* and nods towards the open door where her husband John Christmas Payne grins a greeting. He ushers us inside and asks what our pleasure might be. Given the history of this place, it has to be pale bronze and citrusy *Wethered India Pale Ale*, all the way from Marlow. How did he get his middle name, and how come his broad Norfolk burr doesn't match Mary's Gaelic lilt? The first is easy, he says, I was born at Christmas 1850. And as for the second, it's the way of my trade that you go where the work is and it wasn't until I was nearly 40 that I found myself and the love of my life in Scotland. He smiles enigmatically and takes us on a different tack....

The hotel dates back to the 1780s when **Thomas Wethered** opened it as a coaching inn. Old Wethered was still going strong in the 1830s when **Brunel** began to build the railway and, perhaps fretting what the future would hold once the stagecoach trade ebbed away, by 1834 he had given the old place a new name: ***The Bell & Crown Inn***. Fortune smiled: the ***GWR*** built the original station just 100 yards away. Right there on his doorstep was this new interchange from steam power to horsepower (and vice versa). Dozens of horsedrawn vehicles of every shape and size mingled in the triangle of land across the Bath Road to meet every train: a stagecoach calling itself *The Railway* ran to Reading, a Mr Fry operated a horsedrawn omnibus to *The White Hart* in Maidenhead and locals drove their flys to Burnham and Taplow. **George Butler** built a smithy up to shoe the horses and stables to house them. In 1842 **Richard Cleare** left behind his family's long history as farmers and butchers of Burnham to succeed Sam Morris as landlord of the inn which ***Thomas Wethered & Sons Ltd*** was happy for him to take upmarket as ***The Bell & Crown Railway Hotel*** then – after **John Noble** acquired the freehold in 1852 – as ***Cleare's Hotel*** and finally by 1874 as ***The Dumb Bell Hotel***.

By then, Richard had returned to his roots with a sideline as a farmer and the northern fields of ***Amerden Manor Farm*** had become known as ***Cleare's Farm***. Mr Christmas succeeded him as landlord of *The Dumb Bell* in 1889. He will continue there for at least another 20 years during which he will offer such delights as "River Parties, Masonic Banquets, Beautiful Tea Gardens and Croquet Court, Tennis and Sports Grounds attached" while suffering the personal sadnesses of losing his baby Walter in 1893 and his wife Mary three years later, the joy of marrying a second time to Annie and the birth of John in 1901 and Monica in 1909 either side of the tragic loss of baby Gerald in 1904.

Tall Tale – Ringing Wrong

Dumb Bell Bridge, Bath Road / 7th February 2013

Nobody calls it *Dumb Bell Bridge* anymore. They should. The old hotel was a little way west at the bottom of **Berry Hill** until the late-1950s. By then Malcolm Wallace of ***Taplow Motor Co*** was across the road at *The Old Station Inn* selling cars and petrol where the Portsmouth brothers had begun. In no time the *Dumb Bell* site was divided between ***Dumb Bell Caravans*** and Wallace's ***Maidenhead Autos***. As cars clamoured for sale on both sides on the road, a new *Dumb Bell* built on the adjacent plot quickly became popular with bikers. Fortunes fluctuated. Car sales came and went. The most recent changes occurred in 2001 when ***The Old Station Inn*** was replaced by a purpose-built car showroom and *Mitchell & Butler* reinvented the by then not-so-new pub as a *Harvester* which remembers ***The Dumb Bell*** on its sign.

Folklore has much fun telling tales about how *The Dumb Bell* got its name. Two stories relate to the old station. One recalls the silent bell at the original station after it closed in 1872. Another tale tells of several prospective passengers waiting in the inn for a bell to tell them the train was coming. Much to their annoyance, the bell never rang and they missed their train. Then to their chagrin they learned that the poor porter who was supposed to have sounded the warning had been stuck down by a heart attack. This sad day was remembered by having the tongue removed from the bell before it was hung forever silent in the porch of the pub.

Chronology suggests that tongue might have been firmly in the cheek. The same applies to the idea that *Dumb Bell Bridge* was so-called because it looks like a weightlifter's dumb-bell, a claim that relies upon both an unlikely stretch of imagination and (as with the other tales) a determined ignorance of the evidence that the inn's name preceded the coming of the railway by some distance. It was already *The Dumb Bell* by 1819 when the Parish Register first noted Henry Poulton as a hostler there. And despite its reinvention as *The Bell & Crown*, when the first trains ran from Paddington in 1838, they terminated at ***Maidenhead (Dumb Bell Bridge) Station*** – named after the new railway bridge over the Bath Road which itself was called after the late-18th Century hotel nearby. The *GWR* covered its tracks by quickly calling the station ***Maidenhead (Riverside).*** The hotel did something similar for a while before reverting to being *The Dumb Bell*, perhaps as a result of the 'silent bell' story. However it seems that silence will forever reign on how the place really got its name. If only somebody had thought of asking old **Richard Cleare** before he went to rest in peace.

Noble Arts

Dumb Bell Corner, Bath Road / 7th February 1892

As we emerge into the daylight, a public coach-and-four from Maidenhead pulls up on the hotel forecourt. Ever eager to play the charming gentleman, Jesse dashes forward with a flourish to assist a lady down its steep steps. He introduces us to Susanah Strong of Dorney, caretaker at ***Berry Hill House*** where she rarely sees her master Major **Robert Needham**. He has spent only occasional weekends at the house since his wife Eleanor died in 1884. Not that Susie's complaining, mind. She and her husband James, a stockman, have the run of the place. Their teenage son Herbert and his friend Edward Allen can disappear for hours, fishing in the lake like proper gentry with time on their hands. Edward lives in ***Upper Lodge*** with his parents Sophia & George Allen, he the gardener who keeps the grounds looking delightful with the help of his elder son George and their lad **Albert Clark** in *Garden Cottage*. But you only have to look at the empty ***Lower Lodge*** there on the corner to see things aren't quite what they were 25 years ago when **John Noble** and his wife Lily were lavishing a fortune to make *Berry Hill House* a thing of beauty.

Noble was the heir to a highly successful paint and varnish manufacturer. He had watched quietly in *Garraway's Coffee House* that August afternoon 40 years ago as his agent Edward Grove added three lots in Taplow to his expanding property portfolio in London and in the middle Thames Valley. He was content to play the long game with ***The Dumb Bell*** and with ***Bridge Field***, the triangular close bounded by the Bath Road, the railway and the river. The latter was left an untouched investment and Richard **Cleare** remained tenant landlord of the hotel. It was a different matter at *Berry Hill House*. Noble got busy soon after his sitting tenant **Lady Riversdale** departed in 1855 and in the three years from 1859 a colossal earthen hill was piled 12-feet high to be crowned with his new mansion from which he could admire glorious gardens redesigned and extended by **Robert Marnock**, complete with a huge artificial cliff (to screen the gasworks) with waterfalls and a 20-foot "column of water" by **James Pulham**, three Californian sequoia trees and a brick-arched tunnel to bring cattle from his western slopes to be milked at the dairy.

The "beautifully laid out [15-acre] pleasure grounds" were maturing nicely by the mid-1860s in the care of head gardener Alexander Rogers but the house had become rather too cramped for Noble and his wife Lily, seven children and numerous domestic staff. They toyed with ideas for replacing it with a new, larger and more impressive Rothschild-style home but eventually opted in 1869 to acquire *Park Place*, a larger riverside estate at Remenham near Henley-on-Thames. They continued to enjoy *Berry Hill House* while their architect Thomas Cundy substantially rebuilt their new home with an elegant French Renaissance flavour. It will became the UK's most expensive house in 2011 when it is sold for £140m (£145m) to give its vendor a handsome 333% profit in four years.

When the Nobles departed in 1870, Needham was quick to lease his grandfather's much-enhanced mansion and make it his own. That was fine by her, Susie says, but things haven't been the same since the major lost his wife. Things will soon get better. Next year, at the ripe old age of 77, Robert Needham will marry Alice Dixie and spend his last few years at *Berry Hill House*. After his death in 1899, she will continue to live there until her death four years later when her executors sell the place to the stockbroker **Francis Garner (George) Gledstanes** who will make the house a sumptuous home for his wife Georgiana and their teenaged children Sheldon and Elsie. The beautiful grounds will be luxuriant once more in the care of Fred Milsom and his team of four gardeners living in the various lodges and bothies. He will install a fountain within a fernery surrounded with a small brick circular wall topped by a perforated lead pipe that will send a fine spray of water over the plants. This will last until the 1940s when the lead proves much too tempting for thieves to leave alone.

Lower Lodge, Berry Hill / 23rd May 1952

A few months after their arrival in 1947, **Helen** & **Lincoln Lee** discovered that the electric pump which supplied their water drew from an old well beneath their bed. The surface of the water – complete with a dead mouse floating upon it – was barely ten feet below their pillows. They presumed that their bedroom had been built over an old yard.

White Gables, Berry Hill / 23rd May 2012

Sheila & **Barrie Peroni** are showing off the magnificent sequoias behind *Berry Hill*'s dairy, now split into their home ***White Gables*** and ***Well Cottage*** (formerly *Dingly Dell*), where their daughter **Charlie** lives with her husband **Toby Greeves**. The cattle tunnel collapsed and was filled in long ago leaving its eastern end to be conscripted as a garden store.

The Valley People: Noble Arts

Berry Hill House
/ 1975 & 1948

White Gables **shaded by one of** ***Berry Hill's*** **sequoias**
/ 2012

Chapter Seven

Rolling Along

In which we revel in Taplow's Thames

All Aboard

Old Father Thames

The Secret Illusion

Cliveden Reach / 22nd July 2012

What a glorious day: convivial company, incomparable scenery. Upriver in the morning sunshine under the knowledgeable command of Captain **John Dunleavey** to Cookham and lunch at *The Ferry*, now negotiating Cookham Lock anticipating the green serenity of Cliveden Reach, described in 1538 by **John Leland** as "cliffy ground hanging over [the river with] "busshis growing on it". The song written in 1933 by Raymond Wallace and Betsy O'Hogan springs to mind...

> *He never seems to worry, doesn't care for fortune's fame.*
> *He never seems to hurry, but he gets there just the same.*
> *Kingdoms come and kingdoms go whatever the end may be.*
> *Old Father Thames keeps rolling along, down to the mighty sea.*

At various times, the River Thames has been either or both a boundary or a highway for exploration, invasion, travel and trade. In Victorian times its peaceful beauty united Players from far and wide. So much has been written about these reaches. Some records are simple narratives that speak as much of their times as of the waters. Others are glorious works of fiction such as Jerome K Jerome's ***Three Men in a Boat*** (1889) and Kenneth Grahame's ***Wind in the Willows*** (1908). This book cannot hope to compete with such classics but it can celebrate this treasure with a chapter all the river's own. Yet first it must reveal a secret: the river might not seem to worry or hurry but its apparently timeless tranquillity is an illusion.

Messing About with the River

The third Maidenhead Bridge / 22nd July 2013

It is hard to imagine the dramatic nature and scale of the changes that the five miles of Taplow's western watery boundary has seen over the years. Two bridges survive; four have come and gone. There were once more watermills, ferries and fords aplenty; now there are none. There has been a weir at the head of Ray Mill Island perhaps since the late-13th Century but its single-gated flashlock has been replaced by four successive double-gated pound locks, two on the Bucks bank and two more across the water. And there are fewer than half as many islands as there used to be [*see Maps 29, 30, 31 & 32*].

Much of the story is about rich riverside landowners having their way with rights to fish, ferry, tow, load, unload, carry, cross or crush and yet there are occasional examples of the opinions of everyday folks being taken into account....

Something Else Fishy

Cookham / 22nd October 1634

Fishing the Thames is a big issue. The right to fish officially has always been prized by the lords of 'Topley' and by their mill tenants who, for a share of the spoils, managed day-to-day matters on their behalf. Medieval scribes recorded a series of disputes about rights and wrongs. Locals regularly got themselves into deep water for breaking the strict rules imposed by the Crown. King Edward I ordered unofficial kiddles to be removed in 1297. **King Edward III** had several Taplovians summoned in 1340 for taking out various "engines of the queen's fishermen" and "fish to the value of £10" (£7,500). And **King Richard II**'s officials noted in 1387 that "ten pykes and one troute priced 11s 7d (£420) were illegally caught in Reylake" (upstream from the weir). And in 1562 John Fisher and John Norris were ordered to pull up stakes, piles and 'chalke' with which they had encroached upon the first **Henry Manfield**'s fishery.

Arguments about rights and wrongs continue and it became necessary last year to consider a dozen depositions in order to confirm local fishing rights. Testimony was heard from a millwright, a shepherd and a labourer of Bray, a yeoman, a fisherman and two basketmakers of Cookham, a bargeman's wife, a Wooburn wharfinger and two Taplovians: husbandman Roger Woolward and William Edmonds, Master of Arts. The wharfinger **Roger Holderness the Younger** and the yeoman, his nephew Edward, are descended from father and son **John** and **Roger Holderness** who until 28 years ago were millers of Taplow. The

Maps 29 & 30 – Islands in the Stream

The Changing River – Crossings, Mills, a Coaching Inn and the Buckside Boulter's

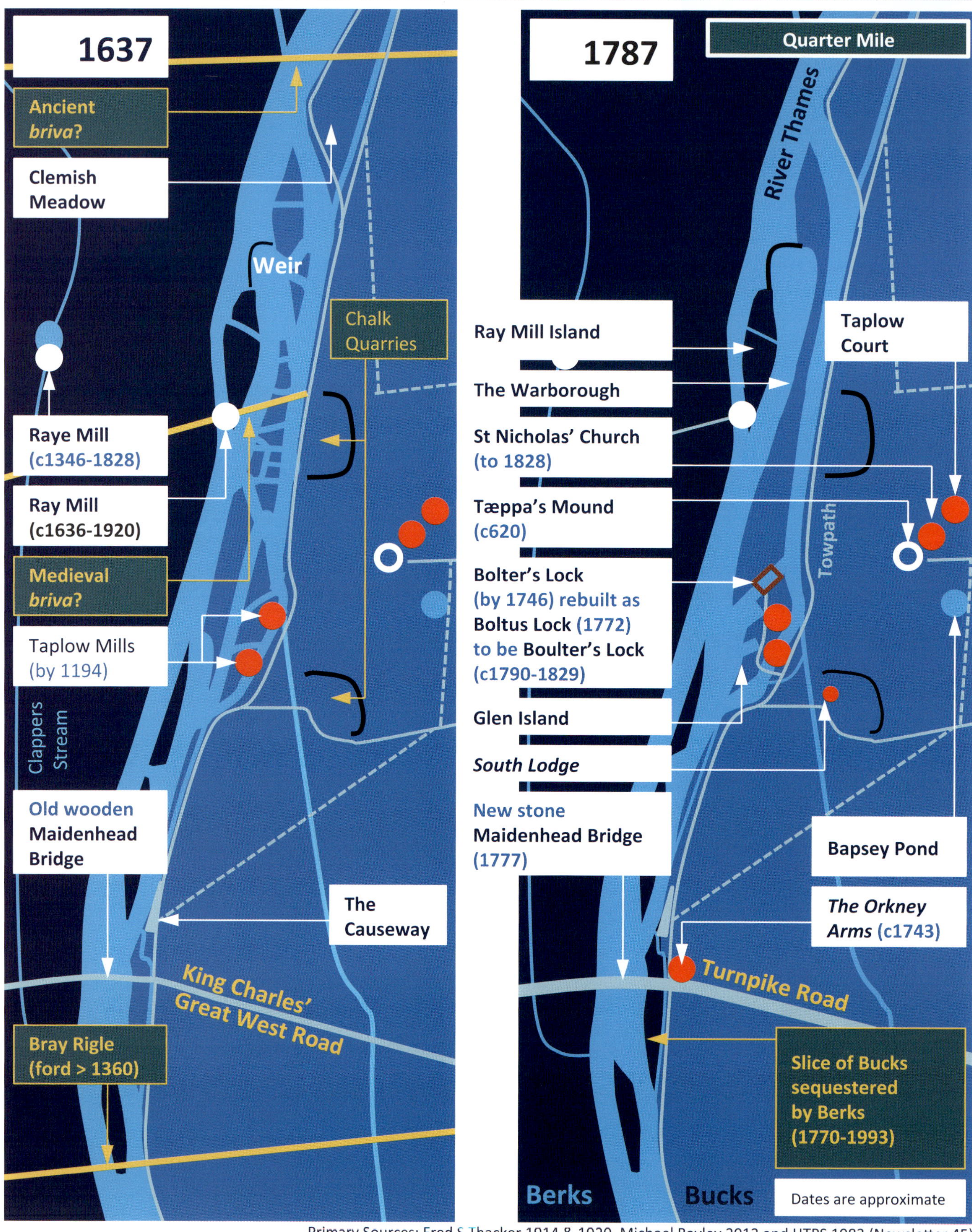

Primary Sources: Fred S Thacker 1914 & 1920, Michael Bayley 2012 and HTPS 1983 (Newsletter 45)

Maps 31 & 32 – Islands in the Stream

The Changing River – Stayers, Players and the Berkside Boulter's

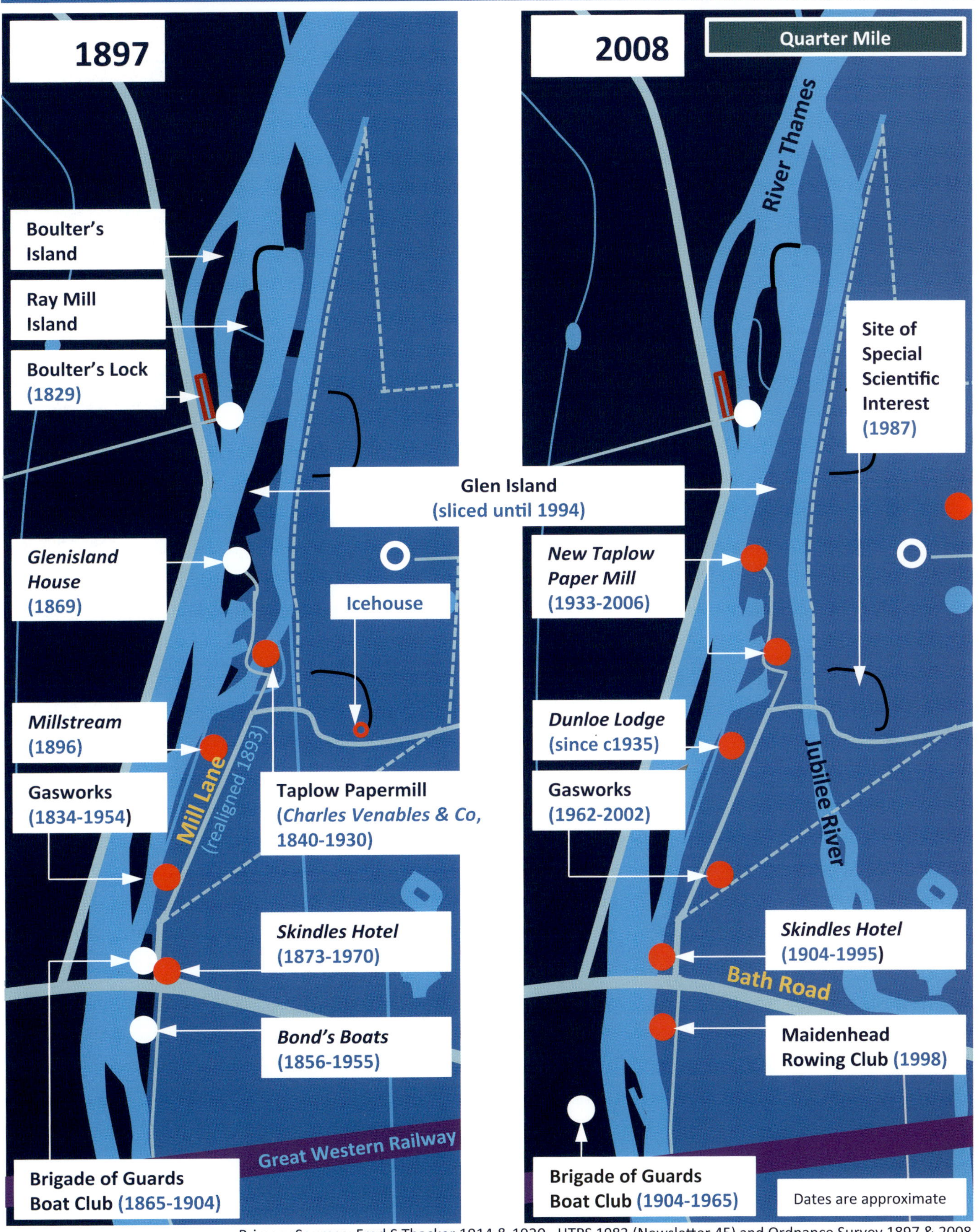

Primary Sources: Fred S Thacker 1914 & 1920 , HTPS 1983 (Newsletter 45) and Ordnance Survey 1897 & 2008

exercise resulted in the definition of five fisheries: four held by the Crown and one by Taplow Mill. That from above Spade Oak to Sashes Island need not concern us. We will explore the others in our travels....

Silent and Secret

Hedsor Wharf / 22nd July 2012

We emerge from Cookham Lock cut but, before we go with the flow downstream, John Dunleavey steers us north into Hedsor Water. This loop of over half-a-mile around **Sashes Island** to Cookham weir is a peaceful, almost private haven as far removed as can be from its past, possibly as a Roman bridgehead, definitely as a Saxon bastion there, a busy port up ahead and notorious rapids right here and a little way upstream.

This reach was described in 1794 as "one of the most difficult and dangerous places on the Thames between Reading and Boulter's Lock" due to its seasonal shallows, shoals, unpredictable currents and "large chalk stones that tumble from the clifts above and lodge in the bottom of the river". Perhaps Jos Gibbins of Abingdon fell foul of one of these boulders on 9th August 1826. He was steering his heavily-laden barge *Mary* through the dark night and low water when he hit an obstruction. *Mary* swung across the stream and broke in two. Her cargo of Bath stone bound for repairs at Westminster was plunged into the river. The poor chap's loss was estimated at £40 (£49,000).

This crisis put the cap on the complaints of a thousand years and more. There had been talk of remedies for 50 years at least. Now it was time for action. George Gyngell was engaged to excavate the cut in 1829 and the lock was opened the following year in the care of Joseph Staniford who was paid a monthly wage of 65s (£4,100). Gyngell's discovery of 9th Century skeletons and weapons added to the evidence that Sashes Island was *Sceaftesege*, a fort of some 28 acres thought to have been built on the orders of King Alfred the Great to resist invading Vikings. By end of the 19th Century, dredging to deepen the various channels had revealed a horse's skeleton and more Danish weapons including an iron spearhead and a winged axe. And mid-20th Century excavations revealed yet more skeletons and barbed spearheads buried on the island. Clearly once upon a time or two, this was a killing field.

The lock made for safer navigation but its opening heralded a 40-year battle of a different kind. The third **Baron Boston** wasn't best pleased that Hedsor Wharf had been bypassed once more. There had been a quay here since medieval times, possibly earlier, and Boston felt justified in 1832 in claiming compensation for a forecast loss of £2,113 (£2.8m) over 30 years. **The Thames Navigation Commission** considered this ill grace and responded that it had been compelled to build the lock by the persistent failure of the lords Boston to remedy the rapids. And yet his lordship was not only successful on appeal in securing £1,200 (£1.6m) in damages and costs, he also returned to court five years later to claim an additional £300 (£367,000) because the wharf had been rendered impossible to let. The Commissioners countered that Boston had no more claim to compensation than an innkeeper from whose house coach traffic had been diverted by a new road. Legal wrangling went on for some years until the Commissioners agreed to pay Boston £75 (£90,000) and to build a flashlock in Cookham weir to offer barges an alternative passage.

Tensions ebbed away until the late-1860s when the fourth Baron Boston tried to acquire Cookham's weirs. Once again a compromise was reached. In 1869 the upper weir was rebuilt to his lordship's liking and he was allowed to keep the eel bucks at the lower end of Hedsor Water which made this reach essentially private, a privilege confirmed by Act of Parliament in 1894. The sixth Baron Boston sold Hedsor Wharf in 1924 and after two further transactions it was acquired in 1968 on behalf of **Roland (Tiny) Rowland** by the *Sugar Corporation of Malawi Ltd*, then a subsidiary of the business conglomerate *London & Rhodesian Mining & Land Company* (*Lonrho*) of which he was Chief Executive. Somehow it became his personal property six years later. This highly successful and equally controversial fellow – 'Tiny' by nickname but by neither stature nor nature – rather enjoyed being accused in 1973 by PM Edward Heath of being "the unacceptable face of British capitalism". We get all sorts hereabouts.

Hedsor Water still has an air of being private – Tiny's widow Josie still lives in their palatial home standing silent and sharing no secrets beyond an impossibly well-manicured lawn – but it isn't. Public rights of navigation were confirmed in 2003 by the Chancery Division of the Court of Appeal.

Beneath Cliveden Cliff

Cliveden Reach / 22nd July 2012

The green wall rises above us as we drift downstream along the left bank. John nods towards a small, grassy shelf where a cottage nestles in the dappled shade. That's **Page's Wharf**, built in the late-1500s by the second **Henry Manfield** to unload goods for ***Manfield Park*** only to precipitate a long dispute with his neighbour **Richard Over**, then owner of **Hedsor Wharf**, which continued with Over's successor Rowland Hynd the Younger. In 1608 Manfield pulled a masterstroke by cutting a channel though Sashes Island to neatly bypass Hedsor Rapids and cut out the competition. His wharf was still in use 250 years later when **Sir George Warrender** built the second Cliveden and his cut still survives as a seemingly natural tributary joining the mainstream just below the lock cut.

And talking of places now more in myth than on maps, here is where **Babham's Ferry** plied its trade for over 200 years from before 1352 until after the death of Arthur Babham in 1561, a time in which it was much used by the Manfields who owned both Cliveden and ***White Place Farm*** (then ***Bullocks***) on either side of the river. It fell out of use for over a century before being revived in 1808 as **My Lady Ferry**, a romantic name which may have derived from its landing on the Berks bank in a close where games were held on 15th August every year to celebrate both the completion of the hay harvest and the Assumption of the Virgin Mary. **Michael Bayley** believes this was *My-Ladres-Clos* (*the enclosure of the sluice or flashlock of the plain*). Other sources have it as *Islade*, which may have been pronounced *Islady*. The toll in 1828 was tuppence (60p) for taking a horse over, in 1866 ferryman Thomas Staniford was paid £2 (£1,470) a month and ferryman S Hamblin was drowned in 1892. Later the ferry enjoyed the Astor replication of the Manfield cross-river landownership and then a period when it was the last ferry operated by the **Thames Conservancy** before slipping into memory once more in 1956.

Continuing downstream, we cross a long-forgotten line that in 1633 marked the end of the Millpond Fishery, which extended from Sashes, and the beginning of the Islade Fishery, which ran down to the lower end of Clemence Mead, variously called Climarsh Meade, Clemarsh or **Clemish**. On our left, families play in the clearing at **Cliveden Spring**. Over our shoulder is the classic sight of **Cliveden** standing proud on high like a monarch of the glen. We slip between **Bavin's Gulls** – the islands in **Slow Grove** named after either Richard Bavin or his son Nicholas, who succeeded the Manfields as lords of Burnham for a time until 1610 – and glance west to see **Battlemead** stretching away to the horizon. **Widbrook** joins the mainstream above the broad waters of **Botany Bay** where the penny drops that many of the observations made 122 years ago by two Victorian academics still ring true today...

Art in the Aid of Nature

Cliveden Reach / 22nd July 1890

The University of Toronto has commissioned Professor John Satterly of Devon to edit a new book which will be published next year. He has engaged various friends and colleagues to contribute to *Rivers of Great Britain: The Thames from Source to Sea*. TG Bonne is out and about today gathering his impressions for the Henley-to-Maidenhead chapter. He believes that the fourth Lord Boston's "imitation castle [at Hedsor] would be improved, pictorially speaking, by a judiciously administered dose of dynamite", and that "the design of Cliefden House could readily be imitated with three or four packing cases". Clearly it is nature not architecture which excites this gentleman, and what a splendid pen picture he paints of the spectacle before him "at the very foot of Cliefden woods"....

"It would be difficult to find a fairer scene on any river within the limits of our island, and not easy did we take a wider range over the surface of the earth. On both sides Art has been called in to the aid of Nature; but that aid has been only bestowed where it is a boon. The chalky upland, which for some miles past has formed a marked feature in the scenery, and has bounded our view in front, now descends to the river brink in steep slopes, sometimes almost in cliffs. Between the foot of these and the water, only here and there does a narrow strip of level land intervene. On two or three of these a picturesque cottage has been built, and the brightest, gayest, trimmest of gardens planted; but the slope itself is one mass of trees and brushwood, through which, though very rarely, gleams forth a little crag of the white chalk rock."

"All the trees of England seem to have congregated on this bank: there are hazel and maple and thorn; there are ash and oak, and beech and elm; there are chestnut and sycamore, and, especially at this upper end, the brighter tints of the deciduous trees, and of the broad-leaved evergreens, are dappled by the sombre hues of Scotch firs, with their ruddy trunks, and of ancient yews, very possibly lineal descendants of trees among which the ancient Britons hunted, before ever a Roman galley floated on the Thames."

"For Cliefden Woods, though doubtless they are in part the result of the gardener's art, are very probably a relic of the primeval forests which once covered so large a part of England. [Here] trees would take root from the time that the slope first was furrowed out by the river, and there would be the 'lurking-place of wild beasts' in days when the huntsman wore skins for clothing, and pointed his arrows with chipped flints. Down by the river's brink what a wealth of beauty is often to be found; the waterside plants grow strong and free, pink willow-herb and purple loosestrife, yellow fleabane and St John's wort, with numbers more which it is needless to mention; while the bank above is green in summer with many a herb, and bright in spring with many a flower. No trim shrabbery this on the Cliefden steeps; nature is left to wanton at will, nay, even to struggle for existence. Ivy and briony and wild bine festoon and sometimes half smother the trees, while the traveller's joy creeps and clings in masses so profuse that from afar it seems to flicker like grey lights among the green shadows."

"The beauty of this part of the river does not so much consist in notable features as in a series of exquisite combinations of subtly varied forms, and in delicate harmonies of colour. There is, of course, the one great effect of wooded slope and of flowing stream, which differs but little from place to place; but there is in addition, at every step, some novel harmony of its minor features, fresh drapery of the aged limbs of trees, a new contrast of sombre yew boughs with the bright green of the sprouting beech or the tender tints of the maple, or of the darkling water beneath the shadow of the wooded hank, with the sparkle of the sun on the ripples of the stream. There float a pair of swans, white as snow; there darts a kingfisher, a flying emerald; there the lilies speckle the stream with gold; there the tall willow-herb forms a pink-tinted fringe to the river, and with its summer splendour alleviates our regret for the many-coloured carpets which in spring-time overspread the meadows."

"Beyond Cliefden, where the plateau begins to slope more gently towards the plain, the river is broken up, and its scenery is pleasantly varied by a group of low islands densely clothed with willows. Near here is Taplow Court, which has a most attractive garden. So also have smaller houses near the river; even some mills, which would be tolerable but for their chimneys, bedeck their bank-sides with flowers."

Cliveden Reach / 22nd July 2012

Given Mr Bonne's proclivities, **Taplow Court** must have been delighted to attract no criticism of its architecture and an outright compliment on its gardens. He concludes his chapter by offering his considered advice that **Maidenhead** is "not in any way remarkable" and that despite having "a well-to-do look [and] not a few pleasant residences in its outskirts [it is] nearly in the blessed condition of a place that has no history". Could this be why you won't find Professor Satterly's book in Maidenhead Heritage Centre?

Islands in the Stream

Cliveden Reach / 22nd July 2012

We come past the Bucks bank bulge of **Clemish** – once a Saxon field, now an almost waterlogged secret world – to the upstream tip of **Glen Island**. The mile between here and Maidenhead Bridge has seen the greatest change of all. Now as in 1637 the river divides into two. Back then, the towpath was on *Bucksyde* where the stream ran to the east of a string of 14 islands to turn the waterwheels of Taplow Mills; these were the waters of the Taplow Mill Fishery. Meanwhile the *Barksyde* stream either went over the weir or powered Raye Mill; the Maidenhead Bridge Fishery extended from *Peacocke Tarrs* below this mill down to the bridge. The fisheries are no longer and now those 14 islands have combined as Glen Island, **Ray Mill Island** was made from two more and **Boulter's Island** has been created alongside it by the 1828 cut. The old *Bucksyde* millstream is now the headwater of the new **Jubilee River** and Grass Eyot, Bridge Eyot and two smaller islands have grown in the mainstream.

This aggregation was the work of many years. It may have been begun by **Sir Charles Doe**, the fellow who we last saw struggling to survive the Great Fire of London. Although his fortune went in flames in 1666, as lord of **Hitcham** and Sheriff of London, he was well placed when some bright spark – possible even Doe himself – came up with a brilliant ruse to fix a longstanding local problem. Many of the islands in the Thames between Cookham and Windsor were all-too-often swamped by high waters until the late-1660s when debris from that awful conflagration was used to link and build them up, not quite into the shape we know today, but a step in that direction. The upstream eleven of the 14 islands were aggregated into two, Turner's Mead and Canon Eyot, which later united as the **Warborough**. The downstream three joined to make Glen Island which retained that name when it eventually merged with the Warborough.

Paper Tiger

The Daily Grind

Taplow Mill / 22nd July 2012

The derelict mill looms on our right, the leafy riverscape's industrial secret hidden behind a screen of greenery, its bedraggled shells of brick and metal cladding exuding mild menace. If it wasn't for its smokeless chimney rising above the trees, the sensitive suburban souls in Berks wouldn't have a clue that the Bucks bank here isn't as thickly wooded as upstream.

It is likely that the first mill began grinding corn and other cereals at the downstream end of the island string in the early-10th Century. The original **William de Turville** had a second mill by 1194. There may have been a third by 1281, when **Merton Priory** operated one as a fulling mill to process wool for cloth-making. There were certainly three by 1304 when William de Clyvedene was granted licence to operate them, which may be why they were noted as **Clevedon Mills**. The fulling mill was let with two islands to John the Dyer in 1315 for 40 shillings (£1,250) a year.

Life by the river wasn't always easy – in 1332, a devastating flood destroyed enough corn for Tappelowe parish to be remitted 10 marks (£4,130) in recompense – but it seems to have been profitable. The fulling mill afforded a prosperous business for 82 years from 1523 to **John Holderness**, his widow Joan (from 1562) and their son **Roger Holderness the Elder** (from 1580). In 1562 their annual rental of £8 10s (£2,500) for the mill and four islands was increased by 50 shillings (£730) per year to cover maintenance costs on Queen Elizabeth I's estate at Windsor. **Sir Henry Guldeforde** acquired the fulling mill from the aged Holderness in 1605 and sub-let it four years later to Francis Phillips and Edward Ferrers. However, his attempt to set up an overshot mill in 1613 wasn't successful, possibly because it caused "damage" (more likely, a reduction in water flow) to the fulling mill estimated at £10 annually (£1,600).

When the mill's gate and fence fell into disrepair in 1621, Sir Henry was obliged to twice summon Widow Phipp (Phillips?) before she put her mind to fixing the problem. Nevertheless, when he became lord of the manor in 1628 **Sir Thomas Hampson** was able to lease the mill to William Warre for a staggering annual rental of £57 (£9,800).

The various mills continued turning in a good profit for grinding, fulling and fisheries. Ray Mill remained with the Manfields of Amerden Manor; it was recorded as a watermill in 1671 and (rather strangely) as a windmill in 1720 by which time it isn't clear if there were still three mills at Taplow or two. The fisheries desposition of 1633 noted two corn mills under one roof "anciently called Clevedon Mills". A corn mill and its orchards were leased to Joseph Darvell in 1698 for £80-a-year (£9,125) and another was let in 1709 to Mr Norris for 50 years at £40 (£4,740). Did Darvell and Norris operate under the same roof or did Darvell have the double mill and Norris another altogether? **John Colsell** of Burnham, copyholder of **Brook End Farm**, held the lease on Taplow Mills by the 1740s and passed it to his son **John Colsell** in 1757. Later the cornmills continued to turn happily for **John Benbow** (from before 1814 to 1824), William Lambert (1824 to about 1828) and then **Charles Benbow**, John's son.

Rags but No Riches

Clifden Paper Mill / 22nd July 1835

The Glory Mill at **Wooburn** converted to papermaking in the 1590s and by 1636 there were at least twelve papermills in Bucks including one at Bourne End – but not yet at **Clevedon**, not unless the record of an unspecified mill in 1579 was a first (and apparently unsuccessful) attempt at such diversification. Now old-fashioned papermakers are hard at work. Having supervised as rags were boiled to pulp, now **Thomas Rutland** watches with paternal pride as his young colleague David Fuller pours the pulp gently into trays where it will dry to become thin sheets of paper.

England's first paper mill began operation near Hertford in 1490. By the Stuart Era plenty of cornmills had been converted to papermaking including a number on the River Wye at Wooburn. A record dating from 1636 might explain why the craft was a long time coming to Taplow. It complained that "through the plague and proximity to Windsor, the mills were dangerous to the royal person; that the noisome smell of the rags spread the infection; that the hammers made a hideous noise day and night and even on Sundays and could be heard two or three miles away"; that "people were afraid to afraid to bring their corn" to the combined mills because they charged too much; that paper mills attracted "many poor and indignent persons" and that "fish were destroyed and hindered". If this was an early conservation group at work, it certainly knew how to make its case.

It was a century before William Church came from Wooburn to try to turn the tide in Taplow and not until 1767 that William & Ann Burnham began to make 'white paper' in one of the mills here. The diversification wasn't a great success. By 1780, the mill had been converted again to make cotton and was still doing soon until at least 1803. However, the development of commerce, newspapers and education was driving a rapidly increasing demand for paper. It was only a matter of time before someone else would have a go and in 1810, undeterred by the Burnham's failure, an enterprising fellow called JB Wise decided to try again. Unfortunately he didn't live up to his name. England's first steam-driven papermill had begun operation seven years before in Hemel Hempstead. Mechanisation was the future and his handmade operation survived only five years. However, perhaps Wise had just been too commercially ambitious because his business did leave a durable legacy. Tom's father **John Rutland** and his uncle George were just two of perhaps a dozen papermakers who came from Wooburn and thereabouts to ply their traditional trade at Taplow either for Wise or after his business went to the wall. Their methods are modest in scale and they have stiff competition from the mechanised papermills in Cookham and the Wye Valley but Tom and David are still going strongly enough to make a modest living.

Revolution Arrives

Clifden Paper Mill / 22nd July 1840

It doesn't look so good for Tom Rutland. He takes Lord Orkney's letter from **Taplow Court** steward John Lowe, breaks the seal and reads his landlord's notice to quit. It is a devastating blow. He has made paper here at Clifden Mills for over a quarter-century, man and boy, but **Charles Venables** has decided to bring the Industrial Revolution to Taplow. Tom had seen it coming. The Venables shadow had been looming ever larger for as long as he can remember.

It had all started in 1719 when William Venables came from Mitcham (Surrey) to High Wycombe. His son William stepped into his papermaking shoes. So did William's son William, at Cookham from 1782. And by 1811 this third William's son Charles was installing a coal-fired steam engine in the mill at Hampton Gay (Oxfordshire) where papermaking tradition stretched back to 1681. The young man quickly established himself in the vanguard of the industrialisation of paper-making in southern England with the foundation of ***Charles Venables & Co***. He soon had at least eight other steam-driven papermills operating around Oxford – all serving *Oxford University Press* – and in 1820 Charles' brother and business partner **George Venables** returned to their father's roots to convert Cookham Mill and take up residence there to make sure mechanisation had the desired effects. Meanwhile their younger brother's stationery company *Venables Tyler & Co* was doing such good business at Queenhithe that the fourth William Venables was honoured as Lord Mayor of London in 1825.

When the elder Venables brothers befriended **Charles Benbow**, Tom Rutland might have worried they had designs on converting the cornmills to papermaking. Any such cunning plan came to naught in 1834 when Benbow and his uncle Joseph died as a result of a mill accident. Tom was sincere in the condolences he offered to the younger fellow's widow Sarah, left alone with two infant boys, yet he heaved a quiet sigh of guilty relief as the reliable **George Norrington** took over the cornmills and kept his fingers crossed that Venables had lost interest in Taplow. It was a vain hope. He just had other fish to fry.

More than three-quarters of all papermaking in the country is mechanised now and *Charles Venables & Co* has converted Lower Glory Mill in Wooburn and perhaps seven more mills along the Wye Valley. The man himself has established a fearsome reputation for being "the authentic voice of thunder [as] a doughty proponent of the rights of employers" quick to argue passionately that "fair and free competition in trade [is] not a new desire". *The Windsor & Eton Express* reported in 1827 that Richard Goodchild, a light-fingered 14-year-old employee, had been whipped and kept in solitary confinement for a week as an example to others who might be tempted to steal brass or other valuable items from a Venables mill. Meanwhile George Venables has upset Cookham with a different lack of scruples. Having taken a liking to the ancient sarsen tarrystone which had for centuries stood at the eastern end of the High Street, he had it removed last year to decorate his garden at the mill. It will stay there for 71 years before being restored to public gaze at the junction of Sutton Road and Odney Lane.

Clearly the Venables brothers were just biding their time until his lordship's need for extra income became critical. Having been here at the papermill for a year or so, now the deal is done. Tom knows it is the end: he has no option but to swallow his pride and accept the offer of employment as a carpenter, a post he will hold for many years while Charles Venables sets Charles Dickens a model for his more unscrupulous fictional businessmen, not least in 1843 when he will respond to a proposed reduction in children's hours of work by writing that the government had "done all that can be done to injure and ruin the papermaking trade in the United Kingdom by the protection and assistance given to foreign manufacture, and further interference would be unjust and arbitrary in the extreme and uncalled for".

Trouble at the Mill

Taplow Paper Mills / 15th April 1881

Charles Venables & Co leased *Clifden Mills* from Orkney in 1840 and converted two of the three to mechanised papermaking. **Charles Venables the Elder** installed his sons George and Charles in the newly-built ***Mill House*** and set about adding workers' cottages, boiler and engine houses, a 'rag house', a 'chop house' and a chemical store. Business was soon booming and the Venables were able to cope with Orkney's opportunistic increase in the rent. Visitors to the 1851 Great Exhibition in Hyde Park saw in all their glory not only old Charles' plate paper (for copperplate printing) and brown wrapping paper but also old George's 'hand paper', made at Cookham. When he became the new freeholder of the mills in 1852, **Charles Pascoe Grenfell** was content to leave things as they were. The younger **George Venables** wasn't. He took holy orders in the early-1860s and set out to make the world a better place as Rector of Burch Castle in Norfolk. His brother **Charles Venables the Younger** stuck to the family way and continued making brown paper in Taplow until his death today. His lot was not always a happy one. Two neighbours from ***Thames Cottages*** tell the tale....

Millwright John Pymm knows all about his employer's travails. He says everything was fine while Charles Pascoe Grenfell was alive. When the old banker died in 1867, his son **Henry Riversdale Grenfell** became Willy Grenfell's guardian and took into his care **Taplow Court** and its many properties [*see Appendix 1, Tree 17*]. Two years later the elder Grenfell wrote to Venables complaining that he "had no right to spend more than was allocated" on repairing the mill stables and "must pay the extra". That was the start of more than seven years of acrimony about their relative rights and responsibilities as landlord and tenant. Uncle Henry was particular about the peace and privacy of Taplow Court. He claimed to be "under the impression that it was [the] wish and desire [of Venables] to assist in ensuring privacy of the millstream" and that consequently he couldn't keep a steamer there, or indeed any boat.

Grenfell lives in London at N° 15 St James's Place. William Bill thinks that, being a city gentleman, he had no appreciation that anyone living and working on an island would need boats to bring in or take away goods. As a waterman who drives steam launches, few know better than Bill that the millstream is the only place which is always deep enough for Venables to float boats safely to his banks. The papermaker has kept various craft there for almost 40 years during which he has tended to its banks, cut weeds and removed obstructions at his own expense while doing his best to prevent public access. Nobody on the river could understand "what possible injury [could be caused by his] pretty little steamer *Iris* [which] you can neither see, hear [nor] smell from the grounds or woods of Taplow Court".

Pymm recalls that Henry Grenfell kept Venables and his wife Harriet "in a state of irritation and annoyance" by disputing the need for and cost of maintenance and enhancements at the mill which in his tenant's view "as landlord [he] should have done". Although Grenfell had raised no objection when Venables substantially rebuilt *Mill House* in 1869, three years later the pair fell out over a new chimney for the mill. They argued in 1874 about replacing the "dangerous" wooden bridge to **Glen Island**, building a new landing stage and a new dock to the mill tail at a cost of nearly £200 (£127,000) including all the associated legal fees. And in 1875 the points at issue were a new oak waterwheel gate costing £60 (£39,300) and the restoration of the second mill. On 28th September that year Grenfell brought matters to a head by declaring: "I will not yield my judgement of what is right to you or any man. You have not acted up to what you agreed because you have not signed the agreement" not to bring a steamer into the millstream. Venables was at his wit's end: although he retained right of access for "punts, skiffs and occasional barges", he "pledged not to navigate" the millstream and to reduce his solicitor's fees from £40 to 30 guineas (£3,450 to £2,890). A kind of peace descended but only because Venables was too exhausted to take issue when Grenfell ignored his requests in 1876, firstly to spend £300 (£200,000) to "build a foreman's residence" at the entrance to the mill or otherwise "make addition to the present untidy, dilapidated and very small cottage" (which is between 50 and 100 years old), and secondly to sell Venables "three or four acres high and dry at Taplow or Boyne Hill [to] build a house [where] for winter months [we can escape the] fearful damp". Venables did rebuild ***Mill Cottage***, possibly at his own expense, but he never got his dream of a home on the hill.

Let's hope, says Pymm, things will be more neighbourly now the papermill has passed to **Christopher Cail** and **Willy Grenfell** has reached his maturity.

Burning Bright

Taplow Paper Mills / 22nd July 1902

Millers made flour here for maybe 900 years. **George Norrington** continued grinding grains until 1864 and Charles Weston, Richard Fry and his son John were content enough at the cornmill until it was devoured by its hungry neighbour soon after Cail took it over in 1881. The census that year counted paper manufacturer William Wallace French at ***Rectory Farmhouse*** but his profession and his proximity are no more than circumstantial evidence of his possible executive involvement. Fortunately censuses reveal some of those who were doing the work. In 1851 Samuel Hancock – son of William, a papermaker of Cores End – was lodging with papermaker Daniel Riddle in Bray. By 1861 Sam was married to a Taplow girl: Mary, daughter of William Simmonds. Later they lived in *Tyrrell's Buildings* (where Maidenhead *Sainsbury's* will be) as he continued at ***Charles Venables & Co*** into the 1880s. Meanwhile John Pim evolved from a 'millinger' in 1861 to John Pymm the millwright by 1881. He was succeeded by his 'engineer' son Charles Pimm with James Hawes a foreman papermaker until after 1901.

This paper tiger emerged to show its strength in 1895 – the company accounts for that year record a profit of £2,083 (£1.34m) from a turnover of £24,631 (£15.79m), a very healthy margin of well over 8% – but today as everyone celebrates the coronation of **King Edward VII**, disaster is in the making. The papermill is in flames. Not even three steam fire engines, two manual ones and the mill's own engine will prevent damage costing £10,000 (£5.47m) to repair. Pymm's hopes will be realised when Willy Grenfell extends a loan to help **Cail** recover. In 1904 he will take into partnership **Charles Mullings** and together they will lease ***Mill House*** from Grenfell together with two cottages, a coachhouse and stabling. The business will soon be back on its feet. **Cail** and **Mullings** will repay their landlord's loan in 1906 and five years later Mullings will be resident at ***Rose Mead*** in River Road. Perhaps either or both he and Cail will be the driving force which reinvents *Charles Venables & Co* in 1918 as a limited company with two machines making brown paper. It will be to no avail: although the tiger will survive a few more years, it will never be quite the same animal again. Grenfell, by then **Lord Desborough**, will see the writing on the wall: on 31st December 1929 he will lease *Mill House* to Barrington Wells for 21 years at an annual rent of £250 (£13,300). *Venables* will go bankrupt within months.

Another Level

Nothing Fishy

Boulter's Lock / 22nd July 2012

A question occurs as **John Dunleavey** eases us gently into the crowded lock: should this be Boulter's or Boulters? Nobody seems to know for certain.

The first record of the name was as Bolter's Lock in 1746 but there never was a Mr Bolter. The word *bolter* or *boulter* derives from the Old French *buletior* meaning a *sifter of meal*. It evolved along two courses to mean either *the offices of the bakehouse* of a nobleman or abbey, where it was the root of *butler*, or a mill worker who would sift meal or flour prior to its being bagged – essentially another word for *miller*. However dictionaries usually define a *boulter* as being *a long stout line with several (fishing) hooks attached*, so maybe there is another etymological angle at work.

Locked Up

The first pond lock / 22nd July 1609

The second **Henry Manfield** must have watched with mixed feelings in the 1580s when the weir and flashlock at **Ray Mill Eyote** was replaced by a new construction slightly downstream from the original and in much the same location and elbowed configuration it will be in 2012. Queen Elizabeth I granted **Rea Locke** to Harry Merry, Yeoman of the Chamber, with Robert Weston its appointed keeper. It was a big responsibility. This was the last lock before the sea for most of the following three centuries. When it was opened the force of water roared so loudly it could be heard two or three miles away. In 1792 it will be said that five feet of water above the weir flows over it with such force to bore a pool 20-foot deep and throw up a ridge 30 yards downstream that rises to barely three feet below the surface. This ridge made for a convenient ford but any paddling traveller had better listen carefully for the lockkeeper's warning horn or risk being washed away. And it's easy to think that the surge may have made survival so hard for the 1461 bridge.

Manfield might have been pleased that the new weir helped maintain water levels but he couldn't rest easy. As lord of **Amerden Manor**, he held the right of drawing ships and boats from **Amerden Bank** to **Ray Mill** and – more to the point – of charging for the privilege, but downstream levels remained too irritatingly variable. Being an innovative sort – especially when he saw a commercial opportunity – he has stuck his oar in by installing the first 'pond lock' on the Thames near Taplow Mill (probably a 'pound lock', a Dutch invention of necessity). This should prove popular because it will allow boats to move between levels easily without upsetting the general levels or flow of the river, and without great delays. However it won't survive for long, perhaps because his tolls are a tad excessive, perhaps because his nemesis **Sir Henry Guldeforde** will win the day. River traffic will have no option but once more to run the risk at the flashlock which will remain in the weir until at least 1865.

Rotten Lock

The Bucks Bank Boulter's Lock / 22nd July 1826

The City of London is complaining again that the height of the lock's cill makes it "inaccessible and impassable at low water", that "the crooked, shallow channel below it [is distant] from the towing path" and that the whole device is "is completely worn out". It is and I am, says 75-year-old **Richard Ray**, but those city folk have got a cheek. They've polluted the river so badly that it is five years since anyone caught a salmon up here. Richard is right, there's a significant chemical barrier downstream, but the increasing number of locks and weirs play their part in preventing salmon getting upriver to spawn. By 1833 there will be none at all in the Thames.

Old Richard has been keeper of the lock for all but the first winter of its 54 years and of the towpath to Hedsor Wharf for almost as long. There's nobody better to tell its tale. Bolter's was the lowest lock on the Thames from 1746 until Romney Lock was built at Windsor in 1797. Meanwhile Bolter's had been rebuilt as Boltus in 1772 to take barges 130 feet long, 18 wide and drawing three; the charge was 4d (£1.90) per ton for each there-and-back voyage. By 1780 the lock was in a bad state but its keeper counts himself lucky: ***South Lodge*** and its stable were built for him in the old quarry, he has had two pay rises – to 12s-a-week (£66) in 1774 and to £5-a-month (£305) in 1814 – and there have been more than a few opportunities to earn extra half-crowns for this and that. I was worth it, smiles Richard. By the 1790s an average 69,285 tons of merchandise was passing through Boulter's every year paying tolls of almost £580 (£60,500) [*see Maps 33 & 34*].

Some of the bargees have been hard to handle. In 1773 the fourth **Lord Inchiquin** complained of barges lying in Taplow millstream and their crews trespassing and causing destruction in his woods where they "very much misbehaved themselves by their indecent Conversations and horrid Oaths and imprecations". His lordship was able to pull strings to secure an Act of Parliament protecting the privacy of his millstream. The lock-keeper had to rely on Thames Commissioners to temper miscreants. Later that year William Webb of Wallingford tried to force his barge through the lock without paying the toll; he was required to pay to repair the damage caused. John Langley of Great Marlow was fined 20s (£86) for doing much the same in 1796. And in 1785 Robert Holmes of Abingdon was obliged to pay five guineas (£580) compensation and to publish an apology in the Reading journal for assaulting poor Richard.

Navigating the lock has always been difficult. Its lower sill was noted as being too high in 1794 and downstream shoals were building above the fishing bucks belonging to Ray Mill miller **Richard Lovegrove**. His three barges and **Charles Benbow**'s two know the waters well but plans have been afoot for a while to build a new lock on the Berks bank. As is the way of things, Bucks bank landowners will claim compensation in 1828 when their towpath is no longer required.

Another question occurs: could be Richard Ray descended from the **John atte Ray** noted at **Ray Mill Island** the small matter of 522 years ago? Ah, nods the lock-keeper with a wink, prob'ly wos me owd granddad. He will be buried by the old St Nicholas' Church on 27th February 1829 just six months before its doors are closed for the last time.

Something Fishy

Boulter's Weir / 19th May 2000

It wasn't until 1975 that the Thames was thought to be clean enough to be replenished with salmon and there was much celebration on 5th August 1993 when the biggest salmon ever caught in the non-tidal Thames – all of 22 inches long and weighing 14.5 pounds – was landed near **Boulter's Lock**. This encouraged the investment of over £3m to construct ladders to enable salmon and other fish to climb past each of 37 weirs between the sea and the favourable spawning and nursery habitat of the upstream River Kennet. Today Arthur Wellesley, 8th Duke of Wellington, and Sir Brian Moffat, Chairman of *British Steel*, are combining their talents to open the new ladder at Boulter's Weir, the final link in a chain to help salmon to find the Kennet where the completion of ladders will shortly be completed.

The scheme will initially seem successful – 338 salmon will be counted swimming upstream in 2003 – but numbers will decline dramatically. Nobody will see any salmon in 2005 and thereafter, despite the release of some 40,000 salmon smolts into the Kennet, only the occasional stray will make it back this far.

Locked Forever

The Berks Bank Boulter's Lock / 19th July 1885

As is the way on most summer Sunday afternoons, the lock is crowded with boats skippered by gentlemen trying to impress their ladies with nautical skills they don't possess. Oars clash, an altercation arises. The bronzed face of the well-built and muscular lock-keeper flashes a sturdy look from beneath the peak of his cap as he sternly calls for the antagonists to go quietly. And so they do. And so they should, for as a retired gunnery and cutlass instructor, former Chief Petty Officer William Turner is used to having his orders obeyed. Not for nothing is he known as 'Chief'.

It is 56 years since the new cut was completed and the new lock was opened on 30th March 1829. It was called Ray Mill Pound until 1842 but so many still called it Boulter's that the old name stuck. Being its keeper is no easy task. The responsibility changed hands six times in the 13 years from 1868, with three fellows being discharged – one for incivility, another for accepting tolls without receipt and the third for intemperance. Thereafter John Moy served for two years, **H Cordery** for three and Moy again for three during which his fine roses drew much compliment. In the early summer of 1881, knowing that the proud lock-keeper would not part with a single bloom, the artist **George Leslie** charmed his wife Lucy to give him one for a young lady in exchange for a sketch of the lock cottage and its garden. Was this why Moy lost his place to Chief later that year?

The white-bearded, wing-collared Chief started well – within a year he was commended for saving a boy from drowning – and nowadays he has everything running smoothly enough for another artist, **Edward Gregory**, to capture the moment in sketches from which he will create a painting to make Boulter's (and himself) famous forevermore. Within three years it will be necessary to introduce a novel solution to reduce congestion. Small boats with their occupants still seated will be able to bypass the lock by means of a moving ramp of wooden slats, with chocks to prevent boats from rolling over, which will carry them up to the higher level. Chief Turner will continue as the keeper of Boulter's until being succeeded in 1905 by John Harrison, formerly a

Maps 33 & 34 – Down by the Riverside: The Mill and Nearby

Rotten Lock & Paper Tiger

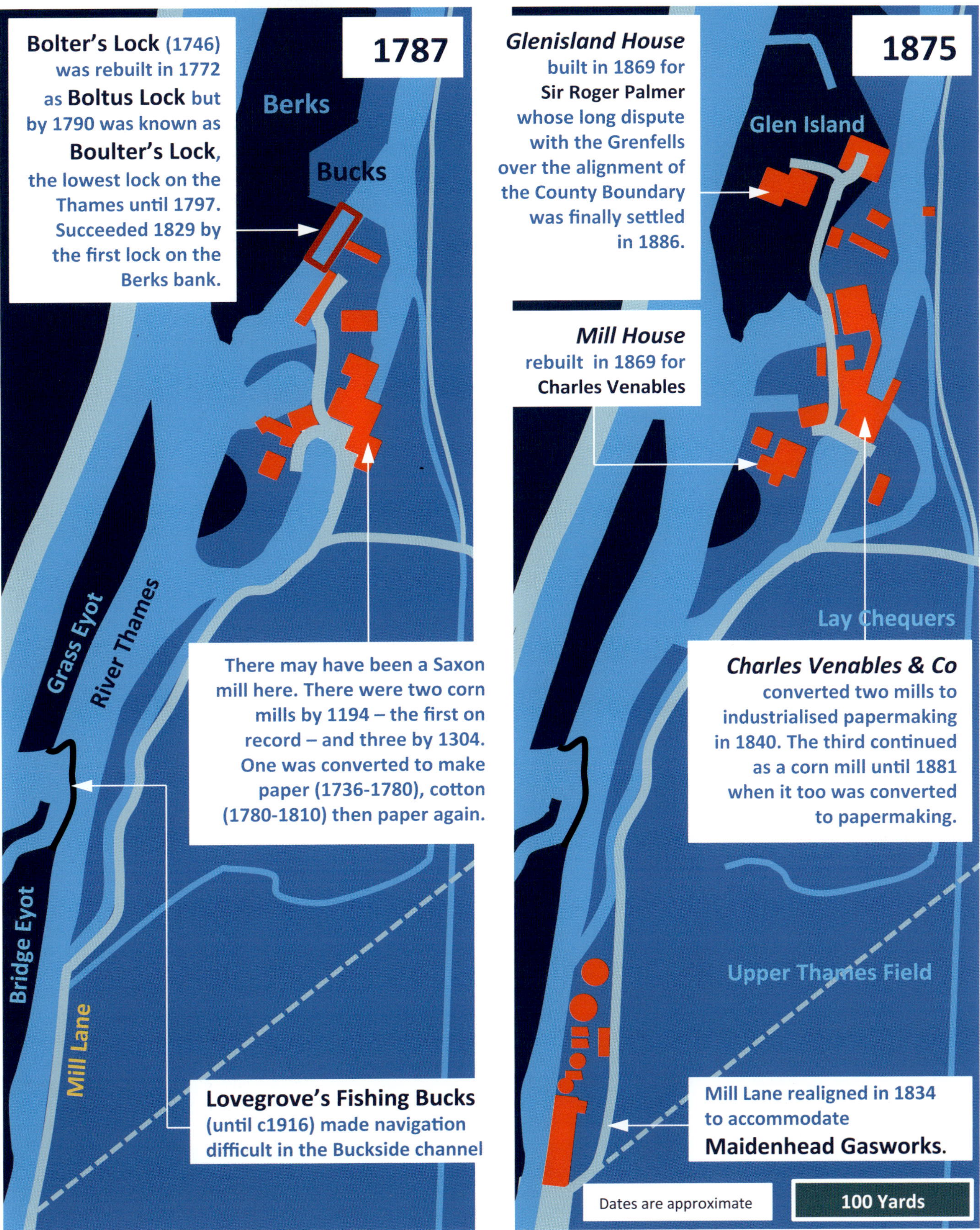

Primary Sources: Inclosure Maps 1779/1787 and Ordnance Survey 1875

Denbighshire coalminer, who during 14 years in charge will preside over the 1909 introduction of an electric motor to power the boat roller and the complete reconstruction of the lock in 1912, a project made possible by the acquisition of Ray Mill Island by the Thames Conservancy three years earlier.

More Rotten Lock

Bray Lock / 22nd July 1892

Teddy Morris is hard at work. The lock-keeper closes the downstream gates, winds open the upstream sluices and looks down his nose at the struggle some inexperienced skippers are having keeping their craft in order as the water swirls into the pound and rises quickly. Life has its ups and downs, he says, which is as it should be for a lock-keeper. He pauses to let his joke sink in before telling his tale.

He can't say why this is Bray Lock when it is actually on the Amerden bank but there may have been a mill here in Saxon times. There were three by 1632. Level's paper mill was noted in 1770. Lavender's corn mill was described in 1794 as being "of little value" yet 50 years later the miller, a fellow called Lewis, could afford to promise £300 (£378,000) towards the construction of a lock because the increased control of the flow would benefit his business. There have always been strong currents and variable levels hereabouts. Various sources say that **Thomas Manfield the Elder** installed a flashlock and weir at *Hameldon* or *Amarsden Ashe* that in 1510 or 1527 was "pluckt up" by order of the "Commission of Scowers" (sewers?). Others tell of "a certain weir between *Olde Field* and *Amarsden Ashe*" in 1672 and of navigation around Headpile Eyot being a risky business due to the shallows and strong currents. Salvation came in 1845 when James Fenemore was appointed to operate his lock "without sides". However, as his fluctuating lock-keeper's income testifies, it was to be a false dawn. His monthly wage was reduced from three guineas (£3,800) at the outset to 47s (£2,200) ten years later because when the river was full he had to leave his gates open and could collect no tolls.

Fenemore's wage had recovered to 52s (£1,960) by the time he retired in 1867 but inflation had eroded its value and the complaints of bargees and successive lock-keepers Charles Roberts, Ralph Lewis, J Croft and Chainey all fell on deaf ears until that Charles Dickens fellow wrote that the lock was "rotten and dangerous". What with him being famous and all, people sat up and took notice, chuckles Teddy. The lock was rebuilt in 1885 and I came from Oxfordshire to keep it. The problem's different nowadays, he sighs. I don't mind at all being busy: it's that people with no appreciation of the river have discovered it. And worse, they think they own it. They hire boats from **Jonathan Bond** by Maidenhead Bridge and treat the Thames between Cookham and Windsor as their playground.

Islands in the Stream

Taplow Woods and Maidenhead Bridge from Cliefden Terrace / 1803

Art in the Aid of Nature: Around Sashes Island

Leaving Cookham Lock / 2012

The real Page's Wharf / 2012

Hedsor Wharf, calm waters below where once rapids ran / 2012

Art in the Aid of Nature: Cliveden Reach

Cliveden Reach / 2012

The Astor-improved quay for My Lady Ferry / 2012

Time for Lunch / 2012

Cliveden on High / 2012

Secret Stream with an Unhappy Ending

The derelict paper mill / 2012

All the Lock

Boulter's Lock / 2012

'Chief' William Turner
Lock-keeper
1881-1905

Below right:
Boulter's Lock, Sunday Afternoon
– Edward Gregory 1897

River Frivolity

Merrily Down the Stream

Timeless Stream, Changing Ways

Bray Reach / 22nd July 1890

There was a time when only the people on the river really knew the river. These proper working watermen may have raced against one another but didn't think to keep records. If there's one thing young Victorian gentlemen like more than making rules, it's keeping records. Once they started rowing, it wasn't long before the competition got serious. The Star Club of Maidenhead held its first regatta on Cliveden Reach in 1839, only for members to be dismayed a few weeks later as it paled by comparison with the grander and ultimately more durable annual sporting and social event which began at Henley. **Willy Grenfell** and his pals revived the tradition in 1876 by founding **Maidenhead Rowing Club** and blessing it with a boathouse sitting snugly by the Berks bank southern flank of Maidenhead Bridge. Nine years later, Grenfell was a founder member of the Thames Punting Club, not least because his home stretch was ideal for racing punts. And in 1893 the rowing club revived Maidenhead Regatta, an annual event held on a course upstream of the bridge.

Properly organised regattas are all well and good. It is the casual amateurs which irritate HS Wilson as he prepares the chapter in Professor Satterly's book on the Maidenhead-to-Windsor stretch of the river. The poor fellow is a sensitive soul who regards Brunel's bridge as "a leading case of engineering versus the picturesque" and is dismayed that the Thames has "undergone disastrous change. It has become crowded, noisy [and] vulgar. Its beauties remain what they ever were but its character has deteriorated. Gone is the pure peace, the cool calm, the tranquil seclusion which twenty years ago rendered it the most charming haunt of the lover of Nature, of the poet who sought mental repose in most lovely and most quiet scenery. [Anyone] who knew the tranquil Thames in the old time, long ago, must find, in its brawling loudness of today, a change which renders sad the heart. I remember it when there were no steam-launches. Now Captain Jinks of *The Selfish* too often troubles the water as he [and] his friends enjoy themselves on the pure river which they pollute with their presence and disturb with their rowdyism. I am credibly informed that one Sunday no less than nine hundred pleasure-craft passed through Boulter's Lock. To what secret ait can the river nymphs now fly for rest and delicate delight?"

Bray Reach / 22nd July 1892

Waterman **Billy Morris** will succeed his father as the keeper of **Bray Lock** for many years. Today he has made us an offer we can't refuse: a ride in his skiff upstream to Maidenhead Bridge. The young fellow is just 24 but he sculls against the headway like a veteran in the brief west-to-east flow past Headpile Eyot.

How little this charming haunt has changed since we met the first Lord Orkney over there on the towing path in 1720. The sun-sparkles dance as the breeze playfully caresses the water. Another barge full of bricks is hauled upriver by a sturdy Clydesdale, the bargee on the tiller and Henry Atkins 'Junior' walking the horse. As ever, the only sounds are the chirrup of birds on the wing, the leaves whispering sweet-nothings, the soft splash of Billy's oars and the faint creak of his rowlocks. Willows still weep with joy at the water's edge. The tower of **St Michael's Church** in Bray proclaims the Lord and all's well with the world. Or it was until that steam-launch heavy with rowdies came into view and, more irritatingly, into earshot. The noise of the engine is enough to shatter the secluded tranquillity. The raucous exchanges between those on board intrude even more unpleasantly. The launch cuts across in front of us and flouts convention by passing on our starboard. Billy brings his bow round to ride the wake muttering that isn't so much the stupidity of these amateurs that is so annoying, it's that they think they're so clever.

Perhaps Mr Wilson was right. What is the river coming to?

This gloomy thought is chased to the back of our minds as the river widens a little and bends with glorious grace around to the north-to-south flow it holds as far as Cookham Lock some three miles upstream. We lie back in the skiff for a thousand yards and admire Billy's smooth sculling almost as much as the scenery.

Bray Reach / 22nd July 2012

Perhaps Mr Wilson wasn't quite so right. Here aboard **John Dunleavy**'s electric launch the river still seems to have a sense of forever about it, a certain magic that blends old and new with artistic flourish and encourages old-fashioned courtesies between its users, such as the friendly waves we've exchanged with the motley crew of that passing pleasure cruiser.

David Long is not so forgiving. He observes scathingly that the Berks bank is lined from Bray to Maidenhead with quiet but unmistakeable proclamations of achievement in styles that might have been "promoted by Mr Toad on his return from perusing the recent architecture of Dallas, Texas". Nobody lives there who hasn't made it. Some mansions are remnants of early-20th Century neo-Tudor extravagance. Many of their more recent neighbours try to appear older than their years; a few are unashamedly modern. No riverbank garden can enjoy complete privacy from the waterborne public gaze – perhaps the price is higher for television personalities Sir Michael Parkinson and the soon-to-be convicted Rolf Harris– but these homes are all highly desirable, not least for having their privileged view of the rural Bucks bank. This has changed too, of course – there would have been no waterside trees or bushes along the towing path – yet it easy to believe it is as it always was until we reach the string of grand houses along River Road, many once of the Whitlaw empire. They ease the mood from rural to select and respectful urbanity with no more than a ripple on the river's serenity.

Local amateur naturalist **Des O'Sullivan** regards the reaches above Maidenhead Bridge as a "jewel of nature". They are home to an amazingly wide variety of wildlife. In the woods on the banks are deer, mice, rabbits, foxes, grass snakes, adders and occasional badgers. The huge insect population provides a feast for resident ducks, geese, grebes, moorhens, herons, swans, cormorants, thrushes, woodpeckers, wagtails, jays, tits, tawny owls, wrens, robins, red kites, kingfishers and both Pipistrelle and Daubenton's bats. The slack waters are safe breeding grounds and nurseries for pinhead fry. Chub, dace, roach, rudd, gudgeon, grayling, flounder, carp, catfish, perch, pike, zander, salmonid, brown trout, barbel, bleak and bream all abound; some even use the Boulter's fish ladder. And then there are the great freshwater snails and the swan, zebra and pea mussels so important to the river's ecosystem. No wonder Des will tell anyone who'll listen that these "high levels of biodiversity [and] ecological value.... must be protected from developer depredations".

The Eel Bucks / 22nd July 1892

Our comfort is disturbed below the Sounding Arch when **Billy Morris** has to break his rhythm to negotiate around a wobbling wherry in which ladies shaded by parasols laugh at the antics of their menfolk in their boaters and brightly-striped jackets. From here to Boulter's the river is crowded with punts, rowboats, dinghies, launches, skiffs and wherries of all shapes and sizes, few crewed by anyone who has a clue what they're doing and everyone wary of the steam launch *Samuel* as her master Walter Pearce pilots her downstream from her moorings by Boulter's Lock.

Billy skilfully manoeuvres his skiff under the western arch. He nods to our right to Oldfield Eyot and says it must be "the little ait after the bridge" noted in the 1570s as being sown with hemp and then barley. He adds that not so many boats go up this quieter channel. The river is funnelled by converging wooden barriers to rush through seven narrow channels in a strange timber framework spanned by a footbridge from the Berks bank to the island where **Brunel** founded the central pier of his arches. The intricate wrought ironwork of the footbridge seems to have been spun by spiders with a fine artistic touch. To the right is a pinnacled boathouse raised on stilts to give the effect of a witch's lair floating on the surface mist. To what sinister purpose does she put the 10-foot long cones of woven willow suspended high above each channel just below the planking of the bridge? We can see why novice watermen might be intimidated, but how will we get past this barrier?

Billy steers us to the left into a pool of still water bounded by the diagonal funnel and pauses to explain that the bucks are lowered into the water every evening from October to December to catch migrating adult eels. The upstream funnels guide them in and once they're in, they can't get out: a bit like a lobster trap. They probably catch over half-a-hundredweight of eels here most nights and can sell them at a shilling-a-pound, so that'd be £3 (£2,025) for a night's work. Talk about being well-eeled, jokes Billy, just like John Collier, a retired barrister for whom he thinks ***Riverside***, that big house up there, was built in the late-1850s. He reckons the bucks were already there well before Collier added the bridge and the boathouse in 1865. That was about the time *Edenall* was built next door for Henry Harrison, a gentleman friend of Collier's. Both places were bought by a Welsh stockbroker called Philip Taylor who lives at ***Edendale*** and in 1889 turned *Riverside* into an exclusive club run by a steward, John Fitzgerald. And having been built six years ago as a private residence, ***The Riviera Hotel*** is now open for business. In five years the rowing club's boathouse will be squeezed between it and the bridge. Oh yes, mark my words, laughs Billy: this is the place to be if you can afford it.

We emerge through a small upstream opening into the congestion below Maidenhead Bridge. Boats trying to leave Bond's landing stage can't get away for others trying to get back there. A steam barge carrying coal to Maidenhead Gasworks looms menacingly through the melee of amateur watermen. Billy shakes his head in quiet exasperation and lays the blame for all this madness on three people: **Henry Hoare** and the two **Jonathan Bonds**, three new Taplovians who he reckons have done more than most to make Maidenhead famous. It is time for the fourth and final leg of our pub crawl....

Jonathan Bond the Elder

Between the Bridges / 22nd July 1892

Bond's main boatyard spreads over two parcels of land. One occupies the whole of the sliver of Berks in Bucks downstream of Maidenhead Bridge and a tad north of it too. The other is across **River Road**. His largest workshop is about 20 years old. It is remarkable for being the first reinforced concrete building in Britain. Could it have been designed and built by **James Rutland**? Can it be a coincidence that soon afterwards Rutland added a concrete extension to the rear of his father's former home (not yet ***The Cottage***) to accommodate blacksmith **Davis Harris**, his wife Charlotte and six children?

Bond is proud to build motor-launches for discerning clients with deep pockets who fancy themselves as watermen. His own fleet of ten elegantly-fitted steam launches includes the 73-foot *Emperor* and the 66-foot *Formosus*, among the best-appointed on the Thames. He also has hundreds of skiffs, punts and canoes. All boats and launches are available for hire by the day, week, month or season with luncheons or teas furnished by ***Skindles Hotel***.

The success of both *Skindles* and *Bond's* depends in part on the aristocracy choosing to believe that it is unnecessary for young ladies to be chaperoned on the river. Neither Henry Hoare nor **Jonathan Bond the Elder** has ever made the mistake of looking this gift horse in the mouth. Some say it all began almost 100 years ago when Bond, then a cattle drover, avoided the toll to cross **Maidenhead Bridge** by buying the adjacent ferry to carry his cows over the river. He quickly realised that it was all the same to him whether his customers had four legs or two and he took to ferrying full-time after 1838 when railway passengers, who had walked from **Maidenhead (Riverside) Station**, preferred to pay a small fee to ride in his wherry rather than the more expensive bridge toll.

Billy Morris isn't convinced this tall tale quite holds water. He thinks it a flight of fancy that buying the ferry would have been cheaper than paying occasional tolls to drive livestock over the bridge. And as Jonathan the Elder was only 19 in 1838, if he had done any droving, it wasn't for long was it? Consequently it must have been his father who started it all. Maybe we should call him Jonathan the Eldest? However, there's no arguing that once the railway arrived the young fellow was quick to catch on to ferrying. And when Bray Lock tamed this stretch of the Thames in 1845, he came up with the clever ruse of renting skiffs to people who wanted to row themselves across. He set himself up on two stretches of river frontage – one with a cottage and boathouse sublet from **William Skindle the Elder** and another leased in partnership with Thomas Wynn – and in no time had boats aplenty on the go. The censuses have him down as a Cookham publican in 1841 and a Bray fisherman in 1851 and 1861 but, says Billy, you have to remember three things. Firstly: Maidenhead doesn't exist as far as census-takers are concerned; people on the west bank are in either Cookham or Bray, an anomaly that will change in 1901. Secondly: although Bond's main boatyard is on the east bank, it is counted as being in Bray, so he is likely to have been there some years before 1857 when Maidenhead Corporation granted him a 99-year lease on the site. And thirdly: whatever he called himself, the boats were his bread-and-butter, business boomed and by the mid-1860s he was living in considerable comfort in Taplow on the Bath Road at ***Cedar Lodge***.

Jonathan Bond the Younger

Sunnyside, Maidenhead Bridge / 22nd July 1904

Twenty years ago the boathouse was a place for Bond's eldest surviving son **Charles** (then of N° 3 ***Thames Cottages***) to learn the ropes before eventually succeeding his father. It was not to be. Sadly he drowned in Bray Reach in 1889 and, having served for many years in the Yeomanry regiment that is now the Queen's Own Oxfordshire Hussars, **Jonathan Bond the Younger** stepped into his big brother's shoes to run the boat hire business. When his father dies at Christmas this year, he will take over the whole concern and invest his considerable energy in building its assets and its reputation.

The junior Jonathan celebrated Queen Victoria's Diamond Jubilee in 1897 by beginning work on the *Empress of India*: at 83-foot long and capable of carrying 250 passengers, the biggest launch the company will ever build. There were whispers of his disappointment that the aging Queen wasn't amused enough to acquire it. He shrugged it all off to commemorate Her Majesty in 1902 with the launch of the 73-foot *Her Majesty's* and build **Bridge Villa** and **Sunnyside** here at the top end of his boatyard, the latter as home for his son George Bond. Now he intends to celebrate the continuing custom of King Edward VII by launching *His Majesty* in 1906.

Electric launches first appeared hereabouts in 1889 and by 1900 they were being operated by six competitors: *Andrews*, ***Bond's***, *Bowen*, *Immisch*, *Thames Valley Launch Co* and *Woodhouse*. Bond was initially content to supplement his fleet by buying electric launches from others until he built *Esperanza* in 1898. Now he has seven including *Kerlew* and *Primate* (both 40-foot) and the 45-foot *Tagus*. He has exercised his considerable influence to have a 4-inch pipe laid from the gasworks to fire the generator he uses to recharge their batteries. The success of this fleet will inspire a further diversification in 1908 when he builds his first electric canoe. He will be succeeded in 1914 by George who will style the company simply as *Bond's* and expand his fleet and reduce his competition by acquiring *Immisch*.

Edward the Third

Riverside Cottages, The Causeway / 22nd July 1904

Edward Andrews is the third of that name hereabouts, which may be why he is called Ned. As a young man he made his living as an angler and his name as a punting champion. His sport became his livelihood in 1870 when he began to hire out punts and skiffs in competition with *Bond's*. His eldest son Edward (the fourth) died in 1890 but nowadays he and his second son Albert must have 200 punts and boats available for hire at their boatyard on the Berks bank just downstream from *Wilder's* boatyard and separated from it by Clappers Creek.

Back in 1841 his grandfather the first Edward, a fisherman of Cookham, lived with his wife Ann and a dozen children in a cottage near to ***The Orkney Arms***. Neither he nor his home stayed long. He moved away to his father Willison Andrews' farm in Harpsden (Oxfordshire) and the cottage was demolished to make way for ***Causeway Cottages***. The second Edward was a fisherman who lived in various locations in Braywick before becoming a waterman on the Thames and by 1891 on the Regent's Canal at St Pancras. In 1847 his wife Mary gave him their first child, the third Edward (Ned), who in the late-1860s moved with his wife Elizabeth from Ray Park to N° 4 *Causeway Cottages*, next door to her parents Elizabeth & Henry Scribbans, a railway policeman. When Ned lost his Elizabeth in 1884, his parents-in-law at N° 3 took in his boys Edward and Albert and also cared for Ellen, Bertha, Elizabeth and Tom while he was at work on the river. Life took a turn for the better in 1887 when he married Louisa Harraway of Devizes who gave him four more children, the last four years ago when he was 53 and she 45. The Scribbans moved to N° 2 *Thames Cottages* enabling the Andrews family to expand into what had become Nos 3 & 4 ***Riverside Cottages***.

Ned's pride and joy is his electric fleet of 12 launches and the *E Andrews & Son* flagship *Angler* which next summer Albert will skipper as King Edward VII, Queen Alexandra and their royal party enjoy the pleasures of the Thames. Sadly tragedy will strike in 1907 when Albert is killed in a river accident. His three half-brothers Harold, Arthur (known by his second name, John) and Frederick will join their father to make the family firm ***E Andrews & Sons***.

Not Page's Wharf

Mill Lane / 22nd July 2013

John Dunleavey lives with his partner **Jane Edmondson** and their daughter **Molly** on ***The Wharf***, a terrace of modern riverfront town houses just south of the kink in Mill Lane. He gets irked when people say this is ***Page's Wharf***. History is on his side. It has always used the name to refer to Cliveden's wharf upstream while this riverbank between the gasworks and the sliver of land acquired in 1852 by James Pearce was ***The Causeway***, a busy quay since before 1814. That would be why the terrace of 13 houses built here in around 1865 was called ***Causeway Cottages*** before being renamed ***Riverside Cottages*** in the 1880s when the southern end made way for a pair of large, semi-detached houses – originally ***Island View*** (by 1950, ***Nº 5 The Causeway***) and ***Causeway House*** (now ***Mallard's Reach***). By 1925 ***The Tower House*** had squeezed between the latter and the remainder of the terrace which was demolished in the 1990s and replaced by *The Wharf*.

William Skindle the Younger

Hamelton Cott, Manor Road, Worthing / 3rd April 1915

Anthony Packe is the 8-year-old grandson of **Charles Pearce-Serocold** of ***Taplow Hill*** [*see Appendix 1, Tree 18*]. Having taken rooms here by the seaside for the Easter holiday, his mother Dorothy has brought him here to meet an old friend. It is strange to think that this old chap is **William Skindle the Younger**. Willy will celebrate his 100th birthday in a few months and yet here he is in his dark sitting-room full of dark heavy furniture talking brightly about the 1820s when he was a post-boy on the stagecoaches and the 1830s when he had a fine reputation with the punt-pole. He nods proudly at all the punting trophies that still adorn the mantelpiece and yet his face darkens when his young visitor asks about the 1840 Henley Regatta when he rowed bow for The Star Club of Maidenhead as it lost narrowly in the coxed-four final heat of the District Challenge Cup against The Albion Club of Henley. It is only with a little difficulty that he is persuaded to tell about his father....

Life's a Picnic

A Taste of Honey

Skindles Hotel / 22nd July 1914

Most people earn less than £1-a-week (£83.74). ***Skindles Hotel*** doesn't cater for most people. It is offering hampers for boating and picnic parties at either 7s 6d (£31.40) or 10s 6d (£42.29) per head including hire of "luncheon baskets, glass, linen, plate, china, etc, etc". The less expensive hampers allow four people to share a cold shoulder of lamb and mint sauce, a fowl, a tongue or a pie (either steak or veal and ham), salad and dressing with bread and cheese. The higher price buys butter for your bread and both a tongue and a choice of pie. The number of fowls and the joint of lamb increase according to the size of the party, and larger parties also can enjoy pressed beef and extra options such as lobster salad and pigeon pie. All customers can order wines and waters at "20% off Hotel Charges".

The Original Skindle

Skindles Hotel / 22nd July 2013

Even as the dark clouds of the Great War were gathering, the legacy of **William Skindle the Elder** had already far exceeded his lifetime achievements. The echoes in today's derelict hotel on Taplow Riverside make it all too easy to assume that he presided over his elite clientele in the late-Victorian and Edwardian Eras when *Skindles* came to mean Maidenhead. He certainly started the ball rolling but was in fact long gone before his name reached the height of its fame.

Little is known of Skindle's first 36 years except he had been a postillion for Sir Thomas Fremantle (then a baronet of Swanbourne in Aylesbury Vale, later Baron Cottesloe) and that when his aspirations to be a King's Messenger came to naught he became a waiter instead. It was probably in this capacity that he first came to work in Taplow before 1826 when his son Henry's baptism first brought him to the attention of the Parish Register. He was quick off the mark in or before 1833 when the opportunity arose to become "keeper of *The Orkney Arms*", but of course that didn't mean he owned the land it stood on....

The Orkney Arms Hotel / 22nd July 1870

In 1846, Skindle agreed a 14-year lease with **Lord Orkney** which made him secure as sitting tenant when **Zadok Jessell** bought the hotel in 1852. By then he had been astute enough to take two tenancies: one on a cottage and boathouse which he sublet to **Jonathan Bond**, the other on **Foxholes**, a close on the north side of the Bath Road about 200 yards east of Maidenhead Bridge. These investments turned out to be nice little nest-eggs but it was his success as an hotelier that attracted all the attention. By a happy coincidence, day-trippers taking a cab or walking from the station could enjoy their day without having to pay the toll to cross Maidenhead Bridge. Here on the Bucks bank is the perfect combination: pleasure boats to hire from Bond and fine fare to buy from Skindle, either in picnic baskets to take out onto the river or in the comfort of *The Orkney Arms*. No wonder that in 1860 William Skindle father and son jointly renewed the lease from Jessell at an annual rent of £160 (£13,100) for 14 years.

The old boy was 83 when he passed away three years ago leaving his eldest son and namesake to continue as leaseholder in partnership with his brothers Henry and George. Now things are changing: today **William the Younger** has jumped at the chance to buy the freehold from Edward and George Jessell for £4,000 (£2.92m), half of which he has borrowed from Edward Cox of N° 25 Gloucester Square, Hyde Park. And yet there will be even bigger changes in 1873: William will repay Cox on 15th April; he will lease the hotel the following day to Alfred Lewis for 31 years at an annual rental of £800 (£62,000); on 23rd August he will allow **Henry Riversdale Grenfell** to exercise his father's reversion to acquire the place for £4,000 (£2.5m); and by 3rd October he and Henry will be the proud owners of *The Marine Hotel* in Worthing. The Skindles' legend will last much longer in Taplow than the half-century or so they lived here [*see Maps 35 & 36*].

Tall Tale – Tiny but Most Desirable

The Old Public Slipway / 22nd July 1892

Billy Morris sculls past our destination to let the current carry us downstream. With delicate flips of his oars, he threads his skiff through a crowd of departing punts to reach the public slipway by the upstream Bucks bank flank of Maidenhead Bridge. He loops his mooring line around a bollard and helps us clamber ashore. A babbling throng mills amok between the two boathouses built here by Bond in 1880. We edge into the quieter shade of the bridge to hear Billy's amusing tale....

In February last year the Corporation of Maidenhead auctioned the lease for this 140-foot strip of river frontage. This was a sales pitch of course for its true measure is 134 feet, 50 of which protrude in front of the riverside bar – ***Skindles Hotel Annexe*** – which now occupies the cottage and boathouse Bond once let from Skindle. What's the story here? Billy believes that the 1461 bridge sprang from this point and that the protrusion was a landing stage for a ferry. And ever since the new bridge was opened in 1777, the public have had right of access to the river and to the ferry which continues to afford passengers an alternative crossing less expensive than the bridge toll.

Apparently **Jonathan Bond the Younger** was keen to acquire the lot, only to be obliged by stiff competition from a stranger to raise his bid to £215-a-year (£12,900) before securing it. Afterwards he furiously challenged his contestant only to be astounded that the stranger thought he was bidding for the freehold. According to *The Financial Times*, "next to the Bank of England and the Mansion House [it must be] the most desirable freehold in the country" at over £50,000 an acre (£4.74m).

The Old Public Slipway / 22nd July 2013

It's a good story but it doesn't add up. Various legal documents relating to the sale of ***Bond's*** in 1937 confirm that the annual rent for the whole holding – the boatyard to the south of the bridge, the slipway north of it and the dry arches under it – was £280 from 1925 until the expiry of the original 99-year lease in 1956. A quick bout of mental arithmetic confirms that 1925 would be roundabout the two-thirds point in this term and 1891 the one-third point. It would be logical for there to be provison in the lease for periodic rental uplifts. All this suggests that the auction in question occurred at the first renewal milestone and the sum related to the whole holding, not just to the slipway. What isn't clear is how, having leased it to **Jonathan Bond the Elder** in 1857, the Corporation had the right to offer any portion of it at auction – but town clerks are notorious clever clogs. Such presumption was still evident in the early-1990s when the National Rivers Authority felt obliged to write to the Berkshire County solicitor to object to unlawful enclosure of this "public water place". However it is amusing to think that "the most desirable freehold in the country" was in Taplow even if it was owned by Maidenhead.

The Old Public Slipway / 22nd July 1892

And how privileged you are to stand upon it, laughs Charles Asplin. He welcomes us with a firm handshake and looks back 26 years in the story of the transformation of Maidenhead (but actually Taplow) into THE place to be....

The Changing of the Guards

The Causeway / 22nd July 1865

Change is in the air. This short stretch of road runs past the west flank of ***The Orkney Arms*** to the gasworks where it kinks to join the southern end of **Mill Lane**. It is a hive of activity with builders hard at work on both sides.

The grand Bath Road frontage of hotel stands as proudly as ever. Meanwhile on **The Causeway** the old taproom and its adjoining cottage where ostler Henry Bowyer now lives are being joined and renovated to create ***The Hotel Tap***. Life is uncomfortable for Bowyer and his family of five but *The Tap* will still be their home once it opens to slake the thirst and sate the hunger of day-trippers while old **William Skindle** and his sons cater for more discerning tastes in *The Orkney Arms*.

Across the road on the riverbank they're building ***Causeway Cottages***. Soon this terrace of 13 houses and the three ***Thames Cottages*** north of the riverside gasworks will be home to 83 people including millers John Fry and Henry Salt, papermakers John Pymm, John Winson, William Whiteman and his brother Thomas, boat builders **Charles Bond** and Sam Rose, fisherman **Jimmy Simmonds**, drayman John Dance and hotel waiter Rhodes Green. Meanwhile villas on the riverbank to the south of the terrace are being converted to accommodate **The Brigade of Guards Boat Club**. The Guards' bent for boats began in the early-1850s when Lieutenant **George Higginson** of the Grenadier Guards relived the joys of his Marlow youth by taking fellow young officers out on the Thames. The distraction was revived on Higginson's return from the Crimean War, only to fall foul of a serious accident as a result of the crowded shipping in London. He has opted for Maidenhead – or to be more accurate, this bit of Berks

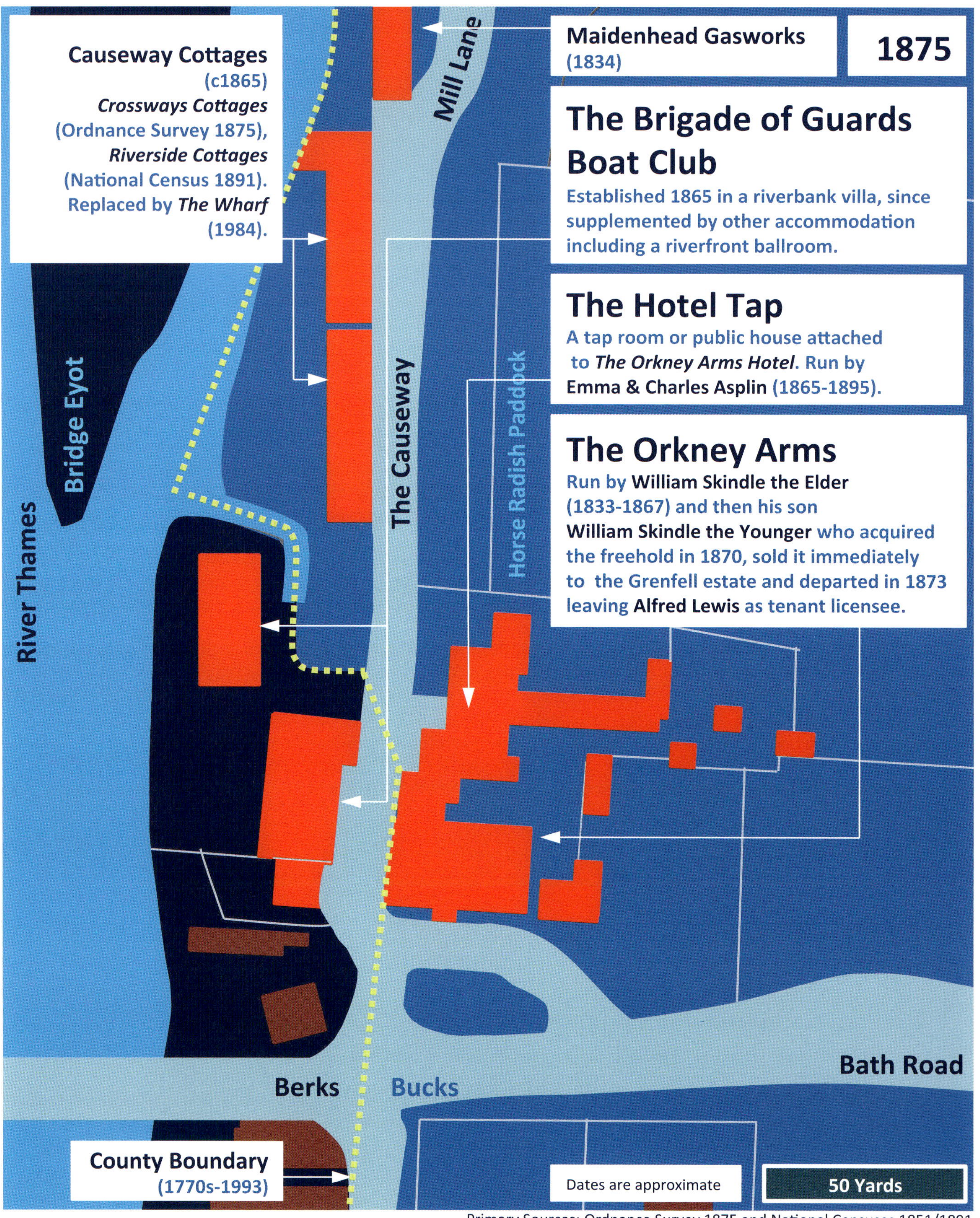

Primary Sources: Ordnance Survey 1875 and National Censuses 1851/1891

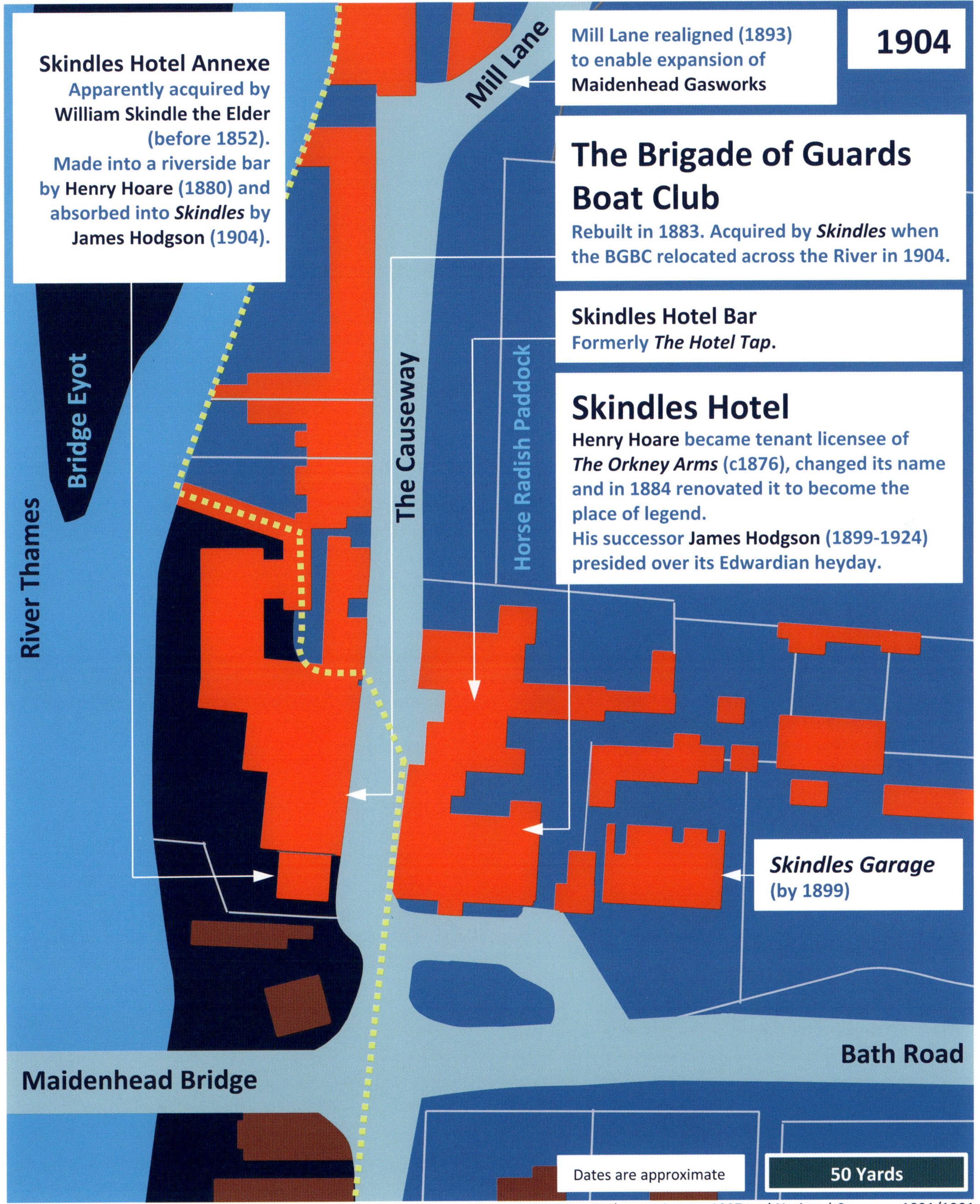

Primary Sources: Ordnance Survey 1897 and National Censuses 1891/1901

in Bucks – as the perfect place for the gallant officers of the Grenadier, Coldstream and Scots Guards to relax on the river. He might have preferred his boyhood home of Marlow but settled on Taplow for its easy access by train from London, by boat from Windsor and on horseback from Pirbright.

The Hotel Tap

The Causeway / 22nd July 1892

Charles Asplin leads the way into *The Hotel Tap* where his wife Emma is pouring us tankards of the famous *Barclay Perkins Russian Imperial Stout* – the king of stouts, says Charles, crafted at *The Anchor Brewery* in Southwark. It is just what the doctor ordered. No wonder the famous Doctor Samuel Johnson allowed his image to appear on bottles of *Anchor* ales.

When did ***The Orkney Arms*** become ***Skindles*** and why isn't it *Skindle's*? What do the Asplins think about the story that, when old **William Skindle** was applying for or renewing his licence, he was asked by the magistrate what name he proposed to give to the place? He hesitated. Somebody whispered, "Call it *Skindles*", and so he did, devoid of any apostrophe. Charles laughs, shakes his head and mutters that's a tall tale if ever he heard one: *The Orkney Arms* was never called *Skindles* when the Skindles ran it. The hero of the story is more likely to be **Henry Hoare**, an ambitious Londoner from Belgravia via *The Balmoral Hotel* on Princes Street in Edinburgh (later *The North British Hotel*). While in Scotland, he met and married Margaret Keith who gave him five children in eight years before she died in 1875. He came south soon afterwards to take over *The Orkney Arms* but when he went to get the licence transferred to him he forgot its name but not that of its previous licensee. With his tenure secured by signing a new lease on 1st September 1884 he immediately suggested that **Henry Riversdale Grenfell** should sell him the freehold. He followed up on 27th October to "impress upon [Grenfell] the necessity of having the front of the hotel put in order [because it was so] dangerous that [he is] obliged to refuse admittance". Grenfell replied the next day that he was unwilling to surrender the lease but will affect the required repairs. Now the old place has a new look. The old white rendering was stripped off to reveal bricks that at Hoare's direction are painted bright red with thick white pointing.

Emma laughs: you can't miss it, can you? Despite *The Orkney Arms* sign still waving in the breeze on the forecourt, everyone knows it is *Skindles* and the heart of what was described not long ago as an "irreproachable venue for boating parties of young people of Ettie Grenfell's class". And yet that same class choose to believe it is unnecessary for its young ladies to be chaperoned on the river. Henry Hoare and **Jonathan Bond** remain the souls of discretion as together they provide perfect opportunities for those seeking amorous adventures.

Charles hastily changes the subject. It isn't only *Skindles* that has changed, he says. Across the river, there's Joe Deadman at *The Ark Inn*, Henry Woodhouse at *The Thames Hotel*, Kerbey Bowen at *The Ray Mead Hotel* and of course ***The Riviera Hotel*** will soon be up and running. Don't forget ***Causeway Cottages***, adds Emma. The Ordnance Survey noted them in 1875 as ***Crossways Cottages*** but perhaps the mapmaker was hard of hearing because everyone including the census-takers called them by their original name until a few years back when they became ***Riverside Cottages***. The middle five are empty, which is partly why just 48 people live in the terrace now. Most of them work locally: for instance, papermakers James Hawes, Charles Pimm and John Holland, boat builders Tom Summers and **Ned Andrews** and watermen Edward Winn and Joey Brooks. And we've got our very own commuter: **Mackworth Bulkeley Praed**, a *Lloyd's Bank* banker if you please and apparently a trustee of the Grenfell estate. Before you ask, says Charles with a wink, that street past Paddington Station was named after his great-great-uncle William Praed, chairman of the company which built the Grand Junction Canal.

More Changing of the Guards

The Causeway / 22nd July 1892

Still in Charles Asplin's wake, we cross the road to a doorway with BGBC 1883 inscribed above it. The door is opened within seconds of him ringing the bell and he introduces us to his namesake Charles Wilkinson, steward of **The Brigade of Guards Boat Club** which finally gave up its piecemeal expansion into neighbouring properties and rebuilt its clubhouse here nine years ago to provide all the luxuries its members expect, including an oak-panelled bar and a well-fenestrated ballroom.

Wilkinson leads the way through the bar and out to the club's riverside garden. What a magnificent view. The sun is low enough now for its reflection to sparkle off the river to silhouette the arches of Turner's graceful bridge. The scene is disturbed by the noise of an altercation at the far end of the bridge. That'll be David Price having trouble collecting the tolls again, reckons Asplin, there's always some visitor refusing to pay up. We don't mind the toll, he adds, because it keeps those who come to this side on this side where we can exchange our hospitality for their cash. Wilkinson reckons the toll will soon be a thing of the past. He's right: the tollgates will finally be done away with in 1903.

The toot of a horn interrupts the conversation, heralding the steam launch *Mars* as she emerges from the central arch heading upstream to Boulter's Lock. She is crammed with passengers and low in the water with their weight. We wave to her master John Chelton. He and half his cargo wave back cheerily, a colourfully-clad party in a skiff join in, a punter does too only to lose his balance and fall in, much to the amusement of everyone but the poor chap himself.

When the laughter dies away, Asplin asks Wilkinson if it's true that a few years ago he entertained General **George Higginson** and a very important gentleman to dinner, and that the general's guest was none other than the Prince of Wales who brought with him a lady that Emma swears was the actress Sarah Bernhardt. Ever the soul of discretion, the steward smiles but says not a word. However he is willing to tell us something of the career of the club's founder who is currently Lieutenant-Governor of the Tower of London. He fought in the Crimea at the battles of Alma, Balaklava and Inkerman, where he had his horse shot from under him, and at the siege and fall of Sebastopol as Grenadier Guards Brigade-Major. He rose to the rank of general and eventually commanding officer of the Brigade of Guards and in the early-1880s played a part in founding and running the Royal Tournament. Perhaps it was in this capacity that he became firm friends with Bertie, the Prince of Wales, who as **King Edward VII** will confer a knighthood upon him in 1903. His royal relationship will extend as friend and mentor to Edward's son and heir King George V.

Tall Tale – Royal Rumours

Ellington Road / 22nd July 2013

Prince Bertie had a reputation for enjoying the company of attractive ladies of character both before and after his marriage in 1863. It is said that his earliest dalliance was in 1861 with the Irish actress Nellie Clifden. Could her surname have been a coded invention inspired by the local wanderings of his youth? The Prince's relationship with another thespian, Lillie Langtry, is the stuff of legend. Some say the Prince and the Showgirl met secretly at ***Redroofs***. This is unlikely. The house on the corner of Ellington Road and the Bath Road wasn't built until more than 20 years after their affair had ended in the late-1870s, and by then she was resident in Monaco. However, Lillie is reputed to have lived for a while at *Bray Lodge* in The Fisheries and she remained friends with Bertie, so who can be sure the thinking is merely wishful? The Prince of Wales was never going to be a Stayer but his being a Player supreme added to Taplow's growing mystique.

Dressed for the Part

Boulter's Lock / 22nd July 1891

Doctor F Campbell Moller is enjoying his visit to England. He writes of "Taking tickets to Taplow [on] one of the specials running 'through' for the accommodation of boating people. At Taplow we engage a fly to carry us over the dusty mile of road to *The Maidenhead Hotel* on the Thames, and shortly our skiff is heading up for **Boulter's Lock**."

Henry Hoare might have interjected that the good doctor should give ***Skindles*** its correct name, but he would no doubt have preferred to be able to offer him some custom. However the American is intent on lunching at *The Compleat Angler* in Marlow and, along the way, on noting how the Players dress for the occasion. He believes the reach above Boulter's to be "happily and aptly named The Ladies' Mile of the Thames" and yet remarks only briefly that "The girls are mostly in white muslin cotton gowns" before waxing lyrical at "the men's white Oxford straw hats, wide white ribbon banded. Some have black or dark blue jerseys, and many have dainty, light-colored covert coats or masculine-shaped shooting jackets of fluffy homespun or checked tweed, as an extra wrap." He continues, "From the crowd of 'swagger' men whose looks, intonations and obvious breeding stamp them as native to the best sets in London, it is evident that white flannel coats and trousers – not knickerbockers – are always in good form. The striped flannels are rather going out and although solid grays or pale lavender serges are worn by some of the ultra-fashionables it is doubtless but a passing fad. The blazer, unless one is a member of some prominent boating, college or tennis or cricket club, is generally left to Johnnie wherewith to emblazon himself. Flannel shirts, even of white, though most comfortable and sensible, are not much worn by those 'in the swim'. White linen shirts, with all the glory of stand-up collar and white four-in-hand tie in silk or duck, are seen, a mass of dazzling white along the unbuttoned coats, for the wearing of vests [waistcoats] is tabooed on the river."

Our transAtlantic cousin's eloquence is getting the better of him. He continues apace by observing the contrasting attire of "the regular river habitué; coatless, his shirt sleeves rolled up to the elbow, his white trousers snugly held about the loins by a large folded bright-colored silk handerkerchief or sash passing through the waist loop, and the turned-up bottoms showing an inch or two of black silk clad ankles above his pipe-clayed buckskin rowing shoes. A little modest-colored cricket cap or flat-brimmed straw hat completes the picture of cool, immaculate freshness in both dress and person, the boating man out for a day's gentle exercise and the various distracting sights of the river."

Valley Valedictory

The Hotel Tap / 22nd July 1893

This has been ***The Hotel Tap*** for years, says Emma Asplin. It will still be our home and our livelihood, says her husband Charles reassuringly. Being *Skindles Hotel Bar* won't change that. Business is booming. Taplow isn't just a good place to go – it's THE place to be. We've got to move with the times and be part of *Skindle's*, not just the pub next door. Mr Hoare knows a thing or two about hospitality and he wants us to carry on as usual, only with a bit more style. Some reckon we had 20,000 people hereabouts on Ascot Sunday this year and it's much the same on other high days and holidays. Most got off the train on this side of the river and plenty of them stayed on this side. Many who couldn't afford to hire a boat or had finished swanning about on the water came in here, bought a drink or two and a bite to eat, talked about all the fun they'd had and felt privileged to be part of it all. All the same, complains Emma, I'm not happy being an annexe.

Taplow has seen so many times to remember. The latest social elites still whirl at Taplow Court and Cliveden and nowadays there is opportunity for old Taplovians and newcomers to join the party or grab a slice of the action if they have a mind to.

Especially down here by the riverside, almost everybody has a chance to taste the honey. The days are long gone when nobody stopped except to pay the tolls. It's not just those who splash a few bob going boating. More than a few spend pounds to stay for the weekend and others come to earn a living helping them do it. There's an unwritten rule that there are no rules except blind-eyed discretion.

Whatever attracts Players, says Charles, attracts Stayers too. Look at all those who are investing a fortune to make their home here. This stretch of the Bath Road is well on the way to becoming somewhere the well-heeled live lives of leisure in splendid new well-appointed residences. **Jonathan Bond** started the ball rolling in the 1860s. Now the old boatman has built himself a little empire. He started with ***Cedar Lodge***, now leased to Captain William Atkinson of the Hussars, and has since added his present home ***Brook Side*** further east and ***Rhone Villa***, home of his son **Jonathan Bond the Younger**.

We're in the dark when it comes to **John Kennedy** – Emma chuckles that he is "of independent means", don't you know – but nobody a clue how he made his money. And yet there he is at ***Elm Cot*** near *Cedar Lodge*, and his son Arthur is in clover as Widow Whitlaw's latest tenant on the riverbank at ***River Bank***.

Willy Grenfell hasn't been slow to realise the opportunity presented at **Foxholes** once the Skindle tenancy ended. He has built there ***Lansdowne House***, the perfect place for **Lady Octavia Harvey** and her four daughters to open a new chapter after her husband Sir John died at ***Springfield*** in 1890. Emma says its name was chosen because Ettie Grenfell's cousin's nephew is the politically powerful Marquess of Lansdowne. Charles reckons that beggars belief. He has heard say that Grenfell will soon build a new mansion called ***Kenmore*** will be built next door to Lansdowne for John Coleman of Marylebone, a retired woollen merchant. Emma asks if he sold wool or woollen garments. What counts is him bringing his money with him, shrugs Charles.

A Fine Table

The Causeway / 22nd July 1892

Are you hungry? It's time for dinner. Mr Hoare aims to attract the kind of people who are generous with themselves. Tonight, let that be us. Let's eat and drink our fill and then sleep it off in comfort in one of the three principal first floor bedrooms.

Our host's eldest daughter **Margaret Hoare** greets us with a smile and ushers us into the dining room where the head waiter Charles Schaper awaits. His accent betrays his German origin and gives the place an international flavour that extends back to Hoare's earliest days when his hotel manager was Antonio Bona, an Italian. The menu presents so many options. We decide to have whatever is recommended by Henrietta Snelling, the hotel's cook, but not until Schaper has served us *Slaughterford Ale*, his choicest pale ale brewed by *Little & Sons* in Chippenham, Gloucestershire. That'll wash the nosh down nicely.

We start with quail stuffed with chicken liver. White soup doesn't sound exciting but it is a tasty stew of veal, fowl, bacon, rice, herbs, ground almonds, eggs and lots of cream. Our fish is baked lamprey and oysters with finochia, an Italian fennel. Our main course is venison slow-roasted in duck fat with baby potatoes served with baked cardoon (a kind of artichoke), skirret (a root vegetable from China) and spinach simmered in chicken broth and garnished with sliced boiled eggs and croutons. And we finish with traditional bread pudding with raisins, stuffed with rum-soaked orange segments and topped with caramelised orange rind.

Henry Hoare invites us to join him in the parlour and calls for something special. He announces with solemn deference that this *Taylor's Old Tawny Port Wine* was made by John Fladgate in 1870 just before the dreaded phylloxera destroyed the vineyards in Portugal's Upper Douro Valley. What better climax could there be to our courageous exploration of Taplow's liquid opportunity?

Our host certainly knows how to keep his customers satisfied. It won't be long before *Skindles* and *The Tap* are synonymous and he has made enough of a fortune to be able to retire across the Bath Road to ***Thames Bank***, one of three new villas he will build looking over ***Bond's Boatyard*** to the river. His tenant neighbours will be **Causton Freeth**, an insurance company manager, at ***River Dale*** and the independently wealthy Herbert Friend at ***Rose Mead***. While these exclusive new residences, with dragon gargoyles made at the Pinkney Green brickworks, are not quite the first of their kind, perhaps they are a sign of times to come. And what heady times they wil be, the Nineties and the Noughties.

Stayers

The Grenfell Five

Bath Road / 22nd July 1905

Grenfell's game has continued. By 1901 he had added three more mansions down by Maidenhead Bridge. Retired Lancastrian seed merchant **Harold King** is on the corner at ***Capenhurst***, originally ***Bridge View***. Next door is ***Bridgefield*** with ***Wargrave Lodge*** tucked behind, its name probably given by its first tenant Grace Crocker, widow of silk merchant Charles Crocker, latterly of Wargrave (Berkshire). Last year these three, *Lansdowne House* and *Kenmore* were offered for sale at auction described as "specially designed by an Eminent Architect (and built) in an unusually substantial manner without regard to cost".

By 1911 *Wargrave Lodge* will be ***The Hermitage Hotel*** in the hands of Welsh hotelier Anne Putley and her husband Frederic, an architect and surveyor from Lambeth. Could it be that the Putleys selected its name because centuries ago tolls were collected at a hermitage on the Bucks side of the river as well as at Chapel Arches in Maidenhead? Mrs Putley will temporarily restore her home's original name only for it to revert to *The Hermitage* before 1928. And that's how it will stay, only not as a hotel.

Bath Road / 22nd July 2013

Capenhurst and ***Bridgefield*** were replaced long ago by the flats of ***Bridge Court***. ***Kenmore*** tried numerous reincarnations. It was *Kenmore Nursing Home* in the care of matrons Margaret Campbell in the late-1920s and Grace Howlett in the early-1930s and then the *Charles Whitlaw Nursing Home*, a dental surgery in the early-1960s and finally ***Old Court Hotel*** only to spend three years threatened with replacement by a block of 11, 14 or 27 flats before being demolished without notice in 2006, possibly to prevent it becoming a squat but more likely because SBDC had just acquired the power to take over unused buildings. Now it is a pile of rubble waiting to be replaced by a block of flats. It is a relief that ***Lansdowne House*** survived such a fate in 1989 to be beautifully converted into apartments and reinvented by Neil Burgess as ***Lansdowne Court***. However worries persist about ***The Hermitage***. This late-Victorian treasure tried being a nursing home and is now the headquarters of *MaST*, a learning and development consultancy, while for 40 years and more it has been coveted by a series of speculators cooking up schemes to knock it down and build townhouses in its place.

The Gradual String

Bath Road / 22nd July 1911

Here is a tale of new homes and new life for old ones. Paper manufacturer **Charles Mullings** has succeeded at ***Rose Mead*** and just east of *Bridgefield* there is Harry Vernon, an American 'dramatic author' at ***Palermo***, Guy Seymour, a Kentish cold storage engineer at ***Kia Ora*** and fruit importer Edmund Thomasett at ***White Cottage***. **Jonathan Bond the Younger** is at ***Rhone Villa*** with his sister Maria nearby at ***Elm Cot***. Their father's homes have found new roles: ***Cedar Lodge*** as a hotel run by Walter le Gros and ***Brook Side*** as ***Silchester House Girls' School*** under its principal **Beatrice Roberts**.

Noble Ambition

Park Place, Remenham / 28th October 1890

John Noble paid £1,500 (£1.65m) for **Bridge Field** in 1852 only to leave the **George Norringtons** father and son grazing their livestock there. He died today without realising the asset. The fact that he left the small matter of £929,044 18s 2d (£600m) suggests it never crossed his mind. His last will and testament reveals a secret long forgotten: his Lily is Eliza Anne. Although the 1861 census noted her given names, she was known to Taplow as Lily and will be so remembered with John in stained glass at **St Nicholas' Church**. She will share her late husband's fortune with their elder sons Wilson and Leonard.

Ellington Road / 28th October 1913

Eliza had today gone to join John. *Bridge Field* is no more. Twelve years ago, just four houses had been completed here, all then empty. Now there is a whole new community. It seems that perhaps the examples of **Willy Grenfell** and **Henry Hoare** encouraged the Noble brothers to guide their mother's hand in reaping their father's investment. Indeed some say Hoare may have had a hand in the deals as they cashed in by constructing houses in **Ellington Road**, a pleasant 90-degree elbow blessed with the old name of its Berkshire neighbour, and **Ellington Gardens**, a short, leafy private cul-de-sac populated from 1902. ***Florence***, ***Southlea***, ***Homefield*** and ***Newlands*** followed in 1905.

Only ***Weymouth Lodge*** is the home of a local: waterman George Saunders of Bray. Most newcomers are from London, a few from far away. Some are here to live lives of leisure: Harry Rawson at ***Corner House*** is a retired merchant and Louisa Cooke at *Newlands* was with the Post Office while Frank Summers at ***Redroofs***, Elizabeth Goodchild at ***Ancora***, Ermyntrude Wiliamson (of County Cork) at ***Little Dene***, Kate Morton at ***Maranoa*** and Alice Phillips (of Cardiff) at ***Briar Bank*** are all 'living on their means'. Others are professionally qualified: Josiah Kilner at ***Attara*** and Percey Cunningham at ***Syringa*** are solicitors, George Emsell at ***The Croft*** is an accountant, Vincent Harman is a medical practitioner at N° 2 Ellington Gardens, Margaret Gleave at ***Pellicks*** is a nurse and Frank Russell at *Homefield* is an architect, estate agent or auctioneer as opportunities arise. Some are in business: Albert Carter at ***Riverway*** is a company secretary and motor engineer **Henry Hewens** is at ***The Laurels***. Others are drawn by local businesses: Joseph Brooks at *Florence* is another waterman, William Baxter at ***The Retreat*** a wharfinger, master shipmaker Arthur Schomberg is at ***The Cottage*** and Peter Rae Mackie (of Aberdeen) at *Southlea* is a papermaker. Charles Bridges is a journalist who commutes to London from ***Rivernere*** [*see Map 37*].

Ellington Road / 28th October 2013

Storytelling hereabouts would be so much easier if it wasn't that the names of so many houses have changed since the 1911 census first counted around here. The application of sequential logic suggests that *Florence* and *Homefield* are now ***Ashbrooke*** and ***River Cottage***. *The Cottage*, *Syringa* and *Attara* are ***Ashling***, ***Fausto*** and ***Riverlea***. *The Laurels* thought better of being ***Laura Cottage***. *Corner House* is ***Cornerways*** and divided into five flats not to be confused with ***Corner Cottage***. ***Copper Beech*** was *Ancora*, *Pellicks* might be ***Ellington Cottage*** and *The Retreat* could be ***Pendeen***.

On River Road, ***Riverdale*** is ***Cherry House***. Out on the Bath Road, *Palermo*, *Kia Ora* and *White Cottage* became ***Bridge End***, ***Arcalaur*** and ***Bridge Cottage*** before merging in 2005 as ***Bridge Cottage Guest House***. ***Tall Trees*** and ***Danehurst*** have appeared next door and, further east, *Cedar Lodge* is ***Norfolk House Hotel***, *Elm Cot* and its semi-detached neighbour were converted in 1987 into four ***Chelsea Court*** apartments, *Silchester House* is the distinctively white-and-pale-blue ***Silchester Manor Day Nursery*** and ***Charlton Villa*** is ***The Walnuts*** [*see Map 38*].

It is likely that some if not all of this guesswork is wrong: answers on a postcard please.

Map 37 – Down by the Riverside: Edwardian Arrivals

Noble Ambition: Elegant Living in Ellington Road

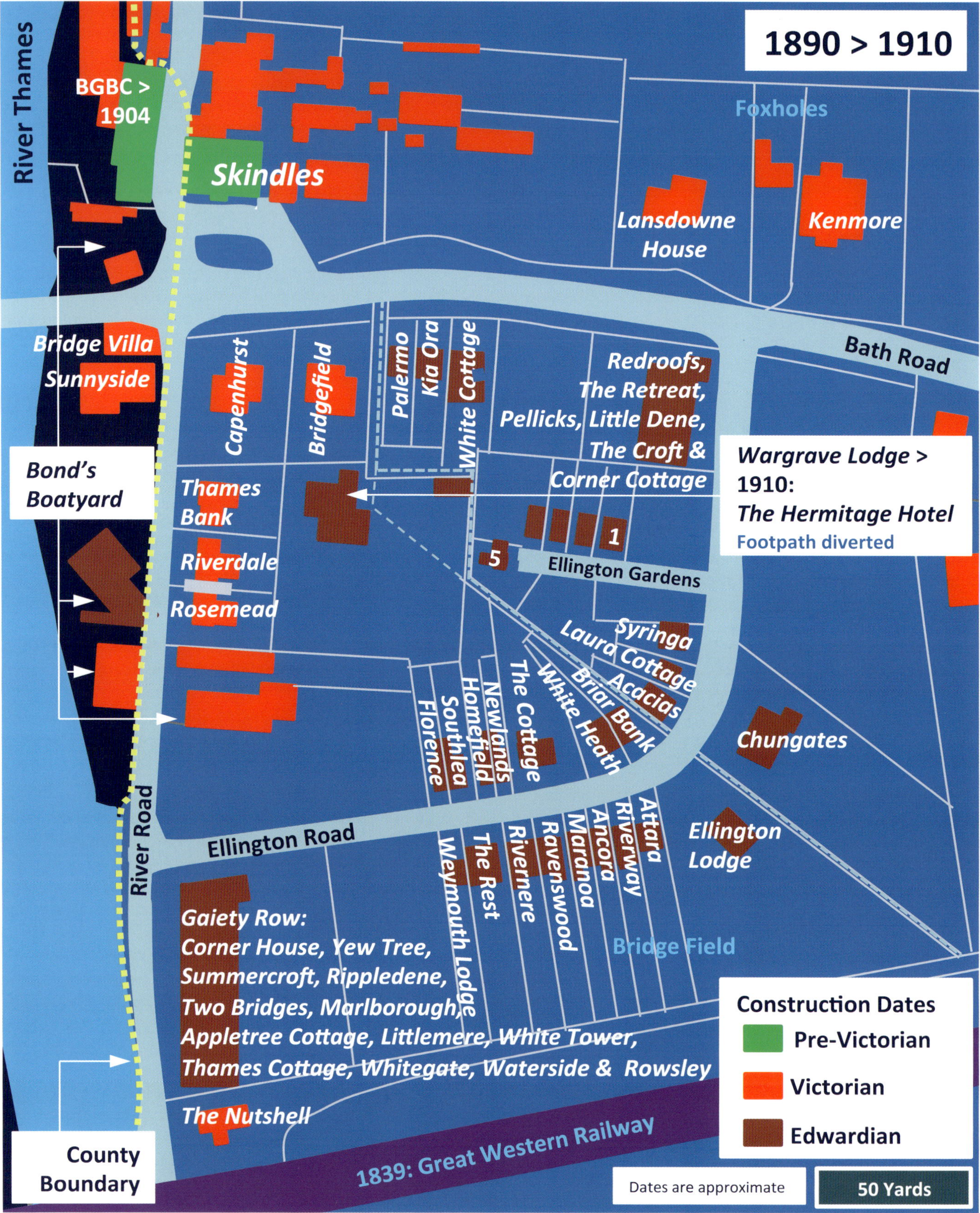

Primary Sources: Ordnance Survey 1897, National Census 1911, SBDC Conservation Area Document 1999 and Joy Marshall 2014

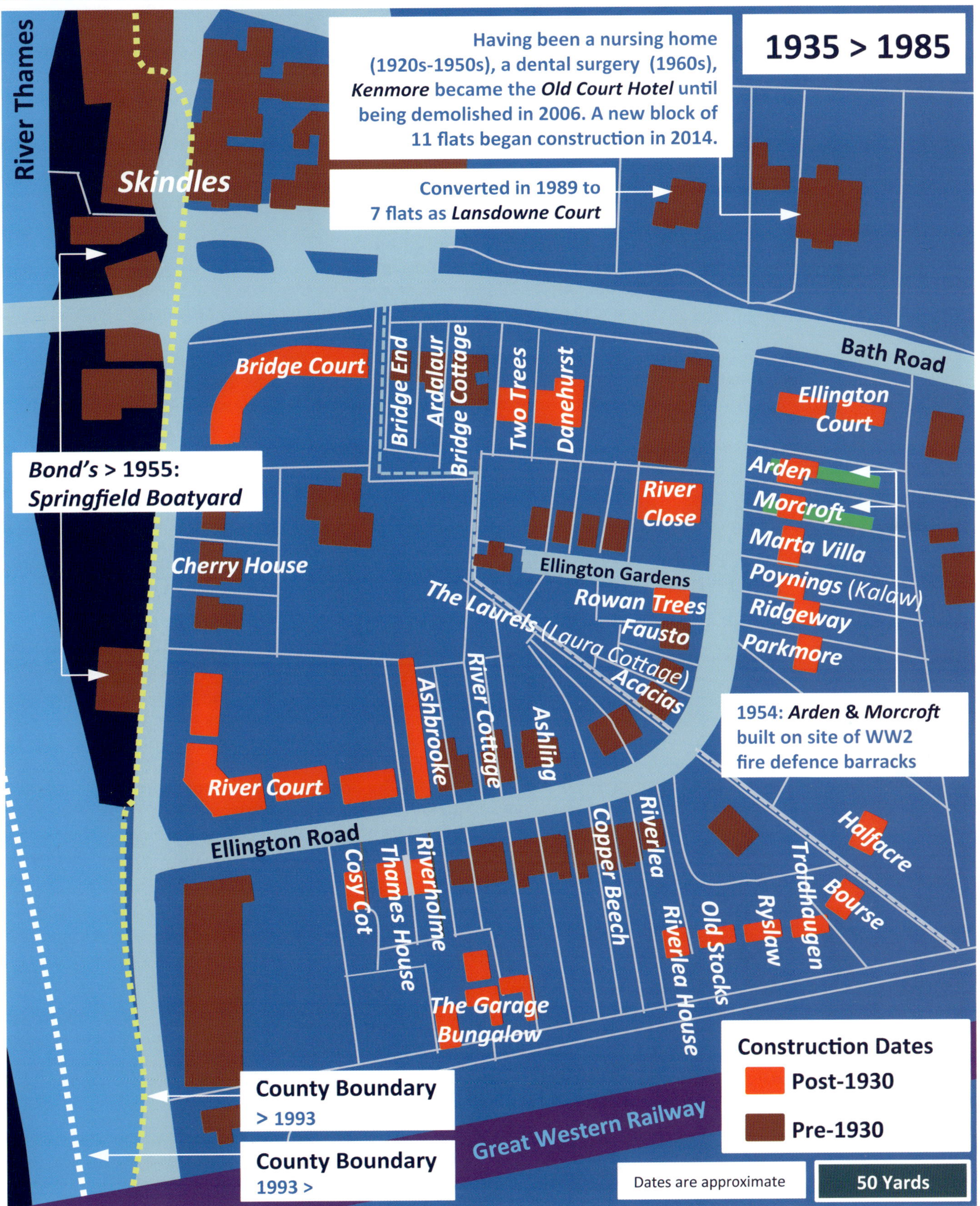
Map 38 – Down by the Riverside: New Neighbours
Gradually infilling Ellington Road
1935 > 1985
Having been a nursing home (1920s-1950s), a dental surgery (1960s), Kenmore became the Old Court Hotel until being demolished in 2006. A new block of 11 flats began construction in 2014.
Converted in 1989 to 7 flats as Lansdowne Court
River Thames
Skindles
Bath Road
Bridge Court
Bridge End
Ardalaur
Bridge Cottage
Two Trees
Danehurst
Ellington Court
Arden
Morcroft
Marta Villa
Poynings (Kalaw)
Ridgeway
Parkmore
Bond's > 1955:
Springfield Boatyard
River Close
Cherry House
Ellington Gardens
Rowan Trees
Fausto
The Laurels (Laura Cottage)
Acacias
Ashbrooke
River Cottage
Ashling
1954: Arden & Morcroft built on site of WW2 fire defence barracks
River Court
Ellington Road
Cosy Cot
Thames House
Riverholme
Copper Beech
Riverlea
Riverlea House
Old Stocks
Ryslaw
Troldhaugen
Halfacre
Bourse
The Garage Bungalow
Construction Dates
Post-1930
Pre-1930
County Boundary
> 1993
County Boundary
1993 >
Great Western Railway
Dates are approximate
50 Yards
Primary Sources: SBDC Conservation Area Document 1999 and Joy Marshall 2014

Ode to Joy

Onyx House, No 1 Ellington Gardens / 20th March 2014

So this house is 112 years old? That's right, says **Joy Marshall**; it's been my home for 63 years and connected to the main sewers only for the past 36. Patience is a virtue, she smiles. Joy began in Datchet, where her family were shopkeepers, and evolved from working in a Slough solicitor's office to become a teacher and then "a full time mum". Once her boys were old enough, she returned to teaching: initially part-time at Boyne Hill Girls' School, eventually full-time after it graduated as Altwood Comprehensive School where she taught English and Business Studies. After her husband Vivian died in 1990, she retired and two years later rose to a new challenge of serving for 21 years as a Parish Councillor. Many know Joy as a stalwart champion of footpaths and trees in particular and Taplow's heritage and countryside in general. She was able to report in 2000 that while Taplow only had one Site of Special Scientific Interest it could boast 11 Sites of Importance for Nature Conservation: Amerden Lakes, Taplow Lake, hedges and trees along Green Common Lane, the neutral grassland of The Old Churchyard, the mixed woodland of Hunts Wood and the broadleaf woodlands of Bristle Wood, Sheepcote Copse and Wooburn Common (all in the far north of the Parish), Homer Wood (by Dropmore), Cliveden and Taplow Court.

Lee Gray of ***Two Bridges*** in **Gaiety Row** paints a neat verbal picture of the familiar sight of Joy and her dog Sammy venturing forth in all weathers: her figure bent against the winter's wind and rain, with scarf flying, one hand firmly on her hat, the other clutching Sammy's lead. Those like Lee who know her well also appreciate her indefatigable diligence as she researches far and wide to unearth historical gems or gather evidence to challenge thoughtless planning applications. But not even Joy can make the complex simple and the deeds of her house defy understanding. The first piece of the jigsaw is all well and good: it adds up that **John Noble**'s widow Eliza (known as Lily to Taplow) should be in on the development. The same can't be said for Lord John Campbell for he died in 1862. However as 2nd Marquess of Breadalbane he warrants a mention for being a trustee of the Orkney estate when Noble acquired the land in 1852. But who was Mabel Campbell? The Marquess had two sisters, Elizabeth and Mary, and two childless wives, Elizabeth and Mary: not a Mabel amongst them. And who might Sir William Brougham be? A barrister and 2nd Baron Brougham & Vaux but also long gone before a sod was turned at Ellington. Have another biscuit, offers Joy.

The guesswork persists where the fate of a neighbour casts a shadow. Joy fears that ambitions to redevelop ***The Hermitage*** have driven the acquisition of two properties at each end of the cul-de-sac and an adjacent patch of woodland where nine trees have recently been cut down.

James Hodgson, Guards and Gaiety

Skindles Hotel / 22nd July 1906

James Hodgson would be surprised if anywhere captures the essence of the joys of the Edwardian Era better than *Skindles*. Although still only 32, he has been the hotel's proprietor for seven years now. His predecessor **Henry Hoare** still lives nearby at ***Thames Bank*** but it is the energy of young Hodgson who has kept the business growing, not least by expanding his premises to match his ambition. Three years ago Grenadier Guards Major-General Herbert Eaton, 3rd Baron Cheylesmore, acquired, converted and extended ***Riverside*** and ***Edendale*** to create a luxurious new home for **The Brigade of Guards Boat Club** complete with a grand ballroom, swimming pool and Oldfield Eyot now the private **Guards' Club Island** with a summerhouse where officers can take tea. Great crowds come to cheer the Thames Derby at the Club's regatta and be entertained by whichever of their bands has the honour of playing and to laugh as the younger set try to climb greasy poles or race gondolas from the lawn by ***Orkney Cottage***.

Hodgson seized the chance to incorporate the old clubhouse into *Skindles* riverside annexe. The ballroom may not be quite as magnificent as the BGBC's new one but it will do very nicely, thank you. And he is more than happy to hear music hall comedians enhance his reputation for modern tolerance with their cheeky question "Are you married or do you live in Maidenhead?"

A highly-irritating roar turns heads to see an amazing sight. A strange vehicle is heading this way along the Bath Road. A driver and his passenger dressed in white flannels and boaters sit behind a pointed cylinder mounted on a maze of pipes. That'll be Algernon Lee Guiness of the brewing family, says Hodgson. Algy had a bet that he and his mechanic 'Snowball' Whitehead could drive his new *Darracq 200* all the way from Datchet and back. They sweep into the hotel forecourt bowing and waving left and right like royalty but they daren't stop for fear of not being able to start again. Algy swings the motor car round in a broad circle and off they go whence they came. Clearly *Skindles* is the place to show off.

Not all of the guardsmen will inherit a baronetcy like Algy but they have all the social advantages, not least the wherewithall and whatever else it takes to cut a gay dash with ladies who like having fun. The only thing that cramps their style is that their club is an exclusively male domain at all times except formal balls. Like Hoare before him, Hodgson is the soul of discretion when it comes to being ready to accommodate the every need of these gentlemen and their lovely lady friends. However, *Skindles* has only so many rooms. The solution is simple: the ladies must have places of their own....

Tall Tale – A Woman's Touch

River Road / 22nd July 2013

The story goes that **Gaiety Row** was built to house *Gaiety Girls* for the convenience of the Guards. This may well be true but other aspects of the saga vacillate from definites to maybes. Those who say the terrace of 13 houses was designed by **Violet Morris** in the 1890s are contradicted by an 1897 Ordnance Survey map and the 1901 census, neither of which note its presence, and by Violet's youth: she was just a teenager at the time.

The descriptions of Violet as "the first female architect of the period" or "one of the first female chartered architects" fall between inaccurate and misleading. These accolades certainly apply to Ethel Charles who at 27-years-old in 1898 was the first woman to become chartered on her election to the Royal Institute of British Architects, a professional acceptance never conferred upon Violet. Although she did style herself an architect it is possible that she never formally qualified like her elder brother Frank. In 1901 he acquired the land on which Gaiety Row was built, or part of it, for £225 (£13,000) and the following year took a mortgage of £1,100 (£65,000) on two "tenements.... known as ***Summercroft*** and ***Rippledene***". Perhaps this mortgage funded the construction of the remainder of the Row.

Violet seems to have been the first resident of *Summercroft* while she and Frank worked in Reading for their father Joseph Morris, Berkshire County Surveyor for 33 years until 1905, on the design of various Berkshire residences and the police stations in Wokingham (1904) and Maidenhead (1906). Although the poet and architectural historian John Betjeman credits her for designing Gaiety Row with two remarkable design features – the first floor balconies affording wonderful views across the river and the interconnecting cellars which just might have enabled friends to reunite privately after entering separate front doors – the established working relationship between the siblings suggests it may have been a joint effort. After Frank died in 1908, Violet and her sisters retained ownership of the Row for some years despite her relocation to Somerset to care for her aged father.

There is another dimension to the intrigue surrounding the origins of Gaiety Row. Could the Levy-Lawson family of *Orkney Cottage* have had some financial interest? After all, Sir Edward's brother Lionel Lawson was one of the investors who funded the 1864 construction of London's *Gaiety Theatre* in *The Strand*. However the seed of the connection between Taplow, the Guards and the *Gaiety* was sown well before the terrace was built. The earliest example is the 1892 marriage of *Gaiety Girl* Constance Gilchrist to **Edmond Fitzmaurice, 7th Earl of Orkney** (grandson of Thomas the fifth who sold Taplow) [*see Appendix 1, Tree 7*]. This gentleman certainly had local connections but his tryst with Connie precedes Gaiety Row by at least a decade. Neither is there any record of him having served in the Guards, an exception that doesn't apply to Geoffrey Taylor, 4th Marquis of Headfort: a Life Guards lieutenant who married *Gaiety* star Rosie Boote in 1901. Perhaps these circumstances have resulted in the assumption that Gaiety Row was built earlier than it seems to have been. It is more appropriate that they add up to reasons why **Frank Morris** thought that, if he built it, people would come.

And come they did. *Gaiety Girls* were considered very respectable and eligible. Gladys Cooper, Cicely Courtneidge, Evelyn Laye and Jessie Matthews became famous actresses and Mabel Russell an MP. Many followed Connie Gilchrist and Rosie Boote by marrying into the aristocracy. Surely the childhood days of John Yarde-Buller, 3rd Baron Churston, at *The Grange* must be the root of his attachment to Taplow that led to his marriage in 1907 to Jessie Smither, a music hall actress, singer and musician better known as Denise Orme of the *Alhambra* and *Gaiety Theatres*. Although life will take her to pastures new, Jessie's infidelity and subsequent divorce from his lordship in 1928 will do nothing to dampen the risqué reputation of Gaiety Row and it was 'case proven' in 1946 when she took for her third husband Edward FitzGerald, 7th Duke of Leinster, who had two Taplow Court connections. His 'official' father was **Gerald FitzGerald**, 5th Duke of Leinster and 5th Viscount Leinster of Taplow, the great-times-three nephew of **William O'Brien, 4th Earl of Inchiquin**, while his biological father was Hugo Charteris, later 11th Earl of Weymss, who knew Taplow well for rather different reasons.

Hidden Gems

Taplow Mill / 22nd July 2012

John Dunleavey is going with the mainstream flow with the balustraded Maidenhead promenade on our right. Suddenly ***Glen Island House*** peeks through the leafy green of Taplow to our left giving a very good impression of being a very special kind of family home rather than the erstwhile headquarters of **Taplow Paper Mill**. Slightly downstream and almost hidden by the foliage are two more Victorian gems. ***Mill Island House*** was merely ***Mill House*** in 1869 when it was rebuilt by **Charles Venables**. ***Dunloe Lodge*** – now sadly an almost burnt-out shell – was built as ***Millstream*** in 1896 for JW Benson by the Maidenhead architects Robert Davy and Stephen Salter. The expansion of the gasworks in 1893 had edged **Mill Lane** eastwards creating enough space on the riverbank for *Millstream*, its lodge (now ***Driftwood Cottage***) and an adjacent boathouse (now ***The Old Boathouse***). For a few years until his death in 1913, the house was home to **George Palmer**, former MP for and mayor of Reading, whose father George Palmer had joined his cousin Thomas Huntley in 1857 to create *Huntley & Palmer*, the famous Reading biscuit manufacturer. Shortly before the Great War, *Millstream* was acquired by **William Frederick le Poer Trench**, **5th Earl of Clancarty**, who changed its name to ***Dunlo Lodge*** spelt free of an *e* to recall his family's seat in Galway.

Dunlo Lodge / 16th February 1929

Clancarty passed away here today leaving his widow Mary with their two youngest children. Their eldest, Brinsley, is at Pangbourne Nautical College developing the belief in 'flying saucers' that in the 1960s will make him a very different public curiosity to his father. Fred was 21 and Viscount Dunlo when in 1889 all the 'High Society' gossip was of his hush-hush wedding to Belle Bilton, a famously risqué music-hall entertainer and mother of an illegitimate son. His father Richard was aghast. He sent Fred abroad leaving Belle pregnant and destitute then later forced him to file for divorce only for accusations of Belle's adultery to prove groundless. And when the young fellow returned to his wife, Richard disowned him only to be twice frustrated – firstly, when she went back onstage with a salary inflated to £200-a-week (£129,000) by her notoriety, and secondly, by his own death in 1891 which prevented him from completely destroying Fred's inheritance. Belle and Fred settled happily in Galway where she gave him five children before her death in 1906. His troubles resumed. He was made bankrupt in Ireland in 1907 and in England in 1910 so it is possible that his second wife Mary may have funded the acquisition of *Dunlo Lodge*. Soon she will sell the house to Captain Philip Hibbert who will never get around to correcting his address after it is inaccurately recorded as ***Dunloe Lodge*** in a 1935 telephone directory.

Hurn's Turn – One of Six Hundred

The National School, Pikels / 22nd July 1869

Freddie Hurn is nearly 6-years-old and goes by this second name Everett. It's a long walk to the village school for his little legs – a mile-and-a-half from his home in the lodge at the gates of **Cliveden**. He is nearly there when young Dickie Cordery bursts out of the front door of a little house which will one day be ***Rose Cott***. As he gabbles his news to Everett, we manage to learn that Dickie's father, the carter **John Cordery**, is already on his way down to a new house by the mill called ***Glenisland*** where he and a party of locals will spend the day carrying furniture into the house off the barges that have brought it from London. The boys wish they knew who this mysterious newcomer is. They will soon find out.

Schoolmaster **John Wright** takes the register before asking who will read a poem to the class. Silence reigns. Mr Wright isn't surprised. He holds up a 15-year-old copy of a newspaper and asks his question again. Every boy does what boys don't normally do when it comes to reading poetry – they volunteer eagerly by trying to reach their hands up nearer to the high hipped ceiling than their classmates. This is no ordinary poem. When Alfred Lord Tennyson's *The Charge of the Light Brigade* was published in *The Examiner* on 9th December 1854, it grabbed the imagination and admiration of the nation, and especially of schoolboys excited by heroic deeds of derring-do. Mr Wright decides that young Hurn had his hand up first. Dickie grimaces in disappointment as Everett comes out to the front of the class and stands nervously waiting for his master's nod. When it comes, he clears his throat and reads in a crystal clear Buckinghamshire burr.... 'Half-a-league, half-a-league, half-a-league onward, all in the valley of death rode the six hundred....' The rhythm of the stanzas has him quickly in his stride like a galloping horse. The words seem to spill out all by themselves. Everett adds a little drama by miming sabre-slashes from a speeding steed. His heart is beating fast as he raises his imaginary sabre in a final flourish and his voice lifts to a triumphant crescendo.... 'Honour the Light Brigade, Noble Six Hundred!' The class bursts into spontaneous applause for both the poem and its orator.

Mr Wright waits a moment then raises his hand for silence. He asks why this poem is appropriate for this very day. It is so quiet you could've heard a pin drop. He is secretly pleased for this presents him with the opportunity to deliver his *coup de grâce* – he announces with a vain attempt at ambivalence that one of the Six Hundred is to become their neighbour. The children gasp in astonishment. After a dramatic pause, Wright confides that he expects we might see **Sir Roger Palmer** in church next Sunday. Everett's eyebrows rise as the light dawns. His friend's father is only lugging furniture about for a real action hero: a cavalry officer in the Light Brigade when it charged into "the valley of death" at Balaklava in the Crimea on 25th October 1854.

Mr Wright continues the lesson by making sure the children do not make the mistake of thinking Sir Roger is related to the Palmers of ***Dorney Court***. The great man's family had hailed from Norfolk in the 1680s when an ancestor was granted lands in County Mayo. Sir Roger had been an MP there for eight years from 1857 during a time of unpopular land clearances by his father Sir William Palmer who, as one of many descended from the infamous Barbara Villiers, may be distantly related to the lords and ladies of Orkney. The schoolmaster uses his cane to point at a map on the wall as he explains that by now the vast Palmer domains spread over something like 115,000 acres here at *Castle Lackin* (Mayo), here at *Kenure Park* (Dublin) and here in County Sligo, and there is also an estate there at *Cefn Park* (near Wrexham, North Wales).

The children's attention is wandering. Mr Wright spins around and adroitly returns to the safer ground of Sir Roger's military exploits. The young Palmer went to the far Crimea as a lieutenant in the 11th Hussars to thwart Russian ambitions towards the Ottoman Empire. He fought at the Battle of Alma and then after surviving 'cannons to the left, and cannons to the right' at Balaklava he captured a high-ranking Russian officer. The schoolmaster neglects to mention that Sir Roger's life had been saved earlier by a Private Jowett whom a few days before he had been obliged to caution for falling asleep at his post, and that the lieutenant is said to have remarked to a friend that Jowett may not have been so inclined to save him had he been flogged for his misdemeanour. Instead Wright is quick to laud Sir Roger's courage at Inkerman and Sevastopol, and to relate that he had succeeded as 5th Baronet Palmer only a few months previously.

Everett leaves school still talking nineteen-to-the-dozen about his hero. He will definitely be in church on Sunday in the hope that Sir Roger will grace it with his presence. Will we see him there often? Mr Cordery suspects not. Sir Roger retired recently on half pay as a Brevet Major in the 2nd Life Guards and will soldier on to be an honorary Major-General next year, a Lieutenant-General (1879) and a Colonel in the 20th Hussars (1881). He will also serve as High Sheriff for County Dublin (1875) and for County Mayo (1888). These responsibilities and the delights of *Kenure* and *Cefn* will mean he'll visit *Glenisland* only when the weather allows him to play tennis with the Prince of Wales and other guests or to jaunt in one of his steam launches. As a member of the **Thames Conservancy**, he will occasionally sit majestically in *Cygnet*, *Comet* or *Swallow* to act as an umpire for the Brigade of Guards Boat Club.

Cordery is of course unaware that last year Sir Roger invested "several thousand pounds" to acquire the land for his house from the Grenfell trust which manages 13-year-old Willy Grenfell's estate. However, the carter could have told the old soldier that the boy's uncle and guardian **Henry Riversdale Grenfell** can be a difficult neighbour and that the meandering longitudinal split of **Glen Island** between Buckinghamshire and Berkshire is an argument waiting to happen. Solicitors acting for Sir Roger have staked out the boundary between his land and that let to the mill but the line is disputed by both Uncle Henry and his tenant **Charles Venables**. Sir Roger will continue to put down deep roots by doubling the size of ***Glenisland House*** and building new stables for his horses and two boathouses for his beloved, slender steam launches but it won't be until 1886 that a two-year negotiation with **Willy Grenfell** finally resolves the matter. Throughout it all, Sir Roger will be oblivious to the dreams of Everett and other young, wide-eyed Taplow lads who keep hoping to catch sight of him. His hero's aura will persist even after his death in 1910, during the further 19 years in which his widow Lady (Gertrude) Millicent will continue to enjoy relaxing occasionally on Taplow's evermore exclusive riverside. In 1919 she will commemorate her late husband by donating £1,000 (£40,000) to fund a motorised fire engine dubbed *Sir Roger*, which will be transferred to the Cookham fire brigade in 1922.

An Exclusive Riverside: Now and Then

The Wharf (once The Causeway, never Page's) / 2012

Sir Roger Palmer – Sir Leslie Ward c1885
....and Glen Island House / 2009

Once the Vortex of Social Whirls

Skindles: Expanding, Evolving....

1883

c1907

c1920

c1925

1949

1962

Skindles: Fading into Memory....

The shell of *Dunloe Lodge* / 2009

The last remnant of the BGBC / 2009

The Brigade of Guards Boat Club dining room / c1900

Skindles forlorn / 2009 & 2012

Sad sights / 2015

Between the Bridges

The *Thames Bank* Dragon....

....watches over Rowing Club Reach / 2012

Gaiety Row – Violet & Frank Morris c1902 / 2012

Upstream and Down, under the Sounding Arch / 2012

And Another

The Whitlaw legacy of fine houses....

....strings the Bucks bank / 2012

Chapter Eight
Setting the Style

In which Taplow showed its naughty streak, did its duty and then lived for today

The Lightness of Being

A Whole New Whirl

Halcyon Days

Skindles Hotel / 18th August 1914

Although Taplow has to grin and bear being thought of as Maidenhead, these are surely its halcyon days. Players who want to be someone come to be seen at ***Skindles*** and those who are already someone enjoy the elite social scene at **Taplow Court** and **Cliveden**. Stayers range from those who can afford to pay for the privilege to those paid to keep them in the comfort to which they aspire. It has been that way for three decades and more. Nobody believes it will ever end. Nobody gives a thought to those silly sabres rattling on the continent.

The roots of this vibrancy extend back to the coming of the railway in 1838, perhaps even before, but the verdancy was assured by two events: the marriage of Willy Grenfell on 17th February 1887, which finally settled him at Taplow Court, and the sale of Cliveden six years later.....

American Dream

The Richest American

Cliveden / 18th August 1893

William Waldorf Astor is a tall man with bright blue eyes, an impressive moustache and a love of classical art which contrasts with his Spartan attitude to life. Having rented Cliveden for a year, Willy has today completed its acquisition from the Duke of Westminster.

The Astors are a German family which made a mint across the pond. Over three generations they have amassed a fortune. Willy's grandfather Johann Jakob Astor was born in 1763, the fourth son of a butcher in Walldorf, a village near Heidelberg. Two of his brothers headed for pastures new. Georg was George by 1779 when he arrived in London to make musical instruments with his little brother, by then John Jacob Astor (JJA), as his assistant. Heinrich became Henry the butcher in New York where JJA followed in 1784, but soon got other ideas. The young man traded in furs, Chinese tea, silk, spices, sandalwood and opium before investing in Manhattan real estate. He died in 1848 the richest man in the USA, worth some $20m (£425m). His son William Backhouse Astor (WBA) expanded his business interests to include railroad, coal and insurance. His sons JJA III and WBA II followed in these footsteps.

The business acumen and generous philanthropy of these Astors defines the American dream and yet it has turned out to be a nightmare for Willy, despite his inheriting from his father JJA III in 1890 the mantle of being the wealthiest man in America. His political career had foundered some ten years previously. During three years as US ambassador to Italy he "found Civilisation" and began to collect it while settling into "a pattern of formalistic behaviour which fell somewhere between that of a Roman emperor and his idea of an English medieval baron (or) a Renaissance prince". This impressed neither the press, which gleefully questioned whether his wealth and privileges exceeded his capabilities, nor his influential socialite Aunt Caroline, wife of WBA II, who had at heart the interests of her own son JJA IV. It was an astute business decision for Willy to commission the construction of a hotel on Manhattan's Fifth Avenue, except for one thing – as it grew to 13-storeys during 1892, the *Waldorf Hotel* overshadowed Caroline's grand mansion next door. She was furious. The compliant press was quick to raise a furore. This was the final straw for Willy. He decided it was time to implement his "English Plan", the first step of which was to disappear. As instructed, his staff let it be known that he had died of pneumonia. The US press mocked him viciously for his subterfuge when he was discovered in fine fettle at *Lansdowne House* in Mayfair's Berkeley Square. It was then he sought refuge by renting Cliveden. Perhaps he would have been less conspicuous at Taplow's more modest ***Lansdowne House***.

Willy will later recollect that "America is good enough for a man to make his livelihood though why travelled people of independent means should remain there for more than a week is not readily to be comprehended". No wonder England's green and pleasant land will be home for the rest of his life. Not even his hotel's signature dish – the *Waldorf Salad*, reputedly created by Oscar Tschirky – will attract him to visit his hotel more than once. His cousin JJA IV will replace Caroline's home next door with the 17-storey *Astor Hotel* but, far from being annoyed, Willy will be happy in 1897 for the hotels to merge. The *Waldorf=Astoria* will set a new benchmark in Manhattan swankiness until 1931 when it moves to Park Avenue to make room for the construction of something even more iconic: the *Empire State Building*.

Last year Willy decided to put his feet permanently under an English table by quietly acquiring **Cliveden**, reputedly for $1.2m (£22.7m). If he is aware that **Queen Victoria** laments her "dear beautiful Cliveden" has fallen into the hands of an alien breed, perhaps he would remark upon their shared Germanic heritage. How it suits him to be a prince of his own delightful domain complete with its new Japanese-style water garden, believed to be the first oriental-inspired garden in the country. Here he can live his highly regimented life hidden away from prying eyes behind a long perimeter wall topped by cut glass. Perhaps it was Arthur Coe of ***The Feathers*** who summed him up wryly as *Waldorf by name, Walled-off by nature*. And yet he is still ill at ease. There are two loaded revolvers by his bed at night. He entertains generously but without *joie de vivre* and with such imperious and inflexible regulation as to stifle enjoyment.

Although he craves acceptance in English society, he isn't easy to like. His idiosyncrasies are one thing, his quick and tactless tongue quite another. And he has been quick to find the means to air his opinions. He bought ***The Pall Mall Gazette*** two years ago and switched the political stance of this London evening newspaper to argue against William Gladstone's second Irish Home Rule Bill. Perhaps he has been influenced by his new neighbour William Grenfell who resigned last year as MP for Hereford rather than support Gladstone on this issue. When his contributions to *The Pall Mall Gazette* were rejected by his editor Henry (Harry) Cust as too artistic for a political journal, he launched ***The Pall Mall Magazine***, an extensively and elaborately illustrated monthly literary magazine that publishes poems, short stories and serialised fiction by such as James Barrie, Hilaire Belloc, Joseph Conrad, Laurence Housman, Rudyard Kipling, Walter de la Mare and HG Wells and artwork by the likes of illustrator EJ Sullivan. It is the perfect vehicle for Willy to share his own stories including several under the pseudonym Andrew Deepgrove, a fictitious 17th Century sage who will obligingly confide his creator's feelings for Cliveden.

The Indulgent Philanthropist

Cliveden / 18th October 1919

Willy Astor became something of a recluse at Cliveden after his wife Mary (Mamie) passed away just before Christmas 1894. He sought solace by investing significant time and money in making his home a wonderful world of its own, where over 30 servants in the house and perhaps 50 gardeners attended to his every whim. Having already acquired an eccentric collection of antiquities during his tours of Europe, he engaged the noted *Gothic Revival* church architect **John Pearson** and his son **Frank** to help him accommodate them in his new home. Together they stripped all trace of Barry from the interior and renovated with imagination, history and skill. In order to accommodate three of **Marlborough**'s ***Art of War*** **tapestries** that Willy had come across by chance in Paris in 1892, the entrance hall was expanded in two directions: east to incorporate the morning room now graced with an early-16th Century chimneypiece from *Chateau Arnay-le-Duc* in Burgundy and west to reveal an imposing new wooden staircase with its carved statues of past Clivedenites. The library was lined in wild tamarind wood panelling from South Africa and the dining room was transformed with particular splendour with Louis Quinze *rococo* panelling transported in its entirety – complete with marks made by bullets fired in 1871 – from Madame de Pompadour's *Chateau d'Asnieres* near Paris.

Sweeping alterations were made in the grounds which were extended by the appropriation of a parcel of common land – where he built that ultimate luxury: an indoor tennis court – and enhanced with a giant maze and many ancient and modern works of art including various 2nd and 3rd Century Roman oil-jars, well-heads and sarcophagi from Italy. The Long Garden was created to accommodate more Italian statuary. The terrace was edged with extensive stone balustrades from the *Villa Borghese* in Rome in 1896. A pagoda built for the 1867 Paris Exhibition was transported in 1900 from *Chateau de Bagatelle* in Paris to be surrounded by a skating pond. A formal grassed area known as The Cabinet was graced with Willy's own sculpture: *The Wounded Amazon*. And Thomas Waldo Story sculpted the *Tortoise Fountain* for the parterre and the *Fountain of Love* for the circus at the far end of Grand Avenue.

It is hard to believe Willy would ever need anywhere better. A London home made sense – he forsook Carlton House Terrace in 1895 to renovate N° 2 Temple Place on Victoria Embankment as a "crenellated Tudor stronghold" – but this wasn't enough. In 1899 he swapped being the richest American for being not quite the richest Briton and, after ten years at Cliveden, he acquired Hever Castle in Kent. Maybe there was method in his apparent madness. While he spent over two years and over £10m (£5,600m) restoring Hever – complete with a mock-Tudor village and lavish landscapes – he stayed on at Cliveden and then made it his wedding present to his eldest son **Waldorf** in 1906. Once Hever was to his taste, he realised an ambition in 1908 when he brought American style and elegance to London by opening the *Waldorf Hotel* in the Aldwych.

Although shy and remote, stern, dictatorial and obsessed with order and punctuality, Willy Astor remained enormously generous to his children, not least in 1908 when he set up **Cliveden Stud** for Waldorf to breed thoroughbred racehorses. His cousin JJA IV went down with the *Titanic* in 1912 but he went up in the estimation of those who count by continuing to make substantial charitable donations to various health and welfare causes. He has also contributed considerable sums to the Gordon Memorial College in Khartoum and to the Women's Memorial to Queen Victoria. His critics are right – his heart was set on a peerage – but King Edward's Hospital Fund, Great Ormond Street Hospital, the Cancer Research Fund, the Red Cross, the Soldiers' & Sailors' Families Association, the National Society for the Prevention of Cruelty to Children, University College and both Oxford and Cambridge Universities have all decided not to look this gift horse in the mouth even if it is a strange beast. They prefer to accept that this awkward, uncomfortable man is simply trying to make the world a better place in the only way he knows how. Despite envious grumbles, he was elevated to the peerage in 1916 as Baron Astor of Hever and then a year later made 1st Viscount Astor. It is likely that **Willy Astor** was never really happy, but he died today a much happier Englishman than he had been an American [*see Appendix 1, Tree 11*].

Tall Tale – The Coming of the Tapestries

The Grand Hall, Cliveden / 20th May 2012

Some say these are three of Orkney's tapestries saved from the fire of 1795. Is this wishful thinking which conflicts with reports that they all went up in smoke? And if not, where had they been for 97 years and how did they find their way to Paris? The likelihood is that these are from one of the other seven sets Marlborough had made for his generals. Nevertheless, the serendipity is sweet: **Willy** bought them because he liked them, not because he knew at the time that they had any connection with Cliveden.

Tall Tale – The Coming of the Redwood

Cliveden / 25th October 1899

It takes but a whisper to start a rumour and a ready ear to hear it as fact....

A little more than two years ago, Willy had a 16-foot-6-inch diameter section of *Sequoia gigantea* (Giant Redwood) shipped from California to be laid at Cliveden. One newspaper reported it was brought from Southampton by rail, but can this be true? Surely bridges over the railway would not have enough clearance for it to pass beneath? Crowds gathered outside ***The Dumb Bell*** to watch as a team of sixteen horses was harnessed to a specially constructed wagon to haul it up the hill. Nobody knew why the then American, now new Briton, went to this immense expense and effort. *The Daily Mail* ran an article under the headline *A Millionaire's Wager* to the effect that Willy had bet **Owen Williams** of *Temple House* in Bisham that he could find a tree of large enough diameter to seat 27 for dinner. Everyone knows that Americans like to do things bigger and by the time this story had crossed the Atlantic the wager was for $50,000 (£1.04m) and the slice of Redwood big enough to seat 50.

Americans have been put right: *The San Francisco Call* reported on 15th January that this "malicious rumour [is] believed to have been spread by the captain of the British ship employed in its transportation". Willy has already sued *The Daily Mail* for libel and, irritated that Britons persist in such gossip, he is today writing to *The Times* to refute the story and to threaten legal action if it is repeated. And yet this inconvenient truth will be ignored and the lie will survive to be posted on the *Weekend Notes* website on 22nd May 2012.

Waldorf's Salad Days

All Soul's Church, Langham Place / 3rd May 1906

It is five months since **Waldorf Astor** met **Nancy** Shaw (née Langhorne) on the New York quayside as they boarded the *SS Cedric* to sail to Southampton. She wasn't husband-hunting. Her first marriage – to the wealthy Bostonian Robert (Bob) Shaw II – had been a disaster due in large degree to his drunkenness. They had a son, **Bobbie**, but nothing else in common. She rejected a divorce for religious reasons rather than to avoid the social shame. They separated. Bob married bigamously and it was to save him from jail that Nancy agreed to divorce on the grounds of his adultery.

Waldorf wasn't on the lookout for a bride but the beautiful, vivacious, exciting, witty and saucy yet insecure Nancy fits the bill to perfection. She has taken some wooing. After her divorce, she escaped to England for the 1904/05 hunting season where she introduced herself as Nancy rather than Nannie, the name with which she had been baptised in 1879, and attracted five proposals of marriage. Two suitors – Sidney Elphinstone, 16th Lord Elphinstone, and John Baring, 2nd Baron Revelstoke – had been particularly persistent. Revelstoke had a fine reputation for rescuing *Baring's Bank* from disaster but Nancy was dismayed by rumours of his affection for **Ethel Grenfell**, Lady Desborough. Elphinstone was sweet but outmanoeuvred by Waldorf who at Christmas resolved to always be wherever Nancy was. His good looks, impeccable social standing, courtesy and old-world charm – and perhaps his wealth and her need for emotional security – proved an ultimately irresistible combination. Nancy whisked Waldorf off to see Arthur Winnington-Ingram, Bishop of London, who agreed that, despite being a divorcée, she would be permitted to marry in church as long as the service wasn't publicly announced.

Willy Astor has sent a message that he is too poorly to be here today to see them married. Some think he had hoped Waldorf would wed a suave English aristocrat rather than a restless, emotional, domineering, religiously devout and almost prudish daughter of America, the country he had rejected. However, even before he met Nancy, Willy reassured both her and Waldorf of his approval and today he has signalled it publicly by giving Nancy the Sancy diamond, a 55-carat Indian jewel dating back more than 400 years during which it has decorated French, Portuguese, English and Scottish royalty. And he has given the happy couple Cliveden as their home. Nancy will waste no time in turning the house topsy-turvy. It will be goodbye to "the splendid gloom" of staid, sedate 19th Century conventionality. The new millennium will arrive at last bringing "books and chintz curtains and covers and flowers.... flooding the house with light and colour", an effect no doubt aided by the wonder of electricity. She is just the spark Waldorf needs to shine.

William Waldorf Astor

The Great Hall / 2014
John Singer Sergant's 1909 portrait of Nancy Astor, the 16th Century chimneypiece and three of Marlborough's *Art of War* tapestries

Indulging in Paradise

William Waldorf Astor / 1914

The Tortoise Fountain – William Waldo Story c1897 / 2009

The Coming of the Redwood / 1899

Hurn's Turn – Parr for the Course

The Feathers / 18th May 1907

Cliveden nightwatchman **Freddie Hurn** now lives at N° 1 ***Triangle Cottages***, **William Parr** the steward a few yards south in a cottage that will one day bear his name. Old Mr Astor took most of the staff with him to Hever, says William. Freddie agrees: there's only a few of us left. But it'll keep Albert Shaw the ferryman busy now young Mr Astor has bought ***White Place Farm*** across the river: as it did for the Manfields of old, it makes sense to have the means to feed themselves as far as possible.

I don't know what the Astors are having done up at the house, says landlord Sam Haydon, but it's good for business. The local tradesmen all come here in on their way home. Itinerants who have found work at Cliveden are only too ready to spend their pay here. Freddie says they don't get much: p'raps seven pence (£1.70), six or even only fivepence an hour. Better than nothing in times like these, reckons William, but it'll be all finished in a few weeks. Then I've got to get everything ready for Royal Ascot week in the middle of June when Mrs Astor is planning her first big house party. She doesn't like racing but she loves horses and parties even more. I don't know how she does it, what with her being six-months pregnant and all, but she's already telling Monsieur Papillion the new chef exactly what she wants. You'll be busy, laughs Sam. That's why I'm taking it easy while I can, smiles William. And I needn't go so easy on my Saturday lunchtime pint today because she and Mr Astor are away in town this weekend. So she doesn't like the drink, asks Sam. William grins: she wouldn't have been happy with my predecessor William Pooley, would she Freddie?

Pooley was old Willy Astor's butler for 13 years. He ran the household smoothly enough except for when temptation got the better of him. Eventually the old man dismissed him for his "bad habits when you're in the drink" with a cheque for £1,000 (£94,410) for his "good habits when you're out of it". Sam laughs: I didn't mind that he spent a good bit of it in here that night!

An Unexpected Blessing

My Lady's Bedroom, Cliveden / 28th August 1907

Although **Willy Astor** always said that he would never return to Cliveden, now he is on his way. His need to see his grandson Bill has made him go back on his word. Horrified that he will be horrified to see what she has done to his old home, Nancy retires to her bedroom. Her father-in-law won't be put off. She agrees to receive him, ready to feign fatigue at the first sign of his dissatisfaction, only to be relieved when he acknowledges that "the joy of possession is to change everything and remould it nearer to the heart's desire" – which is of course exactly what he has done at every residence he has ever owned. Nancy can breathe easily that, although Willy may be rigid in his ways, he is not a hypocrite on the home front.

Waldorf Awakes

Plymouth Hoe / 19th December 1910

Taplow has long been home to a procession of Members of Parliament. Now it has another. After two years cultivating support in a politically hostile environment, **Waldorf Astor** has just been elected as a Unionist MP for Plymouth. He spent his first 12 years as an American, six more as an expatriate and the past 13 as an increasingly enthusiastic and passionate Briton increasingly determined to make amends for what he saw as his father's aloofness from the community that gave him sanctuary. It is well known that he likes to party and it will quickly become clear he isn't the sort to toe the party line. Although in his maiden speech he will argue eloquently for the Conservative Opposition against the Parliament Act (1911), such is his concern about the devastation ill-health causes the poor that he will work with the Liberal Government in the preparation of the National Insurance Act (1911) – some of which will be drafted at Cliveden – and then be one of only eight Tories to vote for it. Prime Minister HH Asquith will be heard to remark that Waldorf has "fine manners, good brains and, rarest of all, high and worthwhile ideals".

At first glance, Waldorf and Nancy seem very different characters – he a reflective visionary quietly seeking behind-closed-doors consensus to do the right things rights, she an instinctive whirlwind of wit and bluster willing to blow down any door to get her way – and yet they share so much. Both have deep religious conviction, both are mavericks determined to use their wealth and privilege for what they see is the greater good. Her energetic optimism has given him the strength to stand up and be counted. Together they are becoming influential forces on the national social and political scene, usually with his feet on the ground and her head in the air. His success in Plymouth was due in no small part to her willingness to campaign not only on platforms but also on doorsteps: they say she overcame her acute fear of cats to knock on more than 20,000 thousand doors.

During his time at Eton and then at Oxford the young Waldorf impressed at polo, rowing, hunting and fencing if not as an academic. In 'Tory' Oxford, the 'city of dreaming spires', he was surrounded by undergraduates born into the upper echelons of a country that thought it ruled the world, or at least a quarter of it. Some with noble ambitions to take on an almost parental responsibility to put the world to rights have played their part in defining a framework to enable four colonies to join together as the Union of South Africa. In the process, they have become known as ***Milner's Kindergarten***. Alfred Milner, 1st Viscount Milner, is a statesman and colonial administrator who, as High Commissioner for Southern Africa, had befriended the far-sighted businessman and politician Cecil Rhodes and built up a body of acolytes, his so-called *Kindergarten*. This intellectual circle includes Robert Brand, Waldorf's Oxford contemporary who has recently joined the investment bank *Lazard Brothers* and will rise to be its managing director. He will become a director of *Lloyds Bank*, the chairman of the *North British & Mercantile Insurance Company* and in 1917 Nancy's brother-in-law when he marries Phyllis Langhorne. Through him the new MP has become acquainted with fellow graduates of New College and All Souls College including Lionel Curtis, Geoffrey Robinson and Philip Kerr who have recently taken to gathering in 'moots' at Cliveden and elsewhere to nurture their heady dreams. Individually and collectively, the *Kinder* will influence British political ideals, ambitions and especially foreign policy for decades.

Curtis is the ultimate visionary. He will be the first to coin the term "a Commonwealth of Nations" to encapsulate Milner's idea for an international movement to promote closer union between the United Kingdom and its self-governing dominions. Kerr is secretary and editor of the organisation's quarterly journal *The Round Table*. Curtis will later promote the idea of uniting not just the Empire but the whole Anglo-Saxon English-speaking world in a federation centred upon the UK. Driven by his aspiration for universal Christian peace and understanding, Waldorf will urge countries to join "as in a great family.... a brotherhood" and summarise his "sole aim [in life as being] to promote by practical means the friendship of nations and peoples". In the meantime, Curtis and Kerr will play their part in the 1919 Paris Peace Conference and in the founding of the League of Nations in the hope that it will be able to broker international accord and thus prevent any future war. The group's efforts to influence British strategy to do just that in the 1930s will see them labelled derogatorily as ***The Cliveden Set***.

Three Equine Queens

Cliveden Stud / 23rd December 1910

The new MP has arrived home for Christmas. As always when **Waldorf** finds time to be at Cliveden, **Nancy** is obliged to share him with his second love: thoroughbred racehorses. He began breeding them for flat races almost by accident. He was a skilled steeplechaser at Oxford where in 1900 he had invested 200 guineas (£114,000) to buy a 5-year-old mare with the intention of breeding hunters and point-to-point horses. *Conjure* had no great pedigree – she, her sire and her dam had won only one race each – but in 1906 she foaled *Third Trick*, a fair racemare, by none other than the great *William the Third*. The same combination of dam and sire produced the outstanding *Winkipop* a year later. All Waldorf needed was somewhere to stable and train them.

This was of course no problem at all for a man of Waldorf's considerable resources. In 1908 he instructed the reliable Captain Pepper to get **Cliveden Stud** into shape and engaged the renowned Willie Waugh to train *Winkipop*. It was a masterstroke. Since she began racing in July last year, the filly has won eight of her 15 races – including *The 1,000 Guineas*, the second of five classic races held in England each season – and been second in four others to pick up a very tidy £11,439 (£5.97m) in prize money. The Stud is off and running.

Conjure has recently been joined by *Popinjay* and *Maid of the Mist*. This trio of broodmares will become regarded by those in-the-know as amongst the greatest ever *Reines-de-Course* (Queens of Bloodline). In the next three decades the bloodlines of Astor's three queens will win £380,000 in 286 races, mostly in his distinctive colours of light blue with pink sash and cap.

Read All About It – Second Edition

Cliveden / 1st August 1911

Waldorf Astor's independence of mind and desire for social reform has prompted James Garvin, editor of ***The Observer***, to suggest that he might like to relieve Alfred Harmsworth, 1st Viscount Northcliffe, of his ownership of the newspaper. Such an investment is beyond his means but not those of his father who has generously acquired *The Observer* and sat Waldorf in the driving seat to steer a path parallel to the Lords Burnham. **Willy** will sell ***Pall Mall Magazine*** in 1914 and within a year will sign *The Observer* and ***The Pall Mall Gazette*** over to his son. Waldorf will soon dispose of the latter to focus on the former, a Sunday paper of some standing. The relationship between the staunchly Conservative Garvin and the liberal, perhaps even Liberal, Waldorf will be prickly but fruitful until 1942 when differences over wartime policy will bring about Garvin's retirement.

Waldorf's son **David Astor** will grow up to be an immensely shy but highly principled young man who in 1931 while at Balliol College, Oxford, will befriend Adam von Trott zu Solz, an anti-fascist German who will be executed in 1944 for his part in the attempted assassination of Hitler. After a spell at *The Yorkshire Post*, David will join *The Observer* in 1937. Once he takes over as its owner and editor in 1948 he will ease it away from an 'independent Tory' stance to become the first British newspaper to declare itself 'non-partisan', only to be persistently just that throughout his 27-year editorship in favour of the liberal agenda he holds dear.

Despite being proved right, his accusing PM Anthony Eden of lying about the Suez Crisis in 1956 will damage the image of *The Observer* and its circulation and advertising revenue will begin to decline. However, David will be about perspective not profit. He will win respect as a brilliant editor, not least for being ahead of his time by playing a leading role in establishing Amnesty International in 1961 and by supporting the African National Congress against the apartheid regime in South Africa. He will resign as editor in 1975 while remaining a trustee until *The Observer* is sold in 1977 to Robert Anderson, the American owner of the *Atlantic Richfield Oil Company*, better known as *ARCO*. And in 1994 he will be made a Companion of Honour before being buried in 2001 alongside his former employee and longstanding friend Eric Blair, better known as George Orwell.

Read All About It – Third Edition

Hever Castle, Kent / 1st August 1923

The erstwhile *Kinder* Geoffrey Robinson became editor of *The Times* in 1912 and Geoffrey Dawson five years later when he inherited his aunt's Yorkshire estates and pedigree. Having fallen out with Lord Northcliffe, he resigned the editorship four years ago only for **John Jacob (Jakie) Astor V** to acquire ***The Times*** on Northcliffe's death last August. Perhaps Waldorf has been at work for now Jakie has restored his big brother's old friend Dawson as editor of *The Thunderer* on his own terms.

This latest JJA has inherited Hever Castle and last November began 23 years as Unionist MP for Dover, but this Kent connection can't diminish the fact that *The Times* is still Taplovian by virtue of his Cliveden upbringing. The same can be said of ***The Observer*** and ***The Daily Telegraph***, steered in strategy and style by Waldorf and his fellow Taplovian Lord Burnham. The Astor brothers and their editors Garvin and Dawson will prove a potent mix. While Jakie will soon branch out to hold long-term directorships of the *Great Western Railway*, *Hambro's Bank* and *Pheonix Insurance*, his influence will be felt mainly through his chairmanship of *The Times* until 1959 when he is succeeded by his son **Gavin**, who will sell out seven years later to the Canadian newspaper tycoon, Roy Thomson.

Milking It

The Feathers, Taplow Common / 1st August 1912

Milking's alright, says John Hillier of *Feathers Lodge*. Looking after the cow on the train and the ferry is all part of the job. Plymouth's alright and the cottage in Kent isn't so bad – last time we were there I enjoyed a round on the miniature golf course while the Mistress was away playing the real one – but Jura really is the back of beyond. The Master goes fishing. I watch the waves roll in. The Master goes deer stalking. I watch the waves roll in. **Arthur Stevens** of ***Green Drive Lodge*** nods knowingly. He feels the same. Landlord Sam Haydon pulls their pints, shakes his head and says they don't know how lucky they are.

Waldorf Astor may have had tuberculosis as a child and he strained his heart while rowing at Oxford. As a result of these worries about his health, he will only drink milk from his own cows at ***White Place Farm***. Whenever he goes to stay at his constituency house at N° 3 Elliot Terrace on the Hoe at Plymouth, to *Rest Harrow*, the Astors' newly-built 15-bedroom 'cottage by the sea' near Sandwich in Kent, or to *Tarbert Lodge*, their remote farmhouse on the isle of Jura off the west coast of Scotland, either Arthur or John travel in the rear carriage of the train with a cow in their care. Their predecessor **Jimmy Sloper** told John the whisky up on Jura was worth all the effort but you had to be careful if you took a dram. The Master doesn't approve but he'll turn a blind eye. The Mistress is a different kettle of fish.

Now they've got a grand house in Westminster at N° 4 St James's Square, says Arthur. I don't suppose the neighbours will be too pleased if we graze the cow there. Don't be daft, laughs John. We'll be sending an urn of fresh milk up every day on the train or in the servant's van. Talking of neighbours, says Sam, did you know that N° 4 has a Taplow connection? The chap the Astors bought it off is the Liberal MP and Cabinet member Auberon Herbert, 9th Baron Lucas, and he's Lady Desborough's cousin. It's been in her family for years. And what's more, N° 15 is owned by Lord Desborough's uncle **Henry Riversdale Grenfell** and N° 5 next door by Lady D's mother's family. Arthur smiles: have they got a cow?

Faith Healing

Cliveden / 1st August 1914

Lady Astor's contradictions are showing again. Such is **Nancy**'s vivacity that many men are a little in love with her: Edward Turnour, 6th Earl Winterton, thinks her "a wonderful woman.... so wild and daring". And yet without warning she can be vexacious and verbally vicious: even the infatuated Winterton confides that she can be "rather quarrelsome and almost shrewish". She will acknowledge that "My greatest battle is with my tongue; it's far too sharp and inaccurate".

The Astors' social whirlwind spins far beyond *Kinder* intellectuals. While the guest lists for dinners and receptions at St James's Square tend to be dominated by politicians and statesmen, those at Cliveden are evermore eclectic. Here such influential men mix with royalty, artists, poets and literary lights, business magnates, celebrities of the moment, peers and their ladies including American heiresses whose fortunes have saved their English husbands from penury. Tonight, as ever, Nancy is quick to assess her guests: King George V's uncle Prince Arthur is "the greatest gentleman", Arthur Balfour "clever", Lytton Strachey "droll and lively" and the American Anglophile novelist Henry James escapes censure but Rudyard Kipling is "dour", James Barrie "spoiled", John Buchan "guilty" of snobbery and Herbert Kitchener, having recently been created 1st Earl Kitchener, is "bothersome". And yet the flattened will accept her next invitation as eagerly as the flattered. Even Waldorf suffers: last August he wrote to her from Plymouth saying he felt that she was "lying in wait [to] discover some fresh delinquency or failure" and yet he finished another letter "you're the only person for me and I just ache to see you".

Nancy's confidence in company contrasts with periods of melancholy when she is alone, bored or spiritually restless. Until recently, such periods have been marked by her being confined to bed by severe bouts of neuralgia....

Rest Harrow, Sandwich / 1st March 1914

It began at Christmas in Virginia and has continued on and off ever since. She can't sleep. She has headaches and backaches and is constantly tired. She came here to recuperate and to contemplate the prognosis of the King's physician [Bertrand Dawson] that she can never hope to be anything but a semi-invalid. Being useless is at odds with her robust Virginian ideals. She sits on her balcony overlooking the sea and thinks "This isn't what God wants. It is not what He meant to happen".

Later her guests arrive. Among them is her sister Phyllis who has brought an American friend. This evening Maud Bull will change Nancy's life by introducing her to Christian Science. Phyllis gave her Mary Baker Eddy's *Science and Health with Key to the*

American Dreams, British Ideals

Waldorf & Nancy Astor / 1908

Summer Evening, Cliveden – Sir Alfred Munnings 1939

***Rest Harrow*, Kent & *Tarbert Lodge*, Jura** / 2014

Cliveden Stud / 2010 & 2012

Maid of the Mist /1911

Scriptures at Christmas but she hasn't paid it much attention. Maud says "Read this book, and I will pray for you". She is inspired by the principle at the heart of Christian Science that 'right thinking can heal'. She embraces the idea that God cannot have created anything evil so purging her mind of evil will vanquish it, and since "God made neither sin nor sickness" she will be sick no more. And indeed she will hardly have another day's illness until the decline at the end of her life. Christian Science is tailormade for Nancy's spiritual need because it accentuates both the zealot in her and the bigot. Doubts are dispelled. She can have things her own way, and she will.

Protestant and nonconformist by nature, Nancy abhors "Roman Candles" for their arrogance of opinion and dictatorial dogma – her friendship with the Catholic poet Hilaire Belloc will break on this rock – and yet she and **Philip Kerr** have become good friends, perhaps because he too suffers from a combination of poor health and a spiritual void, in his case a struggle against the Catholic teachings of his upbringing. Now she has the answer. Next month, as he recovers at *Rest Harrow* from a burst appendix, she will introduce him to Christian Science. As they find the faith they need – he with relief, she with added fervour – their friendship will deepen to be a love affair of heart and soul but not of body. The practical Waldorf will be slower on the spiritual uptake. It will be ten years before he comes to Christian Science, and then mostly to assuage Nancy's persistent indoctrination.

Man for All Seasons

A Fine Citizen

Maidenhead Jubilee Memorial Clock / 1st August 1900

Maidenhead Corporation decided to mark Queen Victoria's Diamond Jubilee by building a clock tower. What a nice idea, but what a long time coming: three years of debate and delay. No wonder no member of the royal family is here to dedicate the finished article. How wonderful to have the next best thing to perform the ceremony. At four o'clock precisely, the charming **Ettie Grenfell** pulls the ornamental chord which starts the clock ticking. She hands the key to Mayor John Truscott and stands back for her husband to give his address. He confides that it gives him special gratification to be here today because he happened to be Mayor of the town during Diamond Jubilee Year.

Modesty becomes **William Grenfell** as usual. This is a man of great natural authority and charisma widely respected not only for his athletic achievements but also more recently for his public-spirited hard work carried out with admirable diligence, integrity and practical good sense. He was elected as a Gladstonian Liberal MP for Salisbury in 1880 and 1885 and for Hereford in 1892. He served as private secretary to Sir William Harcourt, Chancellor of the Exchequer, during his second term but curtailed his third after a year by resigning rather than support William Gladstone's second Irish Home Rule Bill.

Somehow Grenfell has also found the time to be an invaluable servant and a generous benefactor to Maidenhead. He has been its High Steward since 1884 and five years later donated Grenfell Park to the town. The road that runs past it was named after him in gratitude and the park was planted with seeds he has gathered during his travels around the world; they will grow into a most unusual collection of trees. Having spent 1890 as High Sheriff of Buckinghamshire, he was elected as Mayor of Maidenhead in November 1895 – a decision so popular that some 4,000 turned out to witness "a magnificent procession, unique in the history of Maidenhead", to enjoy a spectacular firework display and to cheer as the new mayor, his wife and two curly-headed boys Julian and Billy waved from a Town Hall window. He lived up to the challenge with such energy, ability, usefulness and dignity that he was invited to serve a second term during which he presided over Jubilee celebrations on 22nd June 1897 including a tea for schoolchildren, a dinner "for aged folk", a procession, funfair, sports, illuminations and fireworks.

Grenfell exhibits in abundance both style and substance. The major achievements of his mayoralty included the opening of the new technical school, the installation of mains sewers – he delights in recalling hours spent looking down drains – and the decision to supply mains electricity to the town. These projects will have enduring benefit but right now freshest in the memories of most are his pertinent but always entertaining speeches and his generous hospitality in holding banquets, balls, benevolent fundraising events, fetes, festivities and school treats at Taplow Court.

He will shortly begin five years as Conservative MP for Wycombe but will still find time to serve simultaneously on 115 committees. He is already Justice of the Peace for Buckinghamshire and President of Maidenhead Hospital. He has been on the board of the Thames Conservancy since 1896 and will be its Chairman for 32 years from 1905 when he is elevated to the peerage as 1st Baron Desborough of Taplow, his title taken from the old Buckinghamshire hundred. He is or will be Deputy Lieutenant of Tower Hamlets and of Buckinghamshire, Justice of the Peace for both Buckinghamshire and Berkshire, President of the Royal Agricultural Society, the International Shipping Congress and both the London and British Chambers of Commerce and Chairman of the Pilgrims of Great Britain, a society to promote "goodwill, good-fellowship and everlasting peace" with the USA.

Meanwhile he will continue to be an eminent High Steward of Maidenhead, not least by flicking the switch in 1902 for electricity to illuminate the streets and the Town Hall, and by opening the new Free Public Library in 1904 and the Rifle Club in 1907, the latter formed for the purposes of national defence and built on land he will lease to the town on very advantageous terms. He will be made Honorary Freeman of Maidenhead in 1918 and will strive throughout his life to serve his locality and his nation to the best of his considerable ability. When he passes away at the age of 89 in 1945, *The Maidenhead Advertiser* will mourn the loss of "a fine citizen and a staunch friend".

Siamese If You Please

Taplow Court / 29th April 2009

Most people know the fictionalised versions of the true story that evolved from *Anna and the King of Siam*, a 1944 novel and 1946 film, to *The King and I*, a 1951 stage musical and 1956 film. The real tale has a Taplow connection.

After she was widowed, the English schoolmistress Anna Leonowens (née Edwards) took a post teaching the 39 wives and 82 children of King Mongkut (Rama IV) of Siam. Her life in Bangkok for 6 years from 1862 was not always smooth but she began a firm friendship with Prince Chulalongkorn that they sustained in correspondence throughout their lives despite Anna publishing her memoirs which won her fame in the USA but caused offence in Siam for their imaginative recollection. It was these volumes on which Margaret Landon based her novel and the rest is Hollywood's version of history – except for one thing....

Taplow Station / 6th August 1897

The King of Siam has come to the UK to celebrate Queen Victoria's Diamond Jubilee. Everything is ready for his arrival: the station is lavishly and tastefully decorated with flags from the Siamese Legation, the platform and the concourse outside the station are carpeted. The royal train eases to a halt and emits a gasp of steam. King Chulalongkorn (Rama V) steps down from the comfort of his luxuriously furnished saloon to be welcomed by George Harris, 4th Baron Harris (Lord Harris of cricketing fame), Colonel Sir Frederick Carrington (on a sabbatical from quelling the Matabele Rebellion) and Lieutenant-Colonel Charles Hume, former Military Governor to Crown Prince Vajiravudh who accompanies his father. The King and the Prince leave the station to be heralded by the hearty cheers of hundreds who have gathered to see the spectacle. Many more fringe the route to Taplow Court. Their cheers resound as His Majesty's carriage rumbles past with an escort composed of the 4th Squadron of the Royal Bucks Hussars under the command of Captain **Harry Lawson** and Lieutenant **Willy Grenfell**.

Taplow Court / 29th April 2009

SGI-UK Chairman **Robert Samuels** is welcoming to **Taplow Court** His Excellency Kitti Wasinondh, ambassador of Thailand, and his party together with various local dignitaries. The event marks the time 112 years ago when King Chulalongkorn and his entourage enjoyed two months here courtesy of Ettie & Willy Grenfell. While he was in England, perhaps even right here in this drawing room, Chulalongkorn and Anna were reunited for the first time and only time. And perhaps it was here that he presented ***The King of Siam Cup*** to pupils of the Elementary School as a sports trophy. It is still in use today at St Nicolas' Primary School.

The Life and Soul of So Many Parties

Taplow Court / 23rd April 1904

It serves you right for being late, laughs **Ethel Grenfell**. **Winston Churchill** can take the joke. He had indeed been late for this, Ettie's first party for the boys of Eton to which he had been invited as guest of honour, an example to aspire to. By the time he arrived, everyone else was out on the Thames. The penalty for tardiness was to be flung into the river where he swam with a smile in his greatcoat, spats and top hat. How Ettie relishes the joy of life and shameless egotism of the young MP for Oldham.

During the 1890s the Grenfells had established a reputation for hospitality that was second to none. However, despite knowing Willy Grenfell well – he had been her Groom-in-Waiting in 1882 – **Queen Victoria** took no chances. When she came to stay, an army of servants came with her to make sure she would want for nothing. Her Majesty was the exception. Everyone else was content to enjoy the delights on offer at Taplow Court and the foundation was laid for Ettie to evolve into an Edwardian icon: an intense, intelligent and glamorous woman with an 18-inch waist and impeccable manners, whose public calm and charm conceals contradictions and fragility. Having been orphaned before she was three and bereft of her only brother Johnnie when she was nine and both her matriarchal grandmothers by the time she was 13, she desperately fears losing the security now provided by her devoted husband. And yet his love, devotion and dependability aren't enough. Her lively imagination craves intellectual excitement and amorous adventures. She has found both through ***The Souls***, a small, loosely-knit aristocratic circle that began to gather in 1885 to enjoy stimulating company for "mental and literary pleasure and improvement" that unusually spans the political divide by putting political conversation beyond the pale. Their favoured territory is less the London salon and more the country house weekend, often at Taplow Court. The name of the group of politicians, writers, intellectuals, wits, artists and self-styled cultural sophisticates is said to have been bestowed by Lord Charles Beresford with the observation that "You all sit and talk about each other's souls – I shall call you *The Souls*" [*see Appendix 4*].

Taplow Court's famous house parties from Saturday-to-Monday are a metaphor for the age: glorious gatherings in which no-one is constrained, for it is taken as a matter of course that men and women should compete on equal terms in conversation. The spectrum spans from the gravitas of such as the eminent statesman Lord George Curzon, now Viceroy and Governor-General of India, father-and-son politicians Percy and George Wyndham and the Conservative Prime Minister Arthur Balfour, one of Ettie's greatest friends, to the witty levity of Harry Cust who has introduced to the fold literary doyens Kipling, Oscar Wilde, Wells, GK Chesterton and WB Yeats. While gentlemen like Willy are affiliated to *The Souls* primarily by virtue of marriage, the circle enjoys more than social intercourse. Percy Wyndham's daughters Pamela and Mary married Edward Tennant and Hugo Charteris but they and others are flexible with their affection. The originality and effervescence of the leading ladies gives them a certain privileged emancipation. Norah Lindsay is a country house garden designer who will be celebrated in the 1920s for reinventing the Long Garden at Cliveden. Her sister-in-law Violet Manners, Marchioness of Granby, is bohemian artist of renowned beauty. Although her husband Henry Manners, soon to be 8th Duke of Rutland, is 'officially' the father of her daughter

Diana, everyone knows, but pretends not to, that the supreme socialite Harry Cust was really the man of that particular moment.

Other regular visitors include the noted patron of the arts Lady Ottoline Morrell and the wild, uninhibited author Margot Asquith, sister of Edward Tenant and the second wife of future Liberal Prime Minister HH Asquith. His son Herbert's wife Cynthia (daughter of Mary & Hugo Charteris) will recall that "Even the breakfasts at Taplow Court were more lively than champagne dinners elsewhere". Ettie is perhaps less *avant-garde* than her friends and more intellectually superficial than she seems – she is attracted to authors rather more than their work – but she is the soul of *The Souls* for her bewitching brilliance at putting everyone at ease and making them feel special. She is the same at every party, dinner, ball and function she gives or graces because, according to Margot, "She tells enough white lies to ice a wedding cake". Her smooth discretion will ease the way as *The Souls* evolve into *The Coterie*. Those within won't see the join or be bothered by it for the new blood will flow from the old. The leading lights will be Raymond Asquith (son of HH), Maurice Baring (brother of Revelstoke), the banker and eventual war poet Patrick Shaw-Stewart and Diana Manners, now just 12 but well on the way to becoming an actress considered the most beautiful woman in England by 1919 when she marries Duff Cooper, the future politician and UK Ambassador to France during the Second War.

Many relationships are romantic yet ambiguous about consummation. Ettie's accomplishment as a flirt has led to "vital friendships" with such as George Wyndham, banker Lord Revelstoke and barrister Evan Charteris, brother of Hugo. Later this year she will take under her wing Archie Gordon, the vibrant 20-year-old son of John Hamilton-Gordon, 6th Earl of Aberdeen, who will confide to her that "the truth of my love and trust for you is the truest thing I have ever known". And yet Willy is and will always be her rock and their children her greatest joy. While she enjoys being conspicuous in society, she is content to be seen as a wife by her husband's side and aspires to be the most intimate, attentive and exciting mother. As she gazes out to the lawn, she positively glows to see Julian and Billy, home from Eton for the weekend, playing happily with Monica and Ivo. They will be joined next year by Alexandra Imogen who will be affectionately known as 'Mogs'. Ettie already dreads dying while her children still need her. She will write of Julian "I pray every day to live as long as he needs me." When he grows up, he will write to her "I don't want to see you ever again because after you is like flat soda water".

Eyes of a Child – Billy Grenfell

Taplow Court / 23rd April 1895

Four-year-old Billy is dictating his diary to his Mama: "The company who often comes here, we like George Curzon best, what gives us fruit under the table. We like him very much, he gives us more than we ought to have of fruit. He is merry and very fond of travelling".

The Soul of Discretion

Taplow Court / 26th April 1906

The staff of perhaps 40 can't relax just because the master is away. The mistress keeps them busy with a full diary of dinners, luncheons and weekend parties. Today, Thursday, as on almost every day at 11 o'clock, her ladyship is meeting with her Head Cook and Housekeeper. Menus for smaller or family meals are scribbled in chalk on a slate. More formal functions sometimes take days to plan and prepare for, and the menus are carefully written in a notebook. Rosa Mustoe is feeling rather nervous because, for the first time, it is her responsibility to take notes for the coming weekend's entertainments: an afternoon on the river, a picnic on its bank and later dinner and then breakfast for 12 guests, as usual a carefully selected mix of aristocracy and fashionable intellectuals.

Rosa was 23 when she started making cakes and confectionery as a still room maid six years ago. She loves life at Taplow Court. The work is hard but the Grenfells are kind and considerate to their servants. It is all very exciting to travel by train to London when the mistress goes there 'for the season', or to Scotland to 'open up' the house ready for the master to enjoy the grouse-shooting. Soon Rosa will succeed as Head Cook and eventually Housekeeper during the Great War from which her beau, Head Groom William Duggan, will return an invalid. They will marry and depart to run a market garden in Sydney, Australia. After his death in 1925, she will marry again and move to New Zealand....

Rotorua, New Zealand / 26th April 1966

She has been Rosa Gwilliam for 40 years. Her step-grandson Owen loves her very much despite her being "somewhat autocratic and commanding". Nowadays she enjoys nothing more than sitting by the fire in her lovely cottage by Lake Rotoiti and telling Owen and his children about her life in service....

I was one of eleven children from Siddingford in Gloucestershire, she says. Most of us went into service. I started as a 'Tweeny Maid': a 'Between Maid', meaning I was shared between the Butler, Housekeeper or Cook. It wasn't easy if they didn't agree but "life in service in those days was great if you were lucky enough to be in a good home with good people as long as everyone knew their place. Taplow Court was such a place and the Desboroughs, good people"....

Billy was my favourite. Julian, the poet, was "rather more gentle and feminine". The master was "a fine man, often away. He adored his wife – it was mutual – but she loved.... people, entertaining and clever conversation [while] he was of a quieter nature". The mistress was always particular about schooling her senior staff on the "various idiosyncrasies" of her guests so "they knew who to put next to whom". Mrs [Alice] Keppel had to be accommodated in a bedroom near **King Edward VII**. Oscar Wilde always had a single room with certain young men nearby. Some of those from noble families were "rather foppish".

"Everything good or bad in society which goes on today went on in the big houses of England in those days too but it was never talked about. The servants knew their place and never spoke of it outside the servants' hall". The years, the distance from Taplow and her pride are too much for Rosa to resist showing Owen her *pièce-de-resistance*: a handwritten note from King Edward's queen saying "Compliments to you, Cook, for a lovely meal. Alexandra".

Olympic Spirit – Flying the Flag

Athens Lawn Tennis Club / 26th April 1906

Last year **Willy Grenfell** was awarded the Order of the Redeemer, the oldest and highest decoration of Greece, in recognition for his services in helping to prepare for these Intercalated Games and, on the penultimate day of December, he was created **1st Baron Desborough** of Taplow. Four days ago the Right Honourable Lord Desborough became the first person to carry the flag for Great Britain at an opening ceremony of the Olympic Games. This afternoon he won an Olympic silver medal in the Men's Team Épée. Over the last three days at 50-years-old, he has fought 15 times to win six bouts and draw three as the Great Britain foursome defeated Germany and Belgium and finished all-square in the final against France, only to lose the deciding bout 6-9. There is some disappointment that the judges' eyes weren't sharp enough to score some hits – Desborough might even have conceded his bout against Pierre d'Hugue in unspoken protest – but he will quickly put that behind him to face the new and greater challenge now emerging.

Phaleron Bay, Athens / 29th April 1906

Thomas Scott-Ellis, 8th Baron Howard de Walden, is a fine host. He and his non-playing captain Theodore Cook are staying here on his yacht *SS Branwen* for the duration of the 1906 Olympic Games with three other members of the Great Britain fencing team. Five of them are waiting for the sixth to return from meeting **King Edward VII**.

The International Olympic Committee (IOC) had intended that the 1908 Olympics would be held in Rome but Italy's already very limited financial resources were pushed to the brink a little more than three weeks ago when Naples was badly damaged by the eruption of Mount Vesuvius. The IOC immediately approached Lord Desborough as president of the British Olympic Association to invite London to step into the breach. His Lordship has observed protocol by seeking the view of His Majesty. His smile as he comes aboard signals to his friends that the royal opinion is positive. There will be much to do – not least win the support of the governing bodies of British sport, plan the logistics, raise the funds and build the facilities – but who better to take on the task than Desborough?

His first role in sports administration was as a Royal Henley Regatta steward and management committee member in the 1880s.

He has since or will soon become President of the Maidenhead Athletic & Gymnastic, Bowling, Cricket, Golf and Rowing Clubs, Taplow Cricket Club, the Marylebone Cricket Club, the Amateur Fencing Association, the All England Fencing Club, the Lawn Tennis Association, Wimbledon Lawn Tennis Club, the Achilles Club (for athletes), the Coaching Club, the Four-in-Hand Driving Club, the National Amateur Wrestling Association, the Royal Life Saving Club and the Bath Club, a sports-themed London gentlemen's club. However he will never serve his country more effectively than as Chairman of the Council of the British Olympic Association (BOA) for the IVth Olympiad. His deep commitment to "the actualisation of a dream" and "the cause of international peace" succeeded in winning the support of the governing bodies of British sport, raising the funds and inspiring the planning and construction by George Wimpey of a magnificent multi-purpose stadium in just ten months and ultimately the resurrection of the flagging Olympic movement after its failures in Paris (1900) and St Louis (1904).

Olympic Spirit – Changing the Games

Holborn Restaurant, London / 31st October 1908

The London Olympic Games ended this afternoon at a cool and misty White City Stadium where England won the hockey gold medal with an 8-1 victory over Ireland. William Carter, Mayor of Maidenhead, reflects on the six months since 27th April when King Edward opened the Games and the racquets tournament began at the Queen's Club....

A vast Franco-British Exhibition was already planned for the summer of 1908 on a 140 acre site at Shepherd's Bush in west London. As both BOA Chairman and Managing Director for the sports section of the Exhibition, **Desborough** was able to come to a highly-satisfactory arrangement whereby a new stadium was built alongside the Hungarian entrepreneur Imre Kiralfy's brilliant white marble-clad exhibition buildings which have been nicknamed 'The White City'. Carter believes that this arrangement has brought two substantial benefits. Firstly: these were the first Olympics to have a purpose-built arena. The Great Stadium is certainly something to behold. It has a capacity of 93,000, a 3-laps-to-the-mile cinder running track and a banked concrete cycle track surrounding a 100m swimming and diving pool and a sports field for football, rugby, hockey, lacrosse and archery on which platforms were erected for gymnastics and wrestling. Secondly: the Exhibition subsidised the Games by funding the cost of the stadium, possibly to the tune of £220,000 (£173.3m). At one stage the BOA was relying almost exclusively on funds donated by Desborough's friends. His Lordship tipped the balance by persuading *The Daily Mail* to launch a very successful appeal which resulted in the BOA making a profit of £6,000 (£4.73m) even though £5,300 (£4.17m) – roughly one-third of total expenses – has been spent on entertainments and hospitality such as this evening's banquet.

A total of 2,022 athletes including 44 women from 21 countries have participated in 110 competitions in 24 sports. Every country except the USA has sent letters of thanks and congratulations. Kirafly neglected to fly the *Stars & Stripes* and the Swedish flag at the Opening Ceremony. The Scandinavians accepted his apology in good grace but the Americans chose to take offence.

Life and Souls

Willy Grenfell: Mayor of Maidenhead / 1897

Ettie Grenfell – John Singer Sergant 1909

Willy with Ivo & Monica / c1903

....and Ettie & Mogs / 1908

In the Canadian Rockies / 1884

King Rama V of Siam / 1880

The Thai ambassador with Robert Samuels of *SGI* / 2009

The British Olympic Fencing Team
(Lord Desborough: second right) / 1906

The Desboroughs at Henley: his Lordship opening the rowing events with one of his 139 speeches / 1908

The 1908 Olympic programme

2012 Olympic Volunteers:
Chris Little, Maureen Dennis, Jenny Edmonds, Mike Sharp, Nigel Smales & Heather Piper; Nigel with Rob Williams and his Silver Medal

HRH Queen Elizabeth II & HRH Prince Philip show the way as Phillip Wells takes over as a 2012 Olympic Torch Bearer

Their flag bearer Ralph Rose refused to dip the US flag to the royal box and his compatriots have been tetchy with their hosts ever since, despite Desborough personally paying to replace the gold medals stolen from their shooting team.

One of the earliest events was the rackets tournament. The only competitors were six Britons. Waldorf Astor's brother **Jakie** won a gold medal in the doubles with his partner Vane Pennell and a bronze in the singles. Most events took place in the stadium in the 11 days from 13 July. Attendances were initially low. Desborough responded to press criticism by reducing ticket prices, but not even he could do anything about the awful weather.

His Lordship's intervention in one particular event established a standard that will never change. Until now, the marathon has had no universally accepted distance. The BOA decided the race would be run from Windsor to White City. Desborough ensured the start line was under the royal grandchildren's nursery window at Windsor Castle and the finish line was in front of the royal box in the stadium, and that's why every marathon hereafter will be run over 26 miles 385 yards. Dorando Pietri of Italy looked like he was going to win the punishing race but he entered the stadium in such an exhausted state that two officials assisted him over the line and the gold medal had to be awarded to the next finisher, the American Johnny Hayes. The following day Queen Alexandria presented Pietri with a gilded silver cup in consolation.

The Reverend Robert de Courcy Laffan is the BOA Honorary Secretary. He confides that, but for Desborough's prestige as a sportsman, it would have been practically impossible to have held the Games in London at all. *Throne* magazine declared him "the real hero of the Olympiad" not least for his 139 speeches. Others admired his personal attributes. *Empire* magazine thought him "in every respect an ideal representative of English sport in the best sense – tall, well set up, a commanding presence, yet utterly devoid of arrogance or side which frequently causes Englishmen to be detested by the foreigner" and *Vanity Fair* that "he has a really fine and broad mind [and] that perfect courtesy which springs from a broad and sympathetic humanity".

Neighbours in Name

Taplow Court / 10th July 2012

The Ladies Desborough and Astor had much in common. Both hated music and could love fervently without desire. Both married men of stature who adored them despite being rather overshadowed in social gatherings by their wives' easy charm, energy and excellence at entertaining. And yet they were divided by more than a common language and a hedge.

It probably didn't help that **Ettie Grenfell** first came to **Nancy Astor**'s notice as an apparent rival for Revelstoke's affection. Nor that Ettie's reputation as a fine, attentive and stylish hostess had been established at Taplow Court long before Nancy began to build her own at neighbouring Cliveden. Both circumstances preceded her arrival but Nancy needed to get even or, even better, to get ahead. When the game began, Ettie held the aces of being known and loved by a wide circle of friends. Nancy aimed to trump her hand by any means possible. Disparagement didn't go down well with Ettie's genial friends but Nancy had four distinct advantages: the beauty of Cliveden, the curiosity of being American, the significantly greater wealth of her husband and the fact that those who enjoyed her hospitality didn't realise they were prizes. Nancy may have thought that anyone who came to her was won from Ettie. It is more likely they counted themselves lucky Taplow had two such fabulous places to party [*see Appendix 4*].

If there was any initial reluctance for Taplow Courtiers to venture northwards, any ice that hadn't already melted was broken in the summer of 1908 when **King Edward VII** was lunching with the Desboroughs and thought he might take tea at Cliveden. Ettie telephoned Waldorf who of course immediately agreed, not realising that the King would bring not only Mrs Keppel and the Desboroughs but also 16 others. Nancy took great delight in complaining to her sister Phyllis that "it made us 40 for tea" and in confiding that, although they behaved "nicely", she didn't think the Desboroughs enjoyed the visit. Perhaps she was right, but maybe Ettie had been looking forward to some rather nice crumpets Rosa Mustoe had made for His Majesty's tea at Taplow Court.

Two years later during Waldorf's campaign to be elected as an MP, Nancy mused that the Desboroughs would hate the idea when she held a party at Cliveden in honour of Arthur Balfour. Perhaps she was right, but maybe the Leader of the Opposition saw it not as betrayal but as combining duty with pleasure. Ettie certainly didn't think her sons **Julian** and **Billy** were betraying her when they became good friends with Nancy, although by then she understood her neighbour's game well enough to confide to Billy that she judged Nancy "an excellent friend for her children, but avoided her as best she could".

The evidence seems to suggest that having the Desboroughs on her doorstep rather brought out the worst in Nancy. Could this behaviour have been rooted in a rather unnecessary envy?

By Royal Appointment

Taplow Court / 10th July 2012

Despite it being barely a year since he had invested **Lord Desborough** as a Commander of the Royal Victorian Order (CVO) in 1908 King Edward VII recognised his Olympic achievement by advancing him to Knight Commander (KCVO). After the Great War his lordship went on to be president of the International Shipping Congress, the Honorary Commander of the London Royal Army Service Corps and a major in the 1st Bucks Volunteer Battalion of the Oxfordshire Light Infantry. **King George V** was as overwhelmed as his father by such exemplary and stalwart service that he advanced Desborough further to Knight Grand Cross (GCVO) in 1925 and invested him in 1928 as a Knight of the Most Noble Order of the Garter, since it was founded by King Edward III in 1348, the highest order of chivalry and most prestigious honour that can be bestowed by the Sovereign.

The Olympic Games returned to London in 1948. Now they are back for the third time and the Olympic Torch is touring the country. Just over half-a-mile away, members of **Maidenhead Rowing Club** line Maidenhead Bridge with an avenue of oars as Dominic John, a Bourne End sports coach, carries the Torch into Taplow but not, unfortunately, up Berry Hill to the home of the man who 104 years ago first brought the Games to Great Britain. Taplow Court is now in the care of ***Soka Gakkai International UK***, a lay Buddhist sect which is remembering Lord Desborough with an exhibition celebrating his achievements. Sadly *SGI* has not been able to persuade the Torch to come here to honour this long-ago lordship. Instead it boards a bus to be whisked to Dorney Lake – or 'Eton Dorney' as Eton College's rowing lake has been rebranded ready to stage the Olympic and Paralympic rowing and canoeing events.

Eyes of a Child – Phillip Wells

Windsor Castle / 10th July 2012

Maidenhead netball coach Gina Macgregor carries the Torch into the Castle to be greeted by **Queen Elizabeth II** and Prince Philip. On the southern terrace Gina passes it to 12-year-old **Phillip Wells** of N° 5 **Buffins**, the first child to be baptised at St Nicolas' Church in the new millennium and the first and only Taplovian to be a Torch-bearer. He runs proudly down to the Long Walk Gates where he hands the Torch to Ian Rostance of Leeds who continues onward through crowds marshalled by volunteer 'Ambassadors' including **Maureen Dennis**, **Heather Piper** and **Nigel Smales**. This Taplovian trio will be on duty at Eton Dorney throughout both Games. Three other Taplovians have volunteered as 'Games Makers': **Christine Little** will be meeting-and-greeting VIPs at Heathrow (where she will be interviewed on *BBC Radio 5 Live*), **Mike Sharp** will be driving VIP members of the 'Olympic Family' hither-and-thither in a very swish *BMW* and **Jenny Edmonds** will be at Eton Dorney as a Paralympic hostess.

English Patience

The Cushion Incident

Maidenhead Bridge / 31st October 1903

The English are so patient. Too patient by half, chuckles **George Bond** as he leads a good-natured crowd in throwing the old toll gates into the Thames at midnight. Maidenhead's Town Clerk freely admits that since at least 1400 – when Richard Fruytour and others were charged with "collecting no small sums of money and converting the same to their own uses and not to the repair of the bridge" – proceeds not required to maintain the bridge have been used for anything from the Mayor's Feast to Bonfire Night fireworks. That adds up to 500 years of rot and three to stop it.

It all began with Joseph Fulbrook of Slough, a dealer in the latest *Panhard* cars from France. When he refused to pay to cross the bridge in 1900, the toll-collector confiscated a cushion from his car in compensation. The Corporation sold it for 3s (£14.05) and, after deducting the 8d (£3.19) toll and 2s 1d (£9.74) expenses for sending a telegram and for registered post, returned to Fulbrook the grand total of 3d (£1.12). The incident alerted Joseph Taylor of Eton, who not long before had taken legal action which ended the tolls on Windsor Bridge. In February 1902 he lodged a petition with Charity Commissioners on the basis that the revenue from the tolls had been misused by the Maidenhead Corporation. A public enquiry ensued. The Charity Commission deliberated. Time dragged. Taylor decided to test his right to drive a car across the bridge without paying. On 8th December 1902, watched by a 500-strong crowd, he drove up to the toll gate, which was closed and locked. Under protest he paid the toll and the gates were opened to let him pass.

Eventually the Charity Commission ruled that the tolls were illegal. After failing in an attempt to sell the bridge to Berkshire for £25,000 (£13.96m), Maidenhead referred the matter to Parliament. Once the necessary legislation was finally passed, it was determined that tomorrow would be the first day in over 600 years when folks could cross the bridge for free. The Borough Surveyor had made arrangements to remove the gates in the morning but now Bond & Co have had their fun, he will have to fish them from the river instead.

Called to Account

Taplow Reading Room / 25th April 1907

The Parish Council offers a rather more gratifying example of English patience. The Lords Desborough and Astor have sent their compliments to this august company. The occasion is an annual meeting to finalise the ten accounts through which all the intricacies of Parish business are managed.

Everyone enjoys a delicious cup of tea served with a smile by **Julia Siggers** before Colonel **Oswald Serocold** calls the meeting to order. He opens proceedings by noting that **James Rutland** is indisposed and unable to attend. Our respected Parish Clerk is 78-years-old and ailing. We suspect he will not see another Christmas.

As Honourable Treasurer of seven of the Parish accounts, the Colonel is obliged to report that in the year to Easter, which fell on 31st March 1907, the sum of £618 13s (£57,110) has derived from six sources – donations, subscriptions and collections in church towards Church and Parish costs and charitable donations of £275 16s 1d (£25,460), deposits into the Coal and Clothing Clubs of £156 8s (£14,440), rental of £84 11s (£7,804) for Church houses in Back Lane and Parish poor houses up on the Common, subscriptions and membership fees to the Reading Room and the School of £51 11s 1d (£4,759), charitable grants of £19 6s 4d (£1,783) and hire charges of £31 0s 6d (£2,864) for the Reading Room and School.

The Honourable **Harry Lawson** enquires what these charities might be. Colonel Serocold is good enough to remind us that we benefit from three charities now administered by the Charities Commission. Mrs Morris established an educational charity in 1784 with a bequest of £50 (£5,337) to be used to educate two poor children. Its interest is now enough to contribute £1 5s (£5.30) towards the cost of £5 6s (£489.20) spent on prizes presented to schoolchildren by the Rector. Sharp's Bread Charity uses interest earned from a deposit of £105 (£9,448) made in 1797. It pays £1 12s 4d (£611.40) to fund two issues of bread to the poor supplied by **Flora & Edward Gurney**. Ashford & Moore's Charity utilises interest from an 1867 deposit of £611 9s 4d (£47,240) to provide £15 9s (£1,426) per annum towards the cost of food, clothing and coal for older parishioners who can no long look after themselves.

Serocold continues his introduction by explaining that it has been necessary to expend £631 7s (£58,274) in five areas. Parish expenses amount to £262 2s 10d (£24,200), Church expenses to £89 2s 10d (£8,228) and salary costs were £133 1s 9d (£12,280). In addition, £47 13s 6d (£4,400) has been donated to the National School investment fund and £99 6s 1d (£9,166) to other charities. A deficit on the year of £12 14s (£1,164) is noted but the Colonel is quick to reassure us that all is in order for a most satisfactory sum of £110 18s 2d (£10,240) is retained in hand.

Seymour Grenfell is Treasurer of the Reading Room and its Library. He confirms that costs of £32 7s 10d (£2,988) have been met by subscriptions and membership fees totalling £23 6s 1d (£2,151) and various receipts including £8 8s (£735) paid by those playing billiards. The company chuckles as **John Siggers** challenges Edward Lodge to a game when tonight's business is done. Evidently the Reading Room has become a fundamental aspect of Taplow's society since its founding 13 years ago. Siggers is our man for all seasons, not only our schoolmaster but also secretary to both the Reading Room and the Cricket Club. He allows himself a quiet smile as **Walter Baldwin** explains that despite significant maintenance costs – not least £22 11s 7d (£2,084) spent on repairing the drains – the School continues on a sound footing with £52 16s 4d (£4,875) cash in hand and the sizeable provision for any future rainy days anticipated by Colonel Serocold. Mr Baldwin asks for the record to show his warm appreciation to the 18 subscribers who donated £28 5s (£2,608) to the School fund.

The Reverend **Francis Phillips** echoes this sentiment in thanking the nine donors and the many contributors to collections and missionary boxes in the church to raise £13 18s and thruppence ha'penny (£1,284) which he has been able to remit to the Society for the Propagation of the Gospel in Foreign Parts. The Rector goes on to give thanks that his generous flock has also enabled the Parish to support charities in Africa and India as well as to help locals who need to call on the Poor Rate, the Sick & Needy Fund or the Coal or Clothing Clubs. He observes that **George Webster** does well out of the Parish – to the tune of £48 12s (£4,486) in fact – but thanks him for ensuring his coal is delivered without fuss to the infirm. Webster acknowledges this slightly backhanded compliment with a respectful nod.

Watching these proceedings gives us an insight into what it means to be an Edwardian worthy. These gentlemen rather enjoy pulling the strings and the deference of others but they accept and indeed revel in their duty and responsibility to use their intellect and wherewithal for the common good. It falls to them to set an example of diligent civic pride and of charity beginning at home. We note that the major landowners lead the way; **Waldorf Astor** donated £5 (£461.50), **Lord Desborough** wasn't far behind with £4 12s (£424.60), Elizabeth & Seymour Grenfell contributed £3 (£276.90) and **Selina Whitlaw** gave £2 (£184.60). Wealthy newcomers are quick to emulate their peers; **George Gledstanes** of ***Berry Hill*** matched Astor, **Elizabeth Whaley** of ***Taplow Lodge*** donated two guineas (£193.80), **Mackworth Praed** contributed £2, Walter Baldwin of ***Rectory Farmhouse*** £1 5s (£115.40) and two 'Honourables' – Allan de Tatton Egerton and Harry Lawson – gave a guinea each (£96.92). The rising stars aren't going to be left out; Edward Lodge's wife Matilda, **Tom Horton**, **William Rance the Younger** and William Williams all contributed five shillings each (£23.13); there was ten shillings (£46.25) from Mary & George Webster and £1 each (£92.50) from Reverend Phillips, **Harry Woolfryes** of ***Well Bank*** and **Arthur Kennedy** of ***River Bank***; **John Dykes** of ***Lea Rig Farm*** donated a guinea and **Jonathan Bond the Younger** and his daughter Maria together contributed £1 5s. And those of more modest circumstances put an unaccredited £6 9 3d (£596.50) into charity collection boxes.

The whirl of figures adds up to a simple bottom line: total Parish running costs for 1906/07 were £1,076 18s 6d (£99,400) of which almost 8% has been invested for the benefit of the school and twice that donated to charity.

Another New Beginning

The third (or fourth) St Nicholas' Church / 6th December 1912

The chancel still stands with its altar window, the Grenfell window, another added in 1897 to celebrate Queen Victoria's Diamond Jubilee and a fourth installed the following year. In the corner is a decorated Bishop's Chair carved by **James Rutland**. The tower has been encased in stone and capped with a spire. The rest of the church has been replaced at a cost of £10,149 (£880,000) by the architect **George Fellowes Prynne** to a design that offers a modern nod to the 14th Century. A few years ago Dr Charles Gore, Bishop of Oxford, told parishioners their church was a disgrace, hardly fit to be a house of God. Today he is consecrating the new creation, which has been funded by public subscription and the not inconsiderable private income of the Rector, Reverend Phillips.

Although it is much the same inside, the chancel has been externally reinforced with buttresses. That at the north-east corner incorporates a foundation stone inscribed to reveal that it was laid on 6th July last year by **Elizabeth Grenfell** and acknowledge the efforts of the Rector and two churchwardens, **Charles Seymour Grenfell** and **Oswald Pearce-Serocold**, who led efforts to give St Nicholas another new beginning. The stained glass commemoration of the latter's parents has been retained and another added in memory of James, the infant son of **Youri** & **William Baring du Pré**.

Baron Versatility

Ye Porches / 6th December 1912

This last window was designed by Baron **Arild Rosenkrantz**, son of Baron Iver Rosenkrantz, a Danish diplomat, and Julia McKenzie, a Scot attracted to spiritualism after her husband died when their son was three. Julia has always been a significant influence on Arild's development as a multi-talented artist and on his attitude to life. He travelled widely with her as a child. She encouraged his studies in Rome, Paris and New York and, once he had settled in London in 1898, she arranged for him to marry her niece Tessa McKenzie in 1901. Although their main residence is in London, Taplow is the Rosenkrantz's home from home in the country: for some years here at ***Ye Porches***, shortly at ***Dorl Cot*** and eventually at ***The Old Manor House***.

Rosenkrantz was dismayed last year when the pictures he had painted to adorn the vestibule of the new *Royal Academy of Music* were taken down after only two months because it was thought the displays of nudity would offend female students. He found solace since in directing, choreographing and designing the stage for the ballet *The Gate of Life* set to music by Beethoven, including his *Moonlight Sonata*. And he since his much-loved mother died last year, he has been working to commemorate her with five stained glass windows in the Lady Chapel of **St Nicholas' Church**. Their inscription is revealing: *He that hath an ear let him hear what The Spirits saith unto The Churches*. He met the spiritual philosopher Rudolf Steiner in London recently and as a result has joined the Anthroposophical Society in its mission "to nurture the life of the soul.... on the basis of a true knowledge of the spiritual world".

He will design two more pairs of windows at St Nicholas – one for **Harry Woolfryes** and the last for **Lily & John Noble**, once of ***Berry Hill***, the parents of **Percy Noble**, now of ***The Priory*** – before moving to Switzerland in 1914 to work with Steiner on the design of his Goetheanum in Dornbach, an experience that will introduce him to Goethe's theory of colour and thus change his style dramatically. Although they will only return occasionally to Taplow, he and Tessa will retain roots here by continuing to rent *The Old Manor House* from **Liley Baldwin** until 1918.

The Royal Academy of Music, Marylebone Road / 1st January 2007

After almost 96 years away, Rosenkrantz's paintings have been carefully restored to their rightful place. They were discovered by chance in 2005 crudely pinned to the walls of a neglected upstairs corridor in Rosenholm Castle – the artist's home near Aarhus in Jutland, Denmark – where a collection of his most important works including *The Omnipresent* has been gathered. Those that remain where they were installed include 12 large panels on the ceiling of the dining room at *Claridge's Hotel* in Mayfair, a sculptured bronze war memorial at St George's Church, Camberwell, and celebrated stained glass windows at Berkeley Castle, St Andrew's Church in Wickhambreaux (Kent), St Paul's Church in Kensington, and *Tiffany's* in New York. He also illustrated a Danish edition of Edgar Allen Poe's *Tales of Mystery and Imagination* as well as designing costumes, stage sets and the interior of two anthroposophic theatres.

Hurn's Turn – Jewel in the Cross

The third (fourth) St Nicholas' Church / 6th December 1952

Harry remembers a story told in his family of an emerald being given to the church on its re-consecration. His grandmother Clara was given the task of sewing this jewel into the centre of cross to be set on the white altar frontal. While she was working on the frontal, she hid it in a basket of dirty washing for fear that the gem should be stolen while in her care. The frontal complete with its sparkling green centrepiece was still in use 30 years later, but where is it now?

Eyes of a Child – Hannah Chapman, Willow Kerr & Alex Bainbridge

St Nicolas' School / 23rd April 2012

Hannah's favourite thing about Taplow is the Church. The Church is old but beautiful, she says. When you walk through the gate, along the cobbles when the sun is shining you really can see the beauty of the Church. I also love the pretty ceiling with the wooden beams. When you are watching from the back it is amazing. When we had our school Easter service I loved it just standing and singing. I love to walk around the Church because it is peaceful, calm and beautiful and makes me feel happy. Willow says the Church brings back memories to her and other people. Alex adds that it makes the village feel like a village and he likes the village feeling.

The Fading Day

Taplow Court / 16th July 1914

King George V's brother-in-law Prince Alexander of Teck cannot quite believe it. Archduke Franz Ferdinand of Austria was at Cliveden in the spring? Yes, replies **Lord Desborough**, he brought his wife Sophie to stay with the Astors for a few days on their last visit to England. And now he's gone, says Princess Alice, assassinated in Sarajevo not three weeks ago. The sabres are rattling across Europe. Will there be war? Oh surely not, smiles Lady Desborough.

Ettie & Willy are doing what they always do so well: entertaining in style at home. A special train and a fleet of carriages have brought over 300 guests to this social gathering of The British Imperial Chamber of Commerce. The Prince and Princess are guests of honour. They are joined by local dignitaries including the **Astors**, **Gwendolyn** & **Oswald Pearce-Serocold** of ***Taplow Hill***, his sister **Minna** of ***The Red Cottage***, **Florence** & **Cecil Irby** of ***Hitcham Grange***, **Liley** & **Walter Baldwin** of ***Rectory Farmhouse*** and **John Budgen** of Maidenhead. The band of the Grenadier Guards plays as butler **Barrett Good** directs his staff in serving refreshing fruit tea to all. Everyone is smiling in the sunshine to hide their fears. Few are as optimistic as their hostess pretends to be.

The Fateful Day

Cliveden / 4th August 1914

Charles Hopkins is carefully polishing the *Lanchester*, relieved that it looks as good as new, now the damaged wing has been replaced. He glances up as **William Parr** approaches with a furrowed brow. Have you heard the news? We've declared war on the Kaiser. The chauffeur shakes his head. It's my fault, he says ruefully....

The station telephoned to say the royal train had left Paddington. As instructed, I picked up the Mistress's father, Chiswell (Chillie) Langhorne, to drive him down to Taplow station to welcome the Archduke. We hadn't got to the end of Green Drive when, thinking it was open, the old boy spat onto the window. I looked in astonishment at the spittle trickling down, lost control of a spanking new car and dented its wing on the lodge gatepost. I don't know how I kept my temper while we collected the royal guests and delivered them safely. If my driving had been as wild as my rage that day I might have crashed and maimed Franz Wotsisname badly enough that he wouldn't have been able to go home and get himself assassinated. And now we're at war. William clings to the forlorn hope that it'll all be over by Christmas.

Baron Versatility

St Nicolas' Church: Lady Chapel windows – Arild Rosenkrantz 1913

The Darkness of War

Into Battle

The Pearce-Serocold Brothers

Taplow Hill / 28th August 1914

It is only 24 days since His Majesty's Government decided it had no option but to declare war on Germany. Lieutenant-Colonel **Oswald Pearce-Serocold** has been in Reading all week raising the 1st/4th Territorial Battalion of Princess Charlotte of Wales' Royal Berkshire Regiment. Recruitment is going well. He was delighted to see his Taplow neighbour **Causton Freeth**'s son Richard in the line and has made a mental note that the young man might make a fine officer. Now he has come home for the weekend to put family and personal matters in order before returning to complete recruitment and begin preparing his men for the challenges ahead.

Oswald was commissioned into the 1st Volunteer Battalion of the Berkshires in 1885 soon after **Queen Victoria** had been "graciously pleased" to recognise the Regiment's sterling service in Egypt by blessing it with a royal appellation. He rose to be its Commanding Officer from 1906 until 1908. He then took command of an Army Service Corps until being given his new assignment three weeks ago. Early next year he will lead his men to the front in France and will only be relieved in late-1916 after having seen 779 men lost in action. He will drop his Pearce prefix when he retires in 1924 after 40 years with the Berkshires.

Two of his brothers have also grown up to build military careers which will culminate with their distinguished service during the Great War. Commander **Claud Pearce-Serocold** will be awarded the OBE in 1918 for his service in Royal Navy intelligence and, having taken a commission in the King's Royal Rifle Corps in 1889, serving in the 2nd Boer War in South Africa and rising through many years as a staff officer, Lieutenant-Colonel **Eric Pearce-Serocold** was given command of the KRRC 2nd Battalion two years ago at the rather young age of 42. He is already with the 1st Division of the British Expeditionary Force in France where on 21st October he will be severely injured by shellfire during the 1st Battle of Ypres. He will be promoted to Brigadier-General in June 1915 and be wounded four more times during two further commands. His injuries will weaken his constitution considerably and lead to his early retirement from the army in 1920 and almost certainly to his untimely death from pneumonia in 1926.

Lieutenant-Colonel Lionel Hanbury

Hitcham House / 28th February 1915

Soldiers, soldiers everywhere: the Kent Heavy Battery have been and gone, now the men of the 2nd/4th Territorial Battalion of the Royal Berkshire Regiment are bivouacked in the grounds.

George Hanbury's sons **Lionel**, Robert and Nigel all took commissions in the Royal Berkshire Regiment and by 1906 Lionel was serving in the 1st Volunteer Battalion under his neighbour Lieutenant-Colonel Oswald Pearce-Serocold. Last summer Lionel was himself a Lieutenant-Colonel and on a diplomatic mission in Germany when he received a telegram saying "Family emergency, come home". He heeded the message immediately and arrived back in England days before war was declared; a fellow officer who ignored it was imprisoned by the Germans. He raised this battalion of volunteers in Reading last November and is now supervising preparations for them to transfer for training on Salisbury Plain. During three years at the front from May 1916 the battalion will see six extended periods of action, the worst being at Passchendaele during the 3rd Battle of Ypres in 1917 when 222 men will be killed, wounded or posted missing.

After the Great War, Lionel will command in business as a hop merchant and a director of both a water company and the Bank of England.

Captain Sheldon Gledstanes

Zwarteleen, Flanders, Belgium / 7th May 1915

It is six days since the German surprise attack and two since this small contingent of the 1st Battalion Bedfordshire Regiment was isolated in their trench here on Hill 60 south-east of Ypres. Sheldon Gledstanes of ***Berry Hill House*** was badly wounded yesterday but he and his men have gallantly held their position in spite of being almost completely surrounded by the enemy and dangerously exposed under almost incessant bombardment by asphyxiating gases, bombs, shells and grenades as well as ferocious machine gun and rifle fire. The achievement will be recognised as one of the finest episodes of the war.

The stockbroker's son was educated at Eton, joined the Bedfordshires in 1910 and, having landed with the first wave of the BEF last August, has been at war longer than almost everybody. He has fought at Mons, Le Cateau and Ypres, survived the dreadful winter in the trenches and won a small victory here. He manages a wan smile as his outpost is reached at last and relieved by his fellow Bedfordshires and gives a thumbs-up from his stretcher as the medics carry him to hospital in Bailleul: a sign of hope, but in vain – he will breathe his last in two days time.

Captain Julian Grenfell

Boulogne, Pas-de-Calais, France / 26th May 1915

Lord Desborough had recently returned home from a tour of duty in France on behalf of the Minister of Munitions when he and his wife Ettie received the awful telegram from their daughter Monica, a Red Cross nurse at the British Hospital in Wimereux near Boulogne. They rushed immediately across the Channel to their badly wounded son's bedside. She hoped desperately that a mother's prayer would work wonders. Sadly, it hasn't: **Julian Grenfell** is gone.

Thirteen days ago all was quiet as Captain Grenfell and fellow officers of the 1st (Royal) Dragoons stood discussing strategy not far behind the front line south of Ypres in Belgium. Suddenly a shell exploded nearby sending a splinter of metal one-and-a-half inches into his brain. He was brought here to be cared for by his sister. Before he slipped into a sleep from which he will never wake, he managed to whisper to his mother "Hold my hand until I go". His father Willy was confronted by helplessness, possibly for the first time in his life. Now at least he can busy himself by making arrangements for his son's burial in the nearby cemetery. Nobody will wear mourning. Ettie will write to a friend that "He died radiantly, as he lived. He seems very near to us".

For many, 27-year-old Julian was a famously light-hearted lionheart who personified Triumphant Youth, the lost generation, the best of the nation who gave their lives for freedom. His artistic and literary talents flourished at Eton and at Balliol College where he emulated his father by excelling in every sport. He boxed for Oxford University and in 1909 rowed in the college eight which won the Wyfold Cup at Henley. The following year he obtained a commission in the Dragoons and served in India and South Africa before arriving in France on 6th October 1914. Within weeks he wrote a letter saying "I adore war. It is like a big picnic but without the objectivelessness of a picnic. I have never been more well or more happy". He shrugged off accusations of naivety with a daring feat of individual reconnaissance last November for which he was awarded the Distinguished Service Order. He has since been mentioned in dispatches and wrote his last poem just days before he was fatally wounded. It will be published in *The Times* tomorrow along with his obituary. *Into Battle* advocates "If this be the last song you shall sing, sing well for you will not sing another". His words will sing so well down the years that in 1985 he will be one of 16 poets of the Great War commemorated in Poets' Corner at Westminster Abbey. The historian Sir Arthur Bryant will declare him "A greater poet than Rupert Brooke and a great Englishman".

Lieutenant Billy Grenfell

Hooge, Flanders, Belgium / 30th July 1915

Gerald William (Billy) Grenfell followed his brother Julian through Eton to Balliol where he was awarded an Oxford University 'blue' for tennis. He is perhaps more worldly than his brother but no less eager to strike for glory despite writing to Nancy Astor: "Such a Chamber of Horrors we have passed through, shells thicker than flies, flies thicker than air, and our nearest and dearest neighbours 32 English and 22 German corpses of varying age and savour". He was proud enough to be a second lieutenant in the Rifle Brigade. He was prouder still to be promoted to temporary lieutenant as the 8th Battalion moved into place a week ago to defend the high ground around the Hooge Chateau won from the enemy on 19th July. Two days ago he wrote to Nancy: "Take care of yourself, my pretty, do you hair nicely & do not overload yourself with charitable work in this ungrateful world. *Toujours à toi*. Billy". The battalion is at full strength: 24 officers and 745 men ready, willing and able. Surely he will soon have the opportunity to avenge his brother who was fatally wounded not a mile from the enormous crater in which he now crouches.

It is a quarter after three in the morning. The order to 'stand to' went down the line ten minutes ago. Everyone is on their toes. These wee small hours are when an attack is most likely. Billy peers cautiously over the rim of the crater into the darkness, his heart thumping hard and fast. Suddenly a blast of deafening sound and blinding light explodes from the nearby ruined stables. Simultaneously a hail of machine-gun bullets rains hard and jets of flame stream from the German trenches like water from a hose. Billy is no more. In just a few minutes the 8th Battalion will lose 18 officers and 469 men killed, wounded or missing – mostly missing or, more precisely, completely obliterated by flamethrowers, the first to be killed by such fearsome weapons. Lord Desborough will arrange no funeral for his son. He will immerse himself in his duty as an administrator of a naval hospital at Southend in Essex. When the war is over, Billy's name will be inscribed on the Ypres Memorial and alongside his brother's on the War Memorials at Taplow and at Hertingfordbury in Hertfordshire near his mother's family estate of *Panshanger*.

Margot's Lament

Cavendish Square, London / 3rd August 1915

Margot Asquith has just received news of Billy's death. Her diary reads: "Etty & Willy Desborough have lost their two beautiful sons of 25 and 28.... There is a Shakespearean tragedy in such a double loss as this. They have lost the two beings they loved most on Earth. Billy had everything: courage, brains, good feeling, candour, joy of life. These stupid conscriptionists say you should not take married men, but idle unmarried ones to fight. I think for the sake of the race these splendid boys should have all the children before they are killed".

In addition to the Grenfell boys, 11 more sons of ***The Souls*** will never come home. Field Marshall Kitchener has known them all since childhood and yet his private secretary will recall that "Almost the only time when Lord Kitchener was ever known to break down in office was when news of Billy's death came through".

Hurn's Turn

Carnoy, the Somme Valley, France / 29th June 1916

Freddie Hurn first joined the Royal Berkshires and served in Egypt for three years from 1892 as HM Government strove to secure its influence over the new Khedive Abbas II. While he was there Freddie got news to say that his wife Sophia has passed away and their son Everett was being cared for in Wooburn by her parents Jane & David Wheeler. He returned to find Willy Astor more than happy to engage him once more at Cliveden and eventually to find new happiness himself in 1901 when he married Sophia's sister Clara. Duty called again in September 1914. Freddie enlisted in the Berkshires once more at the ripe old age of 50. His maturity and experience were quickly acknowledged by his being made a sergeant in the 6th Battalion but he had to wait until July last year to be deployed to France.

The barrage has been going on for five days now and Freddie has been in position for two. Incredibly he can stand up here on the trench parapet in broad daylight without fear of snipers – waiting, watching, feeling the most awesome shaking, flashing, crashing and banging that anyone could ever imagine in their wildest dreams. It's different after it gets dark. Casualties come at night. That's when the German artillery retaliates and their aim is pretty good. The officers try to cheer the men by saying how the incessant bombardment will soften the enemy up. Freddie thinks it's doing that to some of our lot too. More than a few of the lads are quaking in their boots already. And instead of launching the 1st Battle of the Somme early today, they've decided the Germans need pummelling for another two days, just to be sure.

Carnoy, the Somme Valley, France / 1st July 1916

Freddie checks his fob watch: it's 07.25. He looks up to exchange nods with a lieutenant who rises and leads their troop silently into No Man's Land. The Berkshires aim to be onto the enemy seconds after the shelling stops at 07.30. They mustn't go too quickly. An enormous mine has been laid under the Casino Point machine gun nest up ahead. Nobody realises that it has been set too shallow until it explodes on schedule at 7.28 and hurls a heavy and horrid rain of earth, burning debris and body bits over the battalion. Freddie hunkers down and hopes. The nightmare cascade peters out and he is up again. The tactics have worked. They reach the first German trench within seconds of the last shell. It takes only ten minutes to secure the trench and start to move off towards the second. That's when they realise that the 8th Norfolks haven't kept pace. The Berkshires' right flank is exposed to merciless machine gun fire. Casualties are heavy but still they advance.

Freddie is left in their wake, his staring eyes seeing nothing. He will never know that his comrades will secure all their targets today and yet their courageous efforts and their sacrifice will be in vain. The survivors will count 259 men wounded and 89 killed or missing – an attrition of just over half – only for the decimation of the Allied left flank to prevent any breakthrough being been achieved. The slaughter by the Somme will continue for four-and-a-half months before the battle ends in stalemate.

Elm View, Church Road / 10th May 1923

Clara Hurn is writing to **Liley Baldwin**. "I felt so overcome yesterday and in fact all night that I feel I must send a line. You have been too good to me. I have never received such generosity from anyone.... With very heartfelt thanks and trusting you feel better today. Yours very gratefully...."

The letter does not reveal what favour the richer widow had done for her neighbour but Liley wasn't Clara's only benefactor. When Freddie went off to the Great War in 1915, Viscount Waldorf Astor quietly provided for his employee's widow by renting N° 2 **Elm View** for her at £14-a-year (£980) plus rates of £12 10s (£875). Liley had the place repaired, redecorated and furnished. When she sold N°s 1 & 2 Elm View to the church organist, choirmaster and gas works official **Percy Goulden** in 1919, she ensured that while he would live at N° 1, he would accept Clara as his sitting tenant of N° 2. Well of course he would, said Liley's companion Obbie Osborn. After all, she is unlikely to default on her rent considering who is paying it. Obbie wasn't mistaken. Lord Astor will continue to rent the cottage from Mr Goulden until Clara's dying day in 1934.

Lieutenant Richard Freeth

Croix Barbee, Pas-de-Calais, France / 13th July 1916

The 2nd/4th Berkshires are supposed to keep the Germans here. The strategy isn't working. Thirteen enemy battalions have already withdrawn to join the battle raging in the Somme valley 50 miles to the south. The Top Brass decided that a raiding party would do the trick. All it has done is give the enemy a late night.

It was 23.10 when four officers led 100 men into No Man's Land and Lieutenant **Richard Freeth** gave the order to fire the first of 185 grenades in support. Two nests of *Spandaus* opened up and the raid quickly ran out of steam. Now 40 minutes later the dozen who reached the enemy wire won't be coming back and many more are pinned down in shell holes. Freeth can't hold back any longer. He has to get the wounded back to safety. After all, he thinks with bitter humour, they probably didn't think to take out life insurance with his father.

Later the cost of this unfortunate episode will be calculated as 18 wounded, 13 missing and 7 dead including the 19-year-old Freeth of ***River Dale*** in River Road. He was mown down by a machine-gun while attempting to rescue others.

Captain John Webster

Ginchy, the Somme Valley, France / 9th September 1916

The 1st/4th (City of London) Battalion of the Royal Fusiliers came here the long way from Southampton via Malta two years ago, Marseilles in January 1915 and Artois two months later when they fought alongside the Indians of the 3rd (Lahore) Division to a dubious victory in the Battle of Neuve Chapelle. That was when **John Webster** was promoted captain. Today the Fusiliers have new partners, the Irishmen of the Royal Munster Fusiliers and the Royal Dublin Fusiliers. Their attack has been one of the most successful in the whole bloody battle for the Somme. The well-fortified village of Ginchy has been taken at the first attempt, depriving the enemy of strategic observation posts overlooking the whole battlefield. How sad the former solicitor of ***The Knowle*** is not alive to enjoy the view.

The Other Skindles

Poperinghe, Flanders, Belgium / 10th October 1917

Before the war, Poperinghe was a small hop-growing town of 12,000 people. Now there must be a quarter of a million here in the only little bit of Belgium not under the Kaiser's heel. Pop was briefly captured three years ago then quickly regained and ever since it's been the gateway to the Flanders front. Those explosions are the Battle of Passchendaele about 10 miles away to the east, just beyond Ypres. It has been banging away for 72 days now and will do so for 30 more. German bombs and shells reach this far now and again but, compared to the trenches, Pop is pure heaven.

When they get a two- or three-day pass, many off-duty officers gather to eat, drink, sing and meet local ladies in the *Hotel Skindles*. This used to be *Hotel de la Bourse du Houblon* until 1916 when (so the story goes) a British officer declared Madame Beutin's fare to be just as good as *Skindles*. The name stuck. Soon it was claiming to be "under the distinguished patronage of HRH Princess Beatrice" and a 'branch' had opened opposite Ypres railway station. The fame of *Skindles* will endure. When the hotel reverts to its original name after the war, its English one will transfer to the former Officers' Club along the street.

Privates John Simmonds & Frederick Malyon

Poperinghe Field Hospital, Flanders, Belgium / 27th October 1917

Passchendaele has just accounted for its second Taplovian. Private Freddie Malyon of the Oxfordshire & Buckinghamshire Light Infantry had been a plumber brought up at N° 1 ***Railway Cottages*** by Elizabeth and Fred, a labourer on the *Great Western Railway*. The 19-year-old was badly wounded two weeks ago. All the doctor and nurses could do was to keep him as comfortable as possible as he slipped away. It had been much the same for 21-year-old Private **John Simmonds** of the Royal Berkshire Regiment who died on 28th August. In 1911 he and his widower father George, a farmhand, and elder brother Alfred, a gardener, were living at ***Leigh Cott*** (later known as *Ye Cottleigh*, eventually *The Old Cottage*).

Flight Lieutenants Herbert Good & John Caudell

Serny, Pas-de-Calais, France / 2nd September 1918

The 19-year-old Flight Lieutenant **Herbert Good** of ***Taplow Court Lodge*** has just touched down in his *SE.5a* biplane fighter. He is eager to claim a *Fokker D.VII* as a 'kill'. His pal James Robb has even better news: the Allies are victorious in the 2nd Battle of the Somme. The Germans have been forced back to the Hindenburg Line from which they launched their offensive in the spring. The pilots might relax with a nice bottle of wine tonight.

It is a year and a day since N° 92 Squadron was founded at London Colney. That makes it exactly seven months senior to the Royal Air Force which evolved from the Royal Flying Corps only on 1st April this year. After scouting in *Sopwith Pups* and *Spads*, the squadron settled on the *SE.5a* before going into action around Dunkirk in July and transferring here in August to help dominate the skies over the battlefield. Bertie the butler's boy and Jimmy the draper's son are two of the squadron's eight 'aces' under the command of Major Arthur Coningham.

Robb and Coningham can look forward to long careers during which both will rise to be Air Vice-Marshalls. Good's future will end in three days. He will have but a fleeting mention in RAF annals while being remembered forever on memorials at Arras in France and in St Nicholas' Churchyard in Taplow.

St Nicholas' Churchyard / 2nd September 2012

Flying was a risky business, and not just because of enemy fire. Good may have been shot down. Flight Lieutenant John Caudell may have been the fellow famed for taking his life in his own hands to skim his plane a foot or so above the river past his home at ***Thames Bank*** and beneath Brunel's Bridge. If he did, his luck ran out on 8th July 1918 when he died in a fatal accident at RAF 211th Training Depot Station near Huntingdon. That's a long way from the front line.

Into Action

Lord Desborough

Taplow Cricket Club / 2nd September 1914

The country is at war. Those at home must be as firm in their resolve as those under fire at the front. An example must be set. Lord & Lady Desborough have risen to the challenge as everyone knew they would. She is organising a sewing society while he has accepted the presidency of the Central Association of Volunteer Training Corps. At **Taplow Grammar School**, the Hitcham & Taplow Unit of the Army Service Corps has been established under Patrol Leader **C Jefferies**. And today his lordship is presenting the colours to the newly-founded **1st Taplow Boy Scouts**. Scoutmaster CA Hunter stands proudly at attention as the Reverend **Phillips** presides over the service of dedication.

Private Charles Hopkins

Grove Park ASC Depot / 24th March 1915

When the war wasn't over by Christmas, Charles Hopkins knew he would have to do his bit. He is relieved not to be heading for the trenches. Having his application to join the Army Service Corps accepted was one thing but he was worried that he might end up like many of his trade who are driving lorryloads of shells to the front. Instead he has been assigned as chauffeur to a London-based Lieutenant-Colonel. He won't trouble himself to wonder if this stroke of luck might be the Astor effect.

Major Waldorf Astor

Cliveden Gages / 17th April 1915

Today's edition of *The British Journal of Nursing* makes interesting reading. Its correspondent reports that "It was difficult to imagine a more peaceful haven, after the storm of shot and shell, the booming of guns, and all the horrors and stress of battle, than the hospital which has been equipped by the Canadian Red Cross, on Mr Waldorf Astor's beautiful estate Cliveden in Buckinghamshire". The article credits "the Canadian Military Sisters, under the superintendence of Miss Edith Campbell, the Matron, and the Commanding Officer, Colonel Gorrell" and adds that "in the course of a very few weeks, huts are to be erected which will increase the beds to a total of 550". This increase has been driven by Charles Hodgett, the London Commissioner for the Canadian Red Cross Society, who believes that the original complement of 131 beds will be far from adequate.

Like his thoroughbred racehorses, **Waldorf Astor** was quick off the mark in August last year. Three days before the UK decided it had no option but to declare war on Germany, he offered the War Office use of Cliveden's indoor tennis court as a hospital. The matter was referred to the British Red Cross Society. While it deliberated, Waldorf volunteered for the army and was immediately made a major, only to discover that he didn't have the heart for it. His illnesses and injuries meant he wasn't fit to serve in combat. Instead he is fighting waste and inefficiency in munitions manufacture and will do so until next year when he becomes Parliamentary Private Secretary to the new Prime Minister, his friend David Lloyd George. Meanwhile he and Nancy will exercise their influence to persuade the USA that neutrality is not in its best interests. Cliveden is the perfect place for British and American decision-makers to consider their political and military options, strategy and tactics in convivial privacy.

The British Red Cross Society dithered. Queen Victoria's daughter-in-law didn't. Princess Louise's husband Prince Arthur, Duke of Connaught & Strathearn, is the Governor General of Canada. Strings were pulled, one thing led to another and soon Cliveden's tennis court was being converted to provide four 25-bed hospital wards for wounded Canadian soldiers with an additional six beds in the gallery above. The matron gets a bird's eye view from her office up there. **The HRH Duchess of Connaught Red Cross Hospital** also has a dispensary and another 25-bed ward in the bowling alley and an operating theatre in the racquets court. Facilities were almost ready on 3rd February when Major Charles Gorrell of Ottawa was appointed commanding officer of what in military parlance is now N° 15 Canadian General Hospital. By the time **Nancy Astor** opened the place in her inimitable style nine days later, Gorrell had been rewarded for his courage by being promoted to Lieutenant-Colonel.

Marquees and bell tents have since been erected to serve as isolation wards, pipes are being laid to supply up to 60,000 gallons of water each day from an artesian well below Widbrook Common via Cliveden's clocktower watertank, a new septic tank has been dug for sewage disposal and ***Taplow Lodge*** across the road has been requisitioned for staff accommodation. Gorrell is now on the polo field south of Gage Close to supervise preparations for the new huts that will provide five pairs of south-facing wards in a "butterfly pattern". His 83 staff includes eight officers and a number of eminent Canadian medical consultants who have been practising in England. Their first patients arrived from France a few weeks ago. There will be plenty more to come.

The Italian Garden War Cemetery, Cliveden / 17th September 2012

As an officer in the Life Guards, **John Astor** served from 1911 to 1914 as Aide-de-Camp to the Viceroy of India, Charles Hardinge, 1st Baron Hardinge. After war broke out, JJA V rose to be a twice-wounded Lieutenant-Colonel who was awarded the Légion d'Honneur as a Chevalier. If Waldorf envied his brother's military career, he could take solace in the benefits brought by the DoCRC Hospital. Its expansion was an astute move. Wounded and gassed soldiers arrived all too soon after the Second Battle of Ypres began on 22nd April 1915. As the casualties mounted, auxiliary accommodation was brought into use in five locations including twelve beds at ***Hitcham House*** and ten more at Maidenhead Cottage Hospital. By the end of 1915 Major Charles

Skipper had added more temporary wards to bring the total number of beds to over 1,000 and some nurses found themselves billeted in Cliveden House itself or in **Taplow Court**, vacated for the purpose by the Desboroughs who settled at *Panshanger* for the duration and later also arranged for nurses to be accommodated in ***Queen Anne's House*** and ***Hill House***. The Astors made their land available rent-free and also funded many building works including the construction of three pairs of semi-detached brick cottages, each housing nine officers. Some of *Winkipop*'s winnings were invested in another cottage set apart for the Sergeants' Mess.

Although it and its successors were always known locally as Cliveden Hospital, the original was named officially for the Duchess who took a great interest in its day-to-day operations and in all things Canadian. She arranged many royal visits to the hospital including those by **King George V** and Queen Mary on 20th July 1915 and 23rd August 1917. However it is likely that she remained blissfully unaware on 20th July 1916 when, as the War Diary records, "the premises known as ***Skindles Hotel*** and the *George Hotel* in Bray were put out-of-bounds to all Officers, NCOs and men of HM Forces". What naughtiness could have caused this prohibition? Perhaps it inspired a certain HJ to pen this ditty, *The Don Juan's Dilemma*....

> There's Gertie of Windsor on Monday. I've promised to meet her at six.
> There's Phyllis of Taplow Tuesday. Now whatever time did we fix?
> There's Mabel of Burnham for Wednesday. She's got curly hair and nice eyes.
> And on Thursday, it's Kitty of Cookham. Her lips are as red as our ties.
> Let me see, on Friday it's Nelly. Where I meet her on chance it depends.
> Saturday brings Dot, my river girl. She comes up from town for weekends.
> Maidenhead calls me on Sunday to Ethel. She's all love and kisses.
> But what's worrying me most at present is what day can I fix for the 'missus'?

Some 24,000 Canadian, British, Australian, American and New Zealand patients were treated at the hospital during the Great War by the 1st Canadian Army Medical Corps, which also researched the effects of chemical warfare and how best to treat its victims. Although as a Christian Scientist not believing in medical practices, the effervescent **Nancy Astor** busied herself by helping on the wards and organising outings and entertainments with unbridled breeziness and good humour, a valuable contribution she shared with many other local ladies including **Minna Pearce-Serocold**. Most of the patients recovered sufficiently to return to the fray or, if they were luckier, back to civvy-street. Some didn't make it. Initially the deceased were buried in the graveyard of St Nicholas' Church in Taplow. Three are still there – one Briton and two British-born Canadians – but the remains of 25 were transferred here to the Cliveden War Cemetery in Willy Astor's beautiful Italian garden after it was ceded to the nation by his son Waldorf and Princess Louise on 9th November 1916. In all 61 were buried in the sheltered serenity of this cemetery.

In accordance with its tradition of repatriating Americans, the USA took 19 home after the Great War – but why not the other five? Perhaps Flight Lieutenant Ray Bray and Privates FB Melsheimer and Carl Russell were regarded as Canadians because they crossed the border to volunteer before the USA joined the war. Poor Russell died on Armistice Day – 11th November 1918 – just two days before Privates George Drake and M Brewer, both of Ohio and the 148th US Infantry. Could this last pair have been forgotten because they breathed their last after peace had been declared?

These five North Americans share their last resting place with 37 others who didn't survive the Great War: one New Zealander, three Australian, six Britons and 27 other Canadians including Nursing Sisters Miriam Baker and Ainslie Dagg who served at Cliveden Hospital and died there in the late-1918 influenza epidemic. Twelve of these unfortunates were new Canadians: eight had emigrated from England and one each from Scotland, Ireland, Sweden and French Algeria. During the Second War they were joined in the cemetery by three others: Nursing Sister Frances Spafford of Canada, Flight Lieutenant SFF Johnson of Australia and Private Ernest Guy, a 60-year-old soldier from Surrey.

The hospital continued to operate for six months after the Armistice, mainly as a clearing station for wounded Canadian troops on their way home. The number of patients peaked at 1,032 in March 1919 but then began to fall away. Edith Campbell's successor Matron E Russell handed over to Matron Cornell on 29th May 1919 and departed for Canada the following day with four of her nursing sisters. By the autumn the huts were being relocated to a Birmingham hospital for tubercular children and Cliveden, its grounds and its tennis court too were all gradually restored to their former glory. And everyone pretended they had never heard of the scandal in 1916.

Major George Bond

Maidenhead Bridge / 3rd June 1915

Last summer the reaches here were crowded with pleasure craft of all kinds going hither and thither. It is an altogether different sight today, one with patriotic purpose. Barge after barge is plying upriver loaded with army supplies for the front in France and Flanders. But wait a minute! They're heading west. Isn't that the wrong direction? **George Bond** smiles at the question.

The gentleman has a rare combination of experience. Having served in the 2nd Boer War in South Africa and spent his life on inland waterways with the people and craft who navigate them, who better for the Royal Army Service Corps to commission as a major in its Inland Water Corps? No wonder he was given the responsibility of assembling a fleet of barges at Teddington and getting them across the Channel to ship supplies along French rivers and canals. He quickly set *Bond's* and other Thames boat-builders to work only to find that, now the barges are ready, the Port of London has been closed for fear of submarines. The

War Office was of course at a loss until George heard what the problem was and told them he had a solution. Under his direction, the fleet will be taken along the Kennet & Avon Canal to Bristol and from there round Land's End to France.

George's intervention will serve the immediate purpose of ensuring that the supplies reach their destination. It will also have the long term effect of preserving the K&A Canal despite inter-war efforts by the *Great Western Railway* to get it closed. Thanks to him, the waterway will still be in use in 100 years.

Sir Maurice & Lady Berta de Bunsen

Old Lodge / 30th June 1915

You can hear it coming all the way up Station Road. The distinguished gentleman at ***Old Lodge*** must be important to have a *GWK* 8-horsepower motor car, one of the latest vehicles off the Datchet production line. As his chauffeur swings it into the drive from Back Lane up to the house, his daughters Cicely, Rosalind and Berta rush out to greet him. Hilda, his eldest at 15, waits at the door with a smile.

Sir Maurice de Bunsen is in the diplomatic service. Although of Prussian descent, he rose to be appointed British ambassador to Spain in 1906 and to Austria-Hungary in 1913. He and his family were withdrawn in haste from Vienna when war was declared last summer. Over the last few months he has chaired a specially-constituted committee which today submitted its report recommending the partitioning of the Arabian domains of the Ottoman Empire to create of the federal states of Syria, Lebanon, Palestine, Transjordan and Mesopotamia. Sir Maurice will be created a baronet in 1919. His retirement years until his death in 1932 will be divided between Taplow and his London home in Hanover Gate. He will play no further part in trying to resolve the increasingly complex strategic conundrum of what will come to be called the Middle East.

Berta is five now. She will soon succumb to polio but will recover to become a female aviation pioneer who in around 1932 will opine that "When present-day landing problems are simplified, the lady owner-pilot upon her daily shopping and visiting rounds is likely to flourish as does her counterpart upon the roads". Later in life she will recall her parents dragging her round hunt dances and balls in the hope of finding a suitable husband, something in short supply after the carnage of the Great War, and remark that she was "far too innocent to realise that, with a lame leg and horn-rimmed glasses, I stood no chance whatever".

Rectory Farmhouse / 30th April 1918

Fifteen-year-old **Daphne Baldwin** opens the envelope to find a handwritten invitation from Lady Berta de Bunsen announcing that "Two Children's Pastoral Plays will be given in the garden of *Old Lodge* on Thursday May 2nd and Friday May 3rd at 3 o'clock (weather permitting)". *Beauty and the Beast* will be performed by the Misses Cicely and Rosalind de Bunsen and *The Enchanted Word* by Adrian Hope. Look Mother, says Daphne, the proceeds will be in aid of The Seamen's Dreadnought Hospital in Greenwich, The Allied Red Cross Workrooms in Belgravia and The Royal Society for Prevention of Cruelty to Animals. We must go.

Liley Baldwin knows her neighbour is trying to keep the children thinking of anything but the war. She takes the invitation from her daughter and notices immediately that tickets are priced differently on each day. Those for Thursday are 2s (£4.24) for adults, 1s (£2.12) for older childen and sixpence (£1.06) for youngsters, tea threepence (53p) extra, while Friday's tickets are 5s (£10.60) for adults and a half-a-crown (£5.30) for children, tea sixpence extra. Clearly the Thursday show will be for those who can afford less. She declares that they shall go to the Friday performance.

Into Trouble

Colonel Charles Gorrell

The HRH Duchess of Connaught Canadian Red Cross Hospital / 29th September 1916

Assistant Adjutant Captain DD Freeze is typing the day's entry into the War Diary of N° 15 Canadian General Hospital. It states simply that "Lieutenant-Colonel DW McPherson CAMC has assumed command of this unit (replacing) Colonel CWF Gorrell". The last mention of the former C/O Charles Gorrell noted his promotion to temporary colonel not three months ago.

It is as expected. The official record makes the reality mundane by being as matter-of-fact as can be. **Nancy Astor** wasn't so circumspect four days ago. She confided then that the "disaster at Cliveden Hospital [was] an awful and miserable story with a tragic end [when] Colonel G committed suicide". It appears that Gorrell and an associate have fraudently benefited from their executive positions at the hospital "to the tune of £11,000" (£651,000). Nancy rued that "Canada's splendid named [had been] besmirched and many local folk [were] involved" and that "It is a great pity the story was hushed up. We all felt it deeply. Colonel Gorrell rang me up, evidently after he knew the worst, and bluntly requested me to send all the convalescents home. I am sure he did it to save my being any way involved".

Unfortunately Nancy left curiosity unsated. She wouldn't say which locals were involved and in what way. And when she spluttered "I daresay [Gorrell was] overthrown by the viper", perhaps she meant Gorrell's partner-in-crime but frustratingly she declined to identify this accomplice beyond an oblique reference to "SM" and an incredulous "she sent me a Christmas card!!" It is unlikely that Nancy will be returning the compliment this year, not even if she could find out in which "gaol" SM now resides.

Into Memory

We Will Remember Them

St Nicholas' Churchyard /11th November 1923

There are about 1,100 people living in the Parish now. Almost everyone is here, wearing poppies in pride and sorrow as they congregate around the War Memorial. The first stroke of eleven has a magical effect. Even the birds in the trees seemed to know not to fly. It is four years since the first two-minute silence was held in London to remember the fallen in the Great War. *The Manchester Guardian* reported that "It was a silence which was almost pain... And the spirit of memory brooded over it all". That spirit has come today to Taplow.

The British Legion was founded two years ago to provide support to those who served and their dependents. This Remembrance service is the first to be held by the Taplow & Hitcham branch. The last stroke of eleven echoes away. The solemn voice of branch president **Lord Waldorf Astor** reads the fourth stanza of Laurence Binyon's *Ode to Remembrance*. All petty social grievances are put aside for a stronger bond unites everyone. How can such a crowd be so still and silent? How sharp are the memories.

The bugler sounds *The Last Post*: still nobody speaks, nobody moves. There are tears in the eyes of even the most stoic as a strange relief washes over the crowd. In years to come some will confuse Remembrance with celebration of victory. How wrong they will be. It isn't victory that fills their hearts but love, regret and a determination never to forget the 28 men whose names are inscribed on the memorial: "Age shall not weary them, nor the years condemn".

Sheldon Gledstanes and **Billy Grenfell** were killed and **Eric Pearce-Serocold** and **Julian Grenfell** wounded (the latter fatally) in Flanders within two miles of each other and but six miles from where 18-year-old 2nd Lieutenant Dennis Theodore Smith of the Royal Engineers was killed in action on 30th August 1915. The Grenfells were not the only Taplovian brothers to fall. Sergeant **Tom Sims** of the Machine Gun Corps and his little brother Lance Corporal **Ted Sims** of the Alberta Infantry Regiment both died of their wounds. Having immigrated to Canada shortly before war was declared, Ted had hardly started to carve his farm from the prairie when he volunteered to join up and was shipped back east only to be fatally wounded on 6th June 1916 in the build-up to the Somme Offensive. Tom made it home to a hospital in Farnborough but survived only until 26th May 1919. He is buried under the walnut tree near the southern hedge. Their father **John Sims** is a gardener, once at ***Taplow Hill*** but now at ***Taplow Lodge***. He and his wife Matilda live across the road at *The Kennels*, formerly the boyhood home of Private George Grantham of the Bedfordshire Regiment who was killed in action at the Somme on 15th July 1916 less than a mile from where Ted Sims had fallen.

John Webster and **Freddie Hurn** died in the Somme Valley within two miles of each other and just three from where the schoolmaster's son Gunner **Gordon Leyster** of the 136th Battery of the Royal Field Artillery (and ***The Nest***) was killed at Albert on 3rd June 1916. Freddie's friend Sapper Willie Waugh of the Royal Engineers (and ***Triangle Cottages***, Cliveden) had been an assistant to his father Thomas, the Astor's resident electrical engineer. And like Freddie, he was awarded the Military Medal but never returned to show it off: he died in Mesopotamia on 8th December 1917. Two others were lost far away: Private **Alfie Portsmouth** of the Royal Fusiliers (a *GWR* fitter of ***The Old Station Inn***) was just 17 when he was killed fighting the Ottomans at Helles Point, Gallipoli, on 27th September 1915 and Private **Alec Hipgrave** of the Royal Army Service Corps (William Rance the Younger's journeyman butcher, son of Flo and Jesse of ***Arch Cottages***) died in the Balkans on 13th August 1917.

Records will not reveal any details of the service or fate of William Cook but others are not so elusive. Brigade Major **Harry Johnson** of the 19th Infantry Brigade of the King's Royal Rifle Corps was 37 when he was buried at Cambrai having died of wounds on 1st January 1915. Private George Wallis of the 6th Battalion, Oxfordshire & Buckinghamshire Light Infantry, died at Ypres on 19th February 1916. Rifleman Charles Penn of the London Regiment, Queen's Westminster Rifles, died on 1st July 1916. Captain George Leake (29) never returned to his post as headmaster of the National School. He died on 2nd June 1917 of wounds sustained while serving with the 2nd/4th Battalion of the Royal Fusiliers, City of London Regiment, and is buried at Rouen along with Private William Grace (32) of ***Coldgrove Cottages***. This son of David was serving with the 6th Battalion, Oxfordshire & Buckinghamshire Light Infantry, when he died of his wounds on 18th January 1917.

Arthur Hooper had begun to learn his father William's trade as a blacksmith in the forge behind ***Sidney Cottages*** in **Station Road**. When he saw the days of true horsepower were numbered, he became a picture framer and then, when war broke out, a private in the 1st Labour Company of the Hampshire Regiment. He died aged 36 on 24th March 1917 and is buried at Hazebrouck, France. Cold storage engineer Guy Seymour of ***Kia Ora*** on the **Bath Road** was a 42-year-old guardsman with the 1st Battalion Grenadier Guards. He survived long enough to be brought to a hospital in Birmingham where he died of his wounds on 18th December 1917. Private Leslie Wingate (20) hailed from *Gilbert Cottage* in Lent Rise to join the 1st Battalion of The Royal Berkshire Regiment. He met his end near Metz in the Moselle Valley on 15th March 1918. In one way, perhaps the unluckiest fellow is Gunner **Arthur Jeffries** of the Royal Field Artillery who died on 31st October 1918 just 12 days before the Armistice was declared. However it is unlikely that Private Arthur Beesley would have counted himself much luckier to survive it by seven days. He was born in **Fairview**, fought in the Machine Gun Corps, died of his wounds on 18th November 1918, was buried near **St Mary's Church** in Hitcham and is mourned by his Taplovian wife Ethel.

Perhaps Taplow's memorial fails to remember Private Walter Sillence of Taplow Lodge because he died on 31st January 1917 under the name of Nolan, but why did its maker forget Air Mechanic Frederick Brittain, who was killed just 17 days before the Armistice? Able Seaman Henry Easden of Dropmore died on 6th November 1917 and others of Hitcham who fell include Lance

Corporals Frederick Slater on 7th August 1915, Francis Slater on 15th September 1916 and E Wells on 11th March 1917. Three soldiers who died at the Duchess of Connaught Hospital remain buried here. Sapper William Buchanan of the Canadian Engineers 1st Field Company died on 31st July 1915, Private Albert Pickett of the 58th Battalion of the Candian Infantry (and Central Ontario Regiment) died on 11th May 1916, and Private George Woods of the Army Service Corps, a former spice worker in a Southall mustard works, died on 27th October 1916.

St Nicholas' Church / 14th November 2010

The Second War left a slightly lighter touch on Taplow. Three fell in 1940: Private Samuel Allen on 25th May, 2nd Lieutenant Desmond Chapman two days later and Sergeant Pilot Frank Edwards on 13th June. Four fell in 1941: Sergeant John Seden on 2nd May 1941, Lance Corporal Stanley Bond (7th July), Pilot Officer William Bloyce (21st August) and Sergeant Peter Ingram (8th November). The next two years saw only four more fall – Sergeant Gilbert Edwards on 4th May and Merchant Navy Chief Steward John Tripp on 7th November 1942, and Bombardier Donald Hilton on 5th March and Sergeant Roy Matthews on 17th August 1943 – but 1944 was less kind: Private Lewis Pearcey fell on 15th February, Major Mervyn Johnson on 11th May, Corporal Gerald Sim of Amerden Grove on 21st July, Private Frank Hammond on 7th August, Sergeant Thomas Wright and Gunner Benjamin Rolfe on 17th and 24th September and Leading Seaman Eric Harding on 6th December. And three more fatalities in 1945 – Private William Poole on 4th March and Lieutenants Edward Richardson and Arthur Akehurst on 15th April and 30th June – brought the toll to 21.

Two soldiers who died at the revived Cliveden Hospital are buried in the churchyard. Little is known of Driver Arnold. Reverend **Alan Dibden** will tell the other's tale. He climbs to the pulpit and pauses to look down on the congregation. The church is packed as it always is on Remembrance Sunday and yet silence reigns supreme until the vicar begins to speak with his usual solemnity and resonance....

In a corner of our churchyard is the grave of Private Joseph Bleakley of the 6th Battalion Queen's Own Royal West Kent Regiment. It is set apart from the graves of other servicemen for some reason we can only guess at. Were it not for the kindness of a parishioner whose father is buried nearby, it might now be overgrown with algae and weed. Private Bleakley was a man of Kent. To mark him being brought into the Taplow family, as it were, we will be laying a cross on his grave today as we commemorate all our other casualties with crosses on our War Memorial.

Bleakley was 18 when he joined up in 1939. His battalion was sent to France in April 1940. Within a month, they were overrun by an enemy armoured division. He was one of only 75 survivors to reach home leaving behind 503 men killed, wounded or captured. The battalion reformed and embarked for the invasion of North Africa, landing at Algiers in November 1942. In the course of the First Army advance on Bizerta and Tunis, it lost 11 officers and 150 men killed, wounded or missing. It transferred to the Eighth Army for the invasions of Sicily in July 1943 and of the Italian mainland two months later. It drove up the east coast to the River Sangro where it is believed that Bleakley – by then 22 and a veteran of four campaigns – was severely wounded, captured and exchanged for a wounded German prisoner of war. He was repatriated to Cliveden Hospital where he died on New Year's Day 1944.

About Grout – One of the Few

Cranford House, Boundary Road / 15th October 2012

Cranford House was the home of **Jim Grout**'s best friend **Eric Williams**. Jim was was 14 when he followed Eric into the Royal Air Force. He began maintaining aircraft at RAF Halton near Wendover, served throughout the Second War, rose to Squadron Leader and became commanding officer of White Waltham Airfield. Eric wasn't so lucky: he died while serving as a pilot with N° 46 Squadron in 11 Group Fighter Command during the Battle of Britain.

Flight Sergeant Williams met his fate exactly 72 years ago today. He was leading a flight of twelve *Hurricanes* on a patrol over the Thames estuary when three developed mechanical problems and had to return to RAF Stapleford in Essex. Almost immediately the remaining nine engaged a much larger flight of *Messerschmitt Me 109*s led by Major Adolf Galland. They shot down one *Messerschmitt* but lost three *Hurricanes* including Eric's which crashed through the roof of a shed on a wharf at Albion Parade in Gravesend (Kent) and buried itself at least 20 feet beneath the earthen floor. His wife Joan was sent a telegram saying he was 'Missing in Action'. It was 47 years before she learned that he remains where he fell. Excavations in 2007 failed to locate either Eric or his *Hurricane* but a memorial to him now stands a short distance away.

Eyes of a Child – Jessica Edmonds

St Nicolas' School / 23rd April 2012

I remember the Remembrance Sunday parade. There were lots of Brownies, Cubs and Scouts plus Guides. Everyone marches down to the church from the car park. Each group had a flag waving high in the sky as they followed the bagpiper. Everyone was wearing a poppy and the church was full of people. We sat in church listening to the Reverend Dibden and sang a couple of songs. Outside, some put reefs on the stone memorial and we stood in silence for two minutes. The atmosphere was quiet and serene. It was a nice day to remember those who died in the war.

Alistair Forsyth says **David Thomas** must be one of the few kilt-wearing, bagpipe-playing Welshmen.

Eyes of a Child – Henry Brothers

The Royal Albert Hall / 10th November 2012

For many years, the Hitcham & Taplow Branch of the Royal British Legion has funded a small party of Scouts and Guides to attend the annual Festival of Remembrance. Tonight the **1st Lent Rise & Dorney Scout Group** is just three rows from the front as Gareth Malone conducts the Military Wives Choir singing *In My Dreams*. When the poppies rain down on the assembled servicemen and women as they stand to silent attention, some fall on Henry Brothers. It all makes him think how lucky he is to be free. This young man will write to Branch Secretary **Laird Mackay** to thank the Legion for "a life-changing experience".

We Will Remember Them

Sheldon Gledstanes & Julian Grenfell / 1915

Homes from home: *Skindles* in Flanders / 1916

Taplow's War Memorial / 2012

Brownies Hannah Irwin, Lyra Cherry & Keira Smales fly the flag / 2010

Piper Keith Thomas leads the parade / 2012

No Tomorrow

Bodies of Influence

No Premature Departure

Taplow Court / 2nd December 1920

The guns have been silent for two years. Survival is a heady feeling. Life must be lived as if there is no tomorrow. There can be nobody better than **Lord Desborough** to show the world the way forward. He has made such a favourable impression at the 9th Congress of the Chambers of Commerce of the British Empire in Toronto that next year he will be invited to become Governor-General of Canada, an offer he will decline for family reasons. Now he is pleased to be home and much amused to read his obituary in *The Times*. Clearly Lord Northcliffe's finest have confused him with Edward Ponsonby, 8th Earl of Bessborough. They really must be rather finer if they are to keep tabs on Taplow....

Next Stop Utopia

Inside the Mind of HG Wells / 1st August 1921

We are characters in the novel *Men Like Gods* riding along in a car driven by Mr Barnstaple of Sydenham. "A little way out of Slough [we see on the left] a low, well-trimmed hedge, scattered trees, level fields, some small cottages lying back, remote poplars, and a distant view of Windsor Castle. On the right [are] level fields, a small inn, and a background of low, wooded hills. A conspicuous feature in this tranquil landscape [is] the board advertisement of a riverside hotel in Maidenhead." A companion remarks "this road is notorious for nursery seedsmen and sometimes they arrange the most astonishing displays". Suddenly there is "a heat flicker in the air and two or three little dust swirls spinning across the road" and we find ourselves in Utopia, an advanced society 3,000 years ahead of humanity which is governed by "the Five Principles of Liberty": privacy, free movement, unlimited knowledge, truthfulness, and free discussion and criticism.

Surely Mr Barnstaple is driving along Bath Road through Taplow, the inn is ***The Dumb Bell*** and the nurseries those of ***Barr's***, ***Rochford's*** and ***William Wood & Sons*** – ideas affirmed by characters referring to Taplow Court and getting "to Taplow on time for lunch with the Windsor people", a reference possibly to the royal family (since **King George V** and Queen Mary come for lunch at least once every summer) but more likely to two of the *The Souls*: Robert Windsor-Clive, 1st Earl of Plymouth (known as 'Lord Windsor' until 1905) and his wife Alberta (known as 'Lady Gay'). Over the years, HG has enjoyed weekends as a guest of the Desboroughs debating the ways of the world with such as Edith Wharton, Henry Irving, Vita Sackville-West and her diplomat husband Harold Nicolson [*see Appendix 4*] and a certain gentleman they knew as Bertie before he became **King Edward VII**. Perhaps the experiences sowed the seed in HG's mind that Taplow is a kind of Utopia. Perhaps his own social insecurity is revealed when Mr Barnstaple is told that the best way he can serve Utopia is to leave it. However Taplow's place in his heart will be confirmed next year when it makes a reprise appearance in his forthcoming novel *The Secret Places of the Heart*.

Tall Tale – The Royal Tipple

Cliveden / 31st August 1923

King George and Queen Mary have arrived for the weekend. Knowing the Astor household is teetotal, the king's equerry discretely delivers to butler **Edwin Lee** a decanter each of port and sherry. Lee smiles his thanks. His Majesty will suffer no deprivation during his stay. When the royal party leaves, Lee will return the decanters still full to the brim. The Astors may not drink and Nancy may rile incessantly against those who do but it seems even she knows where to draw the line.

Many receptions are 'dry' but most guests know to bring hip-flasks of whisky and retire to the cloakroom for sips of sustenance. Dinner parties are different. The Astors expect Lee to buy, care for, prepare and serve the best wines and liqueurs to their guests. He carefully decants claret and port through muslin, briefly heats the port on the hotplate, thoroughly cools champagne in a bath full of ice and always tastes each bottle before serving. And yet despite his discretion and anticipation being well known in the Royal Household, a few days before David, Prince of Wales, first comes to dinner his equerry will telephone to say he will be sending a bottle of brandy which must be available for His Highness at all times. Lee will politely point out that this would be no compliment to the Prince's hosts. And when liqueurs are served after dinner, His Royal Highness will say with a twinkle in his eye: "I'll have a little of your excellent brandy, Lee".

Still Seeing and Being Seen

Boulter's Lock / 21st June 1925

The police will count 10,191 cars driving past Boulter's Lock today. Many have driven down the new Great West Road from London to be part of the Ascot Sunday tradition of seeing and being seen here. Lord Desborough isn't at ease being one of the sights. He has as usual punted his house party guests upstream and as usual they are smiling for the society magazine photographers but something is amiss: the river is so crowded, the riverbank more so, the behaviour is not sedate. His lordship will suffer this downmarket trend only four more times before deciding in 1930 to give tradition a miss. And without him and his ilk, it won't be long before tradition is history.

Tall Tale – Eliot Estranged

The Oak & Saw / 15th July 2014

George Sandy isn't happy. **Alistair Forsyth** is wrong, he splutters: it was the wife of TS Eliot who lived in ***The Porches***, not his sister. There are times when it's best not to argue with George. Best leave that to Alistair. After all, they've had plenty of practice over the past 36 years. And the thing is: he is right. Eliot was born an American and didn't come to England until 1914. If any of his sisters followed him, nobody noticed. His marriage to **Vivienne Haigh-Wood** of Cambridge was not happy. They spent most of it apart so it is perfectly possible that she rented George's house for a period, perhaps in the 1920s. This is hardly Taplow's greatest tale but it still has the potential for getting people hot under the collar.

Farewell to Harm

Taplow Court / 26th September 1926

Lady Desborough continues to be a consummate hostess at **Taplow Court** and her childhood home of *Panshanger*, the Hertfordshire country house she inherited in 1905 from her uncle Francis Cowper, 7th Earl Cowper. When she appears in public, she performs with all her usual poise and elegance. Despite intense private misery at so many tragic losses, grief has revealed the greatness of Ettie Grenfell's spirit. She has never yielded to self-pity and shrugs off sympathy by saying "Life is a series of farewells". Consequently, her fortitude is legend. Some might have shuddered to be satirised as an icon of the decadent and carefree Edwardian age by Max Beerbohm, who in *Seven Men* (1919) observed "exclusive she was but not of publicity. Next to Windsor Castle, [Taplow Court] was the most advertised house in England", and by Maurice Baring, brother of her beau John, who parodied her affectionately as Leila the vamp in his novel *C* (1924). Ettie was shaken not at all.

Of course, this came as no surprise to Margot Asquith, who had already concluded that "Ettie is an ox. She will be made into *Bovril* when she dies". Nor was it to HRH Queen Mary, whom Ettie has attended as a trusted friend and confidante since 1912 and will do so for the rest of her life – including 12 years from 1926 when she will be a Lady of the Bedchamber. Nobody knows more than Ettie about the intrigues, affairs, hopes and grief of the political and intellectual elite but everyone trusts implicitly that her discretion is as adept as it is inviolate. Could this ability to say so little yet mean so much be why her quick-tongued neighbour Nancy finds her hard to take?

Nowadays the Desborough's parties are more relaxed affairs but their guests are no less select. Ettie can count six Prime Ministers past, present and future among her friends. The ailing health of Asquith and of Archibald Primrose, 5th Earl of Rosebery, has prevented their attendance recently but Ettie and Willy are always pleased to entertain Lord Balfour and the present PM Stanley Baldwin. Neville Chamberlain will follow **Winston Churchill**, Rudyard Kipling, King Edward VII and King George V in planting trees in Taplow Court's cedar walk running south-to-north along the top of the ridge[*see Appendix 4*]. Amorous affairs are behind her but Ettie still cannot resist flattering talented younger men such as literary historian Lord David Cecil and poets John Betjeman and Siegfried Sassoon. Another writer, Osbert Sitwell, will remark in admiration that every guest leaving Taplow Court "believed he was the only person she had wished to talk to" and that "his presence had been the very making of the party".

And yet right at this very moment 70 miles away in Kent something is happening that will shake her as never before. Her 28-year-old youngest son **Ivo** has lost control of his two-seater sports car as he rounds a bend. He crashes into a stone gatepost and is knocked instantly into a coma from which he will never awake.

Ivo's death will hit Ettie harder than ever before, not least because his fatal accident is almost identical to that of her young friend Archie Gordon in 1909. Until now, she and Willy have found solace that "our spirits have never capitulated". It will be a year before she confides to him that "this summer mine did" until during weeks of solitude at *Whiteslea*, the Grenfell's house on the Norfolk Broads, "some help came from Ivo himself to set one's spirit free". Sustained by her deep religious conviction that the dead look after the living, she will resume her social round and "the kind of gaiety that has nothing to do with what lies beneath, but makes the actual business of living easier". And it will get easier as between them Monica and Mogs give her five grandchildren to dote upon. Never again will a farewell harm her in the quite same way.

Witch's Brew Too?

Taplow Court / 26th September 1926

Will it cross **Willy Grenfell**'s mind that perhaps fate has been biding its time? His brothers are both long gone and have left no male issue. Claude was killed in action on Spion Kop in 1900 while serving as a lieutenant in Thorneycroft's Horse during the 2nd Boer War. Charles passed away in 1915 leaving just one daughter. His uncle Henry died in 1902, his own sons Julian and Billy fell in the Great War and now Ivo too is no more. His first cousin Edward will go in 1941 and when Willy himself finally slips away at 89 in 1945, the game will be up. There will be no more male Grenfells to inherit Taplow Court. Is it just bad luck? Or have the witches won?

Hurn's Turn – Saving Ways

Taplow Court / 18th July 1952

Harry Hurn has heard that **Lady Desborough** was a real beauty in her youth, a renowned *bluestocking* and – as a member of *The Souls* – folks couldn't help but wonder how much she had in common with her **Willy**. Although **Taplow Court** was not one of the Grand Houses – not like **Cliveden**, Blenheim and Chatsworth – it was however at the heart of Edwardian society for being somewhere that anyone who was anyone – socialite, politician or royalty – could come to stay, have fun and talk politics and scandal.

After their third son **Ivo** died, the Desboroughs spent much of their time at *Panshanger* and made only occasional but usually memorable appearances at Taplow Court. In 1930 Lady Ethel celebrated her birthday by inviting all the women in the Village to tea. My Grannie Clara took me along and introduced me to his lordship as the only other male present. Some years later, at one of the children's parties in the grounds of the Court, I was astonished to hear her ladyship dropping her *aitches* and saying *ain't*, which we were forever being told was not a proper word and that no well-brought-up child would use it. Once each summer the Court held a celebrated tennis tournament when a few envied youngsters were recruited to act as ballboys at five bob each (£9.35). And the 1935 Silver Jubilee of **King George V** and the 1937 Coronation of **King George VI** were celebrated with services in the Church in the morning, sports on the cricket field in the afternoon, tea in the Court's indoor tennis court – where his lordship, just home from his duties and still dressed in his regalia as Gentlemen-in-Waiting to the King or some such, made a patriotic speech and distributed prizes to the winners of various races – and after dark a huge bonfire and fireworks followed by dancing in the tennis court to Jack Gardener's band.

Although the Desboroughs moved in the highest circles it was known in the Village that they were not well off, not in the sense that the Astors were. Her ladyship in particular had "very saving ways". Most famously, she would have her maid buy her a third class ticket knowing that the ***GWR*** staff at Taplow Station would usher her into first class with all ceremony. But once the train was on its way to Paddington she would slip back to third class to avoid being caught having not paid the full fare.

A Formidable Alliance

4 St James's Square, London SW1 / 10th June 1927

Do places influence how people behave or are people attracted to places that match their character? At the dawn of party politics, Taplow Court tended Tory and for the Crown while Cliveden went Whiggish and was for the Country. It is much the same now with a modern twist. The Lords Desborough and Astor have ample common ground politically and yet the older they get the more 18th Century poles of opinion echo in **Waldorf Astor** the principled liberal and Willy Grenfell the loyal monarchist. Neither eschews the other's point of view. It benefits them both to be cordial neighbours and pragmatic, powerful allies when they have a common cause....

The Astors spend the week here at their London home and return on Fridays to Cliveden for the weekends. Astor is writing to his Taplow neighbour Desborough who, he has no doubt, agrees "that it would be a national tragedy – in fact a crime – if our reach of the Thames were ever desecrated by bungalows or villas. We could confer no greater benefit on posterity than by guaranteeing that the wooded banks of Taplow Court and Cliveden on the Bucks side of the river should be protected and preserved from the gerry-builder". As Astor expected, his seed will fall on fertile ground. Even before he joined the **Thames Conservancy Board** (TCB), the then Willy Grenfell had been able to ensure that the 1894 Thames Conservancy Act incorporated a clause which "reserved" as his "private water" the Taplow leat "between the lock in the said stream and a meadow called Clemarsh Mead". Their Ladies might not exactly be the best of friends but these Lords make a formidable alliance.

There is a mood about for those who can to do the right thing for England's countryside. George Peplar has been promoting planning since 1908 and is now Chief Town Planning Inspector at the Ministry of Health. He was supportive when the **Council for the Preservation of Rural England** (CPRE) was set up six months ago to campaign against the sprawl of 'ribbon developments' along main roads. Its secretary is Professor Patrick Abercombie of Liverpool University. He and Peplar wil be leading lights in the gradual acceptance of planning as a concept and in the development of the UK's national town and country planning policies, but what a boon it will be to have Astor and Desborough in the vanguard. By the end of this year, their lordships will have galvanised the high and mighty from Cricklade to Staines to create a Thames Valley branch of the CPRE. Astor as its chairman and Desborough as one of ten vice-chairmen recruited to the cause not only the TCB and major riverside landowners like themselves but also Eton College, Oxford and Reading Universities and all affected public bodies including five County Councils, three Borough Councils and myriad Municipal, Urban and Rural District Councils.

4 St James's Square, London SW1 / 30th July 1929

After a year-and-a-half of surveys, reports and drafting of legalities, the branch has finally succeeded in convincing HM Government to schedule certain Thames riverbanks as 'private open spaces' thus preventing them from ever being built upon. Astor has just received a letter from Eton RDC confirming its agreement to so schedule the Cliveden riverbank. He will shortly conclude a similar agreement with Cookham RDC regarding the Berkshire riverside meadows of ***White Place Farm*** and E**ton RDC** will accede to Desborough's scheduling of the Taplow Court riverbank. **Selina Whitlaw** must be seething. Grenfell made a big play for stayers by expanding his property portfolio on the Bath Road. Desirable residences crept along the Berks bank and she began to match it with ***Harefield***, ***The Red House***, ***Broomcroft***, ***Fair View*** and ***River Bank*** [*see Map 39*] only for her ambition to be frustrated by the economic stagnation stagnation of the Great War and its aftermath. And now its revival has been trumped

Map 39 – The Valley: Playing for Stayers

The Grenfell & Whitlaw Property Portfolios

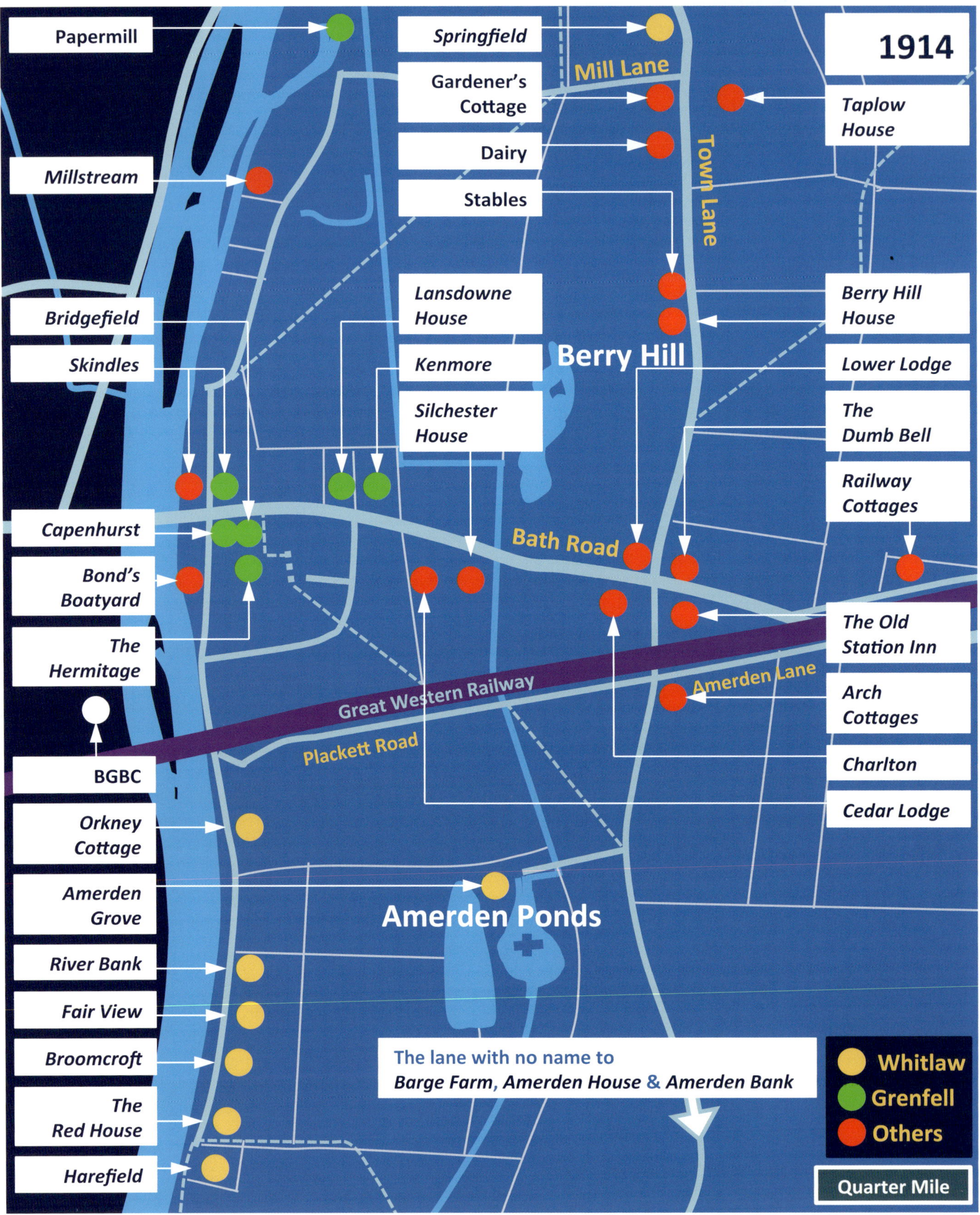

Primary Sources: Ordnance Survey 1897. HTS 2013 (Newsletter 100) and David Long 2014

by her illustrious neighbours. Not forever. *Orkney Cottage* will fragment into three homes. *The Red House* will be split into two (for directors of *Barratt's* and *Woolworth's*) and its stables converted into ***Longacre***. *River Bank* will be reinvented as ***The River Bank House*** and although *Harefield* will remain its southern outpost, **River Road** will see its share of infill over the years as the grounds of the original mansions and the intermittent plots find room for ***Olympia House***, *Pine Lodge*, *Folliots*, *The Anchorage*, *Lamont House*, *Riverholme* and *Kingfishers*.

Cliveden Reach / 22nd July 2012

Now we know why the riverbanks here have changed so little from the descriptions by those academics in 1890. The scheduling of broad riverside strips of their land as 'private open space' in 1929 had an undoubted financial benefit for Astor and Desborough – it exempted them from paying death duties on the value of the land – but the magnificent environmental value for Cliveden and for all river users is still evident 83 years later. However, it would not do them justice to suggest they were driven merely by self-interest. They used their wealth and influence to promote common sense and the common good and with their professional and academic allies laid the foundation for the evolution of the UK's national town and country planning policies. Although they were active in supporting **'Green Belt'** policy when it was pioneered in 1935 with the goal of protecting the openness of the countryside and preventing the merger of towns into one another, neither survived to see the establishment of 'green belts' around major cities in 1955. At least Astor saw Peplar craft the Town & Country Planning Act (1947) and the creation two years later of the UK's first National Parks and Areas of Outstanding Natural Beauty.

No 21 Byways / 22nd October 2013

Euan Felton is preparing an article for the 100th edition of the Society's Newsletter (Autumn 2013). He outlines the evolution of planning as a concept and as government policy to pose the question: "Why is this still important? Imagine for a moment that it had not happened as it did. Taplow would have been a very different place. Without planning there is absolutely no doubt that Taplow would have been subsumed by development stretching northwards to Beaconsfield and southwards to Windsor. Field by field and wood by wood the developers would have advanced into the countryside. Slough and Maidenhead would have merged into a single sprawling city."

A Day at the Races – Horsepower on Four Wheels

Brooklands, Weybridge / 6th July 1907

As the son of a wealthy stockbroker, **Richard D'Arcy Baker** can afford to indulge his passion for speed. Within four years of *Fiat* being founded in 1899 he had secured monopoly rights to import its cars from Turin. Now he is a board member of the *Automobile Association*, founded two years ago to help motorists avoid speed traps. With his encouragement, the AA will soon have a nationwide network of agents, mechanics and legal experts. By 1926 it will have installed thousands of danger, warning, direction and village signs across the country; it won't be until the 1930s that this responsibility passes to local authorities.

That is all well and good in making motoring accessible for the masses but today for the sheer thrill of it D'Arcy Baker (as he likes to style himself) will drive in two races during the inaugural meeting at the world's first purpose-built motor racing circuit. His *Fiats* will come last in one race and fail to finish another but the five meetings here this year will confirm that motor racing is here to stay and that Great Britain is established as a leader in the field and Brooklands as an iconic venue. And next year Baker will win the accolades his adventure deserves when the famous Italian driver Felice Nazzaro drives his *Fiat Mephistopheles* at over 121mph to win a purse of £250 (£23,000).

Hedsor House / 15th August 1932

Baker's pioneering spirit and commercial awareness continued to set the pace that first touched Taplow in 1923 when he settled temporarily at ***The Elms***. After supporting the Astor-Desborough alliance in its efforts to protect the countryside, in 1927 he began to invest £150,000 (£36.81m) in an ambitious restoration of **Hedsor House**. The ornamental domes were removed, a marble and onyx pool installed with matching bathrooms, the ballroom panelled in golden-tinted pine rescued from Orleans House in Twickenham and other rooms panelled in oak from Wingerworth Hall in Leicestershire and the Old Monastery in Isleworth. And yet Hedsor was his home all too briefly. He passed away today leaving just £3,783 (£1.03m) and fleeting memories of his white-and-red *Fiat 514 CA* two-seater sports car stylishly flashing past Cliveden.

A Day at the Races – Horsepower on Four Legs

Epsom Downs Racecourse / 8th June 1929

The three-year-old fillies come under starter's orders for *The Oaks*, the third of the English classics. The warm sunshine is tempered by a pleasant breeze and, though very firm, the going is a tad softer than on Derby Day. It is a surprise to see **Lord Astor** looking rather nervous. This is his race, after all. He has won it four times – first with *Sunny Jane* in 1917 and then with *Pogrom* (1922), *Saucy Sue* (1925) and *Short Story* (1926), all trained by Alec Taylor. Surely he knows that conditions are ideal for *Pennycomequick*.

The starter's gun booms, the horses are off. Astor's eyes tighten in the glare and then relax as *Pennycomequick* pulls clear. But she seems to slow as she approaches the mile post. Her lead over *Golden Silence* is diminishing fast. Her jockey Henri Jelliss gets her back to business and she quickly comes away over the last four furlongs to win with ease. Her time is one of the fastest ever but the look on Astor's face reveals he knows it could have been quicker. He sees our quizzical glance over the shoulder of his trainer Joe Lawson and allows himself a smile of modest celebration. The racing correspondent of *The Evening Standard* asks whether he has a special 'secret formula' for breeding good fillies. After a pause, he replies: "Frankly, I don't know that there is any. I have a variety of theories. All my animals can be traced to three mares: *Conjure*, *Maid of the Mist* and *Popinjay*. Every mare in my stud at present I bred myself except the 24-year-old *Popinjay*. That adds greatly to the interest. I do not believe in buying horses. The pleasure of breeding is that you have always something in anticipation. Since I started racing horses I have bred 89: 74% have been placed in races; 61% have been winners and 28% have been placed in the twelve big events of the English Racing Calendar. That gives me the greatest pride of all." By 1950 his horses will have won 460 races and been placed 547 times to win £487,750.

Sir Alfred Munnings [*see Appendix 4*] captured Astor's pride in his painting *A Summer Evening at Cliveden* which depicts his lordship seated on his shooting stick as five mares and their foals are circled around him for inspection. He certainly has plenty to be proud of, and he will have more. He has had amazingly bad luck in *The Derby*, his horses coming second five times in seven years, but *Saucy Sue* won eight of her ten races and in 1921 *Craig an Eran* won *The 2,000 Guineas*, the first classic of the season. *Plymstock* and *Blink* were winners too and *Buchan* might also have been counted as one of the best racers if luck had gone his way. He had four wins in 1919 and 1920 but was narrowly runner-up in both *The 2,000 Guineas* and *The Derby*, third in another classic, *The St Leger*, and disqualified on a technicality after crossing the line first in *The Ascot Gold Cup*. Astor's consolation was that *Buchan* was declared 'Champion Sire' in 1927 when his daughter *Book Law* won *The St Leger*.

From now on, his lordship will find winning classics more elusive. *Pay Up* (1936) and *Court Martial* (1945) will bring him two more victories in *The 2,000 Guineas* and in 1953 his son Bill, 3rd Viscount Astor, will see Joe Mercer ride *Ambiguity* to victory in *The Oaks*. However, it will him bring quiet pleasure to see his queens' bloodlines succeed for others. *Phar Lap* will have 22 victories in Australia including *The Melbourne Cup* (1930) while *Swale* and *Provoke* will both win major races in the USA. At home, *Tiberius* will take *The Ascot Gold Cup* in 1935, *April the Fifth* (1932), *Bois Roussel* (1938) and *Phil Drake* (1955) will all be victorious in *The Derby* and the line will see success all the way to 1985 when *Shadeed* wins *The 2,000 Guineas*.

The Derby at Last

Epsom Downs Racecourse / 3rd June 1987

New bloodline, new colours, first victory: the master American jockey Steve Cauthen wears the black-spotted yellow silks of 70-year-old **Louis Freedman** to ride the dark bay colt ***Reference Point*** and give **Cliveden Stud** its first Derby winner.

Freedman is a self-made property millionaire – chairman of *Land Securities Ltd* for 19 years until 1977 – who first indulged his love of horseracing in 1965 when his colt *I Say* came third in *The Derby* and won *The Coronation Stakes* the following year. This encouraged him to become an owner-breeder. He acquired Cliveden Stud in 1966 from the estate of Lord Bill Astor and stared well with *Lucyrowe*, *Attica Meli*, *Mil's Bomb* and *Polygamy* all bringing success over the first eight years. It has since been harder to find the winning formula. He invested in a new stable block in 1977 as he harboured dreams of breeding a horse to win the Triple Crown – the *2,000 Guineas*, *Derby* and *St Leger* in the same season – and he thought *Reference Point* might be the answer to his prayers until he caught a cold and had to miss *The 2,000 Guineas* in April. The victory today is a relief, a vindication, but when the colt wins *The St Leger* in September the celebrations will be tinged with a sense of what might have been.

In addition to high position in racing's corridors of power, Louis Freedman's service as chairman, vice-chairman or trustee of four health authorities and especially his 11 years on the Race Relations Board were recognised in 1978 by his being made CBE. When asked what a racehorse-owning property dealer was doing in such a post, he replied: "Had it occurred to you that I might be interested in the dignity of mankind?"

This season will be Louis's last in racing. Early next year, accusations in *The People* newspaper of him making illegal payments to jockey Lester Piggott will damage his dignity sufficiently to influence his decision to cede his bloodstock to his son Philip as the *Cliveden Stud Company*. His receiving substantial libel damages will be little compensation. Perhaps his obituary in *The Independent* might be: on 28th December 1998, it will remember him as a genial man with "no hint of a ruthless streak" who was "fond of humorous understatement". It will laud him as a "natural administrator" whose "boundless energy ensured he pursued an active role in public life". Strangely it will neglect to mention his ten years as a vice-president of the Hitcham & Taplow Preservation Society.

Philip Freedman will celebrate winners including *Daggers Drawn*, *Endorsement* and *Indian Haven* and the latter's dam *Madame Dubois* before selling the Stud in 2006 when retired British equestrian eventer **Tessa Spencer** takes over.

High Society

St Nicolas' Church / 4th August 1932

The Village burghers are assembling here to witness the marriage of **Daphne Baldwin** of ***Rectory Farmhouse*** and **Victor Williams**, a barrister of ***Burwood*** on Taplow Common Road who will one day act as Queen's Counsel for Ian Campbell, 11th Duke of Argyll. Pride of place has of course been allocated to Lord and Lady Desborough and to their daughter Imogen and her husband of 18 months Henry Gage, 6th Viscount Gage. Imogen had her first baby only a few weeks ago but she was determined to be here for she and Daphne have been close friends and tennis partners since they were children.

Although it has been three or four years since the Reverend **Francis Phillips** dropped the 'h' from St Nicolas, a convocation of the more senior local eminent legal eagles can't resist debating the wisdom of it. Two big city solicitors, Sir Henry Kimber of ***Hitcham Place*** and **Noel Dowson**, can see the Latin logic. Barrister **George Bancroft** of ***Elibank*** can't see the point.

Two titled widows are deep in whispered conversation. Lady Florence Dunscombe is now **Selina Whitlaw**'s tenant at ***Springfield***. As daughter of John Montagu, 7th Earl of Sandwich, she has a similar heritage to **Lady Beatrice Pole-Carew** of ***Maryfield***. The latter's daughter Marye is enjoying the less intense company of Grace Howlett of ***Kenmore*** and of **Beatrice Roberts** and **Yvonne Blonay**, respectively principal and tutor of ***Silchester House Girls' School***. **Gwendolyn Serocold** (of ***Taplow Hill***), Gwendoline Romilly (of N° 4 Riverside), Mabel Sainsbury (of N° 6 Riverside) and Wenna Palmer of *Dorney Court* watch indulgently as their husbands Oswald, Frederick, Charles and Charles talk tactics in the way that only retired colonels can.

George Gledstanes of ***Berry Hill House*** looks on quizzically as his wife Monica shares the latest news with four lady friends: **Louisa Rance** and her daughter Mary of ***The Hollies***, **Janie Dykes** of ***Hill Farm*** and Barbara Eastick of *The Chauntry* at Burnham Abbey. **Florence & Cecil Irby** of ***Hitcham Grange*** and **Audrey & Edward Skimming**, a merchant ship-owner of ***Taplow House***, bid welcome to Mr & Mrs Hugh Charrington of the brewing family, now at ***Hill Cottage*** (not-yet ***Hitcham Lodge***), and to **Elfrida & Walter de la Mare** and their son Colin of ***Hill House***. And last but not least here comes **Percy Noble**, red-faced for rushing the few yards across the road from ***The Priory***. Silence falls as the Rector emerges from his vestry to begin "Dearly beloved, we are gathered here today...."

Rectory Farmhouse / 4th August 2002

Liley & Walter Baldwin rented ***Rectory Farmhouse*** from **Willy Grenfell** in about 1892. Daphne took over the lease when Liley died in 1925 and it wasn't until about 1950 that her husband Victor finally acquired the freehold from the Grenfell estate. It passed on Daphne's death in 1988 to their son **Thomas Williams**.

Thomas wasn't an old man, says **Tony Meats**. This was his home for all his 65 years until his death last May. He said his parents didn't have a happy marriage and that he and his mother celebrated with champagne when his father died. Daphne used to see a lot of **Florence Shephard** up at ***Hedsor House*** and I think Florence's son Alexander was a good friend of Thomas but he has kept himself to himself since Daphne died. My boys **Oliver** and **Rupert** used to knock on his door and run away terrified and screaming when he appeared in his ironmonger's smock: poor old Thomas.

Tall Tale – Hill House Horror Stories

The Oak & Saw / 4th June 1999

It is Friday evening. Thirsty neighbours are gathering as usual. Having made it here all the way from ***The Old Manor House*** next door, **Alistair Forsyth** is updating the assembled company on the progress of his photographic history book ***Taplow at the Millennium***. He has heard that the novelist Bram Stoker lived for a while at *Hill House*, perhaps while he was writing *Dracula* in the mid-1890s. Could this Forsyth Saga be true?

Documentary evidence is scant. Censuses find **Dick Grenfell** at *Hill House* in 1891 and Louisa (Lucy) Bourke (Norah Lindsay's sister) there from before 1901 until after 1911, initially with her clergyman brother Cecil [*see Appendix 4*]. Stoker lived at various addresses in Chelsea from before 1880 until his death in 1912 but perhaps he came temporarily to Taplow to feed his muse prior to the arrival of the Bourkes. There is no doubt the famous poet and novelist Walter (Jack) de la Mare lived at *Hill House* for 14 years from 1925....

Lord of Tartary

Hill House, Berry Hill / 23rd May 2014

Giles de la Mare and his wife Ursula have come to unveil a blue plaque commemorating his grandfather's residence here. The ceremony takes seconds. His speech is short and sincere. He reads two poems – *Incomputable* and *All That's Past* – and the assembled company retire for refreshment in Flat N° 5, for two more weeks the home of Penny & Tony Reid.

The event is as brief as it has been long in the making but no less pleasant for that. **Gavin Gordon** thinks it must be 11 years ago that he first had the idea. He recalls that *Hill House* was converted to seven flats in the 1970s. He acquired N° 2 in 1989 and joined with the other owners to create *Tartary Management Ltd*, the company which owns the freehold and has been managed since 2010 by Brian Millin, the admirable fellow who has realised Gavin's dream by having the plaque produced and installed. Giles graces the occasion by reading the poem from which it takes its name. Here is the first verse....

> If I were Lord of Tartary, myself, and me alone,
> My bed should be of ivory, of beaten gold my throne;
> And in my court should peacocks flaunt, and in my forests tigers haunt,
> And in my pools great fishes slant their fins athwart the sun.

Sounds just like Taplow.

Giles is sure he was brought here as a small child but all he remembers is that the house was at the top of a steep hill. His father Richard was the eldest son of Jack and his wife Constance Elfrida (Elfie) who shared with Selina Whitlaw the maiden name

Lord of Tartary

Walter de la Mare / c1919

Hill House / 2012

Gavin Gordon watches as Giles de la Mare unveils the blue plaque / 2014

Giles reads his grandfather's poem *Lord of Tartary* / 2014

Ingpen [*see Appendix 1, Tree 19*]. Their families originated not far from each other in Chelsea, Westminster and Battersea. Were they sisters or more likely cousins? Could this familial link be how Elfie & Jack discovered Taplow? Or was it through mutual friends of their landlords the Desboroughs? His lordship enjoyed Jack's conversation. Her ladyship loved having "a resident genius" at her gates. She would send across pencil notes. One said "Dearest Friend – put one syllable on the exquisite handwriting on a postcard.... How learned you are, how do I ever dare speak to you???" Many others implored him to join to the Saturday-to-Monday parties at **Taplow Court**, at least for Sunday breakfast. It was an ordeal for Jack to set out unfortified to "sing for his breakfast". It was almost a relief early one Sunday morning in August 1930 when a fire badly burned three rooms at *Hill House*. What better excuse could here be for missing his neighbour's aristocratic breakfast?

Jack was much better at home where he and Elfie were often descended upon by friends and family in great number: it wasn't unusual for there to be 20 unexpected guests for dinner. Siegfried Sassoon, Edith Sitwell and Henry Newbolt were regular visitors and JB Priestley, WB Yeats, Max Beerbohm, Thomas Hardy, James Barrie and GK Chesterton almost certainly came to call [*see Appendix 4*]. No arrivals caused a greater stir than those of Lady Ottoline Morrell who cut such a fantastic figure with her gorgeous exotic dresses, marmalade-coloured hair and mouth painted blood-red on her long face powdered dead-white. On one occasion, Jack told **Joyce Grenfell** what she described as "an earthy joke". A lady who was suffering from constipation went to see her doctor and said "I just sit there, but nothing happens". The doctor asked if she was taking anything. "Only my knitting", she replied.

Gavin can't confirm rumours that the house is haunted but he has heard tell that Jack enjoyed sitting in his dining room, now Flat N° 3, thrilling children with tales of two ghosts who haunted the place – a scrabbling old man with a herd of exotic animals and another fellow with a nose protruding from his hat and a mouth on his elbow. Just where does imagination meet apparition? One of those fascinated youngsters was Selina's granddaughter **Anne Whitlaw** (later Young, eventually Milne) who cherished fond memories of Sunday afternoons sitting on Uncle Jack's knee to hear him spin his yarns.

Although during his time in Taplow Jack published two substantial collections of poetry – *The Fleeting and Other Poems* and *Memory and Other Poems* – his muse for verse was temporarily mislaid. He concentrated on writing short stories – including *The Connoisseur*, *On the Edge* and *The Wind Blows Over* – and on compiling three of his most famous anthologies: *Desert Islands*, *Early One Morning* and *Behold, This Dreamer!* Unfortunately his creativity was interrupted all too often by his own and Elfie's bouts of illness. He underwent a prostate operation in *Hill House* and they finally decided to leave for Twickenham in 1939 after she was stricken with pulmonary thrombosis. As they were packing, their daughter Florence rescued from the rubbish pile the greater part of his original manuscript of *Songs of Childhood* (1902) and Jack found in a forgotten notebook verses he had scribbled in his youth, a serendipity that evolved into *Bells and Grass* (1941). He went on to be awarded the *Carnegie Medal* in 1947 for the 17 fantasy and fairy tales in *Collected Stories for Children* illustrated by Irene Hawkins.

Hearing History

Elibank, Rectory Road / Christmas Day 1932

The Grenfell tenure of ***Elibank*** since 1853 has been a complicated affair involving trustees, tenancies and intra-family conveyance presumably designed to keep taxes and duties to the minimum. The title has passed via Anna Matilda Graham of Glasgow to her daughter **Elizabeth Grenfell**, wife of Lord Desborough's half-second-cousin (Charles) **Seymour Grenfell**, and on Elizabeth's death in 1930 to their son **Dick**. After their daughter Mildred married the French-Canadian Brigadier-General Henri Gustave Joly de Lotbinière in 1902, the earthen-floor, single-storey kitchen-and-scullery extension to the rear of *Elibank* was increased to three storeys to accommodate them and their two sons, both of whom have grown up to distinguished careers: Edmond Joly de Lotbinière as a lieutenant-colonel in the Royal Engineers and Seymour Joly de Lotbinière as a barrister and now at the BBC where he is known as 'Lobby' [*see Appendix 1, Tree 16*].

Dick Grenfell had long lived at Welwyn in Hertfordshire and so leased *Elibank* within a year to **George Bancroft**, the barrister son of the renowned Victorian actor-manager Sir Squire Bancroft and his actress wife Marie 'Effie' Wilton. George and his wife Monica have just listened to King George V's very first Christmas message, written by Rudyard Kipling and broadcast live on the wireless to the Empire from Sandringham. She remarks that His Majesty was in good voice. He responds that Dick can be proud of his nephew for it was the 6-feet-8 Lobby who produced the historic royal broadcast. They will laugh when they learn from Desborough that afterwards the king had invited his family to shake hands with the longest man he had ever seen. Lobby Lotbinière will go on take charge of *BBC Outside Broadcasts* for both radio and television. He launched ball-by-ball radio commentary of cricket and was responsible for the historic TV coverage of the Coronations of King George VI in 1937 and Queen Elizabeth II in 1953.

George Bancroft will acquire the freehold of *Elibank* in 1934 and remain there until his death in 1956. With his startlingly white wig and deep theatrical voice, his performances in court have something of his parents about them. Perhaps that is why some will mistakenly claim Sir Squire and Lady Effie lived at *Elibank* despite both being long gone before their son arrived hereabouts.

About Grout – Scouting for Boys

Hitcham Old School / 18th July 1936

My brothers Phil and Jim joined the **1st Taplow Scouts** in about 1923, says **Arthur Grout**. When I joined the Cubs in 1931, we met in **Taplow Reading Room**. Our uniform was a green cap, green woolly jersey, brown neckerchief and black shorts and shoes.

The Cub Master, Mrs Wallis, was very strict. She wouldn't stand any nonsense as she taught us how to keep ourselves clean and tidy. One of our tests was building a fire in the back garden of her cottage on the Bath Road, cooking a stew or porridge over it and then cleaning up afterwards: the pots, pans and even the fireplace had to be left spotless. We always enjoyed her reading from *The Jungle Book* before the end of the meeting.

When I was eleven I moved up to the Scouts under Mr NE Wallis, an ex-Army man. Soon afterwards the Reverend **Phillips** said we couldn't use the Reading Room anymore because some of the boys didn't attend church. The Scoutmaster wanted to keep the Group open to all religions so he arranged for us to meet here instead – **Hitcham Old School** will become ***Cloverdown*** – and that's how we became **1st Hitcham Scouts**. Now our uniforms are khaki shirt, navy blue shorts, a three-pointed hat and a six-foot pole which we use as a measure, a flag pole and for all sorts of useful things like making tables and chairs at camp. In the summer we camp locally most weekends, often at ***Dorneywood***, home of the businessman **Sir Courtauld Thomson** whose sister Elspeth is the widow of Kenneth Grahame, that chap who wrote ***The Wind in the Willows***. But best of all, he says, is the two weeks we spend away at our main camp. We've been to Lechlade and Bridport and next month we're off to Lyme Regis: it costs 15s (£45) but it's the only holiday most of us have. We're looking forward to the District Gang Show in the WI Hall – there'll be about 60 of us involved, aged from 12 to 50 – and to next summer's World Scout Jamboree in Holland.

The Scouts will be camping at Beaulieu Abbey when war is declared in 1939 and civilian travel is forbidden. Arthur won't complain about having to stay an extra week in the New Forest but it won't be much fun when they get home to discover Hitcham Old School requisitioned for evacuees from London. Their only option will be to meet in a draughty old wheelwright's shed at ***Morlew Yard*** in **Marsh Lane**. During the war some of the Scouts will enjoy duties running errands or manning the telephone exchange switchboard at the Canadian Hospital up at Cliveden. Arthur won't know which is better: having the chance to watch the films they show there twice a week or thinking it quite an achievement to have four King's Scouts in the Troop.

Hurn's Turn

Parish Extravaganzas

Taplow Parish Room / 18th July 1952

It isn't much to look at, this large tin hut adjoining the western wall of the Reading Room, but this is where it all happened in the 1930s. **The Parish Room** was originally a corrugated-iron non-conformist chapel acquired and re-erected so that services could be held here while the church was being rebuilt in 1911/12. Thereafter it was used for all manner of functions including charity sales, private and public meetings, parties, the occasional wedding reception and, most memorably, village concerts and plays.

The last typically ran for three nights. Shakespeare did an annual turn. *Henry IV*, *The Merchant of Venice*, *Midsummer Night's Dream* and *The Tempest* were performed by local talent extravagantly costumed by **Agnes Tanner**. Harry had two roles in the last of these but doesn't look back with pride. His thespian qualities were somewhat restricted by costumes so tight that his white underwear could be clearly seen through the stitches of the green knitted elf outfit and through a hole where his hound skin didn't quite meet. He remembers the best-ever show as being a brilliant programme of song, dance and monologues produced in 1938 by Jack Flude, a cobbler of **Nearways** in **Hitcham New Town** (not-yet **Eastfield Road**). It revealed a surprising array of talent as well as a sizeable contribution to the organ fund.

These extravaganzas spiced Harry's teenage years as he was shaped into a grown-up by five Taplovians at the church and the school....

Reverend Francis Phillips – High and Dry

St Nicolas' Church / 18th July 1937

As a choirboy, Harry is able to watch the Reverend Phillips at close-quarters. The 45th Rector's 'High Church' persuasion isn't popular. Many think the full and solemn ceremony, the incense and the oral confessions are to blame for his congregations dwindling from a 'full house' before the Great War to nowadays, when those in the chancel might outnumber those in the nave. Some say it's to do with his old-school, straight-laced, austere and aristocratic manner.

Harry sees all that and more. He will grow up with sad memories of the Rector as a good, sincere and deeply pious man left high and dry in a world that no longer looks to the parish priest for guidance in all things spiritual and most things temporal. Even in his youth, he will silently sympathise with a man left lonely by the loss of his wife not long before coming to Taplow and of his only daughter shortly afterwards. He sees a dutiful and diligent man performing his services, taking scripture lessons and morning prayers at the school and walking the parish from end-to-end to visit his flock, and a quietly generous man who invested a significant proportion of his personal wealth in rebuilding the church, who every Sunday at both Matins and Evensong slips a ten shilling note (£28) into the collection bag – more than a day's wages for Harry's gardener father Everett – and who this coming Christmas, at his own expense, will take all the children in the choir to see *Bertram Mills' Circus* at *Olympia*.

Reverend Phillips never neglects the work of the church overseas. Each year there is a rummage sale in aid of these missions and a missionary on leave from some remote part of the Empire will come to give talks in the school and at the church of his work and adventures among the heathen. And each year he strives to achieve his dream of raising funds to have a new organ installed over the west door and to open the existing organ chamber as a second side chapel. He was desperately disappointed that **Elizabeth Grenfell** was commemorated by ***Elizabeth Cottage*** and not by a new organ that would finally complete the renovation of the church two decades after it began. He was upset with **Lord Desborough**'s offer of a second-hand organ from **Taplow Court** that was in worse condition than the existing organ and arguments became so fractious that Colonel Oswald Serocold only ever attends church on Remembrance Sunday.

Strange to say that the old organ proved itself not to be quite so old as all that by getting a second wind, allowing the money raised to be invested in an electric pump which relieved **Everett Hurn** and many others of the back-breaking work of hand-pumping the organ.

Percy Goulden – Singing the Praises

St Nicolas' Church / 18th July 1937

Harry will cherish the memory of the regular musical and theatrical performances in church such as the nativity play and especially John Stainer's oratorio *The Crucifixion*, an annual highlight at the beginning of Lent. He believes that Taplow has one of the best choirs around thanks to the brilliant organist and choirmaster **Percy Goulden**, a bachelor who lives at N° 1 **Elm View** with his nearly-blind aunt, Miss Mitchell. He earns his living at the gas office down by the river but lives his life at various keyboards and for his 12 boy choristers who practise three times a week. Monday evenings in the school are light-hearted and always finish with story-telling, quizzes or games such as balloon handball. Wednesdays are more serious and the men join on Fridays for a full rehearsal. These fine singers come from near and far: in addition to Frank Flude there's **Bert Hunt** (undertaker and violinist of Coldgrove Cottages), James Glasheen (Cliveden's head gardener), Bert & Wig Trimmings (of Lent Rise garage), Edgar Wingate (retired *GWR* signalman) and Bert Pym who, between bouts of malaria, cycles up the hill from Maidenhead to sing and to be honorary secretary of the Parochial Church Council. Men and boys, the choir takes its responsibilities very seriously until a heel gets caught in the hem of a cassock, and everyone still laughs about the Candlemass service when flames from a loosely held candle rippled up the back of Jack's cotta.

Mr Goulden is always treating the boys by organising cricket matches and outings to Windsor Castle, *The Ideal Home Exhibition* in London or to the seaside and Saturday evening jaunts to one of Maidenhead's three cinemas. Back in the spring, Harry and three other young choristers met by the church to walk down **Old Friend Lane** to ***The Dumb Bell*** where they caught the bus to Maidenhead. First stop was the tobacconists where the choirmaster bought sweets, comics or a *Penny Dreadful* for the lads and a packet of *Player's* cigarettes for himself. Then to the pictures to see George Formby in *Feather Your Nest*. The boys are only vaguely aware that, like others, Mr Goulden is often at loggerheads with the Rector, a friction that early next year will spark into such a serious disagreement that he will up sticks to Bray.

Frederick Gardner – Master of the House

Taplow School / 18th July 1937

After **John Siggers** finally retired in 1919, Fred Milton succeeded as schoolmaster for two years and AG Gomm for ten before Digger Gardner took over in 1931. Digger is a short man with sleeked-back dark hair who always wears a bowtie and walks with a limp since being wounded in the Great War. He has three assistants but is quite able to teach most subjects well, including shorthand to any girls who hoped to become stenographers. He rather fancies himself as a comedian and never fails to take part in every theatrical performance, although his real forte is as musician quite good enough to fill in occasionally as church organist.

The old Victorian school building has survived well enough. The largest of the three rooms is divided into two by a wood and glass screen. The infants have been taught in the Parish Room since 1935, when their old classroom was adapted so woodwork can be taught to the older boys on Tuesday afternoons and cookery to the older girls on Wednesday afternoons. The boys get some fresh air on Friday afternoons, when Digger takes them up to the cricket field for sports – cricket in the summer, football in the winter – and on Wednesday afternoons in the spring and summer they vie with each other as to who can grow the best crop of vegetables in the allotments north of *Church Cottages*. Meanwhile if it's sunny, Mrs Digger might supervise the girls in growing flowers in a ladylike manner.

When Harry was little, everyone used slates and slate pencils. Now the children have steel-nibbed pens which they dip into inkwells on each desk. These are filled on Fridays by trusted elder boys who are also tasked in the winter to bring coal in to stoke the fireplaces in each room. At that time of year, children from Cliveden and the Common are allowed to leave at half-past-three instead of 4 o'clock so they're home before dark, a privilege much-envied by the rest. Next year, Harry will learn a little more about what privilege really means. Like all 11- and 12-year-old schoolchildren, he and his friends will take an exam to determine which of them will go on to secondary education and which will leave school at 14 to make their way in the world. The parents of two or three might be able to afford to send them to private school. Everett and Violet won't have the means to do that for Harry yet the lad will grow up to look back fondly on his schooling for the foundation it gave him in life.

Bob Tanner – Mistress Quickly

The Sweet Shop, Church Road / 18th July 1937

Harry can just about remember the time when this little cottage adjoining ***The Old Manor House*** was Ada West's sweetshop, a veritable seventh heaven for a young boy looking up open-mouthed at shelf upon shelf crammed with jars of gobstoppers, jelly babies, liquorice allsorts, toffees, acid drops, wine gums and aniseed balls. One day it will be ***Mysteria***. Now it is home to **Agnes Tanner**, or *Bob* behind her back. A shilling is a *bob* and sixpence – half-a-bob – is a *tanner*: not much of a joke but it works well enough today, if not after decimalisation in 1971.

Bob never went to college. She trained under the old 'on the job' system as an apprentice teacher and 20 years ago she had a reputation as a tyrant, some say as a result of being crossed in love. Although she may be rather naive to tell children they are fortunate to live today because all things there are to know are now known, she is as good a teacher as Harry will ever meet and more conscientious than most. She is an active member of the Women's Institute, a stalwart supporter of the church and the Rector, a Sunday School teacher and always involved in village concerts and plays, not least by having the girls in their needlework class create costumes which she describes as 'garments'. Harry's mum thinks this a most appropriate term for any clothing of Miss Tanner's design including the selection of knitted creations she keeps on hand for any female who comes to church with her head uncovered.

Harry is looking forward to his confirmation next year with mixed feelings. He doesn't fancy the church convention that he must fast until after he has taken his first communion. As long as he doesn't have to don a 'garment', he relishes the St Nicolas convention that at the Reverend's expense he will then be subjected to bacon, eggs and sausages at Bob's house.

Eyes of a Child – Donald Rosenthaler

Taplow School / 18th July 1936

Donald is a year younger than Harry. He was born in Wraysbury and has lived at *The Railway Hotel* (*The Old Station Inn* by any other name) since 1932. His father works at *Skindles* with his uncle Fred, a tap dancer. His family will move away this summer and change their Czech name to Rose in 1939. His favourite memory of Taplow will be the time his uncle took him to stay overnight at *Skindles* to listen to the music and watch the dancing. His least favourites will be having his knuckles wrapped or his left hand tied behind his back to try to make him write with his right. His most shocking memory will be that time in Miss Tanner's basketwork class when six children caught talking were made to stand at the front of the class with their tongues sticking out as Bob pretended to snip them off, only she made a mistake and actually chopped off the end of one girl's tongue. Donald has never seen so much blood. He never talked out of turn again.

Eyes of a Child – Louise Green

Taplow School / 18th July 1956

Louise is a left-hander. It can be difficult for her because all the scissors and so on are the wrong way around but her parents Yvonne & Frank tell her how lucky she is that children's left hands are no longer tied behind their back to force them to write with their right. That's all very well, thinks Louise, but why can the boys keep their shorts on to do PE lessons in the playground? She is hugely indignant that the girls have to run around in their knickers. At least she is allowed to put her skirt back on to walk across the High Street to her home at ***Victoria Cottage*** (formerly ***The Nest***).

Margaret Rome – Truly Scrumptious

Pax Cottage, High Street / 18th July 1937

Harry's first memory of Miss Rome is as the District Nurse, always capable, caring and wise. Now retired, she is officially sacristan of the church, unofficially of the Rector. **Arthur Grout** has no idea why all his pals call her 'Bogey'. She looks after all the church vestments and accessories, teaches in Sunday School, organises charity sales, entertainments, plays and any else you can think of. And most importantly of all, she is the Rector's right hand and moral support. Theirs is a remarkable partnership for she has qualities he does not. She is a delightful lady who knows all the village children and shows love and many kindnesses to each and every one as if they were her own. Now it's time for a scrumptious Sunday tea in her little home.

St Nicolas' Church / 18th July 1939

It doesn't feel quite right to Harry that the old Rector has retired to Devon without fanfare or appreciation, nor that the lovable Miss Rome has gone with him as his housekeeper. It leaves a hole in the heart of the village just when it needs to be strong in the face of war. Nevertheless all the talk has been of who the new man would be. Canon **Robert Hay** is a more worldly political type from Oxford, which explains his appointment to Taplow as its 46th Rector in readiness for his ascension as Suffragan Bishop of Buckinghamshire in 1944. As the war plays out its last, he will divide his time between his episcopate and his parish where one of his occasional curates will confide to **Violet Hurn** that "Taplow is quite spiritually dead" – in Harry's view, a sad epitaph to Reverend **Phillips**' valiant efforts over three decades.

St Nicolas' Church / 18th July 1999

Harry could never understand why Canon Hay wouldn't allow the choir to sing the verse of the old hymn that goes....

> Time like an ever rolling stream bears all its sons away.
> They fly, forgotten, as a dream dies at the opening day.

In Harry's opinion, we do indeed fly forgotten. Francis Phillips is remembered in the church on a list of rectors. There is no memorial to Margaret Rome. After the Second War, she will be succeeded at *Pax Cottage* by someone Harry thinks almost as deserving of fond memory: **Bert Fowler** was the Verger at St Nicolas' Church for over 40 years and he still led the procession from the vestry even after going blind. Nothing was ever too much trouble for Bert and his wife Gertie. They took it in their stride during the Second War when their little house was packed to bursting with evacuee children. Harry regrets that, as older generations die out, the likes of Margaret, Bert, Gertie and many others such as **Walter Leyster**, **Bob Tanner**, **Julia & John Siggers**, **Digger Gardner** and **James Rutland**, who were important hereabouts in their own time, are inevitably forgotten. Maybe someday someone will put that right by remembering them in a book.

Mills and Boom

The Dumb Bell, Bath Road / 18th July 1940

A rather swish car pulls up outside ***The Dumb Bell***. Freddie Mills steps out. Harry Hurn runs over to get his autograph. Like many prominent boxers, Mills is using the pub as his training headquarters. Our 14-year-old friend is proud to show off the autographs of the American King Levinsky and the British and Empire heavyweight champion Jack Petersen. He will be delighted next month when his hero defeats Jock McAvoy to win the British and Empire light-heavyweight titles.

Freddie's driver is **Edwin Johnson** of ***Station Garage Taplow***. Harry can never look at Mr Johnson without thinking of the moment six or seven years ago when his deaf son came to school wearing the first hearing aid any of the children had ever seen – a huge contraption like a radio speaker which hung in front of the boy's chest by a strap round his neck. Some of the youngsters called the poor lad Deafy Johnson. Harry isn't saying who.

Woman with her Reasons

Three Unequivocal Queens

Cliveden / 1st December 2012

Three women dominated Taplow during the two decades after the Great War, when those who could lived life as if there was no tomorrow. The dowager **Selina Whitlaw** had a reclusive nature but nevertheless ruled the Amerden farmlands and riverside. As **Ethel Grenfell** presided over the social whirl at **Taplow Court** and around her husband, she quietly exercised her gift for getting her way (and his) by being everyone's friend. At **Cliveden**, it was more of a social whirlwind which **Nancy Astor** rode with panache to make friends, enemies and more than a few waves on the national stage. These leading ladies can be summed up simply. History records many quotes by Nancy, more than a few about Ettie and none by or about Selina.

Parliamentary Pioneer

The House of Commons, Westminster / 1st December 1919

Waldorf and Nancy Astor continued to enjoy an enviable social scene even during the Great War when Cliveden was the perfect place to bring British, Canadian and eventually American decision-makers together. Now it is over, their lives are once again a web of interwoven strands – politics, newspapers and philanthropy – spun around entertaining 'Bright Young Things' on a lavish scale. Their abstinence from alcohol doesn't impair their fun one jot. Indeed Nancy is quoted as saying, "One reason I don't drink is because I wish to know when I am having a good time". She certainly had a great time three days ago when she won the by-election in Plymouth Sutton to become only the second woman to be elected to the House of Commons. It was delightful to be welcomed home to Cliveden by cheering retainers at the *Fountain of Love* and to ride with Waldorf in a Victorian carriage along Grand Avenue by the light of bonfires. And today, as the first female MP to be admitted to the House, she is the star of a truly historic occasion. Constance Markievicz (née Gore-Booth) was elected almost a year ago but she was incarcerated in Holloway Prison at the time and, as an Irish republican, has since declined to take her seat.

It was a proud moment for her family to watch from the Distinguished Strangers' Gallery as Nancy was escorted to the Bar by her eminent sponsors Prime Minister David Lloyd George and former PM Arthur Balfour. Of course Waldorf pretended not to notice as she broke all the rules by talking to her sponsors and chatting with Andrew Bonar Law and even to the Speaker, James Lowther. Now she emerges from the chamber into the lobby. The press furiously tries to elicit the kind of witty but sometimes risky one-liners for which she is already famous. Some suspect her career as an MP will be as controversial and exciting as her campaign has been.

While she has never been short of an opinion, it was just six weeks ago that Nancy first really thought about entering the political arena. After serving as MP for the newly-created constituency of Plymouth Sutton for barely a year, the death of his father **Willy Astor** obliged Waldorf to apply for the Chiltern Hundreds in order to give up his seat and enter the House of Lords as 2nd Viscount Astor. He had been horrified when Willy accepted a peerage as Baron Astor in 1916. He was strongly opposed to the principle of honours and titles – he believed fervently that it should not be class distinctions but intellect, ability, character and work that counted in citizenship – and frustrated at the prospect of inheriting a peerage that would put a ceiling on his own political career. His protests resulted in a violent family quarrel. Willy rewrote his will, refused ever to see his son again and caused more dismay by being elevated to Viscount Astor in 1917. Waldorf has tried to disclaim his inheritance but Lloyd George persuaded him otherwise, installed him as Parliamentary Secretary at the Ministry of Health and ensured he will continue to play a prominent role his 'garden suburb' of advisers. This left the question of who should represent Plymouth Sutton, and Nancy just knew it

Parliamentary Pioneer

Nancy Astor campaigning for and winning Waldorf's Parliamentary seat in Plymouth / 1919

"DAILY MIRROR'S" PLAN TO HELP EX-OFFICERS

The Daily Mirror

CERTIFIED CIRCULATION LARGER THAN THAT OF ANY OTHER DAILY PICTURE PAPER

[16 PAGES.] One Penny.

LADY ASTOR'S TRIUMPH: ENGLAND'S FIRST WOMAN M.P.

should be Nancy, not least because, on being elected, she has the opportunity to propose publicly: "Let's abolish titles altogether".

There's no doubt that the campaign tested her. It was hard to find that her idealism was seen as political naivety so she pragmatically moderated her prohibitionist views in public and went carefully on divorce reform. Her quick tongue was taken by some as an indication of instability and yet that same quick wit enabled her to handle hecklers well. She drew laughter and appreciation when a man asked what the Astors had done for him and she retorted with a flirting smile "Why Charlie, you know". Being accused by Markievicz of being "of the upper classes, out of touch" rather baffled her. She believes her work at **Cliveden Hospital** and numerous charities has put her more closely in touch with fundamental social issues than most and, whilst she is no suffragette, she believes she is doing what any woman should: taking her destiny into her own hands and setting out to make the world safe for men since men have made it so unsafe for women. However she is rather pleased to have taken the criticism to heart and worked hard to win the support of female voters. And she is very pleased to have won Plymouth Sutton for the Coalition Conservatives with more votes than the other candidates put together, not least because WT Gay of the Labour Party and Isaac Foot of the Liberals had been formidable opponents.

Nancy is suddenly an international star, effectively not only MP for Plymouth Sutton but for women: a lonely but resolute symbol for her gender. She will be the only woman MP until being joined in 1921 by Margaret Wintringham of the Liberal Party. Their number will rise to eight in 1923 and nine in 1924 before falling in 1925 to five and rising to back to nine in 1929. She will be received in the House with hostile misogynistic prejudice and even humiliation and yet will rise above it to serve as an MP until 1945, a total of 26 years during which she will fascinate, infuriate and offend. Her quick wit is tailormade for the bear-pit of Parliamentary debate. Her style of banner-carrying agitation will work best in tandem with others like Waldorf who are diligent with detail and able to moderate her erratic behaviour for best effect. He knows she hasn't the tactical guile to be a consummate politician, but she will champion her causes with courage, passion, persistence and, in 1924, the simple innovation of making formal introductions unnecessary by requiring guests to wear tags bearing their name, profession and organisation or area of interest. They will unite to introduce the Intoxicating Liquor Act (1923): she the first woman ever to pilot a Bill through all its Parliamentary stages to become law, he steering it through the Lords to raise the age qualification for sale of alcoholic beverages from 14 to 18.

As a divorcee, she will shrug off accusations of hypocrisy to oppose extending the grounds for divorce beyond adultery. Other battles, often in concert with her female colleagues including Wintringham and the Socialists Ellen Wilkinson and Margaret McMillan, will be for various social reforms. Perhaps her greatest success will be working with McMillan to foster a nationwide network of nursery-schools with trained teachers, a cause the pair will pilot with generosity in Plymouth, but she will make a difference on many other matters including women's pension, property, professional and employment rights, equal opportunities and pay for women in the civil service and police, the registration and training of nurses and midwives, the introduction of health clinics, raising the school leaving age from 14 to 16, cheap supplies of milk to young children, legitimacy, adoption and guardianship, slum clearance and modern housing, the protection of prostitutes from unlawful arrest and the abolition of the death penalty.

Meanwhile, having been chairman of the Medical Research Council and of a Government committee on tuberculosis since 1916, **Waldorf** will be instrumental in the founding of the Ministry of Health and an invaluable Parliamentary Secretary to the first minister Dr Christopher Addison. He will go on to help frame legislation on proprietary medicines, factory safety, rent restrictions, slum clearance, juvenile employment, inheritance laws and the sale of alcohol. And he will serve as a British delegate to the League of Nations in 1931. Noble causes all and yet, despite these contributions to a new national social landscape, the Astors will never shake off Markievicz's accusation.

Tall Tale – Witty Lady

The Great Hall, Cliveden / 1st December 2012

Although many stories of Nancy's scathing wit may be of questionable authority and authenticity, remarks attributed to her tend to remain longer in the memory than her political achievements. On her first visit to England before she met Waldorf, one of her hosts in Leicestershire chided "I suppose you have come over here to get one of our husbands". She responded tartly, "If you know the trouble I've had gettin' rid of mine, you'd know I don't want yours". On **Edward VII**'s first visit to Cliveden, she declined to partner him at bridge with the exclamation "Why, I don't even know the difference between a King and a Knave". Despite never being a feminist in the modern sense, she will be quoted as saying, "I married beneath me, all women do" and "the first time Adam had a chance, he laid the blame on a woman". Some in the House of Lords might have less obstructive to her Intoxicating Liquor Bill if she had not called them 'The Beerage'. On foreigners, she may have said "All Latin nations are absolutely rotten.... unprincipled, bibulous and immoral" and "France is nothing but a big brothel", and on education reform, "Real education should educate us out of self into something far finer, into a selflessness which links us with all humanity". If she did, no wonder some thought her idealistic. And perhaps she revealed her own insecure self-awareness with "Pioneers may be picturesque figures but they are often rather lonely ones" and "My vigour, vitality and cheek repel me. I am the kind of woman I would run from".

Her supposed exchanges with **Winston Churchill** are legendary. Here are three favourites. Churchill may have remarked to her that having a woman in Parliament was like having one intrude on him in the bathroom, to which she is said to have retorted, "You're not handsome enough to have such fears". When Churchill asked what disguise he should wear to a masquerade ball, she answered, "Why don't you come sober, Prime Minister?" And possibly the most famous of all such anecdotes reports Nancy as saying to **Churchill**, "If you were my husband, I'd poison your tea," to which he responded, "Madam, if you were my wife, I'd drink it!" Her great-grandson **William Waldorf Astor III, 4th Viscount Astor**, has confided to Maggie Blakeslee of Bergher's Hill that he believes this exchange to be accurate. Whatever the truth of the matter, it seems they both rather enjoyed the game.

Quartet

The Pug's Parlour, Cliveden / 14th August 1928

Rosina Harrison is a matter-of-fact Yorkshire lass, known as Rose. She always knew she'd go into service but, since she had the urge to travel, her mother Rose advised her to be a lady's maid, and for that she'd have to stay on at school until she was 16 and to learn French and dressmaking. The strategy was successful. Her first post was to look after the daughters of Lady Ierne Tufton, 2nd Baroness Hothfield. Her second was to attend to Lady Elizabeth, wife of Robert Gascoyne-Cecil, not yet 5th Marquess of Salisbury. In this capacity she spent every Ascot week at Cliveden where Lady Astor was impressed enough to decide "That's the maid for me". Rose knew Nancy was a difficult mistress and thought "Not if I've anything to do with it". Then she heard that her daughter Phyllis needed a maid. It would be a step down to attend 'Miss Wissie' but the annual salary of £60 (£14,800) was more than twice what she was earning. She applied and got the job without an interview. Does she realise that today is the first day of the rest of her life? She will do so well that Nancy pulls rank and requisitions Rose to attend to her every need. And that's what she will do until My Lady breathes her last in 1964.

Rose will be one of four servants who more than most will define Cliveden in the Waldorf & Nancy years. The others are Nanny Goodwin, **Edwin Lee** and Frank Copcutt.

Nanny Goodwin is first in line in more ways than one. The Australian was first to arrive – in 1907, when Bill was born – and as Lee will recall "Nanny knows best, not just for the children but for the staff as well.... She makes demands on everyone's time and patience and is always allowed to get away with it". And yet even such privileged children as Bill, Phyllis (Wissie), David, Michael and Jakie need a rock of care, consideration and fun to cling to as their busy and self-possessed parents try to change the world. Without her, Nancy will say "Without her I couldn't have done half what I did.... She was my strength and stay and the backbone of my home". She will live on in grace-and favour comfort until her death in 1947.

William Parr took on Shropshire lad Edwin Lee in 1912, initially as a footman, later as Waldorf's valet. On Parr's departure, Lee was elevated to be the Astors' butler in 1919 and has since become quickly become a legend, always distinguished in his navy blue tail coat and black breeches, stockings and pumps. Nobody ever uses his first name, not even here in the senior servants' room: the Pug's Parlour. To the Mistress, he is 'Lord Lee of Cliveden'; to the Master and his guests, he is Lee; to the staff, he is Sir or Mr Lee to his face and 'Skipper' or 'Skip' behind his back. Rose will come to call him 'Father'. She will always be 'Miss Harrison' to him even in their far-off retirement.

Lady Astor expects everything to be just so, including the footmen who Rose thinks look like a swarm of very smart wasps. Their everyday livery is brown with yellow and white striped waistcoats, and red and yellow piping down the side of their trousers. The dress livery is brown jackets, striped waistcoats, breeches, white stockings and black pumps with gold buckles, and of course white gloves. Housemaids too must be immaculate in their brown alpaca uniforms, organdie aprons, high collars and bandeau caps tied with velvet ribbons. Everyone on the staff looks up to Lee with immense respect as he ensures the Astors' every need is provided and that the regular dinners for 60 and the balls for 600 go like clockwork. Just to have been trained by him is a reference in itself.

Lee will tell Rose that her ladyship "is not a lady as you would understand it". Not in the sense that society deems conventional. Rose will decide that Lee and My Lord are well-matched, both being good commanders with discipline, trust and the ability to delegate, whereas My Lady cannot resist interfering and she never says *please* or *thank you*. Frank Copcutt has it right that the Mistress demands while the Master always asks if something is possible. He thought it was a good idea when Mr Camm the Head Gardener suggested that the horses which pull the lawnmowers should wear leather overshoes to avoid bruising the grass. She cries out for flowers and yet won't let him buy many bulbs for his greenhouse. James Glasheen will have his work cut out when he succeeds Camm but things will get better when Frank catches her ladyship's eye....

The Greenhouse, Cliveden / 14th August 1932

Frank will one day be Head Gardener and in charge of perhaps 50 hands. For the present, he is happy not to be George any more. That was the name of her ladyship's previous decorator, he recalls, so that's what she called me for well over a year. I was scared stiff at the prospect of having to fill Cliveden and N° 4 St James's Square with fine displays of cut flowers every day but Nature has a way of sorting things out for you. The following Sunday I was on the way back from church when I saw a most glorious display of wild flowers. That's it, I thought: keep that picture in your mind and you can't go wrong. When I'd done the bowls next day she came in and said "I thought you told me you'd never arranged mixed flowers before". No more have I, My Lady, I replied. "George," she said, "you're a liar". That's the only kind of compliment her ladyship knows how to give, shrugs Frank. She shows neither of us any appreciation for ensuring her impeccable appearance in the House of Commons: always simple and elegant in black and white, always with a fresh, white scented flower in her buttonhole.

The Dining Room, Cliveden / 14th August 1936

Frank shakes his head to recall the times when My Lady sorely tested the patience of the ever-diligent Skip. One evening she returned late from Parliament to find the table set for royal guests arriving the following day. Something wasn't to her liking.

She screamed, kicked her shoes off and climbed onto the table and started to pull my centre-piece to bits. Lee told her with quiet firmess that "if this is the way you want to run your dinner party you must run it yourself. I want no more of it". She paused, stepped down as gracefully as she could and ran after Lee to say "Don't worry. I'm going to change now". On another occasion **Lee** was so exasperated he threatened to tender his resignation. She was ready to counter "Tell me where you're going because I'm coming with you". They both fell about laughing and, of course, he will stay until his retirement in 1960 when, free at last after 48 years on duty, he will marry Emily Blaber, Cliveden's telephonist since before Rose joined the staff.

Lee, Harrison and Copcutt share the strength of character to survive and thrive with the Astors. They and Nanny Goodwin won't be the only ones to serve them faithfully for rest of their lives. Although Rose will never earn more than £80-a-year (£19,000), her peers are generally paid around 10s-a-week (£30) more than the going rate and provided with comfortable accommodation, sickness benefits and a pension scheme. Some of the staff hardly ever leave Cliveden's little world for it has everything they could possibly want in life. They enjoy balls and dances, football and cricket teams, a boat on the river and the use of the tennis court and golf course when the family are away. And there are two really special days each year. The summer party has a flower show, knitting and needlework displays, sports and all the fun of the fair for the children, followed by a big dance in the evening with beer for the men and wine for the women.

Taplow Blue

The Parterre, Cliveden / 14th August 2012

Bees and butterflies flutter about the rounded steel-blue flowers swaying gently on the tall stems in beds of *Echinops bannaticu* – or *globe thistle* to its friends – now the most common of the *Asteraceae* family in England. This robust, upright herbaceous perennial originated in south-east Europe, so how did it come to be called *Taplow Blue*? Perhaps it was first cultivated hereabouts by Holland, Fleming or Frost, Glasheen, Copcutt or Camm.

Tall Tale – The Odd Sailor

The Pug's Parlour, Cliveden / 1st October 1933

Lee is in control as usual. It is a different matter for **Sailor**. This 'odd man' seems to have no name but he can be useful if he stays off the bottle because he knows the ropes of entertaining.

All grand houses have odd men to do anything and everything other staff do not, and some of their tasks too when things get hectic. Cliveden usually has two on the staff and a number of locals that Lee calls in for the big occasions. I can spot such men at a hundred yards, he tells **Rose Harrison**. It's the way they walk: their legs are buckled, their toes turned in and they always look as if they're carrying something heavy. And they do: especially trays full of steaming hot food. Rose thinks they are not as other men. They are often lacking in brain power and have no ambition beyond beer and baccy. She will never know one odd man who marries but most are willing workers and some good friends. Lee and Sailor are like man and dog: Sailor beams at a word of praise and any reprimand is like a whipping. All has gone smoothly this evening but now Sailor is conspicuous by his absence – but not of course by his abstinence: he will be found in the secretary's room sleeping off a few bottles of champagne.

Playing to the Gallery

The Great Hall, Cliveden / Christmas Day 1936

The dark days are gone. The Great Depression nearly reached that doorstep in 1931 when the American real estate market was paralysed and money so tight that **Nancy** and **Waldorf** discussed laying off staff, reducing the wages of those retained and even letting Cliveden to ease the Astor cashflow. It is so good that things are back to normal. And what's more Nancy is still basking in her performance on *BBC Radio* when she was asked to explain the abdication to Canada and the USA. It is not a class issue but a moral one, she said. **King Edward VIII** accepted the Crown as a symbol of the constitution but "Those who will not obey the rules cannot rule". Wallis Simpson cannot be queen, not because she is American, not because she is not of royal blood but because she is divorced.

How convenient that the United Kingdom has someone so well known on both side of 'The Pond' to put the case so well in that slightly-Anglicised, light Virginian accent. Today Nancy's performance will be of an entirely different nature....

Before first light the housemaids are scrubbing, scouring, dusting, working in haste for they must soon be invisible. As always, Lady Astor is up in time to check all is in order. After "doing the lesson" – her Christian Science and Bible readings – she takes a cold bath, touches her toes, stands on her head and does whatever other physical exercises take her fancy. She dresses practically in a sweater over a white silk shirt, a tweed skirt, golf socks and ghillie shoes before touring her domain. The Great Hall is lavishly decorated, its log fire spluttering happily. Frank Copcutt has decorated the sparkling Christmas tree at the foot of the oak staircase and scattered festoons of evergreens and flowers everywhere to meet My Lady's taste for precise chaos. Piles of presents are littered over chairs, sofas and carpets, or stacked on trays and baskets. She reviews the day's menus with Monsieur Gilbert the chef, consults with Lee and issues instructions to Rose. All is as it should be. The day may begin.

At precisely 9 o'clock, Lee strikes the gong to awake the guests for their breakfast. Present-giving lasts until 11 o'clock when those who feel so inclined troop off to **St Nicholas' Church** in **Hedsor**. Although always generous and expecting it in others,

Nancy is quietly pleased that nobody has matched the present of a live pony that her son Bobbie Shaw gave his stepbrother David Astor some years ago. Lunch is served at one o'clock to more than 30 guests who will use only one plate for all courses in accordance with Nancy's consideration for the kitchen staff. In the afternoon there are walks in the grounds and games played on the parterre with rules adjusted according the Nancy's whim.

After tea, everyone assembles in the library for some light entertainment before retiring to don fancy dress for a traditional Christmas dinner of turkey and all the trimmings, plum pudding, sweets, coffee and crackers. "So began 'a characteristic Astorian evening of dance and song all jumbled up in a rollicking way', casual and frivolous. Most of the company [are] run-of-the-mill Arabs, Apaches, cowboys, pirates or gypsies. Not Nancy. She [seeks] to catch the eye, striking poses, playing to the gallery, always theatrical, often melodramatic" as an immaculately attired *nouveau riche* huntsman badgered by his wife, a 'Virginian belle', a snobbish English lady complete with protruding plastic teeth, a racing tout or a 'low-caste Jew'. And now the carpet is being rolled back for charades, yet another opportunity for Nancy to perform. She chatters incessantly, "her timing perfect, her accents accurately pitched". The result is of course "uproarious" as it needed to be to upstage **Rose Harrison**'s hilarious portrayal of the orphan Eliza (as played by British screen sweetheart Betty Balfour in the film *Eliza Comes To Stay*) at the estate Christmas dance, yet another fancy-dress affair also remembered for the contribution of Arthur Bushell, Waldorf's valet. "Cunningly made up as music hall star Nellie Wallace, wearing lorgnettes and a preposterous hat, he [concluded] his sketch by brazenly displaying his 'green knickers with a Union Jack on the behind' to Nancy [who] was not amused", probably because she didn't think of it first.

At about midnight, the revellers retire to bed but not before a hearty sing-song, mostly folk songs and spirituals, to banjo accompaniment. As they fall asleep, **Bobbie Shaw**'s remark rings in everyone's mind: "This house is like a huge liner and that little woman is the rudder".

The Good Ship Cliveden

The Grand Avenue, Cliveden / 16th May 1937

Sunday afternoon in the best of times, the heyday of entertaining. **Nancy** steers the ship with skill as she and **Waldorf** host regular weekend parties of notorious extravagance. The playwright George Bernard Shaw has introduced to the social fold the brilliant, dynamic TE Lawrence (of Arabia). It is perhaps four years since this heroic yet fragile fellow gave his lordship one of the scariest moments of his life. Everyone was taking tea quietly enough when Lawrence and her ladyship suddenly leapt up, rushed outside, jumped on his *Brough Superior* motorcycle and drove off at top speed leaving nothing but a cloud of dust to remember them by. Waldorf was beside himself with worry and embarrassment. They were only away for a few minutes but it seemed like an eternity before they dashed back up Grand Avenue even faster than they'd gone and skidded to a dramatic stop scattering a wave of gravel. "We did a hundred miles an hour" screamed Nancy. Rose silently thanked God for answering her prayers. Waldorf stalked away in fury. His wife was grief-stricken when Lawrence was killed in a motorcycle crash in 1935. At his funeral, she and her nemesis **Winston Churchill** stood silently holding hands in tears.

Today the family has something to celebrate: last Tuesday, Lady Astor was made a Companion of Honour to acknowledge her outstanding achievement in politics. Eventually talk turns to two of the most enjoyable visits to Cliveden, both in 1932: one by Franklin D Roosevelt, now President of the USA, the other by a trio to die for: pioneering aviator Amy Johnson, film star Charlie Chaplin and **GB Shaw** once more. Last year, Harold Nicholson was heard to mutter "There is a ghastly unreality about it all.... I enjoy seeing it. But to own it, to live here, would be like living on the stage of *La Scala* theatre in Milan". And yet still they will come. Next year, one of the most notable guests will be Joseph Kennedy, the USA's new ambassador to the UK (or England, as he will insist on calling it) [*see Appendix 4*].

Driving the Astors

The Garage, Cliveden / 24th November 1938

Charles Hopkins survived the Great War and returned to rise to be the senior chauffeur at Cliveden where he lives very comfortably in *The Doll's House* with his wife Nellie (Helena). It will cost £2,000 (£430,000) to run the garage this year. The various vehicles will cover 88,000 miles of which he will cover 17,000 in the *Phantom II Rolls Royce* and **Albert Jeffries** will do 12,000 in the *Humber Landaulette*. Albert was born here: his father Albert was a gardener for **Willy Astor**. Charles will die here on 16th October 1942 having been in the Astors' employ for 30 years.

Jam, Jerusalem and Joyce

The Women's Institute Hall, Institute Road / 1st October 2009

Nancy Astor didn't invent the **Women's Institute** but the idea was right up her street. It began in 1897 in Canada and took 18 years to arrive in North Wales at Llanfairpwllgwyngyllgogerychwyrndrobwllllantysiliogogogoch. It caught on more quickly in the UK than anyone could say the name of this Anglesey village. Within two years there was a national association and early in 1926 Nancy, by then president of Cliveden & Dropmore WI, suggested to **Audrey Skimming** of ***Taplow House*** that there should be a WI in Taplow. One thing led to another. Lady Kimber and **Lady Pole-Carew** were keen. So was **Eva Davidson** of ***The Gables***, **Elizabeth Grenfell** of ***Elibank***, Miss Lovat of ***The Laurels*** and **Florence Irby** of ***Hitcham Grange***. Taplow & Hitcham WI held its first meeting in March 1926. Christian names were never used. They are now: these seven ladies were Audrey, Irene, Beatrice, Eva, Elizabeth, Lillian and Charlotte.

Muriel King of N° 3 **Wellbank** has long been a member of T&H WI which, many years ago, embraced not only the northern neighbour from which it had sprung but also the Lent Rise Ladies' Club. Early meetings were held in *The Dumb Bell* and then in the Drill Hall built during the Great War at the junction of the Bath Road and Hitcham Road, later used by the Scouts and then the police before being replaced by a purpose-built traffic police headquarters. By 1927 there were 90 members in need of bigger accommodation. Donations enabled the WI to pay the *GWR* an annual rent of £7 10s (£391) for a plot of land – eventually acquired in 1952 – and to build on it a new hall designed by a local architect, **Thomas Salter**, at a cost of £1,340 16 s 3d (£462,000). Lady Astor opened the hall in 1930 into which was placed two proud possessions: the president's chair, late of the Indian Pavilion of the 1926 British Empire Exhibition (courtesy of Mrs Horner) and T&H WI's very own banner (designed by the said Salter) on which Taplow is represented by a swan (for the river) and galleon (from the Orkney arms) and Hitcham by the arms of the **Clarke** family (who upset Good Queen Bess) and the Prince of Wales feathers (for the Black Prince). **William Wood** donated and planted the surrounding shrubs.

The Great Hall, Cliveden / 1st October 1933

Joyce Grenfell smiles to recall her Aunt Nancy's performance last summer when the first County Rally of the Women's Institute was held at Cliveden. A hush had descended upon the 2,000 guests as Nancy rose to speak. True to form, she was dramatic and a little self-centred. She congratulated the Institute for its success in a decade-long campaign to retain the Women's Police Force without failing to mention that she has raised the matter many times in Parliament. And she gave a memorable crescendo by grabbing an umbrella from her friend and guest of honour Sara Roosevelt, mother of the US President, and holding it high to exclaim "It is women of the world not men who make England's green and pleasant land!"

With **Nancy**'s enthusiastic support, the National Federation of Women's Institutes was a founder member of the Associated Country Women of the World, a charity which offers support, friendship and practical help to women and communities and will eventually provide a voice for women at the United Nations. The Triennial ACWW Conference will twice be held at Cliveden: Nancy will host the first just before the Second War and her daughter-in-law Bronwen will host the second in 1965 a little more than a year after she succeeded Nancy as Lady Astor.

The Women's Institute Hall, Institute Road / 1st October 2009

Muriel is pleased to report that the WI Hall is still used almost every day for meetings, talks, demonstrations, drama, arts and crafts, for planning and managing campaigns and for sports including badminton, bowls and table tennis. The hall has had many starring roles. During the Second War, it was an evacuee centre, a ration books station and a canteen and dance hall serving local Army camps and a nearby Prisoner of War camp. Both during and after the War, members staffed a lending library and a child clinic. Later the hall performed as a play group, a venue for public inquiries, political meetings, dog shows, a summer camp for Scouts and Brownies, a catering centre during the making of *Chariots of Fire* (1981) and a film set for the *Most Mysterious Murders* TV series made in 2005 by Julian Fellowes (later of *Downton Abbey* fame). She finishes with a flourish by saying, yes, we do sing *Jerusalem* and make jam but we trust we are maintaining founding ideals of friendship, truth, justice and tolerance.

Courting Controversy

The Library, Cliveden / 28th September 1934

After his mentor Lloyd George was deposed as Prime Minister in 1922, **Waldorf Astor** did his best to help his wife not fall foul of her foibles while directing his energy into *The Observer* and to charitable causes, especially as a governor of both *The Peabody Trust* and *Guy's Hospital*. He and Nancy are great benefactors to Plymouth and to ***The Royal Institute for International Affairs***, an independent not-for-profit organisation founded in 1920 by Lionel Curtis and known by its location, ***Chatham House***. Its mission – to analyse and promote understanding of major international issues and current affairs – suits Waldorf perfectly. It gives him a respected forum for developing grand ideas of the way things should be and influencing governments by the power of intellectual persuasion. And it is conveniently located at N° 10 St James's Square just a few steps from his London home. From next year until 1949 he will serve as chairman of *Chatham House*.

Lady Astor has always been an acquired taste, not least because of her well-earned reputation for "shooting from the lip". Her sharp instinct is often blunted by her sharper tongue. When she forms a view she holds it with a rare passion and can't resist expressing it with force and drama. She deals with her increasing unpopularity by being apparently oblivious to it, which somehow only makes matters worse. She is perhaps most effective when she has practical causes to focus on: Cliveden Hospital during the Great War, and since then the Women's Institute and social reform issues. She would be wise to leave international relations and foreign policy to Waldorf yet such matters are too important for her to ignore. Matters came to a not-so pretty pass in 1931 when two Shaws took centre-stage. Her reputation was already tainted by her son **Bobbie Shaw**'s tendency toward alcoholism and instability. It was further dented when he was arrested for homosexual offences. Perhaps it was fortunate that she was about to embark on a trip to Moscow with Waldorf, her old fast friend and foil **GB Shaw** and her fellow Christian Scientist Philip Kerr, who had recently succeeded as 11th Marquess of Lothian. Despite being politically poles apart, Nancy and GB share a determined non-conformity. They both played true to form. He praised Communism as a great socialist solution. She countered by asking Joseph Stalin bluntly why it was necessary to slaughter so many Russians. She doesn't understand why this question was forgotten and her other vehement and rather courageous criticisms of the Soviet regime were translated innocuously, making it seem she had 'gone soft' on Communism. Nothing could be further from the truth. She and her husband saw all totalitarian regimes as an anathema, whether left or right, but the word spinning gave their political enemies the opportunity to accuse them of being traitors. And mud sticks.

Her credibility took another knock a few weeks ago. Perhaps having seen how heavy drinking damaged her father, brothers and first husband, she has always had a passion for temperance. **Bobbie**'s deeply dismaying troubles have reinforced her hatred of the demon drink. Most who disagreed could ignore her until she declared recently that the defeat of England's cricket team by Australia resulted from their enjoyment of too many beers. Even the Aussies objected. Ridicule rained. Her thick skin continues to be incredibly effective but she has put her head too far above the parapet once too often.

The Cliveden Set

The Library, Cliveden / 28th November 1937

Despite all being fervently anti-German during the Great War, the mood of the moots of the extended *Kindergarten* coterie is to strive for accommodation with Adolf Hitler's National Socialist Party in Germany. Lothian believes the Nazis are an inevitable consequence of the onerous and vengeful financial reparations demanded of Germany after the Great War in treaties he helped to frame but has long since regretted. Hitler's popularity is no more than a natural reassertion of German national identity that will settle down in time. The Astor brothers' newspaper editors, Garvin at *The Observer* and Dawson at *The Times*, have been united in assessing Hitler as being "definitely Christian in his ideals" and exhibiting "moderation and common sense" as he strives to renew "his county's moral life". Bob Brand isn't so sure. Since marrying **Nancy**'s sister Phyllis in 1917, **Waldorf**'s old friend has risen to be managing director of the investment bank *Lazard Brothers & Co*, a director of *Lloyd's Bank* and chairman of the *North British & Mercantile Insurance Company*. This broad business base gives him a more worldly perspective. However, although concerned about the security of France, he wonders if turning a blind eye to the possibility of Germany's eastward expansion might be "a lesser evil" than going to war to prevent it.

Events have brought Nancy's contradictions and prejudices into sharp relief. Although she criticises the Nazis for devaluing women, she supports Germany's re-armament because it is "surrounded by Catholics". And yet she and the Catholic Joe Kennedy agree that Hitler's rise is a welcome solution to the "world problems" of Communists and Jews. Despite having some sympathy with his wife's anti-Semitic tendency, Waldorf will protest personally and with uncharacteristic vehemence to Hitler about Nazi treatment of the Jews, a heated exchange that will result in the Führer having a tantrum or, as Waldorf put it, a "convulsion or spasm". Or was it because he had been told that Nancy thinks he looks too much like Charlie Chaplin to be taken seriously?

Dawson strongly favours direct Anglo-German dialogue and what some call 'appeasement' remains a popular view. **Winston Churchill** and Sir Robert Vansittart, Permanent Under-Secretary at the Foreign Office (and a distant cousin of Taplow's late rector the Reverend **Edward Vansittart Neale**), are among the eminent few to have consistently cautioned against it, but of course it rankles those who see the Nazis as a threat to their beloved Soviet Union. Claud Cockburn knows that mud sticks. When not writing for Communist Party's newspaper *The Daily Worker*, he has begun slinging it in his own hand-delivered four-page mimeographed newsheet *The Week* with the potent mix of facts and supposition he likes to call 'preventative journalism'. Eleven days ago he ran an article exposing the "sensational [but] true facts [of the] sinister affair" at Cliveden on the weekend of 23rd and 24th October – the latest gathering of a supposedly subversive upper-class cabal seeking to exercise covert pro-German pressure – which resulted in Edward Wood, 3rd Viscount Halifax, visiting Berlin on 17th November to indicate informally to Hermann Goering that the UK would give Germany a free hand in central Europe. Today the Sunday newspaper *Reynolds News* has bestowed upon this 'cabal' a new epithet: ***The Cliveden Set*** [*see Appendix 4*].

Cockburn will report that Foreign Secretary Anthony Eden attended that "fateful meeting" unaware he had been invited "in order to associate him with the intrigue". The plot will thicken in stages, not least due to its stirring by the American Communist John Spivak. In a couple of weeks, Vansittart will be 'promoted upstairs' and control of "the extraordinarily powerful British Intelligence Service" will be given to Sir Alexander Cadogan, who was at Cliveden that weekend. In February, Prime Minister Neville Chamberlain will finally do as he is told when "Hitler.... bluntly [demands that Eden] be removed" and replaced at the Foreign Office by Dawson's old friend Lord Halifax, who will do no more than object lamely when the Nazis invade Austria. And at the end of March during a Cliveden weekend in which Chamberlain will take a break from playing musical chairs to agree "six major decisions which will change the face of the world" for they reflect "the conclusion that democracy.... cannot survive and [the UK has] a choice between fascism and communism [and] under fascism [the Cliveden Set] will sit on top of the roost".

Lee laughs at this "balderdash". **Rose** riles against it. As far as she is concerned, it is "poppycock" for anyone to think the Astors believe in what Hitler is doing, would do anything to keep on terms with him, and are plotting to bring about an Anglo-German alliance. It just isn't in her ladyship's nature to plot. She's too open, too quick to tell people they're wrong and why. And his lordship is "straight as a pit-prop, more British than the British, a conventional man" always trying to do the right things right. My Lady's maid concludes that "Clever people may try to make a meal and earn a coin or two out of the Cliveden myth but anyone who really [knows the Astors] can only treat the idea with scorn".

Not Peace for our Time

10 Downing Street, Westminster / 30th September 1938

The Prime Minister has returned home in triumph. Chamberlain believes the accord he and Hitler have signed in Munich secures "peace with honour.... peace for our time". Most are celebrating. **Winston Churchill** is not. In four days he will tell Parliament that "England has been offered a choice between war and shame. She has chosen shame, and will get war".

The atmosphere is poisonous. Nobody wants war but there are sharp differences about how to prevent it. Some say Britain must fight to save democracy from Fascism. Ambassador Kennedy thinks: "That's the bunk. She's fighting for self-preservation" and that "Democracy is finished in England". He advocates strongly that the USA should give the UK no military or economic aid and will persist in this view even after the outbreak of war as he continues in his attempts to meet Hitler "to bring about a better understanding between the United States and Germany". Lothian and Dawson will persist until late next summer in the belief that direct Anglo-German negotiations can groom Germany to play a responsible role in Europe.

Although less culpable than her friends, Nancy Astor's controversial reputation and flamboyant, provocative style ensures she gets much of the flak. Any perceived pro-Nazi on either side of the Atlantic has for some time been dismissed as a 'Clivedenite', a sneer apparently justified by her support for Chamberlain in his efforts to avoid war. She will be derided as "the Member for Berlin" despite accusations not long ago that she was supposedly cosying up to Communism. In a letter to *The Times* on 5th May, Waldorf will write: "For years my wife and I have entertained [at Cliveden] members of all parties (including Communists).... of all faiths, of all countries, and of all interests. To link our weekends with any particular clique is as absurd.... Lady Astor and I are no more Fascists today than we were Communists [when] we supported the trade agreement with the Soviet". She will give her own perspective in the USA's *Saturday Evening Post* on 4th March next year: "Now I'm almost an ancient monument but I'm still a Virginian, and still a democrat, and an ardent believer in women's rights and social reforms. Well, how on earth should such a combination as that believe in Mussolini, or Hitler, or Stalin, or in any dictator?" And a few weeks later, her old friend **GB Shaw** will add that typical 'Clivedenites' include not some elitist cabal but "everybody worth meeting.... of every point of view".

The House of Commons, Westminster / 11th April 1940

Chamberlain faces a motion of confidence. **Lady Astor** rises to tell the House: "I am one of those who criticises the Prime Minister to his face and not behind his back.... Our job [is] to do what is disagreeable if it will help the country.... In wartime we should have no feelings about persons, it is principles that matter". Once again she will be in the minority who will vote against Chamberlain. It will be enough to dislodge him. The Astors will support Churchill as his replacement and continue to do so despite his discomforting but necessary alliance with Stalin next year. Nancy and Waldorf will have their finest hour: she as one of Plymouth's MPs and he as its mayor. They win admiration and affection for their energetic dedication to the city and to its eventual recovery. And yet will still fit the bill nicely for those seeking scapegoats for the folly of pre-war appeasement. In 1944 Nancy will deny accusing the Eighth Army in Italy of being "D-Day Dodgers" but the slur will be accepted as fact. Being a walking joke is irksome but she will somehow always remain above being embarrassed.

The Terrace, Cliveden / 30th September 2012

Cockburn gave vent to an inbuilt social prejudice that the upper classes saw Communism as a threat to their 'behind closed doors' control over the way of things, and that they were therefore natural allies of Fascism. The Nazis didn't see things that way – Nancy was on the *Gestapo* list for immediate arrest as soon as they invaded England – and some (including George Orwell) believed Cockburn was in the pay of the Soviets. This view was given credence 30 years later when Cockburn revealed that his primary source had been Vladimir Poliakoff, a Russian correspondent at *The Times*. So does this mean Rose and Lee were right? Was it all "poppycock" and "balderdash", simply ideologically motivated fabrications with which Cockburn hoped to fuel anti-Nazi feeling and wound Dawson (his former employer at *The Times*)? The ploy was commercially successful – *The Week*'s circulation rose from 1,400 in mid-1937 to 40,000 in 1939 – and the passage of time didn't diminish his penchant for unsubstantiated sensationalism and unabashed contradiction. On the one hand, he claimed in 1967 that Paliakoff's own sources were the British and French Foreign Offices, Churchill's supporters were providing "inside information" and Dawson knew all about it. On the other, he confided that "There was no [Cliveden Set], just people interested in the same objectives [in] a cooperative frame of mind [who] would not have known a plot if you had handed it to them on a skewer". It all goes to show that journalists with axes to grind can never be trusted, but there is a revealing twist. In the USA, Spivak was arrested for criminal libel in 1940 and spent 20 years living under a pseudonym. In the UK, Cockburn was ignored by most but unmolested. He continued spinning yarns until 1947 when he moved to Ireland to combine journalism with writing both fiction and non-fiction.

The individual and collective impact of the Astors and their friends is debatable. They may have yearned to preserve an age of parental imperialism that was fast slipping away but they were not fascists. Perhaps theirs was a think-tank of like-minded friends with a persuasive point of view but little real influence, their only error being adamant if misguided attempts to avoid another bloody World War. However, much to the chagrin of the Astors then and now, the mud stuck. In 1948, the novelist Gore Vidal wrote "The Cliveden-Churchill set are too well-entrenched and I shouldn't be surprised in the least if they created some sort of dictatorship that could never be thrown off without a revolution". The idea of Churchill in such an alliance with 'Cliveden' – meaning the Astors – could only have occurred to someone who had never seen the mutual antithesis between Nancy and Winston. Nevertheless the Astors could never completely shake off the implication that they and their privileged friends aspired to be a secret society running the nation without the inconvenience of a democratic mandate.

ReJoyce

Little Theatre, John Adam Street, London / 21st April 1939

A rather prim 29-year-old lady is standing in the wings of the *Little Theatre* here in the Adelphi wearing the rather fixed toothy smile for which she will become famous. She watches admiringly as the consummate Hermione Baddeley holds the audience in the palm of her hand on this, the opening night of the *Little Revue*. The *Magyar Malady* sketch raises gales of laughter and its closing number *Flotsam and Gypsum* is applauded loudly. How will the nervous debutante follow that?

Joyce Grenfell begins with *Useful and Acceptable Gifts*, delivered as though to a Women's Institute gathering. It goes down rather well, as does *Mothers*, her second monologue later in the show. The revue will run for 415 performances. Joyce's career as a much-loved comic monologist, singer-songwriter and actress on stage and screen will continue for 40 years, the first four of which she and husband Reggie Grenfell will reside a short walk south of ***The Feathers*** at ***Parr's Cottage***.

Could her first monologue have been inspired by listening to talks at the Taplow & Hitcham WI or even first delivered on its stage? Maybe the second was an affectionate tease of her mother Nora, Nancy Astor's little sister and wife of architect Paul Phipps? Perhaps her Aunt Nancy had sowed the seed of Joyce's comic talent and immaculate timing with her "uproarious" mimicry [*see Appendix 1, Trees 11 & 17*].

The WI Hall, Institute Road / 21st April 1949

When it comes to childhood memories, **Harry Hurn** reckons there was little to choose between the Parish Hall and the WI. His eyes gleam as he tells of all the various events here before the war: the children's Christmas parties, the ballet and ballroom dancing lessons for young ladies at 6d-a-time (£2), the Scouts' concerts in the late-1930s and, best of all, the hilarious performances by a posh lady called Joyce. He can't resist humming "We're riding along on the crest of a wave". And what do you know? He's right.

As her married name suggests, Joyce has family connections not only to Cliveden but also to Taplow Court. The link runs up four generations on Reggie's side to **Pascoe Grenfell** and his second wife Georgiana. It cascades down three generations from Pascoe and his first wife Charlotte to **Willy Grenfell**, Lord Desborough. Despite their age difference, Joyce has become such a close friend of her distant cousin's wife Ettie that she will write this poem about her....

ETHEL

I don't understand Ethel.
I don't, I don't really.
She's one of my very best friends,
Just about the best, nearly.
She's an awfully nice girl, Ethel is,
Dainty and refined,
I mean she'd never do or say
Anything unkind.
But get her inside a stadium
And she seems to go out of her mind.

'KILL HIM!' she yells, 'KNOCK HIS BLOCK OFF!'
At ice hockey or football or what.
'KILL 'EM!' she yells, turning purple,
'KILL THE PERISHING LOT!'
'SH-SH!' I say, 'ETHEL!'
'SH-SH!' and I die of shame.
'KILL HIM AND BASH HIS TEETH IN HIS FACE!'
She says,
And calls him a dirty name.

I don't understand Ethel,
I don't, I don't truly.
She is always gentle and sweet,
Never a bit unruly.
She's an awfully shy girl, Ethel is,
Wouldn't say boo to a goose.
You wouldn't think she ever could
Suddenly break loose.
But get her inside a stadium
And her face turns a terrible puce.

'THROW HIM OUT OF THE WINDER!' she yells,
And her eyes go a terrible red.
'SWIPE 'EM!' she says, looking cheerful,
'SWIPE 'EM UNTIL THEY'RE DEAD!'
'SH-SH!' I say, 'ETHEL!'
'SH-SH!' and I nearly die,
'SWIPE HIM AND GRIND HIS FACE IN THE MUD!'
She says,
'AND PUT YOUR THUMB IN HIS EYE!'

I don't understand Ethel,
I don't, I don't, really.
She's one of my very best friends,
Just about the best, nearly.
She's and awfully quiet girl, Ethel is,
That's why I never see
What makes her carry on like that,
Noisy as can be.
Then last Saturday down at the stadium
Well... it suddenly happened to me.

'BREAK HIS SILLY NECK!' I yells, 'IRON HIM OUT!'
Well, Ethel was startled at that.
'IRON HIM!' I says, feeling lovely,
'IRON HIM UNTIL HE'S FLAT!'
'OOH', I says, 'ETHEL!'
'OOH', and I did feel queer.
Then she grinned, and we both of us gave a yell
'BITE A BIT OUT OF HIS EAR!'

A Celebration of Taplow

In 1990-1993, Sheila Horton created a unique historical masterpiece on the walls of the Village Centre's old Reading Room

2004

Three glimpses of her vibrant style: Taplow Horse Show, the Village Green Party and (left) a collection of images

Chapter Nine

A Good Living

In which Taplow retained its character against all odds as it found its place in the modern world

Searching for Something

A Celebration of Taplow

The Village Centre / 22nd June 1993

The vision came to **Sheila Horton** in a dream. Why not brighten the old Reading Room by portraying on its walls the life, times, people and places of Taplow in the early-1990s?

The Parish Council was quickly convinced. Sheila went to work, first observing and sketching, then climbing scaffolds to brush on her acrylic paint. One wall wasn't enough. Her magnificent murals have spread over all four walls to create an absolutely fabulous recollection of her 30 years in Taplow to date. It is justly titled *A Celebration of Taplow*. Here is your house, there is mine. Taplow Court stands proud, *Elibank* too. The Parish Council deliberates. Children mill around the school playground. Others enjoy Thames Valley Adventure Playground or an evening with the Cubs. Still more are maypole-dancing or country-dancing at the Village Green Party while their parents put the world to rights over a glass or two. A naked foursome frolics at Cliveden. *Reference Point* wins *The Derby* for **Louis Freedman** of Cliveden Stud. Nurses come off duty at the Canadian Red Cross Memorial Hospital. Major **Rex Law** welcomes Her Majesty Queen Elizabeth II to Taplow Horse Show. Windsor Castle burns in the distance. **George Clark** tends the *Wickenden* vineyard. A batsman waits as a bowler bowls at the cricket club. There are two churches: St Nicholas no more and St Nicolas now. St Birinus is by Bapsey Pond. A congregation gathers around Tæppa's Mound to be led in thanksgiving prayer by Reverend **Alan Dibden**.

Over 300 people can be recognised. Some will say that the mural should be kept current by the addition of later Taplovians, but who to feature and who not? Better not to tinker with these vibrant, most original and memorable moments in history. Sheila tends to wince when anyone says Taplow is lucky to have its very own Lowry, yet she and the great artist share something of a documentary style that tells tales of recreated reality and captures movement in brief brushstrokes. They differ of course in their subject matter – Taplow has no industrial cityscape – and in their use of colour – he determinedly dour, she as bright and beautiful as her nature. And Lowry never painted with a parrot sitting on his shoulder.

Sunsets and False Dawns

The Passing of Paragons

The Village Centre / 22nd June 2013

For those who were here, the murals bring back memories. For more recent arrivals, they are windows on what went before. Latecomers recognise the Reverend and their houses but did Taplow really have a vineyard, a hospital and a horse show? If so much has changed in 20 years, think what can happen over a longer time span. It is a reminder that the mid-20th Century was a time of endings and of beginnings that haven't stood the test of time.

For hundreds of years a sprinkling of paragons called the shots and employed most people. Their passing was a slow process. The Fortescues seemed to have forgotten **Dropmore** long before the ebb began with the deaths of **Percy Noble** in 1938, **Selina Whitlaw** in 1940 and **Lord Desborough** in 1945. For the first time in over 900 years and probably 1,000, Taplow had no lord of the manor. **Minna Serocold** followed in 1948, her brother **Oswald** in 1951, **Lord Astor** and **Lady Desborough** in 1952, **Lionel Hanbury** in 1954. **Edward & Audrey Skimming** went in the winter of 1957/58 and **Lady Astor** in 1964 two years before her son **Bill, 3rd Viscount Astor**.

These people and their families had led the local tune for so long. This gradual sunset left Taplow searching for a new identity. There were false dawns for boffins at **Taplow Court** and ***The Priory***, animated film-makers at ***Stockwells***, Cold War watchers at ***Hedsor***, Californian universities at **Cliveden** and Dropmore, a country club at ***Berry Hill House***, a Bible college at ***Taplow Hill***, a school of nursing at ***Hitcham House*** and nurses' homes at ***Hitchambury***, ***Taplow Lodge*** and ***Maryfield***.

Serocold Discomfort

11 Boyne Hill Avenue, Maidenhead / 12th January 1943

Gwendolyn Serocold can recall the exact moment she knew the tide was turning: 9th January 1937, the day she invited three 14-year-old village girls to Saturday tea to consider them as domestic servants. Once upon a time, young girls like **Kathleen Hurn**

would have been delighted to have the chance. And yet so confident was the young lady that she could find work in the offices or factories of Slough, she said thank you but no thank you. And when the Second War came, it was even easier for her juniors to do the same.

Society is evolving alright, replies Gwendolyn's husband **Oswald**. Did the gentry's need for servants wane before or because fewer sought a life in service? He can't say which was chicken and which egg but perhaps it all began with the Great War when a generation of young women worked in the munitions factories and enjoyed the independence. Oswald smiles ruefully at the rumours that he and his wife moved here to escape hordes of munitions workers from the new Slough Trading Estate being billeted with them in ***Taplow Hill***. The reality was that the old place had just got too big for them. They keep in touch with Taplow of course but at their advanced years they had little choice but to be amongst the first to seek smaller accommodation requiring fewer staff.

There's a knock on the door. A telegram has arrived. It isn't good news. Oswald's nephew **Arthur Pearce-Serocold**, son of his brother Eric and sister-in-law Blanche, a captain in the Welsh Guards, was killed in action in Tunisia just before Christmas. One less to take on *Taplow Hill*, sighs Oswald. At least the Dutch seem to like it....

Dutch Courage

Taplow Hill, Church Road / 12th January 1943

Taplow rather likes going Dutch. The Dutch High Command was temporarily stationed at ***Maryfield*** in 1940. *Netherlands Shipping & Trading Ltd* paid £5,250 (£666,000) to acquire *Taplow Hill* last year to make it a rest and rehabilitation centre for Dutch merchant seaman who courageously sailed to exile in England – or a covert base for their commandos, if you believe the whispers....

The Schelde Estuary, Netherlands / 1st November 1944

Eddy 'Smiler' Smales is a sergeant cameraman in the Army Film & Photographic Unit. He is covering *Operation Infatuate*, the amphibious Allied invasion of the island of Walcheren to open up the River Schelde to Antwerp. Squeezed alongside him in the landing craft is a Dutch commando. Smiler's ears prick up to hear him reminiscing about *Skindles*. That's my Uncle Cecil's favourite haunt, says Smiler. How do you know it? I was billeted up the hill in Taplow, says the commando, who goes on to tell of being in the Dutch resistance until all his family were executed by the Nazis and how he escaped to England just before his 20th birthday. Suddenly all hell breaks loose: shells exploding, bullets whining. They hit the beach. Dutch leaps forward to liberate this corner of his homeland. Somehow he and Smiler survive. A week later, they will share a beer in Westkapelle. Five-and-a-half years later, Smiler will become my father.

Elibank, Rectory Road / 12th January 1982

Could that commando have been or known Sid Bellafente, this jacket-and-tie attired 'gentleman gardener' of Burnham who divides his time between **Sue & Alan Senior** here at ***Elibank*** and **Josie & Tiny Rowland** at ***Hedsor Wharf***? Sid works hard and well but says little until, over a cup of tea recently, he confided in Sue exactly the story the Dutch commando had told Smiler. He intimated that his escape hadn't been the end of his war but would say no more except how irritated he was to discover a number of Nazi officer prisoners-of-war being kept in comfort at *Hogfair*, then N° 1 Green Lane, now N° 19 Hogfair Lane.

Brash and Biblical

Taplow Hill, Church Road / 19th October 1949

Gwendolyn & Oswald's youngest son **Walter Serocold** has recently published *The History of Watneys*. Some Taplovians recall this *Watney Combe Reid* executive from his childhood here at *Taplow Hill* but now his parents are Maidonians and all other Pearce-Serocold connections are gone. His old home found a new lease of life four years ago as the evangelical **All Nations Bible College** in the care of Henry (Harry) Brash Bonsall and his wife Dosie. In a few years, **Roger** and **Tristan Miall** will join other local children there at *Sunshine Corner*, an evening bible class conducted by theological students who are preparing to be missionaries abroad. The boys will always remember learning to sing "Sunshine Corner, oh it's jolly fine. It's for children under ninety-nine!"

The Red Cottage, Church Road / 19th October 1949

Since Walter's aunt **Minna Serocold** died last year, her home has fallen into line as a hostel for students at the Bible College. Its rooms all have biblical names such as *Nineveh* and *Tarsus*, its bathrooms are *Mediterranean I* and *II* and the college secretary – a Miss Desborough – lives in a caravan in the garden. Any familial connection to Lord Desborough is unlikely. This is the first of four brief incarnations for ***The Red Cottage*** in little more than a decade. The second will be in 1953/54 when it is let to **Lorna & Leonard Miall**. The third will see it sold to Noel Nicholls who will rename it *St Nicolas Lodge*. The last will arrive in the 1960s when **Ann & Anthony Paines** move from ***Rozel*** to make it ***St Nicolas House***.

Boffins About

Taplow Court / 19th October 1959

Taplow is trying on new clothes. Instead of being family homes, two of the grand houses are now places of work where brilliant minds explore innovations in diverse fields.

The Desboroughs departed **Taplow Court** in 1939. It was used to accommodate evacuee children from London until settling down for the duration of the Second War as a girls' school: **St Stephen's College**, relocated from Folkestone. Thereafter it was let to ***British Telecommunications Research Ltd*** under the leadership of Colonel **John Hickman** who presided over the conversion of the *stické* court into a staff canteen. After Lady Desborough died the estate was reduced by 88% with the sale of 645 acres. Taplow Court will moonlight as a medical college in *Night of the Eagle* (1962) before *BTR*, the house and its remaining 85 acres are acquired by ***Plessey Electronics Ltd*** in 1963. During its 24-year tenure, *Plessey* will develop System X (the origins of digital telephony), satellite systems, combat radios and fibre optic telecommunications. Its lasting legacy for Taplow will be the closure of the top end of Church Path, a centuries-old right of way from Mill Lane past Bapsey Pond to the Old Churchyard....

The Oak & Saw / 19th December 1999

Alistair Forsyth recalls that the matter was referred to a public enquiry at which he, as Chairman of **Taplow Parish Council**, fought and unfortunately lost a day-long battle of wits with Queen's Counsel acting for *Plessey*. Much was made of complaints from neighbours about vagrants and vandalism but, with hindsight, he believes that the closure was imposed for security reasons rather than for the convenience of a few disturbed by occasional passers-by. It wouldn't have been unusual for the boffins to have been working on something top secret. *Plessey* covered its tracks by leaving Taplow in 1987 and by amalgamating with *BAE Systems* a few days ago.

The Priory / 19th October 1959

There is a different band of boffins at work in **Percy Noble**'s old home. After his death, ***The Priory*** stood sad and empty for three years until ***Fairey Aviation*** started to use it as a wartime headquarters in 1941. No bombs fell on the village itself but the *Fairey* fellows were pretty sharp in having an air raid shelter built in the garden after one landed not far away in the north-east corner of **Town Field**. The *Luftwaffe* never returned with malicious intent. *Fairey* are still here in the person of its managing director Colin Chichester-Smith, although not for much longer. Back in the late-1940s, Chichester-Smith had been a driving force in pioneering the use of aircraft construction technology to build sailing dinghies and later cabin cruisers. Nowadays his focus with ***Fairey Marine*** is on motor launches and the speedboats that James Bond will enjoy in *From Russia with Love* (1963).

America's Secret

At the gates of Hedsor House / 19th October 1959

It's the height of the Cold War. The USA eyes the Soviet Union with suspicion. The Ruskies warily watch the Yanks. The UK plays piggy-in-the-middle. **Hedsor** is one of the piggies. Everybody knows American Air Force high-flyers are at the end of the half-mile drive monitoring Soviet aircraft with some clever radar kit installed in a building near the house. Everybody knows they're not supposed to know. **Florence & Philip Shephard** know it's best to look the other way. His father Philip bought Hedsor in 1934 and gave it to them as a present. The former Florence David is said to be related to the Sassoon family which may extend back to the Sephardic Jewish community in medieval Al-Andalus (now Andalusia in Spain) and can certainly trace its lineage from eastern Anatolia (modern Turkey) through the Ottoman Empire, in which Sassoon ben Saleh was chief treasurer to the pashas of Baghdad, to Bombay in India, where in 1832 David Sassoon began to build the business empire that he and his eight sons spread to China and South East Asia, Europe, North America and the UK.

Despite the constant temptation to enjoy the company of her childhood friend **Daphne Williams** (of ***Rectory Farmhouse***), Florence found time to give birth at home to her son Alexander in 1938 and to direct the magnificent refurbishment of Hedsor only for it to be requisitioned during the Second War, first for the Army and later for a convent school. The Shephards returned until 1952 when they let the place to the Americans.

At the gates of Hedsor House / 19th October 1989

Florence married **Sydney Dagg** 15 years after she was widowed in 1962. **Maud Johnson** rather enjoys being requisitioned to take the grand lady out to lunch. These adventures have helped introduce Maud to the Taplow community since she and **Ken** settled at ***Elibank Court***. As she drives away, Maud listens as Florence recalls that their transAtlantic tenants left in 1968 and Hedsor became a residential conference and training centre for *International Computers Ltd*. This big business hardly notices its landlord, her son **Alexander Shephard**, living comfortably but discretely at ***Gully Farm***. After *ICL*'s departure in 2003, Alexander's sons Nick, Hamish and Mark will give Hedsor a new lease of life as a luxury location for corporate events, weddings and film-making. Most famously, it will feature in *The Golden Compass* (2007), starring Nicole Kidman, and star itself in *Quartet* (2012) when Dustin Hoffman on his directorial debut will shoot all but two sequences in the House and its grounds. Hedsor will also appear on screen in *The Boat That Rocked* (2009), *Brighton Rock* (2010) and by 2014 on television in *Sense and Sensibility*, *Strictly Dance Fever*, *The Special Relationship*, *Little Dorritt*, *Spooks* and *Hustle*.

Canada's Gift

Cliveden Gages / 5th June 1940

Waldorf Astor has had to develop a thick skin but he still has a kind heart and Cliveden has a Canadian hospital once more. Even before war was declared on 3rd September last year he offered once more to accommodate a hospital in the Gages. An annual rental of $1 was agreed with the Canadian Red Cross Society. Robert Atkinson and AFB Anderson set to work on the design and it has taken *J Jarvis & Sons Ltd* just six months to build a new 600-bed hospital at a cost of £300,000 (£66.15m)

Canadian Red Cross Hospitals, Cliveden

Princess Louise, Duchess of Connaught

WW1: The HRH Duchess of Connaught Canadian Red Cross Hospital

Royal Visits: King George V & Queen Mary / 1915

Queen Elizabeth / 1940

WW2: The Canadian Red Cross Hospital, reinvented in 1947 for the new NHS

Lady Astor opens the hydrotherapy pool / 1956

The Mounties pay a visit / c1970

Professor Eric Bywaters / c1960

Map 40 – Cliveden: Three Times an Angel

The Canadian Red Cross Memorial Hospital (CRCMH)

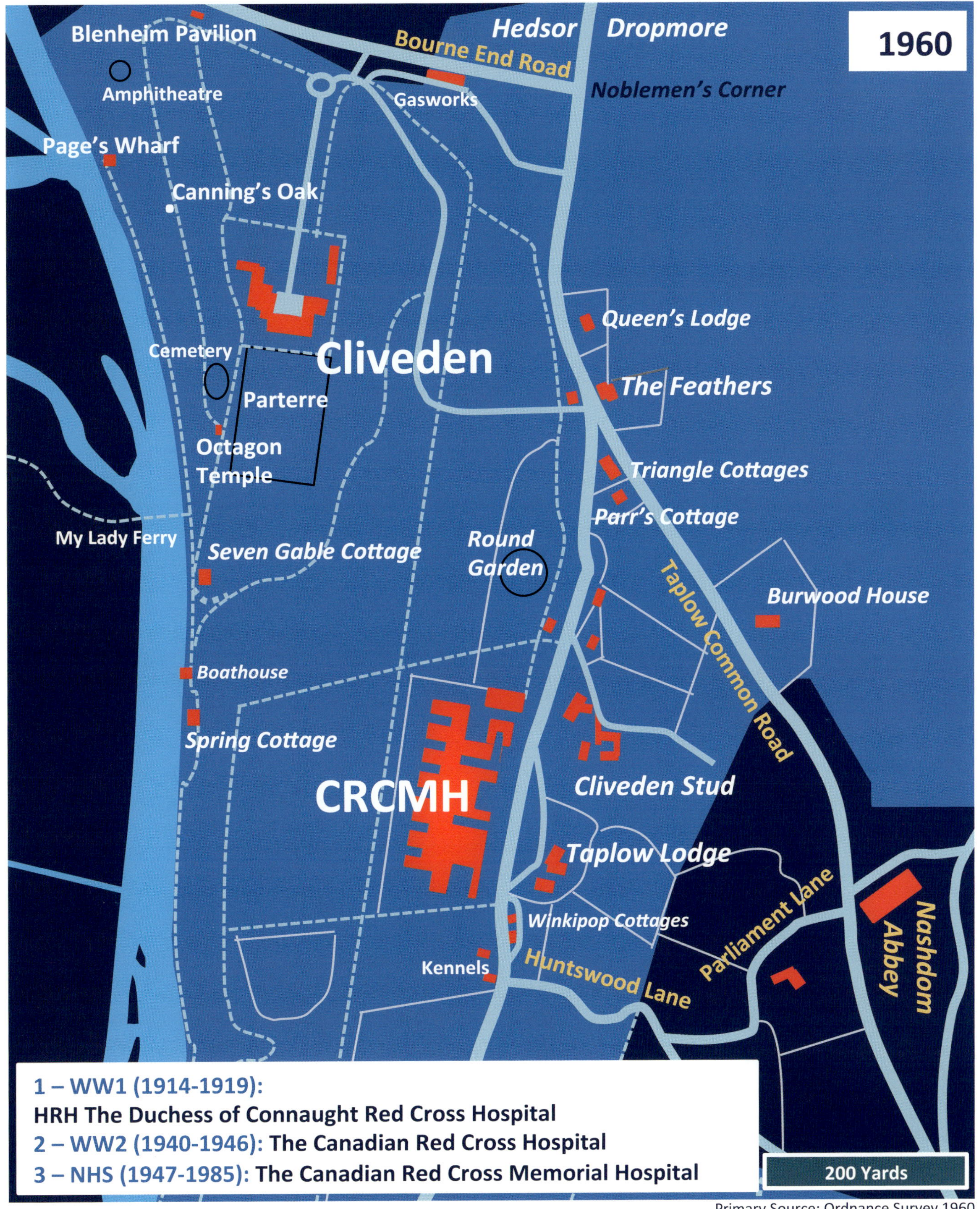

Primary Source: Ordnance Survey 1960

complete with furniture and equipment donated by and shipped from Canada. The 15 wards are arranged in a series of H-shapes with air-raid shelters between them big enough for 20 bedridden patients. The first are being admitted today. August will see two royal visits, first by Queen Elizabeth and her daughters the Princesses Elizabeth and Margaret then the following day by the Duke of Kent, Prince Edward and Princess Alexandra.

The Canadian Red Cross Memorial Hospital, Cliveden / 25th June 1947

Lord Astor donated **Cliveden** to the **National Trust** in 1942 along with a fund of £250,000 (£31.73m) to keep it in good repair. He summarised his reasoning in a letter to National Trust Chairman Lawrence Dundas, 2nd Marquess of Zetland: "Cliveden has such natural beauties and is in many respects so unique that I have already endeavoured to preserve for posterity some of its features. With this in mind, I have given up on my own behalf and on behalf of future owners the right of converting it into a speculators' building estate". He made two provisos: that the house would be home for life to his wife and their eldest son, and that the hospital would remain. The first will sustain the Astors in residence until 1966. The second was more than fulfilled in 1945 when, having treated 25,068 wartime patients, the hospital was presented by Canada to the people of Great Britain for use as a centre for research into juvenile rheumatism under Professor Eric Bywaters. A management committee under Sir Noel Mobbs adapted it for civilian use. The first patient was admitted on 3rd January 1947 and the first baby, Yvonne Cowell, was born the following day to be welcomed by a £5 note (£170) from Sir Noel (of *Slough Estates*). Now the **Canadian Red Cross Memorial Hospital** (CRCMH) is at last being officially opened by Minister of Health Aneurin Bevan. By September, it will have 235 beds including 61 in the Maternity Unit and 90 in the Juvenile Rheumatism Unit complete with a hydrotherapy pool made from a ship's sail. This will be a vital facility but, because canvas keeps rotting, it will need to be replaced every six months until 1953 when Lord Astor's appeal results in Canadians once more coming to the rescue by donating £2,000 (£185,000) to build a proper pool.

A Shaft of Sunshine

The Terrace, Cliveden / 18th June 1957

This is more like it: Cliveden has its sunshine back. The occasion: a 'coming of age' party for Daphne, daughter of American film star Douglas Fairbanks Jnr and his wife Mary. The cast to die for includes **Queen Elizabeth II**, Prince Philip, Princess Margaret, Princess Alexandra and the Duchess of Kent. Dashing society photographer Anthony Armstrong-Jones has come to take the pictures. He and Margaret seem to be getting on rather well. If only Bill's parents were here....

Nancy quit Cliveden after Waldorf died in 1952. **Bill, 3rd Viscount Astor**, has come to realise that old Lord Curzon was right when he said that his childhood home without his mother was "a wedding without a bride". But he knows that things haven't been quite the same here since the early years of the war when the house became less of a home and more a venue where his parents – and especially his mother – would try to get British and American leaders on the same page both socially and militarily. Meanwhile the pressure of work and public scrutiny took its toll on Waldorf's health and on his partnership with Nancy as she drifted to the right politically and he to the left. Although their double-act had seemed strong in Plymouth, Waldorf began to feel too weary to continue as its mayor after the war and that perhaps he didn't have the support to do so. He and their children thought it best that Nancy should also stand down at the 1945 election after 25 years as MP for Plymouth Sutton. She didn't agree and they grew apart.

When **Churchill** put paid to her hopes of being elevated to the House of Lords in her own right, Nancy declared that she would take no further part whatever in public life. She went to America, first with Waldorf then without him, and returned to spend most of her time at *Rest Harrow* or in London while Waldorf remained at Cliveden. Two of their sons served as MPs – Bill for Fulham East (1935/45) then Wycombe (1951/53) and Michael for Surrey East (1945/51) – and one still does. Having held 'the family seat' at Plymouth Sutton since 1951, Jakie will step down in two years. Apart from very brief appearances in their campaigns, Nancy kept clear of their careers. Her relationship with Waldorf thawed after his stroke in 1950 which confined him to a wheelchair and since his death she has reflected that "No two people ever worked happier than we did" before adding some time later "Waldorf was no good without me, and, alas, I am no good without him".

Bill settled at Cliveden only for his first wife Sarah (née Norton) to leave him within a year for Tommy Baring, a cousin of his mother's beau. He married Philippa (née Hunloke) in 1955 and enjoys the stud and entertaining in as near to the old manner as he can – especially when Nancy comes to stay. As this second marriage flounders he will make his mark on Cliveden in 1959 by having Sir Geoffrey Jellicoe reinvent The Cabinet as The Rose Garden, an achievement he will enjoy with his third wife Bronwen Pugh.

Goodnight Nurse

Hitcham House / 5th June 1969

Much of ***Hitcham House*** and its estate were requisitioned during the Second War and the RAF Police occupied part of the house and both its lodges while a camp for Italian prisoners-of-war was established to the north of Hitcham Lane. The Windsor Group Hospital Management Committee (later East Berks Health Authority) acquired the house in 1952 for £17,000 (£1.33m) and within a year it was a home for CRCMH student nurses including Beryl Montague. **Sheila Peroni**'s accommodation was in a nissen-hut alongside Cliveden's tennis court but by the time the *Hitcham House* stables were converted into a School of Nursing a few years ago, the CRCMH ripple had resulted in ***Hitchambury*** and ***Taplow Lodge*** being converted into nurses' homes. The isolation hospital at Cippenham enjoyed the same privilege, as did ***Maryfield*** for a few years in the early-1950s. Somewhere along the way *Taplow Lodge* became ***Orkney Court***, a name it will retain as it descends into other-worldly ruin and is eventually replaced by 16 townhouses in the mid-1990s.

Hitcham House / 5th June 1985

Beryl eventually returned to CRCMH as a nurse then as a nurse teacher living at *Church Lodge*. After the School of Nursing closed in 1982, *Hitcham House* stood empty until a developer acquired it last year for £275,000 (£1.2m) and divided it into nine separate homes with no kitchens, no individual gas or electricity supplies and only such original stairs, water supplies and bathrooms that happened to have survived the cut. And yet each has been snapped up for between £25,000 (£97,000) and £75,000 (£291,500) and is being refurbished by a confusion of contractors fighting for elbow room with each other and with those working for another developer to convert the stables into four dwellings. It is hard to see how but this strange strategy of chaotic creativity will succeed in giving new life to the Victorian grandeur of the old place.

Too Much for Nancy

Spring Cottage, Cliveden / 5th June 1963

It is like watching the last rocket whoosh up and explode on Bonfire Night: so spectacular and yet so final that it takes a moment for everyone to realise it's all over and to begin to wonder what will happen next. There have been political and social fireworks at Cliveden for 300 years but perhaps none with such lasting effect as that set off today by the resignation of John Profumo as Secretary of State for War, as a Privy Counsellor and as an MP. The embarrassment will terminally damage the Conservative government. When it crumbles and falls in October next year, it will be the end of public school patrician governance of the UK.

Spring Cottage, Cliveden / 5th June 2013

The Profumo Affair achieved something incredible: having spent 84 years being apparently immune to embarrassment, **Nancy Astor** was consumed by it. Even after 50 years it is still a tangled web of fact and fiction. They say the truth will always out but 'The Establishment' might not agree.

It all began with Dr Stephen Ward, an osteopath whose practice and personality had brought him into the elite social whirl of the rich, famous and powerful, some of whom were happy to be introduced by Ward to pretty young women from less privileged backgrounds. Two in this circle were MI5 Director General Roger Hollis and **Lord Bill Astor**, who had known Ward since 1949 when **Bobbie Shaw** recommended him. Bill made ***Spring Cottage*** at Cliveden available to Ward who some believe conspired with Hollis to use the charms of Christine Keeler to entrap Yevgeni Ivanov, a naval attaché at the embassy of the Soviet Union, at a Cliveden weekend party beginning on 8th July 1961. At various times, guests included not only Ivanov, Keeler, Profumo and his wife, actress Valerie Hobson, but also Lord Louis Mountbatten, Armenian business magnate Nubar Gulbenkian and Ayub Khan, the President of Pakistan. On the Sunday, Ivanov drove Keeler home to her London flat where they spent the night together. Soon afterwards she began a three-month affair with Profumo. Rumours of this relationship became public in late-1962 at the height of the Cold War. There was considerable concern that the Profumo-Keeler-Ivanov triangle might have compromised British secret security. Even if it hadn't, it was a perfect opportunity to embarrass the Government. Profumo denied the affair in the House of Commons only to be forced to admit some months later that he had lied, and of course misleading the House is an even greater crime for a Minister of the Crown than extra-marital shenanigans.

It was the end of Profumo's political career. He retired from public life to spend 40 years as a volunteer at Toynbee Hall, a charity in London's East End, and thus redeemed his reputation. Ward never had the chance. He was charged with living off the immoral earnings of prostitutes. Mandy Rice-Davies was one of the witnesses at his trial. When counsel remarked that Lord Astor denied having an affair with her or even having met her, she famously responded with the much-misquoted line "He would, wouldn't he?" Ward was found in a coma before being found guilty. He died four days later. It was said to be suicide but some say he was murdered to keep him from implicating establishment figures in sexual naughtiness, exposing one or more as Soviet spies, or both. Perhaps these events contributed to the defection of one spy, Kim Philby, in 1963 and the identification the following year of another, Anthony Blunt, whose royal connections may have been why his treachery was kept secret until 1979. They certainly led to Lord Andrew Lloyd-Webber's 2013 stage musical *Stephen Ward* which casts a sympathetic light on the fellow.

Nancy was convinced that Ward was "depraved, decayed and rotting" for dabbling in witchcraft and meddling with the occult. Early in 1964 she called in Dom Robert Petit-Pierre of ***Nashdom Abbey*** to exorcise the evil from Cliveden. She became ill as he exorcised the house so he advised her not to attend the exorcism of *Spring Cottage*, where it was said that the evil atmosphere was like a physical barrier which almost prevented him from gaining access. Lady Astor died at the beginning of May that year. She was almost 85. The little lady from Virginia left the world a very different place, and some of that was her doing.

About Grout – Old Stamping Grounds

New Scotland Yard / 3rd August 1963

Detective Inspector **Phil Grout** will never say how he felt earlier today when the news came through that Stephen Ward has died. If it was strange to return to his childhood home of Taplow to investigate The Profumo Affair, nobody will ever know. It was the same with the **Hanratty** case, which began at ***The Old Station Inn***. In five days, Phil will begin to investigate the Great Train Robbery at Sears Crossing in North Bucks. He will eventually be promoted to Detective Chief Inspector in charge of Scotland

Yard's Criminal Records Office, the position from which he will retire in 1968 after 32 years in the Metropolitan Police. Of all his many high-profile cases, he will share with his family details of only one: the 1949 murders in Edgware of Esther & Leopold Goodman when he was the most junior Detective Sergeant.

After his retirement, Phil will join *Mowlem Construction* as Head of Security, a responsibility which will include ensuring that nothing goes awry as the 1831 London Bridge is dismantled, transported and reconstructed at Lake Havasu City, Arizona. Its new owner, American oilman Robert McCulloch, will ardently deny he thought he had bought Tower Bridge. Phil will say different.

Not Just Anybody

The Parterre, Cliveden / 11th May 1965

Would any nurses be caring for the patients at CRCMH if they knew Cliveden is currently starring as Buckingham Palace in *Help!*, the second film featuring a certain George Harrison, John Lennon, Paul McCartney and Ringo Starr? During a break on the second day of shooting, ***The Beatles*** have recruited their personal assistant Neil Aspinall and their chauffeur Alf Bicknell to run a relay race against three teams of electricians, carpenters and cameramen. The crew are confident. The Fab Four smoke too much and exercise not at all: they are there for the taking. The crew are wrong. The popstars are adept at escaping from fans. Ringo has a particularly impressive turn of speed. They win easily and are presented with a prize of a bottle of vintage champagne by Lord Bill & Lady Janet Astor. When the group splits in 1970, Paul McCartney and his wife Linda will escape the spotlight at Cliveden. He'll recall **Bill Astor** being "on his last legs" and offering the boys whiffs from an oxygen cylinder which was wheeled in his wake.

All or parts of Cliveden have or will also appear on screen in *The Card* (1952), *The Yellow Rolls Royce* (1964), *Don't Lose Your Head* (a 1966 *Carry On* film), *The Ruling Class* (1972), *Operation Daybreak* (1975), *Death on the Nile* (1978), *Dead Man's Folly* (1986), *Chaplin* (1992), *Carrington* (1995), the *Bollywood* movie *Yaadein* (2001), as Lady Penelope's mansion in *Thunderbirds* (2004), in *Mrs Henderson Presents* (2005), *Made of Honor* (2008), *Sherlock Holmes* (2009), *A Little Chaos* (2014) and on TV in *Nancy Astor* (1982), *Antiques Roadshow* (2000), *Cards on the Table* (2005) and *Marple* (2013). *Scandal* (1989) – the story of The Profumo Affair – will be set at Cliveden and will feature its swimming pool while the house is played by *Longleat*.

Giving up the Ghosts

Eyes of a Child – The Joy of Scary

Maryfield, High Street / 31st October 2013

Groups of Taplow children are Trick-or-Treating around the village. If ghosts and ghouls don't get them first, their Hallowe'en parties will soon converge at ***The Oak & Saw*** for a pumpkin-carving competition. **Keira Smales** and seven girlfriends are at the door of ***Mulberry House***, home of **Lyra Cherry**. **Robbie Lawrence** of **Buffins** and his pal **Tim Pretty** run down the High Street to splutter that they must go to ***Maryfield***. The girls rush to the top of the drive and freeze in their tracks at the scary sight of two skeletons guarding the front door under the gaze of grotesque green faces leering from the windows above.

Suddenly the skeletons leap into life. The girls scream loudly in unison and dash back down the drive scattering its chippings everywhere. At the gate, they hug together in a ruck for courage, their faces glowing with excitement and trepidation. Let's go back, says **Olivia Wrennall**. She and **Lucie Plummer** set off once more, eager for another thrill. Keira follows cautiously with **Nicola Mayo**, **Hannah Irwin** and **Sophie Greenham**, dressed for the part in stunning vampire make-up and costume. **Freya Molony** and **Chloe Plummer** hang back. Their eyes widen as their six friends scream and scramble downhill to safety, but not for long. Let's go again, gasps Lucie breathlessly. This time all seven follow her and their screams are more for show for now they realise the two skeletons are actually men in costume: **Roger Andrews** and his son Max. Congratulations to them for making such special memories.

Eyes of a Child – Richard Forsyth

St Nicolas' School / 31st October 1984

Ten-year-old Richard is wide-eyed as his teacher tells of ghosts in Taplow. She finishes by recounting the tragic and scary story of a man who was minding his own business in his garden one evening when he heard this very strange noise close by. He recognised it as a wolf – it was a time when wolves still roamed down from the Chilterns – and decided to retreat to the house. As he got closer he realised there was a whole pack of hungry wolves making a terrifying noise and clearly intent on catching him. He ran into the house as fast as he could, closely pursued by the pack which cornered him in the front room. His only escape was up the chimney and he scrambled as far as he could up the narrow shaft. The wolves couldn't follow and eventually, having heard the commotion, a neighbour arrived to chase them out of the house with his gun. Sadly the owner did not re-emerge from the chimney. He was never seen again.

The class sits in silence until a boy asks where this house was. The teacher replies that it was *The Old Manor House* next to the pub. Richard screams "That's where I live, Miss!" He bursts into tears and rushes out of the classroom.

Tall Tales – Hauntings Hereabouts

The Old Manor House, Rectory Road / 31st October 1984

Richard's mother Liz decides not to tell him about the old lady her husband Alistair thinks he saw walking past an interior window on several occasions. The lad will have it quite hard enough worrying on windy nights when the fire is lit that the peculiar howling noise coming down the chimney might be the poor man's screaming.

Legend has it that plenty of spirits haunt the houses and countryside in and around Taplow, and not only after closing time. Most are female. There are four capital-L Ladies: the Blue Lady at **Taplow Court**, the Grey Lady at **Dorney Court**, Lady Christiana at **Hedsor** and Lady Hoby at Bisham Abbey. There is also a girl in white at Dorney Court, a woman in a bloodstained dress at Upton Court in Slough and two nuns: Maud at **Huntercombe Manor** and another who was walled up alive at **Burnham Abbey** for breaking her vow of chastity.

That's nine-nil to females who frighten but the two most gruesome ghosts are male. The headless Niddy's haunt is Crown Lane in Burnham. He strangled an old lady and left her body in a cupboard at *Allerds*, the East Burnham manor house demolished in 1837. Moses Hatto haunts the old farmhouse at Burnham Abbey and a nearby footpath. He was trysting in 1853 with his lover, a maid at the farm, when they were discovered by the housekeeper. He battered the poor woman to death. His lover hid him in a wall where perhaps he enjoyed the company of the aforesaid errant nun before being caught, convicted and hanged.

Pax Cottage / 31st October 1994

June is staying with her son **Paul Jeffries** and his wife **Nicki**. As she edges into a deep sleep, she feels someone tucking her into bed and mumbles her thanks. She won't feel quite the same in the morning when she finds that neither Nicki nor Paul performed the good deed. It won't be long before the young couple decide that they share their home with "a benign presence" or two.

It is ten years since Nicki began training as a nurse at Wexham Park Hospital. She lived for three months at the CRCMH but never came into Taplow Village until last year when she and Paul saw in a local newspaper that the Diocese of Oxford was to sell *Pax Cottage* at auction. Paul hadn't even been into the house when their bid of £81,000 was accepted. When he did explore his new domain, it was a bit of a surprise to find the little place was "a wreck still with gaslights upstairs". He will soon discover the front path has been laid over old gravestones relocated from the churchyard. Perhaps one once covered the last resting place of whoever occasionally leaves inexplicable whiffs of lavender or pipe tobacco about the place.

Marsh Lane / 31st October 2004

About 200 yards south of the kink in **Marsh Lane** a footpath angles off to the left. Some say this is one of only two remnants of an ancient track from Taplow to Dorney – the other is **Old Friend Lane** up in the Village – and that not a half-mile down there it forded a stream which ran south-east from the kink. This was little but a trickle most of the time – but not always, not when the flashlock was opened at **Amerden Ponds**. And once upon a time the lock opened, the water surged and the flash took the coachman by surprise. Perhaps the lock-keeper forgot to sound his warning horn. Perhaps the medieval coachman didn't hear it. He and his coach, horses and passengers were swept away and lost. Some say that some used to say that, if on a dark night you walked down the lane to where the ford once was, you might see the ghostly coach and hear the screams of the unfortunate victims above the rush of the water. And that's why the track is called **Devil's Lane**.

The site of the tragic accident is now lost to the **Jubilee River** but – if you're brave enough – walk along Devil's Lane to the footbridge over the flood relief channel, stand still and picture that horrific moment all those years ago. Imagine a flash surging towards you down the Jubilee. If it wasn't for the hum of the M4 Motorway, maybe you might hear those ghostly screams.

Hitcham House / 31st October 2004

The weirdest tale is of hands of death – a bloody handprint on the coat of arms at **Hitcham Manor** that heralded a death in the family, a clammy handprint on new monumental brasses after certain burials at **St James' Church** in **Dorney** which indicated no member of that family would lead a happy life (and that Dorney takes the biscuit for creepiness). The origin of this story might be Ralf, the elder son of Milo Crispin to whom **King William I** granted tenancy-in-chief of Hitcham and Dorney after the Conquest in 1066. When Ralf discovered his wife deep in conversation with his brother Roger, he leapt to the conclusion that they were lovers. The brothers fought furiously. The wife tried to intervene but was killed in error by the frenzied Ralf. His penance was to join the Crusades but he never got further than France. On discovering he had been distracted by Gallic temptation, his confessor cursed him and his family. The murdered woman's ghostly hands are a sign that the curse endures – or not, if you're a sceptic or one of the lucky people who have been shown around Dorney Court by an apparition of a remarkably convivial cavalier.

The Reverend Grimes of Hitcham told the same tale in 1926 but with the twist that, since Milo Crispin died childless, the accursed family is more likely to be that of the Miles Beauchamp who inherited Hitcham in 1292. His Beauchamp, Ramsay and Clarke descendants held the manor until 1660 so had plenty of time for the sore to become lore. However this doesn't explain how it hung around in Dorney, which had a much more chequered ownership throughout the crusading centuries and until 1542, when it was acquired by Sir William Garrard, later Lord Mayor of London and ancestor to the Palmer family which still owns and occupies *Dorney Court* today.

Hill House, Berry Hill / 31st October 2004

Local lore (and **Walter de la Mare**) celebrated the White Witch of Burnham who is said to have used her powers for good in the years before the Great War. Now she is long gone and unable to help the leader of a coven of witches which met in Burnham Beeches on a midsummer night almost half-a-century ago. He drank poison in the belief that his magic made him immune to its effects. He was wrong. He died hours later at CRCMH.

The Flincher and Friendlier Ghosts

Cliveden Gages / 31st October 2003

The old buildings of **CRCMH** have been slipping deeper into decay and dilapidation ever since they were left in 1985. The pillared portico is peeling. The wards are damp, smelly and perhaps even dangerous. No wonder several shades are said to haunt here....

As Hospital Secretary from 1949, Tom Powell was vital in keeping the place ticking for 24 of its 39 years and possibly for fuelling its folklore. Who saw the one-legged soldier roaming the north end of the main corridor and making babies cry when he limped into the maternity ward? Or the dreaded Flincher who appears with a crash and shrieks loudly as he chases anyone alone in the southern part of the hospital? Or the Night Sister on Ward 6 clad in the pale grey, ankle-length shoulder cape and a starched white cap worn during the Great War? In the wee small hours of a 1950 night she was seen by Betty, a student nurse who wondered whether the apparition might be one of the two sisters buried in Cliveden cemetery.

Jeanne Hopkins remembers reality being just as scary – a fellow nurse emerging from a hole in the riverbank with a badger trap embedded in her dress, dead grass snakes found coiled in nurses' beds, boiling her bra and knickers (muddy from swimming in the Thames) in the dormitory milk saucepan until it burnt dry and, having solemnly accompanied a porter pushing a corpse to the mortuary, being grabbed by him and propelled at speed on the morgue trolley down the gravel path to the Grand Corridor.

Over 60,000 people were born here, some of them delivered by **Sheila Peroni** who also had the thrill of riding helmetless on the pillion of her friend's motorbike to attend the 1959 midnight Christmas service at St Nicolas' Church and the pride of winning Pupil Midwife of the Year in 1960 under the renown Doreen Slade, Superintendent Midwife for 24 years from 1950. Other nurses and many patients remember with respect and affection at least one of the six matrons – Miss I Baugham, Miss O Morris, Mrs Hambleton, Miss J O'Toole, Miss O'Connor and Mrs Callaway – and the smart and colourful nurses' uniforms: students in royal blue, staff nurses in buttercup yellow, sisters in mid-green and all in black tights with white aprons. Valerie Kent will never forget her joy in 1956 when the actor Richard Todd signed her staff nurse apron and the despair when, as was expected and accepted without question, she put it in the wash.

Sheila still has the prize, a book, presented to her by the third **Lord Astor**. However, perhaps the greatest prize of all is that there were many children, now grandparents, who would have perished had it not been for the brilliance of the talented teams assembled and inspired by Professor Eric Bywaters. Their achievements in the eradication of rheumatic fever put Taplow firmly on the medical research map [*see Map 40*].

Rheumatic fever was a prevalent and serious illness in 1947. Within little more than ten years it had become a rarity thanks to the pioneering combination of experts in pathology, immunology, orthopaedic, ophthalmology, nursing, physiology and physiotherapy, whose visionary research and treatment demonstrated that powerful antibiotics and improvement in public health and hygiene could prevent and cure the streptococci infections that triggered rheumatic fever. Bywaters was joined in 1962 by Dr Barbara Ansell to focus on Still's Disease, later called Juvenile Idiopathic Arthritis. Using a similarly holistic approach that also embraced orthopaedic and plastic surgery, splint technology, prosthetics, child psychiatry and social work they quickly established Taplow as the world centre of excellence from which sprang a medical diaspora of international significance. By the time the Rheumatology Unit transferred to purpose-built accommodation at Wexham Park Hospital in 1965, Ansell was recognised at the founder of the newly-recognised speciality of paediatric rheumatology and her CRCMH colleague orthopaedic surgeon George Arden was able to pioneer total hip replacement in juveniles who had become wheelchair bound. Later patients were treated in a new hydrotherapy unit funded in part by Taplow Memorial Trust, a charity set up for the purpose by Taplow Parish Council.

Eyes of a Child – Bronwen Renwick

The Hollies, High Street / 3rd April 1947

Bronwen has been given a proper grown-up bicycle for her tenth birthday today. Her excited eyes gleam at the prospect of racing her 17-year-old big sister Tinkle (officially Helen) down Berry Hill to their school at ***Silchester House*** and of playing in the farmyard across the road with her "first boyfriend", **Thomas Williams** of ***Rectory Farmhouse***. It helps push to the back of her mind all the strange goings-on at home. It started the very night her family moved into *The Hollies* a year ago. Her mother Helen hung her father George's portrait on a handy hook in the hall before everyone went to bed. In the morning, the portrait was on the floor leaning against the wall with shards of broken glass piled neatly before it. Nobody had heard any glass breaking. Nothing was said for fear of upsetting young Bronwen and that became the way of things.

Early one evening soon afterwards, Helen heard a door banging. She sent Bronwen to close it but the child found no door unlatched and returned to settle with her parents and sister in the morning room. Two hours later, the banging began again. Once more Bronwen's search was to no avail. This went on day after day. Nobody could ever find the offending door yet nothing was said. She always felt somebody was following her until she got to the warm safety of her bedroom. The girls' upstairs sitting room was always cold, their ponies would never settle in the loosebox outside the back door and when Jet the Labrador was shut in there, the dog went berserk and gnawed her way out. There was something in the house but nothing was ever said.

The eeriness intensified when family friends came to visit. Their young adult daughter suddenly declared she had been here before. No you haven't, she was told. Yes I have, she said, as a child. She described sitting on a swing hanging from a rose archway in the garden. And sure enough, an expedition into the garden revealed an overgrown archway with an old swing tucked into its frame. The friends quickly left. Bronwen wondered if this was connected with the other events. Nothing was said.

The girls are used to their father Captain **George Renwick** taking command of the situation. It runs in the family. His great-uncle Sir George Renwick co-founded the shipping company *Fisher Renwick & Co* in Newcastle in 1872, served for many years as MP for Newcastle-upon-Tyne and paid for the city's war memorial in thanks for all five of his sons returning safely from the Great War. The brothers steered the business very successfully into road-haulage as their cousin, the latest George, joined the Royal Navy. In 1924 he volunteered for the newly-founded Fleet Air Arm and was soon a test pilot landing on and taking off from *HMS Hermes*, the first purpose-built British aircraft carrier. In the three years from 1943 he, Helen and the girls moved home nine times before renting *The Hollies* from **Maurice Rance** (of ***The Porches***). George impressed his landlord and their neighbour Jack **Martineau** (of ***Old Lodge***) sufficiently for him to be invited to join them on the organising committee for this year's Taplow Horse Show.

Keneric Court, Ray Park Road, Maidenhead / 6th May 2014

The Renwicks left Taplow a few weeks later. It wasn't until Bronwen grew up that her mother admitted "something wasn't right" at *The Hollies*. She was amazed to learn that Helen had often been hit by household objects flung at her back, including a cuckoo clock that leapt off its hook above the kitchen door, and that Jack had finally confided a secret: after **Louisa Rance** died her son Maurice's first tenants at *The Hollies* had left within weeks, too scared to stay. However Bronwen was reassured to hear that, when Jack added that he'd heard tell of a butcher's boy having hanged himself in the loosebox, her father had taken command by calling in an exorcist who seems to have put right whatever wasn't.

Three Gloomy Ghosts

Berry Hill / 31st October 1969

Climbing Berry Hill is a strange experience: on the left are three looming ghosts of the more affluent past.

Berry Hill House tried a new career in the 1950s as a hotel and country club set in 30 acres: "one of the most beautiful grounds in Buckinghamshire". Mark Pick was its manager in 1963 when the Bed & Breakfast tariff was one guinea (£19.20) or 14 guineas (£269) per week for a double room. In 1968 he began to build ***Fielden House*** only to leave it half-finished for **Daphne & Derek Walker** to come to the rescue. Nobody could save the country club. There were rumours that it was struggling before it was damaged not long ago by a fire that some suspected of being rather convenient for insurance purposes.

Further up the hill, ***Springfield*** never really recovered from being requisitioned by military during the Second War. Nobody was surprised when, soon after its neighbour's fire, it suffered a similar fate. The remains of these once magnificent mansions are waterproof enough to give shelter to squatters at *Berry Hill House* and tramps at *Springfield* but no itinerants have taken up residence in what was ***The Elms*** and has been ***Stockwells*** for some 20 years, a reversion remembering the ancient close on which it stands. The once beautiful grounds of this sad trio are now overgrown wildernesses save for the riding school paddocks on the lower slopes of Berry Hill.

The tramps will be evicted from *Springfield* next year for a combination of reasons including the death of one, possibly from alcohol poisoning caused by consuming too much methylated spirit, and the arrival of a female or two of their ilk. And one Sunday in 1979 **Morag & Mike Scarlett** in ***Stable Cottage*** will be aghast when, for reasons unknown, the squatters in *Berry Hill House* pile their mattresses in the ballroom, set them alight and watch in delight as the whole place burns to the ground. The fire brigade's attempt to extinguish the blaze will use so much water that the run-off from its hoses will flood the Bath Road.

No Strings Attached

Stockwells / 31st October 1969

Some ten years ago a schoolfriend excited the young **Ginny Miall** with tales of a different kind of ghost he had discovered when trespassing in *Stockwells*. He found the cellar strewn with reels of film, film cans and card models broken and distorted by time but could only guess what magic had been worked in those murky depths.

This was then the home of a television producer known only as 'Smithy' Smith-Morris whose company ***Polytechnic Studios*** employed **Gerry Anderson** in the making of TV programmes such as *You've Never Seen This* which featured people with unusual or bizarre talents. It was well-named for hardly anyone ever did see it: the BBC broadcast the show only once (on Tuesday 4th October 1955) and by 1957 *Polytechnic* was in liquidation. By then, Anderson and friends including Arthur Provis and Sylvia Thamm had founded ***Pentagon Films*** were making some TV adverts, one of which featured Enid Blyton's *Noddy* promoting *Kellogg's Ricicles*. It is likely that this ad, Anderson's first venture into puppetry, was made at *Stockwells* and possible that the detritus was the *Noddy* set. However *Pentagon* went bust soon afterwards and it was the end for the cellar studio.

It wasn't the end for **Anderson**. In fact, it was the beginning. He, Provis and their pals set up *AP Films* in a studio at *Islet Park* in Maidenhead. They struggled financially until Roberta Leigh engaged Anderson to direct *The Adventures of Twizzle*. Despite later confiding that "the idea of working with puppets made me want to vomit", it was his destiny to become a master of the art. He progressed to *Torchy the Battery Boy*, the development of *Supermarionation* for *Four Feather Falls*, the success of *Supercar* and *Fireball XL5*, the move to new studios in Slough in 1964 to make *Stingray* in colour and, of course, the iconic *Thunderbirds*. By then, Sylvia was not only his second wife but the model for and voice of *Miss Penelope*. While Gerry and Sylvia had no visible strings attached to Taplow, it is possible that they first met at *Stockwells* as he stumbled upon what would make him famous.

No Strings Attached

Gerry Anderson, with Troy Tempest / 1966

St Nicolas' Church & Nearby / c1963

Looking south-east

St Nicolas' Church & Nearby / 1963

St Nicolas' Church & Nearby / 1992

Looking east

Looking south-west

Sunrises and Newcomers

Another New Trinity

The Village Centre / 31st December 1969

Right now it feels like *The Swinging Sxities* has brought the curtain down on what was. Let's shake off the dusty old and make a whole new world. It is the Age of Aquarius. Peace will guide the planets and love will steer the stars.

Time will tell that we are kidding ourselves but how good it is to dream that every change will be for the better. And in Taplow, we are turning the corner, finding our feet, looking to the future, thanks to the efforts of three overlapping organisations – two new, one not, each a potent mix of new blood and old. The Association, the Society and the Parish Council are the framework of how our world works. First of the new was the **Taplow & Hitcham Recreation Grounds Association** (THRGA)....

The Association

Hitcham Field / 11th February 1956

The worry is worse that, having swallowed much of Burnham, Slough has a taste for Taplow. And there is the more immediate threat that, now bereft of barbed-wire, **Hitcham Field** may be about to become a caravan site. **Eileen Matthews** and **Catherine 'Cash' Martineau** have galvanised the community into action to beat the developer's site valuation by £50 (£880). Cash's husband **Jack Martineau** has joined with Eileen and five others – **Audrey Skimming**, **Jack Page**, **Ernest Perkins**, Robinson Peter Rigg and **Alexander Sim** – to acquire Hitcham Field with the aim of setting it aside as a green buffer to the seemingly irresistible urban expansion. Today this magnificent seven formally united as THRGA with Jack as Chairman and **Lorna Miall** as Secretary. They will soon be joined on THRGA's Council of Management by **Lord Bill Astor**, GH James (of ***Hitcham Rectory***), **Burnard Morton**, **Maurice Rogers** and **David Morris**. Many others will also quickly join the Association as ordinary members for an initial subscription of one guinea or as life members for a fee of not less than £50 (£1,100) followed by £5 (£110) annually and £100 (£2,180) to be bequeathed in their wills.

The Pit / 11th February 2012

THRGA quickly leased part of the field as a sports ground to ***Flexello Castors & Wheels Ltd***, a company formed in Slough in 1934 and acquired in 2001 by *Colson Castors Ltd* of West Bromwich. Plans to build huts for the Scout and Guides were put on hold in 1959 when Buckinghamshire County Council approached THRGA with an offer of over £10,000 (£530,000) to extract gravel from the site for the construction of the M4 motorway. After much soul-searching, THRGA agreed. It was a wise decision. When excavations were complete in 1961 and founder members generously chose to forego the money due to them, THRGA could afford to repay other interest-free loans, build the huts and landscape what came to be called '**The Pit**' as an open space. It is popular with dog-walkers and especially for sledging when it snows. Scouts, Guides, Brownies, Cubs and Beavers all thrive, the sports ground has been let for many years to **Pheonix & Claires Court Sports Association** and interest on the original investment is still enough to pay for the ongoing maintenance of the Grounds.

Alistair Forsyth is now Chairman of THRGA and **Keith Paskins** is its Treasurer. Alistair's long service on the Council overlapped with that of **Eileen Law** (née Matthews) and Jack Page, MP for Harrow West for 27 years from 1960. Their fellow councillor **Ginny Felton** (Lorna's daughter) believes that The Pit is still as important as it was nearly 60 years ago. She is confident that it will remain forever a "recreation ground for the use of the inhabitants of the ecclesiastical parishes of Taplow and Hitcham".

No doubt **'Bob' Tanner** would be delighted that the buffer seems secure. She may also have been pleased that THRGA has also been able to fund or support a range of community and charitable causes including St Nicolas' Primary School, the Taplow Playgroup, the Women's Institute, Taplow Cricket Club and both St Nicolas' and St Mary's Churches. It paid for the electrification of the clock in St Nicolas' Church spire in 1987, continues to fund the trimming of the churchyard's holly hedge and will this year expand its remit to support the initiative led under THRGA's umbrella by **Roger Andrews**, **Miv Wayland-Smith**, **Malcolm Tait** and **Anthony Harding** to rescue for public use ***Old Priory Garden***, the unkempt woodland that was once **Percy Noble**'s secret in the south-eastern extremity of **Rocque Meadow**.

About Grout – Back to Scouting

The Women's Institute Hall, Institute Road / 11th May 1951

After the war, the wheelwrights wanted their shed back so **Iris & Albert Bovington** – she as Cubmaster, he as Scoutmaster – moved 1st Hitcham Group to Burnham's long-disused scout hut where they became 1st Burnham & Hitcham Scouts with the stalwart help of **Arthur Grout**, David Guire and **Ray Portsmouth**. Today after four years of discussion founders Derek Strickland and Bob Hirons are delighted to watch as Group Scout Leader Les Melbourne of Langley presides over the first meeting of 1st Lent Rise Scout Troop and, in exactly six months time, Mrs M Tomsett of *Garden Cottage* on Cliveden Road will begin many years as Cubmaster of the new Cub Scout Troop. The Group will use the WI Hall and the Drill Hall for meetings until moving to an old galvanised tin hut between Lent Rise Road and the top end of Milner Road.

Gravel Gone, Seeds Planted

Keira Smales, Lyra Cherry & Sophie Greenham / 2012

Hitcham Field, now 'The Pit': in 1956, the seed for the Association / 2013

Boundary Road and some of its 1980s trees / 2013

Hummers footpath: near where the hay ricks burned in 1936 / 2013

***Lea Rig* & *Poplar Farm*:** in 1959, the seed for the Society / 2013

The Scout Hut, Institute Road / 12th June 1965

Les Melbourne approached JR Kemp of ***New Taplow Paper Mills*** and persuaded him to pay £20-a-ton (£402) for waste paper collected by the Scouts. This ruse raised several hundred pounds for tents and camping equipment but Arthur had bigger ideas when he took over as Group Leader. Whist drives, fetes and bazaars were held with one purpose in mind: to raise funds for new headquarters. And then fate took a hand: THRGA made the south-east corner of **The Pit** available at a peppercorn rent and two new huts were built, one for the Guides and Brownies, the other for the Cubs and Scouts. And today they are being opened by Air Commodore Ian Brodie, the County Commissioner for the Scouts Association. Arthur will go on to become a Venture Scout Leader and eventually Assistant District Commissioner. In 2010 he will recall the energy and generosity of the Group's presidents – including Lady **Nancy Astor** and **Louis Freedman** of Cliveden Stud – and reflect on the 59-year history of the Group during which over 2,600 boys have tasted Cubs, Scouts and Venture Scouting in the outdoors and discovered the friendship and brotherhood of the movement. Modesty will prevent him for mentioning his own fundamental role.

Girlguiding

The Guide Hut, Institute Road / 12th June 2014

Dick Humphries and Sheila Birchtnell led the fundraising for the Guide Hut. Both continued for many years: he as chairman of the Guide Hut Supporters, she as Guide Captain for the 1st Taplow & Hitcham Guides which was formed in 1936 by Miss D Hardy. Back then its Brownie troop met in the garage of its founder – Mrs Wiseman (wife of Noel, then of Taplow Lodge) – and in 1948 the sisters Gill and Nancy Treleaven began a Guide Company and a Brownie Pack in the Rheumatic Ward at Cliveden Hospital which gave these isolated handicapped children fun and a sense of belonging to the outside world. Ten years later, Mrs Slow of *Hitcham Grange* and June Thom of Eastfield Road formed the 2nd T&H Brownies which met in the old Parish Room until they joined the 1st T&H Guides and Brownies in the new hut. In 1969, the 2nd T&H Guides moved there too under the leadership of Gillian Hughes. Mrs E Elsey formed the 4th T&H Brownies the following year and Hazel Humphries led the 4th T&H Guides from 1977.

The 1st and 2nd Guides closed in 1999 and 1985 respectively and the 1st Brownies in 1987 but the other units still thrive with Trevor Sheddon as Chairman of the Guide HQ Committee, Susan Silver and Bernadette & Felicity Poole as leaders of the 1st Brownies, Tracy Weeks of the 4th Brownies, Bryony Waters and Nina Heavyside of the 4th Guides and the little Rainbows (founded in 1987) led by Carol Martin. Next month, many girls will enjoy a week at *Wings*, a Jamboree in Windsor Great Park for 7,000 Scouts and Guides.

Eyes of a Child – Olivia Hall & Lauren Murphy

St Nicolas' School – 23rd April 2012

In Taplow there is this hut where lots of little girls go. They call it Brownies, says Olivia. We wear brown and yellow clothes that says Brownies on it. When you join Brownies you get a Brownie Box, inside the box is a Badge Book. In Brownies you can get badges, swimming badges, you can get entertainment, winter challenge, sewing, knitting, friend to animal and tidier. To get badges you have to work hard on a badge you want. We go every Tuesday to Taplow Brownies, says Lauren, and play fun games. We all play all sorts of games like *Princess Got a Headache*, *Twins Jump the River* and *Cut the Cake*. Once a year we help people who shop at Sainsbury's packing their shopping into bags and, if they are happy, they put some money into the pot.

Eyes of a Child – Nicola Mayo & Timothy Pretty

St Nicolas' School – 23rd April 2012

Nicola has only been at Guides a few weeks. I am really enjoying it, she says, because we do all sorts of activities. For example, we did bidding and Lucie Plummer bidded to have a best friend. I like the Scout Hut, says Tim, because we learn different things and survival. This comes in handy when we're older and camping. Your survival skills keep you alive. If you don't have a tent you need to make a briar. In Scouts we do canoeing, flintstone carving, caving, rock climbing, kayaking, zipwire and abseiling.

Something's Brewing – Cash and Carry On

The Old Lodge, High Street / 11th February 2013

Audrey Skimming and her husband **Edward** of ***Taplow House*** had been pillars of local life for over 30 years. Both would soon be gone but THRGA was instrumental in the baton being passed to a new generation. Matthews, Page, Perkins, Rogers and the Martineaus and Mialls all played significant roles in shaping Taplow over many years.

It was during the Second War that the Martineaus made their home here at ***Old Lodge***, then still one house that had gradually expanded eastward from ***The Gables***. Cash, a descendant of the author William Thackeray, was known locally as a passionate patron of the Cookham artist Sir Stanley Spencer and for her stalwart service during the war at CRCMH where she became a close friend of **Joyce Grenfell**. Jack carried on Taplow's tradition as being a home for brewers of renown. He was the fifth or sixth generation of his family to be involved in the management of *Whitbread.* Indeed the company can thank his ancestors John and Joseph for saving it from bankruptcy in 1812 when they amalgamated their Lambeth brewery, *Martineau & Bland*, with that of Samuel Whitbread the Younger. The business struggled at first – Sam cut his own throat in 1815 – but recovered to dominate the brewing industry despite John Martineau's strange demise in 1834 at the Chiswell Street brewery. The inquest decided that his fall into a yeast trough caused "death by visitation of God". The company had its ups and downs. It dominated British brewing by 1900, suffered like its competitors from the Great War restrictions and only began to emerge from another difficult period in 1948 when Jack played a leading role in its listing on the Stock Exchange, a vital step on the road to its modern prowess as a leisure conglomerate.

Jack may have been distantly related to the Grenfells. Sugar refiner **George Martineau** of Esher, possibly Jack's uncle, certainly knew the Desboroughs well enough to be one of their guests at the Taplow Court garden party for the British Imperial Chamber of Commerce in July 1914. Perhaps it was this link which brought him and Cash to the relative safety of Taplow when their Chiswell Street home was bombed in the Blitz. Jack was later to be president of The Institute of Brewing and in 1955 Past Master of The Brewer's Hall, an accolade held just two years before by former Taplovian **Walter Pearce-Serocold**.

Eyes of a Child – Bronwen Renwick

Keneric Court, Ray Park Road / 6th May 2014

Bronwen remembers a trip to the circus at Christmas 1946 when the Martineau boys' laughter at the clowns was cut short by the sight of their father's "po-face". But despite him having "no sense of humour", she was so sad the following winter to hear that the Martineaus' baby daughter had drowned in a pond in the garden of ***Old Lodge***.

The Society

Boundary Road / 11th February 2013

The second of the new organisations began in what became a very big hole. The seed sown in the green pasture to the east in December 1959 grew to be the **Hitcham & Taplow Preservation Society** (HTPS), renamed the **Hitcham & Taplow Society** (HTS) in 2007 but still 'The Society'.

It all started with **Maurice Rogers**, a Doctor of Philosophy (possibly in mechanical engineering) and a director of *ICI Paints* in Slough who was known as Mat (the initials of his Christian names). In 1958 he spent £6,500 (£362,000) to acquire ***Lea Rig*** from John Shepherd whose son, also **John Shepherd**, inherited the farm and gave it a new name: ***Poplar Farm***. All the noise was about **Hitcham Field** until late-autumn 1959 when it was discovered that the M4 was also greedy for the gravel beneath the younger Shepherd's land.

Lea Rig, Poplar Farm / 29th May 1979

Mat Rogers was aghast that his rural idyll would be disturbed. He recalls that "The news was received with horror. Taplow wasn't organised to fight and, by the time it tried to, the battle was practically lost. Some of us met here in December 1959 to consider options. We didn't think an appeal would raise enough to buy the land as we had Hitcham Field. Instead we decided to propose the formation of a Preservation Society so that never again would we be caught unprepared. The support we got at a special meeting in the WI Hall in February 1960 was very encouraging. By then we were organised and ready, with **Viscount Astor** as the Society's president, to ensure that the contractor complied with the conditions of its planning permission and that the land was restored to a proper condition for pasture. The result is there for all to see – the restoration has been pretty successful – but perhaps the most important outcome of the rumpus was that [Buckinghamshire] County Council changed the procedures for contractors seeking gravel extraction rights. Now the opposition stands a chance."

The episode taught Taplow a thing or two. Applications to extract gravel were rejected for sites just north of Taplow Village (1961), at Hunts Wood (1962), *Barge* and *Amerden Farms* (1967), Cookham (1969) and Dropmore (1971). The ambition of ***William Boyer & Sons Ltd*** at ***Barge Farm*** was thwarted with the help of Bray Preservation Society, formed in the 1960s for that very purpose, and by **Ernest Perkins** and then **Giles Sim** taking extended leases of the land. It was possible to reach a reasonable compromise on vehicular access and restoration arrangements to allow ***Summerleaze*** to excavate what became **Taplow Lake**. A three-year fight will succeed in 1980 when *Barge Farm* is once again saved from becoming another big hole. Woodland north of Hedsor will be saved in 1981 and operational compromises will be agreed for extraction at ***Berry Hill Farm*** in 1980 and 2002.

Rogers concludes with the observation that, although it began with a single purpose, the Society has spread its branches "to have a significant influence in maintaining the surroundings to our homes at least as attractive as we found them". It is possible that the younger Shepherd didn't agree. While he had originally been content enough to use the proceeds from the gravel extraction to replace the farm bungalow with a chalet-style home, perhaps he was less satisfied in 1976 when the objections of the Society prevented 146 houses being built on the *Poplar Farm* pasture, a move that would have seen Slough's sprawl spread beyond Burnham to engulf Taplow.

Berinus, No 7 Saxon Gardens / 29th September 1999

With typical quirkiness, **Lincoln Lee** recalls when Mat Rogers announced at an AGM in the early-1960s that "the Scouts.... would pick up all the litter in Taplow and Dropmore". That immortal line works better if said out loud.

Taplow Village Centre / 29th November 2013

Rogers died at the age of 92 in 2004. Nowadays the Society phrases its objectives as being "to protect Hitcham, Taplow and the surrounding countryside from being spoilt by bad development or neglect". Here in a nutshell is what the Society is about – it aspires to make the best of things. It has always lived in the real world – hence its change of name in recognition that its purpose is protection not preservation – while never accepting that poor planning or design, lack of joined-up thinking or no thought at all can ever be acceptable. It took its time – although **John Hanford** suggested the abbreviated slimline 'fit-for-purpose' name in 2003, it was four years before 'Preservation' was finally dropped – but it has always been prepared to ask decision-makers and developers difficult questions, to be their conscience and if it can to hold them to account for the sake of the social and physical fabric of our little corner of the world and its character and quality of life.

The first Annual General Meeting of the Society was held in November 1960. This evening the 54th AGM was addressed by the 8th president, **Eva Lipman**, and the 13th chairman, **Karl Lawrence**. Along with their peers and predecessors in office, on the committee and in the membership, they can be proud that, without any statutory authority, the Society has succeeded in using its energy and influence to press successfully to reduce aircraft noise (1972/73), to establish conservation areas for **Taplow Village** (1975) and **Taplow Riverside** (1990), to extend both (2006) and to have the countryside from Taplow Village to the M40 (including Cliveden, Dropmore and Hedsor) designated an Area of Attractive Landscape (1978) and the Old Churchyard and Tæppa's Mound designated as a National Monument under the protection of English Heritage (1996).

Along the way, the Society has also prevented, or more often moderated for the better, many proposals for changes great and small while embracing two supplementary goals. It encourages local community spirit through such events as the Easter Egg Hunt and the Village Green Party, the latter held complete with ox roast and country dancing on the mid-summer Saturday every year since 1986. And it shares and celebrates our heritage through the execution or funding of or contributing to various renovation, restoration or rescue projects including Bapsey Pond and Taplow Court's cruciform dairy, Boundary Road trees, Burnham Abbey, Cliveden's Hanging Woods, St John's Ambulance Brigade, St Mary's Church, St Nicolas' Church, the Scouts, Maidenhead Sea Cadets (or *TS Iron Duke*), Old Churchyard's Celtic Cross, Old Priory Garden, Sheila Horton's mural, Taplow Station flowerbeds, a bench on the Thames Path by Maidenhead Bridge, Thames Salmon Trust, Thames Valley Adventure Playground, Thames Valley Hospice, the Village telephone box and the Women's Institute. Many of these achievements were recently remembered in the milestone 100th edition of its bi-annual newsletter, a bumper 20-pager which has been delivered not only to members as usual but also throughout Taplow and Hitcham.

Society records have been lost for the first ten years but by 2014 the list of 31 double-decade servants will include **Ernest Perkins** (possibly 26 years), **Helen Lee** and **Leonard Miall** (25 each), **Anne Milne** and **Eileen Law** (both at least 23) and **Andy McKenzie** of *SGI* (22) with Eva Lipman (22) and the record-holders **Barrie Peroni** and **Tony Hickman** (both 33) still counting. **Ivan Snow** served nine of his 15 years as Chairman and founder member **Jack Page** was another of at least ten in the high teens. **Helen Wogan** didn't quite make it into double figures. Two of these remarkable people also achieved national recognition....

The Man from Auntie – Miall's Away

The Red Cottage, Rectory Road / 15th May 1954

When they came home from the USA last year, Lorna & Leonard Miall took a short lease on ***The Red Cottage***. With its proximity to her parents in Bourne End and a reasonably convenient commute for him to London, Taplow suits them to a T. They have just acquired ***Maryfield*** from **Marye Pole-Carew** of ***The Old Cottage*** for nearly £4,000 (£278,500). Leonard is loading belongings into his car to ferry them up the High Street when the Reverend **Christopher Hare** rushes up to accuse him (quite correctly) of being "in the *BBC*" and ask whether the Queen has yet set foot on English soil. She is due back from her six-month post-Coronation tour of the Commonwealth and the Rector intends to ring the church bells just as soon as she is safely home. Leonard is one of the very few people whose car has a radio. He tunes into *BBC Home Service* to discover that Her Majesty has indeed arrived. By the time Leonard reaches *Maryfield*, he can't hear himself think for the joyous pealing of the bells.

Although he has been in Taplow only since the previous August, Leonard is already known for knowing just about everybody and everything to do with news and current affairs. He can certainly count amongst his friends and acquaintances broadcasters, journalists, politicians and personalities on both sides of the Atlantic. And his reputation was enhanced in March when he got a scoop for the *BBC*. He knew before anyone else that two recent fatal crashes had led to the suspension of production of the *de Havilland Comet 1* jet airliner. When asked his source, he revealed with a wink that he had ***Fairey's*** at the bottom of his garden. He had of course heard the news from his next-door neighbours at ***The Priory***. This was typical of his talents for having his ear to the ground, an eye for a good story and a silver tongue.

These attributes were already evident when Leonard was reading economics at Cambridge, President of the Union in 1936 and editor of the undergraduate newspaper *Cambridge Review*. Somebody predicted he would end up at the *British Broadcasting Corporation*. And so he did, in March 1939. It was his fluent German that got him the job of producing talks in its newly-formed German Service which, when war was declared, fell under the direction of the Enemy Propaganda Department of the Ministry of Information.

Leonard's Quaker education had instilled in him a pacifism that had been sorely challenged during mid-1930s visits to Germany where realisation slowly dawned that force might be the only way to stop Hitler. Quite by chance, he had found a way to fight the Nazis peacefully but effectively and will forever count his blessings that his war was psychological and not physical. For two years from 1942 he was with the Political Warfare Executive, mostly in the USA, initially alongside *Voice of America* in New York, later in San Francisco setting up a daily broadcast to the Far East to combat *Toyko Rose* (the Japanese equivalent of *Lord Haw-Haw*). He spent the winter of 1944/45 at *Radio Luxembourg* broadcasting 'white' (persuasive) propaganda and ventured into Czechoslovakia as a correspondent before once more crossing the Atlantic to be *BBC News* correspondent in America. During eight years there listeners at home were treated to two British perspectives on the USA; both Leonard's news coverage and Alistair Cooke's weekly *American Letter* (*Letter from America* from 1950) were delivered in measured, authoritative, clearly well-informed tones with occasional hints of humour.

It was fortunate for Europe that powerful people listened to Leonard. European leaders failed to realise the significance of a speech made at Harvard in June 1947 in which US Secretary of State George Marshall outlined ideas to encourage the economic recovery of Europe in order to prevent the spread of Communism. Leonard didn't miss the point and he made it eloquently in his news report. British Foreign Secretary Ernest Bevin said later that hearing it "was like a life-belt to a sinking man, and I grabbed it with both hands". The Marshall Plan saved Europe. It might never have happened if it hadn't been for Leonard's friendship with Marshall's Undersecretary Dean Acheson, his economic awareness, instinct for news and ability to communicate it succinctly.

The Man from Auntie – The Extra Miall

The Oak & Saw / 27th September 2002

Once again a few neighbours are enjoying Friday night refreshment together, nobody more than Leonard who raises a laugh with his story of how his hearing aid went missing for several months before being found in here. Keen to egg on an anecdote, I ask how long he and Sally have been at ***Maryfield Cottage***. His eyes gleam at the prospect of telling the tale....

Until 1954 it was a barn-cum-coachhouse-cum-cottage where the gardener **Arthur Sims** lived with his wife and son. Arthur had tended the ***Maryfield*** garden all his life. As a youth he had helped plant its yew hedge for George Webster. Under Lady Beatrice's direction he had planted snowdrops from her family home at Shambally Castle in Tipperary, lilacs of many different hues as well as lemon verbena, nicotiana and other sweet-scented plants. There was a rookery in the five huge elms at the top of the garden. In days of old, rectors would lead a procession here to pray for a good harvest. Local lore said that if the rooks ever left Taplow its luck would go too. Things turned out the other way around. The rooks had to go when Dutch elm disease struck in the 1970s but Taplow survived.

When Arthur retired **Marye Pole-Carew** sold the cottage and its appendages to Lieutenant-Colonel **Burnard Morton** JP who brought his wife Judith from *Rookwood* in **Marsh Lane** to combine its parts into the whole he called *Maryfield Cottage*. Meanwhile Leonard and Lorna decided that, even with four children, they rather rattled around in *Maryfield*. The servants' wing was duly converted into a separate dwelling, *Maryfield Orchard*, and let to a series of American servicemen doing that secret stuff up at Hedsor. What with being so busy at the *BBC*, Leonard rather neglected the garden until Arthur turned up on the doorstep one day to make an offer he couldn't refuse. The old fellow was delighted to spend his last years restoring his life's work to its former glory.

Here the story takes a necessary twist. Having had to give up the coachhouse where she kept her car, Marye retained the patch of land in front of *Maryfield Cottage* to build a double garage. She also insisted on keeping a smaller wedge on the other side of *Maryfield*'s drive in case she might want to bring her car right up to the door of ***The Old Cottage***. Leonard had no idea how she thought she could make a drive over a public footpath but he correctly anticipated the headaches her decision would cause for conveyancing lawyers whenever any of the properties were sold.

Leonard gets back on track to explain how *Maryfield Cottage* change hands twice in the winter of 1971/72 when **Jack Page**'s sister Margot Gibbons bought and sold it within months to Jeremy Richards, manager of the *Westminster Bank* in Windsor. He busily set about remodelling it only for the merger of the *Westminster* with the *National Provincial Bank* to have him transferred back to his New Forest origins. His successor Sandy Burgess, publisher of a Windsor newspaper, sold it to Leonard and Sally in 1979 who in turn sold *Maryfield* into what became a twilight existence. It spent four years as a rarely-used executive *pied-a-terre* for *Alltransport*, a South African multi-national freight company, and almost five as a rarely-used summer retreat for Al Mubarak Aiquasi of Bahrain. It was given new life on New Year's Day 1988 with the arrival of **Jane & Jerry Burley**, he a senior tax partner with accountants *Touche Ross*. Jerry played in the youth team at Chelsea Football Club but National Service came first and then a career as a chartered accountant, initially with a bank in Jersey. During severe bouts of illness in the early-1980s, he fell in love with his nurse, married her in 1986 and brought her to Taplow where they have a reputation for being generous hosts. Jerry is a passionate bridge player and the Society's honorary auditor. He will be 77 when he passes away in 2008. By then his successors at *Maryfield* will be opening their garden for the first time to the National Gardens Scheme. Old Arthur would have been delighted to see his domain in the tender loving care of **Jacqueline & Roger Andrews**.

The Man from Auntie – Another Extra Miall

The Oak & Saw / 4th October 2002

Another Friday brings another chance to go the extra Miall. Tonight Leonard's theme is commuters. For many years until the early-1980s, a train left Taplow at seven every weekday morning to speed non-stop to Paddington and a return service arrived back at six-thirty each evening. This rather convenient arrangement was one of the reasons why Leonard and many others settled here. He would like to believe the oft-told tale that it was a legacy of the days when various notable locals were directors of the ***Great Western Railway***. However neither he nor **Michael Bayley** has been able to establish exactly who these influential eminences were. He guesses that Desborough might have been one, simply because his lordship held directorships beyond counting. **George Trumper** might have been a candidate if there were any record that he lived on rather than merely owned the Amerden lowlands once held by **George Whitlaw**.

Our storyteller smiles to recall how he raised certain Taplovian eyebrows in the late-1950s and early-1960s when he would zoom to the station on a moped his children dubbed *The Black Steed* and how even as late as the 1970s two eminent gentlemen always smartly turned out in three-piece suits and bowler hats would march down the hill with brisk precision. The matching attire of **Anthony Paines** and **Eric Pope** belied their very different callings – one a city solicitor with *Allen & Overy*, the other an MI6 spycatcher – which may be why they would nod acknowledgement but not converse.

Alistair Forsyth interjects with the amusing tale of a 1980s commuter. Guy de Pass lived up the High Street at either ***Wee Cott*** or ***Rose Cott***. One evening Guy had his usual tipple at Paddington and as usual fell asleep on the train, trusting his instinct to wake him just before arriving at Taplow. Unfortunately the train stopped at a red signal half-a-mile short of the station. He woke with a start, opened the door and fell onto the track. Everybody was too stunned to react. A moment later, a briefcase appeared followed by a very dishevelled and slightly bruised Guy who brushed himself down, apologised to all for getting out on the wrong side and promptly repeated his trick by falling through the opposite door. Poor old Guy, sighs **Tony Meats**, he used to talk to our twins Oliver and Rupert as if he was at school with them. And do you remember the time he stormed into the Parish Council meeting to demand what did they intend to do about the prostitutes on the High Street? Yes, says Alistair, and you shouted: Where? Where? We couldn't work out if Guy's complaint was that there were too many of them or none at all.

The conversation turns to Taplow's 1960s housing explosion, and especially to **Buffins** which Eton RDC permitted to be built on Green Belt land and yet soon afterwards sent to all constituents a report which trumpeted its determination to protect the Green Belt. As then president of the Society, Leonard wrote to the Eton RDC chairman challenging him "to declare how much ratepayers' money had been spent on this glossy brochure with its mendacious propaganda". Leonard copied this letter to the local newspapers and from there the row got taken up by the national press and the luckless RDC chairman lost his seat at the next election. The resulting fuss led in due course to the Village being made a Conservation Area.

The Man from Auntie – Yet Another Miall

The Oak & Saw / 25th October 2002

Tonight the topic is aircraft noise. Leonard recalls that on 21st July 1972 a new beacon at Lake End came into operation to concentrate what had previously been dispersed aircraft taking off from Heathrow for Scandinavia, the USA and northern UK to fly in a narrow funnel right over Taplow. This was known as the 'Minimum Noise Route', which meant maximum noise for those beneath it.

Tony Field (of N° 18 **Cedar Chase**) was a founder of the 21st July Action Group which advised the Society to make no complaint but instead to write to the Civil Aviation Authority (CAA) asking difficult questions such as "Could you please tell me how many perceived noise decibels a 747 should be emitting when it passes over Taplow Village?" Since these letters expressed no views, the CAA was unable to respond with the standard postcard saying 'the Minister will take note'. And because every letter was copied to a local MP, it was wary that awkward questions might be asked in the House if it had failed to reply to such perfectly reasonable enquiries. Consequently it had no option but to draft over 5,000 individual replies. Meanwhile Ivan Snow, then chairman of the Society, joined Leonard to raise the matter with the Noise Advisory Council and make the point that those living in areas of low ambient noise were more susceptible to being disturbed by aircraft noise than those in urban areas. As a result, early in 1973 over 300 people gathered in St Nicolas' School hall at which the Society's barrister Ronald Bell QC presided over a "vigorous but controlled" debate with representatives of the CAA, the Department of Trade & Industry and the British Airline Pilots Association. The CAA crumbled eventually and installed the Burnham Beacon near Burnham Beeches to enable a fan-pattern of take-offs.

This new 'Split Burnham Route' sounded painful and westward departures from Heathow still spared Maidenhead at the expense of Taplow (same old story in a new dress) but at least Taplow no longer had a monopoly. It's not as bad here as at Windsor – how silly to put a royal castle under the approach to Heathrow, smiles Leonard – but we have to be vigilant. It was necessary to mobilise new pressure to prevent erosion of the night flying curfew in 1992 and **Derek Walker** represented the Society diligently during the Heathrow Terminal 5 Inquiry. After almost seven years of deliberation, the Inspector accepted Derek's evidence that, since Taplow and Hitcham are on higher ground, they are exposed to the sound of passing aircraft for at least 60 seconds, more than half that time at intrusive levels, which meant that at busy times the noise was continuous. His other environmental concerns were also treated sympathetically in the seven-inch thick report which confirmed that a third runway would not be required. So that's alright then. Well, only until 2007 when the argument will once again raise its head and rage for years. Derek will pass away in 2008 and his widow Daphne, long a stalwart of St Nicolas' Church and the Royal British Legion, will return to her roots in Bray six years later.

Tall Tale – Best Friends: Billy Chandler & Sailor

The Oak & Saw, Rectory Road / 23rd April 1986

Sailor and Billy are two of six old folk enjoying later life at ***Desborough Cottages*** (Hill Farm Road). Billy has been at N° 1 since it was built in the late-1950s and a cowman around here since the cows came home. In fact, he says, 'twas me who brought 'em 'ome to 'ill Farm an' milked 'em fer Mr Mewton and before him fer Mrs Dykes. He and Sailor (at N° 5) go way back. Billy and **Anthony Harding** are two of the very few who know Sailor is **Arthur Morrell**, once the Astors' odd man, later of Marsh Lane.

Nowadays the claim to fame of this pair of old boys is propping up the bar and telling tall tales. Sailor drains his pint and asks his pal if he can remember the old village simpleton when they were lads. Village simpleton, grins Billy, wasn't that your job? Sailor ignores him. Back then, he says, all the nobs walked to the station wearing bowler 'ats. The old fella asked the village bobby if 'e could wear a bowler instead of 'is flat cap. The copper shook 'is 'ead slowly and said no, yer wudn't qualify fer a licence. After a dramatic pause, Sailor adds: an' from wot I've 'eard, you won't qualify fer one either. Wotja mean, asks Billy. Well, you 'ad a bit o' trouble getting 'ome the uvver day. You curled up an' fell asleep 'alfway up the 'igh Street an' them Meats twins 'ad to getchya back on yer feet. Is that right? Can't remember, mumbles Billy, who features in the odd slice of local lore tale himself....

Alistair Forsyth says Billy always used to get up every morning at six o'clock and put a cup of tea at this wife Evelyn's bedside before going to work in the fields all day. On his way home, he would drink the evening away in the pub before staggering home and collapsing into bed beside Evelyn who was already fast asleep. One morning he was surprised to see three undrunk cups of tea on her bedside table. It turned out that the poor old girl had been dead for two days and he hadn't noticed.

The Man from Auntie – Miall's Apart

St Nicolas' Church / 8th March 2005

Having graced Taplow for nearly 52 of his 90 years, Leonard passed away on 24th February. Today at a Celebration of the Life, two of his sons are remembering him in affectionate eulogies which include snapshots of his time here....

Tris tells of their childhood – the fat and fearsome **Arthur Mewton** (who had succeeded **Janie Dykes** at ***Hill Farm***), the cows breaking through (from the field where Taplow Horse Show was held) to turn *Maryfield*'s grass tennis court into a quagmire, the day that same field caught fire and **Jack Martineau** in his Leander blazer stood serenely and uselessly as everyone else struggled to put out the blaze and save ***Maryfield***.

Roger picks up the story. After his mother Lorna passed away in 1974, old friends drew up a list of ladies who might match up to a man of Leonard's calibre. Enter **Sally Bicknell** (née Leith), a versatile and vivacious divorcee, author, graecophile and former Bletchey Park codebreaker and trophy-winning rally driver, who he had met in Washington DC in the late-1940s when she was married to UK Air Attaché Nigel Bicknell. They clicked. Her four sons joined his three to dwarf Ginny who was pleased to play the Snow White of their extended family. After moving to ***Maryfield Cottage***, Leonard and Sally decided to herald the festive season by celebrating his birthday with a party on the first Friday in November. Each year the numbers grew despite the occasional clash with Bonfire Night. At his 90th birthday party last year he asked that there be no presents. Instead each guest was to write and read out loud a poem or limerick. Sally's contribution was these immortal lines: "Earth has not anything to show more fair, than Leonard Miall in his underwear". She may have been looking through a glass of *Hunter Valley* red.

St Bride's Church, Fleet Street / 25th May 2005

The *BBC* has arranged this service of thanksgiving for the life of Leonard. **Sir David Attenborough** begins his address with the thought that, in the late-1940s and early-1950s, radio was too dignified to have stars – but if the *BBC* had had stars, Leonard Miall was certainly one of them.

It was during the 1950s that the *BBC* came to be derided as 'Auntie' for its superior 'I know what's best for you' attitude. Leonard may have had the right perfectly clipped voice for *BBC Radio* of the time, but talking down was never his style as he demonstrated consummately in his next responsibility as head of *BBC TV Talks Department*. *Talks* had a broad brief: it covered everything that wasn't drama, light entertainment, news or outside broadcasts.

Sir David poses a question: "How did Leonard, who had no direct experience whatever of television or with managing a department, deal with such a rebellious, fractious, unruly group?" And he answers it: "He succeeded because of his sheer niceness, his kindness, his good humour and straightforward honesty". Leonard's benign encouragement and advocacy created a fertile environment in which innovators could realise their dreams. Cobwebs were blown from current affairs with the launch of truly iconic programmes including *Tonight*, *Panorama*, *Monitor* and *That Was The Week That Was*. The creativity extended to many other programmes, such as *The Sky at Night*, that were the first of their kind anywhere in the world and which have left lasting legacies in the coverage of archaeology, gardening, travel, medicine, the arts, the sciences, do-it-yourself, military history and natural history – which is where Sir David came in to set standards that will never be equalled.

After managing the launch of *BBC2* in 1964, Leonard returned to the USA as Auntie's Man in New York from 1966 to 1971. Lorna's death coincided with another ending. Auntie said he had to retire at 60 like everyone else and so he pretended to. During ten years as consultant research historian for the *BBC*, he assisted Asa Briggs in the production of a history of UK broadcasting, wrote obituaries for *The Independent* and a book, *Inside the BBC*, which comprised pen pictures of 25 icons of the *BBC* from Lord Reith to Sir Robin Day.

Sir David ends his speech by saying that great organisations inevitably influence those who serve them. But then some of those who serve are the very reason why those organisations are great. Leonard was one of those. He didn't say (but perhaps many thought) that it is hard to fathom why this incredible fellow was appointed OBE in 1961 but never knighted like Sir David and other friends such as Robin Day, Hugh Carleton Greene, Ludovic Kennedy, Patrick Moore, Malcolm Muggeridge and **Jack Page**.

Six Mialls

Maryfield / 1954

The Man from Auntie / 1947

Ginny, Lorna with St John, Tristan, Roger & Leonard / 1953

Two Dimensions

Sir John Page / 2005

Bill Astor, 3rd Viscount Astor, with Bronwen / 1960

The Man who knew Maggie

Hitcham Lodge / 3rd November 2008

Although he never held a ministerial post, **Jack Page** was a 'power behind the throne' before and during the prime ministry of Margaret Thatcher. He supported her passionately as a politician and with great sympathy as a personal friend. He and his wife Anne were regular guests of Maggie and Denis at *Chequers*. It was at her recommendation that he was knighted in 1984. Thereafter, he was Jack or Sir John but never Sir Jack.

Sir John passed away four days ago at 89. In its obituary today *The Daily Telegraph* remembers him as a "defender of the little man". Having risen from an artillery gunner to major during the Second War, his energetic attitude to business resulted in the opportunity in 1959 to stand for election as MP for Eton & Slough. It was around that time he discovered Taplow and has lived here ever since. He was narrowly defeated then but recovered to represent Harrow West for 27 years from 1960. He exercised considerable influence as a Conservative backbencher, prepared to rock the boat with his provocative views on a wide range of topics including Rhodesia, Malta, Israel, Northern Ireland, cooperation (or lack of it) in the European Union, excessive red tape, employment and union law, metrification, capital punishment, national security, education, independent schools, immigration, insurance and water supply. The last led to his 15 years from 1986 as chairman of *Three Valleys Water Co Ltd*.

His Parliamentary responsibilities didn't prevent the Pages from enjoying the local social scene: on Burns' Nights, his lines of *Tam o'Shanter* would be given with gusto and at **Leonard Miall**'s 80th birthday party he sang a warm and hilarious self-penned tribute to the tune of *The Red Flag*. It was too much for **Anne Milne**. She walked out muttering I'm not going to stay and listen to that.

Two other amusing stories regularly do the rounds. The first goes that in 1974 Jack sold a 30-acre pasture adjacent to his home and watched curiously as the purchaser pegged out the land in one-sixth acre plots then advertised them for sale making it clear that the price included the cost of a planning application to build a detached house. Minister of the Environment Anthony Crosland advised Sir John that this ruse was not illegal since any such applications could not be pre-judged but of course Green Belt provisions prevailed. Some suspect there's more to this tale than meets the eye but one thing is certain: the pegs remained for many years a memorial to the folly of the fellow who had them staked.

The second story concerns **Karl Lawrence** who recalls getting a glimpse of the security surrounding the PM's pal in the mid-1980s. When his car spluttered to a stop outside Sir John's house, he had no choice but to leave it there and walk home intent on phoning a nearby garage to tow it away for repair. It took him fifteen minutes to get to **Cedar Chase** yet that was time enough for the police to trace his name and address from his car registration number and arrive at his front door ready for trouble. Karl is neither by nature nor stature a threatening fellow but the officers took some convincing. They relaxed only when contact was made with Sir John who confirmed with a smile that Karl presented a risk of no more than a passionate political debate.

Sir John remained for many years on the Association's Council of Management and an active member of The Taplow & Hitcham Royal British Legion. For many years he and his wife Anne invited Poppy Day collectors to a generous thank-you evening at *Hitcham Lodge*. In his last words to them, he said that "bringing to a new generation the awareness of the magnitude of the sacrifices made to preserve our freedoms within democracy was his most worthwhile endeavour". On 4th March next year, 60 locals will travel on two coaches to join 500 family, friends, dignitaries and members of both Houses of Parliament for a Service of Thanksgiving at St Margaret's Church, Westminster. They will hear moving tributes by Sir John's Parliamentary colleague John Gummer and his friend **Sir Terry Wogan**. On the way home, Karl will recall that, although he stepped down as a vice-president of the Society in 1974, Sir John was always willing to provide wise counsel to both it and to the Parish Council....

The Parish Council

The Village Centre / 31st December 1969

Records suggest that Taplow had a parish clerk as far back as the late-18th Century. This implies that a body of locals met regularly to manage church business. By the mid-19th Century **Taplow Parish Council** was also administering parochial care of the poor some time before the 1894 Local Government Act confirmed and defined the secular responsibilities of parish councils in the greater scheme of things. Although the various Town Planning Acts between 1909 and 1947 gave the Council a role in local town planning, few proposals for development found their way onto its agenda for consideration. It rather touched its forelock to Desborough, Astor and Whitlaw and trundled on seemingly in the hope that if it ignored the 1900s they would go away. They didn't.

In the meantime, Taplow simply grew old. Many people had been here for years, left behind when their children moved away to find employment or excitement in the big, wide world or because there was nowhere local to live. The sense of social timewarp was reflected in the fabric. Mains sewers ran under the Valley's spine but cess pits still secretly sprinkled the Village and the Common. The gloom that had descended upon Berry Hill appeared ready to spread when ***Fairey*** left ***The Priory*** and the **Bible College** vacated ***Taplow Hill***. The Victorian school was in urgent need for repair and even more urgent one for children. All the **Reading Room** needed was a little tender loving care but its adjoining **Parish Hall** – still that 'temporary' tin hut of 1911 vintage – was on its last legs.

Clearly Taplow required much more than tinkering. Perhaps the egalitarian examples of the Association and the Society gave the Council confidence to rise to the challenge. Thank Heaven that chairman **Ernest Perkins** and his councillors – including **Jack Martineau**, solicitor **Anthony Paines**, **Eileen Law** and **Anne Young** (née Whitlaw) – had the perception to see what's wrong and the vision and perspicacity to put it right.

Another Formidable Alliance

The Village Centre / 11th October 2006

Local lore tends to think that Eileen and Anne were the leading lights. That's true enough but far from the whole story. Both were staunch Conservatives. Both always thought they knew best. They were social rivals from very different backgrounds – Anne landed, Eileen commercial. Neither was everyone's cup of tea. It was perhaps the greatest achievement of Perkins that these powerful personalities were potent as allies.

By the 1960s, Ernest had moved from ***The Hollies*** to ***Hitcham Close***, next-door to **Jack Page**, and would eventually live at ***Barge Farm***. The committee room at **The Village Centre** bears his name for a very good reason: it was one of the many fruits of his leadership, determination and diplomacy. The old tin **Parish Hall** was demolished to make space for an extension to the Reading Room which accommodated an office for the parish clerk and a kitchen and toilets as well as the committee room. The old school made way for a car park, much to the disappointment of **Harry Hurn** who thought it would have made a fine place to stage concerts, plays and performances like those which excited his youth.

A Law to Herself

Marshmead, Marsh Lane / 11th October 1996

A memorial service is being held today at St Nicolas' Church for Eileen Law, a colourful character with bright red hair and vivid make-up. Her father, a successful London printer and stationer, bought this land at the top of ***Marsh Lane*** and built upon it a grand house called ***Marshmead*** surrounded with paddocks where his daughter could ride and jump her beloved horses. How sad she would be to think that in less than 15 years her home will have been rebuilt with 2,000 egg-laying chickens and an illegal egg packaging and distribution business packed into ***Marshwood Farm*** to the rear. Perhaps it will be some solace that in 2014 an application to build sheds for 40,000 chickens on the northern paddock will be refused.

Eileen Matthews made her name as a young horsewoman in the **Taplow Horse Show**, an event she made her own. In 1963 she married **Frederick Reginald (Rex) Law**, a Justice of the Peace on the Burnham bench – the youngest magistrate ever to be appointed – and President of the Taplow & Hitcham Branch of the Royal British Legion from 1972 until 1978. Together they made a big impression. **Brenda Hickman** remembers Rex as "a Colonel Blimp [who] shouted at people on ponies", which is remarkable given that his wife was always "on ponies". **Sheila Peroni** recalls him being blind in one eye and some saying that – having been first chairman of the Thames Valley Police Authority and sporting the numberplate GBH1 – he would never be stopped by the police.

However it was Rex's wife who had the greater impact. **Sir John Page** will recall that "The Taplow Conservative Committee was reigned over by Eileen Matthews, later Mrs Law, who was on every council and every important committee and whose word was in fact law. She fought every planning application (even for the enlargement of a lavatory window) like a tigress, and it is largely due to her and Anne (Young) that the thin and beautiful Green Belt between Maidenhead and Slough, in which we live, still exists".

Rusty Grant remembers a meeting of the Conservative Association in the 1970s. The most difficult item on the agenda was the menu for a forthcoming dinner at the House of Commons at which Eileen was determined that afterwards they should have not a 'sweet' but a 'savoury'. By the late-1980s the Taplow social scene included extravagant fancy dress parties, often to see in the New Year at ***The Old Rectory*** courtesy of **Sheila & Brian Horton**. It was at one such shindig with a *Great Lovers* theme that **Iris Midlane** first met the "extremely glam" Eileen who was "decked out in oranges". Iris asked who she had come as. Myself, responded Eileen as though it was obvious. She later confided proudly that she never had washed up or cleared up. It seems that she always had people to do such things. That was how she ran the Horse Show, and the Legion too, once she succeeded Rex as branch President. Her energy and willpower made things happen. And only ten days before her death, she still had enough of both left to get up from her bed to entertain 30 Poppy Appeal collectors at *Marshmead*.

Her funeral was a strange affair. It was scheduled for midday at St Mary's (Hitcham). Reverend **Alan Dibden** arrived at ten-thirty to find no grave prepared and the fellow whose job it was still on the other side of Reading. The service went ahead then everyone repaired for refreshment while the gravedigger dug. They returned an hour-and-a-half later feeling in no mood to mourn as the coffin was interred. Her memorial service proceeds in a similar vein.

Riding High

Barge Farm / 29th April 1990

Taplow Horse Show is now the first major event of the equestrian year and biggest one-day show in the country. Last year over 1,000 horses and riders came to Taplow from all over the UK to compete for almost £6,000 (£13,000) in prize money, thanks especially to the sponsorship of *Slough Estates* and to the Guides who volunteered to sell programmes. Fifty classes were held in five rings, each a qualifier for the Royal International Horse Show, the Olympia Horse Show or National Breed Championships. Meanwhile Taplow Horse Show Club has over 200 members who enjoy the annual two-day show at *Marshmead* which involves dressage and showjumping, hunter and cross-country trials – and even gymkhanas, just for fun. Nowadays and for many years Eileen Law has been its heartbeat in concert with **Alan Oliver**, who sets the challenging course, **Madeleine Hewens**, **Joyce Sim** and Miss Smith, who had taught the Princesses Elizabeth and Margaret to ride and by the 1950s ran the riding school on Lower Berry Hill.

The Show has been held at various locations including **Arthur Mewton**'s pasture north of ***Maryfield*** until **Buffins** was built there and now at ***Barge Farm*** courtesy of **Giles Sim**. Over the years, so many of the great British showjumpers have competed at Taplow, from Pat Smythe in the early days through Harvey Smith and his sons Stephen and Robert, David Broome and his sister Liz Edgar and her husband Ted, Michael Whitaker and Alan Oliver to Nick Skelton – and not forgetting Princess Anne who in 1970 rode *Doublet* in the Foxhunter Event watched by her proud mother Queen Elizabeth II. This year the main ring display is the famous Shetland Pony Grand National, sponsored by *Pet Plan* in aid of Great Ormond Street Hospital for Sick Children. Sadly after its fiftieth year the Horse Show will pass with Eileen into history. Although she will leave £3m (£5.9m) to a horse charity, there will be insufficient financial means and nobody with the time, knowledge and determination to continue to organise such an event – which just goes to show that it is her Show. But contrary to what many think, it didn't start out that way....

The First Event

The Paddocks, Crazies Hill / 15th March 2012

Jim Rance smiles to recall coming second in the Children's Trotting Race at the first **Taplow Horse Show & Gymkhana**, then his face clouds a little. I'm a little sad, he says, that people seem to have forgotten it was originally the brainchild of my parents. Florence & **Maurice Rance** invited a few friends to their home, ***The Porches***, in April 1946 to discuss the idea of holding a modest show restricted to local riders in aid of local charities. Enthusiasm for the project exceeded all expectations and on Saturday 7th September 1946 "in delightful surroundings adjoining Taplow Court" a large crowd surrounded the single-ring arena with cars and horse-boxes to provide grandstands (and shelter from occasional showers) from which they watched 150 entrants compete in 14 classes.

Right from the start, remembers Jim, everybody who was anybody wanted to be involved. **Lord Kemsley** accepted dad's invitation to be the event's President and he presented a cup to the Maharaja of Mysore, a very exotic personality. There were three equally eminent Vice-Presidents in **Lord Astor**, Colonel **Lionel Hanbury** and **Lord Courtauld-Thomson** who presented a prize to Pat Moss of Bray for winning the Children's Open Showjumping. Pat also came third in two other events to make a fine start to her career in which she blossomed first as an international showjumper and later as a rally driver, not such a surprising diversion when you consider that her brother was Stirling Moss: one of the greatest motor racing drivers ever.

Jim can't recall if **Eileen Matthews** competed at that first Show. *The Maidenhead Advertiser* of 13th September 1946 confirms her mother presented 12-year-old Pat with a special prize but does not record Eileen being placed in any class. However, it wasn't long before she wasn't only competing but in command, which might be why Maurice stepped out of the limelight.

A Chip off the Block

Priory Cottage, Rectory Road / 23rd May 2012

Selina Whitlaw's son Charles Francis Whitlaw married Gwendoline in 1911. She gave him two children, Francis and Anne [*see Appendix 1, Tree 19*]. Selina had always been a strong woman in a man's world. Perhaps she saw herself in her granddaughter. In 1938, just two years before her death and comfortable in the knowledge that Francis would inherit ***Springfield***, she drafted her will to ensure that three riverside properties – ***Broomcroft***, ***The Red House*** and ***Harefield*** – would pass on her son's death to Anne.

Selina wasn't wrong. **Anne Whitlaw** had her grandmother's steely determination to have things her way. During the Second War – during which ***Amerden House*** saw service as a children's home – Anne was commissioned into the Auxiliary Territorial Service at Bletchley Park doing secret stuff she never revealed. In 1945 she was in Venice to help Jewish refugees get to what would become Israel. It was there she met **Dorrien Young**, a dashing intelligence officer – essentially a 'diplomatic soldier' – who was working with the Americans to identify, arrest and convict Italian war criminals. He would shortly be appointed Allied Commander in Vienna before becoming Defence Attaché at the British Embassy in Moscow.

Dorrien was 20 years her senior but Anne married the spy who loved her in 1947. They had the pick of the Whitlaw properties, chose *The Red House* and punctuated his travels with two sons, John and Allen. Having been exiled from Taplow by his mother or by choice (depending on which story you hear first), Anne's father finally passed away in 1955 after living his last years with her. His son-in-law survived him by little more than four years. Dorrien was 50 when he died of a stroke on the way to the Foreign Office. The Martineaus encouraged Anne to make a fresh start by becoming a Parish Councillor and then, when they left for Suffolk in 1964, by leasing ***Old Lodge*** from them. Anne went on to be both a District and County Councillor and also a Justice of the Peace. This gave her the platform to perform. She and her cohorts surprised the diligent architect **Tony Hickman** with how they virtually "bucked planning law" to push for permissions to build a "proper mix" of housing in and around the Village.

As Anne's star rose so that of her brother **Francis Whitlaw** was a little eclipsed. He didn't seem to mind too much and perhaps a lower profile wasn't such a bad strategy, at least not for him. The sales of *Springfield* and ***Stockwells*** set him up comfortably enough for him to live quietly with his wife Annette in ***Springfield Cottage***, then later in a bungalow behind it with his second wife Phoebe. Some tongues wagged that he had done alright for himself. Most saw it as a reasonable realisation of assets in the context of a bigger picture in which Taplow was rejuvenated without losing its character.

Life As We Know It

Heartbeat

Eyes of a Child – Felicity Humphreys, Freya Molony, Sophie Greenham, Grace Dixon & Ariana Aghoghovbia

St Nicolas' School – 23rd April 2012

Felicity thinks the **Village Green** is the heart of Taplow. She says the scenery is beautiful and there is always something to do with the ox roast in the summer and the Remembrance Parade and the Christmas tree in the winter. Freya and Sophie agree that the Green is the best thing about Taplow. Freya is looking forward to after school when she will play there with her schoolfriends. It makes Sophie feel she is truly part of the community. Grace says it is very vast and a nice clean place to have picnics and carols. Ariana likes interacting with her friends, rolling around on the grass and doing cartwheels.

Eyes of a Child – Kai Cooper, Theo Wayland-Smith, Jamie Ashford, Edward Bennett & Andrew Walker

St Nicolas' School – 23rd April 2012

Kai, Theo and Jamie can't wait to play football on the Green. Edward thinks it is just wonderful to have such a very big space to play on and run around, to sit and relax, to just be calm and free, and to watch and know nature and it is just wonderful. Andrew loves the grass and the fresh air and all the nature and greenery on the Green and the leaves on the trees whooshing in the wind and running so the air goes on his face like paper.

Eyes of a Child – Ciara Williams, Alex Bainbridge, Chloe Plummer, Lucinda Plummer & Willow Kerr

St Nicolas' School – 23rd April 2012

When it is covered in dew, Ciara thinks the Green looks sparkly and magical, and in winter snow it looks like a sheet of white icing. Alex gets a warm feeling inside to see everyone playing there and having fun; the green grass and the buttercups in the summer make him feel happy. Chloe feels the same about all the different coloured flowers in the summer and the huge Christmas tree with lots of fairy lights every winter. Her sister Lucinda loves all the mysterious and weird adventures they have on the Green with their friends Alex, Freya, Sophie, Nicola Mayo and Keira Smales. Willow adds that it is so fun playing on the Green and seeing children have lots of fun.

Eyes of a Child – George Pole, Katie Wrennall, Anna Shanu-Wilson, Jessica Cart, Serena Protopapadakis & Lucy Hill

St Nicolas' School – 23rd April 2012

George, Katie, Anna, Jessica and almost half the children are voting for the Green as their favourite place in Taplow. All of them will grow up with this cherished picture of childhood sharply in their mind. But of course, as Serena says, it's not the School's green, it's the villagers' green to share. Lucy thinks it is lots of years old. At 9-years-old, she can be forgiven for having no idea it hasn't always been like this....

Eyes of a Child – Hurn's Turn

Pater Noster Farmyard – 23rd April 1937

Harry Hurn and his pal **Mike Good** really shouldn't be here. They are on their way to the church where **Percy Goulden** will rehearse the choir for the Good Friday service. But boys will be boys and Harry reckons half the fun of watching the pigs rooting in the mud is that the Reverend **Francis Phillips** thinks them disgusting. Mike chuckles that it's not half as disgusting as at harvest time when Mrs Dykes brings in the steam engine and threshing machines. The racket they make sends rivers of rats running out of the pigsties, barns and briars all over everywhere. That puts the shakes up his surplice.

The boys are leaning over the school wall looking into what was the *Pater Noster* pasture. That means *Our Father*, says Mike. Was it called that because it's across the way from the new church? No, says Harry, the name goes way back. It has always been glebe land – owned by the Church to provide for 'the living' of the Rector – so maybe that's why. The Briginshaws of ***Rectory Farm*** were using it as a farmyard by the time St Nicholas moved east in 1828. It must be more than 60 years since the Websters of ***Hill Farm*** took it over and now their lease has passed to Mrs Dykes. Harry points to where the almond tree by the farmyard gate rises above the long barn. That flowered well this year. Perhaps we'll get to pinch a few pocketfuls of nuts come the autumn. Yes, laughs Mike. Perhaps we'll find a way to break them open without smashing them to pulp like we did last year.

Mike's father Harry is the son of Lord Desborough's former butler **Barrett Good**, now a 76-year-old widower but still estate manager at **Taplow Court**. Harry will step into his father's shoes and pass them eventually to Mike in the days when ***Plessey*** needs a safe pair of hands to look after the place. What will he think to see much of the ground floor of the Desborough home converted to a staff social club complete with a bar and bar billiard tables? In the early-1970s the teenage **David Grout** will be oblivious to its halcyon heyday as he earns a few bob pocket-money as the club's cleaner and general dogsbody.

Eyes of a Child – Ginny Miall

Pater Noster Farmyard – 23rd August 1956

The hay bales piled high in the biggest barn make a fantastic castle to burrow within, climb upon and leap from onto the deep bed of straw. Ginny's brothers are enjoying the company of Dale and Sasha of ***The Hollies***, daughters of **Ernest Perkins**. **Roger** reckons they're "not bad for girls" and **Tristan** will confide that "the Perkins sisters looked good on horses and off them too" but right now they all have something else to worry about in the shape of **Arthur Mewton**. It's the same old story. The farmer fears for his store of winter fodder for Hill Farm. The children are after adventure. Never the twain shall meet. The youngsters scarper behind the gate of *The Hollies* and burst into fits of giggles.

A Whole New World

St Nicolas' School / 31st December 1971

The 1960s were mad. Taplow was a nightmare of demolishing that, building this and digging big holes in the road. **Helen & Aleyn Grellier** survived to tell the tale....

Aleyn hails from Oxford where he worked as a journalist and editor on newspapers and magazines – including a prestige promotional magazine for the *British Motor Corporation* – before becoming a distributor of *Wolsesley* cars. Helen is a teacher, the daughter of the Archbishop of York's chauffeur and proud of being descended from a Lancastrian cotton mills family. They came in 1957 to live at ***Victoria Cottage*** (High Street), formerly the home of schoolmaster, verger and parish clerk **Walter Leyster** and later of **Yvonne & Frank Green**. They found to their surprise that it was unnecessary to have their cesspit emptied because its contents were consumed by the flourishing pear tree in the garden of *The Porches*. They were not amused when the tree was cut down and they had to empty the cesspit every two months. However this wasn't the most dramatic change in Helen's life....

Taplow School / 6th June 1959

The roll rose recently from 93 pupils to 101, roughly the number it has been since 1945 when this ceased to be an all-age school. The 5-to-11-year-olds on the register include well-known local family names such as Bidgood, Bunce, Elliot, Elsey, Grellier, Hales, Hocking, Judge, Miall, Moon, Shuker and Stedman.

As the 47th Rector, the Reverend **Christopher Hare** is Chairman of the managing board which comprises District Nurse **Helen Burley**, Dr Harold Jacques, **Jack Martineau**, **Alexander Sim** and **Victor Williams**. Following Norman Holbrook's six-year tenure and Richard Poole's one-term secondment, they appointed Albert Goodman headmaster as in January. He teaches the upper juniors, the long-serving Mrs Barnett the lower juniors, Mrs McLaughlin the older infants and former 'dinner lady' Mrs Ford the younger ones. Now Mrs Thorne does the dinners, helped by two others. Megan Tolhurst is the visiting music teacher. The secretary Mrs Farrington works a few hours each week in the Reading Room where she keeps the school paperwork (in a single filing cabinet and a pile of boxes), an old-fashioned typewriter and – only since last October – a telephone.

The school's main entrance is at the top of the stairway from the High Street. To the left, the playground is bounded to the south by the Reading Room and to the west by the Parish Room, the 'tin hut' which is used for school meals and the infants' classes during the day and for the 2nd Taplow & Hitcham Guides and Brownies in the evenings. The 1870 classroom is on the right; a folding wooden partition divides the two older classes which enter from the far end. The 1848 and 1854 classrooms are straight ahead and, beyond them, the gabled schoolmaster's house with its charming garden. Classroom windows are set high for maximum light and minimum distraction: no chance for pupils to watch the world go by. The elderly stoves are useful for melting frozen milk in winter but less so for keeping the children warm. Even with your eyes closed, you'd know you're at school. The smell is unmistakable: a rather sickly mix of disinfectant, floor polish, chalk, school milk and wet children stewed to imperfection by perennial problems of ventilation, heat and damp. That's the way it has been for generations. And yet in six years its days will be done.

It has been clear for some time that a new school was required since it would be difficult, expensive and probably impossible to repair the physically decaying and out-dated old buildings. Funding is the problem. The managing board opted for aided status in order that costs and responsibilities will be shared between the board, the Diocese of Oxford and the Department of Education. A house will be built for the headmaster in the hope of attracting the best applicants and, after three years of negotiations begun by Jack Martineau, Victor Williams is pleased to report that Viscountess **Imogen Gage** is "desirous of making over to the school managers a playing field for the school in memory of (her father) **Lord Desborough** by a deed of gift". At the end of the year, the board will be pleased with the Diocesan Inspector's conclusion that "All is well at Taplow".

St Nicolas' School / 6th June 1964

As a young mother teaching part-time at first Taplow School and then at the CRCMH School, Helen was aware of but not party to all the talk around tables, all the applications, persuading and manoeuvring that was going on. But if anyone doubted the purpose of Perkins and pals, they should see what's happening today. Taplow will never be the same again....

The Right Reverend **Robert Hay**, Suffragan Bishop of Buckingham, is joined by Reverend Hare, his successor as Rector of Taplow, to lay a foundation stone for the new Church of England primary school for 5-to-11-year-olds. Debates continue about its size and detailed design but, eventually, the Diocese, the Parish Council and the generosity of **Percy Goulden** will enable £44,000

(£1.78m) to be invested in a bigger school at the expense Mr Goodman's dream of a swimming pool. Even now, many think there won't be enough children to fill it. They reckon without the new blood that will arrive once the sewers are complete. Works began last year and will not be finished until next. Helen's mini-van won't be the only vehicle to suffer from the bumps and ridges of the unfinished business.

Something's Burning – School's Out

St Nicolas' School / 19th October 1965

Everyone was excited ten days ago when the new school was consecrated by the Right Reverend Harry Carpenter, Bishop of Oxford, and opened by Anthony Chenevix-Trench, Master of Eton College. Nobody needed the excitement that has just begun. It is just after seven in the evening. Smoke is billowing from the school. **Aleyn Grellier** has called the fire brigade and alerted new headmaster Colin Blackwell and his deputy, former acting head Mary Alexander, who has lived with her husband Francis at ***The Porches*** while teaching at the old school since 1960.

The fire began in the chair store off the assembly hall. Mr Blackwell braves the smoke to get across the hall to the office where he switches off the gas and electricity supplies before escaping through the window. Twelve firemen wearing breathing apparatus take 50 minutes to extinguish the blaze. Two dozen chairs, a piano and the hall's fibre-glass ceiling have all been badly damaged. The news will spread quicker than the flames. Only 24 of 150 children will turn up tomorrow to be sent home. Most pupils will be given work to do at home on Thursday and Friday while the rest are taught in the Reading Room. The half-term break will be brought forward a week so the school can be made safe. It will reopen in two weeks but it will be another three months before repairs and renovations are completed.

The influx of children to **Cedar Chase** and **Buffins** will increase the register to 214 pupils within a year of Edmund Hancock succeeding as headmaster in 1968. Soon after Helen Grellier begins 22 years as headmistress in 1971, there will be pressure for St Nicolas' to become an infants' school but, in 1973, a parent poll and the efforts of County Councillor **Anne Young** will secure its status as a 'Combined School'. By then, Taplow will have a new heart....

The Heart of Taplow

The Village Green – 23rd April 1987

A mother is bringing her young son to the newly-founded playgroup in **The Village Centre**. She stops outside *The Perkins Room* to admire the view downhill. It could have been so different. This could have been a small housing estate. Instead at not quite 20-years-old, it is surely one of the youngest greens of any vintage village in the country.

The deliberations about where to put the new school were complicated. One option was Grange Meadow, south of ***Hitcham Grange***. Buffins was another. **Pater Noster** was preferred for its easier access. Initially the idea was to build the school in its south-east corner, opposite the church. Second thoughts occurred when Lady Gage gifted the school playing field, which is why it was sited in the opposite, uphill corner to the west of the old school. The question remained: what about the farmyard in lower Pater Noster? Eton RDC was persuaded by its councillors Anne Young and **Eileen Matthews** to offer £50 (£1,880) plus costs to purchase the smaller, western portion from the estate of the recently deceased **Arthur Mewton**. Meanwhile the larger, eastern portion was sold to ***Bunce Brothers*** of Burnham with planning permission to build five houses. There the matter rested for three years during which construction of the new school began, various developments doubled the population in the Village already "very deficient in open space" and **Victor Williams** tried to oil the wheels of a deal....

On behalf of the Parish Council, **Ernest Perkins** returned to Eton RDC in June 1965 with the proposal that the farmyard might be made an open space while a larger council estate could be built at Buffins. It seemed touch-and-go when an exhibition in the Reading Room attracted just one visitor but the children of today and tomorrow can be thankful that these efforts succeeded in persuading a rethink that so nearly went wrong when the Bunce brothers – almost certainly descendants of **Charlie Bunce**, the late-19th Century *Hill Farm* farmhand – threatened to begin construction unless it received £15,000 (£534,000) plus costs for its land by 31st January 1966. With a 'following wind' of a £5,000 (£178,000) grant from Buckinghamshire County Council, the RDC acceded to this demand with just 14 days to spare.

At some point in these years of uncertainty, **Michael Bayley** was commissioned to survey the old barns in the farmyard and came to suspect that trusses from the 12th Century St Nicholas' Church may have found their way into one of them. He was dismayed when it mysteriously burnt to the ground. All but one of the remaining barns was demolished and the Parish Council rejected a tender of £5,000 to create a proper green because it could afford just £85 (£1,400) to have local farmer **John Shepherd** rake the ground roughly and sow grass seed. The following year the Council acquired the freehold of the **Reading Room**, the old tin **Parish Room** and the old school. The latter was demolished to create a car park. The Parish Room was repaired to prolong its life until 1974 when work began to replace it with an extension to the Reading Room which added a committee room, kitchen, toilets and clerk's office. The transformation is almost complete. All that remains to be done now is hang the curtains and draw them to hide from all the complaints about the thin soil on the Green, its sprinkling of clinker, cinder and bricks and how the grass browns off at the first sign of hot weather because, having moved bureaucratic mountains to create it, the Council didn't have the cash to do the job properly. Fortunately in 2000 it will persuade **SBDC** to renovate the remaining barn.

Beginnings

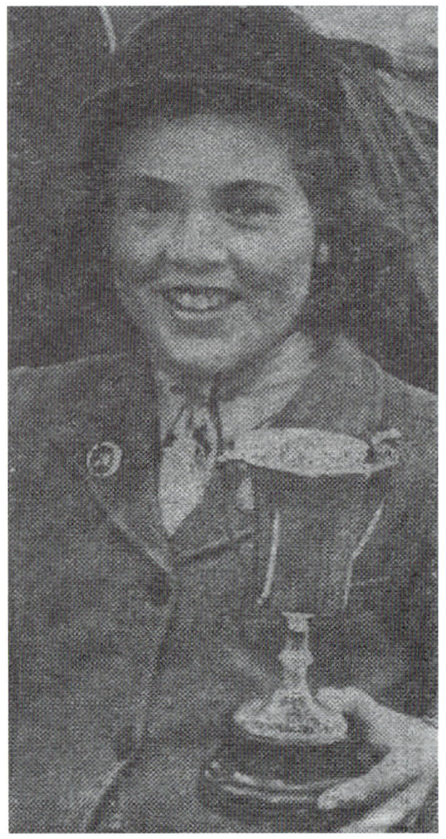

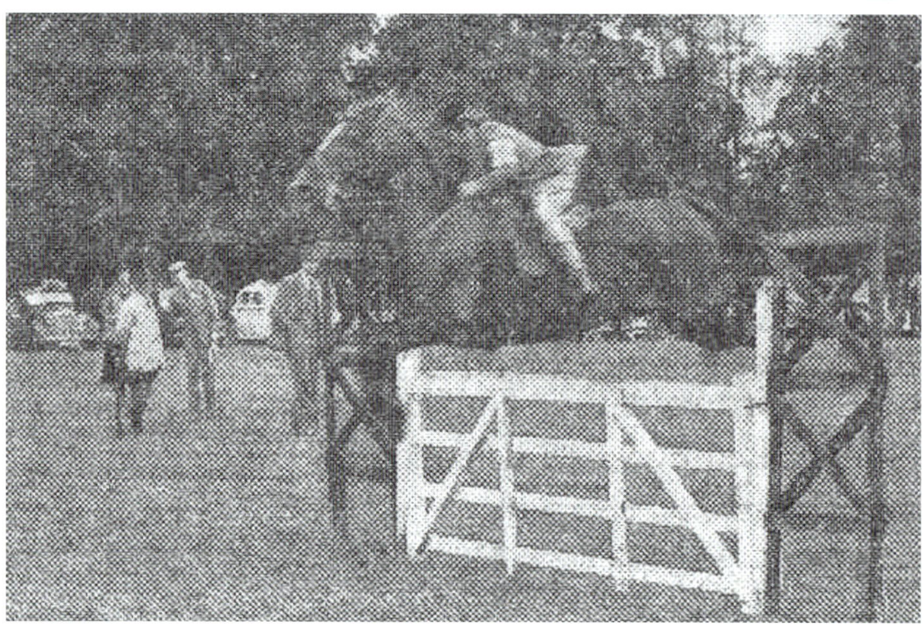

The first Taplow Horse Show & Gymkhana:
Pat Moss (12) rides *Hairpin* to victory in the Children's Open and shows off the trophy presented to her by Lord Courtauld / 1946

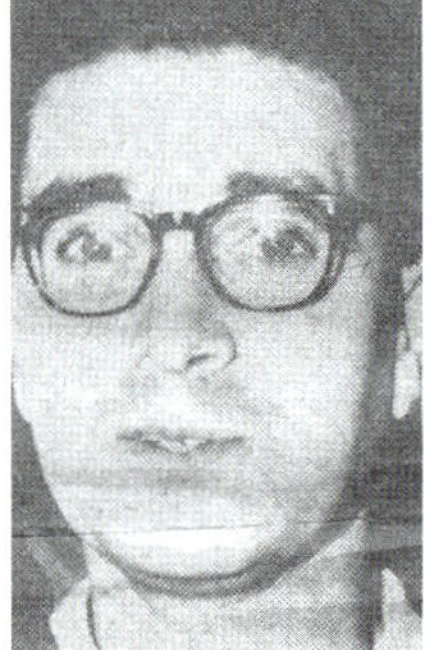

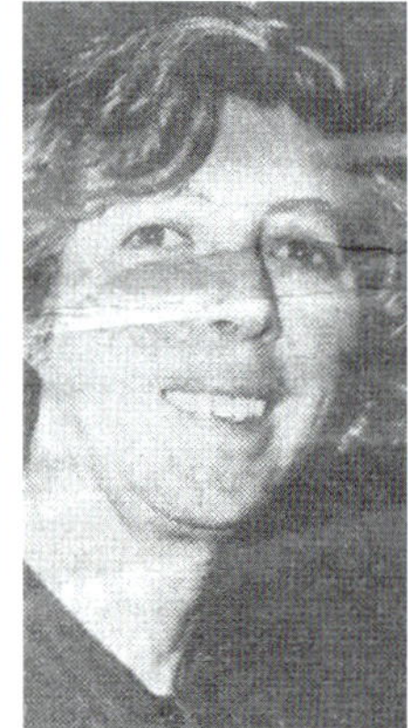

Colin Blackwell, the first Headmaster of St Nicolas School, and his Deputy Mary Alexander / 1965

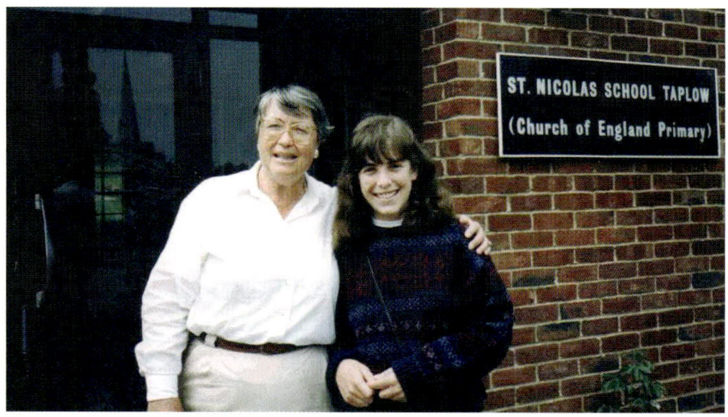

Helen Grellier with a former pupil / 1988

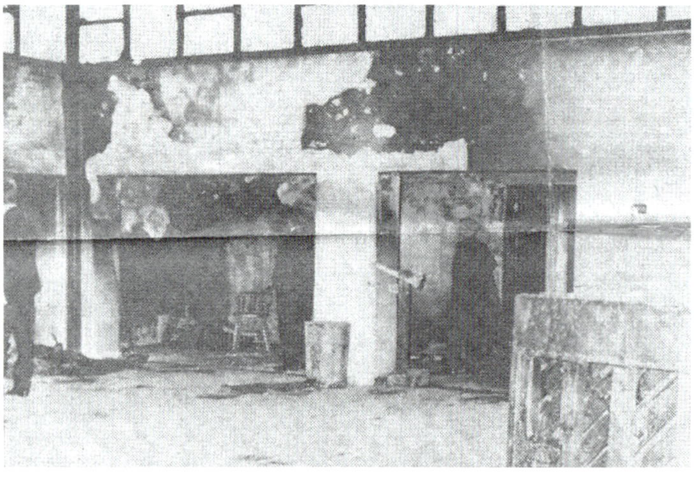

Something's burned: the school hall, after the fire / 1965

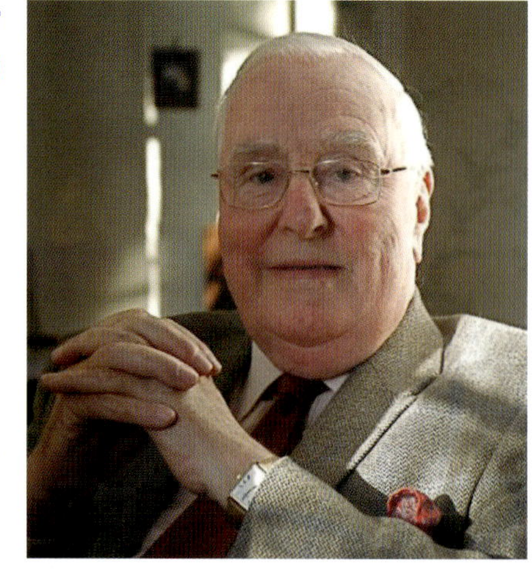

Aleyn Grellier / 2010

Sports Day:
Catherine Oliver shares out PTA lollies / 2009

St Nicolas goes Olympic / 2012

Summer Fete: Maypole Dancing, a tuneful tangle / 2009

Leavers / 2013

Girls – Phoebe Anderson, Ciara Williams, Ronia Falana, Rosie Middleton, Polly Bennett, Lily Messenger, Ariana Aghoghovbia, Willow Kerr, Freya Molony, Hannah Irwin, Nicola Mayo, Lyra Cherry, Chloe Plummer, Esme Maree, Lucinda Plummer, Olivia Wrennall, Hannah Chapman, Sophie Greenham & Keira Smales
Boys – Archie Norman, George Green, Joe Pontin, Renzo Casale, Edward Bennett, Monty Keates, Joshua Stow, Alex Bainbridge, Max Stone, Robbie Lawrence, Timothy Pretty & Arthur Cassells
with Mr Stuart Cook & Kai Cooper relaxing

The Heart of Taplow

The Village Green, our favourite place – Emily Costello & Katie Harris / 2012

The Village Green

For many years, Pater Noster meadow saw service as a farmyard with a colony of barns before becoming one of England's youngest village greens in 1966 / 2012

The Green in white / 2010

The Green in Spring / 2012

Eyes of a Child – Lily Messenger, Willow Kerr, Esme Maree & Eleanor Bunce

St Nicolas' School – 23rd April 2012

Lily likes the school because it gives her lots of history. She says it has been here for centuries even though it has been transferred from the car park to the top of the Village Green, so that makes me feel proud. Willow agrees: they did that to give the school a good view. Esme reckons it's an awesome school because I have really nice friends and teachers. Eleanor likes the Green because of the really fun events held there. Does she know that her forebears had other ideas?

Eyes of a Child – Joshua Stow, Renzo Casale, Arthur Herman-Heynes & Ronia Falana

St Nicolas' School – 23rd April 2012

Joshua reckons St Nic's has been in Taplow for years on end – that includes Victorian times. It's an eco-friendly school now a plastic bottle greenhouse is being built using recycled *Coke* bottles collected by the students. Many of the resources are brilliant such as the computers in the ICT suite. Renzo thinks the equipment is very good. He likes maths, which isn't too hard, PE is active and in science he gets to do experiments. Arthur says: I enjoy going to school to get educated so I can get a good job and when I think about school I realise how lucky we are even to have school. Yes, says Ronia, the teachers and good friends I've got are really friendly and help you when you're sad. The main reason Lily likes school is because of the wonderful good-natured people in the Village who make her feel part of the community.

Eyes of a Child – Lyra Cherry, Joe Pontin, Archie Norman & Freya Molony

St Nicolas' School – 23rd April 2012

Lyra says the school field is her favourite part of Taplow. It's big and luscious and full of nature. The field can be used for sport. It has different tracks and a long jump. It's perfect for events like sports day. Also every year it's where we practice for the Stoat Podges race (an athletic competition in Stoke Poges). And it's the perfect place for nature from the small shrubs and bushes to the tall majestic trees. There are places where in the summer you can watch spellbound as dragonflies hover over the blackberry bush before disappearing. And it's a shortcut to the cricket club, a way of connecting it directly to the heart of Taplow. It's a wonderful place for everyone to enjoy and that's why the field is my favourite place in Taplow.

Joe agrees: there is so much space you can run and run also there's so much fun games you can play with a few people and a ball. Some of the class just walk around talking, says Archie, but the rest play games. I adore the field when me and my friends can play football, we always have a laugh and joke around. Freya likes having her lunch there because there's lots of room and the boys can play football without hitting the girls with the ball. Archie says: my second favourite thing about Taplow is my school because all the teachers are really friendly, nice, caring and good at teaching, especially maths. I also like the school because all my friends here are really funny and kind. The school will help me get a good future.

About Grout – Boys Being Boys

St Nicolas' School / 23rd October 1967

David Grout and **Mike Ness** started at the old school and moved to the new one. They are chuffed little chappies for having circled the school field without touching the ground. The place is ringed in tall elms. If you're careful, says David, you can climb out on the branches until they sag enough for you to swing onto the next tree or onto the roof of the old pavilion. And nobody's snitched to Mrs Alexander. Unfortunately for nine-year-old David his next trick won't escape her attention. He will jump on a dumper truck, release the handbrake and steer it across the school playground straight into her bad books, her very bad books, so bad that he will be asked to leave St Nic's.

Eyes of a Child – Best Friends: Jamie Ashford & Theo Wayland-Smith

St Nicolas' School / 23rd April 2012

Jamie lives at N° 4 **Elm View**. He says it is in the centre of Taplow Village. I and my friends play 'footy' after school. I like to scooter around the block. My best friend Theo, he lives just down the road. Theo is always coming around my house and we play *Lego* or we play on the *Wii*. Theo is always there for me. Last year I got a dog and Taplow is great for walking dogs. Our dog is called Tilly. All my friends have a dog as well. At the back of our garden is a massive horse field, from our garden we can get into the vicar's garden. He is the vicar of St Nicolas' Church. Taplow is a nice environment to live in, even though we are near Maidenhead and Slough.

Theo lives at ***Wellbank Cottage***. He loves the fact that there are loads of friends in Taplow and you get to play with them on Taplow's local space. You meet most of your friends for example at Cubs that is done in the Village Hall and **Taplow United** where most of my friends go. All the friends I've met are all very nice and kind, a lot of my friends go on the Green after school. We would play football or climb on the trees and play *Man Hunt* and usually after that my best friend would come round called Jamie. We would play football or play on the *PS3* or sometimes we would climb my playhouse and jump off the roof into the bush and get scratched badly. Then we would have dinner then after dinner Jamie would go home then I would go to bed. Then the next morning I would see all my friends walking up to school and if I was early I would play on the playground with all my friends. Then I would have my lessons and then I would play on the Green with all my friends again.

Eyes of a Child – Best Friends: Rebecca & Eleanor Jeffries and Stephanie & Charlotte Prestidge

The High Street / 8th January 2003

Snow is falling heavily. This is what they have all been waiting for. Rebecca & Eleanor live at ***Pax Cottage*** right on the Green, or should that be 'the White'? Their friends Stephanie & Charlotte don't have far to come, only from ***Old Lodge*** across the road. The girls have had such a good time building snowmen with noses like their dads. Now, what next? It is pretty spectacular. They start to roll their snowball at the top of the High Street. Halfway down the hill it's so big it gets stuck between a parked car outside ***Number Three*** and the hedge to *Pax Cottage*. They run inside giggling. It is only later that their fathers **Paul Jeffries** and **John Prestidge** realise they had better break up the blockage their daughters have created.

Taking Control – The Parish Plan

The Village Centre / 29th March 2005

There have been various attempts to establish a framework for development control. Overall responsibility passed from Eton Rural District Council via Beaconsfield District Council (1974) to South Bucks District Council (1980) which eventually established a Local Plan in 1989 and replaced it with another ten years later. Some thought Taplow should seek to influence decisions by having its own Parish Design Statement. Others didn't. The wind changed. A Government directive required the production of Parish Plans as the 'bedrock' of Local Development Frameworks. It was time to call for Kennedy....

John Kennedy is a Doctor of Chemistry. He joined *ICI Fibres* in 1954 to work in the development, marketing and sales of polyester fibres including *Crimplene*. After four years in the USA, he and Brenda decided their children needed an English education. They returned home in 1970 for John to begin 29 years with *Trendtex International* in Maidenhead and the rest of their lives at what became ***Olympia House***, a modern home on River Road built on land acquired from ***Broomcroft*** and named after *Olympia Mills*, the company John had been with in America. **Eva Lipman** describes him as someone with strong opinions who gets things done. He has for many years supported *Padstones*, a local charity which helps homeless youngsters.

John began an eight-year stint as a Parish Councillor in 1975. Halfway through this period he succeeded **Eileen Law** as Taplow's District Councillor and served for 24 years during which he held office as chairman of many committees, including the Housing Committee which privatised the housing stock, and eventually of SBDC itself. His retirement as District Councillor in 2003 was perfectly timed for him to be invited to chair a Parish Plan Steering Group "to identify key facilities and services, set out problems that need to be tackled and demonstrate how distinctive character and features can be preserved". Consultation has been wide and extensive with subcommittees, questionnaires, an exhibition and meetings which **John Hanford** thought "depressing [for the] negative nature [of] the Canutes [who] wish to turn back the tide of change [and] the Ostriches who think everything can remain as it is now". Fortunately the diligent and perceptive analysis and significant contributions of Parish Councillor **Mary Trevallion** and her husband **Bernard**, former Professor of Planning at the Kwame Nkrumah University of Science & Technology in Ghana, have made sense of it all and the Parish Council has this evening unanimously agreed Taplow's Parish Plan. It will be the first such plan to be submitted to SBDC.

Despite being quickly commended as a model for others, the Parish Plan will lay dormant during two years of cogitation before being adopted as an 'Advisory' document to the revised Local Plan in 2007 and eventually to the SBDC Core Strategy in 2011 and the National Planning Policy Framework in 2012.

The Heart of Oak

St John's Square, Eton – 23rd April 2012

The one visitor to the 1965 Village Green exhibition was **George Milne**. **Ernest Perkins** saw in this former Royal Navy Lieutenant Commander a potential new recruit to the Council. George served for the best part of four decades. He is 95 now and alone but content. He recalls how he and **Anne Young** "grew together" over time as fellow Parish Councillors and adds with a shy smile that he wishes he had "plucked up the courage sooner" to propose. They settled at *Broomcroft* and forged their own formidable alliance as both served the Parish with distinction: Anne with passion if a little proprietorially, George with a lower profile but no less perception or diligence.

George was born in Warrington, the son of a Lancashire lass and an industrial chemist with *St Helen's Cable & Rubber Co Ltd* which soon relocated to Slough Trading Estate. His father died in a road accident when George was 13 and, having been educated at Slough Grammar School, the young fellow joined the Royal Navy as an 18-year-old midshipman in 1943. He served during the Second War on Atlantic convoys, on minesweepers in the Channel and later in the Mediterranean where, as a Sub-Lieutenant on *HMS Rowena* in 1945, he tried to keep out of Palestine the very Jewish refuges that his future wife was trying to send there from Venice. He retired from the RN in 1965 to care for his mother at ***Ryslaw*** in Ellington Road and commuted to executive positions at the British Institute of Management in the days when management was desperately trying to modernise. George confides that he and **Francis Whitlaw** of ***Springfield Cottage*** were typically English commuters. If their eyes met, they would exchange nods but not much more, not even after they became brothers-in-law in 1976.

The rest is (local) history, which is why nowadays everyone sees George as a pillar of the community, not least for serving many years as a Parish Councillor, a Parochial Church Councillor, a churchwarden and Chairman of the Taplow & Hitcham branch of the Royal British Legion from 1969 until 1986. Few know that on 3rd October 1952 he was an official witness to an earth-shattering event: the first British nuclear test in the Montebello Islands off Western Australia. As a Lieutenant-Commander aboard *HMS Tracker*, he turned his back to the blast and shut his eyes yet still "saw the flash". He watched as the awesome mushroom cloud billowed and the impact rushed towards his ship. Instinctively he steadied himself to take the 'hit' and thought little more of it until the early-1960s, when he was stationed on Clydeside as a military adviser to a team planning how the UK might survive an atom bomb. It was only then that he began to understand the potential effects of nuclear radiation. He smiles to wonder if his exposure might have taken years off his life or whether it added the twinkle in his eye that appealed to Anne.

A Different Kettle

Farm View, Rectory Road – 23rd April 2013

The rise of supermarkets and demise of elite clients like the Astors was a deadly combination for Jack Saunders the butcher, who died in 1969. Nobody remembers the surname of his live-in butcher Harry who struggled on next door until perhaps early-1971 and both his shop and the one in Maidenhead made their last appearance in the 1970 telephone directory. Nobody can recall when Harry's home adopted its imaginative new name – ***The Cottage*** – which was expanded into the shop and then extended in the late-1980s with a garage and room over by Rosalie & Geoff Ideson, he an art teacher and skilled amateur potter who had his workshop and kiln in the erstwhile abattoir.

Their neighbours here were **Gladys & Leslie Kettle**. Few can recall much about Leslie – **Alistair Forsyth** thinks he might have been a former showbiz organist then something with *Woolworth's* – yet everyone has a tale to tell about his wife. Gladys was a different kettle of fish: a longstanding secretary of the local Conservative Party, a staunch supporter of the *Darby & Joan Club* and a great character who could always be relied upon to keep Leslie in the shade by saying exactly what was on her mind.

John Kennedy believes Gladys may have been in sales. She certainly used a rather forceful sales technique to recruit new members for the Conservative Party. In Rectory Road alone she signed up 57 people who probably decided it was the only way to make her go away. She would attend church regularly not because of her faith but in order to see and be seen. **Alan Dibden** adds that, as she approached the communion rail, Gladys would mutter to Gillian Dibden in the choir "Do you want a drink after?" As is often the way with those who are a little deaf, these mutterings never had the intended confidentiality. When it was pointed out that silence would be prudent, Gladys would stand still to catch Gillian's eye before miming an invitation to take a tipple.

Some suspect she liked to shock. Alistair recalls **Dick Nutt**'s 60th birthday party at ***Lea Rig*** when the host proposed a toast to his father who had left him enough money to pay for the party. Everyone raised their glasses to chorus "Dick's dad". In the silence that followed, Gladys held her drink aloft, loudly transposed the words of the toast and drained her glass. **George Milne** believes she was much too proper to do such a thing, and yet when recruiting for the party she knocked on his door at ***Priory Cottage*** to ask bluntly if he would like to meet the member, meaning the local MP.

Gladys lived to be 95 and was equally memorable in death. Her funeral in 1994 was set for the day before a big wedding. The happy couple wanted to have St Nicolas' Church decked with flowers costing £25,000 (£42,000). That's alright, thought Alan, as long as the florists can complete their job before the funeral. It was only when mourners arrived to find blooms everywhere that someone whispered Gladys had stipulated "no flowers" in her will. He hopes she would've seen the funny side.

Up on the Hill

Being Connected

Springfield Cottage / 6th June 1965

The new sewers are already working some kind of magic. The wind of change is blowing strong. It began in the late-1950s when ***Guildersfield*** was split into four apartments, William Barton arrived at ***Pan's Place*** and Thomas Hardwick settled in what had been the garden of ***Hill House*** at ***The Old Malt House*** (Rectory Road) which isn't old, was never a malt house and is not noted as being the site of one.

Nothing now remains of ***Springfield*** except *Springfield Cottage* which preceded it. The grounds had become overgrown as it deteriorated to be a derelict shell occupied by a party of tramps. Despite often being high on methylated spirits these colourful neighbours weren't evicted until females joined the party. Or was it because one chap died, possibly pickled by raw alcohol? Either way the mansion has been demolished and replaced by seven modern detached houses. One retains the name *Springfield House* but don't be confused. The original wasn't hidden in the north-west corner of the estate behind a gate; it stood with proud confidence on the Berry Hill frontage.

Across the road are eight more new detached dwellings. ***Eriska*** is home to James Niven; it faces **Rectory Road** from the northern portion of **Carkins**, the former pasture where ***Taplow House*** grazed its cattle. Three of the homes in **Saxon Gardens** – those in the southern portion of Carkins – are forbidden to build even a garden shed against their western fence in case somebody decides to widen **Berry Hill**. Two of the others fit snugly into the former walled garden of ***Taplow Hill***, which was sold by Edgar Clarke of the *All Nations Bible College* in 1959.

Saxon Gardens / 6th June 1965

John Shilton steers his brand new *Bentley* carefully down the drive from Saxon Gardens to the former ***Taplow House*** kitchen garden and cattle briar. Once peach trees lined the sunny wall to the left and the whitewash on the north-facing wall to the right recalls where gardeners' bothies huddled in the shade. Now in an uncanny repetition of events a century ago on the other side of the wall, the garden is being levelled with tons of topsoil and ***Hiltons***, his brand new luxury home, is being built with some of the £50,000 (£675,000) the lucky man has won on the football pools. He'll also invest in Baylis Lido in Slough only to learn he isn't so lucky. His wife will decide Taplow is too quiet, take their children and leave him to rattle around alone until he sells *Hiltons* in 1968 to **Eva & Max Lipman**. They will rename it ***Upper Bumbles*** and set about a tasteful renovation of house and garden which will include converting the briar as Max's office.

These changes will be small beer compared to what else is afoot. The biggest will be at **Buffins** where next year the close on which **Taplow Horse Show** was held and the three ***Little Coldgrove Cottages*** will make way for **Eton RDC**'s estate of 41 houses. After four years of marriage **Mary & Anthony Harding** will be able to leave his parents' home at ***Caversham*** in **Marsh Lane** to settle in at N° 15 (which they will eventually swap for N° 33). ***Stockwells*** (the mansion) has already been replaced by 12 houses in Stockwells (a cul-de-sac of three neo-Georgian terraces) and soon *Taplow Hill* will be succeeded by 24 houses at **Cedar Chase** and ***The Priory*** by 12 at ***Wellbank*** next to the new, much grander ***Priory Cottage*** just built for **Madeleine & Jack Hewens**, lately of ***Chungates*** in Ellington Road. Jack grew up across the road at ***The Laurels*** and has now inherited his father Henry's Maidenhead garage and car dealership. He and Madeleine will be succeeded in the late-1980s by **Anne & George Milne** and in 2008 by **Jo & Duncan Leftley**.

Eyes of a Child – Rosie Middleton & Chloe Harvey

St Nicolas' School / 23rd April 2012

Rosie likes Buffins road. She says: I like to play with my friends and go on adventures and there's lots of fun areas to play in. I like my house in Buffins, says Chloe. I feel safe with my Mum, Dad and my brother. I go to my room and play lots of games. I like playing on the front lawn with my friends from school. We all get to play catch, scooters and bikes. All the children that live in our road go to the village school which is a five-minute walk. When it's winter we have a snowball fight and then make a funny and different snowman with a tomato nose so that we can just kick it down again and then start again. When it's hot in the summer we play water fights and get our super-soakers out. Sometimes our parents join in as well. And then all laugh at the end of it, adds Rosie. And then we start the water fight all over again and then get freezing then run all around the place. Which is fun for all of us, but we will never put our coats on for too long and much more fun like that and that's why I like Taplow. If Chloe had to move she would move house but in Taplow. Rosie reckons the fact she knows everybody is great but Taplow is even more beautiful too!

Answer to a Prayer

Rectory Road / 6th June 1967

Even the Church of England is in on the act. The Diocese of Oxford is realising its assets in Taplow by dividing the grounds of ***The Rectory*** in two, sacrificing its rose garden to build a new Rectory on the eastern half for the Reverend **Christopher Hare**, and putting what will be recast as ***The Old Rectory*** up for sale for £22,500. His wife Katherine is driving the builders mad by constantly popping in to make sure everything is just so. They will enjoy their new home for 11 years before the Reverend John Kemp arrives to spend five years as Taplow's 48th and last Rector and one as its first Vicar.

Something's Burning – Pipe Dream

Elibank / Christmas Day 1967

Joanna Brooking is relieved to be home again in the top floor flat in the extension behind ***Elibank***. How scary it was earlier this year when the main house caught fire. How grateful the teenager was that her next-door neighbours gave her a calming cup of tea at two in the morning. What a blessing it all happened before **Sheila & Brian Horton** moved to *The Old Rectory*.

Elibank had been acquired in 1956 from the Bancroft estate by LQ Bamber, a Surrey estate agent and developer, who converted the rear extension into three flats and, within a year, sold the house and flats to **Peggy & Derrick Livsey** and the adjacent coach house as ***Elibank Cottage*** to Sheila & Brian. Jo and her mother Kate have been in the top flat since 1962. They are friendly with teachers Sybil & Johnny Hatfield and her mother Blanch Cox in the middle flat but only know the strange fellow on the still earthen-floored flat below as 'Gardener'. Some call him 'Sailor'. Everyone agrees he has green fingers. Who knows his real name?

The Livseys are kind landlords but Jo wonders if it was Derek's yellow-and-black *Rolls Royce* which ran over her white pedigree Persian cat in the *Elibank* driveway. And could it be true that the fire started when Derek set himself alight when trying to light his pipe? The house will be repaired sufficiently for it to be sold in 1970 to **Jane & Ted Wright**, who within two years will demolish the derelict lodge on the frontage to give *Elibank Cottage*, by then reinvented as ***The Old Coach House***, its own access from Rectory Road. When will things calm down? What will the Seventies bring?

The Unfolding Patchwork

Berry Hill / 31st December 1981

After it was sold by Ian Skimming in 1959, ***Taplow House*** tried being RW Lack's guest house for the elderly only to fall empty. Thieves stole the lead from its roof but somehow it survived two proposals to demolish and replace it with a block of either 24 or 18 flats before being acquired in 1974 by CA Jurgens. Within a year he succeeded in converting it to a hotel but later failed to get permission to build detached houses in its garden or a three-storey 19-bed extension. His successors will have similar big ideas: in the five years from 1987 modest plans to expand will be approved but not implemented in the ultimately vain hope of adding up to 28 bedrooms and a swimming pool. The hotel will have to settle for appearing on television in *The Big Game* (1995).

Up the hill, ***The New House*** now stands in the grounds of *Bapsey*. Down the hill, the failed ***Berry Hill Country Club*** has been replaced by the 12 flats of ***Berry Hill Court*** and ***Fielden House*** was joined by ***Redwood*** but the idea of one house or perhaps six between there and ***White Gables*** has come and gone, another idea for four will do the same in 1988/89 and it will be necessary in 1992 to enforce the end of illegal boat building on the site.

Hill Farm Road / 30th September 2014

Hitcham Grange has survived, but only just. Planning applications in the mid-1970s swung from clearing the site to make way for a housing development to converting the house as offices for *Plessey* and then to replacing it with a block of 12 flats. A compromise will see *The Grange* converted to 12 flats, its stables and outhouses to four cottages, its old lodge opposite the High Street junction will be demolished and its entrance moved 100 yards lower down Hill Farm Road without the loss of any significant trees. In 1975, there were planning applications to build two large residential developments: one east of **Marsh Lane** and the other in the triangular field north of the new **Buffins** estate. Both were refused to protect the Green Belt, as was a recent application to create an equestrian centre in the latter.

Cut to the Chase

Cedar Chase / 29th June 2013

Some themes can be traced back to an intruder. Doing so is a risky business. Even after four-and-a-half decades, there are those who might be unhappy with Cedar Chase being given any place in history. Although Taplow cannot claim any distinctive architectural contiguity, it had a certain taste of antiquity which in 1966 was challenged by the angular and monochrome design of *Span Developments*. Its 24 houses of pale-grey bricks, dark-stained vertical timber cladding, horizontal windows, L-shaped plans and mono-pitched roofs caused such offence they were dubbed 'Taplow Toilets'.

Span began in the late-1940s when architect Eric Lyons, architect-turned-developer Geffrey Townsend and landscape architect Ivor Cunningham developed their concept of modern architecture promoting modern communities to 'span' the gap between mass public housing projects and bespoke architectural design. To enthusiasts, their ethos of affordable 'homes within a garden' fitted perfectly into the grounds of ***Taplow Hill***, the old Serocold mansion, and their vision captured the spirit of *The Swinging Sixties* by appealing to young (and young-at-heart) creative professional people and their families: just the kind of people Taplow needed to give it new life. And despite the detractors, that's just what it did, and it did so well that seven couples who came in the early days are still maturing in Taplow's embrace....

It's the last Saturday in June, the evening when Chasers and their guests gather in the private delight of their communal garden to roast an ox, chew the cud and dance a reel. Two of those seven couples still live here. Two more have come from their houses by the Green to relive old times. Three others are otherwise engaged....

Still Chasers – Rosemary & Tony Read

No 7 Cedar Chase / 29th August 1966

The Reads are pioneers: the first family in Cedar Chase and feeling a little lonely. They had responded immediately to a *Sunday Times* advert and waited for three-and-a-half months until their new home was ready. But since moving in a couple of weeks ago, their excitement has turned to dismay. Taplow isn't giving them a good reception. Locals seem to regard them with suspicion, even hostility. Stony faces greet them in the pub, the grocer's and the butcher's. The two couples already in the Chase have no children and no desire to socialise. Emma (4) and Amelia (18 months) have no playmates. Their parents are wondering if they have made a serious mistake

No 7 Cedar Chase / 29th June 2013

Their worries began to dissolve several weeks later when other families began to arrive. Soon there were hordes of youngsters swarming around in the five-acre grounds with complete safety and freedom. The feeling of being 'Beyond the Pale' persisted – when Rosemary was finally invited to a coffee morning, she was paraded as a curiosity as someone who lived in "those houses" – but this rather united the Chasers in adversity. Community spirit grew in the formal arrangements for the management of the site through the Residents' Association and in the social activities such as garden working parties and Bonfire Night celebrations. Emma and Amelia always say they had an idyllic childhood and now it is their children who howl with dismay if Rosemary & Tony even think of leaving for pastures new.

Tony's e-mail address begins *readwrites*, which says it all. His three-month contract with the *BBC* in 1963 turned into ten years as a writer, script editor and eventually producer of *BBC TV* dramas series including *Detective*, *The Indian Tales of Rudyard Kipling*, *Sherlock Holmes* (when he was Peter Cushing), *The Avengers*, *The Troubleshooters* (which began as *Mogul* and twice won BAFTAs for Best TV Drama Series), *This Man Craig* (set in a Glasgow school long before *Grange Hill* and *Waterloo Road*) and *The Lotus Eaters* (1972/73) in which Emma and Amelia starred as Wanda Ventham's children. He went on to write for *Z-Cars*, *Shoestring*, *Quiller*, *Powers of Darkness*, *The Omega Factor*, *The Professionals*, *Hammer House of Horror* and *Sapphire & Steel* and to spend two years as script editor for *Dr Who* (when he was Tom Baker). He earned an award from *The Writer's Guild of Great Britain* for his work on *The Baker Street Boys* (1983) and the novelist John Wyndham's estate considered his adaptation of *Chocky* (1984) to be the best ever. Since then Tony has written many non-fiction history books (often about World War Two), many more TV scripts and a series of children's novels about *The Baker Street Boys*.

After a *Writers' Guild* committee meeting in 1967, Tony declined the offer to go for a drink with **Wilfred Greatorex** because he had a long journey to his new home. Wilfred asked where he lived. You probably won't know Taplow, said Tony. Oh yes I do, laughed Wilfred, Beryl and I are having a house built there. ***Foxwells*** is in the north-east corner of the former ***Taplow House*** estate and just a stone's throw south of Tony's home. The coincidence didn't stop there. They were in direct competition making TV drama series about hardbitten business: Tony with the *BBC*, producing and script editing *The Troubleshooters* (1965/69), and Wilfred (never Wilf, if he could help it) with *Associated Television* (*ATV*), creating and script editing *The Plane Makers* (1963/65) and *The Power Game* (1965/69), at that time with a new producer, **David Reid**, who would shortly move in N° 7 **Wellbank**. Tony smiles to recall "All the lust for power and profit emanating from one patch". David didn't stay long in Taplow but later as *ATV* Head of Drama he was Tony's executive producer on *Hammer House of Horror* and *Sapphire & Steel*. Wilfred remained here until his death in 2002. His other achievements included co-writing the screenplay of the film *The Battle of Britain* (1969) and devising the TV series *Secret Army* (1977/79) and *Airline* (1982).

In those early days, the Chase was also home to two television reporters and a movie art director. **Michael Clayton** was still at N° 14 when he moved from *BBC TV News* to become editor of *Horse and Hound* but it was after he left N° 17 in 1976 that **David Lomax** made current affairs television history with his brave interviews of Robert Mugabe of Zimbabwe, Idi Amin of Uganda and an Irishman who claimed to have murdered Airey Neave, Shadow Secretary of State for Northern Ireland. **Roy Walker** lived at N° 20. Having cut his teeth in television and in the art department on *Doctor Zhivago* (1965), *A Man for All Seasons* (1966), *Oliver!* (1968) and *Diamonds Are Forever* (1971), he rose to be art director on such movies as *Ryan's Daughter* (1970) and *Barry Lyndon* (1975), for which he won an *Oscar*. He moved into production design to win a *BAFTA* for *The Killing Fields* (1984) and great distinction on other notable films including *The Shining* (1980), *Good Morning, Vietnam* (1987) and *Eyes Wide Shut* (1999).

Once Chasers – Anne & John Hanford

No 9 Cedar Chase / 29th November 1967

The Hanfords are not the first Chasers but they can claim to be originals, since earlier this year they moved into the showhouse with its green, orange and purple decor. They enjoyed *Span* living at Blackheath in Kent when John was a biochemist with *Rank Hovis MacDougall* at Deptford. Cedar Chase made sense when *RHM* laboratories transferred to High Wycombe. It was a surprise for John to have two former contemporaries as neighbours: he went to school in Nottingham with **Tony Meats** and to King's College, London, with **Max Lipman**. As a librarian and one of the few wives here who worked, Anne will cycle to the station to take the train to the *BBC Library* at Ealing and later the *BBC Written Archives* at Caversham.

No 9 Cedar Chase / 29th June 2013

Anne & John are two of six former Chasers correct but not present. John's career took him into management consultancy and food licensing before he and Anne went independent as food importers of French toast melba. Eventually their home became too small, or the inhabitants (now three sons and a live-in nanny) had become too big and too numerous. They moved in 1975 to N° 1 **Saxon Gardens** and after 37 years to N° 42 **Cliveden Gages**. Both have served the Society: Anne as Chairman, John as Treasurer. Their eldest son Jonathan has returned with Jane to his childhood domain to settle at No 17 Cedar Chase.

Still Chasers – Rosaleen & Karl Lawrence

No 12 Cedar Chase / 29th August 1970

The Lawrences met in the Bahamas. Karl started there in 1953 managing a bookshop which held various retail franchises. The company expanded rapidly and so did his responsibilities. Within two years he was managing director of its news agency and by 1958 he was group operations and marketing director. The following year Rosaleen flew in as an air stewardess and was soon training cabin crew for *Bahamas Airways*. Within months *British Overseas Airways Corporation* had acquired both her employer and her services. Her high life captured Karl. They married and came back to the UK in 1965. Karl was soon Director of Management Systems at *Granada Publishing* and Chairman of the Publishers Association Distribution Committee and the Book Trade Working Party which developed the international bar code for books preserving the existing Standard Book Number system.

No 12 Cedar Chase / 29th June 2013

Karl and Rosaleen paid £9,000 (£241,000) for their new home; today it might sell for around £460,000. He emerged from mergers in the 1980s to be 'without portfolio' at *HarperCollins* and eventually to an internal management consultant role reporting to the Chairman. During that time he was invited to be interviewed for a detailed taped record of his career for the British Library Book Trade Lives archive. Since retiring at 73 in 2002, his continuing responsibility as a pension trustee left him time to spend the last 11 years on the Society's committee and the last three as its chairman.

Two other early Chasers are still here – Kay Ferguson has been in N° 6 since 1967 and Jan Storey in N° 11 since 1970. They will remember the two cedars which gave the Chase its name. Back in the mid-1970s a limb dropped off one tree slightly damaging a house, demolishing a wall and destroying a car. At the time this was thought to be no more than an unfortunate incident but perhaps it was the first sign of the tree having acquired *Phaeolus Schweinitizil*, a fungal pathogen that has generally worked its fatal spell before anyone is aware of its presence. It wasn't until 1990 that 'fruiting bodies' appeared on the bark of both trees and arboriculturalists recommended they be taken down.

Once Chasers – Brenda & Tony Hickman

No 17 Cedar Chase / 29th November 1971

It was in the summer that the Hickmans discovered Cedar Chase by accident when, having sold their London home and needing another urgently, they came to a children's party. As an architect, Tony was familiar with *Span* and drawn to the ethos but had no idea at the time of his cousin **John Hickman**'s connection with **Taplow Court**. He and Brenda bought the house there and then with the intention of staying only six months or so.

No 17 Cedar Chase / 29th June 2013

Ten years later they moved to ***Allington Cottage***. Although they were well aware by then of how far beyond the pale Cedar Chase was thought to be by some, it was still a surprise when **Ann Paines** (then of ***St Nicolas House***) welcomed them to the Village. Brenda didn't bother to point out that, having returned with her parents from India in 1954 to ***Crosswinds*** (River Road), she could claim a longer history as a Taplovian than Ann. Tony's professional achievements include two commendations from the Civic Trust and one from *The Financial Times*. He designed additions to St George's Choir School in Windsor, the parish room at **St Mary's Church** and the porch of **St Nicolas' Church** where he and Brenda are stalwarts. He has also served as Justice of the Peace on the Burnham and Beaconsfield benches and as the Society's president for four years and its vice-presidential planning guru ever since, for the last decade in tandem with **Euan Felton**.

Once Chasers – Sally & George Sandy

No 22 Cedar Chase / 29th November 1971

Like the Hanfords, the Sandys had also experienced *Span* in Kent, in their case at New Ash Green. When *Wrigley's* relocated from Wembley to Plymouth, George needed to continue sales and marketing in London so a home *en route* to the West made sense.

No 22 Cedar Chase / 29th June 2013

After a while George went into vending machines and eventually became the sole supplier to *London Transport*. Since leaving Cedar Chase in 1978 he and Sally have lived at three addresses in Taplow: ***Rozel*** (until 1983), ***The Dower House*** (1993/2005) and ***The Porches*** (since 2005) interspersed with a decade on Castle Hill in Maidenhead during which they remained active in Taplow social life. Sally served as the Society's secretary and as a Parish Councillor. George is now Taplow's District Councillor and Parish Council Chairman.

Once Chasers – Sarah & Tony Meats

No 15 Cedar Chase / 29th November 1975

The Meats are settling in nicely. As an architect specialising in the grand concepts of urban design, Tony believes Cedar Chase works well both within itself and by giving character and enclosure to Rectory Road. He had been aware of and impressed by the development for some years but Sarah knows Taplow too. As a young teenager living in Ealing some 20 years ago, she and three friends had ridden their horses up the central reservation of the A40 to Taplow Horse Show (with boys cycling alongside) to camp in Buffins. Sarah's first job had been on the production line at *Cote's Perfume* on the Great West Road where **Pamela Bentley**, then Pam Jones, worked in the office.

No 15 Cedar Chase / 29th June 2013

Sarah & Tony are two of the four former Chasers here tonight. One of their twins, **Oliver**, has returned to settle in Cedar Chase, but not in his boyhood home: that belongs to **Chris & George Ormond**. Having been gazumped by **Patty & David Stanning** in their bid to buy ***Bapsey*** in 1978, Sarah & Tony moved the following year to ***Number Three***, High Street. Tony has served the Society as an architectural adviser and briefly on the Parish Council until being ousted by Chairman **Alistair Forsyth** for excessive non-attendance.

Once Chasers – Liz & Alistair Forsyth

No 22 Cedar Chase / 29th November 1978

Earlier this year, the Forsyths came down from Edinburgh for a weekend to look for somewhere to live near Heathrow, having been appointed Software Marketing Director by his employer *Burrough Machiners* (later acquired by *Unisys*). They spotted a personal ad in *The Sunday Times* and came to see Sally & George Sandy's house, which faces Rectory Road. At first glance they didn't like the look of it and drove straight past only to come upon the Village Green with its church and pub. In Alistair's mind, this was a picture of somewhere he had always wanted to live. They turned around, viewed the house and bought it on a handshake. Soon after they moved in, there was a knock on the back door: it was **Tony Meats** claiming right of way through the house to *The Oak & Saw*. Alistair granted passage on condition Tony took him too and bought him a pint.

No 22 Cedar Chase / 29th June 2013

He reckons that might have been the only time Tony did stand a round but it was the start of a long friendship hardly dented at all by Tony's subsequent ousting.

Sarah & Tony had long departed for *Number Three* when the original Cedar Chase leaseholds became freeholds, each with an equal share in the Residents' Society through which communal space is managed. Alistair recalls that this was achieved very late one night in The Reading Room. Every household was represented at a meeting to consider the proposal, which required unanimous agreement. Objectors were gradually won over until only one, Mary Clayton, remained. As Chairman, Alistair said they would all sit there until she agreed. After a long period of silence, she succumbed at about 11 o'clock.

Liz was a teacher, eventually head of a primary school in Bracknell. Alistair's career evolved from software marketing via wine importation to railway coupler manufacturing and sales but somehow he found time to start the ox roast tradition. When they bought ***The Old Manor House*** in 1985 from Phyllida & Richard Sneyd (he of the National Trust), **Anne Milne** made a point of welcoming them to Taplow. Alistair protested that he and Liz had been in Cedar Chase for seven years. After a suitably meaningful pause, Anne gave him an equally meaningful stare and repeated "Welcome to Taplow". Liz is a Parish Councillor. Having been Chairman of the Council for eight years until 1994, Alistair has held the same position with the Association since 2007.

The Forsyth Saga – The Village Green Party

The Village Green / 22nd June 2013

The legacy of Chairman Forsyth is more subtle than that of Ernest Perkins but no less enduring. It was Alistair's idea in the late-1970s for **Cedar Chase** to have a summer ox roast party, which was very successful. And ten years later, whilst he was custodian of the Village Green, somebody – possibly **Bob Hanbury** or **Dick Nutt** – suggested that the Society should hold a similar 'pic-nic' for the whole community on the Green. This quickly became the Village Green Party (VGP) or The Ox Roast, an annual tradition every midsummer Saturday evening. Some call it The Hog Roast despite beef being the meat in question almost every year except during the Mad Cow Disease scare in the late-1990s.

Early this morning, as they always do for both the VGP and the Chase roasts, **Jane Curry** and **Andrew Findlay** were up at the crack of dawn lighting the fire beneath the ingenious spit on which the enormous shoulder of beef (or occasionally pork) is impaled for roasting. This innovative creation was designed all those years ago by Glyn Davies of Cedar Chase, built by his students at Imperial College, London, and improved over the years, the better to keep the meat in one piece and cooked to perfection: crispy on the outside and rare within to suit all tastes.

Tonight almost 400 people are enjoying themselves the 28th VGP. This is **Euan Felton**'s last year as captain of the Society's team of volunteers who make it all happen. The atmosphere is relaxed, convivial and uncommercial if tainted a tad by the few who come without paying the very modest fee of just £3. The aim is to break even and to have fun, not to raise funds. As usual, it is a party of impromptu parties. Folks emerge from their marquees and pergolas circling the Green to mingle with friends. The enormous shoulder of ox has been roasted over a roaring log fire, carved and consumed. Having been lit soon after dawn, the fire now smoulders gently. Children pull their parents into the middle to dance another reel to the merry music of **Mike Anderson's Folk Band** which has played at every VGP. Even those with two left feet can follow the directions of **Tom Browne**, the consummate country-dance caller, who has led the revelry at all but one occasion when, as **Barrie Peroni** remarks, "Oh boy, was his magic missed, especially by the children".

Some dads drift down the south-east slope of the Green to refresh their (plastic) glasses in ***The Oak & Saw***. Few realise that until the late-1980s this slope was as steep as that in the south-west corner. Alistair's Council had the gradient softened and he, Liz and Peter Binstead of ***The Porches*** planted the daffodils, primroses and crocuses which add splashes of colour every spring. Some accused them of "prettifying the Village". How fortunate they responded with shrugs of why ever not. And how lucky Taplow was Alistair & Co were receptive to **Sheila Horton**'s brilliant idea in 1990 to paint the mural. Few know that his wife Liz has a cunning plan to mark the centenary of the outbreak of the Great War next year by planting poppies along the roadside.

Having a Ball – Busy Bill

No 3 Cedar Chase / 29th June 2013

Bill Ball once held the onerous responsibility of being Keeper of the Spit. His other significant contributions to Taplow began soon after arriving with his wife **Marjorie** in 1982. He served for many years on the Parish Council and 20 on the Society's committee, including three as its chairman, yet somehow found the time to rise to become Chief Executive of *Rank Film Laboratories Ltd* whilst also spending 15 years as chairman of the Buckinghamshire Association for the Blind followed by another ten as chairman of the South East Division of the National Association. Bill is no longer with us but Marjorie, author of a book on her US ancestry, is still a good neighbour.

Chasers Reunited

The much-repaired wall of *Elibank* opposite Cedar Chase / 2012

Still Chasing: Alistair Forsyth, Tony Read & Karl Lawrence behind Rosemary Read, Liz Forsyth, Rosaleen Lawrence, Sarah & Tony Meats / 2013

Getting ready to party....

The ox roasts from the crack of dawn until early evening....
Simon Fox starts to slice....
A latecomer seeks somewhere to settle....
Euan Felton & Karl Lawrence take a little lubrication....
And the sun shines on the frivolous / 2014

The shadows lengthen....

Mike Sanderson's Band strikes up....

And the dancing begins under the direction of consummate caller Tom Browne / 2013 & 2014

The dancing continues as Chris Ashford & Alastair Hill barbeque burgers and sausages....

Whatever the weather, Taplovians wile away their Midsummer Saturday evenings shooting the breeze over a glass or two , stepping out in style or sheltering from a shower with smiles like Teresa & Brian Foreman / 2013 & 2014

The Jubilee: Just the Job

No concrete culvert / 2011

The Forsyth Saga – Just the Job

Maidenhead Rowing Club / 9th February 2014

The wettest winter in 250 years has seen the Thames break its banks everywhere from Oxford to Shepperton except here. Although the water laps the door of the Rowing Club boathouse, the rest of Taplow is dry. Cookham is an island. Datchet and Wraysbury are underwater. As the river rose, *The Daily Mail* smirked that the "Celeb's Riviera" would be swamped, only to shoot itself in the foot by painting **Helen & Terry Wogan** as a potential victims, despite their doorstep being 115 feet above mean river level. Not even Michael Parkinson in Bray has got damp. Windsor MP Adam Afriyie says that Maidenhead's "Gin-and-Jag Set" has been saved at the expense of its downstream neighbours, which goes to show the **Jubilee River** has done its job.

There was a lot of argument about whether the Jubilee would be worth it. The National Rivers Authority (NRA) concluded in 1986 that Maidenhead was vulnerable to a 60-year flood event of "devastating consequences" and, since the last "disastrous" flood was in 1947, another one was likely sooner rather than later. A year later the NRA floated ten possible schemes before deciding to spend £32m (£130m) creating an entirely new channel slicing through Taplow and beyond, because it would have the least impact on existing housing. Naturally Taplovians felt aggrieved that they should bear the brunt of a project to protect Maidenhead, where flood plain regulations had been ignored to build thousands of houses, whilst South Bucks had played by common-sense rules.

As Chairman of the Council, **Alistair Forsyth** put together a Taplow Action Group (TAG) of local residents including **Philip Cooley** (of **Cedar Chase**), a retired senior project manager for *Thames Water*, **Derek Walker** who had experience of several large infrastructure projects and **Sir John Page** who had been chairman of one of the river authorities. They registered three main objections: that the scheme would be an environmental disaster both during and after its five-year construction and would leave Taplow with an ugly scar across its landscape, that it was not economically justified and that a far smaller scheme would be less damaging but equally effective.

Whilst the project – by then estimated at £45m (£125m) – was still under review, Maidenhead suffered a flood in 1990 which conveniently provided extra ammunition. The NRA claimed that 123 properties were "damaged" but, according to TAG, only 35 required repairs costing over £1,000 (£2,770) and the two worst cases involved indoor swimming pools. TAG argued that these people would be well insured and that surely "public money should not be spent to protect rich people's extravagances".

Local MP Tim Smith was extremely helpful. He secured an emergency Parliamentary debate in the House of Commons which took place at 11pm in the presence of about six MPs and a similar number of Taplovians. This led to a month-long public inquiry in Reading about a year later. TAG managed to raise £5,000 (£10,300) to engage a barrister for one day to present its case but decided that it would be pragmatic to shift its focus from outright objection to damage limitation and in particular on minimising the environmental impact of the scheme on Taplow's fragile landscape. As a result, the channel is not the concrete culvert eyesore Taplow once feared but an apparently natural river with islands and an interesting variety of flora and fauna.

There was much debate about what the cut should be called. **Lincoln Lee** suggested with perceptive anticipation that it might be either METS (for 'Maidenhead Expects Taplow to Suffer') or LODHIC (for 'Look Out Downstream, Here it Comes'), the latter no joke nowadays for Datchet and Wraysbury. The cut eventually cost well over £100m (£147m) – at the time, the biggest man-made river project ever in the UK – and even its detractors had to admire the civil engineering: not least the freezing of the railway embankment in order that a big enough hole could be created without causing its collapse. The channel's name was selected because the water first flowed through to mark the Golden Jubilee of Queen Elizabeth II in 2002.

Eyes of a Child – Joseph Oliver

St Nicolas' School / 23rd April 2012

I like the scenery in Taplow. The best scenery is by the Jubilee Channel. It has ducks, swans, geese, heron and even cormorants! Also in April the cowslips are in full bloom! And with lots of rabbits, the foxes never go hungry. Also it is very quiet as the sounds of the A4 are drowned out. On cold days the river is covered by a thick sheet of mist: it is very beautiful. But my favourite thing has to be when it is a sunny day when the sun reflects on the water.

Tuppence a Fortnight, Cheap at the Price

Broadcasting House / 18th December 2009

Three years ago, the renowned broadcaster Terry Wogan was challenged over the size of his salary. He responded: "Factoring in my eight million listeners, I cost tuppence a fortnight. I think I'm cheap at the price." Who could disagree?

Taplow has been graced by many national figures. Its latest is today looking forward to a lie-in each morning. After 16 years, the army of *TOGGs* has just heard the last *Wake Up to Wogan*. Terry won't disappear (except occasionally with Helen to his French retreat). He will continue writing his whimsical column for *The Sunday Telegraph* and presenting *Wogan's Perfect Recall* regularly on *Channel 4* and *Children in Need* annually on *BBC1* – and from next year he will return to *BBC Radio 2* with *Weekend Wogan* – but *TOGGs* (*Terry's Old Geezers & Gals*) will have to live with less is more from now on.

Terry (late of Limerick) has been a celebrated fixture on the *BBC* since 1966. His voice, way with words and senses of humour and irony are legendary. Novelist Allison Pearson hit the spot by observing that he is "the Irishman who reminded the British of what they could be at their best". He joined *Radio 1* at its launch (1967) and has completed two long stints on the *Radio 2* breakfast show (1972/84 and 1993/2009). His work on television includes *Come Dancing* (1974/79), *Blankety Blank* (1979/84), *Children in Need* (since 1980) and his chat show *Wogan* (1982/92). For many, his sardonic commentary on radio (1971 and 1974/77) and especially on television (1973, 1978 and 1980/2008) was the saving grace of the *Eurovision Song Contest*. Having been made Knight Commander of the British Empire in 2005, he is proud to be styled Sir Terry.

Second Innings

The first Wickenden / 8th June 1975

Windsor-born **Raymond Lock** is a former RAF 85 Squadron Wing Commander who flew *Hurricanes* in the Battle of Britain. It is nine years since he and his wife Irene bought old ***Bapsey Cottage*** overlooking the northern boundary of the cricket field. They quickly replaced it with a new bungalow they called ***Wickenden***, a name Irene had heard over the loudspeakers at Heathrow and they liked because of the cricketing allusion. The view from their living room is magnificent. **Ten Acres** is glistening green in the early morning sun. Later today **Taplow Cricket Club** will celebrate its 125th anniversary with a match against a team of cricketing and showbiz celebrities led by **Terry Wogan**.

Taplow captain Doug Hatch will lead stalwarts such as record wicket-taker (and current Chairman) Dave Wigmore and record run-scorers Chris Goodrham and Gerry Mills in jovial competition against cricketing legends Denis Compton, Tony Lewis and Brian Johnston, actors Sheridan Morley and Willie Rushton and *BBC Radio* stars Pete Murray, Paul Burnett, Simon Bates, Tony Brandon and Tony Blackburn with his actress wife Tessa Wyatt and TV star Isla St Clair providing a very pleasant echo of the 1888 **Ally Sloper's XI**.

The backdrop to this afternoon's fun will be an opportunity to reflect over a pint or three on the milestones and characters in the club's history....

Taplow CC had 32 enthusiastic members in 1891. After a spell as Taplow Railway Cricket Club in the summer and Taplow Railway Football Club in the winter under President **Harry Lawson**, by 1910 it was struggling for lack of players even before going into hibernation during the Great War. **Lord Desborough** commemorated his eldest son in 1919 by donating the Julian Cup, still played for by local teams, and in 1925 he became President of the club. The first pavilion was erected in 1927, a small cedar construction with two dressing rooms fronted by a veranda. Despite finding himself in a difficult position, Desborough supported the club's stance in the early-1930s when it abstained from the Julian Cup because it doubted that all entrants were *bona fide*. Maybe they didn't speak Latin.

Reverend **Francis Philips** ended his 35-year term as Chairman in 1939 and – much to the satisfaction of **Arthur Mewton** whose cows could graze the cricket field freely – the club once again went into wartime hibernation. The cows were banished to the outfield in 1946 and, in accordance with long-established tradition, the new rector was asked to succeed as Chairman. Canon **Robert Hay** graciously accepted the invitation only to resign two years later in protest at the decision to play on Sundays as well as Saturdays. **Sydney Marriott** of ***The Hermitage*** was elected in his place just in time to lead a ten year battle to save Ten Acres from being turned into a council housing estate by Eton RDC. What a hero, but there was more. He also steered the club though a nervous period when the deaths of Lord and **Lady Desborough** in 1945 and 1952 threatened the club's survival. All was resolved in 1958 when their daughter **Imogen**, **Viscountess Gage**, executed a Deed of Gift that ceded Ten Acres to the club.

Marriott is perhaps the only officer in the British Army ever to be commissioned by two monarchs. Possibly the final regal act of **Queen Victoria** was to sign his commission. Clearly the effort was all too much for the old girl; hours later she breathed her last and King Edward VII was obliged to endorse the document. Marriott served with the Essex Regiment, later the 7th King's Liverpool Regiment, and rose to Lieutenant-Colonel during the Great War before becoming a director of *Limmer & Trinidad Lake Asphalt Co Ltd*, a connection that led to an even greater achievement: the installation (for free) of an experimental artificial practice pitch at Ten Acres. It will still be in use in 2013.

Colonel Marriott presided over the club's centenary celebrations in 1950: a gentlemen's dinner at ***The Dumb Bell***, a Ladies' Night at ***Skindles*** and two matches. One game was between club members dressed in the mode of 1850. Some cycled to the match on penny-farthings. Oh, how they laughed. The film made by Treasurer FT Wilson has been lost but Bray artist John Wilson's commemorative cartoon *The Old Man on the Hill* survived. Over 3,000 people flocked to Ten Acres on 28th May when a Taplow & District XI took on a strong Middlesex County Cricket Club team captained by RWV (Walter) Robins and including England players Bill Edrich and Jack Robertson, then at the height of their careers. Everyone hid their disappointment that a knee injury prevented Denis Compton from playing but the dashing batsman was able to make a fine cut through the marzipan cricket field on the cake baked by **Edith Hunt**, wife of the club's longest serving player. **Bert Hunt** was 16 when he made his debut in 1902. Although he was still playing occasionally at 64, Bert umpired the celebrity match.

Although **Maurice Rance** was 12 years younger, he decided that year to declare his innings closed. At the end-of-season reunion in the Parish Hall, Marriott spoke fondly of the four generations of Rances at the club – **William Rance the Elder**, a co-founder and the first captain of the club, **William the Younger**, Maurice and his 17-year-old son Jim – and club vice-president **Sir George Franckenstein** presented Maurice with a silver salver to mark his retirement after 30 years as club captain. Time moved on and the original pavilion was replaced by a Nissen hut clubhouse in 1954 which was succeeded in 1960 by a timber clubhouse – the Desborough Memorial Pavilion – thanks to the fundraising efforts of Charles Bye. Football twice had a foothold and hockey once but cricket reigned. The First XI won the Julian Cup in 1963 and the Chilterns League in 1975. Further showbiz matches will be held in 1977, 1980 and 1983. And Rachel Heyhoe-Flint will bring the England Women's Team to thrash Taplow in 1982.

The Preservation of Peace

The Paddocks, Crazies Hill / 15th March 2012

Jim Rance smiles to recall that his father wasn't just a cricket captain. As one of the last Taplow Parish Constables, Maurice had the power of arrest and the duties including "the protection of life and property and the preservation of peace" and the onerous responsibilities of reporting "the suspicious movement of strangers" in the village, of quelling any disturbance, of informing the village policeman of any planned offence (as if they would know in advance) and, "in times of trouble or personal anxiety [of giving] counsel and advice". Such constables had been appointed every year from 1842 until 1949, when the Parish Council forgot to appoint anybody. It recovered in 1950 to issue warrant cards to Maurice and three others – **Arthur Mewton**, **Fred Joel** and E Wheeler – only for the tradition to fall away a few years later.

Eyes of a Child – Graeme Paskins

The Orchard, High Street / 4th September 1988

The 16-year-old cricketer awakes to find his arms covered in bramble scratches and nettle stings. How did that happen? His brain clears enough to realise that he must have staggered home from the club last night along the overgrown footpath to the curl of the High Street. It must've been an end-of-season celebration to remember, if only he could.

Graeme's long innings began with Taplow Colts under coaches Brian May and David Thornley. Already he treasures memories of squeezing into David's car to travel to away games with his brother Chris and the rest of the lads and of the wonderful feeling of power when he whacked a ball for six straight through the clubhouse window. He will go on to represent Buckinghamshire 61 times, the last in his son Nick's Minor Counties debut in July 2014. A week later Graeme will captain Marlow Cricket Club in winning the Julian Cup for the first time in 25 years.

Midlanes in the Middle

Taplow Cricket Club / 13th August 1995

Only true cricket-lovers will really and truly understand how proud a father feels when his son joins him in the team. Not a lot can be better in life than for the pair to share a century-partnership. Wraysbury watched helplessly this afternoon as **John Midlane** at 53 scored 53 and young Will at 14 scored 65 as they put on 111 together.

John hailed from Bourne End but started to play for Taplow in the 1970s. After dabbling in road haulage he moved into car rental with *Hertz* and then *Rentco Nationwide* as its managing director. He first met **Iris** when she was with *Hertz* at Belfast Airport. They met again after she transferred to Heathrow, married in 1979 and acquired ***Wickenden*** "for the cricket" in 1987. Four years later it had been rebuilt it in the style of Edwin Lutyens after a very good day at Lord's Cricket Ground. Two stumps frame the portico and a third lies flattened into the stone floor of the entrance hall. Inside there are stumps everywhere: in the stone surround of a fireplace, in the banisters of the galleried landing and on the staircase with cricket ball newels top and bottom. It takes an observant eye to spot the woman's touch: a stone carved iris above the front door.

Taplow Cricket Club / 13th August 2011

Somebody asked John: isn't it a bit risky having a window bigger than a sightscreen overlooking the pitch? He responded by offering a bottle of champagne to anyone who could break it with a six. It was only natural that this cricket buff should succeed Raymond Lock as club President and, given the extent of his network, no surprise that he instigated an annual August Bank Holiday celebrity match involving famous cricketers like England's Derek Underwood and West Indian stars Jimmy Adams, Keith Arthurton, Ian Bishop and Roger Harper. None of them won the champagne before this passionate man played his last innings. It is likely that he would be pleased but not surprised that Iris has stepped into his shoes as President *par excellence* presiding over a golden era during which the club has won the Old Paludians Diamond Jubilee Bowl twice, the Chilterns League twice and the League Cup seven times between 2002 and 2010 (including two 'doubles').

St Nicolas' Church / 30th September 2014

Taplow has gathered in number to remember Iris. **Peter Casey** confides that, ten days before she died, he drove her over to White Waltham to enjoy seeing Taplow's victory make the club Chilterns League champions. She will be warmly remembered at the club where part of her legacy is a fine new tradition of Friday family evenings....

They Don't Like Cricket

Sidney Marriott

Sir George Franckenstein

Four of the Committee / 1950

The oldest club photo / c1888

Maurice Rance

Canon Robert Hay

Centenary Matches / 1950

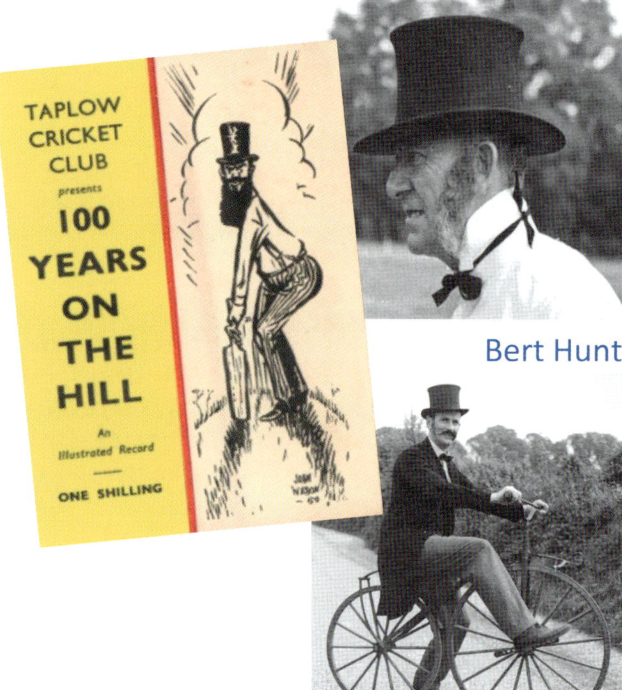

Bert Hunt

Friday Evening Fun – Imogen Wallis / 2012

Celebrity Match / 1980

Raymond Lock is encircled by Tony Lewis, Terry Wogan, Pete Murray & Isla St Clair

Eyes of a Child – Hannah Irwin, Arthur Cassells, Freya Esplun-Evans, Alice Snoxell & Imogen Wallis

St Nicolas' School / 23rd April 2012

My favourite thing in Taplow is the cricket club, says Hannah. Everybody is always chatting and laughing. There's sometimes a barbecue and we eat popcorn. It smells really nice and all the people are tempted to try some. Arthur likes playing games, having a chat and the big groups of colourful flowers. Freya thinks the club was made in 1850. She goes every week with her dad and step-brothers. The boys usually play football, cricket or manhunt or bulldog. She plays with her friends **Katie Hornett**, **Rosie Sellers** or Alice who says it's a kind and joyful place where people come on a Friday night to chill out. There are about 20 children and 30 adults, it's that popular. People are very so friendly. There is a bar where you can get cool drinks. Everybody stares at the TV like a bunch of owls. Hannah laughs at how the dads crowd around the TV biting their nails or jumping up and down. Imogen adds that this is a special part of Taplow. There are competitions and games and you can get anything you want – litterally – like crisps and nuts, orange and blackcurrant J²Os and fizzy pop blackcurrant squash. And you are aloud to rome the field for as long as you want.

Wine to Savour

The second Wickenden / 13th August 1998

It wasn't only at *Wickenden* and with the cricket that the **Midlanes** succeeded the **Locks**. They also took over the vineyard and a cellar of 9,000 bottles of wine.

Most of the land where Taplow Horse Show had been held was **Buffins** by the time Irene & Raymond acquired the last parcel along with ***Bapsey Cottage***. They loved wine almost as much as he loved cricket and so from 1976 planted on this patch several thousand *Sauvignon*, *Merlot*, *Müller Thurgau* and *Seyval* vines. The first vintage in 1983 was not a success but **George Clark** of N° 1 **Buffins** acquired 'on the job' knowledge to gradually improved output and quality. The Reverend **Jonathan Meyrick** took the first press each year for communion wine. ***Wickenden Wines*** were matured in French barrels to win three international competitions and be enjoyed at the House of Commons.

Iris & John knew their wine but not how to make it. George did, so they took up the challenge. They rebranded as ***Taplow Wine***, found retail outlets at Cliveden's Orangery, *The Oak & Saw* and *Majestic Wine* in the Bishop Centre, and won a bronze medal at the English Vineyards Association national festival in 1994 with their white 'oaked' wine. However, viniculture is hard work and very dependent on the weather – the best year produced 12,000 bottles, the worst just 2,000 – and when the vines were approaching the end of their natural life last year, the Midlanes decided to call it a day. The vines have been grubbed out and replaced by woodland with a small lake: an easily-maintained haven for wildlife, a sad loss for Taplovian wine-buffs after a brief but brilliant 14 years. Here's to the Mocks and the Lidlanes. Hic.

A Brand New Morris

Tæppa's Mound / 28th August 1981

They have taken their name from the Mound so it's only right that the lady morris dancers of ***Tæppa's Tump*** should complete their initiation here. The *Ellington Morris Men* of Pinkney's Green declined a request to take lady members so the sisters are doing it for themselves. They are based in Furze Platt and gave their first performance earlier today in Maidenhead town centre dancing not in the Cotswold style of the men but in the North-West style popular in Cheshire and Lancashire. The Taplow connection begins and ends with the name but it serves in a fine cause.

Something's Burning – A Senior Moment

Elibank / Christmas Day 1982

This isn't how **Sue & Alan Senior** had hoped to spend Christmas. The interior of ***Elibank*** is still blackened. The temporary tin roof keeps out the rain but not the cold and damp. At least they can laugh at how surprised **George Sandy** had been to be overtaken on the motorway by Alan, who had begun speeding home from Luton as soon as he got the news that *Elibank* was burning for the second time in 15 years.

When the Seniors bought *Elibank* three years ago, the three flats in the rear extension were separated from the main house only by locked doors and Sue was horrified to hear that **Jane Wright** had allowed a tramp to use a 'hidden' key to get into the ground floor flat to find food she had left for him. No time was wasted in blocking all the doors and converting the extension into ***The Dower House***, a single and separate home for Sandra & Stephen Randall (he a *Lloyds* name) who eventually sold it to Sally & George Sandy.

Sue wasn't too happy to hear that Jane's mother was buried under a walnut tree in the north-east corner of the garden but Alan renewed a lapsed planning permission and the eastern portion of the land was sold to John Blore, a local builder, who constructed ***Elibank Court*** which was acquired last year by **Maud & Ken Johnson**, he something important with *Shell*. They have rented it out for until Ken's foreign assignments are over.

The Seniors will stay at *Elibank* for another 14 years despite calamities continuing in the form of floods not fire. Next winter, heavy snow will bring down the temporary roof and a quick thaw and heavy rain will cause a deluge in the house with water gushing behind recently restored panelling. A burst pipe in 1986 will cause a ceiling to collapse while Sue & Alan are away skiing. And in 1990, when the front wall collapses under the weight of rain-soaked earth, Alan will be obliged to fight off council workmen determinedly trying to cart away all the valuable old bricks. Many will never be saved, which is why the wall is rebuilt using concrete blocks faced externally with what was left of the original bricks.

Secrets and Spies

Queen Anne's House / 13th April 1996

Leonard Miall is doing one of the many things he does so well: writing an obituary. Such recollections are usually for the *BBC* or a national newspaper. This will be published in the Society's Newsletter 66 (Spring 1996). It celebrates **Eric Pope** as "a most versatile [pianist] who loved classical music and played jazz superbly" and mentions in passing that he "worked for MI6 and was posted at different times to Paris, Singapore, India and Brussels". It is likely that there is much more to tell of Eric's career as a spy and that Leonard could do so but of course doesn't. It just wouldn't do. Certain secrets should never be told even when rumour thrives in the silence.

Some say that Eric was recruited to British Intelligence by **Dorrien Young** during or soon after the Second War. Perhaps it was this friendship that brought Eric and his wife Laura (known as Lynn) to Taplow in 1956 when they acquired ***Queen Anne's House***. It was probably 13 years later that they converted the old stable block into *Queen Anne's Cottage* and let it to Roland Boland and then Elizabeth & Glenn Cornelia before making it their own home.

Tall Tale – Talk of York

Queen Anne's House / 13th April 2012

There are still whispers that in the mid-1980s the Popes permitted **Prince Andrew**, **Duke of York**, to secretly tryst in *Queen Anne's House* with his future wife Sarah Ferguson, daughter of the royal polo manager. If they did, their rendezvous was well-chosen for it was never confirmed by snoopers. If they didn't, it makes a good tall tale.

Tall Tale – Not So Dusty

The National Film & Television School, Beaconsfield / 29th June 2012

Intrigue continued at *Queen Anne's House* after the Popes sold it in 1988 to a glittering show-business couple who sought the quiet life. Half of that couple was **Sandie Shaw**, 'the barefoot pop princess of the 1960s' who won the Eurovision Song Contest in 1967 with *Puppet on a String*. The other half was **Nik Powell**, once Richard Branson's partner in a mail-order company, a record shop and a recording studio. In 1972 they and others founded *Virgin Records* and made it one of the UK's major recording labels before Nik left to follow his dream into film with the launch of *Palace Pictures* in 1983. By then he had married Sandie and helped revive her career with an introduction to Martyn Ware and Ian Craig Marsh, formerly of *Human League*, then of *BEF* (*British Electronic Foundation*), eventually of *Heaven 17*.

Once Sandie & Nik settled in Taplow, their children Amie and Jack went to St Nicolas' School and there were stories that not only Ware but also Chrissie Hynde (of *The Pretenders*) had been seen visiting. Even now another tale still does the rounds. It was probably in 1990 that Sandie went knocking on doors to recruit support for a traffic-calming scheme. However, according to Nik, it is "apocryphal" that one in **Wellbank** opened to reveal **Dusty Springfield**, only for neither to recognise the other because they didn't have their specs on. Although Dusty's cat was killed by a car in Rectory Road, Nik can't recall if she signed up for the scheme. Having produced *Absolute Beginners* and *Mona Lisa* (both 1986), he was too busy at the time on *Scandal* (1989), a film about the Profumo Affair in which Longleat played Cliveden. He and Sandie left Taplow in 1991 and divorced in 1994. Since then Nik has divided his time between producing movies including *Fever Pitch* (1997), *Little Voice* (1998) and *Ladies in Lavendar* (2004) and his directorship of the National Film & Television School (since 2003).

Whatever the truth of the doorstep story, it is an amazing coincidence that these two female pop icons shared Taplow for a time. They had their first hits within months of each other: Dusty with *I Only Want To Be With You* (1963) and Sandie with *Always Something There To Remind Me* (1964). They traded chart success with each other, Cilla Black and Lulu for the rest of the 1960s and both enjoyed revivals in popularity in the 1980s: Sandie with *BEF* and *The Smiths* and Dusty with *Pet Shop Boys*. Having been born Mary O'Brien (with such a fine Orkney-Inchiquin name, no wonder she was drawn to Taplow) she earned her nickname as a dusty childhood tomboy and her worldwide fame as a panda-eyed, peroxide blond soul singer with a distinctively sensual voice and a romantic attraction to women which nowadays would raise no eyebrow but did in her heyday.

A New Awakening

Taplow Court / 28th April 1989

Sandie Shaw became a Buddhist in 1978. She was drawn to *Queen Anne's House* because an international Buddhist sect had established its UK headquarters across the road at Taplow Court. It was a little confusing in January last year when news filtered through that ***Plessey*** had sold the grand Grenfell home to *NSUK*, or was it *SGI-UK*?

Indra Adnan explains that the ***Soka Gakkai International*** is a worldwide network of lay Buddhists dedicated to a common vision of a better world through the empowerment of the individual and the promotion of peace, culture and education. The practise of *Nichiren Shoshu* follows the teachings of the 13th Century Japanese priest Nichiren who, on this very day 736 years ago, devoted himself to the Mahayana Lotus Sutra of Buddha Siddartha Gautama, the Awakened One. Members of *SGI* wear no saffron robes. Many eat meat and enjoy the odd drink. They have no public code of behaviour beyond an equanimity achieved by chanting twice daily to draw up natural human qualities of wisdom, compassion, courage and, most importantly, life force. But they do have a motto: Trust through Friendship, Peace through Trust. If the immediate aim of members is to revolutionise their own lives by bringing out the very best of themselves, their broader aim is to do the same in their immediate environment and eventually in the land at large.

One of the first actions of General Director **Richard Causton** was to extend the hand of friendship by inviting the Society's Committee to visit Taplow Court last September to meet his wife Mitusko, Indra and their colleagues, and to learn about *NSUK* and *SGI*'s aspiration to play a valued role in the community. He reassured the visitors that *SGI* fully appreciated the historic importance of its new home and that, although guests would often stay, there will be no commune: only estate manager **Andy McKenzie**, his wife **Annick** and their two boys are resident. Andy accepted a reciprocal invitation to join the Committee and will serve for 22 years during which exhibitions, concerts and 'open days' at Taplow Court will become a regular feature of local life. However his first task is to manage a complex programme of restoration involving challenges such as replacing all of the 150-year-old lead on the roof of Taplow Court and many timber beams ravaged by deathwatch beetle, dismantling and rebuilding 52 decorative chimneys with reproduced stonework and handmade bricks moulded and colour-matched to the originals, and manoeuvring a crane through the gates with half-an-inch to spare on each side.

Andy is one of the very few Britons to have fought in the Vietnam War. When he was 18, his residency in the USA resulted in him being drafted into the army as a tank driver. With typical understatement, he says it was "useful experience for learning to drive a tractor". More importantly, he discovered Buddhism and through it Annick, a young Frenchwoman who will spend a few years as a teaching *assistante* as Desborough School in Maidenhead before fulfilling her lifelong ambition to be an artist. Her vibrant work will be exhibited in London, Reading, Windsor, New York and France while her clients include *Starbucks* and Adrian Moorhouse's *Lane 4* in Bourne End. Meanwhile Andy will support the various archaeological investigations and then supervise the construction of a new 500-seat *butsuma* (chanting hall) which will also be used for conferences and concerts; all this while keeping Taplow Court in trim. Taplow can be grateful that one of its greatest assets is in such good hands.

Taplow Court / 18th July 1998

The *butsuma* is yet to be. There is plenty of room here for over 2,000 people to enjoy a concert in aid of *War Child*, a charity founded five years ago to help children in areas of conflict or post-conflict. Occasional country rockers *The Notting Hillbillies* have taken time out from 18 gigs at *Ronnie Scott's* to entertain Taplow. Can Maidenhead hear the distinctive guitar of Mark Knopfler, once of *Dire Straits*?

Taplow Court / 2nd June 2011

More than 30 **St Stephen's College** 'old girls' have gathered with their husbands and families to enjoy the Ascension Day picnic courtesy of *SGI-UK* and the warm and sunny weather. They are delighted to find that, although **Winston Churchill**'s looks the worse for wear, 'their' trees still stand at the far end of the Cedar Walk.

Our Friends in the North

Read All About It – Fourth Edition

Dropmore / 14th September 1945

The last four years have brought sharp contrast. No longer was Dropmore a half-forgotten Fortescue family treasure. Having been requisitioned by the Army in 1941, suddenly the whole place was a hive of secret soldiery with officers making battle plans in the secluded comfort of the house and their men training in the extensive woodlands. The US Army took full advantage during its preparations for D-Day. Its departure left a feeling of loss and neglect in the house, its unkempt grounds and the empty nissen-huts peeking through the trees on the western boundary, but now Dropmore is about to buck the trend. Unlike other grand houses taking on new roles, it will return to its roots as a rich man's retreat. It is time for Cinderella to go to the ball.

Today's *London Gazette* carries the news that (James) **Gomer Berry, 1st Baron Kemsley** of Farnham Royal, has been elevated to 1st Viscount Kemsley of Dropmore. He and his brother William Ewart Berry, 1st Viscount Camrose, together acquired *The Sunday Times* in 1915 and *The Financial Times* in 1919. They joined Sir Edward Iliffe in 1924 to found *Allied Newspapers* and acquire *The Daily Telegraph* four years later from **Harry Lawson, 1st Viscount Burnham**. Lord Camrose took ***The Daily Telegraph*** and *The Financial Times* in 1937, leaving his brother Lord Kemsley with ***The Sunday Times***, *The Sunday Graphic* and *The Daily Sketch* as the main titles of *Kemsley Newspapers*.

Now Kemsley has succeeded the Astors and Levy-Lawsons as the local newspaper magnate. As prisoners of war reinstate the house and grounds, he plans to restore Dropmore and fill it with furniture, books and paintings. In 1948 he will bring a pair of 19th Century wrought-iron gates from *Farnham Park* to be installed at the main entrance by ***Dropmore Lodge*** and he will live happily behind them until his death in 1968 while slowly divesting his empire. *The Daily Sketch* will be sold to *Associated*

Newspapers in 1952 and *The Sunday Times* to Roy Thomson in 1959; *The Sunday Graphic* will cease publication in 1960. Meanwhile his nephew Seymour Berry, 2nd Viscount Camrose, will sell *The Financial Times* to *Pearson* in 1957 to leave an extremely tenuous Taplow link alive on the board of *The Daily Telegraph* in Seymour and his brother Michael Berry and in Edward and then Hugh Lawson, the fourth and sixth Lords Burnham, until 1986 when the paper is sold to Conrad Black.

California Dreaming

Sotheby's, Mayfair / 20th March 1969

Two illustrious neighbours have recently arrived at similar crossroads. **Cliveden** and **Dropmore** are no longer family homes. Faced with uncertain futures, both are California dreaming.

When the third **Viscount Astor** died three years ago with no heir wanting to take on his home, many wondered whether the **National Trust** could afford to keep Cliveden in trim. The worry worsened last year when the first **Viscount Kemsley** died because Dropmore has no such capable carer. The Berry family has sold 431 acres to *Broadland Property Co* of Scarborough for £59,500 (£1.87m), 288 acres of woodland (complete with its gravel) to ***Summerleaze*** for £77,000 (£2.42m) and 174 acres of Brook End Farm (including Lambourne's Wood) to an undisclosed buyer for £49,000 (£1.54m): a total of 893 acres for £185,500 (£5.83m). Fearing the worst, the Society has done its best by persuading Eton RDC to place a tree preservation order on the woods. It can do nothing to prevent the family selling "the valuable contents of Dropmore" at auction. Today at the third and final day of the sale, the atmosphere has an air of the end of an era. The total value of the sale will be £249,860 (£7.33m).

Hope springs from two universities on the shores of the Pacific. **Stanford University** is near San Francisco. Late last year it leased Cliveden as a campus where some 80 of its students will soon be spending six months of their degree courses. Stanford will stay until 1983 when it will relocate its UK campus to Oxford. The smooth manoeuvring of its Academic Director Sir Jack Rumbold has encouraged a competitor with a less tender touch. The **United States International University** (USIU) of San Diego has acquired 685 acres of Dropmore with the idea of making it the first of perhaps a dozen foreign campuses.

However, in its haste, USIU will tread on a few toes. Firstly: by felling four acres of woodland near ***The Feathers*** subject to certain replanting provisions. Secondly: by selling off about 200 acres including about a quarter of Grenville's Pinetum, ***Cabrook Cottages***, ***Queen's Lodge*** (which will be rebuilt in a grand manner and secreted behind enormous gates), land on the northern perimeter (for gravel extraction), ***Burwood House*** and ***Brook End Farm*** (much of which will be sold in the mid-1980s to become ***The Lambourne Club*** golf course). And thirdly, much to its own detriment: by not obtaining permission to have the site rescheduled for educational use. And yet its first students will arrive in September and it has ambitions to build new accommodation for up to 350 students to reside for a year of their courses. USIU Director Dr Graddon Rowlands will respond to the Society's successful objections to the gravel extraction proposals with a charm offensive and a promise that areas of Dropmore Park would be re-opened to the public, a practice terminated by Kemsley in 1963. The Society will eventually concede that these academic aspirations are "the least unsatisfactory of various alternatives", but in the summer of 1970 Eton RDC will give permission to build accommodation for only 90 students. Rowlands won't give up. However, in the year it will take to negotiate permission for 350 students, his San Diego superiors will quietly buy Ashdon Park in Sussex and put Dropmore (by then with 7 reception rooms, 38 bedrooms but now just 195 acres) up for sale at £280,000 (£6.75m). The Jon Pertwee incarnation of *Dr Who* will take advantage when the four-part serial *Day of the Daleks* is filmed at Dropmore for broadcast in January 1972.

A Saw Point

Abbott's Wood / 23rd June 1969

Meanwhile there is a buzz here at **Hedsor Sawmill**, once Dropmore's carpentry and joinery workshop, now a substantial electrical works until next year when *TW Murphy & Co* receives an order to desist illegal industrial use. After ideas to convert the sawmill for office use come to nothing in 1973, *Summerleaze* will be granted permission to extend it in 1975.

Abbott's Wood / 23rd June 2008

This path – known as Footpath 21 – was blocked for a time during those years of uncertainty. **Mary Trevallion** believes it is the only remnant of a medieval Pilgrim's Way from **Burnham Abbey** to **Wooburn Palace**. Its probable route came up Lake End Road, Lent Rise Road and Taplow Common Road to Rose Hill, through Wymer's Wood to Cabrook Priory, through Dropmore Park and across Heathfield Road to here, and then on past the sawmill onto Wooburn Common Road, along Broad Lane and then down into Wooburn. The northern and southern stretches are now tarmac roads, the middle bit has long been lost in Dropmore and now even this last 300 yards may be diverted on a longer route around a strange new Tudor-Graeco-Roman mansion which has replaced the sawmill. It will be sad if this ancient way is lost but there are benefits: the new route offers a pleasant woodland walk and a new footpath skirting the eastern and northern edges of Abbott's Wood to link two other rights of way: the Beeches Way from Littleworth Common and the footpath running west of Hedsor golf course to Broad Lane and then on to St Paul's Church at Wooburn down either Wash Hill or the footpath from Berghers Hill.

Something's Blowing – Not Again

Cliveden / 26th January 1990

It's ironic, says Head Gardener **Philip Cotton**. Yesterday morning we were congratulating ourselves on a job well done on the recovery of Cliveden's grounds after the Great Storm of 1987. We knew it would be a windy afternoon but had no idea how bad a storm was coming until just after lunch two police officers knocked on my door. A tree had been uprooted and crushed a car. I just thought, not again.

Perhaps 1,000 trees have been blown down in the last 24 hours. Many were rare and important. Some were over 200 years-old and over 90-feet tall. The wind was blowing at 75 mph and gusting even more strongly: not quite as forceful as during the Great Storm but the damage was twice as bad because hollows created then exposed mature trees to killer gusts from angles never before experienced. Many parts of the Woodland were practically decimated. Green Drive suffered badly. It could take 100 years for certain areas to recover. The National Trust will re-open its Tree & Garden Disaster Appeal which raised £2m (£5m) to aid recovery after 1987. Cotton reckons he will need a similar amount to repeat the trick. Meanwhile **Andy McKenzie** anticipates it will take a year to clear the damage at **Taplow Court** where 32 of the trees in the famous Cedar Walk have fallen.

The Trials of Trevallion

Johnson's Coppice / 26th January 1999

This house by Heathfield Road was ***Cedar Lodge***, Dropmore's western guardian recently renamed after the wood around it because **Mary & Bernard Trevallion** became fed up with their post getting lost at Cedar Chase. When they moved here 30 years ago, the Trevallions decided to tame a nearby stream for their children to paddle and sail their boats. They never saw it again: it was swallowed by a new sink hole. We shouldn't have been surprised, says Mary. This is *Droppingwell* after all. And it can work the other way too: ***Cedar Cottage*** next door has a glass-topped well in its conservatory, an attractive feature until the water level rises dramatically after heavy rainfalls.

Where are the cedars now? Unlike Dropmore's finest specimens of *Cedrus Deodora* planted by **Philip Frost** in 1834, the avenue of *Cedars of Lebanon* he added in the late-1840s did not survive January 1990. The storm toppled many trees. The chainsaw gang which arrived to clear them couldn't resist the unsupervised commercial opportunity: it felled those still standing.

Something's Burning – Third Time Lucky

Dropmore / 11th January 2013

Once again, smoke hangs ominously over Dropmore. Surely history can't repeat itself a third time, not when the old place is seems to be about to be back on track? Reassuring news spreads like wildfire: only trees and brushwood are burning – the fire is under control and the house is safe.

Dark Arabian Nights

Dropmore / 11th January 2007

After the departure of *Dr Who*, Dropmore became shrouded in secrecy. It was acquired in 1972 by **Muhammad Mahdi Al-Tajir**, then and until 1987 the United Arab Emirates ambassador to the UK and France. The Bahrain-born, Lancashire-educated Al-Tajir was the most powerful man in Dubai after its Emir, Sheikh Rashid bin Saeed Maktoum. Having won the Emir's favour by running Dubai customs, he evolved into gold and metal trading, property, oil and gas and to enjoy profitable alliances with Mohammed Al-Fayed, owner of *Harrod's*, and with *Costains*, the British construction and civil engineering group.

Al-Tajir invested £220,000 (£4.7m) to make Dropmore his. It was hoped that such a wealthy and influential man might grow to cherish it. It didn't work out like that. He started well with a generous donation towards the repair of St Anne's Church, only to set the tone for his tenure by using his diplomatic immunity to secure planning permission to build 50 houses in the grounds for his staff. **Tony Hickman** wrote to him requesting that he revive the Fortescue and Kemsley tradition of allowing locals occasional access to enjoy Dropmore's woodlands; he didn't reply. Whispers spread of the main house and the aviary having a major restoration, of valuable art and antiques being installed and of opulence. Privacy was paramount: in 1977 the park's wooden fence was replaced by a secure but intimidating chain-link fence topped with barbed wire. Having been rebuilt by Kemsley as *Dropmore Lodge*, ***Queen's Lodge*** was again rebuilt, this time in a grand manner and secreted behind enormous gates.

The one tradition Al-Tajir did revive was the Fortescue habit of visiting Dropmore only intermittently. He was spoiled for choice. By 1976 he also owned the *Sheraton Park Tower Hotel* in Knightsbridge, *Mereworth Castle* in Kent and *Keir House* and its 15,000 acres in Perthshire. He might drop into Dropmore for Ascot week in a motorcade flanked by police motorcycle outriders. Various children and nannies might appear during the holidays to throw peaches from the conservatory at each other. His wife might stay briefly during West End shopping trips: a collision with the Trevallions' flower butts one icy morning left pieces of her pale blue *Rolls Royce* scattered on their verge. Eventually all family visits died away and twin disasters struck in 1990: an armed gang made off antiques worth over £6m (£15m) months before an electrical fault started a fire which blazed for four days. It destroyed the east wing of the house as well as gold and silverware reputedly worth £60m (£150m). Nobody could be sure but it is unlikely Al-Tajir ever returned, and seven years later another fire at the house destroyed the roof and left it entirely uninhabitable. Valuable garden ornaments disappeared and ***Oak Lodge*** was boarded up, its gates stolen and replaced only by a mess of wire.

Al-Tajir vowed to restore the house but, unconvinced that it was adequately weather-protected, the Dropmore Society hired a helicopter to take aerial photographs which showed their fears were well-founded and sparked South Bucks District Council into requiring appropriate measures to be put in place. Sadly these didn't include the provision of any security. Word got around. Dropmore was a hotspot for crime ranging from growing cannabis, poaching and petty vandalism to theft and hostage-taking. Everything from valuable garden ornaments and wrought ironwork to wardrobes and doormats was pilfered. Even Al-Tajir was at it. **Bernard Trevallion** managed to prevent a lorryload of listed stonework being removed to *Mereworth Castle*. Soon afterwards, as a result of being found guilty of defrauding *Dubai Aluminium*, Al-Tajir became the first former ambassador to the UK for more than a century to be declared *persona non grata*. Bernard sums it up succinctly: "Grenville found a wilderness and left a paradise"; Al-Tajir "found a paradise (albeit somewhat run down) and left a wilderness". And yet today, the former Bahraini's business empire still includes a glass-bottling plant in Dubai, a private bank in the Cayman Islands and Scotland's *Highland Spring* bottled water company. How refreshing is that?

The World's Most Expensive Sandwich

Cliveden / 11th January 2007

The veiled mystery, neglect and abuse of **Dropmore** are magnified by the re-emergence of its neighbour onto the international stage. Cliveden's new life began when it was leased by *Blakeney Hotels*, later ***Cliveden Hotel Ltd***, restored, refurbished and opened in 1985 under the direction of company chairman John Lewis and managing director John Tham, husband of actress Jenny Agutter. Somebody asked what Harold Macmillan thought about Cliveden becoming a hotel. The former Prime Minister smiled to recall coming here in his youth as a guest of the Astors and remarked: "But my dear boy, it always has been".

An indoor swimming pool was added in 1990. Four years later conversion of the west wing brought the total number of bedrooms to 37 in addition to the self-contained *Spring Cottage* down by the Thames. The hotel was listed on the London Stock Exchange as *Cliveden plc* in the 1990s before being acquired in 1998 by *Destination Europe*, a consortium led by Bill Gates of *Microsoft*. There were rumours in 2005 that the American singer Michael Jackson coveted Cliveden but it was acquired by *von Essen Hotels* which took pride in offering guests the Platinum Club Sandwich for £100, confirmed by *Guinness World Records* last year as "the world's most expensive sandwich".

Fairy Godfathers

Dropmore / 11th February 2012

There was hope in 2001 that Cinderella might go to the ball again. **Andre Meyers** of ***Corporate Estates*** turned a poor start into promise but was no Fairy Godfather. His first idea was for the house to be a conference and leisure centre with several residential developments scattered about the park. That wasn't the kind of ball anyone else had in mind. He thought again, consulted locally and negotiated planning permission to create 57 luxurious dwellings: 17 in the house, 23 in existing buildings including ***Cabrook Cottage*** and *Oak Lodge* plus another 17 in a new west wing. Although this involved the loss of 42 trees, it wasn't such a bitter pill. Work began in 2006 and was 70% complete by 2008 when the company went into administration. Once more Dropmore was in the doldrums.

At last, hope glimmers again. Last year through his company *Dropmore Park Estate (Jersey) Ltd*, **Richard Livingstone** acquired Dropmore and declared his intention to renovate the house as a single residence, add another new one of complimentary style in the northern meadow, remove all other modern additions and restore historic but neglected garden structures. And now his local commitment increases as he and his brother Ian, through their primary business *London & Regional Properties*, take over the lease on Cliveden Hotel. Can Richard really be the Fairy Godfather that Dropmore so desperately needs?

Dropmore / 18th January 2014

Could the magic coach be ready to appear? Planning permission was secured last June and today **Mary Trevallion** received a report on progress towards meeting its conditions, the most onerous of which relates to the protection of a colony of greater crested newts. It is hoped that various works of demolition and renovation will start shortly and that the good news won't disappear in a puff of smoke when the clock strikes twelve.

Something's Blowing – Huff and Puff

Cliveden Gages / 18th January 2014

A gage is a valued object deposited as a guarantee of good faith, possibly as a security against an obligation, or something such as a glove thrown down by a medieval knight as a challenge to combat. Which of these applied to the closes clustered together to the east of Cliveden's Green Drive: Gage Meadow, Gage Coppice and Gage Copse? That they already had names implies they had ceased to be common land even before the fifth Lord Inchiquin sequestered the rest of the common in 1787. A clearing south of the Gages was the perfect place for the polo field that **Waldorf Astor** sacrificed for a hospital during the Great War. He was probably past polo by the time he repeated this trick in 1939, a generosity which ironically came to frustrate his declared desire to protect the rural character of his domain from speculative developers. He cannot have imagined such a fate has resulted from his ceding it to the **National Trust**.

It wasn't as if it was a surprise when **CRCMH** closed in 1986 and yet it was three years before there was talk of a new chapter in the story. Planning permission was granted in 1990 for a care-based community of 134 dwellings: 99 houses plus 35 apartments in sheltered accommodation with associated medical and community centres. The Trust thought again and decided it didn't like the numbers. Blight descended. The notion revived ten years later. Still it didn't happen. Taplow "felt that the future should echo at least a morsel of the selfless dedication that made [the site] such a successful medical centre". The Trust had other ideas....

Enter ***Countryside Properties*** and an idea for 191 homes with no wisp about it of social or medical care. This wasn't good faith. How could the National Trust of all organisations aspire to overdevelop an isolated site in an environmentally unsustainable, car-dependent manner? Nobody objected to the Trust seeking to replace its rental income from the *National Health Service* but, as **Mary Trevallion** observed, "It did not seem fitting that.... property developers should profit [from a site with a] strong tradition of voluntary work" associated with the charitable and caring ethos of CRCMH and its wartime predecessors. And soon a strange contradiction arose: in December 2003 the developer's Ecological Survey Report ignored the CRCMH site which months later was designated with the rest of Cliveden as a Biological Notification Site worthy of note for its total of 192 species of fauna and flora including nine very rare plant species. Clearly the authors were dancing to different tunes. The incredulity was hard to stomach. Taplow threw down the glove. The *Cliveden No* Campaign united the Parish Council, the Society and others. When it discovered that its launch had been infiltrated by a wolf in sheep's clothing – a *Countryside* employee posing as a landscape journalist – it retaliated with an article in the London *Evening Standard* featuring Parish Councillor **Euan Felton** and Society Chairman **Anne Hanford**. The *No* Campaign staged a counter-exhibition in Cliveden Hotel on the very day *Countryside* exhibited its scheme in The Orangery, with traffic generation forecasts so inaccurate that it was obliged to apologise to the Society member who had pointed out the error (yours truly). And it enjoyed muddling matters further with the discovery that neither Inchiquin's 1787 sequestration nor the walling of Cliveden in the 1890s by **William Waldorf Astor** had enclosed a narrow strip of common land that runs unbroken between the former hospital site and Cliveden Road. This wasn't **Waldorf Astor**'s to give when he donated Cliveden to the National Trust in 1942. Consequently the Parish Council was duty bound to defend this strip against 'encroachment and trespass' or, in practical terms, vehicular access and its requisite 'visibility splays'.

Countryside applied for planning permission for the 191 scheme. District Councillor **George Sandy** was successful in persuading SBDC to refuse it. The Trust decided to appeal. Huffing turned into serious puffing at its Annual General Meeting when **Karl Lawrence** joined Euan to propose a motion condemning this decision. Those present supported the motion by 32,000 votes to 28,000, only for Chairman William Proby to win the day by casting the 19,000 proxy votes he had up his sleeve. It was finally official: this protector of national assets was diversifying into property speculation. Proby did not distinguish himself with the claim that no offers had been received to build a 'retirement village', only to be trumped when Karl produced a copy of a letter from a developer confirming its offer of £14m (£15.3m) to do just that.

SBDC Offices, Capswood, Denham / 7th November 2005

Thoughts race back to earlier this year when two surprises were sprung. *Countryside* 'floated' a scheme for 170 open-market dwellings. The Campaign swithered; might this be the best game in town? Meanwhile the National Trust indicated it would build the 134 scheme if the 191 is refused on appeal; was this too good to be true?

The Office of the Deputy Prime Minister (otherwise known as John Prescott) appointed an Inspector to hear the appeal. He spent eight long days last August listening to the evidence and the arguments over what constituted the developable site, how many cars each dwelling should have, the number of bicycle sheds, the mini-bus timetable and – most importantly (here was the ruse) – that unlike the 191 scheme, the 134 did not comply with more recent planning guidelines. And further, said *Countryside*, it will generate less traffic. Not if you compare them over the same timescale, replied Euan. **Richard Dawson** asked if anyone had tried running buses to the school and the station in accordance with the proposed timetable: deadly silence was the stern reply. Counsel for *Countryside* – by all accounts on a tidy £30,000-per-diem (£32,400) – referred to a document which Euan pointed out related to Taplow Court not Cliveden and had been signed by Desborough not Astor: laughter in the public gallery. **Eva Lipman**, **Bernard Trevallion** and Karl all added to the case that no number of bicycle-sheds and mini-buses could ever overcome the inherent unsustainability of the 191 scheme. But will the appeal be upheld or rejected?

The Inspector announces his decision: the 191 scheme would be unsustainable in terms of traffic generation and "an inappropriate use of the Green Belt". He adds that this finding is not only accepted but endorsed by the Deputy Prime Minister. It takes a moment to sink in: the *No* Campaign has won a famous victory. *Countryside* and the National Trust have no option but to settle for a compromise: 134 dwellings for the Over-55s but without a medical centre.

Cliveden Gages / 18th January 2014

The huffing and puffing wasn't quite done. *Countryside* wanted to call its estate *Cliveden Village*. For Taplow, this had too much of a whiff of a 1950s holiday camp. And as **John Hanford** observed, "There is no church, school or pub, or indeed any other facilities [that] one would normally expect in a village". Mary & Bernard exercised their knowledge of history to suggest *Cliveden Gages*. And that's what it is, despite *Countryside*'s marketing. And recently with its fourth and final phase, *Countryside* accepted what Taplow had long been saying: larger, more expensive properties sell more easily. Consequently the final estate will comprise 128 homes. The Trevallions live happily in one of the ground floor flats, the Hanfords in one of the houses; none of them are in the least embarrassed to have fought so hard and to reap the benefit of *The Gages* being what it should be.

Southern Comfort

The Dancing Dame

The Rectory / 7th July 1956

Peggy Hookham isn't royalty but try telling that to smitten parishioners. Her charismatic presence glides across the lawn with elegant but easy grace. With sparkling-dark eyes and a smile wide and warm, she takes and shakes every extended hand. The prima ballerina was made Dame **Margot Fonteyn** de Arias in February and her company will become *The Royal Ballet* in October, yet not for a second could anyone think that being guest of honour at St Nicolas' Church fete isn't the highlight of the year for this princess of Amerden.

Margot Fonteyn is and will remain the most famous English ballerina yet her story is as exotic as can be. Her Irish-Protestant grandmother Evelyn Acheson met the dashing Brazilian businessman Antonio Goncalvez Fontes at an ice-rink and nine months later in Derbyshire gave birth to a daughter, Hilda, who in her teens decided to be Nita (short for Juanita) and eventually became known as BQ (for *Black Queen*, from the ballet *Checkmate*). She married Yorkshireman Felix Hookham and gave him two children, Felix and Margaret (hence Peggy) who showed a natural aptitude as soon as she went to ballet school in Ealing. Nita saw the future and took control. In 1927 *British American Tobacco Ltd* sent the elder Felix and his ladies to China while the younger Felix remained at boarding school. Nita made sure that her daughter continued to develop her talent in Tientsin and then Shanghai until civil unrest prevented the pair of them returning in 1933 after visiting young Felix in England. This was fortuitous for Peggy. Ninette de Valois took her into *Vic-Wells Ballet* where her dance partner-to-be Robert Helpmann decided the name Peggy Hookham wouldn't look very glamorous on the billboards. She tried Margaret Fontes for a while before settling on Margot Fonteyn. Within six years at just 20 she was prima ballerina.

Her career has since gone from strength to strength. As *Vic-Wells Ballet* became *Sadler's Wells Ballet* and will soon be *The Royal Ballet*, she danced for choreographers such as Sir Frederick Ashton and Roland Petit. Last year Michael Somes was her partner as she performed in the first-ever colour television broadcast of a ballet: Tchaikovsky's *The Sleeping Beauty*. In 1958 they will dance together in the first British televised performance of *The Nutcracker* and in 1961 at the age of 42 she will begin a long and celebrated partnership with Rudolph Nureyev.

It was BQ who, three or four years ago, decided that ***Amerden Bank*** would make a very nice secluded weekend retreat for her famous daughter. Now a bevy of ballet dancers and their friends gather regularly to put their feet up and let their hair down in what has become a private riverside colony. The gentle gentleman Leslie Edwards has a rustic lean-to abutting the main house where he plays 'The Moaning Widow' to perfection, much to everyone's amusement. Gerd Larsen and Pamela May have taken nearby cottages and hidden their medieval features behind smooth modern finishes. Margot's brother Felix presides over the fun from ***Amerden Lodge***. Having restyled himself **Felix Fonteyn** during the war, he is now a fashion, dance and society photographer in well-connected circles. The Fonteyn flexibility with names is reflected by both his second wife Pheobe (usually Feebee) – formerly Joan Turner – and Margot's husband Roberto Arias – once a lawyer then a journalist, now a diplomat, always Tito.

It was love at first sight when Margot and Tito first met in Cambridge in 1937. However he returned to his native Panama where his family is prominent politically. His father and uncle have both held the presidency and much was expected of him. He married and had three children before being sent to New York as Panamanian ambassador to the United Nations. It was there in 1953 that he re-entered Margot's life by arriving in her dressing room just as she was pinning on her head-dress for the third act of *The Sleeping Beauty*. He showered her with roses, diamonds and mink. She was only too ready to be swept off her feet. He divorced, they married last year and now he is Panama's ambassador in London until his cousin is deposed as president in October. She is utterly devoted to him despite his philandering and will remain so, even while he foments revolution at home and survives an attempted assassination in 1964 which will leave him in a wheelchair for the rest of his life.

Felix and Feebee will be fixtures at Amerden until his death in 1998. They will keep their little collection of cottages a treasured family retreat and the haven in which Margot will settle briefly in the early-1970s to write much of her autobiography before she and Tito eventually retire to Panama in 1979.

Eyes of a Child – Ginny Miall & Louise Green

Cyberspace / 9th July 2014

Louise e-mails to say how exciting it was to dance for Dame Margot that day at the church fete. Ginny thinks it was probably the only occasion when she wore a tutu, so it must have been hired or lent. What did we wear for our weekly ballet class? Not the dreaded knickers again! Certainly the word *leotard* hadn't been invented then, let alone *Lycra*.

Through the Keyhole

River Road / 25th June 2012

It is a curious sight: to the right, the open tranquillity of a riverside lawn and Bray Reach stretching downstream; to the left, what hides behind **Sydney Tanfield**'s eight-foot high brick wall? A narrow gate offers answers. Visiting **Liz & Tim Anderson** is like going through a keyhole to a secret world. Their story begins eight miles away as the crow flies....

Loakes Park, High Wycombe / 19th April 1947

There's very good reason why more people than usual are crammed in here today for the Isthmian League game against Corinthian Casuals. Before play starts, having acquired the freehold of *Loakes Park* two years ago from Lord Peter Carrington, **Frank Adams** will present the deeds of the ground to Wycombe Wanderers Football Club, thereby securing its future.

Frank is a successful sports goods retailer and photographer, a longstanding Councillor of the Football Association and stalwart of amateur football. His heart is with the Wanderers, the team that, but for a short spell with Shepherd's Bush FC and a longer one in military service, he has played for and will help to run as its much-loved patron until his death in 1981. Four years later the club will sell *Loakes Park* in 1985 to allow for the expansion of Wycombe General Hospital and use the proceeds to build a new ground – *Adams Park* – thereby ensuring its benefactor will always be remembered in High Wycombe.

Eastbank, River Road / 19th April 2003

Liz is ensuring that Frank is not forgotten in Taplow by writing an article for the Society's Newsletter 79 (Spring 2003) which explains that he and his wife Muriel bought ***White Place*** in 1948. Having been used as the headquarters of the fire service during the Second War – when firemen were billeted east of **Ellington Road** in two rows of huts that survived until 1954 when they were replaced by *Morcroft* and its neighbours – *White Place* was in a bit of a state but the Adams family put soon that right. They lived there happily for 20 years until schizophrenia overtook the grand old house. In fact, it developed not just a dual but a triple personality for it was unceremoniously chopped into three. Jock McElwain bought the eastern third, once the servants' quarters but graced with the original name, ***Orkney Cottage***, and lived there for 33 years. The north-west third remained *White Place* while the south-west corner became ***Eastbank***. Meanwhile Frank's widow Muriel, as upstanding and elegant as ever, continues to enjoy life in one of Tanfield's Cotswold stone flats.

Tim and Liz bought *Eastbank* in 1968 and raised their family here. As a medical student, Tim had competed for Great Britain in the pole vault at the 1952 Olympics in Helsinki. His best leap of 3.8m wasn't enough to qualify for the final, which was won with an Olympic record of 4.55m by Bob Richards of the USA. When he was practising as a general surgeon in Windsor, Tim also worked at CRCMH as a weekend locum. One thing led to another and in 1967 he joined CRCMH as a gynaecological surgeon and stayed until it closed in 1986; he smiles to recall that all the senior CRCMH midwives were battleaxes except Doreen Slade, a lovely person. Meanwhile he continued to work privately in Windsor where his patients included Olivia, wife of ex-***Beatle*** George Harrison, and their son Dhani.

Liz was also a doctor. Once their four children were old enough in 1974 she resumed her professional career to spend 16 years in general practice at ***Rosebank*** in River Road. She recalls scary moments – an old lady being found strangled in her bed at ***River Court***, checking under her car for a bomb convinced that a patient was an IRA conspirator and having a *Coke* can crumpled before her nose by another patient as he threatened "I'm going to get you" – and the best of times playing violin in the Slough Philharmonic Orchestra, being true to her Christian faith within the **St Nicolas' Church** community and enjoying bird-watching and skiing with Tim, often in the company of their friends **Sheila & Brian Horton**.

Liz had been born in Mandalay, Burma, where her father, a deeply religious medical missionary, translated the Bible into Burmese from the original Classic Greek and Hebrew. These early years left in her a love of South-East Asia which was renewed in 1991 when, as new retirees, she and Tim began two years in Voluntary Service Overseas at Phnom Penh, Cambodia. At the time, this was a dangerous place just emerging from the horrors of the dictator Pol Pot and still threatened by the Khmer Rouge remnant hidden in the northern jungle. Their work treating young prostitutes in the heat and squalor was hard but very worthwhile, as she recorded movingly in her vivid book *Red Lights and Green Lizards*. While they were away, they were pleased to hear that *White Place* had been refused permission to build a bungalow in its garden. Spencer, Betty & Jock Barclay will eventually acquire *White Place* and reunite it with *Orkney Cottage*.

Bath Road – The Magnet Mile

Dumb Bell Bridge, Bath Road / 11th August 2012

It is a little more than a mile along the Bath Road from Maidenhead Bridge to the junction with Lake End and Lent Rise Roads. This stretch of busy road has always been a magnet – once for stagecoaches now cars, once for inns now car sales and a petrol station, once for nurseries now supermarkets – but that's not the whole story. By the station there's a new Thames Valley Police Station where the old Drill Hall once stood, a garden centre, a motorhome sales yard and a motorcycle training school. Across the road, closes once held by Newberry, Colsell and the Rector and the western slice of Cowleys Close are now submerged beneath **Taplow Lake** while the remnant of Cowleys and the adjacent glebe allotment is scarred with tracks left by summer weekend car boot sales which clog the Bath Road. Each of these could tell a tale but here are four others to chew on....

Eyes of a Child – Lynette Murray & Ingrid Thomas

Silchester House Girl's School, Bath Road / 30th September 1966

Ten-year-old Lynette was born at the **CRCMH**. She lives across the river in Lower Cookham Road, Maidenhead, and loves coming here to study with Ingrid in this "spacious and welcoming" Victorian building. Her mother's nieces Giane and Antoinette (Toni) Charpentier had been happy here 15 years ago and now she is too.

The Magnet Mile

Lynette Murray's hat with the SHS Crest / 1966

Silchester Manor Day Nursery
(formerly Silchester House School for Girls) / 2014

The new Bishop Centre:
complete with
an aberrant apostrophe
and yet more traffic lights
on the Bath Road / 2014

Taplow United
– Renzo Casale / 2012

Thames Valley Adventure Playground / 2014

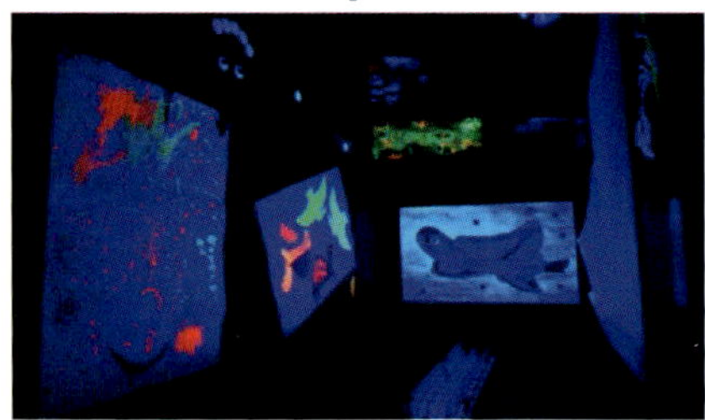

The school is 'mixed' until the age of seven then girls only, mostly day pupils but also a few weekly boarders and some full-timers whose parents are airline crew and often abroad. It can count amongst its 'old girls' Pat Moss and another showjumper, Pat Smythe, who both enjoyed Miss Lemon's tuition. Lynette's own family is international. So are her friends who include French, Swiss, Lebanese, Americans, a Barbadian and (although nobody believed it at first) a Russian princess. As a Rurikid, Princess **Alexandra Obolenksy** must be distantly related to Prince **Alexis Dolgorouki** of Nashdom. Her family fled the 1917 Bolshevik Revolution and her uncle, Prince Alexander Obolensky, is famous for scoring two tries in England's 13-0 rugby union victory over the All Blacks in 1936 and for being killed in action while serving in the Royal Air Force in 1940. Ingrid won't forget her last sports day when the school gate was blocked with screaming girls who thought the handsome actor Warren Beatty was presenting the prizes. The special guest was a film star but the princess's stepfather Robert Beatty doesn't have quite the same heartthrob appeal.

The flavour of the school is set by its principal Mademoiselle **Yvonne Blonay**, a Swiss-born French lady who succeeded **Beatrice Roberts** in 1959 and commemorated her late friend and mentor with a stained glass window in the south aisle of St Nicolas' Church. Mademoiselle lives at the school with two Persian cats. She may have discovered Taplow through her father Baron Godefroy de Blonay who, as a member of the International Olympic Committee (and its president during the Great War), had known **Lord Desborough** from before 1908. When her parents Peter and Daphne first brought her to the school in the spring of 1965, Lynette was rather taken by the petite, elegant, charming, warm and friendly headmistress, only to be surprised by how firm and strict she is once adults are elsewhere. And yet, despite only being allowed to talk French, it is an honour for any girl to be invited very occasionally to sit at her table for lunch, the best part of the school day. The food is delicious, the puddings exceptional: oblong jam or treacle tarts which the elder girl on each table must divide up equally. After lunch, the girls enjoy walking along the lovely veranda at the rear of the school to the gravel playground, although Lynette isn't so keen on skipping there since she fell into the nearby greenhouse, cut her hand and had to be rushed to hospital. She will still have the scar 48 years later.

The tall and capable Miss Forster, the deputy head, also lives at the school. She teaches physical education with great gusto and organises everything from craft fairs and Christmas parties to arranging talks by visiting speakers and the screening of feature films. Captain Parker had a habit of teaching history with the aid of a well-aimed board rubber yet the girls were devastated when he died. Lynette loves searching through her parents' *Encyclopaedia Britannica* to find the answers to the 20 general knowledge questions that are set each week as part of their homework. She isn't so keen on rehearsing her piano pieces or learning poems and yet she can recite Bible passages off-by-heart for the gentle Mistress Gibbons who teaches Scripture. Perhaps that's why she will study theology at Oxford. Mrs Bringes will inspire Ingrid to grow up to write and illustrate her own books.

Silchester Manor Day Nursery, Bath Road / 31st August 2014

Yvonne Blonay was 70 when she passed away in 1967. Silchester House School continued until the 1980s before running out of pupils. After failing in 1991 to get permission to be demolished and replaced by either 11 or 28 flats, it found new life as ***Silchester Manor Day Nursery***, only to come to another crossroads. This testimony to Bond's business acumen and Roberts' determination to give girls as good a chance in life as boys has recently twice survived the threat of being replaced by four houses, the sale of which was intended to fund the construction of a new day nursery to the rear. Can common ground be found between progress and preservation?

Commercial Creep

Bath Road / 30th September 2008

Back in the 1930s, Bob Tanner told Harry Hurn that the spread of urbanisation from Slough wouldn't get beyond *Rochford's*, *Barr's* and *Wood's*. She was wrong. These once large and successful horticultural businesses are long gone. ***Barr's*** was a bulb-grower of national repute until post-war housing on the north side of the Bath Road took priority. ***Rochford's*** supplied vegetables to Covent Garden until *Sainsbury's* thought better of it in 1992 [*see Map 46*]. **Jon Willmore** takes up the story....

William Wood & Sons was a well-respected landscape design and horticultural business on the Bath Road between Hitcham Road and Station Road. It was successful enough to be accorded a Royal Warrant in 1955 for its work at Windsor Castle, almost certainly in the private gardens of Queen Elizabeth II. When Jon left school in 1969 his first job was with this genteel firm. His day began soon after half-seven with the watering of shrubs until ten o'clock when Dick, an accomplished old-fashioned head gardener complete with pipe and pork pie hat, would call him, Hazel and Colin into the potting shed to enjoy Cornish pasties or something similar heated over a paraffin stove. Other colleagues included John, a qualified nurseryman who lived in Lent Rise, and landscape gardener Mr Brett, a gentleman in all senses, whose home was one of the flats in the old grammar school. Jon and his wife Esther live in ***The Lodge*** on Boundary Road, the last remnant of the school since it was replaced by ***Hillmead Court***.

Wood's was taken over in the early-1970s by Jack Bishop, a very different and more dynamic fellow who turned the traditional plant sales business into a retail garden centre in the modern sense while vigorously developing the landscape side. Jon transferred to the drawing office to design such delights as a swimming pool for actor Sid James and a lake for ex-Beatle John Lennon. However celebrity and showbiz clients could only go so far in sustaining the firm and, as times got tighter, ***The Bishop Centre*** forgot its roots to become a drive-in collection of retail outlets. By 1982 a greengrocer and a fishmonger had opened without permission and *Wood's* wares included kitchen utensils, china, glass and household linens as well as plants and gardening tools. And in 1984 *Habitat*, *Payless DIY* and a trout farm were each fined £50 (£140) for trading in prohibited goods.

Bath Road / 30th September 2013

It took a while but the eclectic nature and convenience of *The Bishop Centre* made it a popular feature. There was a cafe, a car wash, a play area and shops selling art and artist materials, party goods, beer and wine, clothes and shoes, double-glazed windows, made-to-measure picture frames, fireplaces, kitchen units, musical instruments, wine and beer, do-it-yourself tools and materials, designer furnishings, antiques, quirky furniture and myriad household bit and pieces. And have I mentioned wine? Many were sad to hear that the site had been acquired by a developer with other ideas. The last plants were sold in 2008 at the *Focus Do-It-All* closing-down sale. The last shop – *Majestic Wines* – closed just after New Year. Now the site has been cleared to make way for *The Bishop's Centre*, a new retail development with an added apostrophe, an unwanted *Tesco* supermarket and the welcome return of *Majestic*. Time will tell but, with *Sainsbury's* expanding down the road, many fear all the extra traffic and the competitive damage to Burnham High Street will be a high price to pay. It has cost the developer over £800,000 in 'sweeteners' to various local authorities and organisations which must now consider how to put it to sufficiently good use to balance the 'quality of life' books....

Taking Control – The Windfall

The Village Centre / 15th July 2014

Taplow Parish Council has £100,000 at its disposal. This 'windfall' is a double-edged sword: an opportunity to leave a legacy, a certainty that the money won't go far enough to suit everybody. The Council invited ideas from parishioners and whittled 56 applications down to just eight which were presented for consideration on 20th May. This evening Chairman **George Sandy** announces that it will support the recording of Sheila's murals, the repair of the Village Green and the roof of St Nicolas' Church, the restoration of Old Priory Garden, the creation of a new map of the Parish footpaths and the strengthening of its influence over development by replacing the 'Advisory' Parish Plan with a Neighbourhood Plan that will have 'Statutory' status.

Sylvia's Vision

Thames Valley Adventure Playground, Bath Road / 11th August 2012

It was 30 years ago today that **Sylvia Livsey** gave them a chance to play. **Barrie Peroni** explains that Sylvia is the wife of **Charles**, son of **Peggy & Derrick Livsey**, then of ***Elibank***. He recalls that her vision was for children with special needs to be able to do things others took for granted. She called **Peter Prior** of ***Summerleaze*** to ask for some sand. He said OK, where do you want it delivered? That was the other problem.

Summerleaze had owned **Taplow Lake** since the early-1960s when it excavated the gravel for use as aggregate in concrete. Peter made available two acres on its northern edge at an annual rent of just £1 (£3). After three years in development, **Thames Valley Adventure Playground** (TVAP) opened in 1982 with just six children coming each day to enjoy its first structure, an aerial walkway for wheelchairs that wobbled like tree branches. Nowadays some 60 children and adults with all kinds of special needs come each day to enjoy the exceptional range of adventurous, therapeutic and educational play activities which offer fun and freedom in a safe, caring and stimulating environment. That adds up to over 13,500 visits a year during which they can spend whole days of fun, playing and laughing together inside and out with their families and carers, who have the opportunity to relax and recharge their batteries by sharing with those who know.

TVAP is a charity funded mainly by voluntary contributions and still enthusiastically supported by *Summerleaze*. As Donations Manager, **Nicky Hutchinson** has a vital responsibility. She arranged a sponsored walk on 19th May, a talk over tea with TVAP patron **Sir Terry Wogan** on 7th July and today's Fun Day. Nearly 300 people have come to see comic actor, broadcaster and charity president **Tim Brooke-Taylor** cut the birthday cake under the watchful eyes of Barrie, chairman since 2004, former chairman **Barbara Prior**, still a tower of strength as one of five trustees, and Sylvia herself, who on 22nd May was presented with the South Bucks District Council Chairman's Community & Voluntary Award for 2012.

The Village Centre / 26th November 1982

The Society's AGM is over. Barbara Prior has just completed a most inspiring illustrated talk about TVAP. **Eric Pope** leaps to his feet and offers his hat to take a collection for the cause. His fellow Taplovians respond by donating over £70 (£216).

Eric will make great contributions to TVAP, not only of money but also of his time and musical talent. For many years until he becomes too ill to continue, he will go two or three times a week to soothe and stimulate children with his music and his humour. He will treasure a most poignant moment when a boy who was unable to speak, having listened with rapt attention to his performance, will take his hands and firmly replace them on the keyboard. He will bequeath his piano to TVAP in the hope that another musician can follow the score.

Old Pals now United

Stanley Jones Field, Berry Hill / 22nd April 2012

The Old Paludians Association was founded in 1915 by former pupils of Slough Secondary School which became Slough Grammar School in 1936. It took its name from the Latin word *palus*, meaning a *marsh*, *muddy mire*, *bog* or *slough*. **The Old Pals** football club was formed in 1924 and in 1955 acquired as its home the old *Dumb Bell* paddock, which it named it after then Chairman and fundraiser-in-chief Stanley Jones. The club built itself a clubhouse by 1958, separated from its parent association in 1988 and ten years later became **Taplow United** under the chairmanship of John Head-Rapson.

Despite the academic connection being broken 24 years ago, club colours have followed those of the school from chocolate to sky blue, navy and amber to maroon and sky blue striped shirts with maroon shorts and socks. Paul Holt has been Chairman since 2007. Like many of those who run the club, he is Taplow-born (at the CRCMH, of course). Three senior sides play on Saturday in the Reading Football League and on Sunday in the Berks Free Press League. In addition there are Under-16 and Under-18 girls' teams and boys' teams all the way from Under-7 up to Under-18. It is in these junior elevens that Taplovians are most evident: youngsters on the pitch, their parents on the touchline....

Eyes of a Child – Renzo Casale, Robert Hutton & Tom King

St Nicolas' School – 23rd April 2012

Renzo likes Taplow United Football Club because he likes to play football. Robert thinks that overall Taplow United is brilliant for all ages with about seven pitches, changing rooms and a clubhouse. It is a place for budding young footballers with a dream. It encourages girls and boy groups, but can be mixed in. Our manager and trainer Gary Jones is kind and good but he can be a little rough sometimes but hardly ever. His training sessions are fun and helpful. Tom likes Taplow United because he really loves to play football. He says I love getting ready for the rest of Sunday by getting muddy and I see all my friends such as Robert, **Louis Ness**, **Louis Plumley**, **Jamie Ashford** and **Theo Wayland-Smith**. There is a bar where you can buy food such as bacon sandwiches and drinks such as *Lucozade* – all very refreshing when you've played football.

Simply Lovely

Amerden Ponds / 26th August 1968

Giles Sim's widow **Joyce** is a dear, kind elderly lady who keeps 'open house' on lazy summer afternoons such as today: August Bank Holiday. **Eva & Max Lipman** have brought their children to learn to swim in her pool. Joyce explains that her home was called ***Amerden Grove*** when **Sir Henry Rae Reid** lived here. When they got older, he and his wife Louisa decided they needed a second pool nearer the house, and this is it. And simply lovely it is too, says Eva. Joyce points to a nearby field where she grows Christmas trees and invites her guests to put a ribbon on one of them to reserve it until just before Christmas, when they should come to chop it down to take home.

This ceremony *en famillie* won't last many years. In 1969 *Amerden Ponds* will survive plans to replace it with a *Futuro* house before finding a new lease of life by being converted into flats, one of which Joyce will rent to Patricia Andrews for a couple of years in the early-1970s. When Patricia pays a nostalgic visit in 1998, she will be sad to see it "rather worse for wear" and not at all surprised to hear a few months later that it had burned down. Various schemes will be proposed before a curved terrace of seven new homes is completed in 2005.

Tall Tale – The Taplow Express

Taplow Station / 7th February 1989

All the buildings have been stripped from Platform 1 which, with Platform 2, has been taken out of service as new and faster trains speed past on the main lines. Nowadays only Platforms 3 and 4 are in use and the fastest diesel-fueled train takes 43 minutes to travel from Taplow to Paddingon. That works out as 30 mph, only fractionally faster than those first steam-driven journeys 151 years ago. Many rue 'the good old days' when Taplow was, as it had always been, the first (or last) stop west of Paddington for 'through-trains' which took just 25 minutes to complete the journey at an average speed of 53 mph.

This very agreeable arrangement ended about ten years ago. Some say it was a remnant of "the time when directors of the *Great Western* lived at Taplow". History doesn't reveal who these influential fellows were. Desborough and Astor had plenty of clout, of course, and the likes of the Serocolds, the Dowsons, the Hanburys, Skimming, Martineau and Page were certainly well-connected but only **George Trumper** fits the bill as a known *GWR* director and yet, although he owned some of Amerden, he doesn't seem to have ever lived hereabouts.

Taplow's many, much-put-upon commuters can only look forward to 2018 when, having been mooted for over 20 years, electrification of the line will allow the launch of *Crossrail*, an advent that could further enhance Taplow's attraction for commuters.

So Long – Saving Amerden House

Amerden House / 19th March 2014

The trustees of ***Amerden Properties Ltd*** were not as trusty in caring for her beloved home as **Selina Whitlaw** might have hoped. ***Amerden House*** had a series of tenants – one cared less for it than he did for his name, which in 1953 he changed by deed pool from Cyril de Lara Bell to Cyril de Lara-Bell (what a relief that must have been) – until it was acquired in the late-1950s by an estate agent who sold it to Michael Brown. His ten years or so here are remembered only for a police raid in about 1960 which discovered 'Miss Whiplash' attending to a Reading dentist who was tied to a bed. Edward Farley Rae bought the place in 1968 and converted it into flats and bedsits for staff working at the John Wyatt Research Laboratory at nearby Huntercombe. That wasn't a success. When **David Long** rented the house in 1971 he was dismayed to find Selina's chapel trying to be a kitchen. This sparked an interest in Whitlaw lore that encouraged him to acquire the house in 1980 and begin a one-man programme of idealistic restoration and preservation that continues today despite occasional visits by members of the Cross family who claim the place was built by their Victorian ancestors. It wasn't: the **George Crosses** father and son lived at and may have built ***Barge Farm House***, long since divided into three flats now in need of tenants as *William Boyer & Sons* seeks to sell the farm itself after sitting on it for over 70 years.

Down by the Riverside

Tales of the Riverbank

Maidenhead Bridge / 31st March 2013

A hundred years ago, this central half-mile of Taplow's riverbank was thriving. Life revolved around *Skindles*, the mill, the boatyards and the big houses. All have seen ups and rather too many downs which, by 20 years ago, had blighted much of it. Some parts have recovered, most haven't yet. The tale starts upstream....

Once More a Paper Tiger

Taplow Paper Mill / 31st March 1933

It has been three years since ***Charles Venables & Co*** folded. Now George Stratton and three fellow directors have left ***Reed & Smith Ltd*** in the West Country to reawaken the Thames-side paper tiger as ***New Taplow Paper Mills Ltd*** [*see Maps 41 & 42*]. As Chief Engineer, George will direct the scrapping of two derelict machines and from the salvaged bits the construction of a single 72-inch machine to turn waste material – mainly cardboard offcuts and bookbinder trimmings – into ticket middles, wrappers and strawpaper for the corrugating industry. When this begins operation at the end of September, it will produce in its first week 16 tonnes of paper with a value of £116 (£4,500). ***Glen Island House*** has been acquired to accommodate offices, its stables are used for storage and a new roll store is being built. Weekly production will rise to 120 tonnes by 1939. The following year *New Taplow* will acquire the freehold of its site from **Desborough** and it will be strong enough to recover from disasters of a serious fire in 1946 and the floods of 1947.

Taplow Paper Mill / 31st March 1978

Reed & Smith acquired *New Taplow* in 1957. This led to new investment which enabled the 1933 machine to be succeeded in 1963 by a 120-inch replacement which uses starch as a size press to recycle container waste to produce fluting medium: the wavy filling in the sandwich of corrugated paper and cardboard from which boxes are made. ***Mill Cottage*** was altered to make space for large vehicles to pass and to be reinvented as the staff canteen. However, having operated discretely and inoffensively for many years, the mill began to cause local considerable upset. In the late-1960s it acquired **Lay Chequers**, the close in the elbow of **Mill Lane**, to create a small car park and a very large concreted area to store its raw material: enormous bales of waste paper. That was unsightly enough but by 1970 it degenerated into an eyesore littered with rubbish and scrap with waste paper blowing across the countryside. And much to everyone's surprise, a warehouse had become a supermarket causing vehicular congestion in the narrow lane. Unauthorised retail use ceased by 1972 but the *Reed & Smith* subsidiary ***Severnside*** began a paper recycling operation and now gigantic trucks are trundling heavily along Mill Lane to deposit enormous sea-going containers in Lay Chequers. This first expansion beyond the mill's semi-secret domain won't be the last: by the mid-1980s these trucks will take to lurking with menace in a concrete lay-by sliced through the wooded grounds of ***Dunloe Lodge***.

At the end of last year, *Reed & Smith* was acquired as a division of the ***St Regis Paper Company*** of Georgia (USA), one of the oldest and biggest paper companies in the world. It will appoint SG Kay as Managing Director of *New Taplow* to execute a major modernisation and expansion. The roll store will become *The Power House*, the stables will be truncated and virtually all the old buildings will be replaced by huge industrial sheds in which annual production will increase from 37,000 to 50,000 tonnes by 1981. JR Kemp has been Commercial Manager of *New Taplow* since the company was founded. When he retires in 1980 after 47 years service he will be succeeded by JR Briggs.

The two years from 1984 will see rapid corporate turnover. First *St Regis* will be acquired by *Champion International Paper* of Ohio. Then a consortium of UK directors will buy out ***St Regis (UK) Ltd*** which within a year will be acquired by ***DS Smith plc***, a London-based group founded in 1940 to manufacture cartons. Having succeeded Kay as Managing Director of *New Taplow*, George's son Sandy Stratton will step up to be Managing Director of ***Reed & Smith (Holdings) Ltd***. And with six mills including *New Taplow*, the *Reed & Smith* division of *St Regis* will quickly become the UK's second largest manufacturer of case materials and a vital element of *DS Smith*'s ambitions to expand into all kinds of paper-manufacturing, packaging, recycling and waste management. The mill will settle into the local business and social community, valued not least for its sponsorship of the Maidenhead Carnival and for staging riverside concerts every summer for the enjoyment of hundreds lining the Ray Mead riverbank. Managing Director Bryan Woodley will be proud to announce in 1990 that the mill is producing 70,000 tonnes of recycled paper each year. And just in case this doesn't sate the thirst for superlatives, he will add that this is equivalent to a ten-foot wide road going around the world five times, saving over a million trees or an area twice the size of Burnham Beeches.

Tranquility playing tricks

Taplow Court looks serenely down on apparently unspoilt countryside but, in fact, is in the middle of a slim rural sliver of Green Belt which prevents Burnham and Slough (top) from merging into Maidenhead (bottom)

The Jubilee River diverges below the ancient wooded slopes which still screen Taplow Court from the derelict mill.... Mill Lane's redundant gasometer and adjacent paper storage site await redevelopment less discretely

Looking north-east

Skindles & Nearby / 1962

Maps 41 & 42 – Down by the Riverside: The Mill and Nearby

So Many Endings

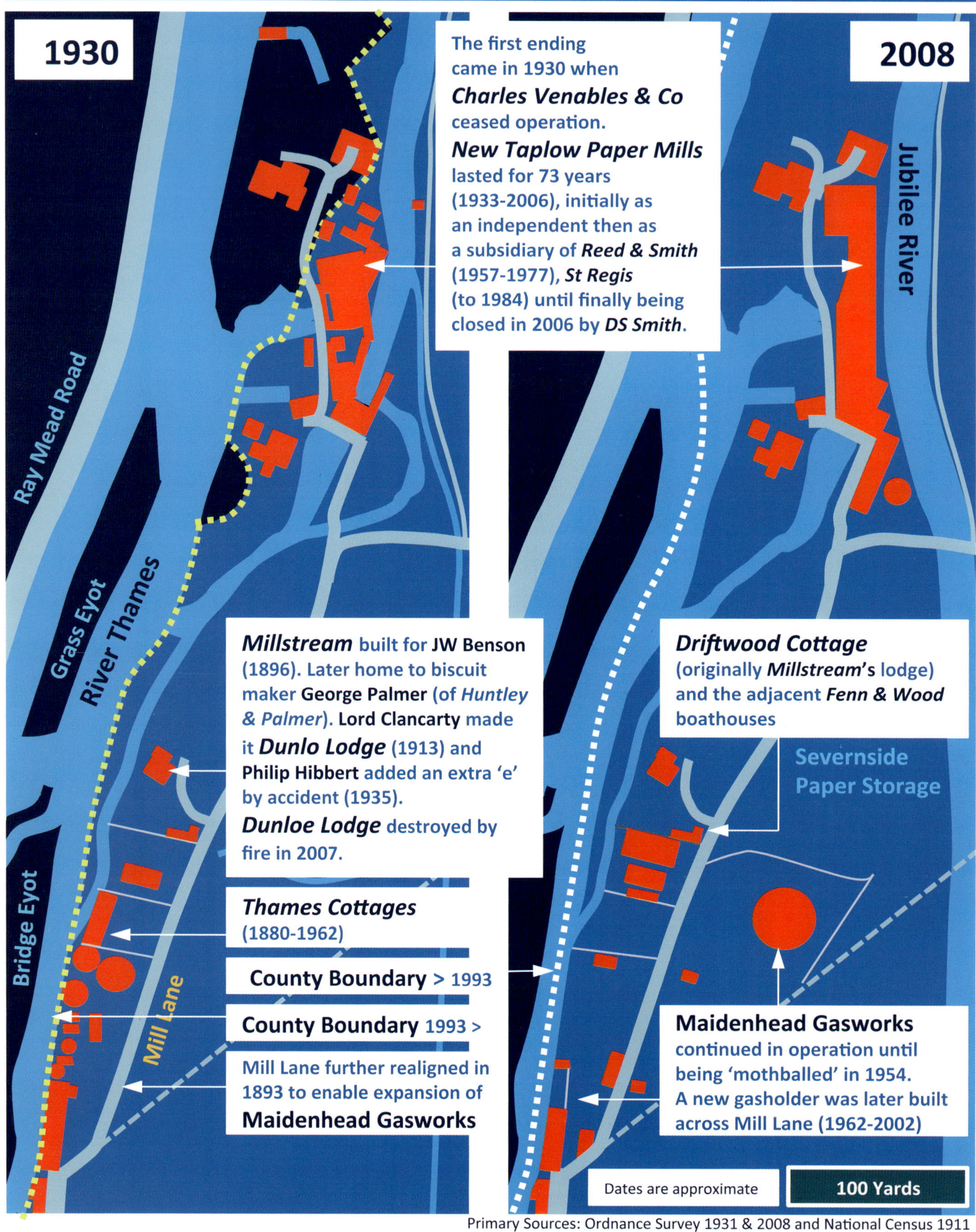

Primary Sources: Ordnance Survey 1931 & 2008 and National Census 1911

Paddy Pause

Maidenhead Bridge / 22nd July 1937

It's a fine view of the boatyard from up here. **George Bond** gives us a wave from the quayside. He's still a director of the company, says **Bill Brown**, but **Paddy Smith** is in charge now – once of Portsmouth and the Merchant Navy. It was autumn last year when we first saw him. There we were, all working hard to complete the conversion of most of our electric launches to petrol. Mr Bond came into the workshop with a party of smartly-dressed gentlemen. One of them was Mr Smith, now the Managing Director. Back on 7th January he invested £6,300 (£1.39m) to acquire the company now called ***Bond's (Maidenhead) Ltd*** under the chairmanship of George Howitt and with Jeph Gillet as company secretary. It was a complicated process, says Bill, because Mr Bond had to get the agreement of our landlord, the Borough of Maidenhead, to assign his lease for the boatyard to the new company. Having uplifted the annual rent to £280 (£14,000) in 1925, the town clerk was all for putting it up again until both vendor and purchaser told him what for.

We were worried for a while, continues Bill. Mr Bond was a popular employer but the business wasn't what it had been. He had already sold off the boatyard east of River Road to become part of the site where ***River Court*** now stands and we were concerned for our jobs. We needn't have been. I was sorry not to be skipper of *Her Majesty's* any more, but being small craft master suits me well enough. The workshops, boathouses and residences have all been repaired and redecorated. I have a new neighbour at *Sunnyside* where Mr Smith and his wife Dorothy (known as Biddy) replaced Mr Bond, who upped sticks to *Rhone Villa*, his father's old home on the Bath Road near to ***Kanellan***, the house he had built in 1934 for his sisters Kate, Ellen (Nellie) and Annie. And most impressively of all, Mr Smith has hung by our boathouse the ship's bell from the original *Mauretania*, a prize he acquired at auction in 1935. What a sight that is. The only other change isn't evident at all to the naked eye: the company pays Mr Bond £20-a-year (£165,000) for a 21-year lease on a triangular section of riverbed between Maidenhead Bridge and Guards' Club Island – or more to the point, the riparian rights that apply to the water flowing over it. And yet Mr Smith will continue the old Bond's tradition that folks can fish here for free as long as they feed some of their catch to the boatyard cats.

Bill recalls that, as well as himself, in December 1936 *Bond's* had skipper George Mitchell, boatman George Truss, driver-cum-fitter **Charlie Johnson** and launchmen Alfred Saw (known as 'Dad'), **Billy Joel** and his brother Harry on the water and foreman **Gilbert Lovegrove** and his brother Albert, an electrician, boatbuilders Tommy Bishop and **Bert Hooper**, fitter Willie Wheeler and clerk Richard Lewcock on land. That's 13 full- and part-time staff in all. **Bert Joel** was no longer on the payroll. He, Billy and Harry had all been born in ***Chalk Pit Lodge –*** probably the house built for lock-keeper **Richard Ray** in the late-1770s and for 40 years from the 1880s the home of their father, **Taplow Court** waterman and watchman **Isaac Joel**, who was usually known by his middle name Fredrick. Weekly wages ranged from Billy's £1 19s (£458) to Willie's three guineas and a ha'penny (£740). And then there was Charles Perry, 'borrowed' from *Skindles* to give everywhere a lick of paint at an hourly rate of 1s 5d (£13) which works out at £3 7s 3d (£517) for a five-and-a-half day week.

All other companies except ***Andrews Brothers*** have given up on electric canoes in the last few years but *Bond's* will continue to offer a few for hire until the company is wound up in 1955. When the actress Beatrice Lillee buys the original 1908 mahogany carvel-hulled canoe in 1946, she will bless it with her nickname, *Beazie*, given to her by Ivor Novello. It will be acquired and restored by Rupert Latham in 1990 and used by his *Steam & Electric Launch Co Ltd* as the master pattern for its new range of glass-reinforced plastic electric canoes.

Not Wanted on the Voyage

Maidenhead Bridge / 22nd February 1941

Nine months ago, 933 'Little Ships' braved the elements and the enemy to rescue over 338,000 troops from Dunkirk. Everybody's talking about how the crews were heroes, says Bill Brown, but it's left a bitter taste at *Bond's*. Mr Smith offered six of our boats and we despatched three as requested only for two – *Flosshilde* and *Esperanza* – to be sent back from Southend for having too much glass and the third – *Good Hope* – to be lost, and I don't mean lost at sea or due to enemy action.

Here's *Flosshilde* now, says Bill as she comes under the Sounding Arch. That'll be Billy Joel at the helm. He still won't talk about him and Bert Childs not being allowed to do their bit. Dad Saw and his son George were aboard the *Esperanza* and they feel much the same. However it's the *Good Hope* that the boss is put out about. As instructed, George Mitchell and Charlie Johnson delivered this 73-passenger launch to Ramsgate where a Royal Navy crew took over. She's never been seen since nor reported missing: all very suspicious. The Ministry of Shipping originally offered £400 (£16,800) in compensation. Mr Smith has succeeded in getting this increased to £600 (£25,200) but it still falls well short of her £900 (£37,800) valuation: all very disappointing.

Fortunately our customers' boats fared better. We offered four with their owners' permission and two were selected. We delivered *Balquhain* to Mr PM Watt at Teddington and he sailed her across, and a fellow called Messum took Mr ET Holme's *Curlew* over with Norman Hinton on board broadcasting for the radio. Mr Hinton lives at *Rowseley* down there in **Gaiety Row**. He knows all there is to know about dinghy racing and such like, and makes his living writing about it.

Young Bayley Lore – The High Life

Skindles Hotel / 1st March 1947

The Nursing Association Ball was one of the big events here in the Thirties, says Norman Smith. *Skindles* was THE spot then, lovely place, right by the river, lovely sprung floor for dancing on, ninepence (£1.30) for a gin-and-tonic and we thought we were

Bond's: Under New Management

Smith (left) **at the Boat Show with his *Mauretania* bell** / 1954

HIRE PRICES 1937 *HIRE CHARGES*

FOR

SKIFFS, PUNTS, DINGHIES, CANOES.

WEEK-DAYS

	£	s.	d.
Per Day		7	6
Per Hour (First)		2	0

1/- per hour after.

SUNDAYS

Per Day		10	6
Per Hour		2	0

Camping Punts & Skiffs

Week-End		17	6
One Week	£1	15	0
Two Weeks	£3	5	0

HOLIDAY WEEK-ENDS—Special Charge.

Cabin Cruisers

(2 and 4 BERTHS)

Per Week ... ... from £5 10 0

The above charge includes full Lock Pass and Insurance

During HENLEY REGATTA WEEK we have a position for Hire of Launches, Punts, etc. Prices on application.

PRIVATE LAUNCHES, BOATS, Etc., HOUSED VARNISHED and PAINTED.

LARGE STORING SHEDS.

Steam Launches

	Week-day	Sat. & Sun.
To carry 150	from 12 gns.	15 gns.
„ 50	„ 6 gns.	9 gns.

Petrol and Electric Launches

	Week-day	Sat. & Sun.
To carry 6	from 3 gns.	4 gns.
„ up to 20	according to size	

Electric Canoes

	Week-day	Sat. & Sun.
To carry 6 ...	from 2½ gns.	4 gns.

We have the largest and smartest fleet of Launches and Electric Canoes on the Upper Thames.

RIVER CRAFT OF ALL DESCRIPTIONS FOR SALE AND HIRE, BOUGHT AND SOLD ON COMMISSION.

EASY PAYMENTS ARRANGED.

Launches inspected, bought & sold on commission.

Bond's boats for hire / 1930s

ESTABLISHED OVER A CENTURY.

Telegrams: "Bond's, Bridge, Maidenhead."
Telephone: No. 16, Maidenhead.

BOND'S,

LAUNCH & BOAT BUILDERS & PROPRIETORS,

MAIDENHEAD BRIDGE, Berks.

Nearest Station (G.W.R.): Taplow.

ELECTRIC CANOES A SPECIALITY.

Slipway for hauling out Launches. Charging Station for Electric Launches.

RIVER CRAFT OF ALL DESCRIPTIONS FOR SALE AND HIRE OR BOUGHT AND SOLD ON COMMISSION.

LAUNCHES & SMALL CRAFT HOUSED, OVERHAULED & REPAIRED.

c1947

Revised List of BOND'S LAUNCHES in Commission.

Name	Comfortable Carrying Capacity	Saloon to Dine	Lavatory	PRICES FOR HIRE Ordinary Day	Saturday	Sunday
				Guineas	Guineas	Guineas
STEAM:						
"Her Majesty"	150	54	Ladies and Gents.	14	18	18
"Good Hope"	50	18	Yes	7	9	10
MOTOR:						
"Flosshilde"	20	15	do.	6	8	9
"Madcap"	10	6	do.	5	6	7
"Emerald Isle"	12	8	No	5	6	7
"Selma"	10	Awning	—	4	5	6
"Wave"	10	do.	—	4	5	6
ELECTRIC:						
"Kerlew"	12	8	—	5	6	7
"Colonial"	10	Awning	—	4	5	6
"Marconi"	8	do.	—	4	5	6
"Cherie"	6	do.	—	3	4	5
"Toni"	6	do.	—	3	4	5
ELECTRIC CANOES:						
"Clarijim"	6	—	—	3	4	5
"Nelson"	6	—	—	3	4	5
"Maruchita"	6	—	—	3	4	5
"Neil"	6	—	—	3	4	5
"B"	6	—	—	3	4	5
"Hermit"	6	—	—	3	4	5
"Gee"	6	—	—	3	4	5
"Woggs"	6	—	—	3	4	5

☞ *These prices do not include Special Days, such as Ascot Sunday, Regatta Days, &c. Terms for these days on application.*

Sidney 'Paddy' Sutton Smith / 1945

Festival of Britain / 1951

Her Majesty's / c1937

Electric canoe *Victoria* / c1950

Silver Javelin / c1950

being done! Mary Rose remembers one night during the war when the Air Auxillary Transport came – all in uniform, of course – and she got to dance with the famous aviator Jim Mollison.

Nanette Garwood thinks ***Skindles*** epitomises the high life. It is the one place you want to go. Before we married, Stanley would save up to stand me tea here. It was all so sophisticated. I would worry that my dress wasn't the right length, or that I didn't have the right gloves. The Garwoods are back for tonight's dinner dance with Nanette's sister Pauline Oppenheimer. It cost seven-and-six each (£12.80) to get in – a ruinous price, says Pauline, but it's fun to properly dress up: long skirts for the girls and dinner jackets or uniform for the men. There is always live music and if you ask they'll come to our table to play a special request. It will be a late night tonight for us girls. I won't be home until half-past-ten or eleven. And if I keep you up too late, smiles Pauline's fiancé **Michael Bayley**, your mother will walk hard across the floor above the drawing room to make the chandelier tinkle.

Harding Happening – Watching the Waters

Caversham, Marsh Lane / 16th March 1947

Ten-year old **Anthony Harding** can't believe his eyes. The river keeps creeping up **Marsh Lane** inch-by-inch. It is almost at the kink in the lane. And here, at the third most northerly house, the water table is already so high that the cess pit is overflowing and dirty water has seeped under the floorboards. How much higher will it go?

The Harding home will not be swamped, not quite. In two days, the river will reach its highest point just north of the kink. Only the southern lowland stretches of Taplow will be flooded. The paper mill will be out of action for five days. *Skindle's* will be a mess. Maidenhead will count the cost as over 2,000 homes are affected. When the water recedes, hundreds of baby pike will be trapped in the furrows of *Withy's*, a close of pollarded willows off ***Devil's Lane***. Anthony and his pal **Michael Mann** will valiantly rescue them in buckets only to fail to improve their lot by pouring them, not into the river, but instead into a shallow pond at the top end of *Ye Meads*.

Water, Water Everywhere

Maidenhead Town Hall / 15th September 1947

As councillor for Oldfield Ward and chairman of most local river associations, nobody is better qualified or positioned than **Paddy Smith** to sit on Maidenhead's Floods Subcommittee as it considers a report on the floods last March by Town Clerk JA Baird and Borough Engineer CT Read. He notes the level of the river and the intensity or speed of flow are the primary factors determining whether the Thames Conservancy grades floods from 'Small' though 'Serious' and 'Major' to 'Disastrous'. He remarks that small floods have been recorded on 939 days in the 63 years preceding 1947. In that time there have also been 84 days of serious floods, 58 major and only five disastrous – all in 1894, and **Thames Conservancy**'s Chief Engineer RVW Stock has "grave doubts" over the accuracy of the records for that supposedly worst-ever flood.

Paddy tables his own graph of levels recorded last March on the gauge at the Sounding Arch. The river there was five-feet deep at midnight on the 12th. It rose rapidly by three-and-a half-feet over four days then after peaking at just over eight-feet-eight-inches on the 18th – almost six inches below the 1894 level – it took ten further days to subside to its original level. He ventures that at this point a depth of seven-feet-six might be considered a disastrous flood when compared to major floods of seven-feet-two in 1940 and six-feet-seven in 1939. Other major floods in 1900, 1915 and 1929 reached lower levels but higher intensity of flow.

The report observes that "the amount of dredging [of the river] would not have made any appreciable difference to the recent floods" and identifies two factors which are most significant in causing floods: the amount and concentration of rainfall or snowfall and the degree to which the ground was frozen and therefore incapable of absorbing water. The first factor was pertinent in 1894 and 1929 while the second factor was more so in 1900, 1928, 1933, 1940 and especially this year when snow fell heavily on frozen ground on 4th March and then melted rapidly on the 10th. Paddy remarks on two other aspects: firstly, the "little knowledge" that Thames Conservancy seems to have "of the amount of free water in its [catchment area of 3,812 square miles] and the amount of flood it will produce [given] land drainage" of 2,382 square miles; and secondly, that Maidenhead "householders seem to have forgotten that they live in a flood area".

The Subcommittee goes on to recommend how and where river levels and flow should be monitored and the need for command and control in erecting elevated plank footways, mobilising boats and amphibious transport and arranging communication, safety precautions, evacuation and emergency "food, necessaries and meals". Although water levels will rise in 1954 to about six-feet at the Sounding Arch, it will be many-a-year before floods rise anywhere near the "disastrous" level of 1947.

Andrews Anew

Ray Mead Road, Maidenhead / 15th September 1947

E Andrews & Sons went from strength to strength until 1937 when 91-year-old Ned died and his sons recast the business as ***Andrews Brothers***. John ran the Taplow yard until he went upstream to build new boats at Bourne End leaving Harold in charge at Taplow. Meanwhile Frederick is here sandwiched between *Bushnell's*, which has taken over *Wilder's*, and ***Bond's***, which built

Bridge Villa in 1926. Jack Bushnell of Wargrave has held a Royal Warrant since before the Great War and ***Bond's*** are well-established but Frederick thinks the boat sales showroom across the road gives ***Andrews*** an edge. His daughter Pamela says it is "new and commodious". Her sister Peggy is married to Peter Farmiloe of Datchet. Recently in a flat above the showroom she gave birth to their son, **Michael Farmiloe**, who will grow up to take over the business.

Fred Horsham was professional punting champion twice before the war but now everyone agrees that two *Andrews* watermen – the Edwards twins, Spider and Wilson – are the ones to beat in the Maidenhead Mile, a race that starts at *Bond's* boatyard and goes half-a-mile downstream and back. It is one of the main events in the annual Maidenhead & Bray Watermen's Regatta which ends with crowds cramming the *Skindles* lawn to down a little refreshment while watching Maidenhead take on Bray at canoe football.

Row, Row, Row the Boat

Henley / 9th August 1948

The stewards won't allow Jack's son Bertie Bushnell to enter the Leander Club. They don't believe he is posh enough to partner Dickie Burnell of Kingston Rowing Club in the Olympic double sculls final. They aren't exactly best friends. Bertie is a former Royal Navy Chief Petty Officer who was involved in the evacuation of Dunkirk. He would lose his amateur status if he worked for his father so he is a marine engineer at *Thornycroft* where his having unpaid time off to compete in the Olympics is "a bloody nuisance". Dickie is an Old Etonian, Oxonian rowing correspondent and author who held a commission with the London Rifle Brigade. Despite these sharply differing backgrounds, they make a formidable pair on the water. A crowd of 20,000 will cheer them on as they power to win the gold medal from the Danes and Uruguayans.

Bertie won't treasure the memory. He will recall "The Olympics didn't feel a big deal. It was like Henley Regatta with a few foreigners thrown in". Instead he will settle down happily to take over his father's yard and rent out cabin cruisers until 1979. He will earn the nickname 'Recirc Bert' for inventing recirculative 'pump-out heads' (on-board lavatories). Now that's a real claim to fame.

The Italian Job

62 King Street, Maidenhead / 12th July 1950

Giulio Trapani can't quite believe it. ***Skindles*** is his. The old place has had a tough time of late. **James Hodgson** (or his brother) finally sold *Skindles* in 1934 to a company with the imaginative name of *Skindles (1934) Ltd*. The high life continued well enough until the disasters of 1947 when first a severe fire and then the floods put the business on the back foot. Despite featuring in *Kind Hearts and Coronets* (1949), it hasn't really recovered. Giulio intends to put that right.

The auction today here at the offices of *Cyril Jones & Clifton* wasn't quite as straightforward as he expected. It is said that Lord Desborough left *Skindles* to his daughter Imogen's daughter Camilla only for her father **Henry Gage, 6th Viscount Gage**, to decide it is too disreputable an asset to be held by someone still not yet 13-years-old. However the complication wasn't to do with the immaturity of the vendor: the land was offered in four lots, each of which took some understanding....

Lot 1 consists of three parcels of land. The first on the east side of **Mill Lane** comprises *Skindles Hotel* itself (formerly *The Orkney Arms*) with ***The Orkney Arms*** (formerly *Skindles Hotel Bar* and before that *The Hotel Tap*) and a small cottage let to Mr Tombs at 15s-a-week (£22). The second to the north of the first was once known as **Horse Radish Paddock**. This pair passed on 5th August 1930 to **Lord Desborough** who on 21st June 1939 renewed its lease to *Skindles (1934) Ltd* for 99 years at an annual rental of £341 (£18,500). Guilio now holds the remainder of that lease. He also holds the freehold of the third parcel west of Mill Lane which having been acquired by the Hodgsons on 5th August 1930 now comprises the riverside *American Bar, Restaurant & Hotel* [*see Map 43*]. The original hotel boasts 14 bedrooms and two bars with another bar and taproom in *The Orkney Arms* to the rear, facing Mill Lane. Its American cousin has another 18 bedrooms (with separate bathrooms and WCs) and a Masonic room together with a sumptuous L-shaped oak-panelled bar, lounge, dining room and ballroom all overlooking the river through full-length windows and doors opening onto the riverside lawn. The special conditions of sale stipulate that a small 50-foot long riverside portion of land "belongs to the Borough of Maidenhead and is held at will from *Messrs Bonds Boathouse*". This is the protrusion that **Jonathan Bond the Younger** leased from Maidenhead in 1891.

It isn't clear when one of *Skindles'* owners acquired ***Nº 5 The Causeway***, formerly ***Island View***, but now it is Lot 2, a "freehold semi-detached riverside house divided into three flats"; one is vacant, the others let to Mrs Huntley at £1 10s (£45) per week and to Mrs Lucas at £1 7s 6d (£41) per week. The freehold of Lots 3 and 4 passed from Lord Desborough to the **Taplow Court** Estate on his death in 1945. Both were offered for sale today under the terms of leases dated 25th March 1939 subsequently incorporated into the lease of 21st June that year. Lot 3 is occupied by *Skindles Garage Ltd* which has 16 years remaining on its tenure at an annual rental of £275 (£8,220). Lot 4 consists of two parcels: the market garden on the Bath Road frontage has 88 years remaining at £15 (£450) per annum and the 1.63-acre paddock to the north – once the southern portion of Upper Thames Field – has 16 years remaining at £10 (£300) per annum.

As owner of *Ye Olde Bell Hotel* in Hurley, Giulio is an old hand at running upmarket destinations. He will recover from all these complications to restore *Skindles* to its illustrious place as a playground for the elite. He will pay **Mick Free**'s brother-in-law John Dean to install electric light standards on Maidenhead Bridge to improve the view from *Skindles* at night. His tea dances and

Map 43 – Down by the Riverside: The Evolving Skindles

As auctioned on 12th July 1950

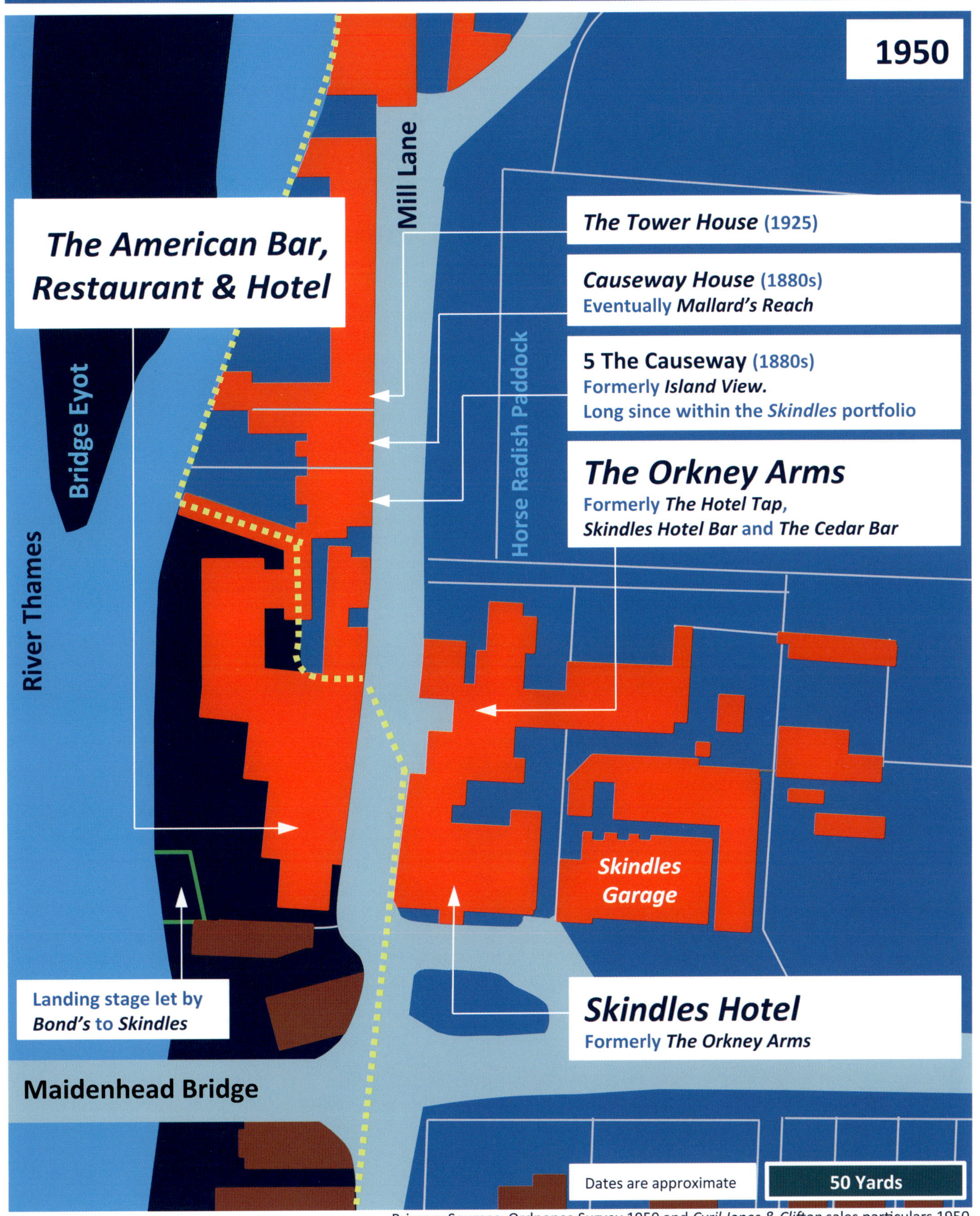

Primary Sources: Ordnance Survey 1950 and *Cyril Jones & Clifton* sales particulars 1950

more private hospitality will be enjoyed by Hollywood stars such as Bette Davis, Boris Karloff and the Marx Brothers, by the Queen's sister Princess Margaret and by visiting dignitaries including US Vice-President Richard Nixon and His Majesty King Hussein of Jordan, who will stay here on almost every visit he makes to London.

Making a Splash

Ray Mill Island / 17th June 1951

The confident and competent **Paddy Smith** is in his element as Honorary Secretary to the Maidenhead & District Festival of Britain General Committee. The aim of the Festival is to give Britons a feeling of recovery in the aftermath of war and to promote Britsh contribution to science, technology, industrial design, architecture and the arts. Other events will be held elsewhere in the town later this summer but, as Councillor for Oldfield Ward and Chairman of most local river associations, nobody is better qualified or positioned than Paddy to preside over this afternoon's spectacular River Pageant in which "a Unique Procession of River Crafts" will "revive the glories Maidenhead's Ascot Sunday".

The author Dorothy Upson is the daughter of Arthur Upson, erstwhile Mayor of **Maidenhead**, and the great-great-niece of Ann & **Richard Cleare** of ***The Dumb Bell***. She recalls in the River Pageant programme the time before the shadow of war fell across the land....

"In the early days of this century, the Sunday after the Ascot race meeting gradually came to be celebrated as a river festival.... by the gayer section of the English people. It was often said that if one sat on the steps of **Boulter's Lock** on that day, one would see everyone of note. An exaggeration, no doubt, but with a foundation of truth for Ascot Sunday came to take its place as one of the definite dates in the social calendar.

King Edward VII often brought a launch party of friends though Boulter's Lock [and] house parties from Cliveden and Taplow Court embarked in launches and punts to see and be seen. Cabinet ministers, peers and peeresses, sportsmen, writers, actors and actresses joined in the water carnival and the hotels were crammed to capacity.

To negotiate Boulter's Lock was a matter of at least an hour's waiting upstream and downstream, but that was a matter of satisfaction to the gaily dressed river throng who rightly regarded themselves as part of a living pageant. The ladies often wore the creations they had flaunted on Gold Cup day in the Royal Enclosure and the men did not lag behind in sartorial splendour for a contemporary journalist wrote the following: 'Young men, clad in all varieties of flannels, some entirely in cream, with gold crests emblazoned on the breast pockets, some with mauve shirts and some with green shirts, but all with the most gay-looking ribbons round their fine straw hats escorted beautifully-dressed ladies'."

Her programme notes continue by explaining that "the people of Maidenhead have tried to recreate some of the glamour and beauty of those days [before the Great War] to prove that some of the gaiety lingers yet in our lovely reaches of the Thames. Austerity is with us, but sunshine and rippling water, music and pageantry, are not rationed and it is good to be gay and carefree, if only for a few hours".

Miss Upson is right. An estimated 20,000 people have come to see the spectacle. As this year's Mayor of Maidenhead, JB Maudsley is of course the official host. He has arrived by launch from *Skindles Hotel* in the company of our guests of honour, stars of stage and screen Cecily Courtneidge, Ronald Howard and Richard Todd: the first a former *Gaiety Girl*, the last currently of ***Neighbours*** in Taplow's newly-named **Hill Farm Road**. They stand on the landing stage to watch the procession pass by. It is appropriate that *Waterlily* leads the way for she has seen service since 1867. Next in line are veteran craft from 1880 to 1910 with crews in period costumes created for the occasion by the ladies of Maidenhead and Taplow. Beyond them are modern craft – but calamity comes first!

The landing stage has collapsed! Miss Courtneidge and two others are in the water! How did that happen? The unfortunate trio are fished out as quickly and with as much as delicacy as possible. The grand actress has hurt nothing but her pride yet clearly this has been wounded deeply. She departs in haste spluttering a threat to sue. **Lady Astor** glances in disdain and signals that festivities will continue by loudly admiring the *Silver Javelin*, a sleek launch designed by Paddy and his friends **John Fenn** and **Charlie Wood**.

The garden party gets under way despite the cloud hanging over the organisers, who gather as casually as they can to consider their position. The stirring music of the band of the Grenadier Guards provides a kind of confidentiality to their whispered deliberation. Paddy thinks Miss Courtneidge should be grateful for the publicity but the view prevails that the Corporation must admit liability. Next week he will accompany Mr Maudsley and town clerk Stanley Platt to the *Saville Theatre* in London's Shaftesbury Avenue to see her star in Ivor Novello's *Gay's the Word*. They will smile to hide their embarrassment at the on-stage quips about the mishap but not when they visit her dressing room after the show to apologise, only for her to sit stony-faced and flanked by solicitors: so much for gaiety.

Bond's No More

Bond's Boatyard / 18th October 1955

How could it come to this, wonders Paddy Smith. He was proud to play a prominent role in arranging the first Boat Show at *Olympia*, opened on 28th December 1954 by the ringing of his *Mauretania* bell, and yet utterly dismayed to be unable to keep *Bond's* afloat.

Selling off the Silver

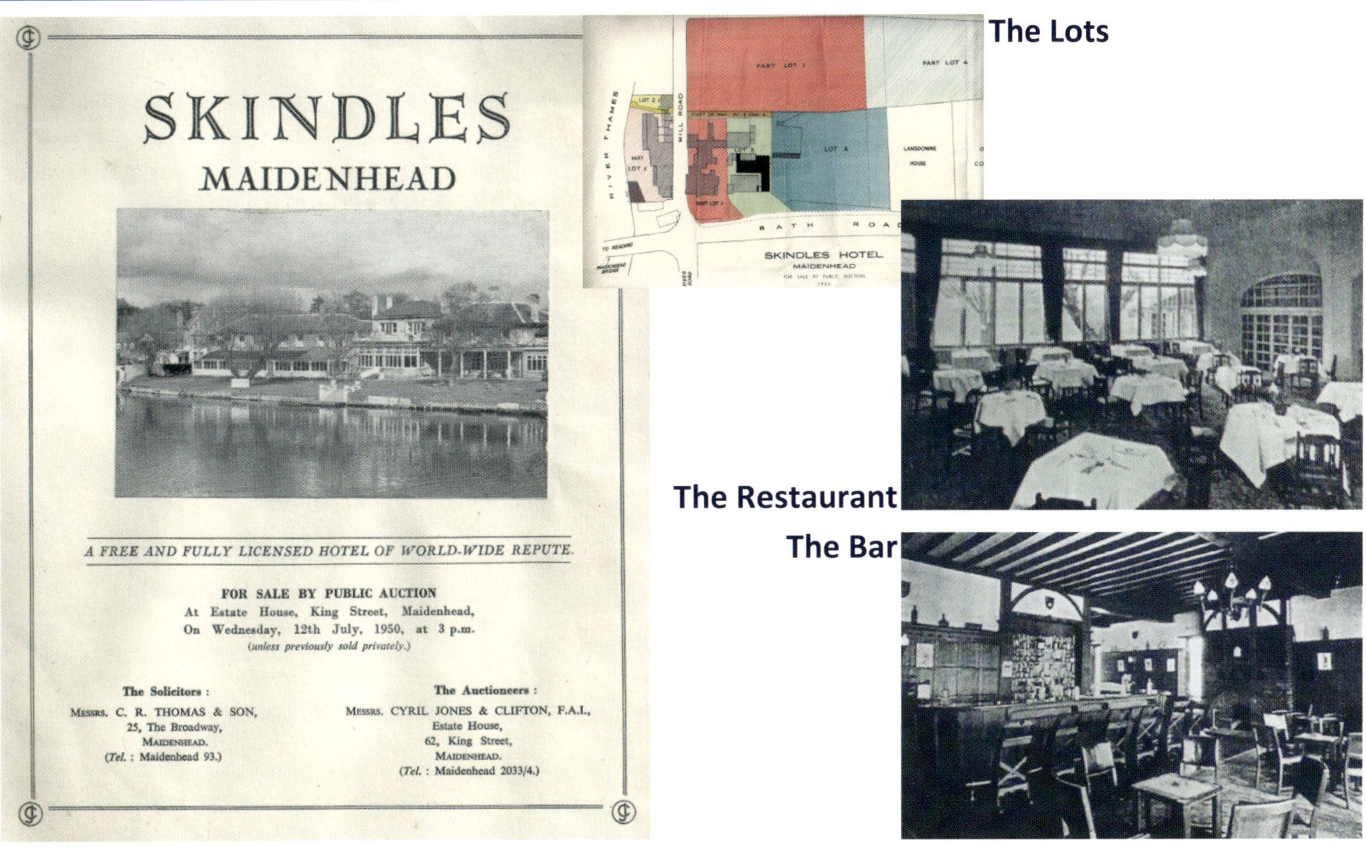

The Lots

The Restaurant

The Bar

***Skindles* for sale in five lots** / 1950

***Bond's* for sale in 690 lots** / 1955

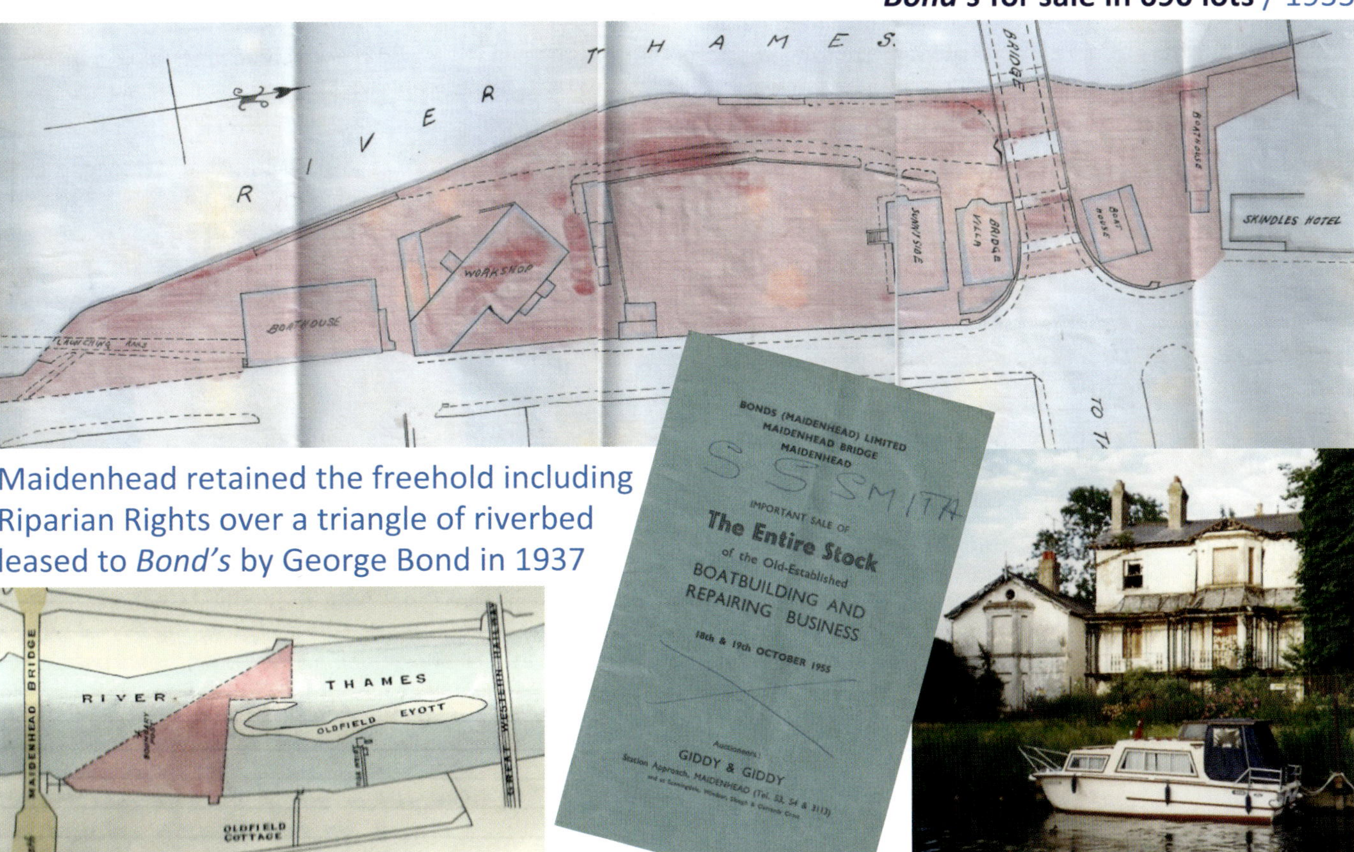

Maidenhead retained the freehold including Riparian Rights over a triangle of riverbed leased to *Bond's* by George Bond in 1937

Bridge Villa & Sunnyside / 1997

The company's lease will expire next March. In January last year Maidenhead Corporation made two offers to extend the lease, the best of which involved more than doubling the annual rent to £600 (£13,700) for a 14-year lease to begin immediately. In addition, the rates were to increase by a similar proportion to £750 (£17,200). Paddy had been astonished. His good relationship with the Corporation over many years clearly counted for nothing. Surely councillors knew that such demands would be the end of the business? And yet when he brought this to their attention, their surveyors compiled a claim for more than £8,300 (£190,000) in dilapidations.

Today the boatyard is swarming with people eager to pore over the remains of the business and to pick up the pieces in an auction of over 600 lots, conducted by *Giddy & Giddy*. Nothing is going for what Paddy expected. The eight cruisers went for £2,750 (£63,000), £600 less than hoped, and now the *Silver Javelin* has fetched £250 (£5,700). This is only £25 (£570) under his value but suddenly the hurt of it all is etched on his face. He will take quiet solace to have sold the *Mauretania* bell privately – it will soon be in the reception of *Lloyd's Registry of Shipping* – as this two-day auction realises £8,147 (£186,500). The company will eventually be liquidated on 29th March 1957. The lease will be taken up by the former motor engineer **Richard Springfield** of N° 4 **River Court**: a character not short of confidence, full of stories about all the clever things he'd done, could do and will do.

Fenn in the Fast Lane

Coniston Water / 4th January 1967

BBC TV News cameraman **Eddy Smales** breathes out slowly as he pans his camera to follow *Bluebird K7* as she accelerates to 328mph on her second run. Suddenly she begins to lose speed dramatically. Eddy instinctively zooms out just in time to keep her fatal somersault in frame. He zooms back in on *Bluebird* as she cartwheels, settles and sinks. It is a tragic end to **Donald Campbell**'s attempt to recapture the world water speed record. It will be over 34 years before his body is recovered from the depths.

Eddy had met and admired Campbell but he didn't know him. **John Fenn** was such a good friend that the speed-king had been his best man, and when Eileen's wedding ring slipped off her finger some years ago, Donald kept on scuba-diving down into the dark waters of Coniston until he found it.

John was born and brought up at *Oldfield House* in Maidenhead. Like his father Bertie – owner of a successful London light bulb factory – he had an eye for the main chance and a love of life. His post-war service in the RAF and a spell as UK agent for an American company introduced him to new aeronautical technologies and sowed seeds which bloomed when he and **Charlie Wood** revived memories of *Bond's*. He acquired ***Driftwood Cottage*** on **Mill Lane** – originally the lodge of ***Dunloe Lodge***, latterly a fisherman's cottage – and added a second riverbank boathouse where he and Charlie crafted boats of cold-moulded plywood. Their innovative *Meteor* motorboats were launched on a double-stand at the 1954 Boat Show. Enthusiasts flocked to admire their stylish hull design, sample the modern creature comforts of their soft-padded weatherproof seats and meet the trend-setting John, the man who claims to have introduced water-skiing to the UK.

Business boomed. Soon ***Fenn & Wood*** had 14 employees building boats for customers in Europe and the USA as well as across the UK. One of them was Campbell. Initially their common ground was a liking of 'live for today' leisure. That changed in 1957 when Donald set the world water speed record at 239mph and declared his ambition to break the land speed record. Suddenly he was a national hero and in such demand that he needed a public relations officer. Who better than his smooth-talking friend Mr Fenn? John was swept into Donald's slipstream. Although *Fenn & Wood* continued to ply its trade, his focus was more and more on living life in the fast lane. He was with Donald at Coniston in 1958 and 1959 when he rescued Eileen's ring before edging the water speed record up to 260mph, in the USA in 1960 during the development of *Bluebird CN7* and in Australia in 1964 when Donald became the first (and in 2014 still the only) person to break both speed records on land (403mph) and on water (276mph) in the same year.

When they had the time, the pals enjoyed relaxing in Taplow. John's riverbank just upstream from *Skindles* is the mooring of choice for Donald's spectrum of showbiz connections. In recent years they have often been seen on the river with the likes of Hollywood film star Diana Dors (who lives across the river at *Woodhurst* on Ray Mead Road) and *The Saint* (who is Roger Moore). And if the wags are to be believed, when they can't be seen, they are partying in private in the way that celebrities do. All his galavanting and globe-trotting came at a cost – *Fenn & Wood* folded and so did his marriage – but John will recover to resume his social whirl for many years. His boathouses are now a depot for *Southwestern Marine Factors* and he will shortly join Warren Curtis in another new venture next door: the first cash-and-carry in England. Curtis will employ **Arthur Grout** to run ***Warren's Warehouse*** only for it to be a shooting star. Long queues of traffic clogging Mill Lane will draw attention to its lack of planning permission for retail use and its brief, spectacular explosion of success will quickly fade in 1972 when it returns to being the warehouse it first claimed to be. Arthur will transfer to the original *Warren's* on Farnham Road

Streets Ahead

Skindles Hotel / 23rd May 1970

There is good reason to celebrate at *Skindles* right now: the hotel features daily on television. ***The Scaffold*** sings a version of their hit *Lily the Pink* to promote *Watney's Pale Ale* in an advertisement directed by the soon-to-be-famous Ridley Scott. **Lesley & Geoff Street** are celebrating too: they got married this afternoon. The young couple are treating themselves by spending the first night of their honeymoon in the famous *Skindles Hotel*. One night is all they can afford, but oh what a night!

That's quite enough of that. The happy couple will do what happy couples do at N° 1 ***Church Cottages*** until 1978 when they begin 35 years at ***East Bapsey***. Their sons Dan, James and Tim will be both cost and consolation.

Tall Tale – The Defenestration of Skindles

Skindles Hotel / 31st March 1971

The Rolling Stones completed their *Goodbye Britain* tour 17 days ago at *The Roundhouse* in London. With the end of the UK financial year fast approaching, later today Keith Richard, Charlie Watts, Bill Wyman and the Micks Jagger and Taylor will all become tax exiles. It's a farewell and a half alright. The party started hours ago and it's still going strong – but what's upset Old Rubber Lips? Two in the morning, the music has to stop. Jagger can't get no satisfaction and, to prove it, he's having a tantrum. Yoko Ono naturally remains detached as John Lennon and Eric Clapton try to calm him down. He's having none of it. Here's a chair and there's a window. The first sails through the second exploding the glass into splinters. Two burly bouncers suggest firmly to Jagger that it might be time to make an early departure for south of France. As he leaves, he shouts over his shoulder "See ya on the Côte d'Azur".

When ***Rambutan Ltd*** acquired *Skindles* in 1966, the plan was to bring its exclusivity within the reach of the middle classes. It rebranded the three venues in search of clear identity. The original 18th Century inn was once more ***The Orkney Arms***, a middle-of-the-road hotel. Having had a taste of being *The Orkney Arms* and then *The Cedar Bar*, the original *Hotel Tap* became ***The Sir Percy Flanagan***, an out-and-out pub which expanded into an area shut off and forgotten during the Trapani years. And the riverside hotel took a gamble as *Skindles Sporting Club*, an elegant casino that opened with a glittering charity ball but lasted barely two years. The second bet is doing better. This live music and cabaret nightspot quickly became hot as a cool place to party, a 'must-play' gig for any band with ambition. That was how *The Rolling Stones* discovered it and plenty of others are doing the same. ***Manfred Mann*** often used to gig here, ***Thin Lizzy*** is doing a set in a couple of weeks and bands will keep coming.

Strawberry Fields

Skindles Hotel / 15th May 1976

The Strawbs are tearing heartstrings with their latest single *I Only Want My Love To Grow In You*. It won't be long before magic music moments like this are gone forever.

Some will say *Rambutan* started the rot as far as ill-founded ideas are concerned. In 1969 the company negotiated a new 99-year lease with **Lady Imogen Gage** as a Grenfell trustee and by 1971 had demolished *The Orkney Arms* and *The Sir Percy Flanagan* to create a car park for *Skindles* [*see Map 44*]. After much talk of extending the hotel, two years later it went for broke with a series of planning applications – one to build either 36 flats in three blocks or 20 townhouses on Horse Radish Paddock and Upper Thames Field, another to build a pub and restaurant on the site of the original inn and, much to the horror of music fans and locals alike, a third to demolish *Skindles* and replace it with ten townhouses. All applications were refused. All went to appeal and rumbled on to a public enquiry in 1974 at which *Rambutan* realised the game was up. Now it is just playing out time until it can find a buyer.

Rambutan wasn't alone in having its ambitions thwarted. Two years ago ***Taplow Developments Ltd*** applied for permission to build 52 houses on the northern portion of Upper Thames Field. That too was refused after an unsuccessful appeal. An application to turn ***Old Court Hotel*** into 11 flats suffered similar frustration. If not a lot is happening in the inner triangle, it's not for want of trying.

Brown Sugar

Studio Valbonne, Skindles Hotel / 15th May 1981

Entrepreneur **Louis Brown** acquired *Skindles* in 1978 and immediately let *Skindles Garage* and the former market garden to *Esso* who replaced it with a petrol station. Meanwhile he formed a management company with the imaginative name of *Skindles Ltd* and spent £2m (£12.36m) restoring the hotel to his idea of its former glory, complete with *The Rocking Horse Bar* at the southern end and at the other *Studio Valbonne*: a riverside version of the first of London's big discos. Nowadays crowds flock in for rocking-horse, disco and roller-skating competitions, beauty contests and jazz sessions. It isn't quite like the old days but once more royalty and the stars of stage and screen revel in champagne lunches on the river and wile away their evenings at glittering parties and their nights in various après-party pleasures.

Brown wants to extend these joys to a wider clientele. Although he shelved his 1979 plan to bridge from *Skindles* across **Mill Lane** to a new 81-bed hotel, now he has submitted a new application to close the southern end of Mill Lane entirely in order to build a 70-bed extension to *Skindles* with an enormous car park behind a larger petrol station stretching across the whole Bath Road frontage. This idea will hang hopefully in the wind as a separate and more modest scheme comes to fruition in 1983 when permission is granted to demolish ***Riverside Cottages*** and replace them with eight townhouses on ***The Wharf***. ***The Tower House*** will remain as will ***Mallard's Reach***, the semi-detached house adjoining what was **N° 5 The Causeway**.

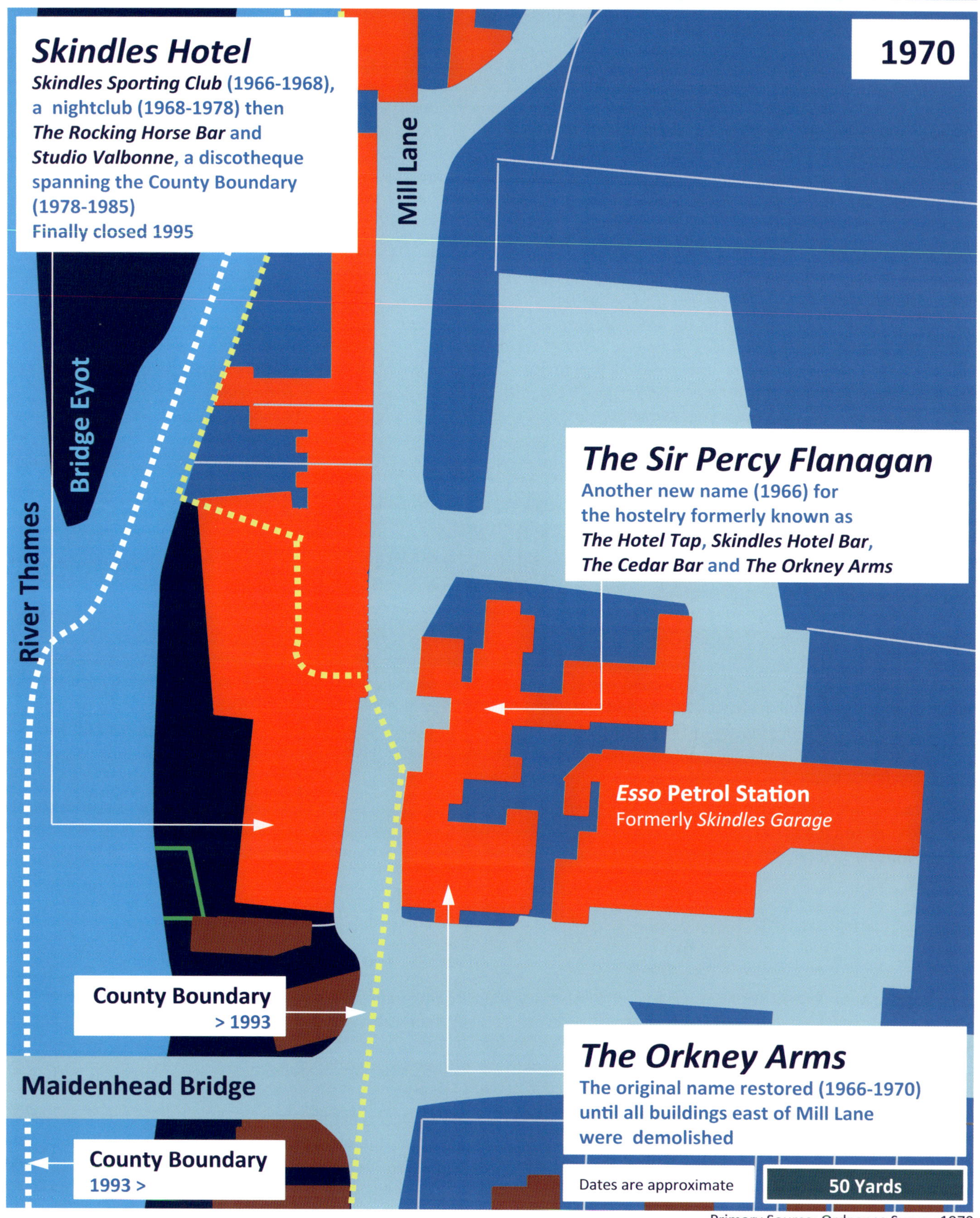

Primary Source: Ordnance Survey 1970

About Grout – Money Laundering

The Rocking Horse Bar, Skindles Hotel / 15th May 1981

It has been a good day for the young Man from the Pru. Perhaps *Prudential* insurance agent **David Grout** would have been wise to take his day's takings home but he trusted to luck that the £4,000 (£13,400) would be safe in his pocket while he enjoyed some light refreshment and admired the extremely pretty waitresses. He reckoned without his mates who decided to chuck him into the inside-outside pool. Now he's off to dry out the wad of notes and safely separate every one with great care. Perhaps the effort will be so great that he will reinvent himself as a postman.

The Dwindling of Boating

Springfield Boatyard / 18th October 1984

Richard Springfield is in his ninth decade. It is all getting a bit too much. He started well enough but, when it came to the crunch, confidence and bravado were never enough. He had moderate success building, maintaining and hiring out cabin cruisers. He invented a novel way of building boats by forging two fibreglass hulls together to create a wider kind of craft. Perhaps the market moved on so small yards can no longer compete. Perhaps Richard lost the energy to keep up. Now the dilapidated old boatyard is in limbo with greedy developers snapping around. Some of the sheds are let for storage, another to *Batt's Sails* for whom Jimmy Janes who keeps the wolf from the door as an old-fashioned traditional sailmaker. What will happen after the yard is sold at auction next year?

Jimmy goes way back. He was with *Bushnell's* and remembers **Mick Free** as a lad in the mid-1950s when he started at ***Andrews Brothers*** hiring out boats from Ray Mead at weekends and helping to build them up at Bourne End during the week. That was about the time Colin Chichester-Smith of ***Fairey Marine*** bought the ***Bridge Villa*** yard from ***Bond's*** to rent out its wooden-hulled cabin cruisers built on the River Hamble. This wasn't such a good idea – there wasn't much headroom in the boathouses; any flood like 1947 would have jammed all the cruisers against the ceiling – but then everyone had a mix of craft for hire. Cruisers gave a better margin yet plenty of folk still wanted to have leisurely picnic on the river – in his teens **Michael Farmiloe** could earn tips of as much as £5-a-time (£100) taking *Andrews'* rowing boats, dinghies, skiffs and punts over to *Skindles*.

Mick left *Andrews* in the early-1970s to work at Windsor Racecourse Marina but Jimmy can't be sure if that was before or after young Farmiloe took over his family firm. What he does recall is Michael's big ideas. He let the old yard to Bertie Bushnell and moved next door into *Bridge View*. And in 1979 he acquired the site of *Warren's Warehouse* and made it another boatyard. That was the year Bertie retired and sold to *Richardson's* (of Norfolk) which sold to *Butlin's* (the holiday camp people), or was it the other way around?

Michael and his wife Carol now live in River Road at ***Longacre***, formerly stables to ***The Red House***. He will recognise that the market is changing and gradually wind the business down. The boat showroom will be recast as a Chinese restaurant, the Taplow boatyard will be sold to Ted Harris and the *Bridge View* boathouses be converted to offices and in 1991 the Farmiloes will move into N° 4 Bridge View, the flat over the northern end. New blocks of flats will proliferate: the *Bushnell's* and the original *Andrews* boatyards will unite as *Chandler's Quay* in 1998, ***The Nutshell*** will be reinvented in the shadow of the Sounding Arch in 2006 and four years later *Chef Peking* will serve its last crispy duck.

Street's Ahead

Skindles Hotel / 18th May 1990

Tim Street has learnt a thing or two from his parents. He and his pals Trevor Bowron and Bruce Craig know how to make the most of Saturday night at *Skindles*. Into *The Rocking Horse* they go, a drink or two, a nod, a wink and they're into *The Boulevard Room* or the *Valbonne* to party party party. Tim won't recall ever having a dip in *Skindles* pool but he will admit to swimming across the Thames and back. What a wonderful way to sober up enough to work out whose round it is next.

Not What it Was

Lord's Cricket Ground / 26th July 1990

It is 50 years since Major Campbell McConnachie of the Cameron Highlanders was evacuated from Dunkirk. On arriving back in Blighty, he hailed a cab and said "Take me to *Skindles*": where better to celebrate his safe return? Hoping to revive fond memories, his stepson **Alistair Forsyth** booked him a room there last night and secured tickets to bring him here to enjoy the first day of England's Test Match against India. Things are not going to plan. Campbell wasn't at all impressed with *Skindles*: the whole building is in serious disrepair and loud music erupted from the *Valbonne* until the wee small hours. Fortunately cricket will calm his troubles. By close of play, England will rattle up 359 for two and Graham Gooch will be 194 not out, well on his way to 333 – the highest ever individual score in a Test Match at Lord's: now that's something to celebrate.

Matchmaker Nessie

Driftwood Cottage, Mill Lane / 4th January 1997

The party's over. **John Fenn** isn't well. He still enjoys claiming that Margaret Thatcher owes him a favour because, a few months before the 1979 election made her Prime Minister, he persuaded her to swing in a jackstay above the water at the *Earl's Court Boat Show*, an escapade which gave the press a glimpse of her femininity. And six years later on a trip to Paris he was swept away by the Alaskan charms of **Heather Lindsey**. He was organising *Operation Deepscan* – a sonar search for the Loch Ness Monster – and she was with *Lowrance Electronics*, an American company which was developing sonar echo-sounders. John and Heather smile to recall that during trial scans in October 1986, there were more journalists on the shores of the Loch than at the Reagan-Gorbachev summit in Iceland that same week. The trials were foiled by bad weather but a year later a more intensive *Deepscan* search recorded sonar contacts with three moving objects "larger than a shark but smaller than a whale".

Sharing all the fun of this nearly-but-not-quite experience brought John and Heather together. They finally married last September and she will care for him until his death later this year when he will leave her the house, the moorings and the boathouses, which were converted to offices about ten years ago for a subsidiary of *General Electric*. Heather will soon extensively refurbish them and by 2013 they will be home to two brand and media companies, *Enigma Graphics* and *BWP Group*, and organic babyfood suppliers *Plum Baby Ltd*.

The Sliver Sorted

Springfield Boatyard, River Road / 19th May 1993

That settles it. The county boundary is now at the centre of the Thames, or at least the centre of its eastern channel. **Mick Free** has no idea of the rights and wrongs of the argument but it all got rather tetchy as it was complicated by a confusion of ambitions. The **Royal Borough of Windsor & Maidenhead** had inherited the land from Maidenhead Borough Council in 1974 and by the mid-1980s seemed content as blight descended on the redundant boatyard and on ***Sunnyside*** and ***Bridge Villa***. Mick's suspicions were confirmed in 1988, when RBWM gave itself planning permission to knock down the old timber-and-corrugated-iron **Maidenhead Rowing Club** on its side of the river, with the idea of putting a brand new one here. Along came *Birmingham Estates* and *Trident Construction Group*, two developers with ideas bigger than their ability to deliver on dreams of refurbishing the boatyard and building up to 26 'residential units'. The Hitcham & Taplow Preservation Society and the Maidenhead Civic Society united with others to fight to keep public right of access to the Thames Path. It looked like things might become clearer on 18th February 1991 when the Department of the Environment decreed that the boundary change would become effective on 1st April that year. However RBWM wasn't happy and within months won support from the Boundaries Commission, only for the arbitrator to confirm today that the sliver is back in Bucks. Now **SBDC** has to decide what's best....

Maidenhead Rowing Club, River Road / 3rd August 2012

Can it be true that *Sunnyside* and *Bridge Villa* were incapable of restoration? Or had the local authorities neglected them for so long that they really were past it? Now they've been replaced by ***Taplow Quay*** and a (by no means modest) grant of £500,000 of public money funded the construction of this new clubhouse which was opened just over 14 years ago by Sir Steve Redgrave, the magnificent quintuple Olympic gold medal winning rower. This admirable knight of Marlow Bottom knows Maidenhead Rowing Club well, having represented it almost 20 years ago when he partnered Eric Sims to victory at Henley Royal Regatta. MRC has grown from a rowing club with 75 members to a social club for over 300. It still runs Maidenhead Regatta, a late-season 500m sprint event held on Bray Reach every year since 1893, except in 2007 and 2008 when it put a toe in the waters of Dorney Lake, and it continues to have plenty to celebrate on the water – especially today for Taplow-born **Rob Williams** has added an Olympic lightweight fours silver medal to the gold and two bronzes he has won at recent World Rowing Championships.

Plunging at the Pecks

Bray Reach / 8th August 2010

This is the spiritual home of punt racing. The tradition of **Willy Grenfell** and the younger **William Skindle** lives on in the Thames Punting Club which is today holding its 25th annual Championship Regatta downstream of Brunel's bridge. Competitors from Dittons Skiff & Punting Club, Wargrave Boating Club, Thames Valley Skiff Club and Wraysbury Skiff & Punting Club have completed 15 Championship races over half-mile and three-quarter-mile courses marked at each end by vertical poles called *rye-pecks* where the punter not the punt turns around. Silver cups dating back 125 years have been presented to the winners. The serious stuff is over, now let the fun begin. The crowds congregate on the riverside lawn to watch the fascinating frenzy of nine shorter inter-club races. Wraysbury will enjoy generous applause for taking the overall prize but the biggest cheers are of course when punters plunge in at the pecks.

The Long Swim

Maidenhead Rowing Club, River Road / 30th June 2012

Somehow neither rowing nor punting are quite so admirably crazy as **The Long Swim**, a race from Boulter's Lock to Bray held annually from the late-Victorian era until 1969 interrupted only by the war years. Huge crowds would gather on Ray Mead Road, on Maidenhead Bridge and along the tow-path to watch the fierce competition in two events: a one-mile course for ladies and two miles for the men. Hundreds have crawled out of bed at a silly hour today to see this wonderful madness revived. And here they come now, the first of 125 swimmers are emerging beneath the bridge. Mike Hughes won in 1967 and 1968: he's 74 now and somewhere in the swim again once again. Cynthia Lockie won in 1950: she's waiting to present the trophies. Some will say it is like surviving in a washing-machine but the event is a hit with both seasoned open-water swimmers and first-timers like **Chris Ashford** of N° 4 **Elm View**. Let him take up the story....

"Weeks of heavy rainfall had made the river level very high and the flow fast and strong. We paddled into the cold, muddy water off Boulter's Island and struggled not to get swept past the start line as we waited for the gun at 6.30am. Finally we were off at an amazing pace with the landmarks flying past. We had been warned that the swirling eddies under Maidenhead Bridge could be dangerous but everyone passed through unscathed to get a fantastic boost from seeing and hearing the supporting crowds as we flew past **Maidenhead Rowing Club**. The river then opened out and it was a push to the finish trying to make the most of the midstream current. My aching arms and legs made it a bit of a mad scramble up the slippery bank opposite *The Waterside Inn* at Bray, but what an exhilarating experience."

Send in the Clowns

The derelict Skindles Hotel / 30th June 2013

Hindsight is a wonderful thing. *Skindles* lost its way on **Louis Brown**'s watch and never really found it again. His ambition was a step too far yet four followed in his footsteps after he sold out in 1985. All stumbled and fell. A *Wynmoss-Savegate* consortium lasted a year. A 1986 mystery buyer remained a mystery. Hope sprang in 1989 when *Birmingham Estates* announced big ideas for a luxury Edwardian-style hotel with conference and leisure facilities. Hope withered and died as *Skindles* went downmarket, fewer and fewer came and those who did raised a cacophony of complaints about litter, noise and vandalism (but not about Tim, Trevor and Bruce, of course). Bankruptcy was inevitable. Swedish-owned *Securum UK* stepped into the breach with plans for a new dawn. In May 1994 it promised "an up-market operation quite different from the one we have inherited". An agreement for the *Valbonne* to open only on Thursday, Fridays and Saturdays until January persuaded SBDC to renew *Skindles* late-night licence only for it to go dark early in 1995, perhaps even before. The lights have been out ever since and the roof fell in last winter.

The triangle bounded by the Bath Road, the River Thames and the Jubilee River has come to be euphemistically dubbed the Mill Lane Development. It is not only to do with **Mill Lane** and, despite years of possibility, no development is yet apparent. Once it was a vibrant area of mixed uses, most derived from the river. Now almost all have had their day. The iconic but increasingly dilapidated buildings are testimony to the blight which has been creeping more than 30 years. The land is industrially contaminated here, biodiverse and ecologically sensitive there and subject to degrees of flood risk almost everywhere. Everyone agrees it is in desperate need of rescue. The sites have individually and collectively been coveted for hotel and residential schemes galore. All have so far come to nought for being of poor design, piecemeal, fragmented, insensitive, over-ambitious or without financial viability. It is such a sorry story; you couldn't make it up....

A Change of Spots

The derelict Taplow Papermill / 30th June 2013

The mill has been awaiting its fate for seven years now. Although it will see a little life over the coming winter as a production office and set for the TV detective series *Endeavour*, it will then return to being a stark and crumbling reminder of what can happen when a tiger changes its spots.

New Taplow Paper Mill objected to the various planning applications for the triangle on the grounds that its access would be impaired or even prevented by the proposed schemes. It adopted a quiet but determined and ultimately irresistible strategy to protect access for its trundling trucks by gradually acquiring more of the land along Mill Lane. Eventually its stifling embrace extended to Horse Radish Paddock and the whole of Upper Thames Field, ***Dunloe Lodge*** (for which the mill failed in 1988 to get permission to convert to offices), the former *Andrews* boatyard, the *Windrush Volkswagen* car sales site (formerly the *Esso* petrol station) and even ***Skindles***. Consequently the mill's patchwork now covers the whole inner triangle except the two redundant gasworks and **Maidenhead Sea Cadets** (all acquired from *British Gas* by *National Grid Company*), ***The Wharf***, ***Lansdowne Court***, the vacant site of ***Old Court Hotel*** and two hints of bygone days: the former *Fenn & Wood* boathouses (now converted to offices) and Heather Fenn's moorings.

This History isn't brave enough to tell the whole story – too many rumours and accusations, too few irrefutable facts – but, after a number of contretemps over such matters as the mill's illegal lorry parking and 'waste transfer station' (recycling metal cans and plastics) and its laxity in obtaining timely planning permissions for changes of use and of fabric, relationships deteriorated to the extent that Taplow wasn't sorry in 2006 when *DS Smith* received an offer that was much too good to refuse. Having until then valued its local property portfolio at a little more than one third of £30.25m (£34.29m) the developer ***Towntalk*** offered, the group was obliged to disclose this whacking great windfall as an unforeseen profit in its annual financial report.

Still the troubles continued. The mill was no more but the 'waste transfer station' remained, now paying a mere 'peppercorn' rent and seemingly set on sneaking through a perverse loophole, which would enable it to become legal by operating illegally for long enough. Its heavyweight vehicles pulverised Mill Lane, crushed gas mains beneath it and subjected residents to constant dust, noise and intimidation. Two mysterious fires broke out in 2007: a portacabin at the mill was destroyed by the first, but why the false report to evacuated locals that it started on a boat? The second reduced *Dunloe Lodge* to an unsafe blackened shell. How could an old house without mains gas or electricity spontaneously burst into flames during extremely wet weather? Neither fire was forensically examined despite CCTV evidence suggesting arson. Could it have been a case of "no arson, no crime: doesn't go on record, no comment"?

Towntalk quickly discovered it had bitten off more than it could chew. When its attempt to acquire the gasworks from *NGC* failed and its planning application for an ambitious housing and hotel development was refused, it cut its losses and sold out in 2007 to another developer. ***Watchword*** funded its acquisition with a massive loan from the *Irish Nationwide Building Society*. At least Taplow could be pleased that, as a result of the *Towntalk* affair, **SBDC** was at last receptive to the Society's plea for a cohesive development brief for the whole site. Its Core Strategy was established accordingly around two important statements: that new-build heights and footprints should be no larger than the existing, and that the site "has potential for around 100 dwellings". What Taplow didn't realise at the time was the consequence of the legal wrinkle left when ***Springfield Boatyard*** was transferred to Bucks. Its northern protrusion had been used by *Skindles* for so long that SBDC must have mistakenly thought it was part of the *Skindles* estate acquired by *Watchword*.

A Pair of Micks

The Old Public Slipway / 16th July 2013

If only they'd asked Old Mick, says **Michael Fletcher**, he'd have put them right. Michael has been 'Young Mick' for 24 years. How strange it feels now to be just Mick, all alone in this old boathouse.

His boss and friend **Mick Free** died three weeks ago. He had been happily maintaining boats here with great care and skill for 28 years. Alan Hockham joined him a year later and he employed Keith the painter on subcontract. He was barely 54 when the boys started to call him Old Mick after he took on Young Mick as an apprentice. It has been just the two Micks since 1998.

Old Mick left Windsor Racecourse Marina for a spell at *John Turk's* at Cookham before deciding to go it alone by launching ***Marlow Boat Services***, named after his home town. This old place probably dates from the early-1870s, was extended in 1880 and widened and an extra storey added in the early-1920s when *Bond's* business was booming. It continued in use for another half-century until *Springfield* began to go downhill. Thereafter it might have been used to store beds, probably for *Skindles*, possibly for sale, and when Old Mick came here in 1985 it was an ivy-covered beer store for an open-air bar on ***Skindles*** riverside terrace. The other boathouse in the upstream curl of the bridge had been demolished not long before.

The Old Public Slipway / 7th April 2014

Young Mick is settling to his task. Old Mick's widow Ann and their son Paul were happy for him to take over *Marlow Boats* and he has plenty of longstanding customers to keep him busy. The boathouse is packed upstairs and down with craft in his tender loving care. Two were built in the 1930s: an electric canoe built by *Buss* at Watford and a slipper stern launch built in 1936 by *Andrews* at Bourne End. And two in the 1920s: there is *Piroska*, a motor launch built by *Bond's* just a few yards away and here is the beautiful *Arethusa*, a 40-foot umpire's launch built at Henley in 1921 by *Hobbs & Sons*. She has served at many regattas including Henley Royal and has carried *BBC Radio* teams covering the Oxford & Cambridge Boat Race, most tragically in 1990 when commentator Peter Jones had a heart attack on board and died the next day.

Marlow Boats may be a one-man-band but Young Mick will take on an apprentice if he can secure his future here. Trouble is, he says, the ownership question is peculiar. Old Mick gave up trying to keep up during the seven-year wrangle between the two local authorities and two developers. All four were happy to take his rent, although Old Mick didn't trust the second developer at all. He always paid by cheque to make sure there was an independent and reliable record of his having done so. It was a wise move: the company went under. That was around the time *Skindles* finally closed and we've lived in limbo ever since, says Michael. SBDC never seemed much interested in sorting out the legalities but now, with the redevelopment of *Skindles* at last a possibility, I'm concerned for the future of my business (the last of its kind hereabouts), the boathouse (a notable heritage asset) and the Old Public Slipway (a valued amenity as a right-of-way for walkers and as the only public access to the river for miles used by perhaps 20 or 30 boat-owners most summer weekends). Currently we can enjoy all three, but for how much longer?

At Last a Possibility

SBDC Offices, Capswood, Denham / 16th July 2013

The **Mill Lane** triangle will see the biggest development ever in Taplow. Any rescue of the blighted sites risks the very high cost of the riverside rural character being destroyed by urbanisation. Worries grew over the last couple of years as SBDC exhibited a strange reluctance to make any meaningful public declaration of what nature and scale of development would be considered appropriate while chaperoning an extended and opaque courtship with a housing developer which had ambitions to build more than 400 dwellings. These concerns were not entirely allayed today when SBDC adopted its Supplementary Planning Document (SPD) for Mill Lane. Why did the SBDC Cabinet do this in private rather than in public at a full Council meeting?

The SPD isn't to everyone's taste but it has some tasty bits. Everyone welcomes the requirements for the refurbishment of historic buildings, the provision of new footpaths and a footbridge across to Ray Mill Island, the protection of the rural Green

Jonathan Bond's old boathouse on The Old Public Slipway....

....where Michael 'Young Mick' Fletcher runs *Marlow Boat Services* / 2014

Belt character and openness of the area and of the special biodiversity in and by the river. However, SBDC has published no documentary evidence to support its claim that there is public support for **Mill Lane** having new junction with the Bath Road and being closed at the **Jubilee River**. In fact, there are sharp differences of public opinion on both matters. The first is favoured by most in Mill Lane but it seems by nobody on or south of the Bath Road. The second is supported by most in Mill Lane and others wishing to prevent the current so-called 'rat run', but a survey of Society members will confirm that the majority is against it for fear of the fragmentation of the Taplow community, increased congestion on **Berry Hill** or simply that it is a sop to enable a developer to charge premium prices for exclusive homes free of passing traffic.

These are all important issues but the primary concern is and has always been about scale. Despite the recognition in the SBDC Core Strategy that some 100 households would offer a developer reasonable profit, the SPD permits a total footprint of 13,917m^2 which could result in more than three times that number with perhaps 650 residents: potentially a 38% increase in the total number of homes and people in Taplow compared with the 2011 census which counted 1,669 Taplovians living in 791 households. Add in just two more prospective developments – perhaps 80 new dwellings on the ***SGT*** site and 11 new flats at ***Old Court*** – and in just a few years Taplow can look forward to a 56% increase in population and dire traffic congestion on and around the Bath Road. No wonder the natives are restless.

SBDC Offices, Capswood, Denham / 17th December 2014

Earlier this year, the administrator acting for Irish government finally agreed to sell the Mill Lane land to ***Berkeley Homes (Three Valleys) Ltd*** which in September submitted planning applications to build 257 homes, including one replacing the derelict ***Dunloe Lodge*** and 17 in refurbished buildings. Although there has been some good news – *Berkeley* responded to public opinion by discarding its unattractive design for the footbridge and opting for the graceful span imagined by Taplovian **Martin Knight**, a bridge architect of international reputation – there are concerns about the scale of the scheme, which would all by itself increase the number of homes in Taplow by one-third. It has been described as "an elaborate housing estate" with "privatised waterfronts" and the feel of being apart from Taplow not a part of it. Some accept the iconic ***Skindles*** name being invested in a new restaurant overlooking **Maidenhead Bridge**. Others can't see why a new boutique hotel wouldn't be viable. And many say the proposals add up to urban over-development in a rural setting and not only "a massive missed opportunity" to enhance the Thames but a threat to its delicate ecology.

Most of the many Taplovians here this evening breathe a quiet sigh of relief as the **SBDC** Planning Committee deliberates and decides to refuse permission for the main scheme. Over the next few days, the odd Maidonian will miss the point and complain about the delay in improving their view across the river. Taplovians will shake their heads in disbelief at such myopia and look forward to February 2015 when *Berkeley* will indicate a willingness to moderate its ambitions. Follow the unfolding saga in forthcoming editions of the Society's newsletter, which will also continue to document how our community spirit evolves....

Eventful

Carols on the Green

The Village Green / 22nd December 2007

Last year after the St Nicolas' School Christmas Bazaar, the Parish Council organised carol-singing by the barn on the Green. Today **Jo Brooking** is the inspiration. She loved Taplow from the moment as a young teenager when she and her mother Kate came to live in the middle flat in what is now ***The Dower House*** behind ***Elibank***. As an adult, Jo worked at **Taplow Court** for ***Plessey*** and moved with Kate to N° 1 **Elm View**. Sadly both ladies passed away at the same age, just 54. When Jo died in 2005 she left a bequest to be used "for cultural or recreational purposes in Taplow Village".

As one of the trustees, **Liz Forsyth** suggested using this legacy to fund a Christmas tree on the Green. The first was installed three weeks ago courtesy of Janet Wheeler of Cookham (who does this every year) and numerous passers-by who lent a hand. Now thanks to Liz, **Gillian & Alan Dibden**, the Parish Council (especially Josie Corio and **Iris Midlane**) and others we are gathering to sing carols by the light of its 400 bulbs. It is a fine turn-out: the Salvation Army brass band is carolling 200 of us towards Christmas, there is mulled wine to wash down mince pies, hot chestnuts and roasted marshmallows, farm animals for children to pet and over £250 is being collected for bowel cancer research.

Hark, the Herald Angels Sing loud in Jo's memory. Let's hope that Carols-on-the-Green continues either as an organised event or a more casual affair. As long as we have the tree, we can make the most of it according to how the Christmas spirit takes us.

Hunting Eggs

Taplow House Hotel / 5th April 2010

Over 100 people spanning 90-something years have gathered to celebrate the Society's 50th Anniversary with an Easter Egg Hunt organised by a team led by **Gilly & Neil Blundell**. More than 30 children are scurrying excitedly about the grounds, the ancient tulip trees and a ridiculously enormous Easter Bunny (yours truly) searching for brightly-coloured eggs. Amazingly, they will miss only one of over 400. Each will be traded in for prizes designed so everyone ends up with the same overdose of chocolate. Soon the adults will have their excitement – a champagne hunt – before we all adjourn inside for a family lunch.

This is a celebration but a more modest (but no less well attended) hunt will continue to be held each Easter Monday, initially at *Taplow House Hotel*, eventually in the grounds of ***White Gables*** and ***Well Cottage*** courtesy of the consummately hospitable **Sheila & Barrie Peroni** and **Charlie & Toby Greeves**.

Racing to the Church

The High Street / 29th April 2011

How often do ideas like this start in a glass of wine? Everybody is certain it happened last December at ***Maryfield*** where many had gathered to wish Merry Christmas to their hosts, **Jacqueline & Roger Andrews**. Nobody is saying who said what when. Perhaps somebody mentioned **Pamela Bentley** riding a horse to the 1977 Silver Jubilee street party in the High Street and somebody else thought, how do we trump that? All we know is that by the end of the evening a gang of four was in charge. In no particular order, step forward **Juliet Lecchini**, **Martin Knight**, **Paul-Ant Viollet** and the aforementioned Jolly Roger to present your manifesto....

"We laugh in the face of technology. We deny the existence of engines, pedals and performance materials. We embrace gravity at the expense of all other forms of propulsion. We support the use of karts made from recycled, reclaimed and re-used parts. The spirit of the event is to purchase as little as possible. We celebrate the amateur and the optimistic, where the heroic arrival at the start-line is vastly superior to the time across the finish-line." Or to put it another way, let's celebrate the Royal Wedding with a Race to the Church in cobbled-together go-karts pushed from the gates of *Maryfield* to whoosh their way downhill to St Nicolas.

And today's the day. Union Jacks flutter across the High Street somewhat softened by bales of hay. Marshalls call 'Clear' into their radios. Paul-Ant snaps 'Go'. Roger repeats. Martin pushes off on a test run. Gravity does indeed take over and, as hoped, the shallower gradient towards the finish slows the kart and he stops short of the hay-bale barrier before ***St Nicolas House***. It's Juliet's turn. She flashes past with her spaniel Daisy on board, the dog's ears flowing in the slipstream. In all 16 karts dash downhill time and again with different age-groups at the helm until they crash, collapse or complete the course. They say that who dares wins. It has certainly left lasting memories....

Eyes of a Child – Thomas Knight

St Nicolas' School / 23rd April 2012

When Prince William and Kate Middleton got married last year, most places had a garden party or whatever. Not us. We had a Go-kart race down the High Street. The hay bales for the chicane were just straightened a bit to prevent crashes (which there was a lot of) and the first Go-kart went down the track – Go-kart after Go-kart, crash after crash, one kart even lost a wheel. And then we had the awards ceremony. Most people were really excited. **Jamie Barnard** won a courgette for the best kart. **Louise Ashford** was Key Stage One winner with my brother **Jack** second, and the Key Stage Two winner was **Jamie Ashford** with me second. The day went on and on and finally came to an end!

Eyes of a Child – Mia Webb, Rosie Sellers & Katie Hornett

St Nicolas' School / 23rd April 2012

Mia liked the Go-kart race because everyone was smiling in it. Loads of people did the event because it was fun, says Rosie. My friends **Katie Hornett** and **Alice Snoxell** and others were there too. On the Green near the race was an ice-cream van. My Dad helped me to build my Go-kart. When we were having the race my Mum crashed into the pavement and at the end my family won the golden spoon award for the most crashing. It was really fun! Katie recalls all the people who came to watch even though they weren't racing. In the pub there was a TV, she says, and on the TV the Royal Wedding was on. I really liked to race even though my Go-kart wasn't very good. Lots of people got an ice-cream. At the end of the race, there were prizes. We got one for the worst Go-kart. It was a really good day.

The Fruit of Balls

St Nicolas' School / 28th June 2011

It's the same every year: **Jenny Dobson** teaches Year 4 to play the African drums. This year the children have a new place to play at the annual St Nic's Open Day. They parade in single file across the playground to the new boardwalk at its top end where they sit and await their cue before banging out a rhythm on their drums. What a performance. And that's the point. Mrs Dobson and her colleagues aim to instil in their pupils a love of and appreciation for music in particular and for performance in general that will never leave them. It's all part of how the School encourages their development not only academically but socially.

If the children are lucky to have St Nic's, it is also lucky to have an active Parents & Teachers Association which regenerates to find new ways to have fun and raise funds. The calendar most years has a Christmas Bazaar and a Summer Fete with Easter Fun Days, campnights and quizzes sprinkled here and there and – most eventfully of all for the grown-ups – a series of seven summer balls over the past 14 years, each of which has raised between £5,000 and £8,500. The latest all-weather boardwalk and covered sitting area on the upper playground replaced an earlier refurbishment of the area. In between, funds have been invested in enhancements such as the Reception Class Play Area, the Music Room and the IT Suite.

The first of these balls was held at Cliveden's Orangery (about 1998), the next four (2000/05) in a marquee erected on the playground, the sixth in a medieval barn at *Foxley Manor* in Holyport (2008) and the most recent a *James Bond* Ball last summer at *Oakley Court*. Those who were there think the last three marquee balls were most memorable for they transformed the School into a Venetian Palace, the Orient Express and Bombay Dreams. Many parents worked so hard to make these happen; most would acknowledge that two people were their heart and soul: **Nicki Jeffries** (of ***Pax Cottage***) and Tammy Mariaux (of *Tummies* restaurant in Station Road, Burnham) who will never take 'No' for an answer.

Paddling around the Leftleys

Taplow Lake / 5th June 2012

If Queen Elizabeth II thinks a Raft Race on Taplow Lake is a funny way for us to mark her Diamond Jubilee she has been too polite to let us know. It is all the idea of **Juliet Lecchini**. Who's that mumbling 'It figures'? Her goal is of course to replenish the Royal Navy on the cheap. The result is a state-of-the-art flotilla created by each of five teams from a ready supply of plastic jerry-cans, lengths of 3-by-2-inch timber and yards of colourful rope. The water reflects the steel grey sky but – as one team will soon discover – it is warmer in the drink than out of it.

Each team nominates a crew of two adults and two children for the first leg. Rafts are launched and lined up for the start. And then off they go on a splash course to circumnavigate the Leftley family (doing a fine impression of a marker buoy) and paddle madly back again. Points are earned by collecting yellow plastic ducks along the way. Teams rotate crews for the second and third legs, if they survive that long. *Team Silver* doesn't. Its crew of Bullocks, Lawsons and Rollinsons sinks on the home run. By now *Oarsome Nuggets* (Bainbridges, Foxes and Stowes) are enjoying a leisurely barbecue lunch, having left everyone else in their wake with such furious paddling it was like watching Redgrave and Pinsent after sprinkling bran on their breakfast porridge. The real race is for the runner's up spot. *Crusaders* (Ashfords, Edmonds, Sharps and Wayland-Smiths) narrowly edge out *Crown Jewels* (Barnards, Bodens, Brownings, Lecchini and Cherry) while *Bluebeard's Revenge* (Knights, Mackays, Webbs, Dunleavey and Edmondson) go forth and come fourth in inimitable style.

The sky starts to drizzle. We laugh it off (the rain stops when it got to the skin) and warm ourselves with the thought that £935 has been raised for the **Thames Valley Adventure Playground**. And we applaud heartily as the victors and duck-collectors are presented with prizes kindly donated by **Simon Fox**, **Duncan Leftley** and their companies. Somebody asks Juliet how she'll follow up next year. She suggests they should see a psychiatrist and (ever smiling) even offers to recommend a good one. **Chris Cherry** does his very best to look vacant. Perhaps he is wondering what on earth Taplow can dream up next to amuse itself....

Three Nuts in a Volvo

Nürburgring, Germany / 10th July 2012

For Taplovians, ***Three Men in a Boat*** is so 19th Century. Here come three nuts in an ancient *Volvo* driving it to Monaco and back on the ninth and last Monkey Run. This endurance rally is so-called because (among various other qualifications) all participant cars must have cost less than a *monkey* (£500). **Jamie Barnard**, **Tim Browning** and **Martin Knight** thought: bring it on! When they got their *Volvo 245GLT* for £387 on *eBay* it already had over 120,000 miles on the clock. By the time they get home tomorrow it will have another 2,484 and the boys will have five days of great memories – not least of completing the second leg from Le Mans-to-Clermont Ferrand 30 seconds quicker than any rival, of a black-tie-and-DJ gourmet dinner in Monte Carlo and of today twice circumnavigating the famous Nürburgring race-track in (as Jamie says) "hysterical disbelief that we are still alive. The elation is so tangible that you could eat it with a spoon". So better than a nice quiet trip down the river, then?

Still Singing After All These Years

The Village Green / 22nd December 2014

We have the tree, its lights sparkling. We have a starry night, a crowd gathering on the Green and two young ladies with bags of initiative. This year, **Sasha Boden** and **Scarlett Wayland-Smith** decided to make it happen. **Sally** and **Lauren Sharp** are leading the carolling and Father Christmas is on his way....

Homeland

Within and Without

The Village Green / 24th June 1989

Taplovians gather to enjoy the fourth VGP. As youngsters merrily join the dance, a small group of parents mulls sagely over a robust red. Their topic is an article in the Society's Newsletter 56 (Summer 1989) in which **Tony Meats** considers "the spirit of [Taplow] and how it works". He makes the case that, since the Village "has no overall consistent unifying form [and the] precious few buildings of any real architectural interest [have] no visual cohesion or relationship [then] what we are trying to conserve therefore must be a myth" without logical explanation, a concept he fully supports. Tony goes on to describe the Village and its "encircling open landscape... in our minds, far wider than actually exists" as "Taplow Within and Taplow Without". As the Hickmans and Forsyths can testify, this myth has narrow bounds and deep roots.

The Taplow Tapestry

The Village Green / 21st June 2014

There are nearly 400 people here at the 29th VGP this evening: friends, neighbours and not, enjoying this recent addition, this modern yet already timeless tradition. Folks are free to share the moment (or not), to make memories (or not): this is community. We are 'within' yet there is no whiff of anyone being from 'without'. Has Tony's terminology had its day? Not quite: some still look askance at the Village and think it aloof on its hill. However, most recognise that everywhere here is somewhere because it should be. There are unsmoothed edges, of course, yet something ties us together. Is it merely sharing the space or is there something deeper, something in a common cultural and historical heritage, the myth that drew us here or keeps us here because here is just that little bit special in the way Tony tried to touch? Whether we relate to each other in communities of neighbourhood or of interest, service, faith or fun, we are all Taplovians and the better for it. Everywhere and everyone here are vital to Taplow's tapestry and each thread past, present and future enhances the whole. This History hopes to play a small part in helping our community of differences to recognise and be united in Taplow's intangible sense of place. I'll drink to that.

The Last Moment

South View Lodge, Piggy Lane, Bicester / 9th March 2015

There were days when I thought I'd never get here, but this is it: the moment to stop. I've come to give Tony Gray my last amendments to the first proof and deliver to him all the maps, family trees and photographs which I have redesigned in full-colour over the past panic-stricken twelve days thanks to the graciously-received last-minute grant from Taplow Parish Council's legacy fund. All that's left is for Tony to produce the final proof and for me to complete the index. Then pre-publication marketing can begin in the hope of attracting enough orders to make a larger print run viable.

It's a strange feeling: I'm still thirsty for knowledge but full to bursting. History has won; it always does. Nothing is ever enough yet this History is as complete as can be. What's done is done and what's not must be left to whoever thinks they can do better. Please form a queue over there....

Map 45 – The Common: Here and Hereabouts

Life As We Know It

Primary Source: Ordnance Survey 2008

Map 46 – The Village and the Valley: Here and Hereabouts

Life As We Know It

Primary Source: Ordnance Survey 2008

The Race to the Church ....

Downhill Racer: Jamie Barnard, coming and going

Crash Champions: Rosie, Rupert, Caroline & Issy Sellers

Setting the style: Juliet Lecchini & Daisy

Those held responsible: Duncan Leftley with Jack, Juliet Lecchini, Paul-Ant Viollet, Roger Andrews & Martin Knight

Going aghast: Marianne Boden

Going for speed: Chris Ashford & Louise

....to celebrate the Royal Wedding / 29th April 2011

Anna Hill, Thomas Knight (both left) **and Marie Tenglund stay on track....**

Lyra Cherry relaxes with a smile....

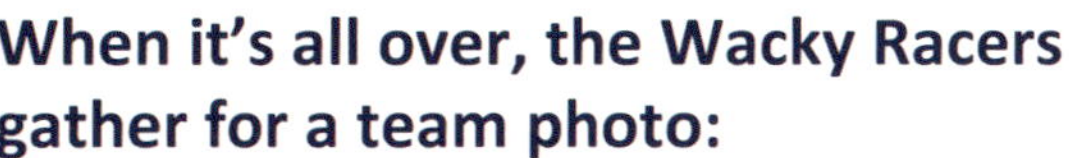

When it's all over, the Wacky Racers gather for a team photo:

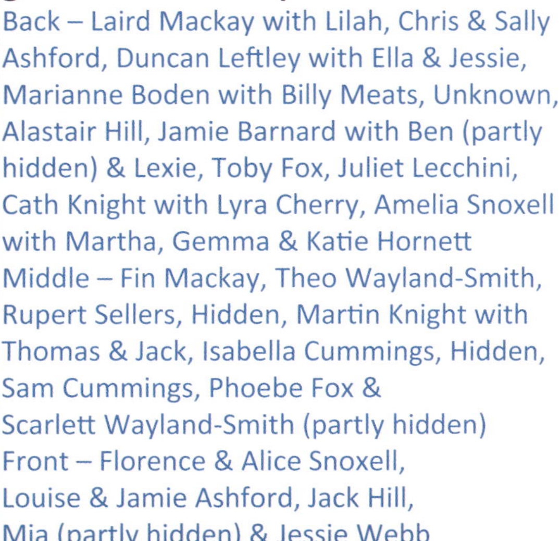

Back – Laird Mackay with Lilah, Chris & Sally Ashford, Duncan Leftley with Ella & Jessie, Marianne Boden with Billy Meats, Unknown, Alastair Hill, Jamie Barnard with Ben (partly hidden) & Lexie, Toby Fox, Juliet Lecchini, Cath Knight with Lyra Cherry, Amelia Snoxell with Martha, Gemma & Katie Hornett
Middle – Fin Mackay, Theo Wayland-Smith, Rupert Sellers, Hidden, Martin Knight with Thomas & Jack, Isabella Cummings, Hidden, Sam Cummings, Phoebe Fox & Scarlett Wayland-Smith (partly hidden)
Front – Florence & Alice Snoxell, Louise & Jamie Ashford, Jack Hill, Mia (partly hidden) & Jessie Webb

The Oarsome Raft Race / 5th June 2012

Ready, steady, go: the five crews get under way....

Tim Browning & Chris Cherry meddle with Sally Sharp's paddling....
Janette Mackay and her son Finlay catch their breath....
John Dunleavey catches Thomas Knight as his parents
Cath & Martin frame Marianne & Marc Boden

Top left – Keith Thomas pipes in Barrie Peroni with the Burns' Night Haggis
Clockwise from top right – Jane Barnard with Marianne Boden & Cath Knight, Brenda Burns (the night is hers), Maud Johnson and Marc Boden, Jamie Barnard & Sally Sharp, Brian Horton, Pamela Viollet & Karl Lawrence, Laird Mackay with Anna Hill & Miv Wayland-Smith, Charlie Greeves & Gilly Blundell, John & Brenda Kennedy and George Sandy, wearing his *Tam o'Shanter* to recite *Tam o'Shanter*

The Usual Suspects / 2012

Above (clockwise from top left) – Jacqueline Andrews, Jenny Edmonds, Marie Tenglund, Jane Edmondson, Nigel Smales, Neil Blundell and Pete Webb

Below (clockwise from top left) – Mike & Sally Sharp, Caroline Smales, Clementine Fox & Victoria Wayland-Smith, Caroline Sellers, Rupert Sellers & George Ormond and Miv Wayland-Smith & Fiona Plumley

Clockwise from top left –
Jamie & Jane Barnard, Duncan Leftley & Marc Boden, Adam Benatar & Pete Webb, Juliet Lecchini with Sam Viollet & Clementine Fox, David Hindle & Mike Sharp, Sally Ashford with Marianne Boden, Victoria Wayland-Smith, Anna Hill & Cath Knight, Tim Browning with Simon Fox, Paul-Ant Viollet & George Ormond, Tony Meats, Marianne Boden & Jo Leftley, Chris & George Ormond, Brian & Sheila Horton, Patrick (& Julia) Shanu-Wilson and Chris Cherry

Clockwise from above – Sally Sharp with Lauren & Ben, Rachel & Clemency Horton-Kitchlew, *Tap L'eau* (created by Jamie Barnard, Tim Browning & Pete Webb to raise funds for TVAP), Ginny & Euan Felton, Alistair & Liz Forsyth, Eva Lipman and Jane Curry & Andrew Findlay

Rescuing Old Priory Garden

Clockwise from left – Simon Fox & Malcolm Tait, Bob Hanbury, Anthony Harding with Roger Andrews, Julia Paskins and Miv Wayland-Smith

Appendix One
Family Trees

Norman Knights

1 – The Conqueror Connection

2 – The Leicester-Lancaster Line

3 – Turville & Bolebec

To the Manor Born

4 – From Piscator to Manfield

5 – From Manfield via Hampson to Orkney

The Royal Ripple

6 – The Dashing Duke and the Pervasive Villiers

7 – The Lords & Ladies Orkney, Inchiquin & Boston

8 – The O'Brien

The Common People

9 – Grenville & Fortescue: In Paradise at Dropmore

10 – The Richest Englishmen: Sutherland & Westminster

11 – Astor and his Cliveden Set

12 – Hurn's Turn

13 – House to House: An Odd Story

The Village People

14 – The Shopkeepers: Gurney, Darling & Rance

15 – The Murrays of Elibank

16 – The Spreading Grenfells (Part 1)

17 – The Spreading Grenfells (Part 2)

18 – The Pearce-Serocolds of Taplow Hill

The Valley People

19 – The Whitlaws in Southern Comfort

The Farmers

20 – Neighbour, Norrington & Briginshaw

21 – Webster & Cross

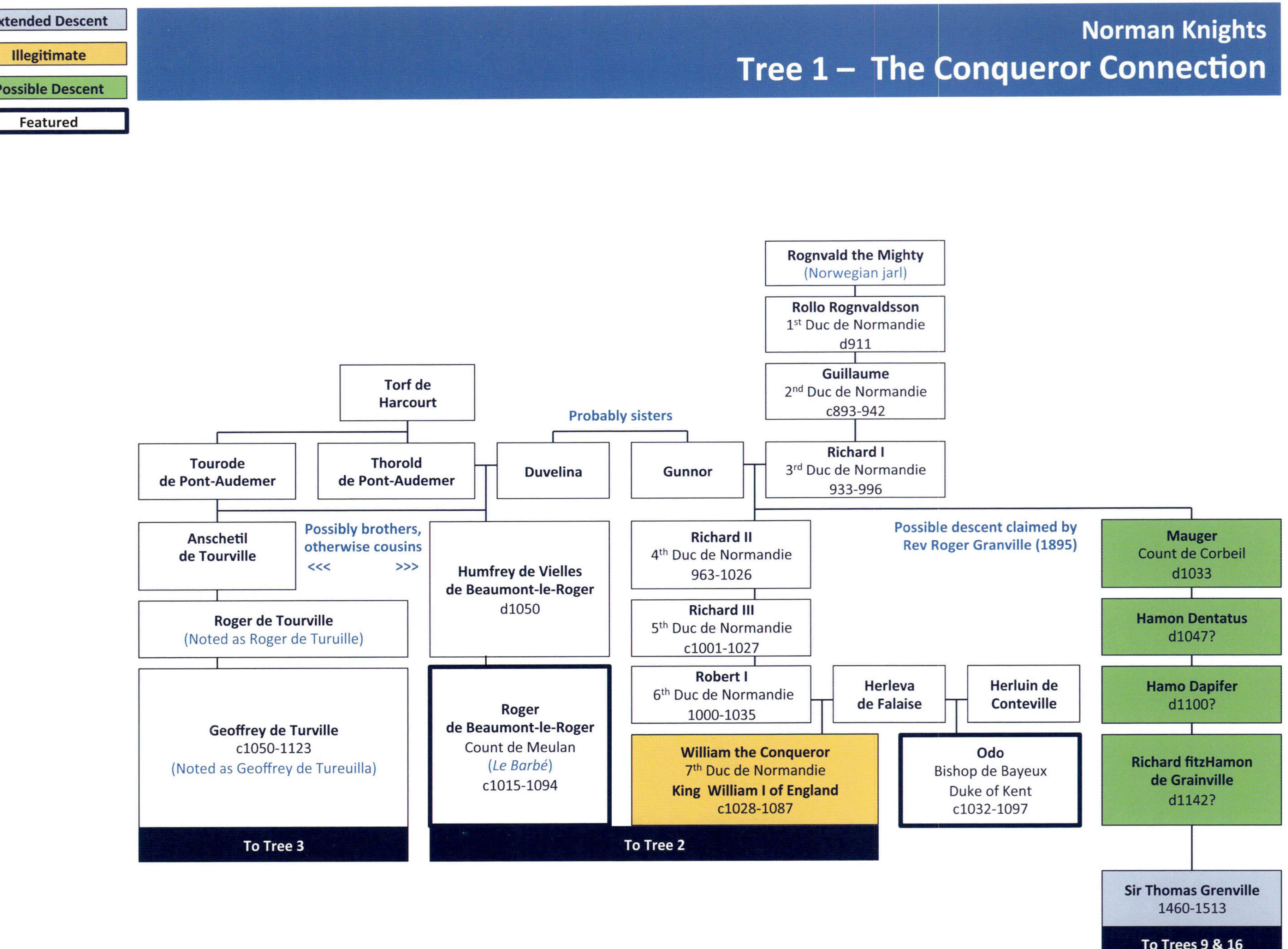
Norman Knights
Tree 1 – The Conqueror Connection
Extended Descent
Illegitimate
Possible Descent
Featured
Rognvald the Mighty (Norwegian jarl)
Rollo Rognvaldsson 1st Duc de Normandie d911
Guillaume 2nd Duc de Normandie c893-942
Richard I 3rd Duc de Normandie 933-996
Torf de Harcourt
Probably sisters
Tourode de Pont-Audemer
Thorold de Pont-Audemer
Duvelina
Gunnor
Anschetil de Tourville
Possibly brothers, otherwise cousins
<<< >>>
Humfrey de Vielles de Beaumont-le-Roger d1050
Richard II 4th Duc de Normandie 963-1026
Possible descent claimed by Rev Roger Granville (1895)
Mauger Count de Corbeil d1033
Roger de Tourville (Noted as Roger de Turuille)
Richard III 5th Duc de Normandie c1001-1027
Hamon Dentatus d1047?
Robert I 6th Duc de Normandie 1000-1035
Herleva de Falaise
Herluin de Conteville
Hamo Dapifer d1100?
Geoffrey de Turville c1050-1123 (Noted as Geoffrey de Tureuilla)
Roger de Beaumont-le-Roger Count de Meulan (Le Barbé) c1015-1094
William the Conqueror 7th Duc de Normandie King William I of England c1028-1087
Odo Bishop de Bayeux Duke of Kent c1032-1097
Richard fitzHamon de Grainville d1142?
To Tree 3
To Tree 2
Sir Thomas Grenville 1460-1513
To Trees 9 & 16

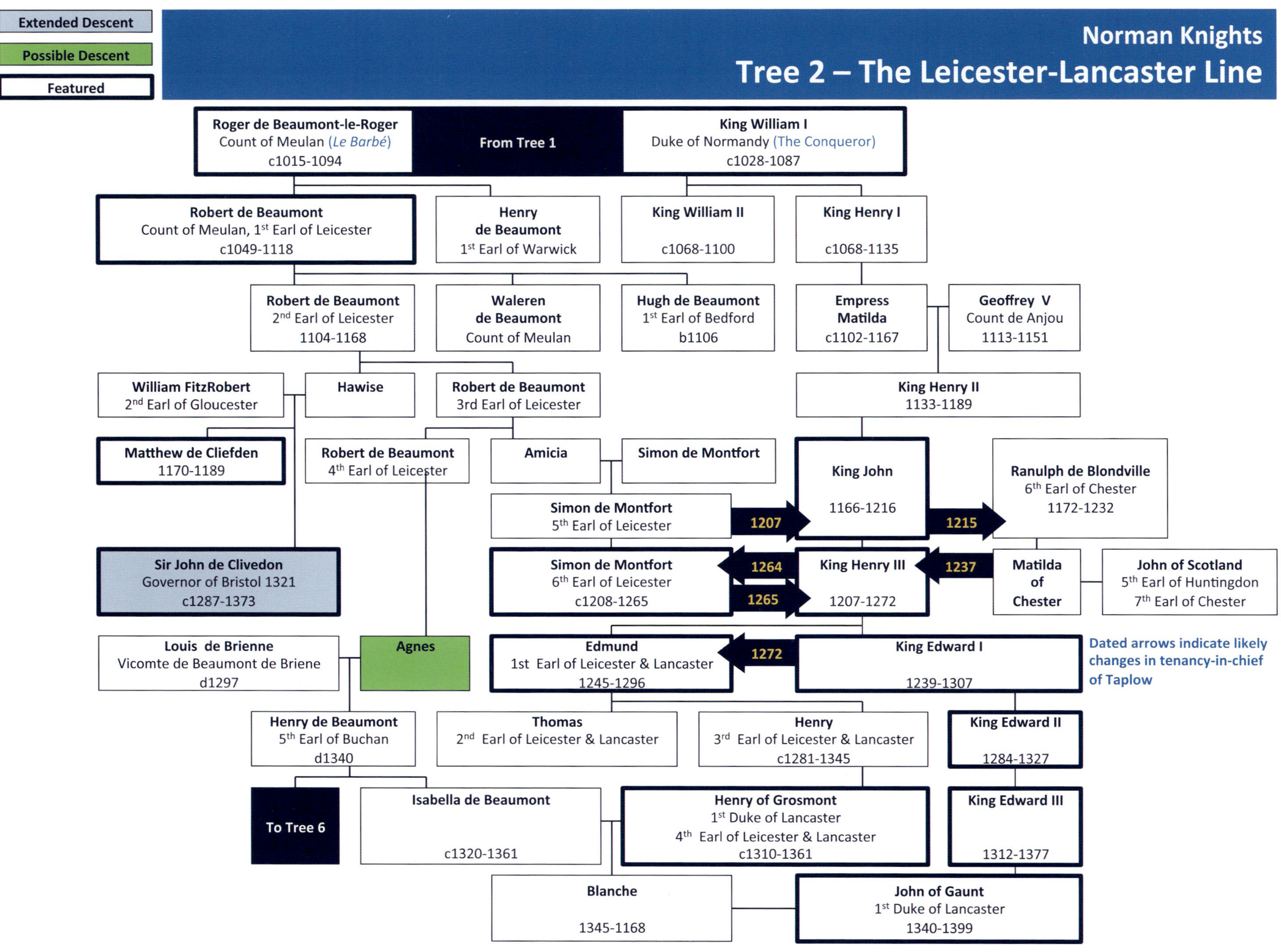
Extended Descent
Possible Descent
Featured
Norman Knights
Tree 2 – The Leicester-Lancaster Line
Roger de Beaumont-le-Roger
Count of Meulan (Le Barbé)
c1015-1094
From Tree 1
King William I
Duke of Normandy (The Conqueror)
c1028-1087
Robert de Beaumont
Count of Meulan, 1st Earl of Leicester
c1049-1118
Henry de Beaumont
1st Earl of Warwick
King William II
c1068-1100
King Henry I
c1068-1135
Robert de Beaumont
2nd Earl of Leicester
1104-1168
Waleren de Beaumont
Count of Meulan
Hugh de Beaumont
1st Earl of Bedford
b1106
Empress Matilda
c1102-1167
Geoffrey V
Count de Anjou
1113-1151
William FitzRobert
2nd Earl of Gloucester
Hawise
Robert de Beaumont
3rd Earl of Leicester
King Henry II
1133-1189
Matthew de Cliefden
1170-1189
Robert de Beaumont
4th Earl of Leicester
Amicia
Simon de Montfort
King John
1166-1216
Ranulph de Blondville
6th Earl of Chester
1172-1232
Simon de Montfort
5th Earl of Leicester
1207
1215
Sir John de Clivedon
Governor of Bristol 1321
c1287-1373
Simon de Montfort
6th Earl of Leicester
c1208-1265
1264
1265
King Henry III
1207-1272
1237
Matilda of Chester
John of Scotland
5th Earl of Huntingdon
7th Earl of Chester
Louis de Brienne
Vicomte de Beaumont de Briene
d1297
Agnes
Edmund
1st Earl of Leicester & Lancaster
1245-1296
1272
King Edward I
1239-1307
Dated arrows indicate likely changes in tenancy-in-chief of Taplow
Henry de Beaumont
5th Earl of Buchan
d1340
Thomas
2nd Earl of Leicester & Lancaster
Henry
3rd Earl of Leicester & Lancaster
c1281-1345
King Edward II
1284-1327
To Tree 6
Isabella de Beaumont
c1320-1361
Henry of Grosmont
1st Duke of Lancaster
4th Earl of Leicester & Lancaster
c1310-1361
King Edward III
1312-1377
Blanche
1345-1168
John of Gaunt
1st Duke of Lancaster
1340-1399

Extended Descent

Featured

Norman Knights
Tree 3 – Turville & Bolebec

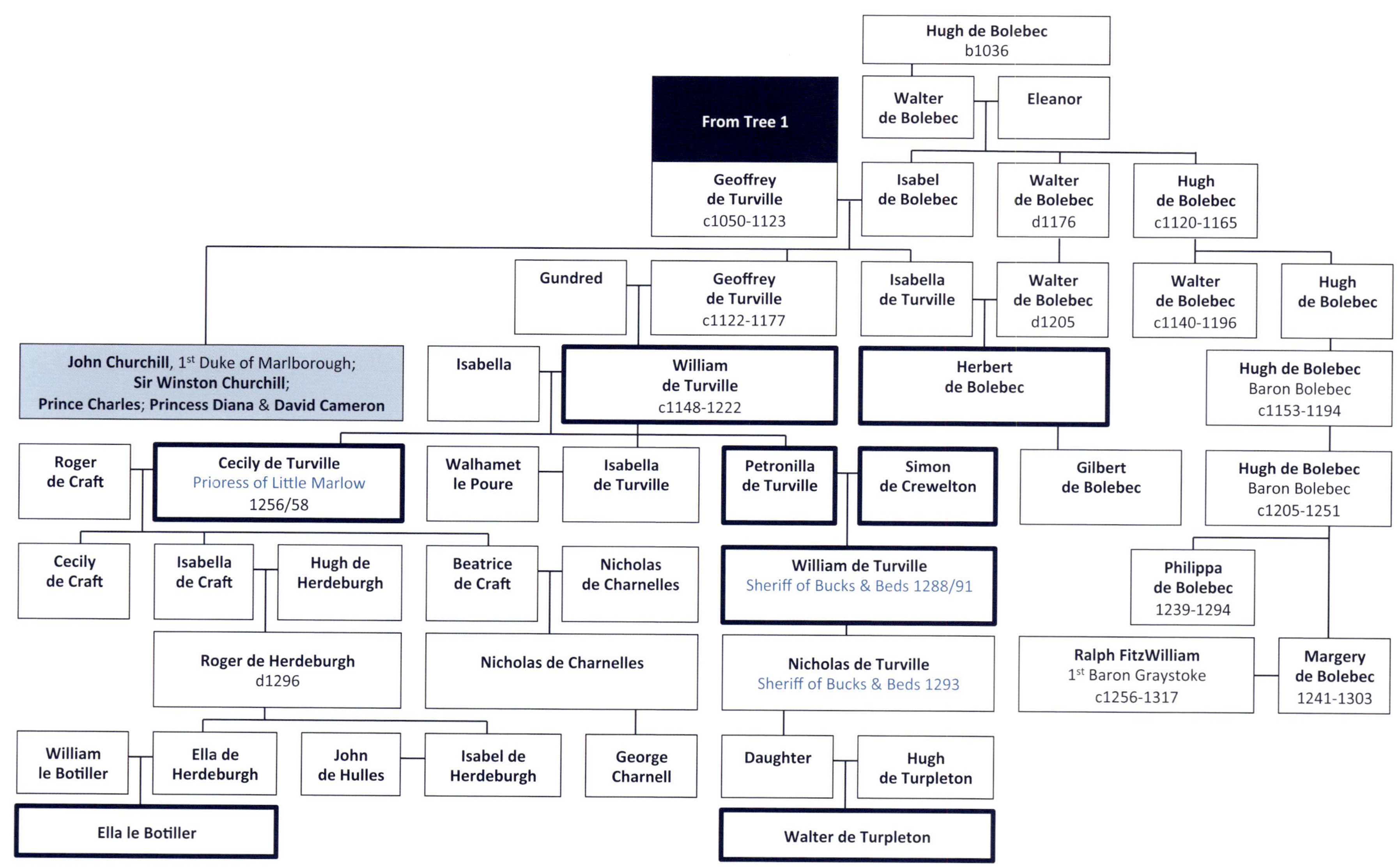

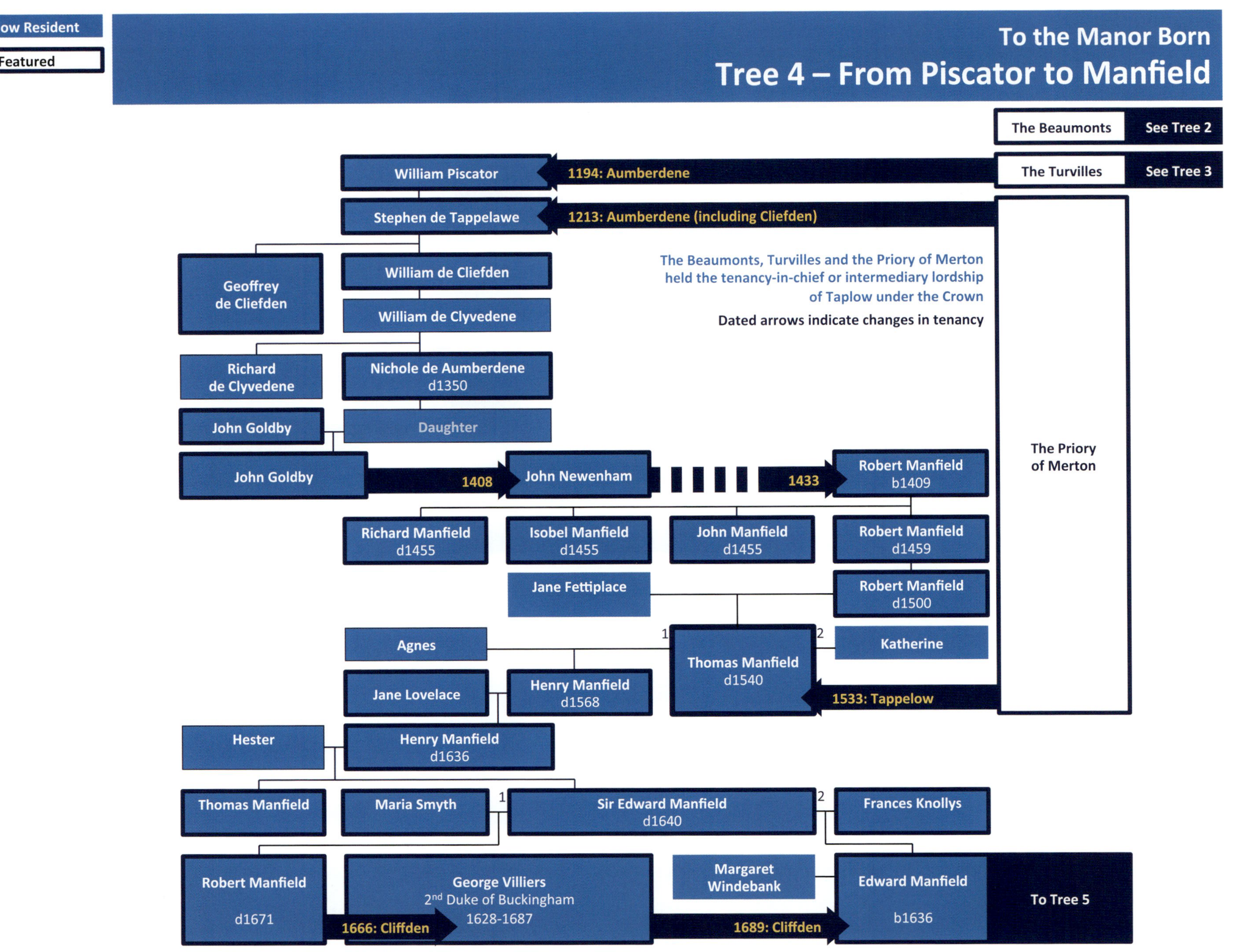

Taplow Resident
Featured
To the Manor Born
Tree 4 – From Piscator to Manfield
The Beaumonts
See Tree 2
The Turvilles
See Tree 3
William Piscator
1194: Aumberdene
Stephen de Tappelawe
1213: Aumberdene (including Cliefden)
The Beaumonts, Turvilles and the Priory of Merton held the tenancy-in-chief or intermediary lordship of Taplow under the Crown
Dated arrows indicate changes in tenancy
Geoffrey de Cliefden
William de Cliefden
William de Clyvedene
Richard de Clyvedene
Nichole de Aumberdene d1350
John Goldby
Daughter
The Priory of Merton
John Goldby
1408
John Newenham
1433
Robert Manfield b1409
Richard Manfield d1455
Isobel Manfield d1455
John Manfield d1455
Robert Manfield d1459
Jane Fettiplace
Robert Manfield d1500
Agnes
1
Thomas Manfield d1540
2
Katherine
Jane Lovelace
Henry Manfield d1568
1533: Tappelow
Hester
Henry Manfield d1636
Thomas Manfield
Maria Smyth
1
Sir Edward Manfield d1640
2
Frances Knollys
Robert Manfield d1671
George Villiers 2nd Duke of Buckingham 1628-1687
Margaret Windebank
Edward Manfield b1636
To Tree 5
1666: Cliffden
1689: Cliffden

Tree 5 – From Manfield via Hampson to Orkney

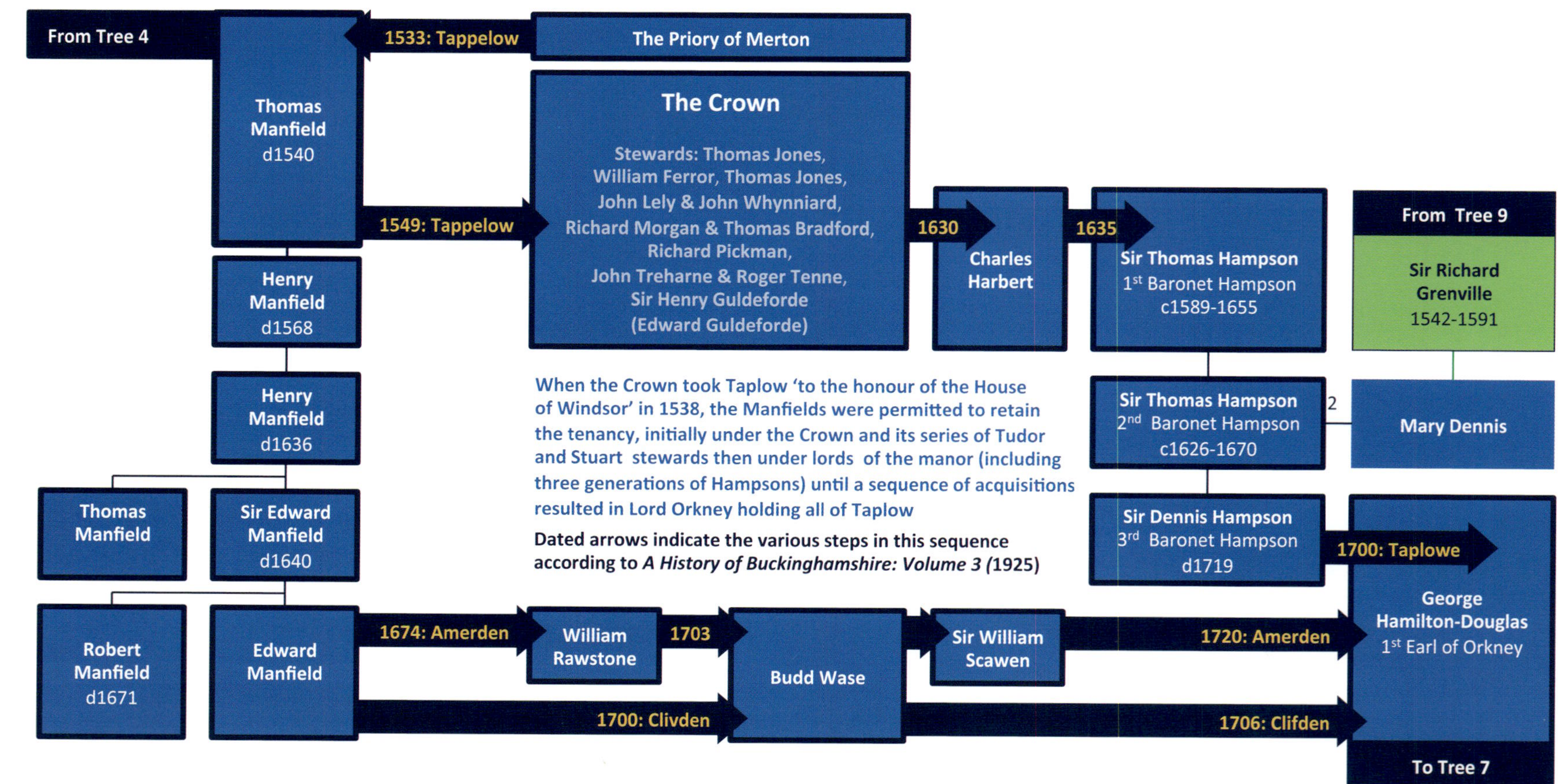

When the Crown took Taplow 'to the honour of the House of Windsor' in 1538, the Manfields were permitted to retain the tenancy, initially under the Crown and its series of Tudor and Stuart stewards then under lords of the manor (including three generations of Hampsons) until a sequence of acquisitions resulted in Lord Orkney holding all of Taplow

Dated arrows indicate the various steps in this sequence according to *A History of Buckinghamshire: Volume 3* (1925)

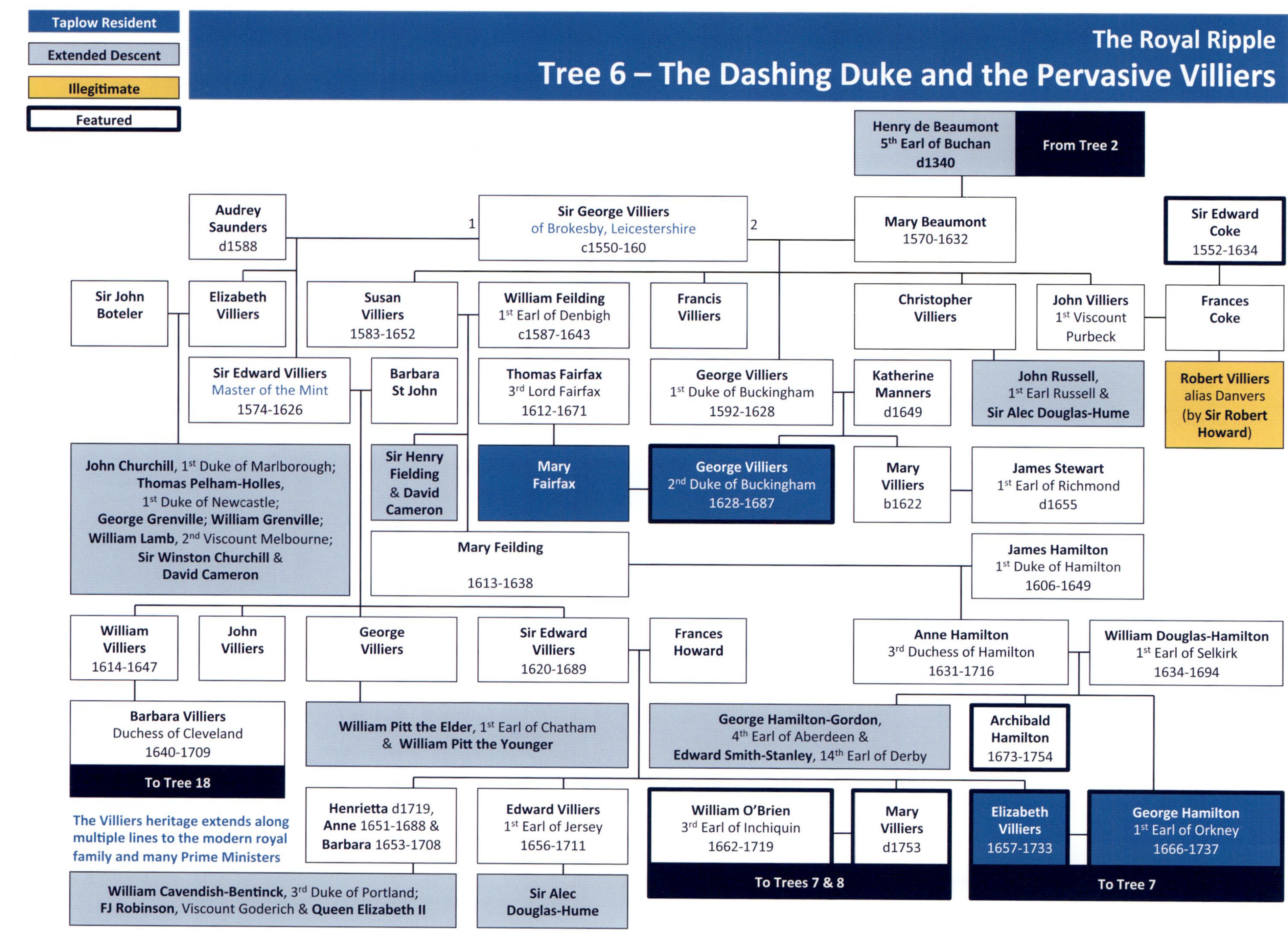
The Royal Ripple
Tree 6 – The Dashing Duke and the Pervasive Villiers
Taplow Resident
Extended Descent
Illegitimate
Featured
Henry de Beaumont 5th Earl of Buchan d1340
From Tree 2
Audrey Saunders d1588
Sir George Villiers of Brokesby, Leicestershire c1550-160
1
2
Mary Beaumont 1570-1632
Sir Edward Coke 1552-1634
Sir John Boteler
Elizabeth Villiers
Susan Villiers 1583-1652
William Feilding 1st Earl of Denbigh c1587-1643
Francis Villiers
Christopher Villiers
John Villiers 1st Viscount Purbeck
Frances Coke
Sir Edward Villiers Master of the Mint 1574-1626
Barbara St John
Thomas Fairfax 3rd Lord Fairfax 1612-1671
George Villiers 1st Duke of Buckingham 1592-1628
Katherine Manners d1649
John Russell, 1st Earl Russell & Sir Alec Douglas-Hume
Robert Villiers alias Danvers (by Sir Robert Howard)
John Churchill, 1st Duke of Marlborough; Thomas Pelham-Holles, 1st Duke of Newcastle; George Grenville; William Grenville; William Lamb, 2nd Viscount Melbourne; Sir Winston Churchill & David Cameron
Sir Henry Fielding & David Cameron
Mary Fairfax
George Villiers 2nd Duke of Buckingham 1628-1687
Mary Villiers b1622
James Stewart 1st Earl of Richmond d1655
Mary Feilding 1613-1638
James Hamilton 1st Duke of Hamilton 1606-1649
William Villiers 1614-1647
John Villiers
George Villiers
Sir Edward Villiers 1620-1689
Frances Howard
Anne Hamilton 3rd Duchess of Hamilton 1631-1716
William Douglas-Hamilton 1st Earl of Selkirk 1634-1694
Barbara Villiers Duchess of Cleveland 1640-1709
To Tree 18
William Pitt the Elder, 1st Earl of Chatham & William Pitt the Younger
George Hamilton-Gordon, 4th Earl of Aberdeen & Edward Smith-Stanley, 14th Earl of Derby
Archibald Hamilton 1673-1754
The Villiers heritage extends along multiple lines to the modern royal family and many Prime Ministers
Henrietta d1719, Anne 1651-1688 & Barbara 1653-1708
Edward Villiers 1st Earl of Jersey 1656-1711
William O'Brien 3rd Earl of Inchiquin 1662-1719
Mary Villiers d1753
Elizabeth Villiers 1657-1733
George Hamilton 1st Earl of Orkney 1666-1737
To Trees 7 & 8
To Tree 7
William Cavendish-Bentinck, 3rd Duke of Portland; FJ Robinson, Viscount Goderich & Queen Elizabeth II
Sir Alec Douglas-Hume

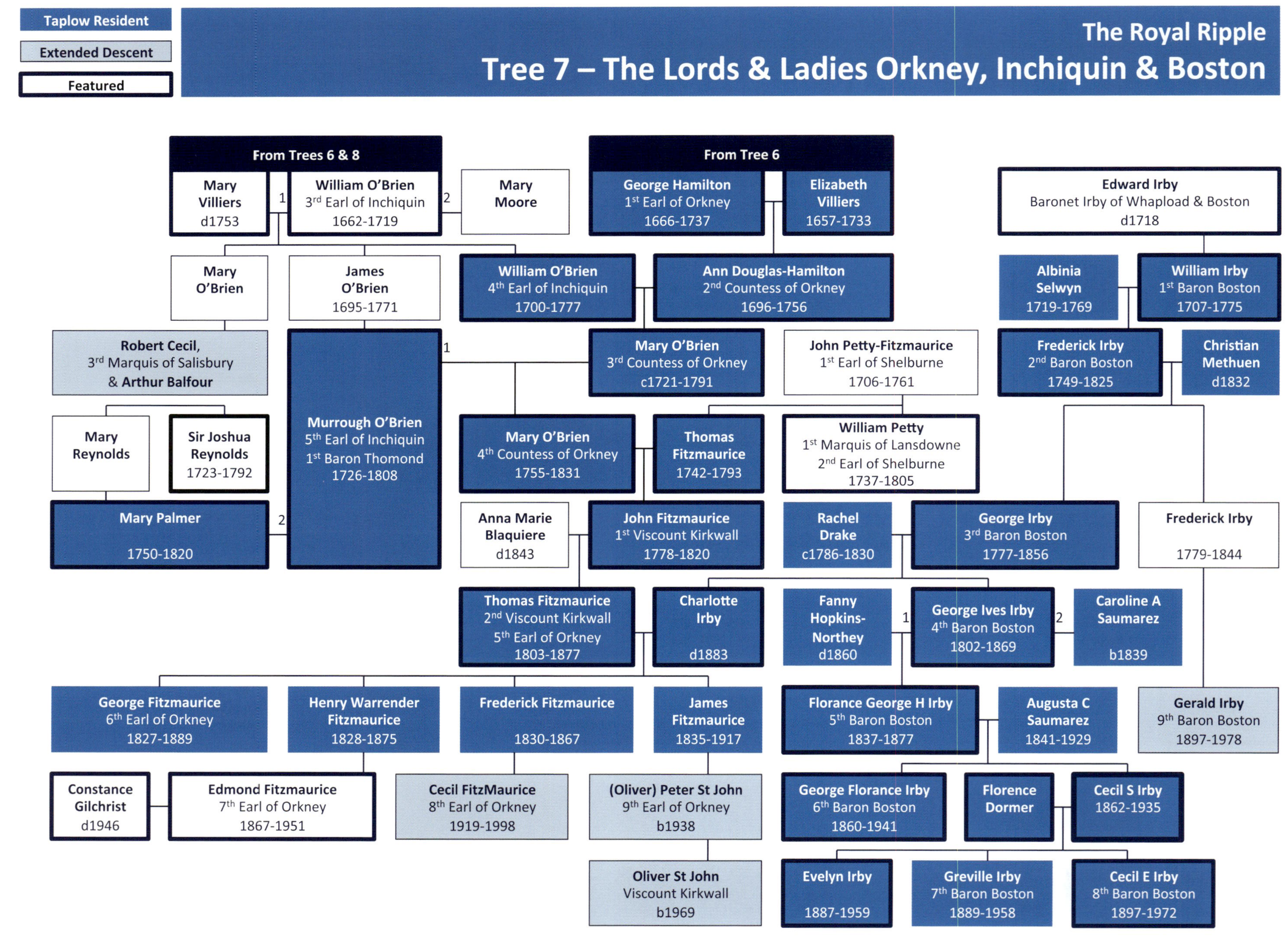

Taplow Resident
Extended Descent
Featured
The Royal Ripple
Tree 7 – The Lords & Ladies Orkney, Inchiquin & Boston
From Trees 6 & 8
Mary Villiers d1753
1
William O'Brien 3rd Earl of Inchiquin 1662-1719
2
Mary Moore
From Tree 6
George Hamilton 1st Earl of Orkney 1666-1737
Elizabeth Villiers 1657-1733
Edward Irby Baronet Irby of Whapload & Boston d1718
Mary O'Brien
James O'Brien 1695-1771
William O'Brien 4th Earl of Inchiquin 1700-1777
Ann Douglas-Hamilton 2nd Countess of Orkney 1696-1756
Albinia Selwyn 1719-1769
William Irby 1st Baron Boston 1707-1775
Robert Cecil, 3rd Marquis of Salisbury & Arthur Balfour
Murrough O'Brien 5th Earl of Inchiquin 1st Baron Thomond 1726-1808
1
Mary O'Brien 3rd Countess of Orkney c1721-1791
John Petty-Fitzmaurice 1st Earl of Shelburne 1706-1761
Frederick Irby 2nd Baron Boston 1749-1825
Christian Methuen d1832
Mary Reynolds
Sir Joshua Reynolds 1723-1792
Mary O'Brien 4th Countess of Orkney 1755-1831
Thomas Fitzmaurice 1742-1793
William Petty 1st Marquis of Lansdowne 2nd Earl of Shelburne 1737-1805
Mary Palmer 1750-1820
2
Anna Marie Blaquiere d1843
John Fitzmaurice 1st Viscount Kirkwall 1778-1820
Rachel Drake c1786-1830
George Irby 3rd Baron Boston 1777-1856
Frederick Irby 1779-1844
Thomas Fitzmaurice 2nd Viscount Kirkwall 5th Earl of Orkney 1803-1877
Charlotte Irby d1883
Fanny Hopkins-Northey d1860
1
George Ives Irby 4th Baron Boston 1802-1869
2
Caroline A Saumarez b1839
George Fitzmaurice 6th Earl of Orkney 1827-1889
Henry Warrender Fitzmaurice 1828-1875
Frederick Fitzmaurice 1830-1867
James Fitzmaurice 1835-1917
Florance George H Irby 5th Baron Boston 1837-1877
Augusta C Saumarez 1841-1929
Gerald Irby 9th Baron Boston 1897-1978
Constance Gilchrist d1946
Edmond Fitzmaurice 7th Earl of Orkney 1867-1951
Cecil FitzMaurice 8th Earl of Orkney 1919-1998
(Oliver) Peter St John 9th Earl of Orkney b1938
George Florance Irby 6th Baron Boston 1860-1941
Florence Dormer
Cecil S Irby 1862-1935
Oliver St John Viscount Kirkwall b1969
Evelyn Irby 1887-1959
Greville Irby 7th Baron Boston 1889-1958
Cecil E Irby 8th Baron Boston 1897-1972

Extended Descent

Featured

The Royal Ripple

Tree 8 – The O'Brien

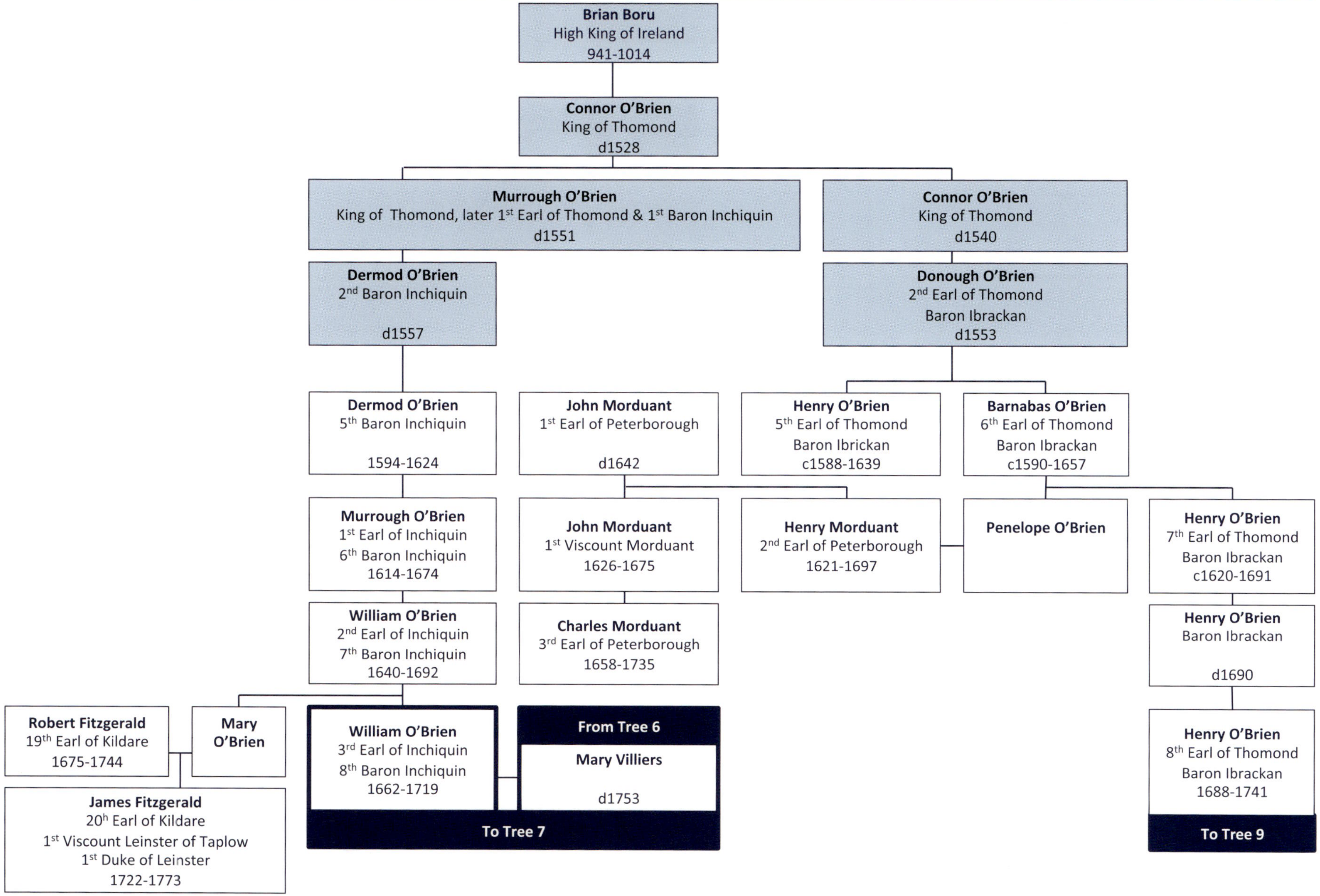

Brian Boru
High King of Ireland
941-1014

Connor O'Brien
King of Thomond
d1528

Murrough O'Brien
King of Thomond, later 1st Earl of Thomond & 1st Baron Inchiquin
d1551

Connor O'Brien
King of Thomond
d1540

Dermod O'Brien
2nd Baron Inchiquin
d1557

Donough O'Brien
2nd Earl of Thomond
Baron Ibrackan
d1553

Dermod O'Brien
5th Baron Inchiquin
1594-1624

John Mordaunt
1st Earl of Peterborough
d1642

Henry O'Brien
5th Earl of Thomond
Baron Ibrickan
c1588-1639

Barnabas O'Brien
6th Earl of Thomond
Baron Ibrackan
c1590-1657

Murrough O'Brien
1st Earl of Inchiquin
6th Baron Inchiquin
1614-1674

John Mordaunt
1st Viscount Mordaunt
1626-1675

Henry Mordaunt
2nd Earl of Peterborough
1621-1697

Penelope O'Brien

Henry O'Brien
7th Earl of Thomond
Baron Ibrackan
c1620-1691

William O'Brien
2nd Earl of Inchiquin
7th Baron Inchiquin
1640-1692

Charles Mordaunt
3rd Earl of Peterborough
1658-1735

Henry O'Brien
Baron Ibrackan
d1690

Robert Fitzgerald
19th Earl of Kildare
1675-1744

Mary O'Brien

William O'Brien
3rd Earl of Inchiquin
8th Baron Inchiquin
1662-1719

From Tree 6

Mary Villiers
d1753

To Tree 7

Henry O'Brien
8th Earl of Thomond
Baron Ibrackan
1688-1741

To Tree 9

James Fitzgerald
20^{h} Earl of Kildare
1st Viscount Leinster of Taplow
1st Duke of Leinster
1722-1773

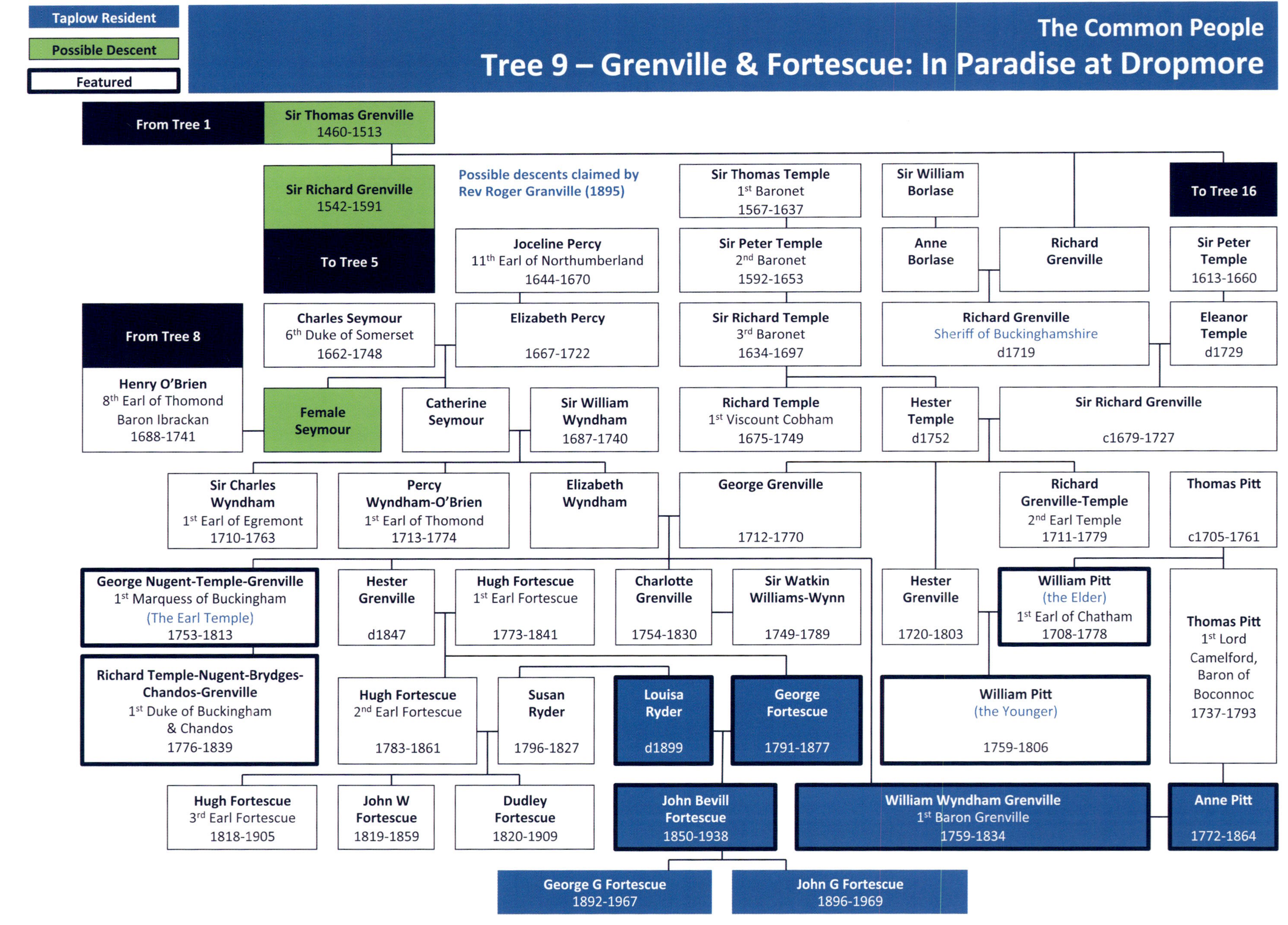
Taplow Resident
Possible Descent
Featured
The Common People
Tree 9 – Grenville & Fortescue: In Paradise at Dropmore
From Tree 1
Sir Thomas Grenville 1460-1513
Sir Richard Grenville 1542-1591
To Tree 5
Possible descents claimed by Rev Roger Granville (1895)
Sir Thomas Temple 1st Baronet 1567-1637
Sir William Borlase
To Tree 16
Joceline Percy 11th Earl of Northumberland 1644-1670
Sir Peter Temple 2nd Baronet 1592-1653
Anne Borlase
Richard Grenville
Sir Peter Temple 1613-1660
From Tree 8
Henry O'Brien 8th Earl of Thomond Baron Ibrackan 1688-1741
Charles Seymour 6th Duke of Somerset 1662-1748
Elizabeth Percy 1667-1722
Sir Richard Temple 3rd Baronet 1634-1697
Richard Grenville Sheriff of Buckinghamshire d1719
Eleanor Temple d1729
Female Seymour
Catherine Seymour
Sir William Wyndham 1687-1740
Richard Temple 1st Viscount Cobham 1675-1749
Hester Temple d1752
Sir Richard Grenville c1679-1727
Sir Charles Wyndham 1st Earl of Egremont 1710-1763
Percy Wyndham-O'Brien 1st Earl of Thomond 1713-1774
Elizabeth Wyndham
George Grenville 1712-1770
Richard Grenville-Temple 2nd Earl Temple 1711-1779
Thomas Pitt c1705-1761
George Nugent-Temple-Grenville 1st Marquess of Buckingham (The Earl Temple) 1753-1813
Hester Grenville d1847
Hugh Fortescue 1st Earl Fortescue 1773-1841
Charlotte Grenville 1754-1830
Sir Watkin Williams-Wynn 1749-1789
Hester Grenville 1720-1803
William Pitt (the Elder) 1st Earl of Chatham 1708-1778
Thomas Pitt 1st Lord Camelford, Baron of Boconnoc 1737-1793
Richard Temple-Nugent-Brydges-Chandos-Grenville 1st Duke of Buckingham & Chandos 1776-1839
Hugh Fortescue 2nd Earl Fortescue 1783-1861
Susan Ryder 1796-1827
Louisa Ryder d1899
George Fortescue 1791-1877
William Pitt (the Younger) 1759-1806
Hugh Fortescue 3rd Earl Fortescue 1818-1905
John W Fortescue 1819-1859
Dudley Fortescue 1820-1909
John Bevill Fortescue 1850-1938
William Wyndham Grenville 1st Baron Grenville 1759-1834
Anne Pitt 1772-1864
George G Fortescue 1892-1967
John G Fortescue 1896-1969

Taplow Resident

Featured

Tree 10 – The Richest Englishmen: Sutherland & Westminster

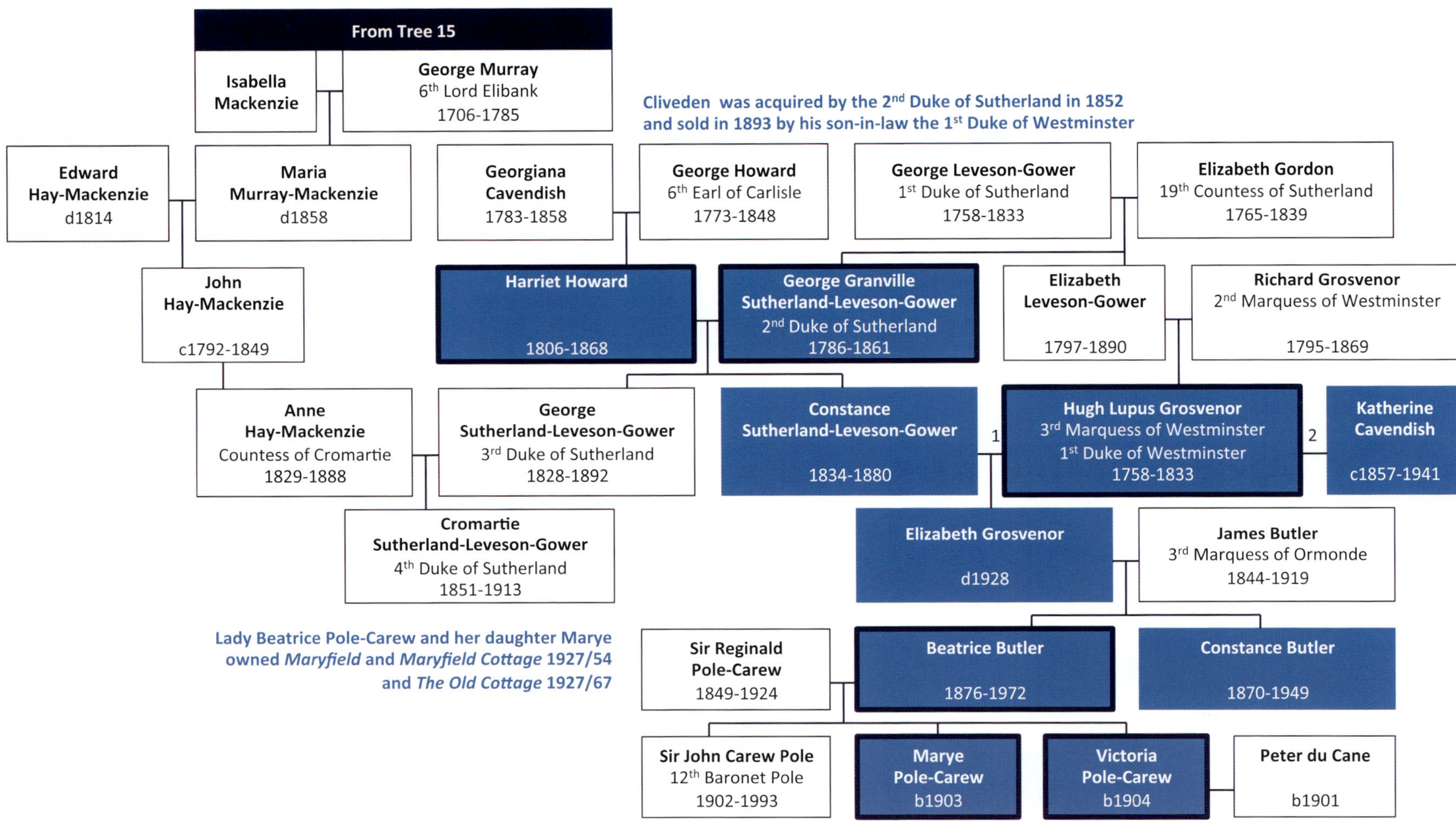

Tree 11 – The Richest American: Astor and his Cliveden Set

Taplow Resident

Featured

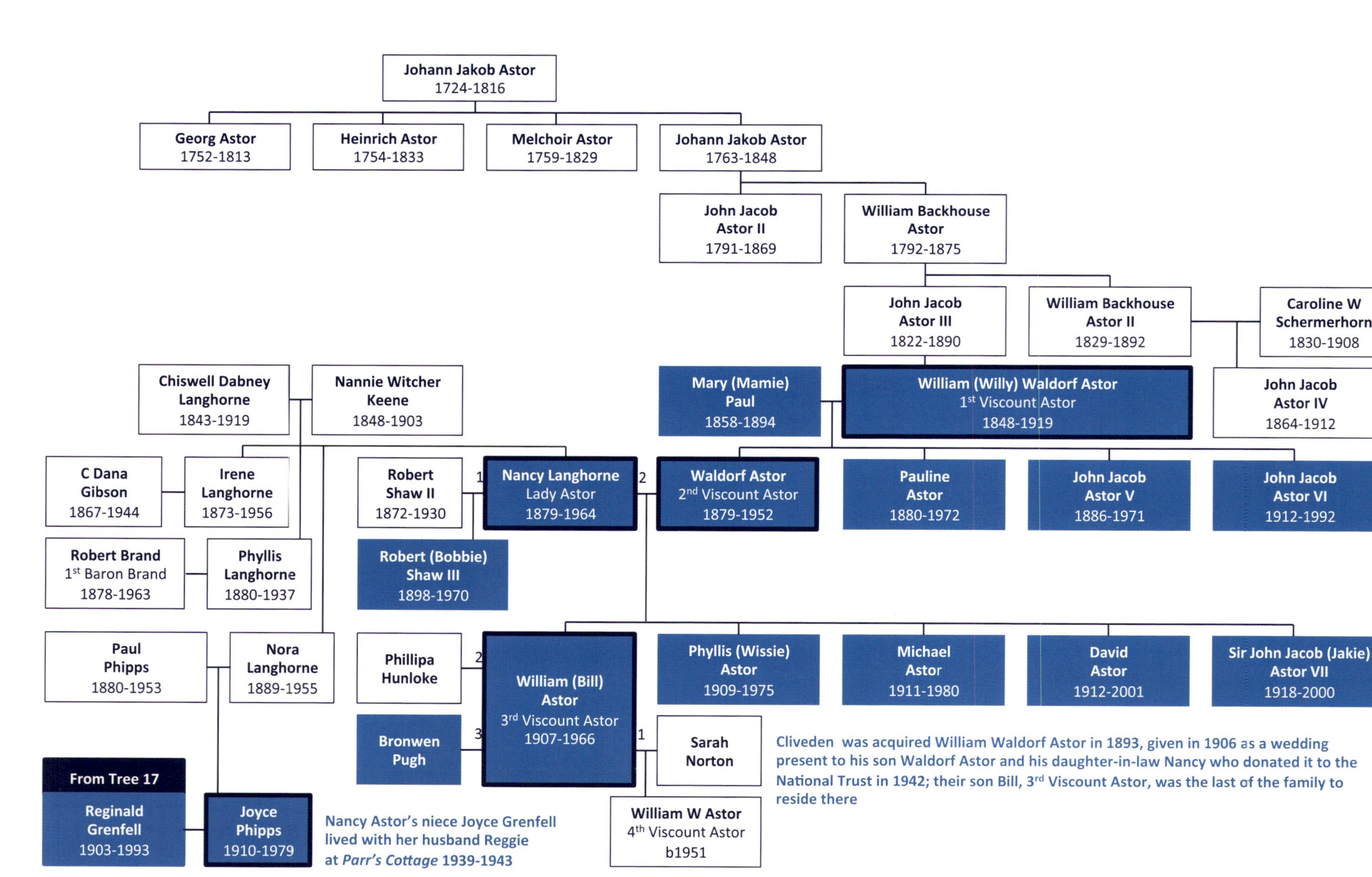

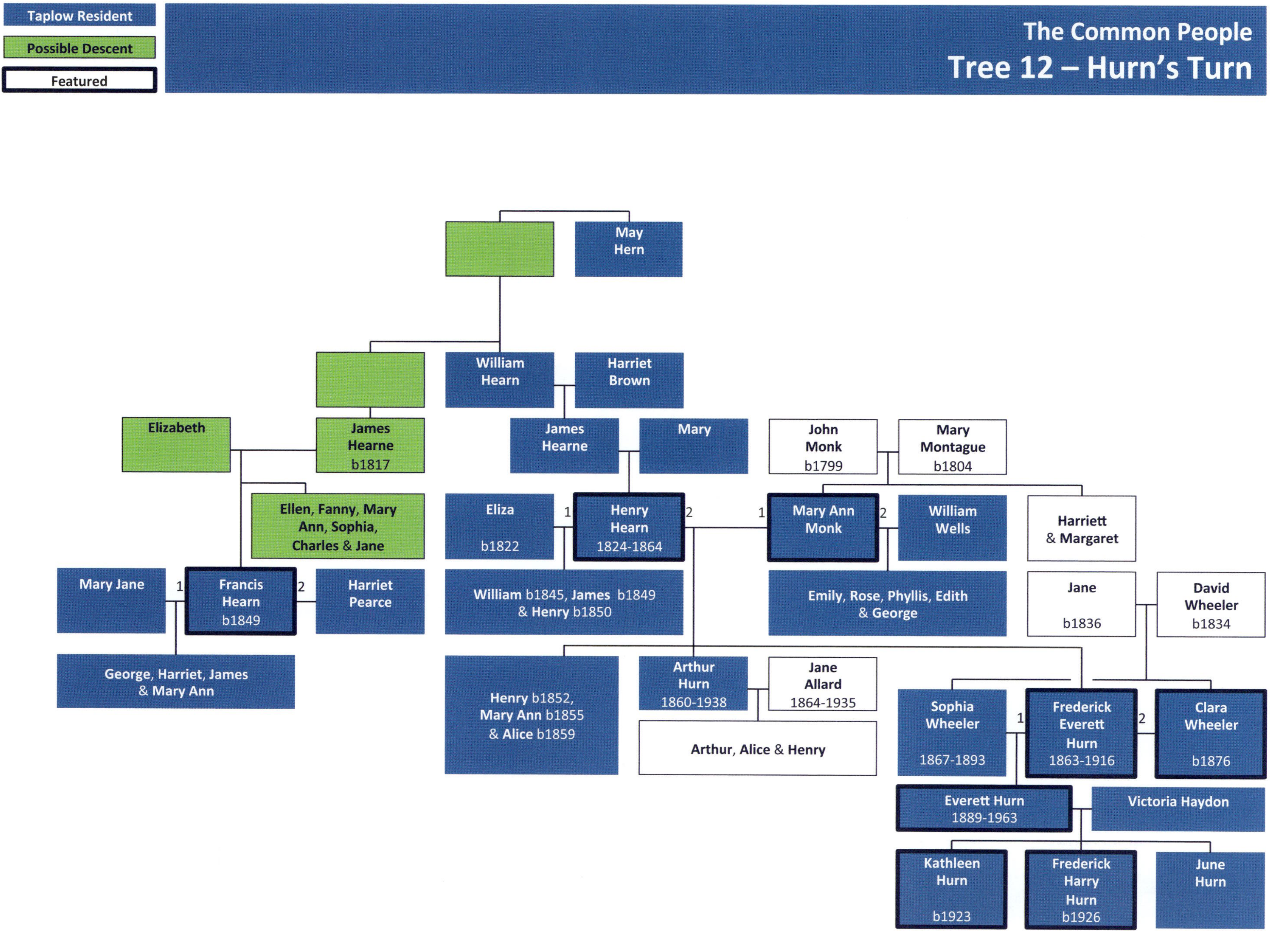

Taplow Resident
Possible Descent
Featured
The Common People
Tree 12 – Hurn's Turn
May Hern
William Hearn
Harriet Brown
Elizabeth
James Hearne b1817
James Hearne
Mary
John Monk b1799
Mary Montague b1804
Ellen, Fanny, Mary Ann, Sophia, Charles & Jane
Eliza b1822
1
Henry Hearn 1824-1864
2
1
Mary Ann Monk
2
William Wells
Harriett & Margaret
Mary Jane
1
Francis Hearn b1849
2
Harriet Pearce
William b1845, James b1849 & Henry b1850
Emily, Rose, Phyllis, Edith & George
Jane b1836
David Wheeler b1834
George, Harriet, James & Mary Ann
Henry b1852, Mary Ann b1855 & Alice b1859
Arthur Hurn 1860-1938
Jane Allard 1864-1935
Arthur, Alice & Henry
Sophia Wheeler 1867-1893
1
Frederick Everett Hurn 1863-1916
2
Clara Wheeler b1876
Everett Hurn 1889-1963
Victoria Haydon
Kathleen Hurn b1923
Frederick Harry Hurn b1926
June Hurn

Tree 13 – House to House: An Odd Story

Taplow Resident

Featured

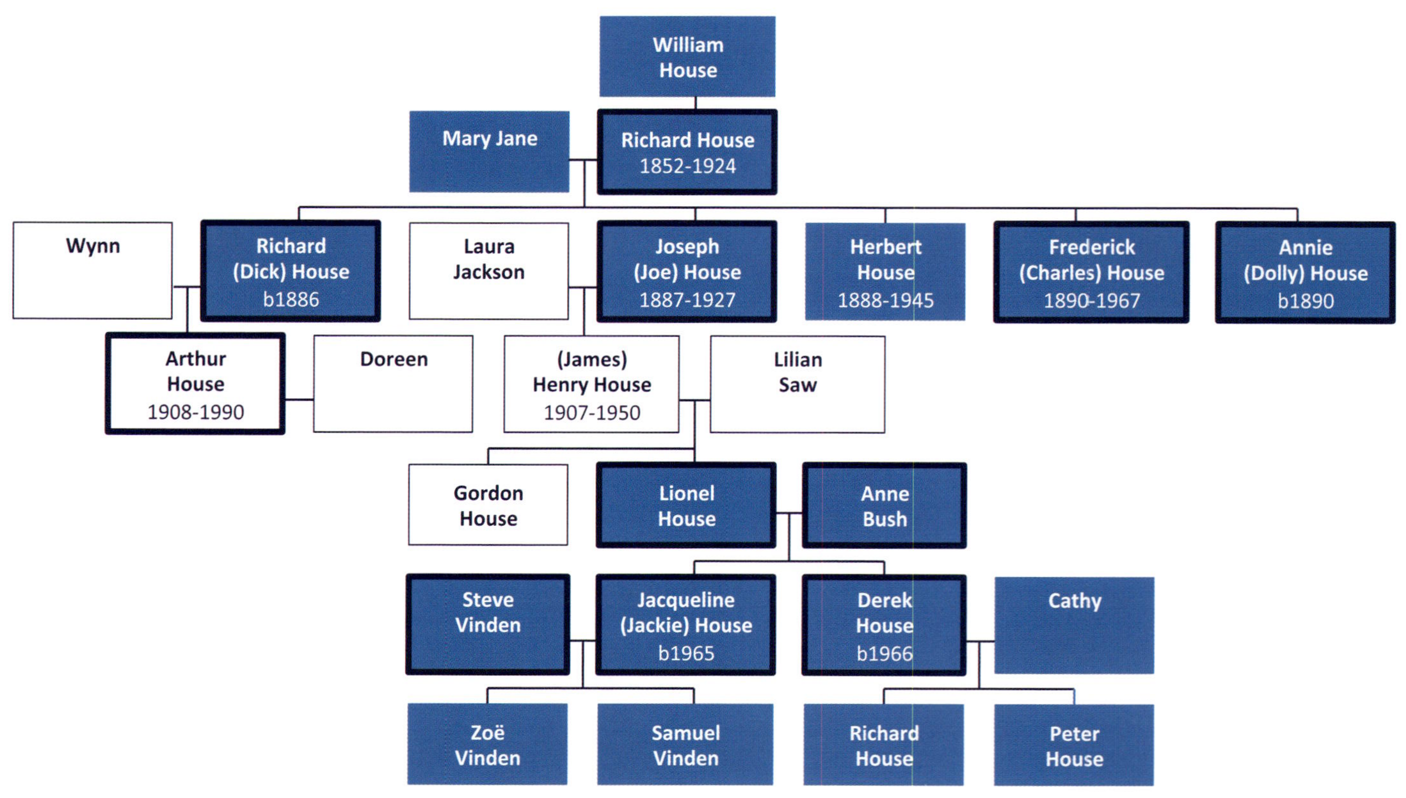

Taplow Resident

Possible Descent

Featured

Tree 14 – The Shopkeepers: Gurney, Darling & Rance

In the early-1800s, Tothill's late Passingham's was a close on the eastern frontage of the modern High Street divided into a patchwork of 'tenements' including a Butcher's Shop and a Bakery

1833: William Rance the Elder tenant of the Butcher's Shop

Late-1830s: Mary Darling (née Gurney) tenant of the Bakery; made it the Village Shop and Post Office

Mid-1840s: Mary Ann Gurney (not yet Darling) and brother George took over the Village Shop and Post Office

1863: Rance acquired the freehold of Tothill's; he built a new house and Butcher's Shop (later *The Hollies*, now *Mulberry House*) and then two cottages (now combined as *Rozel*)

1873: William Gurney married Elizabeth Rance and soon took over the Village Shop; he was joined by his cousins Kate Gurney (as sub-postmistress) and Edward Okey Gurney (as his assistant and successor c1895)

1880-1916: William Rance the Younger succeeded his father at the Butcher's Shop

c1925-1936: Edward Gurney succeeded his father at the Village Shop and Post Office

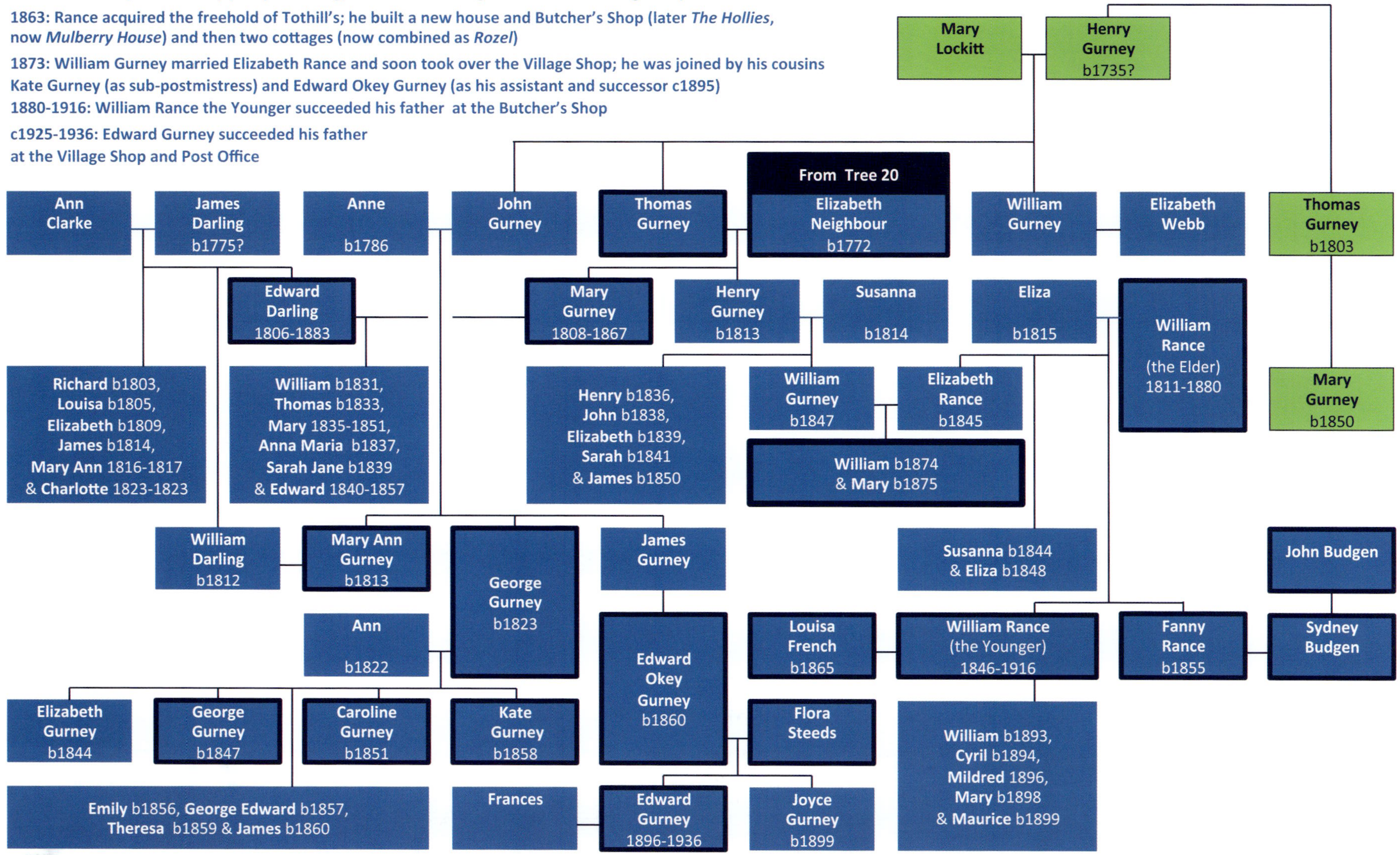

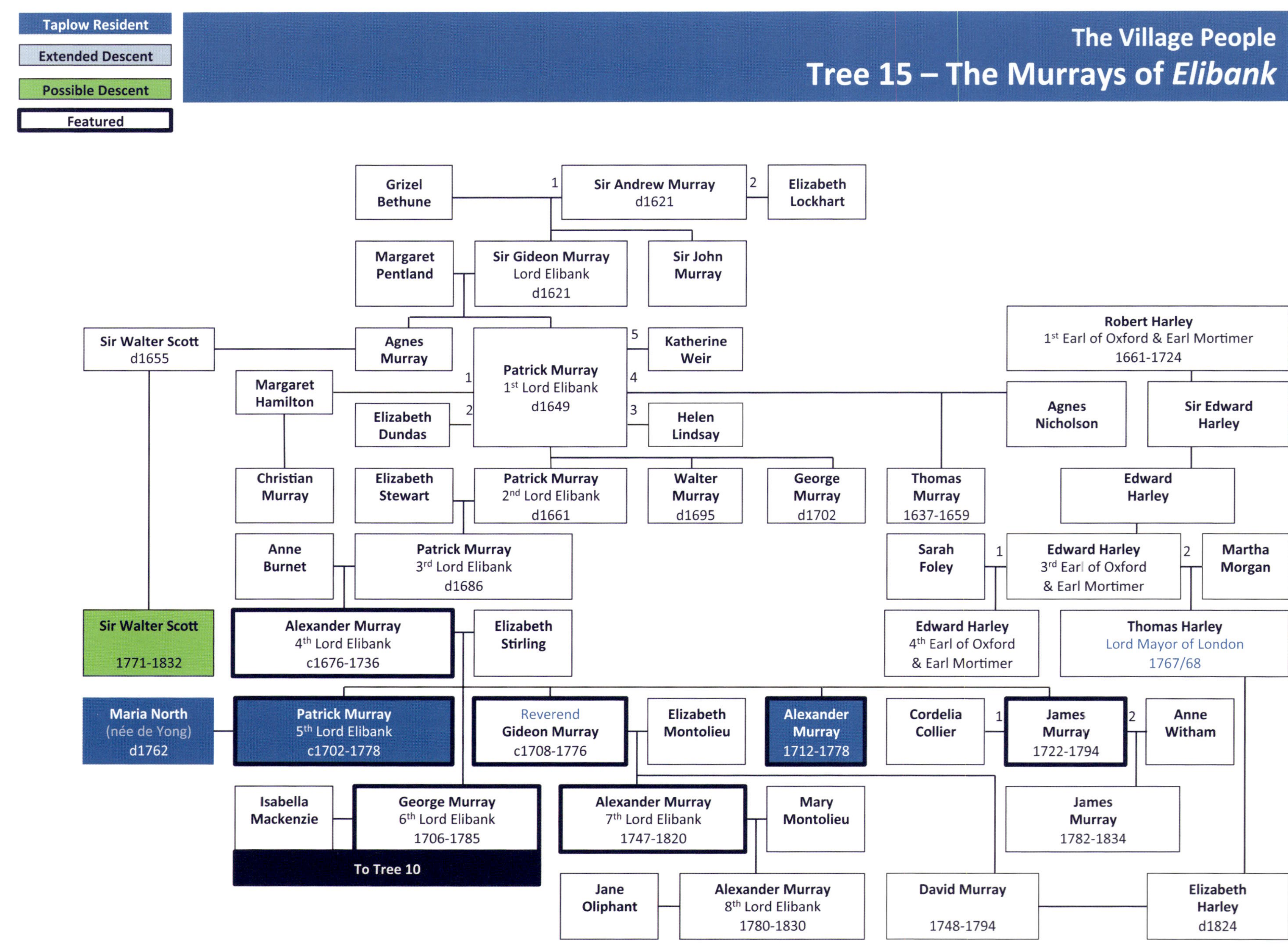

Taplow Resident
Extended Descent
Possible Descent
Featured
The Village People
Tree 15 – The Murrays of Elibank
Grizel Bethune
1
Sir Andrew Murray d1621
2
Elizabeth Lockhart
Margaret Pentland
Sir Gideon Murray Lord Elibank d1621
Sir John Murray
Sir Walter Scott d1655
Agnes Murray
Patrick Murray 1st Lord Elibank d1649
5
Katherine Weir
4
3
Helen Lindsay
Margaret Hamilton
1
2
Elizabeth Dundas
Robert Harley 1st Earl of Oxford & Earl Mortimer 1661-1724
Agnes Nicholson
Sir Edward Harley
Christian Murray
Elizabeth Stewart
Patrick Murray 2nd Lord Elibank d1661
Walter Murray d1695
George Murray d1702
Thomas Murray 1637-1659
Edward Harley
Anne Burnet
Patrick Murray 3rd Lord Elibank d1686
Sarah Foley
1
Edward Harley 3rd Earl of Oxford & Earl Mortimer
2
Martha Morgan
Sir Walter Scott 1771-1832
Alexander Murray 4th Lord Elibank c1676-1736
Elizabeth Stirling
Edward Harley 4th Earl of Oxford & Earl Mortimer
Thomas Harley Lord Mayor of London 1767/68
Maria North (née de Yong) d1762
Patrick Murray 5th Lord Elibank c1702-1778
Reverend Gideon Murray c1708-1776
Elizabeth Montolieu
Alexander Murray 1712-1778
Cordelia Collier
1
James Murray 1722-1794
2
Anne Witham
Isabella Mackenzie
George Murray 6th Lord Elibank 1706-1785
To Tree 10
Alexander Murray 7th Lord Elibank 1747-1820
Mary Montolieu
James Murray 1782-1834
Jane Oliphant
Alexander Murray 8th Lord Elibank 1780-1830
David Murray 1748-1794
Elizabeth Harley d1824

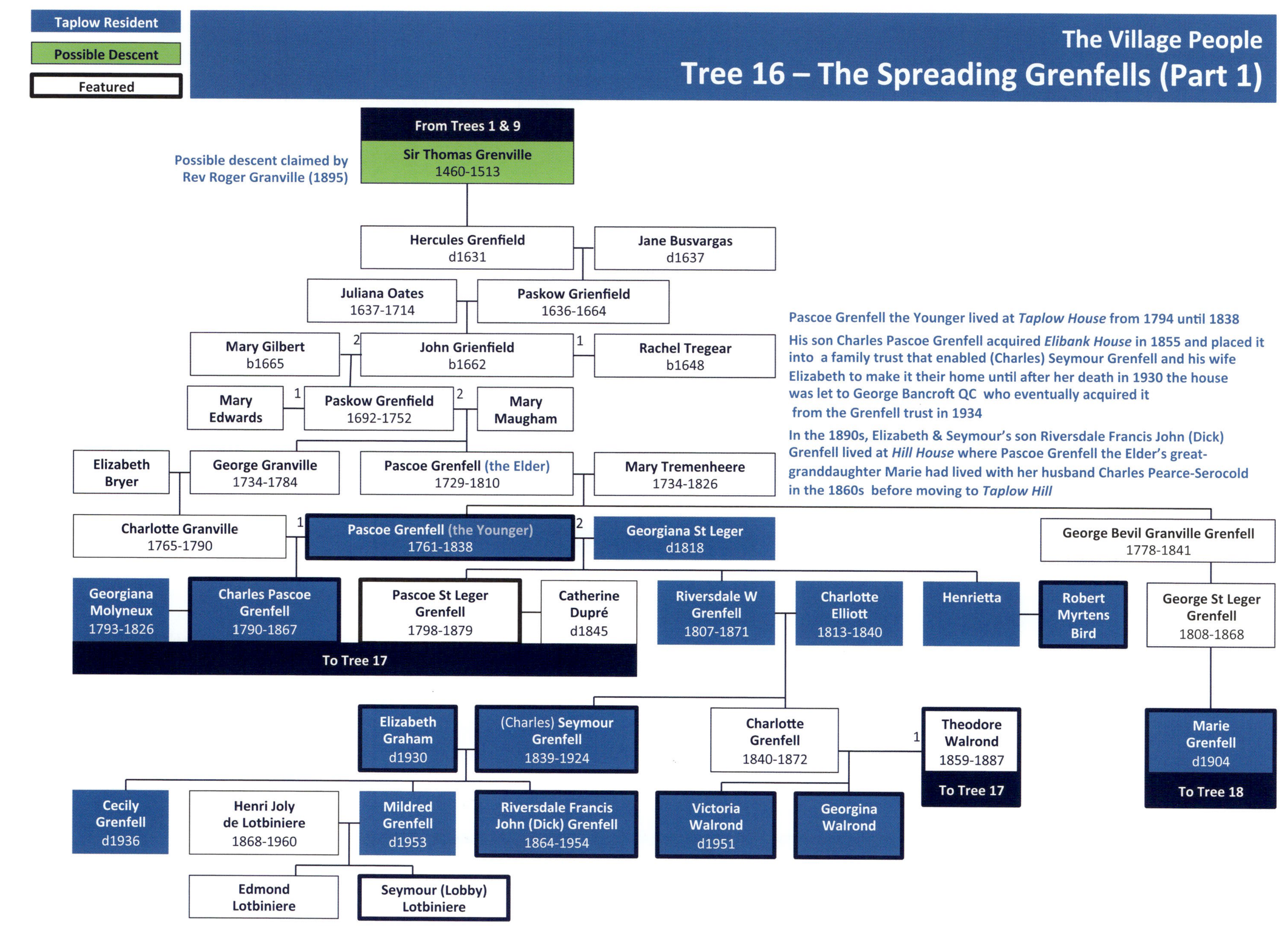

Taplow Resident
Possible Descent
Featured
The Village People
Tree 16 – The Spreading Grenfells (Part 1)
From Trees 1 & 9
Sir Thomas Grenville 1460-1513
Possible descent claimed by Rev Roger Granville (1895)
Hercules Grenfield d1631
Jane Busvargas d1637
Juliana Oates 1637-1714
Paskow Grienfield 1636-1664
Mary Gilbert b1665
2
John Grienfield b1662
1
Rachel Tregear b1648
Mary Edwards
1
Paskow Grenfield 1692-1752
2
Mary Maugham
Elizabeth Bryer
George Granville 1734-1784
Pascoe Grenfell (the Elder) 1729-1810
Mary Tremenheere 1734-1826
Charlotte Granville 1765-1790
1
Pascoe Grenfell (the Younger) 1761-1838
2
Georgiana St Leger d1818
George Bevil Granville Grenfell 1778-1841
Georgiana Molyneux 1793-1826
Charles Pascoe Grenfell 1790-1867
Pascoe St Leger Grenfell 1798-1879
Catherine Dupré d1845
Riversdale W Grenfell 1807-1871
Charlotte Elliott 1813-1840
Henrietta
Robert Myrtens Bird
George St Leger Grenfell 1808-1868
To Tree 17
Elizabeth Graham d1930
(Charles) Seymour Grenfell 1839-1924
Charlotte Grenfell 1840-1872
1
Theodore Walrond 1859-1887
To Tree 17
Marie Grenfell d1904
To Tree 18
Cecily Grenfell d1936
Henri Joly de Lotbiniere 1868-1960
Mildred Grenfell d1953
Riversdale Francis John (Dick) Grenfell 1864-1954
Victoria Walrond d1951
Georgina Walrond
Edmond Lotbiniere
Seymour (Lobby) Lotbiniere
Pascoe Grenfell the Younger lived at Taplow House from 1794 until 1838
His son Charles Pascoe Grenfell acquired Elibank House in 1855 and placed it into a family trust that enabled (Charles) Seymour Grenfell and his wife Elizabeth to make it their home until after her death in 1930 the house was let to George Bancroft QC who eventually acquired it from the Grenfell trust in 1934
In the 1890s, Elizabeth & Seymour's son Riversdale Francis John (Dick) Grenfell lived at Hill House where Pascoe Grenfell the Elder's great-granddaughter Marie had lived with her husband Charles Pearce-Serocold in the 1860s before moving to Taplow Hill

Tree 17 – The Spreading Grenfells (Part 2)

Taplow Resident

Featured

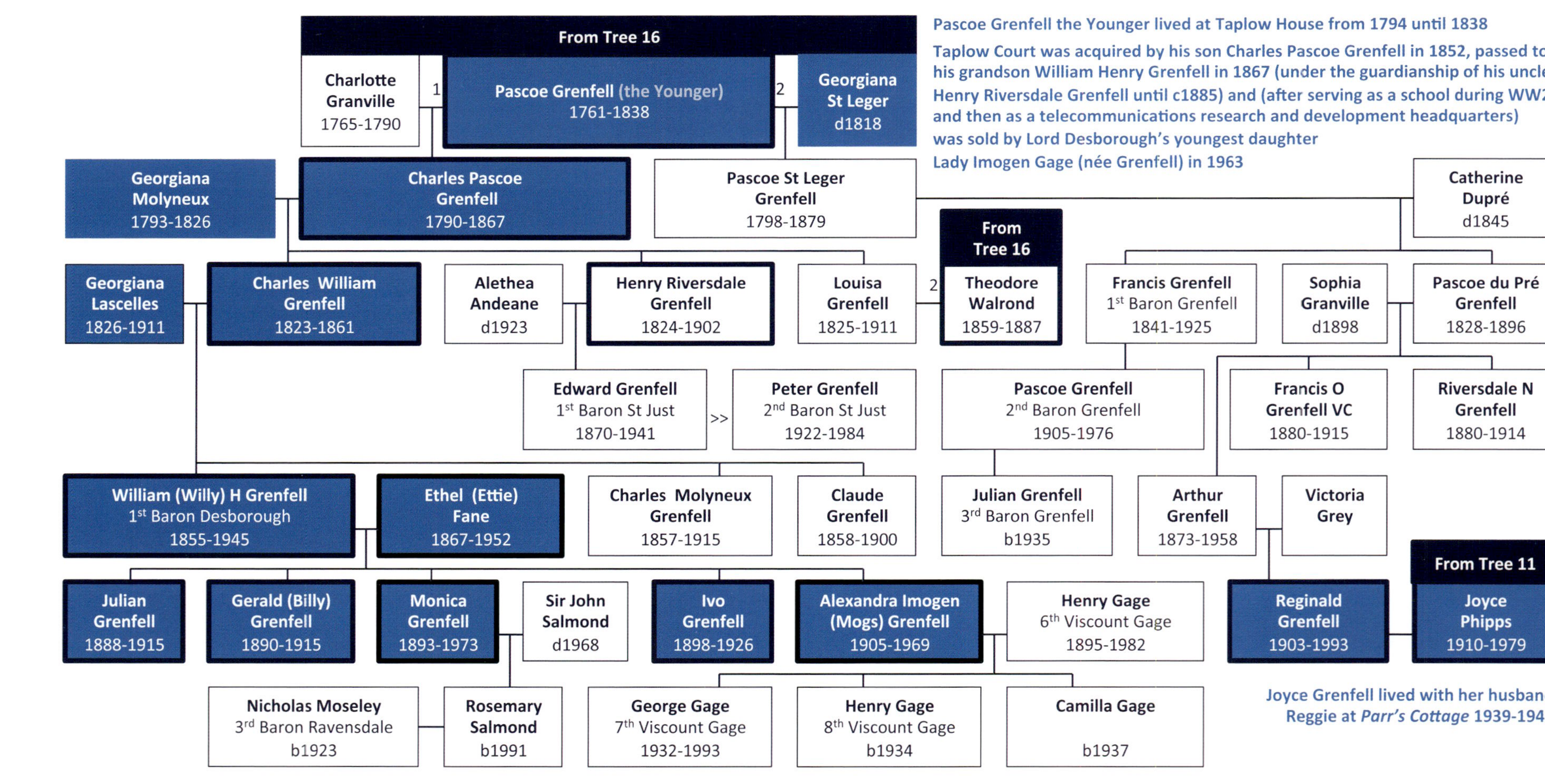

Pascoe Grenfell the Younger lived at Taplow House from 1794 until 1838

Taplow Court was acquired by his son Charles Pascoe Grenfell in 1852, passed to his grandson William Henry Grenfell in 1867 (under the guardianship of his uncle Henry Riversdale Grenfell until c1885) and (after serving as a school during WW2 and then as a telecommunications research and development headquarters) was sold by Lord Desborough's youngest daughter Lady Imogen Gage (née Grenfell) in 1963

Joyce Grenfell lived with her husband Reggie at *Parr's Cottage* 1939-1943

Tree 18 – The Pearce-Serocolds of *Taplow Hill*

and their Royal Connections

Taplow Resident

Illegitimate

Featured

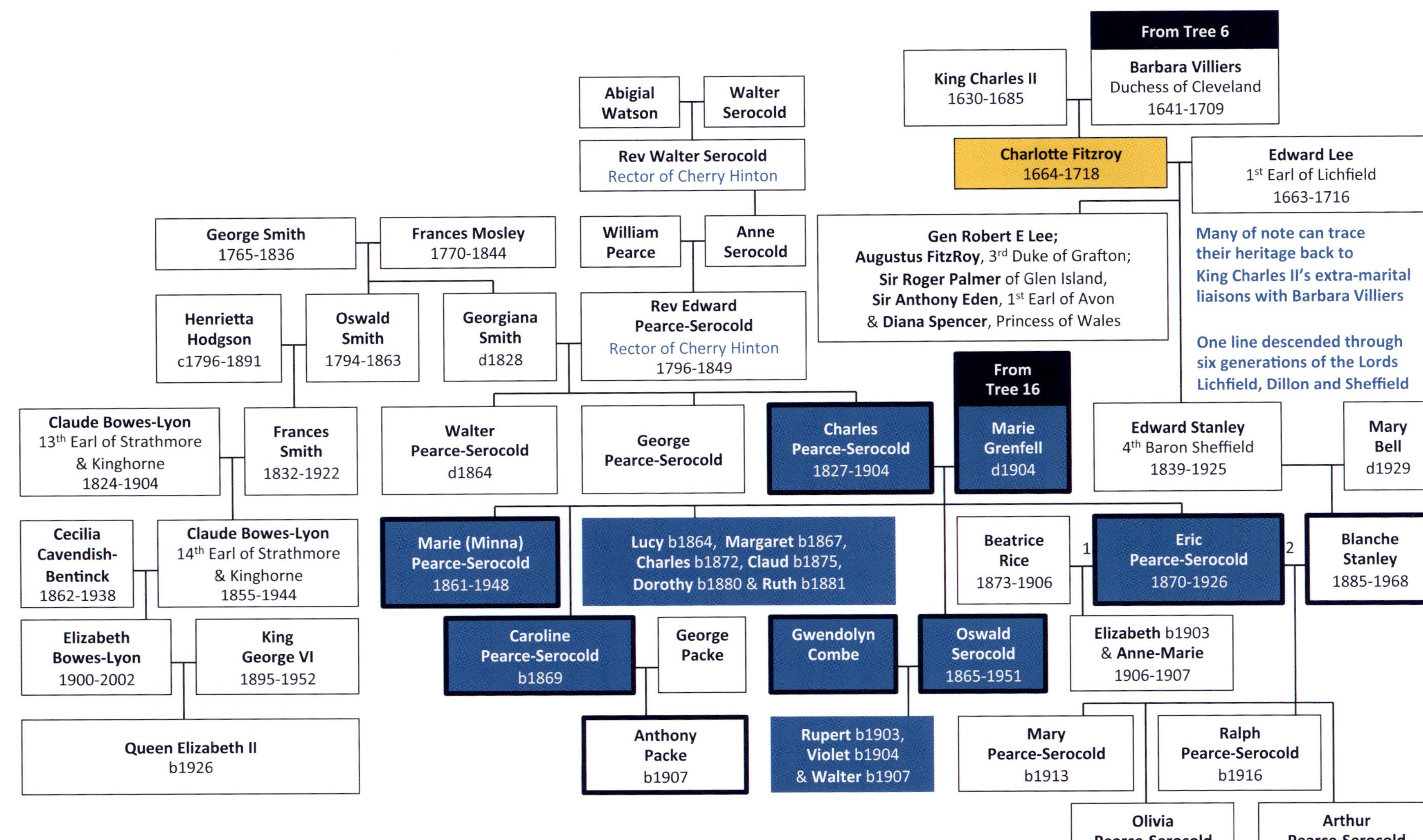

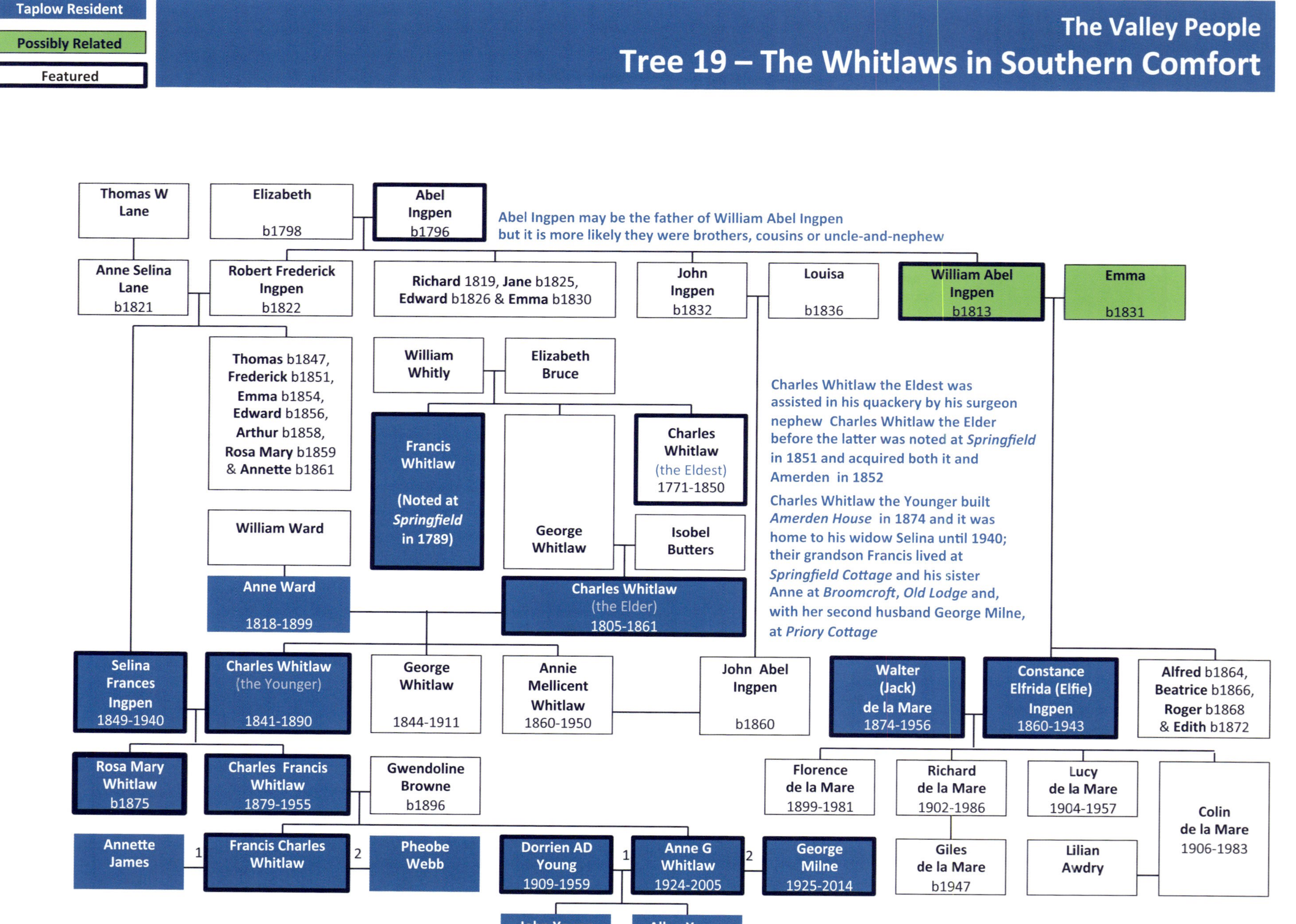

Taplow Resident
Possibly Related
Featured
The Valley People
Tree 19 – The Whitlaws in Southern Comfort
Thomas W Lane
Elizabeth b1798
Abel Ingpen b1796
Abel Ingpen may be the father of William Abel Ingpen
but it is more likely they were brothers, cousins or uncle-and-nephew
Anne Selina Lane b1821
Robert Frederick Ingpen b1822
Richard 1819, Jane b1825, Edward b1826 & Emma b1830
John Ingpen b1832
Louisa b1836
William Abel Ingpen b1813
Emma b1831
Thomas b1847, Frederick b1851, Emma b1854, Edward b1856, Arthur b1858, Rosa Mary b1859 & Annette b1861
William Whitly
Elizabeth Bruce
Francis Whitlaw (Noted at Springfield in 1789)
George Whitlaw
Charles Whitlaw (the Eldest) 1771-1850
Isobel Butters
William Ward
Anne Ward 1818-1899
Charles Whitlaw (the Elder) 1805-1861
Charles Whitlaw the Eldest was assisted in his quackery by his surgeon nephew Charles Whitlaw the Elder before the latter was noted at Springfield in 1851 and acquired both it and Amerden in 1852
Charles Whitlaw the Younger built Amerden House in 1874 and it was home to his widow Selina until 1940; their grandson Francis lived at Springfield Cottage and his sister Anne at Broomcroft, Old Lodge and, with her second husband George Milne, at Priory Cottage
Selina Frances Ingpen 1849-1940
Charles Whitlaw (the Younger) 1841-1890
George Whitlaw 1844-1911
Annie Mellicent Whitlaw 1860-1950
John Abel Ingpen b1860
Walter (Jack) de la Mare 1874-1956
Constance Elfrida (Elfie) Ingpen 1860-1943
Alfred b1864, Beatrice b1866, Roger b1868 & Edith b1872
Rosa Mary Whitlaw b1875
Charles Francis Whitlaw 1879-1955
Gwendoline Browne b1896
Florence de la Mare 1899-1981
Richard de la Mare 1902-1986
Lucy de la Mare 1904-1957
Colin de la Mare 1906-1983
Annette James
1
Francis Charles Whitlaw
2
Pheobe Webb
Dorrien AD Young 1909-1959
1
Anne G Whitlaw 1924-2005
2
George Milne 1925-2014
Giles de la Mare b1947
Lilian Awdry
John Young
Allen Young

Tree 20 – Neighbour, Norrington & Briginshaw

Elinor, Elizabeth & Lydia Neighbour were the matriarchs of Taplow's emerging middle-class of farmers and retailers

1790: Elinor married John Briginshaw the Younger who held *Amerden Manor Farm* while his father John Briginshaw the Elder held *Tythe Farm*

1800: Elizabeth married Thomas Gurney; their daughter Mary married Taplow Court gardener Edward Darling and became the village shopkeeper

1808: Lydia Neighbour married widower William Norrington who by 1825 held *Home Farm* and was steward of the Taplow Court estate; their son George Norrington succeeded him at *Home Farm*

1837: Elinor & John Briginshaw's son Richard held *Rectory Farm* (previously *Tythe Farm*) on his marriage to Lydia & William Norrington's daughter Grace

1841: Elinor & John Briginshaw's son William Davis Briginshaw held *Amerden Manor Farm*; the matriarchal trio's cousin William Davis Neighbour held other land locally

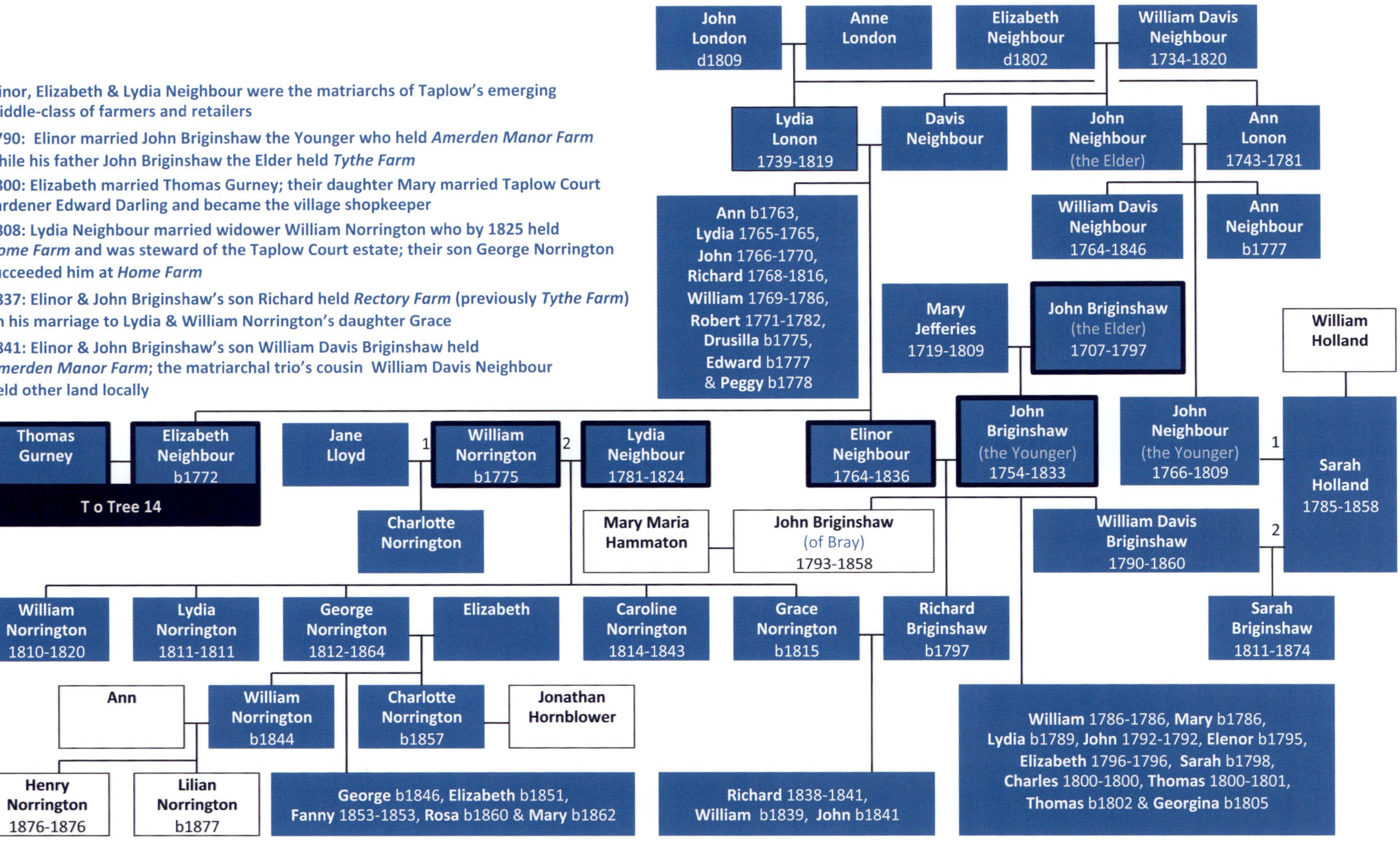

Tree 21 – Webster & Cross

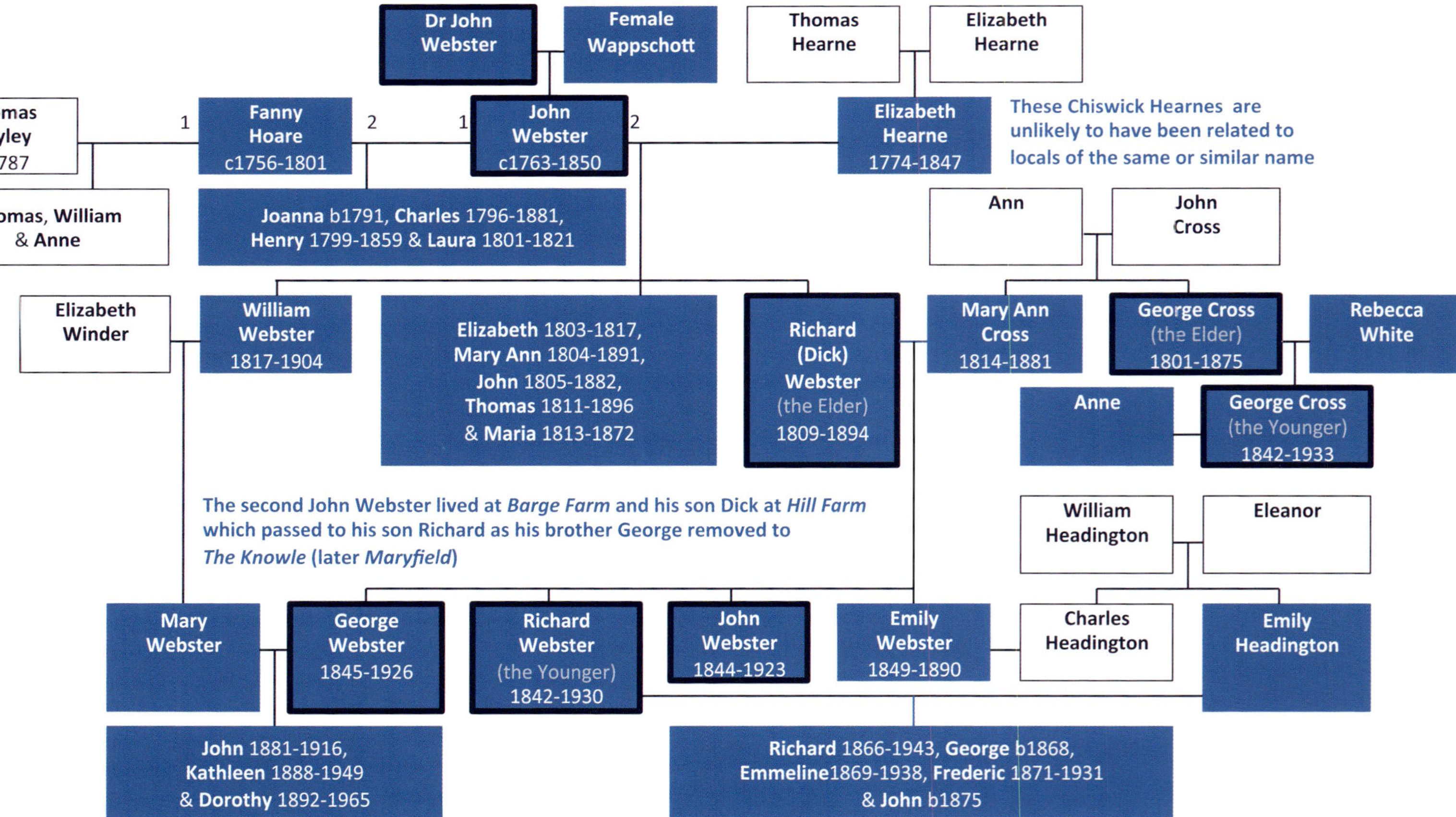

Appendix Two
Maps

Appendix Three
Photographs

Appendix 3: Photographs

All entries note Page / Title / Date [Creator; Source]
All photographs by the Author unless noted

St Nicolas' Churchyard: Gravestone of Francis Hearn d1906 & his wife Harriet Hearn d1935 / 14th November 2012
St Nicolas' Churchyard: Gravestone of Mary Darling d1867 and her husband Edward Darling d1883 / 14th November 2012
St Nicolas' Churchyard: Gravestone of Caroline Norrington d1843 / 14th November 2012
St Nicolas' Churchyard: Gravestone of Martha Springall d1855 and her husband Joseph d1867 Springall / 14th November 2012
St Nicolas' Churchyard: Gravestones of Thomas Hughes d1852, his daughter Elizabeth Castle d1852 and her husband James Castle d1916 / 14th November 2012

150 *The Oak & Saw* / 15th June 2009
The Royal Standard / 26th March 2012
The Feathers / 15th June 2009

158 *Taplow Lodge* / 1994 [Damon Torsten; www.crcmh.com]
Orkney Court / 25th March 2012
Canadian Red Cross Memorial Hospital / 2001 [*King Sturge*; www.crcmh.com]
Cliveden Gages / 5th March 2012

159 *Hedsor House*: From the south-east / 23rd April 2013
Hedsor House: Domed Hall / 23rd April 2013
Hedsor House: From the south-west / 23rd April 2013
The Arms of the Barons Boston / 1790 [Charles Catton: *English Peerage*]
St Nicholas' Church, Hedsor / 11th July 2012

160 Dropmore: Cedar Walk / c1925 [Unknown; The Dropmore Society]
Dropmore: *Cedar Lodge* / c1925 [Unknown; The Dropmore Society]
Dropmore: Evelyn Gates / c1925 [Unknown; The Dropmore Society]
Dropmore House / c1925 [Unknown; The Dropmore Society]

161 *Dropmore House* / 2011 [*Quinlan &Francis Terry LLP*]
Dropmore: Evelyn Gates / 2011 [*Quinlan & Francis Terry LLP*]
Dropmore: The Aviary / 2011 [*Quinlan & Francis Terry LLP*]
Dropmore: From the air / 2011 [Unknown; *Quinlan & Francis Terry LLP*]

162 The House Family: Squirrel shooting / 9th June 1951 [*The Shooting Times*; Anne & Lionel House]
Odds Farm / c1925 (Unknown; Anne & Lionel House]
Odds Farm Park: Farm Park of the Year / 2013 [*Odds Farm Park*]
Steve & Jackie Vinden, Anne & Lionel House / 2013

166 *The Thatched Cottage*, Bapsey Green / c1912 [Unknown; Miv Wayland-Smith]
East & West Bapsey / 5th March 2012
The Thatched Cottage, Berry Hill / 15th June 2009
The second *Wickenden* / 1992 [John Midlane]
May Cottage / 5th March 2012

167 *Queen Anne's House* / 5th March 2012
Queen Anne's House / c1904 [Unknown; www.taplowsociety.org]
Hill House / 5th March 2012
Taplow Hill / c1930 [Unknown; www.taplowsociety.org]

177 *The Old Rectory* / 22nd May 2009
The New Rectory / 8th December 2013
Rectory Farmhouse / 5th March 2012

178 The Site for Saws: From the west / c1912
The Cottage / 27th December 2011
The Site for Saws: From the west / 5th March 2012
The Site for Saws: From the east / 17th June 2009

179 *The Oak & Saw* sign / 31st May 2009
The Hamilton Arms / 27th December 2011
The Orkney Arms / 5th March 2012
The Oak & Saw / c1912

180 *St Nicolas House* / 31st May 2009
Wellbank Cottage / 31st May 2009

191 Through the Church Gate / 31st May 2009
Mulberry House: From the Green / 27th December 2011
Mulberry House: From the north-west / 5th March 2012
The Hollies: From the south-east / c1929

192 *Gurney's Shop & Post Office* / c1890 [Unknown; Alistair Forsyth & Karl Lawrence: *Taplow at the Millennium*]
Gurney's Shop & Post Office / c1910 [Unknown; Miv Wayland-Smith]
Number Three: From the north-west / 31st May 2009
Number Three: From the south-west / 31st May 2009
Number Three on TV / 6th June 2012

In the Canadian Rockies / 1884 [Unknown; *SGI-UK: Olympic Hero*]
King Rama V of Siam / 1880 [Unknown; Wikimedia Commons]
The Thai ambassador with Robert Samuels of *SGI* / 2009 [Simon Adinsell of *SGI-UK*; Hitcham & Taplow Society Newsletter 92, 2009]
285 The British Olympic Fencing Team / 1906 [Unknown; *The Guardian*]
The Desboroughs at Henley / 1908 [Unknown; *Where Smooth Waters Glide* – http://thames.me.uk]
The 1908 Olympic Programme / 1908 (Unknown; *BBC*]
Olympic Volunteers: Chris Little / 30th July 2012 [Unknown]
Olympic Volunteers: Maureen Dennis / 9th September 2012
Olympic Volunteers: Jenny Edmonds / 2nd September 2012 [Nikolas Kominis]
Olympic Volunteers: Mike Sharp / 24th July 2012 [Unknown]
Olympic Volunteers: Nigel Smales & Heather Piper / 2012 [Geoff Lavers]
Nigel Smales with Rob Williams and his Silver Medal / 9th September 2012 [Tony Sutton]
Queen Elizabeth & Prince Philip with Phillip Wells / 10th July 2012 [LOCOG]
290 Arild Rosenkrantz / 1913 [Unknown; http://wn.rsarchive.org]
St Nicolas' Church: Lady Chapel windows / 1913 [St Nicolas' Church]
300 Taplow War Memorial / 14th November 2012
Taplow War Memorial (detail) / 14th November 2012
Two *Skindles* in Flanders / 1916 [Unknown; Leonard Miall]
Sheldon Gledstanes / 1916 [Unknown; www.bedfordregiment.org.uk]
Julian Grenfell / 1916 [*Maull & Fox*; Wikimedia Commons]
Brownies Hannah, Irwin, Lyra Cherry & Keira Smales / 14th November 2010
Keith Thomas leads the Parade into the Churchyard / 11th November 2012
308 Walter de la Mare / 1919 [Unknown ; www.walterdelamare.co.uk]
Hill House / 5th March 2012
Giles de la Mare unveils the blue plaque to his grandfather / 23rd May 2014
The blue plaque / 23rd May 2014
Giles de la Mare reads his grandfather's poem *Lord of Tartary*/ 23rd May 2014
314 Nancy Astor campaigning in Plymouth / 1919 [Plymouth City Museum]
Nancy Astor campaigning in Plymouth / 1919 [Plymouth City Museum]
Lady Astor's Triumph / 1919 [*The Daily Mirror*, 29th November 1919]
Nancy Astor: Parliamentary Pioneer / 1919 [Unknown]
324 Shelia Horton / 29th September 2004 [Andrew Findlay]
A Celebration of Taplow: Taplow Horse Show / c1995 [Unknown; Taplow Parish Council]
A Celebration of Taplow: A Collection of Images / c1995 [Unknown; Taplow Parish Council]
A Celebration of Taplow: The Village Green Party / c1995 [Unknown; Taplow Parish Council]
328 Princess Louise, Duchess of Connaught / 1905 [*Lafayette*; National Portrait gallery]
WW1: The HRH Duchess of Connaught Red Cross Hospital: General view [Unknown; www.crcmh.com]
WW1: The HRH Duchess of Connaught Red Cross Hospital: A typical ward [Unknown; www.crcmh.com]
WW1: The HRH Duchess of Connaught Red Cross Hospital: The converted tennis court
WW1: The HRH Duchess of Connaught Red Cross Hospital: Canadian soldiers [Unknown; Dorothy Blackman & Daphne Chevous: *Around Burnham*]
WW1: The HRH Duchess of Connaught Red Cross Hospital: Royal visit by King George V & Queen Mary (Unknown; www.crcmh.com]
WW2: The Canadian Red Cross Hospital: Royal visit by Queen Elizabeth / 1940 [Unknown; www.crcmh.com]
WW2: The Canadian Red Cross Hospital: From the air / c1942 [Unknown; www.crcmh.com]
The Canadian Red Cross Memorial Hospital: Lady Astor opens the hydrotherapy pool /1956 [Unknown; www.crcmh.com]
The Canadian Red Cross Memorial Hospital: The Mounties pay a visit / c1970 [Unknown; Dorothy Blackman & Daphne Chevous: *Around Burnham*]
The Canadian Red Cross Memorial Hospital: Professor Eric Bywaters / c1960 [Unknown; Dorothy Blackman & Daphne Chevous: *Around Burnham*]
336 Gerry Anderon with Troy Tempest / 1966 [Unknown; www.gerryanderson.com]
337 St Nicolas' Church & Nearby: From the air, looking south-east / c1963 [possibly *Airpic*; via Lincoln Lee to Leonard Miall]
338 St Nicolas' Church & Nearby: From the air, looking north / 1st June 1963 [*Airpic*]
339 St Nicolas' Church & Nearby: From the air, looking north / 28th October 1992 [*Airpic*]
340 The Village: Looking east / 6th June 2014 [Tim Browning]
The Village: Looking south-west / 6th June 2014 [Tim Browning]
342 Keira Smales, Lyra Cherry & Sophie Greenham sledging / 5th February 2012
The Pit (Hitcham Field) / 23rd September 2013
Boundary Road trees / 23rd September 2013
Hummers footpath, looking south-east / 23rd September 2013

Lea Rig & *Poplar Farm*, from Boundary Road / 23rd September 2013
349 *Maryfield* / c1954 [Leonard Miall; Ginny Felton]
Leonard Miall: At the microphone / c1947 [*BBC*; Ginny Felton]
The Miall Family / c1953 [Unknown; Ginny Felton]
Bill Astor with Bronwen / 1960 [Unknown; www.the peerage.com]
Sir John Page / 2005 (Unknown; Hitcham & Taplow Society Newsletter 91, 2009]
356 Taplow Horse Show: Pat Moss / 7th September 1946 [*Maidenhead Advertiser*; 13th September 1946]
Taplow Horse Show: Pat Moss riding *Hairpin* / 7th September 1946 [*Maidenhead Advertiser*; 13th September 1946]
St Nicolas' School: Colin Blackwell / 1965 [*Maidenhead Advertiser*; 21st October 1965]
St Nicolas' School: Mary Alexander / 1965 [*Maidenhead Advertiser*; 21st October 1965]
St Nicolas' School: The fire / 1965 [*Maidenhead Advertiser*; 21st October 1965]
St Nicolas' School: Helen Grellier [Unknown; Helen Grellier]
Aleyn Grellier / 2005 [Unknown; Hitcham & Taplow Society Newsletter 93, 2010]
357 St Nicolas' School: Sports Day / 3rd July 2009
St Nicolas' School goes Olympic / 5th March 2012
St Nicolas' School: Maypole Dancing / 12th June 2010
St Nicolas' School: Leavers / 12th July 2013
358 The Village Green: My favourite place / 23rd April 2012 [Emily Costello; St Nicolas' School]
The Village Green: My favourite place / 23rd April 2012 [Katie Harris; St Nicolas' School]
359 The Village Green: The last of Pater Noster's barns / 23rd April 2012
The Village Green: The southern slope / 23rd April 2012
The Green in white / 19th December 2012 [Eva Lipman]
The Green in spring / 23rd May 2012
368 Cedar Chase: Snapshot / 5th March 2012
Cedar Chase: Snapshot / 5th March 2012
The much-repaired wall of *Elibank* / 5th March 2012
Still Chasing / 29th June 2013
Cedar Chase: Slice / 5th March 2012
369 Village Green Party: The ox roasting / 21st June 2014
Village Green Party: Simon Fox starts to slice / 23rd June 2012
Village Green Party: A latecomer seeks somewhere to settle / 21st June 2014
Village Green Party: Euan Felton & Karl Lawrence, men at work / 23rd June 2012
Village Green Party: The sun shines on the frivolous / 21st June 2014 [Tim Browning]
370 Village Green Party: The shadows lengthen / 21st June 2014 [Tim Browning]
Village Green Party: Mike Sanderson's Band strikes up / 23rd June 2012
Village Green Party: The dancing begins / 21st June 2014
Village Green Party: The consummate caller, Tom Browne / 23rd June 2012
371 Village Green Party: The dancing continues / 21st June 2014
Village Green Party: Chris Ashford & Alastair Hill, burger kings / 23rd June 2012
Village Green Party: Shooting breeze/ 23rd June 2012
Village Green Party: Stepping out in style / 23rd June 2012
Village Green Party: Teresa & Brian Foreman, sheltering from a shower / 23rd June 2012
372 Jubilee River: Looking upstream towards Ye Meads / 21st June 2014
Jubilee River: Tranquil waters / 23rd June 2012
Jubilee River: No concrete culvert / 23rd June 2012
Jubilee River: Under the railway / 23rd June 2012
376 Cricket Club: Sidney Marriott / 1950 [Unknown; Jim Rance]
Cricket Club: Sir George Franckenstein / 1950 [Unknown; Jim Rance]
Cricket Club: Maurice Rance / 1950 [Unknown; Jim Rance]
Cricket Club: Canon Robert Hay / 1950 [Unknown; Jim Rance]
Cricket Club: Bert Hunt / 1950 [Unknown; Jim Rance]
Cricket Club: Penny-farthing / 1950 [Unknown; Jim Rance]
Cricket Club: The oldest club photo / c1888 [Unknown; Iris Midlane]
Cricket Club: Centenary Match v Middlesex CCC / 28th May 1950 [Unknown; Jim Rance] Cricket Club: Centenary Match in the style of 1850 / 1950 [Unknown; Jim Rance]
Cricket Club: Centenary programme / 1950 [Unknown; Iris Midlane]
Cricket Club: Celebrity Match / 1980 [Unknown; Iris Midlane]
Cricket Club: Friday Evening Fun / 23rd April 2012 [Imogen Wallis]
386 Silchester Manor Day Nursery / 2014
Silchester House School hat / 2014 [Lynette Szczepanik]
Silchester House School hat badge/ 2014 [Lynette Szczepanik]
Bishop Centre signpost / 2014
Taplow United / 23rd April 2012 [Renzo Casale; St Nicolas' School]

Thames Valley Adventure Playground: Snapshot / 2014 [Unknown; www.tvap.co.uk]
Thames Valley Adventure Playground: Snapshot / 2014 [Unknown; www.tvap.co.uk]
Thames Valley Adventure Playground: Snapshot / 2014 [Unknown; www.tvap.co.uk]
Thames Valley Adventure Playground: Snapshot / 2014 [Unknown; www.tvap.co.uk]
Thames Valley Adventure Playground: Snapshot / 2014 [Unknown; www.tvap.co.uk]
391 Jubilee River: Looking up to Taplow Court / 10th December 2011
The Mill Triangle: From the air, looking east / 2011 [*Commission Air*; Heather Fenn]
The Mill Triangle: From the air, looking north-east / 2011 [*Commission Air*; Heather Fenn]
392 *Skindles* & Nearby: From the air, looking north-east / 1962 [*Aerofilms*; Adam Smith]
393 *Skindles* & Nearby: From the air, looking north / 1962 [*Aerofilms*; Adam Smith]
396 *Bond's*: The *Mauretania* bell / 1954 [Unknown; Christopher Smith]
Bond's: Hire Charges / 1937 [Unknown; Christopher Smith]
Bond's: Leaflet / c1947 [Unknown; Christopher Smith]
Bond's: Hire Charges / c1947 [Unknown; Christopher Smith]
Bond's: Sidney 'Paddy' Sutton Smith / 1945 [Unknown; Christopher Smith]
Festival of Britain Programme / 1951 [Unknown; Christopher Smith]
Bond's: Boats for Hire / 1930s [Unknown; Christopher Smith]
Bond's: Her Majesty's / c1937 [Unknown; Christopher Smith]
Bond's: Electric canoe Victoria / c1950 [Unknown; Christopher Smith]
Bond's: Silver Javelin / c1950 [Unknown; Christopher Smith]
401 *Skindles*: Sales Particulars / 12th July 1950 [*Cyril Jones & Clifton*; Christopher Smith]
Skindles: The Lots / 12th July 1950 [*Cyril Jones & Clifton*; Christopher Smith]
Skindles: Restaurant / 12th July 1950 [*Cyril Jones & Clifton*; Christopher Smith]
Skindles: Bar / 12th July 1950 [*Cyril Jones & Clifton*; Christopher Smith]
Bond's: Site Plan / 18th October 1955 [*Giddy & Giddy*; Christopher Smith]
Bond's: Sales Particulars / 18th October 1955 [*Giddy & Giddy*; Christopher Smith]
Bond's: Riparian Rights Plan / 7th January 1937 [George Bond's lease; Christopher Smith]
Bond's: *Bridge Villa* & *Sunnyside* / 1975 [Christopher Smith]
409 The Old Boathouse on The Old Public Slipway / 12th July 1950
Michael Fletcher of *Marlow Boat Services*
416 Race to the Church: Downhill Racer – Jamie Barnard coming / 29th April 2011
Race to the Church: Downhill Racer – Jamie Barnard going / 29th April 2011
Race to the Church: Crash Champions – The Sellers Family / 29th April 2011
Race to the Church: Setting the Style – Juliet Lecchini & Daisy / 29th April 2011
Race to the Church: Going Aghast – Marianne Boden / 29th April 2011
Race to the Church: Going for Speed – Chris & Louise Ashford / 29th April 2011
Race to the Church: Those Held Responsible – Duncan Leftley with Jack, Juliet Lecchini, Paul-Ant Viollet, Roger Andrews & Martin Knight / 29th April 2011
417 Race to the Church: Anna Hill / 29th April 2011
Race to the Church: Thomas Knight / 29th April 2011
Race to the Church: Marie Tenglund / 29th April 2011
Race to the Church: Lyra Cherry / 29th April 2011
Race to the Church: The Wacky Racers / 29th April 2011
418 The Oarsome Raft Race: Ready, Steady, Go / 5th June 2012
The Oarsome Raft Race: Janette & Finlay Mackay / 5th June 2012
The Oarsome Raft Race: Paddlers meddling / 5th June 2012
The Oarsome Raft Race: John Dunleavey with Thomas Knight / 5th June 2012
The Oarsome Raft Race: Cath & martin Knight, Marianne & Marc Boden / 5th June 2012
419 The Usual Suspects: Barrie Peroni & Keith Thomas / 20th January 2012 [Miv Wayland-Smith]
The Usual Suspects: Barrie Peroni & Keith Thomas / 20th January 2012 [Miv Wayland-Smith]
The Usual Suspects: Jane Barnard, Marianne Boden & Cath Knight / 20th January 2012 [Miv Wayland-Smith]
The Usual Suspects: Brenda Burns / 20th January 2012 [Miv Wayland-Smith]
The Usual Suspects: Maud Johnson / 20th January 2012 [Miv Wayland-Smith]
The Usual Suspects: Marc Boden / 20th January 2012 [Miv Wayland-Smith]
The Usual Suspects: Jamie Barnard & Sally Sharp / 20th January 2012 [Miv Wayland-Smith]
The Usual Suspects: Brian Horton / 20th January 2012 [Miv Wayland-Smith]
The Usual Suspects: Laird Mackay, Miv Wayland-Smith & Anna Hill / 20th January 2012 [Victoria Wayland-Smith]
The Usual Suspects: Charlie Greeves & Gilly Blundell / 20th January 2012 [Miv Wayland-Smith]
The Usual Suspects: John & Brenda Kennedy / 20th January 2012 [Miv Wayland-Smith]
The Usual Suspects: George Sandy / 20th January 2012 [Miv Wayland-Smith]
420 The Usual Suspects: Jacqueline Andrews / 10th February 2012
The Usual Suspects: Jenny Edmonds / 10th February 2012
The Usual Suspects: Marie Tenglund / 10th February 2012

The Usual Suspects: Jane Edmondson / 10th February 2012
The Usual Suspects: Nigel Smales / 10th February 2012
The Usual Suspects: Neil Blundell / 10th February 2012
The Usual Suspects: Pete Webb / 10th February 2012
The Usual Suspects: Mike & Sally Sharp / 10th February 2012
The Usual Suspects: Caroline Smales / 10th February 2012
The Usual Suspects: Clementine Fox & Victoria Wayland-Smith / 10th February 2012
The Usual Suspects: Caroline Sellers / 10th February 2012
The Usual Suspects: Rupert Sellers & George Ormond / 10th February 2012
The Usual Suspects: Miv Wayland-Smith & Fiona Plumley / 10th February 2012
421 The Usual Suspects: Jamie Barnard / 15TH September 2012
The Usual Suspects: Jane Barnard / 15TH September 2012
The Usual Suspects: Duncan Leftley & Marc Boden / 15TH September 2012
The Usual Suspects: Adam Benetar & Pete Webb / 15TH September 2012
The Usual Suspects: Juliet Lecchini with Sam Viollet & Clementine Fox / 15TH September 2012
The Usual Suspects: David Hindle & Mike Sharp / 15TH September 2012
The Usual Suspects: Sally Ashford, Marianne Boden, Victoria Wayland-Smith, Anna Hill & Cath Knight / 15TH September 2012
The Usual Suspects: Tim Browning, Simon Fox, Paul-Ant Viollet & George Ormond / 15TH September 2012
The Usual Suspects: Tony Meats / 15TH September 2012
The Usual Suspects: Marianne Boden & Jo Leftley / 15TH September 2012
The Usual Suspects: Chris & George Ormond / 15TH September 2012
The Usual Suspects: Brian & Sheila Horton / 15TH September 2012
The Usual Suspects: Patrick (and Julia) Shanu-Wilson / 15TH September 2012
The Usual Suspects: Chris Cherry / 15TH September 2012
422 The Usual Suspects: Sally Sharp with Lauren & Ben / 29th March 2014
The Usual Suspects: Rachel & Clemency Kitchlew-Horton / 9th February 2015
The Usual Suspects: *Tap L'eau* / 29th November 2014
The Usual Suspects: Ginny & Euan Felton / 30th January 2015
The Usual Suspects: Alistair & Liz Forsyth / 30th January 2015
The Usual Suspects: Eva Lipman / 2012
The Usual Suspects: Andrew Findlay & Jane Curry / 30th June 2012
Old Priory Garden: Simon Fox & Malcolm Tait / 17TH January 2015
Old Priory Garden: Bob Hanbury / 6th December 2012
Old Priory Garden: Anthony Harding & Roger Andrews / 6th December 2012
Old Priory Garden: Julia Paskins / 17TH January 2015
Old Priory Garden: Miv Wayland-Smith / 17TH January 2015
423 Nigel Smales / 12th July 2014 [Keira Smales]
Back St Nicolas' Church / 21st June 2014 [Tim Browning]

Appendix Four
Social Whirls

The Scriblerus Club (1714-1745)

The Scriblerus Club was an informal association of authors and intellectuals who would meet to 'put the world to rights'. Eventually they created the fictional persona of Martin Scriblerus, through whose writings they accomplished their satirical aims. Alexander Pope and Jonathan Swift were the hubs around which the whirl revolved. All Scriblerans were known to George Hamilton, 1st Earl of Orkney, who entertained them individually or collectively at Taplow Court and Cliveden....

Joseph Addison (1672-1719) – Politician, Playwright, Poet & Essayist – Co-founder (with Sir Richard Steele) of *The Spectator* 1711 and *The Guardian* 1713

John Arbuthnot (1667-1735) – Satirist, Mathematician & Physician – Invented *John Bull*

William Congreve (1670-1729) – Playwright & Poet: *The Way of the World* (1700)

John Gay (1685-1732) – Poet & Playwright: *The Beggar's Opera* (1728)

Robert Harley; **1st Earl of Oxford & Mortimer** (1661-1724) – Politician: Lord High Treasurer (effectively Chief Minister) to Queen Anne (1711-1714)

Thomas Parnell (1679-1716) – Poet & Cleric

Alexander Pope (1688-1744) – Satirist & Poet: *An Essay on Man* (1734), *The Memoirs of Martin Scriblerus* (1741), translation of Homer's *Iliad* (1715-1720) and *Odyssey* (1726)

Henry St John; **1st Viscount Bolingbroke** (1678-1651) – Politician, Civil Servant, Pamphleteer & Political Philosopher: *The Patriot King* (written 1738, published 1749)

Sir Richard Steele (1672-1729) – Politician, Pamphleteer, Playwright & Journalist – Founder of *The Tatler* 1709; co-founder (with Joseph Addison) of *The Spectator* 1711 and *The Guardian* 1713

Jonathan Swift (1667-1745) – Satirist, Pamphleteer, Poet, Essayist, Cleric & Author: *Gulliver's Travels* (1726)

Sir John Vanbrugh (1614-1726) – Architect & Playwright

Mary Wortley Montagu (née Pierrepoint, 1689-1762) – Aristocratic Lady of Letters from 1717-1719 while in Istanbul with her husband Edward Wortley Montagu, English Ambassador to the Ottoman Empire – Later as a friend of Alexander Pope (and a contemporary of Scriblerians) she was a noted Writer, Poet & Critic

Cliveden (1737-1893)

With Cliveden established as a place for the elite to play, successive residents enjoyed eminent and creative company....

Frederick, **Prince of Wales** (1737-1751)

Thomas Arne (1710-1778) – Composer: *Rule Britannia* (1740)

Henry Carey (1687-1743) – Satirist as a Poet, Dramatist & Songwriter: *Namby-Pamby* (1725)

George Grenville (1712-1770) – Politician: Prime Minister 1763-1765 (enacted the Stamp Act 1765, one of the factors which led to the American Revolution) – Father of George Nugent-Temple-Grenville (1st Marquess of Buckingham) & William Wyndham Grenville (1st Baron Grenville of Dropmore)

David Mallet (c1705-1765) – Scottish Dramatist: *William and Margaret* (1723) & *Alfred* (1740) featuring *Rule Britannia*

William Pitt the Elder; **1st Earl of Chatham** (1708-1778) – Politician: Prime Minister 1776-1778

James Thomson (1700-1748) – Scottish Poet & Playwright: The Seasons (1726-1730) & *Alfred* (1740) featuring *Rule Britannia*

Murrough O'Brien; 5th Earl of Inchiquin (1777-1795)

Lancelot (Capability) Brown (1716-1783) – Landscape Architect: Stowe 1741 (for Richard Grenville-Temple; 2nd Earl Temple) then Warwick Castle, Blenheim Palace, Hampton Court and over 170 other estates and gardens including (perhaps) Taplow Court in the 1770s

James Boswell; 9th Laird of Auchinleck (1740-1795) – Scottish Lawyer, Diarist, Essayist & Author: *The Hypochondriack* (1777-1783), *The Journal of a Tour to the Hebrides with Samuel Johnson* (1785) & *The Life of Samuel Johnson* (1791)

Francis (Fanny) Burney (1752-1840) – Author, Diarist & Playwright: *Evelina* (1778), *Cecelia* (1782), *Camilla* (1796) & *The Wanderer* (1814) – Reported from the Battle of Waterloo (1815)

Edmund Burke (1729-1797) – Irish Author, Philosopher & Politician – Supporter of the American Revolution but not the French – Lived at *Gregories Court*, Beaconsfield

Joseph Farington (1747-1821) – Landscape Artist & Diarist: *History of the River Thames* (76 acquatints, 1794) – Editor: *Memoirs of Sir Joshua Reymolds* (1819)

David Garrick (1717-1779) – Actor, Playwright & Theatre Impressario: *Richard III* (1741), later *King Lear* and other Shakespearian stalwarts

Oliver Goldsmith (1728-1774) – Anglo-Irish Author, Playwright & Poet: *The Vicar of Wakefield* (1766) & *She Stoops to Conquer* (1773)

John Hawkesworth (c1715-1773) – Writer & Editor: *The Adventurer* (1752-1754), *Edgar and Emmline* (1761) & *The Journals of Captain Cook* (1773)

Dr Samuel Johnson (1709-1784) – Poet, Essayist, Moralist, Critic, Biographer, Editor & Lexicographer: *London* (1738), *A Dictionary of the English Language* (1755), *The Patriot* (1774), *A Journey to the Western Isles of Scotland* (1775) & *Lives of the Poets* (1779-1781)

Sir Joshua Reynolds (1723-1792) – Artist: *Sarah Siddons as the Tragic Muse* (1784) & *The Age of Innocence* (1788) – Co-founder and first President of The Royal Academy of Arts 1768

Sarah Siddons (née Kemble, 1755-1831) – Welsh Actress: *Macbeth* (1794), *Hamlet* (1795) and many other Shakespearian and 'tragedienne' roles

Henry Wyndham (1736-1819) – Politician, Author & Topographer

Sir George Warrender (1824-1849)

George Canning (1770-1827) – Anglo-Irish Politician: Foreign Secretary 1807-1809 & 1822-1827, Prime Minister 1827 – Played an important role as Latin American countries asserted their independence from Spain

Dukes of Sutherland & Westminster (1849-1893)

Charles Dickens (1812-1870) – Author & Social Critic: *Oliver Twist* (1837-1839), *A Christmas Carol* (1843) & *Great Expectations* (1860-1861)

William Gladstone (1809-1898) – Politician: Prime Minister 1868-1874, 1880-1885, 1886 & 1892-1894

Rev Charles Kingsley – Cleric, Historian & Author: *Westward Ho!* (1855), *The Water Babies* (1863) & *Hereward the Wake* (1866) – Co-discoverer of Taplow's mammoth 1854

Sir John Lubbock; 1st Baron Avebury (1834-1913) – Banker, Politician, Philanthropist, Scientist, Archaeologist & Polymath – Co-discoverer of Taplow's mammoth 1854

Carlo Marochetti (1805-1867) – Italian-born French Sculptor: *Richard Couer de Lion* (Great Exhibition 1851, a copy at the Palace of Westminster since 1860), *Robert Stephenson* (Euston since 1871) & *Four Lions* (Trafalgar Square since 1867, cast by Marochetti to Sir Edwin Landseer's design)

Sir Joseph Paxton (1803-1865) – Gardener, Architect & Politician: Chatsworth 1823-1858 (Gardens, Conservatories & Greenhouses plus the Emperor Fountion and Edensor Village), *The Crystal Palace* (Great Exhibition 1851) & *Mentmore Towers* (1854)

Alfred Tennyson; 1st Baron Tennyson (1809-1982) – Poet Laureate 1852: *The Lady of Shalott* (1833 & 1842), *Ulysses* (1847) & *The Charge of the Light Brigade* (1854)

Queen Victoria (1819-1901) – Queen of the United Kingdom of Great Britain & Ireland 1837-1902 & Empress of India 1876

Dropmore (1792-1899)

The Grenvilles made Dropmore a parallel attraction which their Fortescue heirs continued. Its social whirl overlapped Cliveden's and Taplow Court's – Queen Victoria visited Anne Grenville & Louisa Fortescue regularly – with the exception of three notable allies of Lord Grenville's....

Thomas Clarkson (1760-1846) – Abolitionist – Lifelong campaign against slavery began in 1785, joined forces with Wilberforce, Pitt the Younger, Grenville and others 1787

William Pitt the Younger (1759-1806) – Politician: Prime Minister 1783-1801 & 1804-1806 – Cousin of both Anne & William Grenville, his political ally during his first ministry and against slavery

William Wilberforce (1759-1833) – Politician, Philanthropist & Abolitionist – Led anti-slavery campaign in Parliament which banned the slave trade (under Grenville, 1807) and finally slavery in the British Empire (in 1833, a month after his death)

The Souls (1885-c1905) and **The Coterie** (c1905-1920)

From their marriage in 1887 until the cost of the Great War was counted in lost friends and family, Ethel & Willy Grenfell made Taplow Court one of the most favoured venues for *The Souls* and their successors in *The Coterie* to wind down at weekends. The honeypot saw the start of many formal relationships and some informal ones too....

Sir Denis Anson (1888-1914) – Barrister – Drowned in the Thames near Battersea Bridge

HH Asquith (1852-1928) – Politician: Prime Minister 1908-1916

His second wife **Margot** (née **Tennant**, 1864-1945) – Author & Socialite

Herbert Asquith (1881-1947) – Lawyer, Poet & Author – Son of HH Asquith and his first wife Helen

His wife **Cynthia** (née **Charteris**, 1887-1960) – Author & Diarist – Daughter of Mary & Hugo Charteris

Raymond Asquith (1878-1916) – Barrister; son of HH Asquith and his first wife Helen – Killed in action in France during WW1

His wife **Katherine** (née **Horner**) – Sister of Edward Horner

Arthur Balfour; **1st Earl Balfour** (1848-1930) – Politician: Prime Minister 1902-1905 – Joint first President of The Royal Institute for International Affairs (1920) – With the Balfour Declaration 1917, established the UK's support for "the establishment in Palestine of a home for the Jewish people"

John Baring; **2nd Baron Revelstoke** (1863-1929) – Banker – Brother of Maurice Baring

Maurice Baring (1874-1945 – Dramatist, Poet, Essayist & Author: *C* (1924), *Daphne Adeane* (1926); brother of John Baring

Bertie, **Prince of Wales** (1841-1910) – **King Edward VII** 1902-1910

Louisa (Lucy) Bourke (d1961) – Tenant at ***Hill House*** 1901 – Sister of Norah Lindsay

St John Brodick; **1st Earl of Midleton** (1856-1942) – Politician – Styled **The Viscount Midleton** 1907-1920

His wife **Hilda** (née **Charteris**, d1901) – Sister of Hugo & Evan Charteris

Evan Charteris (1864-1940) – Barrister, Biographer & Arts Administrator – Brother of Hugo & Hilda Charteris

Hugo Charteris; **11th Earl of Weymss** & **7th Earl of March** (1857-1937) – Politician – Styled **Lord Elcho** 1883-1914 – Brother of Evan & Hilda Charteris

His wife **Mary Charteris** (née **Wyndham**)

Hugo Charteris; **Lord Elcho** (1884-1916) – Soldier – Son of Mary & Hugo Charteris – Killed in action during WW1

His wife **Violet** (née **Manners**, 1888-1971) – Daughter of Violet & Henry Manners

Chulalongkorn (1853-1910) – **King Rama V of Siam** 1868-1910

His former tutor **Anna Leonowens** (1831-1915)

Sir Winston Churchill (1874-1965) – Soldier, Historian, Writer, Artist & Politician: Prime Minister 1940-1945 & 1951-1955

David, **Prince of Wales** (1894-1972) – **King Edward VIII** 1936

Duff Cooper (1890-1954) – Politician, Diplomat & Author – Ambassador to France 1944-1948

His wife **Diana** (née **Manners**) (1892-1986) – Actress & Socialite – Illegitimate daughter of Violet Manners & Harry Cust

Henry (Harry) Cust (1861-1917) – Politician & Editor: *The Pall Mall Magazine*

George Curzon; **1st Baron Curzon of Kedlestone** (1859-1925) – Politician & Statesman: Viceroy of India 1899-1905

Archie Gordon (1884-1909)

Joyce Grenfell (1910-1979) – Entertainer – Related to both the Astors and (by marriage) to the Grenfells

Edward Horner (1888-1917) – Barrister – Descendent of 'Little Jack Horner'; killed in action in France during WW1

King George V (1865-1936) – Reigned 1910-1936

Henry Lindsay (1866-1939) – Soldier – Brother of Violet (wife of Henry Manners)

His wife **Norah** (née **Bourke**) – Socialite Garden Designer: The Long garden at Cliveden

Alfred Lyttelton (1857-1913) – Cricketer, Footballer, Politician & Statesman

His wife (Octavia) **Laura** (née **Tennant**, 1862-1886)

Henry Manners; **8th Duke of Rutland** (1852-1925) – Politician – Father of John & Violet Manners

His wife **Violet** (née **Lindsay**, 1856-1937) – Artist – Sister-in-law of Norah Lindsay; mother by her husband Henry Manners of John & Violet Manners; mother by Harry Cust of Diana Manners

John Manners; **9th Duke of Rutland** (1886-1940) – Patron of Loughborough College – Son of Violet & Henry Manners

His wife Kathleen (née **Tennant**, 1895-1989)

Edward Tennant; **1st Baron Glenconner** (1859-1920) – Politician – Styled **Sir Edward Tennant**, **2nd Baronet** 1906-1911

His wife **Pamela** (née **Wyndham**) – Daughter of Madeline & Percy Wyndham

Robert Windsor-Clive; **1st Earl of Plymouth** (1857-1923) – Politician – Styled **The Lord Windsor** 1869-1905

His wife Alberta (**Gay**) (née **Paget**) (1863-1944)

George Wyndham (1863-1913) – Politician, Stateman & Privy Counsellor – Son of Madeline & Percy Wyndham

Percy Wyndham (1835-1911) – Soldier & Politician

His wife **Madeline** (née Campbell, d1920)

The Company (1870s-1970s)

Friends and family of the Grenfells at Taplow Court (1887-1939) and the Astors at Cliveden (1906-1966) enjoyed the company of a wit parade of artists, artistes, poets, performers, politicians and statesmen, literary lights and royalty, some of whom also discovered the riverside delights of *Skindles* (1876-1971). As the hub of this social whirl shifted slowly from Taplow Court to Cliveden, Walter de la Mare offered a more intimate, less ostentatious diversion at *Hill House* (1925-1939).

Leo Amery (1873-1955) – Journalist, Politician & Statesman – Milner's Kindergarten 1900s

Anthony Armstrong-Jones (b1930) – Photographer & Filmmaker – **1st Earl Snowdon** 1960 on his marriage to Princess Margaret, sister of Queen Elizabeth II

Stanley Baldwin (1867-1947) – Politician: Prime Minister 1923-1924, 1924-1929 & 1935-1937

James Barrie (1860-1937) – Author & Dramatist: *Peter Pan* (Play 1904, Novel 1911)

Sir Max Beerbohm (1872-1956) – Essayist, Caricaturist & Author: *Zuleika Dobson* (1911) & *Seven Men* (1919) – Uncle of Iris Tree

Hilaire Belloc (1870-1953) – Poet, Author & Historian: *Cautionary Tales for Children* (1907) & *The Crusades: the World's Debate* (1937)

Sarah Bernhardt (1844-1923) – French Actress

John Betjeman (1906-1984) – Poet Laureate 1972

Edward Burne-Jones (1833-1898) – Pre-Raphaelite Artist & Designer

Buchan, John; **1st Baron Tweedsmuir** (1875-1940) – Author, Historian & Statesman – Milner's Kindergarten 1900s – *The Thirty-Nine Steps* (1915) – Governor General of Canada 1935-1940

David Cecil (1902-1986) – Biographer, Historian & Academic

Robert Cecil; **1st Viscount Cecil of Chelwood** (1864-1958) – Lawyer, Politician & Diplomat – An architect of The League of Nations 1920 & joint first President of The Royal Institute for International Affairs 1920

Neville Chamberlain (1869-1940) – Politician: Prime Minister 1937-1940

Charlie Chaplin (1889-1977) – Comic Actor & Filmmaker: *The Gold Rush* (1925), *Modern Times* (1936) & *The Great Dictator* (1940)

GK Chesterton (1874-1836) – Author, Poet, Dramatist & Journalist

John Clynes (1869-1949) – Trade Unionist & Politician – Joint first President of the Royal Institute for International Affairs 1920

Joseph Conrad (1857-1924) – Anglicised Polish Mariner 1874-1894 & Novellist: *Heart of Darkness* (1899) & *Lord Jim* (1900)

Nancy Cunard (1896-1965) – Writer & Political Activist – Muse to wordsmiths such as Aldous Huxley & Ernest Hemingway

George Curzon; **1st Baron Curzon of Kedlestone** (1859-1925) – Politician & Statesman: Viceroy of India 1899-1905, Foreign Secretary 1919-1924 – Restored Taj Mahal 1904-1908, partitioned Bengal 1905-1911 & defined Poland's eastern border 1920

Bette Davis (1908-1989) – American Actress: *Jezebel* (1938), *Now, Voyager* (1942), *All About Eve* (1950) & *Whatever Happened to Baby Jane?* (1962)

Walter de la Mare (1873-1956) – Poet & Author: *The Listeners* (1912), *Desert Islands and Robinson Crusoe* (1930), *Early One Morning* (1935) & *Behold, This Dreamer!* (1939)

His wife **Elfie** (née **Ingpen**, 1860-1943)

Anthony Eden (1897-1977) – Politician: Foreign Secretary 1935-1938, 1940-1945 & 1951-1955, Prime Minister 1955-1957

Douglas Fairbanks Jr (1909-2000) – American Actor: *A Woman of Affairs* (1928), *The Prisoner of Zenda* (1937), *Gunga Din* (1939), *Sinbad the Sailor* (1947) & *Douglas Fairbanks Presents* (1954-1956) – WW2 US Navy Officer & Anglophile

Giuseppe Garibaldi (1807-1882) – Italian General & Politician – Leading role in the unification of Italy 1859-1866

James Garvin (1868-1947) – Editor: *The Observer* 1908-1942

David Lloyd George (1863-1945) – Politician: Prime Minister 1916-1922

Edward Grey; **1st Viscount Grey of Fallodon** – Politician & Stateman: Foreign Secretary 1905-1916 – UK Ambassador to the USA 1919-1920 – Joint first President of the Royal Institute for International Affairs 1920

Thomas Hardy (1840-1928) – Author & Poet: *Far from the Madding Crowd* (1874) & *Tess of the d'Urbervilles* (1891)

Laurence Housman (1865-1959) – Playwright, Author & Illustrator: *Victoria Regina* (1934)

Sir Henry Irving (1838-1905) – Actor-Manager: *Lyceum Theatre* 1871-1902

Henry James (1843-1916) – American Author & Critic: *The Portrait of a Lady* (1881)

Hussein bin Talal (1935-1999) – **King of Jordan** 1952-1999

Amy Johnson (1903-1941) – Pioneering Aviator: first woman to fly solo England-to-Australia 1930 – Killed during WW2

Boris Karloff (1887-1969) – Actor: *Frankenstein* (1931), *Scarface* (1932), *Bride of Frankenstein* (1935) & *Son of Frankenstein* (1939) & *How the Grinch Stole Christmas* (1966)

Katharine (née Worsley); **Duchess of Kent** (b1933) – Wife of Prince Edward, Duke of Kent; a cousin of Queen Elizabeth II

Joseph Kennedy (1888-1969) – American Businessman & Government Official – US Ambassador to the UK 1938-1940 – Father of US President John F Kennedy

Alice Keppel (1868-1947) – Socialite; mistress to King Edward VII

Rudyard Kipling (1865-1936) – Poet & Author: *Gunga Din* (1890), The Jungle Book (1894), *Kim* (1901) & *If* (1910)

Herbert Kitchener; 1st Earl Kitchener (1850-1916) – Army Officer & Colonial Administrator: Mahdist War (Sudan) 1884-1899, Second Boer War (South Africa) 1900-1902, India 1902-1909, Egypt 1911-1914, Secretary of State for War 1914-1916

Lillie Langtry (1853-1929) – Actress: *She Stoops to Conquer* (1881) – Mistress of Bertie, Prince of Wales

TE Lawrence (1888-1935), **Lawrence of Arabia –** Soldier: *Seven Pillars of Wisdom* (1922) – Served as TE Shaw in RAF 1925-1935

Richard Nixon (1913-1994) – American Politician: US Vice-President 1963-1961 & US President 1969-1974

Harold Macmillan (1894-1986) – Politician: Prime Minister 1957-1963

Margaret McMillan (1869-1931) – Pioneer of nursery schools and training of teachers and nurses, causes enthusiastically supported by Nancy Astor, her friend GB Shaw and her Taplow neighbours Walter de la Mare and Arild Rosenkrantz, who introduced Margaret to Rudolph Steiner and Anthroposophy

Manfred Mann (1962-1969) – R&B Band featuring Paul Jones until 1966 then Mike D'Abo; succeeded by *Manfred Mann's Earth Band* 1971 and *The Manfreds* 1991

Marx Brothers – American Comic Actors in Vaudeville, on Broadway and in Movies 1905-1949: *Animal Crackers* (1930), *Monkey Business* (1931), *Duck Soup* (1933), *A Night at the Opera* (1935) & *A Day at the Races* (1937)

Ottoline Morrell (née **Cavendish-Bentinck**) 1873-1938) – Aristocratic Socialite & Patron of Artists & Authors

Sir Alfred Munnings (1878-1959) – Equestrian Artist

Henry Newbolt (1862-1938) – Poet, Author & Historian: *Vita Lampada* (1892) & *Drake's Drum* (1897)

Sir Harold Nicholson (1886-1968) – Diplomat, Author, Diarist & Politician – Husband of Vita Sackville-West

George Orwell (1903-1950), in reality **Eric Blair** – Author, Essayist, Journalist & Critic: *The Road to Wigan Pier* (1937), *Coming Up for Air* (1939) featuring a Thames-side idyll (Taplow?), *Animal Farm* (1945) & *1984* (1949) which was mostly written at the Astor's *Barnhill* on Jura – *The Observer* 1939-1946 – Creator of neologisms *Cold War*, *Thought Police*, *Doublethink*, *Room 101* & *Big Brother*; married Eileen O'Shaughnessy 1936 – Buried alongside David Astor

Eileen O'Shaughnessy (1905-1945) – Journalist & Teacher (Silchester House Girls' School 1927-1928) – First wife of Eric Blair (George Orwell) 1936-1945

JB Priestley (1894-1984) – Author, Playwright, Social Philosopher & Broadcaster: *Let the People Sing* (1939), *An Inspector Calls* (1945) & *The World at War* (1973) – In 1940, observed "Nothing [but amateurism] could be more English... both in its beginning and its end, its folly and its grandeur.... We have gone sadly wrong [and] must resolve never, never, to do it again".

Princess Alexandra (b1936) – Cousin of Queen Elizabeth II; widow of Sir Angus Ogilvy

Princess Margaret (1930-2002) – Sister of Queen Elizabeth II; married 1960-1978 to Anthony-Armstrong Jones; 1st Earl Snowdon

Franklin D Roosevelt (1882-1945) – USA President 1933-1945

Sara Roosevelt (1854-1941) – Mother of Franklin D Roosevelt; friend of Nancy Astor

Vita Sackville-West (1892-1962) – Author, Poet & Garden Designer – Wife of Sir Harold Nicholson

Siegfried Sassoon (1886-1967) – Poet, Author & Editor

Patrick Shaw-Stewart (1888-1917) – Banker & War Poet – Killed in action in France during WW1

John Singer Sargent (1856-1925) – American Artist specialising in Society Portraits: *The Wyndham Sisters* (1899), *Mrs Waldorf Astor* (1909) & *George Curzon* (1914)

George Bernard Shaw (1856-1950) – Prolific Irish Playwright, Essayist & Author: *Arms and the Man* (1894), *Man and Superman* (1903), *St Joan* (1923), *The Apple Cart* (1929) & *Pygmalion* (1912) for which he was awarded the Nobel Prize in Literature 1925 and an *Oscar* 1938 – Long-term friend of Nancy Astor

Edith Sitwell 1887-1964) – Poet & Critic – Sister of Osbert Sitwell

Osbert Sitwell (1982-1969) – Poet, Journalist & Art Critic – Brother of Edith Sitwell

Bram Stoker (1847-1912) – Irish Theatre Manager (with Henry Irving at *Lyceum Theatre* 1878-1902), Journalist (*The Daily Telegraph*) & Author: *Dracula* (1897) & *The Lair of the White Worm* (1911) – Lived at various addresses in Chelsea but is said to have written *Dracula* during a sabbatical at *Hill House*

Lytton Strachey – Biographer & Critic – *The Spectator* 1904-1914, *Queen Victoria* (1921)

The Beatles (1960-1970) – Rock Band – From 1962: John Lennon, Paul McCartney, George Harrison & Ringo Starr

The Rolling Stones (from 1962) – Rock Band – 1969-1975: Mick Jagger, Keith Richard, Charlie Watts, Bill Wyman & Mick Taylor

The Strawbs (1964-1980) – Rock Band (featuring Rick Wakeman 1969-1971); reformed 1983

Thin Lizzy (1969-1983) – Irish Rock Band featuring Phil Lynott & Brian Downey; reformed 1996-2001 & 2004

Iris Tree (1897-1968) – Poet, Actress & Artist's Model – Daughter of actor Sir Herbert Beerbohm Tree

HG Wells (1866-1946) – Essayist & Author: *The War of the Worlds* (1897) & *Men Like Gods* (1923)

Edith Wharton (1862-1937) – Author, Poet & Designer – *The Descent of Man* (1903) & *The Age of Innocence* (1920)

James Whistler (1874-1903) – American Artist: *Whistler's Mother* (1871)

Henry White (1850-1927) – American Diplomat – US Ambassador to Italy 1905-1906 & France 1906-1909

Oscar Wilde (1854-1900) – Irish Playwright & Author – *The Picture of Dorian Gray* (1890) & *The Importance of Being Earnest* (1895)

Ellen Wilkinson (1891-1947) – Politician: MP 1924-1931 & 1935-1947 – Peer of Nancy Astor, a pioneer for social reform: supported General Strike 1926, led Jarrow March 1936

Margaret Wintringham (1879-1955) – Politician: MP 1921-1924 – Peer of Nancy Astor, a pioneer for social reform and nurses; through Nancy, she was assisted by GB Shaw and Walter de la Mare and Arild Rosenkrantz who introduced her

WB Yeats (1865-1939) – Irish Poet & Politician – *The Tower* (1929), Nobel Prize in Literature 1923

The Cliveden Set (so-called in 1937)

This circle of friends around Nancy & Waldorf Astor at Cliveden had its roots at Oxford University (1898-1901) where Waldorf met an idealistic group (primarily undergraduates and fellows of New College and All Souls College) who matured within Milner's Kindergarten in South Africa (1901-1910). Some set out to change the world through the League of Nations and The Royal Institute for International Affairs at *Chatham House* (both founded in 1920). As newspaper proprietors, Waldorf (*The Observer*, 1915-1948) and his brother Jakie (*The Times*, 1922-1959) were said to have considerable influence over public opinion. In the 1930s, Waldorf & Nancy debated with their friends the contrast between Nazi fascism, Soviet communism and British imperialism. Critics gave the gathering its derogatory epithet in 1937.

Robert (Bob) Brand (1878-1963) – Civil Servant, Banker & Businessman – Married Nancy Astor's sister Phyllis Langhorne 1917 – Created 1st Baron Brand 1949

Lionel Curtis (1872-1955 – Political Philosopher, Statesman & Author – Founded *Round Table* movement 1910 & The Royal Institute for International Affairs 1920 – Wrote *The Commonwealth of Nations* 1916

Geoffrey Dawson (1874-1944), Geoffrey Robinson until 1917 – Editor: *The Times* 1912-1919 & 1923-1941

Philip Kerr (1882-1940) – Politician, Journalist & Diplomat – Founded and edited the *Round Table Journal* 1910-1916; active in the foundation of The League of Nations 1920 – Succeeded as **11th Marquess of Lothian** 1930 – UK Ambassador to the USA 1938-1940

William Montagu; **9th Duke of Manchester** (1877-1947) – Politician

Edward Wood (1881-1959) – Politician & Statesman – Foreign Secretary 1938-1940 – Styled as Lord Irwin 1925, Viscount Halifax 1934 & 1st Earl of Halifax 1944

Their chief critics:

Claud Cockburn (1904-1981) – Journalist & Author – Editor: *The Week* 1933-1941

Reynold's News (1850-1962) – Owned in the 1930s by the *Cooperative Press* – First to coin the term 'The Cliveden Set' (28th November 1937) subsequently made 'popular' by Cockburn

John Spivak (1897-1981) – American Journalist & Author; funded by the Soviets

Sir Robert Vansittart (1881-1957) – Civil Servant, Poet, Playwright & Author – Private Secretary to Foreign Secretary Lord Curzon 1920-1924, Principal Private Secretary to PMs Stanley Baldwin & Ramsay Macdonald 1928-1930 then supervised the British Diplomatic Service as Permanent Under-Secretary at the Foreign Office 1930-1938 – Strongly opposed to appeasement – Elevated as 1st Baron Vansittart of Denham 1941

Appendix Five
Bibliography

Books and Articles

Tim Allen, **Chris Hayden** & **Hugo Lamdin-Whymark** – *From Bronze Age enclosure to Anglo-Saxon Settlement: Archaeological excavations at Taplow hillfort, Buckinghamshire* (The Oxford Archaeological Unit Ltd, 2009)

BM Ansell, **EGL Bywaters**, **PE Spencer** & **JP Tyler** – *Looking Back 1947-1985: The Canadian Red Cross Memorial Hospital* (Barbara M Ansell, 1997)

Asylum for the Cure of Scrofula & Glandular Diseases – *Report on the Medical Principles of Charles Whitlaw* (25th March 1824)

Sir David Attenborough – Memorial Service tribute to Leonard Miall (Unpublished, 2005)

KA Bailey – *Who Was Who and Who Became Whom: Buckinghamshire Landowners 1066-1086*

The Baldwin Family of *Rectory Farmhouse* – Private documents and correspondence (Unpublished, 1902-1932)

Michael Bayley – *The Unwritten History & Traditions of the Useful Waters of the Middle Thames* (Privately published, c2003)

Michael Bayley – *Finding Maidenhead's Flashlock Canals* (Privately published, 2008)

Michael Bayley – *Maidenhead, its Seal and its Bridges* (Privately published, 2010)

Walter de Gray Birch (Editor) – *Cartularium Saxonicum: a collection of charters relating to Anglo-Saxon history* (Whiting & Co, 1885; University of Oxford Text Archive)

Dorothy Blackman & **Burnham Historians** – *Yesterday's Town: Burnham* (Barracuda Books Ltd, 1984)

Dorothy Blackman & **Daphne Chevous** – *Around Burnham* (Amberley Publishing, 2009)

Angela Bolger, **Colin McGeachie** & **Rob Wermerling** – *Mary Palmer's Inheritance* (SGI-UK, 1988)

Angela Bolger, **Colin McGeachie** & **Rob Wermerling** – *The First Field Marshall and the King's Mistress* (SGI-UK)

Angela Bolger, **Kate Pankhurst** & **Rob Wermerling** – *Olympic Hero: The Sporting Life of Lord Desborough* (SGI-UK, 1994)

Angela Bolger, **Jessica Miller** & **Rob Wermerling** – *Grenfell for Maidenhead* (SGI-UK, 1996)

Angela Bolger, **Joy Garstang**, **Tom McGuire** & **Jessica Miller** – *The Changing Face of Taplow Court* (SGI-UK, 1997)

Bond's (Maidenhead) Ltd – Company archives (Unpublished, 1936-1955), courtesy of **Christopher Smith**

Michael & Eleanor Brock – *Margot Asquith's War Diary 1914/18* (Oxford University Press, 2014)

Burnham Historians – *Both Teams at Plough* (Burnham Historians, 1992)

Burnham Historians – *Dropmore & Littleworth: The Story of a Bucks Parish* (Burnham Historians, 1996)

Burnham Historians – *Lent Rise: A School and its Community* (Burnham Historians, 1998)

Centre for Buckinghamshire Studies, Aylesbury – *The Grenfell Papers* (Ref D-GR)

Daphne Chevous – *Old School Memories* (Article in *Roundabout*, probably late-1970s)

Claud Cockburn – *I Claud* (Penguin, 1967)

James Crathorne – *Cliveden, the Place and the People* (Collins & Brown, 1995)

Meredith Daneman – *Margot Fonteyn* (Penguin Books Ltd, 2004)

Richard Davenport-Hines – *Ettie: The Intimate Life and Dauntless Spirit of Lady Desborough* (Weidenfield & Nicholson, 2008)

Sharon Davis – *A Girl Called Dusty* (Andre Deutsch Ltd, 2008)

Directory & Gazeteer for Oxon, Berks & Bucks (Dutton Allen & Co, 1863)

Michael Farley (Editor) – *An Illustrated History of Early Buckinghamshire* (Buckinghamshire Archaeological Society, 2010)

Eric Fitch – *Unknown Taplow and Environs* (Windsor Publications, 1988)

Adrian Fort – *Nancy: The Story of Lady Astor* (Vintage, 2013)

Alistair Forsyth & **Karl Lawrence** – *Taplow at the Millennium* (Taplow Parish Council, 2000)

Robert Gibbs – *Worthies of Buckinghamshire* (1888)

Peter Lee Goodchild – *Beer and Skittles* (Privately published, 2010)

Kenneth Grahame – *The Wind in the Willows* (Methuen, 1908)

Helen Grellier – *A History of St Nicolas' CE School, 1848-1900* (Unpublished, 1998)

Rev **CDH Grimes** – *Ye Oulde Storie of Hitcham* (1926)

Arthur Grout – *Scouting in Taplow, Hitcham & Burnham* (Unpublished memoirs, 2010)

Jeff Grout & **Liz Fisher** – *Murder Without Motive?* (Shoehorn Media Ltd, 2009)

Owen Gwilliam – *Memories of Taplow Court: Recollections of Rosa Mustoe* (Old St Stephen's Society Newsletter, 2011)

Rosina Harrison – *The Lady's Maid* (Ebury Press, 2011)

Alyson Haymonds – *Letters from a Lady: The Remarkable Life of Jane Vigor* (*Windlesora*, Journal of Windor Local History Group, 2006)

Hitcham & Taplow Historians including **Indra Adnan** (SGI-UK), **Greg Armstrong** (Environment Agency), **Liz Anderson**, **Patricia Andrews**, **TM Balfe**, **Bill Ball**, **Michael Bayley**, **Pamela Bentley**, **Julian Bicknell**, **Angela Bolger** (SGI-UK), **Alison Bromley**, **Henry Brothers**, **Joanna Brooking**, **Phil Catherall** (Environment Agency), **Daryll Clifton-Day** (Environment Agency), **Philip Cooley**, **Philip Cotton** (Cliveden), **Tim Craufurd** (Cliveden), **Ian Dunningham**, Rev **Mervyn Eden** (St Mary's Church, Hitcham), **Ginny & Euan Felton**, **Andrew Findlay**, **Alistair Forsyth**, **Budge Francis**, **Lee Grey**, **Helen & Alleyn Grellier**, **Michael Goss**, **Sally Hayles**, **Graham Hickman**, **Tony Hickman**, **Eddie Hoare** (Hedsor), **Gill & Geoff Holloway**, **Huw Jenkins**, **Roisin Lakings** (née Lawrence), **Peter Lane**, **Karl Lawrence**, **Helen & Lincoln Lee**, **Laird Mackay**, **Susan Mason**, **Andy McKenzie** (SGI-UK), **Tony Meats**, **Leonard Miall**, **George Milne**, **Polly Nissman**, **Dick Nutt**, **Des O'Sullivan**, **Tony Packe**, **Keith Paskins**, **Laura Pope**, **Hannah Purcell** (Cliveden), **Tony Read**, **Fred Russell**, **Alan Senior**, **Richard Sneyd**, **Dan Sousa**, **Brett Thorn** (Bucks County Museum), **Damon Torsten**, **Mary & Bernard Trevallion**, **Derek Walker**, **Miv Wayland-Smith**, **Esther & Jon Willmore**, **Ted Wright** and **Rosemary Zorsa** (Hitcham & Taplow Society Newsletters 19-22, 25-26 and 28-102, 1969-2014)

Karl Hulka – *Initial Archaeological Appraisal: Mill Lane, Taplow* (Heritage Collective on behalf of BDO, 2013)

Harry Hurn – Letter to a friend (Unpublished, 2001)

Jerome K Jerome – *Three Men in a Boat* (JW Arrowsmith, 1889)

Sister **Jane Mary** – *A Short History of Burnham Abbey* (The Society of the Precious Blood, 1988)

SG Kay & **JM Briggs** – *Papermaking at Taplow: A Historical Survey* (New Taplow Paper Mills Ltd, 1980)

Kelly's Directories for Berks, Bucks & Oxon (Kelly & Co, 1891, 1895, 1903, 1911, 1929, 1935, 1939 & 1960)

Alexander Kidd – *Hill Forts and Churches: A Coincidence of Location?* Chapter within *Record of Buckinghamshire* Volume 44 (Editor **John Clarke**, Associate Editor **ME Farley**, Buckinghamshire Archaeological Society, 2004)

Walter Leyster – *A Short History of Taplow* (Unpublished, 1941)

George Lipscomb – *The History and Antiquities of the County of Buckingham* (J&W Robins, 1847)

David Long – *The Chapel at Amerden* (Unpublished, 2010)

Maidenhead Advertiser – Various editions

Maidenhead Corporation – Report to conference on Thames Valley Floods (16th July 1947) and Minutes of Floods Subcommittee (15th September 1947)

Andrew Marr – *A History of Modern Britain* (Macmillan, 2007)

Leonard Miall – *Unfinished Memoirs* (Unpublished, 2002)

Roger & Tristan Miall – Eulogies for Leonard Miall (Unpublished, 2005)

F Campbell Moller – *Boating Life on the Upper Thames* (Volume XVIII N° 4, Outing 1891)

S Neuman, **NC Burgess**, **M Alexander** & **J Urwick** – *St Nicolas' Church, Taplow: A Short History* (Undated leaflet)

Alice Osborne – *Rectory Farmhouse Diaries* (Unpublished, 1906-1926)

Luke Over – *The Story of the Old Station Inn and the Great Western Railway at Maidenhead* (1839-1989) (Luke Over, 1989)

Luke Over – *Villages Around Maidenhead* (The History Press, 2009)

Luke Over & **Chris Tyrell** – *The Royal Hundred of Bray* (Cliveden Press, 1993)

William Page (Editor) – *A History of Buckinghamshire: Volume 3* (St Catherine Press, 1925; reprinted in 1969 by University College of London's Institute of Historical Research)

Philip Purser – *Obituary of Wilfred Greatorex* 1922-2002 (*The Guardian*, 17 October 2002)

IS Rogers – *Robert Manfield* (Unpublished research notes, 2006)

Donald Rose (formerly Rosenthaler) – Letter to St Nicolas' School (Unpublished, 2013)

Norman Rose – *The Cliveden Set: Portrait of an Exclusive Fraternity* (Jonathan Cape, 2000)

Chrissy Rosenthal & **Ann Danks** – *Voices of Maidenhead* (The History Press, 2012)

Royal British Legion – Taplow & Hitcham Branch Minute Books (1949-1991), courtesy of **Laird Mackay**

James Rutland – *Taplow Parish Register 1604-1904*, copied and maintained while Rutland was parish clerk 1885-1906 (Buckinghamshire Family History Society, 2004)

Professor **John Satterly** (Editor), University of Toronto – *Rivers of Great Britain: The Thames from Source to Sea* (Cassell & Co Ltd, 1891; relevant chapters by **TB Bonne** & **HS Wilson**)

Lawrence B Smith – *Oxford Dictionary of National Biography: Hamilton, George, first earl of Orkney* (Oxford University Press, 2004)

Sidney (Paddy) Sutton Smith – Private papers and correspondence (Unpublished, 1947)

Cyril Staley – *Old Lodge* (Unpublished notes, 1988)

WH Summers – *The Lollards of the Chiltern Hills, glimpses of English dissent in the Middle Ages* (Francis Griffiths, 1906)

Fred S Thacker – *The Thames Highway: Volumes I & II* (David & Charles of Newton Abbott, 1914 & 1920; reprinted 1968)

Mary Trevallion – *Taplow Parish* (Unpublished presentation notes, 2013)

Mary Trevallion – *Cliveden Gages: Origin, Creation and What's in a Name* (Unpublished presentation notes, 2013)

Mary Trevallion – *From Wilderness to Paradise and back again: Dropmore House, Taplow's Cinderella* (Unpublished presentation notes, 2014)

Gore Vidal – *The City and the Pillar* (EP Dutton & Co Inc, New York, 1948)

Dr **Lynne Walker**, University of London – *Women Architects in Britain* (a blog posted in 2000 in preparation for a book then with the working title *Gender and Architecture: A History of Women and Architecture in Britain)*

Matthew Wells – *First Stop Maidenhead* (Matthew Wells, 1973)

Francis E Witts – *The Complete Diary of a Cotswold Parson – Volume 7: The Man of Business* (Amberley Publishing)

Brian Benchley Wheals – *Theirs Were But Human Hearts; a local history of three Thameside parishes: Wooburn, Little Marlow and Hedsor* (HS Publishing, 1983)

HG Wells – *Men Like Gods* (Cassell & Co Ltd, 1923)

Theresa Whistler – *The Life of Walter de la Mare* (Duckbacks, 2003)

Charles Whitlaw – Last Will & Testament (Fisher, Dowson & Wasbrough, 18th December 1882; proved 4th July 1890)

RP Wright – A Roman Veterinary Physician from the Thames Valley (Britannia, Volume 8; Cambridge Journals, November 1977)

Electronic Sources

Ancestry & Genealogy

Briginshaw: http://www.briginshaw.net/archive/Letter3.pdf

Censuses & Other Archives: http://www.ancestry.co.uk; http://familytreemaker.genealogy.com; http://www.geni.com/

Peerage: http://thepeerage.com; http://www.cracroftspeerage.co.uk

Prime Ministers: http://en.wikipedia.org/wiki/Genealogical_relationships_of_Prime_Ministers_of_the_United_Kingdom

Taplow: http://forebears.co.uk/england/buckinghamshire/taplow

General Historical Context

Anglo-Saxon Chronicles: http://omacl.org/Anglo/part1.html

Beer: http://www.cambridgebeerfestival.com/viewnode.php?id=108

Claud Cockburn: http://spartacus-educational.com/SPcockburn.htm

Domesday: http://www.domesdaybook.co.uk/

General: http://www.british-history.ac.uk/, http://www.nationalarchives.gov.uk , http://en.wikipedia.org/wiki

Inflation: http://www.measuringworth.com/ukcompare/relativevalue.php

Inflation & Currency Conversion: http://apps.nationalarchives.gov.uk/currency/default2.asp

Maps: http://maps.familysearch.org/

Military / War Casualties: http://www.cwgc.org

Military / Warships: http://www.battleships-cruisers.co.uk

The Virginia Company Charter: http://avalon.law.yale.edu/17th_century/va01.asp

Weather: http://booty.org.uk/booty.weather/climate/1650_1699.htm

Local Historical Context

Buckinghamshire / General:
http://www.buckscc.gov.uk/bcc/archives/Centre_for_Buckinghamshire_Studies; https://ubp.buckscc.gov.uk/

Buckinghamshire / Maps:
http://www.buckscc.gov.uk/leisure-and-culture/centre-for-buckinghamshire-studies/online-resources/historic-maps/

Burnham: http://www.buckscc.gov.uk/media/130492/burnham_draft_report.pdf

Chilterns: http://www.archive.org/stream/lollardsofchilte00summuoft/lollardsofchilte00summuoft_djvu.txt

Cookham: http://widbrook2.blogspot.co.uk

Geology: http://oxoniensia.org/volumes/1945/arkell.pdf

Guards' Club: http://gcra.wordpress.com/guards-club-park/

Military / Royal Berkshire Regiment:
http://www.thewardrobe.org.uk/research/war-diaries, http://www.6throyalberks.co.uk/1stJuly/default.html

River Thames / John Satterly – *The Rivers of Great Britain: the Thames, from source to sea*:
http://www.archive.org/stream/riversgreatbrit00londuoft/riversgreatbrit00londuoft_djvu.txt

River Thames / *Where Smooth Waters Glide*: http://thames.me.uk/s00750.htm
https://ubp.buckscc.gov.uk/SingleResult.aspx?uid=TBC719

South Bucks: http://www.visionofbritain.org.uk/unit_page.jsp?u_id=10084660&x=3286681.55753&y=2802086.66793

Taplow People

Ronald Binge: http://www.rfsoc.org.uk/rbinge.shtml

Bert Bushnell of Maidenhead: http://en.wikipedia.org/wiki/Bert_Bushnell

John Fenn: http://www.nessie.co.uk/htm/searching_for_nessie/deepscan.html

John Freind of Hitcham: http://rsnr.royalsocietypublishing.org/content/61/2/109.full;
http://articles.adsabs.harvard.edu/full/seri/HisSc/0041//0000163.000.html

Sheldon Gledstanes: http://www.bedfordregiment.org.uk/1stbn/1stbtnofficersdied.html

The Hanbury Family of Hitcham: http://www.pennyghael.org.uk/Hanbury.pdf

John Harvey: http://www.jjhc.info/harveyjohnrobert1921.html

The Grenfell Family: http://www.grenfellhistory.co.uk/origins.php

Willy Grenfell, **Lord Desborough**: http://www.la84foundation.org/6oic/OfficialReports/Mallon/1908.pdf

Brian Horton: http://www.messums.com/artist/42/Brian-Horton/

Violet Morris of Gaiety Row (Lynne Walker – *Women Architects in Britain*):
http://www.culture2000.tee.gr/paris/textes/lynwalk.htm

Budd Wase of Datchet: http://www.datchethistory.org.uk

Richard Webster: http://hortonpallister.awardspace.com/we-9-richard%20webster.php

Edward Whaley: http://www.scribd.com/doc/90059870/re-Whaley-IMAGE-03-10-11-234704

Charles Whitlaw: Edinburgh University Press: http://www.euppublishing.com/doi/pdfplus/10.3366/anh.2013.0139;

University of Otago: http://www.otago.ac.nz/library/exhibitions/linnaeus/cabinet15/;

Letter to Thomas Ford, Governor of Illinois (1st May 1844): http://www.usd116.org/ProfDev/AHTC/images/Early-IL-Gov-Letters/gov.html

Eric Williams of *Cranford House*: http://www.forcesreunited.org.uk/britain-at-war.asp

Taplow Places

Berry Hill: http://pulham.org.uk/2013/01/01/20-january-2013-berry-hill-buckinghamshire/

Cliveden / **Canadian Red Cross Memorial Hospital** (The Official Unofficial Cyberspace Shrine): http://www.crcmh.com

Cliveden / **Duchess of Connaught Hospital** (Canadian Army Medical Corps: 1915-1919 War Diary for 15th Canadian Field Hospital): http://data4.collectionscanada.gc.ca/netacgi/nph-brs?s1=15th+hospital&s13=&s12=&l=20&s9=RG9&s7=9-52&Sect1=IMAGE&Sect2=THESOFF&Sect4=AND&Sect5=WARDPEN&Sect6=HITOFF&d=FIND&p=1&u=http://www.collectionscanada.gc.ca/archivianet/02015202_e.html&r=1&f=G

Cliveden / General: http://www.nationaltrust.org.uk/; http://www.weekendnotes.co.uk/cliveden-house/

Cliveden / **Redwood**: http://britishtrees.blogspot.co.uk/2010/01/1-cliveden-redwood.html

Cliveden / **Stud**: http://www.reines-de-course.com/Articles/Articles%20C/Conjure.html

General: http://met.open.ac.uk/genuki/big/eng/BKM/Taplow/index.html; http://www.taplowsociety.org.uk; https://ubp.buckscc.gov.uk/SingleResult.aspx?uid=TBC719; http://www.british-history.ac.uk/report.aspx?compid=42553

General / Domesday: http://www.domesdaymap.co.uk/place/SU9182/taplow/

St Nicolas' Church: http://www.st-nicolas.org.uk/history.htm

Skindles / Rolling Stones: http://www.musictrekker.com/rockpop/rollingstones/rollingstones.html

South Lodge Pit: http://www.bucksgeology.org.uk/sssi/south_lodge.htm

Taplow Court / St Stephen's College: http://www.ststephensbroadstairs.org.uk/documents/Newsletter2011.pdf

Taplow Cricket Club: http://www.taplowcricketclub.co.uk/other/BriefHistory.html

Taplow House / Tulip Trees (The Chilterns): http://www.chilternsaonb.org/ccbmaps/766/137/taplow-s-champions.html

Taplow House / Tulip Trees (The Woodland Trust): http://www.ancient-tree-hunt.org.uk/discoveries/newdiscoveries/2009/Taplow+House+Hotel+Tulip+Tree

Taplow United: http://www.taplow-utd.co.uk/

Tæppa's Mound: http://www.indigogroup.co.uk/edge/Taplow.htm

Index

Over 2,500 individuals appear in *Taplow Moments*: far too many to list here. Decisions on who to include in the **People** section have been influenced by two things: how likely it is that each name will be searched for, and whether searches are more likely to be for **Places** or **Events & Entities**. This results in current, recent and notable Taplovians appearing under **People** alongside historical figures (including architects) that have had an impact locally but not (for example) the leading lights at Cliveden Hospital, who can be found in **Events & Entities**. Unless it is necessary to distinguish between unrelated individuals, surnames refer to all those within a family.

People

Places

Neighbours: Berkshire

Neighbours: Buckinghamshire

Taplow Common

Taplow Court & Nearby

Events & Entities